PASTON LETTERS
AND PAPERS
OF THE
FIFTEENTH CENTURY

British Museum MS. Add. 34888, f. 18

Letter no. 128, written for MARGARET PASTON, 1448

PASTON LETTERS
AND PAPERS
OF THE
FIFTEENTH CENTURY

EDITED BY

NORMAN DAVIS

PART I

OXFORD
AT THE CLARENDON PRESS
1971

Oxford University Press, Ely House, London W. 1

GLASGOW NEW YORK TORONTO MELBOURNE WELLINGTON
CAPE TOWN SALISBURY IBADAN NAIROBI DAR ES SALAAM LUSAKA ADDIS ABABA
BOMBAY CALCUTTA MADRAS KARACHI LAHORE DACCA
KUALA LUMPUR SINGAPORE HONG KONG TOKYO

PRINTED IN GREAT BRITAIN
AT THE UNIVERSITY PRESS, OXFORD
BY VIVIAN RIDLER
PRINTER TO THE UNIVERSITY

PREFACE

THIS edition was undertaken many years ago, at the suggestion of C. T. Onions when he was Honorary Director of the Early English Text Society. It was designed to be one of the Society's publications; but by the time the first part was nearing completion the publishing programme had been committed for several years ahead. I am very grateful to the Delegates of the Oxford University Press for their willingness to adopt the book, and to the Council of the Society for approving the transfer, which has enabled the first part to be brought out with much less delay. Special thanks are due to the Clarendon Press for the generous scale on which the book has been produced and illustrated, and the care with which difficult copy has been printed.

Most of the manuscripts on which the edition is based are in the British Museum, to the Trustees of which I am indebted for permission to publish the texts and to reproduce the illustrations. I am obliged also to the authorities of the Bodleian, Cambridge University Library, Pembroke College, Cambridge, and Norwich Central Library, and particularly grateful to the President and Fellows of Magdalen College, Oxford, for permitting me to print, for the first time in full, documents in their archives. His Grace the Duke of Rutland kindly let me verify the text of the two Paston letters in his muniment room at Belvoir Castle. Captain Anthony Hamond generously lent me the two papers that he owns. Dr. Curt F. Bühler sent me photocopies of the Pierpont Morgan manuscripts he had edited in 1938. I received invaluable help also from two distinguished collectors who have since died, the sixth Earl of Ilchester and H. L. Bradfer-Lawrence.

I wish to thank for their unfailing assistance the staffs of all the libraries in which I have worked, pre-eminently that of the British Museum Students' Room, as well as the officials of the Principal Probate Registry, the Public Record Office, and the Norfolk and Norwich Record Office. For expert advice I am indebted to Dr. A. I. Doyle and Mr. N. R. Ker, and to the late K. B. McFarlane, whose untimely death forestalled the edition, on different lines, which he had planned.

PREFACE

I gratefully acknowledge the important help given by the Leverhulme Trust towards the purchase of photostats of many of the manuscripts, without which the close comparison of so many handwritings could hardly have been made.

N. D.

Merton College
Oxford

CONTENTS

List of Illustrations   xx

INTRODUCTION   xxi

'The Paston Letters': Manuscripts and Editions   xxiv

The Paston Family   xl
    Biographical Summary   lii
    Chronological Table   lxiv

Table of Authors and Clerks   lxxv

Editorial Procedure   lxxx

Abbreviations   lxxxvi

THE LETTERS AND PAPERS

WILLIAM PASTON I

1. To John Staynford, 1425   1
2. To an unidentified lawyer in Rome, 1425, 5 November   2
3. Probably to Master John Urry, 1425, November   4
4. To William Worstede, John Longham, and Piers Shelton, 1426, 1 March   6
5. Memorandum to Arbitrators, 1426–7   7
6. To the Vicar of the Abbot of Cluny, probably 1430, April   13
7. Recipe, probably 1430   14
8. To an unidentified lord, 1436   14
9. To John Berney, 1439–40   16
10. To Philip Berney, 1442, before October   18
11. Inventory, not after 1444   19
12. Testament and Last Will (extracts), 1444, 10 and 21 January   21

AGNES PASTON

13. To William Paston I, probably 1440, 20 April   26
14. To Edmond Paston I, 1445, 4 February   27
15. Indenture of lease, 1446, 30 October   28
16. Indenture of lease, 1446, 10 November   28

CONTENTS

17. Indenture of lease, 1447, 29 November — 29
18. To John Paston I, not after 1449 — 30
19. To John Paston I, probably 1450, 18 February — 31
20. To John Paston I, probably 1450, 11 March — 32
21. To John Paston I, probably 1451, 12 May — 33
22. To John Paston I, probably 1451 — 34
23. To John Paston I, probably 1451, 8 November — 35
24. To John Paston I, probably 1451, 21 November — 36
25. To John Paston I, probably 1452, 16 November — 37
26. To John Paston I, 1453, 6 July — 39
27. Draft indenture of marriage settlement, perhaps about 1454 — 40
28. Memorandum of 'errands', 1458, 28 January — 41
29. To John Paston I, 1461, 1 December — 42
30. To John Paston I, perhaps 1465, 29 October — 43
31. Draft Will, 1466, 16 September — 44
32. Part of Draft Will, probably 1466 — 45
33. Part of Draft Will, probably 1466 — 47
34. Extract from Will, not after 1479 — 49

JOHN PASTON I

35. To John Damme, probably soon after 1444 — 50
36. Petition to Henry VI, 1449, before 16 July — 51
37. To an unidentified person in London, about 1449 — 53
38. Petition to the Chancellor, 1450 — 55
39. To James Gresham, 1450, 4 September — 56
40. Petition to the Lords, 1452 — 58
41. Petition to the Chancellor, 1452 — 62
42. Probably to the Sheriff of Norfolk, 1452, 23 April — 64
43. Probably to the Sheriff of Norfolk, 1452, 23 April — 66
44. Probably to the Sheriff of Norfolk, 1452 — 68
45. To Richard Southwell, perhaps 1452, 20 July — 69
46. Memorandum, 1452, late — 72
47. To John Norwode, not before 1453 — 74
48. Petition, probably 1454 — 75
49. To the Earl of Oxford, 1454, 31 March — 80
50. To Lord Grey, 1454, 15 July — 82
51. To the Duke of Norfolk, probably 1455 — 83
52. To James Gloys, probably 1455, 25 July — 84

CONTENTS

53. To Sir John Fastolf, 1458, 24 May   85
54. Nuncupative Will of Sir John Fastolf, nominally 1459, 3 November   87
55. To Margaret Paston, 1460, 19 June   91
56. To Margaret Paston, 1460, 28 July   92
57. Petition to Henry VI, 1460, 7 October   93
58. To Margaret Paston, 1461, 12 July   95
59. To Margaret Paston, 1461, 1 August   96
60. Petition to the Chancellor, 1461–2   98
61. Statement of Fastolf's intention, after 1459, before May 1466   103
62. Perhaps to Thomas Howes, perhaps 1462, 9 February   104
63. Perhaps to the Sheriff of Norfolk, 1462, March   105
64. Inventory and indenture, 1462, 6 June   107
65. Petition to the Duke of Norfolk, 1462–3   114
66. To John Pampyng, Richard Calle, and John Wykes, about 1463   116
67. Petition to Robert Welles and others, probably 1463–5   118
68. Inventory, probably 1464, not later than April   120
69. Memorandum, 1464, April   121
70. Petition to Edward IV, 1464   122
71. To Margaret Paston, 1465, 14 January   125
72. To Margaret Paston, John Daubeney, and Richard Calle, 1465, 15 January   126
73. To Margaret Paston, John Daubeney, and Richard Calle, 1465, 27 June   131
74. To Margaret Paston, 1465, 13 July   134
75. To Margaret Paston, James Gresham, and Richard Calle, 1465, 7 August   136
76. To Margaret Paston, 1465, 7 August   138
77. To Margaret Paston, 1465, 20 September   140
78. Draft Message from the King to Sir William Yelverton, 1465   145

EDMOND PASTON I

79. To John Paston I, perhaps 1447, 5 July   147
80. Nuncupative Will, 1449, 21 March   148

WILLIAM PASTON II

81. To John Paston I, 1452, 16 June   149
82. Memorandum on French Grammar, probably 1450–4   150
83. To John Paston I, 1454, July   154

CONTENTS

84. To John Paston I, 1454, 6 September 155
85. To Margaret Paston, probably 1458, 10 August 156
86. To John Paston I, 1459, 12 November 157
87. Inventory, probably 1459–60 159
88. To John Paston I, 1460, 28 January 160
89. To John Paston I, 1460, 2 May 163
90. To John Paston I, 1461, 4 April 165
91. To John Paston I, 1462, about 20 July 166
92. To John Paston II, 1467 167
93. To Margaret Paston, probably 1469, 7 April 170
94. Indenture pledging plate, 1470, 15 August 171
95. Indenture pledging plate, 1474, 24 October 171
96. To John Paston II, perhaps 1474–5 173
97. Part of draft deed, perhaps 1474–5 174
98. Memorandum on rent collection, 1477, 22 August 175
99. Memorandum on the benefice of Oxnead, 1478, 31 July 177
100. To Nicholas Goldewell, 1478, 9 October 179
101. To William Pope, 1478, 17 October 180
102. Memorandum on Marlingford manor, 1479, 18 January 181
103. Memorandum to Richard Lee, 1479, March 182
104. Indenture depositing plate, 1479, 7 July 185
105. To Thomas Lynsted, 1479, 11 July 185
106. To Harry Waryns, 1479, 19 July 186
107. To Robert Walsche, 1479, 22 November 187
108. To Richard Roos, probably 1479, 28 November 188
109. To Richard Roos, probably 1479, 19 December 190
110. Memoranda on Knapton, probably 1479–80 191
111. To John Kyng, 1480, 24 February 192
112. Memorandum to the Duchess of Norfolk, about 1480 192
113. Will, 1496, 7 September 194

CLEMENT PASTON

114. To John Paston I, 1461, 23 January 197
115. To John Paston I, 1461, 26 June 198
116. To John Paston I, 1461, 25 August 199
117. To John Paston I, 1461, 11 October 200
118. To John Paston I, 1464, 15 February 202

119. To John Paston I, 1464, 18 April ... 203
120. To John Paston I, 1466, 18 March ... 204

ELIZABETH POYNINGS or BROWNE (*née* PASTON)

121. To Agnes Paston, 1459, 3 January ... 206
122. To John Paston II, probably 1467, 15 December ... 207
123. Will, 1487, 18 May ... 210

MARGARET PASTON

124. To John Paston I, about 1441 ... 215
125. To John Paston I, probably 1441, 14 December ... 216
126. To John Paston I, probably 1443, 28 September ... 217
127. To John Paston I, 1444, 8 July ... 219
128. To John Paston I, 1448, April ... 220
129. To John Paston I, 1448, 19 May ... 223
130. To John Paston I, 1448 ... 226
131. To John Paston I, 1449, 15 February ... 227
132. To John Paston I, 1449, 28 February ... 230
133. To John Paston I, 1449, 2 April ... 233
134. To John Paston I, perhaps 1449 ... 234
135. To John Paston I, probably 1449, 9 May ... 235
136. To John Paston I, 1450, 12 March ... 237
137. To John Paston I, 1451, 3 March ... 238
138. To John Paston I, 1451, 15 March ... 239
139. To John Paston I, 1451, 30 March ... 240
140. To John Paston I, probably 1451, 3 June ... 241
141. To John Paston I, 1451, 1 July ... 242
142. To John Paston I, probably 1451, 6 July ... 243
143. To John Paston I, probably 1452, 21 April ... 245
144. To John Paston I, probably 1452, 5 November ... 246
145. To John Paston I, perhaps 1453, 30 January ... 247
146. To John Paston I, 1453, 20 April ... 248
147. To John Paston I, 1453, 6 July ... 250
148. To John Paston I, perhaps 1453, 15 October ... 251
149. To John Paston I, probably 1453, 14 November ... 252
150. To John Paston I, perhaps 1454, 29 January ... 253
151. To John Paston I, perhaps 1454, 1 February ... 254

152. To John Paston I, about 1459, September   255
153. To John Paston I, probably 1459, 24 December   257
154. To John Paston I, 1460, 21 October   258
155. To John Paston I, 1460, 29 October   260
156. To John Paston I, 1460, 25 November   262
157. To John Paston I, 1460, 1 December   263
158. To John Paston I, probably 1461, 1 March   264
159. To John Paston I, 1461, perhaps 2 July   265
160. To John Paston I, 1461, 9 July   267
161. To John Paston I, 1461, 15 July   268
162. To John Paston I, 1461, 18 July   269
163. To John Paston I, 1461, 2 November   270
164. To John Paston I, 1461, 16 November   272
165. To John Paston I, probably 1461, 20 November   274
166. To John Paston I, 1461, 3 December *Gloys*   275
167. To John Paston I, 1461, 29 December   276
168. To John Paston I, 1462, 7 January   278
169. To John Paston I, 1462, 27 January   280
170. To John Paston I, 1462, March   282
171. To John Paston I, 1462, 18 May   282
172. To John Paston I, 1463, probably 19 January   283
173. To John Paston I, 1463, before 10 April   285
174. To John Paston I, probably 1463, 13 November   286
175. To John Paston II, 1463, 15 November   287
176. To John Paston I, 1464, 6 May   289
177. To John Paston I, 1464, 8 June   290
178. To John Paston I, 1465, 8 April   292
179. To John Paston I, 1465, 3 May   293
180. To John Paston I, 1465, 10 May   295
181. To John Paston I, 1465, 13 May   299
182. To John Paston I, 1465, 20 May   301
183. To John Paston I, 1465, 27 May   302
184. To John Paston I, 1465, 11 June   304
185. To John Paston I, 1465, 24 June   306
186. To John Paston III, 1465, probably 30 June *Gloys*   308
187. To John Paston II, 1465, perhaps 6 July   309
188. To John Paston I, 1465, 12 July   310

189. To John Paston I, 1465, 7 August *Gloys/Calle*   311

190. To John Paston I, 1465, 18 August   314

191. To John Paston I, 1465, probably August   317

192. To John Paston I, 1465, 27 September   318

193. To John Paston I, 1465, 27 September   322

194. To John Paston I, 1465, 17 October *Gloys*   323

195. Inventory of goods stolen, 1465, soon after 17 October   324

196. To John Paston I, 1465, 27 October   329

197. Perhaps to John Berney, before May 1466   332

198. To John Paston II, 1466, 29 October   333

199. To John Paston II, 1467, 11 July *Gloys*   334

200. To John Paston II, 1469, 12 March *Gloys*   336

201. To John Paston II, 1469, 3 April *Gloys, Edm II*   338

202. To John Paston II, 1469, 31 August *Gloys*   340

203. To John Paston II, 1469, 10 or 11 September   341

204. To John Paston II, 1469, 12 September *Gloys*   344

205. To John Paston II, 1469, 22–30 September   345

206. To John Paston III, probably 1470, 6 July *Gloys*   348

207. To John Paston II, 1470, 15 July   349

208. To John Paston II, 1470, 28 October *Gloys*   350

209. To John Paston III, 1471, 5 November   351

210. To John Paston II, perhaps 1470, 15 November   356

211. To John Paston II, 1471, 20 November   357

212. To John Paston III, 1471, 29 November   358

213. To John Paston III, probably 1471, 7 December   360

214. To John Paston II, about 1472 *Gloys*   361

215. To John Paston III, 1472, 5 February   363

216. To John Paston II, 1472, 5 June   364

217. To John Paston III, perhaps 1472, 23 October   366

218. To John Paston III, 1472, 19 November *Gloys*   367

219. To John Paston III, 1472, 23 November   368

220. Probably to James Gloys, probably 1473, 18 January   369

221. To John Paston II, 1475, 28 January   371

222. To John Paston III, 1475, 28 January   373

223. To John Paston III, 1475, 5 March   374

224. To John Paston II, 1475, 23 May   375

225. To John Paston II, 1475, 9 August   376

226. To Dame Elizabeth Brews, 1477, 11 June — 378

227. To John Paston II, 1477, 11 August — 379

228. To John Paston II, 1478, 27 May — 380

229. Indenture of lease, 1480, 1 August — 381

230. Copy of will, nominally 1482, 4 February — 382

JOHN PASTON II

231. To John Paston I, 1461, 23 August — 390

232. To John Paston I, 1462, 13 March — 392

233. To John Paston I, 1462, probably May–June — 393

234. To John Paston I, probably 1464, 5 March — 394

235. To John Paston I, 1465, 27 September — 395

236. To John Paston III, 1467, probably March — 396

237. Indenture of wager, 1467, 1 May — 397

238. To John Paston III, 1468, 9 November — 398

239. To John Paston III, 1469, 17 March — 399

240. To John Paston III, 1469, early June — 400

241. To Walter Writtle, 1469, early September — 401

242. To Walter Writtle, 1469, 10 September — 402

243. To Margaret Paston, 1469, 15 September — 405

244. To John Paston III, 1469, 18 September — 407

245. To Margaret Paston, 1469, October — 408

246. Indenture of sale, 1469, 6 November — 410

247. To Roger Townshend, for another, perhaps about 1470, 12 February — 411

248. To John Paston III, 1470, about 20 February — 412

249. To the Bishop of Winchester, 1470, between February and July — 416

250. Indenture pledging plate, 1470, 3 July — 417

251. Indenture pledging plate, 1470, 8 July — 418

252. Indenture of agreement on Fastolf estate, 1470, 14 July — 419

253. Indenture of release and quitclaim of Fastolf manors, 1470, 14 July — 426

254. Indenture of agreement concerning Fastolf manors, 1470, 14 July — 428

255. To Lord Beauchamp, 1470, July — 429

256. To John Paston III, 1470, 5 August — 430

257. Indenture pledging plate, 1470, 7 August — 431

258. To John Paston III, 1470, 15 November — 432

259. Inventory, probably 1470 — 434

260. Declaration concerning the Fastolf estate, 1471, 12 February — 436

CONTENTS

261. To Margaret Paston, 1471, 18 April   437
262. Schedule to release of lands, 1471, 12 July   439
263. To John Paston III, 1471, 15 September   439
264. To John Paston III, 1471, 28 September   442
265. Inventory of papers, after 1470   444
266. To Margaret Paston, 1472, 8 January   445
267. To John Paston III, 1472, 17 February   447
268. To John Paston III, 1472, 30 April   448
269. To John Paston III, 1472, 4 November   449
270. To John Paston III, 1472, 8 November   451
271. To Margaret Paston or John Paston III, 1472, 22 November   453
272. To John Paston III, 1473, 3 February   455
273. To John Paston III, 1473, 2 April   456
274. To John Paston III, 1473, 12 April   457
275. To John Paston III, 1473, 16 April   460
276. To John Paston III, 1473, 18 May   461
277. To John Paston III, 1473, 3 June   463
278. To Edmond Paston II, 1473, 5 July   464
279. To Margaret Paston, 1473, 30 July   466
280. To John Paston III, 1473, late   467
281. To John Paston III, 1473, 6 November   468
282. To John Paston III, 1473, 22 November   470
283. To John Paston III, 1473, 25 November   473
284. To Margaret Paston, 1474, 20 February   474
285. To Margaret Paston, 1474, probably November   475
286. To Margaret Paston, 1474, 20 November   477
287. To John Paston III, 1474, 20 November   478
288. To John Paston III, 1474, 11 December   480
289. To John Paston III, 1475, 17 January   481
290. To John Paston III or others, 1475, 5 February   483
291. To Margaret Paston, 1475, 22 February   484
292. To Edmond Paston II, 1475, 13 June   485
293. To Margaret Paston, 1475, 11 September   486
294. Petition to Edward IV, 1475   487
295. To Margaret Paston, 1476, 17 January   489
296. To John Paston III, 1476, 27 January   490
297. To John Paston III or Margaret Paston, 1476, 12 March   492

CONTENTS

298. To Margaret Paston or John Paston III, 1476, 21 March . . . 493

299. To Margaret Paston or John Paston III, 1476, 27 May . . . 494

300. To John Paston III, 1476, 30 June . . . 496

301. To Margaret Paston, probably 1476, 30 August . . . 497

302. To John Paston III, 1477, 14 February . . . 498

303. To John Paston III, 1477, 9 March . . . 499

304. To Margaret Paston, 1477, 28 March . . . 500

305. To John Paston III, 1477, 14 April . . . 501

306. To John Paston III, 1477, probably April . . . 502

307. To John Paston III, 1477, 23 June . . . 504

308. To Margaret Paston, 1477, 7 August . . . 504

309. Copy of will, nominally 1477, 31 October . . . 506

310. To John Paston III and Osbern Berney, 1478, 5 May . . . 508

311. To Margaret Paston, 1478, 13 May . . . 510

312. To John Paston III, 1478, 25 August . . . 511

313. To Margaret Paston, 1479, about May–June . . . 512

314. Memoranda, 1479, August . . . 514

315. To Margaret Paston, 1479, 29 October . . . 515

316. Inventory of Books, not after 1479 . . . 516

JOHN PASTON III

317. Perhaps to Thomas Playter, 1461, March . . . 519

318. To John Paston I, probably 1461, 10 November . . . 521

319. To John Paston I, 1462, 1 November . . . 522

320. To John Paston II, 1462, 11 December . . . 523

321. To John Paston I, 1464, 1 March . . . 525

322. To John Paston I, probably 1464, 2 June . . . 526

323. To Margaret Paston, 1465, 14 September . . . 528

324. To John Paston I, 1465, 3 October . . . 529

325. To John Paston II, 1467, 27 January . . . 531

326. To John Paston II, 1467, 7 February . . . 533

327. To John Paston II, 1467, April . . . 534

328. To Margaret Paston, perhaps 1467, about October . . . 536

329. To John Paston II, probably 1468, March . . . 537

330. To Margaret Paston, 1468, 8 July . . . 538

331. To John Paston II, 1469, 7 April . . . 540

332. To John Paston II, 1469, May . . . 541

68. To John Paston II, 1476, 23 January 597

369. To John Paston II, 1476, 3 February 598

370. To Lord Hastings, 1476, 2 March 599

371. To Margaret Paston, 1476, probably late March 601

372. To John Paston II, 1476, 6 May 603

373. To an unknown lady, probably 1476 603

374. To Margaret Paston, 1477, 8 March 605

375. To John Paston II, 1477, 9 March 606

376. Memorandum of marriage terms, 1477 607

377. Memorandum on marriage negotiations, 1477 608

378. To Margaret Paston, 1477, probably 28 June 608

379. To John Paston II, 1478, 21 January 611

380. To Margaret Paston, 1478, 3 February 612

381. To John Paston II, 1479, 6 November 614

382. Account, 1479, after 25 November 616

383. To Margaret Paston, 1479, November 617

384. To Margaret Paston, 1479, December 618

385. Memorandum of complaints against William Paston II, after 1479 .. 620

386. To Margaret Paston, between 1482 and 1484 621

387. Bill of complaint against William Paston II, 1484 622

388. Draft letter from Elizabeth Browne, 1485, before 23 September .. 627

389. To Margery Paston, between 1487 and 1495 628

390. To Lord Fitzwalter, between 1487 and 1495 628

391. To Richard Croft, probably about 1500 629

392. To William Paston III and Richard Lightfoote, probably 1503 .. 630

393. To an unknown knight, after 1485 631

EDMOND PASTON II

394. To John Paston III, 1471, 18 November 633

395. To John Paston III, probably 1472, 16 May 635

396. Indenture for military service, 1475, 7 April 636

397. To John Paston III, 1479, 21 August 638

398. To William Paston III, perhaps after 1480, January 639

399. To Margaret Paston, 1481, 27 January 640

400. To John Paston III, between June 1487 and February 1493 .. 641

401. Claim for allowances, between 1489 and 1492 643

333. To John Paston II, 1469, June 543

334. To John Paston II, 1469, about 25 September 546

335. To John Paston II, 1469, 5 October 547

336. To John Paston II, 1469, after September 548

337. To John Paston II, 1469, December 550

338. To John Paston II, 1470, 23 January 551

339. To John Paston II, 1470, 1 March 554

340. To John Paston II, 1470, 14 May 556

341. To John Paston II, 1470, 25 May 558

342. To John Paston II, 1470, 22 June 559

343. To John Paston II, 1470, 25 June 561

344. Declaration concerning the Fastolf estate, 1470, 27 August ... 562

345. To Margaret Paston, 1470, 12 October 563

346. To Margaret Paston, 1471, 30 April 565

347. To Margaret Paston, 1471, 5 July 566

348. To Margaret Paston, 1471, 22 July 567

349. To Margaret Paston, 1471, 28 October 568

350. To John Paston II, 1471 569

351. Verses, probably after 1471 571

352. To John Paston II, 1472, 5 June 573

353. To John Paston II, 1472, 8 July 575

354. To John Paston II, 1472, 21 September 577

354A. Letter in the name of James Arblaster to the Bailiff of Maldon,
      1472, 20 September 580

355. To John Paston II, 1472, 16 October 581

356. To John Paston II, 1472, 24 November 583

357. To John Paston II, 1472, late November 584

358. To John Paston II, 1472, 18 December 585

359. To the Duke of Norfolk, 1472, late 587

360. To John Paston II, 1473, 8 March 588

361. To John Paston II, 1473, 26 March 589

362. To 'Mistress Annes', 1474, 22 July 590

363. To John Paston II, 1474, 25 July 591

364. To Margaret Paston, probably 1475, 29 March 593

365. To John Paston II, 1475, 10 October 594

366. To John Paston II, 1475, 23 October 595

367. To Margaret Paston, 1476, 21 January 596

CONTENTS

WALTER PASTON

402. To Margaret Paston, before 1479, 19 May   644
403. To John Paston II, 1479, 22 May   645
404. To John Paston III, 1479, 30 June   646
405. Copy of will, nominally 1479, 18 August   647

WILLIAM PASTON III

406. To John Paston III, probably 1478, 7 November   649
407. To John Paston III, probably 1479, 23 February   650
408. To Edmond Paston II, after 1480, 22 February   651
409. To John Paston III, 1487, 7 March   652
410. To the Bailiff of Mautby, 1487   654
411. To John Paston III, 1488, 13 May   655
412. To John Paston III, 1489, April   656
413. To John Paston III, 1489, between 6 and 10 May   658
414. To John Paston III, 1492, 18 February   660

MARGERY PASTON

415. To John Paston III, 1477, February   662
416. To John Paston III, 1477, February   663
417. To John Paston III, perhaps 1481, 1 November   664
418. To John Paston III, perhaps 1481, 4 November   665
419. To John Paston III, 1486, 21 January   666
420. To John Paston III, 1489, 10 February   667

WILLIAM PASTON IV

421. To John Paston III, perhaps about 1495   670

LIST OF ILLUSTRATIONS

British Museum MS. Additional 34888, f. 18.
  Letter no. 128, written for Margaret Paston, 1448   *Frontispiece*

Map of part of Norfolk and Suffolk   *p. 671*

PLATES (*at end*)

 I. B.M. MS. Add. 27443, f. 80
    Letter no. 4, hand of William Paston I, 1426

 II. B.M. MS. Add. 43488, f. 4
    Letter no. 13, written for Agnes Paston, probably 1440

 III. B.M. MS. Add. 34889, f. 9^v
    Letter no. 73, hand of John Paston I, 1465

 IV. B.M. MS. Add. 33597, f. 5
    Letter no. 85, hand of William Paston II, probably 1458

 V. B.M. MS. Add. 34888, f. 191
    Letter no. 116, hand of Clement Paston II, 1461

 VI. B.M. MS. Add. 27445, f. 83
    Letter no. 286, hand of John Paston II, 1474

 VII. B.M. MS. Add. 43491, f. 26
    Inventory, no. 316, hand of John Paston II

 VIII. B.M. MS. Add. 43491, f. 11
    Letter no. 330, hand of John Paston III, 1468

 IX. B.M. MS. Add. 34888, f. 22
    Letter no. 395, hand of Edmond Paston II, probably 1472

 X. B.M. MS. Add. 27446, f. 12
    Letter no. 402, hand of Walter Paston, before 1479

 XI. B.M. MS. Add. 43489, f. 25
    Letter no. 407, hand of William Paston III, probably 1479

 XII. B.M. MS. Add. 27446, f. 52
    Letter no. 418, written for Margery Paston, with autograph subscription, perhaps 1481

INTRODUCTION

It is almost a hundred years since James Gairdner began to publish his edition of fifteenth-century letters and related documents concerned with the Norfolk family of Paston. These are not quite the earliest private letters known in English, but they are far more numerous and more varied in interest than any of the other fifteenth-century series.[1] Gairdner added a large number of papers to those printed by John Fenn when he first edited a selection towards the end of the eighteenth century. Since Gairdner finished his last edition in 1904 important manuscripts not accessible to him have come into the keeping of the British Museum, so that texts which Fenn had printed incompletely or inaccurately can now be corrected (e.g. nos. 88, 136, 245, 351 below). All texts in the present edition rest on completely new transcripts repeatedly collated. They include full texts of some letters and other documents which Gairdner omitted or gave in abstract: of the letters the most important are Margaret Paston's of May 1448 (no. 129), the two at Belvoir Castle (nos. 108–9), and the group in B.M. MS. Add. 45099 (see no. 10); of the other papers those in Magdalen College, Oxford (nos. 67, 252–4, 260, 262, 344), and in the Central Library, Norwich (no. 82). The handwriting of the manuscripts has been specially noticed.

Neither Fenn nor Gairdner was more than superficially interested in these letters as specimens of the English language at an important stage in its history—for the study of which they are scarcely less valuable than they are for the wider field of social history. Records of this kind, written without thought of publication mostly by identifiable persons of whose circumstances something is known, and usually capable of being fairly closely dated and localized, offer evidence more precise than that of most manuscripts of literary works of similar age; and the period of their writing, not long before and immediately after the introduction of printing into England, was of great consequence in the development of the language. The precision of the evidence they give depends in part on recognizing the handwriting of authors and their clerks, for plainly an author's use of language can be seen in an autograph manuscript as it cannot in one written from dictation,

---

[1] Their nearest rival is the Stonor collection, which contains nearly 400 documents, the first one in English of 1420: *The Stonor Letters and Papers 1290–1483*, ed. C. L. Kingsford (Camden Soc., 2 vols., 1919), and 'Supplementary Stonor Letters and Papers' in *Camden Miscellany*, xiii (1924).

or under instruction, by a secretary. The earlier editors did not as a rule say whether letters were autograph or not. Many readers have been misled into assuming that they normally were, and have drawn unjustified conclusions about the state of the language.[1] Identification of handwriting can be important in matters other than linguistic. For example, a letter tentatively dated by both Fenn and Gairdner in 1484, and attributed to Margery Paston, the wife of John Paston III, is partly in the hand of John Daubeney. He was killed in 1469; and this is one of a number of reasons for placing the letter a generation earlier and assigning it to Margery's mother-in-law, Margaret Paston.[2] Again, the eight stanzas headed by both editors 'Verses written by a Lady . . . to an absent Lord with whom she was in love' take on a different aspect when they are observed to be in the handwriting of John Paston III, with running corrections which show them to be an original composition, not a copy.[3] Not all clerks can be named: some wrote only one or two letters, others a considerable number for their employers but none in their own names. Even the negative knowledge that a letter is not autograph is important, but it is obviously more interesting to find out who a clerk was, and it is often possible to do so from letters written on his own account.

My first endeavour in this edition is to present the texts of all the family documents in English completely and accurately, while making reading easier by introducing punctuation and modernizing the use of capital letters. Documents in Latin are printed only when that is the most effective way of presenting essential information which they contain. Since a great part of this material has the special value of displaying the writings of a single family over three generations, I have emphasized this aspect of it by dividing the main body of papers into two parts. The first contains the letters written by or on behalf of the members of the Paston family themselves, including their wives Agnes, Margaret, and Margery. A number of legal and similar papers—leases, inventories, wills—are also included though they cannot have been composed by the persons concerned, because it seems most convenient to have them near other documents to which they are relevant. Each person's letters and papers are brought together, arranged chronologically as far as dates are determinable, to exhibit his or her characteristic language, style, and interests as a whole. The second part contains letters written to the Pastons by correspondents other than members of the family, and in addition some related documents which do not fall strictly within this definition but give relevant information.

This arrangement has the obvious drawback of breaking up the general chronological sequence of the papers; I have tried to mitigate this as far as

---

[1] Some examples are given in N. Davis, 'The Text of Margaret Paston's Letters', *Medium Ævum*, xviii (1949), 12–28. See also 'The Language of the Pastons', *Proceedings of the British Academy*, xl (1955), 119–44.   [2] See no. 153.   [3] No. 351.

possible by cross-reference. The advantage of setting out each author's surviving writings together seems to me to justify this order; and it also enables Part I, the family letters which are generally more important than the rest, to be brought out as a first instalment.

Parts I and II have the limited aim of presenting the texts, with head-notes specifying each manuscript, identifying its handwriting if this can be done, dating it as closely as possible, and briefly giving the evidence for the date assigned. A third part will contain notes on persons and events, some discussion of the language, the text of some associated papers which are outside the classes covered in Parts I and II, a glossary, and indexes.

'THE PASTON LETTERS': MANUSCRIPTS AND EDITIONS

This title, by which the celebrated collection has long been known, is first recorded in the letters of Horace Walpole. Writing on 7 May 1784 to John Fenn, of East Dereham in Norfolk—with whom he had exchanged occasional letters on antiquarian subjects since 1774—Walpole said

> I have brought you back yʳ MSS myself, for I was afraid of keeping them they are so valuable, especially the Paston Letters, which are the most curious papers of the sort I ever saw, & the oldest original letters I beleive extant in this Country. The historic picture they give of the reign of Hen. 6. makes them invaluable, & more satisfactory than any cold narrative. It were a thousand pities they shoud not be published, which I shoud be glad I coud persuade you to do.[1]

The first mention of the collection, without any name, appears to be in another letter from Walpole to Fenn two years earlier, dated 15 May 1782:

> I was extremely pleased with the letter of William of Worcester. . . . It is very curious—indeed I did not know that there was so much as a *private* letter extant of that very turbulent period. This gives me, Sir, a high idea of your treasure. . . . If you could select any new curious facts, Sir, relating to that period . . . you would much oblige literary virtuosos, especially were you to print the letters themselves, or the interesting extracts.[2]

Thus encouraged by Walpole, and by others whom he thanked in his preface, Fenn brought out a selection of the letters in two quarto volumes (dedicated, by permission, to the King), containing 155 letters, related documents, or extracts, and many illustrations of signatures, seals, and watermarks, on 1 February 1787.[3] (He transcribed the texts exactly, adding punctuation, on his left-hand pages, and gave a modernized version on the facing pages.) He did not mention the Pastons in his title, which was *Original Letters, Written during the Reigns of Henry VI. Edward IV. and Richard III. By various Persons of Rank or Consequence*; but from the fact that Hannah More wrote to her sister as early as 31 March of the same year, 'Well, I have got the "Paston Letters" '[4] it appears that the short title was already current. Fenn's first edition sold out in a week, and he issued a second, incorporating some notes and corrections by George Steevens, 'the

---

[1] Original in a volume of letters collected by Fenn, now in the Colman Library, Norwich; published by R. W. Ketton-Cremer in 'Some New Letters of Horace Walpole', *T.L.S.*, 15 March 1957, p. 164.

[2] *Yale Edition of Horace Walpole's Correspondence*, ed. W. S. Lewis, xvi (1952), 243.

[3] Advertisement in *The Morning Chronicle* of that day. (The price was £1. 16s.)

[4] *Memoirs of the Life and Correspondence of Mrs. Hannah More*, ed. W. Roberts (3rd edn., 1835), ii. 50.

learned and ingenious Editor of Shakespeare', in the same year.[1] He added
two more volumes, containing another 220 letters and further illustrations,
in 1789. Fenn died in 1794, in his fifty-fifth year; but he had left the text
of a fifth volume, containing another 110 letters, almost ready for publication, and this was brought out by his nephew, William Frere, Master of
Downing College, in 1823. Fenn had thus edited in all 485 documents,
though a considerable number of them he had abridged.

All these papers were Fenn's own property. He gave a brief account of
their descent, stating that they had been carefully preserved in the Paston
family and were finally in the possession of the Earl of Yarmouth—that is,
William Paston, the second earl, who died aged 78 in 1732, without surviving male issue so that all his honours became extinct.[2] 'They then became
the property of that great collector and antiquary Peter le Neve, esquire,
Norroy; from him they devolved to Mr. Martin, by his marriage with Mrs.
le Neve, and were a part of his collections purchased by Mr. Worth, from
whom in 1774 they came to the editor.' John Worth was a chemist of Diss
in Norfolk, who had bought the documents as a speculation but died 'before
he had completed the sale of his collections'.[3] But, as Gairdner later observed in the preface to his new edition of 1872, the history of the manuscripts was less simple than this. Peter Le Neve died in 1729, three years
before the Earl of Yarmouth. The Earl must have sold him some of his
family papers, presumably when he fell into financial difficulties in the
latter part of his life—as early as 1708 he was described as 'as low as you
can imagin; he hath vast debts, and suffers every thing to run to extremity'.[4]
But he did not sell all of them; for his house at Oxnead—which had been
a family residence since the first William Paston bought it about 1420,
though Clement Paston (1515?–97) had built a fine new house—still contained a great number of documents when he died. The Revd. Francis
Blomefield, then preparing his *Essay towards a Topographical History of the
County of Norfolk*, was given access to the evidence-room at Oxnead and
'spent almost a fortnight among the old writings'. A letter he wrote to Major
Weldon, apparently one of the Earl's executors, on 13 May 1735 shows
something of the extent of the records and Blomefield's attitude to them:

[1] Steevens's intervention was sometimes unfortunate. For instance, Fenn in a letter
from James Gresham to John Paston I, now MS. Add. 43491, f. 2 (his edn., i. 114; G.
257/303; this edn., Part II, no. 534), printed in his first edition the words 'ryfled his houses',
but in the second changed *houses* to *huches*, with a footnote, 'Huche, French, a Coffer, or
Chest standing upon legs'. Gairdner, who could not consult the manuscript, followed the
second edition, and *O.E.D.* quotes the passage accordingly. A note by Steevens now in
MS. Add. 27452, f. 321ᵛ shows that the emendation and explanation were his; but Gresham
plainly wrote *houses*.
[2] *Complete Peerage*, under *Yarmouth*.
[3] *Original Letters*, i. xix–xx. For Le Neve (usually so spelt) and Martin ('Honest Tom
Martin of Palgrave') see *D.N.B.*
[4] Humphrey Prideaux, cited in *Complete Peerage*, xii, Part 2, 892.

There are ten boxes of court-rolls, surveys, extent-books, deeds and other things material to the several manors. . . . There are three trunks and chests full of the ancient and present title-deeds to the manors and estates, all which I carefully put together. There are two boxes of old leases only, which I laid by, not knowing but they might be of some service. . . . There is another box full of the pardons, grants, and old deeds, freedoms, &c. belonging to the Paston family only, which I laid by themselves, for fear you should think them proper to be preserved with the family: they don't relate to any estates. . . . There are innumerable letters, of good consequence in history, still lying among the loose papers, all which I laid up in a corner of the room on a heap, which contains several sacks full; but as they seemed to have some family affairs of one nature or other intermixed in them, I did not offer to touch any of them, but have left them to your consideration, whether, when I go to that part of the country, I shall separate and preserve them, or whether you will have them burnt, though I must own 'tis pity they should; except it be those (of which there are many) that relate to nothing but family affairs only. I have placed everything so that now the good and bad are distinguished and preserved from the weather, by which a great number have perished entirely. I shall be ready to return those things that I have, when you please to command me.[1]

It is usually assumed, with good reason, that the 'innumerable letters' included those contained in these volumes, which Blomefield must have been permitted to remove on terms which are not recorded. There is no doubt that many of these manuscripts were in his collection, for he has left signs of his ownership on them; some have brief notes in his hand (not always accurate) on persons, dates, or handwriting, a larger number only his initials and a small mark in the form of a circle or a square with a cross in it. Similar records of his possession appear on some of the manuscripts of the much later family letters, notably those of Lady (Katherine) Paston,[2] as well as on a number of Fastolf papers formerly in the Phillipps collection and now in the British Museum, and others in the Bodleian and the Pierpont Morgan Library. Blomefield declared his intention of uniting his collection with Le Neve's, which was then in the possession of 'that judicious antiquary, Mr. Thomas Martin, who not only supplies me with whatever occurs in his own large and valuable Collection of Antiquities, but also with the whole Collections of that late industrious and perfect antiquary, Peter le Neve, Norroy';[3] but the plan came to nothing because he died in debt in 1752 and his possessions were sold by his creditors. Some of the manuscripts went to Martin; some to the younger antiquary John Ives, who also acquired certain of Le Neve's and Martin's manuscripts.[4]

[1] S.W. Rix,'Cursory Notices of the Rev. Francis Blomefield', *Norfolk Archaeology*, ii (1849), 201–24, esp. 210–11. Rix modernized Blomefield's spelling. His autograph copy survives in his Entry Book, now MS. Walter Rye 32 in the Norwich Central Library, pp. 33–4.
[2] *The Correspondence of Lady Katherine Paston, 1603–1627*, ed. Ruth Hughey (Norfolk Record Soc. xiv, 1941). See further below p. xxxii. [3] *History of Norfolk*, I. xv.
[4] See *D.N.B.* One such manuscript is MS. Walter Rye 38, which bears inscriptions in

Martin's library was sold after his death in 1771 to John Worth, as Fenn's account given above reports. Ives's was sold in March 1777. Part of it was bought by Richard Gough, part came into Francis Douce's collection and so to the Bodleian. The precise fortunes of particular papers are sometimes obscure; but certainly many of the letters that Fenn bought from Worth had been in Blomefield's hands.

Fenn's collection included only a part of the Paston letters and papers now known, and he printed from it only a selection of the earliest documents. This was a reasonable procedure, because the letters of the fifteenth century present a fairly continuous record of the correspondence of three generations of the family, whereas after the beginning of the sixteenth there is a break in the series and only scattered letters survive until about a century later. The importance of his edition led readers to think of 'the Paston Letters' as a collection of fifteenth-century documents, and the usage has become so settled that an attempt to alter it now would be more confusing than profitable. It is nevertheless worth remembering that many later letters concerned with the family survive.[1]

Fenn's edition brought together—though in an inconvenient order because of its publication in successive selections—a comparatively coherent assemblage of the great majority of the earliest and most interesting of the letters. The later fate of the manuscripts on which it was based is therefore of special importance.

His first two volumes aroused keen attention in literary circles. It appears that, no doubt partly because Chatterton's 'Rowley' poems were fresh in memory, questions were raised about their authenticity. Fenn deposited the manuscripts of the letters in these volumes for a time in the library of the Society of Antiquaries, 'for the general inspection and examination of the Members of that, and of the Royal Society'.[2] In the Preface to his third volume, issued two years later, he said: 'During their continuance in that repository, it was intimated to the Editor that THE KING had an inclination to inspect and examine them; they were immediately sent to the Queen's Palace, with an humble request from the Editor, that, if they should be thought worthy a place in the Royal Collection, HIS MAJESTY would be pleased to accept them; to this request a most gracious answer was returned, and they are now in the Royal Library.'[3] The answer was indeed gracious: Fenn was summoned to the levee at St. James's on 23 May 1787, 'had the honour of presenting to his Majesty (bound in three volumes) the

Blomefield's and Ives's hands: see N. Davis and G. S. Ivy, 'MS. Walter Rye 38 and its French Grammar', *Medium Ævum*, xxxi (1962), 110–24.

[1] In addition to those now in the British Museum (see p. xxviii below), over three hundred letters of the period 1630–79 are in the collection of the late H. L. Bradfer-Lawrence of Ripon, transferred to the custody of the Norfolk and Norwich Record Office in 1967.

[2] *Original Letters*, 2nd edn. (1787), i. xxxiv.

[3] *Original Letters*, III (1789), Preface, p. xvi.

original Letters, of which he had before presented a printed copy', and was forthwith knighted.[1] When Frere published the fifth volume of the *Letters* he wrote, 'The originals of the fifth volume I have not been able to find. Some originals I have, which appear not to have been intended by Sir John Fenn for publication. The originals of the former volumes were presented to the late King, and were deposited in His Majesty's Library.'[2] This last sentence is inaccurate, for it was only the originals of Fenn's first and second volumes, not his third and fourth, that were presented to George III; but the important point is that Frere, though he had 'some originals', had not seen the manuscripts of any of Fenn's five volumes and did not in fact know where they were. They returned to public view in a strange piecemeal way.

In 1865 Philip Frere, son of William Frere, found the manuscripts of the fifth volume, together with some which Fenn had not printed and other letters of the sixteenth and seventeenth centuries, in his house at Dungate in Cambridgeshire. This large collection he sold to the British Museum on 13 October 1866; the fifteenth-century letters and papers are in Additional MSS. 27443–6 and 27450–1, the later letters in MSS. 27447–8. (MSS. 27452–5 contain Fenn's notes and other working material.) It was this discovery that set James Gairdner to work on a new edition of the Letters, 'to be arranged in true chronological order, and augmented by those hitherto unedited'.[3] He suspected that other manuscripts might also be recovered, and asked George Frere, then the head of the Frere family, whether they might be at his house, Roydon Hall near Diss. He tells with much feeling how Frere replied that nothing was known of them, how he eventually went on with his edition, and how after he had sent the third volume to press Frere sent a message that a number of letters had come to light. These turned out to be the originals of Fenn's third and fourth volumes, together with ninety-five others of similar date; and Gairdner added an appendix to his third volume giving a summary account of them. His three-volume edition, which was published from 1872 to 1875, was entitled *The Paston Letters 1422–1509 A.D.* These Roydon Hall manuscripts were sold at Christie's in 1888, and resold by the purchaser to the British Museum in June 1896; they now form Additional MSS. 34888–9. Yet another group of later letters was found at Roydon Hall at the same time, and also sold; it was purchased by the Museum in 1904, and is now Additional MS. 36988. The manuscripts of three of Fenn's five volumes had thus been brought together again, and much new material with them. But the manuscripts of his first two volumes had long been lost

---

[1] *Morning Chronicle*, 24 May 1787. [2] Pp. vii–viii.
[3] The only other edition had been a selection from the modernized texts in Fenn's first four volumes (the fifth being still in copyright) made by A. Ramsay and published in 1840–1. Ramsay retained Fenn's title, but prefixed to it 'Paston Letters'.

sight of. They were supposed to be, as Fenn and William Frere had said, in the Royal Library; but when that was presented by George IV to the British Museum in 1823 they were not there, nor could they be found in any of the royal palaces. They eventually reappeared in 1889, at Orwell Park in Suffolk, after the death on 25 August of Colonel George Tomline, grandson of Pitt's tutor and secretary Dr. George Pretyman, who became Bishop of Lincoln in 1787 and of Winchester in 1820, and took the name of Tomline, in consequence of a legacy, in 1803. An editorial comment in *The Athenæum* sums up contemporary opinion:

> The long-lost original MSS. presented by Fenn to George III have turned up at last. We know on the authority of Fenn himself that they were presented in 1787; and in the preface to his third volume, dated 'St. George's Day, 1789', he says 'They are now in the Royal Library'. But from that day forward, with the exception of a vague tradition that they were once seen by somebody in the hands of one of the ladies of the court, no one seems to have known what became of them; nothing whatever, in short, was known about them beyond the simple fact that they were no longer in the Royal Library, until, shortly after the death of the late Col. George Tomline, they were found in his library at Orwell Park. Fenn's introduction to the king, to whom, on the recommendation of Mr. Pitt, the volumes were permitted to be dedicated, was brought about by the intervention of his friend Dr. Pretyman, at that time Pitt's private secretary (afterwards better known as *Tomline*, Bishop of Lincoln, and subsequently of Winchester); and it is a singular coincidence that the MSS. in question should have come to light just one hundred years later in the possession of one of the bishop's grandsons.[1]

At any rate, the manuscripts were now known to exist, but they were not open to public inspection; and when Gairdner produced a new edition in 1901, with a fourth volume including the new material from Roydon Hall, he could not collate the texts and simply reprinted again Fenn's texts of 1787. In 1931 the Orwell Park manuscripts were the subject of court proceedings in the Chancery Division. The Right Honourable E. G. Pretyman asked the court to decide whether the manuscripts bequeathed by Colonel Tomline 'were included in the chattels settled by the will to devolve as heirlooms, or formed part of his residuary personal estate', and he asked that if they were included in the heirlooms he might be authorized to sell them. The court sanctioned the sale on condition that a minimum price (not made public) was reached, and the manuscripts, in their original binding, were offered at auction by Sotheby's on 1 April of the same year.[2] But the highest bid was insufficient: *The Times Literary Supplement* of the following week reported that 'their fate still hangs in the balance, for the £5,800 at which they were knocked down does not seem to have reached the

---

[1] 29 March 1890, p. 405.
[2] *The Times Law Report*, 30 January 1931; Sotheby and Co.'s *Catalogue*.

undisclosed sum at which Mr. Justice Maugham sanctioned a sale'.[1] In the event they were bought in at £6,500. Two years later they were offered to the British Museum through the Friends of the National Libraries for £3,000, and eventually bought.[2] They are now Additional MSS. 43488–91. In 1947–8 they were taken out of their eighteenth-century binding (but left in the mounts in which Fenn had had them set), partly rearranged, and newly bound with an index of writers, hands, and dates.

By this purchase the manuscripts Fenn had published were at last re-united—except for one letter in the third volume (early, but not particularly important) which somehow found its way to Holland House. Its presence there was recorded, without comment, by Princess Marie Liechtenstein in 1874.[3] The person most likely to have taken it there is John Hookham Frere (1769–1846), brother of William Frere who edited Fenn's fifth volume and eldest son of John Frere of Roydon Hall, Fenn's brother-in-law and inheritor of his library.[4] Hookham Frere often visited Holland House. The single Paston letter was removed to Melbury early in the Second World War (in which Holland House was destroyed) by the sixth Earl of Ilchester (d. 1959), who kindly showed it to me in London in March 1959. It was sold with other Ilchester papers at Sotheby's in February 1964, and was bought for £580 by the British Museum, where it is now Additional MS. 54210.[5]

Apart from the letters which can be traced back to Fenn, the British Museum possesses a number of minor groups. The most important of these is a set of about sixty letters and documents relating to Sir John Fastolf, formerly MS. Phillipps 9735 and earlier in the hands of Blomefield, Ives, and others; it was bought at Sotheby's in June 1919, and is now Additional MSS. 39848–9. Smaller numbers are in Additional MSS. 28212, 33597, and 35251, and there are numerous single deeds and similar papers especially in the series Additional Charters 17217–62 (acquired in 1866)—the most important perhaps the copy of Margaret Paston's will, no. 17253 (no. 230 below). An unusual item is a set of copies of six letters and an indenture all relating to the manor of East Beckham, evidently drawn up for John Paston III.[6] This was presented to the Museum in 1937 by the late R. W. Ketton-Cremer, to whose great-uncle R. W. Ketton, of Felbrigg Hall, it had belonged in the nineteenth century. After the death of the second Earl of Yarmouth, East Beckham passed to the Windhams of Felbrigg about 1740,

---

[1] *T.L.S.*, 9 April 1931, p. 292.

[2] *T.L.S.*, 3 August 1933, p. 525; *Friends of the National Libraries Annual Report 1933–4*, pp. 17–22.

[3] *Holland House*, ii. 198.

[4] On 31 July 1888 Sotheby's sold the Anthony Norris manuscript collections formed by Sir John Fenn, formerly the property of John Hookham Frere.

[5] Fenn, iii, p. 28; Gairdner, 1901 edn., no. 38; 1904, no. 52; this edn., Part II, no. 425.

[6] See no. 10 below.

and the manuscript must have been transferred there.[1] It is Additional MS. 45099.

In Oxford, the principal manuscripts in the Bodleian are Douce 393 and Charters Norfolk a.8. That there may yet be isolated documents to be found is shown by the gift in 1968 by Messrs. Hofmann and Freeman of a fair copy in James Gresham's hand of a text of the inquisition *post mortem* on John Paston I.[2] Magdalen College has many important documents among its muniments, because William Wainfleet, Bishop of Winchester and founder of the college in 1458, finally assumed administration of Fastolf's estate and transferred to his college the foundation of priests and poor men that Fastolf had intended for Caister. The documents are largely concerned with the agreement of 14 July 1470 between the Bishop and John Paston II and with its consequences.[3]

In the Pierpont Morgan Library in New York there are seven letters and documents concerned with the Pastons directly, and three others on related subjects.[4] These were part of the collection made by John Thane (1748–1818), a printseller and antiquary of Soho,[5] who wrote his name on six of them, with the date 1776 except for one which has 1777, and a few notes. Five also bear notes in Blomefield's hand, and it is likely though not demonstrable that they came to Thane through Martin, somehow escaping inclusion in the papers acquired by Worth which Fenn later bought. How the Thane collection came into the Pierpont Morgan Library is not known.

A small group of letters is contained in a volume given to Pembroke College, Cambridge, by the Revd. Charles Parkin, who completed Blomefield's *History* after his death, and himself died in 1765.[6] These again depend on Blomefield; but the two letters from William Paston II to Richard Roos, now at Belvoir Castle,[7] have no doubt been in the family archives without interruption, since the Roos family were among the ancestors of the Dukes of Rutland. These two letters were not printed by Fenn or Gairdner.

Historical and antiquarian interest in the letters has been keen, if intermittent, since the early eighteenth century; but this was not the beginning of it. A surprising feature of many of them, and of associated documents, is that they bear notes, usually endorsed, in a hand of the sixteenth century. It is a small, neat, practised hand; some of the notes are in Latin, most in English. They often simply identify the persons concerned in the document, as a cataloguer might do. For example, Margaret Paston's letter no.

---

[1] So the Museum *Catalogue of Additional Manuscripts acquired in the Year 1937*.

[2] Now Bodl. MS. Don. 3.93.

[3] See no. 252 below, and *H.M.C. Fourth Report* (1874), p. 458.

[4] See C. F. Bühler, 'Some New Paston Documents', *R.E.S.* xiv (1938), 1–14; and no. 396 below.

[5] See *D.N.B.*   [6] *H.M.C. Fifth Report* (1877), Appendix, p. 484; no. 235 below.

[7] Nos. 108, 109 below.

208 is endorsed, 'A lettre to Sʳ J. Paston from his mother'; her no. 227, 'Copia litere Jo. Paston mil. a matre sua'; John Paston II's no. 248 has under its autograph address *To John Paston, esquiere* . . . the note 'From his brother Sʳ John Paston knight'. But sometimes they summarize or comment on the principal contents: so on Agnes Paston's no. 25, 'It appereth by this lettre that Sʳ Jo. Fastolf was of kynred to John Paston ar.'; on Margaret's no. 128, 'Relief demaunded by the Lady Morley for the mannour of Sparham'; on her no. 129, 'Mergeret Paston certifieth her husbond of the falling out of Wyndam with her servaunt Ja. Gloys, and of his slanderous wordes vsed against her mother in lawe & her'; no. 151, 'It appere[th] by this lettre yᵗ Justice Paston had a sonne named Henry who dyed yonge'; no. 187, 'A lettre shewing yᵗ the Duke of Suffolk raised a nomber of people to remove Sʳ John Paston from the possession of Heylesdon & Drayton'; no. 201, 'The L. Scales is now frind to Sʳ J. Paston'; on John III's no. 383, 'A lettre sent from Jo. Paston ar. to his mother touchyng the Buryall of his Brother Sʳ John Paston at London'; on Elisabeth Clere's no. 446, 'A lettre from E. Clere concernyng a mariage betwen Scroop & Eliz. Paston, which neuer toke effect'; on William Jenney's no. 581, 'A frindly lettre of W. Jenney who after became a mortall Enemye'. The same hand endorses papers now separated from the main collection of letters, such as Agnes Paston's deed no. 16, some of the Pierpont Morgan documents, and the record of evidence given in the inquiry into Fastolf's will which is now Bodleian MS. Top. Norfolk c.4, so that when the notes were written the manuscripts must still have been together. But the examples given above are enough to show that the annotator was not simply arranging or listing the documents, but was interested in many particulars of the history of the family. His motive would seem to have been essentially antiquarian, for most of the details he noted are not of a kind that would be of practical use, as for example in a claim to land or other legal affairs. A search of the volumes containing sixteenth-century family papers, MSS. Add. 27447, 33597, and 36988, has yielded no letters written in this hand, which might have given evidence of the identity of the writer. A few endorsements on letters of the third quarter of the century appear to be by this same hand—perhaps not unchallengeably, because it is of a common type and lacks strikingly individual features, but very probably. The latest such entry associated with a firm date is in MS. 36988, f. 11, 'A lettre reporting a bill exhibited into the Starre Chamber by Sʳ Tho. Woodhows against Mʳ John & Clement Paston supposing a Ryott to be comytted by them at Flodgates 1570'. The writer was therefore at work later than this. John Paston IV, the third son of William Paston IV,[1] died in 1575; Clement, the fourth son—a distinguished sailor and soldier, who inherited and rebuilt Oxnead—in 1597. There is no positive evidence to show whether

[1] Blomefield, vi. 487.

the endorsement was made during the lifetime of either; but the writing is not likely to be later than the end of the century, and the anonymous annotator may well have been a member of Clement Paston's household at Oxnead.

Gairdner's three-volume edition of 1872–5 was the first since Fenn's to introduce new material or to be based on manuscripts. Gairdner was unfortunate in being overtaken by rediscoveries twice in the course of his work. He was able to take the texts of Fenn's fifth volume from the Dungate manuscripts, but they had evidently not been foliated when he worked on them and he assigned each letter only to 'Paston MSS., B.M.'. For the letters in Fenn's third and fourth volumes he had transcribed Fenn's texts before the Roydon Hall manuscripts came to light, and printed them with page references to Fenn's edition. A 'new edition' of the three-volume work was issued in 1896. When the manuscripts became available Gairdner collated some of them, and concluded, justly enough, that Fenn's transcripts were on the whole remarkably accurate, though he had omitted parts of some letters and altered the order of others. Gairdner judged that the labour of making new texts of these letters would not be worth while; but he did transcribe an additional 105 letters, mainly from the Roydon Hall manuscripts but a few from others, and these he printed as a Supplement (with separate roman numbering) in the fourth volume of a new edition in 1901. For these supplementary letters he gave precise folio references where they existed. In 1904 he issued a 'new and complete Library edition', the text entirely reset in six volumes, limited to 650 copies. The letters previously in the Supplement were now brought into their places in the general order and numbered accordingly; but even for this edition he did no more work on the manuscripts: 'Notwithstanding the recovery of the originals of the letters printed by Fenn, it has not been thought necessary to edit these anew from the MSS. . . . The letters are here reproduced as they were printed in previous editions, only in a better order. Fenn's text has been followed, where no corrections have been found, in all the letters printed by him except those of his fifth volume.'[1] Thus in 1904, in the edition which has remained 'standard', the texts of the letters in four out of Fenn's five volumes, a total of 375, were presented almost exactly as he had printed them in 1787 and 1789.

Since then there have been numerous more or less popular reprints of selections, but none of them has any independent textual value. No new edition based on the manuscripts appeared until the selection published in the Clarendon Medieval and Tudor Series in 1958.

Form of the manuscripts

Many of the legal documents are on parchment, but all the letters are on paper, in a great variety of sizes. A full sheet measured about 17 by 11½

---

[1] 1904 edn., i. 11, 19.

inches, but not many writers needed as much space as this. The usual practice was to write across the shorter side, and when the letter was finished to cut off the rest of the sheet. Since many letters would not be long enough to reach as far as halfway down the sheet, this would leave a rectangle with the lines of writing parallel to the longer side. This is a very common shape, which must evidently have been generalized from letters begun on a new sheet and cut off short to those written on parts of sheets left over. Especially in the earlier years of the collection paper was often used very economically: William Paston I kept old drafts to use as scribbling paper, and even wrote notes upside down between the lines (no. 7); Margaret let her secretary use a part of a sheet with a quarter cut out, and explained that 'paper is deynty' (no. 142). Sometimes the text of a letter, or a postscript, ran over on to the verso. If the letter was actually to be sent, and not merely a draft or copy, it was folded to form a small packet and secured by stitching with string or by passing narrow paper tape through slits and sealing the ends with wax, sometimes covered by a paper wafer; and the address was normally written on the outside. If a letter has been sent the folds are well marked and the parts that have been outside are soiled by carrying. Such a letter nearly always bears traces of a seal, and usually an address as well; and even if an address is omitted—as it occasionally is—the marks of folding, stitch-holes or tape-slits, and remnants of wax are sufficient evidence that it was a missive and not a file copy. Plate III shows the verso of John Paston I's letter no. 73: it contains a substantial part of the text, in his own hand without a signature; the address also in his hand, on a soiled section of the paper; remains of the sealing wax, with a space in it where the tape was, and slits both there and in the corresponding position on the other side of the sheet; and notes by Fenn.

In setting out the letters the writers naturally differed greatly in their habits, and the same writer varied at different times according to circumstance or mood. Some divided their longer letters up into paragraphs, occasionally with marks of the conventional kind in the margin; but most wrote them continuously, and often without punctuation and without consistent use of capital letters to begin sentences. Sometimes a new topic was introduced by 'Item', but by no means regularly. Corrections were often made not only in drafts but also in final copies: letters or words to be deleted were usually simply struck out—sub-punctuation was scarcely ever used—but occasionally more completely obliterated by overwriting a succession of repeated letters, most often h; words to be substituted or inserted were written above the line, or in the margin, usually but by no means always with a caret at the appropriate point. When punctuation was used at all it was most commonly a single oblique stroke, occasionally a double stroke at more important divisions; but individual scribes sometimes used points, and very occasionally more developed forms resembling a *punctus elevatus.* A formal letter from a nobleman was usually headed, by the secretary, with his title. Familiar letters, or ordinary business letters, opened directly with the 'salutation', without naming the person addressed either at the head or the foot. The date was not put at the head of the page, but incorporated in the final sentence; and the salutation was not written on a separate line but formed part of the opening sentence. On the other hand the signature, whether autograph or in a clerk's hand, and often also the introductory words of the subscription, were normally written separately at the end, sometimes spaced over two or even more lines. Nearly all letters were dated to some extent, though some gave no more than the day of the week, perhaps specified sufficiently for the person addressed but not very helpful today: e.g. John Paston III's no. 358, 'Wretyn at Framly[n]gham the Fryday next aftyr þat I depertyd fro yow.' A few writers gave the day of the month, but by far the commonest method of dating was reference to the nearest important saint's day or other church feast. (This is usually clear enough provided that the year can be discovered from the content of the letter; but one or two saints' days are ambiguous—see the headnote to Margaret Paston's no. 125.) Few writers troubled to record the year in dating their letters; but some did—nearly always the regnal year rather than the year of grace—and an interesting change can be seen in John Paston II's practice from the beginning of 1472. Up to that time he had written, in the usual way, 'wryten at London on Thursday next aftere Seynt Erkenwoldes Day', 'the Thorysdaye in Esterne Weke', 'the daye nex Holy Roode Daye', 'on Mychellmesse Euyn' (nos. 258, 261, 263, 264); but then he adopted the form 'the viij daye of Janeuer A° E. iiij xj°' (no. 266), and used it very frequently, though not exclusively, thereafter.

The forms of salutation appropriate to different correspondents, and to a less extent the forms of conclusion, were well established even at the beginning of this series of letters. They depended ultimately on the rules set out by the professional instructors in letter-writing, the *dictatores*, from the eleventh century onwards; but the rigidity of the rules had been much modified by French practice, and it was evidently from France rather than the Latin treatises that the formulas used in English derived.[1]

Handwriting

There is an obvious distinction between personal letters and legal documents, which except for preliminary drafts are usually in the hands of professional clerks, seldom identifiable. A letter may well be in the hand of the person in whose name it stands; but whether or not it is cannot always be simply determined. If the subscribed name is in a hand other than that

---

[1] For references see N. Davis, 'The *Litera Troili* and English Letters', *R.E.S.*, N.S. xv (1965), 233–44.

of the body of the letter it is, of course, likely to be the author's signature. Many fifteenth-century letters, especially those of noblemen or other magnates, are of this pattern; but of ordinary private letters a large number are not. A series of letters by a single author may be written in several different hands, each having the subscribed name in the same hand as the rest of the letter, so that it does not at once appear which if any of these is the author's signature. It is evident that a clerk who took a letter from dictation, or perhaps composed it largely himself according to a general direction, would often write his employer's name in the place of the signature, not leaving it for his autograph as a modern secretary normally would. A genuine signature is usually enough to enable an author's hand to be identified. When it is not, the author's hand can sometimes be recognized if a draft written by a clerk is corrected in a different writing, for the corrector will normally be the author. The same is often true of a postscript written in a hand different from that of the letter, but it is not invariably so; some postscripts are certainly in the hand of a second clerk.

The manuscripts of the letters in these volumes vary greatly, no doubt largely because of the accidents of preservation of documents, in the evidence they give about the employment of clerks by the different authors. Of William Paston I's surviving papers all but one are drafts. They show three hands, one of which writes corrections and informal notes of such a kind that it must be his own. One complete letter (no. 4, Plate I) is carefully written in this hand. Many of John I's letters are written partly in a neat and regular professional-looking hand, then corrected and completed, and usually signed also, in a coarse and ill-formed hand which is clearly his. Only a few letters are in his own hand throughout. The majority of William II's letters, from the time when he was at Cambridge and would hardly have employed a secretary, are in a single hand, though some of the later ones are not. In this case the writing of the majority must be his. All six of Clement's letters of which the originals survive are in the same hand, strongly characteristic and certainly unprofessional, with no incongruous corrections. This must be his own. In the next generation the great majority of John II's letters are in a single hand, which also signs or initials them; and nearly all John III's in another. Both groups must be autograph. All Edmond II's letters are in one hand, and so are Walter's three, and eight of William III's— which he usefully identified by subscribing 'wyth þe hand of your brodyr'.

All these men, therefore, could write, with differing degrees of competence and elegance. The crudest hand is John I's, the most accomplished, in a rather dashingly careless but fluent way, John II's. The hand best represented is that of John III, which in addition to seventy-five of his own papers appears in three of his father's and eleven of his mother's. The variety of writing styles is conspicuous, especially perhaps between the hands of John II and John III, though they were only two years apart in age. It is worth notice that when any of the men employed clerks to write the copies of their letters that were actually sent they nearly always signed them themselves: the only clear exceptions are among William II's letters, in which nos. 93 and 111 are subscribed by the respective clerks, the former identifiable as William Ebesham.

The circumstances of the women's letters are quite different. In Agnes Paston's name there are thirteen letters and a note of 'errands to London', in addition to parts of a draft will and several indentures which one would not expect to be autograph in any case. Five of the letters and the note are in one hand, two in another, and the rest all different. Margaret Paston sent 104 letters, in an astonishing variety of hands—apparently twenty-nine in all: two each wrote about twenty letters in whole or part, two about a dozen, several four or five, many only one; and some letters are in more than one hand. The subscriptions are all in the same hands as the letters. Margery has left only six letters, the texts in four different hands. There are only two in Elizabeth's name, the hands different. Some of these hands, especially in Margaret's long series of letters, can be seen to be the same as those that appear in other letters in the collection, and a considerable number of these are by their nature manifestly autograph; so that the clerks can be named. But many still cannot, including unfortunately one important and well-represented hand that wrote the group of which the earliest is no. 128. The natural interpretation of this multiplicity of hands in one person's work surely is that the women could not write, or wrote only with difficulty, and so called on whatever literate person happened to be most readily at hand—in Margaret's letters particular hands tend to be concentrated in limited periods. Margery's small group of letters provides two significant pieces of evidence. Three of them, the texts of which are in different hands, have subscriptions 'Be yowre seruaunt (and bedewoman) Margery Paston', all in the same distinctively halting and uncontrolled hand, as of someone beginning to learn to write (nos. 417, 418, 420). These must be by Margery herself, making a rather ineffectual effort to sign her letters in her own hand as the men so often did. She certainly could not have written a whole letter reasonably legibly in a reasonable time; but she is at any rate the only one of the women of the family who can be seen to have been able to write her name—though her husband's aunt Elizabeth was expected to be able to do so (no. 388). (It is sad that the writing of the subscription was no more skilful in 1489 than it had been in 1481.) Evidence of another kind is given by her two earliest letters, the 'Valentines' of 1477 (nos. 415, 416). The former at least of these she wished to be 'not seyn of non erthely creature safe only ȝourselfe'. She would surely therefore have written it herself if she could have; but both were certainly written by a clerk of her father's. Still another indication comes in a letter from John Paston III to his mother, in the course of the negotiations for his marriage to Margery Brews. He

wished Margaret to write to Dame Elizabeth Brews in his interest, and he
provided a draft of what he thought she might most effectively say. He
suggested that before she sent this letter she should have it rewritten 'of
some other manys hand' (no. 378). If she could have written it herself this
qualification would not have been needed.

From these considerations it is legitimate to conclude that the women of
this family whose letters survive were not, or not completely, literate. Since
we have no letters by Anne Paston we cannot tell whether she was better
able to write than her grandmother, mother, and sister-in-law; but she
could presumably read, for she owned a copy of Lydgate's *Siege of Thebes*,[1]
which she would hardly have acquired if it had been unintelligible unless
read out to her. A sentence in a letter of John Paston II's which seems to
imply that Margaret also could read is in fact ambiguous: 'I praye yow
schewe ore rede to my moodre suche thyngez as ye thynke is fore here to
knowe, afftre yowre dyscression.' At this date 'show' could mean 'make
known'.[2]

It is seldom possible to know whether a letter written by a clerk was taken
down verbatim at dictation or composed more or less freely on the basis of
instructions given by the author. In a few places corrected errors are significant: e.g. 'Ser*e* and her*e*' written for 'Ser*e* Andrew', no. 141 n. 11, seems
to depend on mishearing; 'rapere w^t' for 'rape rewith', no. 220 n. 8, is more
likely to be a mistake in copying from a draft. Neither mistake, at any rate,
would be made by anyone composing as he wrote. Some of Margaret
Paston's letters to her husband have been annotated in the margin, usually
in his own hand simply drawing attention to the topics mentioned;[3] but one
or two by his clerk John Pampyng look as if they might have been dictated to
him to serve as a guide in composing a reply.[4]

It remains to consider the relation of final text to possible early draft.
Since nearly all the letters now known were preserved over the centuries
in the archives of the Paston family, those sent to members of the family are
normally actual missives; and this, of course, includes the large number
written by one member to another. The final copies of most letters sent to
persons outside the family are lost, for not everyone receiving a letter would
keep it and fewer would return it for the family records. The two Belvoir
Castle letters are a notable exception. Letters sent away are thus normally
known from 'file copies', which seem nearly always to be drafts, some very

[1] No. 352, l. 58.
[2] No. 248. This corrects the interpretation given in 'The Language of the Pastons' (see
p. xxii n. 1), p. 121. On the literacy of women cf. Caxton's *The Book of the Knight of
the Tower*, ed. M. Y. Offord (E.E.T.S., s.s. 2, 1971), p. 122: 'as for wrytyng it is no
force / yf a woman can nought of hit but as for redynge I saye that good and prouffytable
is to al wymen / For a woman that can rede may better knowe the peryls of the sowle and
her sauement / than she that can nou3t of it.'
[3] e.g. nos. 178–80.
[4] No. 192 nn. 15, 24, 49.

heavily corrected, rather than fresh copies made from the final text. The letters within the family show that by no means all letters were composed first in draft and then copied fair, for some of them, especially John I's, were sent off in a very untidy state. In only one or two cases we have both draft and fair copy, which serve to illustrate the kind of revision that might be made.[1]

For particulars of the principal writers, see the table on pp. lxxv–lxxix below.

[1] Nos. 42, 209.

THE PASTON FAMILY

This section is in three parts: a general outline of the affairs of the family during the period of these volumes; a series of brief biographical notes on each member of it separately; and a comparative table showing the principal contemporary events in public affairs, and in literature as far as the dates can be determined. There is some repetition, to avoid excessive cross-reference. References to evidence for events in the lives of individuals are given in the biographies rather than in the outline.

In the year 1674 Francis Sandford, Rouge Dragon Pursuivant, drew up 'The Genealogie of The Right Honorable Sr Robert Paston of Paston, in the County of Norfolke, Knight and Baronet, Lord Paston of Paston, and Viscount Yarmouth. Together with the Descents of those Familyes, into which the Pastons have married, and of many Illustrious Houses, which branch themselves from this Noble and Antient Family: Collected out of severall Pedegrees & Evidences of this Family, the publick Records of the Kingdome, the Registers of the Colledge of Armes, and other Monuments of Antiquity.' It is an imposing volume handsomely bound and carefully written on parchment,[1] with 260 coats of arms splendidly blazoned, made for Sir Robert Paston the year after he had become Viscount Yarmouth. It was first at Oxnead, later in the library of the Duke of Newcastle at Clumber, and is now in the Cambridge University Library.[2] In it Sandford traced the family back to one Wulstan who 'came out of France to his cosin William Earle Glanvile three years after the Conquest'. This tradition was evidently already current in the fifteenth century,[3] and it was taken seriously in the family in the sixteenth, for the second son of Sir William Paston (1528–1610, grandson of William Paston IV, for whom see p. lxiv below) was named Wolstan. It was also recorded by Charles Parkin in his continuation of Blomefield's *History of Norfolk* (vi. 480–2) as 'said by most historians'. But it cannot be supported by any existing documents, and though there are some early deeds in the names of men called 'de Paston',[4] they cannot be shown to have been ancestors of the later family. The oldest document which has some claim, from the agreement of names, to be in the true line is an indenture of 15 Edward III (1341) concerning a Clement de Paston and William his son; but it tells us nothing about their standing. The earliest certain record is the will of a later Clement, 'Clemens Paston de Paston', made on 15 June 1419 and proved on 2 October of the same year.[5] It is a modest document, leaving sums of a few shillings, or a few pence, to the vicar of Paston and to the church, and to the churches of

---

[1] About 12½ × 17 in.; xii+114 pages.
[2] MS. Add. 6968. A summary of its main contents was given by F. Worship in *Norfolk Archaeology*, iv (1855), 1–55.
[3] Part II, no. 897.   [4] e.g. B.M. Add. Charters 14810–17, 17217–19.
[5] Consistory Court of Norwich, Reg. Hyrning, ff. 51^b–52^a: *Norwich Wills*, ii. 282.

xl

Trunch and Mundesley; the largest bequest was 6s. 8d. to the Prior and Convent of Bromholm. The residue was to go to his sister Martha and his son William, who were named executors; no other child was mentioned. No lands were specified, but the residue must have included some because when Clement's son William Paston I came to make his will in 1444 he included tenements in Paston, Bacton, Edingthorpe, Witton, and Mundesley (all within a few miles of Paston) which had formerly belonged to his father. Clement asked that his body should be buried in the church of St. Margaret at Paston, between the north door and the tomb of his wife Beatrix. He did not describe himself as 'armiger' or in any other way; but again this need not be significant, for such descriptions were used inconsistently: William I, after his distinguished and prosperous legal career, also called himself in his will simply 'Willelmus Paston de Paston'.

A view of the Paston genealogy very different from Sandford's was set out in a document of unknown authorship which from its content must have been composed after William I's death in 1444 but before John I died in 1466. Where this manuscript now is I do not know. Gairdner had not seen it (his no. 524/605), and it is not where it would be expected to be, in the British Museum among the Frere manuscripts acquired in 1866— William Frere had it in 1823; it is likely to be still in existence somewhere. Frere published it when he issued volume v of Fenn's edition of the letters, as a footnote to the last section of the Preface in which Fenn had written (p. xliv): 'I had once an intention of writing a short history of the Paston Family, and had begun to make some collections for that purpose.' Frere added: 'Among the documents collected for this purpose by Sir John Fenn, there remained an original paper, written in an ancient hand, of the date of that period to which it refers; which appears to me so curious, from the picture it gives of the times, particularly the representation of the state of villenage as then subsisting, that I think it right to give it to the public. The author of it was clearly no friend of the family.' I reproduce the text exactly as Frere printed it, only omitting a number of glosses that he inserted. (Gairdner printed it in the introductions to his editions, but modernized it; thus obscuring the important fact that the spelling shows Frere to have been right in assigning it to the fifteenth century. Moreover, a number of the spellings are characteristic of Norfolk, so that it was evidently a genuine local composition of the time.)

A Remembraunce of the wurshypfull Kyn and Auncetrye of Paston, borne in Paston in Gemyngham Soken.

Fyrst there was one Clement Paston dwellyng in Paston, and he was a good pleyn husbond, and lyvyd upon hys lond yᵗ he had in Paston, and kept yᵗon a Plow alle tymes in yᵉ yer, and sumtyme in Barlysell to Plowes.

The seyd Clement yede att on Plowe both wyntᵣ and sōmer, and he rodd to mylle on the bar horsbak wyth hys corn undᵣ hym, and brought hom mele ageyn under hym.

And also drove hys carte with dyv^{rs} cornys to Wynt^{r}ton to selle, as a good husbond ought to do.

Also he had in Paston a fyve skore or a vj skore acrys of lond at the most, and myche y^{r}of bonde lond to Gemyngham-halle w^t a lytyll pore watyr-mylle rennynge by a lytylle ryver y^{re}, as it aperyth y^{re} of old tyme.

Oy^r Lyvelode ne maneris had he non y^{re} ne in none oth^r place.

And he weddyd Geffrey of Somerton (qwhos trew s^{r}nome ys Goneld) Sist^r qwhych was a bond womanne to qwom it is not unknowyn (to ye Pryore of Bromholm and Bakton also, as y^t is seyd) yf y^t men wyll inquire.

And as for Geffrey Somerton he was bond also, to whom, &c. he was both a Pardoner and an Attorney; and y^{an} was a good werd for he gadred many pens and halfpens, and y^{re} wyth he made a fayre Chapelle att Somerton as it aperyth, &c.

Also the seyd Clement had a sone William qwhych y^t he sett to scole, and oftyn he borowyd mony to fynd hym to scole; and aft^r y^t he yede to Courte wyth ye helpe of Geffrey Somerton hese uncle and lerned the lawe, and y^{re} bygatte he myche good and yanne he was made a S^{r}jaunt, and aft^{r}ward made a Justice, and a ryght connyng mane in ye lawe.

And he purchasyd myche lond in Paston, and also he purchasyd the moyte of ye vth parte of ye man^r of Bakton callyd oy^r Latymers or Stywardys or Huntyngfeld qwhyche moyte strechyd into Paston, and so wyth yt and wyth a noth^r parte of ye seyd fyve partys he hath Senery in Paston but no man^r place; and therby wold John Paston sone to ye seyde Wylliam make hym selfe a Lordschype y^{re} to ye Duke of Lancastrs grete hurte.

And the seyde John wold and hath untrewly incressyd hym be one ten^{nte} as wher that the Pry^r of Bromholm borowyd mony of the seyd William for to paie w^t all his Dymes, ye seyd William wuld not lend it hym, but the seyd Pry^r wold morgage to ye seyd Wylliam one John Albon ye seyd Pryowris bondmane dwellyng in Paston, qwhyche was a styffe Cherle and a Threfty mane, and wold not obeye hyme unto ye seyd Wylliam, and for y^t cause and for evyll wyll y^t ye seyde Wylliam had un to hym he desyryd hym of the Prio^r, and nowe aft^r ye deth of the seyd Willm ye seyd John Albon deyed, and nowe John Paston son to the seyd William by force of the seyde morgage sent for the son of the seid John Albon to Norwyche.

Whatever the truth of this—and some of it at least carries more conviction than the descent from Wulstan—two months after the death of John Paston I his son John II was able to secure from King Edward IV a statement that he and his uncles William and Clement had convinced the King and his council that they were 'gentlemen discended lineally of worshipfull blood sithen the Conquest hither'.[1]

Yet it was without question William the justice, making good use of the schooling to which his father and his uncle are said to have set him, who brought the family from obscurity in its little village on a bare coast to a position of respect in Norwich and a substantial holding of lands in the county. To his inherited possessions, which were all in the immediate neighbourhood of Paston, he added numerous manors further afield, such as Snailwell in Cambridgeshire, not far from Newmarket. One of his important purchases was Gresham, near Holt; another was Oxnead, which

[1] Sandford, p. 23. Part II, no. 896.

he settled on his wife Agnes Berry, a Hertfordshire heiress; and she brought into the family Marlingford in Norfolk as well as Stanstead in Suffolk and Orwellbury in Hertfordshire. His early career as a lawyer in Norfolk was by no means free from strife. In the 1420s his acting as counsel for the Prior of Norwich in the matter of the advowson of Sprowston church brought against him the anger of Walter Aslak, who he alleged threatened him with violence; and his advocacy of the Prior of Bromholm's right to his office against the claim of John Wortes (who to make matters worse asserted that he was a Paston) led to a suit in the Roman court in which he was defeated, fined, and excommunicated. But after he became a judge, except for the petition brought against him by William Dalling in 1433, which was rejected, the records suggest a life fully engaged in legal affairs but not abnormally disturbed. Though he was evidently aware that some of his titles to land might be challenged—'he seyde manie tymis that ho so euer schuld dwelle at Paston schulde have nede to conne defende hym-selfe',[1] and he had a statement drawn up to show that John Hauteyn had no right to Oxnead—he seems never to have suffered any attempt at dispossession such as his widow and his eldest son were faced with not long after his death. Perhaps he owed his security to his reputation as 'a grete man, and a wyse man of the lawe'.

After William Paston I died in 1444 his widow Agnes continued to live at Oxnead for a time, and sometimes in Norwich. Hauteyn's claim to Oxnead, on the ground that his ancestors had owned it, caused her anxiety for some years but came to nothing in the end. William and Agnes had four sons from whom we have letters, John I, Edmond I, William II, and Clement II, another named Henry of whom nothing else is known,[2] and a daughter Elizabeth who was evidently the third child unless Henry was older. Edmond I died at the age of 24, and little is known of him. Clement II appears briefly in the care of a tutor to whom his mother commends the efficacy of corporal punishment, and not long afterwards as the writer of seven letters from London over a period of five years. Elizabeth remained unmarried until she was nearly thirty, and suffered much from her mother's displeasure at her living at home. She was twice married, but lost both husbands by violence—the first in battle, the second on the scaffold. The family fortunes were very much in the hands of John, with some support from William II. Both of them had gone to Cambridge, and John later followed his father's profession of the law at the Inner Temple. His marriage to Margaret Mautby brought him new manors, including Sparham of which much is heard in the next generation, and Fritton in Suffolk. It brought him also her extraordinary competence and devotion, which were to be constantly called upon during the twenty-six years of their marriage, and indeed later. Her first severe trial came when the young Lord

[1] No. 14. [2] No. 151, l. 14.

Moleyns, evidently urged on by John Heydon of Baconsthorpe not far away, violently usurped the manor of Gresham. John Paston tried to assert his right, and took up residence in another house of which he left Margaret in charge. Moleyns's men attacked again, 'myned down the walle of the chambre where-in [she] was, and bare here oute at the yates'; but the resilience and determination so characteristic of her later appear already in her uncompromising refusal to accept the case put by Moleyns's agents who came to talk to her.[1] It was through his marriage also that John Paston met Sir John Fastolf, a veteran of the French wars who had acquired great wealth and who, after retiring to England in 1439, was even then building a fine new castle at Caister only a mile and a half from Mautby.[2] The consequences of the meeting were eventually immense, transforming John's life—and no doubt shortening it: 'Remembre it was þe distruccion of your fader', Margaret wrote after his death.[3] And it was the circumstances of John's married life that led to the assembling of the greater part of the collection of letters. From the time before his marriage only occasional papers are preserved; but when he was so much away from home, leaving the management of his property to Margaret and his estate servants, his instructions and their replies came to be important and he evidently thought they ought to be kept. Letters from him are not very numerous: the heart of the collection is formed by letters to him, especially during the busy and anxious years after Fastolf's death. The two eldest sons must also have been well schooled in filing letters, for they kept each other's, and their mother's.

By 1450 John Paston I was acting for Fastolf in matters of business, and by 1456 he was so much in his confidence that he was made one of a new body of trustees to hold Fastolf's lands in Norfolk and Suffolk; and his brother William was also included. In June 1459 Fastolf made his will, in the course of which he enjoined his executors to found at Caister a college of a prior and six monks of the Order of St. Benedict, and seven poor men, to pray in perpetuity for his soul and the souls of his parents, kinsfolk, and benefactors; their maintenance to be provided from the income of certain of his estates. But this will was ostensibly superseded by a nuncupative will dated 3 November of the same year—two days before he died—in which responsibility for the foundation of the college (now simplified to seven monks or priests and seven poor folk) was committed to John Paston alone, who in return for a payment of 4,000 marks was to have in fee simple all the manors, lands, and tenements in Norfolk and Suffolk of which he was a trustee.[4] In addition, administration of the estate was limited to John Paston

[1] No. 131.

[2] See especially K. B. McFarlane, 'The Investment of Sir John Fastolf's Profits of War', *Transactions of the Royal Historical Soc.*, 5th series, vii (1957), 91–116; H. D. Barnes and W. Douglas Simpson, 'The Building Accounts of Caister Castle', *Norfolk Archaeology*, xxx (1947–52), 178–88.

[3] No. 213, l. 18.   [4] No. 54; cf. 60, 61.

and Fastolf's chaplain Thomas Howes, though there were eight other executors including William Wainfleet, Bishop of Winchester, John, Lord Beauchamp, William Yelverton, justice, Friar John Brackley, and William Worcester, who had for many years acted as Fastolf's secretary and agent. The admissibility of this supposed will turned on the testimony of those of Fastolf's household who had been with him during his last illness. Paston acted upon the nuncupative will at once and entered Fastolf's properties, sending his brother William to London to see Wainfleet, who was then chancellor. William reported an encouraging reception; but it was soon clear that the other trustees were far from satisfied. Worcester early showed himself suspicious that he would go unrewarded for his long service to Fastolf, and allied himself with Yelverton to contest Paston's claims. In the disturbed conditions of 1461, too, when Henry VI was deposed after the second battle of St. Albans and driven out of the country after Towton, the Duke of Norfolk took possession of Caister for a time. Yelverton instituted a suit against Paston and Howes in the Archbishop of Canterbury's Court of Audience. Evidence was taken from 1464 to 1466, but no conclusion was reached in Paston's lifetime. Meanwhile his opponents were not idle. Yelverton, with his associate William Jenney, claimed possession of the Fastolf manor of Cotton in Suffolk, and ordered the tenants to pay no rent to Paston. Later they sold the manor to Gilbert Debenham, and it was he who pursued the resistance to Paston there. Thomas Howes turned against Paston.[1] Lord Scales threatened to occupy Caister and Cotton.[2] Worcester says that he did enter Caister in Edward IV's name, on the false pretext that John Paston was a serf of the King's;[3] but there is no mention of this in the letters. Then John de la Pole, Duke of Suffolk, devised a claim for himself to Hellesdon and Drayton, just across the Wensum from his own residence at Costessey. After some weeks of harassing Paston's tenants, he finally sent a raiding force in October 1465 which destroyed the house and lodge at Hellesdon and robbed and damaged houses in the village, and the church as well. John Paston I was in the Fleet Prison at this time, and though Margaret was not at Hellesdon when the attack was made she suffered the shock of the loss of the house and goods and the anxiety of dealing with the tenants. This setback came soon after she had brought off something of a coup at Cotton. Returning from London where she had gone to see her husband, she had entered the manor of Cotton, sent for John III who was at Hellesdon, and left him to collect the rents. Debenham had raised 300 men to take possession again; but his son Sir Gilbert, like John Paston III, was a dependant of the Duke of Norfolk—'he takyth vs bothe for hys men and so we be knowyn well j-now'[4]—and the Duke forbade them to pursue the quarrel. At the beginning of 1466 a new attack

---

[1] Nos. 77, 119. [2] Part II, no. 741.
[3] *Itineraries*, p. 188. [4] No. 324.

came, not on the Fastolf estate but on John Paston I's own property in Norwich. Lord Scales determined to seize his house, goods, and chattels in the King's name, again claiming that Paston was a serf. The mayor and aldermen were embarrassed by this encroachment on the liberties and privileges of the city, but compromised by persuading the assembly to agree that entry might be made by the feoffors to avoid breaking.[1]

After nearly seven years of such contention, with constant anxiety, long absence from home, occasional violence, and the personal distress which imprisonment must have brought, John Paston I died at the age of 45 leaving the lands he had hoped to acquire from the Fastolf estate with a very precarious title. Even without them he was a man of some substance; but there were already signs of dissension between him and his mother about some of the rents, and his brother William soon showed that he felt his own interests to diverge from those of his nephews.[2] John I left five sons and two daughters: John II, John III, Edmond II, Walter, and William III; Margery, and Anne. Of the education of the two eldest nothing is recorded, but it is apparent from the ease with which they write that this at least they had been well taught, and John II was much interested in books. He had been placed in the King's household when he was about 19, apparently with the help of John Wykes, esquire, an usher of the King's chamber and later esquire of the body, who was among other things steward and constable of the castle and lordship of Rising in Norfolk and controller of customs and subsidy in the port of Bishop's Lynn.[3] After an unpromising beginning John II fared well enough, being knighted as soon as he was of age and travelling with the King on various expeditions. His taste for the life of the court and the camp came to seem excessive to his father, who called him a drone among bees.[4] Yet for all his lack of serious application to business it was he who in the end, by his personal connections, managed to save something of the Fastolf inheritance for the family. Though probate of his father's will was long delayed,[5] as early as July 1466 he won from the King recognition of his right to Caister. (Probate of Fastolf's will was granted on 26 August 1467.)[6] The royal warrant was far from giving him undisputed possession; for Yelverton, now joined by Howes, acting as Fastolf's trustees, sold the manor to the Duke of Norfolk in 1468,[7] and this gave Norfolk the pretext for his attack on it a year later. The Pastons had long had some attachment to the Mowbray Dukes—William Paston had been steward to the second duke; John I had employed his bailiff Richard Calle on the recommendation of the third duke,[8] and had placed his second son John III in the household of the young fourth duke now in question.

---

[1] *Records of Norwich*, i. 286–7.   [2] Nos. 180, 198.
[3] No. 116. *Cal. Pat. Rolls, 1461–7*, pp. 23, 123, 124, 188; *Cal. Fine Rolls, 1461–71*, p. 185.
[4] No. 72.   [5] No. 279.
[6] No. 92, headnote.   [7] Nos. 294, 332; Part II, no. 902.
[8] No. 65.

John III served with Norfolk in the north in the campaigns of 1462–4, and despite their later clash of interests, and the ill-will of some members of the Duke's council, he always preserved a relation of a special if uneasy kind with him and the Duchess.[1]

The young men's preoccupation with the cares of estate was agreeably interrupted in 1468 by their journey to Bruges in Princess Margaret's retinue when she married the Duke of Burgundy. John II may have owed his place to his acquaintance with Anthony Woodville, Lord Scales, brother of the Queen. Scales had earlier been an adversary of the Pastons, threatening to seize not only Fastolf manors but also John Paston I's Norwich property in 1466; but by April 1467 John II is found taking part in a tourney with Scales, on the King's side, and some two years later engaged to be married to his cousin Anne Haute. There was perhaps an additional reason for John III's presence in the company in that the Princess's chief lady-in-waiting for the occasion was the Duchess of Norfolk. But in 1469 there was to be no comfort in the name of Norfolk, for the Duke determined to take Caister by force. John II prepared to defend it, and put John III in command, with tried men such as John Daubeney, Osbern Berney, John Pampyng, and John Styll, as well as some specially recruited. Norfolk was too strong. John II tried, with the help of Walter Writtle, who was in the service of the Duke of Clarence, to make the best terms he could while the defenders held out; but they were short of supplies and were forced to capitulate. Daubeney had been killed, and the castle was surrendered. Margaret reproached John II bitterly for failing to support his brother adequately, and despite his protestations it must be admitted that he seems never to have understood the garrison's needs or grasped the seriousness of its danger. On the other hand, John III showed none of his mother's censoriousness. The letter he wrote after the surrender is self-possessed, dignified, and generous.[2]

To the economic blows dealt to the family by the destruction of the Hellesdon buildings and the loss of Caister there was added in the same year 1469 a shock to their opinion of their social position, when Margery Paston fell in love with the bailiff Richard Calle and refused to be dissuaded by mother, brothers, or bishop from marrying him. She was the first of her generation to marry. It must have been about the same time that her uncle, William Paston II, made an impressive match by marrying Lady Anne Beaufort, daughter of the Duke of Somerset who had been a strong opponent of Richard of York and had been killed at the first battle of St. Albans in 1455. But William by now stood somewhat aside from the affairs of his nephews, and this cannot have given them much consolation.

The year 1470 was momentous in the history of the Fastolf lands. Wainfleet, 'considered of the seid grete substance of lond and goodez the grete

---

[1] Cf. nos. 296, 342.   [2] No. 334.

waste, destruccion, and perplexité',[1] with the authority of Archbishop Bourchier[2] took execution of the will into his own hands and made a compromise with John Paston II by which Paston was to relinquish all manors and appurtenances except Caister, Hellesdon, Drayton, and some minor holdings, and the Bishop was to provide for the priests and poor men, whom Fastolf had wished to endow at Caister, at his new college of St. Mary Magdalen at Oxford; at the same time discharging Paston of the 4,000 marks he was to pay under the original bargain, and of any of Fastolf's movable goods which the Pastons might have acquired in the interval. This at last settled the legal position between the Paston claims and the counterclaims of other executors. But to put the agreement into effect was another matter, for the Duke of Norfolk held Caister, and the Duke of Suffolk still claimed Hellesdon and Drayton, so the end was not yet—and in fact the details were later revised.[3] Then came the sudden reversal of fortune when the exiled Warwick brought a Lancastrian force to England, swiftly drove Edward out, and restored Henry VI. Though Warwick was master, Clarence was made joint lieutenant of the realm with him, and Oxford was constable. John Paston II had been in favour with both of them, and he looked forward to a sharp improvement in his position. Though not all his hopes were fulfilled, Norfolk did release Caister. But 'God schewyd hym-selffe marvelouslye, lyke hym þat made all and can vndoo ageyn whan hym lyst'.[4] When the counter-attack came in April the Paston brothers— perhaps partly out of resentment at their ill-treatment by the strongly Yorkist Duke of Norfolk, old patron though he was, partly from their higher hopes of the Lancastrian Earl of Oxford—fought at Barnet for Henry, and lost. Though they were both pardoned after a few months, their standing with the King could obviously no longer be what it had been less than three years before, when they were so much in favour as to be accepted as members of his sister's entourage. On the other hand, John II's engagement to Anne Haute, cousin of Lord Scales and of the Queen, seems not to have been called in question on her side at this time; though John very soon showed a strong inclination to free himself of it, and it was finally cancelled in 1477.[5]

From late 1471 onwards, no doubt in part because of John II's surrender of so many manors from which he might have drawn rents, much is heard of shortage of money. John II borrowed from his mother, who in turn had to borrow from Elisabeth Clere and could not pay the sum back when she was asked for it;[6] he urged his brother to special efforts in collecting rents, but with little success;[7] he mortgaged the manor of Sporle, to his mother's great indignation because she feared he would never redeem it;[8] he borrowed

[1] No. 252.	[2] No. 248, headnote.	[3] No. 277, ll. 30–3.
[4] No. 261.	[5] Nos. 263, 308.	[6] No. 209.
[7] No. 353.	[8] No. 355.	

from his uncle William, who treated him ungenerously.[1] Margaret complained of his extravagance and his carelessness, not only in money matters but in managing his property, and even in attending to his father's gravestone.[2] That she had good reason can hardly be doubted. John II seems to have had little heart for hard bargaining, and little competence in it. Even after the supposedly definitive agreement with Wainfleet, certified by multiple instruments, he continued to lose. Margaret resentfully pointed out in June 1472 that Wainfleet had sold the manors of Saxthorpe and Titchwell to Henry Heydon, and feared that not only Guton but Hellesdon and Drayton might go the same way.[3] By the terms of the agreement Wainfleet would seem to have been within his rights in doing what he liked with Saxthorpe and Titchwell; but Margaret's fears for Drayton, which ought to have been safe, were all too well founded. A year later John II was obliged to report that he had had to give up Drayton because of new negotiations in which the Bishop apparently went back on his bond.[4] Margaret's financial anxieties were not all the fault of John II. In 1472 and 1474 Parliament granted the King the right to raise money by taxation for the invasion of France, and in May 1475 Margaret wrote that 'the Kyng goth so nere vs in þis cuntré, both to pooere and ryche, þat I wote not how we shall lyff but yff þe world a-mend'.[5]

After 1472 John II was not often in Norfolk. He was sometimes in London, at his 'place' in Fleet Street or at the George at Paul's Wharf, but from 1473 to 1477 a great deal at Calais, serving under the command of Lord Hastings. In the meantime John III at first lived at his mother's house in Norwich, and so did Edmond II and doubtless the younger children. The household was not harmonious, because Margaret's chaplain James Gloys, an old servant of the family, had won her confidence at the expense of her sons, and 'many qwarellys ar pyekyd to get my brodyr E. and me ought of hyr howse'.[6] Edmond had been briefly in London, at Staple Inn. In 1473 he went to Calais for perhaps a year, and in 1475 John III and he both went there with the King's army. By this time the young Walter, from whom Margaret hoped for better things than his elder brothers had done,[7] had gone to Oxford, and Margaret had left Norwich to go to live in her childhood home at Mautby.

Soon after the brothers returned with the army from Calais in September 1475 Caister was unexpectedly brought back into John II's hands. Whatever his neglect of other responsibilities he had constantly done all he could to assert his right to Caister, both through intercession by John III with the Duke of Norfolk and his council or with the Duchess, and directly to the King.[8] But the Duke, supported by one or two of his advisers, was

---

[1] No. 271, end.   [2] e.g. nos. 212, 228.   [3] No. 216.
[4] No. 277.   [5] No. 224.   [6] No. 353.
[7] No. 220, ll. 11–12.   [8] Nos. 354, 356–7, 359, 293–4.

Duke of Norfolk

obdurate. Then in January 1476 he died suddenly, aged only 32. John II was evidently at Framlingham at the time, and surprisingly enough offered cloth of gold for the funeral; but within three days he went to London to urge his right to Caister once more, and simultaneously sent a messenger there to make a formal claim.[1] This time he was successful, for the King's council ruled in his favour; and at last, seventeen years after Fastolf's death and ten years after John Paston I's, Caister became the undisputed property of the Pastons.

In the following year John Paston III, who had at intervals expressed an inclination to marry, at last approached the matter seriously. Margery Brews, daughter of Sir Thomas Brews of Sall and Topcroft, was more than willing, but her father demanded a richer jointure than John had intended to offer. John II was not disposed to make any concessions to help his brother;[2] but with the generous support of Margaret, who gave the couple the manor of Sparham, all obstacles were overcome and the marriage took place before the end of 1477. On this marriage, as it turned out, the future of the house of Paston depended; for John II was taken ill in London and died in 1479, still unmarried though not childless, and the succession eventually passed to John III's second son.

In the same year as John III his younger sister Anne was also married, to William Yelverton, grandson of Sir William the judge who had been so determined an adversary of her father. Walter was still at Oxford, and William III was at Eton by 1478. The year 1479 was one of great mortality: shortly before John II's death his grandmother Agnes and his young brother Walter also died, and Anne had a child which died at birth.

John III, as the new head of the family, had to contend with his uncle William II's claims to property which had come into the family as Agnes's dowry in 1420. William had taken his mother to live with him in London for a number of years, in the mansion near Newgate which had once belonged to the Earl of Warwick, and he evidently had reason to hope that he might inherit these manors; but William I's will had left them to Agnes for life and thereafter to the heirs of both of them, so that John III was right in resisting this claim. William II had for some years played a rather equivocal part, lending money on occasion but also pretending a right to part of the family lands;[3] and now his hostility became manifest, even to the length of sending dependants of his to seize goods at Marlingford.[4] The records do not show how the dispute ended. It was still going on in 1487, but a reference to William II in a letter of Edmond's later than that but before 1493 implies that some accommodation had been reached before William died in 1496. The contested manors are not mentioned in his will.[5]

---

[1] Nos. 295, 367, 368.   [2] Nos. 304, 306.
[3] No. 222.   [4] Nos. 111, 384–5, 417–18.
[5] Nos. 400 (l. 21), 113.

1

Edmond Paston II married the widow Clippesby probably in 1480, and went to live at her house at Oby near Ashby. John III began to take a greater part in public life, on the commission of the peace and other commissions, and as M.P. and sheriff in 1485–6. He became a member of the council of his old friend the Earl of Oxford, and brought his youngest brother William III into the Earl's service until a mental breakdown, about 1503, caused him to be discharged. It was doubtless through John III also that Edmond was made receiver of the Scales lands. In the reign of Richard III little is heard of John except for a pardon. In 1487 he took part in the overthrow of the promoters of Lambert Simnel in the battle of Stoke on Trent, and was one of sixty-five men knighted on the field. After his mother's death in 1484 letters in John III's name are few and disconnected, but there is a substantial number addressed to him. Not many of them are concerned with family affairs in the manner of the earlier documents: the correspondent best represented is the Earl of Oxford, with a series of brief business letters. Indeed, much of the life goes out of the collection after the death of Margaret Paston. Margery Paston died in 1495, and John III took a second wife from whom no letters are known. Anne Yelverton died in 1494–5, her sister Margery Calle apparently much earlier. Edmond Paston II's first wife died in 1491; he married again, and himself died shortly before February 1504. William III continued to write occasionally, mainly on Oxford's business, until 1492. He was still living and in Oxford's service in 1503; the date of his death is unknown. John III was the last survivor of his generation of the family, except perhaps William III, when he died in August 1504, leaving his second son William Paston IV as his heir.

The later history of the family was of increasing prosperity and importance for two hundred years, followed by catastrophic collapse. The fourth William married Bridget, daughter of Sir Henry Heydon, whose father had in his day been a strong opponent of John Paston I. He flourished under Henry VIII, and was a knight by 1520 when he was present at the Field of Cloth of Gold. He died in 1554. His eldest son, Erasmus, had died before him, and his heir was Clement (?1515–97), who became a distinguished soldier and sailor. He built a new house at Oxnead which remained the principal seat of the family as long as it endured. His nephew William (1528–1610), son of Erasmus, succeeded him; it was he who founded the Sir William Paston Grammar School at North Walsham. His son Christopher, born in 1554, became insane about 1587; his son Sir Edmund (1585–1632) married Katherine Knyvett, whose letters are the most important of the seventeenth-century records of the family. Their son, yet another Sir William (1610–63), was a traveller and a wealthy collector, but during the Civil War he took the King's side and was heavily punished for it by fines and confiscation. In his time Caister, 'þe fayereeste flowere of owr garlond' for Margaret Paston in 1472,[1] was sold. In the next generation Sir Robert Paston (1631–83) was created, for services to Charles II, Baron Paston and Viscount Yarmouth in 1673, and Earl of Yarmouth in 1679. His son was the last William (?1654–1732), second earl, who lost all his wealth and survived his sons, so that at his death the male line and the title died out. His estates were bought by Admiral Lord Anson.

BIOGRAPHICAL SUMMARY

D.N.B. gives biographies of William Paston I, John I, John II, and William III. The service in Parliament of John I, William II, John II, and John III is recorded in the *History of Parliament, Biographies of Members of the House of Commons 1439–1509*, ed. J. C. Wedgwood (1936). Statements below which coincide with these, and routine records of service on commissions, which depend on the Calendars of Patent Rolls for the years in question, are not supported by detailed references unless they are of unusual interest. Numbers otherwise unspecified refer to documents in this edition.

WILLIAM PASTON I

Born 1378, son of Clement Paston (d. 1419) of Paston, Norfolk, and his wife Beatrix, *née* Somerton. He first appears in public records in Norwich City accounts for 1412, when he was paid by order of the mayor for service as counsel; mentioned again in 1413 and 1415.[2] He appears on the Patent Roll as an executor of Alexander de Totington, Bishop of Norwich, who died in 1413.[3] The next bishop, Richard Courtenay (d. Sept. 1415) made him steward of all his courts. In 1413 he was a commissioner to hold an estate in the King's interest;[4] in 1414 and again 1433 an arbitrator in disputes about election of the mayor of Norwich.[5] In 1415 he became steward of John Mowbray, second Duke of Norfolk. From 1415 onwards, he served on many commissions of the peace, first for Great Yarmouth, from 1418 Norfolk, 1420 Yorkshire, 1422 Suffolk, and thereafter many other counties also; and on numerous commissions of array, assize, oyer and terminer, jail delivery, etc. In 1418 he was one of those charged to inquire into lands held in Norfolk by Sir John Oldcastle (executed 1417).[6] In 1419–20 Norwich City paid 7s. 6d. for three yards of cloth for his vesture that year.[7] In 1420 he married Agnes Berry (settlement dated 24 March),[8] on whom he settled the manor of Oxnead,[9] newly bought. In 1423–4 Norwich paid messengers sent to him for advice, one of them to London.[10] About 1425

[1] No. 216.
[2] *Records of Norwich*, ii. 58, 59, 60.
[3] *Cal. Pat. Rolls, 1416–22*, p. 16.
[4] *Cal. Pat. Rolls, 1413–16*, p. 126.
[5] Blomefield, iii. 126, 148.
[6] *Cal. Pat. Rolls, 1416–22*, p. 202.
[7] *Records of Norwich*, ii. 63.
[8] B.M. Add. Charter 17225 (in his own hand).
[9] No. 32.
[10] *Records of Norwich*, ii. 64.

he acted as counsel for the Prior of Bromholm,[1] and for the Prior of the Cathedral Priory, Norwich,[2] in suits which led to disputes and eventually his excommunication. About the same time, and also later, he was often named by prominent men a trustee of property and executor. He bought the manor of Gresham in 1427 from Thomas Chaucer.[3] On 15 October 1429 he became justice of the Common Bench, with a grant of 110 marks and two robes yearly besides the customary fee. In the same year the monastery of Bury St. Edmunds made him a brother of the Chapter-house.[4] In 1433 William Dalling, in a petition to Parliament, accused him of accepting fees from clients, but the petition was rejected. On 27 August 1437 he was granted exemption for life, 'for good service to the King in the said Bench and as serjeant at law, and for good service to Henry IV and Henry V, and to the King as one of the councillors at law of the duchy of Lancaster and in consideration of his great age', from assizes and other duties outside his own 'country'.[5] Despite this exemption he continued as justice of assize and commissioner in the home counties and London as well as Norfolk. In 1439 and 1442 he was a trier of petitions in Parliament; in 1441 and 1443 a member of commissions inquiring into the administration of Norwich. In 1442 he was granted the keeping of the manor of East Beckham.[6] In January 1444 he was not well enough to ride the south-eastern circuit.[7] He died on 13 August 1444 and was buried in the Lady Chapel of Norwich Cathedral.[8]

AGNES PASTON

Daughter and heiress of Sir Edmund Berry of Orwellbury near Royston, Hertfordshire. Married William Paston I in 1420. She inherited the manors of Marlingford, Stanstead, and Orwellbury[9] from her father (who d. 1433), and was given Oxnead by her husband. Her title to it was contested by a friar named Hauteyn in 1443 and later, but after 1450 his claim seems to have been abandoned.[10] She lived sometimes at Paston, sometimes at Oxnead,[11] often at Norwich, until at least 1469;[12] but before 1474 went to live in London, at Warwick's Inn,[13] with her second son William. About 1451 she was involved in a dispute with the villagers of Paston about the building of a wall.[14] Severe towards her children, she bullied Elizabeth before her marriage[15]

---

[1] No. 2. [2] No. 5.
[3] *Chaucer Life-Records*, ed. M. M. Crow and C. C. Olson (Oxford, 1966), p. 543.
[4] B.M. Add. Charter 17226. [5] *Cal. Pat. Rolls, 1436–41*, pp. 59–60.
[6] No. 10. [7] Part II, no. 432.
[8] See also E. Foss, *The Judges of England*, iv (London, 1851), 350–2; E. A. Robbins, *William Paston, Justice* (Norwich, 1932). [9] No. 32.
[10] Nos. 18, 133; Part II, nos. 453, 871, 874. [11] Nos. 13, 23, 24; 18, 125.
[12] Nos. 14, 19, 20, 203. [13] No. 285.
[14] Nos. 21–4. [15] Part II, no. 446.

and urged Clement's tutor to treat him sternly.[1] She complained in 1465 of John I's intrusion on certain of her property rights,[2] and showed some hostility to him when she drafted her will in 1466.[3] She died in London about 18 August 1479.[4]

Children of William Paston I and Agnes

JOHN PASTON I

Born 1421. Educated at Trinity Hall and Peterhouse, Cambridge,[5] and the Inner Temple, where he later lodged.[6] Married Margaret Mautby about 1440.[7] He was in London, in poor health, in 1443.[8] In 1447 he appears on the commission of the peace for Norfolk. In February 1448 Lord Moleyns, apparently at the instigation of John Heydon, drove him out of the manor of Gresham inherited from his father. He returned in October to another house there, from which Margaret was expelled in January 1449;[9] but he regained possession evidently early in 1451.[10] In 1450 he was a commissioner of array, with John, Earl of Oxford, William Yelverton, Sir Miles Stapleton, John Ferrers, John Berney, John Damme, and William Lomnor. From about this time he became a legal adviser to Sir John Fastolf, who took up residence at his new castle of Caister in 1454.[11] In 1452 Paston was active in protesting against disturbers of the peace in Norfolk.[12] In 1453 he was pardoned, as 'of Norwich, gentleman'. In 1455 he was one of three men who received a majority of votes in the election for knights of the shire, but the Duke of Norfolk insisted on his own nominees being returned.[13] When Fastolf made a new feoffment of his Norfolk and Suffolk lands in 1456 he made Paston one of his trustees, together with Thomas Bourchier, Archbishop of Canterbury, William Wainfleet, Bishop of Winchester, William Yelverton, and others.[14] In 1457 Paston paid a fine (unspecified) in consideration of declining a knighthood.[15] In 1458, together with his brother William, Osbert Mountford, John Berney, John Heveningham, and twenty-three others, he was accused of riotous behaviour; and a commission headed by the Duke of Norfolk and including Sir Thomas Tuddenham, Sir Miles Stapleton, and John Heydon was charged with arresting them.[16] In 1459 Paston was one of a commission to arrest

---

[1] No. 28.   [2] No. 180, ll. 124–34.   [3] Nos. 31, 32.
[4] No. 397. Writ of *diem clausit extremum* issued 5 September (Norfolk, Suffolk, and Hertfordshire): *Cal. Fine Rolls, 1471–85*, no. 513.
[5] Part II, no. 438; no. 124.   [6] Nos. 126, 139, 232, etc.   [7] No. 13.
[8] No. 126.   [9] Nos. 36, 38.   [10] Part II, no. 473.
[11] Nos. 83, 84, Part II, no. 483; B.M. MS. Add. 39848, f. 9 (abstract in G. 123/153).
[12] Nos. 40–4.   [13] Part II, nos. 526, 529.
[14] Inq. p.m., 38–9 Henry VI, no. 48.
[15] B.M. Add. Charter 17246, an account of his expenses from Michaelmas 36 to Michaelmas 37 Henry VI, containing the item 'Pro fine Domino Regi facto quod J. P. non sit miles.'   [16] *Cal. Pat. Rolls, 1452–61*, p. 491.

masters and mariners for ships under the command of Richard, Earl of Warwick. He was one of the ten executors of Fastolf's will as he propounded it, and, with Thomas Howes, charged with administering it.[1] (Fastolf died on 5 November 1459.) He took possession of Fastolf's Norfolk and Suffolk lands, and sometimes resided at the principal manors of Caister and Hellesdon. In 1460–1 he served on commissions, notably 30 January 1461 to arrest persons in Norfolk and Suffolk impeding the King's lieges coming to defend the King's person[2] and 14 May 1462 to place watchmen and beacons for the defence of Norfolk.[3] He was J.P. for Norfolk again in 1460–6, M.P. in 1460–1 and 1461–2. In 1461 he came into conflict with Sir John Howard (then sheriff), and was imprisoned in the Fleet for a short time.[4] In 1464 William Yelverton, justice, and knight since 1461, another of Fastolf's executors, who contested Paston's claim to be the chief executor and legatee, proceeded against him in the Court of Audience of Canterbury.[5] He was also accused in the Suffolk county court of trespass, declared an outlaw, and again imprisoned;[6] and in 1465 he was in the Fleet a third time. At this period he was on bad terms with his son John II.[7] The year 1465 was full of troubles: the manor of Cotton was threatened, the manor of Drayton was seized, and the house and lodge at Hellesdon sacked by the Duke of Suffolk's men in October.[8] In January 1466 Lord Scales forced the Norwich city officials to allow Paston's property to be seized in the King's name.[9] John I died in London on 21 or 22 May 1466, and was buried in Bromholm Priory, Norfolk.

MARGARET PASTON

Daughter and heiress of John Mautby of Mautby, Norfolk, and his wife Margery, daughter of John Berney of Reedham, through whom she was related to Sir John Fastolf.[10] She was born at Reedham. (John Mautby died in 1433, and his widow married Ralph Garneys of Geldeston.)[11] Married John Paston I about 1440. She was in charge of his house at Gresham in 1449 when it was attacked by Lord Moleyns's men and she was expelled.[12] Later she lived mainly in Norwich until after Fastolf's death in 1459, when she was often at Caister or Hellesdon,[13] and managed the property generally in Paston's absence. When John II displeased his father in 1463–5 she interceded in his favour.[14]

[1] No. 54. [2] *Cal. Pat. Rolls, 1452–61*, p. 656.
[3] *Cal. Pat. Rolls, 1461–7*, p. 205. [4] No. 163.
[5] Bodl. MS. Top. Norfolk c. 4; B.M. MS. Add. 27450.
[6] B.M. MS. Add. 27444, ff. 132–6. [7] No. 73.
[8] Nos. 192, 196. [9] See p. xlvi above.
[10] No. 25, and B.M. MS. Add. 27443, f. 118 (G. 132/162), in which Fastolf writes of 'my cosyn John a Berney' (Margaret's uncle) and 'my cosyn Paston'.
[11] No. 126. [12] No. 131.
[13] Nos. 154, 174, 175, 179. [14] Nos. 176, 178.

In September 1465 she visited John I in prison in London,[1] not long before the destruction of Hellesdon. After his death in 1466 she continued to live in Norwich until about 1474,[2] when she moved to her old home at Mautby.[3] In 1469 she was incensed by her daughter Margery's attachment to the family steward Richard Calle, but was unable to prevent their marriage.[4] In the same year she rebuked John II for his failure to defend Caister adequately or rescue his brother and his men there;[5] and in later years she often complained of his extravagance, and his neglect of his father's grave.[6] Yet before he died she was on affectionate terms with him again.[7] In 1477 she took an active part in forwarding John III's suit for the hand of Margery Brews.[8] She was ill in 1478 and made a will,[9] but recovered; her effective will was made in February 1482.[10] She died in 1484, apparently on 4 November,[11] and was buried in Mautby church.

EDMOND PASTON I

Born 1425.[12] He was at Clifford's Inn in 1445,[13] and died in London in 1449, on or soon after 21 March.[14]

ELIZABETH PASTON, later POYNINGS and BROWNE

Born probably 1429.[15] By 1449 there were negotiations for her marriage with Stephen Scrope, Fastolf's stepson and ward (at this time about 50),[16] and about 1450 with Sir William Oldhall.[17] Agnes, who had ill-treated her before, was reported in 1454 to be impatient to be 'delivered of her';[18] and articles were drawn up between Agnes and William Clopton for the marriage of Elizabeth to John Clopton.[19] In July 1454 Lord Grey of Hastings offered to introduce yet another suitor, but John Paston I replied cautiously.[20] None of these moves took effect, and in 1457–8 Elizabeth was at board in London with Lady Pole.[21] She eventually married, evidently late in 1458, Robert Poynings, second son of Robert, fourth Lord Poynings,[22] and had a son who later became Sir Edward.[23] Poynings was killed at

[1] No. 192.   [2] e.g. nos. 199, 264, 284, 353.   [3] Nos. 221–2.   [4] No. 203.
[5] Nos. 204–5.   [6] Nos. 208–9, 212.   [7] No. 221.   [8] Nos. 226, 374.
[9] Part II, no. 782.   [10] No. 230.
[11] Gairdner (881/999) refers to 'the calendar prefixed to an old MS. missal in the possession of Mr. C. W. Reynell'. Writ of *diem clausit extremum* issued 7 Nov. 1484 (Norfolk and Suffolk): *Cal. Fine Rolls, 1471–85*, no. 831.
[12] No. 12.   [13] No. 14.   [14] Nos. 80, 133.
[15] Sandford's Genealogy (see *Norfolk Archaeology*, iv (1855), 21) gives 1 July 1429. Cf. no. 388.
[16] No. 18; Part II, no. 446.   [17] No. 19.   [18] No. 150.
[19] Part II, no. 436.   [20] Nos. 50, 84; Part II, no. 499.   [21] No. 28.
[22] No. 121.
[23] No. 123. At the time of the inquisition on his father, which was not held until 1471 (see next note) Edward was 11 years old.

the second battle of St. Albans in February 1461.[1] In 1471 Elizabeth married Sir George Browne of Betchworth, Surrey,[2] by whom she had a son and a daughter. Browne was executed on 3 December 1483 for rebellion against Richard III, and attainted on 23 January 1484.[3] Elizabeth made her will in May 1487,[4] and died on 1 February 1488.[5]

WILLIAM PASTON II

Born 1436. Educated at Cambridge, where Agnes asked John I to send him books in 1449.[6] He was sometimes in London from 1450 to 1456.[7] He became one of Fastolf's trustees, with John I and others, in 1456,[8] and went to London on John's behalf soon after Fastolf's death in 1459 to try to negotiate administration of the estate.[9] After John's death in 1466 there were some conflicts of interest between him and his nephews over inheritance,[10] and uneasy relations with John II to whom he had lent money.[11] He served on the commission of the peace for Norfolk in 1465–6, 1469–70, and 1473–4, and on a few other commissions. He was pardoned in 1468, as 'of London, of Caister, of Norwich, and of Wymondham, gentleman'.[12] Before 1470 he married Lady Anne Beaufort, third daughter of Edmund, Duke of Somerset (killed on the Lancastrian side at the first battle of St. Albans, 1455), and by her had at least four daughters, one of whom died in childhood.[13] On 9 December 1471 he was pardoned by Edward IV. He was M.P. for Newcastle under Lyme in 1472–5, and for Bedwyn, Wiltshire, in 1478 and 1491–2, and perhaps other parliaments in Henry VII's reign. By 1474 he was living in London at Warwick's Inn near Newgate.[14] After the death in 1479 of his mother, who lived with him, he quarrelled with John Paston III over inheritance of her lands.[15] He was on friendly terms with the Duchess of Norfolk.[16] He died in London in September 1496;[17] his will, dated 7 September and proved 28 November, named distinguished executors, who, however, declined to act.[18]

[1] No. 122. *Inq. p.m.*, 9 and 10 Edward IV, no. 49.
[2] No. 266.
[3] *Cal. Pat. Rolls, 1476–85*, pp. 371, 401, 406; *Cal. Close Rolls, 1476–85*, no. 1301; *Rot. Parl.* vi. 244–9.
[4] No. 123.   [5] *Inq. p.m.*, Henry VII, i, nos. 434, 436.
[6] No. 133.   [7] Nos. 20, 26, 84.
[8] *Inq. p.m.*, 38–9 Henry VI, no. 48.   [9] No. 86.
[10] Nos. 198, 245, 341, 343, 353.   [11] Nos. 271, 285.
[12] B.M. Add. Charter 17248 (G. 586/685).
[13] According to Sandford (see p. lvi n. 15 above) the eldest daughter was born on 19 January 1470. He gives her name as Mary, whereas William's will mentions Agnes and Elizabeth as surviving. Margaret, born on 19 July 1474, died in November of the same year: no. 286.
[14] No. 285.   [15] Nos. 385, 387.
[16] Nos. 108, 109.
[17] Writ of *diem clausit extremum* issued 27 September (Norfolk and Essex): *Cal. Fine Rolls, 1485–1509*, no. 558.
[18] No. 113.

CLEMENT PASTON II

Born 1442.[1] In 1458 he was in London under a tutor, having already been at Cambridge.[2] His surviving letters are all from the period 1461–6, and were written in London. After 1466 he was associated with William II and Agnes in their dispute with John II and John III over property.[3] He was dead by the time Agnes made her final will, that is not later than August 1479.[4]

Children of John Paston I and Margaret

JOHN PASTON II

Born 1442. His father evidently sent him to court in 1461, in the hope of gaining royal favour in his litigation about property; and he travelled with the King in that year and the next.[5] He was home again at the beginning of 1463, and a writ of attachment was issued against him alleging felonies in Suffolk.[6] He was knighted on coming of age in 1463. In November of the same year he left home at Caister, without his father's leave, to join the King in the north; and this began a period of extreme disfavour with his father, who banished him from home in 1464–5.[7] By May 1465 he had returned, and was in charge of Caister during Margaret's absence at Hellesdon.[8] From 1466 onwards he was in London a great deal, seeking probate of his father's will and settlement of the still outstanding disputes over Fastolf's estate. By 27 July 1466 he succeeded in obtaining from the King a warrant restoring to him Caister and other Fastolf lands which had been in the possession of John I.[9] In April 1467 he took part, with the King and Lord Scales, in a tournament at Eltham.[10] He was M.P. for Norfolk in 1467–8. On 26 August 1467 probate of Fastolf's will was granted to John Paston and Thomas Howes;[11] and in January 1468 Fastolf's surviving trustees released to John II a number of manors and lands in Caister and elsewhere in Norfolk and Suffolk.[12] In late June 1468 John II and John III went to Bruges in the retinue of Princess Margaret, youngest sister of Edward IV, for her marriage to Charles the Bold, Duke of Burgundy, which took place on 3 July.[13] About this time John II employed William Ebesham as scribe, partly of legal documents but also of his 'Great Book' of chivalric treatises and other verse and prose texts.[14] Despite his own constant complaints of lack of money he lent a large sum to George Neville, Archbishop of York.[15] Early in 1469 he became engaged to marry Anne Haute, a cousin of the Queen and Lord Scales,[16] but after long negotiations the engagement was

---

[1] No. 12. [2] No. 28. [3] No. 32.
[4] No. 34. [5] Nos. 116, 231, 232. [6] No. 172; Part II, no. 678.
[7] Nos. 72, 175, 178. [8] No. 180. [9] Part II, no. 896.
[10] No. 236, headnote. [11] No. 326, headnote.
[12] Bodl. MS. Charters Norfolk 746. [13] No. 330.
[14] Part II, nos. 751, 755. [15] No. 387, ll. 111–14.
[16] No. 200; Part II, nos. 904, 905.

broken off in 1477.[1] In August 1469 the Duke of Norfolk, who had long claimed Caister, besieged it for five weeks and subdued the defenders under John III.[2] John II was J.P. for Norfolk in 1469–70. During 1470 he reached a compromise with Wainfleet about the Fastolf estate: Paston to retain Caister and some other manors, the rest to go to Magdalen College, Oxford. The agreement was signed on 14 July,[3] but Norfolk held Caister. When Warwick and his associates restored Henry VI in October the Paston brothers took the Lancastrian side.[4] Both served on a commission of oyer and terminer under Clarence. Norfolk released Caister in December. In April 1471 the Pastons fought at Barnet on the losing side.[5] On 23 June Norfolk's men again seized Caister.[6] John II received his pardon on 21 December. In 1472 there is word of his interest in Calais,[7] and in February 1473 he was there,[8] serving under the command of Lord Hastings. He was often there during the next four years, and took the opportunity to visit Bruges[9] and perhaps Neuss.[10] In January 1476 the Duke of Norfolk died suddenly, and John II at once sent a messenger to claim Caister.[11] Though this was not well received, his title was recognized to be valid by the King's council and he regained possession in June.[12] He made his will in October 1477.[13] In 1478 he was M.P. for Yarmouth. In October 1479 he wrote from London 'in fear of the sickness',[14] and died there in November; he was buried in Whitefriars Priory.[15] He left a natural daughter by Constance Reynforth.[16] At some time after 1475 he drew up a remarkable inventory of his books.[17]

Compare with Harley 2253 scribes.

JOHN PASTON III

Born 1444, probably at Geldeston.[18] He appears first as secretary to his mother in letters written from probably 1459 to early 1462.[19] From late 1462 until 1464 he served under the Duke of Norfolk at Holt Castle, Denbighshire,[20] and Newcastle-upon-Tyne.[21] From June 1464 he was at home in Norfolk, helping his mother with the management of the estates, taking her place when she went to London in September 1465,[22] and put in charge of the manor of Cotton after her return.[23] In October 1465 he was invited to attend the celebration of the Duke of Norfolk's coming of age, as 'one of our servants of household'.[24] He went to Bruges with John II for Princess

---

[1] No. 282, 308. [2] No. 334. [3] No. 252.
[4] No. 258. [5] Nos. 261, 346.
[6] Worcester, *Itineraries*, p. 252.
[7] No. 355. [8] No. 272. [9] Part II, no. 769.
[10] No. 289. [11] No. 368. [12] Nos. 299, 300.
[13] No. 309. [14] No. 315.
[15] No. 383. Writ of *diem clausit extremum* issued 30 November 1479 (Norfolk and Suffolk, Cambridgeshire and Huntingdonshire, Hertfordshire): *Cal. Fine Rolls, 1471–85*, no. 515.
[16] No. 230, l. 174; Part II, no. 781. [17] No. 316. [18] No. 346.
[19] Nos. 152, 154, 155, 157, 163–5, 167–70. [20] Nos. 319, 321.
[21] No. 320. [22] No. 323. [23] No. 192.
[24] Part II, no. 784.

Margaret's marriage in July 1468.[1] By the middle of 1469 he was in command at Caister, apprehensive of an attack by Norfolk's men and critical of his brother's inaction;[2] and when the attack came in late August he withstood a siege until forced to surrender about 25 September.[3] His letters in 1470 are mostly dated from Norwich, but he went to Esher in August to take his part in the settlement of Fastolf's estate with the Bishop of Winchester,[4] and he was in London with John II in October.[5] He was on the commission of oyer and terminer for Norfolk appointed the same month. With his brother he fought at Barnet in April 1471, and was wounded.[6] He was pardoned in July, though the pardon was not sealed until the following February.[7] In 1472 he was living in Norwich with his mother, on unfriendly terms with her chaplain James Gloys.[8] He had already begun to try to negotiate with Norfolk's council for the restoration of Caister to John II in return for payment,[9] and repeatedly visited Framlingham on this account. He intended to go to Compostela on pilgrimage in the summer of 1473,[10] but there is no firm evidence that he went. In 1474 he showed interest in young women in London, but to no effect.[11] In 1475 he went to Calais for a short time, but was back in Norwich in the autumn.[12] He was again at Framlingham in March 1476.[13] Early in 1477 he was contemplating marriage with Margery Brews, and after some setbacks in the negotiations married her before the end of the year.[14] His eldest son was born in 1478,[15] the second about a year later. When John II died in November 1479 John III took immediate steps to secure his possession of the estate,[16] but was much obstructed by his uncle William II.[17] He was on the commission of the peace for Norfolk in 1480–2, and from 1483 onwards on various other commissions: to assess subsidies, of array, of jail delivery, etc. He was pardoned by Richard III on 10 March 1484. In 1485–6 he became M.P. for Norwich, and sheriff of Norfolk and Suffolk; and by the beginning of 1487 was 'right trusty and right well beloved councillor' to the Earl of Oxford.[18] On 16 June of that year he fought at the battle of Stoke, and was knighted on the field.[19] Oxford, who was Lord High Admiral, made him his deputy, and a number of letters and commissions about 1490 are concerned with shipping.[20] He was J.P. for Norfolk again in 1494–7. After Margery's death in 1495 he married Agnes, daughter of Nicholas Morley of Glynde, Sussex,[21] who had been married twice before. In 1500 he was commanded by the King to attend on the arrival of Catherine of Aragon (which in fact was postponed).[22]

---

[1] No. 330.
[2] No. 332.
[3] No. 334.
[4] No. 344.
[5] No. 345.
[6] No. 261.
[7] No. 348.
[8] Nos. 353, 355.
[9] No. 354.
[10] No. 278.
[11] Nos. 362–3.
[12] No. 365.
[13] No. 371.
[14] Nos. 374–9, 226.
[15] No. 312.
[16] No. 383.
[17] Nos. 385, 387.
[18] Part II, no. 807.
[19] B.M. MS. Add. 34889, f. 135.
[20] e.g. Part II, nos. 823–7.
[21] No. 392.
[22] Part II, no. 839.

His last commission was dated 15 May 1504.[1] He entered into recogniz-
ances on behalf of a number of men from 1502 to 1504, and had to be replaced on the last occasion because he had died on 28 August.[2] His widow
survived until 1510.[3]

MARGERY PASTON

Daughter of Sir Thomas Brews of Topcroft, Norfolk. Her earliest
surviving letters are of February 1477, the year in which she married
John Paston III.[4] She was living in Norwich about 1481, but at Caister
in 1486.[5] In 1489 she went to London, partly at least on pilgrimage.[6]
She died in 1495, and was buried in the White Friars' church in
Norwich.[7]

EDMOND PASTON II

First mentioned in a letter by Richard Calle datable in November 1461
recommending Margaret Paston to send Edmond 'nouther to Cambregge
nor to non other place' until after Christmas.[8] There is nothing to show
where he then went: he next appears writing part of a letter for his mother
in April 1469,[9] and a month later he was at Caister, hoping soon to go to
London to an inn of court or chancery.[10] He went to Staple Inn, but was back
in Norwich before the end of 1471.[11] In 1472 he was living in Margaret's
house in Norwich, but was unwelcome there and was trying to arrange to
go to Calais with John II.[12] He had left home by September[13] and was in
Calais in July 1473,[14] but the following year in London.[15] In January 1475
he was in Norwich again.[16] In April the same year he was indentured to the
Duke of Gloucester 'to do him service of war with the King' over the sea;[17]
and in June was in London on his way to Calais.[18] He was back in Norfolk
by the beginning of 1478, and John III was looking for a wife for him.[19] In
November 1479 negotiations were in progress with Katherine, daughter of
John Spelman and widow of William Clippesby,[20] whom he married soon
afterwards, probably in 1480, and went to live at her house at Oby.[21]
Perhaps about the same time he was concerned to find a wife for his brother
William.[22] By February 1482 he had a son named Robert.[23] Between 1486

---

[1] *Cal. Pat. Rolls, 1494–1509*, p. 361.

[2] *Cal. Close Rolls, 1500–9*, nos. 131, 135, 361, 419. Writ of *diem clausit extremum* issued
20 October 1504 (Hertfordshire, Suffolk, Norfolk, Essex, and London): *Cal. Fine Rolls,
1485–1509*, no. 804.

[3] Will dated 31 May, proved 19 June 1510: P.C.C. Reg. Benet, 29. Part II, no. 930.

[4] Nos. 415–16.   [5] Nos. 417–18, 419.   [6] No. 420.

[7] J. Weever, *Antient Funerall Monuments* (1631), p. 866.   [8] Part II, no. 650.

[9] No. 201.   [10] No. 332.   [11] No. 394.

[12] No. 353.   [13] No. 354.   [14] No. 278.

[15] Nos. 285, 363.   [16] No. 289.   [17] No. 396.

[18] No. 292.   [19] No. 380.   [20] No. 381.

[21] No. 399.   [22] No. 398.   [23] No. 230.

and 1489 he was appointed by the Earl of Oxford receiver of the lands formerly belonging to Thomas, Lord Scales.[1] Katherine died on 18 April 1491,[2] and Edmond later married Margaret, daughter of Thomas Monceaux and widow of William Lomnor and of Thomas Briggs. He died before 8 February 1504.[3] On 24 November of the same year his widow made her will, which was proved on 15 May 1505.[4]

MARGERY PASTON, later CALLE

Agnes Paston's reference, in writing to John I in 1450, to 'all your sons and daughters',[5] should mean that both Margery and Anne had been born before then; but (unless there was another girl who died young) it is probably only an inclusive phrase not to be strictly interpreted: Margaret, writing probably in 1451, speaks of only one daughter,[6] and since Anne is said to 'wax high' as late as 1470[7] she cannot have been born much before 1455. Margery's birth at any rate was evidently before 1450. The first mention of her by name is by William Paston II, probably in 1458, reporting an offer of marriage;[8] the next is a greeting by John III in 1462.[9] In November 1463 marriage was again being discussed,[10] and when Margery went to London with her mother in 1465 it was still a live question.[11] Another offer was made a year or two later, after John I's death.[12] But in 1469 she shocked her mother and brothers by insisting on marrying Richard Calle, their head bailiff.[13] Though Margaret forbade her the house, and still disapproved of her a year later,[14] she later relented at least so far as to leave a legacy to Margery's eldest son, with reversion to the two younger;[15] and in view of this it is likely that the omission of Margery from the will means that she had died before it was made in February 1482—indeed, since Walter Paston's will also omits her,[16] though he had sent greetings to 'sisters' in his uncertainly dated letter no. 402, and Edmond shortly afterwards uses 'my sister' without distinguishing name,[17] she was probably already dead by 1479.

ANNE PASTON, later YELVERTON

First mentioned by name by John III in 1465, when she was living at Hellesdon.[18] In 1469 she needed neckerchiefs to meet the standards of the household in which she had been placed.[19] This was doubtless that of Sir

[1] No. 401.　　　　　　　　　　　　　[2] Blomefield, xi. 148 (misprinted 144).
[3] Writ of *diem clausit extremum* issued 8 February 1504: *Cal. Fine Rolls, 1485–1509*, no. 786.
[4] *Norwich Wills*, ii. 243; Part II, no. 929.　　　　　　　　　　　[5] No. 20.
[6] Nos. 140, 142.　　　　　[7] No. 206.　　　　　　　　　　[8] No. 85.
[9] No. 320.　　　　　　　[10] No. 174.　　　　　　　　　　[11] No. 323.
[12] Part II, no. 756.　　　[13] Nos. 203, 245, 332.　　　　　　[14] No. 208.
[15] No. 230, ll. 177–85.　　　　　　　　　　　　　　　　　　[16] No. 405.
[17] No. 397. Cf. also John III's no. 386 (later than the will): 'my brethryn and systyr'.
[18] No. 323.　　　　　　　　　　　　　　　　　　　　　　　[19] No. 201.

William and Lady Calthorp, of Burnham Thorpe; for Calthorp, probably in 1470, asked Margaret Paston to make other arrangements for Anne.[1] By June 1472 negotiations were in progress for her marriage to William Yelverton, grandson of the judge.[2] They did not go altogether smoothly, and John II in 1473 was concerned lest her 'old love' for John Pampyng—a family servant no doubt uncomfortably reminiscent of Richard Calle—might revive.[3] In 1476 he suggested a different match;[4] nothing came of this, and in March 1477 Anne appears to have been still living with her mother.[5] Before June of the same year, however, she had married Yelverton.[6] In 1479 she gave birth to a child, which did not live.[7] Margaret's will left her various legacies, but mentioned no children.[8] Anne died in 1494–5, her husband in 1500.[9]

WALTER PASTON

Since he was not 24 years of age in February 1479,[10] the date of his birth cannot have been earlier than 1455 and was probably a year or two later. He is first mentioned in 1472 as having borrowed a book of his brother's.[11] He went to Oxford probably early in 1473,[12] and took the degree of B.A. there on 18 June 1479.[13] He fell ill soon afterwards and had to be brought home to Norwich, where he died on or shortly after 18 August of the same year.[14] He was buried in the church of St. Peter Hungate, which had been repaired by his parents in 1460.[15]

WILLIAM PASTON III

Born probably in 1459.[16] In 1477 Margaret Paston told John II that she would no longer meet William's expenses, and charged him to do so.[17] William was at Eton in 1478 and 1479, intending to leave as soon as he had acquired 'versifying', and considering the marriage prospects of Margaret Alborough.[18] Perhaps in 1481 or soon after he was in London, concerned with his and his brothers' inheritance from John II;[19] and perhaps about the same time Edmond commended a widow to his attention.[20] By 1487 he had entered the service of the Earl of Oxford.[21] He was prevented, in part by illness, from going to Calais in 1492;[22] and in 1503 or 1504 was discharged from the Earl's service because he was 'so troubled with sickness and crazed in his mind'.[23]

[1] No. 206.   [2] Nos. 216, 352.   [3] Nos. 282, 283.
[4] No. 296.   [5] No. 374.   [6] No. 226.
[7] No. 397.   [8] No. 230.   [9] *Inq. p.m.*, Henry VII, ii, no. 353.
[10] Part II, no. 731.   [11] No. 353.   [12] No. 220.
[13] No. 404.   [14] Nos. 405, 397, 382.
[15] E. A. Kent, *The Church of St. Peter Hungate, Norwich* (Norwich, 1932).
[16] No. 282.   [17] No. 227.   [18] Nos. 406–7.
[19] No. 408.   [20] No. 398.   [21] No. 410.
[22] No. 414.   [23] Part II, no. 848.

Sons of John Paston III and Margery

CHRISTOPHER PASTON

Born 1478.[1] Since he is not mentioned in Margaret's will, though his younger brother is, he must have died before 1482.[2]

WILLIAM PASTON IV

Born about 1479. Negotiations with Sir Henry Heydon towards his marriage are mentioned not later than 1493,[3] and he did marry Bridget Heydon. He was at Cambridge, perhaps about 1495.[4] He was sheriff of Norfolk and Suffolk in 1517–18, and was a knight by 1520, when he was present at the Field of Cloth of Gold. He died in 1554.

CHRONOLOGICAL TABLE

DATE	FAMILY AFFAIRS	PUBLIC AFFAIRS	LITERARY EVENTS (many only approximately datable)
1378	William Paston I b.	Richard II king.	
1399		Richard II deposed, Henry IV king.	
1400			Chaucer d. (?).
1412	W. Paston counsel in Norwich.		Lydgate's *Troy Book* commissioned by Prince Henry. Hoccleve, *Regement of Princes* (?).
1413	W. Paston steward of courts of the Bishop of Norwich.	Accession of Henry V.	Prose *Pilgrimage of the Soul* (?).
1414	W. Paston arbitrator concerning mayoralty of Norwich.	Oldcastle's insurrection.	*Chronicles of London* (?).
1415	W. Paston J.P. William Worcester b	Henry V's first campaign in France. Battle of Agincourt.	Hoccleve, *Reproof to Oldcastle*. Charles of Orleans prisoner in England. R. Burton's List of the York Plays.
1417		Henry V's second campaign in France. Execution of Oldcastle.	Lydgate, *Departing of T. Chaucer for France*.
1418	W. Paston commissioner on Oldcastle's lands.	Siege of Rouen.	
1419	Clement Paston I d. W. Paston commissioner to inquire into treasons in Suffolk and Norfolk.	Surrender of Rouen.	J. Page, *Siege of Rouen*.

[1] No. 312. [2] No. 230. [3] No. 400. [4] No. 421.

Sons of John I — John II – at Court (1442-79); John III – Duke of Norfolk (1444-1504); Edmond II – Earl of Oxford (?–1504); Walter – Oxford (1455(?)–1479) B.A.
Sons of Wm I — Wm III – Eton, Earl of Oxford (1459-1504)
Cambridge: John I (1421-66), Edmond I, Wm II (1436-96), Clement II (1442-79); Wm IV (1479-1554) sheriff of Norfolk + Suffolk. Kt at Cloth of Gold.

CHRONOLOGICAL TABLE

DATE	FAMILY AFFAIRS	PUBLIC AFFAIRS	LITERARY EVENTS
1420	W. Paston m. Agnes Berry; buys Oxnead about this time.	Treaty of Troyes. Henry V m. Catherine of Valois.	Lydgate's *Troy Book* completed. Yonge's translation of *Secreta Secretorum*. Friar Daw's *Reply to Jack Upland* (?).
1421	W. Paston serjeant at law. John Paston I b.	Henry (VI) b.	Lydgate, *Siege of Thebes*. Hoccleve, various *ballades* (?).
1422	W. Paston commissioner of assize in the south-west.	Accession of Henry VI, 1 Sept. Bedford Regent.	Caxton b. (?). Lydgate, *Life of Our Lady; Epithalamium to the Duke of Gloucester; Serpent of Division*. Hoccleve, *Complaint* and *Dialogue with a Friend*.
1423			*The Kingis Quair*.
1424	W. Paston in London, consulted by Norwich Corporation. Walter Aslak attacks him in Norwich.	Battle of Verneuil. James I of Scotland (a captive since 1406) released.	Wyntoun, *Original Chronicle of Scotland* (?).
1425	W. Paston's earliest surviving letter. His disputes with Aslak and Wortes. Edmond Paston I b.	Conflict between Gloucester and Beaufort, Bishop of Winchester.	*Castle of Perseverance. Life of Ypomydon. Avowing of Arthur.* Lovelich, *Merlin*. (All approx.)
1426	W. Paston's charter for the manor of Shipden confirmed.		Hoccleve d. Lydgate in Paris; begins *Pilgrimage of the Life of Man*. Audelay fl.
1427	W. Paston buys Gresham.	Beaufort cardinal.	
1429	W. Paston justice, and brother of Bury monastery. Elizabeth Paston b.	Joan of Arc raises siege of Orleans. Henry VI crowned at Westminster.	Lydgate, *Coronation Address to Henry VI*.
1430	W. Paston concerned with the condition of Bromholm Priory.	Joan of Arc captured. Henry VI in France.	Russell, *Book of Nurture* (?). Continuation of prose *Brut* (?).
1431		Joan of Arc burnt. Henry VI crowned in Paris.	Lydgate begins *Fall of Princes*.
1432		Ewelme School founded by Michael de la Pole.	*Book of Margery Kempe*: rewriting begun.
1433	W. Paston commissioner to inquire into administration of Norwich. William Dalling petitions Parliament against him.		Lydgate, *Lives of St. Edmund and St. Fremund*.
1435		Death of Bedford. Fastolf governor of Anjou and Maine. Gloucester gives books to Oxford University.	Misyn, *Fire of Love*.

DATE	FAMILY AFFAIRS	PUBLIC AFFAIRS	LITERARY EVENTS
1436	William Paston II b.	French recover Paris. York appointed lieutenant in France. Scotland at war with England.	*Libel of English Policy.*
1437	W. Paston I exempted from certain duties.	James I of Scotland murdered.	Lydgate, *Horse, Goose, and Sheep.*
1439	W. Paston a trier of petitions.	Fastolf returns to England. Gloucester gives more books to Oxford.	Lydgate, *Lives of St. Alban and St. Amphibalus.* Capgrave, *Commentary on Genesis.*
1440	John Paston I m. Margaret Mautby.	York lieutenant again. Siege of Harfleur. Eton College founded by Henry VI.	Charles of Orleans released. Margery Kempe d. (?). Burgh, *Letter to Lydgate. Eger and Grime. Wedding of Sir Gawen. Gesta Romanorum* tr. *Book of the Knight of La Tour Landry* tr. *Epistle of Othea,* tr. Scrope. (All approx.) *Promptorium Parvulorum.* Manuscripts of the York Plays and of *Dux Moraud* (?). Thornton MS. (romances).
1441		Trial of Duchess of Gloucester. King's College, Cambridge, founded by Henry VI.	
1442	Clement Paston II b. John Paston II b. W. Paston granted the manor of East Beckham.	Duke of Somerset's campaign in France. Sir John Fortescue chief justice.	
1443	J. Paston I ill in London. J. Hauteyn claims Oxnead.		Pecock, *Rule of Christian Religion* and *The Donet* begun. Bokenham, *Lives of Holy Women* begun.
1444	William Paston I d. John Paston III b.	Peace negotiations with France.	Lydgate, *Miracles of St. Edmund.*
1445	Agnes Paston in dispute with vicar and villagers of Paston.	Henry VI m. Margaret of Anjou.	Idley, *Instructions to his Son* (?).
1447	J. Paston I J.P.	Arrest and death of Gloucester.	Bokenham d. (?)
1448	J. Paston expelled from Gresham by Lord Moleyns, but takes up residence again.		
1449	Edmond Paston I d. William Paston II at Cambridge. Margaret Paston expelled from Gresham by Moleyns. Hauteyn still claims Oxnead. Stephen Scrope a suitor of Elizabeth Paston.	War with France renewed. Rouen and eastern Normandy lost.	Lydgate d. (?).

DATE	FAMILY AFFAIRS	PUBLIC AFFAIRS	LITERARY EVENTS
1450	J. Paston commissioner of array. Moleyns indicted. Margery Paston b. before this year.	Duke of Suffolk impeached and soon afterwards murdered. Jack Cade's rebellion. Cherbourg lost.	The Bible printed at Mainz. Harding, *Chronicle* (?). *Dicts and Sayings of the Philosophers*, tr. Scrope (?).
1451	Agnes Paston in conflict with villagers of Paston about a wall. Moleyns acquitted, but J. Paston recovers Gresham.	Gascony and Guienne entirely lost. Complaints in Norfolk against Sir Thomas Tuddenham and John Heydon.	Capgrave, *Lives of St. Augustine and St. Gilbert. Upland's Rejoinder* (?).
1452	J. Paston complains of disturbances in Norfolk.	General pardon on Good Friday. Army under Shrewsbury sent to recover Guienne.	
1453	Margaret Paston's uncle Philip Berney d.	Constantinople falls to Turks. Queen Margaret visits Norwich. Henry VI insane. Edward, Prince of Wales, b.	J. Dunstable, composer, d.
1454	J. Paston I appeals for clemency for Thomas Denyes. Wardship of Thomas Fastolf of Cowhaugh granted to Paston and Thomas Howes. Sir John Fastolf takes up residence at Caister. Elizabeth Paston's marriage discussed: Lord Grey suggests a match, and William Clopton makes draft agreement (?) about this time.	York made protector, and captain of Calais; and commissioned to commit the Duke of Exeter to Pontefract Castle. York's brother-in-law Salisbury chancellor. Somerset in prison. Cardinal Kemp d. Thomas Bourchier Archbishop of Canterbury. Plague in London. Henry VI recovers at Christmas.	Pecock, *Follower to the Donet.*
1455	J. Paston among those with most votes at shire election, but the Duke of Norfolk's nominees returned. Anne Paston b. (?).	Henry resumes power. Bourchier made chancellor, Somerset and Exeter released. York, Warwick, and Salisbury march south. First battle of St. Albans 22 May: Somerset killed, York constable of England and again protector.	Pecock, *Repressor* (?).
1456	J. Paston J.P. He and William Paston II among Fastolf's trustees. Fastolf proposes to found a chantry.	York discharged from protectorship 25 Feb. From September the court in Coventry. William Wainfleet chancellor.	J. Shirley d.
1457	J. Paston pays fine to decline knighthood. Elizabeth Paston in London. Walter Paston b. (?).	The French sack Sandwich. The King and Queen at Hereford. Welshmen indicted.	Pecock forced to resign bishopric of Chichester. Vegetius, *Knighthood and Battle* tr.
1458	J. Paston and others accused of riotous behaviour. Clement Paston in London under a tutor. Elizabeth Paston m. Robert Poynings. Offer of marriage for Margery Paston.	Reconciliation of the lords in London. Warwick at Calais. Magdalen College, Oxford, founded by Wainfleet.	

lxvii

DATE	FAMILY AFFAIRS	PUBLIC AFFAIRS	LITERARY EVENTS
1459	William Paston III b. (?). Fastolf d. 5 Nov. J. Paston I an executor, and on various commissions. W. Paston II and W. Worcester go to London about Fastolf's property.	Battle of Blore Heath: Lancastrians repulsed. Rout of Yorkists at Ludford. York escapes to Ireland, he and supporters attainted in parliament at Coventry.	J. Fisher b.
1460	J. Paston I M.P. Inquisitions on Fastolf's lands.	Rivers captured at Sandwich and taken to Calais. Edward Earl of March, Warwick, and Salisbury invade England. Battle of Northampton: Henry VI taken prisoner. York claims the crown. Battle of Wakefield: York killed.	Pecock d. (?). Skelton b. (?). Dunbar b. (?). MS. of Towneley Plays about this date.
1461	Threat to kidnap J. Paston I and take him before one of the northern lords. Duke of Norfolk (John Mowbray II) seizes Caister. Robert Poynings killed at St. Albans: Elizabeth dispossessed of lands. J. Paston I at court in June; later in scuffle with John Howard at shire hall in Norwich. In October J. Paston I in Fleet prison, but soon released and Howard imprisoned. J. Paston I M.P. again. J. Paston II in royal household. Worcester on bad terms with Pastons.	Battle of Mortimer's Cross. Second battle of St. Albans. Edward IV proclaimed King 4 March. Battle of Towton. Carlisle besieged by Scots. Edward crowned 28 June. Henry VI and Queen Margaret in Scotland. Duke of Norfolk d. 6 Nov.	G. Ashby, *Poems.* Burgh, *Cato* tr. Ostensible date of the events dramatized in the *Play of the Sacrament.*
1462	J. Paston II travelling with the King. J. Paston I petitions the Chancellor against Yelverton and Jenney. J. Paston III serving in the north with the Duke of Norfolk (John Mowbray III).	Margaret of Anjou invades Northumberland. Castles of Alnwick, Dunstanburgh, and Bamburgh besieged by Warwick's forces. Tuddenham executed.	H. Medwall b. (?). Adam of Cobsam, *The Wright's Chaste Wife* (?).
1463	J. Paston II back in Norwich; a writ against him. Offer of marriage for Margery Paston. J. Paston II leaves home again without his father's leave.	Margaret of Anjou retreats to Flanders, with Exeter and Fortescue. Henry VI remains in Bamburgh.	Capgrave, *Chronicle.*
1464	Inquiry into Fastolf's will: witnesses for Yelverton and Worcester examined. J. Paston I petitions the King for licence to found college	Somerset rebels. Battles of Hedgeley Moor and Hexham: Somerset executed. Margaret seeking French help. Edward IV	Capgrave d. Second continuation of the *Brut* begins.

DATE	FAMILY AFFAIRS	PUBLIC AFFAIRS	LITERARY EVENTS
	as Fastolf directed. J. Paston I outlawed and imprisoned. J. Paston II banished from home. J Paston III at home in Norfolk.	m. Elizabeth Woodville privately.	
1465	Manor of Cotton threatened by Yelverton and Jenney. Drayton seized and Hellesdon house and lodge sacked by the Duke of Suffolk's men. J. Paston I in the Fleet again. Margaret goes to visit him, taking Margery with her. Inquiry into Fastolf's will continues. W. Paston II J.P. J. Paston II at Caister. J. Paston III at Norfolk's coming of age.	Coronation of Queen Elizabeth. George Neville Archbishop of York. Henry VII captured in Yorkshire and imprisoned in the Tower.	Hector Boece b. (?). J. Harding d. J. Tiptoft tr. Cicero *de Amicitia* (?).
1466	Lord Scales seizes J. Paston I's Norwich property. J. Paston I d. in London. Draft will of Agnes Paston.	Elizabeth of York b. Warwick's relations with Edward IV begin to deteriorate.	
1467	J. Paston II in tournament at Eltham; M.P. J. Paston III interested in Lady Boleyn's daughter. Probate of Fastolf's will granted to J. Paston and T. Howes.	Warwick on mission to France to negotiate treaty; but Edward accepts offer of marriage of his sister Margaret to Duke of Burgundy's heir. George Neville dismissed from chancellorship.	J. Colet b. (?).
1468	Fastolf's trustees release Caister and other manors to J. Paston II. T. Howes declares Fastolf's will falsified. J. Paston II and J. Paston III in Bruges for Princess Margaret's marriage. William Ebesham writing J. Paston II's 'Great Book'.	Princess Margaret married in Bruges to Charles the Bold of Burgundy. Edward declares war on France. Warwick disgraced. Lancastrian rising in Wales. Burgundy makes truce with France.	Fortescue, *de Laudibus Legum Angliae* begun. Gregory, *Chronicle* begun.
1469	J. Paston II J.P.; engaged to Anne Haute. J. Paston III besieged in Caister by Norfolk's men, and forced to surrender. Margery Paston contracts to marry Richard Calle, and is forbidden her mother's house. J. Paston II sells Beckham to Roger Townshend.	Edward IV visits Norwich. Robin of Redesdale's insurrection. Warwick crosses from Calais and captures Edward after battle of Edgcote. Rivers, his son, and other royal favourites executed. Edward released in October.	Malory, *Morte d'Arthur* finished 9 Edward IV (4 March 1469–3 March 1470).
1470	W. Paston II m. Lady Anne Beaufort before this year. J. Paston III and others	Insurrection of Sir R. Welles in Lincolnshire. Edward IV leads force to	J. Tiptoft d. *Chronicle of the Rebellion in Lincoln-shire. Rauf Coilyear* (?).

DATE	FAMILY AFFAIRS	PUBLIC AFFAIRS	LITERARY EVENTS
	accused of felony in killing men at siege of Caister. J. Paston II compromises with Wainfleet on disposal of Fastolf's lands, many of which pass to Magdalen College. After Henry VI's restoration Norfolk releases Caister to J. Paston II. Edmond Paston II at Staple Inn. Sir W. Calthorp asks Margaret Paston to take her daughter Anne home, and recommends marriage.	crush it, and afterwards attacks Warwick and Clarence, who escape to France. Warwick comes to terms with Margaret of Anjou, invades England with Clarence, Jasper Tudor, Oxford, and other Lancastrians, forces Edward to flee to Burgundy, and restores Henry VI (re-crowned 13 Oct.). Prince Edward (later Edward V) b.	Morality plays *Mankind,* and probably *Wisdom,* composed about this time. MS. of *Ludus Coventriae* (?).
1471	J. Paston II and J. Paston III at battle of Barnet on Lancastrian side. J. Paston III wounded. Caister seized again by Norfolk in June. J. Paston II's pardon signed July, sealed Dec. Margaret Paston complains of his extravagance. Elizabeth Poynings m. Sir G. Browne. W. Paston II pardoned.	Edward IV lands at Ravenspur 14 Mar. Clarence joins him. Battle of Barnet: Warwick killed. Queen Margaret lands, is defeated at Tewkesbury and captured, and her son Prince Edward killed. Edward IV enters London 21 May. Henry VI put to death.	Caxton, now in the service of the Duchess of Burgundy, tr. *Recuyell of the Histories of Troy* (printed 1475). Ripley, *Compend of Alchemy. History of the Arrival of Edward IV.* Fortescue, *Governance of England.*
1472	Sale of Sporle wood negotiated. J. Paston II hoping to go to Calais. J. Paston III and Edmond Paston II on bad terms with James Gloys, Margaret's chaplain. J. Paston II proposed for election to Parliament for Maldon. J. Paston III often at Framlingham, recommends his brother to attend christening of the Duchess of Norfolk's expected child; finds himself out of favour with the Duke. W. Paston II M.P.	Truces with Scotland and France. Clarence and Gloucester given most of Warwick's lands. Gloucester m. Anne Neville, Warwick's daughter and formerly betrothed to Prince Edward. Clarence and Gloucester at odds. Duchess of Norfolk gives birth to daughter (Anne Mowbray).	Worcester, first revision of *Book of Noblesse.* Caxton returns to Bruges from Cologne.
1473	J. Paston II at Calais. He wishes to end his engagement to Anne Haute. E. Paston II at Calais. J. Paston III intending pilgrimage to Compostela. Walter Paston goes to Oxford. J. Gloys d.	Edward IV raises new taxes for an expedition against France, but postpones it. Earl of Oxford seizes St. Michael's Mount, but is besieged there. Treaty with Hanseatic League.	Worcester rev. Scrope's tr. of *Dicts and Sayings,* and presents his own tr. of Cicero *de Senectute* to Wainfleet.
1474	J. Paston II redeems Sporle. J. Paston III looking for a wife. Agnes Paston recovers from illness, but W. Paston II's daughter Margaret dies. Margaret Paston at Mautby.	Earl of Oxford surrenders. Edward makes treaty with Burgundy concerting invasion of France.	Stephen Hawes b. (?). Warkworth, *Chronicle* (?).

DATE	FAMILY AFFAIRS	PUBLIC AFFAIRS	LITERARY EVENTS
1475	J. Paston II at Calais, in poor health. He petitions the King for recovery of Caister, still in Norfolk's hands. W. Paston II has designs on Oxnead. E. Paston II indentured to Gloucester for service with the King. J. Paston III also at Calais.	Burgundy besieges Neuss. Edward IV invades France, but Burgundy fails to co-operate and Edward makes Treaty of Picquigny in return for money payments.	Alexander Barclay b. (?). Gavin Douglas b. (?). G. Ashby d. *The Flower and the Leaf*, and *Assembly of Ladies* (?). Caxton prints in Bruges *Recuyell of the Histories of Troy* and *Game and Play of the Chess*, his own translations.
1476	Duke of Norfolk d. 16–17 Jan., and J. Paston II sends to Caister to claim possession. His title eventually confirmed; he takes over in June. Meanwhile he goes to Calais again with Lord Hastings.	Margaret of Anjou handed over to France for ransom.	Fortescue d. (?). Caxton sets up press at Westminster, and prints *Book of Courtesy, Paruus Cato, Anelida and Arcite, Churl and the Bird, Horse, Goose, and Sheep, Stans puer*, etc.
1477	Negotiations by J. Paston III for marriage to Margery Brews; they are married by end of year. Anne Paston m. William Yelverton III. J. Paston II mortgages Sporle to Townshend. Margaret requires him to pay for W. Paston III's keep and school fees. His engagement to Anne Haute broken off. He makes his will.	Clarence angers Edward IV by numerous acts of defiance; two of his servants executed on charges of necromancy. Duke of Burgundy killed at battle of Nancy; his daughter and heiress Mary m. Maximilian of Austria.	Caxton tr. and pr. *History of Jason*, pr. *Dicts and Sayings of the Philosophers* tr. Earl Rivers (formerly Scales, J. Paston II's friend), and *The Temple of Brass* (Chaucer's *Parlement of Foules*). Norton, *Ordinal of Alchemy*. Makculloch MS. containing Scottish poems, some by Henryson.
1478	J. Paston III suggests a wife for Edmond II. J. Paston II M.P.; at law with the Duke of Suffolk over Hellesdon and Drayton. J. Paston I's tomb at Bromholm not yet made. Walter Paston at Oxford. William Paston III at Eton. Margaret Paston ill, makes will. J. Paston III's son Christopher b.	Richard, Duke of York, m. Anne Mowbray. Clarence attainted of treason, and executed.	Thomas More b. First book printed at Oxford (?). Caxton pr. Chaucer's *Canterbury Tales* and *Boece*, and Rivers's tr. of Christine de Pisan's *Moral Proverbs*.
1479	Walter Paston takes B.A. degree at Oxford in June, but falls ill and dies in August. Agnes Paston d. at almost the same time. Anne (Yelverton) has child which does not survive. William Paston II claims Agnes's manors of Marlingford, etc. J. Morton, Bishop of Ely, offers to mediate between him and J. Paston II. John II d. in Nov., and John	Edward IV negotiating with France for a commercial treaty, depending on his attacking Burgundy; but eventually he inclines instead to Burgundy.	First book printed at St. Albans.

DATE	FAMILY AFFAIRS	PUBLIC AFFAIRS	LITERARY EVENTS
	III asks Edmond to enter Marlingford, etc., in his name. Clement Paston II dead by this year, and probably Margery (Calle) also. J. Paston III's son, William IV, b. (?).		
1480	Edmond Paston II m. Katherine Clippesby; and about the same time looks for a wife for W. Paston III. J. Paston III J.P.	Edward IV planning to attack Scotland.	Worcester, *Itineraries* in preparation. Caxton pr. *Chronicles of England*, *Description of Britain* (tr. of Higden), *Vocabulary in French and English*; and tr. Ovid's *Metamorphoses* from a French version. John Lettou begins to print in London.
1481	William Paston III in London.	English fleet raids Scotland; Gloucester besieges Berwick.	Caxton tr. and pr. *Mirror of the World* (Vincent of Beauvais), *Reynard the Fox* (from Dutch), *Godfrey of Boulogne*; and pr. Worcester's *Tully of Old Age* and Tiptoft's *Tully of Friendship*.
1482	Edmond Paston II's son Robert b. by this time. J. Paston III's son Christopher dead. Margaret Paston makes the will which took effect. W. Worcester d. this year or soon after.	Gloucester captures Edinburgh. Berwick surrendered to England.	Henry the Minstrel, *Sir William Wallace* (?). Caxton pr. Trevisa's tr. of Higden's *Polychronicon*.
1483	J. Paston III on various commissions. Summoned in Oct. by the new Duke of Norfolk (his father's old adversary John Howard) to take part in suppressing rebels in Kent. Sir. G. Browne executed 3 Dec. for complicity in Buckingham's revolt.	Edward IV d. 9 Apr. Edward V aged 12. Gloucester protector. Hastings accused of plotting his death, and executed. Gloucester, with support of Buckingham, assumes throne as Richard III. Edward and his brother murdered in the Tower. Buckingham heads revolt in Oct., is captured and executed.	Earl Rivers d. Caxton pr. Chaucer's *House of Fame* and *Troilus and Criseyde*, Gower's *Confessio Amantis*, Lydgate's *Pilgrimage of the Soul*; and tr. and pr. *Golden Legend* and *Caton*.
1484	J. Paston III petitions for redress of infringements of his property rights by W. Paston II. He is pardoned by Richard III. Margaret Paston d. Nov.	Bill of attainder against many participants in Buckingham's revolt. Parliament confirms right of succession to Richard's descendants, but his only son Edward d. Apr. Henry, Earl of Richmond, in France.	Caxton pr. Lydgate, *Life of Our Lady*, and 2nd edn. of *Canterbury Tales*; tr. and pr. *Æsop's Fables*, *Order of Chivalry*, Chartier's *Curial*, *Knight of the Tower*; and tr. *The Royal Book* (pr. 1486).

DATE	FAMILY AFFAIRS	PUBLIC AFFAIRS	LITERARY EVENTS
1485	J. Paston III M.P. for Norwich, sheriff of Norfolk and Suffolk.	Richmond lands in Wales. Battle of Bosworth 22 Aug. Richard III killed, Richmond succeeds as Henry VII.	Caxton ed. and pr. Malory, *Morte Darthur*, and tr. and pr. *Charles the Great, Paris and Vienne, Life of St. Winifred.* Skelton tr. Diodorus Siculus from Poggio's Latin (?).
1486	J. Paston III on the Earl of Oxford's council. E. Paston II receiver of the Scales lands about this time.	Henry VII m. Elizabeth of York. J. Morton Archbishop of Canterbury.	*Book of St. Albans.* Caxton pr. Love's *Mirror of the Life of Christ.*
1487	J. Paston III knighted at battle of Stoke. W. Paston III in service of the Earl of Oxford.	Lambert Simnel's rebellion crushed at battle of Stoke.	Caxton tr. and pr. *Book of Good Manners.*
1488		Sir Edward Woodville goes to help the Duke of Brittany against the French. James III of Scotland murdered after rebellion by his son, James IV. Duke Humfrey's Library opened at Oxford.	Miles Coverdale b.
1489	J. Paston III ordered to meet the Earl of Oxford at Cambridge with a body of men to do the King service. Margery Paston in London on pilgrimage.	Rising in Yorkshire: Earl of Northumberland killed.	Skelton, *On the Dolorous Death of the Earl of Northumberland.* Caxton tr. and pr. *Blanchardyn and Eglantine, Feats of Arms and Chivalry, Four Sons of Aymon.*
1490	J. Paston III acting as deputy for Oxford as Admiral.		Sir David Lindsay b. Sir Thomas Elyot b. (?). A. Boorde b. (?). Caxton tr. and pr. *Eneydos* and *Art and Craft to know well to die.*
1491	Katherine, wife of Edmond Paston II, d.	Henry VIII b.	Caxton d. His translation of *Lives of the Fathers* (pr. W. de Worde, 1495).
1492	W. Paston III hoping to go to Calais, but unwell.	Columbus discovers the West Indies. Henry VII invades France.	J. Ryman, *Liber ympnorum.* Pynson pr. *Ghost of Guy.*
1493	Proposal for marriage of W. Paston IV to Bridget Heydon.		W. de Worde pr. *Chastising of God's Children.* Pynson pr. *Life of St. Margaret* and *Seven Wise Masters.*
1494	J. Paston III J.P. Anne Yelverton d. 1494–5.		De Worde pr. Hilton, *Scale of Perfection.* Pynson pr. Lydgate, *Fall of Princes.*

DATE	FAMILY AFFAIRS	PUBLIC AFFAIRS	LITERARY EVENTS
1495	Margery Paston d. W. Paston IV at Cambridge about this time; at Sir J. Fortescue's house at Punsborne because of plague at Cambridge.	Perkin Warbeck attempts to land at Deal.	John Bale b. De Worde pr. Trevisa's tr. of *De Proprietatibus Rerum*. Medwall, *Fulgens and Lucrece* (?).
1496	W. Paston II d. Sept.		De Worde pr. *Abbey of the Holy Ghost*. Pynson pr. *Mandeville's Travels* and Stanbridge, *Vocabula*.
1500	J. Paston III commanded to attend on arrival of Catherine of Aragon. William Yelverton III d.		Henryson d. (?). De Worde pr. Lydgate's *Siege of Thebes*, *Bevis of Hampton*, *Guy of Warwick*, *Robin Hood*. *Everyman* (?), *Golagrus and Gawain*, *Lancelot of the Laik*, *Partenay*, *Squire of Low Degree*, and other romances, before this date.
1504	W. Paston III discharged from Oxford's service because mentally ill (perhaps earlier). E. Paston II d. (perhaps late 1503). J. Paston III d. 28 Aug.		Skelton rector of Diss.

TABLE OF AUTHORS AND CLERKS[1]

Papers wholly or partly in the hand of the author (excluding mere signatures)

WILLIAM PASTON I: 1–4, latter part of 6, 7.

JOHN PASTON I: 37, most of 42A, most of 43 and 44, 73–4; short sections of 45–7, 59, 63, 66, 69, 71, 75, 77.

EDMOND PASTON I: 79.

WILLIAM PASTON II: 81–7, 88 PS, 89, 91–2, 110; short sections of 100–2, 106.

CLEMENT PASTON II: 114–16, 118–20.

JOHN PASTON II: 231, 234–6, 238–41, 243–5, 248–9, 256, part of 258, 261, 263–93, 295–308, 310–16.

JOHN PASTON III: 318–43, 345–86, 388–93; short section of 387.

EDMOND PASTON II: 394–5, 397–400.

WALTER PASTON: 402–4.

WILLIAM PASTON III: 406–11, 413–14.

WILLIAM PASTON IV: 421.

Papers in the hand of an identifiable writer other than the author

PASTONS:

CLEMENT II for AGNES: 32.

JOHN II for MARGARET: 177, 188.

JOHN III:
  for JOHN I: 57, 61, part of 63;
  for MARGARET: 152, 154–5, 157, 163–5, 167–70.

EDMOND II for MARGARET: 201 PS, 203, 205, 208 PS, 211–12, 216.

OTHERS: (in alphabetical order):

CALLE, Richard:
  for JOHN PASTON I: 56;
  for MARGARET: 156, 171, part of 189, most of 193, part of 195, 225;
  for MARGERY: 417.

---

[1] For further details see: 'The Text of Margaret Paston's Letters', *Medium Ævum*, xviii (1949), 12–28; 'A Scribal Problem in the Paston Letters' [the hand of no. 128], *English and Germanic Studies*, iv (1951–2), 31–64; 'A Paston Hand' [Edmond II], *R.E.S.*, N.S. iii (1952), 209–21; 'The Letters of William Paston', *Neophilologus*, xxxvii (1953), 36–41; 'Scribal Variation in Late Fifteenth-Century English', *Mélanges F. Mossé* (Paris, 1959), 95–103.

Bailiff of the Paston lands from about 1455,[1] evidently with general oversight of all the properties but not having authority over some other estate employees such as Daubeney and Pampyng. A native of Framlingham in Suffolk, recommended to John Paston I by the third Duke of Norfolk,[2] whose seat was there. In 1469, much against the will of Margaret and her sons, married Margery Paston, and consequently in disfavour for a time.[3] But he worked for them again later,[4] and wrote a letter for Margaret in 1475 and one for his sister-in-law Margery about 1481.[5] Still living in 1503.[6]

DAUBENEY, John:

> for MARGARET PASTON: part of 153, 159–61, part of 169 PS, 172–5, 178, 191;
>
> for JOHN II: 233.

Described by Worcester as 'esquire',[7] by John III as 'my cousin',[8] and by John II as 'Sir'.[9] First mentioned in 1461, as likely to be sent by John I to a muster of troops.[10] Later seems to have been especially entrusted with defence of property: prominent in the altercations with the Duke of Suffolk's men preceding the attack on Hellesdon in 1465,[11] and at Cotton later that year.[12] Killed at the siege of Caister in 1469.[13]

EBESHAM, William, for WILLIAM PASTON II: 93—the only extant letter written by him for a member of the family, but he wrote also a large part of John II's 'Great Book' (B.M. MS. Lansdowne 285) and a number of legal documents: see his letter in Part II, no. 751.

A professional scribe. Several other books written by him have been identified by A. I. Doyle: 'The Work of a Late Fifteenth-Century English Scribe, William Ebesham', *Bulletin of the John Rylands Library*, xxxix (1957), 298–325. About 1475 he had a tenement in the Sanctuary of Westminster, and was still living in 1497.

GLOYS, James:

> for JOHN PASTON I: 36, 41, part of 42A, 42C, part of 43, most of 47, 49;
>
> for MARGARET: 139, 143, 166, 186, part of 189, 194, 199, 200, part of 201, 202, 204, 206, part of 208, 210, 213–15, 217–19.

A priest, in the service of the Pastons for many years, performing general clerical and estate duties[14] as well as acting as chaplain. First mentioned in 1448,[15] and apparently continuously with the family until his death in 1473.[16] A special confidant of Margaret, his influence with whom came to be resented by her sons.[17] Appointed rector of Stokesby in 1472.[18] He may well have been a local man: the name is rare, and a Thomas Gloys(e) was made freeman of Yarmouth in 1472 and bailiff in 1478.[19]

---

[1] Part II, no. 519.   [2] No. 65.   [3] No. 336.
[4] Part II, nos. 728–9.   [5] Nos. 225, 417.   [6] No. 392.
[7] *Itineraries*, p. 190.   [8] Nos. 322, 330.   [9] No. 309.
[10] No. 317.   [11] e.g. nos. 180, 188.   [12] No. 192.
[13] No. 205, and Worcester.   [14] e.g. nos. 36, 52, 59.   [15] No. 129.
[16] No. 282.   [17] Nos. 353, 355.   [18] No. 355.
[19] *Calendar of the Freemen of Great Yarmouth, 1429–1800* (Norfolk and Norwich Archaeological Soc., 1910), p. 10; Blomefield, xi. 326.

GRESHAM, James:

for JOHN PASTON I: 39, 55, part of 63;

for MARGARET: 129, 158, 197.

Described as 'gentleman',[1] of Holt. One of William Paston I's clerks,[2] and continued to act as confidential agent, especially in legal affairs, of John I and Margaret.[3] In November 1471 John II for some reason threatened to sue him, which Margaret deplored.[4] He was then ill, and since he is not mentioned later than this he may have died soon afterwards.

LOMNOR, William, for the Pastons only in 317, apparently nominally for JOHN III.

Described as 'gentleman', of Mannington near Gresham; first appears in the letters in 1450.[5] Often acted for John I in matters of business.[6] Evidently related to the Pastons, but how is not clear: Margaret calls him 'my brother' and John II and John III 'my cousin'.[7] His widow Margaret married Edmond Paston II as his second wife.[8] J.P. often between 1466 and 1474; died in 1481.[9]

MOWTH or MOLET, John, for MARGARET PASTON: 176.

Prior of the Cathedral Priory of the Holy Trinity, Norwich, 1453–71.[10] He supported the Paston interest in the suit about Fastolf's will.[11]

PAMPYNG, John:

for JOHN PASTON I: part of 57, 58–60, part of 63, 64–5, 68, 70 B, C, 71–2, 75–8;

for WILLIAM II: 92 PS;

for MARGARET: 207;

for JOHN II: 237, 247, 249 endorsement, 259.

Described as 'gentleman';[12] first mentioned in the letters on 1 August 1461,[13] but must have been in John I's service the previous year because part of a draft of October 1460 is in his hand.[14] Later accompanied John I on business to London. Continued in family service after John I's death, and was praised by John III for his part in the defence of Caister;[15] but John II feared that Anne Paston was too fond of him.[16] Last mentioned in the letters in November 1473,[17] so cannot be the man of this name whose will was proved on 20 March of that year.[18] Another of the same name appears in a copy of Caxton's *Indulgence* of 1489.[19]

[1] *Cal. Fine Rolls, 1437–45*, p. 323; *Cal. Close Rolls, 1461–8*, p. 230; Blomefield, viii. 175.
[2] No. 388; Part II, no. 432.
[3] e.g. nos. 22, 39, 75.
[4] No. 212, ll. 44–52.
[5] Part II, no. 450.
[6] e.g. no. 192.
[7] Nos. 181, 261, 384.
[8] Her will in Norwich, Reg. Rix 128–9: *Norwich Wills*, ii. 243.
[9] Writ of *diem clausit extremum* issued 17 May: *Cal. Fine Rolls, 1471–85*, no. 614; will proved 1482: *Norwich Wills*, ii. 240.
[10] Blomefield, iii. 604.
[11] No. 327; Part II, no. 693.
[12] Writ copied in MS. Add. 27445, f. 43.
[13] No. 59.
[14] No. 57.
[15] No. 335.
[16] Nos. 282, 283.
[17] No. 283.
[18] *Norwich Wills*, ii. 280 (given as 1472, but 20 March falls in 1473 by modern reckoning).
[19] G. D. Painter in *The Library*, 5th ser., xvi (1961), 229.

PLAYTER, Thomas:

for WILLIAM PASTON II: 88, 90, 95;

for MARGARET: part of 169 PS.

Described as 'esquire';[1] first mentioned in a letter probably of 1456 by Friar Brackley, who called him 'cognatus meus'.[2] A Close Roll reference of 1448 to 'Thomas Playter of the Chancery'[3] probably means this man. Escheator for Norfolk and Suffolk in 1466–7,[4] on commissions in 1473 and 1478.[5] Last mentioned in the letters in 1478;[6] died in 1479.[7]

WORCESTER, William, for JOHN PASTON I and THOMAS HOWES: 53. Servant and secretary to Fastolf from 1436; translator and antiquary. Later joined Yelverton in opposing John Paston's claims to Fastolf property. Died in or soon after 1482. See *D.N.B.*; K. B. McFarlane in *Studies presented to Sir Hilary Jenkinson* (Oxford, 1957), pp. 196–221; N. Davis in *Medieval Literature and Civilization. Studies in Memory of G. N. Garmonsway* (London, 1969), pp. 249–74; *William Worcestre, Itineraries*, ed. J. H. Harvey (Oxford, 1969).

WYKES, John:

for MARGARET PASTON: 179–85, 190, part of 195, 196, 198;

for JOHN II: 232, 242, part of 258.

Distinct from (though perhaps a relative of) the man of the same name who was usher of the King's chamber, etc. (see p. xlvi above), he was evidently an estate servant of comparable status to Calle, Daubeney, and Pampyng. His hand appears first in 1462,[8] and is most frequent in 1465; he disappears after 1471.[9] Certain features of his spelling are characteristic, especially *y* instead of *e* in some words. A man of the same name was bailiff of the manor of Gaywood at Lynn in 1487.[10]

Papers in hands appearing more than once but not identifiable

Hand of beginning of 6, for WILLIAM I: also 13 for AGNES.

Hand of 8, for WILLIAM I: also part of 9.

Hand of 19, for AGNES: also 20–1, 24, 28–9; 100–1 for WILLIAM II, and 418 for MARGERY.

Hand of 22, for AGNES: also 23.

Hand of most of 40, for JOHN I: also 45, and 144 for MARGARET.

Hand of 66, for JOHN I; also 67, 69, and 192, part of 193, 195B for MARGARET.

Hand of 128, for MARGARET: also 129 PS, 130–8, 140–2, 145–51, and addition to 40, 42B, 46, 50–2 for JOHN I.

---

[1] *Cal. Fine Rolls, 1471–85*, nos. 515, 578. [2] Part II, no. 557.
[3] *Cal. Close Rolls, 1447–54*, p. 69. [4] *Cal. Fine Rolls, 1461–71*, p. 192.
[5] *Cal. Pat. Rolls, 1467–77*, p. 408; *1476–85*, p. 112. [6] No. 379.
[7] Writs of *diem clausit extremum* issued 29 September (Norfolk) and 12 November (Suffolk): *Cal. Fine Rolls, 1471–85*, nos. 512, 515.
[8] No. 232. [9] No. 350.
[10] H. L. Bradfer-Lawrence, 'Gaywood Dragge, 1486–7', *Norfolk Archaeology*, xxiv (1932), 146–83.

Hand of 103 fragment, for WILLIAM II: also 104–5, 109.

Hand of 221, for MARGARET: also 222–3.

Hand of 226, for MARGARET: also 227–8.

Hand of 252 draft, for JOHN II: also 255, 260.

Hand of 309, for JOHN III: also 10, 35, and associated documents, and part of 387.

Incidence of hands in Margaret Paston's letters

124, 125, 127 Different unidentified hands

126 Two unidentified hands

128 Unidentified, but frequent, also for John I

129 Gresham

129 PS, 130–8, hand of 128

139 Gloys

140–2 Hand of 128

143 Gloys

144 Unidentified, also for John I

145–51 Hand of 128

152 John III

153 Part unidentified, part Daubeney

154–5 John III

156 Calle

157 John III

158 Gresham

159–61 Daubeney

162 Unidentified

163–5 John III

166 Gloys

167–70 John III

171 Calle

172–5 Daubeney

176 Mowth

177 John II

178 Daubeney

179–85 Wykes

186 Gloys

187 Unidentified

188 John II

189 Gloys and Calle

190 Wykes

191 Daubeney

192 Unidentified, also in 195 B and for John I

193 Mostly Calle

194 Gloys

195 Wykes, Calle, and hand of 192

196 Wykes

197 Gresham

198 Wykes

199, 200 Gloys

201 Gloys and Edmond II

202 Gloys

203 Edmond II

204 Gloys

205 Edmond II

206 Gloys

207 Pampyng

208 Gloys and Edmond II

209 Unidentified

210 Gloys

211–12 Edmond II

213–15 Gloys

216 Edmond II

217–19 Gloys

220 Unidentified

221–3 The same unidentified hand

224 Unidentified

225 Calle

226–8 The same unidentified hand

229, 230 Different unidentified hands

EDITORIAL PROCEDURE

In Part I the letters and papers are arranged under the names of the various authors, who are placed in order of seniority in the family but with wives at the end of each generation. Each author's papers are arranged chronologically. The headnote to each letter gives first the person to whom it is addressed, whether expressly or by inference; if the paper is not a letter its nature is briefly indicated. In Part II the letters to members of the family are arranged under the names of the recipients, and after them are miscellaneous related documents. Here the headnote gives first the name of the writer. In both parts it gives next the date, as closely as it can be determined, with the year placed first. The next line gives the manuscript authority for the text, usually with the size of the sheet—paper unless parchment is specified—in inches (horizontal dimension first); then a note on the handwriting. Manuscripts not otherwise placed—all those marked 'Add.' and 'Add. Charter'—are in the British Museum. Since the edges of the sheets are nearly always uneven, and some of them partly covered by mounts or guards on which they are bound, the dimensions cannot be minutely accurate; they are intended to give a general idea of shape and size in relation to the amount of writing on the page.

The next section describes the essential features of the back of each document. It notes first if the text runs over, or a postscript is added; but the main purpose is to give the evidence showing whether the paper is a missive or a draft or copy. If there is an address, with remnants of a seal, it can be taken to have been sent, and usually no other details are needed. But if there is no address, other particulars, especially marks of folding and soiling such as would be caused by carrying, are recorded. Endorsements in hands approximately contemporary with the document are also noticed; but the numerous annotations of later owners or editors, especially Blomefield and Fenn, are generally ignored.

The body of the headnote gives the evidence for the date assigned, and refers to any other documents that may be closely related. At the end of the note references are given to earlier printings of each text in the editions of Fenn ('F.', with volume and page number) and Gairdner ('G.', with the number of each text in his editions of 1901—in which the Supplement is numbered in roman numerals—and 1904), and in the selection in the Clarendon Medieval and Tudor Series, 1958 ('C.'), or in the other places (such as Historical Manuscripts Commission reports) where a few of the documents were first printed. Editions merely reprinting Fenn or Gairdner are not noticed.

The text preserves the spelling of the manuscripts, including the letters þ and ʒ: these are used commonly, but very variously by different writers and by the same writer at different times, so that they contribute to the characteristic appearance of some hands and can also help towards dating. A few adjustments have been made for the sake of easier reading. The manuscripts do not distinguish in form between *ȝ* and *ȝ*; where the letter is *ȝ* it is so printed. Some writers do not distinguish in form between *þ* and *y*; where the letter has the function of *þ* it is so printed, but a footnote draws attention to the writer's practice—this, like the use of *þ* itself, sometimes changes and may be significant for dating. (A few writers eccentrically use *þ* for *y*; this also is normalized and noted.) Many writers use both short and long forms of *i/j*, and both *u* and *v*, indifferently for both vowel and consonant but sometimes characteristically according to position; the distinctions are therefore preserved in rendering minuscule by lower case. But for capital *I/J* all writers use a single form (usually, until late in the century, like *J*) in both functions; and in printing this is split into the two modern letters in the same way as *ȝ* and consonantal *y*—the pronoun 'I' and the initial letter of 'John', for instance, which are written identically, are distinguished in printing.

Final *-e* standing for etymological *i* or French *é* is marked with an acute accent, as *redé* 'ready', *contré* 'country'.

The common abbreviations are used extensively by most writers, but by some far more than others. Sometimes the correct form of expansion is uncertain because the writers are inconsistent in spelling the same words or endings when they write them in full. This is most easily seen in the treatment of the ending of the plural and the genitive of nouns, which may be written *-es*, *-is*, or *-ys*, sometimes by the same writer in the same document (e.g. by John Paston II in no. 249). This ending is extremely frequently abbreviated by a loop attached to the preceding letter, without sufficient evidence of the writer's preferred form. Mainly because of inconsistency of this kind, but also because the extent of abbreviation itself can be characteristic of a writer's habits, expansions in English are printed in italics. (In continuous Latin texts, where there is usually little doubt, they are not distinguished unless they may give some evidence about the writer's use of the same abbreviations in English.) Exceptional forms of abbreviation are sometimes mentioned in the footnotes. Despite the uncertainties an attempt is made to accommodate the spelling of expansions to that of forms written out in the same writer's hand about the same time. But since the use of italics guards against misinterpretation, identical abbreviations are occasionally expanded differently according to sense: notably the crossed *p* which can stand for either *par* or *per* (more commonly written in full *par* in these texts) is differently treated in 'per*son*' and 'par*son*'. Unhistorical as this is, since the words were not finally distinguished until the seventeenth century, it avoids the still less historical effect, ludicrous to a modern reader, of phrases such as 'a riotous peple to the nombre of a thowsand parsons' (no. 36).

Some writers use abbreviation marks inaccurately, variably, or super-fluously. For example, superior *a*, which normally stands for *au*, or in different contexts *ra*, sometimes appears where the *u* is already written, and can mean no more than *a* on the line; and superior *r*, which normally stands for *ur*, sometimes simply takes the place of ordinary *r*. (John Paston III, however, uses superior *r* in 'our' and 'your' apparently as the equivalent of the spelling -*yr* that he favours in these words especially in his earlier letters—*yowyr*, *youyr*, later often *your*.) Some writers use the abbreviation normally standing for -*us* to represent the second syllable of the name *James*, which is never written in full with -*us*; John Paston II does this often, but writes in full either *James* or *Jamys*. There is sometimes doubt about the significance of a curved line, or a dotted circumflex, above a series of minims: it normally implies the addition of *m* or *n*, but often, when there is no place for any addition, it evidently serves to indicate which of the minims are to be understood as forming *m* or *n* (and even here it is sometimes used carelessly). There is also occasionally doubt about the value of a simple horizontal line above a letter, or a tail on *m* or *n* curved back above it. The line normally implies the addition of *m* or *n*, but is evidently sometimes superfluous. The curved-back tail in most of these writers is a mere flourish—some make -*n* and -*u* both with the tail in precisely the same way, and use them where no additional letter is called for.

Other letters final in words are often written with appendages of various kinds—curls on -*c*, -*g*, and -*t*, tags on -*d*, -*f*, and -*k*, strokes through -*h* and -*ll*, flourishes on -*r*, and others—which have sometimes been understood as representing -*e*. A related use is that of a dotted circumflex above *p* (mainly but not exclusively when final), which is an occasional idiosyncrasy of particular writers (John Paston III especially). It seems that at least in these informal hands most of them have no significance, and they are therefore ignored in transcription. Final -*e* is in any case so irregularly written by most of these writers that it has little importance. An occasional exception is a curl on -*c* in some words which seem to require a following -*e*, as *vnc* 'ounce', which is transcribed 'vnce'. A more frequent and important exception is the common flourish on *r* (usually the long form), which is often used to render a syllabic *re* whether final or not, as 'remembre' or 'contré'. Here the flourished *r* must stand for *re*, and in writers who use such forms it is so expanded; but again there are difficulties in that some writers—conspicuously John Paston II—often so reduce the flourish that the intention is uncertain. Also important, and affecting more than -*e*, is the barred -*ll*. The bar seems nearly always to be meaningless, for it is used indiscrimin-ately everywhere a final -*ll* occurs; but in a few places it apparently stands for -*es* (or -*is*/*ys*)—see, for example, the notes to no. 195, where three plural nouns are so written. Problems of this kind are dealt with as far as possible in the light of each writer's practice in other places, and annotated only if they may be of wider interest.

In expanding abbreviations which are not by conventional signs but by raised letters, only letters that are omitted, not those above the line, are italicized: so $þ^t$ is printed 'þat'. Accordingly the frequent $þ^e$ is not distinguished from þe—which can scarcely ever lead to ambiguity in these papers because the pronoun 'thee' is very rarely used. Ambiguity could arise from the loss of the distinction which writers sometimes, but far from regularly, make between y^e 'the' and ye 'ye'; but the distinction is maintained in another way by printing the former 'þe'.

The word division of the manuscripts is slightly modified. It is in any case often inconsistent, and some writers' spacing is so erratic that their intention is uncertain. But when certain groups now always written separately are fairly regularly run together and immediately intelligible, they are so printed: such are *asfor, aswell, shalbe* in some writers. On the other hand when there is great irregularity, and retention of the manuscript lack of division could check a reader, the words are divided, and if it seems necessary 'No space' is recorded in the notes. This affects principally the numerous cases of *a* written together with the following word. When it is a weakened form of 'have' it is regularly separated and annotated; when it is the indefinite article, which is very frequently joined, it is sometimes silently detached. Some words now treated as single but clearly divided in the manuscripts are hyphenated, as *a-nother, j-now*, since both the fact and the manner of division are sometimes of interest. But complete consistency in these matters is scarcely attainable.

The punctuation and capital letters of the printed text are editorial. This includes the apostrophe introduced to mark off the *th* or *þ* for 'the' occasionally used before nouns beginning with a vowel, and similarly the *t* for 'to' in infinitives. Many of the writers do not punctuate at all, except for marking off numerals, and perhaps indicating larger changes of subject by oblique strokes. Some punctuate irregularly, usually by obliques. One or two of the more practised, such as James Gresham, do use fairly systematic pointing, even to question marks; and of course this is taken into account in the modernization. The writers' use of capital letters is mostly inconsequential, often depending on favoured shapes of particular letters rather than on position; thus *A* and *C* in some hands are commonly of capital form even within words. A particular eccentricity is John Paston II's use of *ff* as equivalent to *f* almost everywhere. Initially it can be regarded as a capital, and so is simplified in transcription where a capital would not now be used; but elsewhere, despite the resulting inconsistency, it is retained because its intention is uncertain. Though this looks strange in a word such as 'afftre' the simplification would look strange in say '*diferent', and there are no grounds in his own practice for distinguishing such cases.

Division into paragraphs is also mainly editorial, though a few letters and documents have it. When they do they usually also mark the beginning of each paragraph in the margin, mostly with the paragraph mark resembling superior *a* (apparently originally *C* for *capitulum*). Many writers prefix the same mark, or some other conventional sign, to each letter they write.

Numerals, and regularly used abbreviations of weights and money terms, are left unexpanded, and in such contexts the ampersand is also retained. Punctuation of these items is standardized, with a point after 'li', etc., though the manuscripts usually indicate the abbreviation by a line above. The treatment of 'marc' sometimes presents a problem: a curl is often attached to the -*c* which might be intended as a mark of suspension, so that it is uncertain whether the word is meant to be inflected or not, and if so exactly how. In printing the curl is represented by a point. The special punctuation associated with numerals is not reproduced: in the manuscripts a point is usually written both before and after letters used as numerals, and also the very rare occurrences of arabic figures. The common bracketing off and underlining of sums of money and weights, and occasionally of personal names, is also ignored because it is no part of modern punctuation. A few Latin abbreviations are left unexpanded, as *A°* for 'anno' and *r.r.* for the double long *r* with flourish standing for 'regni regis' in dates.

Interlineations are enclosed in half-brackets. If they are not in the principal hand of the document a note specifies the hand if possible.

Words miswritten are emended. If the error is only the omission of a letter or abbreviation, it is supplied in square brackets, without a note. If a greater change is needed the manuscript form is given in a footnote. Words apparently unintentionally omitted are also supplied in square brackets, with no note except for a special reason. Square brackets are additionally used in a few drafts to enclose passages of some length which have been written but struck out; these are annotated.

Loss of text due to physical damage to the manuscript is shown by angle brackets. If the missing letters or words can be guessed with fair probability they are supplied; if not, the gap is shown by an arbitrary three points, and some attempt is usually made in the notes to indicate its extent. Most of the writing in these papers is not regular enough in size or spacing to permit a confident estimate of the number of letters missing, so that a line of points to represent the loss could be misleading.

The footnotes record mainly difficulties of reading and alterations in the text which may reveal something of the process of composition or of writing down, or provide additional linguistic forms of interest. Not every alteration is annotated; some are mere miswritings currently corrected, a record of which would burden the notes and throw light on nothing. References are normally to the word immediately preceding the number, but to the whole of an interlineation or lacuna enclosed in half- or angle brackets. Letters at the beginning, middle, or end of the word referred to are shown by hyphens thus: a-, -a-, -a. So 'a- *canc.*' means that an initial *a* was written but cancelled; '-a- *over* o' that a medial *a* can be seen to have been written on top of an earlier *o*; '-a *from* e' that a final *a* is an alteration of an earlier *e*. When no such specific reference is given, a note of a cancellation means that it followed the word to which the number is attached. So in letter no. 2, n. 3, referring to 'matier' in the text, is 'of *canc.*'; which means that William Paston I wrote 'matier of' and cancelled the *of*.

In editorial matter, the spelling of personal names is intended to be consistent. Many names are spelt variously in the texts, and the most frequent form, if it can be discerned, is adopted except that names derived from surviving place-names are given in the modern form. Thus *Pampyng* and *Wykes* are spelt with the *y* that most of their contemporaries preferred, but *Writtle* is so spelt though John Paston II wrote *Wryttyll*, and *Worcester* so though he himself often wrote *Wyrcestre*.

ABBREVIATIONS AND SHORT TITLES USED IN THE INTRODUCTION AND HEADNOTES

Blomefield   Francis Blomefield, *An Essay towards a Topographical History of the County of Norfolk.* Completed by Charles Parkin and published in five volumes from 1739 to 1775. Quoted from the second edition, 11 vols., London, 1805–10.

C.   *Paston Letters*, selected and ed. N. Davis (Clarendon Medieval and Tudor Series), Oxford, 1958.

Cal. Charter, Close, Fine, Pat. Rolls   The Calendars of rolls published by the Public Record Office, the volume shown by dates, the reference to page or number of document according to the arrangement of each.

Complete Peerage   12 vols., 1910–59.

D.N.B.   *Dictionary of National Biography.*

Fenn, F.   *Original Letters, Written during the Reigns of Henry VI. Edward IV. and Richard III.* . . ., ed. John Fenn. London, vols. i and ii 1787, vols. iii and iv 1789, vol. v 1823.

Gairdner, G.   *The Paston Letters 1422–1509 A.D.*, ed. James Gairdner. Four vols., Westminster, 1900–1; six vols., London and Exeter, 1904.

Inq. p.m.   *Calendarium Inquisitionum post mortem sive excaetarum*, vol. iv, 1828, and *Calendar of Inquisitions Post Mortem Henry VII, i–iii, 1898–1955.*

Jacob   E. F. Jacob, *The Fifteenth Century 1399–1485*, Oxford, 1961.

Mackie   J. D. Mackie, *The Earlier Tudors 1485–1558*, Oxford, 1952.

Mayors of Norwich   B. Cozens-Hardy and E. A. Kent, *The Mayors of Norwich 1403–1835*, Norwich, 1938.

Norwich Wills   *Index of Wills Proved in the Consistory Court of Norwich . . . 1370–1550*, ed. M. A. Farrow, Norfolk Record Society XVI, Parts i–iii, 1943–5. (Issued also as Index Library lxix.)

P.C.C.   Prerogative Court of Canterbury, Registers of Wills in the Public Record Office. List in Index Library, x, xi, 1893, 1895.

Records of Norwich   *Records of the City of Norwich*, ed. W. Hudson and J. C. Tingey, 2 vols., Norwich and London, 1906, 1910.

R.E.S.   *Review of English Studies.*

Rot. Parl.   *Rotuli Parliamentorum* [1767].

Scofield   Cora L. Scofield, *The Life and Reign of Edward the Fourth*, 2 vols., London, 1923.

Worcester, *Itineraries*   *William Worcestre, Itineraries*, ed. John H. Harvey, Oxford, 1969.

ABBREVIATIONS

abbr.	abbreviated, abbreviation	*fold.*	followed
canc.	cancelled	*interl.*	interlined
corr.	corrected	*repr.*	represented
eras.	erasure		

WILLIAM PASTON I

1. To JOHN STAYNFORD: draft   1425

Add. 34889, f. 213. $8\frac{3}{4} \times 4\frac{5}{8}$ in. Autograph.

Dorse: Marks of folding, but no seal or address. Along the long side the following memorandum, autograph:

> Sount duez a mon *sir* Will Bardolf de sez gages en lez lyuerés a Caleys de mon *tr*eshonnuré ⌐sir⌐ le Count de Warr*ewyk*,[1] capitayn illeoqes, jusqes al iiij^{te} io*ur* de fevr*ier* l'an de Roy Hen*ri* Sysme tierce ccccxiij li. xvj s. x d. q^a.

Under this a pattern of six lines roughly drawn, the first two beginning parallel, half an inch apart, but opening to a funnel shape, the third fairly close to the second, the fourth and fifth fairly close half an inch below, the sixth again half an inch below—apparently a plan of some kind. At right angles to the memorandum, in a narrow column following a fold, autograph: 'M. Pa⟨. . .⟩ | *tradatur* | *pro* ston | q*uod* capia*tur* | &c.'

The date appears from the memorandum.[2] The third year of Henry VI was 1 September 1424–31 August 1425.
     G. III/7.

> To my weel beloued John Staynford of Furnyvales Inne.

þe instruc*cion* to comune of to John Robynson of Carleton bysyde Snayth.

    T⟨o⟩[3] ⌐enquerre *and*⌐ wyte whether þe stoon may be sawed or nought, *and* whether it wille chippe or chynne or affraye w*ith* frost or weder or water.   **5**

    Al-so þ*at*[4] eu*er*y pece of þe stoon be iij foote longe and þ*at*[5] xv ⌐tunne tygh⟨t⟩⌐[6] of þe[7] stoon be eu*er*y stoon weel bedded in-to þe walle *and* a foote thikke þ*at* it ryse in heighte a foote in þe walle, *and* x stones[8] of ⌐þe⌐ stoon must be ij foote brood[9] *and* at þe leste a foote *and* an half thikke.

---

1. [1] *Abbr.* warr *with flourished* -r.
  [2] *A note on the MS. in Fenn's hand misinterprets it:* '14 Feby. 3 H. 7 1487'.
  [3] *Hole in paper.*   [4] þe *canc.*
  [5] *A number containing* x-, *apparently* xl, *canc., obscured by damp.*
  [6] *Paper rubbed.*   [7] *Only partly visible owing to damage to paper.*
  [8] *A space over half an inch long between this and the following word, filled by a line.*
  [9] þat i *canc.*

10   A stoon wil drawe[10] ⌈þe⌉ wighte of a pipe, as I suppose. þo grete stones
⌈and nought þe smallere stones⌉ shuld be sawed so þat euery pece sawed
shuld holde þe seid lengthe[11] of iij foote *and* þe seid brede of ij foote, *and*
to be, after it is sawed, half a fote or lesse ⌈on thikkenesse⌉; *and*[12] thenne
⌈þo⌉ brode sawed stones shulde euere stonde in þe werk betwen þe seid
15 weel bedded[13] stonys[14] þat shuld rise but a fote in þe walle *and* ben ankered
iche of hem with other; *and* þis werk shal be strong j-nowe, as werkmen
seyn, *and* drawe but litill cariage. I wold haue ⌈swiche⌉[15] stoon a xx^ti
tunne tight caried to Moneslee in Norffolk, betwen Crowmere *and* Bromholm *and* but a myle fro Bromholm.
20   To[16] reporte plein answere of this bylle writen *and* how sone I myght
haue the seid stoon caried to Moneslé a-forn seid, *and* for what price.
    þis werk is for a myll.[17]

p[er][18] W. PASTON[19]

2. To an unidentified lawyer in Rome: draft   1425, 5 November

Add. 27443, f. 78^v. 12 × 14 in. Autograph.

This large sheet has been used for drafts and notes. It has been neither sealed nor
addressed and was obviously never sent away. On the recto is a draft of a long Latin
pleading concerning the Abbey of Bermondsey, in an unidentified clerk's hand
extensively corrected in Paston's hand and preceded by these words also by
Paston:

    Do writen ij copies of þis note in papier wyde writen, *and* gete a copie of þe
writte in þe Eschekyr ageyn ⌈yow⌉.

The verso, all in Paston's hand, contains a short addition to this Bermondsey
draft, then the present text. Below the body of this text, but crowded in above the
subscription, is a line of names apparently unconnected with the subject of the
letter, then the following words: 'A jnstruccion ⌈and informacion⌉ of þe verray
trewe matier betwen þe[1] Priour *and* þe couent of Bromholm *and* þe seyd John[2]
and me as I am enformed *and* as I knowe touchant my persone *and* þe'—which
look like the beginning of a heading for an account of the Wortes affair which
Paston projected but did not write, at any rate here. Immediately under these
words, but still only opposite to the subscription of the present letter, the draft of
no. 3 begins.
    In the top right-hand corner of the verso is the name *Wortes*, and upside down
at the bottom *Wortes* on the right and *Bermund⟨esey⟩* on the left. These are
roughly written but apparently also in Paston's hand. The writing throughout
these drafts is untidy, with many corrections of which only the more important
are recorded in the footnotes.

---

[10] litill lesse þan *canc.*	[11] -t- *over* h.	[12] þ *and another letter canc.*
[13] *MS.* beddes.	[14] of *canc.*	[15] *Interl. above* þis *canc.*
[16] bry *canc.*	[17] *Last word uncertain owing to damage to paper.*	
[18] *At foot; no cross-stroke visible.*	[19] *Last letter only partly visible.*	
2. [1] seyd *canc.*	[2] as I am enformed *canc.*	

2. To an Unidentified Lawyer in Rome, 5 November 1425

Nos. 2 and 3, from their concern with John Wortes's claim to the priorate of Bromholm against Paston's client Nicholas Loddon, must have been written about the same time as no. 4, which is evidently of March 1426. The November of this letter is therefore doubtless that of 1425. A slightly earlier stage of the dispute is seen in Prior Nicholas's letter to Paston, Part II, no. 422.

G. 5/10.

Right worthy *and* worshepefull s*er*, I recom*au*nde me to yow *and* thank yow for þe good, trew, *and* diligent labour ye haue hadde for þe matier[3] betwen þe Priour of Bromholm *and* his commoigne apostata John Wortes, þ*at*[4] namyth hym-self Paston *and* affermith hym ⌜vntrewely⌝ to be my cousyn.[5] God defende þ*at* any of my pou*er*e kyn shuld be of swych 5 gou*er*na*u*nce as he is of. Maister John Ixworth told me þat he hadde lettres fro a frend of yowres in þe court of Rome ⌜þat is of þe seyd Prioures counseill in þis mater as ye be⌝, whos name I knowe nought, specifyeng þat þe seyd John Wortes, adu*er*sarius Prioris, desperat in c*au*sa *et* concordiam querit. It ⌜is⌝ told me sithen þat þe seyd John Wortes is ⌜in þe 10 c⟨ourt⟩[6] of Rome⌝ sacred a bysshop of Irland, vide*l*icet ep*iscop*us Corcagensis; wherby it is seyd here þat ⌜his⌝ p*re*tense ⌜of⌝[7] his title to þe priourie of Bromholm is adnulled *and* voide in yo*w*r lawe. þe seyd John Wortes *and* a contréma⟨n⟩ of myn in þe seyd court, ⌜Maister John Vrry⌝, haue sent me lettres wher-of I send yow copies[8] ⌜*and* a trewe instrucc*io*n 15 of þe seyd matier⌝ closed w*ith* þis bille, þe whiche lettres *and* þe matier ther-of me semyth meruaillous *and* straunge. A p*re*st of Norff*olk* þat spak w*ith* yow[9] in Jull or August last passed told me þat he yede with yow to þe cardinales hous Trikaricen*si*s to espie if any swych p*ro*cesse were sued ageyn me as þe seyd lettres specifien, *and* þat ye told þe same 20 prest at alle ⌜tymes⌝ þer was þan no swich p*ro*cesse sued ne had; þe which relac*io*n I trust *and* beleue bettre þan þe seyd lettres.

I haue, by aduys of counseill, in makyng a p*ro*curacie *ad agend*um *defend*endum *prouocand*um et *appelland*u*m* to yow *and* ⌜þe seyd⌝ Maister John Vrry *and* þe Wynsolaw de Swysco, *and* also a gen*er*al appelle þe 25 engrossyng of wych þe messager of this bill myght nought abide; þe which p*ro*curacie *and* appelle I shal sende to yowr p*er*sone[10] *tantumodo*[11] ⌜with moneye onward⌝ on trust.[12] My wille is ye haue þe chief gou*er*na*u*nce of þis matier *and* ⌜þat⌝ þis article be counseill; wher-vpo⟨n⟩ I prey yow

---

[3] *of canc.*   [4] vntrewely *canc.*

[5] I haue many pou*er*e ⌜men⌝ of my ky⟨n⟩ but so fals *and* so pouere but he was neuere of my kyn *canc.*

[6] *Badly damaged; apparently traces of* -rt.

[7] *Interl. above ampersand canc.*

[8] *and* a trewe instrucc*io*n of þe matier of seyd matier *interl., then canc.;* stet *written in margin, and canc.*   [9] sithe þe date *canc.*

[10] *This word ends a line, and at the beginning of the next are five short words, in a different hand, canc. They seem to have been a casual note or scribble, unconnected with the draft letter.*

[11] c*um* pecunijs *interl. and canc.*   [12] þat *canc.*

3

30 hertily to be saddely auysed in þese matieres¹³ *and*, as nede ⌐is, so⌐ to
gouerne hem by yowr wysdam þat þe seyd Prioures estat *and* honesté,
and myn also, to yowr worshepe be saued, and þat in alle hast resonable
ye lyke to sende me ⌐redé⌐¹⁴ lettres of alle þe seyd matier *and* þe circumstances ther-of, ⌐*and* whou ye wil I be gouerned in þis mater⌐. I was
35 neuere somouned ne ⌐neuer⌐ hadde¹⁵ tydynges of þis matier but by seyd
lettres *and* other ⌐fleyng⌐ tales þat I haue herd sithen, ⌐ne neuere hadde
to do more with þe seyd John Wortes þan is specified in þe seyd instruc-
cion⌐.

Al-myghty God haue yow in his gouernaunce. Writen at London þe
40 v day of Nouembre.

Yowre frend *and* vnknowen

3. Probably to MASTER JOHN URRY: draft 1425, November

Add. 27443, f. 78ᵛ. Autograph.

For the position of this draft on the sheet see the headnote to no. 2. The date
must be very close to that of no. 2.

Since the person addressed has written to Paston about 'Sir John Paston' (i.e.
Wortes, called *Sir* as a priest and 'naming himself Paston'), and is 'our country-
man' and abroad, he is most likely to be the Master John Urry mentioned in no. 2,
lines 14 and 25. Urry was a proctor at Rome at this period (*The Register of Henry
Chichele, Archbishop of Canterbury 1414–1443*, ed. E. F. Jacob (Canterbury and
York Soc. xlv, 1943), I. lxxvii).

In the margin, roughly opposite lines 6 and 7 of the manuscript, is the note
'Ista *litte*ra missa no*n* fuit'.

G. 5/10.

Right worthy *and* worshepefull s*er*, I recomaunde [me] to yow, ⌐preyeng
yow to wite þat I haue resceyued⌐¹ yowr goodly *lett*res² makyng mencion
þat S*er* John Paston³ ⌐vt asserit⌐ hath optyned me condempnyd to hym
⌐in⌐ ccc⁴ marcz⁵ ⌐*and* c s.⌐⁶ *and* þat þe same John, atte reue*r*ence of yo*w*r
5 right worthy p*er*sone, hath cesed of his sute of certeins *p*rocesses ⌐ageyns
me⌐ vp-on þe seyd condempnac*i*on, takyng conti*nu*ance⁷ of þe same matier
vn-to Cristemasse next comyng; ⌐by whiche lettres ye conseille me to
make ende w*it*h þe seyd John ne deterius inde conti*n*gat⌐.

---

¹³ *and* to putte *canc.*
¹⁴ *The reading of the interlined word is not certain. It was evidently first written* redy,
then s *was added, partly covering the* -y. ¹⁵ other *canc.*
3. ¹ *Interl. above* and thank yow w*it*h al my herte of yo*w*r right *canc.*
  ² makyng mencion *canc.* ³ my cousyn *interl. and canc.*
  ⁴ vij *canc.* ⁵ vj s. viij d. *canc.* ⁶ *and* diuerses processus *canc.*
  ⁷ *Abbr. here and in l.* 20 contiance, *in l.* 14 contiaunce, *with stroke above.*

4

I send yow closed w*ith* this bille ⌈copie of vn⌉[8] frendly lettre þat þe
seyd John hath[9] sent to me ⌈late⌉ touchant þe same matier. ⌈þe seyd 10
Priour hath⌉[10] sent also to yow *and* to Mayster Will Swan, which longe
tyme hath be ⌈his⌉[11] procurato*ur*, a procuracie for my p*er*sone *and* v m*ar*cz
of moneye onward.[12] Wher-vp in þe seyd Prioures name *and* in myn
owyn also I prey yow hertily to sette al these matieres in conti*nu*aunce
vn-to yo*wr* comyng in-to Ingeland, *and* be-cause ye arn here ⌈beneficed⌉, 15
owr cuntréman, *and*[13] of worshepe *and* cunnyng worthyly endowed, þe
seyd Priour,[14] his brether,[15] *and* I also willen gladdely in these matieres
be treted by yow; *and* if þis mesure be accepted *and* we may haue knowyng
here ther-of, it shal cause þe attemptac*i*on of diuerses matieres a-geyn
su*mm*e frendes of þe seyd John to cese. *And* if þis conti*nu*ance be refused 20
I prey yow with al my power þat of yo*wr* wysdom *and* good discrecion ye
wille[16] in þe seyd Prioures name *and* myn[17] defenden þe seyd sutes, *and*
alle other þat ⌈þe⌉ seyd John sueth a-geyn þe seyd Priour *and* me, in
yo*wr* best maner, ⌈*and* to be of owr counseill in þese matieres⌉; *and* as
ye lyke resonablely to write to vs so we wil be gou*er*ned in yo*wr* rewarde 25
and al other circumstaunces of þe same matieres.[18]

I conceyve by yo*wr* seyd l*ett*res þat ⌈þe grete of⌉[19] þe matier conteigned
in þe same ye haue of þe informac*i*on *and* assercion of þe seyd John,[20]
and as he hath enformed yow I wot weel ye trewely writen; but I hope
and trust verrayly þe matier of his informac*i*on is vntrewe.[21] Þe Priour 30
of Bromholm sued a-geyn þe seyd John *and* other in Ingeland a wryt of
premunire facias, *and* I was ther-in of þe same Prioures conseill, as þe lawe
of Ingelond[22] ⌈*and*⌉ myn office willen, *and* more I haue nought hadde to do
with þe seyd John; *and* I can nought beleue þat ⌈in þis cas⌉ þe same John[23]
myght by yo*wr* lawe any swich sute ⌈haue ageyn me⌉ as yo*wr* lettre speci- 35
fieth. Also Will, þe prest specified in yowr [lettre], told me þat he, after
þat ye told hym of þis matier lyke as ye[24] wr[i]te, he comuned with
Maister Will Swan, *and* he told þe seyd prest þer [was] no p*ro*cesse in þe
courte ageyn me in no[25] man*er*.

---

[8] *Interl. above* þe *canc.*   [9] sende *canc.*
[10] *Interl. above* and prey yow hertily I haue *canc.*
[11] *Interl. after* þe ⌈seyd⌉ prioures *canc.*
[12] preyeng yow hertily þat ye lyke *canc.*   [13] of worshe|pe *canc.*
[14] *Ampersand canc.*   [15] willen *canc.*   [16] helpe *canc.*
[17] as of owr counseille *interl. and canc.*
[18] ferthermore touchant my p*er*sone I m*er*uaille þat þe seyd ferthermore *canc.*
[19] *Interl. above* part of *canc.*
[20] an / þe which informac*i*on *and* asse[r]cion *canc.*
[21] for he hath no ⌈maner⌉ cause to swe to me / ne I was neure somouned ne cited *canc.*
[22] wille *and* as *canc.*   [23] nother *canc.*   [24] *No space.*
[25] *A letter, probably* n, *canc.*

4. To William Worstede, John Longham, and Piers Shelton
1426, 1 March

Add. 27443, f. 80. 11⅝×8¾ in. Autograph; see Plate I.

Dorse: Traces of red wax. Address autograph:

> *A mez treshonnurés meistres William Worstede, John Longham, et Meistre Piers Shelton soit donné.*

From the reference to 'yowr frere my maister suppriour' it appears that the men addressed were monks of Bromholm.

The fact that Paston could consult officials at Leicester indicates that Parliament was meeting there, as it did from 18 February to 1 June 1426 (*Rot. Parl.* iv. 295). This date also fits what is said of Humphrey, Duke of Gloucester, who married Jacqueline of Hainault in 1423. She began a divorce suit in the Roman court for dissolution of her marriage to John, Duke of Brabant, in April 1421. Preliminary sentence was not given until 27 February 1426, definitive sentence not until 9 January 1428 (*Cal. Papal Registers, Papal Letters*, vii. 28–9).

G. 7/12. C. 1 (part).

Right worthy *and* worshepefull *se*res *and* maistres, I recomand me to yow *and* thank yow wi*th* al my herte of þe gret tendrenesse ye lyke to haue of þe saluac*io*n of my symple honesté, preyng yow eu*er*more of yo*w*r good contin*u*ance.[1] I haue, after þe aduys of yo*w*r lettre, doon dwely
5   examyned þe jnstrument by þe wysest I coude fynde here, *and* in especial by on Maister Robert Sutton, a courtezane of þe court of Rome, þe which is þe chief *and* most chier man with my lord of Gloucestre *and* his matier in þe seyd court for my lady his wyff. *And* here aunswere is þat al þis p*ro*cesse, þough it were in dede p*ro*ceded as þe instrument specifieth, is
10 not suffisant in þe lawe of Holy[2] Cherche, *and* þat hem semyth by þe sight of þe instrument *and* by þe defautes ⟨þat⟩[3] ye espied in þe same *and* other, *and* in man*er* by þe knowelech of þe notarie, þat þe p*ro*cesse in gret part ther-of is fal⟨se *and* vn⟩[3]trewe. I haue taken aduys of Maister Robert Bruus, chaunceller wi*th* my lord of Cantirbury, *and* Maister Nicholl
15 Billesdon, cha⟨unceller⟩[3] of my lord of Wynchestre, *and* Maister John Blodwelle, a weel lerned man holden *and* a suffisant courtezan of þe seyd court; *and* alle þese acorden to þe seyd Maister Robert Sutton.

Nought wi*th*-stondyng þat I herde neu*er*e of þis matier no man*er* lykly ne credible euidence vn-to þat I sey yo*w*r lettre *and* þe jnstrument, yet I
20 made an appell ⌐*and* a procuracie *and* also a prouocacion¬ at London longe beforn Cristemasse by þe a⟨duys⟩[3] ⌐of¬ Maister Dauid Aprys, Maister Symond Kempston, *and* Maister James Cole, *and* sent al þis wi*th* an jnstruccion of al þe matier to my procuratours to Rome by yo*w*r frere my

---

4. [1] *Abbr.* contiance *with stroke above.*   [2] of þe *canc.*
    [3] *Edge of the paper torn, and some letters lost at ends of four MS. lines.*

maister suppriour, *and* gaff hym gold þat he was content. *And* ouermore now here by aduys I make þis day a newe apelle *and* a newe procuracie, 25 *and* vp-on þis alle þe seyd worthy men here seyn *and* informe me pleynly I haue no maner cause in lawe ne in conscience to drede aught in þis matier. Myn aduersarie is become bysshop of Cork in Irland, *and* ther arn ij other persones prouided to þe same bysshopriche yet lyuyng beforn my seyd aduersarie; *and* by this acceptacion of þis bysshopriche he hath 30 pryued hym-self of þe title þat he claymed in Bromholm, *and* so adnulled þe ground of his processe a-geyn me. *And* also þe tyme of his greuaunce pretendid *and* þe tyme of his sute he was apostata, *and* I trowe ⌈is yet⌉, *and* so vnable to sue any swich processe.

I purpose me to come homward be London to lerne more in þis matier 35 if I may. I prey þe Holy Trinité, lord of yowr cherche *and* of alle þe werld, delyuere me of my iiij aduersaries, of þis cursed bysshop for Bromholm, Aslak for Sprouston, *and* Julian Herberd for Thornham. I haue nought trespassed a-geyn noon of these iij, God knowith, *and* yet I am foule ⌈and⌉ noysyngly vexed with hem to my gret vnease, *and* al for my ⌈lordes and⌉ 40 frendes matieres *and* nought for myn owyn. I wot not whether it were best in any sermon or other audience in yowr cherche ⌈or elles-where⌉ to declare ought of þis matier in stoppyng of þe noyse þat renneth in þis case. I submitte me *and* alle þis matier to yowr good discrecion, *and* euere gremercy God *and* ye, who euere haue yow *and* me in his gracious 45 gouernaunce.

I suppose to se yow on Palme Sunday. Writen at Leycestre þe Friday þe thredde wyke of Lente.

Alle þe seyd lerned men telle me trewely þer is nother perill ne doute in þe takyng doun of þe instrument *and* þe bille to no creature,[4] which 50 jnstrument *and* bille I send yow a-geyn by þe berare of this, which I prey yow to kepe as pryué as ye may. I haue preyed my maister Hamond to write yow tydyngges *and* smale lesynges among.

Yowr man, W. PASTON

5. Memorandum to Arbitrators 1426–7

Add. 27443, ff. 75–7. Ff. 75 and 76, $10\frac{1}{2} \times 16\frac{3}{4}$ in., f. 77, $10\frac{1}{2} \times 9\frac{1}{2}$ in. Unidentified clerk's hand, formally written; a few interlineations by Paston.

Dorse blank.

A series of entries on the Close Roll records that John Duke of Norfolk made an award between William Paston and Walter Aslake on the feast of St. Peter and

---

[4] *This was evidently to have been the end of the letter, for the remaining words are crowded at the bottom of the page to the left of the subscription.*

St. Paul 6 Henry VI (29 June 1428): Paston paid Aslake £50 and each party released the other from all personal actions, etc. (*Cal. Close Rolls 1422–9*, pp. 393–4, 406). The present paper is clearly earlier than that. An upper limit is set by the reference to 'the two last parliaments holden at Westminster and at Leicester' (ll. 140–1). The Leicester parliament was that of 1426 (see no. 4); the previous one had met at Westminster from 30 April to 14 July 1425 (*Rot. Parl.* iv. 275). The latest year specified is 4 Henry VI, which is spoken of as if it were over (l. 166); it ended on 31 August 1426. The next parliament had evidently not opened; it did so on 13 October 1427 (also at Westminster: *Rot. Parl.* iv. 316–18). This document thus falls between September 1426 and early October 1427.

Aslak's account of the dispute appears in a petition addressed to the Duke of Bedford (P.R.O., S.C. 8–135–6715); see Part II, no 867.

G. 4/6.

Be it remembred þat where, on þe nyght next biforn¹ þe feste of þe Circumcision of owre Lord Jesu² þe [secunde]³ yeer of þe regne of Kyng Henry þe Sexte, certeyns maffaisours, felons, *and* brekeres of þe Kynges peas vnknowyn, to þe noumbre of iiij^xx *and* more by estimacion, of malice *and*
5 jmaginacion forn-thowght⁴ felonwsly þe dwellyng place of John Grys of Wyghton in Wyghton in þe shyre of Norffolk brokyn, *and* wyth carpenteres axes þe yates *and* þe dores of þe seyd place⁵ hewen, *and* þe seyd John Grys *and* hys sone *and* a seruaunt man of hese by here bodyes tokyn *and* fro þe seyd dwellyng place by þe space of a myle to a peyre galwes ledden,
10 þere hem for to have hangyd; *and* by-cause hem fayled ropes convenient to here felonowse purpos þe seyd John Grys, hese sone, *and* hys man þere felonowsely slowen *and* mordered in þe most orrible wyse þat euer was herd spoken of in þat cuntré. Wher-vp-on Walter Aslak, purposyng *and* jmaginyng to putte William Paston in drede *and* intollerable fere to be
15 slayn *and* mordered in þe seyd forme wyth force *and* ageyn þe Kynges peas, on þe shyre day of Norffolk halden at Norwiche þe xxviij day of August in þe seyd secunde yeer, beyng þere þanne a grete congregacion of poeple by-cause of þe seyd shyre, in hese owne persone *and* by Richard Kyllyngworth, þat tyme hese seruaunt, to þe seyd William Paston swiche *and*
20 so many manaces of deth *and* dismembryng maden *and* puttyn by certeyns Englishe billes rymed in partye, *and* vp-on þe yates of þe priorie of þe Trinité chirche of Norwiche *and* on þe yates of þe chyrche of þe Freres Menures of Norwiche *and* þe yates of þe same cité called Nedeham yates *and* Westewyk yates, *and* in othre places wyth-inne þe seyd cité, by þe
25 seyd Walter *and* Richard sette, makyng mension *and* beryng þis vndyrstondyng þat þe seyd William *and* hese clerkes *and* seruauntes schuld be slayn *and* mordered in lyke fourme as þe seyd John Grys in þe seyd fourme was slayn *and* mordered; conteynyng also þese too wordes in Latyn, '*et* cetera', by whiche wordes commvnely it was vndyrstandyn þat

---

5. ¹ -n *over another letter, perhaps* e.   ² *Abbr.* ihu *with stroke above.*
³ *No gap; see l.* 17.   ⁴ -r- *over* o.   ⁵ *This word in another hand in space left.*

þe forgeers *and* makers of þe seyd billes jmagyned to þe seyd Will*i*am, 30
hese clerkes, *and* seru*au*ntz more malice *and* harm þan in þe seyd billes
was expressed; wherfore þe seyd Will*i*am, hese seyd clerkes, *and* seru*au*ntz
by longe tyme aftyr were in gret *and* intollerable drede *and* fere by þe
seyd maffaisours *and* felons to be slayn *and* mordered, wherfore þe seyd
Will*i*am, hese clerkes, *and* seru*au*ntz ne durst not at here fredom nothyr 35
goon ne ryde. Wher-vp-on þe seyd Will*i*am for hese owyn ⌈persone⌉¹⁶
affermyd a pleynt of trespas ageyn þe seyd Walter *and* Richard. P*ro*cesse
*con*tynued þer-vp-on til þe seyd Walter *and*⁷ Richard were foun*d*en gilty
of þe seyd trespas by an jnquisic*i*on þer-of takyn in dwe *and* lawefull
fourme, by whiche jnquisic*i*on þe damages of þe seyd Will*i*am for þe 40
seyd trespas were taxed to cxx li.; aftyr whiche pleynte affermyd, *and* tofore
ony plee vp-on þe seyd⁸ pleynt pleded, þe seyd Walter *and* Will*i*am by
Thom*a*s Erpyngham, knyght, a myghty *and* a gret⁹ supportour of þe seyd
Walter in alle þese matiers *and* circumstaunces þer-of ageyn þe seyd
Will*i*am, were induced to trete in þe same matier in þe fourme þat folwith; 45
þat is to seyne þat þe seyd Will*i*am schuld sue forth þe seyd pleynt *and* þe
execuc*i*on þer-of at hese owne will, *and* þe seyd Walter schuld defende hym-
self in þe seyd pleynt at hese owne will, except þat he schuld no benefice
take by noon p*ro*tecc*i*on ne wrytte of *corpus cum causa* ne of no lordes
lettres vp-on þe seyd sute. And what-so-eu*er* fortunyd in þe seyd pleynt, 50
þe p*ro*ces, ⌈execuc*i*on⌉, or þe sute þer-of, þe seyd Walter *and* Will*i*am
schuld stonde *and* obeye to þe ordinaunce of certeyns p*er*sones by þe seyd
Will*i*am *and* Walter arbitratores þat tyme named, if þei myghten accordyn;
and ellys of a noounpier¹⁰ also þat same tyme named of all þe seyd trespas,
pleynt, *and* sute *and* all þe circumstaunces þer-of, so þat þe seyd arbitrement 55
and ordinaunce of þe seyd arbitratores, or ellys of þe seyd nounpier, were
made wyth*in*ne xl dayes next¹¹ folwyng aftyr þe jugement yeven in
þe seyd pleynt.

    And aftyrward, þe Thursday next biforn Pentecost þe thrydde yeer of
þe regne of þe seyd Kyng, at London in þe p*re*sence of þe right excellent 60
high *and* myghty prynce þe Duc of Gloucestre, *and* by hese commaundement, atte sute *and* instaunce of þe seyd Thom*a*s Erpyngham it was
accordyd bytwen þe seyd Will*i*am *and* Walter þat þei¹² schuld stande *and*
obeye to þe ordinaunce *and* award of all þe seyd matiers of tweyne of þese
iiij p*er*sones: Will*i*am Phelip, knyght, Henry Inglose, knyght, Oliuer 65
Groos, *and* Thom*a*s Derham chosen on þe p*ar*tye of þe seyd Will*i*am
Paston; *and* tweyne of þese iiij p*er*sones: Symond Felbrygge, knyght,
Bryan Stapilton, knyght, Roberd Clyfton, knyght, *and* John of Berneye of

---

⁶ *Interl. by Paston.*   ⁷ iugement *canc.*   ⁸ sp *canc.*
⁹ *This word over another imperfectly erased, perhaps* busy.
¹⁰ a- *not separated; -*un *repr. by tailed* u, *as in* nounpier *l.* 56.
¹¹ f *and unfinished* l *canc.*   ¹² sculd *canc.*

9

Redeham ⌐chosen on þe partie of þe seyd Water ¬;[13] and elles þe decree
70 and iugement of a nounpier to be chosen by þe same arbitrores. þe whiche
William Phelip, Bryan Stapilton, Roberd Clyfton, Oliuer Groos, John of
Berneye, and Thomas Derham takyng vp-on hem þe charge of þe makyng
of þe seyd award and ordinaunce by ⌐þe assent of þe seyd Thomas Erpyng-
ham¬, þe Fryday next aftyr þe feste of þe Assumpcion of Owre Lady in
75 þe seyd thrydde yeer, at Norwiche[14] tokyn ensurauns of þe seyd William
and Walter by here feyth and here trowthez to stonde and obeye to here
ordinaunce of alle þe seyd matiers; and þe same day biforn noon maden
here full ordinaunce and arbitrement of alle þe same matiers in þe chyrche
of þe Greye Frerys at Norwich, and aftyrward, vp-on þe same award and[15]
80 ordinaunce mad, hadden a commvnicacion þer-of wyth þe seyd Thomas
Erpyngham, and aftyr þe same commvnicacion þe same day aftyr noon
þe same ordinaunce and award wretyn was red byforn þe seyd arbitrores
and þe seyd Walter and William, and examyned, agreed, and assented,
and by þe seales of þe same vj arbitrores and þe seyd Walter and William
85 was ⌐affermed and ¬[13] ensealed and left in þe handes of þe seyd Ser Bryan,
saueliche to be kept in pleyn remembraunce of þe seyd award and
ordinaunce, þe whiche award and ordinaunce þe seyd William was at all
tymes redy to obeye and parfourme on-to þe seyd feste of Michelmesse
þat þe seyd Walter to holde or parfourme þe seyd award pleynly refused.
90 And where þe seyd Walter, by iugement of þe Chaunceller of Inglond
þe xvj day of Jull þe seyd thrydde yeer, was remytted to þe Kynges prison
at Norwich by-cause of þe seyd sute, the seyd Walter yede at large owt
of warde fro þe seyd xvj day of Jull to þe seyd day of þe makyng of þe
seyd arbitrement and award, and fro þat day in-to Michelmesse þanne
95 next aftyr, þe seyd William þat meene tyme euermore supposyng þat þe
seyd Walter wold have holde and parfourmyd þe seyd ordinaunce, arbitrement, and award. And at þe comyng of þe right high and myghty prynce
þe Duc of Norffolk fro hys castell of Framyngham to þe cetie of Norwyche
aftyr þe seyd day of þe makyng of þis arbitrement and ordinaunce, and
100 tofore þe feste of Michelmesse þan next folwyng, þe seyd Walter by hese
sotill and vngoodly enformacion caused þe seyd Duke to be hevy lord to
þe seyd William, where þe seyd William þe tyme of þe seyd enformacion
was, wyth Ser John Jermy, knyght, and othre of þe counseill of þe seyd
Duk of Norffolk in hys lordshipes in Norffolk and Suffolk þanne to hym
105 falle by þe deth of þe right worthy and noble lady hys modyr, occupied
abowte þe dwe seruice of wryttes of *diem clausit extremum* aftyr þe deth of
þe seyd lady; and where as þe seyd William Paston, by assignement and
commaundement of þe seyd Duk of Norffolk at hese fyrst passage ouer þe
see in-to Normandye in þe Kynges tyme Henry þe Fyfte, was þe styward

---

[13] *Interl. by Paston.*   [14] *F. 75 ends.*   [15] *Three minims, probably* iu, *canc.*

of þe seyd Duc ⌐of Norffolk⌐¹⁶ of all hese lordshipes in Norffolk and ₁₁₀
Suffolk fro hys seyd passage vn-to þe seyd feste of Michelmesse.¹⁷ [And
ouer þat as sergeaunt of lawe, thow he be vnworthy, withholdyn wyth
þe seyd Duc of Norffolk all þe tyme þat he was sergeaunt bifore þe same
feste of Michelmesse. And all be it þat þe fees and þe wages of þe seyd
William for hys seyd seruice vnpayed draweth a gret somme to his pouere ₁₁₅
degree, jf þe seyd Duk ⌐of Norffolk⌐¹⁶ lyked of hys noble and plentifous
grace to graunte to þe seyd William in right ony part of þe fauour of hese
good lordship, þe seyd William wold euere be hys pouere and trewe bede-
man and euere in hys herte thenke all hys seyd seruice and all þe seruice
þat euere he dede to ⌐þe seyd [Duke] of Norffolk⌐¹⁸ plentefousely weell ₁₂₀
rewardyd.] And where þe seyd Walter þe tyme of þe seyd trespas and of
þe seyd bylles makyng ne longe tofore, ne neuer aftyr biforn þe seyd
comyng of þe seyd Duc of Norffolk to Norwich, ne no tyme hangyng þe
seyd sute, ne þe tyme of makyng of þe seyd arbitrement and ordinaunce,
neuer was seruaunt to þe seyd Duc of Norffolk at fees ne at wages, ne ₁₂₅
wythhaldyn in hese seruice, ne to hym sued to be supported by hese high
lordship in þis seyd matier, to þe knowleche of þe seyd William¹⁹ ne to no
commvne knowleche in þe shyres of Norffolk, Suffolk, ne Norwiche; the
sute þat þe seyd Walter made for supportacion in þis seyd matier was be
þe meene of þe seyd Thomas Erpyngham to þe seyd Duk of²⁰ Gloucestre, ₁₃₀
by whose reule and commaundement²¹ þe seyd arbitrement and award
was mad in þe fourme aforn seyd.

And not with-stondyng þe seyd trespas and greuaunce by þe seyd
Walter doon to þe seyd William, ne þat þe seyd William ⌐ne is not satis-
fied⌐¹⁶ of þe seyd cxx li. ne no peny þer-of, and hath absteyned hym of al ₁₃₅
maner of execucion, sewyng of godes or catelles þat by force of þe seyd
processe or ony othyr he myght have had ageyn þe seyd Walter or hese
borwes, ne þat þe seyd William hath suffred þe seyd Walter to gon at
large by long tyme whan he myght haue had hys body in warde in lawefull
fourme, the seyd Walter be billes in þe too last parlementz holden at ₁₄₀
Westminster and at Leycestre, and at diuers tymes in diuers other maneres
hath noysed and skaundered þe seyd William vngoodly and othyr wyse
þan othyr gentilnesse or trowthe wolde, and ouermore caused þe seyd
William orribly to be manassed of hys deth, betyng, and dismembryng of
hys persone by certeyns seruauntz of þe Lordes Fitz-wauter and othre ₁₄₅
persones and by ferefull and ouere felle lettres and sondes, wherfore þe
seyd William nothyr hese frendes ne hese seruauntz in hys companye at

---

¹⁶ *Interl. by Paston.*
¹⁷ *Fold. by* va *interl. by Paston, with* cat *l.* 121 making the word Vacat *to cancel the inter-*
vening passage. ¹⁸ *Interl. by Paston above* my lord *canc.*
¹⁹ m *and another partly-formed letter canc.* ²⁰ Glous *canc.* ²¹ in *canc.*

here fredam sithen þe seyd parlement at Leycestre durst not, ne yet ne
dar not, rydyn ne goo abowte swyche occupacion as he arn vsed *and*
150 disposed,[22] to here grete *and* importable drede *and* vexacion in here
spirites *and* gret harme *and* damage *and* losse of here pouere goodes.[23]
[Ouermore þe seyd Walter hath sued, *and* yet rigerously sueth, a wrytte
of *decies tantum* ageyns x persones of þe seyd jnquisicion *and* ij of þe
seruauntz of þe seyd William *and* iiij othre persones, supposyng by hese
155 seyd sute hem to have taken of þe seyd William in hys seyd sute lxij li. *and*
more of moneye; the whiche sute of *decies tantum* þe seyd Walter betwyx
God *and* hym knowith verraly is vntrewe. And also þe seyd Walter hath
sued *and* yet pursuyth Adam Aubré, on of þe seyd jnquisicion, in þe court
of þe seyd Duc of Norffolk of hys manoir of[24] Fornsete by cause *and*
160 occasion of þe seyd matiers, in whiche sute in þe seyd court it is proceded
ageyn þe seyd Adam in other maner þanne othyr lawe, conscience, or good
feyth wolde.]

Ouermore þe seyd William, atte commaundement of þe seyd Duc of
Norffolk, hath submytted hym to stonde to þe ordinaunce of diuers
165 persones of alle þe seyd matiers: ones at Leycestre þe Wednesday next
biforn Palme Soneday þe iiij yeer of þe regne of þe seyd Kyng, a-nothyr
tyme atte Reed Clyf in Aprill þe same iiij yeer, aftyr þe fourme of certeyns
billes endented þer-of made; the whiche submission wyth alle þe circumstaunces þer-of þe seyd William hath be at alle tymes redy to obeye.

170 The cause why þe seyd Walter by þe seyd Englyshe bylles *and* in othyr
fourme putte *and* sette þe seyd William *and* hese seyd clerkes *and* seruauntz
in drede *and* fere intollerable to be slayn *and* mordered, *and* to hem tres-
paced in þe fourme aforn seyd, was onely for as moche as þe seyd William
was wyth þe Priour of Norwich of counseill in hese trewe defence ageyn
175 þe entent of þe seyd Walter in a sute þat he made ageyn þe seyd Priour
of a voweson of þe chyrche of Sprouston in þe counté of Norffolk, wher-to
þe seyd Walter hath nothyr title suffisaunt ne right in no maner wyse by
ony matier by hym declared byforn thys tyme.

Thys scrowe is mad only for þe jnformacion of þe worthy *and* worshepfull
180 lordes þe arbitrores, sauyng euere to þe maker þe benefice resonably to
adde *and* amenuse, &c., his ignoraunce in swiche occupacion *and* defaute
of leyser also tendrely considered.

---

22 *F. 76 ends.*
23 *Fold. by va interl. by Paston, with cat l. 162 cancelling the passage.*
24 Fr *canc.*

6. To the VICAR OF THE ABBOT OF CLUNY: draft
Probably 1430, April

Add. 27443, f. 87ᵛ. 11½×7¼ in. Beginning in an unidentified hand (see also no. 13), remainder autograph.

No seal or address. The text is a draft, but seems to have been begun as a fair copy, for the first ten and a half manuscript lines are carefully written in a professional-looking hand, with a wide margin. It is completed (three and a half lines), with corrections and interlineations, by Paston. The sheet was afterwards used as scribbling paper, and contains a variety of notes mostly in Latin or French. Those on the verso (this side) are in Paston's hand, some of them written between the lines of the draft but upside down (see no. 7). The notes that cover the recto are partly in Paston's hand, partly in another which appears also in nos. 8 and 9.

A note above the draft, evidently written later, is dated 'in crastino Concepcionis Beate Marie' 9 Henry VI (9 December 1430). The first note on the recto is 'in parliamento anno H vjᵗⁱ viijᵒ' (1 September 1429–31 August 1430), and another mentions the twelfth year of the pontificate of Martin V (which ended in November 1429). The concurrence of these dates makes 1430 the probable date of the draft.

  G. 14/20. C. 2.

My ryghte worthy and worshepeful lord, I recomaunde me to yow. And for as meche as Iˡ conseyue verrayly þat ye arn vicar gen*er*al in Ingge-lond of þe worthy p*re*late þe Abbot of Clunie, and have hys powr*e* in many grete articles, and ⌜aˡ-mong² other ⌜in p[ro]fession of monkes⌉³ in Inggelond of þe seyd ordere. And in my cuntré, but a⁴ myle fro þe place 5 where I was born, is þe povr*e* hous of Bromholm⁵ of þe same ordre, in wheche arn diu*er*s vertuous yongge men, monkes clad and vn-professyd, þat have abedyn þer*e*⁶ ⟨wyt*h*ow⟩t⁷ abbyte ix or x yeer*e*, and be lenger delaye of here p*ro*fession many inconuenientez arn lyke to falle. And also þe Priour of ⟨þe seyd hous⟩ hath resigned in-to yowr*e* worthy handes by 10 certeins notables and resonables causes, as it apperyth by an instrument and a symple lettre vnder þe co*mmu*ne seal of þe seyd hous of Bromholm, which þe berare⁸ of this hath redy to shewe yow. Wher-vp-on I prey yow wyt al my herte, and as I eu*er*e may do yow s*er*uice, þat it lyke to y*owr* grace to graunte of y*owr* charité by yowr*e* worthy lettres to þe Priour of 15 Thetford in Norffo*l*k, of þe seyde ordre of Clunye, autorité and powere as y*owr* ministre and deputé, to p*ro*fesse in dwe forme þe seyd monkes of Bromholm vn-p*ro*fessed; and ⌜þat it lyke yow⌉⁹ ouer*m*ore to accepte *and* admitte þe seyd resygnac*i*on by y*owr* seyd autorité and powere wyth þe

---

6. ¹ *Paper damaged, and repaired with adhesive paper which covers* nd for as meche as I. *But the words can be clearly seen, complete except for the top of* I.
  ² *Interlined letter only partially visible.*
  ³ *Interl. in Paston's hand above* in professyng monkes *canc.*   ⁴ *No space.*
  ⁵ to wh *interl., and canc.*
  ⁶ right religiously *interl. by Paston, and canc.*
  ⁷ *Hole in paper, mutilating this and the next MS. lines.*
  ⁸ my clerk *interl. by Paston, and canc.*   ⁹ *Interl. by Paston.*

20 fauour of yo*wr* good lordshepe, in confort and consolacion of yo*wr* pouere
prestes þe monkes of þe seyd hous of Bromholm;[10] *and* ther-vp to graunte
yo*wr* worthy *lett*res wittenessyng þe same acceptacion *and* admyssion of
þe seyd resigna*cion*, *and* al yo*wr* seid *lett*res to delyuere to my clerk, to
wham I prey yow to gyve feith *and* credence touchant þis matier, *and* to
25 delyuere hym in alle þe hast resonable.

And I am yo*wr* man *and* euere will be, by þe grace of God, which euere
haue yow in his kepyng. Writen at Norwich þe [11] of Aprill.

Yowres, WILL*IAM* PASTON

7. Recipe   Probably 1430

Add. 27443, f. 87ᵛ (reversed). Autograph.

See no. 5. This is the only note in English on the page. It begins at the fifth line.

Printed in *Neophilologus*, xxxvii (1953), 37.

P*ur* faire holsom drynk of ale, R*ecipe* sauge, auence, rose maryn, tyme,
chopped right smal, *and* put þis *and* a newe leyd hennes ey in a bage *and*
hange it in þe barell. Item, clowys, maces, *and* spikenard grounden *and*
p*ut* in a bagge[1] *and* hangen in þe barell. *And* nota[2] þat þe ey of þe henne
5 shal kepe þe ale fro sourynge. P*ar* Sibill Boys.

8. To an unidentified lord: draft   1436

Add. 34889, f. 140. 11½ × 5⅞ ins. Hand unidentified.

Dorse: No seal or address. Four memoranda in Paston's hand (see n. 12).

The text is a draft, in a hand apparently the same as that of Add. 27443, f. 88 (see
no. 9), and so probably the hand of a clerk of Paston's. Interlineations are in
Paston's hand. The paper is cut across above the beginning of the draft, leaving
bargeyn and the tails of a few other letters, in the clerk's hand, from what had been
written above.

The date appears from the last of the endorsed memoranda. Cf. Part II, no. 425.
G. VI/30.

Paston recomaund hym to your good lordeship, willyng w*ith* all his herte
to doo yow s*er*uise to his symple power. And as touchyng þe maner of
Walsh*am* he seyth þat at your comaundement he wille be redy to shewe
yow *and* preve þat þe seid maner *and* all þe vesture *and* crop þer-of þis
5 yeer by trewe title in lawe and conscience is his owen, trewly bowth *and*

---

[10] *Rest of letter in Paston's hand.*   [11] *Left blank.*
7. [1] *-s canc.*   [2] *Abbr. no and raised t.*

in gret p*art*ye payed for, and þat John Roys never hadde non estate in þe
seid maner but oonly occupied ⌜it⌝[1] by suffraunce of þe seid Paston *and*
other feffés in þe seid maner, *and* þat ⌜by þe bargayn of þe seid maner⌝
þ'estate þat þe seid Roys shuld have hadde in þe seid maner ⌜*and* in stoor
ther-of⌝ shul have be ⌜condicionel to be voide *and* nought⌝[2] for defaute 10
of payement, *and* þat þe seid John Roys ne kept not his dayes of þe paye-
mentz, &c., and þat þe seid Will Paston, in þe lyve of þe seid John Roys,
for defaut⟨e⟩ of payment entred in þe seid man*er* with ⌜þe seid⌝[3] crop
and þe vesture of þis yeer þer-of þan þer-vpon, and þat þe seid John Roys
never at noo tyme payed[4] to þe seid John Baxtere sith þe seid bargeyn, 15
nether for þe seid bargayn ne for þe dette he aught to hym, more þanne
an c *and* xl marcz, wher-of he borwed ageyn ⌜of þe seid John Baxtere⌝
xl li. *and* over þat he oweth; *and* befor þe seid bargeyn aught by his
obligac*i*on to þe seid John Baxtere of trewe dette of mony borwed other
xl li., *and* hath hadde and taken þe profitz of þe seid man*er* by iij hool 20
yeer befor his deth[5] to þe value of xxx li. and more, *and*[6] he receyved ⌜in
his seid bargayn⌝ of þe seid John Baxtere xl marcz worth of stoor, the
which iiij[xx] li. of dette *and* xxx li. of þe profitz of þe seid man*er and* xl
marcz worth of stoor maketh þe so*m*me of cxxxvj li. xiij s. iiij d. Wher-of,
thogh[7] þe lawe wille it not, were abated, if conscience required it, cxl 25
marcz payed by þe seid John Roys *and* x li. for þe value of þe seid crop
⌜ouer þe value of þe verray ferme of the seid maner⌝ for þis yeer; yet
remaigneth dwe to[8] þe executoures of þe seid John Baxter ⌜liij li. vj s.
viij d.⌝,[9] *and* all þe title and int*er*esse of þe seid John Roys, his heires *and*
assignes, in þe seid man*er* lawfully[10] *and* in conscience extincted[11] *and* 30
adnulled. Wher-vpon þe seid Paston lowly bese*c*heth your good lordeship
þat if it may be p*re*ved þis mater be trewe þat ye wille not be displesed
þogh he desire to have his fre disposic*i*on of þe seid man*er*.[12]

8. [1] *This and all the other interlineations are in William Paston's hand.*
  [2] *Interl. above* with *a reentre canc.*
  [3] *Interl. above* þe *which in error remains uncancelled.*   [4] more *canc.*
  [5] *Paper torn, top half of* his deth *lost.*   [6] r *and part of* e *canc.*
  [7] withoute *canc.*   [8] þes *canc.*
  [9] *Interl., after another correction, above* xxxiij li. vj s. viij d. *canc.*
  [10] ext *canc.*   [11] -ed *crowded in.*
  [12] *Recto ends. On the verso are four memoranda in Paston's hand, mostly in Latin. The first, the top line of which is defective at tears in the paper, begins:* 'Hec billa indentata ⟨. . .⟩ quod Johannes Baxtere vendidit Johanni Roys mesuagium suum vocatum [Baxteres place *canc.*] Walsham place, cum toto stauro ibidem viuo et mortuo, et Bryanes cum omnibus alijs terris et tenementis suis. . . .' *The price was 350 marks,* 'vnde dictus Johannes Roys soluit dicto Johanni Baxtere, die Jouis proximo ante festum apostolorum Simonis et Jude anno regni regis Henrici vj xij [*sc. 22 October 1433*] c m. et habet diem soluendi residuum. . . . Datum die Jouis predicto.' *The second and third were both cancelled, but the second restored; it is a brief note of a payment by Roys. The third is as follows:*

  Hec indentura facta vj die Octobris anno xiiij r.r. Henrici vj testatur quod W. Paston soluet [exec. *canc.*] ⌜Roberto Tebald, Johanni Deyes, clerk, et Johanni Wyllyot, executoribus &c.⌝ alle þe so*m*mes of moneye dw⟨e⟩ to hem by John Roys for a purchas made

9. To JOHN BERNEY 1439–40

Add. 27443, f. 88. 11⅝×9½ in. Headnote autograph, text in the hand of those notes on f. 87^r which are not by Paston (see nos. 6 and 8).

Dorse: Paper seal over red wax. Address in unidentified hand:

> To þe worthy and worshepfull ser, John Berneye of Redham.

Above this, in a rough hand like John Paston I's, litera Willelmi Paston, and below in the same hand, copia statu facture Margerie nuper vxori Johannis Mauteby.

This draft lease is presumably connected with the marriage of John Paston I to Margaret Mautby, whose name appears here for the first time. The date is between the death of John Boys, who died on 21 August 1439 (Inq. p.m., 18 Henry VI, no. 2), and that of John Berney of Reedham in 1440 (will dated 16 June, proved 5 September: Blomefield, xi. 126; Norwich Wills, i. 39).

    G. 26/35 (abstract).

þis note is not made to þ'entent þat dedes acordyng ther-to shuld be engrossed with-oute more comunicacion and sadde aduys of alle þe feffés to-gedere, or elles counseill by here comune assignement. Ferthermore þe note of ⌈þe condicion of þe⌉ reseruacion of the rent is not yet
5 noted.

Sciant presentes et futuri quod nos Simon Felbrygge, miles, Oliuerus Groos, armiger, Johannes Berneye de Redham, armiger, Willelmus Paston ⌈de Paston⌉, Thomas Stodhagh, Rogerus Taillour de Stafford Bernyngham, et Thomas[1] Newport de Runham, iuxta effectum et formam
10 vltimarum voluntatum Roberti Mawteby de Mawteby, armigeri, et Johannis de Mawteby filij sui, ⌈iam⌉ defunctorum, dimisimus, liberauimus, assignauimus, et hac presenti carta nostra tripartita et indentata confirmauimus ⌈Margerie⌉[2] que fuit vxor predicti Johannis Mawteby duas partes maneriorum, &c., ac reuercionem, &c.,[3] que[4] nos prefati Simon,

by hym of the seid John Baxter of þe maner of W⟨. . .⟩ [paper decayed] except clj marcz, and þe [exec. canc.] ⌈same Tebald, Deye, and Wyllyot⌉ shal relese and make þe parson of Crostwheyt, Thomas Walsh, and William Burgh, Henry Lesyngham, William Bakton, and William Paston [breaks off].

The fourth contains the following passages fixing the date:

    Memorandum quod licet esset concordatum quod W. Roys haberet barganium, &c., quod vt credo non ita erit, tunc in festo Natiuitatis Domini anno regni regis Henrici vj xv^o [sc. 1436] debentur executoribus de eodem barganio c marce. . . . Set circa Natiuitatem Domini anno regni dicti regis xiiij^o, ⌈et in quadragesima tunc proxime sequenti⌉ vxor dicti Roys apud Paston ⌈dixit⌉ quod habuit xx marcas paratas ad soluendum. Et sic dixit Johannes Roys tempore quo Domina Skarlet fuit apud Paston, videlicet ix die Januarij dicto anno xiiij^o.

9. [1] Runham de Newport canc.　　　　　　[2] Interl. above Margarete canc.
  [3] habendas canc.　　　　　　　　　　　[4] fuerunt predicti Roberti Mawteby canc.

Oliuerus, Willelmus, Thomas Stodhagh, Rogerus, et Thomas Newport, 15
vna cum Milone Stapilton, milite, Willelmo Argenten, milite, Johanne
Heuenyngham, milite, Johanne Carbonell, milite, Willelmo Calthorpe,
milite, Johanne Boys, armigero, et Willelmo Caston, armigero, iam de-
functis, nuper habuimus ex dono,⁵ feoffamento, remissione, et relaxacione
predicti Roberti Mawteby, prout in quibusdam cartis et scriptis inde 20
confectis plenius continetur, habendas et tenendas predictas duas partes
ac reuercionem, &c., prefate Margerie et assignatis suis ad totam vitam
suam de nobis et heredibus nostris, reddendo inde nobis et heredibus
nostris annuatim   ⁶ legalis monete Anglie ad festa Pasche et Sancti
Michaelis equis porcionibus, faciendi gracia inde et reddendi pro nobis 25
et heredibus nostris, capitalibus dominis feodorum illorum, reddita et
seruicia inde debita et consueta. Ita quod predicte due partes, &c., ac
reuercio, &c., post mortem predicte Margerie integre remaneant⁷
Margarete,⁸ filie predictorum Johannis Mawteby et Margerie, et heredibus
de corpore eiusdem Margarete exeuntibus; videlicet quod si eadem 30
Margareta sine herede de corpore suo exeunte obierit, aut si ipsa aut heredes
sui predicti donum aut talliam predictam, in forma predicta factam per
feoffamentum scriptum siue factum aut alio modo, discontinuarint aut
discontinuari fecerint, quod tunc due partes, &c., integre remaneant
Petro Mawteby, filio predicti Roberti Mawteby et avunculo supradicte 35
Margarete, et heredibus de corpore predicti Petri legitime exeuntibus,
sub certis forma et condicionibus subsequentibus: videlicet quod si idem
Petrus sine herede de corpore suo exeunte obierit, aut si ipse aut heredes
sui predicti discontinuauerint, &c., quod tunc predicte, &c., integre
remaneant Thome Mawteby, fratri predicti Petri, et heredibus de corpore 40
suo legitime exeuntibus, tenende, &c., vt supra, reddendo et faciendo, &c.,
vt supra, sub forma et condicionibus subsequentibus: videlicet quod si
predictus Thomas obierit sine herede de corpore suo legitime exeunte,
aut si ipse aut heredes sui, &c., discontinuauerint, &c., quod tunc predicte,
&c., integre remaneant Alianore que fuit vxor predicti Roberti, habende 45
et tenende sibi et assignatis suis de nobis, &c., ad terminum vite sue,
faciendo et reddendo vt supra. Et quod ex tunc predicte, &c., post mortem
predicte Alianore integre remaneant heredibus de corpore Alianore que
fuit vxor predicti Willelmi Calthorpe, sororis predicti Roberti Mawteby,
legitime exeuntibus. Et si nullus fuerit heres de corpore predicte Alianore 50
que fuit vxor predicti Willelmi Calthorpe legitime exiens, aut si aliquis
huiusmodi heres de corpore eiusdem Alianore legitime exiens donum,
&c., discontinuauerit, &c., quod tunc predicte, &c., ad nos prefatos
Simonem, Oliuerum, Johannem Berneye, Willelmum Paston, Thomam
Stodhagh, Rogerum Taillour, et Thomam Newport et heredes nostros 55
integre reuertantur ad faciendam inde et debite exequendam predictam

---

⁵ et *canc.*   ⁶ *Blank.*   ⁷ predicte *canc.*   ⁸ et he *canc.*

vltimam voluntatem predicti Roberti Mawteby. In cuius rei testimonium duabus partibus presentis carte indentate nos prefati Simon, &c., sigilla nostra apposuimus, tercie vero parti eiusdem carte penes nos et heredes 60 nostros remanenti predicti Johannes Mawteby, Edwardus Mawteby, Petrus Mawteby, Thomas Mawteby, Alianora que fuit vxor predicti Roberti Mawteby, et Willelmus Calthorpe, armiger, consanguineus et heres predicte Alianore que fuit vxor Willelmi Calthorpe de corpore eiusdem Alianore legitime exiens, sigilla sua apposuerunt hijs testibus, 65 &c., data, &c.

10. To PHILIP BERNEY: copy   1442, before October

Add. 45099, f. 2. Hand of the clerk who copied John Paston II's will, no. 309.

The manuscript consists of two sheets of paper (ff. 1, 2), each *c.* 12 × 17¼ in., f. 1 slightly decayed at the edges, especially the top right. They were originally stitched together to form a roll, but are now pasted to a mount of modern paper and bound as a book. The recto contains copies, all in the same hand, of six letters and an indenture, numbered in the left margin *ij* to *viij*, of which this letter is *vj*. The mount is cut to leave visible four endorsements: one, much faded, in a hasty hand probably of the sixteenth century, *Carta de Estbeckham*; the second, which seems to be of the fifteenth century, apparently p^{ia} p^{ia}, which I cannot explain; the third, in a sixteenth-century hand, *Coppies of diuers Letters* and *of an Indenture*; the fourth, in a different hand of similar date, *East Beckham*.

This file of documents relating to the manor of East Beckham is likely to be connected in some way with John Paston II's sale of the manor to Roger Townshend in 1469; see especially no. 246. But the sale was not final: the indenture provided for possible redemption, and John II still recorded 'a bag with evidence of East Beckham' in his inventory no. 265; and the manor was still the subject of 'variance' between John Paston III and Roger Townshend II (son of Sir Roger, who died in 1493) as late as 1503 (see Part II, no. 928). It is remarkable that this file of documents is in the same hand as the copy of John II's will (no. 309), which was drawn up at the end of October 1477, and part of John III's draft petition of 1484 (no. 387). The most probable explanation is that both this file and the will were copied after John II's death on John III's instructions, perhaps about the same time as he made his complaint against William II in 1484.

Since the original of one of these letters is preserved it can be seen that the clerk did not think it necessary to copy his exemplar with minute accuracy; see Part II, no. 431.

A patent dated 22 March 1442 granted to William Paston I the keeping of the manor of East Beckham from 22 February 18 Henry VI (1440) for seven years and thereafter during pleasure (*Cal. Pat. Rolls 1441–6*, p. 44). The present letter is presumably close to Thomas West's letter to Paston numbered *iiij* in this file and datable probably in 1442 (Part II, no. 430), but earlier than the indenture which immediately follows as no. *vij*, and which begins thus:

> Hec jndentura facta die lune proximo post festum Sancti Michaelis Archangeli anno regni regis Henrici Sexti post conquestum vicesimo primo [*sc. 1 October*

1442] inter Willelmum Paston ex vna parte et Simonem Gunnore et Willelmum Shepherd ex altera testatur quod predictus Willelmus Paston tradidit et ad firmam dimisit predictis Simoni et Willelmo Shepherd manerium de Estbecham cum pertinencijs, exceptis toto bosco et subbosco, shredynggis, ac proficuis curiarum et letarum predicti manerij, preter tantomodo spinas pro sepibus in manerio predicto faciendis et fines pro quibuscumque alienacionibus terrarum et tenementorum ad voluntatem dominorum eiusdem manerij tentorum durante termino subscripto factos, habendum et tenendum manerium predictum cum pertinencijs, exceptis preexceptis eisdem Simoni et Willelmo Shepherd . . . vsque finem termini quinque annorum ex tunc proxime sequencium et plenarie completorum; reddendo inde predicto Willelmo Paston, executoribus et assignatis suis, ad festum Sancti Michaelis Archangeli proxime futurum nouem marcas legalis monete Anglie et annuatim postea durante termino predicto decem et octo marcas. . . .

For the other letters in this series see no. 35 (John Paston I) and Part II, nos. 428 ff.
The English documents in this manuscript were printed in a modernized and not wholly accurate text in *H.M.C. Twelfth Report*, Appendix ix (1891), pp. 1–179 ff.

To the ryght wursheful syr and my good frende Phylyp Berney, esquier

Ryght wurshefull ser, I recummend me to yow and prey you to wete þat[1] ye and oder arn enfeoffed in the maner of Estbecham to myn[2] oeps; and thervpon I haue in yowre name *and* otherys take an accion a-yens John Maryete of Crowmer, wherfore I prey you that ȝe make no releasse therof to no man til I speke wyth yow; and God haue yow in hys kepyng. Wrete 5 at London the xxij day of Octobre.

Youres, WYLLYAM PASTON

11. Inventory   Not after 1444

Bodleian, Douce charters 18. Parchment, $11\frac{1}{2} \times 10$ in. (indented, bottom turned up). Unidentified clerk's hand, endorsement in Paston's hand.

Dorse: Summary account: see n. 5.

A note in Blomefield's hand dates this document 1424, but there is no surviving evidence for this or any other date except that it is obviously in Paston's lifetime.
G. 964/49.

Hec sunt hostilmenta et vtensilia domus, bona et catalla, que Willelmus Paston, in indentura presentibus annexa nominatus, tradidit et dimisit Willelmo Joye, in eadem indentura nominato, secundum formam eiusdem indenture ex communi assensu eorundem Willelmi et Willelmi per Robertum Gynne, Johannem Albon de Paston, et alios appreciata, 5 assignata, et specificata modo subsequenti, videlicet: tres equi precij quinque marcarum; quatuor vacce quelibet precij vij s. vj d.; vna juuenca

---

10. [1] þ *in form of* y *throughout.*   [2] op *canc.*

brendit precij v s.; vnus tauriculus precij iiij s.; vna juvencula dowet
precij iij s.; due sues quelibet precij iij s. iiij d.; tres po⌐r⌐culi quilibet
10 precij xvj d.; tres porcelli quilibet precij xij d.; quatuor alij porcelli quilibet precij viij d.; vna carecta precij vj s. viij d.; apparatus carecte, videlicet
vna sella, vnum par des stroppys, duo paria dez trayses precij ij s.; due
caruce cum lez hokys et stappilles, vnum par rotarum, due herpice precij
v s.; quatuor paria dez trayses ad aratrum precij viij d.; due furse fimose
15 precij vj d.; vna vanga precij iij d.; vnus tribulus precij iij d.

Hec sunt blada et alia hostilmenta et vtensilia domus, bona et catalla, per
predictum Willelmum Paston predicto Willelmo Joye secundum formam
dicte indenture similiter dimissa et non appreciata, videlicet: sex quarteria
frumenti; xxv quarteria ordei; viij quarteria auenarum; quidam tassus
20 pisarum in fine australi antique grangie mesuagij predicti, qui est altitudinis
iij virgarum et iij quarteriorum vnius virge, et quidam alius tassus vescarum
in boriali fine eiusdem grangie, altitudinis iij virgarum et j quarterij vnius
virge, qui quidem duo tassi fuerunt vesture xij acrarum et dimidij et dimidij
rode terre; iij vasa vocata kelerys; j gilyngfat; iiij stondes pro seruicia;[1]
25 j stonde in coquina; ij patelle cum ligaminibus ferreis; j parua patella
cum ligamine ferreo; j magna olla ennea; alia olla ennea minor; j parua
olla ennea; j tabula; j par des trostelles;[2] j longum hostium iacens in
boteria; j par des trostelles; j trow; ij bolles; j morter; j thede; j temse;
j mashsterell; j tankard cum ligamine ferreo; j bultyngpoke; j magna trow
30 pro farina; j cista pro farina; j fleshoke; j tripes ferreum; j veru ferreum;
j aundern; j par de tongys; j lachgres ennea; j securis; j magnum laua-
crum pendens; j kynderkyn; ij soos leeke; j par de belwes; j magnum
planke super mensam coquine; ⌐j chargour⌐; iij perapsides; iij disci; iij
sauserys de pewter; iij perapsides; iij disci; j magnus discus; vj sissorij;
35 iij ciphi de ligno; j chayer; duo longa scanna; j scannum mediocre longi-
tudinis; ij scanna vocata buffetstoles; ij bankare; j gladius; ij ferra vocata
aplates; j chirne; j chyrnyngstaf; j curta falx; j candelabrum ferreum; j
paruum salerium; ij beryngsceppes; vnum par dez pepyrquerns; ij vteri;
j cadus cum vergous; j parua cista in boteria; j selura supra seruisiam; j
40 metesetell; j pykforke; iij longe bordclothys; j towayll; j san⟨ap⟩[3] ⌐et⌐ j
walet pro autumpno; j lucerna; ij vomerj et ij cultri que ponderant xvij
li. et di.; j carectula, anglice a carre; j sunvectorium; ij noui rowmtrees[4]
et j curtum lignum in le carthows; ij veteres bige; j par rotarum ferra-
tarum; ij kemell cum hopys ferreis; j frena; j peluis; viij sacci; iiij longa
45 ligna fraxinora in pistrina; j fetyrlok.[5]

11. [1] -c- *apparently over long* s.   [2] j parua tabula *canc.*
[3] *From* bord- *on eras., cramped; last letters smudged.*
[4] *This word on a dark patch, third and fourth letters uncertain.*
[5] *Recto ends. On the verso the following note in Paston's hand:*
Summa catallorum infrascriptorum et appreciatorum 6 li. 19 s. 8 d.

12. Testament and Last Will (extracts) 1444, 10 and 21 January

P.C.C., Reg. Luffenam, 29.

These extracts are given for the information they contain about dates, persons, and property. The parchment of the register has been damaged by damp at some time and a large patch on f. 227ᵛ made illegible, so that the age of Clement Paston, in particular, has been lost. The amount of writing obliterated varies from line to line, but no attempt is here made to indicate these variations. All lacunae due to damage are shown by ⟨. . .⟩; editorial omissions by . . .

    G. 984/Will 2 (complete).

In Dei nomine, amen. Ego Willelmus Paston de Paston, sane mentis et memorie, condo testamentum meum in hunc modum. In primis, lego animam meam Omnipotenti Deo, Beate Marie, et omnibus sanctis, et corpus meum sepeliendum ad finem australem altaris in capella Beate Marie in fine orientali ecclesie cathedralis Sancte Trinitatis Norwici. Et 5 si contingat corpus meum ibidem sepeliri, lego cuilibet monacho sacerdoti ecclesie predicte qui singulis diebus aliqua septimana per septem annos proximo sequentes post mortem meam missam de Spiritu Sancto in capella predicta tempore celebracionis summe misse in eadem ecclesia decantauerit, ad exorandum in eadem missa de Spiritu Sancto et in alijs 10 diuinis per ipsum diebus illis factis pro anima mea et animabus vxoris mee, patrum, matrum, et omnium consanguineorum et benefactorum nostrorum, et omnium quorum debitores sumus, et omnium per nos iniuriam paciencium, et eorum omnium pro quibus Deo est deprecandum, et omnium fidelium defunctorum, septem denarios. Item, lego Roberto 15 nunc priori ecclesie Sancti Andree de Bromholm quadraginta solidos; et cuilibet monacho eiusdem ecclesie conuentus de Bromholm sex solidos et octo denarios; et executoribus testamenti Ricardi Causton nuper vicarij ecclesie de Paston viginti solidos; et executoribus testamenti Ade nuper vicarij ecclesie de Bakton sex solidos et octo denarios, ita quod remittant 20 et relaxent in consciencijs suis animabus predictis si que per earum aliquam sibi debita fuerint. Et si hoc remittere et relaxare recusauerint, de predictis legatis nihil habeant, sed in omnibus que sibi per animas predictas vel earum aliquam deberi racionabiliter aut euidenter, in con- sciencia vel aliter, iuxta discrecionem executorum meorum aut maioris 25 partis eorundem, probauerint aut verificauerint, sibi satisfaciant executores mei. Residuum vero bonorum meorum omnium non legatorum do et

11. [*Note 5 continued*]

    Summa granorum infrascriptorum vltra pisas et vescas iiij li. xviij s. iiij d.; quarterium frumenti ad iiij s., quarterium ordej ij s. iiij d., et quarterium auenarum ad ij s.

    Item, vestura xij acrarum et di. et di. rode pisarum et vescarum.

    Item, dicta vestura pisarum et vescarum ad l s. [*eras., covered by line*] lacr. ad iiij s. de xij acrarum et di. rode non taxatum.

    Summa totalis xiiij li. viij s.

lego Agneti vxori mee, Johanni filio meo, Willelmo Bakton, et Johanni Damme de Sustede, quos ordino et constituo executores huius testamenti
30 mei, vt ipsi inde disponant pro[ut] in iustis consciencijs suis magis viderint Deo placere et animabus predictis prodesse. In cuius rei testimonium presentibus sigillum meum apposui. Datum decimo die Januarij anno regni regis Henrici Sexti post conquestum vicesimo secundo. Huius autem testamenti mei venerabilem in Christo patrem et dominum Domi-
35 num Willelmum Lincolniensem episcopum ordino et constituo super-uisorem.

Extracts from Last Will:

. . . Ita quod eadem maneria de Oxenede, Marlyngforde, Stanstede, et Horwelbury, et terre et tenementa que fuerunt Roberti Salle, Willelmi Clopton et Francisse, seu alicuius eorum, cum pertinencijs, post mortem
40 prefate Agnetis remaneant heredibus de corpore meo et corpore predicte Agnetis exeuntibus. Et predicta manerium de Shipdene et parcella manerij de Latymers ac dicta mesuagia, molendinum, terre et tenementa nuper Clementis Paston et Hugonis atte Fen, seu alicuius eorum, cum pertinencijs, post mortem predicte Agnetis ad predictas personas feof-
45 fatas seu feoffandas, heredes et assignatos suos reuertantur, ad perficiendam inde hanc vltimam voluntatem meam. Et si nullus extiterit heres de corpore meo et corpore predicte Agnetis exiens, quod tunc post mortem eiusdem Agnetis predictum manerium de Oxenede et dicta terre et tenementa nuper predictorum Roberti Salle, Willelmi Clopton et Francisse,
50 seu vnius eorum, cum pertinencijs, ad predictos feoffatos et heredes suos similiter reuertantur, ad perficiendam inde hanc vltimam voluntatem meam. Et quod predicta maneria de Marlyngford, Stanstede, et Horwelbury, cum pertinencijs, remaneant rectis heredibus Edmundi Barry, militis, patris predicte Agnetis, imperpetuum. Item, volo quod predicte
55 persone vt predicitur, feoffate seu feoffande, heredes seu assignati sui, paciantur et permittant Robertum Clere, armigerum, Edmundum Clere, armigerum, Johannem Pagraue, armigerum, Willelmum Bakton de Bakton, et Johannem Damme de Sustede, vel duos eorum per communem assensum eorum quinque, predictum manerium de Snaylwell et predicta
60 alia terras et tenementa in Snaylwell in toto, per communem estimacionem, ad valenciam quadraginta marcarum per annum occupare et exitus et proficua inde percipere et habere a festo Sancti Michaelis proximo sequenti post mortem meam vsque Edmundus filius meus iam etatis xviij annorum peruenerit ad etatem xxj annorum. . . . Et de eisdem exitibus
65 et proficuis predicto Edmundo filio meo, quousque ad dictam etatem xxj annorum peruenerit, racionabiles victum, vestitum, apparatum, et sustentacionem, iuxta gradus sui exigenciam sic quod non superbiat, inueniant, et eum tam ad artis dialectice per dimidium annum, iuris ciuilis per vnum

22

annum, ac iuris regni Anglie postea ad sufficienciam, si fieri poterit, sub
sana tutela prouidenter ponant et ipsum in eisdem continuare et residere 70
faciant prout eisdem melius visum fuerit ipsum Edmundum in hac parte
sapere et intelligere et sibi in futurum prodesse; et domos, muros, edificia,
et clausuras in eodem manerio nostro existencia racionabiliter reparari
faciant, et redditus et seruicia et alia onera inde debita soluant, et hoc
quod de eisdem exitibus et proficuis ad dictam etatem dicti Edmundi 75
remanserit iuxta sanas consciencias suas eidem Edmundo satisfaciant
tempore quo ipse iuxta hanc voluntatem meam statum de eodem manerio
receperit et habuerit. Item, volo quod predicte persone prout predicitur,
feoffate seu f⟨eoffande⟩, heredes seu assignati sui paciantur et permittant
predictos Robertum Clere, Edmundum Clere, Johannem Pagraue, 80
Willelmum Bakton, et Johannem Damme, vel duos eorum per communem
assensum eorum quinque, predictum manerium de Beauchamp et Holle-
welhalle et dicta alia mesuagia, terras, tenementa, tofta, clausuras, redditus
et seruicia quondam Ricardi Doket, Willelmi Thuxton, Johannis Patgris
senioris, Johannis Whynne, et Eustachij Rows, seu aliquorum vel alicuius 85
eorum, in Wymondham, Carleton, Bonnewell, Estodenham, et alijs villis
adiacentibus, per communem estimacionem ad valenciam xxv marcarum ⟨. . .⟩ et proficua inde percipere et habere a predicto festo Sancti
Michaelis vsque Willelmus filius meus iam etatis vij annorum peruenerit
ad etatem xviij annorum, et quod ijdem Robertus Clere, Edmundus Clere, 90
Johannes Pagraue, Willelmus Bakton, et Johannes Damme, vel dicti duo
eorum, quinque marcas annuatim prouenientes de eisdem exitibus et
proficuis per octo annos proximo sequentes predictum festum Sancti
Michaelis, per discrecionem ⟨. . .⟩ predicte Agnetis annuatim distribuant
inter pauperes et debiles predictos et [pro] missis, oracionibus, et suffragijs 95
celebrandis ⟨. . .⟩ in forma predicta et de eisdem exitibus et proficuis
predicto Willelmo filio meo vsque ad dictam etatem xviij annorum ⟨. . .⟩
statum et sustentacionem iuxta gradus sui exigenciam, sic quod non
superbiat, inueniant et tribuant ⟨. . .⟩ scolas ponant et ibidem ⟨. . .⟩ residere
faciant prout predicitur de predicto filio meo Edmundo, et domos, muros, 100
et clausuras ⟨. . .⟩ repararent et redditus et seruicia et alia onera inde
soluant et de residuo dictorum exituum et proficuorum dicto Willelmo
filio meo satisfaciant ⟨. . .⟩ statum de eisdem manerio, terris, ⸢et⸣ tenementis
iuxta hanc voluntatem meam ⟨. . .⟩ heredes seu assignati sui paciantur et
permittant predictam Agnetem ⟨. . .⟩ West Somerton, Hennesby, Martham, 105
et Wynterton, tam illa que fuerunt ⟨. . .⟩ de Reston in toto per communem
estimacionem ad valenciam xxv marcarum ⟨. . .⟩ gaudere a predicto festo
Sancti Michaelis vsque Clemens filius meus ⟨. . .⟩ xviij annorum, et quod
eadem Agnes de eisdem exitibus et proficuis predicto Clementi Paston
⟨. . .⟩ xviij annorum, et Elizabeth filie mee quousque maritetur, racionabiles 110
victum, vestitum ⟨. . .⟩ exigenciam, sic quod non superbiant, et de eisdem

exitibus et proficuis nutriatur honeste ⟨. . .⟩ filiam predictam Elizabeth
prout statui suo conuenit, ac inueniat et ponat predictum Clementem ⟨. . .⟩
scolas grammaticales quam alias et ceteras erudiciones prout predicitur de
115 predictis fratribus suis; et domos, muros, clausuras, et edificia in eisdem
mesuagijs, terris, et tenementis existencia racionabiliter reparari faciat et
redditus et seruicia et alia onera inde debita soluat ac annuatim quousque
⟨. . .⟩ Clemens filius meus ad dictam etatem xviij annorum [peruenerit]
distribuat manu propria in elemosinis iuxta discrecionem suam inter magis
120 pauperes et debiles creaturas, in honore quinque principalium vulnerum
et passionis Domini Nostri Jesu Christi et quinque gaudiorum Beate
Marie Virginis et Matris eius, pro animabus predictis, quinque marcas.
Et de hoc quod de eisdem exitibus et proficuis ad dictam etatem predicti
Clementis filij mei remanserit, satisfaciat eadem Agnes iuxta sanam
125 conscienciam suam eidem Clementi tempore quo ipse iuxta hanc voluntatem meam statum de eisdem manerio, mesuagijs, terris, et tenementis de
predictis personis feoffatis siue feoffandis receperit; et quod dicte persone
feoffate seu feoffande, heredes seu assignati sui, infra xl dies proximo
sequentes postquam ipsi post festum Sancti Michaelis proximum post
130 mortem meam per Johannem Paston filium meum primogenitum racionabiliter fuerint requisiti, per facta sua tripartita et indentata dimittent,
liberent, et assignent predicto Johanni Paston, iam etatis xx annorum
et amplius, predictum manerium de Gresham cum pertinencijs, habendum
eidem Johanni ad totam vitam suam; ita quod si contingat predictum
135 Johannem Paston aliquem exitum vel heredem de corpore Margarete
nunc vxoris sue procreare, quod tunc idem manerium cum pertinencijs
post mortem eiusdem Johannis remaneat dicte vxori sue, tenendum sibi
ad terminum vite eiusdem vxoris. Et si predictus Johannes Paston nullum
exitum vel heredem de corpore dicte vxoris sue procreauerit, tunc imme-
140 diate post mortem eiusdem Johannes idem manerium cum pertinencijs
heredibus masculis de corpore meo exeuntibus integre remaneat. . . .
[*Provision for many contingencies follows.*]
Item, volo quod predicta Elizabeth filia mea habeat ducentas libras legalis
monete ad maritagium suum si ipsa per auisamentum predicte Agnetis
145 et executorum meorum maritetur, prouiso semper quod eadem Elizabeth
pari sexu et etate in bona et competenti consanguinitatis linea maritata
sit, et per maritagium illud habeat statum sufficientem et securum in lege
sibi et viro suo et heredibus de corporibus suis exeuntibus, si fieri poterit,
seu saltem ad totam vitam suam, in terris et tenementis valoris quadra-
150 ginta librarum per annum ad minus. Et si eadem Elizabeth antequam
maritata fuerit obierit, quod tunc dicte pecunie summa pro maritagio eius
limitata in solucione debitorum que me debere contingat et in reformacione
et satisfactione mesprisionum et extorcionum, si quas fecerim, et pro
animabus predictis fideliter distribuatur per discrecionem predicte Agnetis

et executorum meorum. In cuius rei testimonium ego prefatus Willelmus 155
Paston presentibus sigillum meum apposui. Datum vicesimo primo die
Januarij anno regni regis Henrici Sexti post conquestum vicesimo secundo.

Probata fuerunt predicta testamentum et vltima voluntas coram nobis
Alexandro Prowet, decretorum inceptore, ac reuerendissimi in Christo
patris et domini Domini Johannis, permissione diuina Cantuariensis 160
archiepiscopi, commissario generali, &c., vicesimo quarto die mensis
Nouembris anno Domini millesimo cccc^{mo} xliiij^{to}. . . .

AGNES PASTON

13. To WILLIAM PASTON I   Probably 1440, 20 April

Add. 43488, f. 4. 11¾×4 in. Hand of the first part of no. 6; see Plate II.

Dorse: Traces of red wax. Address in hand of letter:

To my worshepefull housbond W. Paston be þis lettere takyn.

The date is evidently not long before the marriage of John Paston I and Margaret Mautby. This had presumably not taken place at the date of no. 9, but a letter from Robert Repps to John Paston I of 1 November 1440 shows that he was married by then (Part II, no. 439).

Deus qui errantibus is the opening of the collect for the third Sunday after Easter; Easter Day in 1440 was 27 March.

The hand, though smaller, is certainly that of the writer of the beginning of no. 6, who can hardly have been Agnes acting as her husband's secretary. If she could write as well as this she would surely not have had her other letters written by clerks. The point of the closing words is therefore obscure.

F. i, p. 2. G. 25/34. C. 3.

Dere housbond, I recomaunde me to yow, &c. Blyssyd be God, I sende yow gode tydynggys of þe comyng and þe brynggyn hoom of þe gentyl-womman þat ye wetyn of fro Redham þis same nyght,[1] acordyng to poynt-men þat ye made þer-for yowre-self. And as for þe furste aqweyntaunce
5 be-twhen John Paston and þe seyde gentilwomman, she made hym gentil chere in gyntyl wyse and seyde he was verrayly yowre son. And so I hope þer shal nede no gret treté be-twyxe hym.

þe parson of Stocton toold me yif ye wolde byin here a[2] goune, here moder wolde yeue ther-to a godely furre. þe goune nedyth for to be had,
10 and of coloure it wolde be a godely blew or ellys[3] a bryghte sanggueyn.

I prey yow do byen for me ij pypys of gold. Yowre stewes do weel.

The Holy Trinité have yow in gouernaunce. Wretyn at Paston in hast þe Wednesday next after *Deus qui errantibus*, for defaute of a good secretarye, &c.

15   Yowres, AGNES[4] PASTON

13. [1] ac *and another letter canc.*
    [2] *No space; so again in all other occurrences of the indefinite article.*
    [3] *MS.* erlys.   [4] *Abbr. by tailed* -n.

14. To Edmond Paston I   1445, 4 February

Add. 34888, f. 13. $11\frac{3}{8} \times 6\frac{7}{8}$ in. Hand unidentified.

Dorse: Remnants of red wax. Address in hand of letter:

> *To Edmond Paston of Clyffordis Inne in London be this lettre take.*

The date appears from the fact that William Paston I was dead when the letter was written, but had been alive in the previous Lent. He died in August 1444 (see no. 33, and Part II, no. 441). Palmer of Trunch appears in the following year in no. 16.

F. iii, p. 32. G. 46/62. C. 6 (part).

To myn welbelouid sone.

I grete yow wel, and avyse yow to thynkke onis of the daie of yowre fadris counseyle to lerne the lawe; for he seyde manie tymis that ho so euer schuld dwelle at Paston schulde have nede to conne defende hym-selfe.   5

The vikarie of Paston and yowre fadre, in Lenttyn laste was, wher thorwe ⌈and⌉ acordidde,[1] and doolis sette howe broode the weye schuld ben; *and* nowe he hathe pullid vppe the doolis and seithe he wolle makyn a[2] dyche fro the cornere of his walle ry3ht overe the weye to the newe diche of the grete cloose. And there is a man in Truntche hy3ht Palmere   10 to, ⌈þat hadde⌉[3] of yowre fadre certein londe in Truntche on vij yere ore viij yere agoone for corn, and trwli hathe paide all the yer*is*; and now he hathe suffrid the corne to ben w*ith*-sette for viij s. of rentte to Gymmyngham, wich yowre fadre paide nevere. Geffreie axid Palmere why the rentte was notte axid in myn husbonddis tyme, and Palmere seyde, for   15 he was a grete man and a wyse man of the lawe, and that was the cawse men wolde not axe hym the rentte. I sende yow the namis of the men that kaste down the pittis that was Gynnis Close ⌈wretyn⌉[4] in a bille closid in this lettre.

I sendde yow not this lettre to make yow wery of Paston, for I leve in   20 hoope; and ye wolle lerne that they[5] schulle be made werye of her*e* werke, for*e* in good feyth I dar*e* wel seyne it was yowre fadris laste wille to have do ry3ht wel to that plase, and that can I schewe of good p*r*efe, thowe men wolde seye naye.

God make yow ry3ht a good man, *and* sende Goddis blessyng *and* myn.   25 Wrettyn in haste at Norwich the Thorsdaie aftir Candelmasse Daie.

Wetith of yowre brothere John how manie gystis wolle serve the parl*our and* the chapelle at Paston, and what lenghthe they moste be and

---

14. [1] that th *canc.*   [2] *No space.*
   [3] *Interl., with caret, above* to *and another letter, apparently* l. *The latter should certainly have been cancelled, and perhaps* to *also; but it may be intended to mean 'too'.*
   [4] *Interl. above* closid *canc.*   [5] -y *crowded in.*

what brede *and* thykkenesse thei moste be; for yowre fadris wille was, as
30 I weene veryli, that thei schuld be ix enchis on wey and vij another weye,
and po*ur*veiithe therfor*e* that thei mow be squarid there and sentte
hedre, for here can non soche be hadde in this conttré. And seye to
⌈yowre⌉ brothir John it weere wel don to thinkke on Stansted chirche;
and I p*ra*ye yow to sende me tydyngg*is* from be-yond see, for here thei
35 arn aferde to telle soche as be reportid.

By yowre modre ANGNEIS PASTON

15. Indenture of lease   1446, 30 October

Add. Charter 14819. Parchment, $4\frac{3}{4} \times 5\frac{1}{2}$ in. (indented). Hand unidentified.

Dorse: In hand of text, *Wood mylle*.

Unprinted.

This byll jndented mad the xxx daye of Octobe*re* wittenessyth that Agnes
Paston hath this daye the xxv^{ti} yer*e* of Kyng H. the Sexte letyn to John
Downyng, myllere,[1] to Rob*er*t Cobbe, *and* to Rob*er*t Eemond my mylle
callede Woodmyll for the t*er*me of v yer*e*, paying there-fore yerly to the
5 seyd Agn*es*, to hire heyres or to hir*e* certeyn attorny, x marke at iiij t*er*mes
in the yer*e*, that is to sey: at the Nat*iuité* of Owre Lord v nobl., *and* at the
fest of the Anunciacion of O*w*r Lady v nobl., and at the fest of the
Nat*iuité* of Seynt John the Baptest v nobl., and at the fest of Seynt Michaell
v nobl.; to hauen *and* to helden to the seyd John, Rob*er*t, *and* Rob*er*t,
10 doyng the cost*es* of the rep*ar*acion, like as the mylle*res* haue do biforn, fro
the fest of Seynt Mychaell last past duryng the t*er*me a-boue seyd.

Item, the seyd Agn*es* hath letyn to the seyd John, Rob*er*t, *and* to Robe*r*t
the clos next the myll, paying to the seyd Agn*es* yerly duryng the t*er*me
a-boue seyd viij s.
15 In wittenesse wher*e*-of the partyes han set her*e* sealis. Yeuen the daye
and the yer*e* a-boue seyd.[2]

16. Indenture of lease   1446, 10 November

Add. Charter 19336. Parchment, $8\frac{5}{8} \times 4$ in. (indented). Hand unidentified.

Dorse: In hand of text, in right bottom corner:

The endenture of Palmer of Trunche.

Printed by L. Morsbach, *Mittelenglische Originalurkunden von der Chaucer-Zeit
bis zur Mitte des XV. Jahrhunderts* (Heidelberg, 1923), no. XVI.

This endenture made the teen day of Nouembre þe yeer of þe regne of
Kyng Henry þe Sexte xxv^{ti} be-twen Anneys Paston, late the wyff of

---

15. [1] of *canc.*   [2] *No seal or signature.*

William Paston, on the ton parte and William Palmer of Trunche on the tothir parte witnessyth þat þe seyd Anneys hathe grauntyd *and* lete to ferme to þe seyd William Palmer a pece of londe, outetake þe medwe in 5 *and* of þe same pece, conteynyng be estimacion ix acres in all, lyyng in Trunche feld, to haue and to hold þe seyd pece, outetake þe seyd medwe, to hym, his heires *and* hys assyngnes, fro the fest of Allehalwyn nowh last paste on-to the terme of teen yeer þan nexte folwyng fully endyd, payyng yeerly there-fore to the lordys of the fee the rentys, seruys and custumys, 10 taxes *and* talagys of all the holl forseyd pece duryng the terme be-foreseyde. *And* the seyd William Palmere schall felle *and* dite the medwe and brynge home all the heie, and stakke it in seche an hous, in þe maner of the forseyd Anneys in Paston, os sche or her debité wyll assyng hym; *and* yf sche kepe houssold there, he schall dyne or suppe there at þe bryngyng 15 home. *And* the seyd Anneys schall warent the lond clere to the seyd William Palmer on-to þe daye of þe makyng of ⌜thise⌝ endenture. *And* yf the forseyd medwe be not dite in good tyme of þe yere, but appeyred or lost throwh þe defaute of þe forseyd Palmer, þat þan it be lawfull to the seyd Anneys or her assyngnes to distreyne op-on the holl forseyd 20 pece of lond on-till the seyd Anneys be satysfyed of the valew of the heye, yf it had well a be dite.

In witnesse where-of eche of them to othirs parte haue set her selys. Youe þe day and þe yeer a-boue seyd.

17. Indenture of lease   1447, 29 November

Add. Charter 17236. $11\frac{3}{4} \times 9$ in. (indented). Hand unidentified; last sentence in a second hand. Remnants of red wax.

Dorse: Marks of folding. On the centre panel, in a formal hand, *Wareyn Baxstere of Knapton*, and two faded lines in Latin.

G. 55/73 (abstract).

This indenture mad on Seynt Andrewes evyn the yere of the regne of Kyng Herry the Sexte xxvj wyttnessyth that it is a-cordyd a-twyx Agnes Paston *and* Waryn Baxtere that the seyd Waryn shall haue to hym *and* his heyres, at the wille of the lord of the maner of Knapton, all the londes *and* tenementes in Knapton that were Richard Redys that he late held to 5 ferme for barly, except a messe conteynyng be estymacion di. acre that was sumtyme Robert at the Medwes, sold to William Boot, *and* iiij acre j rod sold to John Archall the yongere. And the seyd Waryn shall content[1] *and* a-gré wyth the seyd lord for the fyne of the seyd lond, that be estymasion is cxiiij s. vj d., and aquyte the seyd Agnes of all oder duteys dew 10

17. [1] *Dotted circumflex, otiose, above* n *; again in same word and in* lond 19, Lauerans 22, *as well as finally in* Waryn 8, Fen 15 *; above* u *in* Foucke 12.

to the seyd lord or to any od*er* p*er*sone except Will*ia*m Ward that claymyth
xij s., Nicholus[2] Crabbe that claymyth iiij s., *and* Will*ia*m Foucke that
askyth xxviij d. for the seyd lond, be-for the[3] day of the date of this[3]
indenture. And he shall pay xvj s. viij d. to Jone, late the wiffe of the seyd
15 Ric*hard* Rede, *and* xx s. to John of Fen to the vse of the chirche of Knapton,
and viij s. x d. to the same John to his awne vse. Also he shall pay to the
seyd Agnes, on of the executou*r*es of Will*ia*m Paston, xx comb*es*[4] of barly
at Candylmes next comyng in fulle payment for all the ferme of the seyd
lond. And the seyd[5] Waryn knowlachyd that he is alowyd *and* content, as
20 wele for that that he can aske of the seyd Agnes as wele for the seyd lond
as for all od*er* thyng.[6] Yowe the day *and* yere be-forseyd.

Wittnes of Will*ia*m Dalton, Lauerans p*ar*son of Oxnede, John Fen,
and Thomas of Fen. In witness wheroff þe p*ar*tés haue sette her seles.[7]

18. To John Paston I Not after 1449

Add. 34888 f. 33. $11\frac{1}{2} \times 4\frac{3}{4}$ in. Hand unidentified.

Dorse: Traces of red wax. Address in hand of letter:

*To John Paston be þis lett*er* delyu*eryd.*

The date cannot be later than 1449; for Sir Harry Inglose died on 1 July 1451
(see no. 141), and in 1450 the Saturday next after Midsummer, when this letter
is dated, preceded the Wednesday after Midsummer, which is mentioned as the
date of a previous letter.
The friar of l. 20 is John Hauteyn, who claimed Oxnead. Mention of him links
this letter with Margaret Paston's no. 133 of 2 April 1449, and with John I's no. 37.
F. iii, p. 202. G. 70/93.

Soon, I grete 30w wel w*yth* Goddys blyssyng *and* myn; *and* I latte 30w
wette þat[1] my cosyn Cler*e* wrytted to me þat sche spake w*yth* Schrowpe
aftyre þat he had byen w*yth* me at Norwyche, *and* tolde her*e* what cher*e*
þat I had made hym; *and* he seyde to her*e* he lyked wel by þe cher*e* þat I
5 made hym. He had swyche wordys to my cosyn Cler*e* þat lesse þan 3e
made hym good cher*e* *and* 3af hym wordys of conforth at London he
wolde no mor*e* speke of þe matyr*e*. My cosyn Cler*e* thynkyth þat it wer*e* a
foly to forsake hym lesse þan 3e knew of on owdyre as good or*e* better*e*,
and I haue assayde 30wr*e* suster*e* *and* I fonde her*e* neu*er* so wylly to noon
10 as sche is to hym, 3yf it be so þat his londe stande cleer*e*.

I sent 30w a lett*er* by Brawnton for*e* sylke *and* for*e* þis matyr*e* be-fore
my cosyn Cler*e* wrote to me, þe qwyche was wrytten on þe Wednysday

---

2 *Abbr.* Nichus *with dotted circumflex above* u.
3 seyd *canc.*   4 -es *abbr.* 3.   5 lon *canc.*
6 *Stroke over* -ng *evidently otiose.*   7 *This last sentence in another hand.*
18. 1 þ *in form of* y *throughout.*

nex3t aftyr*e* Mydsomer*e* Day. S*er* Herry Ynglows is ry3th besy a-bowt Schrowpe for*e* on of his do3thter*e*s.

I prey 30w fore-3ette no3th to brynge me my mony fro Horwelbery as 15 3e com fro London, edyr*e* all or*e* a grete parte. þe dew dette was at Cryste- messe last paste, no thynge a-lowyd, vij li. xiiij s. viij d., *and* at þis Myd- somer*e* it is v li. more; *and* thow I a-low hym all his askyng it is but xxvj s. vj d. lesse, but I am no3th so avysyth 3ytt.

As for*e* þe frer*e*, he hath byen at Sent Benett*ys and* at Norwyche, *and* 20 made grete bowste of þe sewte þat he hath a-3ens me, *and* bow3the many boxes, to what jntent I wett neu*er*. It is well doen to be war*e* at London in drede 3yf he bryng ony syse at Sent Margaret*ys* tyme.

I kan no mor*e*, but ⌈Almy3ty⌉ God be owr*e* good lorde, who have 30w eu*er* in kepyng. Wryten at Oxnede in grete hast on þe Satyr-[day][2] 25 next aftyr*e* Mydsomer*e*.

By 30wr*e* mody*re* A. P.

19. To J OHN P ASTON I Probably 1450, 18 February

Add. 34888, f. 92. 11¾×4¼ in. Hand unidentified, found in five other letters by Agnes Paston (nos. 20, 21, 24, 28, 29).

Dorse: Paper seal over red wax. Address in hand of letter:

*Thys lett*er *be delyuerd to John Paston, dwellyn jn the Inder*e *In of the Tempyll att London, in hast.*

The date is evidently close to that of no. 20: John Paston is at the Inner Temple in both, the report of Margaret Paston's health at the beginning is in similar terms, and the writing is not only by the same hand but is remarkably alike in detail—extending to the odd spelling *Inder*(e) in the address, which is very rare elsewhere. A date in 1450, when Ash Wednesday fell on 18 February, would mean that this letter was written just three weeks before no. 20. This is perfectly credible; it may well be 'the letter that I sent yow last' mentioned at the end of no. 20.

F. iii, p. 188. G. 197/237 (dated about 1454).

I grete yow well, *and* lete yow wete that thys day I was w*yth* my doughtyr yor wyfe, *and* che was in good hele att the makyn of thys lett*er*, thankyd be God. *And* sche lete yor sustyr *and* me wete of a[1] lett*er* wheche ye sent hyr, that ye haue be laboryd to for*e* Ser*e* Willi*a*m Oldhall to haue y*our* sustyr *and* desyryng in the seyd lett*er* to haue an answer*e*[2] in schort tyme 5 who sche wyll be demenyd in thys mater*e*. Yor suster*e* recomaundyt hyr to yow, *and* thankyt[3] yow hertyly that ye wyll remembyr*e* hyr *and* lete

---

[2] *This comes at the end of a line. The two short oblique strokes used as a hyphen indicate that the writer meant to finish the word in the next line, but forgot it.*

19. [1] *No space, as commonly in this hand.*   [2] in *canc.*   [3] *your canc.*

hyr haue knowleche there-of; *and* p*r*eyt yow that ye wyll do yo*ur* deuer*e*
to bryng it to a good conclusyon, for*e* sche seythe to me that sche trystyt
10 þat⁴ ye wyll do so that it xall be bothe for*e* hyr worchup *and* p*r*ofyt. And
as for*e* me, if ye can thynke that hys lond standyt cler*e*, in as meche as I
fele yo*ur* sustyr well wyllyd ther*e*-to I hold me well content.

And as for*e* the oblygacyon of the person of Marlynferthe, wheche I
sent yow by John Newman, I p*r*ey yow lete it be suyd; and as for*e* the
15 person *and* Lyndesey, they be acordyd.

And God haue yow in kepyn *and* send yow hys blyssyn and myn.
Wretyn att Norwyche on Puluer Wedenesday.

Be yor moder*e* A G N E S   P A S T O N

20. To J O H N P A S T O N I　　　　Probably 1450, 11 March

Add. 34888, f. 40. 11¾×7¾ in. Hand of no. 19, etc.

Dorse: Paper seal. Address in hand of letter:

*To John Paston, dwellyn in the Inder In of the Tempyll att London, be thys
letter delyuerd in hast.*

The date is likely to be 1450 because the report of enemy vessels off the coast
resembles the account in Margaret Paston's letter no. 136, also from Norwich,
which is certainly of 1450, and is dated St. Gregory's Day (12 March).
F. iii, p. 304. G. 80/105.

Son, I grete yow *and* send yow Godd*ys* blyssyng *and* myn; *and* as for my
doughtyr yo*ur* wyfe, che faryt well, blyssyd be God, as a¹ woman in hyr
plyte may do, *and* all yo*ur* sonys *and* doughtrys. *And* for as meche as ye
wyll send me no tydyng*ys*, I send yow seche as ben² in thys contré.
5 Rychard Lynsted cam thys day fro Paston, *and* letyt me wete that on
Saturday last past Drawale, halfe brother*e* to Waryn Harman, was takyn
w*yth* enemyis walkyn be the se syde *and* haue hym forthe w*yth* hem; *and*
they tokyn³ ij pylgremys, a man *and* a woman, *and* they robbyd the woman
and lete hyr gon *and*⁴ ledde the man to the see, *and* whan they knew he
10 was a pylgreme they geffe hym money *and* sett hym ageyn on the lond. *And*
they haue thys weke takyn iiij vessellys of Wyntyrton *and* Happysborough,
and Ecles men ben sor*e* aferd for takyn of mo, for ther*e* ben x grete
vessellys of the enemyis. God yeue gra*c*e that the see may be better*e*
kepte than it is now, or ellys it chall ben a perlyous dwellyng be the se
15 cost.

---

⁴ *This scribe, who uses þ only occasionally, writes it as y.*
20. ¹ *No space.*　　²	h *canc.*　　³ awon *canc.*
⁴ ledde (*smudged*) *canc.*

I prey yow grete well your[5] brethyrne, *and* sey hem that I send hem
Goddys blyssyn *and* myn; *and* sey Willia*m* that, if Jenett Lanton be
nott[6] payd for the krymsyn cors wheche Alson Crane wrote to hyr for*e*
in hyr owyn name, that than he pay hyr *and* see Alson Cranys name
strekyn owt of hyr boke, for che seythe che wyll aske no man the money 20
butt Alson Crane.

And I prey yow that ye wyll remembyr[7] the[8] letter that I sent yow last;
and God be wyth yow. Wretyn att Norwyche the Wedenesday next
before Sent Gregory.

Be yor moder*e* A G N E S P A S T O N 25

21. To J O H N P A S T O N I Probably 1451, 12 May

Add. 27444, f. 10. 11⅝ × 3⅞ in. Hand of no. 19, etc.

Dorse: Remnants of red wax. Address in hand of letter:

To John Paston be thys byll delyuerd in hast.

This is one of a group of four letters by Agnes concerned with a dispute about her
building of a wall in the village of Paston, evidently as part of the diversion of the
'way' mentioned in no. 14. The letters are presumably not far apart in time, but
are difficult to date exactly because only no. 22 mentions a year and that indirectly;
it is at any rate not earlier than September 1450. The present letter seems to be the
earliest of the series: it is dated from Norwich, whereas the others are from Paston;
it speaks of 'Waryn Herman of Paston', who would scarcely need this identification
if nos. 23 and 24 had already been written; and the injunction 'foryete not yor
sustyr' would fit best if it were not too long after the proposal for Elizabeth Paston's
marriage mentioned in no. 19. The last consideration would suggest the year
1450, and this would suit the letter in itself well enough. But it would not suit no.
23, which requires 'the Monday after Hallowmas', the date of the letter, to be later
than 'the Sunday after Hallowmas' on which the events reported took place—this
is of course the normal relation, but it did not obtain in 1450 in which 1 November
fell on a Sunday. This letter does not look as if it were as much as eighteen months
earlier than no. 23, so that both are evidently later than 1450. On the other hand
Agnes's interests here are not those of no. 25. The most acceptable date seems to
be 1451, though it is surprising, if that is right, that the fine for building the wall
should have remained unpaid as late as the date of no. 29, which must be of 1461;
but the present group of letters can hardly be near that time.

G. 161/195.

I spacke thys day wyth a man of Paston syde, *and* he told me that a man of
Paston told hym that Paston men wold nott goo presessyon ferther than the
chyrche-yerde on Sent Markys Day, for he seyd the presessyon wey was
stoppyd in, *and* seyd wyth-in chort tyme men hopyd that the wall chuld

---

[5] bretryn *canc.*
[7] tha *canc.*

[6] payd *canc.*
[8] latter *canc.*

5 be broke doun[1] a-geyn. Item, he seyd that I was amercyid for stoppyng
of the seyd [wey] att the last generall court, butt he cowd not tell who
meche the mercyment was; *and* he that told it me askyd the man that told
it hym if he had the mercyment in hys exstrete for to dystreyn there-fore;
and he seyd nay, but seyd he that chuld do it chuld bettyr dor take it
10 up-on hym than he chuld. Item, the same man told me that he mett
w*yth* a man of Blyclyng hyght Barker*e*, that cam late fro London, *and*
he told hym that I had a sute att London ageyn Waryn Herman of Paston,
and seyd that Roberd Branton was hys[2] attornye *and* seyd he seygh hym
ryght besy for hym att London.
15 And for-yete not yor sustyr, *and* God haue yow in kepyng. Wretyn att
Norwyche the xij day of May.

Be yor modyr A. PASTON

22. To JOHN PASTON I   Probably 1451

Add. 27444, f. 9. 12 × 2⅜ in. Hand unidentified, found again in no. 23.

Dorse: Conclusion of text. Traces of red wax. Address in hand of letter:

*To ⌜Meye⌝[1] Barkere of Synt Clementys parys in Norwych, to delyuer to my
master John Paston in haste.*

On the adjacent fold, upside down, *Paston* in another hand.

The date cannot be earlier than September 1450 because the twenty-eighth year
of Henry VI (1 September 1449–31 August 1450) is spoken of as past (l. 21). Yet
it does not seem likely that a minor dispute of this kind would be reported many
years after it occurred.
    The address need not imply that John Paston was in Norwich at the time, and
not in London as he was when the associated letters were written, for Harry
Barker—at any rate twenty-five years later—was a carrier; see John Paston II's
letter no. 296, l. 52.
    G. 160/194.

On Thurisday þe wall was mad ȝarde hey; *and* a good wylle be-fore euyn
it reyned so sore þat þey wer*e* fayne to helle þe wall *and* leue werke, *and*
þe wat*er* is fallyn so sore þat it standyt ondyre þe wall a fote deppe to
Ballys warde. *And* on Fryday aft*er* sakeryng on come[2] fro cherch warde
5 *and* schoffe doune all þat was þere-on *and* trad on þe wall *and* brake su*m*
and wente ou*er*. But I can not ȝet wete hoo it was.

---

21. [1] *Apparently written first* doū, *then* n *added.*   [2] attory *canc.*

22. [1] *Written above* Herry *canc.*
    [2] *These words here and elsewhere have a stroke above the* m *and* n *which could be intended
to represent a second letter. But the same kind of stroke appears at the ends of words, and even
above* ȝou *ll.* 18 *and* 24, *so that it appears to be a meaningless flourish used by the scribe above
minim groups.*

And Warne Kyng*ys* wyfe, as she went ou*er* þe style, she cursyd Ball *and* seyde þat he had ӡeuyn aweye þe waye, *and* so it p*r*euyt be John Paston is word*ys*; *and* after, Kyng*ys* folke *and* odyr come *and* cryid on Annes Ball, seying to her*e* þe same. Ӡystyrneuyn wan I xul⟨d⟩³ goo to my bede þe 10 vycare seyde þat Warne² Kyng *and* Warne Harman be-twyxte messe *and* matynsse toke⁴ S*er* Roberd i*n* þe vestry *and* bad hym sey to me verely þe wall xullde dou*n* a-gayne;² *and* wan þe⁵ vycore tolde me I wyste þere-of no worde, nor ӡet do, be S*er* Roberde, for he syth he were loth to make any stryfe. *And* wan I cam out of þe ⌈cherch⌉ Roberd Emu*n*d*ys* schewyd me 15 how I was a-mercyde for seute of corte þe laste ӡere vj d., *and* seyd it was xij d. tylle Warne Kyng *and* he gat it awey⁶ vj d.⁷

I send⁸ ӡou word how John Jamys was de-menyd at Crom*er*e, to send⁹ to Jamys Gressh*a*m how he xall be de-menyd. Gaffrey Benchard *and* Alexander¹⁰ Glou*er*, heyward*ys*, tokyn a dystresse of John Jamys on þe 20 bond tene*ment* of A. Paston calde Reynald*ys* i*n* Crom*er* þe xxviij^{ti} ӡere of þys ky*ng*, *and* W. Goodwyn, baly of Crom*er*, wy*th* þe seyd J. Jamys wy*th* forsse toke awey þe dysstres, wech was ij horsse *and* a plowe.

And Good be w*yth* ӡou.

Be ANNES PASTON ӡour*e* modyr 25

23. To JOHN PASTON I   Probably 1451, 8 November

Add. 34888, f. 76. 11¾×3¾ in. Hand of no. 22.

Dorse: Paper seal over red wax. Address in hand of letter:

To John Paston, dwyllyng in þe Tempyll at London, be þis letter delyuerid in haste.

See nos. 21 and 22.
  G. XXVIII/207. C. 16.

I gret ӡou well, *and* lete ӡou wete þat Warne Harman, on þe Sonday aft*er* Hallumes Day aft*er* ensong, seyd oponly¹ i*n* þe cherch-ӡerde þat he wyst wyll þat and þe wall were puddou*n*,² þou he were an hondryd myle fro Paston, he wyste well þat I wolde sey he ded yt *and* he xuld bere þe blame, seyi*ng*, 'Telle yte³ here ho so wyll, þou it⁴ xuld coste me xx 5 nobyllys it xall be puddou*n*² aӡen.' *And* þe seyd Warnys wyfe wy*th* a³

---

³ *Edge of paper torn, most of the* d *lost.*   ⁴ syre *canc.*
⁵ wycore *canc.*
⁶ *Last two letters indistinct.*   ⁷ *Recto ends.*
⁸ w *canc.*   ⁹ ӡow *canc.*   ¹⁰ glou*er* *canc.*

23. ¹ in *canc.*
  ² -n *abbr. by tail on* u *carried back, indistinguishable in form from the tail usually added to* m, n, *and* u *in this hand.*
  ³ *No space.*   ⁴ were *canc.*

lovde vosse seyd, 'All þe deuyllys of hell drawe here sowle to hell for þe weye þat she hat mad!'

And at euyn a sertyn man suppyd wyth me and tolde me þat þe patent
10 grantyt to closse but a perch on bred, and þat I had clossyd more þan þe grant of þe patent is, as men seyd. And John Marchall tolde me þat þere was a thryfty woman come forby þe watteryng and fond þe wey stoppyde, and askyd hym ho had stoppyd þe weye; and he seyd þey þat had pore to ȝeue it, and askyd here wat was freere þan ȝyfte. And ⌈she seyd⌉ she sey
15 þe day þat Paston men wold not a³ sofferyd þat.

And God be wyth ȝou. Wretyn at Paston on Monday after⁵ Hallumys Day.

Be ȝoure modyr ANNES PASTON

24. To JOHN PASTON I   Probably 1451, 21 November

Add. 34888, f. 71. 11¾×7½ in. Hand of no. 19, etc.

Dorse: Paper seal over red wax. Address in hand of letter:

To John Paston, dwellyng jn þe Tempyll at London, be thys lettere delyuerd in hast.

See nos. 21 and 22. The day of St. Edmund, king and martyr, is 20 November. (That of St. Edmund, archbishop, is 16 November, but the other is likely to have been more prominently in mind in East Anglia.)
F. iii, p. 44. G. 162/196. C. 17 (part).

I grete yow well, and lete yow wete that on þe¹ Sonday before Sent Edmond after euyn-songe Angnes Ball com to me to my closett and bad me good euyn, and Clement Spycere wyth hyr. And I acsyd hym what he wold, and he askyd me why I had stoppyd jn þe Kyngys wey; and I seyd
5 to hym I stoppyd no wey butt myn owyn, and askyd hym why he had sold my lond to John Ball; and he sore he was neuyr a-cordyd wyth your fadyr. And I told hym if hys fadyr had do as he dede, he wold a² be a-chamyd to a seyd as he seyd.

And all that tyme Waryn Herman lenyd ouyr þe parklos and lystynd
10 whatt we seyd, and seyd þat þe chaunge was a rewly chaunge, for þe towne was vn-do þereby and is þe wersse by an c li.; and I told hym it was no curtesé to medyll hym jn a mater butt if he were callyd to councell. And prowdly goyn forthe wyth me jn þe cherche, he² seyd the stoppyng of þe wey xulld coste me xx nobyllys, and ȝet it chuld downe ageyn; and
15 I lete hym wete he þat putte it downe chull pay þere-fore. Also he seyd þat it was well don þat I sett men to werke to owle money whyll I was

---

⁵ halm (*at end of line*) *canc.*
24. ¹ þ *in form of* y *throughout.*   ² *No space.*

here, butt jn þe ende I chall lese my coste. Than he askyd me why I had a-wey hys hey at Walsam,[3] seyng to me he wold he had wyst it whan it was karyyd *and* he chuld a lettyd it; *and* I told hym it was myn owyn grownde, *and* for myn owyn I wold holde it. *And* he bad me take iiij 20 acre and goo no ferthere; *and* thus churtly he departyd fro me jn þe cherche-ȝerde.

And syt, I spacke wyth a serteyn man *and* acsyd hym if he herd owt sey why þe dynere was mad att Norfolkys howse; *and* he told me [he] herd sey that serteyn men had sentt[4] to London to gete a comyssyon owt 25 of þe Chaunstré to putt downe ageyn þe wall *and* þe dyke.

I receyuyd yor lettere by Robert Reppys thys[5] day after thys letter wretyn thus fare. I haue red it butt I can yeue yow non aunswere more than I haue wretyn, saue þe wyfe of Harman hathe þe name of Owre Lady, whos blyssyn ye haue, *and* myn.   30

Wretyn at Paston on þe day aftere Sent Edmond.

Be yowyr modyr AGNES PASTON

25. To JOHN PASTON I   Probably 1452, 16 November

Add. 34888, f. 86. $11\frac{1}{2} \times 10\frac{3}{4}$ in. Hand unidentified.

Dorse: Traces of red wax. Address in hand of letter:

This lettre be delyuered to John Paston, beynge at London in the Innere In of the Temple.

The date is earlier than Fastolf's removal from London to Caister in the autumn of 1454 (see William Paston II's letters nos. 83 and 84). It cannot be the same as that of nos. 23 and 24, for Agnes was at Paston in November of that year. It is likely to be not long before no. 26, in which she recommends John to seek another tenant for Orwellbury in place of Gurney (cf. ll. 24–36 below); so that 1452 suits best. (Gairdner's view that it must be later than 1451 because Lady Boys became a widow only in 1450 cannot be sustained. It was her son who died then; her husband Sir Roger had died in 1422, but she was still living in 34 Henry VI (1455–6) (Blomefield, vi. 9, ix. 497, xi. 43; *Norwich Wills*, i. 55).)

F. iii, p. 162. G. 183/222.

I grete you well, and sende you Goddes blissyng and myn; and as touchyng the mater wheche ye desyryd my cosyn Clere shulde write fore, she hath doo, and I sende you the copy closed in this lettre.

As for the enquerré I haue sent by Pynchemour to enquere, and sent myn owen men to William Bakton *and* don hem enquered in dyuerse 5 places, and I can here no word of noon suych enquerans. I wot not[1] what

---

³ seyd *canc.*   ⁴ -tt *over imperfect* d.   ⁵ dye *canc.*

25. ¹ *In these four cases* not *has* t *raised as if it were abbreviated, but this scribe raises other letters which cannot involve abbreviations, e.g.* u *of* you *ll.* 27 *and* 49, e *of* boþe *l.* 30.

it menyth. Roberd Hill was at Paston this wyke, and the man that duelled
in Bowres place is oute there-of, and seid to Roberd he durst no lenger
a-byde there-in for Waryn Herman seyth to him it is his place.

10   As for Coketes mater, my doughter youre wif told me yester-even the
man that suyth him will now stonde to youre a-warde. Bertilmow White[2]
is condennyd in Fo⌐r⌐necet court in xl marc.,[3] ⌐as it is seid⌐.

Item, as for Talfas, the sherevis han be-hest to do all the fauour thei
may. I sente the parson of Seynt Edmundes to Gilberd, and he seide
15 there was come a newe writ for to haue him vp by the xv day of Seynt
Martyn; and how Caly hadde ben at hem and desired to car⌐y⌐e vp
Talfas on his owen cost and yeue hem goode wages.

Item, John Osbern seide to me this day that he supposed thei will not[1]
haue him vp be-forn Estern, and Margerete Talfas seide to me the same
20 day that men tolde hire that he shulde neuer han ende till he were at
London, and asked me counsell wheder she myte yeue the sherevys syluer
or non, and I tolde hire if she dede I supposed she shulde fynde hem the
more frendly.

Item, as for Horwelbury I sende you a bill of all the reseytes syn the
25 deth of youre fadere, and a copy wrete on the bak how youre fader lete it
to ferme to the seide Gurnay.[4] I wulde ye shulde write Gurnay[5] and charge
him to mete wyth you fro London warde, and at the lest weye lete him
purveye x li., for owyth be my reknyng at Myhelmesse last passed, be-syde
youre faderes dette, xviij li. xiiij s. viij d. If ye wolde write to him to brynge
30 suerté boþe for youre faderys dette and myn, and pay be dayes so þat the
man myte leven and paye vs, I wolde for-yeue him of the olde arrerages
x li., and he myte be mad to paye xx marc.[3] be yere.[6] On that condicion
I wolde for-yeuen him x li., and so thynketh me he shulde han cause to
preye for youre fader and me, and was it leten in my faderes tyme. I fele
35 be Roberd his wif is right loth to gon thens; she seide that sche had leuer
I shulde haue all here gode after here day than thei schulde go out there-of.

Item, John Dam told me that þe[7] Lady Boys will selle a place called
Halys, but he seith sche speketh it prevyly and seith it is not[1] tayled;
as John Dam knoweth will, she hath seide as largely of[8] oþer thyng þat
40 hath not[1] be so.

Item, he tolde me as he herd seyn Sere John Fastolf hath sold Heylysdon
to Boleyn of London, and if it be so it semeth he will selle more; wherfore
I preye you, as ye will haue my loue and my blissyng, þat ye will helpe
and do youre deuer that sumthyng were purchased for youre ij bretheren.
45 I suppose þat Ser John Fastolf, and he were spoke to, wolde be gladere
to lete his kensemen han parte than straunge men. Asay him in my name

---

[2] in *canc.*   [3] *Curl on* -c.   [4] I *canc.*
[5] a ye *canc.*   [6] me thyn *canc.*   [7] lay *canc.*
[8] o *and an incomplete second letter canc.*

of suych place*s* as ye suppose is most[9] clere. It is seid in this contré þat my lord of Norfolk seith Sere John Fastolf hath youen hi*m* Castre, *and* he will han [it] pleynly. I sende you a bill of[10] Osbern hand whech was the ansuer*e* of the sheref *and* John of Dam. 50

Item, brynge me my l*ett*re hom with you, and my cosyn Cler*e* is copy of her*e* l*ett*re and the copy of the reseyth of Horwelbury. And[11] recomaunde me to Lomno*ur*, and tell hi*m* his best be-loued fareth well, but sche is not yet come to Norwich, for thei[12] deye yet, but not so sor*e* as thei dede.

And God be wyth you. Wrete at Norwych in right gret hast the xvj 55 day of Nouembr*e*.

By your*e* moder ANNEYS PASTON

26. To JOHN PASTON I 1453, 6 July

Add. 34888, f. 88. $11\frac{1}{2} \times 5\frac{7}{8}$ in. Hand unidentified.

Dorse: Traces of red wax. Address in hand of letter:

To my welbelouyd son John Paston.

The date is fixed by the report of the death of Sir John Heveningham, which occurred on 3 July 1453 (*Inq. p.m.*, 31 Henry VI, no. 7). 'Sent Thomas Evyn' must therefore be the eve of the Translation of St. Thomas of Canterbury, 7 July.

Cf. Margaret Paston's letter no. 147.

F. iii, p. 182. G. 188/227.

Sone, I grete yow well *and* send you Godys blyssy*ng* and myn, *and* lete you wete that Robe*rt* Hyll cam homward by Horwelle-bery; *and* Gurney tellyd hym he had byn at London for mony *and* kowd not spedy*ng*, *and* behestyd Robe*rt* that he shuld sende me mony be you. I p*ray* for-ʒet[1] yt not as ʒe com homward, *and* speke sadly for j nothyr fermo*ur*. 5

And as for tydyng*ys*, Phylyppe Berney is passyd to God on Munday last past, wyt þe[2] grettes peyn that evyr I sey man. *And* on Tuysday Sere Jon Heny[n]gham ʒede to hys chyrche *and* herd iij massys, *and* cam hom agayn nevyr meryer, *and* seyd to[3] hese wyf that he wuld go sey a lytyll deuocion in hese gardeyn *and* than he wuld dyne; and forth-wyth he felt 10 a[1] feynty*ng* in hese legge *and* syyd dou*n*. Thys was at ix of þe clok, and he was ded or none.

Myn cosyn Cler*e* preyt you that ʒe lete no man se her*e* letter wheche is in-selyd vndyr my selle. I pray you that ʒe wyl pay[4] your*e* brothyr Wili*am* for iiij vnce[5] *and* j half of sylke as he payd, wheche he send me by Wili*am* 15

[9] sekyre *canc.*	[10] ⌜þe⌝ answer*e canc.*
[11] g *canc.*	[12] -i *added later.*
26. [1] *No space.*	[2] þ *in form of y throughout.*
[3] the *canc.*	[4] yure *canc.*
[5] *Curl on -c exactly as in l.* 16.	

Tauyrner*e, and* bryng wyt you j quarter of j vnce[6] evyn leke of the same that I sende you closyd in thys letter. *And* sey your*e* brothyr Will*ia*m that hese hors hath j farseyn *and* grete renny*n*g sorys in hese leggis.

God haue you in kepyng. Wretyn at Norwyche on Sent Thom*as* Evyn
20 in grete hast.

Be your*e* modyr A. PASTON

27. Draft indenture of marriage settlement Perhaps about 1454

Add. 34888, f. 98. $11\frac{3}{4} \times 8\frac{1}{2}$ in. Hand unidentified.

Dorse blank except for later notes.

The possible date appears from John Paston I's letter to Lord Grey of July 1454 (no. 50), in which he writes that there have been discussions about his sister's marriage 'dyvers tymys and late'. But since there had been earlier talk of possible marriages to Stephen Scrope and Sir William Oldhall (see nos. 18, 19), and Elizabeth was not in fact married until 1458 (see no. 121), there may well have been other times before the latter date at which negotiations of this kind were in progress. This draft settlement is evidently linked to John Clopton's letter to John Paston I, Part II, no. 493.

F. iii, p. 196. G. 203/243.

This indenture made betwix Anneys that was þe wyfe of William Paston, John Paston hir sone, and John Dam on þe one partie and Will*ia*m Clopton, squyer, on þe other partie witnesseth that accord is take attwyn þe seid parties that John Clopton, sone and heir of þe seid William Clopton be
5 þe gr*a*ce of God, shall wedde Elizabeth, the dought*er* of þe seid Anneys. For which mareage the seid Anneys, &c., shall paye to þe seid John Clopton cccc[th] marc. in hand of lawfull mony of England; and ou*er* that, yf the ⌐seid¬ mareage be holdyn with the seid Anneys, the seid Anneys shall bere þe costages þerof þe day of þe weddyng, w*ith* swech chaumbyr
10 as shall be to þe plesir of þe seid Anneys. And þe seid William[1] Clopton shall do his feffees make a lawfull estate to þe seid Will*ia*m[2] of lond*es*, ten*emen*tz,[3] rentz, *and* s*er*uysez to þe yerly value of xl li. ⟨ouer all chargez b⟩orn to haue and hold to hym t*er*me of his lyfe wi*th*outyn enpecheme*n*t of wast, the remaindr*e* þerof to þe seid John and E⟨lizabet⟩h and to his
15 heir*es* male ⟨of⟩ hir body[4] lawfully begotyn w*ith*oute enpecheme*n*t of wast,

---

[6] of *canc.*

27. [1] *This word partly lost owing to an irregular tear in the paper, affecting also the two following lines. Enough remains here for the reading to be in no doubt; in the next line the gap can be confidently filled by comparison with repetitions of the same phrases in ll. 19 and 28; and Fenn evidently read more than now remains. After this word* Paston *was written and cancelled.*   [2] *Error for* John.

[3] *Abbr. throughout* tentz *with dotted circumflex above; -z may be meant as abbr. for -es, but cf.* seruysez *written in full.*

[4] begot *canc.*

wit*h*ynne xij dayes aft*er* þe seid weddyng. And ou*er* that, wit*h*ynne þe
seid xij dayes the seid John shall do lawfull⁵ estate to be made to þe seid
William of lond*es*, ten*emen*tz, rentz, and s*er*uysez to þe yerly value of xl
marc. ou*er* all charges born, to haue and hold to þe seid William t*er*me
of his lyfe wit*h*oute enpechement of wast, the remayndre therof to þe seid 20
Elizabeth to haue and hold to hir t*er*me of hir lyfe wit*h*oute enpechement
of wast.

Also it is accorded that þe seid William shall make estate of all þe
residue of his lond*es* which he is sesid of, or any other man to his vse, to
swech p*er*sonys as the seid John shall name to þe vse of the seid John. 25
Also the seid John Clopton shall do lawfull estate to be made to þe seid
Elizabeth of lond*es*, ten*emen*tz, rentz, and s*er*uysez to þe yerly value of
xxx li. ou*er* all charg*e*z born, to haue and hold to hir dur*y*ng þe lyfe of the
seid William.

And moreou*er* the seid John promytteth and ensureth be þe feith of his 30
body that he shall leve, ou*er* the xl li. worth lond aboueseid, to his heir*es*
and issue male of þe body of þe seid Elizabeth begotyn, londes in fee symple
or in taill to þe yerly value of xl m*ar*c. in cas þe same issue male be gou*er*nyd
to the seid John as the sone oweth to be to the fadir. And &c.

28. Memorandum of 'errands' 1458, 28 January

Add. 43491, f. 3. 5½ × 10⅝ in. Hand of no. 19, etc.

Dorse: Marks of folding, no seal. The following note in the same hand:

*Eran*d*y*s *to London of Angnes Paston the xxviij day of Jeniu*er *the yere of
Kyng Herry the Sext xxxvj.*

The text is set out in paragraphs, which are here preserved as a matter of interest
even when they do not correspond to the syntax. All but the last are marked by
signs in the margin.

F. i, p. 142. G. 311/362. C. 20.

To prey Grenefeld to send¹ me feythfully word by wrytyn who Clem*en*t
Paston hath do his deve*re in* lernyng.
And if he hathe nought do well, nor wyll nought amend, prey hym that
he wyll trewly belassch hym tyl he wyll amend;
And so ded the last mayst*er*, *and* þe² best that eu*er* he had, att Caumbrege. 5
And sey Grenefeld that if he wyll take up-on hym to brynge hym in-to
good rewyll *and* lernyng, that I may verily know he doth hys deve*re*, I
wyll geue hym x m*ar*c.³ for hys labo*re*; for I had leu*er* he were fayr beryed
than⁴ lost for*e* defaute.

---

⁵ -e *blurred, evidently canc.*

28. ¹ me *canc.*   ² þ *in form of* y *throughout.*
³ *Curl on* -c.   ⁴ than *repeated.*

10 Item, to se who many gownys Clement hath,
And tho that be bare, late hem be reysyd; he hathe a⁵ chort grene gowne,
And⁶ a chort musterdevelerys gowne were neuer reysyd,⁷
And a chort blew gowne þat was reysyd and mad of a syde gowne whan I
was last at London,
15 And a syde russet gowne furryd wyth bevyr was mad this tyme ij yere,
And a syde murry gowne was mad this tyme twelmoneth.⁸

Item, to do make me vj sponys of viij ounce of troy wyght, well facyond
and dubbyl gylt.
And sey Elyzabet⁹ Paston that che must vse hyr-selfe to werke redyly as
20 other jentylwomen don, and sumwhat to helpe hyr-selfe ther-wyth.
Item, to pay the Lady Pole—xxvj s. viij d. for hyr bord.
And if Grenefeld haue do wel hys devere to Clement, or wyll do hys
devere, yeffe hym þe nobyll.

29. To John Paston I   1461, 1 December

Add. 27444, f. 108. 11½ × 3¾ in. Hand of no. 19, etc.

Dorse: Red wax. Address in hand of letter:

> To John Paston at London be this delyuerd jn hast.

The date appears from the mention of John Northales as sheriff of Norwich. The
only year in which he was sheriff was 1461 (P.R.O. *List of Sheriffs*, p. 212).
      G. 426/493.

I grete you welle, and lete you wete that this day Bertholomew Elys of Paston
come to Norwych to me and shewyt me a rentall for the terme of Seynt
Michel¹ the yere of Kyng H. vj xxxix^ti, and jn the ende of the seyd
rentall, of Waryn Kynges hand, is wretyn 'Agnes Paston vij d. ob. Item,
5 the same Agnes for² v acre lond xx d.'
      Item, Aleyn Bayfeld askyth the same rent for the yere last past at
Michelmas.³
      Item, I haue⁴ knowlech be a trew man that whan Sharpe the reseyuore
was at Gemyngham last Waryn Herman was dyuers dayes wyth hym,

---

⁵ *No space, as generally with the indefinite article in this text.*
⁶ achorit *canc.*
⁷ reysyd *begins a line, the rest being blank except for* weryd *twice written and cancelled. It
is marked off as if intended to follow* neuer.
⁸ *Space of half an inch after this line.*
⁹ -bet *abbr.* -bȝ.
29. ¹ *Abbr.* Mich, *with* h *crossed.*   ² v acre lond *canc.*
      ³ *Abbr.* Mich, *exactly as in l.* 3, *but here* Michelmas *must be meant.*
      ⁴ know Item Aleyn Bay *canc.*

and put hym in mynde þat⁵ þe mercyment for makyng of the walle chuld 10
be askyd ageyn *and* be distreynyd þer-for*e*.

Item, I sent you be Doctor*e* Aleyns⁶ man the rescew of Waryn H*e*rman⁷
and seche names as Cullynge *and* Sammys putt in of her owyn fre wylle
be-for*e* John Northales, shereue of Norwyche, vnder her selis.

God be w*yth* you *and* send you his blyssyng *and* myn. Wretyn at 15
Norwych the Tuisday next aft*er* Seynt Andrew.

Item, the seyd Berth*olomew* Elis seyth that þe seyd reseyuor*e* wold not
alowe the rent in Trunche nor the m*er*cyment*ys* for my sute to þe curt.
Gonnor*e* wold suffyr no man to answer*e* for me.

Be your*e* mod*er* AGNES PASTON 20

30. To JOHN PASTON I   Perhaps 1465, 29 October

Add. 34888, f. 135. 12×4 in. Hand unidentified.

Dorse: Remnants of red wax. Address in hand of letter:

   *Tho my wele be-louyd son John ⌐Paston⌐ be þis delyu*e*red in haste.*

The date is uncertain. It cannot be very soon after William Paston I died, for
Clement was then only two years old. Since relations between John and his
mother have evidently been strained, this letter may well be soon after Margaret's
letter no. 180 of 10 May 1465. John was in London in October of that year (see
Margaret's letters nos. 194 and 196), probably still in the Fleet prison as he was
when he wrote no. 77.

   F. iii, p. 40. G. 312/363. C. 44.

Sonne, I grete ȝ0w wele and lete ȝ0w wete þat,¹ for as myche as ȝ0ure
broþir Clement leteth me wete þat ȝe desyre feythfully my blyssyng,
þat blyssyng þat I prayed ȝ0ure fadir to gyffe ȝ0w þe laste day þat eu*er*
he spakke, and þe blyssyng of all seyntes vndir heven, and myn, mote
come to ȝ0w all dayes and tymes. And thynke veryly non oþer but þat 5
ȝe haue it, and shal haue it w*yth* þat þat I fynde ȝ0w kynde and wyllyng to
þe wele of ȝ0ure fadres soule and to þe welfare of ȝ0ure breþeren.

   Be my cou*n*seyle, dyspose ȝ0ure-selfe as myche as ȝe may to haue lesse to
do in þe worlde. Ȝ0ure fadyr² sayde, 'In lityl bysynes³ lyeth myche reste.'
Þis worlde is but a þorugh-fare and ful of woo, and wha*n* we departe 10
þer-fro, riȝth nouȝght bere w*yth* vs but oure good dedys and ylle. And þer

---

⁵ þ *in form of* y *throughout.*
⁶ men *canc.*
⁷ er *in this word unusually abbreviated by a simple stroke through* h.
30. ¹ *This scribe here and often uses* y *for* þ, *and sometimes* þ *for* y.
  ² *Apparently written first* fad *with* -er *abbreviation, then* -yr *added* (y *in form of* þ).
  ³ *Both* ys *here in form of* þ.

knoweth no man how soon God woll clepe hy*m*, and þer-for it is good for eu*er*y creature to be redy. Qhom God vysyteth,[4] hi*m* he louyth.

And as for ȝoure breþeren, þei wylle I knowe certeynly laboren all þat
15 in he*m* lyeth ⌈for ȝow⌉.

Oure Lorde haue ȝow in his blyssed kepyng, body[5] and soule. Writen at Norwyche þe xxix day of Octobyr.

Be ȝoure modir A. P.

31. Draft Will   1466, 16 September

Add. 27445, f. 20. $11\frac{1}{8} \times 15\frac{1}{2}$ in. Hand unidentified.

Dorse blank. Marks of a single fold.

The date is given in the opening sentence. The lines are widely spaced, in a rather neat hand.

G. 555/644.

To all to whom this *pre*sent writting xal come I, Agnes Paston, late the wife of Willia*m* Paston, Justice, send greting in God eu*er*-lasting, lating he*m* know that I, the forseid Agnes, of goode *and* hole mende the xvj day of Septe*m*bre the vj yere of the reigne of Kyng E. the iiij[th], and the yere of O*ur*
5 Lord a m[l] cccc lxvj, make and ordeyn my last will in al the man*er*s, lond*ys*, ten*em*ent*ys*, rent*ys*, s*er*uic*ys*, mes*u*agys,[1] *and* plac*ys* that ony p*er*son or p*er*sonis ben seased of to my*n* vse *and* behof w*yth*-in Norwiche, Norff*olk*, Suff*olk*, Essex, Hertford*s*here, or in any othe*re* shere w*yth*-in Englond, praying *and* desiring al the p*er*sonez so feffed to my*n* vse, aft*er* this my
10 will writtyn and inceled vnd*er* my seale be shewed vnto the*m*, that they wol make astate to the p*er*sones lemitid in my seid will according.

And in asmiche as myn husbond, whos soule God assoile, dyu*er*se tymes *and* specialy among othe*re* the   [2] day of the moneth, rehersed to me that the lyvelod whiche he had assigned to his ij yongest, Willia*m and*
15 Clement, by his will in writting was so littill that they miȝt not leve theron w*yth*ouȝt they shuld hold the plowe be the tayle, and ferthermore seying that he had dyu*er*s od*er* man*er*s, that is to say the man*er* of Sporle, Sweynsthorp, ⌈and⌉ Bekha*m*, which man*er* of Bekha*m* he was p*ur*posed to chaunge w*yth* the man*er* of Pagrave, and if he myȝt bring it abouȝt then
20 xuld on of his ij yongest sones haue the seid man*er*s of Sporle *and* Bekham and no more, *and* the other yongest sone xuld haue al the remen*au*nt, and he that had the man*er* of Sweynsthorp xuld be bound in a[3] gret some to the Pri*or* of the abbey of Norwiche to paie dayly for eu*er* to the monke that

---

[4] *Second* y *is* þ.   [5] -y *is* þ.
31. [1] *Abbr. by final loop.*
    [2] *Space for about four letters left blank.*   [3] *No space.*

44

for that day singeth the masse of the Holy Goste in *Our* Lady chapell in
Norwiche, where he *pur*posed to leye his body, eu*er*y day iiij d. to sing and 25
pray for his sowle *and* myn and al the sowles that he *and* I haue hade any
goode of or be beholdyn to pray for.

And aft*er* that the ___ ² day of ___ ⁴ next folowing my seid husbond,
lying seke in his bed, in the *pre*sens of John Paston, his sone *and* my*n*,
John Bakton, John Dame, *and* of me, declared his will towching cert*ein*⁵ 30
of his childern *and* me, at whiche tyme he assigned ⌐to⌐⁶ the seid John
Paston the man*er* of Gressham in honde, *and* the reu*er*cion of suche
lyvelode as he ȝave me aft*er* my decesse, askyng hy*m* the question⁷ whed*er*
he held hy*m* not co*n*tent, so seying to him in these t*er*mes: 'Sir, and thow
do not I doo, for I will not geve so mekyll to on that the remen*au*nt xal 35
haue to littill to leve on'; ⌐at⌐ the whiche⁸

32. Part of Draft Will   Probably 1466

Add. 27445, f. 7. 4¾×8½ in. in full, but a rectangular piece about 1½×4¼
in. was cut off before this draft was written. Hand of Clement Paston.

The writing, small, cramped, hasty, and much corrected, covers both sides of this
scrap of paper. A few letters have been trimmed away at the right-hand edge of
the verso. The letters *b* and *d* prefixed to the two paragraphs on the recto are
evidently reference marks to show where these passages are to be inserted in
another draft.

In some places the corrections have so confused the construction that it cannot
be put right by any simple alteration. Emendation has therefore been limited to
supplying obvious defects and eliminating careless repetitions.

Though Agnes lived until 1479, the date of this draft cannot be far from that of
no. 31, the last part of which it expands.

G. 556/645.

b And after þat¹ þe ___ ² day of þe³ monethe my seyd husbond, lyyng sek
on hijs bede, sent fore⁴ me, John Paston, Bakton, *and* John a Dame to
here hijs wyll rede. And in owr*e* *pre*sens all he⁵ began to reede hijs wyll,
and spak fy[r]st of me and assynyd⁶ to me ⌐the man*er*is of⌐ Paston,
Latym*er*, *and* Schypden *and* Rop*er*s in Crowm*er* fore term of my lyffe, and 5
the man*er*ys of M*er*lyngforthe, Stonsted, *and* Horwelbury, wyche wasse
myn own enheritans, and Oxned, wyche wasse my jontor*e*; and ⌐seyde⌐⁷
and [he] hadde do to lityll to ony it wasse to me, ⌐for fo[r] me he faryd

---

⁴ *Space for some ten or twelve letters left blank.*
⁵ *Abbr.* cert *with curl on* t.   ⁶ *Interl. above* the maner of Caster *canc.*
⁷ on *canc.*   ⁸ *Foot of page.*

32. ¹ þ *in form of* y *throughout.*   ² *Space for some three letters left blank.*
³ moneth of *canc.*   ⁴ John *canc.*
⁵ re *canc.*   ⁶ -d *over* ng.
⁷ *Interl. above* prayd me to hold me contente so fore *canc.*

45

þe bett*er* and so[8] dede he[9] for noo[n] of hem all⌐,[10] but he hadde more to
10 care for wyche myn as well as hys. And þan he red John p*ar*te and assynyd
to hym ⌐*and* to hys wyffe⌐ the man*er* of Gressam and aft*er* my desesse
the man*er* of Oxned; and he, thynkyng by John Pastons demenyng þat
he wasse not plesyd be-cause[11]
d Swynne of slowthe þat hijs wyll wasse not made vp, 'but wat swm eu*er*
15 cwm of me, dame, I wyll ȝe know my wyll'; and seyd þat swyche[12] lond as
he hadde not wrytyn in hijs wyll, wat xwlde be do w*yth*-all he wolde hijs
ij ȝongest sonnys Wyllam *and* Clement[13] xwlde haue, and owte of Sweynthorpe[14] to haue hijs p*er*petuell masse. And of thys p*ra*yd me to reporte,
record, *and* berre wyttnesse; in qwyche disposici*on* and intent he cont[i]-
20 nuyd on-to þe day off hijs dethe. And I darre rytgh largely deposse þat
that sam wasse hijs last wyll the[15] tym of hijs dethe,[16] qwyche wyll inmediatly
aft*er* my husbond*ys* decesse I hopynd and declaryd to John Paston and
al the other exc*e*ctor*ys* of my husbond, desyeryng hem to haue p*er*formyd
it. And the seyd John Paston wold in no wysse agree ther*e*-to, seyyng þat
25 by the lawe the seyd man*er*ys xulde be hijs, in as moche as my husbonde
made no wyll of hem in wrytyn; and gatte þe ded*ys* owte of my possession
and[17] estat of the feffeez in þe seyde man*er*ys ⌐myn vnknowyng⌐.[18]

And aft*er* þat swyche tresowre of my husbons as wasse leyd in the abbey
of Norwyche by the seyd John Paston, John Bakton, John Dam, and me,
30 to delyu*ere* ⌐aȝen⌐ to vs all ex⟨*cectorys*⟩[19] the seyde John Paston owte of
þe seyde abbey, vnknowyn to þe P*riour* ore ony od*er* p*er*son of þe seyde
abbey, and w*yth*-owte my wetyn[20] *and* assente ore ony of owre felawys,
toke *and* barre awey all, and kepyng it styll[21] a-ȝens ⌐my wyll and⌐ all the
tothere exc*e*ctor*ys* wyllys, nothere[22] restoryng the seyd Wyllam *and*
35 Clement to þe forseyd lond nore ⌐of my husbond*ys* tresore⌐ recompensyng
theim[23] and ordeynyng fore my husbond*ys* sowle in hauyng of hijs p*er*-
petuell masse acordyn[20] to[24] hys wyll. Werefore in as moche as I know and
vnder*e*-stonde[14] v*er*rely þat it wasse my husbond*ys* wyll þe tym of hys
dethe þat the seyd Wyllam *and* Clement xwlde haue the seyd man*er*ys of
40 Sporle, Swey[n]sthorpe, *and* Bekham, and ⌐þe anuyté fore⌐ hys p*er*-
petuell masse ⌐to be goyng⌐ owte of þe seyde man*er* of Sweynthorp, and

8 dede *apparently superfluous but not cancelled.*
9 ded *apparently superfluous, not cancelled.*
10 *This interlineation very cramped and often uncertain.*
11 *Abbr.* cae *with stroke above. Next paragraph at right angles.*
12 s- *over* he.   13 *Names underlined.*
14 *Divided at end of line.*   15 -r *canc.*
16 as I mote awnswer *canc.*   17 gatt *canc.*
18 *Interl. above* before my knowlache and the euydens of hem owte of my *canc. Recto ends.*
19 *At edge; only part of* x *visible.*
20 *At edge; a letter probably lost.*
21 and now *canc.*
22 -re, *repr. by flourished* r, *apparently written over* to.   23 wyth *canc.*
24 *In margin opposite the line beginning with this word is* Nota.

þat they[25] ⌜þat be⌝ possessioners of the seyd manerys ⌜at thys day⌝ wyll
in no wysse by any fayere menez ore spekyng tendere my seyd husbondys
sowle *and* myn, nere perform the wyll of my seyd husbon, I wyll haue *and*
xall—by the grass[20] of swyche lyuelode as I haue in my possession, ⌜þat   45
is for to sey þe[26] maner of Stonsted, Marlyngforthe, *and* Horwelbury⌝,
þat swm tym wasse my faderys and my moderys and cwm on-to me by
them as myn enheritans,[27] and after my decesse if I wolde[28] soffere it to
desend xwld goo to þe wronge posses⟨si⟩oners[29] of the seyd manerys of
Sporle, Swe⟨yn⟩sthorp, *and* Bekham, qwyche xall not be lettyd fore me   50
but if it be thorow here owne defau⟨te⟩, make, sta⟨b⟩lesse, *and* ordeyn myn
husbondys p[er]pet⟨uell⟩ masse *and* myn, and of þe remnaunt as swerly
as can be made by the lawe I wyll the seyd Wyllam *and* Clement be
recompensyd to þe valew of the seyde manerys of Sporle, Sweynthorpe,
and Bekkam 3erly, on-to þe tyme þat they be restoryd to þe forseyd   55
manerys of Sporle, Sweynthorp, *and* Bekkam in lik form *and* lyke estat, as
xall be afterwardys lymytyd in thys my last.[30]

33. Part of Draft Will   Probably 1466

Add. 34889, ff. 44[v]–45[r]. 9¾ × 14⅝ in. Hand unidentified.

Dorse blank except for a note, only partly legible, in a very rough hand
apparently contemporary: . . . *pro voluntate Willelmi Paston justiciarij.*

The content is so like that of part of no. 32 that the date cannot be far distant.
    The text is carefully written, with wide spaces between the paragraphs. It
must be a copy of an earlier draft in which *th-* was represented by *y-* (as, for instance, by Clement Paston in no. 32), for *the* and *this* in lines 35 and 36 must be
wrongly transcribed from *ye* and *yis*; and *dowte* 29 is probably an error for *do yt.*
    A good deal has been lost by decay and staining of the paper a little below the
middle. Some words normally illegible can be read by ultra-violet light.
    F. iii, p. 15 n. G. 558/647 (part).

On the Thurseday at nyght before O*ur* Ladys Day the Assu*m*pcion,
betwixt xj and xij of the clokk, in the yere of o*ur* Lord God m¹ cccc *and*
xliiij, the Sondays lettre on the D, died my husbond, God assoyle his
sowle. And on the Fryday after I sent for John Paston, Willi*a*m Bakton,
and John Dam; and on the Wedynysday after cam John Paston, the   5
Thurseday John Dam *and* William Bakton. And ⌜on⌝ the Fryday John
Paston, John Dam, *and* I yode in-to the chambre whyche was Goodredys,

---

[25] *-y crowded in.*   [26] *MS.* de.
[27] *Abbr. by curl on* t.   [28] *-old- over* yll.
[29] *Two or three letters lost at edge in this and a few words in following lines.*
[30] my last *repeated, followed by this passage cancelled:* chargyng and requiryng the seyd
Wyllam *and* Clement þat after þat they be restoryd to þe manerys of Sporle, Swey[n]s-
thorp, *and* Bekam they restore myn heyrys to Merlyngforthe, Stonst⟨ed⟩, *and* Orwelbury.

and they desyred of me to see the wyll. I lete them see it, and John Dam
redde it. And whan he had redde it John Paston walkyd vp and down in
10 the chamer; John Dam *and* I knelyd at the beddys fete. The sayd John
Dam askyd me what was my husbondys wyll shulde be done w*yth* Sporle,
and I sayd it was his wyll that oone of his ⟨tw⟩ayn¹ yongest sonnys shulde
haue it. He sayd pr*eue*ly to me by his feyth he sayd the same to hym. Than
the ⟨sa⟩me tyme I lete them see the dede of yiffte which as I suppose was
15 councell to all tho this dede was made on-to till I shewyd it them. And soo
they swore all sauf John Paston *and* John Damme. After t⟨hat⟩² my sonne
John Paston had neu*er* ryght kynde wordys to me. And John Dam askyd
me what justice *and* felowe of his my husbond trustyd most, and I
aunsweryd hym as I knewe.

20 ⟨Th⟩an they yede home w*yth* the body in-to Norff*olk and* buryed it
⟨. . . . . .⟩³ys whych I had takyn hym in his fadirs lyue whych oon longyd
to the coffre at Ox⟨nede⟩ wher-in my dedys were that now be forsworn.⁴
Whan my husbondys body was in-to Norff*olk* I went to Berkyng *and*
⟨. . .⟩ Michelmas com to Shipleys hows in London. And thider cam John
25 Paston *and* John Dam and intreted me to put in ⟨. . .⟩ Sweynesthorp *and*
Sporle that John shuld haue it. And I sayd it was neu*er* my husbondys
⟨. . . . . .⟩ the ad⟨uy⟩s of my lord of Lyncoln. And John Dam lenyng vp-on
a stole, I syttyng by hym, say⟨d . . . . . .⟩ to a prest to aske hym councell of
suche a thyng he wolde nat byde⁵ hym dowte, but if he do it *and* go to the
30 prest he wyll asoyle hym. I yede in-to⁶ Seint Elyne chirche and told ⌈to⌉
Will*ia*m Bakton how they had sayde to me, *and* told hym I coude not
fynde in my herte to sette in the wyll that I knewe wel was ⌈the⌉ contrary.
And he sayde he wolde not councell me therto; *and* soo we departed.
After this cam John Damme and askyd me whyche of the justic*ys* my
35 husbond trusted most, *and*⁷ sayde to me, 'Be ye⁸ not reme*m*brid of suche
a day my maist*er* helde w*yth* Maryott at Norwych?' I sayd, 'Yis,⁹ for I
was ther my-selfe.' ⟨He⟩ sayd to me my husbond toke a certeyn man a
thyng wryten *and* insealed of my husbond*ys* hande, but what was in
⟨þer⟩-in he wyste neu*er*.

33. ¹ *Letters lost here and in some following lines where left-hand margin has crumbled.*
² *Paper rubbed.*
³ *A large irregular stain, and two considerable holes, almost in the middle of the sheet*
affect eight lines of writing, three of them losing nearly three inches, about a third of their
length. Six dots indicate a long, but variable, gap.
⁴ *MS.* -swron.
⁵ -e *not clear, because on wrinkle; but not struck out.*
⁶ the *canc.*
⁷ *Fold. by* asked, *which should have been cancelled.*
⁸ *MS.* the.   ⁹ *MS.* this.

34. Extract from Will   Not after 1479

C.U.L. Add. 6968, pp. 11–12.

This extract is given in Sandford's Genealogy of 1674, beside the names of William and Agnes Paston, introduced thus: 'A note taken out of the last Will and Testament of Agnes Berrye, wife to Justice Paston, proving her discent from Gerbredge and Berrye.'

The spelling is obviously in the main of the seventeenth century; the few abbreviations of 'the' and 'which' are here expanded, and capitals modernized.

The date of the final form of Agnes's will is not known. It must have been later than the drafts of 1466 (nos. 31–3), for Clement Paston was there both beneficiary and scribe, but in the present text he is dead.

G. 557/646, printed from *Norfolk Archaeology*, iv (1855), 16.

Also I bequeath to the Whight Fryers of the said city of Norwich, for I am there a suster, to helpe to pay hir debts xx li., which I will be gathered of the arrerage of my lyvelode. Also I bequeath to the auter of Gracion of the said house, wheras mine husband and I have a perpetuall masse, a vestment which they have for a prist to judge in of[1] rede satern. Also to 5 the mendinge of the chappell of Our Ladie within the said place, wheras Sir Thomas Gerbredge my grandfather and Dame Elizabeth his wife and Sir Edmond Berry my father and Dame Alice his wife be buried, and Clement Paston my sonn.

34. [1] *MS.* or.

35. To JOHN DAMME: copy
Probably soon after 1444, copied probably after 1480

Add. 45099, f. 2: see no. 10.

This letter is the last (no. *viij*) in the file of East Beckham documents. It was evidently written after the death of William Paston I in August 1444, but how long after cannot be determined—perhaps the absence of the customary pious formulas (such as 'whom God assoil') may imply that some time had elapsed. Harry Goneld, whose name appears below the letter, was an employee and tenant of the Pastons who is mentioned in 1448 and 1450 (see Margaret's letters nos. 128, 131), but the significance of the name here is in any case obscure. The letter cannot have been later than 1462, when John Damme died (will proved 29 December: Blomefield, viii. 168; *Norwich Wills*, i. 113).

To John Damme

Ser, I recummaund me to you and thank yow of youre grete laboure wyth all myn hert; but as be youre bille my fader shul[1] be bounde to pay all Wyllyam Maryottes dettes, or half at the leest, þat[2] ⌈is⌉ c li., whych wyth
5 the seid xl[3] li. þat John shuld haue is twyes as meche as is owyng as I conseyve; the whyche shuld hurte me more þan avayle. And I was at that tyme at Crowmer, *and* wote[1] well þat it was neythyr Maryottes mevyng ne my faders that he shuld be chargeable of more þan he oweth, ⌈hys paymentes⌉, expences, and hys bargeyn[4] alowed. ⌈I suppose⌉ they shall
10 holde hem payed wyth this bill yf ther be ony more that hard it. I prey help they may enseale; but begyn at thise fyrst and theene send for the toder. I wold we hade vj sealles yf ⌈it⌉ myght easly be.

Ser, Jamys Gressham told me that[5] ȝe thynk the bergeyn were not certen but yf it wer put in[1] certeyn what the dettes be that shuld be
15 content. Me thynketh that the xl li. makyth the[6] bargeyne certen attwyx John and my fader, ⌈and⌉ thow it be not, wyth oder mater þat I haue it shal[1] be certeyn j-now.

My lady Morley, Hastingys,[7] and my moder *and* I, &c., dyned this day at Lyncolne Kokys *and* suppyd this nyȝt to-gedyr also, *and* dyuers persons

---

35. [1] *No space.*   [2] þ *in form of* y *throughout.*   [3] *This sum on eras.*
[4] -s *erased.*   [5] t *canc.*   [6] lenger *canc.*
[7] *Dotted circumflex for* n *over* y *instead of* i.

were disposed to haue seid no good word of you; and aft*er*, or we dep*a*rted, 20
they that haue seid worst of yow seid bett*er* of yow than I herd hem sey
thys twelmoneth day, *and* in substance contrary to all olde tales. Multa
habeo vobis dicere que non sunt in libro hoc.

Be JOHN PASTON

Herry Gunell 25
N Basyngh*a*m
N Matelask[8]

36. Petition to HENRY VI   1449, before 16 July

Add. Charter 17240. Parchment, $21 \times 7\frac{1}{8}$ in. Hand of James Gloys (see p. lxxvi).

Dorse blank.

The date appears from the sequence of events described in the text: Lord Moleyns expelled Paston from the manor of Gresham on 17 February 1448; Paston appealed without success until the following Michaelmas, and then, on 6 October, took up residence in 'a mansion within the seid town'. On 28 January 1449 Moleyns's men drove Margaret Paston and her servants out of this mansion. This petition must have been presented to Parliament during the session of 1449 (Westminster, 12 February–4 April, 7–30 May; Winchester, 16 June–16 July *Rot. Parl.* v. 141–3).

This is the natural interpretation, for if Paston lost patience about Michaelmas 1448 his return to Gresham on 6 October of the same year follows easily. Gairdner thought he did not return until October 1449, but in that case the mention of Michaelmas 1448 would have little point. Nothing in other papers is incompatible with the present dating.

G. 77/102.

To the Kyng oure Sou*er*ayn Lord, *and* to the right wyse and discrete
lordis assemblyd in this *p*resent *P*arlement

Besechith mekly y*our* homble liege man John Paston that, where he[1] *and*
od*er* enfeffed to his vse haue be pecybily poscessyd of the man*er* of Gresham
wi*th*in the Counté of Norff*olk* xx yere *and* more til the xvij day of Februarij 5
the yere of y*our* nobill regne xxvj, that Rob*er*t Hung*er*ford, knyght, the
Lord Molyns, entred in-to the seyd man*er*. And how be it that the seyd
John Paston aft*er* the seid entré sued to the seid Lord Molyns *and* his
councell, in the most louly man*er* that he cowde, dayly fro tyme of the
seid entré on-to the fest of Mihelmes than next folwyng, duryng which 10
tyme diu*er*s co*m*municasyons were had be-twix the councell of the seid
lord *and* the councell of y*our* seid besechere; and for asmych as in the
seid co*m*municasions no titill of right at any tyme was shewed for the seid

---

[8] *These names seem to be intended to follow this letter, and were presumably copied from notes on the original.*

36. [1] *Fold. by eras. about $1\frac{1}{4}$ in. long.*

lord but that was fully *and* clerly answeryd, so that the seid lord*es* councell
15 remitted y*our* seid besecher*e* to sewe to the seid lord for his finall *and*
rightfull answer*e*, and aft*er* sute mad to the seid lord be y*our* seid besecher*e*,
aswell at Salysbery as in od*er* places, to his gret coust, *and* non answer*e*
had but delays, which causyd y*our* seid besecher*e* the vj day of Octobr*e*
last past to inhabite hym in a mansion w*ith*-in the seid town, kepyng stille
20 ther*e* his poscession on-tille the xxviij day of Januarij last past the seid lord
sent to the seid mansion a² riotous peple to the nombre of a thowsand
p*er*sones, w*ith* blanket bendes of a sute as riser*es* a-geyn y*our* pees, arrayd
in maner of werre w*ith* curesse, brigaunder*es*, jakk*es*, salettes, gleyfes,
bowes, arows, pavyse, gonnes, pannys w*ith* fier *and* teynes brennyng
25 ther*e*-in, long cromes to draw dou*n* howsis, ladder*es*, pikoys w*ith* which
thei myned down the walles, *and* long trees w*ith* which thei broke vp
yat*es* *and* dores *and* so came in-to the seid mansion, the wiff of y*our* seid
besecher*e* at that tyme beyng ther-in, *and* xij p*er*sones w*ith* here, the which
p*er*sones thei dreve oute of the seid mansion and myned down the walle
30 of the chambre wher*e*-in the wiff of y*our* seid besecher*e* was, *and* bare here
oute at the yat*es* *and* cutte a-sondre the post*es* of the hows*es* *and* lete them
falle, *and* broke vp all the chambres *and* coferes w*ith*-in the seid mansion,
and rifelyd *and* in maner of robery bare a-wey all the stuffe, aray, *and* mony
that y*our* seyd besecher*e* *and* his s*er*uau*n*tes had ther*e*, on-to the valew of
35 cc li., *and* part there-of sold *and* part there-of yaffe, *and* the remenau*n*t thei
dep*ar*ted among them to the grete *and* outrageous hurt of y*our* seid
besecher*e*; sayng opynly that if thei myght haue fou*n*d ther*e* y*our* seid
besecher*e*, *and* on John Damme which is of councelle w*ith* hym, *and*
diu*er*s od*er* of the s*er*uauntes of y*our* seid besecher*e*, thei shuld haue died.
40 And yet diu*er*s of the seid mysdoer*es* *and* ryotous peple onknowyn,
contr*a*ry to y*our* lawes, dayly kepe the seid man*er* w*ith* force *and* lyne in
wayte of diu*er*s of the frendis, tenau*n*tes, *and* s*er*uau*n*tes of y*our* seid
beseche*r*, *and* greuously vexe *and* trobill hem in diu*er*s wise, *and* seke
hem in her howsis, ransakyng *and* serchyng her shevys *and* strawe in her
45 bernes *and* other places w*ith* bore speris, swerd*es*, *and* gesernys, as it
semyth to sle hem if thei myght haue found hem; *and* su*m*me haue bete
and left for ded, so that thei, for doute of her*e* lyves, dare not go home to
her*e* houses ner occupy her*e* husbondry, to the gret hurte, fere, *and* drede
aswele of y*our* seid besecher*e* as of his seid frendis, tenau*n*tes, *and* ser-
50 uau*n*tes. And also thei compelle pore tenau*n*tes of the seid man*er*, now
w*ith*-in ther daunger*e*, a-geyn ther wille to take feyned pleynt*es* in the
courtes of the hundred ther*e* ageyn the seid frendis, tenau*n*tes, *and*
s*er*uau*n*tes of y*our* seid besecher*e*, whiche dare not apere to answere for
fere of bodily harme, ne can gete no copijs of the seid pleynt*es* to remedi
55 them be the lawe, because he that kepyth the seid courtis is of covyn

² *No space.*

52

wi*th* the seid misdoere*s and* was on of the seid ryseres which be coloure
of the seid pleynt*es* greuously amercy the seid frende*s*, tena*u*ntes, *and*
seruau*n*tes of yo*ur* seid besecher*e* to the[r] outrageous *and* importabille
hurt.

Please it yo*ur* Hynesse, consideryng that if this gret insurreccyon, 60
ryottis, *and* wrongis, *and* dayly continuans ther-of, so heynosly don a-geyn
yo*ur* crowne, dignité, *and* peas shuld not be yo*ur* hye myght be duly
punysshid, it shall gefe grett boldnesse to them *and* alle od*er* mysdoere*s*
to make congregacyou*n*s *and* conuenticles riottously, on-abille to be seysed,
to the subu*er*syon *and* finall distruccyon of yo*ur* liege peple *and* lawes; 65
and also how that yo*ur* seid besecher is not abille to sue the commu*ne*³
lawe in redressyng of this heynos wrong for the gret myght *and* alyaunce
of the seid lord; and also that yo*ur* seid besecher*e* canne haue non accyon
be yo*ur* lawe ageyn the seid riotous peple for the godis *and* catellis be hem
so riottously *and* wrongfully take *and* bore a-wey, be-cause the seid peple 70
be onknowe, aswelle her*e* names as her*e* p*er*sones, on-to hym; to purvey
be the avyse of the lordis spirituall *and* temp*or*all assembled in this
p*re*sent p*ar*lement that yo*ur* seid besecher*e* may be restoryd to the seid
godis *and* catellis thus riottously take awey, and that the seid Lord
Molyns haue suche comaundment that yo*ur* seid besecher*e* be not thus, 75
wi*th* force in maner of werre, hold oute of his seid maner cont*r*ary to alle
yo*ur* statutes mad a-geyn suych forcibille entrees *and* holdynge*s*; and that
the seid Lord Molyns *and* his s*er*vau*n*tes be sette in suche a rewle that
yo*ur* seid besecher*e*, his frendis, tena*u*ntes, *and* seruau*n*tes may be sure
and saffe from hurt of here p*er*sones and pesibily ocupy her*e* londe*s and* 80
tene*mentes* vnd*er* yo*ur* lawes wi*th*-oute oppressyoun or onrightfull vexasion
of any of hem, and that the seid riser*es and* causer*es* therof may be punysshed
that other may eschewe to make any suche rysyng in this yo*ur* lond of
peas in tyme comyng. And he shalle p*r*ay to God for yowe.

37. To an unidentified person in London: draft   About 1449

Add. 27446, f. 41. 8 × 5⅝ in. Autograph.

Dorse: Almost completely filled by text. No marks of folding, seal, or
address.

This is a corrected draft. It was attributed by Fenn and Gairdner to John Paston
III, and dated 1479–80. Gairdner thought it was 'apparently in the hand of
Edmund Paston'; but the hand is John I's.¹ The brother with whose gravestone
he is concerned must be Edmond Paston I, who died in London in March 1449

---

³ *Abbr.* coe *with dotted circumflex.*

37. ¹ *John's hand is always coarse and irregular, making an impression of impatient haste.*
It is characteristic of him to omit abbreviation marks as in among, think, *ll.* 19, 35.

(see his nuncupative will, no. 80). The friar with whom Paston and his mother are in dispute is John Hauteyn (see Agnes's letter no. 18, Margaret's no. 133, and Part II, no. 871).

The person addressed is evidently some confidential agent of Paston's such as James Gresham (cf. no. 39).

F. v, p. 272. G. 851/967.

Ser, I pray yow þat ye will[2] send sum chyld to my lord of Bukingham[3] place, and to þe Crown, wich as I conseiue is callid Gerardis Hall in Bredstret, to inquere whedir I haue any answere of my letter[4] sent to Caleys whech ye know[5] off, and that ye will[6] remembre my broþiris ston so þat
5 it myth be mad er I cumm ageyn, and þat it ⟨be⟩[7] klenly wrowgth. It is told me þat þe man at Sent Bridis is no klenly portrayer, ⟨wh⟩erfor I wold fayn it myth be portrayid[8] be sum odir man, and he to graue it vp.

⟨. . .⟩ It is informyd sum personis in þis cuntré þat ye know þat ⌐þe⌐ frere will sew a-nodir delegaci fro Rome direkt to sum bischop of Ingland to
10 amend his mater, &c., and how be it þat it may not gretly hurt, yet[9] þe seyd personis, ⌐&c.⌐, wold not he shuld haue his entent, in a[s]moch as his suggestion is vntrewe, but raþer þey wold spend mony to lette it. I suppose þe Abbot of Bery shuld labor for him ⌐rather þan anodir⌐ becawse ⟨þ⟩e sey[d] Abbot ⌐is aparteynor⌐ to þe lord þat is þe freris
15 mayntener, &c.; wherfore, ser, my modir[10] and I pray yow ⟨i⟩nquere after a man[11] callid Clederro whych is solisitor and attorné with ⟨M⟩aster Will Grey, þat ⌐late⌐ was þe Kinggis proktor at Rome, and þe seyd Clederro sendith maters and letters owth of Ingeland to his seyd master euer[y] monith, &c. He is well knowe in London and amo[n]g
20 þe Lumbardis, ⌐and with þe Bischep of Winchesteres men⌐, but I wot not wher he dwellit in London; and I suppos[12] if ⌐ye⌐ speke with him he knowith me.[13] Plese yow to comen with him of þis mater, ⌐but let him not wete of þe mater atwix my modir and him, but⌐[14] desir him to wryth to his master to lett þis if it may be; or ell[15] to se ⌐þe⌐ best wey
25 þat he haue not his intent, and to comon with þ[e] proktor of þe Whith Freris at Rome to he[l]p forth.[16] For þe freris here haue laborid to my modir[10] and ⌐praiid her⌐[17] to help to lette his[18] on-trewe intent, and haue wrete to her proketor befor þis; and I suppose if ⌐ye⌐ speke to þe prior of þe Freris at London he will writh to her seyd proktor, &c. But tell ⌐þe⌐
30 prior no word þat I know ⟨þer⟩of, but let him wete if he will wryth

---

[2] at canc.   [3] Abbr. Buk with -k tailed, not the -is loop.
[4] c with curl canc.   [5] c canc. before k-.   [6] me canc.
[7] Here and later a few letters lost at torn margin.   [8] to his canc.
[9] y- corr. from þ.   [10] Abbr. M.   [11] wich is canc.
[12] Long -s crowded in.   [13] w canc.   [14] Interl. in place of &c. canc.
[15] This word, as often elsewhere, written ell with ll barred. Generally this barred -ll means only -ll, but in this word and a few others it might be intended as abbr. of -llis.
[16] Recto ends, except for ex altera parte below.
[17] Interl. above &c., of which the c is canc.   [18] hyn canc.

54

to his pr*o*ktor odir men shall help forth. ⟨M⟩ore-ou*er* þat ye[19] will tell
Cledero þat I am not seker ⌐þat þe frer*e*⌐[20] laborith þus ⟨bu⟩t be talis of
freris *and* odir. Neu*er*theles let him writh to his mast*er* þat[21] whatsumevyr[22]
he[23] do herin he shall be truly cont*en*t for his labor *and* cost*is*. *And* if ye
thi[n]k þat[24] Cledro will writh effectually herin, geff hym j noble. ⟨Le⟩t[25] 35
hy*m* let his mast*er*[26] know[27] þat my lord of Wynchest*er and* Danyell ow
godwill to þe p*ar*t that he shall labor for*e*. *And* if þer*e*[28] be fown no sech
swth be þe seyd ⟨fre⟩r*e*,[29] yet wold I haue sum thi*n*g fro Rome to anull þe
old ⌐bull⌐, &c., or to apeyre ⌐it⌐ ⟨if⟩ it myth be do esily, &c., *and* tydi[n]g
wheder þer be any sech sute, &c. 40

Yo*wr* awn, &c.[30]

⟨. . .⟩ how beit þat it may nowþir avayle ner hurt, yet my m*o*dir[31] will þis
be do. ⟨I⟩ send yow þe copi of þe bull *and* how execuciun[32] was do, *and*
informaciu*n* of þe mat*er* j*n* p*ar*te,[33] &c. I pray yow red it ou*er*, *and* spede
yow homward. *And*, s*er*, I sha[l] cont*en*t yo*wr* nobl[e], &c.[34] Bry[n]g þis 45
lett*er* hom w*ith* yow, &c.

38. Petition to the CHANCELLOR   1450

Add. Charter 17239. Parchment, $18\frac{1}{2} \times 4$ in. Hand unidentified.

Dorse blank.

From the additional detail of resistance to one of the justices of the peace, the
date is evidently later than that of no. 36. This fits the fact that John Kemp,
Cardinal Archbishop of York, became Chancellor on 31 January 1450.
   G. 107/135.

Vn-to the right reue*r*ent fadir in God and my right g*r*acioux lord the
   Cardinal Archebisshop of York, Prymat *and* Chaunceller of Inglond.

Besecheth mekely John Paston that, where Rob*er*t Hungerford, knyght,
Lord Molens, and Alianore his wyff late with force and strength *and* grete
multitude of riottous peple, to þe noumbre of a thousand p*er*sones *and* mo, 5
gadered by th'excitacion *and* procuryng of John Heydon a-yenst the
Kyngg*es* pees, in riotous maner entred vp-on yo*ur* seid besecher *and* othir

[19] wer *canc.*   [20] *Interl. above* the *canc.*
[21] *A caret marks an insertion, but it is partly lost at the tear, partly erased.*
[22] -v- *over* e.   [23] sh *canc.*   [24] ke *canc.*
[25] *This in margin, beginning lost.*   [26] haue *canc.*
[27] -ch *canc.*   [28] *Flourished* -r *over* t.   [29] þer *canc.*
[30] *This subscription, to right of page, marked off and underlined; remainder written even
more hastily to left of this.* y- *here written* þ.
[31] *Abbr.* M.   [32] *This word underlined.*
[33] *MS.* j *fold. by three minims and* parte *without space.*
[34] *This sentence bracketed off, to the right; not only* I *and a* canc. *before last sentence.*

enfeoffed to his vse in the manoir of Gresham, with þ'appurtenauncez in
þe shire of Norffolk; whiche riotous peple brake, dispoiled, *and* drew
10 doun the place of y*our* seid besecher in the seid toun and drafe out his
wiff *and* seruauntes there beyng, and ryfled, took, *and* bare awey alle the
good*es and* catalx that y*our* seid besecher *and* his seruauntes hadde there
to þe value of cc li. *and* more, and the seid manoir after þe seid riottous
entré kept with strong[1] hande in man*er*e of werre, as weel ayenst y*our*
15 seid besecher *and* his feffees as ayenst oon of þe Kyng*ges* justicez of his
pees in þe seid shire that come thedir to execute þe statutes ordeigned *and*
pr*o*uyded ayenst suche forcible entrees *and* kepyng of possessions with
force, as it appiereth by record*e* of þe seid justice certifyed in-to þe
Chaunc*er*ie; and yet þe seid Lord Molens the same manoir kepith with
20 force *and* strengthe ayenst þe fourme of þe seid statutes; please it y*our*
reu*er*ent fadirhood *and* graci*oux* lordship, these pr*e*misses considered,
to gr*a*unte on-to y*our* seid besecher, for his feffees by hym to be named,
a special assise ayenst þe seid Lord Molens, Alianore, *and* John Heidon,
and othir to be named by y*our* seid besecher, and also an oyer *and*
25 det*er*myner ayenst þe seid Lord Molens, John Heidon, *and* othir of the
seid riotous peple in like fo*ur*me to be named, to enquer*e*, here, *and*
det*er*myn all trespaces, extorc*i*ons, riottes, forcible entrees, maynten*a*unces,
champ*ar*ties, embraceries, offenses, *and* mesprisions by hem or ony
of hem doen; als weel atte sute of our souereign lord þe Kyng as of y*our*
30 seid besecher *and* his seid feffees *and* eu*er*y of hem, or of ony othir of þe
Kyng*ges* lieges. Atte reu*er*[en]ce of God *and* in weye of charité.

39. To JAMES GRESHAM: copy   1450, 4 September

Add. 27443, f. 113. 11¼×9¼ in. Gresham's hand (see p. lxxvii).

Dorse: Marks of folding; no seal or address.

This is a copy made by Gresham. He had been one of William Paston I's clerks,
and continued to act for many years as agent and secretary to other members of
the family; cf. especially Margaret's letter no. 212, ll. 44 ff.
    The year is evidently that of no. 38, which is the 'bill' mentioned in the opening
sentence. Moreover, it answers a letter from Gresham (Part II, no. 455) referring
to the loss of Cherbourg, which fell on 12 August 1450.
    G. 108/136.

The copie of þe lett*er* of J. P.

James Gresham, I prey yow laboure forth to haue answer of my bille for
myn especial assise *and* the oyer *and* t*er*myner accordyng to my seid bille
that I delyuered to my lord Chaunceler, letyng hym wete that, as for that

38. [1] *No space.*

his lordship conceyved the gr*a*unt of suyche a special matier myght cause 5
a rumo*ur* in þe cuntré, owt of dowte the cuntré is not so disposed, for it is
desired ageyn suche p*er*sones as the c⟨untré⟩[1] wolde were ponysshid. And
if they be not ponysshid to refourme that they haue do amysse, by likly-
nesse the cuntré wole rise up on th⟨em⟩. Me⟨n⟩[2] talke that a gen*er*al oier
and ter*m*yner is gr*a*unted to the Duke of Norff*o*lk, my lord of Ely, the 10
Erll of Oxenford, the Lord Scales, S*er* John Fastolf, S*er* Thomas Fulthorp,
and William Yeluerton, *and* men be right glad therof. Yet that not with-
stondyng, laboure ye forth for me, f⟨or⟩[3] in a gen*er*al oyer *and* ter*m*yner a
supersedeas may dassh al, and so shall not ⌈in⌉ a special. And also if þe
justicez come at my reque⟨st⟩ they shall sytte als long as I wole, *and* so 15
shall thei not by the gen*er*all. And as for co*m*myssioners in myn, &c.,
S*er* John Fastolf must be pleyntyf als weel as I my-self, *and* so he may not
be commyssioner; and as for alle the remen*a*unt I can thynke them
indifferent j-now in þe matier except my Lord Scales, whos wyff is aunte
to þe Lady Moleyns.   20
　And as for that þe Lord Moleyns hath wretyn, þat he dar put[4] þe matier
in awarde of my lord Chaunceler *and* in what juge he wole take to hym,
&c., whiche offre as I suppose shall be tolde to yow for to make yow to
cesse yo*ur* labour, thanne lete þat be answerid *and* my lord Chaunceler
enfourmed thus. The matier was in treté by th'assent of þe Lord Moleyns 25
atwene his counseil *and* myn, whiche assembled at London xvj dyuers
dayes, *and* for þe more part there was a s*er*geant *and* vj or vij thrifty
apprentisez; at whiche tyme the Lord Moleyns title was shewed *and*
clerly answerid, in so meche þat his own counseil seide they cowde no
forther in the matier, desiryng me to ride to Salesbury to þe Lord Moleyns, 30
pr*o*myttyng of their part that thei wolde moeve the Lord Moleyns so þat
þei trusted I shuld haue myn entent or I come thens; of whiche title and
answer I sende yow a copie that hath be put in-to þe p*ar*lement, the Lord
Moleyns beyng there pr*e*sent, wherto he cowde not sey nay.
　Also by-fore þis tyme I haue agreed to put it in ij juges so þei wolde 35
dete*r*myne by our euydences the right, moevyng nother partie to yeve
oþ*er* by ony mene, but only the right dete*r*myned, he to be fully recompensed that hath right; wherto he wold not agree, but alle tymes wolde
þat thoe juges shulde entrete the parties as they myght be drawe to, by
offre *and* pr*o*fre to my conceyte as men bye hors.   40
　Whiche matiers considerid, my conseil hath alwey conceyved that
the tretees þat he offred hath be to non othir entent but to delaye the
matier, or ellis to entrete me to relese my damages, for title hath he non.
And he knowith weel the title shall neu*er* better be vndirstond thanne it
hath be by his counseil *and* myn atte seid comunycacions.   45

---

39. [1] *This and other words partly lost through a tear at edge.* 　　　[2] -n *rubbed.*
　[3] a general *canc., and also subpuncted.* 　　　　　　　　　　　　　　　[4] th *canc.*

And also ⟨. . .⟩⁵ my lord Chaunceler vndirstond that þe Lord Moleyns men toke *and* bar⁶ away more þanne cc li. worth of my goodes *and* catalles,⁷ wherof I delyu*er*ed hym a bylle of eu*er*y parcell wherto all⟨e⟩ þe world knoweth he canne make no title; and if he were disposed to do right my
50 counsell thynketh he shulde restore þat, for þ*er*for nedith ⌐nowthir⌐ comuny[ca]c*io*n ne treté. And with-owt he wole restore that, I trowe no ⟨m⟩an can thynk that his treté is to no good p*ur*pose.

I p*re*ye yow hertily laboure ye so to my lord Chaunceller that owther he wole gr*au*nte me my desire or ellis that he wole denye it; and lete me
55 haue answer from yow in wrytyng how ye spede. If my lord Chaunceler hath lost my bille þat I delyu*er*ed hym, wherof I sende yow a copie, that thanne ye put up to hym an othir of þe same, takyng a copie to y*ou*r-self.

Recomaund me to my cosyn ⌐William⌐ Whyte, and prey hym to gyf yow his help in this; *and* lete hym⁸ be prevy to þis letter, and lete hym
60 w⟨ete⟩ þat my cosyn his suster hath childe a doughter. Wretyn at Norwich the iiij day of September.

Dyu*er*se men of my freendis auyse me to entre in-to þe maner of Gresham by force of my writte of restituc*io*n, whiche I wole not do by cause þe maner is so decayed by the Lord Moleyns ocupac*io*n that where it was
65 worth to me l marc.⁹ clerly by yeer*e* I cowde not now make it worth xx li.; for whiche hurt *and* for othir hurtis by þis special assise I trust to haue remedye.

40. Petition to the Lords: draft 1452

Add. 27444, f. 18. 12×17 in. Mostly in an unidentified hand which appears also in no. 45 and in Margaret Paston's letter no. 144; corrections and additions by Paston, and a short addition by the scribe of no. 42, f. 14, etc.

Dorse: Last seven manuscript lines. Traces of red wax. No address.

The year appears in part from the complaint against Roger Church, which is essentially the same as that in no. 41. Further, no. 48 is a later version of many of the same charges against Robert Ledham and his associates, in the course of which the attack on Philip Berney (ll. 26 ff. below) is dated in 30 Henry VI (1 September 1451–31 August 1452).
   G. 179/217.

Charlys Nowel, Otywell Nowell, Robert Ledeh*a*m, John the sone of Hogge Ratkleff, Robert Dallyng, Herry Bangge, Roger Cherche, Nicholas

---

⁵ *Edge torn; there would have been room for* lete.   ⁶ away *canc.*
⁷ *Edge torn, but nothing seems missing.*
⁸ wete *canc.*   ⁹ -c *with curl over* k.

Goldsmyth,[1] Robert Taylo*ur*, *Cris*tofore[2] Grenescheve,   [3]Dunmowe,
⌐Elis Dokworth, *Cris*tofir[4] Bradlé, Jon Cokkow⌐,[5] assemblyng *and*
gadderyng to hem gret multitude of mysrewled people, kepe a[6] frunture 5
and a forslet at the hows of the seid Robert Ledeh*a*m and issu ought at
her pleser, sumtyme vj, sumtyme xij, sumtyme xxx^{ti} ⌐and mo⌐,[7] armed,
jakked, and salettyd, wyt*h* bowis, arwys, speris, *and* bylles, and over-ride
the contré *and* oppresse the people and do many orible and abhomynable
dedis lyke to[6] be distruccion of the shire of Norff*o*l*k* wyt*h*oute the Kyng 10
owre sovereyn lord seth it redressid.

Vn Mydlent Soneday certeyn of the seid felechep in the chirche of
Byrlyngh*a*m made afray vpon tweyne of the s*er*uaunt*is* of the reu*er*ent
fadyr in Godde Byshop of Norwiche, the seid s*er*uaunt*is* at that tyme
knelyng to see the vsyng of the masse; and there and than the seid felechep 15
wold have kelled the seid two servaunt*is* at the prestis bakke ne had they
be lettyd, as it semed.

[[8]Item, vn the Moneday next before Esterne Daye sex of the seid p*er*sones
made a saute vpon John Paston and hese two s*er*vau*n*t*is* at the dore of the
Cathedrall cherche of Norweche, wyt*h* swerd, bokeler, and dagareis drawe 20
smet at the seid Paston, on of them holdyng the seid Paston be bothe
armes at hese bakke, as it semeth purposyng there to have morderid the
seid Paston *and* they had not abe lettyd; and also smet on of the servaunt*is*
of the seid Paston vpon the naked hed wyt*h* a swerd and poluted the seynte-
wary.] 25

Item, ⌐on þe Monday next befo[re] Estern Day⌐[9] x of the seid p*er*sones
lay in a wayte in the hey weye[10] vndy*r*e Thorp woode vp-on Phelep
Berney, esquier*e*, *and* hese man, and shet at hem and smet her horse wyt*h*
arwes, and then over-rede hym and brake a bowe vn the seid Phelippis
hed and toke hym presoner, callyng hym trayto*ur*; and when they had 30
kepte hym as long as they lyst þei[11] led hym to the ⌐seyd⌐[12] Byshop of
Norwiche and askid of hym swerté of the peas, *and* forwyt*h* relessed her
suerté and went her way.

Item, iij of the seid felechep lay vn[6] awayte vpon Emond Brome,
jentelman, *and* ⌐with nakid swerdes⌐[5] fawte wyt*h* hym be the space of a 35
qu*a*rter of a owre, and toke hym pr*e*soner; and when they had kepte hym
as long as they lyst, lete hym goo.

---

40. [1] Thom*a*s Iryng *canc.*   [2] *Abbr.* xp-, *with dotted circumflex.*
  [3] *Left blank; the name should have been William—see no.* 48, *l.* 24.
  [4] *Abbr.* xp-.   [5] *Interl. in Paston's hand.*
  [6] *No space, as often with indefinite article and* to be.
  [7] *Interl. by Paston above* sumtyme lx *canc.*
  [8] *This paragraph cancelled by large crosses.*
  [9] *Interl. by Paston, very roughly, above* vn the same day at afty*r*e none *canc.*
  [10] vpon *canc.*
  [11] þ *in form of* y.   [12] *Interl. apparently in Paston's hand.*

Item, xl[ti] of the same felechep come rydyng to Norwiche, jakked *and*
salettyd, wyt*h* bowys *and* arwys, byllys, gleves, vn Mavndy Thursday;
40 and that day afty*re* none when se*r*uice was doo they, in lyke wyse arayid,
wold have broke vp the Whyte Freris dores[13] seying that they come to
here Evesong, howbeit that they made her a-vaunte in towne they shuld
have ⌐sum men owt of town⌐[14] qwhyke or deed; and there made a gret
rumore[15] ⌐where þe⌐[16] Mayre and the aldermen[17] wyt*h* gret multitud of
45 peple asembled, *and* þer-vpond þe seyd feleschep dep*a*rtid.

Item, dyvers tymes serteyn of the seid felechep have take fro John
Wylton, wyt*h*oute any cause, hese net, hese shep, *and* odyre catell, **and**
su*m*me there-of have saltyd *and* eten, su*m*me there-of have aloyned so
that the seid Wylton wot not where for to seke hese best*is*; and vn the
50 morwe next afty*re* Esterne Day last past they toke fro hym xj bestis *and*
kepte hem two dayis wyt*h*owte any cause.

Item, in lyke wyse they have do to John Coke ⌐and⌐ Kateryn Wylton.

Item, in lyke wyse they have take the goodys and catelles of Thom*a*s
Baret and many odyre.

55 Item, certeyn of the seid felechep ⌐late⌐ made a sawte vpon John Wylton
in Plu*m*sted cherche-yerd, and there beete hym so þat he was ⌐dowth of
his liff⌐.[18]

Item, in lyke wyse vpon John Coke of Wytton, brekyng vp hese dores
at xj of the clok in the nyght, and wyt*h* her swerdis ma*v*med hym and gaf
60 hym vij grete woyndis. Item, smet the mody*re* of the seid Coke, a woman
of iiij[xx] yer*is* of age, vpon the crowne of the heed wyt*h* a swerd, wheche
wownde[19] was neuer hol to the daye of her deth.

Item, þe seyd[20] Dunmowe, on of the seid feleche[p] now late[21] beet the
p*a*rson of Hasyngh*a*m and brake hese hed in hese owne chauncell.

65 [[22]Item, iiij[xx] of the seid felechep, arayid as men of werre, now late
enterd wyt*h* fors vpon Phelep Berney and dissesid hym of the man*e*r of
Rokelondtoftys; wheche darnot for feer of mordy*re* reentre hese owne
lond, how be it he *and* hese aunseters have be pesibely possessid there-of
many yeris.]

---

[13] *Fold. by* where [*end of line*] the seid Paston dwellith *all canc. except* where, *left by
mistake.*

[14] *Interl. by Paston above* the seid Paston *canc.*

[15] ⌐*and* noyse⌐ be the space of halff a owre and when they myght not have her intent
they de-partyd seying they shuld purveye a-nodyre meane to have her entent of the
wheche when *canc. fold. by the* which should have been cancelled.

[16] *In margin by Paston.*

[17] of Norwych *interl. by Paston but canc. ;* had knowing they lettyd her intent *canc.; the
rest of the paragraph in Paston's hand, very hasty.*

[18] *From* so *in Paston's hand ;* þat *written* þe.

[19] *Second* w *written, probably by Paston, over partly erased* y.

[20] þe seyd *written by Paston in space left by scribe.*   [21] *MS.* lete.

[22] *This paragraph canc. by rough crosses, and marked by vertical line in margin.*

Item, Alredis sone of Erll Some, fast be Framyngham, vn the Saterday 70
next before Palme Soneday last past was pullid ought of a hows *and* kyllid.
Whedy*re* any of the seid felechep were there or not men kan not sey, there
be of hem so many of wheche many be vnknowe people.

Item, the seid felechep make seche affrayis in the contré abowte the
seid Ledeh*a*ms place, and so frayith the people, that dyvers p*er*sones for 75
feer of mordy*re* darnot abyde in her howses ne ride ne walke abowte ther
ocupacions wyt*h*-owte they take gretter people abowte[23] hem then acordith
to her degré, wheche they wolnot do in evel exaumple gevyng.

Item, the seid felechep of afer-cast maleys *and* purpose[24] now late toke[25]
Roger Cherche, on of the*re* owne felechep, be hese owne assent; wheche 80
Roger Cherche be her assent ⌐had mevid *and* sterid a risi[n]g in þe hundred
of Blofeld *and*⌐[26] hath confessed hym-self to be at þat[27] arysyng *and* hath
enbylled,[28] as it is seid, divers jentelmen and the most part of the trysty
yemen and husbondis and men of good name *and* fame of the hundre[29]
abowte the seid Ledeh*a*ms place, where the seid felechep is abydyng, and 85
nameth hem wyt*h* ody*re* suspecious people for risers, to the entent ⌐to
hide *and* couer her awn gylt *and*⌐[26] to holde them ⌐þat be trw men *and*
innosent ⟨in⟩[30] þat mater⌐[31] in a dawnger *and* feer that they shuld not gader
peopell ner atempte to resiste ther riotows governauns of the seid reotows
felechep. 90

[[32]Item, ⌐it⌐[33] is conceyved that if the seyd riotows felechep and they
that drawe to them were dewly examyned it shuld be knowe that if there
were any seche rysyng it was coniectyd, don, jmagened, *and* labored be
the seid reotows felechep and be ther meanes, for ⌐aswele⌐ the seid Cherche
as dyvers of the most suspeciows p*er*sones be the seid Cherche enbelled 95
for rysers, as it is seid, be *and* have be of long tyme[34] dayly in compeny
wyt*h* the seid reotows felechep.

Item, on of the seid felechep of late tyme, as it is seide, to encresse her
maliciows purpoce hath p*ro*ferid rewardis *and* goode to a-nody*re* p*er*sone
for to take vpon hym to apele certeyn p*er*sones and afferme the seying of 100
the seid Roger Cherche.][35]

In wytnesse of these p*re*messes dyvers knytes and esquier*is* and jentelmen, whos names folwen, wheche knowe this mater be seying, heryng,
or credible reporte to this wrytyng have set her seall, besechyng y*our*
lordcheppis to be meanes to the Kyng owre Sovereyn lord for remedy in 105
this behalve. Wrete, &c.

---

[23] hem, *with* e *over* y, *canc.*   [24] *as it semyth canc.*   [25] on *canc.*
[26] *Interl. in Paston's hand.*   [27] *Crowded in by Paston.*   [28] -y- *over* e.
[29] *Sic:* -re *repr. by flourished* r.   [30] *Paper rubbed.*
[31] *Interl. by Paston;* hem *at beginning canc.*
[32] *This paragraph and the next (which runs on) canc. by a large cross.*
[33] *Interl. by Paston, who also made* Item *from* it *and cancelled* how beit *preceding.*
[34] *Ampersand seems to have been erased.*   [35] *This paragraph inserted later.*

Item, Robert Taylour be[t] T. Baret be-cause his[36]

Memorandum þat Jon, sone of Roger Ratkliff, bet T. Baret, and Beston and Robyn Taylor tok and jmprysonyd[37] Thomas Byrdon of Ly[n]gwode.

110 Item, Robert Dalli[n]g bet[38] Nich[ol]as Chirch at Stromsaw chirch. Memorandum[39] of manassi[n]g of þe quest at Hengham.

Item,[40] Robert Dallyng bete Thomas Dallyng.

Item, Beston and W. Berton asautid Spany in his hows.[41]

þe[42] manassi[n]g and frayng of diuers personis þat þei departid ow[t] 115 of her how[s]is, þat is to sey ⌜T.⌝ Holler to Norwich, Spany to[43] Aylesham, Holler to Yermoth, Wilton to Norwich, Oliuer Knivyte to Norwich, Philip Berney to Caster, T. Siluester to[44] my lord of Norwich.

Roger[45] att Chirche, ⌜Robert Dallyng⌝, and Herry Bang, wyth oþer, went wyth fors and armys[46] and fechid William[47] Clippisby oute of his 120 faderys hous and brought hym to þe town of Walsham, and kept hym þer ij days[48] and ij nytys, and fro thens had hym to Bungey and þer inpresonyd hym and made hym to enseale an oblygacion of c libr. made aft[er] her owyn desyre.

41. Petition to the CHANCELLOR — 1452

Add. Charter 17241. Parchment, 14 × 5¾ in. Gloys's hand.

Dorse blank except for the name *Ledam* in a contemporary hand, and a sixteenth-century note.

The year appears from the reference to a general pardon granted by the King on 'Good Friday last past'. An offer of pardons for all who would apply for them to the Chancery was made by Henry VI on Good Friday, 7 April 1452 (*Registrum Abbatiæ Johannis Whethamstede*, ed. H. T. Riley (Rolls Series), i (1872), 85 ff.).

Though there is no direct evidence that John Paston composed this document, he was active in drawing up similar complaints about this time, as the preceding text and the following four show—the charges against Church in no. 40 (ll. 79 ff.) are partly in his hand. It is therefore likely that he had some part in this one, and the employment of Gloys as clerk confirms this.

G. 180/218.

To the right reuerent fader in God, Cardynale Archebusshop of York and Chauncelere of Inglond.

Please it yowre gode lordeshep to know that oon Rogere Cherche, other-

---

[36] *From* Item *added by Paston, who also wrote most of the rest of the notes on the recto.*
[37] *First* -y- *over* e.   [38] Richard *canc.*
[39] *Ampersand seems to have been erased.*
[40] *This sentence in the hand of the scribe who wrote the final postscript.*
[41] *This sentence written extremely carelessly, the last few words scarcely decipherable. Recto ends here.*
[42] *This paragraph very roughly written by Paston.*   [43] Norwich *canc.*
[44] No *canc.*   [45] *This paragraph in the hand of the scribe of no. 42 B, etc.*
[46] to Bungey *canc.*   [47] Ch *canc.*   [48] -s *crowded in.*

wyse callyd ⌐Roger¬ Bylaugh, ⌐Roger¬ Wryte, *and* ⌐Roger¬ Baly, late[1] was ⌐at¬ a gaderyng *and* assemblé of xv p*er*sones in a feleshep vnd*er* a 5 wode in the town of Possewyke in the counté of Norff*olk*, which feleshep, as it is seid ⌐be hem¬, was procured *and* gaderyd be the seid Roger*e* Cherche *and* be his councelores, ⌐the same Roger*e* seyng to su*m*me of the same feleshep[2] he had reme*m*bred a gode name for her*e* capteyn, that shuld be John A-mend Alle¬. And the seyd Roger*e* aft*er* the seid gaderyng 10 aggreyd hym-self to be take *and* examyned be p*er*sones of his owyn covyne, and be colo*ur* of his seid feleshep of xv p*er*sones ⌐be hym gaderyd¬ enbilled diu*er*s gentilmen *and* many thryfty *and* substanciall yomen, *and* thryfty husbondes *and* men of gode name *and* fame, noysyng *and* diffamyng to the Kyng *and* his councell that the seid gentilmen *and* yomen *and* thryfty 15 husbondes, w*i*th other to the nombre of ccc p*er*sones, shuld haue mad a gaderyng *and* a risyng a-geyn the Kynges peas vnd*er* the seid wode, con-trary to the trought; which is veryly conceyved to be don of malyce to put the seid gentilmen *and* yomen in feer *and* trobill that thei, aswele as alle the contré, shuld not be hardy to attempt ne lette the p*ur*posyd malyce 20 of the seid Cherche *and* his councellores in diu*er*s riottes extorc*i*ouns, forsibil[3] entreys, *and* vnlawfull disherytau*n*s of gentilmen *and* other of the Kynges liege peple in the seid shire that thei dayly vse; which riottes extorc*i*ons, aswele as the seid vntrewe diffamac*i*ons, causyth gret grudgyng, trobill, *and* comocyon in the seid shire. 25

Please it yowre gode grace, thes p*re*mysses considered, not to suffre the seid Cherche to haue no pardon of the comune grac*e* gr*au*nted be the Kyng, owre soue*r*ayn lord, vn Gode Fryday last past vn-to the tyme that he hath fownde sufficient suerté of wel namyd p*er*sones of the seid shire of his gode beryng, and to direct a comyssion vn-to such notabill p*er*sones 30 in the seid shir*e* as please you, to take *and* examyn the seid Roger*e* Cherche, aswele as othre that them semyth necessary to examyn in this behalf, so that thei that be giltles in this may be ⌐so¬ declared and that thei that be gilty may be ponysshed acordyng to her*e* demerytes; and to beseche the Kyng, owre soue*r*ayn lord, in the behalf of the gentilmen of the seid 35 shire that his Hignesse wull not take hem ne any of hem in conceyt to be of such rewle *and* disposicion vp-vn enformac*i*on of such a mysse-rewled *and* encredibill man as the seid ⌐Roger¬.[4] And thei shall p*ra*y to God for you.

---

41. [1] befor Crystmasse last past *canc.*

[2] *Caret here refers to some words in margin, of which only* hundre. me. .nd that *can be made out.*   [3] *No space.*

[4] Chirch is *canc.*

42. Probably to the SHERIFF OF NORFOLK: drafts

1452, 23 April

Add. 27444, f. 15, $11\frac{5}{8} \times 4\frac{7}{8}$ in.; f. 14, $11\frac{3}{8} \times 4\frac{7}{8}$ in.; f. 13, $11\frac{5}{8} \times 5\frac{5}{8}$ in.

A. F. 15 is a rough draft, extremely ill written in Paston's hand except for most of the first two manuscript lines, which are in the hand of James Gloys. The dorse is filled by the draft transcribed as no. 43.

B. F. 14 is a second draft, in the hand of an unidentified clerk who wrote twenty of Margaret Paston's letters (the earliest no. 128) and some other drafts for John (nos. 46, 50, 51, 52, and part of 40). It must be later than f. 15 because it incorporates the corrections there made by Paston. There are a few new additions in Paston's hand, and names of signatories are added. The dorse is blank.

C. F. 13 is a fair copy in Gloys's hand, written more evenly than most of his work, and with a certain flourish. It must be later than f. 14 because it incorporates Paston's additions there, and the misunderstanding of *yet* as *that* in l. 49 indicates that it was copied directly from that text, with its unusual use of þ for y. The dorse bears marks of folding and faint traces of red wax, but no address.

Since these texts briefly illustrate how some clerks treated the exemplars they were copying, all are given in full.

This letter and the following two drafts are obviously closely related. The date appears from the association of Charles Nowell with the offences complained of in no. 40. The sheriff of Norfolk and Suffolk in 1451–2 was John Clopton (see no. 27). A letter from Clopton, in his capacity of Sheriff, to the King and his council (Part II, no. 884, G. 177/214) reports that 'by the commandment of my lord of Norfolk' he had received a 'bill' of confessions made by Roger Church and others. From this it appears that he was the person to whom such a complaint as the present letter could appropriately be sent, and that he would also be in a position to approach the Duke as the appellants request.

G. 174/211.

A

⌜Reuere[n]t *and*⌝¹ Right wurchepfull s*er*, we comaund vs to yow. Please it yow to wete that we *and* othire jentilmen of the shire of Norff*olk* hath be in purpose to² assuyd to ⌜þe hygh *and* migthi³ prens *and*⌝⁴ owr right gode *and* gracyous lord the Duke of Norff*olk* ⌜to Framy[n]gham⌝,⁴ to haue
5 enformyd his Highnesse⁵ of dyu*ers* ⌜assaut*is and*⌝ riott⁶ mad be Charlis Nowell *and* odir ⌜ageyn þe Ki[n]g*is* pees⌝ vpon Jon Paston *and* odir of owr kyn, frend, *and* neybor*is*,⁷ ne had be þat dayly þes x days⁸ jt hath be do vs to vndirstand þat hys Highnes shuld com in-to⁹ Norwich¹⁰ or Claxton,

---

42A. ¹ *These first two words written in the margin.* ² *see canc.*
³ *This appears to be the reading; but the word is very roughly written, and a loop over the t suggests correction.* ⁴ *Interl. words in Paston's hand.*
⁵ *The rest in Paston's hand.* ⁶ *and frayis canc.* ⁷ *in þis canc.*
⁸ *þe we hard canc.* ⁹ *þis town canc.* ¹⁰ *of canc.*

⌐we not being in s*e*rtey[n] yet where¹¹ he shall r*e*meu[e]⌐; prayi[n]g yow,
as ⌐we trust⌐¹² ⌐þat ye tender⌐ þe welfare of þis shyr*e* *and* of the gentilm*e*n 10
þerin, þat ye well let owr seyd lord haue know[ing] of¹³ owr*e* int*e*nt, *and*
aft*er* to send vs¹⁴ answer*e* whedir it plese¹⁵ his Hynes we shuld com to
⌐his⌐¹⁶ p*re*sens ⌐*and* at what plase⌐, or to send owr¹⁷ compley[n]t to
him,¹⁸ trosti[n]g to ⌐his⌐ god lords[h]ep of remedi in þis mat*er*,¹⁹ whech
do²⁰ semith ⌐vs⌐ shall be to owr seyd²¹ lord*is* honure²² ⌐*and* gret rejoy to 15
þe gentilm*e*n of þis shyr*e*⌐, *and* cause þe pese to kep be þe grase of God, ho
haue yow in his blesid kepi[*n*]g, &c.

Wret at Norwych on S*e*nt Georg*is* Day.

B

Right wurchipfull, we¹ co*m*mawnd us to yow.² Please it yow to wete that
we *and* other*e* jentilmen of the shyer*e* of Norff*olk* hath be in purpose to 20
assewyd to the hygh *and* myghty prynce *and* owr*e* ryght gode lord the
Duke of Norff*olk* to Framlyngh*a*m, to have enformyd his Highnesse of
dyuers assaughtes *and* ryottes made be Charles Nowell *and* other*e* ageyn
the Kyng*ys* lawe *and* peas ⌐withowt any cause or occaci*u*n⌐³ vp-on John
Paston *and* other*e* of owr*e* kynne, frendes, *and* neyghborys, ne had be 25
that dayly this x days it hath be do us to wete that his Highnesse shuld
come in-to Norwych or Claxton, we not beyng in certeyn yet whedyr*e* he
shall remeve; p*ra*yng yow, as we trust that ye woll tender*e* the welfare of
this shyer*e* *and* of the jentylmen ther*e*-in, that ye woll lete owr*e* seyd lord
haue knowyng of owr*e* entente in this, and after*e* to send us answhere 30
whed*er* it please his Highnesse we shuld come to his p*re*sens and in what
place, or to send owr*e* compleynt to hym ⌐if mor*e* informaci*u*n be thowth
behoffull⌐;⁴ trosty[n]g to his gode lordshep of remedy in this mater*e*,
whiche do semyth vs shall be to owr*e*⁵ seyd lord*ys* honure *and* gret reioyng
to all the jentylmen of this shyer*e*, *and* cause the peas to be kept here- 35
after*e* be the grace of God, how have yow in hys blyssed kepy[n]g.

Wretyn at Norwyche vn Seynt Georgys Day.

S*er* John Heueny*n*ham, John Ferrers, Tho*mas* Gurnay, John Groos,
W. Rokewode, John Bakon, sen*ior*, John Bakon, jun*ior*, J. Pagraue, Rob*er*t
Mortim*er*, Nichu*las*¹ Appilyard.¹ 40

¹¹ *Uncertain*; -r- *seems to be written over* d. ¹² þe dere *and interlined to be* canc.
¹³ yow canc. ¹⁴ yowre avise whed*er* if is ples his þa canc. ¹⁵ MS. phese.
¹⁶ his high canc. ¹⁷ ent*e*nt canc. ¹⁸ in writing *and interl.* more clerly canc.
¹⁹ MS. mant*er*. *This is followed by* euer eschewi[n]g of sech sch canc.
²⁰ vs canc. ²¹ go ca*n*c. ²² *and* encress of canc.

42B. ¹ MS. wo.
  ² *Initial* y *throughout this draft in form of* þ. ³ *Interl. in Paston's hand.*
  ⁴ *Interl. in Paston's hand:* if it leke canc. *before* if, *and* he desi canc. *after it.*
  ⁵ *Imperfectly corrected by Paston from scribe's* more. ⁶ *Written* Nichu *and flourish.*
  ⁷ *The names of Pagraue and Mortimer in Paston's hand, the last uncertain, but not in the hand of the main draft.*

C

*Reue*rent *and* right wurchepfull s*er*, we recomaund vs to yow. Please it
yow to wete that we *and* othre jentilmen of the shire of Norff*olk* hath be
in purpose to haue sued to the high *and* myghty prynce *and* owre right
gode lord the Duke of Norff*olk* to Framlyngh*am*, to haue enformyd his
45 Highnesse of diu*ers* assaughtes *and* riottes mad be Charll*es*[1] Nowell *and*
othr*e* a-geyn the Kyng*es* lawe *and* peas w*yth*-ought any cause or occasyon
vp-vn John Paston *and* othr*e* of owr*e* kynne, frend*es*, *and* neghbores,
ne had be that dayly this x days it hath be do vs to wete that his Highnesse
shuld come in-to Norwhich or Claxton, we not beyng in certeyn yet[2]
50 whed*er* he shall remeve; p*ra*yng yow, as we trust that ye wull tender*e*
the welfar*e* of this shire *and* of the jentilmen ther*e*-in, that ye wull lete
owr*e* seid lord haue knowyng of owr*e* entent in this, and after to send vs
answer*e* whed*er* it please his Highnesse we shuld come to his p*re*sens *and*
in what place, or to send owr*e* conpleynt to hym if more enformac*i*on be
55 thought behoffefull; trustyng to his gode lordshep of remedy in this
mater*e*, which do semyth vs shall be to owr*e* seid lord*es* honure *and* gret
reioyng to all the jentilmen of this shir*e*, *and* cause the peas to be kept
her*e*-aft*er* be the g*ra*ce of God, how haue you in his blyssid kepyng.

Wretyn at Norwhich v*n* Seynt Georges Day.

43. Probably to the SHERIFF OF NORFOLK: draft

1452, 23 April

Add. 27444, f. 15ᵛ. See no. 42.

This is a rough draft, the first ten and a half manuscript lines in Paston's hand,
written very untidily with a bad pen and much corrected. The remaining five
and a half lines of text are in Gloys's hand. The direction, in the extreme right
bottom corner, is in Paston's hand; it has faded badly and partly crumbled away.
What remains does not suggest that the critical word was 'sheriff' (or 'shreve');
yet the reference to 'the letters written to you from gentlemen of this shire' implies
that it was intended for the same person as no. 42.
   The date is the same as that of no. 42.
   G. 175/212.

*Reue*rent *and* ryth worsepfull s*er and* my god mast*er*, I recom*m*and me to
yow. Plese yow to wete þat Charlis Nowell, with odir, hath in þis cuntr*é*
mad many riot *and* savtis, *and* amo[n]g ⌜othir ⌝ⁱ he and ⌜v of⌝ his felachip set
vp-on me *and* ⌜to of⌝ my s*er*uant*is* at þe Chathedrall chirch of Norwich,
5 he smyti[n]g at me whilis on of his felaws held myn arm*is* at my bak[2]

42c. ¹ *Written* Charll, -ll *barred as it usually is finally* (*exactly as in* Nowell).
   ² *MS.* that, *which destroys the syntax. The scribe of f. 14 wrote* y *as* þ, *which Gloys
transliterated to* th *in the usual way.*

44. ¹ *Interl. above* mong *canc.*   ² be lyklines *and* ba *canc.*

as the berer herof shall more playnly inform yow; whech[3] was to me
straw[n]ge cas, thi[n]k[i]ng ⌐in⌐ my co[n]seyth þat I was my lord*is* man
and his homagere ⌐or Charlis knew hy[s] lo[r]dschipe[4] *and* þat my lord
was my god lord⌐, þat I had be with my lord at London within viij day⟨s⟩[5]
⌐be⌐-for Lent, at which tyme he[6] grantyd me[7] his godlordship so largely[8] þat[9] 10
⌐it must[10] cause me eu*er* to be his trew s*er*ua[n]t to myn pow[er]⌐. I thowt
also þat I had neu*er* geff cawse to non of my lord*is* hous to ow me evill
will, ne þat þer was no*n* of þe hows but I wold haue do fore as I cowd[11]
desir*e* anima*n* to do for me, *and* yet will,[12] except my adu*er*saré. *And*
þus ⌐I⌐ and my frend*is* haff mwsid[13] of þis, ⌐*and* thowt he was hired to do 15
þus, and þis notwithstandi[n]g⌐, assone as knolech[14] was had of my lord*is*
co*m*ing to Frami[n]gha*m*, neu*er* attemptid to p*ro*cede ageyns him as
justis *and* law wuld, but to trust to my seyd lord þat his Hyghnes wold se
þis punischid,[15] *and* ⌐desirid my mast[er] Howar[d], mi cosin Tymp*er*lé,
þe dene, *and* odir to⌐[16] dayly hath be redy[17] w*ith* such jentilm⟨en⟩[18] as dwelle 20
here-a-bought ⌐that can record the trought to haue come compleyn to
my lord⌐, but we haue had contynually[19] tydyng*is* of my lord*is* comyng
hed*er* that causid vs for to a-bide there-vp-vn, besechyng y*our* gode
mayst*er*shep that ye wull lete my[20] lord haue knowlech of my compleynt,
and that ye wull tender the gode spede of the entent of the letter*is* wretyn 25
to you[21] fro jentilmen of this shire,[22] p*ra*yng you that ye woll ⌐yeve credens
to the berer*e* here-of⌐, be ⌐his⌐ gode mayst*er* in cas any man make any
qwarell to hym.

And what that I may do be y*our* comaundment shall be redi w*ith* the
gr*a*ce of God, how haue you in his blissid kepyng. Wretyn at Norwhich vn 30
Seynt Georg*is* Day.

To my lord þe [?]ch⟨. . .⟩
of þis⟨. . .⟩

---

3 *MS.* whes.

4 *MS.* -schide.

5 *MS.* bay *at edge, which has crumbled slightly.*

6 shew *canc.*

7 *MS.* my.

8 *MS.* lagerly.

9 it gladit mi hert eu*er* thyk on it *canc.*

10 *MS.* mast.

11 *Uncertain*: cow *seems to have been written first, then* d *written over part of* w.

12 *MS.* wilt.

13 *Smudged*; -w- *seems to be written over* y.

14 *MS.* knelech.

15 *MS.* punischichid. *After this* & shuld h *written in Paston's hand, then all but* & *cancelled. Paston's hand ends here except for interlineations.*

16 *This interlined passage is very hard to read, and the text given is to some extent provisional. It does not fit the context as it stands, but it would do so if* dayly hath *were cancelled, as the preceding* shuld h *has been.*

17 for *canc.*

18 *At edge.*

19 such *canc.*

20 gode *canc.*

21 of *canc.*

22 of which And s*er* what I may *canc.*

44. Probably to the SHERIFF OF NORFOLK: draft   1452

Add. 27444, f. 16. $11\frac{1}{2} \times 5\frac{1}{4}$ in. Mostly autograph.

Dorse: No seal or address. The names *Ledam* and *Nowell* written apparently in the hand of f. 14 (no. 42B).

This is another draft in Paston's hand except for the last incomplete sentence, which is by Gloys.

As with no. 43, the reference to 'the letter direct to you from certain gentlemen of this shire' recalls the opening sentence of no. 42. This seems therefore to be a supplementary, or perhaps alternative, draft of the complaint to the sheriff in no. 43, couched in less formal terms.

The date appears from the contents, and from the presence of Gloys as Paston's clerk, to be close to that of nos. 42 and 43.

   G. 176/213.

Ryth worchepfull s*er and* cosyn, I recu*m*mand me to yow [and] pray yow
þat ye will in mi behal⟨f⟩¹ inform my lord of þe deme[n]i[n]g of Charlis
Nowell to me ward, ⌈withow[t] occ[a]ci*un gef on mi p*art, as þe berer
her[of] shal rem[em]b*re yo[w]*⌉.² I am *and* was my lord*is* man *and* homager
5 or þe³ seyd Charlis knew my lord, *and* will do my lord sech s*er*uis as I
can;⁴ *and* þat ye will tendre þe god sped of þe mat*er* of ⌈þe⌉⁵ lett*er* direct⁶
to yow from ⌈serteyn⌉ gentilmen of þes shire, with whech jentilme*n and*⁷
odir ⌈to bere recor[d] of riot rowt*is* I haue be purp⟨osed⟩⌉ dayly⁸ toward
my lord to co*m*pleyn to his lor[d]ship. But þe continuall⁹ tydi[n]g*is* of
10 my seyd lord*is* coming heder hath cawsid vs to awayt þeropon;¹⁰ besech-
i[n]g yow, cosine, as my¹¹ trust is in yow, þat ye will ⌈help to kepe⌉ þe
god rewle of þes shire and my por*e* honestté, *and* geff credens to þe berer
herof *and* be his god mast*er* if any querel be mad to him.¹² And what I
may do for you, I am *and* eu*er* shall be redi to do it, be the grace of God,
15 hoo

44. ¹ *Paper crumbled at edge.*

   ² *The interlined words from* as *onwards are so cramped and confused as to be scarcely legible, and the reading given is tentative. For* shal *the MS. has* shar. *The half-dozen letters following the interlineation are obliterated by over-writing.*

   ³ þe *repeated.*

   ⁴ *Three words, the last two as* he, *canc.*

   ⁵ *Interl. above a canc. word, perhaps* open.

   ⁶ *Abbr.* direc *with stroke above.*

   ⁷ *A word, perhaps* mo, *canc.*

   ⁸ *This passage uncertain. It was first written* I haue dayly be, *of which* I haue *and* be *were cancelled and replaced by the interlined words. These are hastily scribbled and in part doubtful:* riot *was first written with* -h, *over which the* r *of* rowtis *was heavily written;* -is *is an expansion of a tail on* -t. *Whatever the precise forms intended, these appear to be the words meant to be read:* OED *records their association in legal use from 1429 on. Still in the interlined passage* dayly *is canc. after* haue; *of* purp⟨osed⟩ *only* p- *is reasonably clear, but the word may fairly be supplied from the parallel passage in no. 42.*

   ⁹ *Abbr.* cotiall *with strokes above* o *and* ia.

   ¹⁰ pray *canc.*   ¹¹ sengler *canc.*

   ¹² for þis *and perhaps three more letters canc. Paston's hand ends here.*

45. To RICHARD SOUTHWELL: draft   Perhaps 1452, 20 July

Add. 27444, f. 86. $8\frac{3}{8} \times 11\frac{1}{2}$ in. Autograph for a few lines at beginning and end, the rest in the main hand of no. 40, with corrections by Paston.

Dorse: Continuation of text. No seal or address.

This is a rough draft, much corrected, and becomes rougher as it goes on. The alteration of 'yow' to 'Sothwell' in lines 42 and 46 does not mean that Paston changed his mind, in the course of composition, about the person to whom he would send the letter. It comes in a list of 'proofs' evidently designed to be separate from the letter itself—'a bill closed herin' (l. 20).

The year is uncertain. Gairdner notes that it cannot be later than the death of Osbern Mundford, who is mentioned in the penultimate paragraph. He was executed on 25 June 1460 (Scofield, i. 76), so that the latest possible date is 1459. But it is likely to be much earlier. The main hand appears elsewhere only in no. 40, which is certainly of 1452, and in Margaret Paston's letter no. 144, which is probably of the same year—an agreement which, for a hand so seldom found, is probably significant. A like date would fit the reference in the opening sentence to Lee: Southwell and Lee were both in the service of the Duke of Norfolk at Framlingham, but the second sentence of no. 46 says that Lee is out of favour; the present draft is therefore probably earlier than that.

G. 375/440.

Brothir Suthwell, I coma*n*d me to yow, sertifij[n]g yow þat on Thursday be þe morwe I spak with my cosine Wichi[n]gha*m* at London, where he lete me wet of yo*w*r lett*er* sent to Lee, ⌐wherby I⌐¹ conseyve þe stedfast godlordship *and* ladiship of my lord *and* my lady ⌐in þis mater⌐² &c.,³ whech geuith cause to all her s*er*uant*is* to trost verily in þem⁴ *and* to do 5
hem trew s*er*uise.⁵

I lete yow wete that the seyd Wychyngha*m*, whan I dep*ar*tid from hym, had knowleche that Jane Boys shuld that nyght be come to London, and ⌐he⌐⁶ put jn a⁷ bylle to the lordis for to have delyuerauns of hyr ⌐and to haue⌐⁸ hese adu*er*sarys ⌐arestid⌐;⁹ and¹⁰ this nyght at Norwiche was 10
told me newe tydyngg*is* that she shuld vn Thursday ⌐after my dep*ar*ti[n]g⌐⁶ a⁷ be before the lordis, and there a⁷ sa⌐i⌐de ⌐u*n*trewly of her-selff⌐,¹¹ as the berer hereof shal informe yow if ye know⁷ it not before; of wheche tydyngg*is*, if they be trew, I am sory for her sake, and also I fere that¹² her frendys shuld sew the more feyntely, wheche Godde defende;¹³ for 15

---

¹ *Interl. above* be whech he *canc.*   ² *Interl. above* of *canc.*

³ *The following canc.* : wherof I all þat owe to þem her seruise have cause to be wherfor all þer seruant*is* hau cause to do þem trew *and* stedfast s*er*uise *and* verily may trost on þem in all trew mater*is* the I lete yow w*e*te, *and two illegible groups of letters.*

⁴ in all trew *canc.*

⁵ *Paston's hand ends except for interlineations, etc.*

⁶ *Interl. in Paston's hand.*   ⁷ *No space.*

⁸ *Interl. by Paston above* and that *canc.*

⁹ *Interl. by Paston above* myght be arestyd *canc.*   ¹⁰ now sith I *canc.*

¹¹ *Added by Paston,* untrewly *in margin, rest interl.*

¹² Wychyngham *canc.*   ¹³ for my symple avys is *canc.*

her seying vntreuly of her-selff may hurt ⌐þe mat*er* in⌐[16] no man but her-
selff, and thow she wol mescheue her-selff it were gret peté but if the
mat*er* were laborid ⌐forth—not for her sake but for the worchepe of⌐[14]
the estatys and other that have laboryd therin and in ponyshing of the gret
20 oryble dede, wherfore I[15] send yow dyuers articljs ⌐in a bill closed herin⌐[16]
wheche p*re*ue that she was raveshid ayens hyr wel,[16] what so ever she sey.

þes[17] be p*ro*uis that Jane Boys was rauischid[18] ageyn her wil, *and* not
be her[19] own assent:

On is that she, the tyme of her takyng whan she was set upon her hors, she
25 revylid Lancaster*other and* callid hym knave, and ⌐wept *and*⌐[20] kryid
owte upon hym ⌐pitow[s]ly to her⌐,[6] and seid as shrewdly to hym as coud
come to her mende, and fel doune of her hors vnto that she ⌐was⌐[16] bound,
and[21] callid him fals t[r]ayt*ur* þat browth her þe rabbett*is*.

Item, whan she was bounde she callid vpon her mody*re*, wheche folwyd
30 her as far as she myght on her feet, and whan the seid Jane sey she myght
goo no ferther she kryid to her mody*re* and seid that what so ever fel of
her she shuld neu*er* be weddyd to that knave, to deye for it.[22]

Item, be the weye at Shraggarys hous in Kokely Cley, and at Brycheham-
well and in all other places wher she myght see any people, she kryid owte
35 vpon hym and lete people ⌐wete⌐[16] whos dowty*re* she was and how she was
raveshid a-yens her wyll, desyeryng the people to folwe her and reskew
her.[23]

Item, Lancaster*otherys* prest of the Egle in Lyncolne-shire, wheche
⌐shroff⌐[24] her, seid that she told hym in confession that she wold neu*er*
40 be weddyd to hym to deye for it, and the same prest seid he wold not
wedde hem to-gedy*re* fo[r] m[l] li.[25]

Item, ⌐she sent diu*ers*⌐[26] tokenes of massage[27] to ⌐Sothwell be⌐[28] Robert
Inglose, wheche p*re*vith welle at that tyme she louyd not Lancaster*other*.

Item, a man of the master of Carbrokes come dyuers tymes in the[29]
45 weke before she was raveshid to Wychyngh*ams* hous[30] and inquerid of her
mayde whedy*re* her mastras was insuerid to ⌐Sothwell⌐[31] or nay, ⌐the⌐[16]
wheche p*re*uyth well that Lancaster*other*[32] was not sure of her ⌐godwill⌐,[6]

---

[14] *Interl. by Paston above* forthe for *canc.*
[15] avy *canc.*
[16] and þat *and another word interl. by Paston but canc.*
[17] *This heading inserted, preceded by paragraph mark and indented about an inch, by Paston in space left by the scribe.* [18] *MS.* -ig.
[19] *MS.* ber *for* be her. [20] *Interl. by Paston above* all that nong *canc.*
[21] *This and rest of this sentence in Paston's hand.*
[22] Item *in space at end of line.* [23] and proferd *inserted by Paston but canc.*
[24] *Interl. by Paston above a heavily canc. form which may have been* shreve.
[25] *Recto ends. At top of verso* To my, To, me, *apparently pen trials.*
[26] *Interl. by Paston above* remembre yow what *canc.* [27] she sent *canc.*
[28] *Interl. by Paston above* yow be my cosyn *canc.* [29] the *repeated.*
[30] to jnque *canc.* [31] *Interl. by Paston above* yow *canc.*
[32] hese master *canc.*

ne knew not of her counseyl,³³ for if he had he ne nedid not to haue ⌜sent⌝
no spyes.³⁴

⌜Whech seen⌝,³⁵ I avyse yow to move my lord and my lady to ⌜do⌝³⁶ 50
in this mater as affettualy as they have do before, for this mat*er* touchyth
hem, consideryng that they have be-gonne. And ⌜dowt not⌝,³⁷ what so
eu*er* falle of the woman, well or evel, my lord *and* my lady shal have worchep
of the mat*er* if it be wel laborid; *and*³⁸ also ye shall³⁹ auayl þerof⁴⁰ *and* þe
adu*er*s ⌜parte⁴¹ chall⌝ gret trobil. Also, it were necessarie that Wychyngham 55
were sent to and co[n]forted in hese seute, and that he a-vysid hym ⌜of⌝
seche articlis *and* pr*e*ues of the mat*er* as I haue sent to yow *and* put hem
in wr[i]ti[n]g, but not ⌜to⌝ disclose non⁴² þe preues to non creature vnto
the⁴³ tyme that ⌜it fortune þe mater⌝⁴⁴ to be tried be enquest or other wyse
take end; but avyse hym ⌜for to seye to þe lord*is and* all . . .⌝⁴⁵ in gen*er*all 60
term*es* that what so euer*e* Lancaster*other* or hese dout*er* seyn ⌜nowh⌝¹⁶ it
shal be wel pr*e*uyd she was reveshid ayens her wyll, ⌜*and* let him desir*e*
of þe lord*is* þat his dowt*er* mith be in his kepyng and at large fro Lancaster-
other vn-tylle the mater were duly examynd⌝.⁴⁶

I wold ⌜þis mat*er* sped⌝¹⁶ the betyr*e* be-cause my lady ⌜sp⟨a⟩ke⌝⁴⁷ so 65
feythefully ⌜to me⌝ therin, and that mevyth me to wryte to yow this long
symple lettyr*e* of myn jntent.⁴⁸ [Wh*er* ye be informyd that vj men of
Osbern Monforthes shul a⁷ be at the seid raueshing,⁴⁹ I s*er*tifie yow verely it
was not soo, for Osbern Mondeford wol do in the mater all that ever he
can or may⁵⁰ to ⌜help to⌝ punish⁵¹ þe doer, *and* desirith to know þe grownd 70
of þat tale, of wheche I pray send me word,⁵² *and* what ye will ellis.]

God kep yow. Wret at Norwich þe Soneday nex before þe fest of Sent
Margere[t].⁵³

³³ so that they myght werke be asent as *canc.*
³⁴ *From* if *in Paston's hand.*
³⁵ *Interl. by Paston above* W *and incomplete* h *canc.*
³⁶ *Interl. above* labour *canc.*
³⁷ *Interl. by Paston above* doutyd not *canc.*
³⁸ asso as *canc.*
³⁹ *Illegible word in Paston's hand above* haue *canc.*
⁴⁰ *This word and rest of this sentence by Paston.*
⁴¹ *Interl. in place of the ending of* aduersares *canc.*
⁴² he[r] of *canc. From* and *to* creature *by Paston.*
⁴³ that *written in error, not canc.*
⁴⁴ *Interl. by Paston above* come to the ende *canc.*
⁴⁵ *All but* for *by Paston, last word unintelligible.*
⁴⁶ *From* and let him *written vertically in margin, marked for insertion here ; by Paston as far as* kepyng.
⁴⁷ *Interl. above* seide *canc.; third letter obscured by a blot.*
⁴⁸ Also I sertyfye yow *canc. Following sentence cancelled, apparently by Paston, by a loose roughly 8-shaped curve and a few cross-strokes.*
⁴⁹ *Next seven words by Paston.*
⁵⁰ *Clerk's hand ends.*
⁵¹ *MS.* punisd.
⁵² if *canc.*
⁵³ *Last paragraph one MS. line. Below, after space of half an inch, one or two illegible words and under them* chypman. *Then after another space, still in Paston's hand :* Item she had be of hes assent affter þe time she was in hes possesciu*n* in Lynkoln-shire hit had be bett.

46. Memorandum   1452, late

Add. 27444, f. 19. $8\frac{1}{4} \times 11\frac{3}{8}$ in. Mostly in hand of no. 42B, etc., corrections and additions by Paston.

Dorse: Continuation of text. No seal or address.

'The good lord' is the Duke of Norfolk.

The reference to Roger Church and his associates shows this paper to be similar in date to no. 40 and the related documents, but later in the year because it is after harvest. The main scribe's spelling also shows a significant development, for he uses *y-* normally instead of the eccentric þ- characteristic of no. 42B— except in *yere*, l. 8, where he wrote þ and added a tail to make it *y*. On the other hand he uses *-gth* in *rygth*, l. 20, *mygth*, l. 38, whereas letters in his hand datable in 1453 have *-ght* predominantly and *-gth* not at all (see the reference under no. 128).

G. 181/219.

Itt is to remembre vndere hos rule that þe gode lord is at this day, *and* whiche be of his new cownseyll.

Item, that Debenham, Lee, Tymperlé, *and* his old cownseyl *and* attendans, as well as þe gode ladijs servawntys, be avoydyd, and Tymperlé of malys
5 apelyd of treson.

Item, that þe sescionys of þe[1] pees wyth-owte cawse was warnyd in þe myddys of hervest, to grette trobill of the contré, whiche was nevere se in Norffolk at seche tym of the yere;[2] *and* itt was vnlawfully warnyd to appere wyth-inne iiij or v days aftere þe warnyng, howbeitt þe contré was before
10 warnyd at þe shyere ⌐day⌐ to have had þe sescionys the Tewysday before Michelmes.

Item, þat at þe seid sescionys was non othere cawse of[3] settyng thereof declaryd but a[4] commysyon beryng dat before Estern, &c., to arest, take, *and* expungne traytorys *and* rebellys, of which be Goddis grace is no
15 nede in this contré at þis tyme, &c.[5]

Item, ⌐be⌐ þe demenyng of þe seyd sescionys was verily conseyvid be þe jantylmen of þe shyere ⌐þat it was set⌐[6] of purpose to have be indytementys defowlyd seche personys as were of þe old cownseyl wyth þe seid lord, and seche as kepe Wodhows lond, or seche as help or confort Osbern
20 Munford, Marchale of Kalys, in his rygth of the manere of Brayston, of whiche he is now late wrongfully dyssesyd; and generally to have hurt all othere that wold not folwe þe oppynyons of þe seyd new cownseyll,[7] &c., whiche malysiows purposid oppynyon þe jantylmen of þe seyd shyere þat were sworyn att þe seyd sescions ⌐kowd not fynde in her conciens

46. [1] pese *canc.*   [2] y- *from* þ.   [3] syttyng *canc.*   [4] *No space.*
  [5] *Last four words are in Paston's hand.*
  [6] *Interl. by Paston above* do *canc.*
  [7] whiche oppynyonys be not good *canc.*

to[18] observe, but dede þe contrarye as it apperyth be here verdyte if itt be 25
shewed,[9] &c. Remembre þe verdyt of Brayston, &c.

And where on Rogere Chirche, wyth on Robert Ledham, Charlys
Nowell, John son of Hodge Ratcleff, and on Robert Dallyng had þe rewle
and kepyng of þe seyd manere of Brayston to the vse of Thomas Danyell
aftere þe dyssesing of þe seyd Osbern Monford, the seyd Rogere, be þe[10] 30
comon ascent of his seyd felashep, be þe colowre of xv personys[11] gadderid
be þe exitacion of þe seyd Rogere Chyrche and his felashep, accusid many
notable and thryfty men that were ⌜well willid to þe seyd Munford⌝[12] for
þe seid maner of Brayston to be ryseris, where as þe seyd ⌜thrifti⌝[13] men
aswell as all þat contré hath at all tymys be pesyble and ⌜of⌝ non seche 35
disp[o]sicion.

It[14] was purposid after þe seid sescions, whan þe intentys of þe seyd new
cownseyl mygth not be executyd be indytementys, than to have had þe
seyd Roger Chirche owte of þe Kyngys gayle, seying þat he shuld appele
for þe Kyng, and wold have do þe sheryff delyverid hym owte of preson 40
howbeit he was comyttyd thiddere be þe justyse of assyse and gayl delyveré
be-cawse he was indytyd of fellonye and þat þer apperid not suffycient
inquest to delyuer hym.

Item, Day seth ⌜þey⌝ labour feynid materis to hurt jentilmen and odir
be soch acusementis, &c.[15] 45

Memorandum, as itt ⌜semyth be þe confescion⌝[16] of dyvers of þe seid xv
personys þat þei were innocent and knew not whi þei assemelyd but only
be þe excitacion of þe seyd Chirche and his menys, and after þe tym[17] þat
þey conseyvid itt was do to no good intent þei neuer ⌜medillid forþer in þe
mater⌝.[18] 50

Item, to remembre how suttely þe seyd Chirche was be his owyn assent
led to my lord of Norffolk be his owyn felashep, to þe entent to accuse
and defame seche as they lovyd nott.

Memorandum of þe sescion at Norwich. Memorandum of my lord of
Somerset and of þe Blakfrers.[19] 55

Item, to remembre þat Charlys Nowell is baly of Brayston and hath there ij
d. on þe day, and ⌜of⌝[20] þat matere growyth his malys.

---

[8] *Interl. by Paston above* wold in nowyse *canc.*
[9] *Rest of this paragraph by Paston.*   [10] *From* þere.
[11] of wech þe more part were inosent men *interl. by Paston, canc.*
[12] *Interl. by Paston above* contrary to there oppynyon As *canc. Also interl. by Paston, but
canc., is* of þe seyd Chirch and his felechip as, *to suit which the preceding* there *was corrected
to* the.
[13] *Interl. by Paston.*   [14] *Cross-stroke curled as if for* Item.
[15] *This paragraph (one line inserted at the foot of the page) in Paston's hand.*
[16] *Interl. by Paston above* apperyth be ȝe, *and another word confused by over-writing, canc.*
[17] of *canc.*
[18] *Interl. by Paston above* come thidder aftere *canc.*
[19] *This paragraph (one line) in Paston's hand.*   [20] *Interl. above* for *canc.*

Item, *Memorandum* of them[21] that for[22] fer of disclosid of her false-
nes acusid odyr þat þey shuld ⌜not⌝ be thowth gilti hemselff, *and* labour
60 to haue þe matere handlid be her frend, þat þe trowth shuld not be trijd
owt.

47. To JOHN NORWODE   Not before 1453

Add. 27444, f. 20. 9 × 7¾ in. Mostly in Gloys's hand, additions and signature by Paston.

Dorse: Traces of red wax. Address in Paston's hand:

To John Norwode.

Also endorsed is a series of notes in Latin, in Paston's hand, of payments made to
Hach by Paston, Tolle, Howes, and Norwode. The first three items are headed
A° xxx (which was written *xxxj* but corrected), the last *A° xxxj*. From this it is
clear that 30 Henry VI was past, and 31 at any rate well advanced if not also past.
31 Henry VI was 1 September 1452–31 August 1453.
    G. 186/225.

I lete you wete that Hache hath do no werk of myn where-⌜fore⌝ he aught
to haue receyvid any mony savyng only for the makyng of the litill hous
a-bove the halle wyndownes, for the remenaunte was that fell down in his
diffaute. And as for the makyng of that litill hous, he toke that in a come-
5 naunte *with* makyng of[1] too chymnyes of S*er* Thom*a*s Howys for xl s.,
which comenaunte may not hold be-cause that I must haue thre chymnyes
and in a-nothere place.

Item, the seid litill hows drawyth not v thowsand tyle, which aft*er* xvj
d. the thowsand shuld drawe vj s. viij d. Notwithstandyng, if S*er* Thomas
10 thynk that he shuld be a-lowyd m⟨o⟩,[2] he shall be. And[3] ye must remembre[4]
how that he[5] hath receyvid vj s. viij d. of you, and[6] of Robert Tolle be-fore
Halwemesse, as apperith in his accompt, ⌜viij s.⌝[7] And[8] he hath receyvid
of Tolle sith Halwemesse ⌜v s. iiij d.⌝[9] And than be this rekenyng he
shuld be ⌜xiij s. iiij d.⌝[10] a-fore hand, which I wuld ye shuld gadere vp
15 in this newe werk as wele as ye myght, for I am be-hold to do hym but
litill favo*ur*.[11]

---

[21] *Here the main scribe ends; that for* by Gloys, *the following evidently by Paston, though
the last two MS. lines (from* acusid*) are more upright and legible than most of his corrections.*
[22] *Three or four words, very faint, canc.; for repeated.*

47. [1] the *canc.*
  [2] *Paper crumbled at edge; mo is Gairdner's reading.*
  [3] *Interl. above* but *canc.*   [4] in this newe werk *canc.*
  [5] for the seid ⌜werk⌝ nobill *canc.*   [6] viij s. *canc.*
  [7] *Interl. by Paston.*   [8] what *canc.*
  [9] *Interl. above* Tolle can telle you I suppose it is x s. *canc.*
  [10] *Interl. above* xviij s. *canc.*
  [11] *Rest of letter and signature in Paston's hand.*

It*em*, be war*e* þer leve no firsis[12] in þe deke þat ye rep*are*, *and* þat þe wode be mad of fagot *and* leyd vp forthwith[13] as it is fellid for tak*in*g away. I wold ye wer*e* her on Satirday at euy[n] thow ye red ageyn on Moneday.

J O N P A S T O N

48. Petition: draft   Probably 1454

Add. Charter 16545. $11\frac{1}{2} \times c.38\frac{1}{2}$ in. (two and a half sheets stitched together). Hand unidentified; some corrections in a different hand.

Dorse: Blank except for *Robertus Ledam* in another hand, and a note by Blomefield.

This document is concerned largely with the same events as no. 40, but is considerably later because Philip Berney is reported to have died partly as a result of his injuries (l. 51), and his death can be firmly dated 2 July 1453 (see Agnes Paston's letter no. 26). Since his death is not spoken of as if it were very recent, 'the v day of Novembre last past' seems likely to be November 1453. If the lord addressed in the final paragraph is the Duke of York, as appears probable, Gairdner was doubtless right in believing that the paper was probably drawn up in 1454, after York had been made Protector (27 March).

As with no. 41, there is no direct evidence in this paper of Paston's part in its composition, though he is mentioned twice in it. But much of it follows no. 40 so closely, even to details of expression, that it must have been based in part upon that or a related draft. (The variations in spelling in different parts of the text suggest that it may in fact have been compiled from preliminary notes in more than one hand.)

G. 201/241.

Thees be the p*er*sons that enformyd the justicez of the Kyngis Benche the last terme of suche ryottis as hath be don be Rob*er*t Ledh*a*m: the Lord Skales, S*er* Thom*a*s Todenh*a*m, S*er* John Chalers, Edmond Clere, Water*e* George, John Alyngton, Gilbert Debenh*a*m, John Denston, Will*i*am Whit, William Alyngton, Reynald Rows, John Berney, Ric*hard* 5 Suthwell, John Paston, John Henyngh*a*m, Raff Shelton, Henry Grey.

These be the names of the knyghtes and esquyers that endittyd Rob*er*t Ledh*a*m: Thom*a*s Todenh*a*m, knyght, Androw Ogard, knyght, John Heny[n]gh*a*m, knyght, William Calthorp, esquyer*e*, Bryan Stapelton, esquyer*e*, Osbert Mondford, esquyer, John Groos, esquyer*e*, William 10 Rokwod, esquyer*e*, Thomas ⌐Morlé⌐,[1] esquyer*e*, Thom*a*s Sholdh*a*m, esquyer*e*, John Wyndh*a*m, esquyer*e*, John Berney, esquyer*e*, William Narbow, esquyer*e*, John Chippysby, esquyer*e*, William ⌐White⌐,[2] esquyer*e*, John Bryston, esquyer*e*, John Paston, esquyer*e*.

---

[12] mo *canc.*   [13] *MS.* -woth.

48. [1] *Interl. in different hand and ink above* Mole *canc.*
[2] *Interl. above* With *canc.*

15   These be dyvers of the ryottis and offensis don in the hundred of
Blofeld in the counté of[3] Norffolk, and in other townys, be Robert Lethum,
otherwyse callyd Robert Ledham, of Wytton be Blofeld in the counté of
Norffolk, and by his ryottys men and by othere of his affinitéz and knowleche, whos names folowyn, and that they contynually folow and ressorte
20 vnto his hous and ther be supported and maynteynet and confortid.

These be the principall menealle men of the sayd Robert Ledham ys
hous be the whiche[4] the sayd ryottys haue be don, that vse in substaunce
non oþer occupacion but ryottys: In primis, ⌜John⌝[5] Cokett, Thomas Bury,
Thomas Cokowe, Cristofere Bradlee, Elys Dukworth, William Donmowe,
25 Cristofere Grenesheve, Rogere Chirche. Notwythstondyng the sayd Robert
Ledham kypith dayly many mo in his house and ⌜chaungeth⌝[6] suche as
haue be opponly knowyn for riottis and takith oþer for hem as evill as
they. And these be the moost principale persons comyng and resortyng
vnto the house of the sayd Robert Ledham, and ⟨t⟩her[7] be supportid and
30 mayntened in ryottis, be whom the sayd ryottes haue be don, that ys to
sey: In primis, Robert Taillour, Henry Bang, Robert Dallyng, John
Beston, Charles Navell, John the sone of Rogere Ratclyff, Robert Berton;
notwythstondyng ther be money moo whos names ben vnknowyn. With
the which persons and many moo vnknowyn the sayd Robert Ledham
35 kept atte his hous in maner of ⌜a forcelet⌝[8] and issith ouute atte here
pleaysoure and atte his lust the sayd Ledham to assigne; somtyme vj and
somtyme xij, somtyme xxxti and moo, armyd, jakkid, and salettyd, with
bowys and arrowys, speris, billys, and over-ryde the countrey and oppressid
the Kyng[is] peple, and didde mony[9] oryble and abhomynable dedes like
40 to haue be destruccion of the enhabitantes in the sayd hundred, in the
forme that folowyth, and warse:

In primis, on the Monday next before Ester Day and the shire day, the
xxx yere of oure souerayne lord the Kyng, x persons of the sayd riottours,[10]
with a brothere of the wyff of the sayd Robert Lethum, laye in awayte
45 in the hyght way vnder Thorpe wode vppon Phillip Berney, esquyere,
and his man comyng from the shire, and shette atte hym and smote the
hors of the sayd Phillipp with arowes, and than over-rode hym and toke
hym and bette hym and spoillid hym. And for thayr excuse of this ryot
they ledde hym to the[11] Bysshopp ⌜of Norwiche⌝, axyng severté of the
50 pees, wher they hadde never waraunt hym to areste. Which affray shorttyd
the lyffdayes of the sayd Phillippe, whiche dyed withynne shorte tyme after
the said affray.

---

3 Norff canc.

4 they and oþer of canc.

5 Interl. in second hand above Robert canc.

6 Interl. above cherith canc.

7 First letter lost at hole.

8 Interl. in second hand above affrutoure canc.; no space after a.

9 ory canc.

10 Altered from riottes.

11 sayd lord the canc. The interlineation by the second hand.

Item, iij of the sayd riottys feloshipp, the same day, yere, and place, laye on awayte vppon Edmond Broune, gentilman, and with naked swerdes and oþer wepyng faght wyth hym be the space of on quarte[12] of an houre, 55 and toke and spoillyd hym, and kepte[13] hym as long as them lyst and after that lette hym goo.

Item, xl[ti] of the sayd riottys felowshipp, be the comaundement of the same Robert Lethum, jakket and saletted, with bowes, arowys, billys, and gleyves, oppon Mauyndy Thursday atte iiij of the clokke atte affter noune, 60 the same yere, comyn to the White Freres in Norwyche and wold haue brokyn thayre yates and dorys, feynyng ⌜thaym⌝ that they wold hire thayre eveson; where they ware aunswered suche seruice was non vsed to be there, nor with-yn the sayd citee, atte that tyme of the daye, and prayd them to departe. And they aunswered and sayd that affore thayre 65 departyng they wold haue some persons ouute of that place qwykke or dede, in somoch the sayd freris were fayn to kype thaire place with forsse. And the mayre and the sheriffs of the sayd cité were fayn to arere a powere to resyst the sayd riottis, which to hem on that holy tyme was tediose and heynous, consedryng the losse and lettyng of the holy seruice of that 70 holy nyght. And theroppon the sayd ryotours departid.

Item, the sayd Robert Lethum, on the Monday nest after Esterne Day the same yere, toke from on John Wilton iiij neet for rent arere, as he said—[14]and killid hem and layd them in salte and afterward ete hem.

Item, the sayd Robert Lethum, with vj of his sayd ryottis, the same yere 75 made assaute vppon John Wilton in Plumstede churche-yerde and theer so bete hym that he was in doute of his lyff; and also dede to hym many grete wronggys and oppression, vnto the vndoyng of the sayd John Wilton.

Item, in lyke wyse the sayd Robert Lethum and his men assauted on 80 John Coke of Witton, in brekyng vppe his dorys atte a xj of the cloke[15] in the nyght; and wyth thaire swerdys maymed hym and gaff hym vij grete wondys, and toke from hym certayn goodys and catalls,[16] of the whiche he hadde, nor yitte hath, no remedy nor restitution.

Item, the same day and yere they bete the moder of the same John Coke, 85 she beyng[17] iiij[xx] yere of age and more, and smote hure vppon the crowne of here ⌜hed⌝ with a swerd; of the whiche hurte she myght never be helyd into the day of hure deth.

Item, John the sone of Hodge Rat[c]leff, and oþer of the sayd felowshipp, toke on Thomas Baret of Byrly[n]gham out of his house, and bete hym 90 and wondid hym that he kept his bedde a month, and toke from hym certayn goodes and catells.

12 *MS.* qaurte.
14 *Space, filled with three dashes.*
16 of all that he hadd *canc.*
13 and k *canc.*
15 atte *canc.*
17 of age *canc.*

Item, the sayd Robert Taillour, be-cause the sayd Thomas Baret com-
playned of the same betyng, lay in awayte oppon hym, with oþer of his
95 feloushipp, and bete hym agayn.

Item, John Beston and the sayd Robert Taillour, and oþer of the sayd
riottis felowshipp, toke on Thomas Byrden[18] of Lyngewod and bete hym
and prisoned hym till vnto suche tyme that he was delyuered by the mene
of my lord of Norwych;[19] and for that sorow, distres, and grete payne ⸢and
100 betyng⸣ the sayd Thomas Byrden[18] toke suche syknesse[20] that he dyed.

Item, the sayd Robert Dallyng and Herry Bange,[18] and oþer of the sayd
felowshipp, toke and bete on Nicholas Chirche atte Strumpeshawe, beyng
in the church of the same towne, that he was[21] dout of his lyff.

Item, the sayd Robert Dallyng lay on awayt vppon on Thomas Dallyng
105 and hym grevously bete.

Item, on Middleynt Sunday the xxx[ti] yere of oure soueraigne lorde the
Kyng that now ys, Robert Dallyng, Robert Churche, Robert Taillour,
Herry Bang, Adam atte More, with other vnknowyn, be the comaundement and assent of the sayd Robert Ledham, made affray vppon Herry
110 Smyth and Thomas Chambre atte Suthbirly[n]gham, the sayd Herry
and Thomas at[22] that tyme knelyng to see the vsyng of the masse, and
than and there wold haue kyllyd the sayd Herry and Thomas atte the
prestys bakke, ne had they be lettyd.

Item, the sayd Robert Lethum, with his sayd ryottis felawshipp, the
115 same yere dide and made so many ryottis in the hundred where he dwellyth
that dyuers and many gentilmen, frankeleyns, and good men durst not
abyde in here mansyon place ne ryde noþer walke[23] aboute thaire occupa-
cions without mo persons arrayd in maner and forme of werre attendyng
and waytyng vppon them[24] than thayr lyvelode wold extende to fynde hem.
120 And so, for sauacion of thaire lyves and in eschewyng[25] of suche inordinat
costys as neuer was seen in that countrey befor,[26] many of them forsoke
and leffte thare owyn habitacion, wyff and childe, and drewe to forteresses
and good townes as for that tyme: in primis, Phillipp Berney, esquyer,
Edmond Broom to Castre; Thomas Hollere, John Wylton to Norwych;
125 Oliuere Kubyte to Seynt Benettis; Robert Spany to Aylesham, Thomas
Baret with many othere to Meche Yermouth and to oþer placys of strenght.

Item, the sayd Robert Ledham, contynuyng in this wyse, callyd vnto
hym his sayd mysgoverned felowshipp, consydryng the absence of many
of the well-rewlyd people of the sayd hundred of affere[27]-cast malice, and
130 congected, purposed, ⸢and⸣ labored to the sheriff of the shire that the
sayd Rogere Chirche, on of the sayd riottous felawshipp, was made bailly

---

[18] *Surname inserted later in space first left blank.*   [19] no *canc.*
[20] *MS.* kynesse   [21] *No gap; cf. no. 40, l. 57.*   [22] *MS.* and.
[23] aboute *canc.*   [24] vnto costys them to pay and *canc.*
[25] an *canc.*   [26] and *canc.*
[27] *Perhaps an error for* affore; *but perhaps a modified form; cf. no. 40 l. 79.*

of the hundred, and affter causid the same Rogger to be begynnere of
arysyng and to take oppon hym to be a captayn, and to excite the peple
of the countrey þerto; and ther-oppon, be covyne of the sayd Robert
Ledham,[28] to appeche all these sayd well-rewlyd persons ⌜and⌝ aswell 135
oþer diuers substanciall men of good fame and good gouernaunce that were
hated be the sayd Robert Ledham,[28] and promittyng the sayd Rogger
harmeles and to sew his pardon be the mene of Danyell. To the which
promyse the sayd Roggere aggreed, and was arested and take be the sayd
Ledham be covyne betwixt hem, and appeched suche persons as they lust 140
to the entente that the sayd substanciall men of the countré shuld be by
that mene[29] so trowblyd and indaungered that they shuld not be of powere
to lette and resist the mys-rewle of the sayd Ledham and his mysgouerned
felawshipp; the whiche mater ys confessid by the sayd ⌜Roger⌝[30] Chirch.

Item, William Berton and John Berton and othere of the sayd ryottis 145
come into the place of on Robert Spany of Poswyke and ⌜serched⌝[31] his
housez, hous be hous, for to haue bete hym yf they myght haue founde
hym.

Item, William Donmowe, seruaunt of the sayd Robert Ledham, and by
his comaundement, the same yere bete the parson of Hashyngham and 150
brake his hede in his owyn chauncell.[32]

Item, the sayd Thomas Bery, Elys Dukworth, Thomas Cukowe, George
of Chamer, the v day of Novembre last past, with diuers oþer onknowyn
men onto the nombre of xx persons, and noman of reputacion among hem,
come[33] vndur colour of huntyng and brake vppe gatys and closys of 155
Osburne Monford atte Brayston. And xij persons of the same felowshipp,
with bowys bent and arowys redy in thaire handys, abode alone be-twixt
the manere of Brayston and the chirche, and there kept hem from vij of
the clokke on þe mornyng vnto iij of the clokk after none, lyyng in awayte
oppon the seruauntez of the sayd Osburne Monford, lorde of the sayd 160
maner, so that nonne durst come[33] ouut for doute of thaire lyves.

Item, viij of the sayd felowshipp, on the Wennesday next affter, prevely
in an hole layn in awayte oppon William Eworth *and* Robert Camplyon,
seruauntz to the sayd Osburn Montford, comyng from Okyll market,
till that tyme that the said William Owell[34] *and* Robert come vppon hem 165
onwarre, and theruppon chasid hem so that yf they had not be well
horssyd and well askapped they had ben dede and slayne.

Item, vj or vij of the sayd Ledamys men dayly, boyth workeday and
haly day, vse to goo aboute in the countrey with bowys and arowys,

---

[28] *Name first written* Lethum, *then* -t- *changed to* d *and superior* a *added above* -u-.
[29] be *canc.*   [30] *Interl. above* Robert *canc.*
[31] *Interl. above* sechild *canc.*   [32] whiche was therfore *canc.*
[33] *Stroke above entire word, which might mean doubling of* -m- *or addition of* -n, *but since this scribe affects otiose flourishes is probably meaningless.*
[34] *So MS., despite* Eworth *above.*

170 shotyng *and* playng in mennys closis among men[nys][35] catall,[36] goyng
from alhous to alhousez and manassyng suche as they hated, and soght
occasion and quarels and debate.

Item, notwithstandyng that all the lyvelod that the sayd Ledham hath
passith not xx li., be-sydes the rep*ar*acion *and* outchargez, and that he
175 hath no connyng ne trew mene of getyng of any good in this countré as
fer[37] as any man may conceyve, and yette kypith in his house dayly xx men,
besydes women and gret multitude of suche mysgoverned peple as ben
resortyng to hym, as ys aboue sayd, to the whiche he yevith clothyng, and
yitte bysyde that he yevith to oþer men that be not dwellyng in his house-
180 hold. And of the said xx men ther passith not viij that vse occupacion
of husbondrye; and all they that vse husbondrye, as well as oþer, be
jakked and salettid redy for to werre, ⌐which ⌐[38] yn this countrey ys thoght
ryght st*r*ange, and ys verely so conceyved that he may not kepe this
counten*au*nce be no good menes.

185 Item, the sayd Ledh*a*m hath a *supersedias* oute of the Ch*au*ncerie for
hym and diu*er*s of hys men, that no warant of justi*c*e of pees may be
s*er*ued agayn hem.

Item, please vnto yo*ur* lordshipp to remembre that the sayd Ledham and
his sayd mysgoverned feloushipp be endited of many of these articles, and
190 of many moo not comp*r*ehendit here, and in especiall of the sayd rysyng
agayn the Kyng. Wherfore, though the sayd Ledh*a*m can[39] p*r*ove the sayd
enditement of treson voyde in the lawe for symplenesse of them that gaffe
the verdit, that it lyke you, for the Kyng*is* availl, not redely to suffre the
sayd Ledham to dep*ar*te atte large vnto the tyme that the mat*er* of the sayd
195 enditement be bett*er* enquered of for the Kyng*is* avayll, and that the sayd
Ledham fynde surté of his good aberyng. And the inhabyt*au*ntz of the
sayd hundred of Blofeld shall p*r*ay for you; and els they be lyke to be
destruyd for eu*er*.

49. To the EARL OF OXFORD   1454, 31 March

Add. 27444, f. 25. 12×6⅝ in. Gloys's hand.

Dorse: Marks of folding; no seal or address.

This looks like a fair copy, but does not seem to have been sent.
    The date appears from a letter to Paston from Thomas Denyes which was
clearly the occasion of the present appeal (see Part II, no. 491). Denyes's letter
reports the death of Cardinal Kemp, which occurred on 22 March 1454.
    G. 200/240.

Right wurchepfull *and* my right especiall lord, I recomaund me to yow*re*

---

[35] *No gap; but inflexion seems essential.*   [36] a *canc.*   [37] *MS.* for.
[38] *Interl. above* wyth *canc.*   [39] *Stroke above entire word, of doubtful meaning.*

gode lordshep, besechyng youre lordshep that ye take not to displesauns thow I write you as I here sey: that Agnes Denyes, be the meanes of your lordshep *and* of my lord the Cardynall, hos sowle God assoyle *and* for-geve,[1] was set in preson beyng with child; which, *and* the sorough *and* shame there-of, was nygh here deth, *and* yet dayly is vexed *and* trobled, *and* here seruauntes in like wyse, to the vttermest distruccion of here person *and* godes. In which, my lord, at the reuerens of God, remembre that she was maried be you, *and* be my meanes be your comaundment *and* writyng, *and* drow there-to full sore a-geyn here[2] entent in the be-gynnyng, *and* was worth v c marc. *and* better, *and* shuld haue had a gentilman of this contré of an c marc. of lond *and* wele born, ne had be your gode lordshep *and* writyng to here *and* me. *And* this considered in your wise discrecion, I trost, my lord, thow here prisonyng were of oderes labore ye wuld help here; *and* if she be distroyd be this mariage my conscyens thynketh I am bownd to recompense here after my pore *and* sympill power.

My lord, ye know I had[3] litill cause to do for Thomas Denyes, savyng only for your gode lordshep. Also, my lord, I know wele that Watere Ingham was bete, the matere hangyng in myn a-ward, right fowle *and* shamefully; *and* also how the seid Thomas Denyes hath this last terme, a-geyn your nobill estat, right vn-wysely demened hym to his shame *and* grettest rebuke that euer he had in his lyve; where-fore it is right wele do his person be ponysshed as it pleaseth you. But this not withstondyng, for Goddes loue, my lord, remembre how the gentilwoman is accombred only for yowre sake, *and* help here; *and* if aught lyth in my powere to do that that myght please yowre lordshep, or cowde fynde any wey for Water Ingham a-vayll *and* wurchep, I wull do it to my powere, and the rathere if your lordshep support the jentilwoman, for I know the matere *and* that longe plee is litill a-vayll, *and* euery thing must haue an ende.

I haue told my brothere Mathew Drury more to enfourme yowre lord-shep than I may haue leysere to write for his hasty departyng.

Right wurchepfull *and* my right especiall lord, I besech Allmyghty God send you asmych joy *and* wurchep as euer had any of my lordes yowre aunceteres, *and* kepe you *and* all yowres. Wretyn at Norwich the iiij Sonday of Lent.

Yowre seruaunte to his powre, JOHN PASTON

---

49. [1] hym *canc.*   [2] wille *canc.*   [3] lil *canc.*

50. To LORD GREY: draft   1454, 15 July

Add. 34888, f. 104. $11\frac{3}{4} \times 5$ in. Draft in hand of no. 42B etc., corrections by Paston.

Dorse: No seal or address. Between punctuation marks, probably in the same clerk's hand,

Dominus de Grey.

The date depends on that of a letter to Paston from Lord Grey to which this is an answer (see Part II, no. 499). A note in Paston's hand at the foot of Grey's letter records its receipt on 14 July 32 Henry VI (1454). Cf. also William Paston II's letter no. 84.

F. iii, p. 216. G. 210/252.

Right worshipfull *and* my ryght gode lord, I reco*m*mand me to yowre godelordship; and where as it pleasyd yowre lordship to dyrecte yowr lettere to me for a¹ maryage fore my pore suster to a jantylman² of yowre ⌐knowlech¬³ of ccc marc. lyflod in cas she were not maryd, wherfore I am
5 gretely bownd to do your lordship servyse, forsoþe my¹ lord she is ⌐not¬⁴ marijd ⌐ne jnsurid¬⁵ to noman. Ther is, *and* hath be⁶ dyvers tymys ⌐and late¬⁵ comunycacion of seche maryagys wyth dyuers jantylmen not deter-mynyd as yett; and wheddere the jantylman þat yowre lordchip menith of ⌐be on of hem¬ or nay I dowth. And ⌐where¬⁷ as your seyd lettere specyfyith that I shuld send yow word wheddere I thowght ye shuld
10 labour ferthere in the matere or nay, in that, my lord, I dare not preswme to wryte so to yow wythowte I knew the gentylmans name.

Notwythstandy*n*g, my lord, I shall take uppe-on me, wyth the avyse of othere of here frendys, that she shall nothere be marijd ner inswryd to no creatwre, ne forthere *pro*sede in no seche matere, before the fest of the Assu*m*pcion of Owre Lady next comy*n*g; dwry*n*g whyche tyme yowre
15 lordship may send me, if itt please yow, certeyn informaci*o*n of the seyd gentylma*n*nys name, *and* of the place *and* contrey where hys lyfflod lyth, *and* wheddere he hath ⌐any¬⁵ chyldere. And ⌐after¬⁸ I shall demene me in the matere as yowre lordship shall be pleasyd. ⌐For¬ jn¹ gode¹ feyth, my lord, it were to me grette joy that my seyd pore sustere were,
20 ⌐acordi[n]g to her pore degré¬,⁵ marijd be yowre avyse, trusty*n*g thanne that ye wold be here gode lord.

Ryght wurchipfull *and* my ryght gode lord, I beseche Almyghty God to haue yow in his kepy*n*g. Wrete att Norwych the xv day of Jull.

50. ¹ *No space.*   ² *of c marc. lyfflod canc.*
³ *Interl. in Paston's hand above* aqueyntans *canc.*
⁴ *Interl. by Paston above* nothere *canc.*
⁵ *Interl. by Paston.*   ⁶ late *and canc.*
⁷ *Interl. above* also *canc.*
⁸ *Interl. by Paston above* that do *canc.*

51. To the DUKE OF NORFOLK: draft   Probably 1455

Add. 27444, f. 33. 11⅝ × 5¾ in. Draft loosely written in hand of no. 42B, etc., corrections by Paston.

Dorse: No seal or address. Notes, apparently of rents of manors belonging to Sir John Fastolf, in Paston's hand.

The date appears from the dealings in the wardship of Fastolf of Cowhaugh's heir. John Paston and Thomas Howes were granted the wardship on 6 June 32 Henry VI (1454) (*Rot. Parl.* v. 371). A letter from Sir John Fastolf to the Duke concerning the same dispute is dated 2 April, evidently of 1455 (G. 234/278), so that the present draft is probably to be placed early in the same year. It seems to have been drafted by Paston for Sir John Fastolf to send.

     G. 233/277.

Right hy *and* myghty prynce, my right gode *and* gracyous lord, I recomand[1] me to yo*ur* godelordship, &c.; *and* please itt yo*ur* Hyghnesse to wete þat S*er* Philip Wentewurth[2] p*ur*chasid þe Kyng*is* patentis of the ward of the ⸢heyere *and*⸣ londes ⸢of⸣[3] a[4] pore kynnesman of myne[5] called John Fastolf of Cowhawe, ⸢late passed to God⸣, to þe grett hurte ⸢*and* distrucion[6] as- 5 well⸣ of þe inheritance of þe seyd heyer ⸢as⸣[7] int*er*rupcion *and* brekin*g* of the last will of the seyd John, *and* also to my grett troble *and* dammage. *And* for asmeche as it fortowned ⸢be grase⸣[8] the seyd patentes to be mystake so þat they ⸢were⸣[9] not laufull ne suffycyent,[10] be avyce of conceyll certeyn p*er*sones to myn vse p*ur*chesid be the Kyng*is* lett*er*es patentes 10 suffycyent *and* laufull of the ward of the seyd londes,[11] *and* the ⸢rigth of these bothe pate*nt*is⸣[12] hath be putte in ⸢juges *and*⸣[13] lerned men,[14] affor hom the seyd S*er* Philipp ne his conceyll cowd neu*er* ⸢prove hes tytill lawfull be his seyd pat[enti]s⸣;[15] *and* þis notw*yth*standin*g*, intendith ⸢be fors, as I vnderstand,⸣[16] to take þe profytes ⸢of þe seyd lond*is*⸣[17] ageyns 15 all lawe *and* concyence; besechin*g* yo*ur* lordchip to tender ⸢me in⸣[18] myn age *and* sekenesse þat[19] may not ryde ne help myself,[20] *and* of yo*ur* habundant grace to supporte me in my right þat I be not be fors, ageyns lawe *and*

---

51.   [1] *to* canc.   [2] *late* canc.
[3] *Interl. above* that late wer *canc.*
[4] *No space.*   [5] *late* canc.
[6] *and* dammage *canc.*
[7] *Interl. in Paston's hand above ampersand canc.*
[8] *Interl. by Paston; following* that *canc.*
[9] *Interl. by Paston above* be *canc.*
[10] I dede s*er*teyn p*er*sones *canc.*
[11] of whiche mat*er* canc.
[12] *Interl. by Paston above* this mat*er*, *of which* this *is corrected to* the *and* mat*er* canc.
[13] *Interl. above* dyuers *canc.*   [14] *and* juges *canc.*
[15] *Interl. by Paston above* shew laufull tytell *canc.*
[16] *Interl. by Paston, except* be fors.   [17] *Interl. by Paston.*
[18] *Interl. by Paston;* my *in also interl. but canc.*
[19] causeth me þat I *canc.*   [20] in my right *canc.*

concyence, kepte from²¹ þe possescion of þe seyd londes in this contré
wher ye be prynce *and* souereyn next owre souereyn lord.²²

52. To JAMES GLOYS: draft   Probably 1455, 25 July

Add. 27444, f. 36. 11½ × 5¾ in. Draft in hand of no. 42B, etc.; corrections
by Paston.

Dorse blank.

This answers a letter from Gloys dated the same day, reporting rumours that
Paston and Yelverton intended to 'put in to the parlement a bille of diuers tresons
don be my lord of Norwich, Ser Thomas Tudenham, and John Heydon' (Part II,
no. 532). There is no satisfactory evidence of date. Most of the complaints against
Tuddenham and Heydon belong to 1461, but Paston was in London in July of
that year (see nos. 159–62). It cannot be later, for Tuddenham was put to death
in February 1462. Gairdner suggested with great probability that the only July
during the later years of Henry VI's reign in which an intention to impeach such
influential Lancastrians as Tuddenham and Heydon might be plausibly imputed
to their opponents was that of 1455. In consequence of the first battle of St. Albans,
the Yorkists controlled the parliament which sat from 9 to 31 July of that year.

The grammatical construction is in places defective, but no attempt has been
made to correct it.

G. 255/301.

To Ser Jamis Gloys

Ther be dyuers thyngis in your letter, ⌜sent to me⌝,¹ on that ⌜a slaw[n]-
derus⌝² noyse shuld renne ageyns Yeluerton, Aly[n]gton, *and* me to brynge
us owte of the conceytis of the puple be Heydon *and* his dyscyplis of a bill
that shuld haue ⌜do⌝ put uppe in-to the parlement ageyns my lord of
5 Norwich ⌜*and* odir. I lete yow wete⌝³ this is the furst day þat⁴ I herd of any
seche, but I wold wete the namys of hem that vttere this langage *and* the
mater of the bill. As for my lord of Norwych, I suppose ye know I haue not

²¹ þat I or other men to ne *canc.*
²² *On the verso are the following notes in Paston's hand:*

Br⟨. . .⟩
Br⟨adwe⟩ll iux*ta* Jern⟨e⟩mut
Kirley iux*ta* Leystoft viij *li.*

Foxhole
Cowhaw in Nakton [on þis sy *canc.*] ⎫
on þis side Yepiswich iij myl ⎬ xviij *li.*
                                ⎭
Langston in Brustall   ⎫
ij myle [fro *canc.*] beyond Yepiswich ⎬ viij *li.*
                                   ⎭
Bentelé ij myle beyond   ⎫
Brustall   ⎬ x mark
                            ⎭

52. ¹ *Interl. above* on yo *canc.*
     ² *Interl. above* anoyse, a *canc.*; a not separated, as often below.
     ³ *Interl. above* of which *canc.*   ⁴ euer *canc.*

⌐vsid to ¬5 meddel w*yth* lord*is* mater*is* meche forther than me nedith. *And* as for S*er* Thom*as* Todynh*a*m, he gaff me no cawse of late tyme to labo*ur* ageyns hym, *and* also of⁶ seche mat*er* I know non ⌐deffaut in ¬7 hym. 10 *And* as for Heydon, when I putte a bill ageyns hym ⌐I suppose ¬8 he shall ⌐no cause have ¬,⁹ ne his discyplis nother*e*, to avante¹⁰ of so short a remedy þ*er*-of as ⌐ye wrygth ¬8 they sey now.

As for that ye desyre¹¹ þ*at* I shuld send yow word what ye¹² shuld sey i*n* this mat*er*, I p*r*ay yow to¹³ i*n* this *and* all oþ*er* lyke ⌐ask þe seyer*is* if 20 þei will abyd be þ*er* langage, *and* as for me ¬ sey I p*ur*pose me to take no mat*er* uppon me butt þ*at* I woll abyde by, ⌐*and* in lek wys for Yelu*er*to[n] *and* Ali[n]gton ¬.¹⁴ *And* that ye send me the namys of them that ye¹⁵ wryte þ*at* ⌐herd this langage *and* ¬ seyd shrewydly, *and* what they seyd, *and* that ye remembr*e* what men of substance wer ther that herde itt; for if this 25 ⌐can ¬16 be dreve to Heydon or his dissyplis, as ye ⌐wryte ¬,¹⁷ it wer a gode p*r*eve þ*at* they fere to be appelyd of seche mater*is*.

⌐*And* I thank yow for y*our* godwill. ¬ Wrete att Norwych on Seynt James Day, &[c].

53. To Sir John Fastolf from Paston and
Thomas Howys   1458, 24 May

Add. 39848, f. 46. 10⅜×8½ in. Hand of William Worcester, secretary to Fastolf (see p. lxxviii, and nos. 496, 498, 506 in Part II); subscription in Paston's hand; both signatures autograph.

Dorse: Traces of red wax. Address in unidentified hand:

*To my Maister Fastolf at Castre in Norff*olk.

The date appears from a roll (in Latin) of Paston's expenses between Michaelmas 36 and Michaelmas 37 Henry VI (29 September 1457 and 1458) (Add. Charter 17246, 6×46 in., extracts in G. 321/373). One item records 3*s*. 4*d*. paid for knives given to Fastolf's servants and his own at Doncaster.

G. 316/368 (abstract).

Ryght worshypfull s*er* and my ryght gode maist*er*, I reco*m*maund me to yow. Please ⌐yov to wete ¬1 that yerstenday² I and othyr of your*es* were at

---

⁵ *Interl. by Paston;* meddel *first written* meddelyd, -yd *canc.*
⁶ of *written by Paston over* in.   ⁷ *Interl. by Paston above of canc.*
⁸ *Interl. by Paston.*   ⁹ *Interl. above* not nede *canc.*
¹⁰ that the *canc., followed by* as ye writh he doth *interl. by Paston, but canc.*
¹¹ ye that ye sh *canc.*
¹² *Written* I *by the scribe, corr. to* y, *with raised* e, *by Paston.*   ¹³ sey *canc.*
¹⁴ *Interl. by Paston, after cancelling previously interlined* and þat ye can not I wold be besi in sech mater*is*.   ¹⁵ wy *canc.*
¹⁶ *Interl. above* cowde *canc.*   ¹⁷ *Interl. above* sey *canc.*
53. ¹ *Interl. in Paston's hand.*   ² we were *canc.*

your manere of Bentlay, whych ys ryght a fayre manere, and yn the shrew-
dest reule *and* gouernaunce that euer I sawe.[3] Ye hafe had[4] so manye
5 officers *and* reulers there whych hafe caused dyuers parties kept yn your
toune, to grete trouble of your tenauntes, and som for[5] ylle wylle hafe be
put owte of her landes, and your land leten by your officers to your hurt
and othyr men ys grete avaylle. And there ys owyng yow by som man for
vj yeere, som man for vij yeere, *and* som lesse *and* more to the somme of c
10 li. before Myghellmasse; and besyde that for Estern pay drawyth xl li.
owyng.[6] The worst mater for yow that we hafe to doo ys that there ys so
grete debt lyeng vppon your tenauntes at ones to rere, but we shall do the
best that we may; for ⌜we⌝[1] be sure of gentlemen of the contree to wayt
vppon ws *and* to help ws yn that at nedeth.

15 And yerstenday there were many wyth ws; *and* Herry Sotehill of your
lerned councell was there *and* hath tolde ws the weyes yn the lawe for
remedye. Your tenauntes *and* accomptantes be full obedyent to ws, but
they be ferd off debt; but we shall entrete hem as feyre as we can till we be
sure. And yn asmoch as Barker sent me word that the atteynt hald not,
20 we shall tarye the lenger; for I purpose to take a full conclusyon or[7] I
com thens.

The Lord Egremont sent for ⌜my⌝[8] brother *and* tolde hym he wold see
yow homward as he supposed; and therfor be ye avysed whate grauntes
ye make, for ye hafe made to manye. Also y may lete Bentlay and hafe
25 seurtee and it drew v c marc a[9] yeere, but I can not take vppon me till I
speke wyth yow because of ⌜þe trobill of þe leti[n]g of⌝[1] Wyghton, and
also till Scrope hath spoke wyth yow, whych wille be wyth yow at thys
tyme, as he seyd to me.

Ser, please your maistershyp that som seruaunt of youres may survey
30 my stabler yn my close at Maltby, as Robert Lynne or W. Eton ⌜or som
othyre⌝; but y wold hafe none of Rauff Wodreffes kynnesmen, for here ys
hys eme, as lyke hym of condicions *and* contenaunce as euere I sawe onye.[10]

And Ovr Lord have yow in his kepi[n]g. Wret at Doncaster þe Wednisday in Pentecost Weke.

Yowres to his power, JON PASTON   T. HOWYS

---

[3] the *canc.*   [4] there *canc.*   [5] hi *canc.*
[6] which is *interl. by Paston, but canc.*   [7] we *canc.*
[8] *Interl. above* your *canc.*   [9] *No space.*
[10] *Worcester's hand ends; the rest, except Howes's signature, in Paston's hand.*

54. Nuncupative Will of SIR JOHN FASTOLF
Nominally 1459, 3 November

Add. 22927. Parchment, 20 × 18½ in. at full extent; part cut away from about half-way down for binding, text not affected. Hand unidentified.

Dorse blank except for *Copia voluntatys Fastolf*, very faint except for the middle word, which must have been freshened up at some time.

This text is placed here because it conveniently presents the grounds of Paston's claims to the Fastolf estates with which many later documents are concerned. Though it is not formally in Paston's name, he must evidently have been its principal author. No doubt it was drawn up after Fastolf's death, which occurred on 5 November 1459 (*Inq. p.m.*, 38 and 39 Henry VI, no. 48, etc.), but there is no indication of the exact date. The hand is not that of any of Paston's known clerks. It is formally written, with the opening date and the beginning of each important clause larger than the rest, and altogether makes an official impression.

Another form of Fastolf's will, of the same nominal date, appears in MS. Add. 39849, a fair copy on parchment, about 20½ × 48 in., of a draft preserved in MS. Add. 27444, ff. 60–6 (G. 332/385). It purports to be the will composed by Fastolf himself, revising his earlier will dated and sealed on 14 June 1459 (now Magdalen College, Oxford, Fastolf Paper 65):

> In the name and the wurship of the holy blissydfull Trinité, the yeer of the incarnacion of Oure Lord Jesu Criste m¹cccclix and in the xxxviij yeer of the regne of my souerayn lord Kyng of Engelond *and* of Fraunce Herry the Sexte, the thridde day of the moneth of Nouembre, I, S*er* John Fastolf of Castre be Gret Iernemuth in the counté of Norffolke, knyght, beyng in good remem-brance albe it I am gretly wexid w*yth* syknesse *and* thorwh age infeblyd, bryngyng to mende and oftyn reuoluyng in my soule how this world is tran-scitory *and* how that among*ys* alle erthely thingis that is present or for to come there is noo thinge in this onstable world so s*er*teyn to creature of man to knowe as is departyng out of this world be dethe, the soule from the wrechyd body, and noo thyng erthely so oon-certeyn as the oure *and* tyme of dethe, therfore I, wylling *and* desyring that of suche goody*s* of substaunce worldly, mevable and on-mevable, that God of hise bounteuous grace hathe sent me in my lif to dispose *and* ocupie, that they be disposed as it may be thought best for the helthe of my soule *and* to the plesaunce of God, and also for the relyf, socour, *and* helpe of the soulys that I am most obliged to preye *and* doo prey fore, and for the soules of John Fastolf my fadyr, Dam Mary, doutir of Nicholas Park, squyer, my modyr, and the soule of Dam Mylcent my wif, the doutir of S*er* Robert Tebetot, knyght, and for the soules of othir of myn auncetrys and kynsefolk *and* special frendy*s*, I ordeyne *and* dispose *and* make this my last wyll in fourme *and* maner folwyng: . . .

It provides for the founding of a college at Caister in essentially the same terms as the present text.

G. 333/386.

Anno Domini millesimo quadringentesimo quinquagesimo nono, mensis Novembris videlicet die Sabbati proximo post festum Omnium Sanctorum, Johannes Fastolff, miles, de comitatu Northfolchie, Norwicensis diocesis,

in manerio suo de Castre, dicte diocesis, quoad bona sua immobilia suam
5 vltimam declarauit voluntatem prout sequitur:

John Fastolff, knyght, the secunde and þe thirde day of the moneth of
Nouembre, the yere of the reigne of King Henry the Sexte aftir the
Conquest xxxviij yers, being of longe tyme, as he said, in purpos and
wille to ⟨fo⟩unde[1] and stablissh withynne the gret mansion at Castre by
10 hym late edified a college of vij religious men, monkes or seculer prestes,
and vij porefolke, to pray for his soule and þe soulys of his wife, his fad⟨ir⟩
and modir, and other þat he was beholde to, imperpetuité; and forasmuch
as he had, as he rehercid, a very truste and loue to his cosyn John Paston,
and desired the parfourmyng of the purpoos and wille forsa⟨i⟩d to be
15 accomplisshed, and that the said Sir John shulde not be mevid ne sterid
in his owne persone for þe said accomplisshing of þe said purpoos and
wille, ne with noon other worldly maters but at his oune request and
plesire, wolde, graunted, and ordeyned that the said John Paston shalle,
withynne resonable tyme aftir þe dissese of þe said Sir John, doo founde
20 and stablissh in þe said mansion a college of vij monkes or prestes and vij
porefolke, forto pray for the soulys abouesaid imperpetuité; so that one
of the said monkes or prestes be maister, and haue x li. yerely, and ich oþir
monke or preste x marc. yerely, and ich of the porefolke xl s. yerely, and
þat the said John Paston shalle make sure to the said collegions a sufficient
25 roume and a competent and an esy duelling place in the said mansion, the
said collegions nor her successours bering no charge of reparacion therof.
For which, and for othir charges and labours þat þe said John Paston hath
doon and take vppon hym, to þe eas and profite of þe said John Fastolf,
and for othir consideracions by hym rehercid, the said Sir John Fastolff
30 wolde, graunted, and ordeyned that þe said John Paston shalle haue alle
þe maners, landes, and tenementes in North[folk], Southfolk, and Norwich
in which the said John Paston or any other are or were enfeffed or haue title
to þe vse of the said Sir John Fastolf; and at alle þe feffees infeffed in þe
said maners, londes, and tenementes shalle make and deliuer astate of þe
35 said maners, landes, and tenementes to such persones, at such tymes, and
in such forme as þe said John Paston, his heirs, and his assignes shalle
requere thaym or any of thayme. And that the said John Paston shall pay
to othir of the said Sir Johns executours iiij m[l] marc. of laufulle money of
England in þe fourme þat folweth, that is to say: where þe said Sir John
40 hadde apointed and assigned that his executours shalle, þe firste yere aftir
his disses, dispoos for his soule and parfourmyng his wille a m[l] marc. or
a m[l] li. of money, and yerely aftir viij c marc. tille þe goodes be disposed,
the said John Paston shalle pay iche othir yere þe said summe of viij c
marc. tille þe summe of iiij m[l] marc. be paid, so þat þe said mevabill[2]

---

54. [1] *Parchment decayed, in various patches.*
[2] *Abbr.* mevall *with stroke above.*

88

goodes shalle þe lenger endure to be disposed, by þ'avise of his executours, 45
for þe said soulys.

And also þe said Sir John said, forasmuch as it was the very wille and
entent of þe said Sir John þat the said John Paston shulde be thus³ avaun-
taged and in no wise hurte of his propir goodes, therfore þe said Sir John
wolde [and] graunted that if the said John Paston, aftir the dissese of the 50
said Sir John, by occasion and vnlaufulle trouble in þis reame, or by
mayntenaunce or myght of lordes, or for defaute of iustice, or by vnreson-
able exaccions axid of hym for þe licence of þe said fundacion, withoute
coveyne or fraude of hym-selue, be lettid or taried of þe making or stable-
sshing of þe making of þe said fundacion, that thanne he fynde or doo finde 55
yerely aftir þe first yere of the⁴ dissese of the said Sir John vij prestes to
pray for þe said soulys in þe said mansion, if he can purvey so many, or
els for asmany prestes as faile yeue yerely aftir þe said first yere, by þ'auise
of his executours, to bedredmen and othir nedy true pepille asmuch money
in almose for the said sowlys as the salary or findyng of the prestes so 60
faillyng is worthe or amounteth to, vnto the tyme he may laufully and
peasably founde the said college and doo his true devir for the said fundacion in the meane tyme. And the said Sir John Fastolf wolde, graunted,
and desired faithfully alle the resedewe of his executours and feffees to
shewe the said John Paston fauoure in the said paymentes and daies, and 65
help hym for the Kinges interesse and the eschetours, and furthir hym in
that thay may in alle othir thinges as they wolde doo to hym-selue, and
not vex ne inquiete hym for the said fundacion in the meane tyme.

Ande where the said Sir John Fastolf made his wille and testament the
xiiij day of June in somer last passed, he wolde, graunted, and ordeyned 70
that this his wille touching thes premissez, aswelle as the said wille made
the said xiiij day, except and voided oute of his said wille made the said
xiiij day alle that concerneth or perteyneth to the fundacion of a college,
priory, or chauntery, or of any religious persones, and alle that concerneth
the sale or disposing of the said maners, landes, and tenementes, wherof 75
this is the very declaracion of his full wille, stand and be ioyntly his very
enteir and laste wille, and annexed and proued togedir.

Also the said Sir John Fastolf, knyght, the Tuysday next before the
fest of All Saintes, and in þe moneth of Septembre the said yere, and the
iij day of Novembre, and diuerse other tymes, at ⟨Ca⟩stre aforesaid, wolde, 80
ordenyd, and declared his wille touching the making of the said college,
aswelle as the graunte of the said maners, landes, and tenementes in
Norffolk, Suffolk, and Norwich, in fourme, manere, and substance
aforeseid.

Also the said Sir John wolde and ordeyned that, if the said John Paston 85
by force or myght of any othir desiring to haue the said mansion were

---

³ *Fold. by* be, *superfluous.*   ⁴ *This word rubbed, apparently written* theis.

letted to founde the seid college in the said mansion, that thanne the said
John Paston shulde doo poule doun the said mansion and euery stone and
stikke therof, and do founde iij of the said vij prestes or monkes at Saincte
90 Benettes, and one at Yermuth, one at Attilbrugh, and one at Sainte Oloves
church in Southwerk.

Also the said Sir John Fastolf, the iij and the iiij daies of the moneth of
Nouembir aforesaid, desired his said wille in writyng touching the fundacion of the said college and the graunte of the said maners, landes, and
95 tenementes to the said John Paston to be redde vnto the said Sir John; and
that same wille redde and declared vnto hym articulerly, the said Sir John
Fastolffs wolde, ordeyned, and graunted that the said John Paston shulde
be discharged of the payment of the said iiij m¹ markes, and noght pay
therof in case he did execute the remenaunte of the said wille.

100 Also the said Sir John Fastolf, knyght, aboute the tyme of hervest the
yere of þe reigne of King Henry the Sexte xxxvᵗʰ yere, at Castre faste by
Mikel Yermuth in the shire of Norffolk, in presence of diuers persones that
tyme called to by the said Sir John, did make astate and feffement and
liuerey of the season⁶ of the maner of Castre aforesaid, and othir maners,
105 landes, and tenementes in Norffolk, to John Paston, squier, and othir; and
at that lyuerey of season therof deliuered, aswelle by the handes of the
said Sir John as by other, the said Sir John Fastolfs by his owne mouth
declared his wille and entente of that feffement and liverey of season made
to the vse of the said Sir John asfor during his live onlye, and aftir his
110 decese to the vse of the said John Paston and his heirs. And also the said
Sir John said and declared that þe said John Paston was the best frende
and helper and supporter to the said Sir John, and that was his wille that
the said John Paston shulde haue and enherite the same maners, landes,
and tenementes and othir aftir his decese, and there to duelle and abide and
115 kepe householde; and desired Davn William Bokenham, Priour of Yermouth, and Raufe Lampet, squier, Bailly of Yermuth, that tyme present,
to recorde the same.

Also the said Sir John Fastolf, the vj day of July next aftir the tyme of
the sealing of his wille made the xiiij day of June the xxxv of King Henry
120 the Sexte, and aftir in þe presence of Davn William Bokenham, that tyme
Prioure of Yermouth, and other, wolde, ordeyned, and declared ⟨his⟩
wille that the said John Paston shulde haue alle thynges as the said Sir
John had graunted and declared to the said Prioure and othir at the tyme
of the said ⟨asta⟩te and feffement⁷ made to the ⟨said⟩ John Paston the said
125 xxxv yere of King Henry the vjᵗʰ, the said Sir John seyng that he was of
the same wille and purpoos as he was and ⟨decla⟩red at the tyme ⟨of th⟩e
said astate takyng.

⁵ *Final loop as if for* -es. ⁶ *This word smudged, beginning perhaps* sei-.
⁷ *MS.* feffemement.

Also the said Sir John wolde that John Paston and Thomas Howes, and noon othir 'of his executours, shulde selle alle mane⟨rs⟩, landes, and tenementes in whiche any persones were enfeffed to the vse of the said Sir 130 John, excepte the said maners, landes, and tenementes in Norfolk, Suffolk, and Norwich; and the same John Paston and Thomas Howes shalle take and receyve the profites, ysshueys, and emolumentes commyng of the said maners, landes, and tenementes, excepte before except, tille thay may resonably be solde; and that the said John Paston and Thomas the money 135 commyng of the same sale, aswelle of the said proufites, ysshuys, and emolumentes, shulde dispoos in dedys of almose for the soule of the said Sir John and the soulys aforesaid, and ⟨in⟩ executyng of his wille ande testament.

And also the said Sir John wolde that alle the feffees enfeffed in the 140 said maners, landes, and tenementes assigned to be solde, whanne thay be required by the said John Paston and Thomas Howes, shalle make astate to persone or persons as the said John Paston and Thomas shalle selle to the said maners, landes, and tenementes, or any parte therof; and that noon othir feffé nor the executours of the said Sir John shall make any 145 feffement, relece, ne quitaunce of any londes before assigned to be solde þat wer at any tyme longing to the said Sir John, withoute þe assente of the said John Paston and Thomas Howes.

Datum anno Domini, mense, die, et loco supradictis.

55. To MARGARET PASTON   1460, 19 June

Add. 27444, f. 75. 11½×3⅞ in. Gresham's hand, signature autograph.

Dorse: Traces of red wax. Address in unidentified hand:

To my trusty cosyn Margaret Paston at Norwich be this delyuered.

Below this, apparently in Gloys's hand:

To Richard Calle at Castere be this deliuerid in hast.

The date is evidently in the summer following the death of Sir John Fastolf (see no. 54).
   G. 352/408.

I recomaunde me to you, letyng you witte þat I sent a letter to[1] John Russe *and* Richard Kalle that thei, by th'aduyse of Watkyn Shipdam *and* William Barker, shuld send me word of whom alle the maneres, londes, *and* tene-mentes þat were Ser John Fastolffes wern holde, preyng you þat ye wole do them spede them in þat matier. And if my feodaryes whiche lye in þe 5 tye of my gret cofyr may ought wisse ⌜ther⌝[2]-in, lete them se it.

55. [1] you *canc. and subpuncted.*   [2] *Interl. above* þere *canc.*

Item, I wolde that William Barker shulde send me a copye of þe olde *trauerse* of Tychewell and Beyton. And lete Ric*hard* Kalle spede hym hidderward, and come by Snaylwel *and* take suyche mony as may be
10 getyn there; *and* þat he suffre not þe mony þat þe ten*au*ntes owe to come in þe fermo*ur*s hand*es*.

Item, þat he come by Cambrigge *and* bryng w*ith* hym Maist*er* Brakkelés licence from þe p*ro*uynciall of þe Grey Freres. I p*rey* you recomaunde me to my modir.

15 Wretyn at London the Thursday next to-fore Middesom*er*.

JOHN PASTON

56. To MARGARET PASTON 1460, 28 July

Add. 34888, f. 150. 11⅝×6 in. Hand of Richard Calle (see pp. lxxv–lxxvi), except for subscription and postscript by Paston.

Dorse: No seal. Address in Calle's hand:

*To my wurschipfull coosyn[1] Margaret Paston be this delyu*erd in haste.*

The date appears from the mention of John Berney's death. He made his will at Caister on 2 June 1460, 'compos mentis et sane memorie quamvis infirmus existens', naming John Paston and Thomas 'Holdre' of Moughton (doubtless Moulton near Acle) executors, and requiring his body to be buried in the north porch of Reedham church (P.C.C., Reg. Stokton, 24). Probate was not granted until 1 December 1461 (with administration to Thomas 'Hooler'), but since Margaret writes of his approaching 'year-day' in no. 159, which can be dated 1461, he must have died in July 1460.
  F. iv, p. 36. G. 973/412.

I recomaunde me vnto you, letyng you witte that y*our* vnkyll John Berney is deed, whoos soule[2] God haue m*er*cy; desyryng you to sende for Thom*as* Holler and enquere of hym wher his goode is and what he is wurthe, and that he take goode[3] eede to all suche good*es* as he had, bothe meveable
5 and on-mevable, for[4] I vndre-stande that he is wurthe in money v c marke and in plate[5] to the valwe of other v c marke, beside other good*es*. Wherfor I wolde ye schulde not lete hym wete ⌐of his dissese⌐ vnto the tyme that ye had enquered of the seide Thom*as* Holler of all suche maters as be a-bovyn wreten. And whan he hathe enformed you therof, than lete hym
10 wete verely that he is deede; desiryng hym that no man come on-to his place at Redham but hym-selfe vnto the tyme that I come.

Item, I lete you witte that ⌐gret⌐[6] p*ar*te of his goode is at Will*ia*m Tau*er*ners, as I vndrestande. Thom*as* Holler woll telle you justely the

---

56. [1] *Second o over* y.   [2] h *and part of another letter canc.*
  [3] hee *canc.*   [4] my *and incomplete* m *canc.*
  [5] other *canc.*   [6] *Interl. in Paston's hand above* the moste *canc.*

trouthe, as I suppose; and desyre[7] hym on my behalfe that he doo soo.
And ther is writyng therof, and telle Thom*a*s Holler that I and he be[8] **15**
executo*ur*s named. And therfore lete hym take heede that the good*es* be
kept saffe, and that no body knowe wher it shall lie but ye and Thom*a*s
Holler. ⌐And⌐[9] Thom*a*s Holler, as y*o*ur vnkyll tolde me, is prevy wher all
his goode lithe, and all his writyng; and so I wol that ye be prevy to[10] the
same for casualté of deethe, and ye too schalbe his executo*ur*s for me as **20**
longe[11] as ye doo trewly, as[12] I trowe verely ye woll.
    Wreten at London the xxviij[ti] day of Jule.[13]

Yowr*e* J ON PASTON

    I requer yow be of god cu*m*ffoort *and* be not heuy[14] if ye wil do owth
for me.

57. Petition to Henry VI: draft   1460, 7 October

Bodl. MS. Tanner 95, f. 82. $11\frac{1}{2} \times 10\frac{1}{2}$ in. English text mainly in the hand
of John Paston III, corrections by John Paston I.

The English text covers four manuscript lines (excluding interlineations). It is
followed by a Latin draft of twenty-two lines, of which the first ten and a half are
in John Paston III's hand, heavily corrected and interlined by John I. The rest
of this draft is by John I. Under it are some four lines, in John Pampyng's hand,
of a fuller version of the part of Paston's draft dealing with pasture; these lines
are not here transcribed. (Gairdner's attribution of the handwriting of the whole
draft to William Worcester is unacceptable.)
    The dorse bears marks of folding and stitch-holes, but no seal or address.
    At the right-hand bottom corner, apparently in John Paston I's hand, is the
note *parlia*mentum *ap*ud *Westm' vij Octobr. A° xxxix°* (1460). This date agrees well
with that of the early letters written by John III for Margaret Paston.
    G. 965/59.

To þe Kyng ou*y*r soue*r*ayn lord[1]

Ples yo*wy*r[2] Hyghnes of yo*wy*r abu*n*dant gr*a*ce in consyderac*i*on of þe
seruys *and* plesu*r* þat ⌐yo*wy*r Hyghnes knowyth[3] to yow don by⌐[4] Willi*a*m
Paston, late on of yo*wy*r jugys and old seru*a*unt to þat nobyll pr*i*nse yo*wy*r
fadyr,[5] to gr*a*unt on-to John Paston, ⌐esquyer⌐, sone *and* heyir of the seyd

---

[7] *-y- seems to have been written over incomplete* e.   [8] his *canc.*
[9] *Interl. by Paston above* wheche *canc.*   [10] helpe hym *canc;* to *repeated.*
[11] ay *canc.*   [12] *Corr. from* and.
[13] *Calle's hand ends here, the rest by Paston. The postscript is written, as one line, above the
letter.*
[14] *Last two words corr. from* of no heuynes.
57. [1] *Heading with different pen and ink, but also by John Paston III.*
    [2] hynes *canc.*   [3] by *canc.*
[4] to yow don by *in John I's hand.*
[5] done ⌐to yow⌐ in tyme past *canc. in same ink as the previous correction.*

93

5 Wyll*iam*, *yowyr* lettry*s* patent*ys* ⌐vnder þe seel of yow[r]¬ Duché of Lan-
caster⁶ being in þe kepi[n]g of Tho*mas* Tresham⌐⁷ aftyr affecte ⌐of note¬⁸
folowy*ng*; *and* he schall pray to God for yow.

Rex &c. Sciatis quod de gracia nostra speciali et ex mero motu nostro ac
10 pro bono et laudabyli seruicio quod ⌐dilectus et fidelis nobis¬ Willelmus
Paston, nuper vnus justiciariorum nostrorum, ⌐defunctus¬, nobis in vita
sua jnpendydit, consessimus et hac presenti carta nostra confirmauimus,
in quantum in nobis est, Johanni Paston, armigero, filio et heredi dicti
Willelmi, viginti tria mesuagia, quingintas triginta et ⌐iiij¬⁹ acras pasture,
15 bruere, et marissy in villis de Paston, Edythorp, et Bakton in comitatu
⌐nostro¬ Norff' quas diuersi tenentes ⌐nostri¬ ibidem de nobis separatim
⌐natiue¬ tenent ad uoluntatem nostram per virgam ⌐siue¬ copiam ⌐et per
serta redditus et seruissia ⌐natiua¬ annualia inde nobis reddenda que ad
valorem novem librarum annuatim extendunt vel infra. Concessimus eciam
20 eidem Johanni curiam lete seu visus franciplegij nostri in villis de Paston et
Edithorp predictis,¹⁰ que est annui valoris viij solidorum per estimacionem¬,
ad quatuor libratas, quatuor solidatas, et octo denariatas redditus.
⌐Redditum¬ octo boschellorum auenarum et trium caponum, cum per-
tinensij in villis predictis ac in villis Wytton et Casewyk in comitatu
25 predicto, percipiendum anuatim de omnibus et singulis liberys tenentibus
nostris ibidem pro tenementis suis qui de nobis separatim tenent in eisdem
villis vna cum ⌐fidelitatibus et alijs¬ seruicijs eorundem tenentium et
eorum cuiuslibet¹¹ de seu pro tenementis ⌐illis¬ et eorum qualibet parcella
nobis debitis siue pertinentibus.
30   ⌐Concessimus etiam eidem Johanni ⌐et heredibus suis¬ officium parcarie
ac costidie parci nostri de Gymy[n]gham in comitatu nostro predicto vna
cum ⌐proficuo¬ agistamenti ⌐bestiarum¬ eiusdem parci ⌐pro vadijs suis
pro officio predicto anuatim percipiendo¬, saluis ⌐nobis et heredibus
nostris sufficienti¬ pastura ferarum nostrarum ⌐ibidem¬ vt tempore nostro
35 prius¹² vsitatum fuit, quod quidem proficuum agistamenti ad valorem
x marcarum extendit per annum¬;¹³ habenda, tenenda, et percipienda
predicta messuagia, tarram, pasturam, brueram, mariscum, ⌐curiam ⌐lete
et¬ visus franciplegij¬, redditus et seruisscia, ⌐officium et agistamenti

---

⁶ of diu*ers* man*er*[is] late put in feffement *and three or four other words heavily canc.*

⁷ *Interl. by John I above* of serteyn londys, te*nementys* rent*ys* seruy*s* in Paston *and* othyr townys in þe scher of Norfolk to be mad aftyr, *canc. except for* aftyr, *which has been missed by mistake.*

⁸ *Interl. by John I above* of anote cañc.

⁹ *Interl. by John I above* tres *canc. Corrections and interlineations following are all by John I. Cancelled passages are not recorded.*

¹⁰ *MS.* predictam.   ¹¹ *John III's hand ends.*

¹² *The corresponding passage in Pampyng's draft of the sentence runs:* vt tempore nostro et progenitorum nostrorum antiquitus vsitatum fuit.

¹³ *This sentence written below the rest of the draft, but marked for insertion here.*

proficuum⌐, cum pertinencijs, prefato Johanni et heredibus suis de nobis
et heredibus nostris per fidelitatem et redditum vnius rose rubie ad 40
festum Natiuitatis Sancti Johannis Baptiste annuatim ⌐nobis⌐ solvendum,
si petatur, pro omnibus seruicijs, exaccionibus, et demandis. Eo quod
messuagia, terra, pastura, bruera, mariscus, ⌐curia lete⌐, redditus, seruicia
predicta, ⌐officium et agistamenti proficuum⌐ valorem supra specificatum
[non] excedant vel valorem illam non attingant, aut aliquo actu, restriccione, 45
⌐seu mandato⌐ facto, edito, aut proviso non obstante. Volumus eciam et
assignavimus quod omnes illi qui per nos seu ad vsum nostrum jus, titulum,
seu statum in premissis seu aliquo premissorum habuerunt seu habent,
nobis ante hec non relaxatum, jus, titulum, et statum illa prefato Johanni
et heredibus suis dimittent et relaxent. In cuius.[14] 50

58. To MARGARET PASTON   1461, 12 July

Add. 34888, f. 184. 11⅜×3½ in. Hand of John Pampyng (see p. lxxvii),
signature autograph.

Dorse: Traces of red wax. Address in Pampyng's hand:

To my cosyn Margret Paston.

The date appears from a letter from Berney to Paston complaining of the 'lyght
demeanyng' of the under-sheriff in the election, and dated 17 July 1 Edward IV
(1461) (see Part II, no. 639). Relic Sunday was the third Sunday after Midsummer.
This letter is answered by Margaret's no. 161.
F. iv, p. 20. G. 402/468.

I recomaund me to yow, letyng yow wete þat[1] the vndershreve doughtyth
hym of John Berney; wherfore I pray yow bryng hem to-gedyr and set
hem acord if ye can, so þat the seyd vndershreve be sure þat he shall not
be hurt be hym ner of hys cuntrymen. And yf[2] he woll not, lete hym verely
vndyrstonde þat he shall be compellyd to fynd hym suerté of the pes, 5
magry in hys heed; and þat shall nowther be profitabyll ner worchepfull.
And lete hym wete þat there have be many compleyntes of hym be þat
knavyssh knyght Ser Miles Stapilton, as I sent yow word before; but he
shall come to hys excuse wele jnow so he have a mannys hert, and the
seyd Stapylton shall be[3] vndyrstand as he ys, a fals shrewe. And he and 10
⌐hys wyfe and⌐ other have blaveryd here of my kynred in hodermoder,
but be þat tyme we have rekned of old dayes and late dayes myn shall be
found more worchepfull thanne hys and hys wyfes, or ellys I woll not for[4]

---

[14] *Imperfect; letters after I blotted.*

58. [1] þ *in form of* y; *so regularly in Pampyng's practice when he uses the form, but he does so
only intermittently.*
[2] y *over* e.   [3] *Indeterminate stroke after* -e, *not* n.
[4] all *canc.*

hys gilt gypcer. Also telle the ⌜seyd Berney þat the⌝[15] shreve ys in a dought
15 whedyr he shall make a newe eleccion of[6] knyghtes of the shyre be-cause
of hym and[7] Grey, where-in it were bettyr for hym to have the shreves
good wyll.

Item, me thynkyth for quiete of the cuntré it were most worchepfull
þat as wele Berney as Grey shuld get a record of all suche þat myght
20 spend xl s.[8] a yere þat were at the day of eleccion, whech of them þat had
fewest to geve it vp as reson wold. Wretyn at London on Relyk Sonday.

Item, þat ye send a-bought for syluer acordyng to the old bylle þat I
sent yow from Lynne.

JOHN PASTON

59. To MARGARET PASTON   1461, 1 August

Add. 27444, f. 102. $11\frac{3}{8} \times 11\frac{3}{8}$ in. Mainly in Pampyng's hand, completed
by Paston.

Dorse: Traces of red wax, and paper tape piercing the letter, which has
been folded small. Address in Pampyng's hand:

To my mastres Paston and Richard Calle.

This letter is much corrected, and looks like a rough draft; but it must nevertheless
have been sent.

The year appears from the reference to the election already mentioned in no. 58.
G. 408/475.

j.[1] First, that Richard Calle fynde the meane that a distresse may be taken
of such bestes as occupie the ground at Stratton, and that cleyme and
contynuan⟨s⟩[2] be made of my possession in any wise and that thei be not
suffrid to occupie with-owt thei compoune with me; and that aftir the
5 distresse taken the vndirshreve be spoke with-all that he make no replevyn
with-out agrement or a-poyntement taken, that the right of the lond may
be vndirstand.

ij. Item,[3] I here sey the peple is disposed to be at the shire at Norwich
⌜on Sen Lauerauns Day⌝ for th'affermyng of that thei have do afore,
10 wherof I hold me wele content if thei do it of her owne disposicion; but
I woll ⌜not⌝ be the cause of the labour of hem ⌜ner ber no cost of hem at

---

5 *Interl. above* shreve *canc.*   6 ky *canc.*
7 Berney *canc.*   8 are *canc.;* ayere *without space.*

59. 1 *The numbers j to ix are set out in the margin opposite the beginning of each of the main
'items' of the text. The first five of these are written continuously, but are here divided into
paragraphs.*
2 *Last letter lost owing to tear at edge;* -ua- *abnormally repr. by superior* a.
3 Item *in margin as well as text;* as *for* canc.

96

this tyme, for be þe lawe I am suer befor⌐,⁴ but I am wel a-payed it shall be on han halyday for lettyng of the peples werk. I vndirstand ther shall be labo*ur* for a coroner that day, for ther is labo*ur* made to me ⌐for⌐⁵ my good wyll here, and I wyll no thyng gr*au*nt with-owt the ⌐vnder⌐-shreves assent, for he *and* I thought that Richard Bloumvyle were good to that occupac*i*on. I*te*m, ye shall vndirstand that the vndirshreve was some-what flekeryng whill he was here, for he informyd the Kyng that the last⁶ elecc*i*on was not peasibill, but the peple was iakkyd *and* saletted *and* riottously disposid, ⌐*and*⌐⁷ put hym in fere of his lyfe;⁸ wherefore I gate of hym the writte whech I send yow ⌐herwith⌐,⁴ to that entent thow any fals shrewe wold labo*ur* he shuld not be sure of the writ. And therfore ye most se⁹ that the vndirshreve have the writ at the day in case the peple be gadered, and thanne lete th'endentures be made vp ⌐or⌐¹⁰ er they departe.

iij. I*te*m, that ye remembyr Thomas Denys wyfe that her husbond had diue*r*s billes of extorc*i*on don be Heydon *and* other, whech that he told me that his seid wyfe beryid whan the rumo*ur* was, so that thei were ny roten. Bidde her loke hem vp and take hem yow.

iiij. I*te*m, as for the seyd distreynyng at Stratton, I wold that Dawbeney *and* Thomas Bon shuld knowe the ⌐closes *and* the⌐ ground, that thei myght attende ther-to that Richard were not lettyd ⌐of⌐¹¹ other occupac*i*ons; and I wold this were do as sone as is possibill or I come home. Not with-standyng I trowe I shall come home or the shire, but I woll nat it be knowe till the same day, for I woll not come there with-owt I be sent fore be the ⌐peple⌐¹² to Heylisdoune. Not withstandyng, *and* the peple were wele aue*r*tised¹³ at that day they shuld be the more redy to shewe the oribyll extorc*i*ons *and* briborys that hath be do vpon hem to the Kyng at his comyng, desyring hym that he shuld not have in fauo*ur* the seyd extorc*i*oners but compelle hem to make amendes *and* sethe to the pore peple.

v. I*te*m, that Berney *and* Richard Wright geve such folkys warnyng as wyll compleyne to be redy with her billes if thei list to have any remedy.

vj. vij. I*te*m, that the maters ayens S*er* Miles Stapilton ⌐at Aylesham⌐¹⁴ may be remembyrd. Also if ye can be any craft get a¹⁵ copy of the bille that S*er* Miles Stapilton hath of the corte rolles of Gemyngham, that ⌐ye⌐ fayle not but assay *and* do yow*r*e devyr, for that shuld preve some men

---

⁴ *Interl. in Paston's hand.*
⁶ shire *canc.*
⁸ *and* I *canc.*
¹⁰ *Interl. above* her ther *canc.*
¹² *Interl. by Paston above what looks like* peple, *with second letter smudged, and heavily cancelled.*
¹³ *MS.* -od.
¹⁵ *No space, as sometimes below.*

⁵ *Interl. by Paston above* of *canc.*
⁷ *Interl. above* to *canc.*
⁹ bere *interl. above this, but canc.*
¹¹ *Interl. above* in *canc.*

¹⁴ *MS. has caret wrongly after* may.

shamefully fals. Master Braklé seyd he shuld a get oon of Freston. I wold
he shuld assay, or ellys *par*auenture Skypwith or ellys Master Sloley, for
50 if Stapilton were boren in hande that he shuld be founde fals *and* ontrewe
and first founder of that mater, he wold bothe shewe the bille *and* where
he had it.[16]

viij. It*em*, I wold the prestis of Caster wer content for Midsom*er* term.

ix. It*em*, ther is a whith box *with* evidens of Stratton[17] in on of the canvas
55 baggis jn the gret cofir or in the spruse chestt—Ri*chard* Call knowith it
well; *and* therin is a ded of feffement *and* a lett*er* of atorné mad of þe
seyd lond*is* in Stratton to John Dam, W. Lomno*ur*, Ri*chard* Call, *and* John
Russe. I wold a new dede *and* letter of atorn[é][18] were mad ⌈owth theroff
be tho feffees⌉[19] of þe same land to [20]⌈Thome Grene⌉, Th[o]me Play*ter*,
60 ⌈þe p[ar]son of Heylisdon⌉, Jacobo Gloys, klerk,[21] Joh[ann]i Pampi[n]g, and
that the ded ber date nowh *and* þat it be selid at þe next shire; for than I
suppose þe seyd feffés will be ther*e*, if it may not be don er that tym.[22]
I wold haue þe seyd dedis leyd in a box, both old *and* new, *and* left secretly
at Ri*chard* Thornis hows ⌈at Stratton⌉, þat whan I com homwar[d] I
65 mygh[t] fynd it ther *and* mak seson *and* stat to be take whil I wer ther*e*.
Wret at London on Lammes Day.

60. Petition to the CHANCELLOR: drafts   1461–2

Add. 27444, ff. 120, 121. Both $11\frac{7}{8} \times 17$ in. Mainly in Pampyng's hand.

These folios are written on both sides, without seal or address, but f. 121 bears two
notes endorsed in different unidentified hands: *Bill of subpena; byllys of suppena.*

They contain two distinct corrected drafts of the same text, a 'bill in Chancery'
applying for writs against Yelverton and Jenney requiring them to answer for
having entered some of Sir John Fastolf's lands. Both drafts are in Pampyng's
hand. In f. 120 the interlineations also are in his hand, but in f. 121 they are
mostly in Paston's. Evidently Pampyng wrote two copies, Paston corrected f. 121,
and Pampyng then copied the corrections into f. 120; but the passage beginning
at l. 80 was again recast at the end (see n. 40).

F. 121 is the basis of the following text, and variants in f. 120 are given in the
footnotes. (Minor differences in spelling are ignored.) Unless the notes say otherwise interlineations are to be taken as in Paston's hand in f. 121 but in Pampyng's
in f. 120.

[16] *On a new line, the following in Pampyng's hand, canc.* : Item I send yow a writ direct to
the meyer and shreves of Norwich for to receyve of hem an c mark yerly for suche iowellys
as the Kyng hath of me. *The rest of the text in Paston's hand.*

[17] lyt *canc.*

[18] *So hastily written that only a roughly horizontal stroke follows the* r.

[19] *Interl. above* be hem *canc.*

[20] ⌈Jamis Gloy klerk⌉ John Grenfeld Thom*as* Playter Water Wrottislé squier *canc.*

[21] *C*ristofero Grenac*re canc.*

[22] *Above this line* John Pampi[n]g *canc.; after it,* Item þer be her many artiklis/ *and* if it
myg be do be tym *canc.*

98

The date is uncertain. It cannot be earlier than the deposition of Henry VI in March 1461. A letter from Pampyng to Paston, datable (from an endorsement on a related letter) 6 September 1461, reports interference with Cotton by Yelverton and Jenney (see Part II, no. 643). A letter from John Russe reports in September 1462 that a commission is said to have been granted to Yelverton and Jenney by virtue of which they have entered Cotton and held a court (Part II, no. 675). Either year, therefore, would suit the present document; 1462 perhaps better.

G. 461/530.

Shewyth and lowly compleynith on-to yo*ur* good lordship John Paston the older, squier, that where S*er* John Fastolff, knyght, cosyn to yo*ur* seid besecher, was seasid of diu*er*s maners, lond*es and* tenem*ent*es in Norffolk, Suff*olk*, and Norwich the xxvij yere of Kyng Herry that was, and therof infeffid diu*er*s p*er*sones to execute and p*er*forme his will, and mad his will 5 in especiall that a college of vij monk*es* shuld be stabilisshed, founded, and indewed wi*th*-inne a plase late be the seid S*er* John edified at Caster be the see in Norff*olk*, and certeyn[1] livelode to be inmortesid therto to pray for his sowle, his fader*es* and moder*es*, in forme and maner as in his will mad at that tyme more pleynly specifith, whech will and feffement con- 10 tinued till the xxxv yere of the seid late kyng; and aftir, vpon diu*er*s comuni-cacions had be diu*er*s p*er*sonys w*ith* the seid S*er* John Fastolff, and[1] vpon diu*er*s considera⟨cions⟩[2] mevid to hym, the seid S*er* John Fastolff conceyvid that such monk*es*[3] be hym there to be indewed ⌈shuld not be of power⌉[4] to susteyne and kepe the seid plase edified or the lond that shuld be in- 15 mortesid therto acordying to his ⌈seyd⌉[5] entent and will;[6] whe[r]fore, and for good will that the seid S*er* John Fastolff had to the p*ro*ferryng[7] of yo*ur* seid besecher, mevid hym to haue the seid plase and certeyn of his livelode of gretter valew than the charge of the seid college shuld drawe, and to found the seid college[8] and to bere the rep*ar*acion[9] and defens 20 therof. Vpon whech mocion the seid S*er* John Fastolff and yo*ur* seid besecher apoynted be word, wi*th*owt writyng at that tyme mad, that yo*ur* seid besecher shuld, aftir the decese of the seid S*er* John Fastolff, haue the seid plase in Caster and all the maners that were the seid S*er* John Fastolff*es*, or any other to his vse in Norff*olk*, Suff*olk*, *and* Norwich, vp 25 trust that the same John Paston shuld founde ther a college of vij monk*es* or prest*es*, havyng a certeyn pension ⌈for her sustentacion⌉ payid clerly in mony wi*th*owt any ⌈charge⌉, cost, rep*ar*aci*on*, or jop*ar*dé of defens of the seid plase, or of any other livelode ⌈to be bore be þe seyd colegians⌉,

---

60. [1] *In f. 120 interl.* [2] *End lost at torn edge; complete in f. 120.*

[3] *Spelt out* -ys *in f. 120.*

[4] *Interl. in both copies, the same words canc. after* therto *following.*

[5] *Interl. above* good, *which is not canc. in f. 120.*

[6] *The following passage* wherfore . . . that *interl. in f. 120.*

[7] *The following* of . . . hym *interl. in f. 120.*

[8] and to inhabite in the same plase *canc. in both copies.*

[9] *The following* and defens *interl. in f. 120.*

30 and more-over to pay a certeyn somme of mony ⌐of þe revenus¹⁰ of þe
seyd maneris, londes, *and tenementes*⌐ to be disposed yerly be certeyn
yeres for the sowle of the seid Ser John Fastolff ⌐till þe som of v m¹ mark
wer so disposid⌐. Vpon whech apoyntement it was acordid be-thwyx¹¹ the
seid Ser John and your seid besecher, for asmoch as your seid besecher
35 had non astate in the seid maners, londes,¹² *and tenementes*, that for his
more suerté¹³ ⌐*and* vp-on trust that the seyd Ser Jon had to yow[r] seyd
besecher¹⁴ in this behalve that a newe⌐ feffement shuld be mad of the
seid plase and of the maner of Caster and all the seid maners, londes, *and*
tenementes¹⁵ to your seid besecher *and* diuers other personis, ⌐to the vse of
40 the seyd Ser John term of his liff *and* after his deses to the vse of yowr
seyd besecher⌐.¹⁶ And moreouer, for asmoch as your seid besecher was
in dowte whedir God wold send hym tyme of lif to execute the seid
apoyntement, intendyng that th'effect of the old purpose of the seid Ser
John Fastolff shuld not be all voyded, thow it so fortuned your seid besecher
45 cowd not performe the seid apoyntement, mevid the seid Ser John Fastolff
that not withstandyng the seid apoyntement that he, aftir the seid feffement
mad, shuld make his will for the seid college to be mad in all maner wise as
thow ⌐the sey[d] Ser Jon Fastolff *and*⌐ your seid besecher shuld ⌐not
make⌐¹⁷ the seid apoyntement, ⌐and that, aftir that, the seid apoyntement
50 to be ingrosid *and* mad so that the seyd colege⌐¹⁸ shuld hold be the same
apoyntement of your seid besecher, and ellis this seid will ⌐of þe sey[d]
Ser Jon Fastolff⌐ to stand in effect for executyng of his seid purpose.

And sone aftir this comunicacion and apoyntement, the seid feffement
⌐was made acordi[n]g⌐¹⁹ and season deliuerid to your seid besecher at the
55 seid plase edified in Caster, aswell as at the seid maners, londes, *and*
tenementes, the seid Ser John Fastolff beyng present at deliuery of season
mad to your seid besecher of the seid¹ plase and maner of Caster, where
the seid Ser John, more largely expressyng the seid will and entent,
deliuerid your seid besecher possession with his owne handes, declaryng

---

¹⁰ *Spelt* revenews (*by Pampyng*) *in f. 120.*
¹¹ *So spelt in both copies.*
¹² *The following and* tenementes *interl. in f. 120.*
¹³ on this behalfe that a newe *canc. in both copies.*
¹⁴ That a newe *canc.; not in f. 120.*
¹⁵ aswell of all other maners that were the seid Fastolffes *underlined, evidently for cancellation; canc. in f. 120.*
¹⁶ *Interl. above* whech were in trust with the seid Ser John Fastolff or with your seid besecher or with hem bothe *underlined; canc. in f. 120.*
¹⁷ *Interl. by Paston, who also wrote the preceding* shuld *over original* left; *in f. 120 all three words interl. by Pampyng above* left *canc.*
¹⁸ *Interl. above canc.* to be made so that this purpose, *by Pampyng as far as* apoyntement, *thereafter by Paston. In f. 120* aftir that . . . college *interl. by Pampyng above* aftir that the seid apoyntement to be mad so that his purpose *canc.*
¹⁹ *Interl. by Paston above* was mad *canc. Before this* as weel as þe seyd will *interl. and canc.; in f. 120 only* acordyng *interl.*

to notabill personys there the same feffement to be mad to the vse of the 60
seid Ser John as for terme of his lif only, and aftir his decese to the vse of
your seid besecher and his heyres; and diuers tymes, in diuers yeres aftir,
declared his entent in like wise to diuers personys, and aftir, be ⌈gret
deliberacion *and* oft⌉[20] comunicacion of the[21] seid mater, the seid Ser
John Fastolff and your seid besecher comenauntyd and apoynted ⌈be 65
writi[n]g⌉ thoroughly for the seid mater, so that your seid besecher shuld
haue the seid plase and all the seid maners, londes, and tenementes in
Norffolk, Suffolk, and Norwich to hym and to his heyres, and that he
shuld founde a college of vij monkes or prestes with-inne the seid plase
perpetually, as is before seid, and to pay iiij m¹ mark to be disposed ⌈in 70
serteyn yeris⌉[22] for the sowle of the seid Ser John Fastolff. The whech
apoyntement, declared and red before the seid Ser John Fastolff, be good
deliberacion ⌈was⌉[23] be the seid Ser John[24] fully concludid, ⌈agreid, *and*
stab[l]yshid for his last will in that be-halve. *And* also⌉[25] the seid come-
nauntes eftsonis callid to remembraunce be the seid Ser John Fastolff, the 75
same Ser John for certeyn consideracions movyng hym, be his word
withowt writyng¹ dischargid your seid besecher of the seid somme of
iiij m¹ mark, desiryng hym so to ordeyn that ich of the seid monkes or
prestes shull yerly haue as the prestes of the chauntry of Heylesdon had,
and that vij pore men shull also be founde yerly in the seid plase inper- 80
petuité[26] to pray for the sowles abovesayd.[27]

And aftir, that is to sey the Satirday, Sonday, and Monday next before
the decese of the seid Ser John, the same Ser John, remembryng ⌈the
diuersité of þe forme of þe fundacion of þe seyd colege in hes former
willis wret[28] and in þe seyd appoyntement,[29] also reme⟨mbryng⟩⌉[30] diuers 85
maters and intentes in his mynd necessary for ⌈the⌉ wele of his sowle[31]
not expressid ⌈in writi[n]g in any will be hym mad before, nowithire⌉ in
the seid[32] apoyntement ⌈deklarid⌉,[33] wold haue on will mad and wrete
⌈after þe effecte of⌉[34] the seid apoyntementes ⌈towchi[n]g the fundacion
of þe colege⌉ aswell as the seid other maters[35] [not] declarid in his intent *and* 90

[20] *Interl. above* long proces *and* canc. *in both copies.*
[21] *A second* the *interl. by Paston; not in* f. 120.
[22] serteyn *spelt* certeyn *in* f. 120.
[23] *Interl. above* aswell canc. *in both copies.*
[24] as be your seid besecher was *canc. in both copies.*
[25] *Interl. above* and sith that *canc. in both copies.*   [26] *MS.* im- ; f. 120 in-.
[27] *The following passage as far as* ingrosid and wrete *canc. by large crosses in* f. 120, *re-drafted at the end; see n.* 40. *Paston's corrections are not copied into* f. 120 *in this passage.*
[28] *At edge; other letters may have been lost.*
[29] *MS.* appeyntement.
[30] *Only* reme *and a mark of abbreviation visible at edge.*
[31] whech were *canc.*   [32] will and *canc.*
[33] *Interl. above* nowther in his testament and that he *canc.*
[34] *Interl. above* conteynyng *canc.*
[35] not expressid *canc.; f.* 120 *reads* not declarid *with no alteration.*

will acordyng, comaundid to haue it so ingrosid and wrete, and ⌜wher⌝36
your seid besecher hath don his part acordyng to the ⌜seyd⌝37 will and
apoyntementes of the seid Ser John, aswell in fyndyng of the seid prestes
and poremen as in all other thynges that to hym belongyth to do in that
95 behalfe.

And this notwithstandyng, William Yeluerton, knyght, and William
Jenney, whech be inffid joyntly with your seid besecher in diuers of the
seid maners, londes, and tenementes, ⌜haue⌝37 mad a sympill entré in all the
seid maners in Suffolk, and chargid the baylifs, fermores, and tenauntes
100 of all the seid maners to pay hem the profitez and reuenews of the same
maners, londes, and tenementes, and thus contrary to th'entent of the seid
feffement38 and contrary to the will of the seid Ser John Fastolff thei
trobill and lette your seid besecher to take the profitez of the seid maners,
londes, and tenementes, of whech your seid besecher hath no remedy at39
105 the comon lawe. Wherfore please your good and gracious lordship to
direct seuerall writtes of sub pena to the seid William and William, chargyng
hem seuerally vpon a peyne conuenient to appere before your lordship in
the Chauncery at a certeyn day be your lordship to be limityd, to answer
to these premisses and to do as right and consiens requirith. And your seid
110 besecher shall pray God for yow.40

36 Interl. above that canc. in both copies; f. 120 where. In f. 121 only it replaces not with
standi[n]g interl. and canc.
37 Interl. in f. 121; not in f. 120.
38 F. 121r ends here; verte in Pampyng's hand at the foot, in the middle.
39 F. 120r ends here; verte at foot in the middle.
40 After a space of about an inch f. 120v contains a rough draft of a revision of the passage
cancelled at ll. 82 ff. (see n. 27). It is in Pampyng's hand, with many cancellations and
interlineations by Paston. The first form appears to have been:

and aftir, late before the discese of the seid Ser John Fastolff that the seid apoyntement
and will made with your seid besecher to be better to his pleasir [thanne any other]
thanne aftir any other forme be the seid Ser John ordeynid in his former willes, remembring also diuerses articles conteynid in his seid former willes and not in the seid
apoyntementes, and also remembring diuers maters necessary for his sowle whech were
nevir expressid in writyng before, ordeynid and wold that on writyng shuld be mad of
all this joyntly to-geder, expressyng his hole will and intent in all maters levyng and all
maters [whech] in his former willes whech were omissed wherof his will was chaunged.

After correction it appears thus:

and aftir, late before the discese of the seid Ser John Fastolff, ⌜he wold and ordeyni[d]
that on writi[n]g shuld be mad of the fundacion of the seid college aftir the forme of
the seid⌝ apoyntement mad with your seid besecher, ⌜and of⌝ diuerses ⌜othir⌝ articles
conteynid in his seid former willes ⌜not conserning the seyd colegge⌝ and also ⌜of⌝
diuers maters ⌜whech he remembrid⌝ necessary for ⌜the wele of⌝ his sowle ⌜that⌝ were
nevir expressid in writyng before joyntly to-geder ⌜in⌝ expressyng his hole ⌜and inter
and last⌝ will and intent in all.

After another space of an inch the first twelve words are copied again.

61. Statement of FASTOLF'S intention: draft
After 1459, before May 1466

Add. 27444, f. 67. 8⅜×11⅝ in. Hand of John Paston III, interlineations and conclusion by John I.

Dorse blank except for note in unidentified hand: *Causa festine barganie inter Fastolf et Paston.*

This paper is very crudely written by both writers, with many corrections of which the less important are not recorded in the footnotes.

The date cannot be closely limited within the years between Fastolf's death and Paston's, though it is likely to be earlier rather than later in that period. In appearance—a Latin draft by John III corrected by John I—the text is nearest to no. 57; but since the content resembles no. 60 it may conveniently be placed here. (John III was still writing drafts for his father in 1462, as no. 63 shows.)

G. 337/390.

Vltima exitacio domini Johannis Fastolf ad concludendum festinanter cum Johanne Paston fuit quod vicecomes Bemond, dux Somerset, comes Warwyk, voluerunt emere et quod intendebat quod executores sui desiderabant vendere et non stabilire colegium; quod totaliter fuit contra intencionem sui dicti Johannis Fastolf. Et considerabat quod certum medium 5 pro licencia Regis et dominorum non prouidebatur, et sic tota fundacio colegij pendebat in dubijs. Et idio ad intencionem suam perimplendam desiderauit dictum barganium fieri cum Johanne Paston, sperans ipsum in mera voluntate perficiendi dictum colegium et ibidem manere ne in manibus dominorum veniat.[1]   10

Item, plures consiliarij sui dixerunt quod licet fundaret ⌈regulos seu⌉[2] presbiteros, aut eicientur per clamia falsa aut compellantur aderere dominis pro ⌈man[u]tenencia⌉[2] sostentacione qui ibidem ad costus colegij permanerent et morarent[ur] et colegium distruerent; et hac de causa consessit eos ditari in pencionibus certis ad modum cantarie Heylysdon, 15 sic quod dictus Johannes haberet ad custus proprios conceruacionem terrarum erga querentes et clamatores, et ⌈ne⌉ executores diuersi propter contrarietates et dissimulaciones seu favores[3]

Item, considerabat quod vbi monechy vel canonesi haberent terras seu tenementa ad magnam valorem, scilicet m¹ vel ij m¹, tam si[n]gulares 20 monachi vel canoneci tantum per se resiperent xl s. per annum et prandium, et quod abbas, officiarij, et extraequitatores expendirent residuum in mundanis et riotis, et idio ordinauit dotacionem predictam in annuetatibus.

Et quod non fuit intencio dicti Johannis Fastolf ⌈in conuencione predicta⌉[2] mortificare ccc marcas terre, quia prima conuencio Johannis Paston 25

---

61. [1] *sat written small by John III.*   [2] *Interl. by John I.*
[3] *From* sic quod *in John I's hand between paragraphs (left unfinished).*

est soluere v m¹ marcas in tribus annis et fundare colegium quod in intencione dicti Johannis Fastolf constaret m¹ li., et semper dedit Johanni
Paston mancionem suam in manerio et tota terra in Northefolk et Sowthefolk assessa ad v c marcas annuatim; tunc Johannes Paston emeret reuer-
30 cionem cc marcarum terre que valet predictas⁴ iiij m¹ marcas ad suam
propriam aduenturam pro vj m¹ v c marcis.⁵

Item, pro tranquillita[te] et pace tempore vite, ita vt non perturbetur
per seruos hospicij, balliuos, firmarios seu attornatos placitorum.

Item, quod abbas de Sente Bede⁶ potuit resistere fundacioni, intencione
35 vt tunc remaneat sibi et suis.

62. Perhaps to THOMAS HOWES: draft

Perhaps 1462, 9 February

Add. 27444, f. 115. 12 × 5¾ in. Hand unidentified.

Dorse: Paper seal over wax. Address in Daubeney's hand:

*To my most reuerent and worchepfull maister, John Paston þe eldest, esquier,
be this deliueryd in hast.*

Seal the same as that on Daubeney's letter in MS. Add. 34888, f. 208
(Part II, no. 668), of July 1462.

The person addressed is a servant of Fastolf's responsible enough to have been
entrusted with the formal handing over of property on his behalf, and on good
terms with Paston. Howes seems the most likely. It is not clear what the address
to Paston, and the seal, may imply. This can in any case hardly be the actual missive,
which Paston would not be able to recover from Howes (or another) as easily as
he could collect his letters to his own family; so it can hardly be that this was sent
as a draft to him which he was to approve or correct and then forward. It seems
most likely to be a draft, written on a blank piece of paper which had been sent to
Paston enclosing other documents.
   The date is uncertain. Gairdner suggested 1462 as the first year after Fastolf's
death in which Paston was in London at the beginning of February.
   G. 439/508.

Right trusty *and* welbeloved, I grete yow hartily well, and will ye wyte
þat where hit is so þat Ser John Fastolf, wham God assoyle, wiþ oþur,
was sum tyme by Ser Herry Inglose ⌐enfeffed⌐ of trust of his maner offe
Pykewurþe in Rutlande, þe which made his wille, proved, þat þe seid
5 maner sholde by solde by Robert Inglose *and* Edmunde Wychingham his
executours, to whom þe seid Ser John haþ relesed as his duté was to do;
now it is so þat for ⌐John Brow[n]e⌐¹ þer is shewed a dede vnder seall of

---

⁴ *Reading uncertain.*   ⁵ *Remainder by John I.*
⁶ -d- *over another letter; apparently an error for* Benet.
62. ¹ *Interl. by Paston above* Herry Inglose *canc.*

armes² berynge date byfore his reles made to þe Duk of Norffok, Henry
Inglose, *and* oþur, contrarie to þe wille of þe seid Ser Herry *and* þe trust
⌐of þe feffement⌐ þat þe seid Ser John Fastolf was enfeffed jnne,³ and a 10
letter of atto*ur*ney vnder þe same seal of armes to yow to deliuer seison
acordynge to þe same feffement, to þe gret disclaundre of þe seid Ser
John *and* all his, yef þis be true. Wherfore I preie yow hertili þat ye feithfully *and* truly rescribe to me in all þe hast ye may what ye knowe in þis
mater such as ye wull stonde by wiþ-outen glose, *and* how ye can jmagine 15
þat þis crafte shulde be practised, and specially wheþer ye yo*ur*-self
deliu*er*ed seison in Rutland or noo. And þis *and* what incidentes⁴ ye knowe
I preie yow by wrytinge certifie me⁵ in all hast, þat I may be þe more ripe
to answer to þis to þe wurship of þe seid Ser John þat was yo*ur* maister,
so þat þorowh yo*ur* defaute yo*ur* seid maist*er*s soule þer-for lie not in 20
perell, but þis disclaundre may be eesed *and* cesed as reson requireþ,
to þe wurship of hym *and* all þat longe to hym.

And þis I p*ray* yow faile not offe, as I truste yow.⁶ Wret at Londo[n]
þe ix day of Februar.⁷

Yowr frend JON PASTON

63. Perhaps to the SHERIFF OF NORFOLK: draft 1462, March

Add. 43489, f. 13. 8½×4⅜ in. Draft in five different hands: in order of
appearance John Paston III, James Gresham, John Pampyng, John Paston
I, and an unidentified clerk. (The main hand is Gresham's, not Lomnor's
as the manuscript index says.)

Dorse: Continuation of text.

This is a very rough draft obviously in an unfinished state. From the appearance
of John Paston I's hand in two places (see nn. 15 and 21) it seems that the responsibility for it was his.

The year appears from the references to the Duke of Somerset and the Earl
of Oxford. Henry VI and Queen Margaret had escaped to Scotland after the
battle of Towton in March 1461. Somerset went with them, and he was later sent by
Margaret to France to appeal for help. Oxford, who was discovered to be in correspondence with her, was arrested and beheaded on 26 February 1462. The part
of the draft written by Gresham was dated 'on Our Lady's Eve', that is the eve of
the Annunciation (Lady Day), 24 March; but this was struck out when the text was
extended (n. 13). The third week of Lent mentioned in John Paston III's heading
was presumably (counting from Ash Wednesday) from 17 to 23 March.

F. i, p. 250. G. 443/512 (part).

² by *canc.*
⁴ *Third and fourth letters uncertain.*
⁶ *All after this in Paston's hand.*

³ to litel wurship *canc.*
⁵ þat *canc.*
⁷ *Last three letters uncertain.*

Memorandum,[1] thys is the confescyon of xvj Frenshemen wyth the mastyr takyn at Sheryngham[2] þ[e][3] iij wek of Lent.[4]

Right[5] worshipfull ser, I recomaund me to you and lete you wytte þat I haue be at Shiryngham and examyned þe Frenshmen, to þe nombre of xvj, with þe maister. And þei telle þat þe Duk of Somerset is in-to Skotlond, and þei sey þe Lord ⌐Hungyrforthe¬[6] was on Moneday last passed a-fore
5 Sheryngham in-to Skotlondward in a kervyle of Depe, no gret power with hym ne with þe seid Duk neyther. And þei sey þat þe Duk of Burgoyn is[7] poysened and not like to recouere.[8] And as for powers to be gaderid a-geynst our weelfare, þei sey þer shuld come in-to Seyne cc gret forstages owt of Spayne from þe kyng þere, and ccc shippes[9] from þe Duk of[10]
10 Bretayne with þe navy of Fraunce, but þei be not yet assembled ne vitayll þere purveyd, as þei sey, ne men. And þe Kyng of Fraunce is in-to[11] Spayne on pilgrymage with fewe hors, as þei sey; what þe purpose is þei can not telle certeyn, &c. In hast at Norwich.[12]

Ther[13] ⌐wer¬[14] vpon the costes of Norfolk and Suffolk a xiiij seyle of
15 Depe, Ewe,[15] Hareflew, wherof vij be smalle and passe nott xxiiij men a pese, and the remnawnt be of a vij^{xx} men a pese, wherof ij be in-to Scotland ward. On is lade with wyne and whete and a-nother with iij c menes harneys, white and bregaunders.

Item, ther be passed before tyme a vj or vij shippes in-to[16] Scotland[17]
20 ward in the maner of marchaundes lade with wyne and whete.[18]

Memorandum of Burdews.[19] The Kyng of Frauns hath comittid the rewle of Burdews on-to the marchaundis of the to[wn][20] and the sowiours tha[t] be therin to[21] be at ther wages; and like as Caleys is a stapill of wolle here in England, so is that made stapill[22] of wyne.

63. [1] *This sentence roughly written at the top of the sheet by John Paston III, except for the last four words which are added by John I.*
[2] *Uncertain: abbr.* Sher *with flourished* -r, *then some letters which seem to be* ngha *above line at top edge of paper and imperfect* m.
[3] þ- *imperfect,* e *om.*   [4] *At edge.*
[5] *Gresham's hand begins with this word.*
[6] *Interl. by J. Paston III above* Moleyns *canc.* (Robert Hungerford was Lord Moleyns *before he became Lord Hungerford in 1459.*)
[7] po *and beginning of long* s *canc.*
[8] and Floket poysened *and* ded *canc.*   [9] owt *canc.*
[10] Breyn *canc.*   [11] Bretayn *canc.*
[12] on Our Lady Euyn *canc. Recto, and Gresham's hand, end here.*
[13] *Pampyng's hand begins with this word.*
[14] *Interl. by John Paston I.*   [15] E- *over* h.
[16] -o *over* h.   [17] -a- *apparently from* o.
[18] *Pampyng's hand breaks off here. In next line, in unidentified hand,* Item the lorde Moleynes in Seland *canc.*
[19] *These three words by J. Paston I; remainder of paragraph hastily written by Pampyng, crowded in after the next item was written.*
[20] *Written* to *fold. by dot, perhaps accidental.*
[21] *Written over* be.   [22] *End not clear; written over something else.*

John[23] Fermer, presoner, seyth on John Gylys, a clerk þat was wyth the   25
Erle of Oxforthe wych was some tym in[24] Kyng Herrys hows, was a
prevy secretary wyth the Erle of Oxforthe, *and* if ony wrytyng wer mad
by the seyd Erle the seyd Gylys knew ther-of in[25] thes gret materys, &c.

64. Inventory and indenture: draft   1462, 6 June

Add. 39848, ff. 50–3. Ff. 50 and 51, $6 \times 17\frac{3}{8}$ in.; ff. 52 and 53, $6 \times 8\frac{5}{8}$ in.
Pampyng's hand.
Ff. 50 and 51 written on both sides. Ff. 52 and 53 blank on dorse except
for note by Blomefield on f. 52.

The order in which the parts of the draft are meant to stand is uncertain. F. 50^r
begins the draft indenture, and f. 51^r follows on; f. 51^v begins the inventory of
plate etc., and f. 50^v follows on. From the mention on f. 50^v of 'a note of an indenture wretyn vpon the bak of this bille', it appears that the inventory was regarded
as primary. The two smaller sheets do not fit particularly well after either of the
other parts, but the addenda to the inventory on f. 52 are nearer to the jewels of
f. 50^v than to the arms of f. 51^r, and the receipts of f. 53 deal with matters similar
to those of f. 51^v. The contents of the six sides are therefore arranged here in the
following order: 51^v, 50^v, 52, 53, 50^r, 51^r.
    G. 450/519 (note only).

A remembrauns of the goodes[1] that somtyme were Ser John Fastolffes,
mad be John Paston aftir such examinacions *and* writyngges as he can fynd:

First, in goold *and* siluer coyned—   m^{l}m^{l}dcxliij li. x s.
Item, in plate of siluer gilt *and* ongilt
xiij^{ml}lxvij vnc. price gilt ij s. x d.   ⎫
ongilt ij s. vj d. amountyng to the somme   ⎬ m^{l}dcxv li. sterlynges   5
of a   ⎭

Item, in plate at London of siluer gilt   ⎫
and ongilt[2] m^{l}m^{l}dxxv vnc. prised, &c.   ⎪
wyth a cuppe *and* a peson of gold weyng   ⎬ ccciiij^{xx}ij li. xx d. sterlynges   10
xlvj vnc. prise the vnc. xx s. in all,   ⎪
amountyng to the somme of—   ⎭

                Summa totall of coyne ⎫ iiij^{ml} dcxl li. xj s. viij d.
                and plate prised—   ⎭

Item,[3] jowelis, nowches, and presious stones not prised: 15
ij cuppes of goold and ij ewers weyng—lxxv vnc.

---

[23] *J. Paston III's hand resumes with this word and continues to the end.*   [24] h *canc.*
[25] *Apparently what is meant; only two minims with flourish.*

64. [1] *The plural abbreviation in this text is regularly so expanded; when written in full the*
plural varies between -es, -is, (-ys), and -s, none strongly predominating.   [2] w *canc.*
    [3] *In left margin opposite this line is* Jocalia non appreciata.

Memorandum of a flaket *and* ij prekett*es* of siluer weying lxv vnc. lying
w*yth* the seid cuppes.

Item,[4] jowellis leyd to plegge be my lord of York to S*er* John Fastolff for
20 vj*c* m*a*rk, that is to sey

A gret diamant in a white rose.

A ragged staff w*yth* diu*ers* *p*resious stones deliu*er*id to the Kyng by the
assent and comaundem*en*t of my lord of Caunt*er*bury.

Item, a gret crosse of gold w*yth* a flatte diamant, a flat rubye, ⌐*and*⌐ iiij gret
25 perlis.

Item, a litell nowche of gold mad chernell wise, w*yth* a poynted dyamant,
a rubie, *and* iij perlis.

Item, a-nother nowche mad fawcon wise, enamelid w*yth* white, a bukle of
gold.

30 Item, an other nowche mad treyfowle wise, w*yth* an emerawd in the
middes w*yth* a long perle hangyng.

Item, a ryng of Sent Lowes w*yth* a ston therin.

Item, a litell cheyne of gold w*yth* a perle hangyng therby *and* ij spangell[5] of
gold.

35 Item, a powche of blew velwet w*yth* pearlis therin ensealid.

Item, a litell purse sealid, *and* therin c*er*teyn seales of siluer broken, *and*
a signet of gold.

Item, a nowche of gold of the fac*i*on of a busshell, w*yth* a baleys, a safer
loseynge, a greet orient pearle, *and* a square diamant, losenged w*yth* a
40 strike of gold, garnysshed w*yth* iij rubies *and* iiij pearlis w*yth* iij pendaunt*es*
of gold.[6]

Item, a box of blak leder, a nowche of gold after the fac*i*on of a rote, w*yth*
a gret safer *and* a gret perle set therin.

Item, an nowche of gold after the fac*i*on of an aungell, w*yth* a flat dyamaunt
45 loseyngewise w*yth* a dyamant flou*r*rid, a rubye in the midd*es*, *and* ij gret
moder perlis on eyther side of the aungell.

Item, an other nowche of gold mad aftir the fac*i*on of a jentilwoman, *and*
therin a dyamant poynted square, a rubye *and* an emerawde in the midd*es*,
and ij gret orient p*er*lis.

50 Aras.[7]

Item, on hooll bed of aras of the largest assise, seler, tester, and coue*r*yng,
w*yth* a jentilwoman[8] sittyng in a chayer.

Item, viij costers of aras, wherof somme grete and some smalle, wherof

---

[4] *The five MS. lines of this item bracketed in left margin, and annotated* Dominus Rex
habet.

[5] -ll *barred as usual when no abbreviation is meant (as* litell *above); but it may occasionally
stand for* -lles.

[6] *F. 51*v *ends; continued on f. 50*v.   [7] *Boldly written in left margin*.

[8] *MS.* -wowan.

on is of the sege of Phalist, an other of the shepperd*es* and her wif*es*, an
other of the Morys daunse, an other of Jason *and* Launcelet, an other of 55
a batayle, on of the coronac*i*on of *Our* Lady, a-nother of the Assumpc*i*on
of *Our* Lady.

As for an jnue*n*tary of ⌈the warderobe *and* of⌉ beddyng ⟨and⟩[9] all stuffe
of howsold remaynyng at Caster, the seid Paston hath no very knowlech
⌈ner⌉[10] informac*i*on therof except of such p*ar*cellis as he reseyvid[11] at the 60
tyme of his first dwelling at Caster, wherof the p*ar*cellis be specified in a
note of an inde*n*ture wretyn vpon the bak of this bille.
It*em*, the seid John Paston giueth[12] like answer*e* as for an jnue[n]taré of
spendyng mony, ryngg*es* and jowellis, clothes, silk, lyne, wollen, <u>bok*es*</u>
<u>Frenshe, Latyn, *and* Englyssh remaynyng in the chambre of the seid</u> 65
<u>Fastolff.</u>[13]

Item, in like wise as for an jnue*n*tarie of the warderobe, beddyng, and all
other stuffe of howsold remaynyng at Southwerk,[14] the seid Paston hath
no certeyn informac*i*on therof, ner non cam to his hand*es* except on bed
specifijd on the bak of this bille. 70

Item, as for ⌈an jnue*n*tarie of⌉ quykke catell, ⌈ther*e* were goyng upon the
maner*s*⌉[15] iij^ml shep be estimac*i*on[16] prised[17] ich m^l at an c m*ar*k, except
certeyn shep were taken a-wey be fors.

Item, as for all hors *and* other catell, the ⌈seid Paston⌉ hath non informac*i*on of it except of on ambelyng hors whech was[18] shuld*e*rid *and* 75
marrid.

It*em*, as for an jnue*n*taré of all dett*es*, aswell be obligac*i*on or be acompt
⌈or otherwise⌉ diew to the seid S*er* John Fastolff, the seid[19] John Paston
hath no certeyn informac*i*on therof, ner he neuir reseyvid ⌈any⌉ part
therof. 80

Here is as moch as the seid Paston can make at this tyme[20] touchyng the
seid jnue*n*tarie w*yth*-out sight *and* exam[in]ac*i*on of old jnuentaries and

---

[9] *A few letters obliterated by blot.*
[10] *In left margin.*   [11] wre *canc.*
[12] *Second and third letters obscured by wrinkle.*
[13] *The last sentence small and ill written, crowded into space left between items.*
[14] *MS.* -werh, -h *over partly formed* k.
[15] *Interl. above* the seid Paston answerith of the prise of m, *all cancelled except* of the
evidently missed in error. Maners *again interlined above* grownd *canc.*
[16] remaynyng vpon *canc.*
[17] be *canc.*   [18] lost of an *canc.*
[19] seid *repeated.*   [20] w*yth* *canc.*

remembrauns and obligac*ions* of creditores whech he hath not in ⌐his⌐
possession.[21]

85 Item, of old pec*es* of velwet, reed *and* roset, to make of jakett*es*.
I*tem*, a furre of martirs to the valew of xviij s. be estimac*ion*.
Item, as for the remnaunt of the stuffe, plate, coyne, *and* jowellis conteynid
in the seid jnue*n*tari, Paston hath no maner of knowlech where it is kept
or lyght[22] at this day, except only of the seid ij cuppes and ewres of gold,
90 and the seid iij nowches conteynid in the seid blak box of leder; whech
cuppes, ewres, and nowches remayne in such plase as thei we*re* first leyd
be the seid John Paston *and* S*er* Thomas Howes.[23]

Here folowen the reseyt*es* of John Paston of the parce⟨lles⟩[24] aboueseid:
M*emorandum* of the sommes and p*ar*celles of coyne *and* plate w*yth*inne
95 wretyn come to the hand*es* and sole kepyng of w*yth*inne wretyn John
Paston: in coyne—m^{l}xliij li. vj s. viij d.
Item, in plate in Norf*folk*—iij^{ml}dcccclxviij vnc. valewed after the p*ri*se
w*yth*inne wretyn—dxij li. x s.
I*tem*, in plate at London—cccxxxiiij vnc. dj. after the valew *and* p*ri*se
100 w*yth*inne wretyn—xliiij li. ij s. vj d.

Sum*m*a m^{l}diiij^{xx}xix li. xix s. ij d.

Item, of the ⌐prise of⌐ shep w*yth*inne wretyn, after the nombre that
remayned ⌐not take awey⌐[25]

Item, as for all stuffe of howsold w*yth*inne wretyn or any[26] other stuffe
105 that was the seid S*er* John Fastolff*es*, of gonnes[27] or artillrye[28] remaynyng
in the plase at Caster, the seid John hath reseyvid the p*ar*cellis vndir
wretyn to the valew of xl or l m*ar*k be estimac*ion*, *and* nomore to his

---

[21] *Below this, after a space, is* Item to remembir, *the last two words cancelled; then the
following cancelled by large crosses:*

I*tem*, as for the jnue*n*tary of c*er*teyn coyn ⌐for dayli exspenc*es*⌐, ryngg*es* [broches *canc.*]
or jowellis, clothes of silk, lynen, and wollen, and also diu*ers* bok*es* of Frensshe, Latyn,
and Englyssh [beyng kept in *canc.*] remaynȳng in the chambre of the seid S*er* John
Fastolff at his deyng in the kepyng of his seruaunt*es* Nicholas Newman ⌐and⌐ [*above*
or covered by ampersand] Robard Boteler, the seid Paston hath no certeyn informac*ion*
therof, ne nought therof com to his hand*es*. Cf. n. 13 above.
F. 50^v *ends; continued on f.* 52^r.

[22] *Loop above* -t *perhaps meant as abbr.*

[23] F. 52 *ends except for* Inuentar' vlt. *written upside down about 2 in. from foot. Continued
on f.* 53^r.

[24] *Edge slightly torn.*

[25] *Space for figures left blank.*

[26] wyth *canc.*

[27] *A minim too many.*

[28] -r- *roughly inserted.*

knowlech; whech good*es*[29] the seid S*er* John Fastolff ⌐neuer int*e*nded⌐ to
voyde from the seid John Paston ner owt of the seid plase, but to haue
left it bettir stuffid, as it is wele knowe.[30]   110

This endenture mad at Castre the vj day of June the yere of the reigne of
Kyng Edward the iiij[th] the second witnessith that there remaynid in the
place at Caster c*er*teyn stuff of housold,
that is to sey in the warderobe—xj peyr*e* blankett*es*.   115
It*em*, xvj peyr*e* shet*es and* on old shete, wherof iij peyr*e* be of iij webbis.
It*em*, viij wovyn cou*er*lit*es*.
It*em*, ij dong*es*.
It*em*, v smale fetherbedd*es*.
It*em*, vj traunsomes.
It*em*, v carpett*es*.   120
It*em*, ij coster*es* of tapsery werk of huntyng, for the gret chamber ou*er*
the halle.
It*em*, on coster of taps*er*i for the somer halle.
It*em*, ij costeris of reed tapsery pleyn.
It*em*, j cou*er*yng of pleyn tapsery.   125
It*em*, iij white beddis w*yth* the selo*ur*s *and* tester*es*.
It*em*, ix curteyns.
It*em*, iij p*ur*poyntes[31] of white lynen cloth.
It*em*, a selo*ur*, j tester of white lynen cloth.
It*em*, j coster of taps*er*i of jentilwom*e*n pleyng at the card*es*.   130
It*em*, j pece of grene say poudrid w*yth* levys.
It*em*, j curteyne.
It*em*, j pece of grene say.
It*em*, iij old shet*es*.

In Inglose chambre   135
It*em*, j fedirbed.
It*em*, j traunsom.
It*em*, j selo*ur*, j tester aras, w*yth* a cou*er*yng to the same.
It*em*, iij redde curteyns of say.
It*em*, j banker of taps*er*i.   140
It*em*, iiij costers of taps*er*i werk.
It*em*, j peyr*e* blankett*es*.
It*em*, xij koshyns of taps*er*i.

In my M*aster* Fastolff*es* chambre
It*em*, j fedirbed.   145

[29] was neuir thentent of *canc*.   [30] *F. 53 ends; continued on f. 50*[r].
[31] *First syllable repr. by the usual abbr. for* pro.

Item, j traunsom.
Item, j selo*ur*, j tester of taps*eri* w*yth* jentilme*n and* jentilwomen.
Item, j coster of taps*eri*.
Item, j coster party white *and* grene w*yth* mapill levis.

150 Item, in the warderobe
Item, ij towaylis of diap*er* werk ich x yard*es* long.
Item, iiij napkyns of diap*er*.
Item, iiij tabill clothes of diap*er*.
Item, v pleyn clothes.
155 Item, j towayle of pleyn clothe.
Item, ij old clothes.
Item, iiij cuppebord clothis.
Item, vj pillows of diu*ers* sort*es*.
Item, iij old pillows coue*ryd* w*yth* lynen cloth.
160 Item, ij lavendre pokes.
Item, ij litill pillows stuffid w*yth* downe.

Item, in the white chambre.
Item, j fedirbed, j traunsom.

Item, in the warderobe chambre, j fedirbed, j traunsom.
165 Item, j selo*ur* reed.
Item, j peyre blankett*es*.

In the chambre next the somyr halle, j fedirbed, j traunsom.
Item, j selo*ur*, j tester.
Item, a coue*ryng* of reed taps*eri* w*yth* iij curteyns of tarteryn.
170 Item, j peyre fustiens.
Item, iiij costers of coors taps*eri*.
Item, j fedirbed for a paylet.
Item, j peyre blankett*es*.
Item, j cuppebord cloth.
175 Item, ij pillows.[32]

Item, in the inner chambre
Item, j fedirbed, j traunsom.
Item, j selo*ur*, j tester, j coue*ryng* of boord Alisaundre w*yth* iij curteyns of
white lynen clothe.
180 Item, j coster of taps*eri*.

In the vtter ward in Bokkyngg*es* chambre
Item, j fedirbed, j traunsom.

[32] *F. 50^r ends; continued on f. 51^r.*

Item, j selour, j tester, wyth popeleres.
Item, j peyre blankettes.
Item, ij couerlytes.   185

Item, in the kechyn
Item, vij pottes of brasse, wherof iij grete, iiij smale.
Item, j chafor of laton.
Item, iij spittes.
Item, ij rakkes.   190
Item, a ladill of brasse.
Item, ij chaforis of brasse.
Item, ij lache pannys.
Item, ij chariours of peutir.
Item, xj disshis.   195

All whech Ser Thomas Howes, be the handes of John Russe, hath deliuerid
to Richard Calle to deliuer to hise mastir John Paston the older, squier, at
his comyng to housold to Caster. ˙
Wretyn the day and yere a-boueseid.

Item,[33] of the stuffe of howsold in Southwerk deliuered to John Paston, a   200
bed of white lynen cloth wyth shetes and blankettes *and* a bed[34] *and* a
curyng.

Item, ij gonnes wyth viij chambers shetyng a stone of vij inch thyk, xx vnch
compas.[35]
Item, ij lesser gonnes wyth viij chambers shetyng a stone of v inch thyk,   205
xv vnch compas.[35]
Item, a serpentyng wyth iij chambers shetyng a ston of x inch cumpas.
Item, a-nother serpentyn shetyng a ston of vij inch cumpas.
Item, iij fowlers shetyng a ston of ⌐xij¬[36] inch cumpas.
Item, ij short gonnes for shippes wyth vj chambers.   210
Item, iij smale serpentynges to shete pellettes of leed.
Item, iiij gonnes lying in stokkes to shete pellettes of leed.
Item, vij hande gonnes wyth other apparell longyng to[37] the seid gonnes.
Item, xxiiij paveyz of elm bord, ij of baleyn.[38]
Item, viij white harneys of old facion.   215
Item, x[39] peyre breganders, febill.

---

[33] *This item (bracketed in left margin) evidently written later into space left between
paragraphs.*   [34] *MS.* fedirbed *underlined and* fedir- *canc.*
[35] *Last three words added later in different unidentified hand.*
[36] *Interl. above* vij *canc.*   [37] wyth *canc.*
[38] *Under this line* Item *and part of another letter canc.*
[39] *Indeterminate stroke to right of* x.

Item, xiiij jakkes of horn, febill.

Item, j white jak.

Item, x basenettes, xxiiij salettes, vj gorgettes.

220 Item, xvj malles led.

Item, ix billes *and* other ⌈peces⌉⁴⁰ harneys *and* wepon, *and* cappis of spelter⁴¹ *and* wyer of litell valew.

Item, iiij gret crossebows of stell, ij of baleyn, iiij of ew.

Item, ij haberions *and* a barell to skore hem.

65. Petition to the DUKE OF NORFOLK: draft 1462-3

Add. 34889, f. 182. 11½ × 11½ in. Pampyng's hand.

Dorse: No seal or address, but marks of folding, soiled.

This is part of a corrected draft, evidently lacking the beginning of the petition—in the first sentence the name of the manor in question is not given. It emerges later as Cotton (l. 14), which is associated with Nacton again in John Paston III's letter no. 324, ll. 65–6.

The person addressed is certainly the Duke of Norfolk (not Suffolk as Gairdner suggested). The Debenham who was 'waged man' to the Duke (l. 10) was Gilbert Debenham, Esq., of Wenham in Suffolk, an agent of Norfolk's and a member of his council (see no. 46). Paston's son who was 'a seruaunt of my lordes' (l. 46) was John III (see, for example, nos. 319–21). Richard Calle, who was 'put to [Paston] by my lordes fader' (l. 47) came from Framlingham (see no. 332), which was Norfolk's seat.

The date appears partly from Paston's possession of Cotton for three years and more (l. 25) after Fastolf's death, which brings it to at least November 1462, partly from the reference to the imprisonment of Richard Calle 'at Mighelmesse the yere passed' (l. 45). A letter to John Paston II signed 'Richard Calle, presoner' can be dated in late October 1461 (see Part II, no. 738). If the phrase 'the yere passed' is to be strictly interpreted, therefore, the present paper must be earlier than 25 March 1463.

G. LI/534.

That it please my lordes good grase to be good lord *and* supporter to Paston in his right *and* possession of the maner till his right can be lawfully, or be treté, dispreved by his aduersaries, consideryng that the seid Paston is my lordes homager and was neuir ayens his lordship, and that my lord is 5 not gretly behold to do for the seid Pastons aduersaries, as he vndirstandith.

And in¹ case my lord woll not supporte the seid Paston in his right, but be indifferent athwyx bothe parties, that thanne it please my lord to haue consideracion to the right of the mater as folowyth² in articles, *and*

---

⁴⁰ *Interl. above* broken *canc.*   ⁴¹ *MS.* spleter.

65. ¹ *No space.*   ² *Ampersand canc.*

therupon to be remembird whedir it be resonably desired by Will Jenney or by Debenham as his waged man, or for his sake, that Paston shuld leve 10 the possession or the takyng of the profitez of the seid maner.

First, to be remembird that the seid maner, aswell as the maner of Nakton, were Ser John Fastolffes, and that the seid Paston of the seid maners toke estate at Cotton and atornement of the tenauntes viij or ix yere goo, in such wise as the tenauntes can reporte, and continued there in possession 15 aswell in the live of the seid Ser John as sithen, and hath take the profitez therof sith the discese of the seid Fastolff except for the terme of Mighelmes a yere passed, whech tyme the tenauntes were compellid by fors of distresses to pay ayens ther willes³ part of the seid profitez.

And that also the title of the seid Paston to the seid maner is not all only 20 by the seid feffement, but aswell by a graunt *and* bargeyn mad a-thwyx the seid Fastolff *and* the seid Paston as by the last will of the seid Fastolff, ⌈whereby⌉⁴ the seid Paston ought to take the ⌈hole⌉ profitez of the seid maner. And⁵ also it ⌈is⌉ lefull to the seid Paston to kepe the seid maner with fors, consideryng he hath be in possession iij yere and more; hough 25 be it the seid Paston intendyth to kepe the seid maner pesibly *and* non otherwi⟨se⟩.⁶

And that the pretense *and* cleyme of the seid Jenney is that he shuld be infeffed with the seid Paston in the seid maner, by whech pretense, if it were trewe, yet the seid Paston by reason shuld not be put out of the seid 30 maner; for who som evir had titell therto by feffement or by executrie, Paston shuld be on that had title. Hough be it the seid Paston cleymyth not in that forme, but by the titell of his bargeyn and by the seid Fastolffes will.

Item, to be remembird whech tyme as my lord had wretyn his lettirs 35 ⌈and sent his seruauntes⌉ for the eyde *and* supporte of the seid Paston to take the profitez of⁷ the seid maner⁸ ⌈of Nakton as of the maner of Cotton, desyry[n]g the tenauntis to⌉⁹ the seid Paston, the seid Jenney wold haue no consideracion therto; hough be it, though he were a¹⁰ feffé he had no titell to take the seid profitez, consideryng he is non executor; but pre- 40 sumptuosly, havyng no consideracion to my lordes lettir ⌈ner sendyng⌉, compellid the tenauntes by distresses to pay hym more besely thanne any

³ of *canc.*
⁴ *Interl. by Paston above* and that *canc.*
⁵ *This and the rest of the paragraph added later.*
⁶ *Last two letters, except for the tail of long s, lost at edge.*
⁷ bothe *canc.*   ⁸ -r *over* -rs.
⁹ *Interl. above and* desiryng the tenauntes *canc.; from* desyry[n]g *in Paston's hand.* (*Construction still incomplete.*)   ¹⁰ feffer *canc.*

feffé or executor, and ⌜now⌝¹¹ at this same tyme hath be at Nakton *and* reseyvid as moch mony as he coud gader there.

45 I*tem*, where at Mighelmesse the yere passed the seid Paston sent his sone, a s*er*ua*u*nt of my lord*es*, and also Ri*char*d Calle, s*er*ua*u*nt to the seid Paston put to hym by my lord*es* fader, to reseyve the p*ro*fitez of the seid maner as thei had do many yeres ⟨befo⟩re,¹² the seid Jenney ded arest the seid Calle for a thef, and as a thef caried hym, to th'entent that the ten*auntes* 50 shuld be discoraged to pay the seid Paston; whech tyme, at the request of the seid Calles kynred, it pleased my lord to write to the seid Jenney *and* Debenham for the deliu*er*auns of the seid Calle, ⌜to whech letteris⌝¹³ they nouther toke hede ner reputac*i*on ⟨bu⟩t by that sotilté reseyved the p*ro*fitez of the seid maner, the seid Paston havyng non help by my seid 55 lord*es* writyng ner sendyng.

Wherfore, please my lord*es* good lordship to supporte the seid Paston in kepyng of his right *and* possession till it be dispreved or knowe onlawfull, and the seid Paston will applye to such meanes as it pleasith my lord to take wherby the right of the mater may be vndirstand *and* determ*i*ned.

60 And also that it like my lord to remembir that it is not behofefull for any prinse lightly to geve trust or to applye to the desires of any p*er*sones that haue geve hym cause of mistrust.¹⁴

66. To JOHN PAMPYNG, RICHARD CALLE, and JOHN WYKES
About 1463

Add. 27444, f. 124. 8¼ × 11½ in. Mainly in unidentified hand (appearing also in nos. 67, 69, and three of Margaret Paston's letters: see no. 192), with address at head and a brief addition by Paston.

Dorse: Long notes in the same clerk's hand. No address, but traces of red wax and marks of folding.

The text looks like a draft, but must have been sent.
     A dispute with Debenham about Calcot is implied in a letter from Richard Calle to Paston datable in 1463 by the copy of a writ which it includes (see Part II, no. 678). This letter is probably of the same period. Cf. nos. 173, 192.
     G. 468/540 (abstract).

To John¹ Pamping, Ri*char*d Call, *and* John Wikes
I grete yow well, dyssyryng yow to re*membre* þe¹ junstr[u]ccion þat I made

---

¹¹ *Interl. by Paston.*
¹² *This and but l. 53 partly obliterated by damp.*
¹³ *Interl. by Paston above* wherto *canc.*
¹⁴ *Fold. by* and *and some ten other words, heavily canc.*

66. ¹ Past *canc.*   ² þ *in form of* y *throughout.*

yow for byllys *and* acciou*n*ys to be takyn ayenst Debnh*a*m by myn ten*a*untys
at Calcot, wherine on thyng I haue forgete: ⌜þat⌝¹³ ʒe moust make a⁴ reme*m*-
brau*n*ce ap*a*rte, besyde þe byllys, in what howse, ⌜place, or close,⌝ or pece of 5
grownde eu*er*y trespace or stres was done or made, and also whedre þat
wer*e* of⁵ myn londes in ferme of aney of myn ten*a*untys, or ell*y*s vpon
ther owyn ten*a*untrys holdyn of me by copye or ell*y*s holde of me frely,
and by what rent as neye as ʒe maye, *and* whedr*e* it was holdyn of me by
Calcote⁴ Halle fee or ell*y*s by Freton Halle fee; *and* yf⁶ þe trespace wer*e* 10
don in aney othyr*e* manys grownde or fee, telle hooys it was *and* by what
coullour*e* myn ten*a*untys best*y*s went þer as þei wer*e* dreuyn, as p*ar*auen-
towr⁷ by-cause of ⌜comu*n*e in⌝ chacke tyme or by-cause of her tenowr⁷
þat they hylde of othyr*e* men, for w*y*th*oute* I knowe þis⁸ my ten*a*untys myt
be dysseyuyd in þer plee, for p*ar*aunt*ure* Debnh*a*m wylle of suttl⟨té⟩⁹ 15
justifie he toke them in suche a place as he dede not, *and* w*y*th*o*wte I
knowe þe s*er*teynté I chal not con*n*e answer*e* hym. Also¹⁰ I woulde Deb*n*-
ham schulde haue as lytell knoweleche þat ʒe wer*e* abowte suche acciou*n*ys
as myght be, yf ʒe maye do other-wyse.

Also jn leke wyse, wher*e* as dyu*er*s of myn ten*a*untys *and* fermors at 20
Cotton haue be compellyd by force *and* dystress*c*ys to paye Jenney *and*
Debnh*a*m meche money ayenst þe wylle of myn ten*a*untys, I woulde, as
I haue tolde John Paston þe you*n*gere, that he *and* Ric*h*ard Calle, w*y*th
suche frendchyp as þe seyd John cane gete in þe same cou*n*tré, schulde
ryde to Cotton askyng myn hole duté exeppte of suche p*er*sons as wer*e* 25
compellyd to paye *vt sup*ra and þat they chulde make bylles lyke myn
seyde ten*a*untys at Calcote, and þei to take acciou*n*ys þis nexte terme
ayenst Debunham,¹¹ &c. *vt sup*ra, and I wylle respyte them ⌜for þis onys⌝
al þat þei¹² haue in þis forme payed tylle it maye be recuryd by þe lawe,
so þat they wylle dyssyre this and abyde therby; *and* ellys I woulde by 30
myn fryndys poletekely put them in jup*ar*té of losse of þer fermes *and*
tenowr as they holde of me, *and* of þer catell. Item, at þe same jurné I
woulde Ric*h*ard Calle chulde haue redy a bylle in a longe rolle of þe
⌜tenore⌝¹³ of eche of myn ten*a*untys *and* fe⌜r⌝morrys, as well of þe quan-
tité of þe londe as rent *and* ferme, wretyn to-gyddre and su*m*yd w*y*th a 35
gret spase folowyng, þat¹⁴ ʒe maye, whane ʒe come to Cotton, redely
write what catell of eche man was dystreynyd, *and* wher*e* *and* what daye,
and whoo meche money þei payed,¹⁵ *and* respit þat *and* ask þe remnant.

---

³ *In margin.*   ⁴ *No space.*   ⁵ þe *canc.*
⁶ *MS.* yt.   ⁷ -r *repr. by usual* -ur *abbr.*   ⁸ I maye *canc.*
⁹ *End of this word blotted and illegible.*   ¹⁰ wher *canc.*
¹¹ *Or* Debnnham.
¹² *Written first* þei þat; þat *canc. and inserted before* þei.
¹³ *Interl. above* duté *canc.*   ¹⁴ y *canc.*
¹⁵ *Scribe's hand ends; the rest in Paston's hand, crowded into the small space at foot of*
page, partly illegible owing to smudging, partly lost at edge.

þis bill is god inow to take acciouns by, *and* vnder this Ric*hard* Call may
40 rekkon wi*th* eu*er*[y] p*er*sone for[16]

The Statute of Westm*inster* þe furst, the xxxviij chappe*ter*.
That no man be so hardy to seye ne to telle oney false noueltés or tydyng-
ys whero⟨f⟩ aney dyscorde or slau*n*dre may ryse or growe atuyxe þe Kyng
and hys pepul o⟨r⟩ the grete men of hys londe, and yf aney doo þat he be
45 takyd *and* putt in p*re*son tylle he hath fou*n*de hym that tolde þe tale.
The secu*n*de *and* þe xij yere of Kyng Ric*hard* the ij^de.
That no man be so hardy for to seye, telle, ne cou*n*trefet oney false
noueltés, massonges, or othre falsse thyng*ys* of p*re*lates, duk*ys*, erlus,
barou*n*ys, and othy*re* nobles of the reaulme, ne of þe chau*n*celere, tresor*ere*,
50 clerk of þe p*re*uy seall, stuard of the Kyng*ys* howse, justice of þe co*mun*
banke or of þe thothyre, ne of hothr*e* grete offycer*ys* of þe realme wher-
thourowe[17] oney dyscorde or sklau*n*dre myght ryse w*yth*[i]nne þe realme;
and yf he doo that he be inp*re*sonyd tylle he fynde hym of hwome þe tale or
mat*er* was meuyd, and yf he cane not fynde hym þ*at* he be pu*n*ychyd be þe
55 awyse of þe Kyng*ys* cowncell.
And in þes statute is rehersyd þe cauce of þe makyng therof, for as
moche as be þe menys of suche teller*ys and* cou*n*tre-feter*ys* of tydyng*ys*,
noueltés, *and* false mesag*ys* dyu*er*s lord*ys and* othrys were dysslau*n*dryd
of thyng*ys* þ*at* they neu*er* thowte ne dede, wherthorowe debate *and*
60 stryf grewe as well be-tuyxe lord*ys* as betuyx lord*ys and* comu*n*ys.
Yf a lorde do an extorcion to me or entre in-to myn londe *and* make
hym a tytell by coulloure of purchace or of kynrede whech is falsse *and*
vntrue, I[18] and myn s*er*uauntys may laufully seye that he doth me wronge
and vntrowth *and* telle þe trowthe of my mat*er and* þe vntrowthe of hys
65 mat*er* as it is, and neu*er* offende þe statute.

67. Petition to Robert Welles and others: draft

Probably 1463–5

Magdalen College, Oxford, Fastolf Paper 74. 11⅜×12⅛ in. Hand of no.
66.

Dorse blank except for *Fastolf* in a rough, apparently almost contemporary,
hand.

The date must be between the death of Fastolf in November 1459 (see no. 54)
and that of John Paston I in May 1466. The Willoughby in question is Robert,
sixth Lord Willoughby, about whom Fastolf wrote to Paston in 1456 (Part II,
no. 541). He died in July 1452 without male issue. His nephew Robert Willoughby
took possession of some of his property, but his heir was his daughter Joan, who

---

16 *Recto, as far as legible, ends.* 17 dys *canc.* 18 challe *canc.*

married Richard, son of Lionel, sixth Lord Welles, and whose son was Robert Welles (*Complete Peerage* under *Willoughby* and *Welles*; *Cal. Pat. Rolls 1452–61*, p. 396). Robert Welles was still 'esquire' in February 1465 (*Cal. Close Rolls 1461–8*, p. 261), but later knighted.

The approximate date suggested would suit Paston's complaint about 'ten years and more' (l. 27)—though in any case until 1459 the loss would be Fastolf's, not his—and also his employment of this clerk.

Unprinted.

To my Mast*er* ⌈Robert⌉¹ Wellis, cosyn *and* heyr*e* to S*er* Robert Wylloughby,² knyght, late lorde of Erisby, and to the discrete executor*es* and feffés of the seyde S*er* Robert *and* to euery³ of them.

Compleynyth on-to yow John Paston, esquier, that the seyd S*er* Robert, dyuers tymes faylyng sufficenté of good*es* to susteyne hys astate, opyned 5 that to his trusty frynde S*er* John Fastolff, knyght, and of hym hade *and* cheuysched dyuers tymes grete soummys of money, and in speciall cc marke in money at on tyme, for whech cc mark the seyd S*er* Robert gaff *and* graunted to þe⁴ seyd Fastolff, *and* to hys heyrys *and* assignes, c s. of anuell rennt *and* odre⁵ seruice perteynyng to þe seyd S*er* Robert be hys 10 inherytaunse goyng owt of the maner of Heynforde in Norffolk, and also the seyd S*er* Robert gaff, grauntyd, *and* obliged his maner of Walcot in Norffolk to the seyd Fastolff, his heyr*es* *and* assignes, for her surté *and* jndemnité in case it fortuned the seyd c s. of rennt to be recouered or hade from hym,⁶ hys heyres or assignes, whos estat *and* tytill⁷ therof the seyd John 15 Paston hath; ande that Robert Wylluby, esquer*e*, as cosyn and heyre male to the seyde S*er* Robert, hat recouered *and* opteyned the seyde c s. rent *and* othere seruice wyth the maner of Parham in Suffolk be þe vertue of a tayle of olde⁸ tyme therof made, be wheche he is inheritable as heyre male to þe seyd S*er* Robert Wyllouby. And also ye, my seyd Mastre Wellys, 20 as cosyn and heyre generall to þe seyd S*er* Robert, cleyme *and* pretend to haue the s[e]yde maner*e* of Walcotte frome the seyd Paston, howbeit the seyde maner*e* was of late tyme purchased be þe fadr*e* of þe seyd S*er* Robert in fee⁸ symptle and ys⁹ not tayled; be whiche cleyme *and* pretence the seyd Paston taryeth *and* is lettyd *and* inqueetyd of the takyng of þe 25 profett*es* of þe seyd maner*e* of Walcotte, and hath forbore *and* lost the seyde c s. of rent *and* odre seruice x yer*e* *and* more, to þe summe of l li., wytoute aney recoumpence or satisfac[c]ion hade therfore, ⌈whych is⌉¹⁰ contrarye to seyde graunt*es* *and* gyft*es* made be þe seyde Sere Robert vndre the seall*es* of hys arm*ys*,¹¹ ⌈to hym⌉¹⁰ and his blode werdly dy[s]honoure 30

67. ¹ *Interl. apparently by Paston, abbr.* Robt *without the usual stroke above which all later occurrences have.*

² -g- *over* b.   ³ iche *canc.*   ⁴ þ *in form of* y, *as throughout*; e *raised.*

⁵ seruisec *canc.*   ⁶ or *canc.*

⁷ -s *canc.*   ⁸ *No space.*

⁹ *Written* hys, h- *canc.*   ¹⁰ *Interl. by Paston.*

¹¹ wheche is *canc., then several words obliterated by tear, then* Ser Robert *canc.*

and to hys soule grett *p*erille, to yow*r* seyde supplyau*n*t grete wronge *and* damage*s*;[12] beschechyng yow to reme*m*bre *and* consed*r*e that ye[13] forseyde feffe*s and* executore*s* be bou*n*de to redresse wronge*s* don *and* co*m*myttyd be yow*r* seyde feffow*r and* testatow*r* or be hys menys, and more-ouere
35 yow*r* seyd feffow*r and* testato*w*r by expresse[14] wrytyng declarid his last wylle, that his dett*es and* wronge*s* by hym don schoulde be by yow satys- fyed and payed and that hys f*ᵊr*ᵊlynd*es*, offi[c]er*es* and s*e*ruaunte*s* schuld be made sure of alle *p*rofites, annuyté*s*, *and* fees to hem or anney of them by hym grau*n*tyd, afte*r*e[15] the trewe intent *and* effect of thoo grau*n*tes, and that
40 heys[16] heyres schuld ratyfye *and* make the seyde gr*a*untes sue*r* befor*e* anney astate to hem made of any *p*arte of hys lyflode, as in the seyde wylle mor*e* expressly apperyth; wherfor plese yow*r* gret wysdomys *and* goode con- sienses so to *p*rouide that yow*r* seyd suppliaunt may pesibeli[17] haue *and* jngoye the seyd man*e*r of Walcott*es* that of ryght to hym belongyth be
45 reson of the seyde grau*n*t of the seyd S*e*r Robe*r*t, wyth resonable satis- faccion for the hurte that he hath hadde *and* sufferyd in that behalue.

68. Inventory: draft　　　　Probably 1464, not later than April

Add. 27446, f. 117. $8\frac{1}{8} \times 4\frac{3}{4}$ in. Pampyng's hand.

Dorse blank.

This is a draft of the 'bille drawin jn Englyche' of which a Latin version is given in the latter part of no. 69. The letter with the enclosed inventory cannot have been written much earlier than no. 69, since the instructions in it had evidently not been acted upon when no. 69 was written.
G. 976/562.

This is the plate þat was in my cofir at Norwich.

A chaleys of goold playne, weyng ij pound.
Item, a-nother chaleys of goold w*it*h this writyng, *Cali*cem salutar*is*[1] *accipiam*, weyng xix vnc.
5 Item, on table of gold w*it*h an jmage of Sen James set w*it*h precious stonys, weyng xiij vnc. iij qu*a*rt.
Item, on peyre of sensers of siluer *and* gilt w*it*h scripture, viz. in[2] the first part *Datum est eis*, &c., and in the second *p*arte *Ascendit fum*us, weying xiij li. *and* x vnc.

---

12 dyssyryng *canc.*
13 *Written with* e *on line, not raised; so* 'ye' *not* 'the'.
14 -s *canc.*
15 the *canc.*
16 seyd *interl. by Paston but canc.*
17 -erely *canc.*
68. 1 *MS.* salutular*is*.
2 prima *canc.*

It*em*, on box of siluer *and* gilt for the sacreme*nt*, w*it*h a crosse in the heyght 10
and chased w*ith* lilijs, weying v li. iij vnc. di.

Item, on ⌐potte callid⌐[13] a crismatorie to put in holy creme ⌐*and*⌐[14] oyle
⌐of⌐ siluer *and* gilt, weying j li.

69. Memorandum   1464, April

Add. 27444, f. 129. About $6\frac{1}{2} \times 11\frac{1}{2}$ in. (right edge irregularly torn).
Mostly in the hand of no. 66, but all the notes to the left of the main column,
a few lines at the end, and some interlineations, by Paston.

Dorse blank.

See no. 68.
  The fourth year of Edward IV began on 4 March 1464.
  G. 487/561.

This is[1] þe p*ar*cell be indent*ur* rece*iu*ed by Ric*har*d Calle of⟨. . .⟩[2] day of[3]
Ap*r*ile[4] þe forthe yer⟨. . .⟩ as ⌐it apperit⌐ by þe copye þ*at* þe seyde Ric*har*d
sendyth me by John Threccher:

	vnam cistam rubeam cum xvij bundelliss[5] evidenc-	
	⟨. . .⟩	5
	jn eadem cista content'[6]	
	quadraginta libras argenti in grossis et iiijxx	
	nobil⟨. . .⟩	
	duo turribula argenti et deaurata	
	vnam pixidem argenti et deauratam	10
	vnum osculatorium cum jmagine Sancti Jacobi	
	et⟨. . .⟩	
I left no cruet in þe cofer	vnum cruett argenti et deauratum	
	vnum crismatorium rotundum M^d[7]	
I left non soch in þe cofer but chalis of gold	⎧ vnum calicem argenti et deauratum	15
	⎨ vnum alium calicem cum jmagine Sancte	
	⎩ Trini⟨. . .⟩	

---

³ *Interl. above* box *or canc.*   ⁴ *Interl. above* or *canc.*

69. ¹ þe copy *of canc.*
  ² *An unknown amount of writing lost through the whole length of the sheet at irregularly
torn right-hand margin. The English text shows that in some places several words are missing.*
  ³ Marche *canc.*
  ⁴ wherine þe seyde Ric*har*d writte *canc.*
  ⁵ *Abbr. by* -ll *barred.* (*This is relevant to the interpretation of this group in English.*)
  ⁶ -t *has suspension mark, but correct expansion is uncertain since it is not clear whether the
reference is to what precedes or what follows. After* content' (quadraginta *written in the same
line, and canc.*
  ⁷ *This note in Paston's hand.*

This is þe coppy of a bille ⌐drawin⌐[18] jn Englyche that I sent home⟨. . .⟩
main of suche stuff as w[a]s in myn coffre in þe abb⟨ey[9]. . .⟩ by a letter
20 sent wyth þe same bylle that he chowlde take hede that⟨. . .⟩ yf he fonde
aney more well be it, as it aperit in þe seyd lett⟨. . .⟩ woulle be lokyd vppe.

Thes to chalis after the[10] vnc. xx s. ar worth xliij li.	⎧ vnum calicem de auro playne ponderis duas li⟨. . .⟩ ⎨ ⎩ vnum alium calicem de auro cum scriptura Cal⟨. . .⟩
This is worth ⎱ 25 xiij li. xv s. ⎰	vnam tabulam de auro cum jmagine Sancti J⟨. . .⟩ ponderis xiij vnc. et iij quart.
Thes be worth after xxx d. þe vnc. xxviij li. xiij s. ix. d. 30	⎧ vnum par turribulorum argenti et deaurat'[11] cum⟨. . .⟩ ⎪ et in secunda parte *assendit fumus* ponderis xiij lb. ⎪ et⟨. . .⟩ ⎨ vnum pixidem argenti pro scacramento deaurat'[12] ⎪ cum cruce⟨. . .⟩ lilijs ponderis v lb. et iij vnc. di. ⎩ vnum ampullam argenti deaurat'[12] ponderis j lb.

All þis was put in a[13] panere togyddre and⟨. . .⟩ forto ber[14] it in-to þe
coffre.[15]

Item, xl mark in noblis and xl li. in gro⟨. . .⟩
35   Item, euydens.

70. Petition to EDWARD IV   1464

Three copies, with variant texts:

A. Bodl. MS. Charters Norfolk a. 8, no. 727. $16\frac{3}{8} \times 4\frac{3}{8}$ in.
B. Ibid., no. 726. $14\frac{3}{4} \times 3\frac{7}{8}$ in.
C. B.M. Add. 27444, f. 131. $16\frac{1}{2} \times 4\frac{7}{8}$ in.

All three on parchment, carefully written, though none entirely without
correction: A in an unidentified clerk's hand, B and C in Pampyng's hand.
All dorses blank except for brief Latin descriptions in the sixteenth-
century annotator's hand.

A, the shortest text, seems to have been written first, then C, which retains the
opening formula of A but adds the details of the manors incorporated into B,

---

[8] *Interl. by Paston, followed by* of Pampi, *and top of* g, *canc.*
[9] *Tail of* y *and part of* e *remain.*   [10] *Some letters, perhaps* ow, *canc.*
[11] -t *has heavy curl added later, intention uncertain.*
[12] *In view of confusion of gender at beginning of entry expansion of abbreviation uncertain.*
[13] skepe *to canc.*   [14] *No space.*
[15] *This line crowded in after the remaining two, in Paston's hand, were written, the first
four words by Paston. At foot, to the left, is a hasty scribble that looks like* the endentwr &c.

and in spelling and some details of wording has links with both.[1] A and B are given in full, with the variants of C compared with B.

The date appears from a royal grant evidently made in response to this petition in one of its forms, and dated 10 September 4 Edward IV (1464) (Part II, no. 686).

G. 492/569.

A

To the Kyng owre sovereyn Lord

Please it yowre Highnes to graunte vn-to yowre humble seruaunt John Paston the older, squier, yowr gracious lettres patentz of licence to fownde, stabilysh, and endewe in the gret mancion of Castre be Mekyll Yermowth in Norffolk, that late was John Fastolffes,[1] knyght, cosyn to yowre seyd besecher, a colage of vij prystes, wheroff on to be master, and vij pourmen,   5
to praye for your noble astate and for the sowle of the ⌐said⌐ Fastolff and suche othir as he was be-holde to inperpetuité, and to jnmortese and gyve to the seyd prystes and to ther successours, for the sustentacion of hem and of the seyd pourmen, c marke of annuité and rent charge yerly goyng owt of all maneres, londes, and tenementz that were the seyd   10
Fastolffes with-in the shyres of Norffolk and Suffolk, and vj acres of londe in the sayd town of Castre, and the iiij parte of the sayd mancion for the habitacion of the sayd prystes and pourmen to be repared at the costes of your seyd besecher and hys heyres and assignes for euer, as suerly and lawfully as your seyd besecher can devise; and also be your letteres   15
patentz to graunt the same prystes to be on bodie incorperate and to have succession perpetuall and a comon seall, and to be persones abyll to plede and be impletid,[2] and to purchase and alienyn ⌐all maner⌐[3] londes, tene-mentes,[4] godes, and catell, be the name of the master and hys brethyrn of the collage of Saynt John Baptiste of Castre afore sayd; and also be your   20
letteres patentz to licence the sayd prystes to take and receyve and to holde to theym and to ther successours the sayd annuité,[5] rente charge, vj acres of lond, ⌐auowsons⌐,[3] and the seyd iiij parte of the said mancion for euer, with-owte eny fyne or fe to be payde for the sayd lettres patentz, ⌐licens⌐, or grauntes be your sayd besecher or be the said pristes. And thei shall   25
pray hertly to God for you.

B

To the Kyng oure liege Lord

Besechyth lowly youre humble seruaunt John Paston the older, squier, that it please youre good grace, for such a fyne as youre Highnes hath

---

[1] e.g. *lettirs* with B but *patentz* with A, *prestes* with B but *Castre* with A; also *pourmen* with A against *porefolk* B.

70A. [1] -es *abbr. added later.*   [2] -tid *on eras.*   [3] *Interl. roughly by Paston.*
   [4] *Stroke on eras. of about four letters.*   [5] *MS.* annanuite.

apoynted youre seid besecher to content yow, wherof ye be put in suerté,
to graunt on-to youre seid besecher youre gracious lettirs patentes of
5 licence to found, stabilissh, and endewe in the gret mancion of Caster
in Flegge in Norffolk, that late was John Fastolffes, knyght, cosyn to
youre seid besecher, a college of vij prestes, wherof on to be master, and
of vij porefolk, to pray for youre noble astate and for the soule of the seid
John Fastolff and such other as he was behold to inperpetuité, aftir
10 ordinauns by youre seid besecher in that behalff to be made; and to
inmortese, geve, and graunt to the seid prestes and to ther successours,
for the sustentacion of hem and of the seid porefolk, cxx mark of annuité
and rent charge, or annuités and rentes charge, yerly goyng out of the
maners callid Redhams, Vaux, and Bosomes in Caster forseid, Begviles
15 in Wynterton, Reppis in Bastewyk, Spencers in Heryngby, Loundhall in
Saxthorp, Heylesdon, Drayton, Heynesford, Guton in Brandeston, Beyton,
Techewell,[1] and of the thrid part of the maner of Runham, with th'apportenauns, in the shire of Norffolk, and of the maners of Hemnalis in Cotton,
Burneviles in Nakton, Akthorp in Leystoft, Calcotes, Havelound, Spit-
20 lyngges, with th'apportenauns, in the shire of Suffolk, and out of any part
of the seid maners, with a clause of distresse for defaut of payment of
the seid rente, and vj acres of lond in the seid towne of Caster, and the
avowsons of the chirches of the same town, and the fourth part of the
seid mancion, or any part therof, for the habitacion of the seid prestes and
25 porefolk, to be reparid at the costes of youre seid besecher and his heires or
assignes for evir; and also by youre seid lettirs patentes to graunt the same
prestes to be on body incorperate and to haue succession perpetuall and
a comon seall, and to be persones abill to plede and to ⌈be⌉ impletid, and
to purchase and alienyn all maner londes, goodes, and catell, by the name
30 of the master and his brethyrn of the college of Sen John Baptist of Castre
aforeseid; and also by youre seid lettirs patentes to licence the seid prestes
to take and reseyve and to hold to them and to ther successours the seid
annuité, rent charge, vj acres of lond, avousons, and the seid—[2]part of
the seid mancion for evir, and to geve youre chaunceler of Inglond for the
35 tyme beyng comaundement, power, and auctorité that where as in this
petision is not comprehendid the certeynté of termes, maters, clauses,
and other circumstaunces conuenient and requisite after forme of lawe
for licens of the seid fundacion, that youre seid chaunceler, that notwithstandyng, do make youre seid lettirs patentes in forme of lawe effectuall
40 and sufficient in that behalff after the very entent aforeseid, not excedyng
the valew and somme before specifijd, without any fyne or fee other
thanne is afore specifijd to be paijd for the seid lettirs patentes, licens, or
grauntes by youre seid besecher or by the seid prestes. And thei shall pray
hertly to God for yow.

70B. ¹ -ll *obliterated by modern blot.*　　　　² *Stroke on erasure of about six letters.*

Principal variants in C

1–4. *No heading*

Please it you*re* Highnes to graunte on-to you*re* humble s*er*uaunt John Paston the older, squier, you*re* gracious lettirs patentz

5. Castre (*also* 14)
6. Flegg by Mekyll Yarmowth
7, 30. collage
8, 12, 25 pourmen
10. behalve
11. *and* gra*u*nt *interl.*
12. c mark
13. rentz
14. forsayd *cf.* aforesayd 31, 40
20–1 Suff*olk* w*y*th a clause
22–4. Castre and the iiijth part of the seid mancioun for the habitac*io*n
25–6. heyres *and* assignes
26, 29, 31, 43. be
26, 31, 42. patentz
28. be *on line* inpletid
29. lond*es*, tenem*entes*, god*es*
31. you*re* lettirs
33. vj acres of lond *and* the seid iiijth part
36. sertinté
38–9. that he be auctorité of this bille signed by yo*ur* Highnes do make yo*ur* seid lettirs patentz
41–2. wyt*h*owt eny fyne or fee to be payid
43. pray *interl.*

71. To M*argaret* P*aston*   1465, 14 January

Add. 34889, f. 183. 11⅜ × 6½ in. Mainly in Pampyng's hand, with five lines added by Paston.

Dorse: No address, but traces of red wax and marks of folding, soiled as by carrying.

The text looks like a draft (as Gairdner took it to be), but must have been sent.
From the contents of the opening paragraph this seems to have been written about the same time as no. 72, which is dated the next day.
G. LIII/535.

I recomaund me to yow, and haue reseyvid yo*ur* lettir, which causith me to write in the lettir þat I send to yow, Daubeney, *and Richard* Calle certeyn articles touchyng the rewle of myn hows *and* myn livelode, as ye shall vndirstand whanne ye see hem. Also I send yow in the same[1]

71. [1] bille *canc.*

5 lettir a bille of all the malt þat remaynid at Mighelmes. I suppose ye haue
non such of it; neuirthelesse it had be conuenie*nt* it had be had among*es*
your seruauntes *and* yow.² Also I woll þat ye warne both Daubeney *and*
Ri*char*d Calle þat thei disclose nat what malt I haue, ne what I shall selle,
ne þat on marchaunt knowe nat what an other hath; for ther ⌜is⌝ gret
10 spies leid here at London for ingrosers of malt to heyghne the prise,
hough be it myne is not but of myn owne growyng *and* my tenauntes.

Also I lete yow wete I faile mony here and must nedys haue vp mony
at this tyme for sped of my maters, so þat it may come vp savely whanne
James Gresham *and* other attornés come vp at the begynny*ng* of this
15 terme, wi*th* whom Ri*char*d Calle may come the same tyme. And p*ar*aventure some trusty carier may c⟨ome⟩³ at this tyme, and w*ith* hym myght
some mony come trussid in some fardell, not knowyng to the carier⁴
þat it is no mony but so⟨m⟩e⁵ other clothe or vesteme*nt* of silk or thyng
of charge. Wherfore take avise of such as ye tr⟨ust⟩,⁵ and purvey þat I
20 may haue vp at this time j c li. of gold aftir the old coynage and xx li. in
grot*es*.⁶

It*em*, j[f] I might haue sur*e* cariage I wold haue heder⁷ all þe gylt plate
þat Ri*char*d Call leyd vp—he can tell wer*e*, *and* I trowe ye know also; *and*
ij potell pottis *and* a rosti[n]g jron ⌜of⌝ silu*er* lyth at þe same place;⁸ for it
25 shuld⁹ stand me in gret ste[d]¹⁰ her if it mygth be do closly *and* suerly
⌜an⌝¹¹ take trew me[n] of yowr cowncel.¹²

Wret þe morwe next aft*er* Sent¹³ Hillary.

It*em*, leve a bill ⌜indorcid⌝ what ye take ⌜a⌝-wey, if ye take any.

Yowr own, &[c].

72. To MARGARET PASTON, JOHN DAUBENEY, and RICHARD CALLE 1465, 15 January

Add. 34889, ff. 15–16. $11\frac{1}{2} \times 23\frac{3}{8}$ in. (two sheets formerly stitched together,
now pasted to form a long sheet folded so as to make the two folios).
Pampyng's hand.

Text begins on f. 15ᵛ, continues to 16ʳ, 15ʳ, 16ᵛ.

---

² *and* me *and some six more letters canc.*
³ *Partly obliterated by damp at edge.*   ⁴ *but canc.*
⁵ *Hole in middle of paper.*   ⁶ *Pampyng's hand ends here.*
⁷ *þe canc.*   ⁸ *and* also *canc.*   ⁹ *Followed by* shul, *not canc.*
¹⁰ *Clear space between* ste *and* her; *from Paston's habit of omitting letters it is most likely that he meant* sted (*third letter is* e *rather than* o). *Gairdner's* stoher (*unique in O.E.D. under* store, 6c.) *is not acceptable.*
¹¹ *Interl. above what seems to be an ampersand canc.*
¹² *From* for it *evidently written last, as it is crowded into the space remaining above the subscription.*   ¹³ il *canc.*

Dorse: Continuation of text, first on lower part to the foot, then from top, leaving a space of some 5 in. No seal, but marks of folding, and address in Pampyng's hand:

To my mastres Margrete Paston and to my welbelovid frendes John Daubeney and Richard Calle.

The date appears from the reference to Edmond Clere as escheator (ll. 157-8). He was escheator of Norfolk and Suffolk from November 1464 to November 1465 (*Cal. Fine Rolls 1461–71*, p. 129).

G. LIX/575. C. 33 (part).

I praye yow[1] see to the ⌐god⌐ gouernaunce of my housold and guydyng of other thynges touchyng my profite, and þat ye, with Daubeney and Richard Calle and with other such of my frendes and seruauntes as can avise yow aftir the mater requirith, wekely take a sad communicacion of such thynges as be for to do, or oftenner and nede be; takyng avise of the master and of the viker[2] and Ser Jamis ⌐in⌐[3] þat[4] is for to say, aswell for provision of stuffe for myn howsold[5] as for the gaderyng of the reveneus of my livelode or greynes, or for settyng awerk of my seruauntes, and for the more poletik meane of sellyng and carijng of my malt and for all other thynges necessarj for to be do, so þat whanne I come home I haue not an excuse seying þat ye spoke to my seruauntes and þat Daubeney and Calle ⌐exkuse hem þat þei⌐ were so besy thei myght not attende; for I woll haue my mater so guided þat ⌐if⌐ on man may not attende a-nother shall be comaundid to do it. And if my seruauntes faile I had lever wage some other man ⌐for a iorny or a season⌐ thanne my mater shuld be on-sped.

As for my livelode, I left with Daubeney ⌐a⌐[6] bille of many of my dettes, wherby ye all myght haue be indused whedir ye shuld haue sent for siluer.

It[7] liketh me evill to here ⌐þat⌐[8] my prestes and poremen ⌐be⌐ onpaijd, and ⌐þat⌐ no mony sent to me more thanne x mark be Berney of alle this season. And yet therof telle Richard Calle he sent me viij nobills in goold for v mark and þat as longe as gold was bettir payment thanne siluer I had neuir so moch gold of hym[9] at onys; and telle hym þat I woll nat þat he shall kepe þat vse, for I trowe my tenauntes haue but litell ⌐gold⌐[10] to pay.

Also, remembir yow in any howsold,[11] felaship, or company þat will be of good rewle, purvyauns must be had þat euery persone of it be helpyng

5

10

15

20

25

---

72. [1] -w *imperfect; these two words apparently touched up.*
[2] if nede be *canc.*
[3] *Interl. above* if nede be *canc.*
[4] þ *in form of* y, *as usual in Pampyng though not in l. 2 above and a few places below.*
[5] af *canc.*
[6] *Interl. above* of many *canc.*   [7] *Corr. from imperfect* Item.
[8] *This and the two following interlineations, in the same line of the MS., in Paston's hand.*
[9] in my live *canc.*   [10] *Interl. above* siluer *canc.*
[11] or *canc.*

and fortheryng aftir his discrec*i*on and powyr*e*,[12] and he þat woll not do so *with*out he be kept of almes shuld be put out of the houshold or felachep.[13]

Item, where ye desire me þat I shuld take yo*u*r sone to grase, I woll for
30 yo*u*r sake do the bettir, and will ye knowe þat he shall not be so oute of my favo*u*r that I ⌜will⌝ suffir hym to mischefe *with*out ⌜be eftsones⌝ his owne defaut. And hough be it þat in his *p*resumptuose *and* ondiscrete demenyng he gaf bothe me *and* yow cause of displeasir, and to other of my *ser*ua*u*ntes ille exsaumple, and ⌜þat⌝ also guided hym to all mennes
35 vndirstondyng þat he was wery of bidyng in myn hows, ⌜and he not insurid of help in any other place⌝,[14] yet þat grevyth nat me so evill as doth þat I neuir coud fele[15] ner vndirstand hym poletyk ner diligent in helpyng hym-self, ⌜but⌝ as a drane among*es* bees whech ⌜labo*u*r for⌝ gaderyng hony in the feld*es* and the drane doth nought but takyth his
40 part of it. And if this mygt make hym to knowe the bettir hym-self, and put hym in remembrauns what tyme he hath lost and hough he hath leved in jdelnes, and that he coud for this eschewe to do so heraftir, it mygt fortune for his best. But I here yet ⌜neuir⌝ from no plase þat he hath be in of any poletyk demeny*n*g or occupac*i*on of hym; ⌜and in þe Kyngis
45 hows⌝[16] he coud ⌜not⌝ put hym-self[17] foorth to be in favo*u*r or trust w*ith* any[18] men of substauns þat mygt forther hym. Neuirthelesse, as for yo*u*r house *and* myne, I purpose not he shall come there, ner be my will non other, but if he can do more thanne loke foorth *and* make a fase *and* countena*u*ns.

50 Item, send me word whedir my glasier hath do at Bromholm *and* at the Friers of the south towne, *and* whedir he be paijd such mony as I sent home word he shuld be paijd; *and* if he haue do all[19] he must haue more ⌜mony⌝, but I remembir nat *ce*rteynly what till I come home, for I remembir nat what his bargeyn was for þe ⌜werk⌝ at the south[20] towne. I trowe
55 M*a*ster Clement can telle, and also fele hym-⌜selff⌝ and send me word.[21] Also, þat ⌜ye⌝[22] *and* Rich*ar*d Calle ⌜and Daubeney⌝ see þat M*a*ster Clement *and* M*a*ster Braklee, which hath gret nede I wote well, *and* my prest*es and* poremen be paijd, *and* also all other men; and þat ye see þat I be not callid on for þat is my dewté. Also þat ye see among*es* yow þat
60 that is owyng me be not lost ne forborn for lewdnes, for þat shall bothe hurt me *and* do my tena*u*ntes harme. Lete Rich*ar*d Calle remembir þat my fermo*u*r of Sweynesthorp is falle in gret dette for defaut of callyng

---

12 *This word written over another, not now legible.*
13 *Last two words added by Paston, below end of line. He also began a line before the next paragraph with* It ; *but cancelled it.*
14 *Interl. by Paston.*   15 hym yet *canc.*
16 *Interl. by Paston above* wherby *canc.; the following interl. not also by Paston.*
17 in trust fa *canc.*   18 of gret *canc.*
19 *Apparently corr. from* ell.   20 *No space.*
21 *Two roughly horizontal dashes and two oblique lines here mark off the next passage.*
22 *Interl. above* ye speke *canc.*

vpon but ⌐be¬ on²³ yere, and I deme þat bothe John Willeys *and* my newe fermo*ur* of Snaylewell arn like to be in the same case, *and* p*ar*aventure Aleyn of Gresham, *and* other. 65

Item, remembir yow or evir I had a-doo w*ith* Fastolffes livelode, whill I toke hede to my livelode my-self it bothe servid myn exspenses at home *and* at London *and* all other charges, *and* ye leid vp mony in my cofirs every yere as ye knowe. And I wote ⌐well¬ that the payme*nt* of my prest*es and* other charges þat I haue for Fastolff*es* livelode is not so gret 70 as the livelode is, thow part therof be in trobill. And thanne consider that I had nought of my livelode for myn exspenses at London this thwolmonyth day. Ye may verely vndirstand þat it is not guided wittely ner discretly, and therfore I pray yow hertly put alle yo*ur* wittes to-gedir and see for the reformac*i*on of it. *And* ye may reme*m*bre be þis how ye shuld do if þis 75 wer yowr*es* alone, *and* so do now.²⁴

And þat ye woll remembir I haue sent yow ⌐all¬¹⁴ many lettirs touchyng many maters, and also a bille now last by Pecok of erand*es*, desiryng yow to see hem alle to-gedir and send me an answere articlerly, ⌐*and* such as ¬²⁵ ye can²⁶ not spede at this tyme, lete hem be sped as sone as ye may. þat 80 ye se ou*er* my seyd lett[er]s oft tymis til þey be sped.²⁷

Item, I remembir þat myn heygh at Heylesdon the last yer*e* was spent *and* wasted foull reklesly, *and* colored vnd*er* my shep. I pray yow see þat I be not servid soo this yere.

Ite*m*, Pecok told me of a fermo*ur* þat wold haue had Mautby Me*r*ssh, 85 paying xij m*ar*k, as it went afore; and Ric*har*d Calle told me of on þat wold pay more. Burgeys paijd me first xij m*ar*k vj s. viij d., and I ⌐had¬¹⁴ the reed *and* the russhis and he fond the shepherd*es* hyre in shakke tyme for my fold; and sithen he brigged awey the shepherd*es* hyre *and* thanne the nobill, *and* I trowe ⌐he¬²⁸ occupijth no lenger hym-self, and I remembir 90 he told me vij yere goo þat my me*r*ssh shuld alwey apeyr till the prime were past the nombre of xix and thanne it shuld amend a ix or x yer*e*, p*ro*mittyng me he wold þanne²⁹ amend my ferme. I pray yow help to lete ⌐it¬ aswell as ye can, rather to hym þanne a-nother man if he woll do aswell, *and* þat ye comon w*ith* Pecok.³⁰ 95

Item, as for the mater þat I wrote of to the viker *and* other goode felaws, desire hem þat thei ⟨be⟩³¹ not to ⌐excessiue hasty¬³² in the mater for non ⌐nede¬,³³ but to do þat thei may ⌐do¬ þerin ⌐mesurably¬³⁴ *and* wittely

---

²³ *MS.* en. ²⁴ *This last sentence added by Paston.*
²⁵ *Interl. above* of such as *canc.* ²⁶ and the rem *canc.*
²⁷ *This sentence in Paston's hand,* þ *in* þey *in form of* y.
²⁸ *Interl. above* impenetrable blot. ²⁹ *Written* ynne *with superior* a.
³⁰ *Recto ends; text continues on f. 15ʳ.*
³¹ *Almost obliterated by damage to paper; only the bottom of* b *clear.*
³² *Interl. above* diligent *canc.* ³³ *Interl. above* hast *canc.*
³⁴ *Interl. above* goodly *canc.*

as ⌈sone as thei may⌉; and as for the respite of the mater ⌈here⌉ lete hem
100 not care therfore, I shall do wel jnough. Telle³⁵ hem for certeyn the mater
is in³⁶ as good case as any such mater was this xx wynter, as my counsell
tellyth me; but I woll be sure of all weyes þat I may ⌈haue⌉, *and* specially
of the declaracion of the trought³⁷ of my mater *and* of my frend*es*.

Item, as for the mater ⌈athwyx the p*ar*son of Mautby, Constantine,
105 *and*⌉³⁸ the viker of Derham, whedir it were small mater or gret I care not,
but I am sure þat too witnesse which I knowe were apposed þ*er*in before
a juge sprituall,³⁹ whech as I suppose was M*aster* Robe*r*t Popy or some
other. The viker ⌈of Derham⌉ can telle, and so I trowe can John Wynter
of Mautby or other parysshons telle where the sute was athwyx hem, and
110 I can thynk it was in the chapitell. If ye can safely gette me what the witnesse seid I wold nomore, but do no gret cost on it.

Item, recomaund me to M*aster* Robe*r*t Popy *and* telle hym as for any
thyng seid ayens hym in my mater, thow myn adu*er*saris ment ontrewly
thei prevyd nought but þat he is a good man *and* a worshipfull *and* a trewe.
115 Item, if I haue any⁴⁰ ot*es* beside my stuffe, or may any bye aftir xiiij d.,
spare not *and* take good mesure or bartirre for some other chafare, *and*
send me word hough moch ye may bye.

Item, it is told me ye make no wood nouther at Caster ner Mautby,
wherof I m*er*veyle. Remembir yow we must brenne wood a-nodir yere.
120 Item, I send yow a titelyng⁴¹ þat I mad whill I was at home, what malt
I had by estimac*i*on, set at the lest. Wherfore see þat Brigge make a reknyng of his malt, *and*⁴² cast ye my book *and* loke what ye can amend it;
and apeyre it shall not if alle folk*es* haue do trewly, but I suppose fewe of
yow haue take any heed at it asmoch as I ded.
125 Item, I may selle here for vj s. viij d. a qu*ar*ter clene-fyed after Royston
mesure, whech is lesse thanne the water mesure of London. Cambrigge-
shire malt is here at x s. Cast ye what I may selle of newe *and* old, savyng
stuffe for myn hows. Item,⁴³ to remembir þat Guton malt must be shipped
at Blakeney. Item, Lynsted*es* malt at Walcote may be shipped there;
130 therfore cast among*es* yow what malt may best be sold.

Item, if on man may not attende to gader siluer, sende a-nother; *and*
send me word what hath be reseyvid and spent.

Item, þat I haue an answere of alle my lettirs *and* of euery article in
hem.

³⁵ *Opposite the line beginning with this word, at the centre of a bracket embracing the*
paragraph, þe viker *in margin.*
³⁶ *Three words, unintelligible, heavily canc.*
³⁷ *First written with flourish on* -h, *then* t *added.*
³⁸ *Interl. above* of the mater of *canc.*
³⁹ and *canc.*   ⁴⁰ oth *canc.*
⁴¹ wh *canc.*   ⁴² s *and incomplete letter canc.*
⁴³ *This sentence and the next crowded into the space between this and the following para-*
graph. These two paragraphs bracketed together, malt *in margin.*

Item, but if ye make such purvyauns þat my prestes be paijd *and* pore- 135
men, beside other charges, ⌐*and* purvey mony for me beside¬, outher[44]
ye gader shrewdly or ellis ye spend lewdly.[45]

Item, I sent a lettir by Rauff Greneakyr to James Gresham *and* to yow,
which he promised me shuld be at Norwich on Wednesday aftir Thwelth
Day. And therin were diuers maters, and inespeciall of a mater þat shuld 140
be in comunicacion on Tuisday last past bithwyx Yeluerton *and* Robert
Wyngfeld ⌐for Caster¬[46] as in the seid lettir is specifijd. It is so þat the
seid Robard[47] shall be here with-inne this ij dayes; if any thyng ye haue
aspied of it send me word. Item, yong Knevet tellith me þat he is my good
frend, and he is come ridyng homward on Friday last was. I pray yow ley 145
wetche whedir ye here any thyng þat he medillyth hym ⌐in¬ þat mater,
and send me word;[48] for I wold vndirstand whedir he were iust ⌐*and*
trew¬[14] or nought, *and* that do, it shall not ligh in his power to hurt me.
But take ye hed *and* inquere, *and* knowe other mennes purpos, *and* kepe
your intent as close as ye can; and what some evir boost be mad, ⌐werk ye 150
wisely *and*¬ set not by it but send me word what ye here.

Item, Calle sendyth me word þat Ser Thomas Howes is seke *and* not
like to askape it, *and* Berney tellyth me the contrary; wherfore I pray yow
take hed therat *and* lete me haue knowleche, for though I be not behold
to hym I wold not he were ded for more thanne he is worth.   155

Item, take the viker the bille þat I send yow herwyth.[49]

Item, þat ye, ⌐if ye¬ can, fynd the meane to aspie what goodes Edmond
Clere eschetith of any mannes.

Item, remembir well to take heed at your gates on nyghtes *and* dayes for
theves, for ⌐thei ride¬ in diuers contrés with gret felaship like lordes, *and* 160
ride out of on shire in-to a-nother.

Wretyn at London the Tuisday next aftir Sent Hillary.

Item, þat Richard Calle brynge me vp mony so þat my prestes be paijd,
and þat he come vp suerly with other men *and* attornis.

73. To MARGARET PASTON, JOHN DAUBENEY, and RICHARD CALLE
1465, 27 June

Add. 34889, f. 9. 11½ × 10¼ in. Autograph; see Plate III.

Dorse: Continuation of text. Traces of red wax. Address autograph:

To my cosyn Margret Paston and to Jon Dawbeney and Richard Call.

This is a characteristic specimen of John Paston's hand—energetic, but extremely
coarse and careless, with many letters ill formed and some left out altogether.
There is consequently doubt about the precise form of some words.

---

⁴⁴ the *canc.*   ⁴⁵ *F. 15ʳ ends.*   ⁴⁶ *These two words in margin in Paston's hand.*
⁴⁷ *This is the only form written in full in this letter; elsewhere the name is abbr.* Rob *with*
stroke through b.   ⁴⁸ a *canc.*   ⁴⁹ -wyth *from* in.

The year is shown to be 1465 by the reference to Paston's dispute with the Duke of Suffolk about the manors of Drayton and Hellesdon, which culminated in the Duke's attack on Hellesdon on 14 October of that year (so dated in Bodl. MS. Charters Norfolk 738; see no. 195).

G. LXI/591. C. 36 (part).

⟨I⟩¹ recumma[n]d me to yow, *and* haue rec*ey*vid a lett*er* from yow² *and* a-nother fro³ Ric*hard* Call be John Colma⟨n⟩ *and* on⁴ be Roos, *and* I haue rec*ey*vid of Colma*n* the plate *and* mony acordi[n]g [to] Ric*hard* Callis letteris.

5   It*em,* I can yow thonk ye send me word the pr[i]se of corn.

It*em,* as for yowr*e* sone: I lete yow ⌜wete⌝ I wold he dede wel, but I vnderstand in hym no⁵ dispocici*on* of polecy⁶ ne of gou*er*nans as man of the werld owt to do, but only leuith, ⌜*and* eu*er* hath⌝, as man ⌜disolut⌝,⁷ with-owt any pro*u*icion, ne that he besijth hym nothi[n]ge to vnderstand
10   swhech materis as a⁵ man of lyuelode must nedis vnderstond. Ne ⌜I⌝ vnderstond nothi[n]g of what dispocici*on* he porposith to be, but only I kan thynk he wold dwell ageyn in yowr hows *and* myn, *and* ther ete *and* drink *and* slepe. þerfor I lete yow wete I wold ⌜know⌝⁸ hym or ⌜he⌝ know myn ente[n]t, *and* how wel he ⌜hath⌝ ocupijd his tym now he hath had
15   leyser.⁹ Eu*er*y ⌜pore ma*n*⌝¹⁰ þat hath browt vp his chylder to¹¹ the ⌜age⌝ of xij yer waytyth¹² than to be ⌜holp *and*⌝ profitid be his¹³ childer,¹⁴ *and* eu*er*y gentilma*n* that hath discreci*on* waytith that his ken ⌜*and* seruantis⌝ þat levith ⌜be⌝ hym *and* at his coste shuld¹⁵ help hym forthward. As for yowr sone, ye knowe well he neu*er* stode yow ne me in¹⁶ profite, ese, or
20   help to valew of on grote, sauy[n]g at Calcot Hall whane [he] *and* hes brothir kept it¹⁷ on day ⌜ageyns Debenh[a]m⌝, *and* yet was it at iij þe coste that¹⁸ eu*er* Debenha*m* sones put hym to; for be her policé they kepe Cotton at my cost *and* with the¹⁹ profit*is* of the same. Wherfor geff hem no favor tyle ye feel what he⁵ is *and* will be.

25   It*em,* Call sendith me word that Mast*er* Phylip hat entrid in Drayton in my lord of Suff*olk*²⁰ name, *and* hat²¹ odir purpose to entre in Heylisdon, *and* he askith my*n* auyse; whech is that ye conforte my tenant*is* *and* help hem til I come hom, *and* let hem wet I shall not lese it; *and* that the Dewk of ⌜Suff*olk*⌝²² that last dijd²³ wold haue bouth it of Fastolff, *and* for he mygth

---

73. ¹ *Lost at torn edge.* ² *-w imperfect.* ³ *MS. for.*
⁴ *Not clear, written over something else.* ⁵ *No space.* ⁶ *Ampersand canc.*
⁷ *Interl. after* fownd *of canc., and above another illegible word canc.;* haui[n]g nothi[n]g *to also interl., but canc.*
⁸ *Interl. above* er stan *canc.* ⁹ *I canc.* ¹⁰ *Interl. above* on *canc.*
¹¹ *to repeated.* ¹² *From* wayth. ¹³ *his repeated.*
¹⁴ *-l- over* r. ¹⁵ haue *canc.* ¹⁶ *a canc.*
¹⁷ *MS.* id, *not separated from* kept. ¹⁸ *Repeated as* þat.
¹⁹ *Repeated as* þe.
²⁰ *In view of the possessive* Debenham, *without ending, in l.* 22, *this may be the form intended here.*
²¹ *From* that. ²² *In margin.* ²³ wh *canc.*

not haue it so he[24] claymyd þe man*er*, seyi[n]g it was ⌐on⌐ Polis, *and* ⌐for⌐   30
his name was Poole he claymid to be eyr. He was ansueryid þat he com
nothi[n]g of that stok, *and* how someu*er* were[25] kyn to the Polis þat owth it,
it hurt not for it was laufully bowth *and* sold; *and* he neu*er*[26] kleymid it
after.

It*em*, I am in purpose to take assise ageynse hem ⌐at tis tyme⌐, *and* ell[27]   35
I wold haue sent ⌐theder⌐ streyt be a[5] lett*er* of atorney to entre ⌐in my
name⌐. Neu*er* the les ye be a[28] gentilwoman, *and* it ⌐is⌐ worshep for yow to
confort yowr tenant*is*;[29] wherfor I wold ye myth ryd to Heylisdon *and*
Drayton *and* Sparh[a]m, *and* tari at Drayto[n] *and* speke with hem, *and*
byd hem hold with ther old master[30] til I com, *and* that ye haue sent me   40
word[31] but ⌐late, wherfor ye may⌐[32] haue non answer yet. *And* informe
hem as I ha[33] wrete to yo[w] with-in, *and* sey oupinly[34] it is a shame that
any man shuld set anny lord on so ontrwe a[5] mat*er*, and speciall[35] a p*re*ste;
and lete[36] hem wete as sone[37] as I am ⌐com⌐ hom I shall see hem.

It*em*, ⌐that⌐ as for distreyn for[38] rent or ferm, thow the Dewk ⌐had⌐   45
tytill, as he hath not, he may non ask til the next rent day ⌐after his entré⌐,
that is Michelmes. ⌐*And* seye þat[39] ye will be paijd euer*j* pené, *and* aske
hem it⌐, *and* make mech of men of Cossey becawse þey wer owr wel-
willer*is* when᷑ we wer neybor*is* ther; *and* lete hem wete þat þe begynner*is*
of shech mat*er* had neu*er* worchip ner p*ro*fite of me, ne shall, *and* desyr   50
god will of yowr neybor*is*, &c., *and* fyn[d][40] all othir men*is* þat ye kan to
plese þe pepill. *And* lete yowr tenantes ⌐wete⌐[41] that þe Dewke may neu*er*
be[42] lawe compel hem to torn from me, *and* do all so well as ye can. *And*
if any entyr ⌐be mad⌐ in Heylisdo[n], shuff him owt *and* set sum ma*n* to
kepe þe pla[c]e if ned be, ⌐not w*ith*-standi[n]g it longith not to þe man*er*⌐.   55

It*em*, I wold fayn haue sum man to be baylé of Heylisdon *and* Drayto*n*,
&c., þat mygth go amo*n*gis the tenant*is*; *and* ell[35] I wolld han Rich*ard*[43]
Charllis[44] to go among[45] hem tyl I com hom, *and* also Ric*h*ard Call ⌐whan
he may⌐.

It*em*, he sent me word that the tenant*is* of Drayton wold not come to   60
the Dewkis cort, *and* if þey will be ⌐so⌐ ste[d]fast to me *and* kepe hem

---

²⁴ ch *and part of another letter canc.*   ²⁵ ey *canc.*
²⁶ *Written* kneu-, k- *canc.*
²⁷ *Barred* -ll *in this word might be meant for* -llis, *but cf. l.* 57.
²⁸ -r *added later, wrongly.*   ²⁹ *Recto ends.*   ³⁰ *Ampersand canc.*
³¹ -r- *written over* l.   ³² *Interl. above* ye *canc.*
³³ *Probably a characteristically incomplete writing for* haue; *but possibly a genuine form*
³⁴ *The reading (Gairdner's) seems right but is uncertain.*
³⁵ *No bar through* -ll.   ³⁶ yow *and part of another word canc.*
³⁷ *From* for.   ³⁸ *From* of.
³⁹ þ *in form of* y, *as occasionally later in this letter.*
⁴⁰ *This word uncertain, but Gairdner's* suyn *unacceptable.*
⁴¹ *Interl. above ampersand canc.*   ⁴² k *canc.*
⁴³ Call *canc.*   ⁴⁴ *Botched; apparently* -r- *over an incomplete* a.
⁴⁵ *MS.* amond.

strawnge *and* froward from the Dewkis cowncell, ⌐all⌐ this mat*er* shall turn to a jape *and* not hurt ⌐hem ner⌐, *and* if þe[y]⁴⁶ be waue*ri*[n]g it shall hurt hem.

65 It*em*, I lete yow wete þis is do to cause me to see*se* my labor ayens hym for Dedh*a*m, wh[e]ch I wil not for it.

God kepe yow. Wret the Thursday be-for Sent Petris Day.

It*em*,⁴⁷ tel Ri*chard* Call jf [I] haue witten[e]ssis redy I wol spede this mat*er* spirituall befor Estern.

74. To MARGARET PASTON   1465, 13 July

Add. 27444, f. 147. 11⅜×13 in. Autograph.

Dorse: Continuation of text. Traces of red wax. Address autograph:

To my cosyn Margret Paston.

Note in Calle's hand; see n. 24 below.

The year must be the same as that of no. 73. The exact date appears from a letter of Richard Calle to Paston describing an abortive attempt by the Duke of Suffolk's men to take possession of Hellesdon 'on Monday last past', and dated 10 July (see Part II, no. 690). See also Margaret's letter no. 188, written the day before this.

Calle's memorandum was no doubt added later, perhaps about the time of the inventory no. 195 which contains similar (not identical) particulars in his hand.

G. 514/595. C. 39.

I rec*um*mand me to yow *and*¹ thank² yow of yow*r* labo*wr* *and* besynes *with* þe vnruly felechep that cam befor yow on Monday last past, wherof I herd report be John Hobbis; *and* in god³ feyth ye aquyt yow rygth wel *and* discretly, *and* hertyly to yowr wurchep *and*⁴ myn⁵ *and* to þe shame of

5 yow*r* adu*er*sarijs. *And* I am wel content þat ye avowid þat ye kept posses-cion at Drayton, *and* so wold doo; wherfor I pray yow make yowr word god if ye may, *and* at þe lest let myn aduersarijs not haue it in pees if ye may.

Jon ⌐Hobbys⌐ tellith me þat ye be seekly, whech me lekith ⌐not⌐ to

10 here, prayi[n]g yow hartyly þat ye take what may do yow⁶ eese *and* spare not, *and* in any wyse take no thowth ⌐ne to moch labor⌐ for þes mate*ris*, ne set it not so to yowr hert þat ye fare þe wers for it. And as for þe mat*er*, so þey oue*r*come yow not with fors ne bosting I shall have þe man*er* sewrlyer to me *and* myn þan þe⁷ Dewk shall haue Cossey, dowt ye not.

---

⁴⁶ *Probably so intended; though* þe *is frequent at this date it is not John Paston's form.*

⁴⁷ lab *canc.*

74. ¹ *Ampersand over I.*   ² *Followed by* of, *which should have been canc.*

   ³ *No space.*   ⁴ profyt *canc.*   ⁵ wher I *canc.*

   ⁶ *Indeterminate mark looks like incomplete* -r, *but the idiom requires* yow.

   ⁷ þ *in form of* y.

And jn cas I come not hom within thre wekis, I pray yow come to me; 15
and Wykes hath promisid to kepe the plase in yowr absens.[8] Neuertheles,
whan ye come set it in sech rewle as ye seme best *and* most suer bothe for
Castre *and* Heylisdon, if þe werre hold. In cas ye haue pees, send me word.

As[9] for that it is desyrid I shuld shew my tytill *and* euyde[n]s to þe
Dewk, me thi[n]kyth he had euyll cowncell to entre in opon me trusti[n]g 20
I ⌈shuld⌉ shew hym euydens. ⌈And ye seme it may do yow god or eese⌉,
lete my lord of Norwich wet[10] that þe maner of Drayton was a marchantis
of London callid Jon Heylisdon[11] ⌈longe⌉ er any of þe Polis þat þe seyd
Dewk comyth of wer borne to any lond in Norffolk or Suffolk; *and* if þey
wer at that tyme born to no lond, how may þe ⌈seyd⌉ Dewk klaym Drayton 25
be þat pedegré? As for þe seyd John Heylisdon, he was a[3] por man born,
and from hym þe seyd maner dessendid to Alise his dowtyr, hos estat I
haue; *and* I suppose þe seyd Dewk comyth not of hem.

Item, as for the pedegré of þe seyd Dewk, he is sone to William Pool,
Dewk of Suffolk, sone to Mychell Pool, Erl of Suffolk, sone to Mychel 30
Pool, þe[12] furst Erl of Suffolk of þe Polis, mad be King Richard seth my
fader was born. *And* þe seyd furst Mychell was sone to on William Pool
of Hull, whech was a wurchepfull ⌈man⌉ grow be fortwne of þe werld, *and*
he ⌈was⌉ furst a marchant *and* after a knygth, *and* after he was mad baneret.
And if any of þees hadde þe maner of Drayton I woll los c li., ⌈so þat any 35
persone for þe Dewk will be bond in as mech to proue þe contrary⌉. *And*
I wot weel þe seyd Dewkis cowncell wil not claym þe seyd maner be þe
tytill of þe fader of þe seyd William Pool. *And* what þe fader of þe seyd
William was, ⌈as⌉ be þe pedegré mad in þe seyd ⌈last⌉ Dewkis fadiris
daijs, I know[13] rygt weell; wherof I jnformyd Herry Boteler to tell my 40
old lady of Suffolk, be-cawse he is of her cowncell, *and*[14] more will I not
tell in þes mater but if I be desyrid or compellid.

Item, let[15] my lord of Norwich wete þat it is not profitab[l]e ner þe
comen well of gentilmen that any jentilman shuld be compellid be an
entré of a lord to shew his evidens or tytill to his lond, ner ⌈I⌉ nil not 45
begine þat exsample ne thralldam of gentilmen ner ⌈of⌉ othir. It is god a
lord take sad cowncell or he begyne any sech mater.

And[16] as for þe Poolis that owth Drayton, if þer were c of hem leuyng,
as þer is non, yet haue they no tytill to þe seyd maner.[17] God kepe yow.
Wret þe Satirday, &c. 50

Yowr JON PASTON

I pray yow be as mery with yowr feluchep as ye kan.[18]

[8] Item þe sey *canc.*	[9] *Text runs on, but paragraph mark in margin opposite.*	
[10] that *canc.*	[11] or þ ⌈any⌉ *canc.*	[12] *Crowded in.*
[13] *Fold. by* I, *which should have been canc.*	[14] morw *canc.*	[15] lete *canc.*

[16] *From this point the writing is crowded in at the foot of the page.*
[17] shew nomor þe nede *canc.*
[18] *This sentence at the foot, evidently written after the signature. Recto ends.*

Item,[19] I send hom writt *and* proses for yow[r] seruant*is and* myn.

Item, I may sell yow[r] woll for xl d. þe ston redi mony, as Arblast*er* can tell yow, *and* malt for iiij s. þe q*uart*er at daijs[20] xxj for xx deliu*er*id of Yermoth mesur. If ye fayle mony ye most make it of yowr wole or malt.

55 I send yow hom writt*is* ⌐of repleuin⌐ for[21] þe shep *and* þe hors þat wer take, *and* avise ⌐yow⌐[22] lete þe writtis be deliu*er*d be-for my lord of Norwich *and* god rekord;[23] *and* if ye may make men with fors to take þe catell agey[n] be waran of repleuyn, spar not rather than fayle.[24]

75. To MARGARET PASTON, JAMES GRESHAM, and RICHARD CALLE 1465, 7 August

Add. 27445, f. 3. $11\frac{1}{4} \times 11\frac{3}{4}$ in. Mainly in Pampyng's hand, with additions by Paston.

Dorse: Traces of red wax. Address in Pampyng's hand:

*To my mastresse Margret Paston, James Gresham, and Ric*hard *Calle.*

This is evidently the letter mentioned at the beginning of no. 76, and is of the same date.

G. 520/601.

I recomaund me to yow, and haue reseyvid ij lettirs from John Russe wherin he remembirth me that I shuld owe hym xix li. or ther-upon for diu*er*s p*ar*celles whech he seith he shuld haue deliu*er*id in-to myn hows, wherof he seith ⌐xiiij li.⌐ was deliu*er*id in-to myn howse ij yere g⟨oo⟩[1]
5 and that I had a bille deliu*er*id me therof, and the remn*au*nt sithen, and desireth of me paym*en*t of the seid xix li.; wherfor I certi⟨fye⟩[2] yow as I vndirstand in the mater. Ye may lete John Russe come to yow and take such a direcc*i*on in the mater as reason *and* trought woll.

I[3] lete yow wete that abought ij yer*e* goo the seid John Russe deliu*er*id
10 me first a bille of the seid xiiij ⟨li.⟩, and I examin*ed* the p*ar*celles; and as I remembir xj li. was my dewté, wherof the certeyn somme is writen in my blak book of foreyn reseyt*es* ⌐that yere⌐, and the remn*au*nt was Ric*hard* Calles dewté, wherof he was allowed, savyng a[4] part was Elys dewté. And

---

[19] *Writing on verso hasty and careless, sometimes defective.*
[20] *with* la *canc.*   [21] my sh *canc.*   [22] *MS.* yowr.   [23] -k- *over* g.
[24] *Paston's hand ends here, except for the address. Also on the verso, written upside down near the foot in Calle's hand, is the following:*
M*emorandum* there lefte be-hynde of Heylesdon folde of my mastre schepe xlj modreschep.
Item, of lambes xxxiiij. Item, of my mastres xij modreschep. Item, of her lambes xij.

75. [1] *End lost at tear at edge; cf.* goo l. 9.   [2] *End lost at edge.*
    [3] *Paragraph mark in margin opposite.*   [4] *No space.*

as for the seid xj li., I offerid the seid John Russe payment in hand at
þat tyme and desired hym he shuld nomore send in-to myn howse, and 15
warnyd yow ⌜and Richard⌝ that ye shuld nomore stuffe take in-to myn
hows without ye paijd in hand, nowther of hym ner of non other. And
the seid John Russe praijd me to remembir that I had graunted hym the
maner of Akthorp in Leystoft at a certeyn prise, as it apperyd by writyng
vndir my seall, and desired me that I wold take the seid somme in party 20
of payment. And I told hym that, as for such mony that shuld come from
hym for that lond, I wold take it ⌜of hym⌝ and ley it vp by the self, that
I myght purchase other lond therwith, bicause I wold lesse Fastolffes
lyuelode for the college; but I wold pay hym his dewté without any stop-
page. And he thanne desired me to take þat same xj li. and ley it vp to the 25
same vse, seying to me that it was as good to do so as I for to take it hym
and he to take it me ayen. And thus he and I agreed and departed, *and*
thanne he praijd me to take more chafar of hym, whech I denyed.

And[3] nough I merveyll what shuld cause hym to aske mony for that
dewté. Neuirethelesse I deme he supposith that he coud not opteyne 30
his bargeyn by me bicause of the trobill that it standyth in, and for that
or for some other cause he repentyth his bargeyn *and* woll nomore of it.
Wherfore send for hym, and take James Gresham or some of your frendes
and Richard Calle, and fele what he menyth; and if ye can fynd hym disposed to leve his bargeyn, yet though I myght kepe stille the seid mony, I wold 35
he shuld not lese therby. Neuirthelesse, if he woll refuse his bargeyn, thanne
take ayen the writyng that he hath of that bargeyn and a writyng of his
hand that he dischargyth me of the graunt that I mad hym of that same
bargeyn. And thanne loke[5] that ye enquere what mony he hath reseyvid
of the seid maner in my tyme, wherof the ferme is vj li. yerly, ⌜whech I 40
suffird hym to occupie to his owne vse by fors of the seid bargeyn all my
tyme⌝;[6] and aftir the parcellis cast what I haue had of hym, abbate þerof
the mony that he hath reseyvid of the seid maner and also as moch of
the xiiij li. as the seid Richard Calle *and* Elys owen, wherof he is allowid,
and thanne see that the seid John Russe be content of the remnaunt of 45
his parcellis that is dew by me; but loke ye pay non other mennes
dewtés.

Also[7] the seid John Russe ⌜writyth⌝ in his lettir that, rather thanne he
shuld fayle this mony, that I wold lend hym asmoch to pay ayen at Cristemasse; wherfore, ⌜if he leve his bargeyn⌝, I woll ye lend hym asmoch 50
mony over his dewté as shall make vp xx li., takyng of hym suerté to pay
ayen at Cristemasse, as he writyth. In[4] case be that he will kepe stille his

---

[5] what mony *canc.*

[6] *Interl. above the following canc.:* and that he hath reseyvid ij yere in my tyme at the
leste I suppose he reseyvid that as long as Richard Calle hath gaderid the remnaunt.

[7] *New line, and paragraph mark in margin as well. This paragraph more hastily written.*

bargeyn, thanne ye may answere hym it is no reason that he shuld aske me any part of that mony ayen, for he owyth that *and* moch more.[8]

55 It*em*, the seyd John Rus sent me heder a[4] man for þis mat*er* only w*ith*-in thes ij daijs, wherfor let him know an ansue[r] betym*es*,[9] for I fel[10] well he[11] hath mad a gret bargen but late wherfor he hath mor nede of mony now; *and* I wol do for hym that I may resonably. Neu*er*theles his wryti[n]g merweylith me that ⌐he⌐ askith þis mony as dewté whech he toke me for 60 p*ar*te of my paym*ent*. I deme it comith not all of his owne disposic*i*un.

Inquier ye that ye ca[n] what it menith.[12]

God kepe yow. Wret þe Wednisday nex Lammes.

Yow[r]*is* JOHN PASTON

In cas ye han Drayton in any quiete, take sewerté of yowr tenant*is* for paiment, as I haue wret befor.

76. To MARGARET PASTON   1465, 7 August

Add. 27445, f. 2. $11\frac{3}{8} \times 8\frac{1}{2}$ in. Pampyng's hand.

Dorse: Traces of red wax, and paper tape piercing the letter. Address in Paston's hand:

To my cosyn Margret ⟨P⟩aston,[1] *at Heylisdoune.*

The reference to 4 Edward IV proves the date to be not earlier than 1465, and Paston died in May 1466. (*Inq. p.m.*, 6 Edward IV, no. 44: inquisitions at Acle, Norfolk, on 18 October and at Bungay, Suffolk, on 16 October found that he died 'xxj die mensis Maij'. But other copies (e.g. B.M. Add. Roll 17258 and Bodl. MS. Charters Norfolk 744) give 22 May.)

G. 519/600.

I recomaund me to yow, and as for the letter that I send yow touchyng John Russe, I woll that ye *and* y*our* counsell see it openly, and kepe this bille to y*our*-self ⌐or to some secret frend of your⌐.[2] And I pray yow rem*em*bir ij thyng*es*: on, if ye fynd hym in any maner wise disposed to 5 leve his bargeyn, take it at his offer and take ayen the wrytyng that he hath of that bargeyn, or a wrytyng of his owne hand of relesyng his bargeyn to me;[3] for p*ar*aventure at this tyme he woll be glad to leve his bargeyn, as I vndirstand, and whanne he sethe that I haue peas he woll calle ther-on ayen, wherfore I pray yow werk wisely herin, for he may in no maner 10 wise aske the mony ⌐of me⌐ and kepe his bargeyn, ⌐for he hath diu*er*s

---

[8] *Pampyng's hand ends here; the rest in Paston's hand, very hurried.*
[9] *-es abbr.* 3.   [10] f- *over* w.   [11] hath *canc.*
[12] *The line from* I deme *to this point inserted later.*

76. [1] *First letter destroyed by tape-slit.*
   [2] *Abbr. exactly as* your *above; but possibly meant for* yours.
   [3] *These two words smaller, crowded in at end of line.*

tymes desired me to haue take of hym more stuffe þerfore[1]; a-nother, as sone as ye may, or ye breke this mater with John Russe, make due serche with the fermours at Akthorp what mony ⌈Russe⌉[4] hath reseyvid there ⌈in⌉ my tyme: that is to sey for Mighelmes the first, the ij, iij, iiij yeres of Kyng E., of whech he hath reseyvid ij paymentes, that is 15 xij li. at the lest, or er the maner was trobelid by Jenney or Yeluerton. And I deme that he hath reseyvid some sithen, but that he kepith counsell.

Item, for asmoch as Ser Thomas Howes gaderid for the xxxix yere of Kyng Herry, the seid John Russe woll, vnder colour of that, surmytte that he reseyvid in my tyme was therfore; wherfore ye must make a serche 20 what he hath reseyvid sith Ser John Fastolff dyed, and what tyme, and therupon ye shall vndirstand what he hath reseyvid for me and what ⌈for⌉ hym. And in[5] case he hath reseyvid xij li. and Richard hath paijd hym his duté as he promised, thanne[6] growyth nat to John Russe past iiij or v li. Notwithstandyng,[7] fare fayre with hym and resonabilly, so þat he leve 25 his bargeyn, and lend hym the remnaunt of the ⌈xx li.⌉[8] vpon suerté for xx li. he desireth to haue outher by dewté or borowyng at this tyme.

Item, he that shall speke with the fermours of Akthorp, whos name is Langham, he must inquere generally[9] what mony he hath paijd to all men sith Ser John Fastolff dyed, and see his billes of payment and take 30 therof a titelyng. Richard Calle hath a bille of parcellis of euery mannes ferme, and he can serche this best in[5] case he be not to favorabill to John Russe; wherfore I remitte this to your discrecion. But I suppose John Russe woll telle yow what he hath reseyvid, for [I] haue bifore this tyme wretyn by his seying what he had reseyvid, and I suppose and he 35 remembird that he seid to me he wold not aske his mony in this forme. Neuirthelesse it shall do good so he leve his bargeyn by this meane.

I merveyll that I here no tidyngges from yow hough ye haue do at the assises. The berer of this lettir is a comon carier and was at Norwich on Satirday, and brought me lettirs from other men; but your seruauntes 40 inquere nat diligently after the comyng of cariers and other men.

Wretyn at London the Wednesday next after Lammes Day. Ye shall haue lettirs of me this weke.

JOHN PASTON

.

---

⁴ *Interl. above* he *canc.*   ⁵ *No space.*   ⁶ com *canc.*
⁷ fayre *canc.*   ⁸ *Interl. above* mony *canc.*   ⁹ who hath *canc.*

77. To MARGARET PASTON   1465, 20 September

Add. 34889, f. 33. 10½ × 17 in. Pampyng's hand, a few additions by Paston.

Dorse: Continuation of text. Some red wax. Address in Pampyng's hand:

To my cosyn Margret Paston.

Note in Calle's hand; see n. 63 below.

    The date appears partly from Margaret's reply to this letter (no. 192), partly from the escheatorship of Edmond Clere (see no. 72). 'This house' of l. 185 is the Fleet Prison, to which John Paston had been committed—the evidence he gave to the commission inquiring into Fastolf's will was taken in the Fleet on 28 August (B.M. MS. Add. 27450, f. 4). From Margaret's letter no. 184 it appears that he was in prison as early as June.

    F. iv, p. 90. G. 528/609 (part). C. 40 (part).

Myn owne dere souereyn lady, I recomaund me to yow and thank yow of the gret chere þat[1] ye mad me here, to my gret cost *and* charge *and* labour. Nomore at this tyme but that I pray yow ye woll send me hedir ij elne of worsted for doblett*es* to happe me this cold wynter, and that ye inquere
5 where Will*ia*m Paston bought his tepet of fyne worsted whech is almost like silk; and if that be ⌜moch⌝ fyner thanne þat ye[2] shuld bye me after vij or viij s., thanne bye ⟨m⟩e[3] a qu*arter and* the nayle therof for colers, thow it be derrer thanne the tother, for I wold[4] make my doblet all worsted for worship of Norf*olk* rather thanne like Gonnores doblet.
10   Item, as for the mater of the ix[xx] li. askyd by my lady of Bedford ⌜for the maner of Westthurrok⌝, where as S*er* Thom*as* Howes seith that he hath no writyng therof but þat S*er* John Fastolff purchased the seid maner *and* paijd *cer*teyn mony in ernest, and aftirward gr*au*ntyd his bargeyn to the Duc of Bedford, *and* so the mony þat he toke was for the mony that
15 he had paijd; p*ar*aventure S*er* Thom*as* hath writyng therof and knowyth it not, for if ther be any such mony paijd vpon any bargeyn he shall fynd it in Kyrtelyngg*es* book*es* ⌜þat was S*er* John Fastolff*es* reseyvo*ur*⌝. And it was abought such tyme as the Duc of Bedford was last in Inglond, whech as it is told me was the viij yere of Kyng Herry the Fift or the viij yere of
20 Kyng Herry the Sext, and the somme that he paijd for the seid bargeyn was ccc m*ar*k. Also he shall fynd, the xxij yere of Kyng Herry or ther-abought, in the acompt*es* of on of Fastolff*es* reseyvo*ur*s at London, that ther was take of S*er* Thom*as* Tyrell *and* of the Duchesse of Excestre, that was wif to S*er* Lowes John, fermo*ur*s of the seid maner, *cer*teyn mony for
25 repayme*nt* of ⌜part of⌝ the seid ccc m*ar*k. Also he shall fynd in yeres after þat, or in that yere or ther*e*-aboutes, that S*er* John Fastolff reseyved mony of my Lord Revers þat now is,[5] by the name of Richard Wydevile,

77. [1] þ *in form of* y *throughout.*

    [2] *The first letter unusually formed, but certainly* y *rather than* h, *as Fenn read.*

    [3] *Beginning faded, replaced by three modern dots.*

    [4] not *canc.*   [5] for mony *canc.*

for his owne dette dew to Ser John Fastolff. Wherfore if Ser Thomas be trewe to his master lete hym do his devoir to make þat Worseter, whech is vphold be hym with the dedes goodes, to be trewe to his master; or ellis 30
it is tyme for Ser Thomas to forsake hym and help to punyssh hym, or men must sey that Ser Thomas is ⌐not trewe⌐.[6] And more-ouer lete Ser Thomas examine what he can fynd in this mater that I sent hym word of, whech mater he shall fynd in the seid reseyvours bookes, if he list to seke it. Item, wete of hym whedir any writte[7] of *sub pena* cam to hym therfore. 35
Item, I send hym a bille whech on ⌐Edmond Carvyle for⌐ Robert Otteley askyth of Ser John Fastolff, of whech, aswell as of a bille askyd by on Fraunses for makyng of houses in Southwerk, lete send hedir an answere; for and I coud answere hem I wold not send to hym. And that Richard Calle, or who so evir goo to hym of my seruauntes, ⌐lete hym⌐ vndirstand 40
that such brethelles as be abought Ser Thomas wene that I sent to hym for maters of myn owne, and that I myght not forbere[8] his frenship, whech is no-thyng so; and if it lay in his power to avayle me an c li., as he can not avayle me xx s., I wold [not][9] send to hym whill he ⌐is⌐[10] cuppilled with such felaship as he is. Wherfore he that shuld speke with ⌐hym⌐ were 45
best to mete with hym at a sodeyn, where he were with some substanciall man that coud informe hym what were his trought to do in the mater; for it grevyth me full evill to send often to hym till he be of a sadder demenyng. Item, if any answere I shall haue in this mater[11] I must haue it at the ferthest by that tyme as James Gresham shall come hedir, for that tyme must I 50
geve an answere; and if ye can get it ere, send it.

Item,[12] if the seid ⌐Ser⌐ Thomas be of good ⌐disposicion⌐[13] lete hym be spoke to that he be ware of the evidens of Dedham. He told John Pampyng that he had byd John Russe deliuere hem me, and nough he is turnyd and kepyth hem stille; and I dought lest by such as be abought hym it shall 55
rather be appeyrid thanne amendyd,[14] for this xx wynter hath Worseter vsed to bye and selle evidens. And ye can get hem of hym, take hem.

Item,[15] get yow copys of the jnquisicions take bifore Master John Selot for Drayton chirch and bifore ⌐Edmond Clere⌐,[16] exchetour, if any such were takyn; and also inquere what day Emond Clere satte, for he is 60
bound to put ⌐in the inquisicion with-in⌐[17] a monyth after it is taken in the peyne of xl li.

<hr>

[6] *Interl. above* fals hym self *canc.*
[7] *Opposite the line beginning with this word, roughly in the centre of a bracket embracing the paragraph,* Howes *in margin.*
[8] hym and so *canc.*
[9] *This, or another negative, seems essential to sense.*
[10] *Interl. hastily by* Pampyng.
[11] it *canc.*
[12] send me a copy *canc.*
[13] *Interl. above* mood *canc.*
[14] and ye can *canc.*
[15] *Opposite this new paragraph* Drayton *in margin.*
[16] *Interl. above* the *canc.*
[17] *Interl. above* it in with *canc.*

Item, I sent yow word[18] ye shuld inquere what bribes or rewardes ⌐Edmond Clere⌐[19] toke of outlawed men in Norffolk, or any other fals
65 prattes that he hath doon. Dought ye nat he woll not answere of half[20] the good that he hath taken of outlawed men, ⌐if it were well inquered⌐. James Gresham shall cone telle where ye shall best inquere, and such as ye can[21] knowe send me iustly word.

Item, that the exspence mad by Daubeney for myn howsold be mad vp,
70 and that Daubeney be charged with all such somes as ye or I or Richard Calle haue paijd for hym, ⌐and ye for that he hath paijd for yow⌐. As for that I paijd of that was Daubeneys charge, I toke Calle therof a bille, wherof lete Calle send me ayen a[22] copy, and also send me the copy of the bille of your reseytes whech ye haue hom with yow from hens; and that
75 Daubeney ⌐and ye and Call⌐ send me a remembrauns of the exspensis of myn housold and yowres, your children, ⌐and the college⌐, and all other foreyn paymentes,[23] and that in the makyng of Pecokkes acompt such thynges as he hath paijd for the college or the housold be mad as mony deliuerid to Calle or Daubeney, and that in ther acompt thei to aske
80 alowaunce of the paymentes by the handes of Pecok, for I woll no-thyng haue charged[24] nor discharged withinne the acomptes of any maners but[25] only such as longyth to the exspensis of the seid maners.

Item, that ye see all acomptes be mad vp, and in[22] especiall for ⌐my⌐[10] barly. Notwithstandyng, inasmoch that ye haue had in moch barly and
85 greynes for dettes of your tenauntes of Mautby, therfore Pecokes acompt must be mad first,[26] that such greynes as he hath deliuerid may be charged vpon the maltster or vpon any other that haue reseyved it. Item, lete Pecokkes acompt be mad aftir ⌐the forme of⌐ Norwodes acompt, as I suppose is wretyn in your bille of erandes.

90 Item, ⌐take good heed⌐ at the[27] charge and discharge of the acompt of Fastolffes barly in all plases, for ye shall haue other increse there thanne ye shall haue at Mautby; for the mesure of the barly in diuers plases is gretter thanne the busshell at Caster, and also ye take an hepe at the comb ⌐of fermes⌐, whech in a gret somme castith out a gret. Also the maltster
95 must answere of the increse of maltyng acordyng to old acomptes of Fastolffes, ⌐and⌐ if Calle can not vndirstand þat wele thanne ye may send for Barker; and ye shall,[28] whan[29] ye haue mad all thyng[30] redy[31] to the acompt,[32] for xl d. haue hym a day or ij, and he can as good skyll theron

---

[18] wha canc. [19] Interl. above he canc. [21] fynd canc.
[20] Opposite the line beginning here Clere in margin.
[22] No space. [23] as prestes canc.
[24] with canc. [25] acomptes in margin opposite.
[26] Edge of paper repaired for half an inch after this word, but no trace of writing remains.
[27] barly canc.
[28] for xl d. haue hym canc. [29] he h canc.
[30] An unusual mark above -g, but it does not resemble the -es abbreviation.
[31] MS. redyng. [32] ye canc.

as Bernard can on his sheld. Notwithstandyng, the precedentes of Fastolffes
acomptes can telle it aswell as he if ther were any man coud vndirstand it.[33]   100
    Item, on the day after your departyng I reseyved lettirs by William
Roo from your sones to me *and* to yow *and*[34] to Richard Calle, wherby on
of hem writyth þat[35] my lord of Norwich, by the meane of Master John
Selot, had geue a jugement in the mater of the presentacion for the chirche
of Drayton ⌐or Eue⟨r⟩et[36] cam thedir⌐. Neuirthelesse I wote well the   105
Bisshop may geve no jugement, for ther longyth no jugement to the mater.
Paraventure he may amitte the Dukes presentacion and leve myn, in which
case I and Ser Thomas Howes must take an accion ayens the Duc *and*
the Bisshop *and* the prest, or ellis I shuld lese the patronage. Neuirthelesse,
as for the Bisshop, so[37] ye lete hym haue wetyng aforn ⌐secretly *and*⌐ in   110
jentil wise, he woll take no displeasir; for it must be do for ⌐eschuyng⌐[38]
of a gretter hurt. Notwithstandyng he shall bere no losse but if he woll.
Wherfore send me word betymes the very certeynté what is doon in this
mater *and*[39] what is the prestes name that the Duc presentid, *and* what is
the prestes name that I presentid; and that Ser Thomas Howes be[40] felt   115
of his disposicion, whedir he be of hert to take and abide by an accion, as
it is told me he woll. And if ye may fynd the meane that he may write a
lettir to yow or me therfore, or to speke to James Gresham therfore, and he
be thorougly felt in these maters aswell as in the maters wretyn in your
bille of erandes. Me thynkyth and he ⌐were⌐ comond with-all bifore the   120
prior of the White Freres, or some other frend of yours, it shuld cause hym
to be the more substanciall in his answere. Item, beware *and* remembir
hough Master John Selot hath deseyvid yow in this mater. Lerne wisdom
therby *and* forgete it neuir.[41]
    Item, your seid sones write hedir þat thei wold put some man in Cotton   125
betymes, and þat your yonger sone seith he wold haue do it or this tyme
but that he hath no mony in his purs to pay for his costes thedir, wherfore
he desirith to haue some mony therfore till he myght gadir it vp. Wherfore, if thei be go or[42] whan thei goo, remembir hem that thei haue diuers
tymes had mony thedirward *and*[43] do right nought, and myn aduersaries   130
sent thedir men without mony and had ther intent. Item, hough be it
that Mighelmesse payment may not be askyd till the day, yet ther is arerages
jnough to gader more thanne xx li., as it is told me.
    Item, lete your sone John the yonger wete þat I reseyved his lettirs
and billes for the thyng þat he serched fore, vndir his seall. Neuirthelesse   135

[33] *Recto ends.*   [34] whe *canc.*   [35] or *canc.*
[36] *Blotted.*   [37] he *canc.*   [38] *Interl. above* losse *canc.*
[39] Drayton *in margin slightly above the line beginning here.*
[40] warned *canc.*
[41] *This last item added later in the space between paragraphs.*
[42] *Written over ampersand.*
⌐ Cotton *in margin just above.*

143

I remembir I fayle certeyn writyngges and skrowes on paper and parchemyn touchyng the same mater, and in²² especiall of the obites ⌈and beryi[n]gis⌉¹⁴⁴ of diuers of the Poles and of on ⌈Pole⌉¹⁴⁵ was a wolle marchaunt paijd gret customes to the Kyng; but I am in dought whedir your seid sone

140 lokyd not iustly ther ⌈in the box and bagge þat⌉ I bad hym, or ellis þat it were medelid with some other skrowes in the same, or ellis þat it be in a bagge of like maters in my reed chyste at Caster. Wherfore, if he may easely come ther-to without tarying of his gretter maters, lete hym assay.⁴⁶ Item, he shall ⌈fynde⌉ a²² dede how my fadir wass infeffid in þe maner

145 of Heylisdon and Drayton, whech I suppose be among þe euidens of Heylisdon wher I wole haue þe copy.⁴⁷

Item, he sendyth me word that ther is a prest callid   ⁴⁸ told Ser William Barbour that he hath speciall evidens longyng to the manoir of Drayton, and that he seid he wold I had hem, but he wold speke with me.

150 Wherfore I pray yow lete Ser William Barbour, with some other frend of yours, goo speke with the seid prest and to fynd the meane that he wold deliuer yow the seid evidens; and in²² case he woll not deliuer hem till [he] hath spoke with me, thanne⁴⁹ desire ye⁵⁰ with some frend of yours to see hem, and if ye seme thei be licly ⌈desire hym⌉⁵¹ to come to⁵² London

155 with on of my men, and to pay for his ⌈costes⌉⁵³ to come hedir to me, and quite his labour. But and ye may, take hem of hym, though ye⁵⁴ apoynt to take hem hym ayen or ellis to agree with hym therfore. Neuirthelesse, in the begynnyng lete hym be told þat ye merveyll þat he shuld haue any evidens of that maner, for ye herd me sey þat I had all the evidens

160 of the maner. And lete this be do by-tymes and wittely, and⁵⁵ be ware þat this be not do of a sotilté to fele whedir þat I wold inquere aftir any evidens for faylyng.

Item, I pray yow remembir and rede often my bille of erandes, and this lettir, till it be don; and⁵⁶ all⁵⁷ such maters or articles as ye spede

165 herof, crosse hem þat ye may knowe hem from tho þat be not sped; and send me answere of your good speed.

Item,⁵⁸ send me hedir the avise⁵⁹ what your counsell thynkyth best for the remedy of the chirch of Drayton.

---

⁴⁴ *This and the other interlined words in this paragraph by Paston, who also wrote* John Paston þe yonger *in margin opposite.*

⁴⁵ þat *interl. but canc.*   ⁴⁶ and ellis *canc.*

⁴⁷ *This sentence added between the paragraphs in Paston's hand.*

⁴⁸ *Left blank; room for about fifteen letters.*

⁴⁹ ye *canc.*   ⁵⁰ to see hem *canc.*

⁵¹ *Interl. above* of *canc.*   ⁵² evidens *in margin opposite.*

⁵³ *Interl. above* labour *canc.*

⁵⁴ agree *canc.*   ⁵⁵ in such *canc.*

⁵⁶ *Three letters, apparently* ach, *canc.*

⁵⁷ Erandes *in margin opposite.*

⁵⁸ Drayton *in margin just below.*   ⁵⁹ of *canc.*

Though I write right certeynly, if ye[60] loke hem lightly *and* see hem seld
thei shall sone be forgete.   170

> Item, I shall telle yow a tale:
> Pampyng *and* I haue piked your male,
> *and* taken out pesis v,
> for vpon trust of Calles promise we may ⌈sone⌉ onthryve.
> And if Calle bryng vs hedir xx *li.*,   175
> ye shall haue your peses ayen good *and* round;
> or ellis[61] if he woll not pay yow the valew of the peses there,
> to the post do nayle his ere,
> or ellis do hym some other sorough,
> for I woll nomore in his defaut borough;   180
> and but if the reseyvyng of my livelod be bettir plyed,
> he shall Cristes curs and myn clene tryed.
> And loke ye be mery and take no thought,
> for this ryme is cunnyngly wrought.
> My Lord Persy and all this house   185
> recomaund them to yow, dogge, catte *and* mowse,
> *and* wysshe ye had be here stille,
> for the sey ye are good gille.
> Nomore to yow at this tyme,
> but God hym saue þat mad this ryme.[62]   190

Wret þe vigill of Sent Math[ew] be yowr trew *and* trusti husbond,

J. P.[63]

78. Draft message from the KING to SIR WILLIAM YELVERTON   1465

Add. 27445, f. 11. $8\frac{1}{8} \times 4$ in. Pampyng's hand.

Dorse blank.

This is evidently a draft prepared by Paston. The year appears from the reference
to the Duke of Suffolk's entry into Drayton (see no. 73).
   G. 535/618.

This is the instruccion for the messenger

That ye grete well Ser William Yeluerton, letyng hym wete in our behalf
⌈we be informed⌉ that certeyn persones in the name of the right worshipfull

---

[60] se *canc.*   [61] lete hym *canc.*
[62] *These lines written as prose. Pampyng's hand ends here.*
[63] *At foot of page, upside down, the following in Calle's hand:*
Parsonage of Drayton
Item, John Paston hathe presented Ser Thomas ⌈Hakon⌉ [*interl. above* Hogon *canc.*] to
the chirge of Drayton.

oure cosyn the Duc of Suffolk, haue enterid in the manoir of Drayton
5 that was Fastolffes, and haue dreven from the seid manoir and other xiij^c
shep and other bestes pastured vpon the seid manoir, notwithstandyng we
merveyle gretly that the¹ ⌜seid Ser William, his⌝ sones and seruauntes,
as it is seid, assiste and counfort the seid persones soo entryng and with-
drawyng the seid catell, seying that ⌜he is named⌝² bothe feffé and execu-
10 tour; and all be it so that there is variaunce bithwene ⌜hym⌝³ and oure
welbelovid John Paston in oure coort, consernyng aswell the seid manoirs
as other goodes that were Ser John Fastolffes, whom God assoyle, yit it
may not acorde with worship and consiens for ⌜the seid Ser William⌝³ to
assiste the distruccion of the seid ⌜manoirs and⌝ goodes in the meane tyme.
15 Wherfore we desire ⌜hym⌝³ that he woll do ⌜his⌝⁴ devour effectually to help
to save the⁵ seid manoirs from all such pretense or titell, and to cause the
seid catels to be restored to the manoirs aforeseid and not to be with-
drawen and distroyed as they be; ⌜and þat he do his⌝⁶ feithfull part in
this behalf acordyng to the trust þat ⌜he was⌝⁷ put in, as we may do for
20 ⌜hym⌝³ in tyme to come.

78. ¹ *From* ye; *a following* your *canc.*   ² *Interl. above* ye be *canc.*
³ *Interl. above* yow *canc.*   ⁴ *Interl. above* your *canc.*
⁵ f *canc.*   ⁶ *Interl. above* doyng your *canc.*
⁷ *Interl. above* ye were *canc.*

EDMOND PASTON I

79. To JOHN PASTON I   Perhaps 1447, 5 July

Add. 27443, f. 99. $11\frac{3}{4} \times 6$ in. Probably autograph.

Dorse: Paper seal over wax. Address in hand of letter:

Tradatur Johanni Past[on] of þe Inner In in the Temple att London.

The date, as Gairdner suggests, must be before the Marquis, later Duke, of Suffolk could be said to 'rewle in this schere' without rival. From Margaret Paston's letter no. 128 it appears that Suffolk was in control, and Daniel out of favour, in the spring of 1448. Edmond Paston's nuncupative will (no. 80) is dated 21 March 1449, when he was 'languens in extremis'; so that this letter cannot be later. For Hauteyn (l. 9) cf. Agnes's letter no. 18.

There are no other documents with which the hand may be compared. But, though fluent enough, it has the loose and untidy appearance characteristic of unprofessional writers, and is probably Edmond's own.

G. 53/69.

Ryth worschipfull brothir, I recomaund me to yow, &c. I preye write to myn modre ⌜of your owne hed as for to consell her⌝ howh þat sche kepe her preuye *and* tell no body ryth nowth of her counsell, for sche woll tell persones many of her counsell this day *and* to-morwe sche woll sey be Goddis faste þat the same men ben false. I haue seen parte of þe euydence 5 *and* þe maner hathe be purchasid be parcell *and* certeyn feffementis mad of the auowson *and* certeyn pecis of lond¹ enterlessant þe maner, *and* I wote ⌜well⌝ ye haue ⌜on⌝² collaterall rellesse wyth a warente of on of þe wyffys of³ Hauteyn of all þe holl maner.

Steward, þe chiffe constable, told me he was enpanellyd vp-on þe assise⁴ 10 be-twex yow *and* Frauncesse. He axyd me counsell what he myth do þer-jnne, for he told me it was take in Ser Thomas Tudham name. He wold fayne be chalengyd. I concellyd him swere the trowthe of the issue þat he schuld be swore to, *and* þanne he nedyd neuer to drede hym of noon atteynte. I yaue him this counsell *and* noon othir. I enqueryd me 15 of the rewle of myn master Danyell *and* myn lord of Suffulke, *and* askyd wheche I thowte schuld rewle in þis schere, *and* I seyd bothe, as I trowh,⁵

---

79. ¹ wyth all *canc.*   ² *Interl. above* j *canc.*

³ seyd *canc. preceded by* the left *uncanc. in error.*

⁴ *Abbr.* assie *with stroke above;* a yeens yow *canc.*   ⁵ *Two words heavily canc.*

and he þat suruyuyth to hold be þe u*er*tue of þe suruyuyr, *and* he to thanke
his frendes *and* to aquite his enmyys. So I fele by hi*m* he wold forsake his
20 mast*er and* gette hi*m* a newh yf he wyste he schuld rewle. *And* so wene I
meche of all þe contré is so disposyd.⁶

þe Holy Trenyté kepe yow. Wrete at Norwiche on þe Wednysday aft*er*
Seynt Pet*er*, in hast.

Yo*ur* broth[er] E. PASTON

80. Nuncupative will: draft   1449, 21 March

Add. 27443, f. 101. 11½ × 4¼ in. Hand unidentified.

Dorse: In an approximately contemporary hand: *Copia vltime voluntatis
Edmundi Paston.*

From the numerous corrections and interlineations (not recorded here) this is
evidently a draft rather than a copy. 21 March 1448 falls in 1449 by modern dating.
    G. 64/85.

Omnibus Christi fidelibus ad quos presens scriptum peruenerit nos,
Willelmus May, magister Noui Templi London', Johannes Bakton,
gentilman, Thomas Parker, ciuis et sissor London', et Johannes Osbern,
salutem in Domino sempiternam. Sciatis quod xxj die Marcij Anno
5 Domini m¹ccccxlviij Edmundus Paston de comitatu Norff', armiger, in
bona memoria ac sana mente existens, languens in extremis, in nostra
presencia condidit et declarauit testamentum suum nuncupatiuum in hunc
modum. In primis, legauit animam suam Deo Omnipotenti, Beate Marie
Virgini, et omnibus sanctis, corpusque suum ad sepeliendum in ecclesia
10 Templi predicti siue in ecclesia Fratrum Carmelitarum London'. Item,
dictus Edmundus, pro eo quod noluit circa bona siue negocia temporalia
mentem siue animam suam affligere seu ocupare, set ad eternam felicitatem
se preparare, dedit, legauit, ac comisit omnia bona et catalla sua predilecto
fratri suo Johanni Paston, ex magna confidencia in ipso habita vt ea
15 disponeret pro bono anime sue pro vt melius videret Deo placere ac anime
sue prodesse. Et dictum Johannem Paston ordinauit et constituit executo-
rem suum. In cuius rei testimonium presentibus sigilla nostra apposuimus.

79.   ⁶ he sey *canc.*

WILLIAM PASTON II

81. To JOHN PASTON I   1452, 16 June

Add. 27443, f. 103. $11\frac{1}{4} \times 6\frac{3}{4}$ in. Autograph.

Dorse: Traces of red wax. Address autograph:

*To my*n *most reue*rent and ⟨w⟩*urchepful*[1] brod*er Jon Paston.*[2]

The approximate date, as Gairdner noted, appears from Margaret Paston's letter
no. 133, which shows that William was at Cambridge in 1449. But the dating on
Friday a week before Midsummer Eve must mean that Midsummer Eve itself
was a Friday; and in the acceptable period this occurred in 1447 and 1452. The
report that John Paston had been rumoured to be among 'ryserse in Norfolk'
tells decisively in favour of 1452, a year in which the disturbed state of Norfolk
is amply displayed in Paston's own writings: see nos. 40-6. In particular, no. 41
says that Roger Church and his associates had falsely accused respectable men of
'a risyng ageyn the Kynges peas'; and a copy of a report by the sheriff, John Clopton,
records that in interrogating one of Church's men he asked specifically 'if thei,
whan thei were to-geder, spoke of Paston and othre gentilmen named in the seid
bille to haue assisted hem' (Part II, no. 882; G. 177/214).

   G. 69/91.

To my*n*[3] most reue*rent* *and* wurchepful brodur. I re*cum*mend me hartely
to 30w, desiry*ng* speciali to he*re* of 30w*re* wellefare *and* prosperité, qweche
Almyty God *con*tenu to 30w*re* gosteli hele *and* bodili welfare: *and* if it
plese 30w*re*[4] goode brodorod to he*re* of my*n* wellefare, at þe[5] makyng of
þis bylle I was in good hele. *And* if it leke 30w*re* good brodorod to re*me*mbre   5
þe[6] lett*er* þat I sent to 30w[7] of þe noyse þat was telde of 30w, þat[8] 3e
schuld a[9] be on of þe capetayns of þe ryserse in Norfolk, *and* how þat j
schol*ere* of Cambryg, qweche is *p*ar*sone* of Welle, schuld an vtteryd ferthere
to 30w*re* grete[10] schalndyr, besechyng 30w to vndyrstond þat þe seyde
*p*ar*sone* of Welle was sone þat tyme at Lundon, we*re* he harde sey of j   10
swyre of ij c.[11] marc[12] be 3e*re* þat 3e *and* Mast*er* Thomas Wellys wolde

---

81. [1] *First letter destroyed by slit for tape.*   [2] *dwellyng canc.*
   [3] *This word normally written by W. Paston II* my *with stroke above, which may perhaps
be a mere habit of writing without phonetic significance; but since he uses an exactly similar
stroke very commonly for* n, *it is so transcribed here also.*
   [4] b *canc.*   [5] þ *in form of* y, *as always in W. Paston II.*
   [6] *Corr. from* þat.   [7] *of canc.*   [8] *Ampersand canc.*
   [9] *No space.*   [10] hurte sch *canc.*
   [11] *MS.* cc, *another* cc *above line struck out.*   [12] *Written* mac, -c *flourished.*

sewe þe seyd parsone Welle for ȝowre schalndyr. *And* the seyde parsone come to Cambryg sothyn, *and* hathe pekyd a qwarell to on Mastyr Recheforthe, a knythys sone of Norfolke,[13] and[14] seyd to[15] Rychefor[the][16]
15 þat he had be cause that ȝe schuld sewe hym. *And* the seyd parsone Welle thretyd Rycheferthe þat wat some euer þat ȝe causyd parson Welle to lese be ȝowre sewtys, þat Rycheforthe schul lese þe same to þe par⌐son⌐ of Welle. Were-fore thys jentylman[17] Rycheforthe taket grete thowt, *and* pray me to wrythe to ȝow þat ye wulde sese ȝowre suthe tylle þe
20 tyme þat ȝe[18] wulde asyne þat I mythe speke wythe ȝow, *and* odyr sundry ⌐haue⌐[19] speke wyth ȝow of þe same mater; for yt ware pithé þat[20] Rycheforthe chuld haue ony hurthe there-by.

I beseche ȝow holde me excusyd thow I wryt⟨h⟩[21] no better to ȝow at thys tyme, for in good feyth I had no leysere. þe bry[n]ggar of[22] thys letter
25 can telle ȝow þe same.

God haue ȝow in hys[23] kepyng. Wretyn at Cambryg on Fryday senyth[24] nexste[25] be-fore Mydsomer Euyn. In case ȝe come be[26] Cambryg I schal telle ȝow mo of it. I am sory I may wrythe no bettyr at þis tyme, but I trvst ȝe wyl be[27] pacient.[28]

30   Be ȝowre pore broder W. Paston

82. Memorandum on French Grammar   Probably 1450-4

Norwich Central Library, MS. Walter Rye 38, ff. 64-6. $4\frac{1}{4} \times 5\frac{3}{4}$ in. Autograph.

These notes appear in a book of 72 leaves containing coats of arms of Norfolk families and some obits of Pastons and Barrys. The notes immediately follow the obits. The latest of the obits, in the same hand and style as the notes, is that of Edmond Paston I, who died in 1449 (see no. 80). The notes thus cannot be earlier than that. The style of the writing has features in common with both no. 81 and no. 83. It is most likely that the notes were written while William was at Cambridge. He was there in 1449, and had left by 1454. For a full description of the manuscript see N. Davis and G. S. Ivy, 'MS. Walter Rye 38 and its French Grammar', *Medium Ævum*, xxxi (1962), 110-24, where this text was first printed.

Memoorandum þat ho hath affeccion to lerne þis langage must first considre viij thinggis qweche byn full nessessarij to knowe to come to þe ⌐tru⌐ profescion[1] of þis langage—

81. [13] *MS.* Norforfolke.   [14] de *canc.*   [15] hym *canc.*
    [16] *MS.* Rychechefor.   [17] *MS.* jeltylman.   [18] wuls *canc.*
    [19] *Interl. above* wulle sw *canc.*   [20] þe ryth *canc.*
    [21] *At edge; only part of top and tail of* h *visible.*   [22] thys *canc.*   [23] kepp *canc.*
    [24] *Second letter first written* a, *but a stroke through the lower part seems intended to change it to* e.   [25] *Written* nex, *then* ste *crowded in.*
    [26] come be *repeated.*   [27] *MS.* wylle.
    [28] *This last sentence added in space between end of letter and subscription.*
82. [1] *First syllable abbr. by crossed* p *as if* per; *and* f *uncrossed.*

Frist, because it is not sownid as it [is] wretyn ʒe must considre þat
this lettre s sondit neuer but qwan it stondit be-fore j of þis v letteris 5
qweche ben callid wowellys, þat is to say a, e, i, o, v, and neuer þis letter
sownit but in cas.

The ij rewle is þis, þat þere byn many wordis wretyn at the last ynd
with an z, and oder with j s. Qwan ony word with j z, than þe vowel be-fore
þe sey[d] z sownit long, example as buuez, venez, alez, portez, priez, amez. 10
Item, alle þe wordis qwech jnd with þis letter s, þe wowell be-fore þe s
is schort,[2] as bonnes, belles, mauuaises,[3] rouges, blanches, verdes, noires,
sanguines,[4] blues, grises, gaunes.[5]
Item, þere is a deferens be-twyn þe writyng of þis word il and jlz, for
il seruit fore þe singlere now[m]ber and ilz for the plure noumbre, and þe 15
z sownit neuer, neithere the[6] l, but be-fore j vowell; example as il est
moun bon amy; here þe l sownyt be-cause of þe e qweche folowyt; example
of jlz, ilz mayment bien la leur bonne mercy; here sownyt of[7] ilz but only
j mayment, &c. This z neuer sownit, and þe l[8] sownit not be-cause an m
folowyt here; and this is a general rewle. 20

Item, were two ar iij vowellis come to-geder þe vowell jn þe myddis is
set a-side and is neþ[er] wretyn neithere sownyd, example as[9] jayme; þat
is as muche as je ayme, quantum breuyus tantum melyus.[10]

Item, were ony verbe of plurell noumbre[11] endit w[ith] an n and t, the
n sown[i]th not; example as jayme, tu aymes, jl ayme, nous amons, vous[12] 25
amez, jlz ayment;[13] this ayment sownit as[14] aymet, and all suche oder.

Item, as in Latyn distjnccion is be[15]-twix þe femynyn gender and þe
masculyne gender, so is jn this langgage; were-fore[16] rith nessessary it is
to knowe þe pronons and þe declinacionis of þe verbis jn þe maner here-
after folowyng: 30

je or moy	tu	il	nous	vous	ilz
I	thow	he	w[e]	ʒe	thei

mg	Ces	choses	sount	nostres
	The	th[i]nggis	byn	owres

et	lez autres	choses	sount	vostres	35
and	þe oder	thinggis	byn	ʒowr[17]	

mg	Ce cheval[18]	est moun	et	la cell	est tenne	fg
	þis horse	is myn	and	þe sadil	is thyn	

---

[2] bonnes *canc.*   [3] *The group* uu *a minim short.*
[4] *The group* uin *a minim short.*   [5] *F. 64^r ends.*   [6] *Written* thel, l *canc.*
[7] f *uncrossed.*   [8] neuer *canc.*   [9] jaj *canc.*
[10] *F. 64^v ends.*   [11] ed *canc.*
[12] ames *altered to* amez *and canc.*   [13] *Over* ame.   [14] amet *canc.*
[15] thu *canc.*   [16] *Repeated as* qwere *fore.*   [17] *F. 65^r ends.*
[18] *Abbr.* chal *with stroke above.*

40 fg Ce jument est mon et la veel tien mg
This mare is myn[19] *and* þe calfe thyn

Cest escriptori est nostre *et* tout taunt
This pener[20] is owre *and* all aswell

caniuet poinson forchett*es*[7] *et* plumes
penk[n]yf boitkyn cher*is* and pennes

45 sou*n*t v*o*strez a faire du tout v*o*stre frank volu*n*té
be ʒowr*is* to do[21] w*ith* all ʒowre fre wylle

Tiell vn ad faith moy tort *et* je luy null
Such on[22] hath don me wrong *and* I hy*m* non

Je r*e*porth moy du tout a deu qui congnoist tout
50 I r*e*porth me of all to God qwich know*it* all

Cest chastell est mou*n* Ce ma*n*syu*n* est tenne
This castell is my*n* þis howse is thyn

Je ayme bien ma dame *et* ⌜mieulx⌝[23] mou*n* s*eu*r
I loue wyll my*n* lady *and* better my*n* lord

55 myen teyne syene n*o*stre v*o*stre loure
my*n* thyn hys howre ʒowre thers[24]

je dor tu veiles il song songer*e*
I slep[25] thow wakyst he dr*e*myth to dr*e*me

nous petrons vous courres ils saylent
60 we walk ʒe renne they lepe

ainsi sum*us* nous toutz s*er*uiz solonc pleser*e*
thus be we all s*er*uyd after plesansse

je suy tu es il *et* nous sum*us* u*o*us[26] estez ils sont
I am thow art he is we ar*e* ʒe ar*e* thei arn

65 je estoie tu estoies il estoit nous estoioms u*o*us estiez ilz estient
I was thow wer*e* he was we wer*e* ʒe wer*e* they wer*e*

je serroi[27] tu[28] s*er*res il serra nous serrons[29] u*o*us serrez
il sarront

---

[19] *Stroke above, perhaps intended for* mon *above (to form* moun*)*   [20] e *canc.*
[21] *Miswritten* de.   [22] o- *over* j.
[23] *Written* mieulxu *above* miexu *with* l *over* x *and all canc.*
[24] F. 65[v] *ends.*   [25] *Miswritten* chep.   [26] *Second* u *a minim short.*
[27] il *canc.*   [28] seroit *canc.*   [29] n *a minim short.*

I³⁰ chal be   thow chall be   he chall b[e]   we chall be   ʒe chall be
   thei chall be   70

I chuld be   thow schuldyst be   he schul be
je sarroi   tu   serrois   il sarroit³¹

nous serrons   vous serrez   ilz sarroient
we   schull be ʒe   schull be thei schuld [be]

jeusse   esté   tu   eussez   esté   il vst esté   75
I schuld haue be   thow schuldist haue be,³² &c.

nous vissomus esté   vous eusses esté   ilz   vessent esté
we schuld haue be   ʒe   schuld haue be   thei schul haue b[e]³³

je veul tu   veulez il veult
I wyll thow wylte   he wyll   80

nous voilleimus   uous voilez   jlz   voilent
we   wyll   ʒe   wyll   they wyll

je vouldrai   tu   vuldres   il vouldra
I schall wyll   thow schalt   he chall wyll

nous voldroms   uous vouldres   ilz vouldrunt   85
we   schall will   ʒe   schall wyll   thei schall

je vouldroi   tu   voul[d]rois   il vouldroit
I wold   thow woldist   he wolde

nous vouldroms   uous vouldroies   ilz vuldroient
we   wolde   ʒe   wulde   thei wulde   90

Je confie in du   qe tout serra   bien
I   trust jn God þat all   schall be wyll

et   qe nous aueroms   bones nouelles dez totes nous   améz
and þat we   schall haue good tidinggis of all   howre frindis

et   qe la miere serra   ben   gardé ⌐et⌐ nous enméz   95
   discounfitéz
and þat þe ce   schall be wylle kepth and owre enmis
   disconfith

³⁰ chall *canc.*   ³¹ *MS.* sarrot.
³² he *canc.*   ³³ *F.* 66^r *ends.*

83. To John Paston I 1454, July

Add. 43488, f. 19. 11¾ × 6½ in. Autograph.

Dorse: Two lines of postscript. Paper seal over wax and tape. Address autograph:

To hys wurchypfull brodyr Jon Paston.

The date appears from the report of the arrest of the Duke of Exeter. On 24 July 1454 the Privy Council required the Duke of York to 'bring' Exeter 'to Pountfrete' (H. Nicolas, *Proceedings and Ordinances of the Privy Council of England*, vi (1837), 217).

F. i, p. 72. G. 211/254. C. 18 (except postscript).

Ryth wurchypfull broder, I recomande [me] to ȝow; and as for tedyng, myn lord of ȝorke hathe take myn lord of Exsater jn-to hys a-warde. The Duke of Somerset js styll jn preson, jn werse case than he was.

Syr Jon Fastolf recomande hym to ȝow, &c. He wyll ryde jn-to Norfolke
5 ward as on Trusday, and he wyll dwelle at Caster, and Skrop wyth hym. He saythe ȝe are the hartyest kynysman and frynd þat he knowyt. He wulde haue ȝow at Mawdeby dwellyng.

I had gret chere of Byllyng be þe way, and he told me jn cownsayle wathe he sayd to Ledam. Ledam wulde a do hys wyse to a mad a complent
10 to Pry[s]othe jn þe schere howse of ȝow, and Byllyng consallyd hym to leve and tolde Ledam ȝe and he were no felawys, and sayd to Ledam, 'Yt is the gyse of ȝowre contré-men to spend alle the good they haue on men and leuery gownys and hors and harnes, and¹ so ber² yt owth for j wylle, and at the laste they arn but beggarys; and so ⌐wyll¬ ȝe do. I wylde ȝe
15 schull do wyll, be-cause ȝe³ are a² felaw jn⁴ Grays In, were I ⟨t⟩o⁵ was a felaw. As for Paston, he ys a swyre of wurchyp, and of gret lyuelode, and I wothe he wyll⁶ not spend alle hys good at⁷ onys, but he sparyt ȝerely c mark or j c li. He may do hys ennemy a scherewd turne and neuer fare the warse jn hys howsholde, ner the lesse men a-bowthe hym.⁸ ȝe may not
20 do so, but if yt be for j sesun. ⌐I consayll ȝow¬ not ⌐to¬ contenu long as ȝe do. I wulle⁹ consalle ȝow to seke reste wyt Paston.' And I thankkyd ⌐Byllyng¬¹⁰ on ȝowre behalfe.

God haue ȝow in hys kepyng.

Be ȝowre pore brodyr WYLLYAM PASTON¹¹

25 Meche odyr thyng I can telle and I had lesur. Recomande me to myn suster Margeth [and] myn cosyn Elyzabet Clyre, I pray ȝow.

---

83. ¹ to *canc.*   ² *No space.*   ³ w *canc.*
⁴ gary *canc.*   ⁵ *First letter obliterated by blot.*
⁶ now *canc.*   ⁷ *MS.* as.   ⁸ he *canc.*
⁹ wul *canc.*   ¹⁰ *Interl. above* hym *canc.*
¹¹ *Subscription vertically in margin. Postscript on verso.*

84. To JOHN PASTON I   1454, 6 September

Add. 34888, f. 107. $11\frac{1}{2} \times 5\frac{3}{4}$ in. Autograph.

Dorse: Traces of red wax. Address autograph:

*To my*n *rith wurchipfull brod*er *Jon Paston be þis delyu*eryd.

The date is fixed by several events. Thomas Bourchier became Archbishop of Canterbury in April 1454, and William Grey, who succeeded Bourchier as Bishop of Ely, received his temporalities by patent issued on 6 September 1454 (*Cal. Pat. Rolls 1452–61*, p. 204). The report of Lord Grey's offer to marry his ward to Elizabeth Paston connects this letter with no. 50, and the reference to Sir John Fastolf's going to Caister, later than he had intended, follows the earlier statement in no. 83.

F. iii, p. 220. G. 216/260.

Ryth wurchypfull brod*er*, I recomande me to 30w, desiryng[1] to he*r*e of 30wr*e* willefar*e*. Byllyng þe s*er*iant hathe byn in his contré, and he come to Lundon þis weke. He sent for me and ast me how I fard. I tolde hym he*r*e is pestelens, and sayd I farid þe bett*er*. He was in good hele, for it was noysyd þat he was ded. A toke me to him and[2] ast how my*n* sust*er*   5
dede, and I anssweryd wyll, neu*er* bett*er*. He seyd he was w*yth* the Lord Gray, and they talkyd of j jantilma*n* qweche is ward to my*n* lord, ⌐I⌐ reme*m*bre he sayd it was Harry Gray that thei talkyd of. And my*n* lord sayd, 'I was besy w*yth*-jn þis fewe days to a[3] maryd hym to a jantyll-woma*n* jn Norfolke that schall haue iiij c marc. to hyr mariage, and now a wyll not   10
be me, for iiij c marc. wulde do me hese and now[4] he wulde haue his mariage mony hy*m*-self; and there-fore', q*uoth* he, 'he schall mary hym-self for me.' þis wurd*ys* had my*n*[5] lord to Byllyng, as he tollde me. He vnd*er*stod þat my*n* lord labor*yd* for his owne a-vayle, and co*n*saylyd to[6] byd he*r*e be wyse. And I thankkyd hym for hys good co*n*sayll.   15

I sent 30w an ansswere of[7] 30wr*e* lett*er* of S*er* Jon Fastolf comyng hom, as he told me hem-self. Neu*er* the lesse he bode leng*er* than he sayd hym-self he schull a do. He tolde me he schulde make j ende be-twix Skrop and my*n* sust*er* wulle he is in Norfolke. Many wulde it schulde not pr*eu*e, for thei say it is an onlykkely mariage. In casse Cresse*ner* be talkyd of ony[8]   20
more, he is countyd a jantylma*n*ly ma*n* and a wurchepfull. 3e knowe ho is most wurchipfull bett*er* than I. At the reu*er*ens of Good,[9] drawe to su*m*me co*n*clusyu*n*, it is[10] time.

My*n* lord Chanseler*e* come not he*r*e sone I come to Lu*n*dun, ner*e* my*n* lord of Jorke. My*n*[11] lord of Cantirbury hathe rec*e*yued hys crosse, and I   25

84. [1] 3 *canc.*   [2] tol *canc.*   [3] *No space.*   [4] he wulde *canc.*
    [5] h *canc.*   [6] warne *canc.*   [7] w *canc.*   [8] m *and another letter canc.*
    [9] g *canc.*   [10] tyme *smudged and canc.*   [11] lorid *canc.*

was w*yth* hym in the Kynggys cham*er* qwan he mad hys¹² homage. I tolde Harry Wylton¹³ þe demeny*ng* betwix the Kyng and hym; it war*e* to long to wrythe.

As for the prist þat dede areste ⌈me⌉, I can not vnd*er*stond þat it is þe 30 pryste þat 3e mene. Her*e* is gret pestelens. I purpose to fle in-to the contré. My*n* lord of Oxforthe is come a-3en fro the se and he hath geth hym lytyll thank in this countré. Muche mor*e* thyng I wulde wrythe to 30w, but I lak lysore. Harry Wylton sey the Kyng. My*n* lord of Ely hathe do hys¹⁴ fewthé.

35 God haue ⌈30w⌉ in hys blyssyd kepyng. Wr*e*tyn at Lu*n*do*n* on the Fryday be-for*e* Owr*e* Ladys Day the Natyuité in gret hast. I pray r*e*comand me to my*n* sust*er* and to my*n* cosyn Cler*e*.

Be 30wr*e* brod[er] W. PASTON

85. To MARGARET PASTON   Probably 1458, 10 August

Add. 33597, f. 5. 8¾ × 5⅞ in. Autograph; see Plate IV.

Dorse: Traces of red wax. Address autograph:

To his rythe worchypffull and *harthy wellebelouyd* sust*er* Margeré Paston, dwellyng jn Norwyche.

From no. 121 it appears that Elizabeth Paston was married to Robert Poynings not long before January 1459. William's handwriting varies a good deal over the years, and the style of this letter most closely resembles that of no. 86, which is certainly of 1459. The date suggested suits both these facts well.
G. LXXIX/255.

Rythe harthely well belouyd sust*er*, I r*e*comand me, &c.; *and* I haue r*e*ceyued 30wr*e* letteres. *And* as for*e* my*n* nevewes, they lerne¹ rythe well bothe, *and* there gownys and there gere schall be mad for hem acordyng to þe enthenthe of 30wr*e* lett*er*, *and* all od*er* thynggys² that behouyth on-to 5 here p*r*ofythe harddely to my*n* power*e*. *And* sust*er*, God 3elde 30w for 30wr*e* labore for*e* me for gaderyng of my*n* mony. And I p*r*ay as sone as ⌈3e⌉ receyuyth, send it hed*er* be some trusty ma*n*, *and* þat it plese to calle þere-on, &c.

My*n* sust*er* and my*n* brod*er* r*e*comand hem to 30w bothe, and I may say 10 to 30w jn³ counsayll sche is op-on poyn of mariage so þat mod*er* *and* my*n* brod*er* sett frendely *and*⁴ stedfastely there-on, leke as I wothe well 3e wolld and it lay in 30w as it dothe jn hem, &c. I p*r*ay 30w do 30wr*e* parthe to kall there-on. It were to long to wrythe on-to 30w all þe man*er* of demenyng of þis mat*er*, *and* there-for I haue spoke to Wyllya*m* Worsetere *and* to

---

¹² hys *repeated*.   ¹³ *Ampersand canc.*   ¹⁴ f *blotted out.*

85. ¹ th *canc.*   ² *Ampersand canc.*   ³ counsayd *canc.*   ⁴ skedf *canc.*

Wethewell to tell it ʒow holly as it is. I wothe ryth well ʒow[r] good labore 15
may do moche; *and* send me word how ʒe here as hastely as ʒe may.

Item, Howard spak of a mariage be-twex his sone *and* myn nece ⌈Margeré⌉
ʒowre dothere. It were well do suche materes were nawthe sclawfully
laboryd; it is wurchypffull, &c. Send me word.

⌈*And*⌉ God⁵ haue ʒow in his kepyng. Wretyn at London⁶ ⌈on⌉ Sent 20
Lawrens Day in hast.

Be ʒowre brodyre Wyllya[m] Paston

Item, [I] send ʒow a letter directyd to Wollysby. I⁷ pray ʒow lethe it be
delyuered hym as hastely as ʒe may, *and* if ʒe come to þis contré I am leke
to se ʒow⁸ *and* ⌈we schall⌉⁹ make ryth mery, I trust.   25

86. To John Paston I   1459, 12 November

Add. 34888, f. 140. 10⅝×4½ in. Autograph.

Dorse: Traces of red wax. Address autograph:

*To myn master Jon Paston in Norffolk.*¹

The date appears from William's account of the action he has taken to secure
possession of Sir John Fastolf's property, on behalf of his brother as executor.
Fastolf died on 5 November 1459 (see no. 54).
    F. iii, p. 352. G. 338/391. C. 24 (part).

Rythe willbelouyd broder, I recomand me to ʒow, sertefyeng ʒow þat
on Friday last was, in þe mornyng, Wurceter *and* I were come to London
be viij of þe clok; *and* we² spak wyth myn lord Chancelere, and I fund
hym well dysposyd in all thyng, *and* ʒe schall fynd hym ryth profytabyll³
to ʒow, &c. *And* he desyryd me to wrythe ʒow a letter in hys name *and* 5
put trust in ʒow in gaderyng of þe good togeder; *and* pray ʒow to do so
and haue all his good owthe of euery place of his, his awne place, qwere
so euer they were, *and* ley it secretly were as ʒe thowth best at ʒowre
assynement, &c.,⁴ tyll þat he speke wyth ʒow hym-selff; *and* he seyd ʒe
schulld haue all la⌈w⌉full fauore. I purpose to ryde to hym þis day fore 10
wrythis of⁵ *diem clawsit extremum*, *and* I sopose ʒe schall haue a letter sent
from hym-selff to ʒow. As fore the good of Powlis, it is safe j-now; *and*

---

⁵ *MS.* Gog.
⁶ on þe Fryday next affore *canc.*, *then* Sent Lawrens *interl. and canc.*
⁷ þa *canc.*
⁸ *First letter originally* j, *botched to resemble* ʒ; *a final* r *canc.*
⁹ *Interl. above to canc.*

86. ¹ *Below the address, in the same ink, is a figure composed of four lines, one curved inter-
secting two straight and another curved.*
² haue *canc.*   ³ *MS.* profytalbyll.
⁴ *Flourished* c *of* &c. *replaces* of *canc.*   ⁵ dye *canc.*

þis day we haue grant to haue þe good ⸢owthe⸣ of Barmunsey wyth-
⸢owthe⸣ avyse of any man sauyng Worseter, Plomer, and I myn-selff, and
15 no body schall know of it but we[6] thre.

Myn[7] lord Tresorere spekyth fayre, but ȝet many avyse me to put no[8]
trost in hym. There is laboryd many menys to intytill þe Kyng in his good.
Sothewell is eschetore, and he is rythe good and will disposyd. Myn lord
of Exsater cleymyth tytill in myn master plase, wyth þe aportynantys, in
20 Sothewerk, and ueryly had purposyd to haue entrid; and his[9] consayll
were wyth us, and spak wyth Wurseter and me, and now afterward they
haue sent vs word that they wold meve myn lord to sue be menys of þe
lawe, &c. I haue spoke wyth myn lord of Canterbury and Master Jon
Stokys, and I fynd hem rythe will disposyd bothe, &c.

25 Item, to-morow are þe nexst day ȝe schall haue a-noder letter, for be
that tyme we schall know more than we do now. Myn lord Chancelere
wold þat[10] myn master schulld be beryed wurchyply, and c mark almes done
fore hym; but þis day I schall holly know his enthent. Master Jon Stokys
hathe þe same consaythe and almes geuyng. Harry Fenyngley is nat in
30 this towne, nere þe Lord Bechamp.

Item, we haue gethe men of þe speretuall law wyth-haldyn wyth[11] vs,
qwat casse some euer hap. We haue Master Roberd Kenthe. But in any
wyse haue all þe good there ⸢to⸣-gedyre, and tary for no lettyng thow ȝe
schuld do it be day a lythe opynly; for it is myn lord Chancelere full in-
35 thenthe that[12] ȝe schuld do so.

As for Wyllyam Worceter, he trustythe veryly ȝe wold do for hym and
for his avayll ⸢in reson⸣, and I dowthe natt and he may[13] ueryly and feythefully vnderstand ȝow so disposyd to hym ward ȝe schall fynd hym feytheffull
to ȝow in leke wysse. I vnderstand by hym he will neuer haue oder master
40 but his old master, and to myn consaythe it were peté but iff he schull
stand in suche casse be myn master that he schuld neuer[14] nede seruyce,
co[n]se[de]ryng how myn master trusted hym and þe long ȝerys that he
hathe be wyth hym in, and many schrew jornay fore his sake, &c.

I wrythe ȝow no more, be-cawse ȝe[15] schall [haue] a-noder letter ⸢wretyn⸣
45 to-morow. Wretyn at Lundon þe[16] xij day of Nouembre in hast.

Be WILLYAM PASTON

---

6 iij canc. 7 M apparently from ay. 8 th canc.
9 counsay canc. at edge. 10 he canc. 11 w canc.
12 Ampersand canc. 13 ueryre canc. 14 neder canc.
15 ȝe repeated. 16 xx canc.

87. Inventory

Probably 1459–60

Add. 27446, f. 118. $5\frac{7}{8} \times 8$ in. Autograph except for appended notes by John Paston I.

Dorse: No seal or address. Note in unidentified hand: *Episcopus Cantuariensis.*

The date is uncertain. A list of this kind, in William's hand (not Richard Calle's as Gairdner said) and annotated by John, is most likely to date from soon after Fastolf's death when they were both concerned with assembling his property, as no. 86 shows. The style of the writing, which is nearest to nos. 86 and 89, is in keeping.

    G. 977/563.

An jmage off Owre Lady wyth ij awngellis sensyng gilthe viij^{xx} vnc.[1] vz xiij li. *and* iiij vnc.[2]

Item, a crosse wyth a fott ⌈lx vnc.⌉ gilthe in to cassys gilt viij^{xx} *and* xvij vnc. vz xiiij li. *and* ix vnc.

Item, an jmage off Sent Jon Vangelist gilthe weyng vij^{xx} x vnc. vz xij li. vj vnc.

Item, an jmage of Sent Jon Baptist gilthe wyth þe lamb lviij vnc. vz iiij li. x vnc.[3]

Item, an jmage off Sent Jamis wyth his staff gilthe weyng xxxvj[4] vnc. vz iij li.

Item, an jmage off Owre Lady gilthe wyth a crowne *and* a lely weyng[5] iij^{xx} vj vnc.[3] vz v li. vj vnc.

Item, an jmage off Sent Denys gilthe weyng l vnc. vz iiij li. ij vnc.

Item, an jmage off Owre Sauyowre gilt wyth his crosse, his diademe, *and* his fane v^{xx}[6] xj vnc. vz ix li. iij vnc.

Summa vnc. xl^{xx} viij vnc. Summa lxvij lib. iiij vnc.
    Sum in markis cj mark ij vnc. di.
    Memorandum j lib. continet xij vnc.
        j marc. continet viij vnc.[7]

---

87. [1] *-c flourished throughout.*
  [2] *The final weight in each paragraph underlined.*   [3] *MS.* vnnc.
  [4] vnnc. *canc.*   [5] iij^{xx}vnc. *and canc.*   [6] vnc. *canc.*
  [7] *Last four lines in John Paston I's hand, the indented lines small and hasty.*

88. To John Paston I   1460, 28 January

Add. 43491, f. 4. 12 × 17½ in. Hand of Thomas Playter (see p. lxxxiii), signed by him as well as by Paston. Brief postscript in Paston's hand.

Dorse: Continuation of text. Traces of red wax. Address in Playter's hand:

To his right worshipfull brother John Paston ⟨be pi⟩s¹ lettre delyuered.

The date appears from the report of the capture of Lord Rivers at Sandwich, which occurred on 15 January 1460 (Scofield, i. 51).

F. i, p. 186. G. 346/400 (part).

After dewe recomendac*i*on had, please you to wete that we cam to London vppon the Tewysday by non nexst aft*er* oure depa*r*tour fro Norwich, *and* sent oure men to jnquyre aft*er* my lord Cha*u*nceler *and* Maist*er* John Stokys *and* Malmesbury. And as for my lord Cha*u*nceler, he was dep*arted*
5 fro London ⌈and⌉² was redyn to þe³ Kyng ij dayes or we were come to London; and as we vnderstand he hasted hym to þe Kyng by-cause of my Lord Ryu*er*s takyng at Sandwyche, &c. And as for Maist*er* John Stokys, he was at Mortelak, wheder we yede *and* spak wyth hym, and fond by hym by the begynnyng that he had ben labored a-yens you, but by whom
10 we coude not knowyn ⌈for he wold not telle⌉; but he sayd he was spoken to by on whiche he coude not remembr*e* þat he schuld take good heed vppon the p*r*obat of my maist*er*s wyll⁴ how his lond*ys* schuld ⌈be gyded⌉⁵ by-cause there was a thyng ensealed as his wyll which was forged aft*er* my maist*er*s decesse, &c. But or we had thus moche of his confessyon we⁶
15 were resonably well jn credens wyth hym; but it was long or we coude fynd hym feythfully dysposed in oure conceyt*ys*. And whan we had hym resonably aft*er* oure entent, we enfou*r*myd hym of ⌈Yeluerton⌉⁷ nedeles wastyng of my m*aister* godys *and* the mystrust that he had jn hem hom my maist*er* most erthely trustyd, and how his desyr*e* was⁸ synglerly to
20 have had the kepyng of Castre *and* all stuffe w*yth*-jnne it, *and* there to have lodged hym-self; *and* also hou he dede meve my Lady Hevenyngh*am*, &c. Wherfor he avyseth you, for ony wrytyng ⌈or citacion⌉ that cometh fro my lord of Caunt*er*bury or fro hym, that ye y*our*-self kepe the good*ys* stylle *and* lete hym a-lone for the p*ur*vyans of all suche wrytyng*ys* ⌈or
25 cytacions⌉. We assked⁹ hym ⌈that⌉, if Yelu*er*ton wold not be refou*r*med, wheder for the dyscha*r*ge of all y*our* concyens a mene mygth be found to a-voyde hym owte of the testament. And he sayd if he be fals to the dede it is a cause resonable, and per-jur*é* is a-noþ*er* cause; and if ye woll Maist*er* Stok*ys* com to Norwiche for the p*r*obat, &c., he woll com hym-self or make

---

88. ¹ *Some letters cut away at slit for tape.*   ² *Interl. above* ij da *canc.*
    ³ þ *in form of* y *throughout.*   ⁴ *Ampersand canc.*
    ⁵ *Interl. above* goo *canc.*   ⁶ had *canc.*
    ⁷ *Interl. above* the gre *canc.*   ⁸ to *canc.*   ⁹ *MS.* asshed.

a comyssyon to oþer persones as ye woll assigne, or ell[10] as many as woll 30
take charge wyth you to make a proxi, be it to me or to sum oþer, *and* send
it hym ⌈*and* ye wyll ther-wyth⌉, *and* it schall be proved by that mene. And
all the fauour þat may be don for you schall be don.

And to your bargeyn he woll owe[11] *and* do all the fauour that he may
wyth trouthe, and it schall not nede no wytnesse to youre bargeyn wyth- 35
oute ther be a contradiccion; and if ther be a *contradiccion* iij or iiij wytnesse
is j-now. And he hath no conceyte in Yeluerton as now, and also but lytyll
jn Fenyngley for the seruyce that he oweth to my lord Tresorer, ⌈*and*
oþer causes⌉ whiche we expresse not for cause of long wrytyng. And he
avysed vs to go speke wyth my lord Chaunceler *and* Lord Beauchamp to 40
wete wheder they woll take ony charge or not, *and* to lete hym have
knoweletch of ther dysposycion. And he geveth you leve wyth ⌈a⌉-noþer
executour, or wyth youre owyn clerk, to mynystre *and* geve almesse at his
perill. And if he schuld com ⌈heder he⌉ had lever to com thes Fastegong
tyde or after Esterne than jn Lenton, but jn Lenton he schall com if ye 45
thynk it expedyent. And ther-for send vs word as ye woll we desyre hym
jn that poynt if it lyke you.

Item, ser,[12] Willeam Worceter was com to London ij dayes or we were
com, but[13] we can not aspye openly that he maketh ony labour, nor prevely
nouther, be no maner of harkenyng nor be no maner of talkyng; for I, 50
Playter, have comonyd wyth hym *and* he seyth rygth not, savyng that he
woll be rewarded for his long trewe seruice of my maisters good *and* lyke
as my maister promyssed hym by his lyffe. And euer more whan I sey vn-to
hym that it may not be gaynseyd but as touchyng to al my maister lond
jn Norffolk *and* Suffolk it is ⌈his⌉ wyll *and* suffycyant prove ther-vppon 55
that ye schuld have it, &c., and than he answereth *and* prayeth me no
more to speke of that mater for he vnderstand no⟨. . .⟩[14] covenaunt, &c.;
and more can I not[15] gete of hym. But for God I fele by hym jn my conceyte
that he may help to save *and* gete a m¹ marc or to m¹ marc which wyth-oute
his help may not be saved, as he seyth. And to fele hym wheder he lyed 60
or seyd soth, I asked hym wheder he wold take that which mygth not be
saved wyth-owte his help for his reward, and he sayd ya, wyth good wyll;
and therfor wey ye all, &c.

Item, Ser Phelyp Wentworth acte is passed the Kyng, whiche I doute
not mygth not a be with-oute my lord Chaunceler good wyll[16] *and* assent; 65
and Willeam Worceter sueth to have a copy therof, whiche he mygth have
had of me if he had lyst, &c.

Item, ser, I Playter speke wyth Maister Yeluerton, and he taketh it

---

[10] ll *barred, as regularly when no abbreviation can be intended.*
[11] fauo *canc.*   [12] will *canc.*   [13] wha *canc.*
[14] *Some letters lost at tear at edge.*
[15] geve **canc.**   [16] &c. *canc.*

gretely to dysplesour that it was noysed[17] that he *and* William Wayte
70 schuld have labored to an endyted Maister Th. Howys; for he seyth for
ony anger he wold not do so, and if ⌐he⌐ mygth wete that W. Wayte
labored it he schuld neuer do hym seruice. And as touchyng to the pro-
vokyng that my Lady Hevenyngham schuld sewe forth for Castre, he seyth
he neuer thougth it, but the sendyng to my seyd lady was by a[18] man of
75 his, *and* [a]-noþer of Fenyngley, to wete if sche hard ony tydyngys fro
Coventré, *and* no oþer maner of langage. How be it I vnderstand he woll
not be straunge to falle jn wyth you a-geyn, *and* also that he woll not
hurte you jn your bargeyn if ye coude be frendely dysposed to hym ward
as ye have ben; for wyth-oute a frendelyhood of your parte hym semeth
80 he schuld not gretely help you jn your bargeyn, so I fele hym. He leueth
sum-qwhat a-loffe, *and* not vtterly malycyous a-yens you. The cyrcum-
stans of oure talkyng were to long to wryte, *and* ther-for I expresse the
substauns as I conceyve, &c.

As for my lord Fortescu, we comond wyth hym seuerally, and for to
85 wryte all thyng of oure comonyng it were to long; but jn conclusyon
we vnderstand his good lordschip to you wardys, and all his fauour wyth
trouth, for that is his seyng. I desyred William Jeney to calle vppon the
maters jn lawe for the ward, &c., and he avyseth me to leve this terme *and*
to take avysement a-yens the nexst terme, &c.; and also I thynk it so best
90 whyll my lord Chaunceler hath take it jn rewle, &c., to whom we purpose
to ryde *and* comon wyth jn all maters, &c.

As for tydyngys, my Lord Ryuers was brougth to Caleys *and* by-for the
lordys wyth viij^xx torches, *and* there my lord of Salesbury reheted hym,
callyng hym knaves son that he schuld be so rude to calle hym *and* these
95 oþer lordys traytours, for they schull be found the Kyngys treue liege men
whan he schuld be found a traytour, &c. And my lord of Warrewyk
reheted ⌐hym *and*⌐[19] seyd that his fader was but a[18] squyer *and* broute vp
wyth Kyng Herry[20] the v^te, *and* sethen ⌐hym-self⌐ made by maryage *and*
also made lord, *and* that it was not his parte to have swyche langage of
100 lordys beyng of the Kyngys blood. And my lord of Marche reheted hym
jn lyke wyse, and Ser Antony was reheted for his langage of all iij lordys jn
lyke wyse.

Item, the Kyng cometh to London ward, *and* as it is seyd rereth the
pepyll as he com; but þis is certayn, ther be comyssyons made jn-to dyuers
105 schyres that euery man be redy jn his best aray to com whan the Kyng
send for hem. Plus jn tergo.[21]

Item, my Lord Roos is com fro Gynes. No more, but we pray to Jesu[22]

[17] by *canc.*
[19] *In margin.*
[21] *Recto ends.*
[18] *No space.*
[20] *Abbr.* Hrry *with stroke above.*
[22] *Abbr.* Jhu *with stroke above.*

have you jn his most m*er*cyfull kepyng, amen. Wretyn[23] at London the Monday[24] next aft*er* Seynt Powle Day.

ȝwr*e* brod*er* WILLYAM PASTON[25]
THOM*A*S PLAYTER[26]

It*em*, send us hed*er* a lett*er* be-tymys, þ*at* it may be he[re] be that tyme we come a-ȝen, for to-morwe ⌜we⌝ ryde toward my*n* lord Chancelere. Lethe us haue a lett*er* be that we come a-ȝen, *and* that will [be] v days fore[27] he is at Leyset*er*. Ȝelu*er*ton wold be glad to fall in to ȝow be soposyng, for Mast*er* Markam hathe sayd playnneley j-now to hym.

89. To JOHN PASTON I — 1460, 2 May

Add. 27444, f. 74. $11\frac{7}{8}\times 9\frac{1}{2}$ in. Autograph.

Dorse: Traces of red wax. Address autograph:

⟨*T*⟩*o*[1] *hys rythe wurchyp*⟨*ffull*⟩ *brod*er *Jon Paston*, ⟨*dwell*⟩*yng at Cast*er.

The date is evidently soon after the death of Sir John Fastolf in 1459, and, from the reference to the Queen, before the deposition of Henry VI in March 1461. Further, Elizabeth Paston's husband Robert Poynings is still alive (l. 21); he was killed at the second battle of St. Albans in February 1461 (see no. 115). 1460 is the only possible year.

G. 350/406.

Brod*er*, I comand me to ȝow, certhefieng ȝow that Playt*er* is r*e*dy*n* to Lundon ward þis day a-bowthe ij aft*er* non, and he taryed her*e* and schulde abedyn styll till he had had an horse þ*at* Mast*er* Thomas Howys schuld haue lent hym; *and* so I thowthe he schuld haue taried to long, *and* so he hathe bowthe on of my*n* hors. And iff it nede he schall send ȝow word be his man ⌜fro Lundon⌝ how he felythe þe disposycyu*n* off men ther*e*, &c., and he schall send his man hom be Newmarket wey. And I haue nfur myd hym acord*in*g aft*er* þe ententhe of ȝowr*e* lett*er*.

I spak þis day w*y*t*h* Bokkyng.[2] He[3] had but few wurd*y*s, but I felt be hym he was rythe ⌜euyll⌝[4] disposyd to þe p*ar*son *and* ȝow; but couerthe langgage he had. I wene he be assentid to þe fyndyng of þis offyce ⌜takyn at Bokynh*am*⌝, *and* Recheman schall bryng ȝow þe namys of þe[5] men that mad þe verdythe on Soneday nexst comyng. I pray send to my*n* brod*er* Clement[6] fermor*e* of Som*er*ton for*e* mony for*e* my*n* brod*er* Clem*en*t ⌜for

[23] the *canc.* [24] aft*er* *canc.* [25] *This line in Paston's hand.*
[26] *This in Playter's hand. Postscript in Paston's hand.*
[27] *Flourished* r *over* w.

89. [1] *Letters destroyed by slits for tape; restored after no. 85.*
[2] of me *canc.* [3] har, *with* -r *partly changed to* d, *canc.*
[4] *Interl. above* wyll *canc.* [5] *A short word, perhaps* man, *heavily canc.*
[6] *No abbr. for* -ys *as might be expected.*

15 to haue sent to hym to Lundon⌐. I schuld haue done it qwan I was at
Caster—myn moder desyryd me, *and* I sent a lett*er* aft*er* to þe p*ar*son *and*
pr*ay*ed hym to *re*ceyue it, &c.

Item, I pr*ay*d þe p*ar*son to wrythe a lett*er* in his name to myn sust*er*
Ponyngg*ys*, as ȝe and I comunyd onys to-ged*er*, cownsellyng her*e* to take
20 good auyse ⌐be-fore⌐[7] sche sold her*e* wood at Wrenham, and he schuld
knowe there-by wed*er* Ponyngg*ys* wer*e* in Kent are nat, &c. I vnd*er*stond
that this Bokkyng *and* Worcet*er* haue grett trust in there awne ⌐lewd⌐
consaythe, wathe some eu*er* it menythe, &c. Bokkyng told me þis day[8] that
he stood as well in consaythe w*yth* myn mast*er* Fastolff[9] iiij days be-fore
25 he dyed as any man in Englond. I sayd I soposyd nay, ner*e* iij ȝer*e* before he
dyed. I told hym that I had hard dyu*er*es talkyng*ys* of hym as men sayd,
qweche I soposyd schuld nat easly be browthe a-bowthe; *and* he swore that
⌐he⌐ talkyd neu*er* w*yth* no man in no mat*er* þat schuld be a-ȝen ȝow, &c.
It is he þat makythe William Wurcet*er* so froward as he is. I wold ȝe had
30 a witnesse of Roberd Ingglows, thow he wittnessyd no mor*e* but þat myn
mast*er* had his witthe, be-cawse he was so lathe w*yth* myn mast*er* Fastolff.
Worcet*er* sayd at Cast*er* it schuld be nessessary for ȝow to haue goode[10]
witnesse,[11] as he saythe it schuld go streythe w*yth* ⌐ȝow wythe⌐-owt
ȝowre wittnesse wer*e* rythe sofycyent. Myn cosyn Berney can tell ȝow,
35 &c.

Item,[12] remembre[13] to make þe p*ar*son to make an jnstrument up-on
his sayyng; I funde hym rythe good qwan I spak w*yth* hym at Caster. *And*
remembre[13] þe newe euydens.

Item, Arblast*er* *and* I spakk to-ged*er*. I felle hym rythe feythefully
40 disposyd to ȝow ward, and he schall mow do myche ⌐good⌐ and he go to
Lundon, for*e* he can labor*e* will a-monge lord*ys*. He and I comunyd[14] to-
ged*er* of myn Lord Awbré. Lethe hym tell ȝow qwat it was, for he will
speke w*yth* ȝow to-morow. It is full nessessary to make ȝow strong be
lord-chep[15] *and* be od*er* menys. Myn[16] Lord Awbry hathe weddit þe Duke
45 of Bokyngham dowt*er*, *and* he was lathe w*yth* Mast*er* Fastolff[17] be-for*e* he
dyed, ⌐*and* he is gret w*yth* þe Qwene⌐.

Gode[18] haue ȝow in his kepeng. Wretyn at Norwyche þe secund day
of May.

Omnya p*ro* pecunya facta sunt.[19]

50   Be ȝowre brod*er* W. PASTON

---

[7] *Interl. above* here *canc.*   [8] yth *canc.*
[9] -ff *over* d.
[10] *Unusual curl on* d *seems to intend* -e.   [11] halss *canc.*
[12] that *canc.*   [13] *MS.* remenbre.
[14] a mo *canc.*   [15] *Divided at end of line.*
[16] M *of* Myn *over* he. *This word preceded by* I trow *canc.*
[17] also *canc.*   [18] *No space.*
[19] *This sentence evidently inserted later, to left of subscription.*

164

90. To John Paston I   1461, 4 April

Add. 43489, f. 4. $11\frac{1}{2} \times 4\frac{1}{2}$ in., and a separate slip, $5\frac{1}{2} \times 4\frac{1}{4}$ in. The letter in Playter's hand, signed by him as well as subscribed by Paston; the slip in a different, unidentified, hand.

Dorse: Paper seal over wax and tape. Address in Playter's hand:

> *To my maist*er *John Paston jn hast.*

The date is fixed by the report of the battle of Towton, which was fought on 29 March 1461 (Palm Sunday).
    F. i, p. 216. G. 385/450. C. 26 (part).

Please ⌐you˥ to knowe *and* wete of suche tydyng*ys* as my lady of York hath by a *lett*re of credens ⌐*vnd*er the signe manuel of⌐[1] oure sou*er*ayn lord Kyng Edward, whiche *lett*re cam vn-to oure sayd lady this same day, Est*er*ne Evyn, at xj clok, *and* was sene *and* red be me, Will*i*am Paston. Fyrst, oure sou*er*ayn lord hath wonne the feld, *and* vppon the Munday 5 next aft*er* Palme[2] Sunday he was ress*e*yued in-to York w*ith* gret solempnyté *and* processyonz. And the maire *and* comons of the said cité mad ther menys to haue g*ra*ce be Lord Montagu *and* Lord Barenars, whiche be-for the Kyng*ys* comyng in-to þe said cité desyred hym of grace for þe said cyté, whiche g*ra*unted hem g*ra*ce.   10

On the Kyng*ys* parte is slayn Lord FitzWater, and Lord Scrop sore hurt. John Stafford, Horne of Kent, ben ded, *and* Vmfrey Stafford, Will*i*am Hastyng*ys*, mad knyght*ys*, with oþ*er*; Blont is knygth, &c. Vn the *cont*ra*ry part is ded Lord Clyfford, Lord Nevyle, Lord Welles, Lord Wyllouby, Antony Lord Scales, Lord Harry *and* be supposyng þe Erle of 15 Northumb*er*land, Andrew Trollop w*ith* many oþ*er* gentyll *and* comons to þe nomb*re* of xx m*l*.

It*em*, Kyng Herry,[3] the Qwen, the Prince, Duk of Som*er*set,[4] Duke of Excet*er*, Lord Roos, ben fledde in-to Scottelond, *and* they ben chased *and* folwed, &c.[5] We send no er vn-to you be-cause we had non cert[eyn 20 tyd]yng*ys*[6] tyl now; for vn-to þ*i*s day London was as sory cité as mygth, *and* be-cause Spord*a*uns had no c*er*teyn tydyng*ys* we though ye schuld take them a worthe tyl more c*er*tayn.

It*em*, Thorp Waterfeld is yoldyn, as Spord*a*uns can telle you.

90. [1] *Interl. above* fro *canc., the* above *his* canc.
  [2] *No space.*
  [3] *Abbr.* Hrry *with stroke above.*
  [4] *Abbr. by curl on* -s.
  [5] be a *canc.*
  [6] *MS.* certyngdys; *cf. l.* 22.

25 And Jesu spede you. We pray you that this tydyngys my moder may
knowe.

Be 30wre broder W. PASTON⁷

TH. PLAYTER

Comes Northumbr'⁸

30 Comes Deuon'

Dominus de Beamundo

Dominus de Clifford

Dominus de Neuyll

Dominus de Dacre

35 Dominus Henricus de Bokyngham

Dominus de Welles⁹

Dominus de Scalis Antony Reuers

Dominus de Welluyby

Dominus de Malley Radulfus Bigot, miles

40 Millites

Sir Rauff Gray

Sir Richard Percy

Sir Harry Belyngham

Sir Andrew Trollop

45 With xxviij m¹ nomberd by harraldys

91. To JOHN PASTON I   1462, about 20 July

Add. 27444, f. 119. 5×8¼ in. Autograph.

Dorse: Remnants of red wax. Address autograph:

To myn wurchipfull broder Jon Paston.

The date appears from the report of Christopher Hanson's death. A letter to
John Paston I from Thomas Playter (Part II, no. 674) reports that Hanson died
on the Saturday before St. Margaret's Day 2 Edward IV, that is 17 July 1462.
    G. 457/526.

Ryththe wurchipfull broder, I recomand [me] to 30w. Lekit it 30w ⌈to
wethe⌉ Jon off Dam is come to towne and purposit hym to tary here a day
are ij, are lengar, I can thynk, and he be desyryd; were-⌈fore⌉ I¹ pray 30w,
⌈and⌉ as I haue a-fore þis tyme desiryd 30w þe same, that suche materis as
5 hathe be comunyd now lathe be-twyx myn moder, 30w, and hym may take

---

⁷ *This subscription in Paston's hand, Playter's signature autograph.*

⁸ *This list is on a separate slip of paper, said by Fenn to be 'pinned to the above letter',
and now mounted below it.*

⁹ *Abbr. Well with bar through -ll.*

91. ¹ *pa canc.*

some good² conclucyon be-twyx owre-selff here at hom. And jn myn consayt, sauyng ʒow[r] better avyse, it were so most conuenyent and wurchipfull for us all and comforthe to all owre fryndis. And for þis ententhe I wold tary here the lengare, for I wold be as glad as any man a-lyue that suche an ende mythe be take be-twix vs ⌈that⌉ jche off us all schuld jnyoy þe 10 wylleffare off odyr, qweche I³ trust wyth ʒowre good help schall be rythe wyll. And I dowthe nat myn mastyr Markam wyll be will plesyd thus.

I haue tydyngys from London, and a-monge odyr tydyngys I haue knowlage that Cirstofre Hanson is passid to God on Saterday last past at ij off clok after mydnythe. It is good to take hede there-to, &c. 15

Item, I sent ⌈to ʒow⌉ to haue had ʒowre auyse qwat menys were best to make for þe mater towchyng þe Lord Scrop, qwere-jn I had an answere; but me thowthe it⁴ was⁵ nat to þe poynthe. I sopose, *and* I purposyd to make the labore that ʒe sent me word I schuld do towchyng me, I can thynk I schuld sone be answerid,⁶ sonare than he. I must send some⁷ 20 answere to hym were-jn I wold haue ʒowre consayll, for he desirid þe same *and* I wold not he schold thynk that he were for-gotyn be us.

Be ʒowre pore broder WILLIAM PASTON

I can thynk and he were here he wold be a feythfull frynd to ʒow; but and so were that ʒe thowthe þat it were for to labore for any oder man, me 25 thynkit it were for ʒow to remembre myn nevew that were somewat lykly, and there-to wold I be glad to help *and* lene to þe toder. For as for me, I know so moche that sche will non haue but iff he haue, ar be leke to haue, meche more lond than I haue; and iff I knewe þe contrary it schuld nat be left for þe labore, but I wold ⌈nat⌉⁸ be in a folis paradyce. 30 And ʒe be myn good brodir I trust thow to do rythe will, &c.⁹

92. To JOHN PASTON II   1467

Add. 33597, f. 8. 5¾ × 17 in. Autograph except for postscript in Pampyng's hand.

Dorse: Postscript of four lines. Paper seal over red wax and string. Address in Pampyng's hand:

To my right worshipfull nevew Sir John Paston, knyght.

This is not set out as a letter, but as a series of memoranda, unsigned. Each paragraph is spaced off from the preceding, with a paragraph mark in the margin.

² clucyon *canc.*   ³ t *and part of* h *canc.*   ⁴ *MS.* is.
⁵ to *canc.*   ⁶ me *canc. by diagonal stroke through and* de *above line.*
⁷ and *canc.*   ⁸ *Very cramped,* a *uncertain.*
⁹ *Postscript crowded in beside and below the subscription, from which it is marked off by lines.*

The date is after the death of John Paston I in May 1466, and before the settlement of the Pastons' dispute with Sir William Yelverton and others about the disposal of Sir John Fastolf's property. Litigation continued for several years, until sole administration of Fastolf's estate was granted to William Wainfleet, Bishop of Winchester, on 13 February 1470 (Magdalen College, Oxford, Fastolf Paper 93; cf. John Paston II's letter no. 248 and later documents of his). But the first major event was the grant of probate of Fastolf's will to John Paston and Thomas Howes on 26 August 1467 (Magdalen College, Chartae Regiae et Concessae 50.8.ii: *H.M.C. Fourth Report* (1874), p. 458, and K. B. McFarlane, 'William Worcester: a Preliminary Survey', *Studies presented to Sir Hilary Jenkinson* (Oxford, 1957), p. 202), after which Wainfleet, Yelverton, and other trustees released Caister and other manors which had been Fastolf's to Sir John Paston (Bodl. MS. Charters Norfolk no. 746, dated 11 January 7 Edward IV, i.e. 1468). In the present document 'the will' (l. 35) must surely be Fastolf's, since the whole context concerns the dispute with Yelverton. (It might otherwise have been taken to be John Paston I's, but that was not proved until 1473—see John II's letter no. 279.) This reference therefore places the paper before probate was granted.

G. LXXI/664.

Myn¹ sust*er*, Arblast*er*, *and* I haue apoyntyd þat we schall kepe no*n* howsold þis terme but go to borde, were-fore we auyse ʒow to puruay for us a logynge ner*e* a-bowt my*n* lord Chanseler*e* þ*at* be honest, for Arblast*er* will no*n* od*er*.²

5 Item, as for ʒow, we auyse ʒow jn any wyse gete ʒowr chamer assynyd wyth-in my*n* lord*ys* place, *and* gete chamer a-lone iff ʒe may, þat Arblast*er* *and* I may haue a bed ther-in ʒiff³ it fortune us to be late ther*e* wyth ʒow.

Item, take hed to gete suyrtés for þe por*e* me*n* þat come up, *and* þat þey may be sent hom a-ʒen forthe-wyth wyth-owt taryyng; and take auyse 10 so þat þe proses may so go forthe þat⁴ þey may be qwett at þe nexst assysys. Take auyse off Townysend.

As for ʒelu*er*ton, fynd þe menys þat he speke nat wyth my*n* lord till we come.

Iff any labor*e* be mad to my*n* lord to asyne me*n* to her*e* þe mat*er* jndeffer-15 ently,⁵ make labor*e* to my*n* lord þat tho me*n* be nat namyd till we come, for ⌈we⌉ can jnffurme hym⁶ soche as be p*ar*ciall⁷ be ther*e* ded*ys* here-affor*e* qweche p*ar*aue*n*ture my*n* lord⁸ wold thynk wer*e* jndefferent j-now till he be jnfurmyd. It may be answerid be my*n* lord þat he will nat prosede no ferthar in þe mat*er* till Arblast*er* comyng *and* my*n*, for we can 20 best jnfurme þe mat*er*.

Item, send a lett*er* to Rychard Kall *and* to Se⌐r⌐ Jamys Gloys⁹ to come up to London in any wyse, for ther*e* is no man can do in dyuers mater*ys* þat they can do jn answeryng suche mat*er* as ʒelu*er*ton wyll ley a-ʒens¹⁰ ʒow;

92. ¹ M *from* Ar, *as if* Arblaster *had been started.*
² *Last five words crowded in later.*   ³ *From* yff.
⁴ ʒe *canc.*   ⁵ lete nat tho *canc.*   ⁶ sche *canc.*   ⁷ qwe *canc.*
⁸ wold *canc.*   ⁹ *and* to Call *canc.*   ¹⁰ -n- *lacks a minim.*

and also þey can best mak þe bill þat ȝe schuld put a-ȝens hem, *and* ther-
for remembre.[11]   25

It*em*, wrythe a lett*er* to my*n* sust*er* for þe c mark for my*n* Lady Soffolk,
for we haue no uerry dyrect answer off her wed*er* sche wyll send it ar nat.

It*em*, speke to ȝowr atorney in þe Kyngy*s* Benche þat[12] he take hed[13]
to all man*er* jndytament*ys*, both old *and* new, *and* to all od*er* mater*ys* þat
hangyng ther*e*.   30

It*em*, do Pampyng comy*n* w*yth* owr sperituall concell suche mat*er* as
nedyn ther*e*, *and* haue newe wretyn þe attestac*i*on þat lakkyn. þe same
man þat wrott þe od*er* may wrythe that. For ȝelu*er*ton mad gret auawnt
þat ȝe schuld be hyndrid in that.[14]

Wrythe a lett*er* to my*n* nevew Jon ȝong*er* to come up to pr*e*ue þe wyll. 35
Speke w*yth* S*er* Gilberd Debenham qwill he is in cownt[15] to leue up*er*
Cotton.

It*em*, ȝelu*er*ton, Howys, *and* Worcet*er* make meche þat we haue put
hem owt off possesscyon ⌐off the lond⌐, qweche þey ⌐say⌐ is *con*trary to
my*n* lord Chanseler comandement. *And* jn trowth S*er* Jamys *and* Call 40
meche spokyn to þe tenant*ys* in my*n* lordy*s* name, fore ȝelu*er*ton thynkyt
þat he may now breke þe treté; qwer-for take auyse here-in off M*aster*
Tresham *and* off Mast*er* Staueley, *and*[16] jnfurme my*n* lord how my*n*
brod*er* qwas all-way in possec*i*on till he was put owt for þe mat*er* off
bondage,[17] *and* how ȝe fynd þe colage,[17] *and* qwat an hurt it wer*e* to ȝow 45
in noyse of contré iff[18] any od*er* man schuld now receyue any pr*o*ffity*s*
off þe londy*s*. They will[19] labore þat jndeferent me*n* schuld receyue, *and*
þat wer nat good; my*n* lord may say[20] þat he will end þe mat*er*, but as for
þe possescyon he will nat put ȝow owt. Labor þis[21] in all hast possible.[22]

I pray yow send me an answer*e* of all such thyng*es* as requirith an 50
answer*e* in this contré, for Arblaster p*ur*posith to be w*yth* yow on Sonday
sevenyght, *and* I p*ur*pose to be w*yth* yow ij dayes afore.

---

[11] *This last sentence, from* & also, *crowded in later; MS.* remenbre.
[12] ȝel *canc.*
[13] *Curl on*-d, *as if for* -der, *evidently in error.*
[14] *Last sentence crowded in.*
[15] *Curl on* -t, *apparently without significance.*
[16] *Fold. by* j, *which should have been canc.*
[17] -e *repr. by curl on* -g.
[18] j *canc.*
[19] labr *canc.*
[20] say *canc.*
[21] h *and another letter canc.*
[22] *Recto ends, and Paston's hand; verso all by Pampyng.*

93. To MARGARET PASTON   Probably 1469, 7 April

Add. 34889, f. 215. 10¾×6⅛ in. Hand of William Ebesham (see p. lxxxi).

Dorse: Paper seal over wax and tape. Address in Ebesham's hand:

To my right worshupfull suster Margaret Paston.

The last sentence implies that Margaret was at Mautby when the letter was written. She does not seem to have lived there continuously until perhaps 1474, but she may well have spent short periods there earlier. The fact that the letter is in Ebesham's hand connects it with John II's letter to Margaret of October 1469 (no. 245), which implies that Ebesham was working for William in Norwich in that year; and this is in keeping with Margaret's letter of 3 April of the same year (no. 201), which from its mention of a man of Yarmouth as a messenger seems most likely to have been written at Mautby.

G. XC/869.

Right worshupfull sustir, I recomaunde me to you, prayng you to vndir-stonde the Priour of Bromeholme hath sent ayen to me for xx li., and my cosyn William Whyte desired me to wryte to you for the rewarde that was offird hym to his churche, and xx li. of my brothirs goodys to be lent
5 hym vpon sufficient suertee and by a yeeris ende ⌜payd⌝¹ ayen. He hath and may doo for you, and for my nevewe Sir John, in many thynges, and is his kynnesman; and it were a gode frendely dede and no jopardy nor hurt.

The Abbot of Wymoundham hath sent to me too tymes. Frendship may
10 not hang by the wynde, nor for faire eyne, but causis must be shewid. Men wene that I hadd your coffers and my brothirs and Maistir Fastolff in myne awarde, and that ye wote wele, &c. Sende your avise to my nevewe Sir John by the next messynger. Ye sent to me oonys for the same mater, but I may not leene my money to defende othir men is causis. Your
15 discrecion² thenkith that it were no reason. I haue tolde them your saying, and as it is ⌜s[o]⌝³ that ye may nat come to the coffers but all be togedir, therfor ye must sende to my nevewe and to Arblastir hou ye will haue this answerd; for the Abbot will be heere on Monday at the sene, and labour must bee desirid the next terme. Hit nedis nat to put you in remembraunce
20 of my mater touchyng my fadirs soule, my modir, and me.

And God kepe you. Wreton at Norwich the vij^th day of Aprill.

I haue tolde thes folkis, as ye haue⁴ seide to me all-weys, ⌜that your will is gode⌝ but that ye may not come theretoo withoute th'assent of all your felowes.⁵

25 Item, I pray you remembre the obligacion that Wix hath, and that I may haue my money of the parsone of Maudeby.

By your brothir WILLIAM PASTON

---

93. ¹ *Interl. by Paston.*   ² *Last few letters faded.*
   ³ *Roughly interl. in Paston's hand.*   ⁴ *sede canc.*
   ⁵ *Fold. by* I, *which should have been canc.*

94. Indenture pledging plate   1470, 15 August

Add. 27445, f. 44. 4 × 5⅝ in. (indented).

Text and postscript in different unidentified hands, signature autograph.
Dorse blank.

G. 651/756, no. 2 (abstract).

This bill endentid made the xv day of August the xth yer of King Edwarde
þe iiij^te betwixt William Paston,[1] esquyer, on þe ton *partie and* Thomas
Vyall of Norwich, payntur, witnessith þat þe saide Thomas Vyall hath
borowid of þe saide William Paston v li. of lawfull mony, vpon plege of j
par of corall bedys with xxj gaudys of siluer *and* gilte weyng vj vnc. with 5
þe lace *and* þe knopp, xx siluer sponys weyng xvj vnc., j standyng pes of
siluer with a couer weyng x vnc., a large maseer parcell gilt weyng, þe
tymber *and* all, xv vnc., j maser siluer *and* gilt weyng viij vnc., a maser
weyng vij vnc. dj. *and* j quarter *and* a mase[r] with þe fote broken, not
weyde. And the saide Thomas Vyall byndith hym-silff, his eyres *and* 10
executours to pay to þe saide William Paston the saide v li. of lawfull mony
at þe fest of þe Natiuité of Our Lorde next commyng affter þe date of this
present writyng.

In witnesse wher-of þe parties beforsaide enterchaungeably haue set to
ther seallys. Writen þe day *and* yer above saide.   15

WYLL[IA]M PASTON[2]

This jndenture had William Paston ⌈of⌉ William Bride, quinere, at such
tyme as he delyuerd hym Viallys plegys *and* ressayuyd of hym v li. þe last
day of September in þe presens of William Paston, Richard Lynsted,
Gerer⌈d⌉ Bowen, John Clargenet, Richard Lee, Thomas Martyn, Richard 20
Halle, George Venabuls.

95. Indenture pledging plate   1474, 24 October

Add. 27445, f. 77. 8¼ × 5¾ in. (indented). Playter's hand. Red wax seal at
foot, broken.

Dorse: Some scribbled notes of sums of money, cancelled.

Copy in Add. 27451, f. 1. 5¾ × 8¼ in. Hand unidentified, no seal. Endorsed *Copia*.
G. 740/851 (abstract).

This bille jndented made þe[1] xxiiij day of Octobre the xiiij yer of þe regne
of Kyng E. þe iiij^te witnesse that William Paston, squyer, hath delyuered

94. [1] *Dotted circumflex over -n each time the name occurs.*
      [2] *Signature autograph. The following in a different hand.*

95. [1] þ *in form of* y *throughout.*

and leyde vn-to plegge to ⌈Elizabeth⌉² Clere of Ormesby thise p*arcelles*³
folwyng, that is to wete: a standyng coppe gylt w*yth* a cover ther-to
5 plumyd weyng—⁴xxiiij vnc. & di.; a standyng cuppe couered ⌈gylt⌉ weyng
xxxvj vnc.; a-no*þer* standyng cuppe couered gylt of—xv vnc. iij q*uart*. &
di.; a gobelet couered gylt of xiiij vnc. j q*uart*. & di.; a-no*þer* gobelet couered
gylt of xij vnc. & j d. weyte; a-no*þer* gobelet gylt of vij vnc.; a standyng white
pece ⌈w*yth* a cou*er* w*yth*-ought a knoppe⌉ of—xxij vnc.; a salt w*yth* a pale
10 couered of xiiij vnc. & j q*uart*.; a round salt couered of xix vnc. j q*uart*. &
di.; a round salt oncouered of viij vnc.; a bason of xxxv vnc. & j qrt.;
an ewer to þe same of xv vnc. & di. q*uart*.; j ewer of xiiij vnc. & di. q*uart*.;
vj siluer spones w*yth* oke cornes *and* long stalk*es* of v vnc. & di. & di.
q*uart*.; vj syluer spones w*yth* square scharp knoppes of v vnc. iij q*uart*. j d.
15 weyte; a spone for grene gyng*er* of iij q*uart*. & ij d. weight; which s*umm*a
in all is xij^xx & x vnc. & iiij d. weyte. Vppon whiche pleg*ges* the sayd⁵
Elizabeth hath delyuered to þe said Will*iam* xl *li.*, to be payed a-yen w*yth*-
ought delay by þe fest of *Crist*emes⁶ next folwyng þe date her-of. And if it
be not payed by þe said fest of *Crist*emes, than þe said Will*iam* by þ*is*
20 *present* gr*aunteth* that þe said Elizabeth schall selle ⌈al⌉ þe said plate for
hir repayment, or kepe it to hir owen vse at hir plesure.

In witnes of whiche þe said Will*iam* to þ*is* jndenture hath sette to his
seale, remaynyng w*yth* þe said ⌈Elizabeth⌉². Yoven þe day *and* yer a-bove.

MS. Add. 27451 f. 1 contains the following copy of the counterpart of the above,
with minor variations, in a different hand:

This jndentur mad the xxiijj day of Octobr*e* the xiiij^th yer of the reigne of
25 Kyng E. þe iiij^th witnessith that Will*iam* Paston, squyer, hath deliuered
and laide to plege to Elizabeth Clere of Ormesby these parcell*ys* folowyng,
that is to wete:

a standyng cupp couered gilte weyng—xxiiij vnc. & dj.
a-nod*er* standyng cupp couered gilt of—xxxvj vnc.
30 a-nod*er* standyng cupp couered gilte of—xv vnc. iij q*uart*. & dj.
a goblet couered gilte of—xiiij vnc. j q*uart*. di.
a-nod*er* goblet couered gilte of—xij vnc. & j d.
a-nod*er* goblet gilte of—vij vnc.
a standyng white pes couered w*yth*out knopp—xxij vnc.
35 a salte w*yth* a pale⁷ couered of—xiiij vnc. j q*uart*.

---

² *Interl. above* Margret *canc.*
³ *Abbr.* -ll *with bar through, which here must mean* -es; *cf. the copy.*
⁴ *The dash represents a manuscript punctuation mark formed rather like a figure* 2. *The weights of the individual items are underlined (often including the preceding* of*), but the total in l.* 16 *is not.* ⁵ Margret *canc.*
⁶ *Abbr., here and below,* Xpemes *with curve above* -pem-. ⁷ *MS.* plale.

a rownde salte couered of—xix vnc. j quart. & dj.
a rownde salte vncouered of—viij vnc.
a basyn of—xxxv vnc. j quart.
an ewer to þe same of—xv vnc. & di. quart.
an ewer of—xiiij vnc. & dj. quart.   40
vj siluer sponys wyth oke cornys *and* long stalkys of—v vnc. & dj. di. quart.
vj siluer sponys wyth square sharpe knoppis of—v vnc. iij quart. & j d.
a spone for grengynger of—iij quart. & ij^d weight
which summa in all is—xij^{xx} x vnc. iiij^d weight.

Vpon which plegys the saide Elizabeth hath deliuered the said William 45
xl li., to be paide ayen wythout delay by the fest of Cristenmas next
folowyng the date herof. And if it be not paide by the saide fest of Cristenmas, than the saide William by these presentz grauntith þat the saide
Elizabeth shall sell all þe saide plate for hir repayment, or kepe it to hir
own vse at hir pleasur.   50
   In witnesse of which Robert Clere, by þe commandement of the saide
Elizabeth his moder, hath to this jndenture set to his seel, remaynyng
wyth the saide William. Yoven the day *and* yer above.

96. To JOHN PASTON II   Perhaps 1474–5

Add. 27445, f. 80. Two fragments, remaining from six irregular parts into
which the sheet must have been torn; original size about $7\frac{1}{2} \times 6\frac{1}{4}$ in.
Clerk's hand, appearing again in MS. Add. 27446, f. 44 (see Part II, no.
922), which is subscribed 'Be your frende George, seruaunte to Master
W. Paston', but cannot be closely dated.

Dorse: No seal, but marks of folding. Upper fragment contains remnants
of address, in hand of letter:

⟨To⟩ *my* rig⟨ht⟩ *worshipfull neview* ⟨J⟩ohn Paston, knyghte, be ⟨this lettr⟩e
                            deliuered in hast.

Upside down, in different hand: *To Ser J. P. kn.*

The date is uncertain. Since this letter implies delay on the part of John II in
repaying a loan made to him by William, it may perhaps be connected with other
references to such things in 1474 and 1475, e.g. in nos. 221, 285, 291.
   Since nearly two-thirds of the sheet is lost, there are many long gaps in the
text which cannot be even roughly estimated. In the transcript, therefore, three
dots indicate a lacuna of whatever length.
   G. 743/854.

⟨. . .⟩ worshipfull neview, I recommaund me to you. And, ser, I pray you
⟨. . .⟩ þat there was none obstacle ner lettinge þat ye found in me to ⟨ . . .⟩
saue me harmeles at whiche tyme it was thought aswel ⟨. . .⟩ Johns by

obligacioun was not jnow to saue me harm⟨. . .⟩n the meane seasoune for
5 as youre reasoun will give ⟨. . .⟩ght fell of yow but goode. And if the caas
so fill þat ⟨. . .⟩ys will take it on them ⌈than⌉ I to bere the losse wherup-
po⟨. . .⟩ound to me to saue me harmeles. And for asmuche ⟨. . .⟩m by
obligacioun of statute merchaunt for you the⟨. . .⟩ in myne oune kepinge
for my discharge *and* after a⟨. . .⟩estorid me ageyn at this Michelmas and
10 m⟨. . .⟩ till Candilmas and me thinke it is ⟨. . .⟩ con⟨. . .⟩ I shuld hange
⌈still⌉ ⟨. . .⟩ as I did at þe begynn⟨. . .⟩ obligaciouns paiable at⟨. . .⟩ will
kepe still the ⟨. . .⟩ or sufficient and þat ⟨. . .⟩ as wold pay at th⟨. . .⟩ *wyth*
me þan thus n⟨. . .⟩ jndenture wherby ⟨. . .⟩ for be cawse þat ye w ⟨. . .⟩
experyens.
15 Also I wold auyse you ⟨. . .⟩ my lord of Norffolk.

Also, nevew, þer is onne Fr⟨. . .⟩ but hym-silf *and* his wif and ⟨. . .⟩
wherfore I haue writin to ⟨. . .⟩ in this matier and I trust ⟨. . .⟩ And I pray
yow þat I may ha⟨. . .⟩

97. Part of draft deed   Perhaps 1474–5

Add. 27445, f. 81. $5\frac{7}{8} \times 16\frac{3}{8}$ in. Main hand unidentified, corrections by
Paston.

Dorse blank.

This draft mortgage may be connected with the business disputes between William
and John II in 1474 and 1475 (see no. 96). It must in any case be earlier than 1479,
when John II died.
   G. 744/855 (abstract).

squyere and there heierez for euer. And also more-ouer the seid John Paston,
knyght, and John Paston, squyere, by this presentes graunten that thei
schall, by theire wrygtyng suffycient or othere-wyse, make notyse and yeve
knowleche of thes seid ⌈graunte⌉, bargeyne, and sale to all the seid now
5 feffés and to all othere persones hauyng estate or interest in the seid
maneres, londes, *and* tenementes or in ony parcell of them, requiryng them
to stonde *and* be feffés therof to the vse of the seid Maister John Morton,
William Paston, Thomas ⌈Playter⌉[1] and Thomas ⌈Louell⌉[1] and to there
heierez[2] in forme aboueseid *wyth*-owte ony reles, estate,[3] feffement, or ony
10 graunte of rent charge or annuyté of them or of ony of them ⌈a-for thys
⌈mad ar⌉ had are here-after⌉[4] desyryng to be had or made to ⌈ar by⌉[1]
them or to ony othere[5] contrarie to this presentes. And also the seid John
Paston, knyght, and John Paston, squyere, by thes presentes graunten

---

97. [1] *Interl. by Paston, as are all later corrections except those in nn. 9 and 11.*
   [2] aboue *canc.*   [3] or *canc.*
   [4] *Caret written first after* desyryng, *and canc.*; mad ar *above first interlineation.*
   [5] of them *canc.*

that thei or one of them schall delyu*ere* to the seid Will*ia*m Paston a bill of
all the names of them that now ⌐at þis pr*esent* tyme haue⌐16 estate and be 15
enfeffed in the seid man*ere*s, lond*es*, *and* tenem*ent*es ⌐wy*th* þe aportynance*s*⌐,1 wy*tho*wte frawde or deseyte, be-for the fest of ⌐Mydsom*er* nexst
comyng⌐,7 ⌐specyfyyng in þe seid ⌐bill⌐ þat þey stand jnffeffid from hens
forth to such jntent as is specifyed in þis jndentur *and* yff it⌐18 happyn the
seid John Paston, knyght, and John Paston, squyer*e*, to fayle of payment 20
of the seid so*m*me of c ⌐*and*⌐ xiiij li. in forme afore seid to be payed or ony
p*ar*cell therof at the seid daye of payment, the seid John Paston, knyght,
and John Paston, squyer*e*, by this *pres*ent*es* gr*au*nten that then the seid
Maist*er* John Morton, Will*ia*m Paston, Thom*as* Playter*e*, and Thom*as*
Louell schall ⌐fro*m* thense forthe⌐1i haue and take th'issuez and pr*o*fytez 25
of the seid man*ere*s, lond*es*, *and* tenem*ent*es ⌐wy*th* þe aportena[n]ces⌐1i to
their*e* owne vsee, and that thei nor ony of theym schall not be vexed,
troboled, nor int*er*upted to take ⌐*and*⌐19 perceyue ony of the seid issues
and pr*o*fytes of the seid man*ere*s, lond*es*, *and* tenem*ent*es, rent*es* *and* ser-
ui[c]es ⌐wy*th* þe aportynance*s*⌐1i aft*er* any suche defaute of payment made 30
by the seid John Paston, knyght, and John Paston, squyer*e*, nor by ony of
them, nor by ony other*e* p*er*son or p*er*sons for them or ony of them in
ther*e* names;10 and that then the seid John Paston, knyght, and John
Paston, squyer*e*, schall delyu*ere* ⌐ore⌐1i cause to be delyu*ere*d to the seid
Will*ia*m Paston all man*er* of chartou*r*s, evidenc[e]z,12 monyment*es*, rolles 35
of accomptes and courte rolles conc*er*nyng onely the seid lond*es* and
tenem*ent*es, rent*es* *and* s*er*u[ic]es ⌐wy*th* þe aporten*a*nce*s*⌐,1 or ony p*ar*cell
therof which the same John Paston, knyght, and John Paston, squyer*e*,
haue or eyther*e* of them hath, or ony man to ther*e* usee ⌐hathe⌐, and of all
suche evidencez and wryghtyng*es* conc*er*nyng as well the seid man*ere*s, 40
lond*es*, *and* tenem*ent*es.

98. Memorandum on rent collection 1477, 22 August

Add. 27446, f. 3. 5¾ × 16⅝ in. Formal secretary hand, unidentified.

Dorse: No seal or address. Note in the same hand:

The names of the maners of Agnes Pastons and William Paston in Norffolk,
how thai shulde be taken hede to this haruest anno xvij°.

6 *Interl. above* hathe *canc.; last word at edge, slightly torn, so that* -e *is doubtful.*
7 *Interl. above* Ester next comyng *canc.*
8 *Interl. below* And if it *canc.; very cramped, so that the further interlineation* bill *is hard*
to read.
9 *Interl. above* of *canc.*
10 haue and take thissues and pr*o*fites of the seid man*ere*s lond*es* and tenem*ent*es *canc.*
11 *Interl. above* and *canc.*
12 -z *evidently not abbr. but miswritten for* -ez *as in l.* 40.

And a copy of the same send to Richard Lynstede the xxij day of August anno xvij° per Bacheler Water.

Ten of the items are marked in the margin by paragraph marks of 'superior *a*' form. These are represented here by ⁋.

G. 805/919.

⁋ Paston maner	— Se that the fermo*ur* jn his corn on my moders fe, seale dor*is and* distrayne, *and* put in a newe fermour.
Wodemyl	— Distrayne.
5 Latymers	— Gadir the rente.
Sewardbys	— Gadir the rente.
⁋ Trunche	— Distrayne on þe grounde aft*er* it is fellid while it lieth on my moders fe.
Spriggeis	— Gader the rente.
10 Knapton fe[1]	—
Crowmer	— Gadir the rente.
Owstronde	— Distrayne.
⁋ Rowton	— Distrayne *and* arest the fermo*ur*.
Riston	— Lete Lynsted*is* brother gader the rente.
15 ⁋ Oxned maner	— Se the fermo*ur* in his croppe *and* after seale doris and distrayne, *and* lete hym not renne in dette as other fermo*urs* did.[2]
⁋ Oxned mylle	— Se the fermour in hi⌈s⌉s croppe *and* after seall dor*is and* distrayne *and* lete hym not renne in dette as other fermo*urs* did.
20	
Cast*er* Cleres	— Aske the ferme.
Holkh*a*ms ten*emen*t	— Aske the ferme.
25 The m*e*rsh in Cast*er*	— Aske the ferme.
Caster Bardolf	— Aske the ferme a[nd] rent.
Caster Clere rent*is*	— Distrayne ten*auntis*
Holh[a]m rent[1]	—
Ormysby my*n* fe[1]	—
30 ⁋ Somerton	— Se that he jn his corn *and* seall dor*is* and distrayne till he fynde suerty.
Thirn	— Aske the ferme.
Sowth Walsham[1]	—
Haluyrȝat[1]	—
35 Todenh*a*m	— Aske the rente and areste Smyth.

98. [1] *Inserted in Paston's hand.*
[2] *This is followed in the next line by* Oxned mylle—Se th *canc.*

Cokfeld*is*	— Aske the rente.
¶Apawys	— Se he jn his corn *and* seall do*ris and* distrayne.
¶Marlyngfor[d] man*er*	— Sele doris and distrayne.
¶Marlyngford mylle	— Seale doris and distrayne. 40
Merlyngforde ten*auntis*	— Distrayne.
¶Melton	— Se the croppe jnned *and* seale doris and distrayne.
Bonwell	— Aske rente.
Carleton	— Aske rente. 45
Thuxstons	— Aske rente.

Lynghall nup*er* Dokkyng*is* — Aske rente fro Mich. xvj till xvij° *and* distr*a*yne.

Bulmans nup*er* Dokkyng*is* — Aske rente fro Mich. xvj° til xvij° *and* 50 exorte Martyn to kepe the ferme still, *and* if he woll not praye hym to gete a-noder.

Yeaxh*a*m nup*er* Dokkyng*is* — Aske rente fro Mich. xvj° till xvij° *and* gete a newe fermour, *and* increse the rente and make a newe terrar *and* rentall. 55

Styberd nup*er* Dokkyng*is* — Aske rent fro Mich. xv° till Mich. xvij° and distrayne, *and* allowe no dewty of Dokkyng*is* in abatyng my rente.

Thymbilthorp nup*er* Aske rente fro Mich. xv° till Mich. xvij° Dokkyng*is* — and distrayne, *and* allowe noo dewty of 60 Dokkyng*is* in abatyng my rente.

These maners that ar trahid take gode hede that ye be in gode suertye of them this haruest tyme.

99. Memorandum on the benefice of Oxnead   1478, 31 July

Add. 27446, f. 14. 5¾ × 16 in. Mainly in an unidentified clerk's hand, with corrections by Paston and a fifteen-line addition in another unidentified hand.

Dorse: No seal or address. Fragment of note in hand of end of text (some words lost at trimmed edge):

Parsonage of Oxnede made xxxj Julij A° xviij° E. iiij^{ti}.

The beginning is carefully written as if intended to be a fair copy, but turns into a corrected draft; both Paston's corrections and the additions are hasty. This paper was evidently at first meant to be in the name of Agnes Paston (see n. 5).

G. 819/934.

The comodytys off the parsonage and the
valew off the benyfyce off Oxned

⟨Euer⟩y[1] new parson off Oxned, whan he is jnst[it]ute and jnducte, at the first ⟨e⟩ntré in-to the chyrch and benefyce off Oxned must off
5 awncyent custom long contynued with-in the dyosesse off Norwych pay to the Byschopp off Norwych for the first frutes off the seyd benefyce xiiij marke; for wyche xiiij ⌐merke⌐, iff the new parson be wytty and haue fauour a-bowt the Byschops offycers, he schall haue days off paiment to pay the seid xiiij marke in xiiij yere, that is a marke a yere till it be payd,
10 so that ⌐he⌐ can fynd suffycyent[2] men to be bownd to þe Bischopp be obligacion to kepe his days off payment.

And the Chyrch is but litill and is resonable plesaunt and reparyd ⟨. . .⟩ dwellyng[3] place of the parsonage is a-yoynyng to the ⟨. . .⟩d well howsyd and reparyd, hall, chamberys, barn, doffhowse, and all howsys off offyce.
15 And it hath a doffhows worth a yere—xiiij[4] s. iiij d.

And it hath ij large gardens with frute, and is yonyng to the place and chyrch-yard, wher-off the frute is worth yerly— xxvj s. viij d.

And ther longith to the seid parsonage in frelond, arable, pasture, and medowe a-yonyng to the seid parsonage xxxij[ti] acre or more, wher-off euery
20 acre is worth ij s. to latyn—iij li. iiij d.

And ⌐William Paston, justice, qwan he⌐[5] cam fyrst to dwell in the maner ⌐of Oxned⌐ paid to the parson that was than for the corne growyng on the parsonage londys, and for the tythyngys ⌐ondely but in corn⌐[6] whan it was jnned in-to the barn—xxiiij li.
25 And the same yere the parson had all the awterage and oder profytys be-syde þe seyd xxiiij li.[7]

It is yerly worth, as the world goth now—x li.

And it is butt an esy cure to kepe, for þer ar natt past xx[ti] persons to be yerly howselyd.
30 The parsonage stant be a fresch ryuer syde.

And ther is a good markett town callyd Alysham with-in ij myle off the parsonage.

And the cyté off Norwych is with-in vj myle off the parsonage.

And the see is with-in x myle off the parsonage.
35 And if a parson cam now and warre presentyd, institute, and inducte, he shuld haue by the lawe all the cropp that is now growyng þat was eryd and sowyn off the old parsons cost, growyng on the parsonage landys now, as his own good, and all the tyth off all maner graynys ⌐off þe maner

---

99. [1] *Letters lost at tear here and in next line.*   [2] suyrte *canc.*
   [3] *Hole in paper;* dwelly *incomplete.*
   [4] *An additional -j apparently erased.*
   [5] *Interl. in William Paston II's hand above* my hosbond and I whan we *canc.*
   [6] *Interl. by Paston.*   [7] *All after* be syde *in Paston's hand.*

lond*ys and* tenant*ys* lond*ys*⌐16 towardys his chargys off the fyrst frutes; and
if it ware jnnyd it war, ⌐þis crop now growyng⌐,6 worth his first frutes.8   40
He þat hath þis benefice, and he were a pore man, myght haue lycens
to haue a seruice be-side.

The9 Beshop oght not to haue þe valew of þis cropp for þe arreragys
of þe fyrst fruttys þat Ser Thomas Euerard, last parson of Oxned, oght to
þe Bysshop whan he died; for þe said Ser Thomas Euera[r]d was bond to   45
þe Bisshop in an obligacion for þe said frutys, and þe said Ser Thomas
Euerard, for to defraude þe Bysshop and oder men þat he owid mony to
gaff a-way his gooddys to serten persons, qwech persons toke a-way þe
said goodys, and also durrys and wyndois of þe said parsonage, and it is
though[t] þat both þe Bysshop and þe patron myght take accions a-gayns 50
þe said persons.

100. To NICHOLAS GOLDEWELL: draft   1478, 9 October

Add. 27446, f. 16. 6×6½ in. Beginning in hand of six of Agnes Paston's
papers (see no. 19); extensive corrections, cramped and hasty and often
scarcely legible, and continuation of about eight manuscript lines, by
Paston; the final *of Octobre* in a different hand.

Dorse: No seal or address. Note in the hand that wrote *of Octobre*:

*The copy of a lettre to Master Nicholas Goldewell, broder to þe Busshopp of
Norwich, ixº Octobris Aº xviijº E. iiijti, by Ser William Vbgate, vicar of
Castre.*

This is a very rough draft, preserved for record.
   G. 822/937 (abstract).

Ryght wurchupfull sere, I recomaund me ⌐hartely on⌐1-to you. Plese it
you to be remembryd ⌐how⌐2 that I spacke ⌐on⌐1-to you on the Soneday3
for a4 lytill benyfe[s] of the cherch of Oxned, where-to my moder had5
presentyd a4 clerke ⌐of hyrse⌐,6 whech presentacyon was delyuerd to
Mayster John Bulman, ⌐mi lord deputé, wyth-in þe tyme lymytid be þe 5
law⌐.7 Sere, ⌐I vnderstond⌐1 this clerke is not admyttyd nor ⌐can nat
be amyttyd be no labor þat he can make⌐,8 where-in I vnderstond that my

---

8 *All after this in Paston's hand.*
9 byx bysh *canc.*

100. 1 *Interl. in Paston's hand.*
  2 *Interl. by Paston, replacing* of *interl. by the scribe and canc.*
  3 *MS.* Seneday.   4 *No space.*
  5 *From* hath.
  6 of hyr *interl. by scribe*, se *added by Paston.*
  7 *Interl. by Paston above* whech is on of the secretories of my lord of Norwych And *canc.*
  8 *Interl. by Paston above* not Mayster Bulman willnot admytte hym *canc.*

mod*er* is in wrongjd ⌈for⌉⁹ cause ⌈off nown amyttans⌉;¹⁰ where-fore,
⌈sere⌉, ⌈I desyre ʒow to be þe mene to my*n* lord⌉¹¹ that ⌈the seyd⌉¹² clerke
10 may¹³ haue¹⁴ ⌈in p*re*mys þat þat þe lawe requyrith⌉. For who be it that
the benyf*ys* is small *and* of lytill valew,¹⁵ yet ⌈my*n* mod*er*⌉¹⁶ wolde be
⌈full⌉ loth to lose ⌈here⌉¹⁷ ryght.¹⁸ ⌈ʒowr wysdam demyt þe same, *and* I
can nat *con*ceyue qwat⌉ þe delay off þe mat*er* schuld auantag*e* my*n* lord;
and, sere, such ⌈dyrecc*io*n⌉¹⁹ as shall ples ʒow to take in þis mat*er*, þat it
15 lyst ʒow to schew²⁰ yt wy*th* ʒow[r] good ⌈*and* favorabil⌉ auyse to S*er*
Will Vpgat, veker off Castre, bryng*er* of þis por byll.

And I p*ra*y Owr Lord ⌈send ʒow mech wyrchyp an⌉ ⌐as wellto far ʒe
as I wold my*n*-selff. Wretyn at Norwich þe ix day of Octobre.²¹

Be hy*m* þat is jowr to his power, WILL PASTON

20 To þe ryth wyrchipffill *and* honorabbill
sir, M*ayster* Nicolas Goldewell

101. To WILLIAM POPE: draft   1478, 17 October

Add. 27446, f. 17. 6×7⅜ in. Beginning in hand of no. 19, etc., corrections
and conclusion by Paston (cf. no. 100).

Dorse: No seal or address. Note in hand of endorsement to f. 16 (no. 100):

*The copy of a lettre to William Pope of Bacton þe xvij day of Octobre A⁰
xviij⁰ E. iiijᵗⁱ, by William Dam of Rughton.*

This is a draft similar to no. 100, but considerably less untidy.
   The dating is a useful example of 'St. Edward' meaning the Translation of
Edward the Confessor, 13 October.
       G. 823/938 (abstract).

Welbelouyd, I grete you welle, letyng you wete that I may nott be att the
court att Paston on Monday next comyng, nor no man for me, ⌈nor I
will haue no court kepte þere þat day⌉.¹ Where-fore I pray you that ye

⁹ *Interl. by Paston above* bj *canc.*
¹⁰ *Interl. by Paston, very carelessly, above* hyr clerke is not admyttyd *canc.*
¹¹ *Interl. by Paston above* I I besech you, *of which only* I besech *canc.*
¹² *Interl. by Paston above* my modre *canc.*
¹³ be *canc.*
¹⁴ the lawe wy*th* *canc. followed in the next line by* fauore, *which must also have been meant
to be cancelled.*
¹⁵ *MS.* valow.
¹⁶ *Interl. by Paston above* we *canc.*   ¹⁷ *Interl. by Paston above* oure *canc.*
¹⁸ thou it schuld cost vs rathe*re* more than the benyf*ys* shalbe worth this ij yere *canc.*
The following interlined sentence, and the rest of the letter, are in Paston's hand.
¹⁹ *Interl. above* fauore ordyr *canc.*   ²⁰ jowre *and another word canc.*
²¹ of Octobre *in third hand.*
101. ¹ *Last four words of interlineation crowded in by Paston.*

wille warne all the tenont*y*s to kepe her*e* day att Paston, ⌜for² þe court
schall be ther suyrly⌝³ on Friday next comyng, and warne eu*er*y man to 5
bryng thed*er* his rent *and* his⁴ ferme, for I will ⌜be⌝ there att the ⌜seyd⌝³
court my-selfe. And I pray you that ye wyll warne all the tenont*y*s of
Bakton ⌜to-morow opynly in þe chyrch⌝⁵ of þe ⌜seyd⌝³ court ⌜to be kept
on⌝⁶ Friday next comyng⁷ *and* warne⁸ all od*er* tenant*y*s off Swaffeld,
Monysley,⁹ Edyngthorp, Wytton. 10

Wr*e*tyn at Norwych þis Sat*er*day aft*er* Sent Edward þe¹⁰ day off Octobyr.

Be WILL PASTON

102. Memorandum on Marlingford manor   1479, 18 January

Add. 27446, f. 19. 5¾×5½ in. Beginning in unidentified clerk's hand;
corrections and continuation by Paston.

Dorse: No seal or address. Note, in the clerk's hand to end of date, the
rest by Paston, all cancelled by large cross:

*Erandy*s *to Merlyngford þe xviij day of Januar A° xviij°, wer-off a copy was
⟨d⟩elyuerid ⟨. . .⟩ Sent Edmu*n*dys þe same d⟨ay⟩.*

G. 825/940.

Do Gerald of Marlingford com to me,¹ *and* know wer*e* he ys be-come;
in qwa⟨t⟩² place he hydyt hym he dothe but distroyh hy*m*-selff.

Do ⌜on⌝ Steward ⟨of⟩² Colton,³ a ten*a*unte of Marlingford, com to me.

[Do⁴ Sir John Chapma*n*, p*a*rson of Our*e* Lad*y*s chyrche, send hid*er* the
bill of rekenyng of Richard Hervy shewyng what stokke was deliu*er*ed be 5
Richard Hervy to Harry Hervy.

And also a bill what costy*s* þat Richard H⟨ervy . . .⟩⁵ of at that tyme]

Do John Brigg com to me⁶ *and* bryng me suyrté for hys dett*e*, *and* know
qwat wey⁷ þe parson off⁸ Melton takyt w*y*th hym.

Do⁹ þe p*a*rs⟨on⟩¹⁰ off Melton come to me to Norwych, for tell ⟨h⟩ym 10
⟨þat⟩ *and* he come nat hastely he schall nat¹¹ fynd me her*e*.

---

² att *canc.*   ³ *Interl. by Paston.*   ⁴ *Over* there.   ⁵ agey *canc.*
⁶ to be kept *interl. by Paston above* ageyn *canc.;* to be kept on *written by him in margin of
next line.*
⁷ *The scribe ends here; the rest by Paston.*   ⁸ *and* warne *canc.*
⁹ *First four letters hastily written, doubtful.*   ¹⁰ *Date left blank.*
102. ¹ *The rest of this paragraph in Paston's hand.*
² *Letters lost at hole.*   ³ *Dislocated but legible.*
⁴ *The two paragraphs beginning here canc. by a large cross.*
⁵ *Extensive tear at edge; room for perhaps 15 letters.*
⁶ *All after this in Paston's hand.*   ⁷ w- *over* q.
⁸ marlyngffor *canc.*   ⁹ *MS.* de.
¹⁰ *Paper here and in next line decayed in patches.*
¹¹ *Only lower part of* a *and* t *visible.*

Item,[12] pray þe parson off Melton to call vp-on þe ⌈parteculer⌉ tenantys off Melton þat haue ⌈had⌉ parteculer fermys[13] fro Michelmas[14] xvij till Michelmas[15] xviij to pay þere fermys.

103. Memorandum to Richard Lee 1479, March

Add. Charter 17251. Three sheets of paper joined at the top by a strip of parchment stitched to them, partly mounted on gauze, and rolled. The mounting appears to be modern. F. 1 mounted upside down, badly mutilated; average width 5 in., extreme length $5\frac{1}{4}$ in., reducing to $3\frac{3}{4}$ in. F. 2, $5\frac{5}{8} \times 16$ in. F. 3, $5\frac{5}{8}$ in. $\times$ c. $11\frac{3}{4}$ in. extreme length, reducing to 10 in.

Text begins on f. 2^r. F. 2^v covered by mounting cloth. Text continues on f. 3^r, then, after some damage, on f. 1^r. All these are in the same unidentified, rather unskilled, hand. The obliquely torn, and partly decayed, foot of f. 3 corresponds in shape approximately to the obliquely torn top of f. 1. If these were fitted together the sheet would be almost the same length as f. 2. The link between them is established not only by the handwriting but also by the name Re(e)de among the legible vestiges at the foot of f. 3^r and its recurrence on f. 1^r. Clearly f. 1 is in fact the bottom of the sheet now numbered 3. It follows that Gairdner, in printing f. 3^v between f. 3^r and f. 1^r, disrupted the order.

F. 1^v contains a nine-line addition in a different hand, under which are a few more almost illegible lines in yet another hand. F. 3^v contains another addition of some eight lines, only partly legible, perhaps in the hand of f. 1^v. The manuscript seems to have deteriorated slightly during the last century, since Gairdner printed a few words which can no longer be made out.

A fragment in the collection of Captain Anthony Hamond, of Norwich, (paper, $5\frac{1}{4} \times c.$ $6\frac{1}{4}$ in.) contains a copy, neatly written in the hand of no. 104, of ll. 30–43, beginning where f. 3^r of Add. Charter 17251 begins. The wording is identical and even the spelling differs little from that of this text; some divergences are given in the footnotes, marked H. N. 27 shows that the fragment is the later.

The year 18 Edward IV ended on 3 March 1479. This paper was written after 24 February in that year, but before the end of March: MS. Add. 27446, f. 15, is endorsed 'A copy of a presentacion of the cherch of Oxened send be my moder vnder seall be M. Symond Rede of Norwich the [blank] day of March anno xix°'.

G. 828/943.

Memorandum, the day þat the lapse went out, which is such day vj monethes as the seid parson died, was on Tewesday, Our Lady Day the Natiuité, the viij^{te} day of Septembre last past, anno xviij°.

The day of vj monethes affter Our ⌈seide⌉ Lady Day the Natiuité was

5 on Seint Matheus[1] Day the Apostell last past, whiche was the xxiiij day of Februare; and so I deme eythere the Bisshoppe of Norwiche hath presented

---

[12] speke wyth canc.   [13] to come pay canc.

[14] Abbr. M, followed by a mark like superior a.

[15] Abbr. Michms, with a mark like superior a after M.

103. [1] 24 February is St. Matthias; but the word is written Mathe with the -us abbr.

or els it is in the gifft of my lord Cardinall nowe. Inquere this mat*er*, for the Bisshoppe of Norwich lyth in London, and shall doo till O*u*r Ladys Day ⌐this Lenton⌐, as it is said here.

My mod*er* deliu*er*ed Sir Will*ia*m Holle his p*re*sentac*i*on the xiij day of 10 August anno xviij°, which was nere a² monethe or the day of the vj monethes went out and past; wherfore the Bisshoppe ought to p*re*sent my mod*er*s clarke. Neu*er*thelesse the Bisshoppys office*re*s aunsware this³ sayng þat ⌐if⌐ ij sond⌐r⌐y p*er*sones deliu*er* ij sondrye p*re*sentac*i*ons ⌐for to diu*er*se clark*es*⌐ to the Bisshopp*es* office*re*s for one benefice, þat than the seid 15 p*ar*tyes shuld sue to the Bisshop⁴ at ther cost to haue out an jnquerré to inquere *de vero patrono*, sayng forther-more þat if they sue nat out this jnquerré ⌐with⁵ affect⌐ *and* þat the lapse fall, þan it is lefull for the Bisshop to p*re*sent.

And⁶ it is told me þat the lawe is this, that the Bisshop, ⌐be his office 20 w*ith*out any sute of the p*ar*ties⌐, shall call an jnquerré afore hym to inquere *de vero patrono, and* he shall assign them a day to bryng in a verdett. And he shall warne bothe p*ar*tyes to be ther-at, and he shall amytte his clarke þat is founde patron.⁷

3et the Bisshopp vseth nat to do this but ther*e* as bothe p*ar*tyes that 25 p*re*sent ar*e* myghty⁸ to sue þe Bisshoppe if he did them any wrong, and wher*e* as ther is a doubtable mat*er*; but in this case the prest⁹ þat⟨. . .⟩¹⁰ my mod*er* is but a simple felowe and he is appostata, fore he was ⌐somtyme⌐ a White Frere, and of simple repetac*i*on and of litill substans, as my mod*er* can tell; wherfor*e* bisshoppys vse nat in suche litill casys¹¹ to take so streyte 30 an jnquerré, and¹² specyally wher*e* as¹³ one hath contynued patron w*ith*out int*er*upc*i*on so long as my mod*er* hath don, for she hath contynued more than¹⁴ l wynter*e*. Wherfore I pray you¹⁵ shewe my cousyn Louell this¹⁶ bill and fynde som meanes¹⁷ to jntrete the¹⁸ Bisshopp by the meane¹⁹ of James Hobard,²⁰ which is grete with the Bisshop and is nowe Reder*e* of 35 Lyncoln Inne this Lent. And late my lady speke to James Hobard in the mat*er* if it please²¹ my mod*er*. There²² is a prest callid Sire   ²³ which is thought by the ten*au*ntes of Oxned a metely man to be p*ar*son ther*e*, the most thyng þat I dowte bi-cause Sire Will*ia*m Holle, whom my mod*er* presented, is ronne away.²⁴ If the Bisshop²⁵ will nat p*re*sent my mod*er*s 40

---

² *No space.* ³ sayng *canc.* ⁴ to h *canc.*
⁵ *Written* witht, -t *canc.* ⁶ my counsell *canc.* ⁷ 3 *canc.*
⁸ and where as he thynketh it ware a iop*ar*dy to hym w*ith* *canc.*
⁹ þat *canc.* ¹⁰ *Paper decayed. Gairdner read* troubleth.
¹¹ *F. 2ʳ ends. The Hamond fragment begins at the same point as f. 3ʳ.*
¹² wh *canc.* ¹³ aman *canc.* ¹⁴ *H* þan. ¹⁵ *H* 3ew.
¹⁶ *H* þis, *as below.* ¹⁷ *H* menes. ¹⁸ *H* þe, *as regularly.*
¹⁹ *H* menes. ²⁰ *H* Jamys Hobarde, *here only.*
²¹ *H* plese. ²² *H* þer, *as below.* ²³ *Left blank in both texts.*
²⁴ *Gairdner read* and; *not now visible, and not in H.*
²⁵ was *canc.*

clarke²⁶ in here title, þan I wold that the labour myght be made to the Bisshopp þat he myght present my moders clarke, ⌜suche on as she will name⌝,²⁷ in his one²⁸ title.

Richard Lee, like as ȝe may vnderstand be this writing, where as I²⁹
45 vnderstod þat the Bisshopp myght haue kept the benefice but vj monethes after the patrons vj monethes ware worn out, now I vnderstand the contrary; for I vnderstand he may kepe it a twelm⟨. . .⟩ and ⟨a⟩ day⟨. . .⟩ if ⟨. . . . . .⟩ by law ⟨. . .⟩ fall ⟨. . .⟩ Also, Richar⟨. . . . . .⟩gner here-of is ⟨. . .⟩ s⟨. . .⟩nd Reede ⟨. . .⟩ of the consistoré in Norwich ⟨. . .⟩³⁰ hath a broder
50 in the Towre is master of the mynt vnder Brice, called Bartilmew Rede, and a-nothere broder is a² goold-smyth dwellyng in the Chepe side called   ³¹ Reede; and he is eyther loged with on of these his breder or els at the Jor⟨ge in⟩ Lumbard Strete, ore els at þe Cok and þe Bell at B⟨e⟩linges³² Gate, a brue hous, for þe sei⟨d⟩ gold-smyth hath m⟨ari⟩ed
55 a bruewif and kepeth þe brue hou⟨s⟩.³³ And he can good skylle to helpe in this mat⟨er⟩ of³⁴ the benefice of Oxned.³⁵

Also, Richard Lee, who so euer sh⟨all. . .be⟩nefice³⁶ of Oxned ȝe muste tell hym he³⁷ must pay xiiij marc. to the frutes, and therfore shall he haue ⟨da⟩yes of payment to pay³⁸ a marc a² ȝer if he ⟨may. . .⟩³⁹ And also,
60 Richard, at the makyng of this letter I wend to haue ⌜ben⌝ sure of a prest, and now I am nat⟨. . .⟩ fore if⁴⁰ it please my moder me thynke it ware well don Ser William Storour had it, for I can non gete ȝe⟨t⟩⁴¹

þat⁴² setteth billis vpon Powlys dorre par aue*n*tur wold be glad to⟨. . .⟩⁴³
65 it and wold be glad also to⟨. . .⟩⁴⁴ my lady and my moder for it for a season. I can no more sey, but purvay a² mean to the Bisshop þat som mon may be put in by my moders title.

---

²⁶ *H* clerke, *as below.*   ²⁷ *H writes this interlineation*
on the line.
  ²⁸ *H* owyn   ²⁹ vnderstand *canc.*
  ³⁰ *Paper decayed at foot of f. 3ʳ and top of f.1ʳ.*
  ³¹ *Left blank.*
  ³² *Gairdner read* Billinges; *not now complete.*
  ³³ Cok *to* brue hous *crowded in between two lines already written.*
  ³⁴ *At line end; superfluous* ⟨o⟩f *follows.*
  ³⁵ *F. 1ʳ ends, torn and perhaps incomplete; f. 1ᵛ follows.*
  ³⁶ *Gairdner read* shalbe [presented to the] benefice.
  ³⁷ *MS.* he must tell hym ȝe.   ³⁸ *M canc.*
  ³⁹ *Gairdner read* d[o] gete hym frendschip; *only uncertain traces remain, but the space is insufficient for this. In any case* do *is syntactically unlikely at this date.*
  ⁴⁰ *An indecipherable word canc.*
  ⁴¹ *Originally followed by at least 7 lines, now so faded and mutilated that only scattered words remain; e.g.* Sir John ⟨. . .⟩ore þat is now parson at Seint Edmund; must purvay anoder.
  ⁴² *F. 3ᵛ. Originally preceded by two lines, of which Gairdner read the second:* Also if ȝe knew any yong preste in London; *only occasional letters remain.*
  ⁴³ *Gairdner read* have.   ⁴⁴ *Gairdner* serve.

104. Indenture depositing plate   1479, 7 July

Add. 27446 f. 21. 5¾×7 in. (indented). Hand unidentified, found in several other papers of William II's about this time: see nos. 103, 105, 109. Two seals of red wax on recto over paper tape.

Dorse blank.

G. 832/947 (abstract).

Thys bille jndentyd mad þe¹ vij day of Julij A° r.r. E.iiij^ti xix° be-twyx William Paston *and* Jeffrey Hunt on þe ton partie *and* John Davy *and* Alice hys wyf, late þe wyf of John Gyggys of Burnham, on þe oder partie, witneseth þat² þe seyd William Paston *and* Jeffrey Hunt, by þe handys of þe seyd Jeffrey Hunt, ⌐hath delyuered⌐ to þe seyd John Davy 5 *and* Alice hys wyf, be þe presept of þe seyd William Paston, a rounde salt couered parcell gylt as þe borderys, weying xix vnc. j quarter di.,³ *and* also vj syluer sponys, square sharp knoppys, weying v vnc. iij quarter on peny weight, whiche seyd salt *and* sponys þe seyd John Davy *and* Alice hys wyf bynd them-self, þer² heyrys, *and* executorys by thes presens to þe 10 seyd William Paston *and* Jeffrey Hunt savely to kepe þe seyd salt *and* sponys to þe vse of þe seyd William Paston, *and* ferthermore to delyuer them a-geyn to þe possessyon *and* handys of þe seyd William Paston or⁴ Jeffrey Hunt bi-fore þe fest of Sent Feyth þe Virgyn next commyng after þe date of þis² present bille jndentyd. 15

In wetnesse where-of þe parties a-forn seyd alternatly haue sette þer² seall þe day *and* ȝere a-bove wretyn.⁵

105. To THOMAS LYNSTED: draft   1479, 11 July

Add. 27446, f. 25. 5⅞×2 in. Letter in hand of no. 104, corrections by Paston; postscript apparently in main hand of no. 103.

Dorse: No seal. The postscript runs lengthwise, and at right angles to it are two notes in different unidentified hands:

A letter to Thomas Linst⟨ed⟩¹ the   ² day of Julij a° xix E. iiij^ti.
To Thomas Lynsted.

The postscript is accommodated to the position of these notes, so must have been written later.
G. 833/948 (abstract).

Thomas Lynsted, I gret ȝow wele, *and* it is do me to vnderstond þat ȝe haue fellyd wood *and* fyrrys, *and* also ⌐ser,³ wer-off I wold be answerid⌐,

---

104. ¹ þ *in form of* y, *as usually in this hand.*   ² þ *of correct form.*
   ³ *Weights marked off and underlined.*   ⁴ *Over ampersand.*   ⁵ *Two seals below.*
105. ¹ *At edge.*   ² *Blank.*   ³ *Cramped, reading doubtful.*

Jull*is*[4] hath do mad ⌜fall⌝ ʒatt*ys and* þei ⌜and þe wood þere⌝[5] be broke up
ageyn. þerfor I p*ray* ʒew fynd ʒe þe menys þat þe ʒong spryng may be
5 sauevyd *and* þe wood fensyd, ⌜*and* jnquere ho broke[6] þe jat*ys*⌝, *and* also
late me be answeryd both for þe hold ⌜payment⌝[7] *and* ⌜þe⌝ new ⌜off wood
sale⌝.[8]

And God kepe ʒew. Wretyn þe xj die Julij.

Be W**ILLIA***M* P**ASTON**[9]

10 If Jullis haue made a gate it is the bett*er* for the spring, and as for the key
it is accorded bitwix hy*m* and me þat it shall be lefft w*yth* the millar*e*, þat
insomoche as ye haue felled wood w*yth*-in ye may haue resorte to the key
and deliu*er* it to the millar*e* ageyn.

106. To H**ARRY** W**ARYNS**: draft   1479, 19 July

Add. 34889, f. 133. 5¾ × 12 in. Beginning in a practised clerk's hand,
unidentified, much corrected and completed by Paston.

Dorse: No seal or address. Note in different clerk's hand:

*A lett*er *to Herry Waryns the xx day of Jule A° xix° E. iiij*[ti] *by John Ancell;
off Paston* added in Paston's hand.

G. XCIII/949.

Harry Waryns, I grete you well, and I thanke you for youre labo*ur*. And
as for the ten*au*ntez of Knapton, I vnd*er*stand by youre writing that they
take non od*er* consideraci*on* ⌜to my*n* sendyng but⌝[1] that I call so fast on
my fee, ⌜for cawse þei thy*n*ke⌝[2] that I am aferd lest I shuld haue it no
5 longer*e*; and as for that ⌜I pray ʒow⌝[3] tell them for ther*e* vngentilnes I
woll haue ⌜my*n* fee ⌜off them⌝ *and* in þat man*er*⌝[4] and ⌜in⌝[5] non od*er* place,
and ⌜forthermor*e* I schall fy*n*de þe mene⌝ that they shall paye it more
hastely here-afft*er*. And as for the money ⌜þat þey offyre to pay⌝[6] at the
fest of Advinc*u*la S*an*cti Petri, ⌜receyue je yt off them⌝ and I shall assign
10 one to receyve it ⌜aʒen⌝ of yow.[7] ⌜I fele be ʒowr wrytyng þey will no*n*[8]
sonnar pay it thow þer catell schuld dye for fawth off mete; wer-fore⌝
as for the deliuer*é* of the catell ⌜affor⌝[9] the mony be paid, I putt þat in

---

[4] *Written* Jull, *with* -ll *barred, as often without significance; but in the postscript* Jullis *is
written out.*   [5] *All but* þere *in margin.*
[6] *Last three letters uncertain.*   [7] *Interl. above* wood fyrrys *canc.*
[8] *Interl. above and* þe fyrrys *canc.*   [9] *Recto ends. Postscript on verso.*

106. [1] *Interlineations by Paston throughout.*
[2] *Interl. above but canc.; MS.* þ[ie] *for* þei.   [3] tell he *also interl., but canc.*
[4] *Interl. above* it of them *canc.*   [5] *Interl. above* of *canc.*
[6] *Interl. above* receyue *canc.*
[7] And *canc. and replaced by the following interl. passage.*
[8] erthe *canc.*   [9] *Interl. above* till *canc.*

yo*ur* discresseon whed*er* ye will deliu*er* them or nay. As ʒe do I hold me
content.[10]

Also, as for ⌐Thom[a]s¬ Child, I vnd*er*stand ⌐be ʒowr wrytyng¬ he will **15**
nat seale the jndenture[11] ⌐be-cawse þer is no some ⌐of mony¬ sertayn ⌐ne
days of payme[n]t¬ sett in þe jndentur, *and* as for þat I will neyther sett
some ner days aft*er* his will¬, and if he will nat seale that he shall neu*er*
seale non[12] for me. *And* at last I am sur*e* he schall sell. I send ʒow a-ʒen
þe same jndentur þ*at* ʒe sent me, þ*at* ʒe may kepe it still as long as Thom[a]s **20**
Chyld abyde ⌐now¬ at Paston, in auentur*e* þe casse may hap þat he will
sell yt her-aft*er*; *and* yff he be on dep*ar*tid, than send me ⌐both¬ þe jndentur*e* to London be some masseng*er*.

As for Waryn Kyng, wer[13] I vnd*er*stond be ʒowr wrytyn þat he seyth he
delyu*er*[id] me all euydens, I vnd*er*stond nat þ*at*; *and* as for rentall I am **25**
suyr he deliu*er*[id] me non. *And* yff so be þat he can make þe rentall be
hart, I wold he ded make on, for it war nessessar*é* for me, for ⌐I vnd*er*stond
be jow þat¬ þer was no rent gaderid þis xv ar xvj ʒer for deffawth off a
rentall, *and* reson yt is I had on. Call on þe Prior off Bromholm for þe
xxx comb malt þat ʒe toke hym. **30**

Wretyn at Norton ye xix day off Jull.

By W. PASTON

107. To ROBERT WALSCHE: draft   1479, 22 November

Add. 27446, ff. 38, 31, 37. F. 38, $5\frac{3}{8} \times 4\frac{1}{8}$ in.; f. 31, $5\frac{1}{8} \times 3\frac{3}{4}$ in.; f. 37, $2\frac{1}{2} \times$
$\frac{3}{4}$ in. Ff. 38 and 31 autograph, f. 37 in an unidentified clerk's hand, appear-
ing also in no. 111.

Dorse: F. 38 blank; f. 31 autograph note: *A let*ter *to Robert Walsche of*
Colby þe   1 *day of Nouemb*re *Aº xix*; below which are a few odd words,
evidently pen-trials, in the same hand as f. 37. F. 37 is a small slip now
attached to f. 38, bearing only a neatly written note: *A let*ter *fro William*
*Paston to Robert Walsch and Rob*ert *Fouk of Knapton.* Dorse blank except
for a few meaningless letters.

Ff. 38 and 31 are scarcely more than scraps of paper. They are very similar in
physical appearance, and in the hasty and untidy style of the handwriting. The
subject-matter is also similar, being concerned with Paston's abandonment of
a distress at Walsche's desire, and with the expectation of the coming of certain
people. F. 38 begins with the conventional opening of a letter but has no formal
ending; on the other hand f. 31 ends with the usual form of date but opens abruptly
and is clearly a fragment. All this suggests that they are the first and second parts
of the same rough draft; and the way in which sense and syntax run on naturally

---

[10] *Last seven words added by Paston at end of line.*
[11] I pray you kepe it still *canc. and replaced by the following interl. passage.*
[12] of myn me *canc. Rest of letter in Paston's hand.*   [13] he s *canc.*
107. 1 *Blank.*

from the end of f. 38 (at l. 14) to the beginning of f. 31 makes it certain. Neverthe-less, the two pieces of paper were separate at the time when the draft was written—the width differs slightly, and the spacing of the writing changes on f. 31; and they remained separate, for f. 38 bears stains from folding which are not matched on f. 31.

G. 848/964 (abstract) and 842/958.

I recomand me to jow, marvaylyng gretly þat I am nat payd off myn fe acordyng to þe promysse þat ȝe *and* Fouke of Knapton mad on-to me[2] wan ȝe war wyth me at Norton. þis demeny[n]g off jow ⌐in brekyng ȝor promyss⌐ me thynk ys nat comendabyll. All thow þe tenantis lak vnder-
5 standyng off such jnconuenyens as may jnseu þere-by, I maruayll þe lasse for lak off conyng. As for jow, ⌐be þat knowlach þat I remembre off jow⌐ ȝe haue be so brokyn þat ȝe owth to vndersta[n]d mor þan they. I had a dystres *and* left yt for ȝowr sake.[3] Such a dede awth to be consederyd be any dyscret man. As for þe tenantis, I haue sent to hem for myn fe[4] *and* I
10 fele[5] rythe well, all thow þey say yt nat, þey[6] delay yt indely[7] for comyng off those persons[8] that schuld com to þis awdyth, thynkyng par auentur yff þey wold bid nat to pay me to do after ther comune demening, all thow þe sequell þer-off schuld insew to ther hurte. *And* yf y knew those persowns that schuld com to þis awdyt schuld be[9] her wyth-in[10] a day ar tweyn,[11]
15 yet wold I tary, all be þat I haue taryd þer comy[n]g þis halff ȝer, for I deme hem suche men as schall well vndyrstond myn titill good.[12] Yff any man haue ⌐good⌐ tytyll I am suyr þat myn is god. I dar well juparde to take a dystres, wedyr they come a[r] nat, *and* so I wyll ȝe know. Wer-for, in so much as I left myn distress for jowr dysyr, se þat I be answerid off
20 myn mony acordyng to myn ryth, ar else send me answer on ar oder, *and* lett me take þe auantage þat þe Kyng[13] lawys will ȝeff[14] me be dystress, qweche I haue delayd me thynk to long for any thank þat I haue.

Wretyn at Norwich þe xxij Nouembre.

108. To RICHARD ROOS   Probably 1479, 28 November

Belvoir Castle MSS. Letters I, f. 29. 11¼ × 6¾ in. Hand of letter unidentified, subscription autograph.

Dorse: Paper seal over red wax and paper tape. Address in hand of letter, faint and only partly legible:

T⟨o m⟩y Master Ros ⟨at⟩ Refham ⟨be þis lett⟩re deliuerd.

The date is shown by the reference to the Duke of Buckingham's business with the Duchess of Norfolk to be shortly before that of no. 109.
H.M.C. *Twelfth Report*, Appendix IV, i (1888), p. 11.

² at *canc.*   ³ yt *canc.*   ⁴ *MS.* me.   ⁵ be *canc.*
⁶ tary f *canc.*   ⁷ *First two letters uncertain.*   ⁸ so *canc.*   ⁹ be *repeated.*
¹⁰ few days *canc.*   ¹¹ *F. 38 ends.*   ¹² neuer þe lesse send me *canc.*
¹³ *Curl on -g, as used elsewhere without significance.*   ¹⁴ and sch *canc.*

108. *To Richard Roos, 28 November, probably 1479*

Master Ros, I recommand me to you as humbly as I can, thankyng you nat allonly for⟨. . .⟩¹ which ben grete deynté in this contré, and for your brawne and your crane, but also for the ⟨. . .⟩² labour that ye toke for me in commyng hider to Wodnorton to your grete disese. For I vndirstonde be Master ⟨. . .⟩³ þat was her with me agein yisterday þat ye cam home both colde and late and causid hym and his broder b⟨oth to ab⟩ide⁴ with you al⁵ nyght and made them ful goode chier, as he saith.

Sir, your seruauntes Symond Gonnour and Mils, whan they⁶ cam last from you, tolde me þat ye desired me to com by you to Norwiche⁵ wardes, and þat if I wolde so do ye wolde ride forth to Norwich. And morouer, ser, I remembe[r] þat ye tolde me the last tyme þat I was with you at Refham þat ye wolde dispose your-silf affore this Cristenmas to take a journey to se my lady of Norffolk; which if ye will parfourme nowe I wolde be verrey glade to awaite vpon you *and* to accompany with you thider. And ye coude not take your journey thider in a better season, for ther is commyn hider to me a seruaunte of my lord of Bukynghams, which hath abiden her this iij or iiij dais *and* wil not departe hens till he haue me forth with hym to my lady of Norffolk for a serten mater touching my said lord of Bukyngham, which mater I trust if ye com I shal handill it so þat ye shal do both my lorde *and* hir a plesure. And ser, if ye wil take this journey I wi⟨l awaite⟩⁷ vpon you and com homewardes ageyn with you be my Lady Beaumont *and* my cousyn Ser William ⟨. . .⟩⁸ jntende to take this journey I pray you to sende me aunswer by the brynger herof, for my lor⟨des seruaunte *and* I purp⟩ose⁴ to take our journey from hens on Monday in the mornyng *and* to ly at Norwiche that nyght, *and* vpo⟨n Te⟩wisday⁴ to ride forth to my lady of Norffolk. And, ser, I wil assay to com by you as I ride to Norwiche *and* I may b⟨. . .⟩⁹ doute of it, for my lordes seruaunte callith so sore vpon me to go forth *and* to lese no tyme.

Also, ser, if so b⟨e þat William Bar⟩ker¹⁰ of Bloofeld be with you I wolde fayn speke with hym, wherfor I besiech you þat ye wil sende h⟨. . .⟩¹¹ he shal not tary. Also, ser, I wolde pray you to convey me a lettre to Thomas Bettes of Ermyngham⟨. . .⟩¹² Lord preserue you *and* my mastres your wif.

Writen at Wodenorton the xxviij day of Nouembre.

Be 3owre owne ⌐seruaunt⌐ WILLIAM PASTON

---

108. ¹ *Large hole and tear in paper have caused loss of many words and parts of words through-*
out; here there is room for about 12 letters.

² *Room for 15 letters.*   ³ *Room for 9 letters.*
⁴ *H.M.C.'s conjecture.*   ⁵ *No space.*
⁶ *to canc.*   ⁷ *Room for 8 letters: cf. l. 14 above.*
⁸ *Room for 18 letters.*   ⁹ *Room for 8 letters.*
¹⁰ *H.M.C.'s conjecture; cf. no. 109, l. 18.*   ¹¹ *Room for 14 letters.*
¹² *Room for 11 letters.*

109. To RICHARD ROOS   Probably 1479, 19 December

Belvoir Castle MSS. Letters I, f. 30. $5\frac{7}{8} \times 12\frac{1}{4}$ in. Body of letter in hand of nos. 104, 105; closing phrase in another unidentified hand. Subscription autograph.

Dorse: Remnants of red wax. Address in hand of closing phrase:

To my Master Roos at Refeham be this deliuered.

The date appears partly from the reference to 'my lord of Ely', who must be John Morton, later Archbishop of Canterbury and cardinal. (He was one of William Paston II's executors.) Morton was provided to the bishopric of Ely by the Pope on 30 October 1478 (*Cal. Papal Reg.*, *Papal Letters*, xiii, pt. ii, p. 657) but finally appointed only in January 1479; he became archbishop in 1486 (*D.N.B.*). Further, the Heydon whose father had some 'matter hanging' with Roos must be Henry Heydon, son of John Heydon of Baconsthorpe who is often mentioned in earlier letters (e.g. Margaret's no. 167). It appears that the father had lately died. John Heydon died on 27 September 1479 (*Inq. p.m.*, 19 Edward IV, no. 72); so that this letter is probably of the same year.

    H.M.C. as no. 108.

Mayster Roos, I recomaund me to ȝew in myn most humbill maner. Syr, myn lady ⌈of⌉ Norffolk faryth welle *and* recomaund her to ȝew, *and* gladly wold se ȝew. We sped all myn Lord Bokyngham intent with hyr grace. Syr, þe delyueraunce was at Derham on[1] Thursday, *and* here was
5 Syr William Alyngton, Heydon, Fyncham, *and* many odyr, *and* I spake with Heydon for þe mater hangyng be-twyx ȝew *and* hys fader, *and* I fownd hym ryth conformable to do ȝew plesore *and* ryght reuerent[2] in hys utteraunce, with all dew[3] reueraunce acordyng. *And*, syr, he told me þat he was at Reffham, to seke after ȝew *and* ȝe ware[4] nat at hoom; *and* ⌈in⌉
10 conclusyon he told me þat þe mater was put in Townnysend *and* Fyncham. *And*, syr, he prayd me to wryte to ȝew, *and* to meve ȝew to send to them to a-poynt a day to here þe mater, þe soner þe leuer,[5] *and*[6] ȝe schal fynd hym resonable, as he seyth, *and* be glade to do ȝew plesore; *and* he hym-self spake to Fyncham to be redy qwanne ȝe sent for hym. Me thynk at Norwich
15 were good metyng, *and* yf þe ⌈comminicacion be had will⌉[7] I am here I[8] wolle help þat I can. As ȝe wolle do here-inne send me knowlache be þe brynger here-of.

    Syr, I pray ȝew send me knowlach yf William Barkare be com[9] do hym com to me to Norwich on Munday. And Owre Lord preserue both ȝew
20 *and* myn masteras *and* all ȝowres, as welle fare ȝe as I wold do myn-self.

---

    109. [1] thursy *canc.*   [2] formable *canc.*   [3] remem (*end of line*) *canc.*
    [4] -r- *written over* s.   [5] to *canc.*   [6] he *canc.*
    [7] *Interl. above* contynuaunce be how *canc.*, comminicacion *in clerk's hand*, be had will *in Paston's.*
    [8] *MS. ampersand.*   [9] *Ampersand canc.*

109. *To Richard Roos, 19 December, probably 1479*

S*yr*, my*n* lord of Ely, be þe menys of my*n* Lady Norff*olk and* my*n* lady Anne, *and* my*n* cosyn Southwell þat was masengar*e*, sent me a *suppena* to a-per*e* a-forn þe Kyng in þe peyn of a m¹ li. be-for*e* Crystmes; *and* I wold nat be in þe case þat I was in to dayes, tyl I knw þe mat*er*, nat for xx li. *And* my*n* lady of Norff*olk* wold nat dyscou*er* þe mat*er* tyll I had wretyn ₂₅ *and* sent my*n* seruau*n*tes¹⁰ to London; *and* qwan thei wher*e* gon, than my*n* Lady Norff*olk* told me þe mat*er and* tornyd to a jape þat was ernest w*ith* me a-for*e*, &c.

Written at Estdereham this day Set*ur*day the xix day of Decembr*e*.¹¹

3owr*e* ser*u*ant W. Paston

110. Memoranda on Knapton Probably 1479–80

Add. 27446, f. 34. 5¼×8¾ in. Autograph.

Dorse: No seal or address. At edge, in a clerk's hand like that of f. 37 (see no. 107), fragment of a note the beginning of which has been cut off:

*mat*er *tochyng Knapton for my fee.*

These memoranda are probably to be dated during the last reeveship mentioned, from Michaelmas 1479 to Michaelmas 1480.

G. 844/960.

M*aster*¹ Thom[a]s Pasche off Wynsowr toke þe astat *and* retorne to þe Den *and* colage of Wynsowr jnffra Castru*m*.

   And on   ² Holme, atornay off corte, is receyuor *and* was at stat takyn.

Rob*er*t Walsch, off Colby, j myle *and* di. fro Blyklyng, is steward.   5

Her folow reuys off Knapton:

Fro M*i*chelmas³ xvij till xviij°—Martyn⁴ Smyth⁵
F[ro] M*i*chelmas⁶ xviij till xix°—Roberd Fuuk, his plac*e* bonde
Fro M*i*chelmas xix till xx°—Thom[a]s Frank, his place fr*e*.

---

¹⁰ *MS.* seruu*antes.*
¹¹ *From* Written *in another hand, apparently added later than the subscription.*
110. ¹ *Preceded by paragraph mark, as next two sections.*
² *Room for some six letters left blank.*
³ *Abbr. by flourished* M *undistinguished from* Master.
⁴ M- *flourished.*   ⁵ -m- *lacks a minim.*
⁶ *Abbr. by flourished* M *and superior* c.

111. To JOHN KYNG   1480, 24 February

Add. 27446, f. 43. 6⅛ × 5½ ins. Hand of f. 37 (see no. 107).

Dorse: Remnants of red wax. Address in hand of letter:

To John Kynge, fermour of my maner of Harwelbury in Kelsall be Royston, be this delyuerid.

This must have been written soon after the death of John Paston II in November 1479 (see no. 383).
     G. 854/970.

John Kyng, I grete yow hartely well, and I vnderstond, as well by my frende Syr William Storar as by Richard Browne, that as well my kynnesman Syr John Paston that dede is as my kynnesman John Paston that now leveth have ben wyth yow and yovyn yow many grete thretis for that ye,
5 acordyng to the trowth, tolde vn-to them that ye ocupyed my maner of Harwelbury be my leese *and* be my ryght. And furthermore I vnderstond, not wythstondyng the seyde grete thretis, that ye, lyke a full trwe, harty frende, have delyd *and* fastely a-bedyn in my tytill *and* wolde not retorne to none of them. Wherfor I hartely thank yow, and furthar-more to corage
10 yow in yowr fast dealyng I schew on-to yow that I have ryght bothe in law *and* in concience, wher-by I promyse yow on my feythe to de-fende yow *and* save yow harmeles for the occupacion of the londe, or any thynge that ye schall doo in my titill a-gaynst hym, and it schulde cost me as moche as the maner is worth; and also a-nother tyme to doo asmoche for
15 yow and it ly in my powre, yf ye have ony mater to doo ther, as I may doo for yow. And also I here say by my seid frende Syr William Storar and by Richard Brown that ye ar of suche substaunce *and* of suche trust and suche favor in the contré ther that it lithe in yowr powre to do a goode turne for yowr frende.
20   Wretyn at London the xxiiij^ti day of Februari.

                                        Be WILLIAM PASTON

112. Memorandum to the DUCHESS OF NORFOLK   About 1480

Add. 27446, f. 59. 6 × 15¾ in. Secretary hand, unidentified.

Dorse blank.

The lady to whom this memorandum was addressed must be the Duchess of Norfolk, whose interest in the manors of Stanstead and Orwellbury is apparent from a letter written by John Paston III to Margaret Paston immediately after the death of John Paston II (no. 383). 'My nephew' of the present document is evidently John III, and the date is probably soon after that of no. 111.
     G. 882/1000 (abstract).

The man*er*e of Stanstid is in the countie of Suff*olk*.[1] The astate of this
man*er*e passid nat by the dede that the astate was taken by at Huntingfeld
⌐in Norff*olk*⌐,[2] for it was nat in that shire; but I clayme this man*er*e by my
modi*r*es gifft by anothi*r*e titill sufficient jnow in[3] the lawe.

This man*er*e is but a myle from Cloptons, and nat fer fram Smalbrigge 5
where y*our* grace is now.

This man*er*e is nere[4] vp-on the value of xx li.

Oon John Barell is fermo*ur* of this man*er*e.

This same John Barell cam *with* me whan I com to youre grace in-
continent afft*ur* my modirs decesse, at whiche tyme the seid John Barell 10
confessid afore[5] Piers Roidon, Rumbold, and ⌐William⌐[6] Smyth, youre
s*er*ua*u*ntez, that he was prevy of myn astate of that man*er*e in my modirs
daies ⌐*and* that he herd my mod*er* speke it in hir persown⌐ and that he
retorned to me[7] and at that same tyme he toke the ferm of me, wherupon
y*our* seid s*er*ua*u*ntez sealid me a[3] testimonia⟨l⟩[8] in the pres*en*ce of youre 15
grace.

⌐Madam, this is the man*er*⌐[9] ye sent y*our* s*er*ua*u*nte W. Smyth to, for to
kepe the possession ther*e*, and aff*ter* he had taried there a[3] while he toke a
pr*o*mise of the fermo*ur* that he shuld paie noo mony to no bodie without
comaundem⟨ent⟩[8] from y*our* grace,[10] contrary to whiche pr*o*mise, by the 20
favo*ur* of som folke*s* that y*our* grace can deme, he hath paide my nepueu[11]
a x li. er a[12] xx li.

Madame, I[13] suppose itt shall nat nede to haue noo man to kepe possession their*e*. I thinke, madame, itt is jnowgh if it pleased y*our* grace to sende
a[3] s*er*ua*u*nte of yo*ur*s thider and to shew vnto ⌐the fermo*ur* *and* tena*u*ntes 25
oponly⌐[14] y*our* displease*r* in alsmeche as he hath[15] brokun his pr*o*mise to[16]
y*our* grace ⌐and also consedering afore y*our* s*er*ua*u*ntes he witnessid in his
own p*er*sown myn astate *and* toke the ferme of me *and* retornd to me bothe in
hir lif *and* aff*ter* hire decesse⌐,[17] and to shewe vnto hym that y*our* grace will
distreyn for itt and make hym to paie it ayen that he myght be put in 30
suche a[3] feere that he mygh⟨t⟩[8] thinke that ⌐they of whom he hath his⌐[18]
prevy comforth myght nat cownt*ur* with y*our* displeasure; and thus doon
I trow he shulde contynue trew j-now heraff*ter*.

---

112. [1] *In a line by itself* This Manere passid *canc.*

[2] *Interl. in a different style but apparently by the same hand.*

[3] *No space.*

[4] *Obscured by stain, but legible.* [5] Rumbolde *canc.*

[6] *Interl. above* Richard *canc.* [7] and he *canc.*

[8] *At edge.* [9] *In margin.* [10] whiche *canc.*

[11] *Spelling uncertain;* -u- *has a minim too many.* [12] -x *canc.*

[13] hope *canc.* [14] *Interl. above* hym *canc.*

[15] made his *canc.* [16] *Written* vnto, vn *canc.*

[17] *This whole passage inserted between two of the original lines, consequently very small,*
cramped, and hard to read.

[18] *Interl. above* there *canc.*

The man*ere* of Harwell⌐bury⌐[19] in the countie of Hertford, iiij myle
35 from y*our* man*ere* of Weston Baldok ⌐and⌐ ij myle from Roiston.

This man*ere* passid nat by the astate ⌐þat⌐ was taken ⌐in Norff*olk*⌐[20] for
itt is nat in the same shire.

Of this man*ere* he receyued no mony, for the fermo*urs* are trewe ⌐and
herty⌐ j-now ⌐and fere nat his thretes⌐. I nede no grete helpe there.[21]
40 This man*ere* is worthe an viij li.

113. Will   1496, 7 September

P.C.C., Reg. Horne, 12. Two hands, record of probate in the second.

G. 988/Will 7.

In Dei nomine, amen. The vij[th] day of the moneth of September in the
yere of our Lord God m¹cccclxxxxvj I, William Paston of London, gentilman, being of hooll mynde and in good memory, laude and praysing be
vnto Almighti God, make and ordeigne this my present testament and last
5 wille in maner and fo*ur*me folowing, that is to sey: Furst, I geue and
bequeith my soule vnto my saide Lorde God, to our blessed Lady Sainte
Marye Virgyne, and to all the holy companye of heven. And I will that
my body be buried in the church of Blak Frerez in London at the north
ende of the high altar there by my Lady Anne, late my wife.
10 Also, I will that there be yeuen vnto the saide church of Blak Frires,
where my saide body shall lye, to be praide for and for the place of my
saide burying to haue a large stone vpon the saide Lady Anne and me, a
conuenient rewarde by th'advise and discrecion of myne executours
vnderwriten.
15 Also, I will that all my dett*es* be wele and truely contente and paide.

Also, I wille that xx li. in money be geuen and disposed for my soule
and all *Crist*en soules in dedes of pitee and charitee the day of my saide
burying, that is to sey emonges pouer people and prisoners within the
citee of London and withoute.
20 Also,[1] I will that I haue a preste of honest conu*er*sacion to synge bothe
for me and for suche as I am chargid to do syng for at Cambrige, as my
s*er*uant Thomas Andrew can shew by the space of viij yeres.

Also, I will that for eu*er*y wronge by me done in my life tyme a dewe
recompence be made there-fo*re* by th'enformacion of my saide s*er*uante
25 Thomas Andrew in that behalf.

Also, I will that all my landes and tenement*es*, with th'appurtenanc*es*, be
deuyded bytwene my ij doughters Agnes and Elizabeth, by the discresion

of my executours vnderwritten and after th'enformacion of my saide
seruaunte Thomas Andrew, to whome I haue shewid my entent and mynde
in the same manye tymes and often, to haue to theym and to the heires of 30
theire ij bodies lawfully begoten.

Also, I wille that all the reuennuyes of my fee symple landes ouer and
a-boue the reparacions and charges of the same that shalbe due at Mychel-
mas next after my deceasce be takyn of my tenauntes and fermours there
by fauoure, and that the same reuenues go to the contentacion and pay- 35
ment of my saide dettes assone as it can be conuenyently gadred and levied,
&c.

Also, I will that none of my tenantes nor fermers suche as be of grete age
and fallith in pouerté be in any wise vexid or t[r]oublid after my deceasce
by my executours vnderwritten for no maner of olde dettes due vnto me 40
before the day of my deces.

Also, I will that nether my heires, executours, nor non other person for
theim nor in theire names in any wise vex, sue, or trouble the saide
Thomas Andrew my seruaunte after my deceasce of or for any maner
of rekenynges or other maters bitwene hym and me in all my life tyme, 45
but vtterly thereof I discharge hym and will[2] that he be therof acquyte
and discharged in that behalue, as I haue shewid and declared in my life
vn-to my doughter Elizabeth, Mastres Hide, Master Vrsewik, Archedecon
of Richemonde, Master Doctor Myddelton, Master Thomas Madies,
chapeleyn to my Lorde Cardinall, Master John Shaa, alderman of London, 50
Master Reede, Master Cristofer Middelton,[3] proctours of the Courte of
Canterbury, and many other honorable folkis and to my seruauntes in
my life tyme, consideryng that he hathe ben my trewe and feithfull
seruant these xix yeres or more, in which seasone he hath had dyuers
grete paynfull besynes and labours in my causis, by whose gode policie 55
and meanes I haue purchased moche of my saide fe symple landes, which
also canne geve best enformacion how all suche landes as I haue purchased
stonden and what consciens is there-in, and howe euery thyng shalbe
ordred.

Also, I will that the churche of Saynte Petre in Wodenorton haue a 60
hole vestyment of the price of v merc.

Also, I will that Elizabeth Crane be wele maried at my costis, or ellis by
the menes of my doughters, vn-to suche a persoune as may dispende by
yere xx merc, or ellis to a gode marchaunt or other craftisman.

Item, I will that Cristofer Talbot be treuly contentid and paied of his 65
yerely annuyté of v merke by yere duryng his life.

Item, I will that Thomas Dokkyng have surely his annuyté of xl s.
by yere duryng his life.

---

[2] and will *repeated.*
[3] *MS.* Mildel-.

Item, I wille that the bargayne of Adam Sowter be recompensid after
70 th'enformacion had of my saide seruaunte Thomas Andrew.

Also, I will that euery of my seruauntes be rewarded for theire good
and diligent laboure and attendance had a-bowte me after the discresion
of my executours vnderwritten.

Also, I will that all suche of my godes moveable in Warwikes Inne and in
75 my place callid Castre Clere in Norffolk and in my place in Norwiche be
solde by the discresion of my executours tawarde and for the contentacion
and payment of my saide dettes and performance of this my present will.

Also, I will that the vicare of Fyncham be recompensid of his bargayne
betwene hym and me after th'enformacion of the saide Thomas Andrewe.
80 Item, I will that all my seruauntes suche as be behynde of theire wages
and dueties be trewly content and paied.

Also, I will that all other my godes not bequethid, this my will fulfilled,
my dettes paied, and all my wronges recompensed by th'enformacion of
the saide Thomas Andrew, be departid bytwixte my ij doughter beforesaide
85 after the discresion of my saide executours.

And also, for as moche as I haue not sufficient redy money and that
my dettis cannot be redely levied, þerfore I will that money be made of all
suche plate as I haue for the haste of contentacion of my dettes that I owe
of my buriallis.

90 And of this my present testament and laste will I make and ordeyne and
constitute my executours the moste reuerend fadre in God my Lorde
Cardinall, the right high and myghty prynces my Lady the Kynges modre,
my Lorde Dawbeney, and Sir Edwarde Poynynges, knyght, my nevew,
whome I hartely beseche in executyng and performyng this my laste will
95 to do and dispose concernyng the same in euery thyng as they shall thynke
best to the pleasure of Almyghty God and for the helthe of my sowle and
all Cristen sowles.

Probatum fuit suprascriptum testamentum coram domino apud Lamehith
xxviij° die mensis Nouembris anno Domini millesimo cccc° nonagesimo
100 sexto, juramento Thome Andrew et Laurencij Canwike testium, quibus
Thome et Lawrencio commissa fuit administracio per viam intestati pro
eo et ex eo quod executores in suo testamento nominati ex certis causis
legitimis refutarunt de bene et fideliter administrando eadem iuxta et
secundum ⌐vires¬ ipsius defuncti testamentum siue vltimam voluntatem,
105 ac primo de soluendo es alienum in quo idem defunctus huiusmodi mortis
sue tempore extitit obligatus, deinde legata in huiusmodi suo testamento
contenta quatenus bona et debita &c. ad sancta &c.

CLEMENT PASTON

114. To JOHN PASTON I   1461, 23 January

Add. 43488, f. 55. 11½×8½ in. Autograph.

Dorse: Paper seal over wax. Address autograph:

To hijs rythe worchypfwll brodere John Paston.

The date appears from the reference to the 'field' and the consequent threat to the south. The letter must have been written soon after the Battle of Wakefield, which was fought on 30 December 1460. Sir Andrew Trollope was killed at Towton on 29 March 1461 (*D.N.B.*).

F. i, p. 202. G. 367/430.

Rythe reue*r*ent *and* worchypfwll brod*er*, I recomawnde [me] to ӡow, certyfyyng ӡow þat[1] ӡowre lett*er* was delyue*r*yd me þe xxiij day of Januari abowthe no⌈o⌉ne seiso*n*, *and* Rychard Calle rode in þe mornyng, *and* þerefore I brak ӡowr*e* lett*er* if þere were ony asti mat*er*. *And* I dede *C*ristofyre[2] Hanswm goo to my lord of Cawnt*er*buri to tell him as ӡowr*e* lett*er* rehersyd, 5 *and*[3] my lord seyd he hadde spokyn w*yth* ӡowr*e* man þere-of þe day before, *and* if[4] þe Byssope of Norwyche wold not doo so mwche for him he hijs þe les be-hold to him. Not w*yth*stondyng he sayd he wold saue ӡow harmelez a-ӡens John ӡowng; but, *and* ӡe do well, remembir*e* thys lord*ys* haue many mat*er*ijs to thyng on, *and* if it be fore-getin þe harm is ӡowr*ys*. 10 *And* also if þe word torn John ӡong will not doo at hijs p*r*ayere.

And my Lord FitzWatere is rydyn northe-ward*ys*, *and* it is sayd in my lord of Cawnt*er*berijs howse þat he hathe takyn ij c of Andrew Troloppys men. And as for*e* Colt *and* Sire Jamys Strangwysse *and* Sire Thomas Pykeryng, þey be takyn or*e* ellys dede;[5] þe comyn voysse is þat þey be 15 dede. Hopton *and* Hastyng*ys* be w*yth* þ[e] Erle of Marche, *and* wer not at þe fewlde.[6] Wat word þat eu*er* he haue fro my lord*ys* þat be here, it is well doo *and* best for*e* ӡow to see þat þe contré be all-weys redy to com, bothe fote men *and* hors men, qw⌈a⌉n they be sent for*e*; for*e* I haue hard seyde þe forthere lord*ys* will be here sonere þan[7] men wen, I haue arde 20 sayde or*e* iij wek*ys* to an ende; and also þat ӡe xwld com w*yth*[8] more men

---

114. [1] þ *in form of* y, *as regularly in Clement's hand.*
  [2] *Abbr.* xpitofyre *with stroke above.*   [3] h *canc.*   [4] *MS.* of.
  [5] hopt *canc.*   [6] A *canc.*   [7] *MS.* þat.   [8] a clenrye *canc.*

and clenliere arayed þan a-nodere man of ȝowre cwntré xwld, fore it lythe
more vp-on ȝowre worchyp *and* towcheythe ȝow more nere þan odere men
of þat cwntré, *and* also ȝe be more had in fauore ⌈wyth my lordys here⌉. In
25 thys cwntré euery man.is well wyllyng to goo wyth my lordys here, *and*
I hope God xall helpe hem, fore þe pepill in þe northe robbe *and* styll
and ben apoyntyd to pill all thys cwntré, *and* gyffe a-way menys goodys *and*
lyfflodys in all þe sowthe cwntré, *and* that wyll ask a myscheffe. My lordys
þat ben here haue as moche as þey may doo to kep down all thys cwntré,
30 more þan iiij ore v scherys, fore þey wold be vp on ⌈þe⌉ men in northe, fore
it ys fore þe welle of all þe sowthe.

I pray ȝow recomawnde me to my modere, *and* þat I prayed here of here
blyssyng. I pray ȝow exscwse me to here þat I wryte here no letter, fore thys
was y-now a-doo. I dare not pray ȝow to recomawnde me to my swster
35 ȝowre wyff, and þe masangere, I trow, be so wysse he can not do yt. Ȝe
mwst pay him fore hijs labour, fore he taryd all nyt in thys town fore thys
letter.

Wrytyn ye xxiij day of Janwari in haste, wan I was not well at hesse.
God haue [ȝow] in hijs keping.
40
By CLEMENT PASTON, ȝowre broder

115. To JOHN PASTON I   1461, 26 June

Add. 27444, f. 97. 12×4½ in. Autograph.

Dorse: Paper seal over wax. Address autograph:

To my rythe worchypfwll broder John Paston be thys delyueryd in haste.

The date appears from the report of the dispossession of the writer's sister by the
Countess of Northumberland. Elizabeth Paston was married to Robert Poynings
in 1458 (see no. 121), and he was killed at the second battle of St. Albans on 17
February 1461 (*Inq. p.m.*, 9 and 10 Edward IV, no. 49). Eleanor, Countess of
Northumberland, was Baroness Poynings in her own right (*Complete Peerage*,
x. 665).
    G. 395/461.

Brodere, I recomawnde me to ȝow, desyeryng to here of ȝowre welfare,
þe qwyche I pray God maynten. Plesse ȝow to wette þat[1] I haue sent my
moder a letter fore mony fore my swster, and if ȝe wyll agré þat I may
haue xx^ti li. I xall ȝeue ȝow acowmptys þere-of and ȝe xall be payyd aȝen
5 of þe obligacion þat my moder hathe, or ellys I xall tak a swerté of my
suster. I-wysse obligacion mwste nedys be swyd, and a doseyn accions
more in her name and sche doo well thys terme,[2] and it wyll be doo wyth-
in fowrtenynt. The Cowntas of Northumberlond and Robarde Fenns

---

115. [1] if *canc.*   [2] -r- *flourished in error.*

ocupie all her lond, and þat is a gret myscheffe. I pray ȝow spe[ke] to my
moder her-of, and lat me haue a awnswere wyth-in þis seuenynt.   10

Also, broder, Wymdam is com to town, and he seyd to me he wyll goo
gett hym a mayster; and me thowte by hym he wold be in þe Kyngys
seruise. And he saythe þat he wyll haue Felbryg a-ȝen ore Myhelmes, ore
þere xall be v c hedys brok þere-fore.

Brodere, I pray ȝow delyuer þe mony þat I xwld haue in-to swm 15
priore of swm abbey, to swm mayster of swm colage, to be delyueryd
qwan I can espy ony londe to be purchasyd. I pray ȝow send me word
wyder ȝe wyll doo thus ore no.

No more, but Owre Lord haue ȝow in hys kepyng. Wrytyn on Fryday
nexst after Seynt John is Day.   20

By ȝour broder CLEMENT PASTON

116. To JOHN PASTON I   1461, 25 August

Add. 34888, f. 191. 11¼×8¼ in. Autograph; see Plate V.

Dorse: Remnants of red wax. Address autograph:

To hijs rythe reuerent and worchypfwll[1] broder John Paston.

The date appears from a letter of John Paston II's which also mentions Howard's
attack on John I, and which is datable from Edward IV's going to Wales (see no.
231).
F. iv, p. 52. G. 411/478. C. 28 (part).

Rythe reuerent and worchypfwll broder, I recomawnde me to ȝowre good
broderhood, desieryng to herre[2] of ȝoure welfare and good prosperité,
the qwyche I pray God encresse to his pleswre and ȝowre hertys hesse;
certyfyyng ȝow þat I haue spok wyth John Rwsse, and Playter spak wyth
him bothe, on Fryday be-fore Seynt Barthelmw. And he told vs of 5
Howardys gydyng, qwyche mad vs rythe sory tyl we harde þe conclusion
þat ȝe hadde non harme. Also I vnderstond[3] by W. Pekok þat my nevew
hadde knowlache þere-of also vp-on Saterday nexst be-fore Seynt
Barthelmwe, in þe Kyngys howse. Not wyth-standyng vp-on þe sam day
Playter and I wryte letterys on-to him rehersyng al the mater, fore cause[4] if 10
þere were ony questionys mevyd to hym þere-of þat he xwlde telle þe
trowthe, in cas þat þe qwestions were meuyd by ony worchypfwll man,
and namyd my Lord Bowchere, fore my Lord Bowchere was wyth þe
Kyng at þat tym.

I fele by W. Pekok þat my nevew is not ȝet verily aqweyntyd in þe 15
Kyngys howse, nore wyth þe officerys of þe Kyngys howse. He is not

116. [1] John *heavily canc.*
[2] *First r flourished, as if for -re final; second r and full e added.*
[3] þat *canc.*   [4] *Abbr.* cae *with stroke above.*

takyn as non of þat howse, fore þe cokys be not charged to[5] serue hym
nore þe sewere to gyue hym no dyche, fore þe sewere wyll not tak no men
no dischys till þey be comawndyd by þe cownterrollere. Also, he is not
20 aqueyntyd wyth no body but wyth Wekys, and Wekys ad told hym þat he
wold bryng hym to þe Kyng; but he hathe not ȝet do soo. Were-fore it
were best fore hym to tak hijs leve and cum hom, till ȝe hadd spok wyth
swm body to helpe hym forthe, fore he is not bold y-now to put forthe
hym-selfe.
25 But þan I consyderyd þat if he xwld now cum hom þe Kyng wold thyng
þat wan he xwld doo hym ony seruice sum were, þat þan ȝe wold haue
hym hom, þe qwyche xwld cause[4] hym not to be hadde in fauore; and
also men wold[6] thynke þat he were put owte of seruice. Also W. Pekok
tellythe me þat hijs mony is spent, and not ryotesly but wysly and dis-
30 cretly, fore þe costys is gretter in þe Kyngys howse qwen he rydythe þan
ȝe wend it hadde be, as Wyllam Pekok can tell ȝow. And þere wee mwst[7]
gett hym i c s. at þe lest, as by Wyllam Pekokys seyyng, and ȝet þat will
be to lytill. And I wot well we kan not get xl d. of Cristofyre Hanswm, so
I xall be fayn to lend it him of myn owne siluer. If I knew verily ȝour entent
35 were þat he xwld cum hom I wold send hym non. There I wyll doo as me
thynkithe ȝe xwld be best plesyd, and þat, me thynkythe, is to send him
þe siluer. þere-fore I pray ȝow as hastely as ȝe may send me[8] a-ȝen v
mark, and þe remnawnte I trow I xall gett vp-on Cristofire Hanswm and
Lwket. I pray ȝow send me it as hastely as ȝe may, fore I xall leue my-selfe
40 rythe[9] bare; and I pray ȝow send me a letter how ȝe woll þat he xall be
demenyd.
Wrytyn on Twsday after Seynt Barthelmwe, &c. Christus vos obseruet.
By CLE⟨MENT PASTON⟩[10]

117. To JOHN PASTON I: copy   1461, 11 October

C.U.L. Add. 6968, pp. 19–20.

The original letter is lost; this is the text as given in Sandford's Genealogy of
1674 (cf. nos. 34, 230).

The transcript obviously does not consistently preserve the original spelling,
yet does not bring it wholly up to date. The fifteenth century is most apparent
in the sporadic preservation of the archaic x- in xall and xulde—though in three
places its unfamiliarity defeated the copyist and he wrote p, and once y. The frequent
use of y for þ is also probably due to the original, though it was still current in
abbreviations in Sandford's time. These spellings with x and y, as well as th in
rythe and d in oder, etc., are characteristic of Clement Paston's own usage, and are

---

[5] servy canc.   [6] thyng canc.   [7] mak scheffte canc.
[8] it canc.   [9] barre twice written and canc.   [10] Lost at torn corner.

enough to show—despite the elimination of his equally characteristic ʒ—that Sandford's exemplar was an autograph.

Though he did not trouble to reproduce all details of spelling, Sandford seems to have followed the words of his originals faithfully enough. An extract which he gives from Margaret Paston's will (no. 230), about a hundred words long, alters one or two forms in minor ways and makes one more important change, *provide* instead of *purveye*. It is reasonable to suppose that this represents his usual treatment of documents, so that the present copy no doubt preserves essentially what Clement Paston wrote.

The address, doubtless on the dorse of the original, is given by Sandford at the head of the letter in the following form:
To his R^t reverent and worshipfull broder, John Paston, Esqr, be this delivered in great haste.
In the letter itself Sandford's punctuation and capitals have been slightly modified.

The date appears from the reference to John Paston's dispute with Howard; (cf. no. 116).

G. 417/484, printed from *Norfolk Archaeology*, iv (1855), 26.

Brother, I recommende me to you, after all dewe recommendacions, &c. Sir, it was tolde me by rythe a worshipfull man that loveth you rythe well, and ye him, and ye xall[1] knowe his name here-after, but put all things out of doubt he is such a man as will not lye. On the xj^th day of October the Kinge seid, 'We have sent two privy sealys to Paston by two yeomen of our chamber, and he disobeyeth þem;[2] but we will send him a-noder to-morrowe, and by Gods mercye and if he come not then he xall dye for it. We will make all oder men beware by him how they xall disobey our writinge. A servant of our hath made a complainte of him. I cannot thinke that ⌐he⌐ hath informed us all truely, yet not for that we will not suffer him to disobey our writinge; but sithen he disobeyeth our writinge we may beleve the better his gydinge is as we be informed.' And þerwith he made a gret a-vowe that if ye[3] come not at the third commandement ye xulde[4] dye therefore.

This man that tolde me this is as well learned a man as any is in England. And the same xj^th day of October he advised me to send a man to yow in all the hast that might be to lett yow have knowlache, and that ye xulde not lett for none excuse, but that ye xulde make the man good cheere and come as hastily ye might to the Kinge, for he understandeth so much that the Kinge will kepe his promise. Notwithstanding, by mine advice, if ye have this[5] letter or the messenger come to you, come to the Kinge wards or ye meete with him, and when ye come ye must be suer of a great excuse. Also, if ye doe well, come right stronge, for Howards wife made[6] her bost that if any of her husbands men might come to yow þer xulde[7] goe noe penny for your life; and Howard hath with the Kinge a great felloweship.

---

117. [1] *MS.* pall, *again in next two occurrences of this word.*   [2] *MS.* y *regularly for* þ.
[3] *MS.* he.   [4] *MS. has* x *correctly here and in next two occurrences.*
[5] *MS.* his.   [6] *P. 19 ends.*   [7] *MS.* yulde.

This letter was written the same day that the Kinge said these words, and the same day that it was told me, and that day was the xjth day of October as abovesaid; and on the next morning send I forth a man to yow with this letter, and on the same day send the Kinge the third privye seale
30 to you.

Alsoe he þat tolde me this seid that it were better for yow to come upp then to be fotte out of your house with streingth, and to abide the Kings judgement þerin, for he will take your contumacy to great displeasure. Also, as I understand, the Duke of Norffolk hath made a great complaint
35 of yow to the Kinge, and my Lord of Suffolk and Howard and Wyngfelde helpe well to every day and call upon the Kinge against yow.

The Kinge is at this day at Grenewich, and þer will be still till the Parliament beginne. Some say he will goe to Walsingham, but Master Sotyll seid in the Aulle in the Temple that he harde no worde of any such
40 pilgrimage.

No more, &c. Written the xjth day of October at midnight.

My nevew John tolde me also that he supposed þer were out proclamacions against yow, &c., the same day.

By CLEMENT PASTON, your broder

118. To JOHN PASTON I   1464, 15 February

Add. 34889, f. 2. 11⅞×4½ in. Autograph.

Dorse: Remnants of red wax. Address autograph:

To hijs rythe worchypfwl broder John Paston the heldere, sqwyere, be thys delyueryd.

The date appears from the report of Edward IV's expedition to Gloucestershire. He was in Gloucester from 4 to 10 February 1464 (Scofield, i. 318).
   G. LV/557.

Brodere, I recomawnde me to ȝow after all dew recomendacions, &c. Az fore Hew Fennys obligacion, ȝeluerton knowlacheyd it to be¹ Sire John Fastolfe is dede opynly in þe Eschekere, *and* there he hadde is jugement to receyue þe mony *and* x li. fore damagys, *and* they² report here þat they
5 haue a schreve after here entent þat wyll mak hem execucion, ore ellis return þat ȝe haue wastyd þe godys of þe dede, so þat they wyll haue execucion of ȝowre own³ goodys ore ellys a wryt to tak ȝowre body. Thus ȝe may se they ȝeue no fors wat they doo, thow they xwld lesse *and* stroy all þe goodys of þe dede. And there-fore, fore sauacion of þe goodys of þe
10 dede better it were to⁴ tak sum treté þan to suffe[r] þe goodys thus to be

---

118. ¹ ȝowr *canc.*   ² *From* there.   ³ goddys *canc.*   ⁴ suffer *canc.*

lost. Also, ȝeluerton hathe ben at all þe tenauntys in Sowthewerk *and* chargid hem to pay no mony but to hym.

Also, the Kyng hathe ben in Glowceterschere *and* pwnyssede hijs rebellious a-ȝens[5] þe lawe, *and* so he entendithe to doo in Norfolk, and after þat in odere contreez. God ȝeue grasse *and* good spede in hijs 15 jornay.

No more, but I pray Gode haue ȝow in hijs kepyng. Wretyn on Hasse Wednysday in haste.

Also, I pray ȝou send me xl s. þat I tok Jamez Gressam *and* John Pampyng fore ȝowre materys. Also, there is no man þat hathe contentyd ony 20 thyng in þe Kyngys Benche of all thijs term for ȝour materys, and þat makythe the clerkys *and* ȝowre aturnay wery. I trow I xall be fayn to contente hem ore ellys they xall be vnpayyd.

ȝowre brodere CLEMENT PASTON

119. To JOHN PASTON I   1464, 18 April

Add. 34889, f. 7. 8¼ × 8 in. Autograph.

Dorse: Remnants of red wax. Address autograph:

*To my rygth worchypfull brod*er *John Paston, sqwyer*e.

The date appears from the report of Edward IV's visit to Kent and his intention to go to York. He was in Kent in April 1464, and reached York on 23 May (Scofield, i. 332, 335). Further, the examination of witnesses in the suit brought by Sir William Yelverton and William Worcester against John Paston I and Thomas Howes ('the parson of Blofield') concerning the disposal of Sir John Fastolf's property began on 28 April 1464 (Bodl. MS. Top. Norf. c. 4).

G. LVI/564.

Ryght worshypfull brothyre, I recomawnde me to ȝow after all dew re-comendacions, &c. Plesse it ȝow to wett þat after þat I harde say þat þe parson of Blowfelde wasse com to town I went to hym to hys jn, *and* he bade þe masenger say þat he wasse not wyth-in. And I bad hym say a-gayn þat I com thyder to hym fore hijs own worchype *and* auayle, and 5 þat I wasse sory þat I com so fere[1] fore hym.[2] And after þat he sent fore me *and* he cowde not fynde me, and I harde say there-of; *and* þan I wrott a letter resytyng how þat he wasse sworn ȝesterday fore to say þe trowthe of al maner of materis consernyng Sire John Fastolfe, auysyd hym to[3] remembere qwat hijs wytnesse hadde sayd fore hijs sake *and* wat schame 10 it xwlde be to hym to say þe contrary, and also if he sayde þe contrary ȝe wold here-after proue þe trowthe *and* con[t]rary to hys sayyng, *and* proue

---

[5] y *written over two letters, perhaps* be, *apparently as cancellation.*

119. [1] *MS.* fore.   [2] fore he x *canc.*   [3] y *canc.*

hym in a *periuri*. And also I badde hym remember*e* w*yth* wat man*er* of men he delt wythe, and I rehersyd how vntrwly they hadde don. And not
15 w*yth*-stondyng thys, aft*er* I met w*yth* hym in þe strett *and* spak w*yth* hym, *and* I fownde hym passyng strawngely disposyd, *and* sor meuyd w*yth* co*n*siens þat ʒe xwld haue þe lond *and* fownd þe colage but w*yth* an c marc. not w*yth*-stondyng he myth fynde in hijs co*n*siens rythe well þat þe colage xwld be fowndyd in a-noder plasse but w*yth* an c marc., *and* þe
20 remnaunt⁴ of þe lylode sold so þat he myth pwrce þe mony. So I felt by hym þat all hijs strawngenes from ʒow is for*e* he demythe þat ʒe wold p*ar*te from no thyng, and I told hym þe co[n]tr*ar*y ther*e*-of to be trwe. Az thys day he is exayminid vp-on a bok to sey þe trowthe of all thyng*ys* as þe juge wyll⁵ aske hym for*e* þe jugeis jnformac*i*on, wych I trowe wyll not
25 be good.

Also they haue pwt jn *testes* aʒens ʒow iijˣˣ or*e* iiijˣˣ men. Mayst*er* Robard Kent wold fayn þat ʒe xwld gett ʒow ij lycens of þe p*ri*oris of ʒowre wytnes Mayst*er* Clement *and* þe monke,⁶ w*yth* on⁷ a datt beyng⁸ be-fore þe comyng vp, for*e* þat must ʒe nedis haue. Also he wold fayn þat
30 ʒe xwld com to thys towne. Me thowte by Sir*e* Thomas þat they haue a swerté in man*er* þat ʒe xall haue no lycens for*e* ʒo*ur* fundac*i*on, and they be abowte to gett a lycens to fownde þe colage in a-noder place. Me thynkythe þat wold hurte. Here colo*ur* is for*e* caus*e*⁹ ʒe can gett no lycens to fownde it at Caster*e*,¹⁰ werfor*e*, thow ʒo*ur* wyll wer*e* trwe, they myth
35 lawfully fownde it in a-nod*er* place.

My lord Chawncel*er*e is gone to ʒork *and* wyll not be her*e* of all thys term. Wrytyn on Wednisday nexst be-for Saynt George.

The Kyng hathe ben in Kent, *and* ther*e* ben endityd many for*e* Isleis dethe; *and* he wyll com to town thys¹¹ day a-ʒen, and he wyl not tary her*e*
40 but forthe to ʒork straytt.

By CLEMENT PASTON

120. To JOHN PASTON I   1466, 18 March

Add. 27445, f. 12. 8¾ × 7½ in. Autograph.

Dorse: Traces of red wax. Address autograph:

*To hijs rythe worchypfwll mayst*er *John Paston, sqwyer*e.

Above the address, but on a part of the paper that was folded inside: 'The man wold not tak my lett*er* but I wass fayen to gyue hym ij d. for*e* þe beryng.'

---

⁴ *MS.* re + *seven minims* + at, *with superior* a.   ⁵ *MS.* wyth.
⁶ fore y *canc.*   ⁷ *MS.* an.   ⁸ *MS.* beryng.   ⁹ *Abbr.* cae *with stroke above.*
¹⁰ wrytyn on Wednesday be-for Seynt Georgys Day *canc.*   ¹¹ ny *canc.*

The date must fall between 30 May 1465, when Edmund, Lord Grey of Ruthin, was created Earl of Kent (*Cal. Charter Rolls*, vi. 207), and May 1466, when John Paston died.

G. 540/627.

Rythe worchypfwll brodere, I recomawnde me to 30w; and as fore 30ur letter to my lorde Chawncelere, I haue not delyueryd it, fore I askyd auysse þere-in *and* I was aunsweryd þere-in þat sythe he was takyn to baylle the Chawncelere[1] cowde not compelle þe swertys to bryng hym in be-fore hijs day. Also me thowte 30ur letter was not most plesauntly wrytyn to tak to 5 swyche a lorde.

And as fore[2] þe Tresorere, hijs name is Sire John Fooge; but he is not in London nore wythe þe Kyng, so I kan [not] haue þe letter sent hym but if I hyeryd a[3] man to bere it.

And as fore 30ur question of þe patentys, Grenfeld *and* Catesby *and* 10 Sterkey holdyn it a good question, fore þe statut is *Patentes dez tenementes dount null titill est troué* þur *le roy de recorde sount voydez—A° xviij° H. vj ca° vj°.*[4] But I trow in 30ur cas, *and* be there opiniounis, þe acte of þe parlement is a tytyll of recorde. It is seyd to þe contrary intent, thow þe londys be forfetyd of record yet þere is no certificacion of recorde qwat 15 londys they be, nore were, nore in qwat place þey lye; but and thys clawse be in þe patent, *Non obstante* quod *nulla inquisicio pro nobis inde est inuenta*,[4] by Grenfelde is consayte þe patent xwld be clerly goode. But me semythe þat amendyt not þe mater, fore be-fore þe makyng of þe statut aboue sayde patentys graunttyd of londys be-fore inquisicion were goode *and* effectuell 20 *and* þe statut is generall, quod *patentes dount null tytill, &c. sount voydez.* þan it folowyt well if þe acte of parlement be no tytyll for þe Kyng,[5] þan is þere no tytyll fore þe Kyng of recorde, fore þat clawse in þe patent is no tytyll. þan if þere no tytyll, *ergo*[6] þe patent voyde. My suster standythe in þe same casse wyth my lord of Kent. 25

Broder, I pray 30w send more mony fore my neuew John, fore he mwst ellys com hom a-3en, fore þe Kyng gothe in-to Scotlonde *and* he is nowthere horsyd nor harneysyd, fore hijs grett horse is lykly to dye. And if 3e wyll sende it to me, ore to *Cr*istofyre Hany[n]gton, it xall be saue fore hym. I send 30w a letter[7] from hym closyde her-in. And I pray spek to my moder 30 þat my hors faylle not[8] on Passyon Swnday, fore þan xall I be redy *and* þan xall owre redyng be don.

Wrytyn on Twsday nexst after Seynt Gregory is Day.

30wre[9] broder CLEMENT[10] PASTON

---

120. [1] *MS.* chawncelerere.   [2] Syre John *canc.*
   [3] *No space.*   [4] *Quotation and reference underlined.*   [5] þe *canc.*
   [6] *Abbr.* g°.   [7] for *canc.*   [8] at þe day *canc.*
   [9] -r *followed by loop, as if* -ys *meant, and by a flourish. Evidently* broder *added as an after-thought.*
   [10] *Preceded by* by *canc.*

ELIZABETH POYNINGS

or BROWNE

(née PASTON)

121. To AGNES PASTON   1459, 3 January

Add. 34888, f. 136. $11\frac{7}{8} \times 6\frac{5}{8}$ in. Text in two unidentified clerks' hands, the first writing two manuscript lines and two words over; three small interlineations in a third, much rougher, hand.

Dorse: Traces of red wax. Address in second hand:

> *To my right worshypfull moder Agnes Paston.*

Elizabeth Paston was not married in January 1458 (see no. 28), and her husband Robert Poynings was killed in 1461 (see no. 115). During the interval 3 January fell on a Wednesday only in 1459.
   F. iii, p. 328. G. 322/374. C. 22.

Right worshipfull and my most entierly beloude mod*er*, in the most louly man*er* I reco*m*maund me vnto yo*ure* gode moderhode, besekeyng¹ you dayly and nyghtly of y*our* moderly blissing, eu*er*-more desiryng to here of y*our* welfare and p*ro*sperité, þe which I p*ray* God to contynw and encresce²
5 to your*e* hert*es* desyre; and yf it lyked your*e* gode moderhode to here of me and how I do, at the makyng of thys *lett*re I was in gode hele of body, t[h]anked be Je*s*u. And as for my mayst*er*, ⌈my⌉³ bestbeloved that ye call, and I must nedes ⌈call⌉⁴ hym so now, for I fynde noon oþ*er* cause, and as I trust to Je*s*u neu*er* shall; for he is full kynde vnto me, and is as
10 besy as he can to make me sure of my joyntore, wherto he is jbounde in a bonde of m¹ li. to you, moder, and to my broþ*er* John, and to my broþ*er* Willi*am*, and to Edmund Clere, the which neded no such bond. Wherfore I beseke you, gode moder, as our*e* most syngler trost ⌈is⌉⁵ yn your*e* gode moderhode, that my maystr*e*, my best beloved, fayle not of the c m*ar*c at
15 the begynnyng of this t*er*me the which ye p*ro*mysed hym to his mariage, wy*th* the remanent of the money of my faders wille. For I have p*ro*mytted

---

121. ¹ you *canc.*   ² *First hand ends.*
   ³ *Interl. in another hand above* be, *which is not cancelled though it clearly should have been.*
   ⁴ *Interl. in same hand as* my (*n. 3*) *above* tell *canc.*
   ⁵ *Interl. in hand of notes 3 and 4.*

faithfully to a[6] gentilman called Bain, that was oon of my bestbeloved suertees and was bounde for hym in cc li., of which he reherseth for to resseyve at the begynnyng of thys terme cxx li. And yf he fayle þerof at this tyme he wille clayme the hool of vs, the which were to vs to grete an hurt. And he con not make an ende wyth noon of hys oþer suertees wythoute this seyd syluer, and that con my broþer John telle yow wel j-nough and it lusteth hym to do soo.

And in all oþer thynges, as to my LadyPool wyth hom I soiourned, that ye wil be my tendre and gode moder that she may be payde for all the costes doon to me before my maryage; and to *Crist*ofre Hanson as ye wrote vnto my broþer John that it shuld have ben so. And þat it plese youre gode moderhode to yeve credence to Willi*am* Worcestre.

And Jesu for his grete mercy save yow. Written at London the Wendysday the iij day of Janyuer.[7]

By youre humble doughter E L Y Z A B E T H   P O N Y N G G E S

122. To J O H N P A S T O N II   Probably 1467, 15 December

Add. 34889, f. 69. 11⅜ × 11¼ in. Clerk's hand, unidentified.

Dorse: Slits for tape but no remaining wax. Address apparently in hand of letter:

To the worship⌈ful⌉ Sir John Paston, knyght, be this delyueryd jn hast.
Note evidently in John II's hand: *Lett' A° quarto E. iiijᵗⁱ A° quinto et vj et vij.*[1]

The date must be appreciably later than that of no. 115, for the Earl of Essex has taken over the lands that the Earl of Kent then occupied. It must be earlier than 1471, for Elizabeth was married to Sir George Browne before 8 January 1472 (see John II's letter no. 266); and, as Gairdner notes, it is probably before the restoration of Henry VI in 1470, since the Yorkist Essex would not then have much power. If John II's endorsement can be taken to show that this was the outermost and latest of a file of letters, it cannot be earlier than 7 Edward IV (1467) and is probably of that year.
F. iv, p. 266. G. 593/692. G. 594/693 abstracts no. 122A.

Worshipfull and with all myn hert interly wilbeloued nevoue, I recomaunde me to yow, desyryng to here of your prosperité *and* wilefayre, which I pray all-myghti God maynteyn *and* encres to his plesour *and* your hertes desire, thankyng God of your amendyng *and* helth; forthermore certefying yow þat Sir Robert Fenys hath doon grete hurte in þe lyuelode whiche perteyned to my husbond *and* me in þe shire of Kent, wherin Willi*am* Kene *and* oþer persones arn enfeffid, *and* gretly troubleth hit *and* receyueth

---

[6] *No space.*   [7] *By youre doughter E. Ponyngges canc.*
122. [1] *Another j canc.*

þe issuez *and* profitez of gret p*art* of theym. *And* as of my seid husbond*es*
lyuelode aswell in þe same shire as in o*þer* shirez, besyde myn jount*ur*, my
10 seid husbond whan he departyd towarde þe feld of Saint Albons made
and ordeyned his wille þ*at* I shuld haue þe rewell of all his lyuelode, *and*
of Edwarde, his soon *and* myn, *and* to take þe issuez *and* profitez of þe
seid lyuelode to þe fyndyng of his ⌈*and*⌉ myn seid son, to paie his detteez
and to kepe þe right *and* title of þe same lyuelode which I myght nat
15 accordyng occupie for S*er* Edwarde Ponyng*es*, myn seid husbond*es* brother.
And so, sith myn seid husbond*es* dep*art*yng, I assigned þ*at* þe seid S*er*
Edwarde for c*er*teyn yereez shuld haue *and* take þe reuenuez of þe
man*er*s of Westwode, Estwell, Leuelond, Horsmonden, Totyndon, Eccles,
Staundon, *and* Comebesden, p*ar*cell of þe seid lyuelode, which arn clerely
20 yerely worth lxxvj li. xiij s. iiij d., to þe entent þ*at* þe seid S*er* Edwarde
shuld paye myn husbond*es* detteez, for he wold not suffer me to be in
rest w*ith*out þ*at* he myght haue a rewell in þe lyvelode. And after þe seid
assignem*ent* made, þe seid Robert Fenes, contr*ar*y to trowth *and* w*ith*oute
cause of right, int*er*rupted me *and* þe seid S*er* Edwarde aswell of *and* in
25 þe seid man*er*s as of o*þer* man*er*s vndirwretyn, wher-vppon þe same S*er*
Edwarde suet vnto þe Kyng*es* highnesse *and* hade þe Kyngez honorable
*lett*res vndir his signet directed to þe seid S*er* Robert Fenys, þe tenour
wher-of I send vnto yow herin inclossid. And as for residue of þe lyuelode
of myn seid husbond*es* *and* myn w*ith*in þe same shire of Kent wherin þe
30 seid Will*ia*m Kene *and* o*þer* arn enfeffed, that is to say þe man*er*z of
Tyrlyngha⟨m⟩,[2] Wolu*er*ton, Halton, Newyngton, Bartram, Rokesley, *and*
Northcray, w*ith* th'app*ur*tenauncez, I of them by myn seid husbond*es*
wille shuld haue residue *and* take þe issuez *and* profitez of theym. Contr*ar*ye to right *and* conciens, takyng away my ryght *and* brekyng my seid
35 husbond*es* wille þe seid Robert Fenys hath doon gret wast *and* hurte ther,
and longtym hath take vpe þe reuenuez *and* profitez of þe same, wher-
thorough I haue not my ryght *and* þe seid wille may not be p*ar*fourmed.
Wherfor I hertely pray yow þ*at* ȝe will laboure vnto þe Kyng*es* highnes
at yt lyketh hym addres his honorable *lett*res to be directed to þe seid
40 Robert Fenys, dischargyng hym vtterly of þe menuraunce, occupac*ion*,
and receyt of þe reuenuez of þe said man*er*s of Tyrlyngham *and* o*þer*,
accordyng to þe teno*ur* of þe *lett*res[3] labored by S*er* Edwarde for þe man*er*s
assigned to hym from þe Kyng*es* highnes directyd to þe same Robert
Fynez, or strayter if hit may be, *and* þ*at* I *and* myn assignez may peasseblé
45 reioce theym; and if eny p*er*son wold attempt to do þe contr*ar*ye þ*at* a
com*m*aundement, yf it ples þe Kyng*es* highnes, by hym myght be yevyn
to my lorde Chaunceller to seall writtyng*es* sufficiaunt w*ith* his gret seall
in eydyng *and* assistyng me *and* myn assignez in þe same. And ⌈*as*⌉ for

---

2 *At edge, slightly torn.*
3 *MS.* lret *with stroke above, in error for* lres.

þe maners of Esthall, Faukham, Asshe, *and* Chelsfeld, w*ith* th'appurtenauncez, in þe said schire of Kent, wherof ⌐my⌐ husbond at his dep*ar*tur   50
was seassed, *and* my son sethens vnto þe tyme þat þe Erle of Kent, without eny jnq*u*is[i]sion or title[4] of right for þe Kyng, by colour of þe Kyng*es*
*lett*res patentes entret in-to theym *and* hym ther-of put owte; *and* now
myn lorde of Esse*xe* occupieth them in lyke man*er and* fou*r*me. Yf eny
remedy therin wilbe hade I pray yow attempt hit.   55

Also forther-more I hertely pray yow þat, if eny gen*er*all p*ar*don be
gr*a*untyd, þat I may haue on for John Dane my s[e]ru*a*unt, whom þe
said Rob*er*t Fenys of gret malice hath endyted of felonye; and þat ȝe
secretly labour þis *and* send me an aunsewer in writtyng in as godly hast
as ȝe may. As soon as yt may ples yow to send me passels of costez *and*   60
expenc*es* ȝe bere *and* pay for þe said causez I will truely content yow hit
of þe same, and ou*er* þat rewarde yow to y*our* plesso*ur*, by þe gr*a*ce of
Je*s*u, quo haue yow in his blessed keping.

Wrettyn in Suthwerk the xv^te daie of Decembyr*e*.

By your awnt ELIZABETH PONYNG*ES*   65

122A. Copy of writ to SIR ROBERT FYNYS

Add. 27445, f. 31. 11 × 5¼ in. Hand of letter above, more openly written.

Dorse blank, but marks of folding correspond to the soiled panel on the
dorse of Add. 34889, f. 69, and tape-slits are in exactly the same positions
as those in that sheet.

This must be the very copy of the writ mentioned in the letter above.

By þe Kyng

Tursti *and* welbelouyde, we grete yow wele; and for asmuche as we been
enfou*r*med þat ȝe entend in hasti tyme to[1] lewey *and* gader vpe the reuenuez
and profitez co*m*myng *and* growyng of *and* vppon þe man*er*s of Westwode,
Estwell, Levelond, Horsmonden, Totyngdon, Eccles, Stondon, *and*
Comebesdane w*ith*in[2] our counté of Kent, we for c*er*teyn co*n*sid*er*acions   5
vs nowe moeuyng wol *and* charge you þat from hensse furth ȝe laye off
y*our* hond*es and* in no vise ent*er*met of or in þe ⌐seid⌐ maners or of eny
p*ar*cell þerof, in gad*er*yng of rent*es* ther or other-wise, eny co*m*maunde-
me*n*t or writtyng by vs to you yeven or made herbefore to þe contraré
herof natwithstonding; receyui[n]g þeis our*e lett*res towardes you for your   10
sufficiaunt discharge in þat p*ar*tie, nat failing herin as ye wol aunsewer
vnto vs at y*our* parilie. Yevyn

To SER ROBERT FYNYS, KNYGHT

The copie of[3] þe *lett*re myssyue
endossid by þe Kyng*es* awn hand*es*   15

[4] *MS.* tille.

122A. [1] *One or two letters, the first like* l, *lost at edge.*   [2] *your canc.*   [3] h *canc.*

ELIZABETH POYNINGS

123. Will

1487, 18 May

P.C.C., Reg. Milles, 12. Two clerks' hands, the first writing the first page and the other the remaining two; the second much smaller so that it includes proportionately more material.

G. 988/Will 6.

In Dei nomine, amen. The xviij[th] day of the moneth of May in the yere of oure Lord God m[1]cccclxxxvij and in the secund yere of the reign of King Henry the vij I, Dame Elisabeth, late wife of Sir George Brown, knyght, being of hoole mynde and in good memorye, thanked be Allmyghty
5 God, make and ordeign this my present testament and last will yn maner and fourme folowing, that is to say:

First, I bequeith my soul to Allmyghty God, our Lady Saint Mary, and to all the holy company of hevon, and my body to be buried withyn the churche of the Blak Freris within Ludgate, with my forsaid housband
10 Sir George; to the whiche place I bequeith xxj li. for my said housbandes soul and myne, our fadres and modres soules, and for all Cristen soules to be praid for; and for xiij trentalles of Saint Gregory to be said and songyn for us and thaym by the freris of the said place, as in diriges and masses with all other obseruaunces belongyng to the same in maner and
15 fourme folowing, that is to wete: in the day or morow after my discesse vij trentallis, and euery weke folowing vnto my monthes mynde oon trentall, and iij trentalles at my monthes mynde biside the solempne dirige and masse that is to be requyred for me at that tyme. And I charge myne executours to see that the premisses be done and perfourmed, and
20 also the said freris to feche me from the place where I die vnto thair said place where I haue lymyted afore to be buried.

Also, I wull that, as sone as my body is buryed and th'expenses therof done and paid, that myn executours provide and see that my dettes be contented and paid.
25 Also, I bequeith to the vicare of the churche of Dorking in the county of Surré for my forsaid housbandes soul *and* myne, oure faders and modres, and for all the soules that we be bound vnto to be praid for within the yere after my discesse, as in diriges and masses to be said or song by hym or his deputie, and to haue us specially[1] in remembraunce in thayr memento by
30 oon hole yere, xx s.

Also, I bequeith to the reparacion of the forsaid churche of Dorking xx s.

Also, I bequeith to the parson of Saint Albans in Wodstrete within London, for diriges and masses to be said or song by hym or his deputie in like wise as the vicare of Dorking is charged as is afore rehersed, xxs.
35 Also, I bequeith to the reparacion of the stepull of the said churche of Saint Albans xx solid.

123. [1] *Abbr.* spially *with stroke above.*

Also, I bequeith to the prisoners of Newgate, Ludgate, Kinges Benche, *and* Mershallsee, to euery of those places, to be praid for, xx d.

Also, I bequeith to bedred folkes and other poure housholders, aswell men as women, dwelling within London and without in the suburbis of the same, and moste specially souche as haue knowen me and I thaym, xl s., as by the discrecions and advises of myne executours it shall be thought best to be done.

More-ouer, I geue and biqueith to my doughter Mary, to the promocion of her mariage, all my plate and other juelles, with all myne hole apparell and all my stuff of houshold being within my dwelling place or any other within the citee of London or suburbes of the same, that is to say: first a standing cupp of siluer gilt chaced with plompes, weyeng *with* the cover, knopp, and devise xlij vnces *and* di.; jtem, a standing cupp of siluer² and gilt chaced with flowres, weying with the cover, the knopp, and devise xxvij vnc. *and* di.; a playn standing cupp of siluer gilt,³ weing with the cover, the knopp, and the devise xxx vnc.; a standing cupp of siluer and gilt chaced with half plompes, weying *with* the couer, knopp, and devise xx vnc. *and* di.; a playn standing cupp of siluer gilt, weying with cover⁴ and the knoppe and the deuyse xxvij vnces and an half; a standyng cuppe of siluer and gilt, weyng with the couer, the knoppe, and the deuyse xxvj vnces; a saltseler of syluer and gilte, weying with the couer, the knoppe, and the deuyse xxiij vnces; a saltseler of syluer and gilt without a couer weying xxij vnces and an halfe; a litill saltseler of syluer and gilt, weying with the cover and the knoppe and the deuyse xv vnces and an half; a litell saltseler of syluer and gilt without the couer weyng viij vnces and an halfe; and vj bolles of syluer parcelles gilt weying iiijˣˣ xviij vnces; and ij peces of syluer *with* a couer weying xlviij vnces; a dosen and a half of siluer sponys weying xxiij vnces; and iij sponys of syluer and gilt weying iij vnces and iij quartrons; and a long spone of syluer and gilt for ginger weying j vnce and iij quartrons; jtem, a chafing disshe of syluer weying xxvj vnces; and two litell crewettes of syluer weying viij vnces; a chalese of syluer and gilt with the paten weying xj vnces; an haly water stok of siluer *with* the lid, handill, and spryngill weying xij vnces; an Agnus *with* a baleys, iij saphires, iij perlys, *with* an jmage of Saint Antony apon it; and a tablet with the Salutacion of Our Lady and the iij Kingis of Collayn; a bee with a grete perle, a dyamond, an emerawde, iij grete perlys hanging apon the same; a-nother bee with a grete perle with an emerawde and a saphire weying ij vnces iij quarters; a pece of the Holy Crosse, crosse-wise made, bordured *with* siluer aboute; iij brode girdilles, oone of tawny silke *with* bokill a[nd] pendaunt, a-nother of purpill *with* bokyll and pendaunt, and the iijᵈᵉ of purpill damaske *with* bokell and pendaunt and vj barres of siluer and gilt; and iij brode harnysed girdilles, oone white

---

² *MS.* suluer.   ³ chaced *canc.*   ⁴ *First page and hand end.*

tisshew, a-nother red tysshewe gold, and the iij^{de} a playne grene coorse;
80 a muskeball of gold weying halfe an vnce; and ij bokilles and two pen-
dauntes of gold, oone playne and the other pomisyd, weying an vnce and
a quart*er*; and a harnysed girdill enameled with rowsclare weying halfe
an vnce; a dymysoynt *with* a rubye and an amatyste weying j vnce and
an halfe; an harnysed girdill of golde of damaske, *with* a long pendaunt
85 and a bokill of golde chekkyd, weying j vnc*e*; a grete bed of a-state⁵ of
verdure and a counterpoynt to the same; and iiij curteyns of grene tartron;
a grete federbed; a bolster*e*; and vj fetherbeddys ouer-woren; vj bolsters;
and iiij mattarasses lytyll ouer-woren; xij pellowes of downe; v newe
carpettys of ij ellys in lengeth and yarde and halfe brode; iij fyne pelow·
90 beres; and a grete counterpoynt of tapstery werk of v yardes and a quarter
longe and iiij yardes brode; a hanging for a chamber of grene say borduryd
with acrons of xxxv yerd*es* longe; a whyte spervyour; ij counterpoyntes;
an hanging bed *with* a lyon thereapon and the valence white, grene, and
red, and iiij blew courtens to the same; and two couerlett*es* with lyons;
95 a blak testour for a bed with iiij blak curtens and vj pecys of blak hanging
to the same; ij cusshens of blak velvet; a cusshyn of blak damask; a cusshen
of grene worstede; a long cusshen of blewe saten figur*e*; a blak coueryng
for a bed of borde Alisaunder; and xj pec*es* of grene saye borduryd *with*
acorns to hang *with* a chambr*e*; a vestment of blak velwet with orfrayes
100 browderyd *with* my saide husbondys armes and myne; an awbe; j chesyppill
with a stole and all that belongeth therto; ij corporas casys of cloth of
gold; j olde vestment; an awbe; an awter clothe wyth the jmage of Our
Lorde; a corporas case of blewe cloth of golde, a-nother of blewe saten
and russet; an awter clothe of staynyd werke; and iij stenyd clothes with
105 jmagis in them to hang a chapell; ij awter clothes of white sylke *with* red
crosses; and ij curtens with white frengis and red; and iiij curtens, ij
of rayed sarsenet and two of grene; an awter clothe; a litell pece of grene
tartron; a payer of fustyans of iiij breddys iij yerdys iij quarters long; a
paire of fyne shetys ouerworne of iiij yerd*es* brede; an hede shete; and iij
110 payer of newe shetys of iij levis of iij ellys and an half long; and two payer
of shetys of ij levis and an half long; and iij hedshetys of ij bredys; and vj
paier*e* of shetys ouer-worne of ij levis; and vj paier of houshold shetis;
and two paier of wollen blankett*es*; and a violet gowne furryd *with* martrons; a blak gowne furryd *with* gray; a blak gowne furryd with white; a
115 blak gowne furryd *with* ma[r]trons; and a nyght gowne of blak furryd with
martrons; a kirtill of tawny chamlet; a purfill of ermyns of ij skynne depeth
and iij yardys and an half long; a purfill of martrons of j skynne deppeth
and iiij yardis long; a purfill of shank*es* of ij skynne deppeth and iiij yardis
long; a bonet of poudred ermyns; and a pece of cloth of golde with dropis
120 which was of a duplade; and a dosen of diaper napkyns of flour*e* delyce

⁵ *Divided at line end.*

werke and crownes; and a dosen and a half of naptkyns of playne clothe
with blew pelowers; and a pece of clothe of diaper werke to make with
a dosen naptkyns; a bordecloth of floure delice werk and crownes of x
yardis and an half long and iij yardis brode; and a-nother bordecloth of
floure delyce werk and crownes viij yardes and a half long, ij yardes and 125
a quarter brode; a towell of diaper of flower delice werke and crownys of
xxᵗⁱ yardys long and iij quarters brode; a-nother towell of flower delice
werke and crownys of iij quarters brede and xviij yardes long; a-nother of
latise werke and diaper of iij quarter brede, xiiij yerdes di. long; a-nother
towell of iiij greynys and a fret of viij yerdes di. long; a-nother towell of 130
latise werk and crownys vj yerdes and di. long and iij quarters brede; and
two towellis of great diaper werke iij yerdes and a quarter long and iij
quarter brode; and a pece of new creste clothe conteygnyng xxiij ellys;
and two towellys of great diaper werkes of xiiij yerdes long and iij quarter
in brede; and vij grete cofers, v chestis, ij almaryes like a chayer, and a blak 135
cofer bounden with jron; vj yoyned stoles; iiij kaskettys; v litell ioynyd
stoles; a litill table ij yerdys long; a rounde table; ij trestelles; ij garnysshe
and di. of pewter vessell counterfete, wherof j garnysshe and di. is newe;
and vj great kandelstikkis newe of laton, and iiij newe bellyd kandelstikkis; ij litill kandelstikkes; vij basens of pewater; and v brasse pannys, 140
of the which oon is xvj galons and two of them of viij gallons a pece; and⁶
the other ij more lesse; a grete standing chafere of laton with a lyon apon
the lydde; ij chafers of brasse, and ij litill brasse pottys; ij grete cobardys
and ij othere cobardys more and lesse; ij fyer pannys; a lityll skelet; a ladill
and a scomer of laton; ij colondyrs; ij spyttys; ij dreping pannes of jron; 145
iiij dressing knyfys; ij lechyng knyfys; ij choppyng knyfys; a tryvet; a
brasen morter with a pestell of jron; ij stone morters; ij gredyrons; j
payer of potte hokys, a flesshe hoke, and a kolerake.

Prouydid alwey that myn executours, by the aduyse of myn ouerseers,
ordeigne and put in safegarde, to be kept after my discease in-to som relig- 150
ious place vnto the day of my said doughters mariage, and to the behofe
and promocyon of the same, all and euery part of the forsaid plate and
juelx, with all other stuffe of houshold by me to her as is aboue written
yoven and bequethed, except souche stuffe as canne not be kept from
mowghtes, which I will she haue the rule and gouernaunce of for the 155
safegarde of the same and for her wele.

And if my saide doughter Mary dye vnmaryed, then I yeve and bequethe all the forsaid plate, with all other stuffe of housholde, to my soon
Mathewe her brothere. And if it fortune that he dye vnmaryd, as God
forfende, then I yeve and bequeth all and euery part of my forsaid plate, 160
juelx, and stuffe of housholde vnto my soon Sir Edward Ponyngis. And
yef if fortune the said Edward to dye, as God defende, that then all the

⁶ *Second page ends.*

213

forsaid juelx and other stuffe aboue written, except a playne standing
cuppe of syluer and gilt with the couer, the knoppe, and the deuyse of the
165 same, with gryffons hede in the botom wrought apon blewe asure, weying
xxvj vncis, which I geve to my doughter in lawe Dame Isabell Ponyngis,
be dyuydyd by th'advice of the ouerseers of this my present testament and
last wille, and euynly to be departid vnto Antony Browne and Robert
Browne, my brethern-in-lawe, they to do with it thaire fre wille. And as
170 touching myne Agnus, tablettes with dyamondys, saphires, perlys grete
and small, crosses, gurdillis, dymyseyntes, gownys, with all other thingis
longing to myne apparayle as is aboue written, yef it fortune my said
doughter Mary decease I geve and bequethe all and euery part of it to my
kynnyswoman Margaret Hasslake. And if the said Margaret dye, that
175 then all the said apparell particularly written before remaigne to my said
doughter-in-lawe Dame Isabelle Ponyngys.

Also, xx merc. which I lent vnto my son Ser Edward Ponynges I woll
that it be destributyd by the discrecion of myn executours and ouerseers
among souche as been knowen my seruauntys at the day of my discease.
180 The residue of all my singuler goodes, catallys, and juellys, after my
dettys payde and my bequestes parfourmed and fulfyllyd and burying
done, I geve and fully bequeth to my sonnys Ser Edward Ponyngis and
Mathew Browne, and theym to dispose and do theire fre wille to pray and
to do for my soule as they wolde I sholde do for them, as they will aunswere
185 afore God.

And of this my testament and last wille I make and ordeigne myne
executours my forsaid sonnes Ser Edward Ponyngys and Mathew Browne,
and theire superuysours Humfrey Conyngesby and Richard Tuke. And
I bequeth to euery of myne executours for thaire labour lx s., and to euery
190 of myne ouerseers for thaire labours xl s.

In wittenesse hereof I, the said Dame Elizabeth, to this my present
test[a]ment and last wille haue put my seale. Youen at London the day and
yere abouesaide.

Probatum fuit suprascriptum testamentum coram domino apud Lamehith
195 xxvj^{to} die mensis Junij anno Domini supradicto, ac approbatum, &c. Et
commissa fuit administracio &c. Matheo Browne, filio eiusdem et executori, &c., de bene, &c. Ac de pleno jnuentario, &c. citra festum Sancti
Petri quod dicitur Aduincula, reseruata potestate committendi &c.
Edwardo Ponynges, militi, executori, &c.

MARGARET PASTON

124. To JOHN PASTON I · About 1441

Add. 34888, f. 7. 11¾×3½ in. Hand crude and unpractised, unidentified.

Dorse: Slight traces of red wax. Address in a skilled hand:

To my worshepfull husbond John Paston, abidyng at Petyrhous in Cambrigg.

This letter cannot be exactly dated. As Fenn says, Paston's residence at Peterhouse suggests that it was written early in his life and soon after his marriage; no other letters are addressed to him there. He was married not later than 1440 (see no. 13). John Maryot is not mentioned elsewhere until 1442 (see William Paston I's letter no. 10), and John I had dealings with him probably in 1444–5 (no. 35); but this letter is likely to be earlier because Margaret says nothing about her children, in contrast to nos. 125–7. 'Wetherby's matter' must refer to the great dispute about the administration of Norwich known as 'Wetherby's Contention'. Thomas Wetherby, alderman of Norwich and J.P., mayor in 1427 and 1432, M.P. in 1429, 1431, and 1436, was accused by opponents of acting against the interests of the city. Dissension continued in various forms, sometimes violent, from the end of his mayoralty in 1433 until 1443, when the city was judged—by a court on which William Paston I sat—to be at fault. Wetherby was supported by the Duke of Norfolk, two letters from whom, dated 9 October and 28 December but without year, are in the city records. The former requires the city to give Wetherby free passage, the latter complains that this has not been obeyed: 'We haue conceyued weel be credible informacion that ye haue shewid him no fauoure for oure sake but euer faynyd newe causes of malice aȝens him; wherfor we lete you haue very knowelage that we be his right good lorde and wil supporte him in his right.' The 'quest' in the present letter could possibly be the inquiry into a complaint against the mayor and aldermen by the Prior of the Holy Trinity of Norwich for encroachment upon his rights of jurisdiction, which was eventually held at Thetford in July 1441, before John Fray, William Paston, and Sir Thomas Tuddenham. See most recently W. J. Blake, 'Thomas Wetherby', *Norfolk Archaeology*, xxxii (1961), 60–72; also *Records of Norwich*, i. lxxxiii–xciii and 347; *Mayors of Norwich*, pp. 20–2; Blomefield, iii. 144–55.

F. iii, p. 18. G. 29/38.

Ryth reuerent *and* worsepful husbon, I recomawnde me to ȝow w*yth* alle myn sympyl herte, *and* prey ⌜ȝow to wete⌝ þat there come up xj hundyr Flemyns at Waxha*m*, qwere-of were takyn *and* kylte *and* d⌜r⌝onchyn viij hundyrte. *And* þa[t]¹ had nowte a be ȝe xul a be atte home þis Qwesontyde, *and* I suppose þat ȝe xul be atte home er owte lo*n*gke.5

124. ¹ *Written þᵃ, probably in error for þᵗ.*

I thanke ȝow hertely for my lettyr, for I hadde non of ȝow syn I spake wyth ȝow last² for þe matyr of Jon Mariot. þe qwest pasyd nowte of þat day, for my lorde of Norfolke was in towne for Wedyrbys matyr; qwerefore he wolde nowt³ latyd⁴ pase. As⁵ for-furþe os I k[n]owe Fynche ne
10 Kylbys⁶ makeþe no purwyauns for hys gode.

No more I wryte to ȝow atte þis tyme, but þe Holy Trenyté hawe ȝow in kepyng. Wretyn at Norweche on Trenyté Sunne-day.

ȝow[r] MARKARYTE PASTON

125. To JOHN PASTON I   Probably 1441, 14 December

Add. 43490, f. 34. 7½×7 in. Hand unidentified.

Dorse: Traces of red wax. Address in hand of letter:

To my ryth reuerent and worscheful husbond Jon Paston.

This letter is wrongly attributed by both Fenn and Gairdner to Margery Paston, and consequently misdated. The B.M. MS. index notes that the epistolary forms are characteristic of Margaret, not Margery; and see *Medium Ævum*, xix (1949), 15 n. 2. The child expected must be John Paston II, who was born before 15 April 1442. Bodl. MS. Charters Norfolk no. 740, of that date (an indenture by which the feoffees of Robert Mautby, Margaret Paston's grandfather, grant certain manors to John Paston—abstract in G. 962/43), refers to the birth of a son John to John and Margaret: '. . . pro eo quod ijdem Johannes Paston et Margareta iam habent exitum quendam filium Johannem de corporibus suis legitime exeuntem . . .'. The date is in winter, and St. Thomas's Day seems likely to be St. Thomas Apostle, 21 December, rather than St. Thomas of Canterbury, 29 December, since there is no mention of Christmas.

F. ii, p. 256. G. 809/923. C. 4.

Ryth reuerent and worscheful husbond, I recomav[n]de me to yow, desyryng hertyly to here of yowre wylfare, thankyng yow for þe tokyn þat¹ ye sent me be Edmunde Perys, preyng yow to wete þat my² modyr ⌜sent⌝ to my fadyr to London for a govne cloth of mvstyrddevyllers to make of a govne for me;
5 and he tolde my modyr and me ⌜wanne he was comme hom⌝ þat he cargeyt yow³ to bey⁴ it aftyr⁵ þat he were come ovte of London. I pre yow, yf it be not bowt, þat ye wyl wechesaf to by it and send yt hom as sone as ye may, for I haue no govne to werre þis wyntyr but my blake and my grene a Lyere, and þat ys so⁶ comerus þat I ham wery to wer yt.

---

² of *incompletely erased.*   ³ *No space.*   ⁴ jt p *canc.*
⁵ *Apparently from* of.   ⁶ *Initial not certain.*

125. ¹ þ *in form of* y, *as usually below.*   ² do *canc.*   alle *canc.*
⁴ *No space, as with* it/yt *after verbs throughout.*   ⁵ he *canc.*
⁶ cov *canc.*

As for þe gyrdyl þat my fadyr be-hestyt me, I spake[7] to hym þer-of a   10
lytyl be-fore he ȝede to London last, *and* he seyde to me þat þe favte was
in yow þat ȝe wolde not thynke þer-vppe-on to do mak yt; but I sopose þat
ys not so—he seyd yt but for a[8] skevsacion. I pre yow, yf ye dor tak yt
vppe-on yow, þat ye wyl weche-safe[9] to do mak yt a-yens ye come hom; for
I hadde neuer[10] more nede þer-of þan I haue now, for I ham waxse so fetys   15
þat I may not be gyrte in no barre of no gyrdyl þat I haue but of on.

Elysabet Peverel hath leye seke xv or xvj wekys of þe seyetyka, but sche
sent my modyr word be Kate þat sche xuld come hedyr wanne God sent
tyme, þoov sche xuld be crod in a barwe.

Jon of Dam was here, *and* my modyr dyskevwyrd me to hym, *and* he   20
seyde be hys trovth þat he was not glaᶠdᶦder of no[11] thyng þat he harde
thys[12] towlmonyth þan he was þer-of. I may no le[n]ger leve be my crafte,
I am dysscevwyrd of alle men þat se me. Of alle odyr thyngys þat ye
deseyreyd þat I xuld sende yow word of I haue sent yow word of in a let*ter*
þat I dede wryte on Ovwyr Ladyis Day laste was.[13]   25

þe Holy Trenyté haue yow in hese kepyng. Wretyn at Oxnede in ryth
gret hast on þe Thrusday next be-fore Seynt Tomas Day.

I pre yow þat ye wyl were þe reyng wyt*h* þe emage of Seynt Margrete
þat I sent yow for a rememrav[n]se tyl ye come hom. Ye haue lefte me
sweche a rememrav[n]se þat makyth me to thynke vppe-on yow bothe day   30
and nyth wanne I wold sclepe.

Yowre ys, M. P.

126. To JOHN PASTON I   Probably 1443, 28 September

Add. 34888, f. 8. $11\frac{1}{2} \times 5\frac{3}{4}$ in. Hand unidentified, postscript in different
unidentified hand.

Dorse: Postscript. Traces of red wax. Address in hand of postscript:

To my rygth worchepful husbond Jhon Paston, dwellyng in þe Innere Temple
at London, in hast.

The date is after the birth of John Paston II (l. 44), which was before 15 April
1442 (see no. 125), and before the death of William Paston I in August 1444 (see
no. 33). 'My mother' in l. 22 means Margaret's own mother, but in ll. 4–5 and
the postscript it means Agnes Paston, with whom Margaret must have been living
at Oxnead. Margaret's mother (Margery, daughter of John Berney of Reedham)
had married as her second husband Ralph Garneys of Geldeston ('Gerlyston' in
l. 14), which is just across the Norfolk border from Beccles in Suffolk. Cf. the
indenture referred to in no. 125 headnote: 'post mortem . . . Margerie vxoris
Radulfi Garneys armigeri, matris predicte Margarete, quondam vxoris predicti

---

⁷ -k *in this word, and in a few others, has a flourish so prominent that it probably stands*
for -e; *similarly* -f *in* safe 14.   ⁸ scev *canc.*   ⁹ *Divided at line-end.*
¹⁰ *No space.*   ¹¹ ty *canc.*   ¹² tel *canc.*   ¹³ þe *canc.*

Johannis Mauteby'. B.M. Add. Charter 17739, of 12 May 13 Henry VI (1435) calls her 'vxor Radulfi Garneys, nuper vxor Johannis Mawteby'. (John Mautby died in 1433: *Cal. Fine Rolls, 1430–7*, p. 162; *Inq.p.m.*, 12 Henry VI, no. 47.)

The token that Margaret had promised to send her mother is likely to indicate a second pregnancy. John Paston III was evidently born in 1444 (Sandford's Genealogy, p. 26), so that 1443 is a more likely date than 1442.

F. iii, p. 20. G. 36/47. C. 5 (part).

Ryth worchipful[1] hosbon, I recomande me to yow, desyryng hertely to here of yo*ur* wilfar*e*,[2] thanckyng God of yo*ur* a-mendyng of þe grete[3] dysese þat ye have hade; *and* I thancke yow for þe lett*er* þat ye sent me, for be my trowthe my mod*er and* I were nowth in hertys es fro þe tyme þat we woste
5 of yo*ur* sekenesse tyl we woste verely of yo*ur* a-mendyng. My mod*er* hat be-hestyd a-nodyr ymmage of wax of þe weytte of yow to Oyu*r* Lady of Walsyngham,[4] *and* sche sent iiij nobelys to þe iiij orderys of frerys at Norweche to pray[5] for yow; *and* I have be-hestyd to gon on pylgreymmays to Walsyngham *and* to Sent Levenardys for yow. Be my trowth, I had
10 neu*er* so hevy a sesyn as I had fro þe tyme þat I woste of yo*ur* sekenesse tyl I woste of yo*ur* a-mendyng, and ȝyth myn hert is[6] in no[1] grete esse, ne nowth xal be tyl I wott þat ȝe ben very hol.

Yo*ur* fad*er and* myn was dys[1] day sevenyth at Bekelys for a matyr of the Pryor of Bromholme, *and* he lay at Gerlyston þat nyth and was þer tyl it
15 was ix of þe cloke *and* þe tod*er* day. And I sentte thedyr for a gou*n*ne, *and* my mod*er* seyde þat I xulde non have dens tyl I had be þer a-ȝen; *and* so þei cowde non gete. My fad*er* Garneyss sentte me worde þat he xulde ben here þe nexth weke, *and* myn emme also, *and* pleyn hem here wyth herre hawkys; *and* ⌈þei⌉ xulde ⌈have⌉ me hom wyth hem. And, so God help me,
20 I xal exscusse me of myn goyng dedyr yf I may, for I sopose þat I xal redelyer have tydyngys from yow herre dan I xulde[7] have þer.

I xal sende my mod*er* a tokyn þat sche toke me, for I sopose þe tyme is cum þat I xulde sendeth here yf I kepe þe be-hest þat I have made—I sopose I have tolde yow wat it was. I pray yow hertely þat [ye] wol wochesaf
25 to sende me a lett*er* ⌈as⌉ hastely as ȝe may, yf wrytyn be non dysesse to yow, and ⌈þat⌉ ye wollen wochesaf to sende me worde quowe yo*ur* sor dott. Yf I mythe have hade my wylle I xulde a[8] seyne yow er dys[1] tyme. I wolde ȝe wern at hom,[9] yf it wer*e* yo*ur* ese *and* your sor myth ben as wyl lokyth to here as it tys þer ȝe ben now, lever dan a new gou*n*ne, þow it wer*e* of
30 scarlette. I pray yow, yf yo*ur* sor be hol *and* so þat ȝe may indure to ryde, wan my fad*er* com to London þat ȝe wol askyn leve *and* com hom wan þe hors xul be sentte hom a-ȝeyn; for I hope[10] ȝe xulde be kepte as tend*er*ly herre as ȝe ben at London.

126. [1] *No space.*   [2] th *incomplete, and A, canc.*
[3] þ[t] *canc.* þ *in form of y throughout first hand.*
[4] *Initial* w *at end of line, rest of word in next line.*
[5] *MS.* pary.   [6] not *canc.*   [7] do þer *canc.*
[8] sende *canc. and following* s- *written over* y.   [9] ȝy *canc.*   [10] but for your sor *canc.*

I may non leyser have to do wrytyn half a quarter so meche as I xulde seyn to yow yf I myth speke wyth yow. I xal sende yow a-nothyr letter as 35 hastely as I may. I thanke yow þat ȝe wolde wochesaffe to remember my gyrdyl, *and* þat ȝe wolde wryte to me at þis tyme, for I sopose þe wrytyng[11] was non esse to yow.[12] All-myth God have yow in hys kepyn ⌐and sende yow helth⌐. Wretyn at Oxenede in ryth grete hast on Sent Mihyllys Evyn.

Yourrys, M. PASTON[13] 40

My modyr gretit ȝow wel *and* sendyt ȝow Goddys blyssyng *and* here, *and* ⌐sche⌐ prayith ȝow, *and* I pray ȝow also, þat ȝe be wel dyetyd of mete *and* dryngke, for þat is þe grettest helpe þat ȝe may haue now to your helthe ward. Your sone faryth wel, blyssyd be God.

127. TO JOHN PASTON I 1444, 8 July

Add. 34889, f. 199. 11¼×5¾ in. Hand unidentified.

Dorse: Traces of red wax. Address in hand of letter:

To myn ryth worcepful husbonde Jon Paston.

Margaret wrote this letter while staying at Geldeston (see no. 126). Since she was with her mother and stepfather her reference in l. 21 to 'my father and my mother' must mean, as often, William Paston I and Agnes. William died in August 1444 (see no. 33). At the time of this letter Margaret and John had more than one child, and their second son was born in 1444. These facts can be fitted in if 'St. Thomas' is taken to be the Translation of St. Thomas of Canterbury on 7 July; and this is confirmed by the reference to St. Peter's Day (29 June) in terms which show it to be lately past.

G. XLVI/435.

Ryth reuerent *and* worcepfful husbonde, I recomand me to yow, desyryng hertely to here of yowre welle-fare, thankyn yow for[1] yowre letter and for[2] þe thyngys þat ye sent me þer-wyth. And towchyn Jon Estegate, he com nowdyr non sent hedyre nowt ȝyt, were-for I sopose I must borrowyn mony in schorte time but ȝyf ye come sone home, for I sopose I xal non 5 haue of hym. So Godd helpe me, I haue but iiij s., and I howhe nerre as meche mony as com to þe for-seyd some.

I haue do yowre herrendys to myn modyr *and* myn hunckyl, and as for þe feffeys of Stokysby myn hunckyl syth þat þer be no mo þan he wrot to yow of þat he knowit. And also I hauwe delyuyrit þe todyr thyng[3] þat ye 10 sent me ⌐in-selyd⌐ in þe boxe as ye comaundit me, and þe man seyt þat

---

[11] -g *added later.*   [12] *A flourish, rather like a capital S.*
[13] *Recto ends. Postscript on verso in different hand.*
127. [1] þe *canc.;* þ *in form of* y *throughout.*   [2] alle o *canc.*   [3] in selyd *interl., canc.*

I delyuerid[4] it to þat he wylle nowt of þe bargeyne[5] but sweche thynggys be do or he come þere þat ye sent hym worde of. He seyth he wold nowt be noysyd wyth no sweche thyngys os þat is ⌐þat it were⌐[6] do in hesse time
15 for xx marke. I sopose he xal send yow word in schorte time ho he wylle do.

I pray yow þat ye wylle weche-saue to beyn for me swech lacys os[7] I send yow exsaunpyll of in þ[i]s letter, and j pesse of blac lacys.[8] As for cappys þat ye sent me for þe chylderyn, þey be to lytyl for hem. I pray yow bey
20 hem feynere cappys and largere þan þo were. Also I pray yow þat ye wille wech-saue to recomaunde me to myn fadyr and myn modyr, and tellyth herre[9] þat alle herre chyldyrryn[10] ben in gode hele, blyssyd be Godd.

Heydonnis wyffe had chyld on Sent Petyr Day. I herde seyne þat herre husbond wille[11] nowt of here, nerre of here chyld þat sche ⌐had⌐ last
25 nowdyre. I herd seyn þat he seyd ȝyf sche come in hesse precence to make here exkewce þat he xuld kyt of here nose to makyn ⌐here⌐ to ⌐be⌐ know wat sche is, and yf here chyld come in hesse presence he seyd he wyld kyllyn. He wolle nowt be intretit to haue here ay[e]n in no wysse, os I herde seyn.
30 þe Holy Trinité haue yow in hesse kepyn and send yow helth. Wretyn at Geldiston on þe Wedynisday nexte after Sent Thomas.

Be yowrys, M. PASTON

128. To JOHN PASTON I   1448, April

Add. 34888, f. 18. 11⅝ × 11 in.

The hand is unidentified, but it is the most important of all the hands in which Margaret's letters are written.[1] Twenty complete letters, and the postscript to no. 129, are written in it; the next most numerous group contains nineteen complete letters and part of another written by James Gloys. The hand is characterized by a number of unusual spellings, and by striking changes of habit in the course of a few years; but certain expressions and corrections show that it is not Margaret's autograph.[2] It appears also in six drafts written for John Paston I (nos. 40, 42B, 46, 50, 51, 52). See frontispiece.

[4] -d over t; no space.
[5] at ye sent hym worde of in no wysse canc.
[6] Interl. above weche xuld be canc.
[7] as and canc.
[8] Interl. above of canc.
[9] First r blotted, but the space shows it to have existed.
[10] MS. chyrdyrryn.
[11] nomore o canc.

128. [1] See 'A Scribal Problem in the Paston Letters', English and Germanic Studies, iv (1951–2), 31–64.
[2] Ibid., p. 41 n. 12.

128. To John Paston I, April 1448

Dorse: Traces of red wax. Address in hand of letter:

To my ryth wurchypful hwsbond Jon Paston be þis lettyre delyveryd jn hast.

In one corner, note apparently in John Paston I's hand: *litere termino Pasche aᵒ xxvj.*

Diagonally opposite, and upside down, two other notes in different unidentified hands:

litere tangentes Oxenede Swensthorp Sparham
ante [?] Mych. xxxiiij H. vjᵗⁱ.

Though this large sheet evidently served as a wrapper for files of letters for many years, its own date is presumably indicated by the first endorsement in John I's hand. Easter Term in 1448 began on 10 April, and John would doubtless go to London on his legal business early in the term. The reference to 'your matter touching Gresham' suits the same year, for Lord Moleyns's usurpation of the manor of Gresham is shown by John Paston's petition (no. 36) to have begun on 17 February 1448. It is perhaps surprising that Margaret's agents should still be able to collect rent in April; but it is not until May that she reports rent-collecting by Moleyns's man (see no. 129).

F. iii, p. 54. G. 56/75.

Ryth wyrchypful hwsbond, I recomawnd me to ʒw,[3] desyryng hertyly to heryn of ʒwr wel-fare, prayyng ʒw to wete þat I was wyth my Lady Morley on þe Satyrday nexst after þat ʒe departyd from hens, and told here qhat answere þat ʒe had of Jon Butt; and sche toke jt ryth straw[n]gely *and* seyd þat sche had told ʒw *and* schewyd ʒw j-now qhere-by ʒe myth have 5 knowleche þat þe releve owyth to ben payd to here. And sche seyd sche wyst wel þat ʒe delay jt forþe þat sche xuld nowth have þat longyth to here ryth. And sche told me hw jt was payd in Thomas Chawmberys tym, qhan here dowter Hastyngys was weddyd; and sche seyd sythyn þat ʒe wyl make none end wyth here sche wyl sew þer-fore as law wyl. I conseyvyd be here þat 10 sche had cwnsel to labore aʒens ʒw þer-jn wyth-jn ryth schort tym. And þan I prayd here þat sche wuld vwche-save nowth to labowre aʒens ʒw jn þis matere tyl ʒe kom hom; and sche seyd nay, be here feyth sche wuld no more days ʒeve ʒw þer-jn. Sche seyd sche had sett ʒw so many days to a-kord wyth here *and* ʒe had broke þem þat sche was ryth wery þer-of; and sche 15 seyd sche was but a woman, sche must don be here cownseyl, *and* here cwnseyle had avysyd here,[4] *and* so sche seyd sche wyld do. þan I prayd here aʒyn þat sche wuld teryn tyl ʒe kom hom, *and* I seyd I trostyd veryly þat ʒe wuld don qhan ʒe kom hom as jtt longyth to ʒw to don; and jf ʒe myth have very knowleche þat sche awyth of ryth for to have jtt, I seyd I wyst 20

---

[3] *In this letter the scribe writes* ʒw *and* ʒʷ *indifferently, and the latter form is therefore transcribed* ʒw. *Similarly* ʒwr *appears to be the correct expansion of the possessive.*
[4] to don so *canc.*

221

wel þat ȝe wuld pay jt wyth ryth gode wyl, and told here þat ȝe had sergyd
to a fownd wrytyng þer-of and ȝe kwd non fynd in non wyse. And sche
sayd sche wyst wele þer was wrytyng þer-of j-now, and sche hath wrytyng
þer-of hw Syre Robert of Mawthby and Ser Jon and myn grawnsyre, and
25 dyverse oþer of myn awnceterys, payd jt and seyd nevyre nay þer-to. And
jn no wyse I kwd not getyn no grawnth of here to sesyn tyl ȝe kom hom.
And sche bad me þat I xuld don an erund to my moder; and qhan I kam
hom I dede myn erund to here, and sche axyd me jf I had spokyn to my
lady of þis forseyd matere, and I told here hw I had do and qhat answere I
30 had. And sche seyd sche xuld gon to my Lady Morlés on þe nexst day, and
sche xuld speken to here þer-of and a-say to getyn grawnt of here to sesyn
of þe forsayd matere tyl þat ȝe kom hom. And truly my moder dede here
devere ryth feythfully þer-jn, as myn cosyn Clere xal tellyn ȝw qhan þat he
spekyth wyth ȝw, and sche gete grawnt of my seyd lady þat þer xuld nowth
35 ben don aȝens ȝw þer-jn and ȝe wold acordyn wyth here and don as ȝe
owyn to do be-twyx þis tym and Trinyté Sunday.

Laveraw[n]ce Rede of Mawthby recommaw[n]dyth hym to ȝu and
prayith ȝw þat ȝe wyl vwchesave to leten hym byn of ȝw þe ferm barly þat
ȝe xuld have of hym, and jf ȝe wyl laten hym have jt to a⁵ resonabyl pris he
40 wyl have jt wyth ryth a⁵ gode wyl. And he prayit ȝw, jf ȝe wyl þat he have
jt, þat ȝe wyl vwche-save to send hym wurd at qhat pris he xuld have þe
kowmb as hastyly as ȝe may, and ellys he must be purvayd in oþer plase.

As twchyng oþer tydyngys I sopose Jon of Dam xal send ȝw wurd jn
a⁵ letter. As jt js told me veryly, Heydon xal not kom at London þis term.
45 It is seyd jn þis contré þat Danyel js owth of þe Kyngys gode grase, and he
xal dwn and all hys mene and all þat ben hys wele-wyllerys. þer xal no man
ben so hardy to don noþer seyn aȝens my lord of Sowthfolk nere non þat
longyth to hym; and all þat han don and seyd aȝens hym, þey xul sore
repent þem.⁶

50 Kateryn Walsam xal be weddyd on þe Munday nexst after Trinyté
Sonday, as it is told me, to þe galaw[n]te wyth þe grete chene; and þer js
purvayd fore here meche gode aray of gwnys, gyrdelys, and atyrys, and
meche oþer gode aray. And he hathe purcheysyd a gret purcheys of v mark
be ȝere to ȝevyn here to here joynture.

55 I am aferd þat Jon of Sparham js so schyttyl-wyttyd þat he wyl sett hys
gode to morgage to Heydon, or to sum oþer of vwre gode frendys, but jf I
can hold hym jnne þe better ere ȝe kom hom. He hath ben arestyd sythyn
þat ȝe went, and hath had moche sorw at þe sewte of Mayster Jon Stokys
of London for x mark þat Sparham owyth to hym; and jn gode feyth he
60 hath had so moche sorow and hevynesse þat he wyst nowth qhat he myth
don. I felt hym so disposyd þat he wold a⁵ sold and a⁵ sett to morgage all
þat he hath, he had nowth rowth to qhom so þat he myth an had mony to

---

⁵ *No space, as often with* a *in this hand.*   ⁶ *MS.* þen.

an holpyn hym-self wyth. And I entretyd hym so þatt I sopose[7] he wyl
noþer[8] sellyn nere sett to morgage noþer catel nere oþer gode of hese tyl
he speke wyth ʒw. He soposeth[9] þat al þat js don to hym js att þe request 65
of þe parson of Sparham and Knatylsale. I sopose jt is almas to confort
hym, for jn gode feyth he js ryth hevy and hys wyf al-so. He js nowth nw
vnder arest, he hath payd hys feys and goth att large. He was arestyd att
Sparham of on of Knetysalys men.

Hodge Foke told me þat Sym Schepherd ⌈js⌉[10] styl wyth Wylly, and jf 70
ʒe wyl I xal purvey þat he xal be browth hom ere ʒe kom hom. It js told
me þat he þat kepyth ʒwr schep was owth-lawyd on Munday ⌈at þe swth
of Ser Thomas Todynham⌉, and jf jt be so ʒe arn nowth lyk to kepe hym
longe. And as twchyng þat þat ʒe bodeyn me spekyn for to Bakton, he seyth
he js wel avysyd þat sche seyd sche wuld neuer have to done wyth all, 75
nere he kan not þenk þat sche hath non ryth to have jt. And he wyl say
lyche as he hath herd here seyd, and jf sche speke to hym þer-of he wyll
raþer hold wyth ʒw þan wyth here.

I pray ʒw[11] þat ʒe wyl vwche-save to send me wurd hw ʒe spede in ʒwr
mater twchyng Gressam, and hw Danyel js jn grace. Herry Goneld hath 80
browth to me xl s. of Gressam syn[12] ʒe ʒede, and he seyth I xal have more
or Qhythson tyd jf he may pyk jt vp. I sopose Jamys Gressam hath told ʒw
of oþer thyngys þat I have sped syn ʒe ʒedyn hens. If I here any straw[n]ge
tydyngys in þis contré I xall send ʒw wurd. I pray ʒw þat I may ben
recommaw[n]dyd to my lord Danyel. 85

þe Holy Trynyté have ʒw jn hys kepyng and send ʒw helth and gode
spede jn all ʒwr materys twchyng ʒwr ryth. Wretyn at Norwyche on þe
Wedenys-day nexst after þatt ʒe partyd hens.

ʒwrys, MARGARETE PASTON

129. To JOHN PASTON I   1448, 19 May

Add. 39848, f. 2. 11⅜ × 11 in. Letter in hand of James Gresham, postscript
in hand of no. 128.

Dorse: Postscript. Marks of folding, stitch-holes, and traces of red wax,
but no address.

The date appears from Lord Moleyns's occupation of the manor of Gresham (see
no. 36). 'The Lady Hastings' (l. 32) is Wymondham's wife: she was Margery,
daughter of Sir Robert Clifton of Buckenham Castle and widow of Sir Edward
Hastings of Elsing, who died in 1438 (*Complete Peerage*, vi. 359).

G. 59/77 (abstract). Transcript in the New Palaeographical Society, *Facsimiles of
Ancient Manuscripts*, 2nd series, iii (1921–4), pl. 133. C. 7 (part).

---

[7] *MS.* sopese.   [8] þ *in form of* y.   [9] *Corr. from* I sopose jt.
[10] *Interl. above* was *canc.*   [11] *MS.* þᵂ.   [12] *MS.* sym.

Ryght worshipfull husbond, I recomaund me to yow, and prey yow to
wete þat on Friday last passed be-fore noon, þe parson of Oxened beyng
at messe in our parossh chirche, euyn atte leuacion of þe sakeryng, Jamys
Gloys hadde ben in þe tovne and come homward by Wymondams gate.
5 And Wymondam stod in his gate and ⌐John Norwode⌐[1] his man stod by
hym, and ⌐Thomas Hawys⌐[2] his othir man stod in þe strete by þe canell
⌐side⌐. And Jamys Gloys come with his hatte on his hede betwen bothe
his men, as he was wont of custome to do. And whanne Gloys was a-yenst
Wymondham ⌐he⌐ seid þus, 'Couere thy heed!' And Gloys seid ageyn,
10 'So I shall for the.' And whanne Gloys was forther passed by þe space of
iij or iiij strede, Wymondham drew owt his dagger and seid, 'Shalt þow so,
knave?' And þerwith Gloys turned hym and drewe[3] owt his dagger and
defendet hym, fleyng ⌐in-to my moderis place⌐; and Wymondham and his
man Hawys kest stonys and dreve Gloys into my moderis place. And Hawys
15 folwyd into my moderis place and kest a ston as meche as a forthyng lof
into þe halle after Gloys; and þan ⌐ran⌐ owt of þe place ageyn. And Gloys
folwyd owt and stod with-owt þe gate, and þanne Wymondham called
Gloys thef and seid he shuld dye, and[4] Gloys seid he lyed and called hym
charl, and bad hym come hym-self or ell þe best man he hadde, and Gloys
20 wold answere hym on for on. And þanne Haweys ran into Wymondhams
place and feched a spere and a swerd, and toke his maister his swerd. And
with þe noise of þis a-saut and affray my modir and I come owt of þe
chirche from þe sakeryng; and[5] I bad Gloys go in ⌐to my moderis place
ageyn⌐, and so he dede. And thanne Wymondham called my moder and me
25 strong hores, and seid þe Pastons and alle her kyn were ⌐⟨. . .⟩myngham⌐[6]
⟨. . .⟩e seid he lyed, knave and charl as he was. And he had meche large
langage,[7] as ye shall knowe her-after by mowthe.

   After non my modir and I yede to þe Priour of Norwich and told hym
al þis cas, and þe Priour sent for Wymondham and þerwhyle we yede hom
30 a-geyn and Pagraue come with vs hom. And whil Wymondham was with
þe Priour, and we were at hom in our places, Gloys stod in þe strete at my
moderis gate and Hawys aspyed hym þere[8] as he stod on þe Lady Hastyngis
chambre. A-non he come doun with a tohand swerd and assauted ⌐ageyn⌐ þe
seid Gloys[9] and Thomas my moderis man, and lete flye ⌐a strok⌐ at Thomas
35 with þe sword and[10] rippled his hand with his sword. And as for þe latter
assaut þe parson of Oxened sygh it and wole a-vowe it. And moche more
thyng was do, as Gloys can tell yow by mouthe. And for þe perilx of þat

---

129. [1] *Interl. above* Thomas Hawys *canc.* [2] Interl. *above* John Norwode *canc.*
   [3] h *canc.* [4] s *canc.* [5] we with our shrykes *and canc.*
   [6] *Some words lost at hole in paper, room for about a aozen letters. The relation of the interlined and mutilated name -myngham to the rest of the sentence is not clear.*
   [7] of *canc.* [8] And co *canc.*
   [9] a-geyn *and* þanne Pagrave come owt *and* departed theym *canc.*
   [10] Thomas *canc.*

myght happe by þese premysses *and* þe circumstances þerof to be[11]
eschewed, by þ'aduyse of my modir *and* oþer I send yow Gloys to attend
up-on yow[12] for a seson, for ease of myn owen hert; for in good feyth I 40
wolde not for xl li. haue suyche an-oþer trouble.

As touchyng my Lady Morlé, she seith þat she atte hir*e* will wole haue
þe benyfyce of hir*e* obligac*io*n, for hir counseyll telleth hir, as she seith,
þat it is forfayt. And she wole not haue the relif til she hath yo*ur* homage,
&c. 45

The Lord Moleyns man gaderyth up þe rent at Gresh*a*m a gret pace,
and Jamys Gresh*a*m shall telle yow more pleynly þerof at his comyng.

Nomore at þis tyme, but Almyghty God haue yow in his kepyng. Wretyn
in hast on Trynyté Sunday at euyn.

Yo*ur*s, MARGARETE PASTON 50

As touchyng Rog*er* Foke, Gloys shall telle yow all, &c.[13]

Qwhan Wymdh*a*m seyd þat Jamys xuld dy I seyd to hy*m* þat I soposyd
þat he xuld repent hym jf he schlow[14] hym or dede to hym any bodyly harm;
and he seyd nay, he xuld nev*er* repent hym ner have a[15] ferdy*n*g w*ur*th of
harm þow he kelyd ʒw *and* hym bothe. *And* I seyd ʒys, *and* he sclow þe[16] 55
lest chylde þat longyt*h* to ʒwr kechyn, *and* jf he dede he wer*e* lyke, I
sopose, to dy for hym. It js told me þat he xall kom to London jn hast. I
p*r*ay ʒw be war*e* hw ʒe walkyn jf he be þer*e*, for he js ful cursyd-hertyd
and lwmysch. I wot wel he wyl not set vp-on ʒw ma*n*ly, but I be-leve he
wyl styrt vp-on ʒw or on su*m* of ʒwr men leke[17] a thef. I p*r*ay ʒw hertyly 60
þat ʒe late not Jamys kom hom aʒen in non wyse tyl ʒe kom home, for myn
hertys ese; for be my trwth I wold not þat he wer*e* hurt, ner non man þat
longyt*h* to ʒw jn ʒwr absens for xx pwnd. *And* in gode[18] feyth he js sore
hatyd both of Wy*m*dam *and* su*m* of hys men, *and* of oþer þat Wy*m*dam
tellyth to hys tale as hym lyst, for þer as Wy*m*dam telly*th* hys tale he 65
makyt*h* hem be-levy[n] þat Jamys js gylty *and* he no þy*n*g gylty.

I p*r*ay ʒw hertyly her*e* masse *and* oþer servys þat ʒe arn bwn to her*e* ⌜wyt*h*
a devwt hert⌝, *and* I hope veryly þat ʒe xal spede ryth wele in all ʒwr
materys, be the gras*e* of God.[19] Trust veryly in God *and* leve hym *and* s*er*ve
hym, *and* he wyl not deseve ʒw. Of all oþer materys I xall sent ʒw w*ur*d 70
jn hast.

---

[11] *From* by. [12] til ye *canc.* [13] *Recto ends. Postscript in hand of no. 128.*
[14] *MS.* scholw. [15] *No space.* [16] *Abbr.* þ *with stroke above.* [17] *MS.* lehe.
[18] *MS.* gede. [19] *and* put ʒwr *canc.*

130. To John Paston I 1448

Add. 34888, f. 29. 8⅝ × 5¼ in. Hand of no. 128.

Dorse: Last sentence of letter. Marks of folding, one section soiled. Paper seal, no address.

The approximate date may be deduced from John Paston's petition (no. 36). At the time of writing Margaret was evidently established in the 'mansion' at Gresham, and taking precautions against the sort of attack which was in fact made on 28 January 1449.

F. iii, p. 314. G. 67/88. C. 8 (part).

Ryt wurchipful hwsbond, I recomawnd me to ȝu¹ *and* prey ȝw¹ to gete som crosse² bowis, *and* wyndacis to bynd þem wyth, *and* quarell,³ for ȝwr hwsis here ben so low þat þere may non man schete owt wyth no long bowe þow we hadde neuer so moche nede. I sopose ȝe xuld haue seche thyngis of
5 Sere Jon Fastolf if ȝe wold send to hym. And also I wold ȝe xuld gete ij or iij schort pelle-axis to kepe wyth doris, *and* als many jakkys ⌜and⌝⁴ ȝe may.

Partryche and his felaschep arn sore aferyd þat ȝe wold entren aȝen up-on hem, *and* þey haue made grete ordynaw[n]ce wyth-jnne þe hwse, as it is told me. þey haue made barris to barre the dorys crosse-weyse, *and*
10 þey han made wyketis on euery quarter of þe hwse to schete owte atte, bothe wyth bowys *and* wyth hand gunnys; *and* þo ⌜holys⌝ þat ben made forre hand gunnyss þey ben scarse kne hey⁵ fro þe plawnchere, and of seche⁶ holis ben made fyve. þere can non man schete owt at þem⁷ wyth no hand bowys.
15 Purry felle *in* felaschepe wyth Willyam Hasard at Querles, *and* told hym þat he wold com *and* drynk wyth Partryche *and* wyth hym, and he seyd he xuld ben welcom; *and* after none he went þedder for to aspye qhat þey dedyn *and* qhat fela-schep⁸ þey hadde wyth þem. *And* qhan he com þedder þe doris were fast sperid *and* þere were non folkis wyth hem but Maryoth
20 *and* Capron *and* his wyff *and* Querles wyf a[n]d anoþer man *in* ablac⁹ ȝede sumqhate haltyng; I sopo[se]¹⁰ be his wurdis þat it was Norfolk of Gemyng-ham. *And*¹⁰ þe seyd Purry aspyde alle þis forseyd thyngis,¹¹ and Marioth *and* his felaschep had meche grette langage þat xall ben told ȝw qhen ȝe kom hom.
25 I pray ȝw þat ȝe wyl vowche-saue to don bye for ⌜me⌝¹² j li. of almandis *and* j li. of sugyre, *and* þat ȝe wille do byen summe ⌜frese⌝¹³ to maken of

---

130. ¹ -u, -w *in this word raised; cf. no. 128 n. 1.*   ² bw *canc.*
³ -ll *crossed, as usually when final; here it may be intended for* -llis.
⁴ *Inter. above* as *canc.*   ⁵ for *canc.*   ⁶ *Apparently altered from* soche.
⁷ MS. þen.   ⁸ *Divided at line end.*
⁹ *Beginning damaged by sealing tape, not quite certain: no space after* a-.
¹⁰ he *canc.*   ¹¹ þat I haue seyd here be fore *canc.*
¹² *Interl. above* j *canc.*   ¹³ *Interl. above* fryse *canc.*

ȝwr childeris gwnys; ȝe xall haue best chepe *and* best choyse of Hayis wyf, as it[15] is told me. And þat ȝe wyld bye a[16] ȝerd of brode[17] clothe of blac for an hode fore me of xliijj d. or iiij s. a ȝerd, for ⟨per⟩[18] is n[o]there gode cloth nere god fryse in this twn. As for þe childeris gwnys, and I haue cloth I xal do hem maken.[19] The Trynyté haue ȝw jn his keping *and* send ȝw gode spede *in* alle ȝwr materis.

30

131. To John Paston I 1449, 15 February

Add. 27443, f. 105. 11½ × 16½ in. Hand of no. 128.

Dorse: Continuation of text. Remnants of red wax. Address in hand of letter:

To my rytȝ wurchipful mayster Jon Paston be þis delyueryd in hast.

The date is apparently soon after Margaret's expulsion from the 'mansion' at Gresham on 28 January 1449 (see no. 36). Sustead, about a mile from Gresham, was the property of John (of) Damme, M.P. and recorder of Norwich in 1450 and a friend of the Pastons (see, e.g., nos. 25, 35, 125); and she evidently took refuge there.

G. 78/103. C. 10 (part).

Ryt wurchipful hosbond, I recommawnd me to ȝou,[1] desyryng hertyly to heryn of ȝowr wele-fare, preyi[n]g ȝou to weten þat I commawndyd Herry Goneld to gon to Gunnore to have copys of þe pleyntys in þe hundrede. *And* Gunnore was not att hom, but þe seyd Herry spake wyth ⌐his⌐[2] clerk, *and* he told hym pleynly he wost wele his mayster wuld not late hym have 5 no copys, þow he wer att hom, tyl þe nexst hundred; qher-for I send ȝou þat byl þat was wownd abowt þe relefys. Custans Mak *and* Kentyng wold a[3] dysavowyd here swtys rytȝ fayn þe last hundred, as I herd sayn of rytȝ thryfty men; but þe Lord Moleynys men thrett hem þat bothe þey xuld ben betyn *and* lesen here hws *and* lond *and* all here goodys but if þey wold 10 avow it. *And* after þat Osborn was gon, Hasard intretyd Kentyng *and* Mak[4] to avow þe swtys after þat þey hadde disavowyd itt, *and* ȝave hem mony to ȝef to þe clerkys to entren aȝen þe pleyntys. But jf ȝe seke a remedy in hast ⌐for to remeve[5] itt⌐ I soppose þey wyl distreyn for þe mersymentys er þe nexst hundred. As for Mak, he gate respyt þat he xuld 15

---

[15] MS. is.   [16] *No space, as below.*   [17] clos *canc.*
[18] *Lost at torn corner.*
[19] *Recto ends; from* cloth *to* maken *crowded in at foot.*
131. [1] *MS.* ȝᵘ, *as throughout; but the scribe's habit has changed from No. 128 etc., in that* w *is seldom used as equivalent to* ou *or* ow, *except* hws *l. 10—cf.* ȝow *written out l. 30. The correct expansion thus seems to be* ȝou. *Similarly* ȝowr *is now rendered as in the subscription.*
[2] *Interl. above* Gunorys *canc.*   [3] *No space, as usually with* a *in this hand.*
[4] *and* ȝaf *interl. but canc.*   [5] hem *canc.*

not sew tyl þe nexst hundred. As for Herry Goneld, he was dystreynyd
ȝysterday for rent and ferm, and he must pay it to-morn, xxij s., or ell⁶ lesyn
his dystresse. þey gadder mony fast of all þe tenawntys. Al þe tenawntys
ben chargyd to pay al here rent and ferm be Fastyngong Sonday.

20   It ys told me þat þe Lord Moleynys xuld kepe his Fastyngong att Jon
Wynterys plase.⁷ The seyd lordys men haddyn a letter⁸ on Thursday last
past; qhat tydyngys þey hadde I wote nott, but on þe nexst mornnyng⁹ be
tymys Thomas¹⁰ Bampton, a man¹¹ of þe Lord Moleynys, rod wyth a letter
to his lord, and þey þat ben att Gressam waytyn after an answere of þe
25 letter in hast. Barow and Hegon and all þe Lord Moleynys men þat were
att Gressam qhan ȝe departyd hens ben there styll, save Bampton, and in
his stede is kom anothere, and I here sey þei xul abyd here styll tyl¹² here
lord kom ⟨. . .⟩¹³ to Barow as ȝe komawndyd me, to weten qhatt þe cawse
was þat þei thrett¹⁴ men ⟨. . .⟩. Goneld and other of ȝowr servawntys and
30 wele-willerys ⌐to ȝow⌐ þe qheche were namyd to hym þat were thrett
⟨. . . s⟩wore pleynly þatt þey were never thrett; but I know veryly þe
contrary, for of his own felaschep lay⟨.⟩¹⁵ in awayt sondery dayis and
nytys abowt Gunneldys, Purrys, and Bekkys plasys. And som of þem
ȝedyn in-to Bekkys and Purrys ⟨h⟩wsys,¹⁶ bothen in þe hallys and þe
35 bernys, and askyd qher þei were; and þei were answeryd þat þey were
owth, ⌐and⌐ þei seydyn aȝen þat þey xuld meten wyth hem anoþer tym.
And be dyuers oþer thyngys I know if þei mytȝ a³ ben kawt oþer þey xuld
a³ ben slayn or sore hurt.

  I sent Kateryn on þis forseyd masage, for I kowd geten no man to do
40 it, and sent wyth here Jamys Halman and Herry Holt; and sche desyryd
of Barow to have an anshere of here masage, ⌐and if þese forseyd men
mytȝ levyn in pese for hem, and seyd þer xuld ell⁶ ben purveyd other
remedy for hem⌐. And he made here grett chere, and hem þat were þere
wyth here, and seyd þat he desyryd for to speken wyth me ⌐if it xuld ben
45 non displesans to me⌐. And Kateryn seyd to hym þat sche supposyd þat
I desyryd not to speken wyth hym. And he seyd he xuld com forby þis
plase on huntyng after non, and þer xuld nomore com wyth hym but Hegon
and on of his owyn men, and þan he wold bryng seche an answere as xuld
plese me. And after none þey com hydder and sent in to me to weten if þei
50 mytȝ speken wyth me, and praying þat þei mytȝ speken wyth me; and

⁶ -ll crossed, in this word perhaps for -llis.
⁷ hys canc.   ⁸ þis canc.
⁹ First written morn, with tail of -n brought back as horizontal stroke, as commonly with
-m and -n in this hand; then nyg, with flourished g, added.
¹⁰ bāton canc.   ¹¹ þat was here canc.   ¹² þe canc.
¹³ Some words lost in three lines owing to a hole in the paper; room for ten to fifteen letters.
¹⁴ seche canc.
¹⁵ Last letter caught by the hole, and only the bottom visible; it may have been n—apparently
not d, as Gairdner suggests.
¹⁶ Beginning lost at a small hole; cf. hws l. 10.

þey abedyn styl wyth-owt3 þe 3atys, *and* I kam owth to hem *and* spak
wyth hem wyth-owt, *and* prayid hem þat þey wold hold me exkusyd[17] þat
I browth hem not in to þe plase. I seyd in as meche as þei were nott wele-
wyllyng to þe godeman of þe plase I wold not take it up-on me to bryng
hem in to þe jantylwoman. þey seyd I dede þe best, *and* þan we welk forthe 55
and desyryd an answere of hem for þat I hadde sent to hem fore. þei sayd
to me þei had browt3 me seche an answere as þei hopyd xuld plese me,
and told me how þei had comownd wyth all her felaschep of seche materis
as I had sent to hem fore, and þat þei durst under-take þat þer xud no
man ben hurt of hem þatt were rehersyd, nere noman þat longyth to 3ou 60
noþer, for hem nere non of here felaschep; *and* þat þey inswryd me be
here trowthis. Nevere lese I trest not to here promese in as meche as I fend
hem on-trew in oþer thyngys.

I conseyvyd wele be hem þat þey were wery of þat þei haden don. Barow
swor to me be his trowth þat he had lever þan xl s. *and* xl þat his lord had 65
not commawndyd hym to com to Gressam, *and* he seyd he was ryt3 sory
hidderward in as meche as he had knowleche of 3w be-fore; he was ryt3
sory of þat þat was don. I seyd to hym þat he xuld haue compascion on 3ou
and oþer þat were dissesyd of her lyvelode, in as meche as he had ben
dissesyd hym-self; *and* he seyd he was so, *and* told me þat he ⌐had⌐ sewyd 70
to my lord of Suffolk dyuers tymys, *and* wold don tyl he may gete his gode
a3en. I seyd to hym þat 3e had sewyd to my Lord Moleynys dyuers tymys
for þe maner of Gressam syth 3e wer dissesyd, *and* 3e cowd neuer gete no
resonabyl answere of hym, *and* þer-fore 3e entred a3en as 3e hopid ⌐þat⌐
was for þe best. And he seyd he xuld neuer blame my lord of Suffolk for 75
þe entré in his lyvelode, for he seyd ⌐my⌐[18] seyd lord was sett þer-up-on be
þe informacion of a fals schrew. *And* I seyd to hym in lyke wyse is þe mater
be-twyx þe Lord Moleynys *and* 3ou: I told hym I wost wele he sett neuer
þer-vp-òn be no tytyl of ryt3 þat he hadde to þe maner of Gressam, but
only be þe informacion of a fals schrew. I rehersyd no name, but me thowt 80
be hem þat þei wost ho I ment. Meche oþer langage we hadde qhyche
xuld taken long leysyr in wrytyng. I rehersyd to hem þat it xuld a be seyd
þatt I xuld not ⌐longe⌐ dwell so nere hem as I do;[19] *and* þey for-swere it,
as þei do oþer thyngys more, þat it was neuer seyd; ⌐and⌐[20] meche thyng
þat I know veryly was seyd.[21]   85

I here seyn þat 3e and Jon of Damme ben sore thrett alway, *and* seyn
þow 3e ben at London 3e xul ben met wyth there as wele as þow 3e were
here; and þer-for I pray 3ou hertyly be ware hw 3e walk þere *and* haue a

---

[17] þat *interl. but canc., above* þow þei com not *canc.*

[18] *Interl. above* þe *canc.*

[19] *The sentence has been remodelled. It was first written* I xuld not adwellyd so nere hem
as I dede*; then* longe *was interlined,* a- *and* -yd *canc., and what is apparently a smudged* o
written over the middle of dede.

[20] *Interl. above* nere *canc.*   [21] *Recto ends.*

gode felaschep w*yth* ʒou qhan ʒe xul walk owtʒ. ⌐The⌐[22] Lord Moleynys
90 hathe a cu*m*pany of brothell w*yth* hym þat rekk not qhat þey don, and
seche ar*e* most for to drede. þei[23] þat ben at Gressam seyn þat þey haue
not don so moche ⌐hurt⌐ to ʒou as þei wer*e* co*m*mawndyd to don.

Rab*er*t Laverawns is wele ame*n*dyd *and* I hope xall recure. He seyth
pleynly he wyl co*m*pleyn of his hurt, *and* I suppose Bek wyl co*m*pleyn also,
95 as he hath cause. Bek *and* Purry dar*e* not abyd att hom tyl þei her*e* oþ*er*
tydy*n*g*ys*. I wold not Jon of Da*m*me xuld com hom tyl[24] þe cu*n*tré be
storyd oþ*er*wyse þan it is. I p*r*ay Godde grawnt þat it mot sone ben
oþ*er*wyse þan it is. I pray ʒou hertyly þat ʒe wil send me w*ur*d how ʒe don
and how ʒe spede i*n* ʒowr mat*er*is, for be my trowth I kan not ben wel att
100 ese i*n* my hert, ner not xal ben, tyl I her*e* tydy*n*g*ys* hw ʒe don.

þe most part of ʒowr stuff þat was at Gressam is sold *and* ʒovyn away.
Barow *and* his felaw spak to me i*n* þe most plesaw[n]t wyse, and me semyth
be hem þei wold fayn plese me. þei seyd þei wold do me serv*y*se *and*
plesans, if it lay in her*e* powr*ys* to don owth for me, save only in þat þat[25]
105 long*yth* to her*e* lord*ys* rytʒ. I seyd to hem, as for seche serv*ys* as þey hadde
do to ʒow *and* to me I desyr*e* nomore þat þei xuld do noþ*er* to ʒow n*er* to
me. þei seyd I myt an had of hem at Gressam qhat I hadde desyryd of hem,
and had as moche as I desyryd. I seyd nay, if[26] I mytʒ an had my desyr*e* I
xuld noþ*er* a dep*ar*tid owth of þe place ner*e* from þe stuff þat was þ*er*-in.
110 þei seyd as for þe stuff, it was but esy. I seyd ʒe wold not a ʒoven þe stuff
þat was i*n* þe place qhan þei com jn not for a c li. þei seyd þe stuff þat
þei sey þere was skars w*ur*th xx li.

As for ʒowr mod*er* *and* myn, sche faryth wel, blissid be God, *and* sche
had no tydy*n*gys but gode ʒett, blissid be God.

115 The blissyd Trynyté have ʒou in his kepy*n*g *and* send ʒou helt *and* gode
spede in al ʒowr mat*er*ys. Wretyn at Sustede on þe Satyrday nexst aft*er*
Seynt Valentynys day. ⌐Here⌐[27] dare noman seyn a gode w*ur*d for ʒou i*n*
þis cu*n*tré, Godde ame*n*d it.

ʒowr*ys*, M. P.

132. To JOHN PASTON I   1449, 28 February

Add. 34888, f. 24. 11⅝×17 in. Hand of no. 128, etc., but especially like
no. 131.

Dorse: Marks of folding, soiled. Traces of red wax and stitch-holes, but
no address.

[22] *Interl. above* my *canc.*   [23] seyn *canc.*   [24] it be othe *canc.*
[25] *In margin.*   [26] I had *canc.*   [27] *Interl. above* þer *canc.*

Note in the same hand as the corresponding endorsement to f. 18 (no. 128):

litere pertinentes manerio de Gresh [broken off at lost corner].

The date is a little later than that of no. 131. Margaret had by this time left Sustead owing to rumours of threats of kidnapping, and had gone to Norwich.

G. 992/83 (abstract). C. 11 (part).

Ryt wurchypful hosbond, I recommawnd me to 3ou, desyryng hertyly to heryn of 3owr wele-fare, be-seching 3ou þat 3e be not displesyd þow I be com fro þat place þat 3e left me in; for be my trowth þer were browth me seche tydyngys be dyuerys personys qhiche ben 3owre wele-willerys and myn þat I durst no lengere abyd there, of qhyche personys I xall late 3ou have 5 wetyng qhan 3e com hom. It was done me to wete þat dyuerys of þe Lord Moleynys men[1] saydyn jf þei myt gete me þey xuld stele me and kepe me wyth-jnne þe kastell, and þan þey seyd þei wold þat 3e xuld feche me owth. An þei seydyn it xuld ben but a lytyll hert-brenny[n]g to 3ou. And after þat I herd þese tydyngys I kowd no rest have in myn hert tyl I was here,[2] 10 nere I durst nowt owt of þe place þat I was jn tyll þat I was redy to ryden; nere þer was non in þe place wist þat I xul com þens save þe godewyf not[3] an owre be-fore þat I kam þens. And I told here þat I xuld com hedder to don maken seche gere as I wold haue made for me and for þe childer, and seyd I sopposyd þat I xuld be here a fowrtennythe or iij wekys. I pray 3ou 15 þat þe caws of my komyng ⌈away⌉[4] may ben kownsell tyl I speke wyth 3ou, for þei þat lete me haue warnyng þer-of wold not for no good þat it were diskuryd.

I spac wyth 3owr modyr as I kam hidderwardys, and sche profyrd me, if 3e wold, þat I xuld abydyn in þis town. Sche wold wyth ryt3 a good 20 will þat we xul abyde in here place, and delyueryn me seche gere as sche myt for-bere, to kepen wyth hwsold tyl 3e myt3 ben purvayd of a place and stuff of 3owr owyn to kepe wyth howsold. I pray 3ou send me word be þe brynger of þis how 3e wil þat I be demenyd. I wol ben ryt3 sory to dwel so nere Gressam as I dede tyl þe mater were fully[5] determynyd be-twix þe 25 Lord Moleynis and 3ou.

Barow told me[6] that þer ware no better evydens in I[n]glond þan þe Lord Moleynys hathe of þe maner of Gressam. I told hym I sopposyd þat þei were seche evydens as Willyam Hasard seyd þat 3owr were: ⌈he seyd⌉ þe sellys of hem were not 3ett kold. I seyd I sopposyd his lordys evydens were 30 seche. I seyd I wost wele, as for 3owr evydens, þer myt3 no man haue non better þan 3e have, and I seyd þe selys of hem were to hundred 3ere elder þan he is. þe seyd Barow sayd to me if he com to London qhil 3e were there he wold drynk wyth 3ou, for any angyr þat was be-twyx 3ow. He

---

132. [1] madyn *canc.* [2] þer *canc.* [3] to *canc.*
[4] *Interl. above* awas *canc.* [5] deterny *canc.* [6] as I ka *canc.*

35 seyd he dede but as a servaw[n]t, *and* as he was commawndyd to don. Purry
xall tell ʒou qhat langage was be-twyx ⌐Barow *and* me⌐⁷ qhan I kam fro
Walsy[n]gham. I pray ʒou hertyly, at þe *reverens* of God, be ware of þe
Lord Moleynys *and* his men, þow þei speke neu*er* so fayr to ʒou trost hem
not, ⌐ne ete not ner*e* dry*n*k w*yth* hem⌐, for þei ben so fals it is not for to
40 trost i*n* hem. And also I pray ʒou be war*e* qhat ʒe eten ar dry*n*k w*yth* any
other*e* felaschep, for þe ⌐pepyll⌐¹⁸ is ful on-trosty.

I pray ʒou hertylye þat ʒe wil vowche-save to send me word how ʒe don
and how ʒe speden in ʒo*wr* mat*eris* be þe bry*n*g*er* of this. I merveyl meche
þat ʒe send me nomor*e* tydy*n*gys þan ʒe haue sent.

45 Roger*e* Foke of Sp*ar*ham sent to me *and* seythe þat he dare nott gon owt
of his hows for be kaws*e* of þe sewte þat Heydon and Wymdam haue aʒens
hem, for he is thrett þat if he may be gette he xal be ladde to preson.
Heydon sent Spendlove *and* oþ*er* to wayte qhere he wer*e*, *and* to arest hym
to þe kastell, and þe forseyd Rog*er* is so aferd þat his drede makyth hym
50 so seke þat but ⌐if⌐¹⁹ he haue sokowr sone it is lyke ⌐to⌐ ben his dethe.
Qhere-for I pray ʒou, *and* he bothyn, þat ʒe wil p*ur*vay a remedy for hym,
þat he may gon at large, for it¹⁰ hurtit bothen ʒo*wr* katel *and* hym. Ʒo*wr*
closys *and* ʒo*wr* pastowr lythe all opyn be-kawse he may not gon abrodde
to don hem amendyn, and ʒo*wr* schep ar not lokyd at as þey xuld ben for
55 þ*er* is no schepeherd but Hodgis sonys, for oþ*er* schepherd dare non abyd
þ*er* n*er* com up-on þe comown be-kause þat Wichy*n*gh*am* men thretyn hem
to bete if þei comen on her*e* komon. And but if ʒo*wr* besty*s* mown comown
þ*er* jt¹² xall ben grette hurt ⌐to⌐ hem but if þe haue mor*e* pasture þan þei
haue be-syd þatt.

60 Watkyn Schipdam recommawndyth hym to ʒou, *and* prayt ʒou þat ʒe
woll speke to Ser*e* Jon Fastolf for þe harneys þat ʒe hadden of hym, *and*
tellyn hym how it is þat som þ*er*-of is gon, and speke to hym þat þei þat
arn bownd þ*er*-for ner*e* þei þat delyu*er*yd it ben no hurt.

I haue ʒove P*ur*ry a gown; I pray ʒou take heed qhat it is and send me
65 word if ʒe wil þat I purway all ʒo*wr* leuer*e*s of þe same. þe pris of a ʒerd
þ*er*-of is xiij d. ob., and so me semyt it is wele worth.

The p*ar*son of Sp*ar*ra*m*mys dowt*er* and oþ*er* talkedyn largely, and seydyn
þat ʒe haue hadde on schote *and* but if ʒe ben war*e* ʒe xall haue more
or Estern¹³—ʒe xall for-ber*e* Sporyl *and* Sweynysthorp also but if ʒe ber*e*
70 ʒou wele, er ʒe haue do¹⁴ w*yth* þe mat*er* of Gressam. It is told me as for
Gressam þe Lord Moleynys xuld not cleym it now noþ*er* be tayl ner*e* be
evydens, but be infefment of on of his anset*eris* qhiche dyid sesy*n*nyd, and
i*n* þe same wise it is seyd þat Sweynysthorp xul¹⁵ be cleymyd. In qhat wyse
Sp⌐o⌐ryl xuld ben cleymyd I wote not; but if þ*er* be any seche thi*n*g to-ward

---

⁷ *Interl. above* us *canc.*   ⁸ *Interl. above* world *canc.*   ⁹ *Interl. above* is *canc.*
¹⁰ hortyd *canc.*   ¹¹ br *canc.*   ¹² xald *canc.*
¹³ bot *and part of* h *canc.*   ¹⁴ *MS.* de.   ¹⁵ d, *after a space, canc.*

I send 30u wor[d] here-of þat 3e may taken hede the ⟨. . .⟩¹⁶ Thomas 75
Skippi*n*g seyd qhan he kam fro London to a man þat he wend xuld not a
dis⟨kuryd⟩¹⁷ it þat þ⟨. . .⟩yke¹⁸ to for-gon þe man*er* of Sporyll w*yth*-in ryt3
schort tym. As for þe pleynt*ys* in þe ⟨hundred⟩¹⁷ Purry xa⟨ll tell⟩¹⁶ 30u
qhat is don *and* of oþ*er* thi*n*g*ys* more.

The Holy Trynyté haue 30u in his kepi*n*g. W⟨retyn at⟩¹⁷ Norwyche on 80
þe Fryday nexst af*ter* Puver Weddenysday.

133. To JOHN PASTON I   1449, 2 April

Add 27443, f. 102. 11½ × 6¼ in. Hand of no. 128.

Dorse: Traces of red wax. Address in hand of letter:

*To my ryt3 wurschipful mayst*er *Jon Paston be þis delyverid in hast, dwelli*ng
*in þe Inner*e *Tempill.*

The date is after the death of Edmond Paston I in March 1449 (see no. 80). It cannot be later than 1449, for the Duke of Suffolk is still considered powerful. He
could not have been so a year later, for he was impeached in February 1450, was
exiled, and was murdered at sea on 2 May (*D.N.B.*).
  For the friar's claim to Oxnead cf. Agnes Paston's letter no. 18.
  G. 66/87.

Ryt3 wurschipful hosbond, I reco*mm*awnd me to 30u, prayi*n*g 30u to
wete þat my kosyn Cler*e* dynyd w*yth* me þis day, *and* sche told me þat
Heydon was w*yth* her*e* 3ister*e*vyn late. *And* he told her*e* þat he had a lett*er*
from þe Lord Moleynys, *and* schewyd her*e* þe same lett*er*, prayi*n*g hym
þat he wold seyn to his frend*ys and*¹ wele-willerr*ys* in þis contré þat he 5
thank*yth* hem of her*e* godewill *and* for þat þei haue don for hym, *and*
⌐also⌐² prayi*n*g Heydon þat he wold sey to Rychard Ernold of Crowm*er*
þat he was sory³ and evyl⁴ payd þat his men maden þe afray up-on hym,
for ⌐he seyd⌐ it was not be his will þat his men xuld make afray on noman
in þis contré w*yth*-owth ryt3 grett cawse; and as for þat was don to 30u, 10
jf it myt3 ben prevyd þat he had don oþ*er*wise to 30u þan ryt3 wold as for
30wr mevabyl godis,⁵ 3e xuld ben *con*tent so þat 3e xuld haue cawse to
kon hym þank. *And* he prayd Heydon i*n* þe lett*er* þat it xuld ben reportid
in þe kontré þat he wold don so if he had don oþ*er*wyse þan he awth to don.

  The frere þat cleymyth Oxned⁶ was i*n* þis town 3ustyrday *and* þis day, 15
and was lodgid⁷ att Beris; *and* þis after-non he rod, but qhedd*er* I wote

---

¹⁶ *About six letters lost at hole.*   ¹⁷ *Letters lost at torn corner.*
¹⁸ *About eight letters lost at hole.*

133. ¹ his *canc.*
  ² *Interl. above* he, *which is evidently meant to be canc. ; praying also altered from* prayid.
  ³ for *canc.*   ⁴ *No space.*   ⁵ it *canc.*   ⁶ he *canc.*   ⁷ *MS.* ledgid.

not. He seyd pleynly in þis town þat he xal haue Oxnede, and þat he hath
my lord of Suffolkys good lordschip *and* he wol ben his good lord *in* þat
matere.[8] There was a persone warnyd my moder wyth-in þis to days þat
20 sche xuld ben ware, for þei seyd pleynly sche was lyk to ben servyd as ӡe
were servyd at Gressam wyth-in rytӡ schort tym. Also þe Lord Moleyns
wrott *in* his forseyd letter þat he wold mytyly wyth his body *and* wyth his
godis stand be all þo þat had ben his frendys[9] *and* his wel-willerys in þe
mater towchi*ng* Gressam, *and* preyd Heydon þat he[10] wold sey to þem þat
25 þei xuld not ben aferd in non wyse, for þat was don it xuld ben abedyn by.

My moder prayith ӡou þat ӡe wil send my broþer Willyam to Kawm-
brege a nomynale *and* a bok of sofystré of my broþer Emundys, þe qheche
my seyd broþer be-hestid my moder þe last tym he spak wyth her þat he
xuld a sent to my broþer Willyam.

3   þe blisseful Trinyté haue ӡou *in* his kepi*ng*. Wretyn at Norwyche *in* hast
on þe Wedenysday nexst be-fore Palm Sonday.

ӡowrys, M. P.

134. To JOHN PASTON I   Perhaps 1449

Add. 34889, f. 150. $5\frac{5}{8} \times 4$ in. Hand of no. 128.

Dorse: Continuation of text. Marks of folding, stitch-holes. Paper seal
over wax and string, but no address.

Though there is neither address nor signature this note must, from its handwriting
and contents, have been written by Margaret to her husband. This is confirmed by
the seal, which bears the fleur-de-lis commonly found on surviving seals of
Margaret's letters (e.g. nos. 130, 137, 138).

    The date is difficult to establish. The reference to a lawsuit between Wyndham
and Agnes Paston connects this note with a letter from James Gloys to John Paston
which is datable in 1451 (Part II, no. 474), but the style of the handwriting of the
present note is so like that of nos. 131–3 that it seems unlikely to be so much later.
There is no record of any appointment of Thomas Daniel which would justify the
report that he was 'made amerel'. A possible origin of the report is the grant to him
on 27 July 1449 of a commission for the safe keeping of the sea (*Cal. Pat. Rolls,
1446–52*, p. 270). See *English and Germanic Studies*, iv (1951–2), 57–8.

    G. XXI/165.

I prey ӡou if ӡe haue any old gownys for lyny*ng*ys *and* old schetys *and* old
schertis þat may non le*ng*ere se[r]ven ӡou, I prey ӡou send hem hom in hast,
for I must okupye seche thy*ng*ys in hast. Wymdam hath medyd[1] þe
jvryorys ⌐*and* ӡaf hem mony⌐ þat[2] xuld passe on þe qwhest be-twyn ӡowr
50 modyr[3] *and* hym. If þer myt ben purveyd any mene þat it myt ben dasched

---

[8] M *canc.*   [9] in *canc.*   [10] wor *canc.*

134. [1] his *canc., and following* þ *corr. from* j.   [2] ӡ *canc.*
     [3] *First written with tailed* d, *representing* -er; *then* yr *added.*

in cas were þat⁴ it xuld passe aȝens ȝowr moder it were a good sport, for þan he wold ben wode. He sent wyth his men to þe afray iij gunnys, in very trowth. I haue jnquiryd veryly þer-after. He is wode wroth þat Danyel is amrel, for it is told me þat on of his men is indytyd in þe amrellys cort sythyn þat Danyel was made amerel. 10

I pray ȝou beware in qhat felaschep ȝe ryd⁵ qhan ȝe com homward, for þer gon many fals shrewys ⌈and thevys⌉ in þe contré.⁶ Thomas Skippyng rod to Londonward on Fryday last past in gret hast, *and* purposyd hym for to ben at London on Sonday be none on erundys of his maysterrys. Qhat þe cawse is I wote nott. On sent me wurd here-of þat knowyth ⌈it for⌉⁷ 15 trowth.

135. To JOHN PASTON I Probably 1449, 9 May

Add. 34888, f. 215. 11½ × 11 in. Hand of no. 128, but especially like no. 136.

Dorse: Traces of red wax. Address in hand of letter:

To my rytȝ wurchepfull mayster Jon Paston in hast.

Dating is difficult, partly because there is no record of any 'Fynys' ever being Speaker. Gairdner suggests that John Say, who was Speaker in 1463, may have been a relation of William Fenys, Lord Say. This was evidently not so (J. C. Wedgwood, *History of Parliament, Biographies* (1936), pp. 744–6), but Margaret may have confused the names. But this hand is found nowhere else later than 1454, and in details of style and language this letter is closest to no. 136, so that 1463 is much too late. The same John Say was Speaker in 1449 also (*Rot. Parl.* v. 141), and the Duke of Suffolk's patronage might still be of value in that year (see no. 133).

Crouchmas is the feast of the Invention of the Cross, 3 May, not the Exaltation of the Cross, 14 September.

F. iv, p. 188. G. 472/544.

Ryt wurschipfull hosbond, I recommand me to ȝou, desyrjng hertyly to here of ȝowr wellfare, prayi[n]g ȝou to wete þat I haue spoken wyth Strawngys wyf of þe mater þat ȝe spoken to me of. And sche seyth pleynly to me, be here feyth, þat sche knew neuer non seche ner never herd of non scheche; *and* told to me in lyk wyse as sche had seyd to Jamys Gloys. And sche seyd 5 to me if sche kowd jnquire of any oþer þat sche þingkyth xuld haue knowleche of any seche sche xuld wetyn of hem *and* letyn me haue knowleche þer-of. And¹ jf ȝe soppose þat any oþer be jn þis contré þat ye² thyng xuld haue knowleche of þis forseyd mater, if ye wyll send me word there-of I xall do my part there-in. Also, I haue ben att Sweynysthorp *and* spoken 10

---

⁴ if *canc.* ⁵ wyth *canc.* ⁶ *Recto ends.* ⁷ *Interl. above* þe *canc.*
135. ¹ also *canc.*
² *All cases of initial* y- *in this letter are written* þ *; see next note.*

wyth Kokett, *and* he seyth þat he woll don lyche as ȝe³ bad me þat I xuld
sey to hym for to don. And I haue spokyn wyth þe sexteyn *and* seyd to hym
as ye bad me that I xuld don, *and* he axid me ryt feythfully hw ye sped jn
ȝowr materys. I told him þat ȝe haddyn fayre be-hestys, *and* I seyd I hopyd
15 þat ȝe xuld don rytȝ well þer-jn; and he seyd he supposyd þat D. wold don
for ȝou, but he seyd he was no ⌐hasty⌐¹⁴ laborere jn non mater. He seyd be
hys feyth he wost qhere a man was þat laboryd to hym for a mater ryth a
long tym, *and* alwey he be-hestyd þat he wold labore itt effectualy, but
qhyll he sewyd to hym he kowd never haue remedy of his mater; *and* than,
20 qhan he þowth þat he xuld no remedy haue to sew to hym, he spak wyth
Fynys þat is now Speker of þe Parlment, *and* prayid hym þat he wold don
for hym jn his mater, *and* ȝaf hym a reward, and wyth-jnne ryth schort
tym after his mater was sped. *And* þe seyd sexteyn⁵ *and* oþer folkys þat ben
yowre ryth wele willerys ⌐haue⌐ kownselyd me þat I xuld kownsell ȝou to
25 maken oþer menys þan ye haue made to other folkys þat wold spede yowr
materys better þan ⌐they⌐¹⁶ haue don þatt ye haue spoken to þer-of be-for
this tym. Sondery folkys haue seyd to me that they þynk veryly but if ȝe³
haue my lord of Suffolkys godelorchyp qhyll þe werd is as itt is ye kan
neuer leven jn pese wyth-owth ye haue his godelordschep. Therfor I pray
30 you wyth all myn herth þat ye wyll don yowre part to haue hys godelordschep *and* his⁷ love jn ese of all the⁸ materis that ye haue to don, *and* jn
esyng of myn hert⁹ also. For be my trowth I am afferd ellys ⌐bothen⌐ of
these matery[s] the qhyche ye haue jn hand now, *and* of othere that ben
not don to yett but if he ⌐wyl don for ȝou and⌐ be yowr godelord.
35 I pray ȝow³ hertylye send me word how ȝe don *and* how ye speden jn
ȝowr materys; *and* I pray you, as for seche thyngys as Jamys hath a byll of,
þat I may haue hem as hastyly as ȝe³ may, *and* þat ȝe wyll vowchesave to
bey a pese of blak bukram for to lyn wyth a gown for me. I xuld bey me a
murrey gown to gon in¹⁰ this somer, *and* leyn in the kolere the satyn þat ȝe¹¹
40 ȝeve me for an hodde, *and* I kan gettyn non gode bokeram jn þis town to
lyn it wyth.

The Holy Trinyté haue yow in his kepyng *and* send ȝou helth *and* good
spede in all yowre materis. Wretyn att Norwyche on þe Fryday nexst after
Crowchemesse Day.

45   ȝowrys, M. P.

³ ȝ *corrected from* þ *by addition of small tick.*   ⁴ *Interl. above* sadde *canc.*
⁵ kownseylyd me *canc.*
⁶ *Interl. above* othere folkys *canc.*
⁷ *Some four letters, apparently* gode, *heavily canc.*   ⁸ reme *canc.*
⁹ *Several letters, apparently beginning* there, *canc.*
¹⁰ þis *canc.*   ¹¹ þaf *canc.*

136. To John Paston I   1450, 12 March

Add 43488, f. 11. 11⅝×8¾ in. Hand of no. 128.

Dorse: Traces of red wax. Address in hand of letter:

To my ryt3 worchypful maystyr Jon Paston be this delyveryd in hast.

The date is fixed by the report that 'the Duke of Suffolk is pardoned'. This was not accurate, but it was true that after Suffolk's impeachment in February 1450 he submitted himself to the King's mercy, and instead of being sent for trial by his peers he was exiled for five years (*D.N.B.*).

F. i, p. 28. G. 81/106 (part). C. 13 (part).

Ryt3 worchipful hosbond, I recommawnd me to 3ow, desyring hertyly to here of 3owr well¹-fare, thankyng for þe letter þat 3e sent to me, praying 3ow to wete þat I haue sent Henry to Maltby þis weke to do seche thyngys as 3e commaw[n]dyd in 3owr letter. *And* as towching þe dyche a3ens the maner gate,² 3owr tenawntys haue nere made itt as 3e desyryd þat it shuld 5 ben made qhan 3e were þere, *and* it is made up-on þe old dyche. *And* as for mony, I cowd haue þer at þis tym butt xxj s. viij d. And as for the flete, þe man is not in þis contré þat shuld make itt. 3ow[r] tenawntys *and* oþer men seyn þat³ it shal ben als gode makyng þer-of after Estern as it shuld ben be-fore Estern.   10

I have spoke to Jon of Damme to do as 3e sent me word in 3owr letter, *and* he seyth he wol don his part as 3owr desyre is wyth all his hert. Jamys Gloys was in þat contré sythyn he kom from London, *and* he spak wyth Henry Goneld; *and* þe seyd Henry told hym þat he herd seyn þat Partriche hath⁴ sent a lettyr to þe lym-brennere byddyng hym þat he shuld fell þe 15 rede att Gressam, *and* so it is fellyd *and* karyid to Mariottys plase att Bekkam. And þe seyd Henry seyth how it is seyd in Gressam that Partryche sent hom word þat he⁵ shuld not com hom tyl he com wyth his lord, *and* þat he seyd shuld ben wyth-jnne short tym,⁶ ⌈and þat⌉ he shuld ben lodgyd at Jon Wynterys plase. And as for Capron, he dwellyth styl in 20 Gressam, *and* he seyth, *and* oþer þat ben a3ens 3ow,⁷ thow 3e entre in-to þe manere þat 3e shul nevyre haue it ⌈long⌉ in pesebyl wyse.

Wyllyam Butt, the whiche is wyth Sere Jon Hevenyngham, kom hom from London 3esterday, *and* he seyd pleynly to his mayster *and* to many othere folkys þat the Duke of Suffolk is pardonyd *and* hath his men a3en 25 waytyng up-on hym, *and* is ryt3 wel at ese *and* mery, *and* is in the Kyngys godegrase *and* in þe gode conseyt of all þe lordys as well as ever he was.

There ben many enmys a3ens 3ermowth *and* Crowmere, *and* haue don moche harm *and* taken many Englysch-men *and* put hem in grett destresse *and* grettely rawnsommyd hem, *and* the seyd enmys ben so bolde that they 30

---

136. ¹ ful *canc.*   ² it is *canc.*   ³ is *canc.*   ⁴ send *canc.*   ⁵ shud *canc.*
⁶ *and* he shuld þe tym þat he shuld ben in þis contré *canc.*   ⁷ þat *canc.*

kom vp[8] to þe lond *and* pleyn hem on Cast*er* sond*ys and* in othere plas*es*[9] as homely as they were Englysch-men. Folk*ys* ben ryt3 sore aferd þ*at* they wol don moche harm þ*is* som*er* but if þ*er* be made ryt3 grett purvyans a3ens hem. Othere tydy*ng*ys know I non att þis tym.

35 The blysseful Trinyté haue 3ow in his kepy*ng*. Wretyn at Norwyche on Seynt Gregorys Day.

3owr*ys*, M. P.

137. To John Paston I 1451, 3 March

Add. 34888, f. 64. 8⅝ × 3¾ in. Hand of no. 128.

Dorse: Paper seal over wax and string. Address in hand of letter:

To my rith wurshepfull hosbond Jon Paston.

The date appears from the reference to Tuddenham and Heydon. A memorandum by William Worcester (Add. 27443, f. 108, abstract in G. 92/119) records a commission of *oyer and terminer* dated 1 August 28 Henry VI (1450) (cf. John Paston I's letter no. 39) which held sessions in Norfolk on various dates from 17 September 1450 to 3 May 1451, including one at Norwich on 2 March. A letter from Fastolf to Thomas Howes dated 20 December 1450 (Add. 27443, f. 118, G. 132/162) says that Tuddenham and Heydon are to appear before it.

F. iii, p. 288. G. 148/180.

Rith worchipfull hosbond, I reco*m*mawnd me to yow,[1] prey*i*ng you to wete that there is a gret noyse in þis town þ*at* my lord of Oxforth *and* Yelv*er*ton *and* ye ben endytid in Kent for mayntenyng of þe oyrdet*er*myn*er, and* Jon Da*m*me is endytyd þere also of treson[2] be-cawse þ*at* he dede Heydon

5 endytyn ⌈of treson⌉[3] for takyng down of þe quart*er* of the man. And the pepyll ⌈þ*at*⌉ ben ⌈ayens Sere Thomas Todenham⌉[4] *and* Heydon ben sore aferd be-cawse of þis noyse *and* of oþer langage that is had boþe in þis town *and* in þe contré þ*at* þese seyd Todenham *and* Heydon shuld ben as well at ese *and* haue as grett rewill as eu*er* they hadde. Jamys Gloys tellith me

10 þat he hath sent yow word of Heydonys hors, *and* of oþer thyng*ys* more, of whiche I was ⌈purposid⌉[5] to a[6] sent yow[7] word of.

The Holy Trinyté have yow in kepyng. Wretyn at Norwiche the Weddenysday next aft*er* Seynt Mathy.

Yowr*is*, M. P.

[8] on Cast*er canc.*
[9] *Ending abbr. by long* s *crossed, as if for* -ser.

137. [1] *Initial* y- *in form of* þ *throughout, and also medial* -y- *in* ayens *l.* 6.
[2] for that Heydon *canc.* [3] *Interl. in another hand, perhaps Gloys's.*
[4] *Interl. above* sore aferd be cawse *canc.*
[5] *Interl. above* avysid *canc.* [6] *No space.*
[7] of *canc.*

138. To John Paston I   1451, 15 March

Add. 34888, f. 55. 12×7¼ in. Hand of no. 128.

Dorse: Paper seal over wax and string. Address in hand of letter:

To myn ryth worshipfull hosbond Jon Paston.

The date appears, from the account of rumours of Tuddenham's and Heydon's renewed power, to be close to that of no. 137. Handwriting and linguistic forms support this.

G. XXVII/182.

Rith wurchipfull hosbond, I recommawnd me to yow[1], desiring hertily to here of yowre welfare, preying yow to wete that Herry Halmannys wyf sent to me word on Saturday last past that Prentys thretyth here hosbond sore, *and* Jon Robynys, for seche thingys as Prentys seyth þat þey haue don ayens hym. He seyth he shall make hem so besy or he leve hem that he shall[2]   5 make hem not wurth a peny, *and* they ben aferd þat he woll hold hem connawnt if he have powyre there-to.

It is seyd here þat the Kyng shuld com in-to this contré, *and* Ser Thomas Todenham *and* Heydon arn well cheryshid wyth hym; and also it is seyd they shall have as grett rewill in þis contré as evyre they hadde, *and* many   10 more folkys arn sory þerfore than mery. Ser Thomas Todenhamys men *and* Heydonys sowyn this sedde all abowte þe contré, þat here maysteris shull cum hom in hast in here prosperité *and* be als well att ese as euer they were.

As for that ye desyryd þat I shuld enquyre where any stuff is of yowrys,   15 I wot not how to don þer-wyth, for if on were aspyid þat hath of yowr stuff, *and* we had it from hym, oþer þat have more þer-of wold ben ware be hym *and* avoyd seche stuff as they have of yowris. I suppose Jon Osbern shall tell yow whan ye com hom a gode meen to wete where meche þerof is becom.   20

Jamys Gloys is ayen to Gressam, *and* I suppose Jon Damme shall tell yow what he hath don there. Yowre tenawntys wold fayn þat summe ⌈mene⌉[3] of yowris shuld abyde amongis hem, for they ben in gred diswyre what they may do, the langage is so grett on the toþer party that it makyth þe tenawntys sore afferd that ye shuld not regoyse itt. I send to yow a letter   25 be Colynys of Frawnceys Costard, what dedis he woll don. It was told me also that the Lord Molyns was lyke to have a day ayens yow att Thetford at the next assyse. On þat louyth yow ryth[4] well told me how it was told hym so, *and* warnyd me þerof in secrete wyse. Itt is gode to ben ware of there falsed.[5]   30

138. [1] *Initial* y- *in form of* þ *throughout, and medial* -y- *in* ayens *as l. 5.*
   [2] not *canc.*   [3] *Interl. above* man *canc.*   [4] *No space.*
   [5] that is *canc.*

I pray yow þat ye woll send me word in hast if ye woll have red to yowr levery as ye were avysid, *and* if ye woll not, &c. And also I pray yow þat ye woll do bey ij gode hattis for yowr sonys, for I can none getyn in þis town.

More tydyngys can I not send[6] yow yett.

35 The Holy Trinyté have yow in his kepyng. Wretyn att Norwiche on þe fyrst Monday of Lent.

Yowrys, M. P.

139. To JOHN PASTON I   1451, 30 March

Add. 27444, f. 5. $11\frac{3}{4} \times 5\frac{3}{4}$ in. Hand of James Gloys.

Dorse: Paper seal over wax and tape. Address in Gloys's hand:

To my right wurchepfull husbond John Paston, beyng in the Innere Tempill, be this deliuered in hast.

The year appears from the reference to Tuddenham and Heydon to be the same as that of nos. 137 and 138.
     G. 150/184.

Right wurchepfull husbond,[1] I recomaund me to you, prayng you to wete that myn vnkyll Phylyp Berney was at Lynne this last weke. And he was at jnne at the balyffes hows of Lynne, *and* Partrych came in-to the same place whill myn vnkyll was there. And the seid Partrych was wele aqueyn-
5 tyd with the balyffe, and the balyffe told hym that he sent a letter to the Lord Molyns, *and* that the Lord Molyns had sent hym a-nothere letter letyng him wete that he purposyd hym to be[2] at Lynne thes weke. Than Partrych seid that he had word that thes[3] seid lord purposyd hym to be there at that tyme, but he said summe men supposyd that he wuld not come
10 here; and the balyffe seid that he was right glad that he shuld come in-to this contré. On of myn vnkyll men herd all this langage *and* told it myn vnkill. The baly nere Partrych knewe not at that tyme what myn vnkyll was to vs ward.

Also, I purposyd me to haue sent to Stapylton as ye sent me word be
15 James Gresham, and it is told me that he is to London.

Item, it is noysed a-bowte Gresham *and* all that contré that the Lord Molyns shuld be there in hast.

Item, Gonnore had right gret langage, *and* he trostyd that the word shall turne sumwhat after there entent. Othre tydynges haue we non but that

---

     [6] to *canc.*

139. [1] *Dotted circumflex above the second syllable, apparently without significance. Similar marks above* n *of* letyng, *l.* 7, contré, *l.* 11, *and* Sonday *l.* 23, *and above* p *of* Phylyp *l.* 2. *These marks are especially frequent in Gloys's earlier letters.*

    [2] with *canc.*   [3] *From* he.

Tudenham *and* Heydon shuld haue a-geyn the rewle in this contré assmych 20
as eu*er* thei had, or more.

The Holy Trynyté haue you in kepyng. Wretyn at Norwhich vn the
Tuesday next be-for*e* Mydlente Sonday.

Yowr*e* M. P.

140. To JOHN PASTON I Probably 1451, 3 June

Add. 34888, f. 72. 11⅝×6⅜ in. Hand of no. 128.

Dorse: Traces of red wax. Address in hand of letter:

To my rygth worshipfull hosbond John Paston be þis delyverid in hast.

The date is shown to be later than 1450 by two references: Thomas Daniel's entry
into 'Brayston' (now Bradeston) is known from William Worcester's memorandum
mentioned in the headnote to no. 137 to have occurred in that year; and Lady
Boys's management of her own estates implies that her son Robert, heir to his father
and elder brother, was already dead—he died in December 1450 (Blomefield, xi.
43; *Norwich Wills*, i. 55; Letter from Sir John Fastolf to Thomas Howes of 20
December 1450, MS. Add. 27443, f. 118, G. 132/162). But the Bradeston incident
does not sound very remote; and the style of the writing, in this variable and
quickly developing hand, is so strikingly close to that of no. 141 that it is likely to be
only a month earlier rather than nearly a year later.

F. iii, p. 424. G. 163/197.

Rygth wurchipfull hosbond, I reco*m*mawnd me to yow,[1] desyri*n*g hertyly
to her*e* of yo*w*r welfare, preying yow to wete that itt was told me þis weke
that þer is a[2] fayr*e* plase to sell in Seynt Laveransis parysch, *and* stant ner*e*
the chirche *and* by þe water*e* syde, þe whiche place Toppis hath to sell.
⌜Pyte⌝, a[2] lyster*e*, bowgth itt of Toppis, *and* now for defawt of payme*n*t 5
Toppis hath enterid ayen þer-inne and shall selle itt in hast, as it is told me.
The seyd lyster*e* dwellyth þer-inne at þis tym, but he shall owte, for he is
hald rygth a pore man. I suppose if ye lyke to bye itt when ye com hom ye
shall mou have itt of Toppis als gode[2] chepe or better*e* than anoþer shuld.

Als for tydyng*ys*, we have none gode in þis contré; I p*ra*y God send us 10
gode. Itt was told me that Rychard Sowthwell[3] hath enterid in þe maner*e*
of Hale, þe whiche is þe Lady Boysys, *and* kepyth itt w*yth* strength w*yth*
seche another*e* felashep as hath be att[4] Brayston, *and* wastyth *and* dispoy-
lyth all þat þer is. And þe Lady Boys, as it is told me, is to London to con-
pleyn to þe Kyng *and* to þe lordys there-of. Itt semyth it was not for nowgth 15
þat he held w*yth* Charlys *and* his felashep.

I prey yow þat ye wol vowchesawf to speke to Jamys Gloys to bye þe
vngwentum album þat I spake to hym for*e*, and þat ye woll rememb*re* yo*w*r

140. [1] *Initial* y- *in form of* þ *throughout, and medial* -y- *in* ayens *l. 6.*
[2] *No space.*   [3] -h- *crowded in.*   [4] Bl *canc.*

fayre dowgteris gyrdyl. I hope ye shull be at hom so sone that I woll do
20 wryte nomore tydyngys to yow.

The blyssid Trinyté have yow in his keping and send yow gode spede
in all þat ye woll spede well inne. Wretyn at Norwyche on þe Ascencion
Day.

Yowris, M. P.

141. To John Paston I   1451, 1 July

Add. 34888, f. 74. 11⅝ × 8½ in. Hand of no. 128.

Dorse: Remnants of red wax over string. Address in hand of letter:

To my rygth worshypfull hosbond Jon Paston be this deiyveryd in hast.

Also a hastily written and partly illegible Latin note, apparently in John
Paston's hand, which seems unconnected with the subjects of the letter.

The date is fixed by the report of the death of Sir Henry Inglose. He died on 1 July
1451 (*Inq. p.m.*, 29 Henry VI, no. 9), and his will, dated 20 June, was proved on
4 July the same year (*Norwich Wills*, ii. 214).
    F. iii, p. 124. G. 167/201.

Rygth worchypfull hosbond, I recommawnd me to yow,[1] desyryng hertyly
to here of yowre wellfare, preying yow to wete that I have spoke wyth my
Lady Felbrygg of that ye bad me speke to here of. And she seyd[2] pleynly
to me that she wold not ne nevyr was avysyd[3] noþer to lete þe Lord Moleyns
5 ne non oþer to[4] have ther intentys as for þat mater whyll þat she levyth.
And she was rygth evyll payd wyth Sawtre that he shuld reporte as[5] itt was
told yow þat he shuld have reportyd, and she made rygth moche of yow
and seyd þat she wold nowgth þat no servaw[n]te of herys shuld reporte no
thyng þat shuld be ayens yow oþerwyse þan she wolld þat yowr servawntys
10 shud do ⌐or⌐[6] seyn ayens here. And jf oþer yowr servawntys[7] dede ayens
here, or any of here ayens yow, she wold þat itt shuld be reformyd be-twyx
yow *and* here, and þat ye mygth ben all on, for she seyd in[8] good[8] feyth she
desyryth yowr frendshep. And as for þe report of Sawtre, she seyd she
supposyd þat he wold nowgth reporte so; and if she mygth know þat he
15 dede she wold blame hym þer-fore. I told here þat itt was told me syth þat
ye reden, *and* þat itt grevyd me more þat þe seyd Sawtre shuld reporte as
he dede þan itt had be reportyd of anoþer, in als moche as I had awgth

141. [1] *Initial* y- *in form of* þ *throughout, and medial* -y- *in* ayens.
    [2] *Crowded into small space on eras.*   [3] *that the canc.*
    [4] *Crowded in later.*   [5] *he de canc.*   [6] *Interl. above ampersand canc.*
    [7] *of canc.*   [8] *No space.*

hym goodwyll befor*e*. And she pr*a*yid me þat I shud not beleve seche
report*y*s tyll I knew the trowth.[9]

I was at Toppys att dyner*e* on Seynt[10] Peter*y*s Day. There my Lady 20
Felbrygg *and* oþer jantyll-women desyryd to have hadde yow ther*e*; they
seyd they shuld all a[8] be þe meryer*e* if ye hadde ben ther*e*. My cosyn Toppys hath moche car*e* tyll she her*e* goode tydyng*y*s of her*e* broþeris mat*er*.
Sche told me þat þer shuld kepte a day on Monday next komy*n*g be-twyx
her*e* broþ*er and* Ser*e*[11] Andrew Hugard *and* Wymdh*a*m. I pr*a*y yow send 25
me word how they spede *and* how ye spede in yowr*e* owyn mat*er*ys also.

Also, I pr*a*y yow hertyley that ye woll send me a potte w*y*th triacle in
hast, for I have ben rygth evyll att ese, *and* yo*w*r dowghter*e* boþe, syth þat
ye yeden hens. *And* on of þe tallest you*n*ge men of þis parysch lyth syke
and hath a grette myrre; how he shall do God knowyth. I have sent myn 30
vnkyll Berney the potte w*y*th triacle þat ye dede bey for hym. Myn awnte
recom*m*awnd*y*th her*e* to yow *and* pr*a*yith yow to do for*e* her*e* as the byll
mak*y*th menc*i*on of that I send yow w*y*th this lett*er*, *and* as ye thynk best
for[12] to do þ*er*-inne.[13]

Ser Herry Inglose is passyd to God this nygth, hoys sowle God asoyll, 35
and was caryid forþ[14] this day at ix of þe clok to Seynt Feyþis, *and* there
shall be beryid. If ye desyer to bey any of hys stuff I pr*a*y yo*u* send me word
þ*er*-of in hast, *and* I shall speke to Robe*r*t Inglose *and* to Wychyngh*a*m
þ*er*-of. I suppose þei ben executor*y*s.

The blyssyd Trinyté have yo*u* in his kepy*n*g. Wretyn att Norwyche in 40
hast on þe Thursday next aft*er* Seynt Pet*er*.

Yowr*y*s, M. P.

I pr*a*y yow trost nott to þe sheryve for no fayr*e* langage.[15]

142. To JOHN PASTON I   Probably 1451, 6 July

Add. 34888, f. 84. Written on about three-quarters of a sheet originally
$8\frac{3}{4} \times 9\frac{1}{2}$ in. The lower right-hand quarter has been cut away before the
letter was written, so that the right-hand side is only $5\frac{1}{2}$ in. long instead of
$9\frac{1}{2}$ in. Hand of no. 128.

Dorse: Traces of red wax. Address in hand of letter:

To my rygth wurchipfful hosbond John Paston be þis delyverid in hast.

The date seems likely, from Margaret's repeated request for a girdle for their
daughter, to be close to that of no. 140. The style of the writing is very like that of

---

[9] *Rest of this line and following seven lines written much smaller and more closely spaced,
with a finer pen.*   [10] pt *with curl above canc.*
[11] and here *canc.*   [12] do *canc.*   [13] *From this point the writing larger again.*
[14] *First written* fore (*flourished* r), *then* þ *written over the flourish.*
[15] *Postscript crowded in at foot.*

nos. 140 and 141. Since St. Margaret's Day (20 July) is not far ahead (l. 5) St. Thomas's Day must be 7 July; cf. nos. 127, 160.

For Roger Church of Burlingham see John Paston's complaints in no. 40 and related documents of April 1452. Gairdner would date the present letter after rather than before those, but in handwriting and some details of spelling its affinities are especially with no. 141, the date of which is fixed.

F. iv, p. 14. G. 178/216.

Ryth worshipfull hosbond, I recommawnd me to yow,[1] desyryng hertyly to here of yowr welfare, praying yow þat ye woll send me word in hast how ye be agreid wyth Wychyngham and Inglose for þat mater that ye spake to me of at yowr departyng; for if I shuld purvey oþer wood or hey it shuld
5 be bowgth best chepe be-twyx þis and Seynt Margretys masse, as itt is told me. As for Applyard, he com not yett to this town syn he com from London. I have sent to Ser Bryse to lete me have knowleche when he comyth to town, and he hath promysid þat I shall have knowleche; and when he comyth I shall do yowr commawndement.
10 My moder bad me send yow word þat Waron Herman hath dayly fyshid hyre watere all þis yer, and þerfor she prayith yow to do þer-for whill ye be att London as ye thynk best. Chyrche of Byrlyngham was take and browte to þe castell yisterday be þe Beshopys men, and ┌all┐ his godys ben seysid for þat he owyth to þe Boshop. And þe seid Chirche seyth as for þat he
15 hath seyd of hem þat he hath appelyd before þis tym, he woll ┌awow itt and┐ abyd þerby; and seyth þat he woll appele on þat hath more nobelys þan they have all þat he hath spoke of yett, and þat shall avayll þe Kyng mor þan þey have all þat he hath speke of yett; but whatt he is he woll not name tyll he know more. I trow but if þer be the gretter labowr made ayens hym
20 he is lyke to have grett favowr of hem þat have be his supportorys. Men thenk þat have spoke wyth hym þat he hopyth to haue good helpe.

I pray God that þe trowth mote be knowyn.

I pray yow þat ye woll vowchesaff to send me an oþer sugowr loff, for my old is do. And also þat ye well do make a gyrdill for yowr dowgtere,[2] for
25 she hath nede þer-of.

The blyssid Trinyté have yow in his kepyng. Wretyn at Norwyche in hast on þe Tewysday next before Seynt Thomas Day.

Yowrys, M. P.

Paper is deynty.

142. [1] *Initial* y- *in form of* þ *throughout, and medial* -y- *in* ayens.
[2] that *canc.*

143. To JOHN PASTON I   Probably 1452, 21 April

Add. 34888, f. 66. 8½×7½ in. Gloys's hand.

Dorse: Paper seal over wax and string, stitch holes. No address.

The date is not quite clear. John Paston I was found by the inquisition *post mortem* on his father in November 1444 (23 Henry VI, no. 3) to be 23 years old and Gairdner accordingly dates this letter 16 April 1451. But 'upon the age of xxx winter' (l. 9) could well mean 'just thirty' rather than 'not quite thirty'. 1452 is the more likely year because in 1451 St. George's Day was Good Friday, and it would be surprising if Margaret chose to date her letter by St. George's Day, a week ahead, rather than by Palm Sunday. (In 1452 Easter Day was 9 April.)

F. iii, p. 84. G. 153/187 (part).

Right wurchepfull howsbond, I recomand me to yow, *pr*ayng yow to wete that the *p*arson of Oxened told me that Wymdham told hym that Sweyn-nysthorp is hold of the Kyng be the thred *p*art or the fourt *p*art of a knyt fye; *and*[1] ho so eu*er* had the man*er* of Sweynsthorp, he shuld fynde an armyd man in tyme of werre in the Castell of Norwhic[2] xl days to his owyn 5 cost, *and* that ye shuld pay xxx s. to the Kyng yerly owth of the seyd man*er*; *and*[3] it is fond also that yo*ur* fad*er* shuld a died seysyd, *and*that ye shuld a entyrryd ther-in as heyre aft*er* yo*ur* fad*er* dysseys *and* that ye shuld be now vp-on the age of xxx wynt*er*. It semyth be that he seyd that he is preuy[4] to ⌜the seyd mater*e*⌝. Also the seyd Wymdham seyd to the seyd 10 *p*arson that the Kyng hath yovyn it[5] to the Provost of Eton. I suppose that it myth not be gra*u*nted so hastyly aft*er* that it was seysyd.

It is seyd here that it is lyke that there shall be mad more affrays at Lynne w*yth*-in short tyme. I herd sey that Bosvyle cam in-to Lynne w*yth*-in this vij ny3t *and* mad affray vp-on a man of Lynne *and* yaffe hym a 15 buffette, *and* ⌜that⌝ shall t*ur*ne to non esse or aft*er*. In gode feyth I here no man sey but that Bosvyle is ⌜right⌝ a mysgouernyd yong man, *and* he hath many word*es* myth wele be left. I suppose but if his mayst*er* voyd hym he shall repente hym be-cause of his mysgou[ern]auns w*yth*-in short tyme. His mayst*er* hath[6] many moo elmyes than he shuld haue be-cause of his 20 mysgou*er*nauns. I wold fayn that ye myth conceyle hym that he myth a-voyd hym[7] assone as he myth w*yth* his wurchep, for he shall ell repent hym.

The Trinité haue yow in his kepy*ng*. Writen at Norwhic[2] the Friday next a-fore Seynt George.   25

Yow*res*, M. PASTON

---

143. [1] that y *canc.*

[3] that *canc.*   [4] there *canc.*   [5] *Crowded in.*

[6] the *canc.*   [2] *Curl on -c, significance doubtful.*

[7] *In margin, before* asso *canc.*

144. To JOHN PASTON I Probably 1452, 5 November

Add. 34888, f. 85. 11½×8 in. Hand unidentified, found also in part of
John Paston I's petition no. 40 and letter no. 45.

Dorse: Continuation of text. Traces of red wax. Address in hand of letter.

To my right worchepful husbond John Paston be this delyverid in hast.

Philip Berney of Reedham died in July 1453 (see Agnes Paston's letter no. 26), and
this letter probably refers to his last illness.
F. iii, p. 168. G. 182/221 (part).

Right worchepful husbond, I comaund me to yow, desieryng hertely to
here of your welfare,[1] praying yow to wete that, as for your werk at Mauteby,
it is not lyke that there shal nomore be made there-of this yer but the gabels
of the chambere and the chapel wyndows, and the reder hath don wel hese
5 part to the halle. As for the lytel hows that ye wrete to me for, my vncle
and Ser Thomas sey it is not for your a-vayle for to have werkmen vn it[2]
tyl wyntere be passid. The masons faylyd tyle more than fortenyght
aftyre[3] that I cam thens. And as for ⌐men of⌐ Sparham, they wer not
recompensid[4] the last weke ⌐for her comon as the master promysid yow⌐,
10 as Folcard sent me word; for I sent to Folcard for to know the trowght.[5]

My vncle Phelyppe comaund hym to yow, and he hath be so seke sith
that I come to Redham that I wend he shuld never an[6] askapid it, nor not is
leke to do but if he have redy help; and therfor he shal into Suffolk this
next weke to myn aunt, for there is a good fesician and he shal loke to hym.
15 I cam to Norwiche vn Sowlemesday, and I shal[7] abyde in Talvas place tyl
ye come hom; but as for yowre being there when ye come hom, the howses
be to smale[8] for your men *and* your hors, and therfore ye had nede come
hom the soner to purvey yow of a-nodyre place. And as for stuff of howsold,
I can non bye at Inglos nor in non odyre place yet; and as for mony, it
20 cometh slauly jn. Gerrardys wyff is deed, and there is a fayre place of hers
to selle in Sent Gregorys parysh, as it is told me. I suppose if ye leke to bye
it ye shuld have it worth the mony.

There is falle a gret debate be-twen Heydon *and* Wymondham, as ye
shal here aftyre this; in good feyth, if it be trewe that my Lady Hastynges[9]
25 ⌐and other⌐ report, Heydon hath falsly deseyved hym after that he trustyd
hym. Also, my Lady Hastynges told me that Heydon hath spoke to Geffrey
Boleyn of London, and is a-greid wytht hym that he shuld bargeyn wyth
Ser John Fastolff to bye the maner of Blyklyng as it were for hym-selff, and

---

144. [1] and *canc.* [2] this wynter *canc.*
[3] -re *repr. by flourish on tail of* y, *as several times below.*
[4] *A caret originally here, partly erased; a bold caret after* weke.
[5] Ab *canc.* [6] exc *canc.* [7] have *canc.* [8] MS. snale.
[9] -es *repr. by an upward curl; the two later cases of the name have the usual full loop.*

if Boleyn byet ⌜in trowght⌝ Heydon shal have it. My Lady Hastynge*s* prayid
me that I shuld wryte to yow to lete yow have knowleche there-of, and that 30
ye myght let it; for Heydon hath lost her good *grace*, lest as long as it maye.
John Wodhows shal telle yow more of[10] the mater if he speke wy*th* yow.[11]

I pray yow that ye wol do[12] bye ij doseyn trenchors, for I can none gete in
this town. Also, I pray yow that ye wol send me a booke wy*th* chardeqweyns
that I may have ⌜of⌝ in the mo[r]nyngg*es*, for the eyeres be not holsom in 35
this town. Therfore I pray yow hertely lete John Suffeld bryng it hom wy*th*
hym.

Nomore, but the blyssid Ternyté have yow in hese kepyng and send yow
good sped in all yowre maters. Wrete[13] vn Sent Leonard Even. I pray yow
hold me excusid that I sent yow non ear non ansuer*e* of seche thyngg*es* as 40
ye desierid to have ansuer of, for in good feyth I myght not.

Yo*ur* M. P.

145. To JOHN PASTON I   Perhaps 1453, 30 January

Add. 34888, f. 91. $11\frac{1}{2} \times 5\frac{5}{8}$ in. Hand of no. 128.

Dorse: Traces of red wax over paper tape. Address in hand of letter:

To my right wurshipfull hosbond John Paston be þis delyueryd in hast.

The date is very doubtful. The latest year in which this hand appears is probably
1455 (no. 52), and the state of it seen in the present letter is close to that of no. 147,
which is firmly dated in July 1453. Further, no. 150, mainly from its handwriting,
seems likely to belong to 1454, and its date, 'the Tuesday next after the Conversion
of St. Paul', would be identical with 'the Tuesday next before Candlemas' of this
letter. The two letters cannot have been written on the same day, and this is probably a year earlier. Fenn and Gairdner date it after no. 146, on the ground that it
repeats Margaret's request for a necklace; but 'remember' need not refer to the
particular request in the letter.

F. iii, p. 170. G. 196/236.

Right worshippffull hosbond, I reco*m*mawnd me to yow,[1] prayi*n*g yow to
wete þat I spak yistirday wy*th* my suster*e*, *and* she told me þat she was sory
þat she myght not speke wy*th* yow or ye yede. And she desyrith, if itt
pleased[2] yow, þat ye shuld yeve þe jantylman þat ye know of seche langage
as he myght fele by yow þat ye wull be wele willy*n*g to þe mat*er* þat ye 5
know of; for she told me þat he hath seyd before þis tym þat[3] he co*n*seyvid
þat ye haue sett but lytil þer-by. Wherefor*e* she prayth yow þat ye woll be
here gode brother*e*, *and* þat ye myght haue a full answer*e* at þis tym[4]
wheddere it shall be ya or nay. For here moder*e* hath seyd to her*e* syth þat

---

[10] there *canc.*   [11] *Recto ends.*   [12] *No space.*   [13] the T *canc.*

145. [1] y- *in this and later letters in this hand of normal form.*
[2] -d *apparently inserted later.*   [3] ye have *canc.*   [4] how *canc.*

10 ye redyn hens þat she hath no fantesy þer-inne, but þat it shall com to a
jape;[5] and seyth to here þat þer is gode crafte in daubyng, and hath seche
langage to here þat she thynkyth right strange *and* so þat she is right wery
þer-of. Wherefore she desyrith þe rathere to haue a full conclusyon þer-
inne. ⌐She seyth here full trost is in yow, *and* as ye do þer-inne she woll
15 agré here þer-to.¬

Mayster Braklee was[6] here yisterday to haue spoke wyth yow. I spak
wyth hym, but he wold not tell me what his erond was. It is seyd here þat
þe cescions shall be at Thetford on Saturday next komyng, *and* there shall
be my lord of Norffolk *and* othere wyth grette pupill, as it is seyd. Oþer
20 tydyngys haue we none yett.

The blissefull Trynyté haue yow in his kepyng. Wretyn at Norwyche on
þe Tewysday next before Candelmesse. I pray yow þat ye woll vowchesawf
to remembre to purvey a thing for my nekke, *and* to do make my gyrdill.

Yowris, M. P.

25 My cosyn[8] Crane recommawndyth here to yow *and* prayith yow to remembre her mater, &c., for she[9] may not slepe on nygtys for hym.

146. To John Paston I   1453, 20 April

Add. 43488, f. 18. 8⅝ × 8¼ in. Hand of no. 128.

Dorse: Traces of red wax over tape. Address in hand of letter:

To my right wurshipfull maystere John Paston be þis delyueryd in hast.

The date depends on the presence in Norwich of the Queen and one of the King's
two half-brothers, Edmund, Earl of Richmond, and Jasper, Earl of Pembroke.
Blomefield says that the Queen visited Norwich in 1452; that before she came the
Mayor summoned an assembly at which the commons resolved to advance 100
marks as a loan to the King, and the aldermen to make the Queen a present of £40,
which the commons made up to 100 marks; and that £10 was also voted for the
King's brothers, who were with her. In a volume of records of the City of Norwich,
bearing the title 'Old Free Book and Memoranda 1317 to 1549', there is an inciden-
tal record of these proceedings. The book is mainly occupied by elections of City
officers and enrolments of freemen; but on ff. 17–19ʳ, which had been left blank
between earlier entries, there are lists of names with sums of money evidently
contributed. The opening of ff. 18ᵛ–19ʳ is treated partly as a unit, some of the items
running across the two pages. The relevant entries are apparently all by the same
hand, ill-formed and hasty. On f. 18ᵛ is a column of names headed 'Nomina alder-
mannorum qui prestiterunt summas subscriptas erga adventum Regine'. The list
begins with John Drolle, Mayor, and contains twenty-two other names, with sums
opposite. Most of f. 19ʳ is taken up with notes of the receipt of various amounts,
nearly all from Thomas Ellis but a few from John Drolle, under the heading:

⁵ Aga *canc.*   ⁶ *MS.* we.   ⁷ gr *canc.*
⁸ *Abbr.* cos *with flourished* -s.   ⁹ myth *canc.*

'Memorandum quod iste parcelle resolute per Thomam Elyes sunt medietatis summarum per eosdem aldermannos nomine comitatis domino Regi mutuatarum.' Below these receipts is a note beginning 'Memorandum quod Thomas Elyes, ciuis et aldermannus Norwici, mutuauit domino Regi nomine comitatis lxvj *li*. xiij *s*. iiij *d*.', and recording an additional payment of £3. 6*s*. 8*d*. to the King's brothers. A further note at the end runs: 'Item, dat' Regine lxvj *li*. xiij *s*. iiij *d*.' The memorandum states that Ellis promised that the money would be repaid half at Martinmas and the other half at Martinmas A.D. 1454. There can be no doubt that these accounts refer to the events described by Blomefield—the King and Queen each receive 100 marks, though only 5 marks of the earls' £10 is accounted for. But the date must be 1453. This is shown partly by the terms of repayment, for the second half would normally be paid a year after the first and no year is given for the first— only Martinmas; but even more plainly by the presence of John Drolle as Mayor (*Mayors of Norwich*, p. 26). (Ellis, who managed the loan, was a prominent Norwich merchant, sheriff in 1452, mayor in 1460, 1465, and 1474, M.P. 1463–5: ibid., pp. 28–9.) Blomefield's date of 1452 for the visit is not gravely wrong, for of course he still dated the year from 25 March and most of the preparations must have been made before that, though the Queen did not arrive until 17 April; but his comments on the consequences are incompatible with the dates.

Gairdner observed that this letter could not have been written in 1452 in any case, because John Paston I was in Norwich on St. George's Day of that year (see no. 42). He found the memorandum mentioning the King's half-brothers, but strangely missed the two references to the Queen in the same record, for he said 'As to the Queen's visit I find no direct evidence'.

F. i, p. 68. G. 187/226 (part).

Right wurshippfull hosbond, I reco*m*mand me to yow, p*ra*yi*n*g yow to wete that þe man of Knapton þ*at* owy*th* yow mony sent me this weke xxxix s. viij *d*.; and as for þe p*re*menant of þe mony, he hath p*ro*mysid to bri*n*g itt at Wytsontyd. And as for þe p*re*st, Howard*ys* sone, he yede to Canbryge þe last weke *and* he shall nomor*e* come hom tyll itt be mydsom*er*, *and* therfore 5 I myght not do yo*w*r eru*n*de.

As for tydyngys, þe Quene come in-to þis town on Tewysday last past aft*er* none *and* abode her*e* tyll itt was Thursday iiij aft*er* none, *and* she sent aft*er* my cosy*n*[1] Elysabeth Cler*e* be Sharynborn to come to her*e*. And she durst not dysabey her*e* co*m*mandment, *and* come to her*e*. And when she 10 come in þe Quenys p*re*sens þe Quene made ryght meche of her*e*, *and* desyrid her*e* to have an hosbond, þe which ye shall know of her*e*-aft*er*; but as for that, he is non nerrer*e* than he was befor*e*. The Quene was right well pleasid wy*th* her*e* answer*e*, *and*[2] reportyht of her*e* in þe best wyse, *and* seyth be her*e* trowth she sey no jantylwo*m*man syn she come into Norffolk 15 þat she lyky*th* bett*er* þan she doth her*e*.

Blake, þe baylé of Swaffham, was her*e* wy*th* þe Kyng*ys* broþ*er*, *and* he come to me weny*n*g þat ye had be at hom, *and* seyd þat þe Kyng*ys* broþ*er* desyrid hym þat he shuld p*ra*y yow in his name to come to hym, for he wold right fayn that ye had come to hym if ye had be at hom. And he told me þat 20

146. [1] *Abbr.* cos *with flourished* -s.   [2] report *and incomplete* h *canc.*

he wost wele þat he shuld send for yow when he come to London, boþe for
Cossey *and* othere thyng*ys*. I p*ray* yow þat ye woll do yo*wr* cost on me
ayens Witsontyd, þat I may haue somme thyng for my nekke. When þe
Quene was her*e* I borowd my cos*yn*[1] Elysab*et* Cleris devys, for I durst not
25 for shame go w*yth* my bed*ys* among so many fresch jantylwo*m*man as here
wer*e* at þat tym.

The blissid Trinyté have yow in his kepy*ng*. Wretyn at Norwych on þe
Fryday next before Seynt George.

Be yowr*ys*, M. PASTON

147. To JOHN PASTON I   1453, 6 July

Add. 34888, f. 89. 11½ × 6¾ in. Hand of no. 128.

Dorse: Remnants of red wax over tape. Address in hand of letter:

To my ritht wurchipfull mayster John Paston be þis delyueryd in hast.

The date is fixed by the report of the death of Sir John Heveningham, which occurred on 3 July 1453 (see Agnes Paston's letter no. 26).
F. iii, p. 186. G. 189/228.

Rytht worchipfull hosbond, I recommawnd me to yow, p*raying* yow to
wete þat I haue spoke w*yth* Newman for his plase, *and* I am thorow w*yth*
hym þerfore, but he wold not lete it in nowyse lesse than v marc.[1] I told hym
þat sekyrly ye shuld not know ⌐but⌐ þat I hyrid it of hym for iij li. I seyd
5 as for þe noble I shuld payt of myn owyn purse, þat ye shuld no knowlech
haue þer-of. And þis day I haue had jnne ij cartfull of hey, *and* yo*wr* stabyl
shall be made I hope þis next weke. I kowd not gette no grawnt of hym to
haue þe warehows. He seyth if he may in anywyse forber*e* itt her-aft*er* ye
shall haue itt, but he wull not grawnt itt in no co*n*naw[n]t. He hath
10 grawntyd me þe hows be-twyx þe vowte *and* þe warehows, and þat he seyd
he grawntyd not yow.

And as for þe cham*er* þat ye assygnyd to myn vnkyl, God hath p*ur*veyd
for hym as hys will is: he passyd to God on Monday last past at xj of þe
clok before none,[2] *and* S*er* John Heveny[n]gham passyd to God on Tewys-
15 day last past; hois sowlys both God assoyle. His sekenesse toke hym on
Tewysday at ix of þe clok before none, *and* be too aft*er* none he was dedd.[3]
I haue be-gonne yo*wr* jnventaré þat shuld haue be made or þis tym if I
had ben well at ease. I hope to make an ende þer-of, *and* of oþ*er* thyng*ys*
boþe, þis next weke, *and* ben in þat oþ*er* place if God send me helth. I must
20 do p*ur*vey for meche stuff or I come ther*e*, for þ*er* is noþ*er* bord*ys* ne oþ*er*
stuff þat must ned*ys* be had or we come ther*e*. And Ric*hard* hath gadderid

147. [1] *Curl on* -c.   [2] ho *canc.*   [3] -d *over* e.

butt lytill mony syth he come from yow. I haue sent John Norwod þis day to Gresham, Besi[n]gham, *and* Matelask to gete als meche mony as he may.

The blissid Trinyté haue yow in his kepi*ng*. Wretyn at Norwych on þe vtas day of Pet*er and* Powll.

Yowr*ys*, M. P. 25

148. To John Paston I   Perhaps 1453, 15 October

Add. 34888, f. 65. $11\frac{1}{2} \times 4\frac{3}{4}$ in. Hand of no. 128.

Dorse: Traces of red wax. Address in hand of letter:

To my right wurchipfull hosbond John Paston be þis delyverid in hast.

The date is doubtful. Handwriting and language relate this letter to others written in 1453 and 1454, and the writing suits 1453 better. Fenn and Gairdner associated the purchase of herrings with Lent; but, especially since drink is also to be bought, this is unnecessary. Margaret was probably laying in provisions for the winter, and the association should be rather with the herring fishing season. A letter from Richard Calle to Margaret (Part II, no. 729) shows that the practice was to buy herrings in bulk in the 'fishing time'. On the Norfolk coast in the Middle Ages, as today, the season ran from September to November; in particular, the Great Yarmouth 'Free Fair' or 'Herring Fair' was held from Michaelmas to Martinmas (see H. Manship, *The History of Great Yarmouth*, ed. G. J. Palmer (Great Yarmouth, 1854), p. 178; Blomefield, xi. 348). Cf. a letter from Ralph Neville, Dean of Lichfield, to G. Salvage, before November 1222: 'Mementote de allece quem prior Norwicensis mihi dedit, scilicet quinque millia; ad quem recipiendum oportet quod sitis apud Norwicum, vel tertia die ante festum S. Martini vel tertia die post festum S. Martini.' (*Royal and other Historical Letters, . . . Henry III*, ed. W. W. Shirley (Rolls ser.) i (1862), 191.) The Translation of St. Edward the Confessor is 13 October.

F. iii, p. 238. G. 149/183.

Right wurchipfull hosbond, I reco*m*mawnd me to yow, besechi*ng* yow that ye be not displeasid w*yth* me thow my symplenesse cawsed yow for to be displeasid w*yth* me. Be my trowth it is not my will noþ*er* to do ne sey that shuld cawse yow for to be displeasid, and if I haue do I am sory þ*er*-of ⌈*and* will amend itt⌉; wherefore I beseche yow ⌈to forgeve me *and*⌉ þat ye bere 5 none hevynesse in yo*wr* hert ayens me, for yo*wr* displeasans shuld be to hevy to me to indur*e* w*yth*.

I send yow the roll that ye sent for*e*, in-selyd, be þe bryng*er* here-of; it was fownd in yo*wr* trussi*ng* cofore. As for heri*ng*, I haue bowt an horslode for iiij s. vjd.; I can gett none ell yett. As for bever*e*, þ*er* is p*r*omysid me 10 somme, but I myt not gete it yett.

I sent to Jone Petche to haue an answer*e* for þe wyndowis, for she myt not come to me, *and* she sent me word that she had spoke þ*er*-of to Thom*as* I[n]gham. *And* he seyd þat he shuld speke w*yth* yow hymself *and* he shuld

15 accord wyth yow wel jnow, *and* seyd to her it was not her part to desyr[1] of
hym ⌐to stop þe lytys⌐. And also he seyd itt was not his parte to do itt,
be-cawse þe place is his but for yeris. And as for all oþer erondys that ye
haue commandid for to be do, þei shall be do als sone as þei may be do.

The blissid Trynyté haue yow in his kepi*ng*. Wretyn at Norwyche on þe
20 Monday next aft*er* Seynt Edward.

Yowris, M. P.

149. To JOHN PASTON I   Probably 1453, 14 November

Add. 33597, f. 2. $11\frac{7}{8} \times 6\frac{3}{4}$ in. Hand of no. 128.

Dorse: Paper seal over red wax and tape. Address in hand of letter:

To my right wurshipfull hosbond John Paston be this delyueryd in hast.

The contents give no precise evidence of date. The reference to 'Herry Inglose',
without title, implies that it is later than the death of Sir Henry Inglose in 1451 (see
no. 18); his son and heir was also named Henry. In handwriting and language this
letter is nearest to nos. 150 and 151.

    G. LXIII/620.

Right worchipfull hosbond, I recomand me to yow, prayi*ng* yow to wete
that I have receyvid the mony that Maystere Braklé had of yow, wherof he
hath agey*n* v m*ar*c. uppon pledgis of the too basonys þat ye had of hym tyll
ye come hom. As for cloth for my gowne, I can non gete i*n* this town bett*er*
5 than that is þat I send yow an exsample of, whiche me thynk*yth* to symple
bothe of colo*wr and* of cloth; wherfor*e* I p*ray* yow þat ye woll vouchesauf
to do bey for me iij y*er*dys *and* j q*ua*rter of seche as it pleasith yow þat I
shuld have, *and* what colo*wr* þat[1] pleaset[2] yow, for in[3] gode[3] feyth I haue do
sowte all the drapery*s* shopis i*n* this town *and* here is right febill cheys. Also
10 I p*ray* yow þat ye woll do bey a loff of gode sugo*wr and* di. j li. of holl
synamu*n*, for þ*er* is non gode i*n* this town. *And* as for mony, þ*er* is non of
yo*wr* tenanty*s* ne fermory*s* bryng*yth* non as yett.

As for tydyng*ys* in this contré, Herry Ingloses men have slayn ij men of
Tonsted on Thursday last past, ⌐as⌐ it is seyd, *and* all þat contré is sore
15 trobelid þ*er*with; *and* if he had abedyn at hom he had be lyke to have be
fechid owte of his owyn hows, for the peple þ*er*-abowgth[3] is sor*e* mevod
wi*th* hym. *And* on Saterday last past he come rydi*ng* thorow this town
toward Framy[n]gham, *and* if he had abedyn i*n* this town he shuld haue
ben arestyd; for men of Tonsted *and* of the contré pusewid after hym i*n*-to
20 þis town *and* made a grett noyse of hym *and* required þe mayr*e and* sheryves

148. [1] itt *canc.*

149. [1] it *canc.*   [2] -t *crowded in.*   [3] *No space.*

that he ⌜ne his men⌝ shuld not pas the town but that they shuld do as it longed to here parte to do, *and* told hem the cause why. *And* as it is seyd, the sergeant*ys* wer*e* fals *and* lete hym have knowleche þer-of, *and* he hythid hym hens *in* hast, &c.

The blyssyd Trynyté have yow in his kep*ing*. Wreten att Norwyche on 25 the Weddenesday next after*e* Seynt Martyn.

Be yowr*ys*, M. P.

150. To JOHN PASTON I — Perhaps 1454, 29 January

Add. 34888, f. 87. $11\frac{1}{4} \times 7\frac{7}{8}$ in. Hand of no. 128.

Dorse: Paper seal over red wax and tape. Address in hand of letter:

*To my right worchippfull hosbond John Paston[1] be thys delyu*er*yd in hast.*

The contents give no precise evidence of date, though it must be before 1460 since Sir John Fastolf is alive, and cannot be in 1455 because John Paston I was in Norwich in January and February of that year; see letters to him from Edmond Clere and Fastolf, Part II, nos. 512, 514. The handwriting is closest to that of the draft no. 50 written for John Paston in 1454, and tending towards the style of nos. 51 and 52. See no. 145.

F. iii, p. 324. G. 185/224.

Right worchipfull hosbond, I recomand me to yow, desyr*ing* to here of your welfar*e*, pr*ay*ing yow to wete that S*er* Thomas Howes hath purveyd iiij[2] dormant*ys* for the drawte cham*er and* the malthouse *and* þe browern, wherof he hath bought iij; *and* the forte, þ*at* shall be the lengest *and* grettest of all, he shall haue from Heylesdon, whiche he seyth my mayst*er* 5 Fastolf shall geue me be-cause my cham*er* shal be made þer-w*yth*. As for þe ley*ing* of the seyd dormant*ys*, they shall be leyd this next weke be-cause of the malthous; *and*[3] as for the remenant, I trow it shall abyde tyll ye come hom be-cause I[4] can nother be p*ur*veyd of joyst*ys* ne of bord not yette. I haue take the mesure in the draute cham*er* þer as ye wold y*our* cofor*ys and* 10 y*our* cowntewery shuld be sette for the whyle, *and* þer is no space besyde the bedd, thow the bed wer*e* remevyd to the dore, for to sette bothe y*our* bord *and* y*our* kofor*ys* there *and* to haue space to go *and* sitte be[5] syde. Wherfore I haue[6] p*ur*veyd that ye shall haue the same drawte cham*er* that ye had befor, ther*e* as ye shall ly to yourself; *and* whan y*our* gerre is remeved 15 owte of y*our* lytil hous the dore shall be lokkyd *and* youre bagg*ys* leyd in on of the grete koforis so þ*at* they shall be sauff, I trost.

Rich*ard* Charles *and* John Dow haue feched hom þe chyld from Rokelond Toftes, *and* it is a praty boy; *and* it is told me þ*at* Wyll is att Blyklyng w*yth*

150. [1] esquyer*e* *heavily canc.*   [2] jo *canc.*
[3] af *canc.*   [4] cam *canc.*   [5] twyx *canc.*   [6] purvey *at edge canc.*

20 a pore man of þe town. A yonge woman that was somtyme wyth Burton of
this town sent me word þer-of. I pray yow send me word if ye woll þat any
thyng þat ye woll be do to hym or ye come hom. Richard Charles sendyth
yow word þat Wylles hath be at hym here and offerid hym to make hym
astate in all thyngys according to there in-denture, and if he do the contrary
25 ye shall sone haue word.

My modere prayith yow for to remembre my suster, and to do your
parte feythfully or ye come hom to help to gette here a gode mariage. It
semyth be my moderys langage þat she wold neuer so fayn to haue be
delyueryd of her as she woll now. It was told here that ⌜Knyvet⌝ the heyer
30 is for to mary; bothe his wyff and childer be dede, as it was told here,
wherfor she wold þat ye shuld inquyre whedder it be so or no, and what hys
lyvelode is, and if ye thynke þat it be for to do to lete hym be spoke wyth
þer-of. I pray yow þat ye be not strange of wrytyng of letterys to me[7] be-
twix þis and þat ye come hom; if I myght I wold haue euery day on from
35 yow.[8]

The blyssed Trinyté haue yow in his kepyng. Wrete att Norwyche on
þe Tesday next after þe Conuercion [of] Seynt Poull.

Be yourys, M. P.

151. To John Paston I   Perhaps 1454, 1 February

Add. 34888, f. 23. $11\frac{1}{8} \times 5\frac{3}{8}$ in. Hand of no. 128.

Dorse: Remnants of red wax over tape. Address in hand of letter:

To my ryght worchippfull hosbond John Paston be this delyueryd in hast.

The date is very doubtful, and depends on the similarity of language and handwriting to those of no. 150 and the associated group. In these respects this letter is
so like no. 150 that there can be no reasonable doubt that that is the letter 'written
on Tuesday last past'; and both are certainly among the latest in the hand of this
clerk.

F. iii, p. 408. G. 62/82.

Right worchipfull hosbond, I recommand me to yow, praying yow to wete
that I haue receyved your letter ⌜this day⌝ þat ye sent me be Yelvertonys
man. As for your signette, I fond itt uppon your bord the same day þat ye
went hens, and I send it yow be Richard Heberd, brynger herof. As for
5 your erondys þat ye wrete to me fore, Richard Charles is owte abough[t]
your erendys abowte Gresham, and for his awyn materys also, and I suppose he komyth not hom tyll it be Tesday or Weddenesday next komyng.

---

7 tyll ye *canc.*
8 *Some three or four words heavily canc., only* þis, *the last, legible.*

And alssone as he komyth hom he shall go abowte yo*ur* erond*ys* þat ye wrete to me fore.

I sent yow a lettere wreten on Tesday last past, whiche as I suppose 10 Roger Ormesby delyu*er*yd yow. I toke it to Alson Pertryche; she rod w*yth* Clyppysbys wyff to London.

I p*ray* yow if ye haue an othere sone that ye woll lete it be named Herry in remembrans of yo*ur* brother Herry. Also I p*ray* yow that ye woll send me dat*ys and*[1] synamu*n* as hastyly as ye may. I haue speke w*yth* John 15 Damme of that ye bad[2] me sey to hem to sey to Thom*as* Note, *and* he sey[d] he was well payd þat[3] ye seyd *and* thowgh[t] þ*er*-in as ye dede. Nerles I bad hym þat he shuld sey to the seyd Thom*as* þ*er*-in as it wer*e* of hymself, w*yth*-owte yo*ur* avys or any other*ys*; *and* he seyd he shuld so, *and* that it shuld be purveyd for this next weke at the ferthest. 20

The blyssed T*r*inyté haue yow in his kepy*ng*. Wretyn att Norwyche in hast the Fryday next before Candelmesse Day.

Be youre grony*ng* wyff, M. P.

152. To JOHN PASTON I   About 1459, September

Add. 27444, f. 21. 11⅞×6¾ in. Hand of John Paston III.

Dorse: Marks of folding, paper seal over red wax and string, but no address.

The date is doubtful, but cannot be as early as 1453 which Gairdner suggested. 'My cousin Heveningham', it is clear from the projected negotiations for the remarriage of his mother, is John Heveningham, son of Sir John who died in 1453 (see no. 26). But Wymondham's first wife Margery, formerly Lady Hastings (see no. 129), lived until 1456 (Blomefield, iv. 89). Even at this date John Paston III, who wrote this letter, was only twelve years old, and is unlikely to have been able to write even as well as this for some years to come—the writing, though irregular and awkward, is reasonably competent and gives evidence of some practice. Most of the letters he wrote for his mother fall in the years 1460 to 1462. In one or two details of language the present letter differs from the rest,[1] and is likely to be slightly earlier.

G. 190/229.

Ryth worchepfull housbonde,[2] I recome*n*de me on-to yow. Plesyt yow to wete þat I sent Tom*as* Bon to Edwarde Coteler to haue on ansuer of the mat*er* þat ye spak to hym of, *and* he sent me worde þat he hade spok to hys man þ*er*-of; *and* he tolde hym that he hade no wrytyng[3] nor euide*n*s of no

---

151. [1] the *canc.*   [2] mey *canc.*   [3] þ *in form of* y.

152. [1] *e.g.* qwyche, qwan, *instead of later* whyche, wyche, when; *complete absence of* -n *in strong past participles.*
  [2] *Third letter corrected, evidently from* v; *stroke over the second syllable.*
  [3] *Part of a letter, perhaps* o, *canc.*

5 swyche thyng as ye spak to hym of, ner not wyst were he scholde haue cnowlage of no swyche thyng, saue he tolde hym þat he receyvyd onys j c s. of
þe same rent. But *and* he may ⌜haue⌝ cnowlage of ony man þat havyth
ony wrytyng or ony thyng þat may out prevayle, he schal late yow have
cnoulage ther-of.

10 As for Wylliam Yellverton, he come here never syn ye yede. As for my
Lady Stapullton, att⁴ þe wrytyng of thys letter sche was not come home.
Wyndhamys erend to my lady of Southefolk was to desiyr hyr gode lady-
chep, *and* to beseche hyr þat sche wolde spek to my cosyn Evenyngham
þat he myt have hys gode wyll. For he levith jn hope to have hys modyr,
15 *and* ⌜he⌝ hath made menys to have hyr by John Gros *and* hys wyf, *and* by
Bokynham *and* by odyr dyuers, *and* profiryth hyr ⌜to find suereté⌝ to aquitt
hyr⁵ housbondys dettys ⌜þe qwyche is ccc marc⌝ *and* to pay itt doune on
j day. *And* by thys mene, as he seyth, he hathe bargeynid wyth j marchande
of London *and* hath ⌜solde⌝⁶ to hym þe mariage of hys son, for þe qwyche
20 he scal have vij c marc; *and* of þat þe iij c marc schoulde be payd for ⌜þe
forseyd⌝⁷ dettys,⁸ *and* also he proforyth to yeue hyr þe maner of Felbryg to
hyr joyntour, *and* odyr la[r]ge proforys, as ye schal here erafftter. As for þe
good wyll of my cosyn Heuenyngham, he seyth ⌜Wyndh⟨am⟩⌝⁹ he schall
neuer have hytt, nott for to have hyr gode. Konyth he¹⁰ hys soull hevy
25 ther¹¹-of, for he¹² js a–ferde þat *and* ⌜if⌝ þe large proforys may be per-
for[m]yd þat sche wyll have hym. My seyd cosyn preyith yow, att þe
reuerens of Gode, þat¹³ ye wyll do yowyr [part]¹⁴ þer-in to brec it *and* ye
can. He schall be here a-yen on Mychaell-mas Evyn; he was full sory þat
ye were outt att þis¹⁵ tyme, for he hopyd þat ye schoulde have¹⁶ do myche
30 goode att þis tyme. He hathe seyde as myche þer a-geyns as he dar do to
haue hyr gode modyrchep. My lady of Southefolce sent j letter to hyr
yester-day by Stanlé, ⌜þe⌝¹⁵ qwyche is callyd j well cherysyd man wyth¹⁷ my
seyd lady, *and* desiyryng hyr in þe letter þat sche wolde owe hyr godde
wyll *and* favor to Wyndham in þat þat he desyiryd of hyr, *and* of more
35 matterys þat ye schall here er-after, for I suppose sche wyll schew yow þe
same letter *and* mak yow of hyr counsel in many thyngys. *And* I schall do
my part as feythfully as I can to lett Wyndhamys porpose tyl ye come home.
I pray yow sende me a copy of¹⁸ hys petygré, þat I may schew to hyr how
worcheppfull¹⁹ it is, for in goode feythe sche is informyd bi hyr gentyll son
40 Gros *and* Bokenham þat he is mor worcheppfull in berthe *and* in lyuelode

---

⁴ y *canc.*   ⁵ hovs *and two imperfect letters canc.*
⁶ *Interl. above a cancelled word which seems to have been* soulde.
⁷ *Interl. above* hys *canc.*   ⁸ *thus* large proforys he *canc.*
⁹ *End lost at crumbled edge.*   ¹⁰ abydyth *canc.*
¹¹ *Incomplete* f *canc.*   ¹² b *canc.*   ¹³ *Imperfect* j, *not canc.*
¹⁴ *For this restoration cf. l. 37;* part *was presumably dropped because it resembled following*
þer.
¹⁵ þ *in form of* y, *unusually in John III's hand.*   ¹⁶ hade *canc.*
¹⁷ hyr *canc.*   ¹⁸ ye pe *canc.*   ¹⁹ *MS.* worchepphll.

þer-to than they or ony odyr can p*r*eue, as I suppose. I p*r*ay yow lett nott thys mat*er* be discuyryd tyl ye her more ther-of, or aft*er*, for my cosyn Heue*n*y[n]gh*a*m tolde myche here-of in secret wyse, *and* of odyr thy*n*gis qwyche ye schall haue c[n]oulage of qwan ye come home, &c.

In hast, all jn hast. 45

153. To JOHN PASTON I   Probably 1459, 24 December

Add. 43490, f. 52. 12 × 5½ in. In two hands, the first unidentified, the second John Daubeney's.

Dorse: Marks of folding, tape-slits, and traces of dark wax, but no address visible. Badly stained by damp, but no address seems to have existed even before this.

This letter is wrongly attributed by both Fenn and Gairdner to Margery Paston. The index to the manuscript notes that the epistolary forms are characteristic of Margaret, not Margery, and that the reference to Caister suggests the year 1459. It seems most likely that the letter was written on the eve of the first Christmas after Sir John Fastolf's death in that year, when John Paston, as one of his executors and claimant to the property, might well have been at Caister. In any case the presence of Daubeney's hand requires a date earlier than 1469, when he was killed (see no. 205). (See also *Medium Ævum*, xix (1949), 15 n. 2.)

F. ii, p. 330. G. 881/999. C. 25.

Ryght wvrschipful husbond, I recomaund me on-to yov. Plese it yov to wete that I sent yov*r* eldest svnne to my Lady Morlee to haue knolage qwat sporty*s* wer*e* husyd in here[1] hows in Kyrstemesse next folloyng aftyr the deceysse of ⌐my lord⌐ her*e* husbond. And sche seyd that þere[2] wer*e* non[3] dysgysynggy*s* ner*e* harpyng ner*e* lvtyng ner*e* syngyn, ner*e* no*n* lowde[4] 5
dysporty*s*, but pleyng at the tabylly*s* *and* schesse *and* cardy*s*, sweche dysporty*s* sche gave her*e* folky*s* leve to play, and no*n* odyr. Yov*r* svnne dede hese heyrne ryght wele, as ye xal her*e* aftyr þis. I sent yov*r* yonger*e* svnne to the Lady Stabylton, *and* sche[5] seyd ⌐acordyng to⌐[6] my Lady Morlees ⌐seyng in⌐[7] that, *and* as sche hadde seyn hvsyd in plac*ys* of wvrschip þer*e* as 10 sche hathe beyn.[8]

   I pray you that ye[9] woll asay to gett sume man at Caster*e* to kepe yo*ur* botry, for the mane that ye lefte w*yth* me woll not take vp-on hym to breve dayly as ye co*m*mandyt. He seyth he hath not vsyd to geve ⌐a⌐ rekenyng nothyr*e* of bred nor alle tyll at the weky*s* end, and he seyth he wot well that 15 he xuld not con don[10] yth; and therfor I soposse he xhall not abyd. And I

---

153. [1] hvs *canc.*   [2] þ- *in form of* y *throughout this hand.*
   [3] dysporty*s* *canc.*   [4] sporty*s* *canc.*   [5] acordyt in he *canc.*
   [6] *Interl. above* as *canc.*
   [7] *Interl. above* seyd *canc.*, -s *of* Morlees *added.*   [8] *First scribe ends.*
   [9] y- *in form of* þ.   [10] *No space.*

trowe ye xall be fayne to porveye¹¹ another man for Symond, ⌈for⌉ ye hare
nevere the nerer a wysse man for hym.

I¹² am sory that ye xall not at hom be for Crystemes. I pray you that ye
20 woll come as sone as ye may. I xhall thynke my-selfe halfe a wedowe be-
cause ye xal not ⌈be⌉ at home, &c.

God haue you in hys kepyng. Wretyn on Crystemes¹³ Evyn.

By your M. P.

154. To John Paston I   1460, 21 October

Add. 34888, f. 155. 11⅝×8⅝ in. John III's hand.

Dorse: Continuation of text. Paper seal over red wax. Address in John
III's hand:

To my ryth worchepfull husbond Jon Paston be thys delyueryd in hast.

The date is fixed by the report of the inquisition 'this day' at 'Okyll' (Acle) on Sir
John Fastolf's lands. This was held on the Tuesday after St. Luke (18 October) 39
Henry VI (*Inq. p.m.*, 38 and 39 Henry VI, no. 48; Bodl. MS. Charters Norfolk,
no. 723).
    The mayor (l. 51) was Thomas Ellis (see no. 146).
    F. iv, p. 194. G. 361/423.

R⟨yth⟩¹ worchepfull husbonde, I recomand me to yow. Plesyth it yow to
wet that I receyuyd yowyr letter þat² ye sent³ me by Nycolas Colman on
Sonday last past; *and* as for the mater⁴ þat ye desyiryd me to breke of to my
cosyn Rokwode,⁵ it fortunyd so þat he came to me on Sonday to dyner sone
5 aftyr þat I had yowyr letter, *and* when we had dynyd I mevyd to hym
ther-of in couert termys, as Playter schall informe yow eraftyr.⁶ *And* as I
thowt by hym, *and* so ded Playter also by the langwage þat he had to vs,
þat he wold be as feythfull as he kowd or myte be to that good lorde þat
ye wrot of, *and* to yow also, in onythynge þat he kowde or myte do in case
10 wer þat he wer set in offyse so þat he myth owte do. *And* ther-to he ⌈seyd
he⌉ wolde be bownde in a m¹ li., *and* he wer so myche worthe. As for the
todyr þat ye desyiryd I scholde meue to of the same mater, me semyth he
is to yonge to take ony swhyche thyngys vp-on hym, *and* also I knowe

---

¹¹ por- *repr. by the abbr. normally meaning* pro.   ¹² h *canc.*
¹³ ey *canc.*

154. ¹ *Letters lost at tear.*   ² þe *corr. to* ye *canc.*
    ³ *Most of last letter lost at tear, but it was apparently* t.
    ⁴ *From this letter onwards John III usually curves back the offstroke of his final* -r. *Some-*
times this must mean -re, *as* contré *l. 20; but there is a wide gradation of form, and in other*
words no regular intention is discernible— -m *and* -n *have similar final curves. Unless, there-*
fore, the curve is exceptionally strong it is ignored.
    ⁵ it *canc.*   ⁶ I felt h *canc.*

veryly þat he schall neuer loue feythfully the todyr man that ye desyiryd
þat he schuld do for when he rem[em]bryth the tyme þat is paste; *and* 15
ther-for I spak not to hym ther-of.

Thys day was holde a gret day at Okyll befor the vndyr-schreue *and* the
vndyr-exch⟨etor, for⟩[7] the mater of Syr Jon Fastolfys londys, *and* there was
my cosyn Rookwod *and* my cosyn Jon Berney of ⟨Red⟩ham[7] *and* dyuers
odyr jentylmen *and* thrfty men of the contré; *and* the mater is well sped 20
aftyr yowyr intent, blyssyd be God, as ye schall haue knowlage of in hast.
I suppose Playter schall be wyth yow on Sonday or on Monday next
comyng, if he may.[8]

Ye haue many good prayers of the poer pepyl þat God schuld sped yow
at thys parlement, for they leue in hope þat ye schold helpe to set a wey 25
þat they myte leue in better pese in thys contré thane they haue do befor,
and þat wollys schold be purueyd for þat they schuld not go owt of thys[9]
lond as it hathe be suffryd to do be-fore; *and* thane schalle the poer pepyll
moue leue bettyr thane they haue do by her ocwpacion ther-in.

Thomas Bone hathe solde all yowyr wole her for xx d. a stone, *and* goode 30
swerté fownd to yow ther-for to be payid a Myhellmas next comyng; *and*
it is solde ryth well aftyr þat the wole was, for the moste part was ryte
febyll.

Item, ther be bawt for yow iij horse at Seynt[10] Feythys feyr, *and* all be
trotterys, ryth fayir horse, God saue hem, *and* they be well kepyd. 35

Item, yowyre myllys[11] at Heylysdon be[12] late for xij marke *and* the myller
to fynde the reparacion, *and* Rychard Calle hathe let all yowyr londys at
Caster; but as for Mawtby londys, they be not let yet. Wylliam Whyte
hathe ⌜payid⌝ me a-geyne thys daye hys x li., *and* I haue mad hym a
qwetans there-of be-cause I had not hys oblygacion. 40

Ther is gret talkyng in thys contré of the desyir of my lorde of[13] York.[14]
The pepyll reporte full worchepfully of my lord of Warwyk. They haue no
fer her but þat[15] he *and* othyr scholde schewe to gret favor to hem þat haue
⌜be⌝ rewyllerys of thys contré be-for tyme.

I haue done all yowyr erendys to Syr Thomas Howes þat ye wrote to me 45
for. I ame ryth glade þat ye haue sped welle in yowyr materys be-twyxe
Syr Fylyp Wentworthe *and* yow, *and* so I pray God ye may do in all othyr
materys to hys plesans. As for ⌜the wrytyngys⌝ þat ye desyiryd þat Playter
schulde sende yow,[16] Rychard Call tolde me þat they wer at[17] Herry
Barborys at the Tempyll gate. 50

The meyir *and* the meyires sent hedyr her dynerys thys day, *and* Jon
Dame came wyth hem, *and* ⌜they⌝ dynyd her. I am beholde to hem, for

---

[7] *Letters lost at hole.* [8] sp *canc.* [9] contre *canc.*
[10] feythys, *crowded at edge, canc.* [11] ys *written over* -e.
[12] *In margin, replacing two letters canc.* [13] j *canc.*
[14] men reporte he *canc.* [15] he sch *canc.* [16] *Recto ends.* [17] her *canc.*

they haue sent to me dyue*rs* tymys sythe ye yed[18] hense. The meyr seyth þat ther is no jentylman in Northefolk þat he wolle do more for thane he
55 wole for yow, if it laye in hys poer to do for yow.

Perse is stylle in p*r*esone, but he wolle not confese mor thane he ded when ye wer at home. Edmond Brome was w*yth* me *and* tolde me þat Perse sent for hym for to come spek w*yth* hym, *and* he tolde me þat he was ⟨wy*th* h⟩ym[19] *and* examynyd hym, but he wold not be a-knowe to hym þat
60 he had no knowlage wher no goode was of hys maste*rys* more thane he hade knowlageyd to yow. He tolde me þat he[20] sent for hym to desyir hym to labore to yow *and* to me[21] for hym if ye had be at home, *and* he tolde me þat he seyd to hym a-yen þat he wold neu*er* labor for hym but he myth know þat he wer trwe to hys mastyr, thow it lay in hys power to do ryth
65 myche[22] for hym. I suppose it schulde do none harme thow the seyd Perse wer remevyd ferther. I p*ray* to Gode yeue g*ra*ce þat the trowthe may be knowe, *and* that the dede may haue part of hys[23] owne goode.

And the blyssyd Trinyté haue yow in hys kepy*ng*. Wretyn ⌈in hast⌉ at Heylysdon the[24] Tuesday next aftyr Seynt Lwke.

By yowyrs, M. P.

155. To John Paston I   1460, 29 October

Add. 27444, f. 83. 10⅜ × 8¼ in. John III's hand.

Dorse: Paper seal over red wax and tape. Address in John III's hand:

*To my ryth welbelovyd brodyr ⟨C⟩lement Paston, for to delyue*r ⟨t⟩o hys*
brodyr Jon jn hast.[1]

The date is fixed by the reference to the inquisition on Falstolf's lands in Suffolk to be held on the following day. It was at Bungay on the Thursday before All Saints, 39 Henry VI, that is 30 October 1460 (*Inq. p.m.*, 38 and 39 Henry VI, no. 48). The letter written 'on the Tuesday next after St. Luke' is obviously no. 154.

G. 365/427.

Ryth w⟨orchepfu⟩ll[2] husbonde, I recomande me to yow. Plesyth yow to weet þat I receyvyd a lettyr on Seynt Symondys Evyn *and* J⟨w⟩d þat c⟨a⟩me frome Jon Paston, in the wyche lettyr he wrot þat ye desyiryd þat I scholde do Jon Paston or Thom*as* Pl⟨ayt⟩*er* looke in the gret standy*ng*
5 chyste in on of the gret canvas baggys whyche standyth a-geyns the lokk, for the copys of the fals inqwest ⌈of ofys⌉ þat was fownde in Northefolk,

---

18 hen *and heavy* s *canc.*
19 *Letters partly lost at hole, but parts of* w, *raised* t, *and the bow of* h *remain.*
20 d *canc.*   21 if ye *canc.*   22 in *canc.*   23 godys go *canc.*   24 twe *canc.*
155. 1 *Letters lost at tape-slit.*
2 *Some letters lost at jagged tear in three MS. lines.*

and for the kopy of the comyssyon þat came to Jon Andrewys *and* Fylpot *and* Heydon, *and* othyr thyngys towchynge the same mater. I haue do[3] Jon Paston sowte all iij grete baggys in the seyd kofyr at ryth good leyser, *and* he can non swhyche fynde. Plesyth it yow to remembre ye sent me worde in the fyrste lettyr þat ye sent me þat ye wolde þat Playter scholde a sent hem vp to yow to London, *and* I schewyd hym yowyr wryttyng howe þat ye wrote to me ther-in.[4] I suppose be-cawse he purpoosyd to come vp to London hym-selue hastely, he sent yow none answer ther-of. Rychard Calle told me þat all swhyche thyngys wer lefte[5] wyth Hery Barbore at the Tempyle gate[6] when the laste terme was doo, *and* so I sent yow worde in a lettyr whiche was wretyn on the Twesday next aftyr Seynt ⌐Lwke⌐, *and* ther-in was an answer of all the fyrst lettyr þat ye sent me. ⌐I sent it yow by yonge Thomas Elys⌐,[7] *and* I sent yow a-nothyr lettyr by Playter the whyche was wretyn on Saterday last past.

Item, I receyvyd a lettyr frome yow on Sonday, of the wyche I sent yow an answher of ⌐in a lettyr⌐ on Seynt Symondys Euen *and* Jwde by Edmu[n]de Clere[8] of Stokysby, *and* as sone as I hade the seyd lettyr on Sonday I sent to Syr Thomas Howes for the mater þat ye desyiryd þat he scholde inqwer of to Bokyng. *And* I sent a-yene sethe to the seyd Syr Thomas for to have knowlage of the same mater yestyr-daye, *and* I haue non answher of hym yet. He sent me worde he scholde do hys part ther-in, but othyr answer have I none yet of hym.

I sende yow in a canvase bage inselyd by Nycolas Colman as many of Crystofyr Hansonys acomptys as[9] I *and* Jon Paston cane fynde ther as ye sent worde þat they wer.[10] Rychard Harbard recomawndyth hym to yow, *and* prayth yowe þat ye wole wyche-saue to remembre the lettyr that scholde be sent fro my lorde of Warwyk to a man of hys beyng at Lowys-tofete, *and* if it be not sent to hym þat it plese yow to do purvey þat it may be sent to hym in haste if it maye be.[11] As tomorow ther schall be keppyd a day at Bownggey[12] for Mastyr Fastolfys[13] ⌐londys⌐ be-for the exchetore, *and* ther schall be Wylliam Barker *and* Rychard Call. ⌐Ye⌐[14] schall haue[15] knowlage in haste what schall be do ther.

And the blyssyd Trinité haue yow in hys keppyng. Wretyn in haste at Norwyche on the Wednysday next aftyr Seynt Symond *and* Jwde.

By yowyr M. P.

---

[3] *Followed by a caret mark, but nothing interlined.*   [4] he *canc.*
[5] at *canc.*   [6] th *canc.*   [7] *Interl. above* Item I re *canc.*
[8] *First written with tailed* r *as if final, then* e *added.*
[9] Jon P *canc.*   [10] Ry *canc.*   [11] go/ *and* a *canc.*
[12] *This seems to be the form intended. There is a dotted circumflex above the* n, *which could therefore be read* u *to give* Bowunggey. *But John III often uses the dotted circumflex above undoubted* n, *apparently to distinguish it from* u.
[13] -ys *crowded in.*   [14] *Interl. above* I *canc.*   [15] -ue *crowded in.*

156. To John Paston I   1460, 25 November

Add. 34888, f. 122. 11½×7⅜ in. Hand of Richard Calle.

Dorse: Traces of red wax. Address in Calle's hand:

To my right wurshipfull husbonde John Paston be this deliuerd in hast.

The date of this letter, as Fenn observed, depends on St. Andrew's Day's falling
on a Sunday (ll. 4–5). The next letter is closely related—the box inscribed *falce carte*
about which Margaret is to ask William Worcester in this letter doubtless contained
the 'false forged evidence' that she is to see him about in no. 157, and that is dated
'the Monday next after St. Andrew'. The only two years during the married life
of John and Margaret Paston in which St. Andrew's Day was a Sunday were 1455
and 1460. Gairdner chose the former; but Worcester's avoidance of Margaret
Paston fits the strained relations between him and the Pastons after Fastolf's death
(see for example William Paston II's letter no. 89), and in addition John III, who
wrote no. 157, first appears as an amanuensis for his mother in no. 153, and his
writing in no. 157 is very like that in no. 155. Both letters must therefore be placed
in 1460.

F. iii, p. 252. G. 260/306.

Right wurshipfull husbonde, I recomaunde me vnto you. Plesith you to
witte that myn avnte Mondeforthe hath desiryd¹ me to write to you besechyng you that ⌈ye⌉ wol wechesafe to chevesshe for her at London xxᵗⁱ
marke for to be payed to Mastre Ponyng*ys* outher on Saterday or Sonday,
5 weche schalbe Seint Andrwes Daye, in discharchyng of them that be bounden
to Mastre Ponyng*ys* of the seide xxᵗⁱ marke for the wardeship of here
doughter; the weche xxᵗⁱ marke she hath delyuerd to me in golde for you
to haue at y*our* comyng home, for she dare not aventure here money to be
brought vp to London for feere of robbyng for it [is] ⟨sei⟩de² heere that
10 there goothe many thefys be-twyx this and London, weche causeth here to
beseche you to content the seide money in dischargyng of the matre and of
them that be bounden, for she wolde for no goode that the day were broken.
And she thankyth you hertely for the greet³ labo*ur* and besynesse that ye
haue had in that matre, and in all others touchyng her and hers, wherfore
15 she seithe she is ever bounden to be y*our* bedwoma*n* and ever wolbe whyle
she levethe. My cosyn, her sone, and hese wife recomaundethe them vnto
you, besechyng you that ye woll weche-safe to be her goode mastre, as ye
haue ben a-fore tyme. For they be enformed that Danyell is comen to
Rysyng Castell and hes men make her bost that her mastre shal be a-yene
20 at Brayston wyt*h*inne shorte tyme. Ferthermore, as for the matre that my
sone wrote to me for, the boxe wheron ys⁴ wreten 'Falce carte Sproute'⁵ that
I shulde enquere of Willia*m* Wurcestre wher it were, the seide Willia*m*

156. ¹ -d *over* -th.   ² *Letters lost at tear, but no room for* is.
³ de *canc.*   ⁴ *Written over something now illegible.*
⁵ *This Latin phrase marked off and underlined.*

was not at home sen that I had hes letter, but as sone as⁶ he comethe home
I shall enquere of hym and sende you an answere.

As towchyng for yo*ur* leveryes, ther can noon be gete heere of that 25
coloure that ye wolde haue of nouther murrey nor blwe nor goode russett*ys* vndrenethe iij s. the yerde at the lowest price, and yet is ther not
j-nough of on clothe and coloure to s*er*ue you. And as for to be purveid in
Suff*olk* it⁷ wolnot be purveide nought now a-yenst this tyme w*yth*oute they
had had warnyng at Michelmesse, as I am enformed. 30

And the blissed Trenyté haue you in his kepyng. Wreten at Norweche
on Seint Kateryn Day.

Be yo*ur* MARGARET PASTON

157. To JOHN PASTON I   1460, 1 December

Add. 34889, f. 198. 11⅜ × 6½ in. John III's hand.

Dorse: Paper seal over red wax. Address in John III's hand:

*To my ryth worchepfull husbond Jon Paston be thys ⟨le⟩ttyr¹ delyu*er*yd in
haste.*

The date depends on that of no. 156.
G. LII/553.

Ryth worchepfull husbond, I recomand me to yow. Plesyth it yow to wet
þat Jon Jeney was her w*yth* me thys daye *and* told me þat ye desyiryd þat
I schold do make a dyche at Heylysdon; *and* the seson is not for to do make
no new dechys nor to repare non old tyll it be aftyr Crystmas, as it is told
me, *and* so I sent yow word in a lettyr more thane a monythe goo. I wot 5
⌐not⌐ whedyr ye had the lettyr or not, for I had non answer ther-of fro yow.

Jone Dyngayne recomandyth hyr to yow, *and* prayith yow for Goddys
sake þat ye wole be hyr good mastyr *and* þat ye wole wychesaue to spek to
Hwe of Fen for hyr; for it is so þat serteyn lyuelod whyche hyr husbond
had in Engh*am* was cast in the Kyngys hand in hyr husbondys lyue, *and* 10
as sche vndyrstondyth it was do in hys fadyrys lyue, of the whyche hyr²
husbond spak to Hwe of Fen ther-of in hys lyue, to helpe þat he myth be
dycharchyd ther-of. *And* Hwe of Fen p*ro*mysyd hym v*er*ily þat he had mad
an ende ther-in *and* dychargyd hym, *and* þat he schold³ neu*er* be hurt nor
trublyd ther-for; *and* now⁴ the laste⁵ wek Barnard the vndyr*e*-scheryfe 15
sent downe a warant to sese the lond for the Kynge. *And* so, but he haue
xx s. ⌐for⌐ a fyne w*yth*-in schorte tyme, he wol not suffyr hyr to haue the

---

⁶ I *canc.*   ⁷ is to late *canc.*

157. ¹ *Beginning lost at tape slit; the missing letters must have been written on the tape.*
² husband *canc.*   ³ not be *canc.*   ⁴ wyth in t *canc.*   ⁵ wek *canc.*

auayle of the londys; wher-fore sche p*r*ayth ⌐yow⌐ for Goddys sak þat ye
wole p*ur*uey a mene þat Hwe of Fen may saue hyr harmeles, in as myche
20 as he p*r*omysyd hyr husbond to p*ur*uey the[r]fore in hys lyue. *And* if it
plese not yow to spek to hym ther-of, þat it plese yow to do Jon Paston or
Thom*a*s Playter[6] or sume othyr þat ye thynk þat cane vndyr-stonde the
mat*er* for to spek to the seyd Hwe of Fen ⌐ther-of⌐ in hyr name, *and* to
serge the Ky*n*gys bokys ther-fore, if ye thynk þat it be for to do, *and* sche
25 woll[7] ber the cost ther-of.

As for the mat*er* þat ye wold I schold spek to Wyll*ia*m Worcest*er* of
towchy*n*g the false forgyd euydens, I can not spek w*yth* hym yet; hys wyfe
seyth allwe þat he is owte when þat I send for hym. Yowyr[8] fermore of
Sweynysthorpe hathe fownde suerté for yowyr duté,[9] as Rychard Calle
30 tellyth me,[10] so þat ye schall be plesyd when ye come home.

And the blyssyd Trinité haue yow in hys kepy*n*g. Wretyn in hast on
the Monday next aftyr Seynt Andrew.

By yowyr M. P.

158. To John Paston I   Probably 1461, 1 March

Add. 34888, f. 173. 11¾×5¼ in. Gresham's hand.

Dorse: Marks of folding. Paper seal (Margaret's usual fleur-de-lis) over
red wax and tape, the sealing paper linked to the surrounding part of the
letter by an irregular design in ink. No address.

From the expected power of the lords in the north it seems that this letter was
written when the supporters of Margaret of Anjou appeared likely to succeed. This,
as Fenn suggested, would suit the situation soon after the second battle of
St. Albans, 17 February 1461—though Edward IV was in fact enthroned at
Westminster on 4 March.
 F. iii, p. 412. G. 369/432.

Please it you to wytte that it is lete me witte by on þat owith you good wyll
that þer is leid awayte up-on you in þis cuntré yf ye come here at large, to
bryng you to þe p*r*esence of suyche a lord in the north as shall not be for
yo*ur* ease, but to iop*ar*die of yo*ur* lyf or gret *and* importable losse of yo*ur*
5 good*es*. And he that hath take up-on hym þis ent*er*prise now was vndre-
shireff to G. Sayntlowe; he hath gret fauour herto by the meanes of the
sone of Will*ia*m Baxter that lyth beryed in the Grey Freres. And as it is
⌐reported the⌐ seid sone hath geue gret sylu*er* to þe lord*es* in the north to
bryng þe matier a-bowte, and now he *and* alle his olde felaweship put owt
10 their fynnes *and* arn right flygge *and* mery, hopyng alle thyng is *and* shalbe

---

  [6] to s *canc.*   [7] be *and imperfect third letter canc.*
  [8] be *canc.*   [9] u *evidently over* e.   [10] *Written* mee, -e *canc.*

as they wole haue it. Also it is tolde me that the fadre of the Bastard in this
cuntré seid that now shuld this shire be made sewir for hym *and* his heires
hens-forward, *and* for the ⸢Baxsteris⸣[1] heyres also; wherby I conceyve they
thynke that they haue none enemy but you, &c. Wherfor like it you to be
þe more ware of y*our* gydyng for y*our* p*er*sones sauf-gard, and also that ye 15
be not to hasty to come in-to þis cuntré til ye here þe world more sewer.
I trowe the berar of this shall telle more by[2] mowthe, as he shall be enfourmed, of the revell in this cuntré.

God haue you in his kepyng. Wretyn in hast the secund Sunday of Lent
by candel light at euyn. 20

By yours, &c. M.

159. To JOHN PASTON I   1461, perhaps 2 July

Add. 27444, f. 98. $11\frac{1}{2} \times 7\frac{1}{2}$ in. Hand of John Daubeney.

Dorse: Paper seal over red wax. Address in Daubeney's hand:

*To my right worchepfull hosbond John Paston be þis lett*er *deliuer*yd *in hast.*

The approximate date appears from the report of the attack on Thomas Denys,
coroner of Norfolk. From several letters (e.g. William Lomnor's no. 636 in Part II)
it is clear that Denys was murdered early in July 1461. Gairdner notes that the
records of the King's Bench show that he was taken from his house on 2 July and
killed on 4 July (G. Introd. p.ccxxxiv/205). From the mention of the parson of Snoring
in connection with the murder in nos. 161 and 162 it seems likely that the attack
recorded in the present letter was the abduction of 2 July; but it may have been
a slightly earlier occasion. Denys was at the second battle of St. Albans on 17
February, and at York with the King in May (see Part II, no. 629).

Further, Margaret's uncle John Berney died in July 1460 (see no. 56), so that
preparations for his 'year-day' would be in her mind at the beginning of July 1461.

G. 396/462.

Right worchepfull hosbond, I reco*mm*and me to you. Please you to wete
þat thys day in þe[1] mornyng the p*ar*son of Snoryng came to Tho*m*as Denys
and fechyd hym owt of hys hows, and beryth hym a hand that he shuld a
mad byllys ⸢ageyns⸣[2] Twyer *and*[3] hym, ⸢*and* hathe aleed hym forthe wy*th*
hem, hys wyf hathe no knowlege wer⸣. Ferthermore[4] þe seyd p*ar*son 5
seythe that þe seyd Tho*m*as Denys shuld a take[5] sowdyors owt of hys felachep whan he went to Seynt Albons; that hys a-nother of hys co*m*pleynt*ys*.

---

158. [1] *Interl. above* basteris *canc.*   [2] more by *repeated, canc.*

159. [1] þ- *in form of* y, *as regularly in this hand except in* þat; *in this letter* y^e *'the' is distin-*
guished from ye *'ye'.*

  [2] *Interl. above* on *canc., and after* of *interl. but canc.*

  [3] on *canc.*   [4] h *canc.*   [5] p *written and not canc.*

Item, a-nothyr of hys compleyntys ys, a beryth þe seyd Thomas a hand þat
he had a-wey a hors of John Coppyng of Bryslee *and* a-nother of Kyng ⌈of⌉[16]
10 Donham, þe wyche hors wer stole be þe seyd ⌈ij⌉ personys; wher-fore þe
seyd Thomas toke hem as a comyshaner, *and* delyueryd hem to þe exchetore Frances Costard, and on of them he bowt of the seyd Fraunces.
And þe seyd parson hathe a[7]-wey þe seyd[8] hors and[9] seyth þat ⌈he
wolle⌉[10] þe seyd theuys shuld be recompenst be Thomas Denys. Thys I
15 am enformyd of all thesse maters be hys wyffe;[11] and sche prayythe yow in
þe reverence of God ye wolle be[12] hyr good maister *and* helpe þat hyr
hosbond may have sum remedy be your labore in thys mater ⟨. . . se⟩ythe[13]
⌈syn⌉ that hyr hosbond ys þe Kyngys offycere that they owt to spare hym
þe rathere. But they þat hathe hym take no ⟨. . .⟩ told me þat they hope to
20 haue a newe chonge in hast.

Item, Perys that was wyth my vnkyll Barney sent you a l⟨etter . . .⟩er
desyryng to have your good masterchep, and he woll fyynd sufficient
suerté for hym for to conn⟨. . .⟩ys whan som euer ye woll require hym. I
good feyth it ys told me hys leggys ar[14] all⟨. . .⟩ me word, en[15] cas þe suerté
25 be sufficient,[16] in what sum ye woll have ⌈hem⌉ bownd for hy⟨. . .⟩te in
bayle.

Item, it ys told me that ther be many Freynche shyppys of se a-geyns
Yarmothe an⟨. . . t⟩hey woll do harme on þe coste. I pray yow hertely þat
ye woll send me word in hast howe þat ye do wyth my ⟨lord⟩ of Norffolk
30 *and* wyth your aduersaryys.

Item, I have do purveyed in thys wareyn xj[xx] rabetys, and sent vp[17] be þe
berer her-of.

The blyssyd Trinité have yow in hys kepyng, and send you þe better of
all your aduersarijs and good sped in all your maters. Wretyn in hast, þe
35 same ⌈day⌉ that ye departyd hens.

Item, I pray yow þat ye wolle remembre my vnkyll Barneys maters
tochyng þe executyng of hys wylle, *and* howe ye wolle þat we be demeny⌈d⌉
for kepyng of hys yerday; *and* þat it lekyth you to send me word be Maister
John Smy⟨th⟩.[18]

Your M. P.

[6] *Interl. above a* canc.   [7] geyn *canc.*   [8] Denys *canc.*
[9] on *canc.*   [10] h *canc.*   [11] w *canc.*   [12] good *canc.*
[13] *Some words lost here and in the following seven MS. lines owing to a large irregular hole in the paper. The top of a long* s *can be seen before* ythe.
[14] ny *canc.*   [15] *No space.*   [16] þat he wo *canc.*   [17] to you *canc.*
[18] *End lost at torn edge. The last paragraph was added later, beginning in the space before the subscription and running on to an additional line after it.*

160. To John Paston I 1461, 9 July

Add. 27444, f. 101. 11½ × 7 in. Daubeney's hand.

Dorse: Traces of red wax. Address in Daubeney's hand:

To my ryght worchepffull hosbond John Paston be thys deliuerid in hast.

The date must be soon after the murder of Thomas Denys (see no. 159). 'St. Thomas' must therefore be the Translation of St. Thomas of Canterbury, 7 July; cf. nos. 127, 142.

G. 400/466.

Right worchepful ⌐hosbond⌐,[1] I recommand me to yow. Please yow to wete þat I have spoke wyth Thomas Denys wyffe, *and* she recommand hyr to your good masterchep. And she prayeth[2] yow to be here good master, *and* prayet you of your good masterchep þat ye wolle geve her your advice howe to be demenid for hyr person *and* hyr goodys; for as towchyng hyr   5 owne person she dare not goo home to hyr owne place, for she is thret if þat she myght ⌐be⌐ take she shuld be slayne or be put in ferfull place in short- tyng of ⌐hyr⌐ lyve-dayes, *and* so she standyth in gret heuynes, God her helpe. Ferthermore she is nowe ⌐put be⌐[3] hyre broder in Norwich[4] ⌐wyth Awbry⌐ *and* she thynkyth þe place is right conuersaunt of pupyll for hyr to   10 a-beyd in, for she kepyth hyr as close as she may for spyyng. Item, as I went to Seynt Levenard ward I spake wyth Maister John Salet *and* com- monyd wyth hym of hyre, *and* me thowgt be hym ⌐that⌐ he howyth hyre ryght good wylle. And than I haskyd hym howe she myght be demenyd wyth his goodys ⌐and hyr⌐. He cownseld me þat she shuld get hyr a trosty   15 frend þat ware a good trewe poore man þat had not moche to lese, *and* wold be rewlyd after hyr, *and* ⌐to⌐ have a letter of ministracion; *and* so I told hyr. Than she s⌐e⌐yd she wold have hyr broder[5] ad-vice therin. Item, she seyth ther be nomore feffés ⌐in hys londys⌐[6] but ye *and* Rokwood, *and* she prayeth yow þat it please yow to speke to Rokwod þat he make no   20 relesse ⌐but be your advice⌐[7], as she trostyth to your good masterchep.

Item, þe last tyme þat I spake wyth hyre she mad suche a[8] petows mone, *and* seyd þat she wost ner howe to do for mony, *and* so I lent vj s. viij d.[9]

Item, I sent my cosyn Barney þe bylle þat John Pampyng wrot be your commanddement to me, *and* he hath sent a letter of hys entent to yow *and*   25 to Rokwod therof; *and* also[10] but ⌐yf⌐ it please yow to take better hed to

---

160. [1] *Interl. above* ser *canc.*

[2] h *canc.*   [3] *Interl. above* wyth *canc.*

[4] *A final curl on the* -c *is presumably meant as an abbreviation; Daubeney often uses this form.*   [5] av *canc.*   [6] *Interl. above* in hys *canc.*

[7] *Interl. above canc.* in to þe tyme þat she hathe comonyd wyth yow bothe.

[8] *No space, as commonly with* a *in this hand.*

[9] *The sum underlined, apparently by John Paston, and the passage marked by a bracket in the margin.*   [10] yf *canc.*

hys mat*er* than he can ⌈do⌉ hym-selff I can thynk he shall ellis far*e* þe wors, for j feyth he standyth daly in gret fer*e*[11] for þe false co*ntra*ry *pa*rty ageyns hym.

30 It*em*, at þe reu*er*ence of God be war*e* howe ye ryd or go, for nowgty *and* euyll desposyd felachep*ys*. I am put en[12] fer*e*[13] dayly for myn a-bydyng here, *and* cownsellyd be my mod*er and* be other good frend*ys* þat I shuld not a-beyd her*e* but yf þe world wher in more quiete than it is.

God for hys merci send vs a good world, *and* send yow helthe in body 35 *and* sowle *and* good speed in all yo*ur* maters.[14] Wreten in hast þe Thursday next aft*er* Seynt Thom*as*.

By yo*ur* M. P.

161. To John Paston I   1461, 15 July

Add. 34888, f. 185. 11½ × 3⅝ in. Daubeney's hand.

Dorse: Last two lines of text. Marks of folding, but no seal or address.

The date appears from the reference to Denys's death (see no. 159). This letter clearly answers John Paston I's no. 58, which is dated on Relic Sunday.
    F. iv, p. 24. G. 403/469.

I reco*mm*and me to yow. Please yow to wete that I ⌈have⌉ sent to my cosyn Barney acordyng to yo*ur* desyr*e* in þe lett*er* þat ye deed wright on Relec Sonday to me, wher*v*pon he hathe wreten a lett*er* to yow *and* a-nothyr bylle to me þe wyche I send yow. ⌈He⌉[1] tolde þe masang*er* þat I sent to hym þat 5 þe vnd*er*-shereve nedyth not to fer*e* hym nor non of hys, for he seyd aft*er* þe aleccion was doo he spak w*yth* hym ⌈at þe Grey Fryers⌉ *and pr*ayyd hym of hys good mast*er*chep, and seyd to hym þat he feryd no man of bodely harme but only[2] Twyer ⌈*and* hys felachep⌉.

Item, S*er* John Tatersalle *and* þe baly of Walsyngham *and* þe co*n*stabyll 10 hathe take þe p*ar*son of Snoryng *and* iiij of hys men *and* sett hem fast in þe stokkys on Monday at nyght, *and* as it is seyd they shuld be caryyd vp to ye Kyng in hast. God defend[3] yt but they be shastysyd as þe lawe wolle. Twyer *and* hys felachep beryth a gret wyght of Thom*as* Denys dethe in þe contry a-bowght[4] Walsynham, *and* it is seyd ther yf John Osberne ⌈had⌉[5] 15 owght ⌈hym⌉ as good wylle as he deed be-for þat he was a-quey*n*tyd w*yth* Twyer he shuld not a dyyd, for he myght[6] rewlyd all Walsynham as he had lyst, as it ys seyd.

---

[11] in þe contre *canc.*   [12] *No space.*   [13] *and* cownsellyd *canc.*
[14] wli *canc.*

161. [1] *Interl. above* I *canc.*   [2] Th *canc.*
    [3] *No space.*   [4] war *canc.*   [5] *Interl. above* ad *canc.*   [6] rewy *canc.*

Item, Will Lynys, þat was wyth Maister Fastolff, and swyche other as
he is wyth hym, goo fast abowght in þe contré and ber ⌈men⌉⁷ a hand, ⌈pres-
tys and other⌉, they be Skottys, and take brybys of hem and let hem goo 20
a-geyn. He toke the last wek þe parson of Freton, and but for my cosyn
Jarnyngham þe yonger, they wold a led hem forthe wyth hem. And he told
hem pley[n]ly⁸ yf they mad any suche doyngys ther, but they had þe letter
to schewe for hem they shuld a-bey on her bodyys. It wer welle do þat
they wer met wyth be tymys. It⁹ is told me þat þe seyd Will reportyth of 25
yow as shamfully as he can in dyuers place.

Jesu have yow in hys kepyng. Wreten in hast þe Wednysday after
Relec Sonday.

By your M. P.¹⁰

Yf þe vndershereve come home I woll a-say to do¹¹ for hym as ye desyryd
me in your letter. As for mony, I have sent abowght and I can get non but
xiij s. iiij d. syn ye went owght. I wolle do my parte to get more as hastely
as I¹² may.

162. To John Paston I   1461, 18 July

Add. 34888, f. 187. 11½ × 3⅜ in. Hand unidentified.

Dorse: Paper seal over red wax and tape. Address in hand of letter:

To my worchepful hosbonde Jon Pastun þis letter be delyuer⟨d⟩¹ in hast.

The date appears from the reference to the murder of Denys (see no. 159).
   F. iv, p. 30. G. 406/472.

Ryth worchepful husbond, I recomawnd me to yow. Plesyt yow to wete þat
I am desyrid be Ser Jon Tatersale to wryte to yow for a comyssion or a
neyre in termyner for to be sent down in-to þis cuntré to sit vppon þe
parsun of Snoryng and on soche as was cause of Thomas Denyssys dethe²
and for many and gret horebyl robryys. And as for þe costys þere-of, þe 5
cuntré wele pay þere-fore, for þey be sore a-ferd but þe seyd dethe be
chastysyd, and þe seyd robryys, þey ar a-ferde þat mo folkys xal be seruyd
in lyke wyse. As for þe prest and vj of hese men þat ben takyn, þey³ be
delyueryt to Twyere and iiij be⁴ wyth hem of þe cuntreys cost for to be sent
wyth to þe Kyng. And yf þe⟨y⟩⁵ be browt vp, at þe reuerens ⟨of⟩⁵ God do 10

---

⁷ *Interl. above* hem *canc.*   ⁸ ther *canc.*   ⁹ is *canc.*
¹⁰ *Recto ends.*   ¹¹ my d *canc.*   ¹² *MS.* ye.
162. ¹ *At edge.*   ² and the dethe of hodyrrys *canc.*
   ³ þ- *in form of* y.   ⁴ *MS.* b *with stroke through ascender.*
   ⁵ *Letters lost here and below where paper has decayed.*

yowre parte þat þey schape not but þat þey may haue þe jugement of þe
lawe and as þey haue deseruyd, and be comyt⟨ty⟩t to preson, not to departe
ty⟨l⟩ þey be in-queryd of here forseyd robery be soche a comyssiun þat ye⁶
can get, þat þe Keng and þe lordys may hondyrstonde wat ⟨r⟩ewle þey
15 haue ben of, not hondely for þe morderrys and þe robbryys but as wele
for þe gret in-surrexsiun þat þey were lyke a⁷ made wyth-in þe schyre.

þe prestys of Castyr þey be streytely take hede at be Roberd Harmerer
and hoder,⁸ so þat þe seyde prestys may haue no thyng owt of þere ⌈owne⌉
ne of hodyr mennys but þey be ransakyt, and þe plase ys watchyd bothe
20 day and nyth. þe prestys thynk ryth longe tyl they [haue] tydynggys from
yow. At þe reuerens of God be ware how ye goo and⁹ ryde, for yt ys told
me þat ye [be] thret of hem þat be nowtty felawys þat hathe be in-clynyng
to them þat hath be yowr hold aduersaryys.

The blyssyd Trenyté haue yow in hys kepyng. Wretyn in hast þe
25 Saterday nex be-fore Sent Margarete.

B[e] yowrys, M. P.

163. To John Paston I   1461, 2 November

Add. 34888, f. 195. 11⅝ × 12½ in. John III's hand.

Dorse: Marks of folding. Paper seal over red wax and tape, but no address.

The date, from Paston's relations with Thomas Howes and William Worcester,
must be later than Fastolf's death in November 1459. It cannot be after 1461, for
Sir William Chamberlain died early in 1462—his will was dated 3 March and
proved on 21 April 1462 (Blomefield, i. 321). Nor can it be 1460, for Margaret's
letter no. 155 of 29 October 1460 speaks of Playter's having gone to London a few
days earlier, whereas in the present letter he has not yet left. Further, other letters
show that Paston's dispute with Sir John Howard came to a head in 1461 (see, e.g.,
nos. 116, 231).

F. iv, p. 232. G. 421/488. C. 29 (part).

Ryth worchepfull husbond, I recomand me to yow. Plesyt yow to wet that
I receyvyd yowyr lettyr þat ye sent me by John Holme on Wednysday last
past. And also I receyvyd a-nothyr lettyr ⌈on Fryday at nyt⌉¹ þat ye sent me
by Nycolas Newmanys man, of the whyche lettrys I thanc yow, for I
5 schold ellys a thowt þat it had be wers wyth yow than it hathe be, or schall
be by the grace of almyty God. And yet I kowd not be mery sethyn I had
the last lettyr tyll thys day þat the meyir sent to me and sent me word þat
he had knowlage for very trowthe þat ye wer delyueryd owt of the Flet and
þat Howard was comytyd to ward for dyuers gret compleyntys þat wer

---

⁶ y- in form of þ.   ⁷ No space.   ⁸ þat be canc.
⁹ Interl. above and brede canc.

163. ¹ Interl. above on canc.

mad to the Kyng of hym. It was talkyd in Norwyche *and* in dyuers othyr 10
plasys in þe contré on Saterday last past þat ye wer[2] comytyd to Flet, *and*
in good feyth, as I herd say, the pepyle was ryth sory ther-of, bothe of
Norwyche *and* in the contré. Ye are ryth myche bownde to[3] thank God,
and all tho þat loue yow, þat ye haue so gret loue of the pepyll as ye haue.
Ye ar myche behold to the meyir *and* to Gylberd, *and* to dyuers othyr of 15
þe aldyrmen, for feythfully the owe yow good wyll to ther porys.

I haue spoke w*yth* Syr Thomas Howys for swyche thyngys as ye wrot
to me for, *and* he promysyd me þat he schold labour it aftyr yowyr intent
as fast as he kowd; *and* in good feyth, as my brodyr *and* Playter kan telle
yow, as be hys seying to vs he is *and* wole be feythfull to yow. *And* as for 20
Wylliam Wyrcestyr, he hathe be set so vp-on the hone, what by the parson
and by othyr, as my brodyr *and* Playter schall telle yow, þat they hope he
wole do well inow. The parson seyd ryth well *and* pleynly to hym. The
parson tolde me þat he had spook w*yth* Syr Wylliam Chambyrleyn ⌈*and*
w*yth* hys wyfe⌉, *and* he thynkyth þat they wole do well j-now aftyr yowyr 25
intent, so þat they be plesantly intretyd. The parson told me þat he wyst
well þat Syr Wylliam Chambyrleyn cowd do more ese in swyche materys
⌈as⌉[4] ye wrot of towchyng my lord of Bedford than ony man kowd do þat
leueyth at thys day. Also he told me þat he felt by hem þat they wold owe
yow ryth good wyll so þat[5] ye wold owe hem good wyll. The parson hopyth 30
uerily to make yow acordyd when he comyth to London.

Item, my brodyr *and* Playter wer w*yth* Calthorp to[6] inquer of the mater
þat ye wrot to me of. What answer he gaue hem they schall tell yow. I sent
the parson of Heylysdon to Gurnay to spek to hym of the same mater, *and*
he seyth feythefully ther was no swyche thyng desyiryd of hym, *and* thow 35
it had be desyiryd he wold nowthyr a seyd nor done a-yens yow. He seyd
he had euer fownde you louyng *and* feythfull to hym, *and* so he seyd he
wold be to yow to hys power, *and* desyiryng me þat I wold not thynk hym
the contrary. As for John Gros, he is at Slolé; ther-for he myth not be
spok w*yth*.   40

I pray yow þat ye wole send me word whedyr ye wole þat I schall
remeue frome hens, for[7] it begynyth to wax a cold abydyng her. Syr Thomas
Howys *and* John Rus schall make an end of all thyngys aftyr yowyr intent
as myche as they can do ther-in þis wek, *and* he purposyth to come[8] forward
to yow on þe Monday next aftyr Seynt Leonardys Day. My brodyr *and* 45
Playter schold a[9] be w*yth* yow er thys tym, but þat they wold a-byd tyl thys
day wer past be-cause of the schyer. I spak to my brodyr Wylliam as ye bad
me, *and* he told me, so God hym help, þat he hyryd ij horse ij dayis be-for
þat ye redyn, þat he myth a ryde forthe w*yth* yow; *and* be-cause þat ye

² in *canc.*   ³ God *and a canc.*   ⁴ *Interl. above ampersand canc.*
⁵ they my *canc.*   ⁶ inquer *canc.*   ⁷ the *canc.*
⁸ pr *canc.*   ⁹ *No space.*

50 spak not to hym to ryde wyth yow he seyd þat he wend ye wold [not] haue
had hym wyth yow.

Thomas Fastolfys modyr was her on þe next day aftyr ye wer redyn, to
haue spok wyth yow for hyr sone.[10] Sche prayith yow, at the reuerens of
God, þat ye wole be hys good mastyr, and to help hym in hys ryth, þat he
55 may haue[11] hys lyuᶜeᵓlod owt of ther handys þat haue had it in hys nown-
age. Sche seyth þat they wold mak him a yer yonger than he is, but[12] sche
seyth þat he is more than xxj and vpon þat sche dare take an othe.

And the blyssyd[13] Trynyté haue yow in hys kepyng and send yow good
sped in all yowyr materys, and send þe vyctory of all yowyr enmyis. Wretyn
60 in hast on Sowlemas Daye.

By yowyrs, M. P.

164. To John Paston I   1461, 16 November

Add. 27445, f. 13. 11¾×8⅜ in. John III's hand.

Dorse: Traces of red wax. Address in James Gloys's hand:

To my right wurchipfull husbond John Paston be this deliuerd in hast.

The date appears mainly from the reference to John Paston's having been in the
north country. A letter addressed by Thomas Playter to him or to Margaret shows
that he was in the north with the King in May 1461 (Part II, no. 628). The Duke
of Norfolk took possession of Caister for a time in that year (see Part II, no. 632),
but evidently did not keep it long. He died on 6 November of the same year (*Inq.
p.m.*, 1 Edward IV, no. 46; *Complete Peerage*, ix. 608). The date cannot be 1462, when
several references prove that Caister had been restored to Paston (see, e.g., no. 319
and Part II, no. 670), for John III was in Wales in November of that year (nos.
319–20).

G. 542/630.

5 ⟨R⟩yth[1] wo[r]chepfull husbond, I recomande me to yow. Plesyth yow to
weet þat Thomas Grene was wyth me as on Saterday last paste, and let me
haue knowlage þat the scherre schold be as thys day at the gylde-hall in
Norwyche; and he desyiryd me þat the swte þat ye have a-geyns Thomas
Jeryng and othyr myth be sesyd as for thys schere. And I seyd þat I durste
10 do ryth not ther-in,[2] and he tolde me þat Thomas ᶜJeryngᵓ was wyth yow
ᶜinᵓ Flegge the laste tyme þat ye wer ther, and ye seyd to hym þat he
scholde not be hvrte by the swte. And Thomas Grene tolde me þat if[3] ᶜthe
seyd Jeryng and othyr in the same wryteᵓ mad not an end wyth yow by the
nexte schere, þe whyche schall be thys day monyth, þat[3] the seyd Thomas

---

[10] he *written, not canc.*   [11] haue *repeated.*   [12] y *canc.*   [13] ter *canc.*

164. [1] *First letter lost at tear.*   [2] tyll ye came home *canc.*   [3] he *canc.*

Grene wole purchese a new wryte of hys owne coste ⌐ayens þat daye⌐. I 15
woste not þat the scher schuld be so sone when I wrote ⌐to⌐ yow yowyr
laste lettyr. *And* he remembyryd the trobulus werd þat is nowe, *and* also[4]
þat they wer nowtye felawys þat[5] ye svyd, *and* ther-fore he thowte þat[6] it
wer best to let it be respyte at thys tyme; *and* so they schall be respyth at
thys tyme. 20

I haue sent to Jaferey Spyrlyng for the bokys þat ye sent to me fore, *and*
he seyth þat he hathe none ther-of, for he seyth he lefte hem wyth yow
when he was wyth yow in the northe contré, for he seyth ye left hym behynd
yow at Lynkcolne; he supposyth they be at Kaster.

Item, my cosyn Crane recomandyth ⌐hyr⌐ to yow *and* prayith yow þat ye 25
wole wychesaue to spek to Jamys Gresham for to swe forthe the mater
betwyx Dame Margaret Spurdans *and* hyr; *and*[7] sche prayith yow at the
reuerens of God þat ye wole tendyr þat mater well, for all hyr troste is in
yow.

Item, the tenauntys at[8] Sweynysthorp prayid me for to wryte to yow for 30
to pray yow for Goddys sake þat ye wole help forto get hem a good baly of
the hu[n]dyryd þat they be in, for they sey þat they haue be gretly hurte by
swyche offyserys as they haue had ther be-for tyme.[9] Folk wold fayne in
thys[10] contré þat Heydon scholde be purveyd for þat he goo not so at large
as he dothe, for he is in thys towne ner euery wek, *and* hathe be euer syne 35
ye y[e]d hens. *And* also it is seyd in thys towne þat ye haue be good master
thys terme to Yatys, *and* many be ryth sory ther-of, *and* þat he dothe so
well as it [is] seyd[11] her þat he dothe. It is seyd þat he is scapyd all dangerys,
and he hathe tak new accionys ageyns hys neyborys, as it is seyd. Othyr
tydyngys haue we none here but þat ye haue more pleynly ther. 40

And the blyssyd Trinyté haue yow in hys kepyng, *and* send yow good
sped in all yowyr materys. Wretyn[12] in haste at Norwyche the Monday next
be-for Seynt Edmu[n]de the Kynge.

By yowyr M. P.

My modyr wold ryth fayne know how þat[13] ye *and* my brodyr Wylliam wer
a-cordyd; sche wold ryth fayne þat all wer well be-twen yow.

---

[4] they *canc.*   [5] the swt *canc.*   [6] it *canc.*   [7] he *canc.*

[8] swy *canc.*   [9] fol *and imperfect* k *canc.*   [10] cont *canc.*

[11] her *canc.*   [12] at *canc.*   [13] my *canc.*

165. To JOHN PASTON I   Probably 1461, 20 November

Add. 27444, f. 106. $10\frac{3}{8} \times 5\frac{1}{4}$ in. John III's hand.

Dorse: Paper seal over red wax. Address in John III's hand:

To my ryth worchepfull ⟨hus⟩bond[1] John Paston be this delyueryd in hast.

From the reference to Howard's hostility the date is most likely to be 1461 (see
no. 163, and also Clement Paston's letter no. 116 and John II's no. 231).
    G. 422/489.

Ryth worchepfull husbond, I recomand me to yow. Plesyt yow to wet þat
I receyvyd yowyr lettyr þat ye sent by the gold-smyth as thys day in the
mornyng. As for Syr Thomas, he sent me word he schold to yow ward as
on Twysday last past. If he fayle ony thyng þat ye sent word he schold
5 bryng wyth hym it is not for no lak of remembrans, for I sent to hym thryis
or[2] fowyr tymys ther-for, *and* þat he schold hast hym ther-in. As for
Rychard Call, he was not at hom thys fortnyth. When he comyth I schall
do yowir erendys to hym. *And* as for all yowyr odyr erendys, I schall do
hem as well as I can.

10   I sent yow a byll yestyrday by old Tauerham, *and* a byll of Jone Gaynys
mater, the whyche bylle I pray yow may be delyueryd to Thomas Playter. I
spak to hym of the same mater or he yed hens, and I pray yow, if it plese
yow, to geue hym yowyr avyse[3] what ye thynk is best to do ther-in. Sche
seyth sche is ryth sory[4] if hyr old mastyr demene hym not well to yow. Sche
15 prayith yow þat ye wole be hyr good mastyr, *and* þat sche fare neuer the
werse for hys defawtys; *and* also I pray yow þat ye wole be John Lysterys
good mastyr in hys mater. He spak to Playter ther-of, *and* Playter seyd he
hopyd to fynd a mene, aftyr þat he had spook wyth yow, þat schold ese hym
ther-in.

20   I thank yow hertly for yowyr lettyr, for it was to me gret comfort to her
fro yow. God knowyth my[5] modyr *and* I thowt ryth longe tyll we herd
tydyngys fro yow.

    And[6] the blyssyd Trinité haue yow in hys kepyng. Wretyn in hast on
Seynt Edmu[n]dys Day the Kyng.

25   By yowyr M. P.

The pepyll was nevyr bettyr dysposyd to yow than they be at thys owyr.
The byll þat Howard hathe mad a-yens yow *and* odyr hathe set the pepyll
in thys contré a rore. God yeue grace it be no werse than[7] it is yet.

---

165. [1] *Letters lost at tape-slit.*   [2] *MS.* of.   [3] ther in *canc.*
    [4] j *written and not canc.*   [5] my *canc.*   [6] Jechu (?) haue *canc.*
    [7] it *canc.*

166. To John Paston I   1461, 3 December

Add. 34888, f. 199. 11⅝ × 8½ in. Gloys's hand.

Dorse: Marks of folding, stitch-holes, and traces of red wax, but no address.

The date appears from the reference to John Pampyng's sureties in Ipswich (ll. 24–5). A letter from Pampyng to John Paston I, written at Ipswich and datable on 6 September 1461 (Part II, no. 643), reports that he was imprisoned there at the instance of Yelverton and Jenney, 'with a clog upon my heel for surety of the peace'.
    F. iv, p. 106. G. 429/496 (part).

Right wurchepfull husbond, I recomaund me to you. Please it you to wete that myn awnte is dissesid, whos sowle God assoyll. And if it please you to send word how ye wull þat we do for the lifflode that she had at Walcote, wheder ye wull þat any body take possession ⌈there⌉ in yowr name or not, and if it like you to haue wyth you my cosyn William, here sone, I trow ye 5 shuld fynde hym a necessary man to take hede to yowre howshold *and* to bye all maner of stuffe nedefull þer-to, *and* to se to þe rewle *and* gode gidyn þer-of; it hath be told me be-fore þat he can gode skill of such thynges. And if ye wull þat I send for hym *and* speke wyth hym there-of I shall do as ye send me word, for in feyth it is tyme to crone yowr old officere for diuerse 10 thynges, where-of I haue know parte be Dawbeney *and* more I shall telle you whan ye come home.

    Also it is thought be my cosyn Elisabeth Clere *and* þe vikere *and* othere þat be yowr frendes that it is right necessary for you to haue Hew of Fen to be yowr frende in yowr materes, for he is callid right feythfull *and* trosty to 15 his frendes þat trost hym. And as it is reported here he may do myche wyth the Kyng *and* þe lordes, and it is seid þat he may do myche wyth hem þat be yowr aduersaryes. And þerfore, for Goddes sake, if ye may haue his gode wille forsake it not. Also it is thought the more lerned men that ye haue of yowr owyn contré of yowr councell the more wurchepful it is to you. 20

    Richard Callys brothere sent a letter heder to you which I send you be Dawbeney. I wuld, if it pleasid you, that ⌈he⌉¹ myght haue an answere there-of as sone as ye may. Also, me semyth, savyng yowre better avyse, þat it were wele do þat ye sent a letter to Yepeswhich to them þat were John Pampynges borwys, thankyng them for there gode will, letyng hem 25 wete þat thei shall be savyd harmles; for, as I² herd say, thei marveyle that thei here no word from you, ner that he come not a-geyn to saue them harmles.

    Also, if ye be at home this Cristmes it were wele do ye shuld do puruey a garnyssh or tweyn of pewter vesshell, ij basones *and* ij heweres *and* xij 30 candilstikes, for ye haue to few of any of thes to serue this place. I am a-ferd

---

166. ¹ *Interl. above* I *canc.*   ² hed *with* -r- *crowded in, canc.*

to purvey mych stuffe in this place till we be suerrere þer-of. Asfor the wode
at Mauby, I shall haue heder but litill till ye come home, þat ye may chese
where ye wull haue it. I hope it shall not be longe till ye come home, be the
35 grace of God. Asfor othire tydynges of þis countré, Dawbeney shall tell you.

I pray you þat ye wull vochesaf to be gode mayster to Loveday, and þat
he may haue mony of you to bye such thynges as be necessary for hym, for
I wote wele he shuld go right evill or he shuld compleyne. And if it pleasid
you to purvey for hym þat he myght be in sum gode seruyce ye myght do
40 gret almesse vp-on hym, and so ye haue do be-fore this tyme, which I trost
God shall reward right wele.

The blissid Trinyté haue you in his blissid kepyng. Wretyn the Thursday next after Sent Andrew.

Be yowr M. P.

167. To John Paston I 1461, 29 December

Add. 27443, f. 119. 11½×8½ in. John III's hand.

Dorse: Continuation of text. Well-preserved red wax seal (fleur-de-lis)
over string. Address in John III's hand.

To my ryth worchepfull husbond Jonhn Paston be thys delyueryd in hast.

The date cannot be later than 1461, for Sir Thomas Tuddenham was executed in
February 1462 (Scofield, i. 233). The message from the King is clearly appropriate
to the beginning of Edward IV's reign, and the sheriff who was a knight in the
King's household was Sir Thomas Montgomery, made a 'King's carver' on 22 July
1461 and appointed Sheriff of Norfolk and Suffolk on 7 November 1461 (*Cal. Pat.
Rolls, 1461–7*, p. 125). (A letter from Thomas Playter to Paston (Part II, no. 654)
describes the same sessions.)
    G. 134/497.

Ryth worchepfull husbond, I recomande me to yow. Plesyt yow to wet þat
I receyvyd the lettyr þat ye sent me by a man of Seynt Mychell parysche on
Fryday next aftyr the Consepcion of Owyr Lad[y], and a-non as I had it I
sent my modyr the lettyr be-cause of swyche materys as longyd to hyr in
5 þat same lettyr; and sythyn þat tyme I kowd gete no¹ massanger to London
but if I wold haue sent by the scheryfys men, and I knew nowthyr her
mastyr ner them nor² whedyr they wer well wyllyng to yow or not, and
ther-ᵣforᵣ me thowt it had be no sendyng of no lettyr by hem.

And ᵣasᵣ for swyche materys as John Geney and Jamys Gresham spak to
10 me of, I³ sped hem as well as I kowd; and they bothe told me þat ye schold
veryly a ben at home be-for Crystmas, and that causyd me that I wrot not
to yow non answer. For if I had know þat ye schold not haue⁴ ben at home

---

167. ¹ mass *canc.*   ² *MS.* not.   ³ haue *canc.*   ⁴ he *canc.*

er thys tyme I schold a sent some man to yow, for I thynk ryth ⌐longe⌐ tyll
I haue some god tydyngys fro yow. I fer me þat it is not well wyth yow þat
ye be fro home at thys good ⌐tyme⌐. And many of yowyr contré-men thynk 15
the same, but they be hertty j-now to yow ward and⁵ full fayn wold her god
tydyngys fro yow.

    The[r] wer no byllys put to the scherryf at hys beyng her, ner non opyn⁶
playnt mad ⌐that I ⟨. . .⟩⌐⁷ of no person be-cawse they had so lyttyll knowlage of hys comeyng in-to thys contré. He demenyd hym full ⟨. . .⟩ and 20
jndeferently, as it was told me, and Yeluerton mad a fayir sermone at the
sesschyonys and seyd þat ⟨it was⟩ so that the Kyng was informyd þat ther
was a ryotows felawschep in thys contré, wer-for the Kyng was gretly dysplesyd; and þat the Kyng vndyrstood well þat it was not of ther owne
mosyon boot of cownselyng of one or ij þat ben evyll dysposyd folk. And 25
also he seyd if ony man wold put vp ony byllys of compleyntys of ony
extorcion ⌐or⌐¹⁸ brybery don be ony men of thys contré to them they wer
redy to⁹ receyue them and to make a-kord be-twyx hem; and if they cowd
not mak the acord, þat than they scho⟨ld⟩ tak the byllys to the Kyng and
he schold set hem thorow. And the scheryfe seyd that he wold h⟨. . .⟩ them 30
that wold compleyne ⌐and⌐¹⁰ dorste not for fer put vp ther byllys. And
Yelverton preyid the scheryfe þat if he had forget onythyng that the Kynge
seyd to hem at ther departtyng, þat he wold rehersyt ther. And than the
scheryf seyd þat he had seyd all that he remembryd saue only ⌐the Kyng⌐¹¹
⟨re⟩h⟨er⟩syd to hem ⟨. . .⟩ ij personys,¹² ⌐Syr⌐ Thomas Todenham and 35
Heydon; and than Yeluerton seyd, 'A, that is trowthe', as thow ⟨. . .⟩ that
⟨. . .⟩ Dame told me that he spak wyth the scheryfe aftyrward and let hym
haue k⟨nowlage⟩ o⟨f t⟩he rewylle ⟨and⟩¹³ demenyng of thys contré and
what cawsyd the pepyll for to grwge a-yens swyche¹⁴ folkys as had the
rewyll be-fortyme;¹⁵ and he was pleyne to hym in many thyngys, as he told 40
me, and he fond the scheryfe ryth pleyne ayen to hym¹⁶ and well dysposyd
in that þat myth growe to the welfar of the scher. The scheryfe seyd he
vndyr-stood by swyche in-for-macion as he had syne he came in-to thys
contré that¹⁷ they had not all gydyd hem well þat had the rewyill of thys
contré be-for, and ther-for he seyd feythfully, and swore¹⁸ by gret othys 45
that he wold nowthyr spar for good nor loue nor fer, but þat he wold let
the Kynge haue knowlage of the trowthe and þat he wold do asmyche for

---

⁵ full *canc.*
⁶ *A word canc., apparently* claimour. *The following* playnt *seems to have been corrected
from the same word repeated.*
⁷ *Some letters and words obliterated by damp at the edge, not recoverable even by ultra-
violet light.*
⁸ *Interl. above* of *canc.*   ⁹ receyd *canc.*
¹⁰ *Interl. above* if they *canc.*   ¹¹ *Interl. above a word obliterated by damp.*
¹² *These two words added in margin.*   ¹³ *Recto ends.*   ¹⁴ foly *canc.*
¹⁵ *First written with* m *tailed as if final ; then* e *added.* ¹⁶ in that þat he thowt *canc.*
¹⁷ thy *canc.*   ¹⁸ *First written with* tailed r, *then* e *added.*

thys contré as he cowd or myth do to the welfare ther-of, *and* seyd þat he
lekyd the contré ryth well. And John of Dame seyd if the contré had had
50 knowlage of hys comyng, he schold haue had byllys of compleynt*ys and*
knowlage of myche mo*re* thyng than he myth haue knowlage of that tyme,
o*re* myth haue be-cause of schort aby[dy]ng; *and* he seyd he wold not be
longe owt of thys contré. And also Yelu*er*ton seyd opynly in the seschyons
they to come downe for þe same cause to set a rewyll in the contré. And
55 yet he seyd he woste well þat the Kynge myth full evyll haue for[19]-bor ony
of hem bothe, for as for a knyth the*re* was non in the Kyngys howse þat
myth werse a be for-bore than þe scheryfe myth at that tyme.

I haue myche mor to wryt to yow of than I may haue leyser at thys tyme,
but I troste to God þat ye schall be[20] at home yowyr-selfe in hast, and than
60 ye schall knowe all. And but if ye come home in haste, I schall send to
yow; *and* I p*ray* yow hertly but if ye come home[21] send me word in hast
how ye do.

And the blyssyd T*r*inyté haue yow in hys kepyng. Wretyn in hast on
Seynt Thom*as* Day in Crystmas.

By yowyr MARGARET PASTON

65

He*re* was an evyll rewlyd felawschep yestyrday at the schere, *and* fard ryth
fowle w*yth* þe vndyr-scheryfe, and on-resnably as I herd sey.

168. To JOHN PASTON I 1462, 7 January

Add. 27444, f. 111. 11½×8½ in. John III's hand.

Dorse: Paper seal over wax and tape. Address in John III's hand:

*To my ryth worchepfull ⟨h⟩usbond[1] John Paston be thys delyu*er*yd in hast.*

This letter refers to the same state of affairs as no. 167, which is clearly the earlier
letter mentioned in the second sentence.
  G. 435/504.

Ryth worchepfull husbond, I recomand me to yow. Plesyt yow to wet þat I
sent yow a lettyr by[2] Barneys man of Wychy*n*gham wyche was wretyn on
Seynt Thom*as* Day in Crystmas, *and* I had[3] no tydyngys nor[4] lettyr ⌐of⌐[5]
yow sene the weke[6] befor Crystmas, wher-of I mervayle sore. I fere me
5 it is not well w*yth* yow be-cawse ye came not home or sent er thys tyme. I

---

[19] for *canc.*   [20] h *canc.*   [21] in ha *canc.*
168. [1] *First letter lost at tape-slit.*   [2] my cosyn *canc.*
[3] mo *canc.*   [4] -r *crowded in.*   [5] *Interl. above* frome *canc.*
[6] -e *probably intended by unusual flourish on* -k.

hopyd verily ye schold haue ben at home by Twelthe at þe ⌈ferthest⌉.[7] I
pray yow hertly þat ye wole wychesaue to send me word how ye do as
hastly as ye may, for my hert schall nevyr be in ese tyll I haue ⌈tydyngys⌉[8]
fro yow.

Pepyll of this contré begynyth to wax wyld, *and* it is seyd her þat my
lord of Clarans *and* the Dwek of Suthfolk *and* serteyn jwgys wyth hem
⌈schold come down⌉ and syt on syche pepyll as be noysyd ryotous in thys
contré. And also it is[9] seyd her þat ther is retornyd a newe rescwe vp-on
þat that was do at the last scher.[10] I suppose swyche talkyng comyth of false
schrewys þat wold mak a rwmor in þis contré. The pepyll seyth her þat
they had leuyr go vp hole to the Kyng *and* compleyne of siche fals
sc[h]rewys as they haue be wrongyd by a-for than they schold be compleynyd of wyth-owt cause *and* be hangyd at ther owne dorys. In[11] good
feyth men fer sor her of a comone rysyng but if a bettyr remedy may ⌈be⌉
had to ⌈pese⌉[12] the pepyll in hast, and that ther be sent swyche downe to
tak a rewyll as the pepyll hathe a fantsy in that wole be jndeferent. They[13]
loue not in no wyse the Dwke of Sowthfolk nor hys modyr.[14] They sey that
all the tretourys *and* extorsyonerys[15] of thys contré be meyntynyd by them
and by syche as they get to them wyth her goodys, to that intent to meynten
suche extorsyon ⌈style⌉ as hathe be do by suche as hathe had the rewyll
vndyr them be-for-tyme.[16] Men wene and the Dwke of Sowthfolk come
ther schall be a schrewd reuell, but if ther come odyr that be bettyr belovyd
than he is her. The pepyll feryth hem myche the mor to[17] be hurt be-cause
þat ye and my cosyn Barney come not home. They sey[18] they wot well it is
not well wyth yow, *and* if it be not well wyth[19] yow they[13] sey they wot well
they þat ⌈wole⌉ do yow wronge wole sone do them wronge, *and* that makyth
them all-most mad. God for hys holy mersy geue grace that ther may be
set a good rewyll *and* a sad in thys contré in hast, for I herd nevyr[20] sey of
so myche robry and manslawt in thys contré as is now wyth-in a lytyll tyme.

And as[21] for gadyryng of mony ⌈I sey⌉[22] nevyr ⌈a⌉ werse seson, for Rychard
Calle seyth he can get but lytyll in substans of that is owyng, nowthyr of
yowyr lyuelod nor of Fastolfys.[23] And John Paston seyth they that may
pay best, they pay werst. They fare as thow they hopyd to haue a newe
werd.

And the Blyssyd Trinité haue yow in hys kepyng *and* send vs good
tydyngys of yow. Yeluerton is a good thredbare frend for yow *and* for odyr

---

[7] *Interl. above* ferthe *canc.*   [8] *Interl. above* word *canc.*   [9] seyd *canc.*
[10] *MS.* icher; but *canc.*   [11] gode *canc.*   [12] *interl. above* plese *canc.*
[13] -y *crowded in.*   [14] *and* he come downe *canc.*   [15] b *canc.*
[16] I *canc.*   [17] h *canc.*   [18] thy *canc.*   [19] yow *at edge canc.*
[20] sey *and incomplete* d *canc.*   [21] for gadryg *et edge canc.*
[22] *Interl. above* ther was *canc.*
[23] *Followed by* they *and another cancelled letter. The whole word should evidently have
been cancelled.*

in thys contré, as it is told me. Wretyn in hast on the Thorsday nex aftyr Twelthe.

By yowyr MARGARET PASTON

169. To JOHN PASTON I 1462, 27 January

Add. 27444, f. 112. $11\frac{7}{8} \times 8\frac{5}{8}$ in. Letter in John III's hand, postscript partly in Daubeney's and partly in Playter's hand.

Dorse: Continuation of text. Marks of folding, traces of red wax, and tape-slits, but no address.

The date cannot be earlier than 1461, for the first report of Perse's imprisonment is in October 1460 (see no. 154); but the situation in January of that year, after the battle of Wakefield, excludes the possibility of a general pardon. It cannot be later than 1462, for John Damme died in that year; see no. 35.

G. 436/505.

Ryth worchepfull husbond, I recomand me to yow. Plesyt yow to wet þat Perse was delyueryd owt [of] preson by the generall pardon that the Kynge hathe grantyd, whyche was opynly proclamyd in the gyld-hall.[1] A-none as he[2] was delyueryd he cam ⌐hedyr⌐[3] to me, God wote in an evyll plyte, and he
5 desyiryd me wepyng þat I wold be hys good mastres and to be mene to yow to be hys good mastyr, and swore sor þat he was nevyr defawty in þat ye haue thowte hym defawty in. He seyd þat if ther wer ony ⌐coyne⌐ in the cofyr þat was at Wylliam Tauernerys it was ther wyth-owt hys knowlage, for hys mastyr wold neuyr lat hym se what was in þat cofyr; and he tolde
10 me þat the keyis wer sent to Thomas Holler by Mastyr John[4] Smyth. What Holler leyd in or took owte he wot not, as he sweryth. He offyrd me to be rewlyd as ye and I wold haue hym, and if I wold comand hym to go a-geyn to preson, whedyr I wold to þe castyll or to the gyld-hall, he wold obey my comandment; and seth that he cam of hys owne fre wyll wyth-owt
15 ony comandment[5] of ony man or desyir. I seyd I wold not send hym ageyn to preson so þat he wold a-byde yowyr[6] rewyll when ye came home, and so he is her wyth me and schall be tyll ye send me word how ye wole þat I do wyth hym; wher-for I pray yow þat ye wole let me haue knowlage in hast how ye wole þat I do wyth hym.
20   Item, I haue spok wyth John Dame and Playter for the lettyr testy-monyall, and John Dame[7] hathe promysyd to get it, and Playter schall bryng it to[8] yow to London.

---

169. [1] *and on canc.*   [2] *wad s canc.*   [3] *Interl. above to Heylysdon canc.*
[4] *Smyth canc.*   [5] *and dysy interl. but canc.*   [6] *rewyr canc.*
[7] *First written with tailed m, then e added.*
[8] *yo and imperfect w canc.*

Item, I haue p*ur*veyd yow of a man that schall be her in Barsamys sted *and* ye wole, the wyche can bettyr cherysche ⌜yowyr⌝[9] wood bothe in felly*ng and* fensy*ng*[10] ther-of than Barsam can; *and* he schall mak yow 25 as many hyrdyllys as ye ned for yowyr fold[11] of yowyr owne wood at Drayton, *and* schall tak as lytyll to hys wagys as Barsam dothe. And he is holdyn a trew man.

Item, Playt*er* schall tell yow of a woman þat compleynyd to the Dwk of Sowthefolk of yow, *and* the sey[d] Playt*er* schall tell yow of the demeny*ng* 30 ⌜*and* answery*ng*⌝ of þe scheryfe ⌜for yow⌝, *and* also of the demeny*ng* of[12] the seyd Dwke ⌜*and* of othir mat*erys*⌝ wyche wer to longe mat*er* to put in wryttyn. The pepyll of thys[13] contré be ryth glad þat the day yed w*yth* yow on Monday as it ded. Ye wer nevyr so welcome in-to Norfolk as ye schall be when ye come home, I trowe. 35

And the blyssyd Trynyté haue yow in hys kepy*ng*. Wretyn in hast on Wednysday next aftyr Seynt Angnet the fyrst.

By yowyr M. P.[14]

Item, Rich*ard* Calle told me that he hathe sent you a answer of all erand*ys* þat ye wold shuld be do to S*er* Thom*as* Howes. S*er* Thom*as* Howis 40 cam nowther to me nor sent[15] syn þat he cam home from London.[16]

Will Worcetr*e* was at me in Cristemes at Heylysdon, *and* he told þat he spak w*yth* you dyu*er*s tymys at London þe[17] last terme[18] and he told ⌜me⌝ þat he hopyd þat ye wolle be hys good master, *and* seyd he hopyd ye shuld have non other cause but for to be hys god maist*er*. I hope, *and* so do my 45 mod*er and* my cosyn Cler*e*, þat he wolle do well j-nowe so þat he be fayr*e* fare[19] w*yth*.[20]

Dawbeney *and* Playt*er* avise me to lete[21] Peers go at large, *and* to take a prom*ys* of hym to com to me a-mong vn-to yo*ur* comyng hom; *and* in the mene while his demenyng may be knowyn *and* espyed in mo thyng*ys*.[22] 50

⁹ *Interl. above* yow *canc.*   ¹⁰ of yowyr wood *canc.*   ¹¹ at *canc.*
¹² yowyr older sone *canc.*   ¹³ *From* the.
¹⁴ *John Paston III's hand ends here. First paragraph of postscript written, in Daubeney's hand, in the space to the left of the subscription.*
¹⁵ he *canc.*   ¹⁶ *Recto ends.*   ¹⁷ þ- *in form of* y.   ¹⁸ h *canc.*
¹⁹ *First written with flourished* -r, *then* e *added.*
²⁰ *Daubeney's hand ends here; the rest in Playter's hand.*
²¹ hym go at large *and canc.*   ²² t *and incomplete* h *canc.*

170. To JOHN PASTON I   1462, March

Add. 43490, f. 40. 10½×4 in. John III's hand.

Dorse: Remnants of red wax. Address in John III's hand:

To my ryth worchepfull husbond John Paston be þis delyueryd in hast.

The date is evidently between the imprisonment of Sir John Howard late in 1461
(see no. 163) and John III's leaving home, which took place before November 1462
(see no. 318). Edward IV was at Cambridge on 2 and 3 March 1462 (Privy seals,
noted by Gairdner).
    F. ii, p. 288. G. 441/510.

Plesyt yow to wet þat John Wellys *and* hys brodyr told me thys nyth þat
the Kyng lay at Cambryge as yestyr-nyth to Sandwyche ward, for ther is[1]
gret dyuysyon be-twyx the lordys *and* the schypmen ther that causyth hym
to goo thedyr to se a remedye ther-for. I[2] thank God that John Paston
5 yed non erst forthe, for I trust to God all schall be do er he comyth. And it
is told me that Syr John Howard is lek to lese hys hed. If it plese yow to
send to the seyd Wellys he schall send yow mor tydyngys than I may
wryt at thys tyme.
    God haue yow in hys kepyng. Wretyn in hast at Thetforthe at xj of the
10 clok in þe nyth the same day I dep*ar*tyd fro yow.
    I thank Pampyng of hys good wyll,[3] and them þat wer cause of changyng
of my hors, for they ded me a bettyr torne than I wend they had do; *and* I
schall aqwyt them a-nothyr day and I maye.

By yowyr M. P.

171. To JOHN PASTON I   1462, 18 May

Add. 27444, f. 117. 11½×5½ in. Calle's hand.

Dorse: Paper seal over red wax and tape. Address in a different style from
that of the letter, but nevertheless probably in Calle's hand:

To my ryght wurschipful maistre John Paston.

The date is evidently later than the murder of Thomas Denys in July 1461 (see no.
159). The reference to 'Joan Gayne's matter' shows it to be not much later than
no. 165.
    G. 448/517.

I recomaunde me vnto you. Plesith it you to witte that I haue spoken w*yth*
Furbuscho*ur* and other of the matre that ye spake to me off, and they haue
p*ro*mysed me to be as feytheffull in it as it where for he*m*-selfe. Also I haue

spoken w*yth* my modre *and* seide to here as ye desired me to doo; and sche
seide sche knewe the massache weele j-nowe be-fore be other p*er*sones, in 5
like wice as ye comaunded hem to sey to her, and sche seide she wode fayne
that ye dede weele, what so eu*er* ye sey, and fille forthe in other talkyng.
Me semethe che is displesed that ye came not to her or than ye roode
foorthe. I schall telle you more whan that ye come home.

Thom*as* Denys wyff whas at me and desired me that I schulde[1] sende 10
to you and desire you that che myght haue knowleche from you how ye
woll that sche schall doo w*yth* her matre. Sche seithe her brother *and* other
of her frend*es* thynke that she schulde vp to London and calle vppon her
matre there, but she seithe pleynly sche woll nought doo therin w*yth*oute
y*our* advice. 15

It whas toolde me that Bacon and Gonno*ur* whas here to speke w*yth* me
for the matre that Bacon spake to you of, and at that tyme I whas at Norweche *and* I herde no more ⟨o⟩f[2] hem sethen. And as for my brother
Willi*am*, he is not p*ur*posed to come to London tyll aftre Pentecost, but my
brother Clement is p*ur*posed to come forward on Monday or on Twesday 20
next comyng at the ferthest.

Nomore at this tyme, but the blissed T*r*inité p*r*eserue you. Wrete*n*[3] the
xviij day of Maij.

Y*our* M A R G A R E T   P A S T O N

I prey you that ye woll wetesafe to remembre Johane Gayne matre, *and* 25
that ye woll take John Paston þat he remembre you of it, for Dawbeney and
⌐Pampyng⌐ woll sone for-gete[4] it.

172. To J O H N   P A S T O N I   1463, probably 19 January

Add. 34888, f. 213. 11½×11¾ in. Daubeney's hand.

Dorse: Traces of red wax. Address in Daubeney's hand:

*To my right worchepful John Paston be þis lett*er *deliueryd in hast.*

The date is certainly in the reign of Edward IV, for the Duke of Suffolk married
Edward's sister Elizabeth (l. 24). The only election during Edward's reign at this
time of year was in 1463: Parliament was summoned first for 5 February, then for
7 March, and finally for 29 April (Scofield, i. 268–70).

The mutilation at the end of the letter makes it impossible to be sure whether
the Wednesday on which it was written was before or after St. Agnes's Day

171. [1] *Uncertain:* shulde *seems to have been written first, and* c *then written almost over
the* h.
[2] o *mostly destroyed by tape piercing paper.*
[3] -n *repr. by a superscript stroke, written after instead of above* -e, *above at* canc.
[4] *No space.*

(21 January, a Friday in 1463). The former is more likely, for the Wednesday following would be the day after the important feast of the Conversion of St. Paul and would probably be dated by reference to it.

F. iv, p. 150. G. 465/536.

Right worchepfull hosbond, I recommand me to you. Please you to wete þat I receyvyd a letter frome you on þe[1] Sonday next after Twelthe Day weche was sent be a prest of Seynt Gregorys paryche of Norwich;[2] and wher as ye[1] mervaylyd I sent you no wrytyngs of suche letters as ye sent me be-fore, 5 I sent you a answer of þe substauns of suche maters as ye have wretyn of to me be-fore, be Playter,[3] þe weche he told me a sent hem to you to London. And as towchyng þe[4] erandys þat ye sent to me for to do to Richard Calle, I have do as ye command me to do and callyd vp-on hym therfore bothe be-fore your writyng and sithyn. He thare have non excuse for ⌐de⌐favte 10 of leyser, for he hathe be but ryght litill her syn ye departyd hens.[5] He is owght at this tyme, and whan þat he comythe home I shall make hym make yow a clere ⌐bylle of þe receyt⌐ of your lyvelod and Fastolff bothe, and I shale send yow a clere bylle of my receytys and also of[6] my paymentys owght therof ageyn. And as for suche[4] erandys þat shuld be do to Ser 15 Thomas Howys,[7] I have shewyd Richard Calle your writyng and told hym your entent as ⌐for suche⌐[8] thyngys as ye wold he shuld sey to hym on ⌐hys⌐[9] owne[10] heed. Also I have do your erandys to my moder and to my cosyn Clere after your writyng.

Item, I have spoke to John Adam and to Playter of your entent of þe last 20 bylle þat ye sent me, and they sey they wolle do after your entent as moche as they ⌐may⌐ and ye shalle have a answere therof in hast. Item, Ser Robert Coniors dinid wyth me[11] thys day and shuyd me a letter þat came frome þe Kyng to[12] hym, desyryng hym þat he shuld a-wayt vpon hys welle be-louyd broder þe Duk of Suffolk at Norwich on Monday next comyng for to be at 25 þe aleccion of knyghtys[13] of þe chyer; and he told me þat euery jentylman of Norffolk and Suffolk ⌐þat arne⌐ of any repetacion[14] hathe writyng frome þe Kyng in lyke wysse as he had. I felle hym be hys seyyng þat he ys right welle disposyd to you ward. He seythe ther shall no man make hym to be a-geyns you in no maner.[15] Skypwyth shall telle you suche tydyngys as bethe 30 in þis contré, and of Thomas Gorney and of hys man: hym-self is clerk convicte and hys man is hangyn.[16] Ye shalle here here-after what they and oder were purposyd to a do to her master.

172. [1] *In this letter and the next Daubeney uses* ye *without distinction for 'the' and 'ye'.*
[2] *Curl on* -c, *as below.*
[3] *These two words marked off by a roughly curved line before* be *and an oblique stroke after* Playter.
[4] a *canc.*   [5] but *canc.*   [6] f *canc.*   [7] þe entent *canc.*
[8] *Interl. above* forsum *canc.*   [9] *Interl. above* your *canc.*
[10] ede *canc.*   [11] *In margin.*   [12] me *canc.*
[13] *Written* knygt- *with circumflex over* g; *so also* knigt- *l. 48.*
[14] sul suld be ther as that day *canc.*   [15] ye s *canc.*   [16] -g *written but erased.*

I thank you hertely of yo*ur* writyng to me be-for*e* þat John Paston came home, for God knowith I thowght right longe tyle I hard frome you. I shalle send word in writyng of suche[17] tyding*ys* as we have here[18] on Monday in 35 hast. Daubeney deseyryht to wet[19] what tyme þat it please you þat he shuld come ageyn to you. My mod*er and* many other folkys makyth moche of yo*ur* son John þe old*er*, and right glad of hys comyng hom, *and*[20] lekyth reght welle hys demenyng.

Heydon son hathe bor*e* owght þe syyd stowtly her*e* þis Cristemes, *and* 40 whan þat he rydyth he hathe iiij or v men ⌐wyth hym⌐ in a clothyng, but he hathe but lytyll fafor*e* in þis contré but yf it be of þe Bischop *and* ⟨of⟩[21] þe Prior*e* of Norwic*h*. þe seyd Prior*e* hathe grau*n*tyd[22] hym þe steward-chep[23] þat hys fad*er* had ⟨. . .⟩ he hathe it vnd*er* þe covent seale, *and* Spylman his tutor*e* to lerne hym howe he shuld be dem⟨enyd . . .⟩ it is seyd 45 a-bowght Bakynstorp þat Herry Heydon shuld a seyd þat it wer*e* welle do þat men of ⟨. . .⟩ shuld make[24] redy her bald batt*ys and* her[25] clot shois *and* go feche hom her knig*h*t*ys* of c⟨. . .⟩[26] Barney and it is pr*o*mysyd hym þat he shall be met w*yth*[27] be-cause of hys lan⟨. . .⟩[28] vs a good world *and* a pesybyll. I shall p*ur*vey for all thyng*ys* þat ye have sent to me for so ⟨. . .⟩[26] 50 be pleasyd.

The blyssyd Trinité have you in hys kepyng. Wretyn in hast þe Wednys-day ⟨. . .⟩ Seynt Agnet.

Yo*ur* M. P.

173. To John Paston I   1463, before 10 April

Add. 27446, f. 116. 12×6½ in. Daubeney's hand.

Dorse: Marks of folding. Traces of red wax, and tape-slits, but no address. Latin accounts in Calle's hand.

The date is before Easter, since surety is to be found for payment at Easter. The election mentioned must therefore be that of 1463 (see no. 172); Easter Day was 10 April. The report of Paston's dispute with Jenney and Debenham connects this letter with no. 66, which is also probably of 1463, though no. 192 shows that the trouble continued as late as 1465.

    G. 975/539.

Please you to wet þat Will Jeney *and* Debham came to Calcote on Wednys-day be-for*e* non, *and* ther they spake w*yth* Rysyng *and* John Smythe, *and* haskyd hem rent *and* ferme; *and* they seydyn they had payed you *and* so

---

[17] tyty *canc.*   [18] after *canc.*   [19] of *canc.*   [20] they *canc.*
[21] *Here and in the rest of the letter some words lost at large tear in corner.*
[22] hy *and imperfect* m *canc.*   [23] of þe *canc.*   [24] hem *interl. but canc.*
[25] cr *and incomplete letter canc.*   [26] *Room for about fifteen letters.*
[27] *Three letters, the last two* be, *canc.*   [28] *Room for about eighteen letters.*

they myght not paye hem also. Ferthermore they told hem that ye had hold
5 a corte ther syn þat they enteryd there. Than Jenney answerd ageyn,
'Be-cause he held a corte here we mad hym hold corte at London, *and* so
shall we make the to hold a corte at Ipysweche *wyth*-owt thowe wolt pay
vs þe rent *and* ferme.' 'S*er*', qu*od* Rysyng, 'I toke þe ferme of my mast*er and*
of S*er* Thom*a*s Howys.' ⌈Jenney seyd⌉, '*And* as for S*er* Thom*a*s, he
10 *and* we shall acord well j-nowe'.[1] *And* so they hathe[2] seled vp þe berne dor*ys*,
and woll dryve a-wey þe catell, bothe of þe fermor*ys and* of þe tenaunt*ys*,
wyth-owt þe fermor *and* John Smythe woll fynd hem suerté to pay hem at
Esterne. *And* Jenney *and* Debham woll [be] bownd ageyn to hem in a
obligacion of xl li. to save hem harm-lese ageyns you. *And* so as yet Rysyng
15 standythe vnd*er* award at Leystofte, so[3] Rysyng hathe sent word to[4] me þat
I shall knowe thys nyght or ellis to morowe what end they hathe mad.

It*em*, as towchyng þe burges of Yermothe, they were[5] chosyn on Wednysday. The baly Wydwell ys on, *and* as for the todyr þe Bischop sent to
þe towne for to have a man of hys owne. *And* so they be not a-cordyd yit
20 of hym; en[6] cas they may not a-cord John Rus shall be the todyr.

It*em*, as towchy*n*g Grene, a came not to Cast*er* on Thursday, for he went
to Norwi*ch* þe same day, *and* so he is yet ther. Daubeney hathe spokyn
wyth Watkyn Shypdam for to be at Beyton on Monday to kepe a corte ther,
and so he woll be at Cast*er* on Sonday[7] *and* spek *wyth* you, for he seythe þat
25 Fastolf hathe mad a cleyme ther-to. That is þe cause he wolle comon ⌈*and*
spek⌉ *wyth* you therof[8] hym-selff.

It*em*, I can not, ner Daubeney nowther, fynd yo*ur* wyght boke; it is not
in þe trussyng cofyr ner in þe[9] sprucheste nothyr. Jon Walsham toke me a
quayere—I suppose it lo[n]gythe to þe same boke; þat same I send you *and*
30 þe byllis of Walcote *wyth* ale sealyd.

Wretyn þ*is* day.

By yo*ur* M. P.

174. To JOHN PASTON I   Probably 1463, 13 November

Add. 34888, f. 220. $11\frac{1}{2} \times 4\frac{3}{4}$ in. Daubeney's hand.

Dorse: Paper seal over red wax and string. Address in Daubeney's hand:

*To my ryght worchepfull hosbond John Paston be thys lett*er *delyueryd in hast.*

Since this letter is written from Caister in Daubeney's hand, it is most probably of
the same year as no. 173.
    F. iv, p. 88. G. 479/551.

Right worchepfull ⌈husbond⌉, I reco*m*mand me to you. Please you to wet
þat I was at Norwi*ch* this wek to p*ur*vey suche thyng*ys* as nedythe me

---

173. [1] thys *canc.*   [2] *MS.* hahte.   [3] he h *canc.*   [4] my *canc.*   [5] chosyng *canc.*
     [6] *No space.*   [7] h *canc.*   [8] -r- *inserted later.*   [9] spruc *canc.*

ageyns thys wynt*er*. And I was at my mod*ers*, *and* wille I was ther ther
came in on Wrothe, a kynnysman of Elysabet Cler*ys*, *and* he sey yo*ur*
dowt*er and* pre⌈y⌉syd hyr to my mod*er*, *and* seyd þat she was a goodly yong 5
woma*n*. And my mod*er* pr*ay*d hym for ⌈to⌉ gett ⌈for⌉ hyr su*m* good mariage
yf he knewe any.[1] And he seyd he knewe on shuld be of a ccc mark be yer,
þe wyche is S*er* John Cley son[2] that is chamb*er*leyn w*yth* my lady of York;
and he ys of age of xviij yer old. 3yf ye thynk it be for to be spok of, my
mod*er* thynkyth þat it shuld be get for lesse mony nowe in thys world than 10
it shuld be[3] her-aft*er*, owthyr þat j or su*m* other good mariage.[4]

It*em*, I spake w*yth* Mast*er* John Estgate for Pekeryng*ys* mat*er*, aft*er*
⌈your⌉[5] entent of þe mat*er* of þe lett*er* þat ye sent home; *and* he seyd to me
he shuld write to yow howe he had don ther-in, *and* so he sent you a lett*er*
þe wyche was sent you be John Wodows man w*yth* other lett*ers*. As for 15
⌈answer⌉ [of] other mat*er*, Daubeney tellythe me he wret to you.

I be-seche alle-myghtty God have you[6] in hys kepyng. Wretyn at Cast*er*
þe Sonday next aft*er* Seynt Marteyne.

By yo*ur* M. P A S T O N

175. To J OHN P ASTON II 1463, 15 November

Add. 34888, f. 221. $11\frac{1}{4} \times 8\frac{7}{8}$ in. Daubeney's hand.

Dorse: Traces of red wax. Address in Daubeney's hand:

To my welbelouyd son Ser *John Paston be this deliueryd in hast.*

The date cannot be earlier than 1463, when John Paston II was knighted, or later
than 1465, for John I died in May 1466. 1465 is unsuitable because John Paston I's
sons were evidently with him, and not at home, at the end of October of that year
(see no. 196 below). (Only the two sons named John were by then old enough to be
in question.) Gairdner suggests with great probability that Sir John had gone north
(for he passed through Lynn) to join the King. Edward IV was in Yorkshire in
November 1463, but at Reading in 1464 (Scofield, i. 310–11, 364).
F. iv, p. 168. G. 480/552. C. 30.

I gret yow welle, and send yow Godd*ys*[1] blissyng *and* myn, latyng yow wet
that I have rec*ey*vyd a lett*er* from you þe wyche ye deliu*er*yd to Mast*er*
Rog*er* at Lynne, wherby I conseyve that ye thynke ye ded not well that ye
dep*ar*tyd hens w*yth*-owt my knowlage. Wherfor I late yow wett I was
ryght euyll payed w*yth* yow.[2] Yo*ur* fad*er* thowght, *and* thynkyth yet, þat I 5
was asentyd to yo*ur* dep*ar*tyng, and that hathe causyd me to have gret

---

174. [1] for hyr *canc.*   [2] wyth *canc.*   [3] nowe *canc.*
[4] *Some six words heavily cancelled and illegible.*   [5] *Interl. above* ye *canc.*
[6] *From* alle *on eras.*

175. [1] *No space.*   [2] therfor*e canc.*

hevinesse. I hope he wolle be your good fader her-after yf ye demene you welle *and* do as ye owe to do to hym. And I sharge you vpon my blyssyng þat in any thyng towchyng ⌜your fader þat⌝ shuld be hys worchep, profyte,

10 or avayle, that ye do your deuer *and* dylygent labore to þe fortherauns therin, as ye wolle have my good wille; *and* þat shalle cause your fader to be better fader to you. It was told me ye sent hym a letter to London. What þe entent therof was I wot[3] not, but[4] thowge he toke ⌜it⌝ but lyghtly I wold ye shuld[5] not spare to write to hym ⌜ageyn⌝ as lowly as ye cane, besecheyng

15 hym to be your good fader, and send hym suche tydyngys as bethe[6] in þe contré ther ye bethe in, *and* ⌜that⌝ ye be ware of your expence bettyr *and* ye have be before thys tyme, *and* be your owne purse-berere. I trowe ye shall fynd[1] yt most profytable to you. I wold ye shuld send me word howghe ye doo *and* howghe ye have schevyste for your-self syn ye departyd

20 hens, be sum trosty man, ⌜and⌝ that your fader ⌜have⌝[7] no knowlage ther-of. I durste not late hym knowe of þe laste letter þat ye wrot to me be-cause he was so sore dyspleasyd wyth me at þat tyme.

Item, I wold ye shuld speke wyth Wekis *and* knowe hys dysposysion to Jane Walsham. She hathe seyd[8] syn he departyd hens but she myght have

25 hym she wold neuer [be] maryyd;[9] hyr hert ys sore set on hym. She told me þat he seyd to hyr þat ther was no woman in þe world[10] he lovyd so welle. I wold not he shuld jape hyr, for she menythe good feythe, *and* yf he wolle not have hyr late me wete ⌜in hast⌝ *and* I shall purvey for hyr in othyr wysse.

30 As for your harneys *and* gere that ye left here, ⌜it ys in⌝ Daubeneys kepyng. It was neuer remeuyd syn your departyng be-cause that he had not þe keyes. I trowe it shall apeyer but if it be take hed hate be tymys. Your fader knowythe not wher[11] it is. I sent your grey hors to Ruston to[12] þe ferrore, *and* he seythe he shall neuer be nowght to rood nowthyr ryght

35 good to plowe nore to carte; he seythe he was splayyd *and* hys shulder rent from þe body. I wot not what to do wyth hym. Your grandam wold fayne her sum tydyngys from yow. It were welle do ⌜þat⌝ ye sent a letter to hyr howe ye do as astely as ye may.

And God have you in hys kepyng *and* make yow a good man, *and* ⌜3yf

40 yow grace to⌝ do as well as I wold ye shuld do. Wretyn at Caster þe Tewisday next be-for Seynt Edmond þe Kynge.

Your[13] moder M. PASTON

I wold ye shuld make ⌜meche of⌝[14] þe parson [of] Fylby, þe berer her-of, and make hym good cher yf ye may.

---

[3] nere *canc.*   [4] thoge *canc.*   [5] nos *canc.*
[6] in *interl.*, *with caret, between* be *and* the *; evidently a mistaken correction based on the following clause.*   [7] *Interl. above* hathe *canc.*
[8] synd *canc.*   [9] she is *canc.*   [10] she *canc.*   [11] it *canc.*
[12] ye *and raised* e *canc*   [13] Y- *corr. from* þ.   [14] *Interl. above* good cher *to canc.*

176. To JOHN PASTON I   1464, 6 May

Add. 43488, f. 47. $11\frac{5}{8} \times 5$ in. Hand of Friar John Mowth (see p. lxxvii).

Dorse: Traces of red wax. Address in unidentified hand, certainly not Mowth's:

Tho my ryt worschopffull hossebond John Paston, in hast.

Fenn and Gairdner dated this letter in 1459, the latter on the ground that the only years in the later married life of John and Margaret Paston in which the Sunday before Ascension Day fell appreciably before 10 May were 1456 and 1459, and in 1456 the King could not have been at Leicester on 10 May. But the King who addressed 'more specyal termys' to John Paston II would be Edward IV, not Henry VI, for the young John appeared at court first in 1461 (see no. 116) and was knighted in 1463. Edward IV was at Leicester in May 1464 (Scofield, i. 333 and n. 2). In that year the Sunday before Ascension Day was 6 May, so that, as Gairdner says, Margaret could hardly hope for an answer from her husband in time to send John II to Leicester by 10 May; but in spite of this difficulty the date must stand. John I's displeasure with his son may be connected with no. 175 of November 1463. Gairdner's further objection that no. 232, which is probably of the same year as this, would be signed *John Paston K.* if it were after John II was knighted, is shown to be invalid by the subscription of no. 235; for that is identical with the form in no. 232 and must be dated 1465. See also no. 177.

F. i, p. 174. G. 325/377. C. 32.

Rythe wo*u*rchepfwl hosbond, I reco*m*mawnd me onto ʒow. Plesyth ʒow to wete þat[1] on Thoris-day last was þer wer*e* browt on-to þis towne many prevy selis; *and* on[2] of hem was i*n*dosyd to ʒow *and* to Hastynggys *and* to fyve ore sexe odyr*e* g*en*tylme*n*, *and* a-nodyr was se*n*t o*n*-to ʒow*re* sone *and* i*n*-dosid to hym-selfe alone, *and* asynyd wyth-i*n*ne wyth þe Kynggys howyn hand, *and* so wer*e* bwt fewe þat wer*e* se*n*t, as it was told me, *and* also þe⌈r⌉[3] wer*e* more specyal termys i*n* hys þa*n* wern i*n* oderys. I sey a copy of þoo þat wer*e* se*n*t o*n*to odyr g*en*tylme*n*. þe i*n*tent of þe wrytyng was þat þey schwlde be wyth þe Kyngg at[4] Leycestr*e* þe x day of May, wyth as many p*er*sonys defensabylly arayid as þey myte, acordyng to her degré, *and* þat þey schwld[5] bryng wyth hem for*e* her*e* expe*n*sys for*e* ij monythis. As for þe lettyr þat was i*n*dosyd to ʒow *and* to odyr, it was delyveryd to Welya*m* ʒelvyrton, for þere aperyd no more of þe remwlawnt. Hastyngys js forthe i*n*-to ʒorke-schyre. I prey ʒow þat ʒe vowchesaf to send word i*n* hast how ʒe wyl þat ʒore sone be demenyd her-in. Men thynk here þat byn ʒowre wel-wyllerys þat ʒe may no lesse do þan to send hym forthe. As for*e* hys demenyng swn ʒe departyd, i*n* god feythe it hath byn ryth good *and* lowly, *and* delygent i*n* ovyrsythe of ʒowre servawntys *and* odyr th[i]nggys þe weche I hope ʒe wold a be plesyd wyth *and* ʒe had be at hom. I hope he wyl

5

10

15

---

176. [1] þ- *in form of* y *throughout.*
    [2] to *and beginning of* ʒ *canc.*   [3] *Interl. with caret.*
    [4] leces *canc.*   [5] *MS.* schwldld *following* schwd *canc.*

be wel de-menyd to plese ȝow her*e*aftyrward. He desyryd Alblaster*e*[6] to be[7] mene to ȝow for*e* hym, *and* was ryte hevy of hys demenyng to ȝow.[8] I sent ȝo⌜w⌝ word also be Alblaster*e* how I dede to hym aftyr þ*at* ȝe wer*e* go, *and* I be-seche ȝow hartyly þ*at* ȝe wochesaf to be hys god fadyr, for*e* I hope he is[9] schastysyd *and* wil be þe warher*e* her-aftyr. As for alle odyr t[h]ynggys at hom, I hope þ*at* I *and* odyr*e* schal do howre[10] part þer-i*n*ne as wel as we may; bwt[11] as for mony, it comyth bw[t] slawly i*n*.

God have ȝow i*n* hys kepyng *and* se*n* ȝow good sped i*n* alle ȝowr*e* materis. Wretyn i*n* hast at Norwece on þe Sonday next be-for*e* þe Assencyon Day. Ser*e*, I wold be ryte glad to he[re] swmme gode tydynggys fro ȝow.

Be ȝorys, M. P.

177. To John Paston I — 1464, 8 June

Add. 34889, f. 8. $11\frac{1}{4}\times8\frac{3}{8}$ in. Hand of John Paston II.

Dorse: Conclusion of letter. Paper seal over red wax. Address in John II's hand:

To myn ryght worshypful hosbond John Paston be thys delyueryd in haste.

The date must be shortly after the summonses to the King mentioned in no. 176. No record of a commission in the terms specified seems to survive. The year 1464 is confirmed by the report of the death of Reginald Rous, of Denington in Suffolk, who died in that year (John Weever, *Ancient Funerall Monuments* (1631), p. 782 (recording a memorial in Denington church): 'Raynold Rowsse, son and heyre of Robart Rowsse . . . which dyed in *Anno* Mcccclxiiii').

F. iv, p. 176. G. 490/567.

Ryght worshypful hosbond, I rekomaund me on-to you. Pleasyth you to wete that I sent yist*er*day Louedaye to Norwyche to speke wyth the vykyr*e* of Derh*a*m for*e* the mater*e* betwen Mast*er* Constantyn *and* hym. And he seyth þ*at*, as for*e* that mater*e*, Mast*er* Constantyn sewyd hym for*e* feyth *and* trowth brekyng, ⌜*and*⌝ he sewyd Mast*er* Constantyn in the temp*or*al[1] curte vppon an oblygacion of x li.; *and* ther*e* was made appoyntment betwen hem by the aduyce of bothe ther*e* conceylis be-for*e* Mast*er* Rob*ert* Popy þ*at* eche of hem shuld relece othyr*e*, *and* so they dede *and* the sewtys wer*e* wythdrawyn on both p*ar*tyes *and* jche of hem aquytauncyd[2] othyr*e*; *and* as for*e* ⌜any⌝ copy ⌜of the plee⌝[3] he had neu*er* non, ner*e* he ner*e* Mast*er* John Estegate, þ*at* was hys at*ur*nay, remembryth nat þ*at* it was regestryd.

[6] ryth *canc.* [7] *No space.* [8] *Two letters, perhaps* at, *canc.* [9] sch⌜a⌝stysyd *canc.* [10] i*n*tent *canc.* [11] af *canc.*

177. [1] -por- *repr. by crossed* p. [2] -aun- *written out, and superior* a *added.* [3] *Interl. above* there of *canc.*

And Master John Estegate seythe if it schuld be scergyd in the regester it wold take a fortenyght werk *and* yit parauenture neuer be the⁴ nere. Syre Thomas Howes hathe ben ryght besy thys weke at Bloofeld in wrytyng *and* lokyng vppe of gere, *and* John Russe hathe ben wyth hym there the moste 15 parte of alle thys weke. And thys daye was Robert Lynne there wyth hym; what they haue do I wote nat, but I schal wete if I may. It was told me þat Syre Thomas desyryd of John Russe to make hym a new jnventory of Syr John Fastolffys goodys. John Russe myght not be spoke wyth yit fore the letter þat he shuld a wretyn whych ye sente me word of.   20

Item, it is tolde þat the Dwke of Suffolk is kome home, *and* owthyre he is ded ore ellys ryght seke *and* not lyke to eskape. And Syre John Howard is kome hom, *and* it is seyd þat the Lord Skalys *and* he haue a comyssyon to enquere whye they of thys contré þat were sent fore kame noon⁵ hasty-lare vppe afftyre they were sent fore. It is reportyd þat the Kyng is gretly 25 dyspleasyd there-wyth.

At the reuerence of God, arme yowre-selue as myghtyly as ye kan⁶ ageyn yowre enmyes, fore I know verrayly þat they wyl do ageyn yow as myghtyly as they kan wyth all there powere. It is told me þat Syre Thomas shal kom vppe in haste, *and* othyre suche as he kan make for hys partye. Also, fore 30 Goddys sake be ware what medesynys ye take of any fysissyanys of London. I schal neuer trust to hem be-cause of yowre fadre *and* myn onkyl, whoys sowlys God assoyle.

The blissyd Trynyté haue yow in hys kepyng *and* sende yow helthe *and* good spede in all yowre materris. Wretyn in haste on the Fryday next 35 before Sceynt Bernabye.

By yowrys, M. P.⁷

Alle the gentylmen of thys contré þat went vppe to the Kyng are contre-maundyd² and are com home ageyn. It is told me þat Rowse of Suffolk is ded. If John Gayn myght haue any relese of hys sone, if it myght do hym 40 ese it were a good torne fore hym.

---

⁴ r *canc.*
⁵ *This seems to be what is meant, but the last two letters are not clear; perhaps corr. from* not.
⁶ fore I know verraly þat *canc.*
⁷ *Recto ends.*

178. To JOHN PASTON I   1465, 8 April

Add. 27444, f. 138. 11⅞×8½ in. Daubeney's hand. Notes in margin by John Paston I.

Dorse: Traces of red wax. Address in Daubeney's hand:

To my ryght worchepfull hosbond Jon Paston be þis deliueryd in hast.

The reference to the Duke of Suffolk's claim to Drayton and Hellesdon connects this with many letters of 1465, and the report of Suffolk's purchase of 'Brytyeff's' title links it closely with no. 180.

G. 499/578. C. 34 (part).

Right worchepfull hosbond, I recommand me to you. Please you to wet that I send you a copy of ⌐a⌐ deed that Jon Edmondys of Taueram sent to me be þe menys of Dorlet. He told Dorlet that he had suche² a deed as he supposyd that wold don ease in prevyng of þe tytyll that the Duk of
5 Suffolk cleymythe in Drayton, for þe same deed that³ he sent me⁴ þe seale of armys is lyke on-to þe copy þat I send you, and noo thyng leke⁵ to the Duk of Suffolk auncesters. Item, þe seyd Edmond seythe yf he may fynd any other thyng that may do yow ease in þat mater he wolle doo hys part therin. Item,⁶ Jon Russe sent me word that Barker and Herry Porter told
10 hym in councell that þe Duk of Suffolk hathe bowght on Brytyeff ⌐ryght⌐, þe wyche makythe a cleyme on-to Heylysdon, and þe seyd Duke is purposyd⁷ to entere wythin shorte tyme after Esterne; for in so moche þe seyd Russe felte⁸ be þe seyd Barker and Porter that all þe feffees wolle make a relees on-to þe Duk and helpe hym þat they can in-to her power,
15 for to have hys good lorchep.

Item, yf it please you, me thynkythe it ware ryght nessessary þat ye send word howe þat ye wolle your old malte be purveyd fore, for and any hote weder come affter þat it hathe leyne þis wynter season it shall be but lost but yf it be sold be tymys. For as fore þe pryse here, it is sore falle.⁹ I have
20 sold a c comb of malt ⌐þat came fro Guton⌐ to Jamys Golbeter, clenefyed and strek met and non jument [?], for ij s. ij d. þe comb,¹⁰ and to be payeed at Mydsomer and Lammes.

Item, ther be dyuers of your tenauntrys at Mauteby that had gret ned for to be reparyd, but¹¹ þe tenauntys be so pore that they are not a power to
25 repare hem; wherfor yf [it] leke you I wold that þe marche ⌐þat Bryge had⌐ myght be kept in your owne hand þis yer, that þe tenauntys myght have ruschys to repare wyth her howsys. And also ther is wyndfall wod at þe maner þat is of noo gret valewe, þat myght helpe¹² hem wyth to-ward þe

178. ¹ *Interl. over e of* yᵉ, *the* y *canc.*   ² on *canc.*   ³ I send you a *canc.*
⁴ ys *canc.*   ⁵ þe Duk of Suffolk armys *canc.*   ⁶ it is to *canc.*
⁷ *MS.* pro-.   ⁸ *MS.* felle.   ⁹ Item *canc.*
¹⁰ *This price underlined, apparently by John Paston in connection with his marginalia.*
¹¹ *MS.* at.   ¹² hy *and part of* m *canc.*

rep*a*racion yf it leke you to late hem have it þat hathe most need therof. I
have spoke w*yth* Borges that he shuld heyne þe pric*e* of þe mershe or¹³ ellis 30
I told hym þat he shuld no leng*er* have it for ye myght [have]¹⁴ other
fermors therto that wold geve ther-fore as it was late be-fore; *and* yf he
wold geve therfore as moche as a-nother man wold, ye wold þat he shuld
have it be-for any other man. And he seyd he shuld geve me answer*e* be a
fortenyght aft*er* Estern*e*. I can get non other fermor ther-to yet. 35

It*em*, I vnd*er*stand be Jon Pampy*ng* that ye wolle not þat yo*ur* sone be
take in-to yo*ur* hows ⌜nor holp be you⌝ tylle suche tyme of yer*e* as he was
put owt therof, the wiche shalle be a-bowght Seynt Thom*a*s messe. For
God*ys* sake, s*er*, ⌜a pety on hym *and*⌝ remembre yow¹⁵ it hathe be a long
season syn he had owt of you to helpe hym w*yth*, *and* he hathe obeyed hym 40
to yow *and* wolle do at all tymis, and wolle do that he can or may to have
yo*ur* good fad*er*hood.¹⁶ And at þe reu*er*ence of God, be ye hys good fad*er*
and have a fad*er*ly hert to hym. And I hope he shall eu*er* knowe hym-selff
þe bett*er* her-aft*er* *and* be þe more war*e* to exchewe suche thyng*ys* as shuld
dysplease you, *and* for to take hed ⌜at⌝ þat shuld please you. Pecoke shalle 45
telle you be mothe of mor*e* thyng*ys* than I may write to you at þis tyme.

The blysyd Trinité have yow in hys kepyng. Wretyn at Cast*er* in has[t]e
þe Monday next aft*er* Palme Sonday.

Your M. P.

In margin, notes roughly written by Paston opposite brackets marking off the respective paragraphs, in the following order (no punctuation):
Carte Drayto[n]; Heylisdon, Brythyeve, Barker, Port*er*; bracium; sirpis *pro*
rep[ar]ac*ione* ten*e*mentor*u*m de Mautby; Burgoys mariscus Mauteby; *pro* recup-
[era]c*ione* Joh[ann]is Paston.

179. To JOHN PASTON I   1465, 3 May

Add. 27444, f. 139. 11¼×9½ in., a piece *c.* 5×3½ in. torn off. Hand of John
Wykes (see p. lxxviii).

Dorse: Traces of red wax. Address in Wykes's hand:

*To my ryght wyrshypffull husbond John Paston be thys delyu*er*yd in hast.*

In corner, in unidentified hand: *liter*e.

The report of events at Drayton shows a situation very like that in no. 180, which
can be dated firmly 1465. This letter evidently precedes no. 180: Margaret is here
at Caister, intending to go to Hellesdon, and no. 180 is written from Hellesdon.
'Holy Rood Day' must therefore be 3 May, the feast of the Invention of the Cross,
not 14 September, the feast of the Exaltation of the Cross; the name was used for

¹³ I *canc.*   ¹⁴ *No space or defect; end of line.*   ¹⁵ for *canc.*
¹⁶ *Written* faderood, *then a very small* h *inserted.*

both (see *O.E.D.* under *Rood day*). Margaret would go to Hellesdon on the following Wednesday or Thursday, and write no. 180 on 10 May, the next Friday. The
reference to malt and barley recalls John I's letters nos. 71, 72.

G. 500/579.

Ryght wyrshypful husbond, I recomaunde me vn-to you. Pleasyd you to
wyte that I have spoken thys wyke wyth dyuers of youre tenauntys of
Drayton *and* put hem in confort that all shalbe well hereaftere, by the
grace of God; *and* I fyle well by hem that they wylbe ryght glad to haue a-
5 yen there olde mayster, *and* so wold they all except j or ij that be fals
shrewys.

And thys next wyke I purpose on Wensday or Thursday to be at Haylesdon *and* to a-byde ther a wyke or ij *and* send oure men a-bovte to gedere
money at Drayton *and* Haylesdon, *and* yf ye¹ wyll I woll do kepe a corte at
10 Drayton or I com thens. I pray you send me word how ye wyll that I doo
there-in. I recevyd ij letters ⌈from you⌉ of Nicholl Colman yestere-day,
wer-in ye desyre that we² shuld purvey for your malte *and* barley, *and* soo
shall we doo as well as we cann *and* send you word howe that we may doo
there-wyth in hast.

15 Item, yester-day Maister Phylyp toke Dorletys hors vppon Drayton lond
as they went to the plowe, for the hol⟨e⟩³ yere ferm; *and*,⁴ as it ys told me,
the tenauntys of Drayton told hym that he dyde hym wrong to make hym
pay for the hole yere, for non of the tenauntys had payd hym but for the di.
yere. *And* he say[d] thohg they hadnot payd but for the di. yere Paston
20 shuld pay for the othere di. yere, *and* for moo yerys also yf he lyvyd. But I
trow to gyte Dorlet a-yen hys hors, or els Maister⁵ Phylyp ys lyke to be
vn-horssyd ons, *and* we lyve all.

Youre son shall com ⌈hom⌉ to moryn, as I trowe, ⌈and⌉ as he deme[n]yth
hym hyre-aftere I shall lete you haue knowlych; *and* I pray you thynk not
25 in me that I wyll supporte hym ne fauour hym in no lewdnesse, for ⌈I
wylnot⌉. As I fynd hym⁶ here-aftere soo I wyll lete you haue knowlych.

I haue put youre evydens that com owte of the abbay in a seck, *and* en-
seylyd hem vndere Richard Call ys seall, that he shalnot say but they
⌈eryn⌉⁷ as he left hem. But as for the place where they ern kypt, he hath no
30 knowlych⁸ *and* ⟨. . .⟩ tyll ye ⟨. . .⟩.

As fore the gentylwoman that ye wrote to me fore yn youre lettere, I
⟨. . .⟩ there yf it lykyd all folkys as well as it shold doo me I trow ⟨. . .⟩
a-bowte yf here frendys were as well a-gryed therto⁹ as they ⟨. . .⟩ parte. Yf

179. ¹ thyn *canc.* ² w *over* y.
³ *Cramped at edge;* laste, *at beginning of next line, canc.*
⁴ th *canc.* ⁵ Phyp *canc.* ⁶ so w *canc.* ⁷ *Interl. above* were *canc.*
⁸ *From this point much has been lost by the tearing off of the right-hand bottom corner of the
sheet. At its widest the jagged tear reaches half-way across the paper, and it is impossible to
estimate with any accuracy how many letters may have been lost in each line.*
⁹ *Ampersand canc.*

ye wyll that it be movyd of more here-aft*er* I wyll ⟨. . .⟩ wyll make a newe
p*ar*son at Drayton. Also it ys sayd that th⟨. . .⟩ ther*e* by-cause it hath stond 35
so long voyd. Yet *and* any sh⟨. . .⟩ had lever that he com in by the Byshop
then by a⟨. . .⟩ doo ther*e*-in yf ye wyll send hom any pr*e*sentac*i*on selyd
⟨. . .⟩ we shall a-say to gyte som gode pruste *and* sette hym ⟨. . .⟩.

Wryten in haste at Caster*e* on Holy Rode Day, &c.

As ⟨. . .⟩ doo ther*e*-in as well as I cann. I haue gyte a replevyn ⟨. . .⟩ cc 40
shype, *and* yf thay may not be hadde a-yen then he gra⟨. . .⟩. We¹⁰ fynd
hym ryght gode in that we desyre of hym for you, *and* ther-fore yf it lyk
you I wold he wer*e* th⟨. . .⟩.

In margin, notes roughly written by Paston opposite brackets marking off the
respective paragraphs, in the following order:

Drayton ten*aun*tes bony pr*e*ter ij; malt, barly; Dorlet *et* verb[a] M.P.; J.P. sen.;
rotuli in prioria; [some notes lost at tear]; data subvic' r*e*plev*i*n pr*o* ouib*us*.

180. To John Paston I 1465, 10 May

Add. 27444, f. 141. 11⅝ × 16¾ in. Wykes's hand.

Dorse: Continuation of text. Traces of red wax. Address in Wykes's
hand:

*To my mayster*e *John Paston the oldest be thys delyu*er*yd in hast.*

The beginning of trouble at Hellesdon places this letter in 1465 (see especially
John I's letter no. 73). This year also fits the report that Thomas Ellis had been
elected mayor of Norwich. He was mayor in 1460, 1465, and 1474 (see no. 146);
and of these only 1465 suits the other circumstances.

G. 502/581. C. 35 (part).

Ryght wyrshypfull husbond, I recomaund me vn-to you. Pleysed you to
wyte that on Wensday last passyd Dabeney, Naunton, Wyk*ys*, *and* John
Love werr*e* at Drayton for to speke w*yth* your*e* ten*aun*ty*s* there, to put hem
in confort *and* for to aske money of hem also.

*And*¹ Pyrs Waryn, otherwyse callyd Pyrs at Sloth, whych ys a flykeryng 5
felowe *and* a besy w*yth* M*a*ister Phylyp *and* the bayly of Cosshay, he had a
plowe goyng in your*e* lond in Drayton, *and* there your*e* seyd s*er*uaunty*s* at
that tyme toke hys plowe-ware, that ys to say ij mary*s*, *and* broght hem to
Haylysdon, *and* there they be yet. *And* on the next mornyng aftere M*a*ister
Phylyp *and* the baylly of Cosshay com to Haylysdon w*yth* a grete nombere 10
of pepell, that ys to say viij*ˣˣ* men *and* more in harnysse, *and* there toke

---

¹⁰ *This last sentence crowded in at the foot, beginning in the margin.*
180. ¹ *Two oblique strokes, evidently by John Paston in connection with his marginalia.*

from the parsouns² plowe ij hors, prise³ iiij marc., *and* ij hors of Thomas
Stermyns⁴ plowe, prise xl s., sayng to hem that there was taken a playnt
a-yenst hem in the hunderd by the seyd Pyrs for takyng of the forseyd
15 plowarre at Drayton, *and* but thay wold be bond to com to Drayton on
Tewysday next comyng to awnswere to such maters as shalbe sayd to them
there they shold ⌈not⌉ haue there bestys a-yen; whych they refusyd to do
on-to the tyme that they had an awnswere from you. *And* so they led the
bestys forth to Drayton, *and* from Drayton forth to Cosshay.
20   *And* the same aftere-non folwyng the parson of Haylesdon send hys man
to Drayton wyth Stermyn for to speke wyth Maister Phylyp, to know a way
⌈yf they shuld haue a yen there catell or not⌉.⁵ *And* Maister Phylyp awn-
sweryd them yf that they wold bryng hom there destresse a-yen ⌈þat was
taken of Pyrs Waryn⌉, that then he wold delyuer hem thers, or els not. *And*
25 ⌈he⌉ lete hem playnly wyte that yf ye or any of youre seruauntys toke any
dystresse in Drayton, that were but the valew of an hen, they wold com to
Haylesdon *and* take there the valew of an ox there-fore; *and* yf thay cannot
take the valew therof there, that then they wyll do breke youre tenauntys
howsys in Haylesdon ⌈and take as moch as they cowd fynd there-in⌉. *And*
30 yf they be lettyd ther-of—wych shall neuer lye in youre powere for to do, for
the Duck of Suffolk ys abyll to kype dayly in hys hows more men then
⌈Dabeney⌉⁶ hadde herys in ⌈hys⌉⁷ hede yf hym lyst, ⌈and as for Dabeney he
ys a lewde felow *and* so he shalbe seruyd here-after, *and* I wold that he were
hyre⌉¹⁸—*and* therfore ⌈he seyd⌉ yf ye take vppon you to lette them so forto
35 do, that then they ⌈wold⌉ goo in-to any lyflode that ye had in Norffolk or
Suffolk *and* to take a destresse in lyke wysse as they wold do at Haylysdon.
And othere awnswerre cowde they non gyte, *and* so they departyd.
   Richard Calle axid the parson *and* Stermyn yf they wold take an accyon
for there catell, *and* the parson seyd he was agyd *and* syklow *and* he wold
40 not be trobelyd herafter; he sayd he had leuer lose hys catell, for he wyst
well⁹ yf he dyde so he shold be endytyd *and* so vexid wyth hem that he
shold neuer haue rest by hem. As for Stermyn, he sayd at that tyme he
durst not take no sute a-yenst hem nothere, but aftere that ⌈Richard was
rydyn⌉ I spake wyth hym ⌈and⌉ he sayd he wold be rulyd as ye wold haue
45 hym; *and* I fond hym ryght herty *and* wel dysposyd in that matere. *And* he
is bownde to you an obligacyon of x li. sengyll wyth-outen condycyon that

---

² *Not certain that this is the form meant: dotted circumflex above* u*; but the letter might
equally be* n, *and the mark only a diacritic.*
   ³ -e *evidently intended by curl on* -s.
   ⁴ *First written with tailed* n *as if final; then* s *added.*
   ⁵ *Interl. above* for hys bestys and how he *and* Stermyn shuld be demenyd therin *canc.*
   ⁶ *Interl. above* ye *canc.,* hadde *corr. from* haue.
   ⁷ *Interl. above* youre *canc.*
   ⁸ *From* and I wold *evidently added to the interlineation later for the last two words are
crowded in, above the line of the interlineation, before the following interlined* wold.
   ⁹ he shold be *canc.*

he shall a-byde by such accyons as shalbe takyn by youre advyse in hys name. Wherfore I haue send you a tytelyng therof in a byll closyd herin.

I axyd Thom*a*s Gryne avyse[10] when they had take the dystresse hyre,[11] *and* he avysyd me that herre destresse shold be delyu*e*ryd a-yen to them so that we my3t haue a-yen our*ys*; *and* me[12] thoght it was non awnswer*e* aft*er* myn entent, *and* wold not therof but axyd avyse of Skypw*yth* what[13] hym thoght that wer*e* best to doo ther*e*-in *and* most wyrshypfull. He seyd by hys avyse that I shold send to you in al the hast that I cowde, *and* that ye shuld fynde a mene therfore a-bove by the avyse of ⌐youre⌐ lernyd counsell to haue a wrytte from a-bove for to delyu*er* yt, of lesse then the vndershyrff werre otherr*e* wysse dysposyd to you then we fynde hym; for it symyth that he ys made of the other*e* party. *And* as for the replevyn for the cc shype ys not yet s*er*vyd. Skypw*yth* thynkyth that ye my3t haue a wrytte both for*e* the shype *and* the destresse now taken at Haylysdon. I p*r*ay you that ye wyll send word in hast how[14] [ye] woll that we doo in thys maters.[15]

Skypw*yth* went w*yth* me to the Byshop of Norwych, *and* I lyte hym haue knowlych of the ryotous *and* evyll dysposicyon of M*aister* Phylyp, desyryng hys lordshyp that he wold see a mene tha[t] a correccyon my3t be hadde,[16] in as moch as he was ⌐chyf⌐ justic*e* of the peas *and* hys ordynare, *and* in asmoch as he was a prest *and* vndere hys correccyon that he sholde haue vnderstondy*ng* of hys dysposicyon; *and* I made Dabeney to tell hym all the mater*e* how[17] it was. *And* he seyd he wold send for hym *and* speke w*yth* hym, *and* he told me of dyu*er*s thyng*ys* of the demenyng of hym wherby I vnderstode he lykyd not by hys ⌐dysposicyon nor⌐ demenyng[18] ⌐in thys mat*er* nor in no nothyre⌐, for it symyd he had p*r*ovyd hym what he ys in other*e* maters.

My lord seyd to me that he wold ryght fayn that ye had a gode conclusyon in your*e* maters, *and* seyd by hys trouth that he ought you ryght gode wyll *and* wold ryght fayn that ye wer*e* com hom, *and* seyd to me that it shold be a grete confort to your*e* frend*ys* *and* neghbors *and* that your*e* p*r*esens shold do more a-mong*ys* hem ⌐than⌐ a c of your*e* men shold do in your*e* absens, *and* more your*e* enmys wold ferre to do a-yens you yf ye myght be at home *and* steryng a-mong*ys* hem; *and* seyd full playnly in meny other*e* thyng*ys* ⌐it⌐[19] wer*e* to long*e* to wryte at thys time, ⌐as⌐[20] Skypw*yth* shall tell you when he comy3t to you.

I p*r*ay you thanke Skypw*yth* of hys gode wyll, for he was ryght well wyllyd to go w*yth* me *and* yeve me hys avyse. Me thynkyth he ys ry3t well wyllyd to you.[21]

---

[10] howe we my3t *canc.*   [11] *and* he ⌐sayd⌐ we my3t do there-fore *canc.*
[12] *A caret, but nothing interlined.*   [13] how *canc.*   [14] that *canc.*
[15] *Following section marked off by brackets, by John Paston.*
[16] for *canc.*   [17] *MS.* howt.   [18] nothyre *interl. but canc.*
[19] *Interl. above* the *canc.*   [20] *Interl. above* but *canc.*
[21] *Recto ends; verte folium written at the foot in the middle.*

85   Item, I pray you send hastely word how that ye wyll that we be gydyd
wyth thys place, for as it ys told me it ys lyke to stond in as grete jupardy in
hast as othere don.[22] On Thursday al day there were kypt in Draton logge
in-to lx persons, and yet, as it ys told me, there be wyth-in dayly and ny3tly
in-to a xvj or xx persons.

90   Item, it ys told me that Thomas Elys of Norwych, whych nowe ⌈ys⌉
chosyn mayere, seyd at Drayton that yf my lord of Suffolk nede a c men[23]
he wold purvey hym ther-of, and yf any men of the town wold go to Paston
he wold do lay hem faste in preson. I wold youre men mygh[t] haue a supersedias owte of the Chaunceré and be ovte of the dangere of there men here,
95 and I pray you letnot Wyll Naunton be for-yete there-in. Richard Call and
othere can tell you of hys demenyng, and I pray you that ye be not dysplesyd[24] for hys a-bydyng wyth me, for in gode feth he hath ben a grete
confort to me syn ye departyd hens, as I wyll lete you wyte herafter. I pray
you yf hys brothere com to you for a relesse of ⌈hys⌉ londe, lette hym non
100 haue on-to the tyme that ye see hys faderys wyll, the whych I wote where
it ys, and ⌈þat⌉ it like you to desyre hym to be gode brothere to hym.[15]

    Item, I haue left John Paston the oldere at Castere to kype the place
there, as Richard can tell you, for I had levere, and it pleasyd you, to be
captenesse[25] here then at Castere. Yet I was nothyng purposyd to a-byde
105 here when [I] com from hom but for a day or ij, ⌈but⌉ I shall a-byde here
tyll I here tydyngys from you.[15]

    Item, it ys told me that the Duck of Suffolk hath boght, or shal by in
hast, the ry3t that on Bryghtylhed hath in Haylesdon, &c.[15]

    Item, as for the evydens that Watkyn Shypdam hadd, he delyueryd to
110 hys wyffe a box enselyd wyth hys owyn seall by hys lyffe, for to be delyueryd
to you, whych box she delyueryd to Richard Call vndere the same seall aftere
hys dessesse. Richard can tell you of the gydyng of the cofere, wyth othere
bokys that were at Shypdams. And as for ⌈all⌉ youre ⌈othere⌉ evydens, ye
ther not feere as fore the sy3t of hem, for there hath nor shall no man sen
115 hem tyll ye com hom. I can not fynd that ye send to me fore to haue ovte
of the rolle.

    Item, I hyre no word of Colte of New Castell, nor of no nothere from
you that shold haue youre malte; but I haue spoken to the vikere, John Rus,
and Robert Botelere to help for to sell youre malte, and as we can do there-in
120 we shall send you word.

    The provest of Cambrygge ys com in-to thys contray, and Dabeney shall
receve of hym that longyth to you on Monday or Tewysday, and he shall
haue hyt[26] delyueryd accordyng to youre wrytyng.

    Item, my modere told me that she thynkyth ryght strange that she may
125 not haue the profectys of Clyre ys place in peasabyll wyse for you. She seyt

---

[22] and th canc.   [23] I shuld p canc.   [24] wyth me canc.
[25] -n- lacks a minim.   [26] MS. hys.

it ys hers *and* she hath payd most therfore yet, *and* she sayth she wyll haue the p*r*ofecty*s* therof or ells she wyll make more folk to speke therof.²⁷ She seyth she knowyt not what ryght ne titell that ye haue ther-in but yf ye luste to trobell w*yth* herr*e*, *and* that shold be no wyrshep to you; *and* she sayth she wylbe ther*e* thys som*er and* repayre the housyng ther. In gode feyth I hyre moch langage of the demenyng be-twene you *and* herr*e*. I wold ⌐ryght⌐ fayn, *and* soo wold many moo of youre frendy*s*, that it wer*e* other-wyse by-twene you then it ys, *and* yf it wer*e* I hope ye shold haue the beter*e* spyde in ⌐all⌐ other*e* maters.

I p*r*ay God be your*e* gode spyde in all your*e* maters *and* yef you gr*a*ce to haue a gode conclusyon ⌐of hem⌐ in haste, for thys ys to wyry a lyffe to a-byde for you *and* all your*e*. Wryten in haste at Haylysdon the x day of May. The cause that I send to you this hastely ys to haue an awnswer*e* in haste from you.²⁸

Youry*s*, M. P. 140

In margin, notes roughly written by Paston opposite brackets marking off para-graphs, in the following order:

dist*r*i*n*ctio Petri Warin; dist*r*i*n*ctio Sturmyn *et* rector*is* de Heylisdon; crak; accio rector*is et* Sturmyn; replevin; ep*iscop*us Norwic'; ep*iscop*us Norwic'; Skipwith; p*er* [? *for* periculum] Heyli[s]d[on]; Elys; sup[er]sedeas, Naunton; J. Paston at Castre, M.P. at Heylisdon; Brigtled; evidens Pekeri[n]g; euidens Norwic'; Colt malt; p*r*epositu*s* de; mater, Clere.

181. To JOHN PASTON I 1465, 13 May

Add. 34889, f. 26. 10½ × 5¾ in. Wykes's hand.

Dorse: Postscript of one line. Traces of red wax. Address in Wykes's hand:

*To my ryght wyrshypfull mayst*er *John Paston the oldest be þis delyu*eryd in haste.

The date appears, from the mention of Philip Lipyate and the bailiff of Costessey, to be close to that of nos. 180 and 182. The connexion is confirmed by the fact that Margaret here writes from Hellesdon and speaks of having lately been at Caister (see no. 180). Finally, John Jenney was a member of the Commission of the Peace for Norfolk appointed on 1 April 1465 (*Cal. Pat. Rolls 1461–7*, p. 568).

F. iv, p. 164. G. 503/582.

I recomaund me, &c.¹
Yf it pleasyd you I wold ryght fayn that John Jenney werre putt ovte of the comyssyon of the peas *and* that my brother*e* Wyll Lumn*er* were set yn

---

²⁷ *Some writing partly lost through damage to paper; apparently* it.
²⁸ *This last sentence crowded in after the subscription was written.*

181. ¹ *These words slightly smaller than the rest, alone in the line; evidently added later.*

in hys stede, for me thinkyth it were ryght necessere that there were such
a won in that countray that oght you gode wyll, *and* I knowe verely he
5 owyth you ryght gode wyll. He was w*yth* me at Castere but late. Yf there
be made any labo*ur* for Docto*ur* Alyn to be justice of the peas, I p*r*ay you
for God*ys* sake let it be lettyd yf ye may, for he wyll take to moch apon hym
yf he werre. I woldnot that he were remembyrd of youre parte[2] but yf he
be spokyn of of othere party*s*.[3] He ys ryght grete w*yth* M*aister* Phylyp
10 Lyp3ate *and* the baylyff of Cosshay.

Yf it please yow to wyte that Wyk*ys* dyde a-reste on Wyll Bylmyn of
Norwych, as Pampyng can enforme you of, for sertyn harnys wych he
delyu*er*yd hym at Newcastell for to cary to Yarmoth by watere *and* there
to delyu*er* it to hym a-yen, whych harnys he kypt styll *and* may not be
15 delyu*er*yd; *and* now ther ys com down an *habeas corpus* for hym, *and* most
appyre at the Comyn Place on Fryday next comyng. Wher-fore yf it
pleased you that there myght be taken an accyon in Wyk*ys* name of trespas,
vndere such forme as there may be a *capias* a-wardyd a-yenst hys comyng,
for aftere that he was arestyd he dyde Dabeney to be arestyd for maynten-
20 yng. *And* as for the harnys, Wyk*ys* delyu*er*yd it to hym the x day of Januare
the ij yere of Kyng E. in Pylgryme Strete at Newcastell: In p*r*im*is*, a payre
brygandyrs, a salet, a bore spere, a bawe, xviij arwys, ij payre polrond*ys*, a
standerd of mayle, a payre slyvys of plate to the valew of v marc. *And*, at
the reuerens of God, slowth not youre maters nowe, *and* make an yend of
25 hem other p*ur*uey you to make hym or to marre hem in haste, for thys ys
to orybyll a coste *and* trobell that ye haue *and* haue had for to endure any
whyle, *and* ⌈it ys⌉ grete heuenys to youre frend*ys and* welwyllers, *and* grete
joy ⌈*and* confort⌉ to youre ennemyes. My lord of Norwych seyd to me that
he wold not ha byd*en* the sorow *and* trobell that ye haue a-byden to wyn
30 all S*er* John Fastolf ys gode.

And God be your spyde in all yore maters. Wryten at Haylesdon the
xiij day of May.

Youre M. P.[4]

I thynk ryght long to hyre tydyng*ys* tyll I haue t[y]dyng*ys* from you.

---

[2] but *canc.*   [3] for *canc.*   [4] *Recto ends.*

300

182. To JOHN PASTON I   1465, 20 May

Add. 34889, f. 27. 11¾×10¼ in. Wykes's hand.

Dorse: Continuation of text. Paper seal over red wax. Address in Wykes's hand:

*To my ryght wyrshypfull husbond John Paston by thys delyue*ry[d] *in hast.*

The date appears from the situation at Drayton and Hellesdon, which closely resembles that described in no. 180.

F. iv, p. 200. G. 504/583.

Please it you to wyte that on Satour-day last you*re* seruaunt*ys* Naunton, Wyk*ys, and* other*e* wer*e* at Drayton *and* ther*e* toke a dystresse for the rent *and* ferm that was to pay, to the nombere of¹ lxxvij nete, *and* so broght them hom to Hayllesdon *and* put hem in the pynfold, *and* so kept hem styll ther*e* from the² seyd Satour-day mornyng in-to Monday at iij at clok 5 at after*e*-non. Fyrst on the same Satour-day the tenaunt*ys* folwyd vppon, *and* desyryd to haue ther*e* catell a-yen, *and* ⌐I¬³ awnnsweryd hem yf thay wold do pay such dewt*ys* as they oght for to pay to you, that then they shold haue ther*e* catell delyue*ryd* a-yen; or els, yf they were not a power*e* to pay redy money, that then they to fynd suffycyant suerty to pay the 10 money at such a day as they mygh[t] agrye wyt*h* me, *and* there-to to be bonden to you by obligacyon. *And* that they seyd they durst not for to take vppon hem for to be bonden,⁴ and as for money they had non for to pay at that tyme; *and* there-fore I kept stylle the bestys. Harleston was at Norwych *and* send for the tenaunt*ys* the seyd Satour-day at after*e*-non, *and* there 15 by the menys of the bayllyff of Coshay put the tenaunt*ys* in such feer*e*, ⌐sayng¬ that yf they wold pay such dewt*ys*, or ells for to⁵ be bonden to pay, that then they wold put hem ovte of such lond*ys* as they huld bondly of the lordshyp, *and* so to dystrayn hem *and* trobell hem that they shold be wery of ther*e* part. *And* that put hem such feer*e* that they drust nothere pay nor 20 be bonden. *And* on the sam day at⁶ evynsong tyme Harleston com to me to Haylesdon, desyryng me that I wold delyue*r* a-yen the seyd dystresse, *and* as for such dystressys as they had taken here of you*re* tenaunt*ys* shold be delyue*ryd* a-yen in lyke forme. *And* I seyd I wold not delyue*r* hem soo, *and* told hem that I wold delyue*r* hem as ye wryten a-fore, *and* othere-wyse 25 not; *and* othere-wyse I wold not delyue*r* hem but by the form of lawe. *And* other*e* comynycacyon was had by-twene vs at that tyme of dyue*rs* maters whych wer*e* to long to wryte at thys tyme, but ye shall haue knowlych therof in hast.

And on Monday next after*e* at ix at clok ther*e* com Pynchemore to 30 Haylesdon wyt*h* a replevyn whych was made in Harleston ys name as

---

182. ¹ lvij nete *canc.*   ² the *repeated.*   ³ *Interl. above* yf *canc.*
⁴ nor *canc.*   ⁵ pay *canc.*   ⁶ ny3t *canc.*

vnderstewerd of the Duché, sayng that the best*ys* were taken vppon the
Duché fee; wherfor*e* he desyryd me to mak hym lev[er]y of the seyd best*ys*
so taken, *and* I seyd I wold not delyu*er* hem on-to the tyme that ⌜I⌝ had
35 examenyd the ten*auntys* of the trough. *And* so I send theder*e* Wyk*ys* w*yth*
Pynchemor*e* to vnderstond what they wold⁷ say, *and* the ten*auntys* seyd
that ther*e* was taken non vppon the Duché⁸ at ther*e* knowlych, saue only
Pyrs Waryn ⌜the yongere⌝ *and* Paynter*e* seyd that ther*e* catell was taken
vppon the Duché, whych they con not prove by non record saue only by
40 ther*e* awyn sayng; *and* so we wold not a-bey that replevyn, *and* so they
depa*r*tyd. *And* at iij at clock at after*e*-non Pynchemor*e* com to Haylysdon
a-yen w*yth* ij men whych broght w*yth* hem a replevyn from the shyryff,
whos nam*ys* be John Whycherley *and* Robert Ranson, whych requyryd me
by the same replevyn to make them delyu*e*ry of the seyd best*ys* taken at
45 Drayton. *And* so I, syyng the shyryff*ys* replevyn⁹ vnder*e* hys seall, bade my
men delyu*er* hem, *and* soo they wer*e* delyu*e*ryd. *And* as for all other*e* maters
that ye haue wryten to [me] of, I wyll spede me to send you a awnswer*e* as
hastely as I may, for I may no leysou*r* haue to wryte no more to you at thys
tyme.
50 The blyssyd Trynyté haue you in hys kypyng. Wryten at Haylesdon
the xx day ⟨of May⟩.¹⁰

By your*ys*, M. P.

183. To JOHN PASTON I   1465, 27 May

Add. 34889, f. 28. 11⅞ × 8⅝ in. Wykes's hand.

Dorse: Traces of red wax. Address in Wykes's hand:

> To my ryght wyrshypfull husbond *John* Paston be thys delyu*e*ryd in haste.

The date appears from the situation at Drayton and Hellesdon. The reference in
the last paragraph to Philip Lipyate and William Lomnor is clearly to the opening
paragraph of no. 181.
F. iv, p. 206. G. 505/584.

Ryght wyrshypfull hosbonde, I recomaunde me to you. Please it you to
wyte that I haue send to M*aister* John Smyth *and* to M*aister* Stephyn to
haue a-vyse for the church of Drayton, *and* they send me word that ther*e*
moste be had a comyssion from the Byshop ⌜to calle in the person Flowre-

---

⁷ *Recto ends. At the top of the verso is the following line canc.:* John Whycherley, Rober*to*
Ranson, Will*elmo* Whyte *and* Thome [Whyte *canc.*] Hemyng—thys be nam*ys* þat ser*uyd*
þe replevy[n].
⁸ *-e evidently intended by crossed* h, *though elsewhere this means nothing, as in* Duché *l.* 39.
⁹ *Ampersand canc.*
¹⁰ *Fenn read* of May; *now obliterated by a repair to the paper.*

dew⌐, *and* that most be proclaymyd in the church of Drayton iij tymes by   5
a deen; and after*e* that, yff he appyre not w*yth*-in vj monthys after*e* the
fyrst p*r*oclamacion, that¹ then he for to be depryvyd *and* the² patron to
p*r*esent wham he luste; *and* ells youre p*r*esentacyon ys not sufficyant. *And*
I haue so p*ur*veyd þ*at* a comyssyon ys hadde, *and* shalbe se*r*uyd as hastely
as it may be. As for John Rysyng, I haue sent to hym³ to wyte the cause   10
that he ys not broght vp to London; *and* he sayth that he callyd vppon the
shyrff that he myght be had vp for [to] com to hys awnswer*e*, *and* the
shyrff told hym that he wold not bryng hym vp at hys owyn coste. *And* John
Andres seyd that he wold not haue hym vp, *and* so he ys styll in p*r*ison at
Ipswych *and* so shall he be but yf ye canne fynde the beter*e* mene for to   15
haue hym ovte. I haue sent to hym xiij s. iiij d. to help hym-sylff there-w*yth*.
He payth for hys borde wykely xx d.; *and* Hopton *and* Smyth be ther*e* styll
allso, *and* thay haue money y-nogh, where som eu*er* that they haue it.
Rysyng dymeth that they haue confort of the other*e* p*ar*ty. *And* I send you
a copy of the warant that they wer*e* a-restyd by, &c.   20

I spake not w*yth*⁴ my moder*e* syn Ry*char*d Calle broght me the lett*er*
from you tochyng her*e* mater*e*, for I myght haue no lesou*r*. When I speke
w*yth* her*e* at leysure I wyll remembere her*e* in that mater*e* acordyng to
youre wrytyng. *And* as for youre tenau*n*tys of Drayton, as I canne vnderstond by hem they be ryght gode *and* trew hertyd to you to ther*e* powers,   25
and full fayn wold that ye had it a-yen in peasse; for they had as leff*e*
al-most be tena*u*ntys to the Devell as to the Duke, except Wyll Herne,
Pers at Sloth, *and* on Knott of the same towne, for they be not gode. All
youre tenau*n*tys at Haylesdon *and* Drayton except thes iij be ryght glad
that we err*e* ther*e* a-mong*ys* hem, *and* so be many other*e* of our*e* old   30
nebors *and* frend*ys*.

And but yf ye com hom by Wensday or Thursday in Wytson Wyke, I
p*ur*pose me to see⁵ you in secrete wyse by Trynyté Sonday, but yf ye send
to me contr*ar*y comaundement er*e* that tyme. *And* I p*r*ay you send me
youre avyse how ye wyll that we doo a-yenst the next shyr*e*, whych shalbe   35
the Monday next after*e* Trynyté Sonday, as for callyng vppon the replevyn
that the best*ys* of Drayton wer*e* delyu*er*yd by.

Item, Ri*char*d Calle told me that ye desyryd to haue M*aister* Phylyp⁶ ys
name; *and* hys ⌐name ys⌐ Phylyp Lypȝeate *and* I send you a letter*e* by
Henr*é* Wylton ys man wherin I wrote M*aister* Phylyp ys name, *and* in the   40
same lett*er* I wrote to you for Wyll Lumnour. I p*r*ay you send me word
yf ye haue it.

And the blysshyd Trynyté haue you in hys kypyng. Wryten the Monday
next after*e* Assencyon Day.

By your*ys*, M. P.   45

---

183. ¹ h *canc.*   ² par *canc.*   ³ *Ampersand and two letters canc.*
      ⁴ y *canc.*   ⁵ *MS.* ssee.   ⁶ lypȝate *canc.*

184. To John Paston I

Add. 27444, f. 142. 11⅝ × 14½ in., a piece *c*. 4 × 2½ in. torn off. Wykes's hand.

Dorse: Continuation of text. Traces of red wax. Address in Wykes's hand:

To my ryght wyrshypfull hosbond John Paston be thys lettere delyueryd.

The date appears from the situation at Drayton and Hellesdon (see especially no. 180). Margaret's expressions in ll. 15–17 must mean that John had already been imprisoned in the Fleet, where he certainly was in August (see no. 77).

G. 506/585.

Ryght wyrshypfull husbond, I recomaunde me vn-to you. Please it you to wyte that I recevyd letters from you on Wensday laste passyd the were wryten the Monday next be-fore, wherof I thanke you of the lettere that ye send to me. I wolde fayn doo well yf I cowde, *and* as I canne I wol doo to
5 youre pleasure *and* profet, *and* in such thyngys as I cannot skyle of I wyll take avyse of such as I know that be youre frendys, *and* doo as well as I canne.

Where as ye wrote to me that Lydham told you that I told hym that the Duckys men werre not so besy as thay had be by-fore, no more thay were
10 not at that tyme; but sythen they haue be bysyere. What confort that thay haue I canne not haue no knowlych as yet, but I suppose, *and* all youre felshyp were gode, thay sholdnot haue so grete confort as thay haue,[1] or ells thay wold not be so besy as thay haue be. Grete bost they make that the Duck shold haue Drayton in peas, *and* aftere thys Haylesdon, *and* that
15 wyth-in short tyme. Thay ere moch the boldere, I suppose, by-cause that ye be where as ye be. At the reverens of God, yf ye may by any wyrshypfull or resonabell mene, com ovte ther-of as sone as ye may, *and* com hom a-mongys youre frendys *and* tenauntys, *and* that shold be to hem the grettyst confort that thay my3t haue *and* the contrary to youre enmys.
20 It ys sayd here that the Duck of Suffolk shall com to Coshay in haste *and* logge there for a season. I fyle well by youre tenauntys that[2] yf ye were peaseabyly possessyd *and* youre cort holden in peaseabyll wyse, *and* that thay my3t ⌈be⌉ in pease a-yenst the othere many, than they wold take accyons a-yenste hem for[3] such wrongys as haue be don to hem. *And* ells
25 thay say that they thernot take it vppon hem, for they dwelle so ney to the othere many that thay knowe well thay shold neuer be in ease yf thay dyde soo whyle that thay dele a-mongys hem.

On Thursday last John Doket, ⌈the bayly ys son y lawe⌉, *and* Thomas Ponte, wyth othere, erly in the mornyng ⌈an ovre⌉ by-fore the sonne rose
30 com to youre fold[4] *and* drove away the flock at Drayton, both colyet *and* othere, in-to Coshay fee or euer that the sh[y]pherd myght haue knowlych

---

184. [1] I su *canc.*   [2] thay *canc.*   [3] ells *canc.*   [4] *and* brake it *canc.*

therof. *And* than he fowlyd on *and* desyryd to haue hem a-yen, *and* thay
wold not suffer*e* hym to haue them, no more but the colyet;[5] *and* ther*e* wer*e*
c *and* j of your*ys*, *and* tho had thay forth w*yth* hem to Coshay. *And* the
same day we had a replevyn for the cc shype *and* replevyn for the hors that 35
wer*e* taken at Haylesdon, *and* how that thay were obbeyd Ric*hard* Call shall
enforme you, *and* of other*e* maters also the whych I may not wryte to you
of at thys tyme.

Item, I haue spoke w⟨*yth* John⟩[6] Strange of the mater*e* that ye wrote
to me of, *and* in gode feyth I[7] fynd hym, as me symyth, ryght well dysposyd 40
to you ward*ys*; *and*[8] he hath acordyng to your*e* desyre spoken w*yth* Yeluerton yesterday to fyle hys dysposision in that mater*e*, *and* Yelu*er*ton, as it
symyth by hym, roght not gretely thogh the mater*e* brake so that he myght
haue any resonabell colo*ur* to breke. He ys so callyd vppon by Wayte *and*
other*e* of the Duck of Suff*olk* ys counsell that he ote not where to hold hym, 45
and he ys put in so grete confort, as I am enformyd, to receve money for
the lond; *and* that temptyth ⌐hym⌐ ryght sore, for w*yth* money he wold fayn
be in handelyng,[9] as ye know he hath nede therof. He told John Straunge
that it ys informyd hym that ye haue vp an enquest to deprove ther*e*
wytnesse, *and* ther*e*-w*yth* ys he sore movyd.[10] ⟨. . .⟩ that yf any thyng*ys* be 50
don in temperall maters other*e* in spyrytu⟨all . . .⟩ maters tochyng executours or feoffeys or wyttnes tyll the day of ⟨. . .⟩ trety be passyd he wyll not
abyde no trety ther-in but do as ⟨. . .⟩ thynkyth best for to do ther*e*-in.
I told John Straunge that I kn⟨ew . . .⟩ thogh it were soo þat shold passe
any such enquest it shol n⟨ot . . .⟩[11] of them in pro*v*yng of her*e* trothys, the 55
whych[12] shold be no hurt ⟨. . .⟩ fore John Straunge desyryd me that I shuld
send to you in al haste tha⟨t . . .⟩ any such folky*s* that thay shold not doo in
the mater*e* tyll the day of ⟨. . .⟩ may haue knowlych how he *and* other*e* wold
doo in such maters as sh⟨. . .⟩ he wold be loth that he shold haue any colo*ur*
to breke for any thyng ⟨. . .⟩ *and* Yelu*er*ton sayth it shall not breke thorf hys 60
defaute yf ye wyll n⟨ot . . .⟩ be ryght glad to haue your*e* gode wyll *and* to
goo thorgh in all man*er* mate⟨rs . . .⟩ eschewyng of wastfull expens of the
dede ys god*ys* *and* that the god*ys* my3t be dyspendyd to the welle[13] of the
dede. Straunge desyryd to knowe what appoyntement*ys* he desyryth to
haue in the trety, *and* he sayd he wold not let that be vnderstond tyll the 65
tyme of trety cam.[14] Me symyth, saue your*e* beter*e* avyse, it were wel do
that thay that be com vp for you my3t be kypt in som secryte place *and*

---

5 *and of your*ys* thay canc.*
6 *Hole in paper; most of w and part of raised t remain.*
7 *MS.* in.   8 haue yev *canc.*   9 as ye kno *canc.*
10 *Right-hand bottom corner torn off, so that words are lost in six lines of recto and seven of
verso. At its widest the tear is nearly four inches, so that the number of letters missing cannot
be estimated.*
11 *Recto ends.*   12 w *canc.*
13 *Only the lower parts of these last three words visible.*
14 *Two letters, apparently* it, *canc.*

not do in the matere tyll the tyme of the trety were passyd. The cost there-of shall not be grete to that it my3t hurte yf the trety were broken by that meane. 70 *And* ⌐there⌐15 ye may haue hem nyere, ⌐*and* yf⌐16 ye thynk it be to doo ye may haue hem to go to there matere aftere the seyd tyme, for ⌐of⌐ ij hurt*ys* the grettyst ys best to be eschewyd.

Item, as for youre houshold at Castere, sauyng youre betere avyse me thynkyth that v or vj of youre folk*ys* such as ⌐ye⌐ wyll assyngne were 75 ⟨. . .⟩17 kype the place, *and* thay for to go to bord w*yth* the prustes *and* ye not to kype no houshold there yet,18 *and* that ye shall fynd more profettabyll than for to doo as we do nogh; for there expens, as I vnderstond, haue not be moch the lesse by-fore Wytsontyde than it shold be thogh I had be at hom, by-cause of resortyng of pepell thedere. *And* yf the houshold ⌐were 80 broke⌐ thay my3t haue a gode excuse in that, who som euer com. Ri*ch*ard Call shall enforme you of thys maters *and* mo othere more playnly than I may do wryte at thys tyme. It ys necessary that possessyon be kypt hyre yett tyll ye be more forthere forth in othere maters.

The blessyd Trynyté haue you [in] hys kypyng *and* send you gode spyde 85 in all youre maters, *and* send you grace to haue a gode conclusyon19 in hem in haste. Wryten on the Tewysday nex be-fore Corp*us* Cri*sti*.20

By youre faynt houswyff at thys tyme, M. P.

185. To JOHN PASTON I   1465, 24 June

Add. 27444, f. 145. 11½ × 12½ in. Wykes's hand.

Dorse: Traces of red wax. Address in Wykes's hand:

To my ryght wyrsh[y]pfull husbond John Paston be thys delyueryd in hast.

The date is shown by the references to Costessey and Drayton (see especially no. 184).

G. 510/590.

Ryght wyrshypfull hosbond, I recomaund me to you. Please it you to wyte that the same ⌐Wens⌐day that Ri*ch*ard Call departyd hens I send Ri*ch*ard Charlys to speke w*yth* the vndershyrf, requyryng hym that he shold *se*rue the replevyn for the shype *and* hors that were take, &c.; *and* the shyrf sayd 5 playnly that he wolnot nor derst not *se*rue it, not thogh I wold yeve hym xx li. to *se*rue it. *And* Ri*ch*ard Charlys axhyd the cause why, *and* he sayd for he woldnot haue to doo w*yth* that felshyp; *and* so it ys yet vnservyd. I suppose that Ri*ch*ard Calle hath told you what revell ther was ⌐by the

---

15 *Interl. above* yf *canc.*   16 *Interl. above* that *canc.*
17 *Hole in paper; room for about eight letters.*   18 y *and the lower parts of* et *visible.*
19 of *canc.*   20 *Abbr.* xpi.

bayllyf of Coshay *and* hys felaw¹ vppon youre men that shold haue s*er*uyd
the replevyn.   10

It*em*, the same Wensday that Ric*hard* Call rode from hens the[r] were
endytyd v of [youre] men by the enquest of Fovrhoo hundere, as Crome
can enforme you. *And* on Fryday last paste John Paston ⟨t⟩he¹ yongere,
Wyk*ys*, *and* Thom*a*s Honeworth were endytyd at Dyram, by what menys
the beru*r* herof, Crom, shall ⟨en⟩forme¹ you. I send thede*r*e Ric*hard* 15
Charl*ys*, John Seve, *and* iij or iiij othe*r*e gode felows for to haue don othe*r*e
folk*ys* as gode a torne, but it wold not be for the juge ys soo parcyall w*yth*
the othe*r*e party that I trowe the*r*e shalbe sped no maters be-fore hym
for you nor for non of your*ys* tyl it be otherwyse by-twene you than it ys.²
Crom shall tell you of hys demenyng at the last sessyons at Dyrh*a*m. I send 20
you a copy of both the endytement*ys*. Youre son John Paston the yong*er* I
hope shal be w*yth* you thys wyke, *and* enforme you of mo thyngys, *and*
howe myn hors *and* hys sadell *and* harnys ys prysone*r* at Coshay halle, *and*
haue ben eu*er* syn Wensday last.

It*em*, I recevyd a lettere from you on Satorday last whych was wryten on 25
Monday next be-fore, *and* I haue sent to S*er* Thom*a*s Howys the same day
for such maters as ye wrote to me of, *and* he sent me word that Wyllyam
Worceter had a boke of remembraunce of recaytys that hath be recevyd by
S*er* John Fastolf or any of hys sythen the iiij^te yere [of] Kyng Harry both
of hys awyn lyflode or of any othe*r*e mannys that he had to doo wyth all. 30
He sayd yf ye wold send to Wyll Worcetere³ to loke therfo*r*e he sayd he
wyst well he wold lete you haue knowlych yf any such thyng may be
founde; *and* also he sayd that he wold send to the seyd Wyll⁴ to serche
therfo*r*e. *And* as for such bokys as he hath hyre at hom, he wol doo loke
yf any remembraunce canne be founde therof, *and* ye shall haue knowlych 35
therof as he hath p*r*omysyd ⌐by⌐⁵ Sato*ur*day next comyng. *And* as for the
woman that made the clayme that ye wrote of, he ys wellwyllyd that she
shold be seyn to in the way of almys, *and*, as⁶ I here say, it symyth by hym
that in any thyng that he canne doo tochyng the savacyon of the dedys
gode,⁷ othe*r*e in lyflode othe*r*e in othe*r*e godys, he sayth that he wyll doo. 40

I canne not haue no knowlych that Haydon mellyth in the mate*r*e of
Drayton. Yf he do⁸ oght therin he doyth it closely, as he ys wont to doo,
and wayshyth hys hondys therof as Pylate dyde. It shalnot be long to or
that I send to you of such tythyng*ys* as we haue⁹; I shall lete you haue knowlych therof. I fynd Crom ryght welwyllyng to you in such thyngys as lyth 45
in hym for to do. I p*ra*y you lete hym be thankyd¹⁰ therfore, *and* that shall
cause hym to be the bete*r*e wyllyd. He hath not be rewardyd as yet but by
Ric*hard* Call, as he canne tell you.

---

185. ¹ *First letters lost at torn edge.*   ² Cror *canc.*   ³ ther *canc.*
    ⁴ therfore *canc.*   ⁵ *Interl. above* vppon *canc.*   ⁶ it symyth by hym *canc.*
    ⁷ he *canc.*   ⁸ he do *canc.*   ⁹ to *canc.*   ¹⁰ *MS.* thankynd.

The blyssyd Trynyté haue you in hys kypyng *and* send you gode spyde
50 in al you*re* maters. Wryten in hast on Mydsom*er* Day. As for Rysyng, but
yf ye p*ur*vey for hym he canne no helpe haue at home.

By your*ys*, M. P.

186. To John Paston III   1465, probably 30 June

Add. 34889, f. 208. 11½ × 4 in. Gloys's hand.

Dorse: Paper seal over wax and tape. Address in Gloys's hand:

*To John Paston the yonger*e.

The form in the address means John III, not John II, who had been knighted in
1463 and was afterwards addressed accordingly (e.g. nos. 175, 198). From 1462
onwards John III often appears as a dependant of the Duke of Norfolk, and especially the Duchess, who is certainly 'my lady' of this letter. The date is indicated
by features of both no. 185 and no. 187. In no. 185 Margaret told John I, who was
in London, that 'John Paston the younger' would be with him 'this week'; in no.
187 she wished him to ride 'again' to the Duchess, which implies that he had seen
her lately. If the expectation of no. 185 was fulfilled, the probable date of the present
letter is the following Sunday, which is still sufficiently before the warnings of
attack described in no. 187.
    G. LXV/623.

I grete you wele, letyng you wete that asfor y*our* sustrys beyng w*yth* my
lady, if y*our* fader*e*[1] wull aggrey ther-to I hold me right wele pleasyd, for
I wuld be right clad þ*at* she shuld do her*e* servyse be-for any othe*re*, if
she cowde do that shuld pleas my ladyes good g*race*. Wherfore I wuld
5 that ⌐ye⌐[2] shuld speke to y*our* fad*er* þerof and lete hym wete þ*at* I am
pleasid þ*at* she shuld be ther*e* if he wuld. For I wuld be right glad *and* she
myght be proferrid be mariage or be s*er*vyce so þ*at* it myght be to her*e*
wurchep *and* pr*o*fight in dischargyng of her*e* frend*es*, *and* I p*ra*y you do
y*our* p*ar*te ther-in for y*our* owyn wurchep ⌐*and* herys⌐.
10   And assone as ye may w*yth*-ought daunger*e*, p*ur*uey þ*at* I may haue
ageyn the vj m*ar*c þ*at* ye wote of, for I wuld not þ*at* y*our* fader*e* wust it.
    Item, if ye pas London send me ageyn[3] my chene, *and* þe litill chene þ*at*
I lent you be-for*e*, be su*m* trusty p*er*son. And if ye wull haue my good wille
eschewe such thyng*es* as I spake to you of last in owr*e* p*ar*issh chirch.
15   I p*ra*y God make you as good a man as eu*er* was any of y*our* kynne, and
Godd*es* blissyng mote ye haue *and* myn, so þ*at* ye do wele, &c. Wretyn
the Sonday next aft*er* y*our* dep*ar*tyng. And I p*ra*y you send me su*m*
tydyng*es* as sone as ye may aft*er* þ*at* ye be comyn to London how y*our*
fad*er* spedyth *and* y*our* brother*e* in her*e* mater*es*.
20   Be y*our* mod*er*

186. [1] w*yth* canc.   [2] *Interl. above* she *canc.*   [3] the *canc.*

187. To JOHN PASTON II   1465, perhaps 6 July

Add. 27444, f. 146. 11½ × 5½ in. Hand unidentified.

Dorse: Second postscript. Marks of folding, remnants of red wax over string, and stitch-holes, but no address.

The date appears from Margaret's fear of imminent attack by the Duke of Suffolk. The 'place' is Hellesdon, of which John II was in charge; 'John Paston the younger' is John III. Gairdner plausibly suggested that this letter might have been written on the Saturday preceding the Duke's first attempt on Hellesdon, which was on 8 July (see Richard Calle's letter to John Paston I of 10 July, Part II, no. 690).
    G. 511/592.

I grete yow wele, letyng yow wetyn þat[1] I am informyd for certeyn þe Duc of Suffolk reysyth grete pepyl bothe in Norffolk and Suffolk to comyn doune wyth hym to putte vs to a rebeuc and þei may; querfor I wold in ony wyse þat ȝe make yow as strong as ȝe can wyth-inne [þe] place, for I and other moo[2] suppose that ȝyff they fynd ȝow not here they wyl seke ȝow   5 þere ȝe arn. I wold John Paston þe ȝonger schuld ryde aȝyn to my lady of Norffolk and be wyth hyr stylle tyl we haff other tydyngys, and þer may he do sum good,[3] after þat he heryth tydyngys, in goyng forth to hys fadyr or in-to sum other[4] place quere ⌈we⌉ may hafe remedy. For yt [ys] told me þat þere ar come to Cossey omward more than ij hundred, and þer ys   10 comyng, as yt ys seyd, more than a thowsand. I wold þat ȝe sende hyder lytyl John, that I mygth sende hym abowte on myn errandys. Sende me worde how that ȝe doo by summe of the tenantys þat be not knowyn.

    Item, byd Ric⌈h⌉ard Calle send me word in a[5] bylle of how many materys that he hath ⌈sent⌉ myn husbond an answere of, þe quych he sendt hom in   15 diuers letters for to be sped here; and of þe fermours of Tychwelle.

    Item, ȝyf Ser Iamys Gloys may come to Norwych to Adam Talyurs hows I wold he come on Munday ⌈by tymys and⌉[6] I schal sende to hym thyder.

    God kepe yow alle. Wretyn in hast on Satyrday.   20
                                    By your modyr

    Item, yt ys told me þat ȝong Heydon reysyth mych pepyl in þe sokyn and in othe[r] place.[7]
    Item, I wold ȝe schuld do Rychard Calle hye hym of makeng of alle the acountys, and ȝyf nede lete hym gete help; and kepe Thomas Hunworth   25 stille wyth yow, and be war of pykyng.

187. [1] þ- *in form of* y *throughout*.   [2] *Followed by* I *not canc.*
    [3] j *and part of another letter canc.*
    [4] *Abbr.* oth *followed by a vertical stroke and a dot, like an exclamation mark.*
    [5] *No space.*   [6] *Interl. above* yat *canc.*   [7] *Recto ends.*

188. To John Paston I   1465, 12 July

Add. 34889, f. 30. $11\frac{3}{8} \times 12\frac{1}{8}$ in. John Paston II's hand.

Dorse: Paper seal over red wax and tape. Address in John II's hand:

To my ryght worschipfull husbond John Paston, in hast.

The date appears from the account of the Duke of Suffolk's attack on Hellesdon, where this letter must have been written. The letter from Richard Calle to John Paston to which Margaret refers is no. 690 in Part II. See also no. 187. The situation is that on which John comments in no. 74, having heard of it independently. His letter must have been written the day after the present one, and so cannot be a reply to it.

For St. Thomas's Day cf. no. 160 and references there.

F. iv, p. 218. G. 513/594. C. 38.

Ryght worshypful husbond, I recomaund me to yow, preyeng you hertyly þat ye wyl seke a meen þat yowre seruauntys may be in pees, for they be dayly in fere of there lyvys. The Duke of Suffolk men thretyn dayly Dawbeney, Wykys, *and* Richard Calle þat where so euere they may gete
5 them they schold dye. And affrayes have ben made on Rychard Calle thes weke, so þat he was in gret jupperte at Norwych among them. And gret affrayes have ben made vppon me *and* my felashep here on Monday last passyd, of whych Rychard Calle tellyth me þat he hath sent yow word of in wryghtyng more pleynly than I may doo at thys tyme, but I shal jnforme
10 yow more pleynly heraftyre.

I suppose there schal be gret labore ageyn yow *and* yowre seruauntys at the assysis ⌐*and* cesciouns¬ here, wherfore me semyth, sauyng yowre better advyce, it were wele do þat ye shold speke wyth þe justicys or they com here. And yf ye wol þat I compleyn to them or to any othere, if Good for-
15 tune me lyfe *and* helth I wol do as ye advyse me to do, for in good feyth I haue ben symply intretyd amonge them. And what wyth syknesse *and* troble þat I haue had I am browte ryght lowe *and* weyke, but to my powere I wyl do as I can or may in yowre materys.

The Duk of Suffolk[1] *and* bothe þe duchessys schal com to Claxton thys
20 day, as I am informyd, and thys next weke he schal be at Cossey; whethere he wol come ferthere hyddyrward ore not I wot not yit. It is seyd þat he schold com hyddyre; and yit hys men seyd here on Monday þat he cleymyd no tytyl to thys place. They seyd there comyng was but to[2] take owt such ryotus peple as was here wyth-in thys place, and suche as were
25 the Kyngys felonys, *and* jndytyd *and* owtlawyd men. Neuer the lesse they wold schew no warauntys wherby to take non such, thow ther had ben suche here. I suppose if they myght have com in pesably they wold haue made an othere cawse of there comyng. Whan alle was doo *and* they scholde

188. ¹ schal *canc.*   ² hat *canc.*

departe, Harlyston *and* othere desyryd me þat I schold com³ *and* se myn
olde lady *and* sewe to my lorde, *and* if any thyng were amysse it schold be 30
amendyd. I seyd if I scholde sewe for any remedye þat I scholde sewe ferthere, *and* lete the Kynge *and* alle the lordys of thys londe to haue knowlech
what hathe be don to vs, if so were that the Deuk wolde maynten þat hathe
be don to vs ⌈by⌉ hys seruauntys, if ye wolde geue me leve. I pray yow sende
me worde if ye wyl þat I make any compleynt to the Duke or the Duchesse; 35
for as it is tolde me they know not the pleynesse that hathe ben don in⁴ such
thyngys as hathe ben don in here namys. I schold wryght muche more to
yow but for lak of leysere.

I comaundyd my mayster Tom thys day to have com⁵ ageyn by me from
Norwych⁶ when he had spokyn wyth Rychard Calle, but he cam not. I⁷ 40
wolde he were qwyte of hys jndytment, so þat he were qwyte of yowre
servyce, for by my trowthe I holde the place þe more ongracyous þat he
is in for⁸ hys dysposycion in dyuerce thyngys, þe whych ye⁹ schal be
jnform⌈id⌉ of here-affter.

The Trynyté haue yow in kepyng. Wretyn the Fryday next after Seynt 45
Thomas.

By yowre M. P.

189. To John Paston I   1465, 7 August

Add. 27445, f. 1. 11⅝ × 16 in. (two pieces joined). First 25 manuscript lines
in Gloys's hand, the remaining 27 on the recto and all 19 on the verso in
Calle's hand.

Dorse: Continuation of text. Paper seal over red wax. Address in Calle's
hand:

To my ryght worschipful husbond John Paston be this delyuerd in hast.

The date is fixed by the dispute with the Duke of Suffolk about Drayton and Hellesdon.
G. 518/599.

Right wurchepfull husbond, I recomaund me to you. Please it you to wete
þat I sent on Lammesse Day to Drayton Thomas Bonde *and* Ser James
Gloys to hold the court in your name *and* to clayme your tytill, for I cowde
gete non othere body to kepe the court ner that wuld go theder but þe seid
Thomas Bonde, be-cause I suppose thei were a-ferd of the pepill þat shuld 5
be there of þe Duke of Suffolk parte. The seid Thomas *and* James, as the

---

³ to *canc.*   ⁴ thys mater *canc.*   ⁵ b *canc.*
⁶ a *and incomplete* f *canc.*   ⁷ *No space.*   ⁸ dyve *canc.*
⁹ *Written over* I; *the* be *after* schal *is similarly written over* I.

311

Duke of Suffolk men, þat is to sey Harlesdon, þe parson of Salle, Mayster
Phyllip, and William Yeluerton, þe which was styward, wyth[1] a lx persones
or more be estymacion, ⌐and the tenauntes of the same town⌐, sum of hem
10 hauyng rusty pollexis and byllys, comyn in-to þe maner yard to kepe the
court, met wyth them and told them that thei were comyn to kepe þe court
in your name and to clayme your titill. Wherefore the seid Harlesdon,
wyth-ought ⌐any⌐ more wordes or occasion yovyn of your men, comytted
the seid Thomas Bonde to þe kepyng of þe ⌐new⌐ baly of Drayton, ⌐William
15 Dokket⌐, seyng þat he shuld go to my lord and do his herand hym-self,
notwyth-stondyng þat Ser James dede the erandes to them and had the
wordes; where-fore thei toke ⌐þe seid Thomas[12] wyth-ought occasion. Thei
wuld haue mad the seid Thomas to haue had the wordes, and þe said James
told hem that [he] had ⌐hem⌐ be-cause he was the more pesibill man, wham
20 afterward thei bode avoyde, and[3] sithen led forth Thomas Bonde to Cossey,
and bownde his armes[4] be-hynde hym wyth whippe-cord like a theffe, and
shuld haue led hym forth to þe Duke of Suffolk ner had be þat I had spokyn
wyth ⌐the⌐ juges in ⌐the⌐ morwyn or þei yede to the shire hous, and enformed[5] hem of such ryottes and assaugthis as thei had mad vp-on me and
25 my men, the baly of Cossey and all þe Duke of Suffolk councell beyng there
present and all þe lerned men of Norffolk and William Jeney and my⟨che⟩[6]
pepill of þe contré; the juge callyng þe baly of Cossey be-for them all and
yaffe hym a gret rebuke, comaundyng the shereffe to ⌐se⌐[7] what pepill thei
had gadred at Drayton,[8] which came after to Helesdon to se þe pepill there,[9]
30 wyth ⌐weche⌐[10] [pe]pill he ⌐held hym⌐[11] wele content. And fro thens he rode
to Drayton to se there pepill which were avoyded or he came, and there he
desired to haue deliuered þe seid Thomas Bonde to hym. And thei excusid
hem and seid þei had send hym to the Duke of Suffolk; notwythstandyng[12]
afterward thei sent hym to Norwhich to hym, desiryng hym þat he shuld
35 deliuere hym ⌐not⌐[11] wyth-ought he mad a fyne be-cause he trobilled the
Kynges lete, for which thei mad l⟨. . .⟩[6] to juges; but after þat I vnderstod
it I sent Danyell of Mershlond and Thomas Bonde to[13] enforme the juges
how the seide Thomas was intreted amonges hem, and so he ded, and
the juges were gretly ⟨. . .⟩ wyth the Dukes men and forwyth comaunded
40 the scheryf to delyuer the seide Bone wythoute any fyne m⟨ade⟩, seyng that
he out non to make. And in goode feythe I founde the juges ryght gentell

189. [1] as and the first stroke of x canc.　　　[2] Interl. above hym canc.
[3] let canc.　　　　[4] Written harmes, h canc.　　　[5] of canc.
[6] Letters lost at torn edge.　　　[7] Interl. above sey canc.　　　[8] what came canc.
[9] which canc.
[10] Interl. in Calle's hand, correcting Gloys's whipill; but pe- not supplied.
[11] Interl. by Calle.　　　　　　　　　　[12] -a- apparently from o.
[13] þe justice and he canc. The text continues, in Calle's hand, on a new sheet which was
sewn to the first. This overlapped a line of writing which can be partly read, though the first
words (apparently five) are almost entirely cut away. It is a continuation, in Gloys's hand:
. . . thei toke þe seid Thomas wyth-ought warant Asfor trobillyng of the lete. Calle repeats to.

and forberable[14] to me in my matres notwythstandyng the Dukes
councell had made her compleynt to them or I come in ther werst wice,
noysyng vs of gret gatheryng of peopell and many riotes[15] thynges don be
me and[16] your men. And ⌜after⌝ I enformed the juges of ther vntrouthe 45
and of ther gidyng, and of oure gidyng in like wice, and after the juges
vndrestod the trouthe he gaue the baly of Cossey be-for me and many
other a passyng gret rebuke, seyng wythoute he amended hes condicion
and gouernaunce thei w⟨old⟩[17] enforme the Kyng and helpe that he schuld
be punyschet.   50

And wher as ye avyced ⌜m⟨e . . .⟩⌝[18] a felaschip to kepe the coorte at
Drayton wyth easy cost,[17] it was thought be your councell it ⟨wer⟩ better
otherwice and not to gather no people, for it was told ⌜me⌝[19] that the Dukes
men had to the nombre of v[20] c men, and ⌜your councel⌝[21] aviced me to gete
a felaschip to kepe my place at Heylesdon, for it was told me that they[22] 55
schuld come and pulle me out of the place, weche cauced me to kepe the
place the strenger at that tyme.

And as for kepyng of any coorte for you at Drayton, I can not wete how[23]
it cowde be brought a-boute wythoute helpe of other but if ther schuld
growe gret inconuenyence of it. And[24] at the ass⟨ises . . .⟩[25] made gret 60
labour to endite your men; notwythstandyng[26] it was letted. And as for the
writtes of replevyn they were delyuerd openly be-for the juges to the scheryf,
and also other writtes wech Jamys Gresham brought, and aftre that
Richard Calle spake wyth the high scheref for the servyng of hem, and so
he promysed to serue it and to send men of hes owne to serue it. And so he 65
sent ij of hes men wyth Richard Lynsted and wyth ij of [your] scheperdes
to Cossey for the schepe, and ther they were answer[d] þat[27] Yeluerton
cleymeth the properté, and so wer they answerd in all other places wher as
any catell was; and so they departed and come to the scheryf and enformed
hym, and I vndrestande the scheryf taketh it for an answere. Notwyth- 70
standyng, I send hym word wythoute that Yeluerton had ben ther in hes
owne persone he myte not cleyme the properté, and aviced hym to be ware
what retorne he made þat he were not hurte by it; and so he hathe made no
retorne yet. What he wol doo I wot nere. He is stylle in this contré yet, and
schal be this iiij or v dayes, but your councell[28] thynketh it were wele don 75
that ye gete an allias and a plurias that it myght be sent don to the scheryf,
and than he can make non excuce but nedys ⟨to serue⟩[29] it or ell to make
a retourne as he wol a-bide by. I can not wete how the catell wol be goten

---

[14] *The first e not clear.*   [15] -es *abbr. in the usual way, as also in* thynges *following.*
[16] myn *canc.*   [17] the *canc.*
[18] *Edge torn. Only* m *remains of word interl. above* vs *canc.*
[19] *Interl. above* vs *canc.*   [20] c *interl.*   [21] *Interl. above* they *canc.*
[22] if they had *canc.*   [23] wyth helpe of other *canc.*   [24] as *canc.*
[25] *Hole in paper; room for about nine letters.*   [26] they wer *canc.*
[27] þ- *in form of* y.   [28] *Recto ends.*   *Foxed reading uncertain.*

ayen wythoute other processe be had more than we haue yet.[30] Item, on
80 Twesday next comyng schal the sescions of the pees be at Wolsyngham.
What schal be do ther I wot[31] not yet, for as for any jndytementes that we
schuld labor a-yenst them, it is but wast werk, for the scheryf ner the jurrours
wol no thyng do a-yenst them.

Item,[32] wher as ye desire to knowe what gentelmen wolde doo for you at
85 this tyme, jn[33] goode feythe[34] I founde Herry Greye, Lomnour, Alblastre,
Wech⟨yngham⟩, Berney of Redham, Skyppewyth, and Danyell of Mershe-
lond ryght weele disposed to you ward at this tyme in helpyng and in
gevyng ther goode avice to me for suche maters as I had to doo. Ye schal
haue more pleyne vndrestondyng of all thynges her-after than I may write
90 to you at this tyme.

Item, the supersedias and the supplicauit is delyuerd to Alblastre and to
Wechyngham, and they haue mad out bothe warantes and supersedias;
neuertheles ther is non seruyd yet.

Item, I receyued the box wyth the writte and the letter that Berney sent
95 to me on Friday last past and non er.[35]

Item, as for the pris of malte, it is fallen here sore for it is worthe but ij s.
viij d. j quarter at Yermoth.

Item, as for your wolle, I may selle a stoone for xl d. so that I wol geve
halfe yer day of paymen⟨t⟩.[36] I prey you sende me word how I schal do in
100 this matre and in all other, &c. And God kepe you. Wreten in haste the
Wednesday next aftre Lammes Daye.

Your M. PASTON

190. To JOHN PASTON I

1465, 18 August

Add. 34889, f. 31. $11\frac{3}{4} \times 11\frac{3}{4}$ in. Wykes's hand.

Dorse: Continuation of text. Traces of red wax. Address in Wykes's hand:

*To my ryght wyrshypfull maystere John Paston be thys lettere delyueryd
in haste.*

Note in Pampyng's hand: 'Thomas Bosewell dwellyng at the newe abbey
at Toure Hill in my Lord Revers plase.'

The date appears from the reference to assizes at Norwich and sessions of the peace
at Walsingham, which connects this letter with no. 189. That must, indeed, be the
letter Margaret had sent on the Thursday after Lammas (l. 6). She is evidently
replying to her husband's rebuke at the end of no. 76, which is also concerned with
the assizes. 'John Russe's bargain' connects this letter with no. 75 as well.

F. iii, p. 370. G. 523/604 (part). *Medium Ævum*, xix (1949), 25–8.

[30] Item yesterday the sescions were at Derham *canc.*
[31] *Second letter uncertain.*　　　　　[32] as *canc.*　　　　　[33] *No space.*
[34] he *canc.*　　　　　[35] *Written ere, -e canc.*　　　　　[36] *Hastily written, at edge.*

Ryght wyrshypfull husbond, I recomaund me to you. Please it you to wyte that I recevyd a letter*e* from you send by Laurens Rede on Fryday laste past, wherby I vnderstond that ye had no¹ tythyng*ys* from me² at that tyme that your*e* letter*e* was wryten; wherof I mervayll, for I send you a letter*e* by Chyttock ys son that ys prenteys in London, the whych was delyuer*y*d to 5 hym vppon the Thursday next after*e* Lammas Day, *and* he pr*o*mysyd to ryde ⌜forward⌝ the same day *and* that ye shold haue it as hastely as he my3t after*e* hys comyng to London. *And* ⌜in⌝ the seyd letter*e* was of the demen-yng at the assyses at Norwych *and* of dyu*e*rs othere maters. I pray you send me word yf ye haue it. As for the replevyns, Ric*h*ard Call sayth he hath send 10 you an awnswer*e* of hem *and* also the copys of them. As for the hygh shyrf, he demenyd hym ryght well her*e* to me, *and* he sayd to me as for the replevyns he wold aske counseyll of lernyd men what he my3t doo there-in *and* as largely as he my3t doo there-in, or in any other*e* mater*e* twochyng you, sauyng hym-sylf harmlys, he woll doo for you¹ *and* for your*ys* that he 15 my3t doo.

The cause that I wrote to you non er*e* than I dyde after*e* the sessyons was by-cause that Yelu*e*rton held sessyons at Dyrham *and* Walsyngham the next wyke after*e* the assyses, *and* to haue knowlych what labour that was made ther*e*, *and* to haue send you word therof. There was grete labour 20 made by the bayly of Coshay *and* other*e* for to haue endytyd your*e* men both at Dyrham and at Walsyngham, but I p*u*rvayd a mene that here p*u*r-pose was lettyd at thos ij tymes. I haue send to S*er* Thomas Howys yester-day Ric*h*ard Call, for the mater*e* of my lady of Bedfford, but he my3t not speke w*y*th hym nor I haue non awnswer*e* therof yet, but I shall send to hym 25 a-yen thys wyke.

It*em*, I haue do layd in the pr*e*sentacyon of Drayton, *and* haue pr*e*sentyd S*er* Thomas Hakon, p*a*rson of Felthorp, the whych ys hold ryght a gode man *and* wel dysposyd; *and* the Duck of Suff*olk* hath layd in a-nother*e*, *and* there shall be take an inquisicyon ther-vppon, *and* M*aister* Styven ys 30 your*e* a-voked ther*e*-in.

M*aister* John Estgade ys passyd to God on Thursday last passyd, whos sawle God assoyle; wherof in gode fayth I am ryght sory, for I fond hym ryght faythfull to you. They dyy³ ryght sor*e* in Norwych. M*aister* John Salet *and* M*aister* Godfray *and* M*aister* John Estgate ys brothere of London 35 ben hys excecuto*u*rs, as it ys told me. Yf ye thynk it be to doo, me thynkyth it wer*e* well doo that ye spake w*y*th hys brother*e* at London or he com in-to Norff*olk*, yf he had any thyng*ys* of your*ys* in kypyng towchyng your*e* maters, *and* I shall send to M*aister* Godffray in lyke wyse.

I was at Castere all the last wyke for dyu*e*rs thyng*ys* there the whych ye 40

---

190. ¹ th *canc.*   ² sy *canc.*
  ³ *Before the first* y *is a small mark which might be taken for the beginning of* e, *abandoned in favour of* y; *Fenn's reading* deyy *cannot be sustained.*

shall haue knowlych of heraftere, ⌐and I cam not hom tyll yester yevyn
late⌐. As for the matere that ye wrote to me of for John Rus twochyng the
bargyn, me thynkyth he wylnot in no wyse leve it, wherfore I haue made
purvyauns that he shall haue the money, as ye shall haue knowlych herof

45 heraftere. As ⌐for⌐ any money that he hath recevyd therof to hys awyn vse,
he sayth playnly that he neuer recevyd peny therof yet. As for the examyn-
acyon of the fermours, thay myght not be spoken wyth ⌐yet⌐ sythen I
recevyd youre lettere, but I sall do hem examyn here-aftere as hastely a[s]
y may.[4]

50 John Rus sayth the profetys that hath be taken of that same maner syn
Ser John Fastolf deyd hath be take by Ser Thomas Howys and Jenney.
Hugh a Fen ys in Flegge. Richard Call spake wyth hym thys wyke, and he
sayd to Richard that he ⌐and hys wyff⌐ wold be wyth me here thys wyke
toward a place of hys that he hath purchasyd of Godehredys. Yf he com I

55 shall make hym gode chyre, for it ys told me of dyuers folkys that haue
spoke wyth hym sythen he com in-to Norffolk as thay fele by hys[5] sayng
that he awyth you ryght gode wyll.

Item, as for my comyng to you, yf it please you that I com ⌐y hope⌐ I
shall purvey so for althyngys or I com that it shall be sayff y-nogh, by the

60 grace of God, tyll I com a-yen. But at the reuerens of God, yf ye may purvey a mene that ye may com hom youre-sylf, for that shall be most profect-
abell to you; for[6] men cut large thongys here of othere mens lethere. I shall
wryte to you ⌐a⌐-yen as hastely as I may.

God haue you in hys kypyng. Wryten in haste at Haylesdon the Sonday
65 next aftere the Assumpsyon of Oure Lady.

Item, ⌐my⌐[7] cosyn Elysabeth Clere ys at Ormesby, and youre modere
purposyth to be at here place at Castere thys wyke, for þe pestylens ys so
feruent in Norwych that thay there no lengere a-byde there. So God help,
me thynkyth by my modere that she wold ryght fayn that ye dyde well, and

70 that ye myght spyde ryght well in youre mater⌐s⌐,[8] and me thynkyth by my
cosyn Clere that she wold fayn haue youre gode wyll and that she hath
sworyn ryght faythfully to me that there shall no defaute be founde in
here, nor noght hath be yf the trogh myght be vnderstond, as she hopyth it
shall be heraftere. She sayth there ys no man a-lyff that she hath put here

75 truste in so moch as she hath doon in you. She sayth she wote well such
langage as hath be reportyd to you of here othere-wyse then she hath
deseruyd causyth you to be othere-wyse to[9] here then ye shold be. She had
to me thys langage wypyng, and told me of dyuers othere thyngys the
whych ye shall haue knowlych of heraftere.

By yourys, M. P.

---

[4] Recto ends, except for verte written at foot.   [5] lan canc.
[6] othere canc.   [7] Interl. above youre canc.
[8] -s is apparently meant, but is crowded above the line at edge of paper.
[9] you canc.

191. To JOHN PASTON I   1465, probably August

Add. 27444, f. 148. 11⅜×4⅜ in. Daubeney's hand.

Dorse: Marks of folding. Traces of red wax, and tape-slits, but no address.

The approximate date appears from Margaret's plan to join her husband in London, which she did in September 1465 (see no. 192). Since the same intention is expressed in no. 190 this must be close to it in date; and since in that letter she mentions having sent only no. 189, this must be after rather than before it.

    G. 515/596.

Right worchepful hosbond, I recommand me to yow and pray you hertely¹ at þe reverence of God that ye be of good comfort *and* trost veryly be þe grase of God that ye shall ouercome your enemys *and* your trobelows maters ryght welle, yf ye wolle be of good comfort *and* not take your maters to heuely, þat ye apeyr not your-self, *and* thynk veryly that ye be 5 strong j-nowe for all your enemys, be þe grace of God. My moder is your good moder *and* takyth your maters ryght hertely, and 3yf ye thynnk þat I may do good in your maters yf I come vp to you, after I have knowlage of your entent it shall not be longe or I be wyth you, be þe grace of God. And as for any othyr thyngys of sharge that be in þis contré, I hope I shall so 10 ordeyn therfore þat it shall be safe. I have delyueryd your older sonne xx mark that I have receyvyd of Richard Calle, *and* I kowd [get] nomore of hym syn ye departyd.²

    And I pray God ⌜hertely⌝ send vs good tydyngys of yow,³ and send þe victory of your enemys. Wretyn in hast on Saterday.   **15**

                                    Yours,⁴ M. P.

Item, I take your sonne of your ⌜faders⌝⁵ ode⁶ mony þat was in þe ⌜lytyll⌝ trussyng cofyr x mark, for my broder Clement seythe þat xx mark was to lytyll for hym.

191. ¹ and *canc.*
  ² and I send yow another bage of mony that was in your square cofyr *canc.*
  ³ *and* of wretyn in hast *canc.*
  ⁴ *The usual abbreviation* yʳo *has its o altered to* s.
  ⁵ *Interl. above* [?] *flourished* m *canc.*
  ⁶ *Beginning of this word not clear; Gairdner's* oode *not excluded.*

192. To JOHN PASTON I 1465, 27 September

Add. 27445, f. 8. 11¾×17 in. Hand unidentified, appearing also in nos. 193 and 195 B, and in John I's letter no. 66 and petition no. 67. Marginal notes mostly in Pampyng's hand, three by John I; and in top left-hand corner, in John I's hand, *iiij*.

Dorse: Completely covered with latter part of text. Marks of folding, but no seal or address. See no. 193.

This and no. 193 are virtually one, written on the same day and mainly by the same clerk. But John's numbering distinguishes them as 'iiij' and 'v', evidently of a series the beginning of which is lost.

G. 529/610. C. 41 (part).

Ryght wourchipful husbonde, I recoumaunde me to yow, dyssyryng hertely to here of yowr welfare, thankyng yow of yowr grett chere that ye made me *and* of the coste that ye dede on me.¹ Ye dede more cost thanne myn wylle was that ye choulde do, but that it plesyd yow to do so. God gyf me grase
5 to do² that³ may plese yow.

Plesyt yow to wett that on Fryday⁴ after myn departyng fromme yow I was at Sudbury *and* spake wyth the schreve, *and*⁵ Richard Calle toke hym the ij writtys *and* he brake them, *and* Richard hathe the copés of them. *And* he seyd he wollde⁶ sende the writtys to hys vndreschryf *and* a⁷ l[e]tter ther-
10 wyth chargyng hym that he ⌐schowlde⌐⁸ do ther-jne as largely as⁹ he ⌐owt⌐¹⁰ to do.¹¹ And I ⌐*and* Richard⌐ informyd hym of the demenyng of hys vndr[e]-chryf, how parciall he hade be wyth the other partye, bothe in that mater *and* also for the acciounys beyng in the schere; *and* he was nothyng wel plesyd of the demenyng of hys vndresch[r]ef, *and* he hat wretyn to hym
15 that he choulde be indeferent for both partyes acordyng to the lawe bothe for that materys *and* for alle othere. What þe vndreschryf wylle do þer-in I wot nere, for he is not yet spokyn wyth.

Item, as for Cotton, I entryd in-to þe plase as on Sunday last was, *and* ther I a-bode tyll vn¹² Wednysday¹³ last pasyd. I ⌐have⌐ left ther John
20 Paston þe youngere, Wykys, *and* other¹⁴ xij men for to receyve the profyttys of the manere. And ayenst the day of kepyng of the corte I hope ther chall be more to streynkyth them, yf it nede. John Paston hath be wyth myn lorde of Norffolk ⌐seyth we entryd⌐, *and* dyssyryd hys good lorchypp to strey[n]th

192. ¹ yowr *canc.* ² so *canc.* ³ it I *canc.* ⁴ last *canc.*
⁵ *In margin, in John I's hand,* vic. Norff. pro ovibus. ⁶ *From* wyll.
⁷ *No space.* ⁸ *Interl. above* myght *canc.*
⁹ *In margin, in Pampyng's hand (as other marginalia unless specified),* answere of the writtys *and* of the replevyn.
¹⁰ *Interl. above* myght *canc.* ¹¹ *and* he and I lett *canc.* ¹² Sunday *canc.*
¹³ after *canc. In margin,* Margareta Paston intrauit in Cotton die dominica proxima ante festum Michaelis.
¹⁴ to þe *and* other *canc.*

hym[15] wyth hys howsolde men *and* other yf nede be, *and* he hath promysyd
he woulde do so. *And* I sent Richard Calle on Tusday to Knevett, dysyryng 25
hym that he woulde sende to hys baley *and* tenantys at ⌐Mendlesham⌐[16]
that[17] thei[18] choulde be redy to coume to John Paston whan he sent for them;
and he sent a[7] man of hys forthwyth, chargyng them in aney wyse that they
choulde do so. *And* he sent me wourde ⌐be Richard⌐, *and* hys soune also,
yf ⌐wee⌐[19] were nott stronge jnough that owther he or hys soune, or bothe 30
yf nede were, woulde come wyth suche feleschipp as they coude gett a-bowt
them *and* that þei woulde do as feythfully as ⌐they⌐[20] kowde for yow, bothe
in that mater *and* in alle other.

Item, on Saterday last was Jenney ded warne a corte at Calcotte to be
holde ther in hys name as on Tusday last was, *and* Debunham de[d] 35
charge an other court ther þe Sunday next after[21] to be holde ther þe same
Tusday in hys name. *And* Daubeney had knowleche ther-of, *and* he dede
send on Sunday at nyght to yowr eldere soune for to have soume men fro[7]
thens, *and* so he sent Wykys *and* Bernay to hym[22] on Munday[23] in þe
mornyng. *And* assone as thei were coume to Caster þei sent for men ther in 40
þe contré, *and* so they gett them in-to a iij[xx] men; *and* Daubeney *and* Wekys
and Bernay rod to Calcott þe same Munday at nyght wyth ther felechypp,
and ther kept them prevye in þe pl[a]se so that non of alle þe tenauntys[24]
kneve them ther saf Rysyngys wyff *and* her howsolde[25] tylle the Thevsday
at x of þe cloke. And ⌐than⌐[26] Ser Thomas Brewys,[27] Debunham þe fadre, 45
and[28] þe knyt hys soune, Jenney, Mykelfylde, younge Jermyn, *and* younge
Jernyngham *and* þe baley of Motforde, wyth other to þe nombre of a
iij[xx] persones, coum fro ye sessiounys at Becklys[29] þe whech þei hade keppt
ther on þe day byfore, coume to Seynt Olovys,[30] *and* þer thei teryed *and*
dynyd; *and* whan thei hade dynyd Ser Gylberde Debunham came to Cal- 50
cott wyth xx hors for to wett whatt felechipp ther was in þe plase. *And*
than Wekys aspyed them commyng, *and* he *and* Bernay *and* ij wyth them
rode owt to a spoke wyth them; *and* whan Ser Gilberd aspyd them commyng[31] he *and* hys felechipp flede *and* rode ayen to Seynt Olovys.[32] And
than ⌐they⌐ sent yovng Jernyngham *and* the baley of Mottforde to yowr 55
men, lettyng hem wete that the justice of þe pese wer coum doune wyth

---

[15] *In margin*, I thank yow of your demeny[n]g at Cotton.
[16] *Interl. above* Rendlesam *canc.*   [17] *In margin*, remembir Nakton.
[18] myg *canc.*   [19] *Interl. above* they *canc.*   [20] *Interl. above* he *canc.*
[21] be *canc.*   [22] þe *canc.*
[23] *In margin*, mokcage of Jenney *and* Debenham at Calcote the Tuisday next bifore
Sen Mighell.
[24] kneve *at edge canc. In margin*, now your cost is doon consideryng your frendys be
coragys *and* your enemys discoraged gadir up the profitys in all goodly hast [*ampersand
canc.*] that I may see acompt for this trobill tyme.
[25] and þer *canc.*   [26] *Interl. above* so *canc.*   [27] -y- *crowded in.*
[28] Deb *over* þe *canc.*   [29] to seyn *canc.*   [30] þe seyd *canc.*
[31] they *canc.*   [32] ayen *canc.*

Debunham *and* Jenney to se that þe pese choulde be kepte, and that þei
choulde entre *and* kepe þe courte in pesible wyse. *And* yowr men answeryd
and seyd that they knewe noman was possessyd ther-in[33] ner hade no ryght
60 ther-in but ye, *and* so in yowr name *and* in yowr ryght they seyd they
woulde kepyt. *And* so they yede ayen w*yth* thys answer*e*, *and* wer put[34]
from*m*e ther purp[o]se that day; *and* all þe ten*aun*tys best*ys* wer put ⌜fro⌝[35]
Calcott[36] fee *and* challe be tylle other remedy maye be hadde. Yow*r* men
woulde not kepe ther a cort that daye[37] by-cause it was warnyd by the
65 tother p*a*rte, but we wyl do warne a corte *and* kepyt, I hope in hast. Ye
wyll laugh for to her*e* alle þe p*r*ocesse of the demenyng ther, wheche wer*e*
to longe to writt at thys tyme.[38] Bernay challe telle yow whane he cou*m*e, but
he challe not cou*m*e to yow tylle aft*er* Seynt[39] Feythesmesse,[40] that he maye
bryng yow answer*ys* of other mat*er*ys.[41]
70 It is tolde me the sessiou*n*ys choulle[42] be her at Norwiche on Tusday
next cou*m*yng, *and* in Suffolk ⌜the sessiou*n*ys⌝[43] challe be the same Tusday
owther at Dou*n*wyche or at Ypswyche. I suppose ther challe be labowr*e*
ayenst sou*m*e of ow*r* folk*ys* ther, but we challe assaye to lett ther pourp[o]se
yf we maye. ⌜It is told me⌝ yf ther hade no folk*ys* a be left her*e* in thys
75 plase whyll[44] I haue be owt ther choulde a be nev*e* mastr*ys* her*e* by thys
tyme. Therfor it is not good to leve it alone yett.
It*em*,[45] Arblast*er* hathe sent a[7] lett*er* to myn lorde of Oxnefordy*s* ten*aun*-
ty*s* that be nerrest a-bowt Cotton to help John Paston yf they be sent to, &c.
It*em*, I was thys daye w*yth* my*n* lorde of Norwyche at Thorppe, *and*
80 informyd hym ⌜of the demenyng⌝ of the mat*er*[46] for Drayton chyrche,[47]
and of alle þe demenyng *and* p*a*rcialté of Mast*er* John Salatt *and* Ypswell, *and*
also I[48] informyd [hym] what disposission that they wer*e* of that wer*e* vpon
þe quest; and jn[7] good[7] feyth me thynkyth by hym that[49] he is ryght ille
plesyd that the mat*er* was so gydyt. He seyde to me ryght pleynly that þe
85 jugis dedenot ther-in as thei owght to do, and he seyd thowe I hadde hade
noo cou*n*cell that[50] he howght of ryght to ⌜have⌝ assyngyd me cou*n*cell suche
as I hadde dyssyrid; but he seyde he wyst well he ⌜dede⌝[51] in that mat*er* as

---

33 -e *canc.*   34 for *canc.*   35 *Interl. above* for *canc.*
36 *MS.* Calcalcott.   37 *Recto ends.*   38 but *canc.*
39 *In margin, in Paston's hand,* veneat Barney.
41 *Next two sentences marked off by roughly written oblique strokes.*   40 *MS.* feyther-.
42 *In margin,* sessio[n]es Norwici *et* Donwici Mart*is* prox*imo* post fest*um* Micha*elis.*
43 *Interl. above* they *canc.*
44 *In margin,* de pr*u*dencia custod*iendi* Heylesdon.
45 *In margin,* tenent*es* com*itis* Oxonie pro custod*ia* Cotton.   46 an *canc.*
47 *In margin,* Episcop*us* Norwici p*r*o ecclesia de Drayton.   48 n *canc.*
49 that *repeated. In margin,* lete yo*ur* counsell comon w*yth* hym but thei may sey they
knowe not myn evidens nor titell ner haue nomore to do by my writyng þat I sent yow
thanne to avise hough I shull take myn acc*i*on and þat in þat acc*i*on I haue as good titell
as [any man in Norff*olk* myght haue ayens *canc.*] my lord of Norwich hath for the chirch
of Thorp.
50 *MS.* the.   51 hadde do so *canc.*

320

he have ⌜do⌝ in other mat*er*ys byfore. Me thynkyth by suche thyng*ys* as I
harde the*r*e that þe seyd Mast*er* Johon ner the tother is not grettly in conseyt
at thys tyme, *and* so tolde me[52] Aschefylde in cou*n*cell. What þe cause was 90
he myght have no leyser*e* to telle me. I mevyd my lorde in the mat*er*,
acordyng to the jntent of yow*r* wrytyng, yf aney axcion wer*e* take, *and* he
seyd feythefully yf it myght p*r*ovayle yow he woulde w*yth* ryght good wylle
that it choulde be doo, *and* ellys he woulde not in noo wyse that it choulde
be doo. *And* he dyssyryde me to sende to hym suche as be of yow*r* cou*n*cell 95
lernyd, that they myght comu*n*e w*yth* hym þerin, for he seyd he woulde
not ye choulde take no*n* axcion ther-in w*yth*owt it myght p*r*ovayle. He was
well payed that I tolde hym that ye woulde not do therin w*yth*owt hys
knowleche *and* assent, *and* he seyd he woulde do þerin as he woulde do yf
the mat*er* wer*e* hys owne. Be avyse of ⌜yow*r*⌝ cou*n*cell I purpose to sende 100
Lou*m*nowr *and* Playt*er* to[53] comou*n*e w*yth* hym ther-in. He seyd he woulde
fayne that ye wer owt of troble, *and* he seyd yf he myght doo owght to
helppe yow forwarde in aney of yow*r* mat*er*ys he swore by heys feythe he
wode do hys p*ar*te feythfully ther-in. He purp[o]syth to[54] be at Lou*n*don
thys t*er*me, *and* thanne he seyd he woulde speke w*yth* yow of maney 105
thyng*ys*.[55] He wycheyd herteley that he myght have spoke w*yth* yow on
owre. He mevyd to me of a mat*er* of a[56] jentyllman ⌜of⌝ Cornale. He seyd he
woulde speke w*yth* yow therof her-aft*er*; yf it myght be browt to it myght
do meche good in maney thyng*ys*. I harde yow onys speke of the same—ye
tolde me ye hade be mevyd to therof by other. 110

Item, I rec*e*yvyd a lett*er* frome yow yest*er*day, wherof I thanke yow
hertely, *and* I praye yow that I maye be as ye writt. *And*[57] as for suche
mat*er*ys as S*er* Thom*a*s Howys choulde be spoke to fore, I sent R*ich*ard
Calle þis day to speke w*yth* hym, but he myght not speke w*yth* hym. But
as hastely as I may I challe do my*n* p*ar*te to spede the erand*ys and* other. It 115
is tolde me that S*er* Thom*a*s wyll ressyng Mautby chyrche,[58] *and* yf it plesyd
yow to geve it to on S*er* Thom*a*s Lyndis I truste verely that ye ⌜choulde⌝[59]
leke hym ryght well, for he is ⌜rit⌝ a prystly man *and* vertusly dysposyd. I
have knowe hym þis xx yer*e and* more; he was brother to þe good p*ar*sone
of Seynt Michellys that ye lovyd ryght well. *And* yf he myght havyt he 120
woulde kepe an howsolde þervpon *and* bylde[60] well þe pl⌜a⌝se,[61] *and* þerof
have it grete nede for it is now rit evyll reparyd; and I wott well he woll be
rulyd *and* gydyt as ye wyll[7] have hym. I praye yow, yf it plese yow that
he have it, ⌜that it⌝ lekyth yow to sende me an answer*e* by the berrer
herof. 125

---

[52] in *canc.*   [53] hym *canc.*   [54] *In margin,* Ep*i*scop*u*s ap*u*d Lond*o*n.
[55] he *canc. here, at the end of a line, but written in margin at the beginning of the next,*
apparently in Paston's hand as he annotated the paragraphs.
[56] *In margin,* Cornwayle.   [57] *Crowded in.*
[58] *In margin,* ecclesia de Mautby.   [59] *Interl. above* challe *canc.*
[60] *First letter not quite certain ; written over another.*   [61] *MS.* p*a*lse.

Item,[62] I haue do spoke for yowr worstede, but ye may not haue it tylle Halowmesse; *and* thane I am promysyd ye challe haue as fyne as maye be made. Richard Calle challe bryng it vp wyth hym.

Wretyn the Fryday next byfore Michelmas Day.[63]

193. To JOHN PASTON I   1465, 27 September

Add. 27445, f. 9. 11¾×5⅜ in. First eleven words, and approximately the latter half, in hand of no. 192; the rest in Calle's hand. Marginal notes in Pampyng's hand. In top left-hand corner, in John I's hand, *v.*

Dorse: Remnants of red wax over string. Address in Calle's hand:

To my ryght worschipfull husbond John Paston, in haste.

This is a postscript to no. 192. Since this sheet alone bears an address it was presumably, in spite of its much smaller size, used as the wrapper—there was no room left for an address on either side of f. 8. The 'lodging' of l. 11 is the Fleet Prison; cf. John I's letter no. 77, Margaret's no. 184, and the address of John II's no. 235.

G. 530/611.

Item, it was tolde me thys day that Master John Salatt hathe[1] made a serge in the regestre this monethe[2] aftre the wylles and testementys of suche as hought the maners of Heylesdon and Drayton this c yere, and be that hathe they founde suche evidence as schal be gret strenghthyng to[3] the
5 Dukys tittle, as it is seide. I vndrestonde verely that Mastre John Salet is all on that partye and no thyng wyth you. Item, as for the bill[4] that ye sent to Ser Thomas Howys touchyng on Edmond Carvyll *and* on Fraunces, I wote ner whether he had hem or nought, for he is not spoken wyth yett in tho maters.[5] As wee spede owr materys ⌐we⌐[6] chall sende yow answerys of
10 them as hastely as we maye. At the reuerense of God, spede ye yowr materys that ye maye coume owte of that loggyng that ye are in as hastely as ye maye, for I haue non fansey wyth soume of þe felechipp. I tolde yow as me thowth. I praye yow be ware, &c.

I praye yow yf it plese yow that I maye be recoumaundyd to my Lorde
15 Percy *and* to myn mastres *and* to myn lorde Abott, *and* I pray God bryng yow *and* them owt of troble *and* send yow good spede in alle yowr materys. Wretyn in hast þe Fryday next afore Michellmes.

Be yowr M. P.

Yf it plese yow to send aney thyng by the berer herof, he is trusty jnough.

---

[62] *In margin by Paston,* Wurstid.   [63] *This last line written vertically in margin.*

193. [1] *Calle's hand begins with this word.*

   [2] *In margin,* ⟨. . .⟩ to get a copy ⟨. . .⟩ þat he hath ⟨s⟩erched.

   [3] *In margin,* ⟨n⟩otwythstandyng ⟨I⟩ wote well the haue found non such evidens as ye wene.   [4] ye w *canc.*   [5] *Calle's hand ends.*   [6] *Interl. above* I *canc.*

194. To JOHN PASTON I   1465, 17 October

Add. 27445, f. 10. $11\frac{1}{2} \times 10\frac{1}{2}$ in. Gloys's hand. Four paragraph marks in margin apparently in John Paston's hand.

Dorse: Marks of folding. Paper seal (fleur-de-lis) over red wax and string, and stitch-holes. No address.

The date appears from the report of the destruction of the buildings at Hellesdon (see no. 196).
    G. 533/616. C. 42.

On Tuesday in the morwyn whas John Botiller*e*, o*þer*wyse callid John Palmer*e*, and Davy Arnald y*our* cook, *and* Willi*a*m Malthows of Aylsh*a*m taken at Heylesdon be the balyf of Ey, callid Bottisforth, *and* led for to Cossey, *and* ther*e* thei kepe hem yet w*yth*-ought any warant or autoryté of justice of peas; and thei sey thei wull carie hem forth to Ey pr*e*son, and 5 as many as thei may gete mor*e* of y*our* men *and* ten*aun*tes þat thei may knowe that owe yow good wyll or hath be to you ward, thei be thret to be slayn or pr*e*soned.

    The Duke came to ⌈Norwich⌉[1] on Tuesday at x of clok w*yth* þe nombr*e* of v hundred men,[2] and he sent aft*er* þe meyr*e and* alderman w*yth* þe 10 sheref*es*, desiryng hem in the Kyng*es* name þat thei shuld take an enquer-aunce of þe constablys of eu*er*y ward w*yth*-in the cyté what men shuld a go on y*our* p*ar*ty to haue holpyn or socowryd y*our* men at any tyme of þes gaderyng*es*, and if any thei cowde fynde þat thei shuld take and arest hym *and* correct hym, *and* also certifie hym the names on Wyndenesse-day be 15 viij of clok; which the meyr*e* dede *and* wull do any thyng þat he may for hym *and* his. And her*e*-vp-on the meyr*e* hath arestid on þat was ⌈w*yth*⌉ me callid Roberd Lovegold, braser*e, and* threte hym þat he shall be hanged be the nek, wherfor*e* I wuld þat ther*e* myght come down a writ to remeve hym, if ye thynk it be to do. He was not w*yth* me, not saue that Harleston *and* 20 other*e* mad þe assault vp-on me at[3] Lammesse. He is right good *and* feythfull on-to you, *and* ther*e*fore I wuld he had help. I haue non man at this tyme to avayte vp-on me þat dar*e* be avowyd but litill John. Willi*a*m Nawton is her*e* w*yth* me,[4] but he dar not ben avowyd for he is sore thret.[5] It is told me þe old lady *and* þe Duke is set fervently a-geyn vs be the enformac*i*on of 25 Harlesdon, þe baly of Cossey, *and* Andrewys, *and* Doget þe balys sone, *and* suych other*e* fals shrewys the which wuld haue thes mater*e* born ought

194. [1] *Interl. above* this town, *of which only* town *is canc.*
  [2] where of yed a certeyn felesship to Heylesdon *canc.*
  [3] *MS. ampersand.*
  [4] h *canc.*
  [5] *After this word a square bracket, evidently made by Paston, marks off the following passage, which is also distinguished by a line in the margin extending over six lines (as far as* doggeboltes).

for there owyn plesere; the which causith an[3] evyll noyse[6] in this contré *and* othere plac*es*.

30 And as for S*er* John Hevenyngh*am*, S*er* John Wyndefeld, *and* othere wurchepfull men ben mad but here doggeboltes, the which I suppose wull turne hem to diswurchep here-after. I spake w*yth* S*er* John Heueny[n]gham *and* enformed hym w*yth* the trough of þe matere, *and* of all owyre demenyng at Drayton, and he seid he wuld þat all thyng were wele and þat he wuld
35 enforme my lord as I seid to hym, but Harleston had all þe wordes *and* þe rewle w*yth* the Duke here and after his avyse *and* Doctour Aleynes he was avysed here at this tyme.

The logge *and* the remenaunte of your place was betyn down on Tuesday *and* Wednesday, *and* þe Duke rode on Wednysday to Drayton[7] *and* so for
40 to Cossey whill þe logge at Heylesdon was in þe betyng down. And þis nyght at mydnyght Thom*as* Sleyforth, Grene, Portere, *and* ⌈Joh[n] Botes-forth⌉[8] the baly of[9] Eye *and* othere had a cart *and* fetched awey fether-beddes *and* all þe stuffe þat was left at þe p*ar*sones *and* Thom*as* Wateres hows to be kept of owres. I shall send you billes er-after as nere as I may
45 what stuffe we haue forborn.[10] I pray you send me word how ye wull þat I be demened, wheder ye wull þat [I] a-bide at Caystere or come to you to London.

I haue no leysere to write nomore. God haue yow in his kepyng. Wretyn at Norwich on Sent Lukes Evyn.
50   M. P.

195. Inventory of goods stolen   1465, soon after 17 October

A. Bodl. MS. Charters Norfolk a. 8, no. 738. Folded to form two leaves $8\frac{1}{4} \times 11\frac{1}{4}$ in., a strip $2\frac{1}{2}$ in. wide and varying from $6\frac{1}{2}$ to $4\frac{1}{2}$ in. long torn from foot of second leaf, not affecting text.
First leaf both sides in Wykes's hand, second leaf recto about first half in Calle's hand, the rest in unidentified unskilled hand; dorse blank.

B. Ibid., no. 739. $5\frac{7}{8} \times 17$ in. Hand of no. 192.
Dorse contains last eight lines of text.

These are evidently drafts of the inventory of losses that Margaret, in her letter of 17 October (no. 194), promised to send to her husband. 14 October 1465 was a Monday. The attack presumably began then, and continued with the destruction of the lodge and other buildings on the Tuesday and Wednesday.

In view of the considerable differences in spelling, arrangement, and substance, both versions are given in full.

G. 978/615.

---

[6] to here *canc.*
[7] *and* kept þer a court *canc.*   [8] *Interl. in a different hand.*
[9] hey *canc.*   [10] at leysere *canc.*

A

Thys be the p*arcellys*[1] vnderwryten of such godys as were taken *and* boren a-way at Haylesdon of John Pastons, hys sones, *and* hys s*eruauntys* by the Duk of Suff*olk* s*eruauntys* *and* ten*auntys* the xiiij day of Octobe*r* the v yere of Kyng E. the iiij^{te}, the whych day the place of Haylesdon was broken *and* pullyd dowyn, &c.   5

In p*r*imis, the*re* was lost of John Pastons the*re* at that tyme in beddyng ij federbedd*ys* w*yth* ij bolsters, iiij materas w*yth* iiij bolsters, a grete seleur[2] w*yth* the testou*r* *and* iiij corteyns of whyte lynen cloth, *and* a coue*r*lyte of whyte worstede, longyng thereto.
It*em*, a sele*u*re[2] w*yth* a testou*r* *and* iij corteyns of blewe bokeram w*yth* a   10
coue*r*yng of blew worstede longyng therto, v pylowys of dowyn, vj coue*r*lyt*ys* of werk of dyu*er*s colou*r*s, vj payre blankett*ys*, ij payre shytes of iij webbys, ij hedshytes of ij webbys, vj payre shytes of ij webbys, ij basons of pewter*e*, *and* iij candelstykk*ys* of latyn for the chambe*re*.

The Boter*é*   15

It*em* in p*r*imis, vj bord clothys, vj towellys, xij napkyns, vj candelstykk*ys* of laton, ij saltsalers of sylu*er*, ij saltsalers of pewter*e*, ij basons of pewter*e* w*yth* ij ewers, a barell of vynegere, a barell of vergyous, xij ale stondys, ij pantré knyves, a pyce of sylu*er*, a pype for brede, a ale stole, xij spones of sylu*er*, &c.   20

The Browhern

It*em*, a grete lede to brew v comb malte w*yth* ons plawyng, a mayshfate, ij kylyng fates, vj kylers, ij clensyng fates, a taptrogh, a temps to clense w*yth*, a scyppe to bere malte, a syff to syft malte, a bultyng pype, ij knedyng fatys, a moldyng bord.   25

The Kychyn

It*em*, ij dosyn pewter*e* vessell*ys*, iiij grete bras pannes, iij pott*ys* of bras, j greddyron, ij broches, j dressyng knyff, j morter*e* of marbell w*yth* a pestell, j litell panne of bras of di. galon, ij pothok*ys*, ij rakk*ys* of yron, ij brende-lett*ys*, a almary to kepe in mete, j axe to clyve wode, ij saltyng fatys to   30
salte in flesh.[3]

Gere taken owte of the Chyrch

It*em*, in the stepell, ix sheffe arwys, ix bawys, ij handgonnes, iiij chambers for gonnys, ij mallys of lede, ij jakk*ys*. It*em*,[4] in the church, a purs *and* iij

195A. [1] -ll *crossed, as also in* vessellys *l. 27 and* tabellys *l. 41, must evidently stand for* -llys.
[2] *Written* seler(e) *with superior* r.
[3] *Recto ends.*   [4] *In margin opposite this line* Wykys.

35 gold ryngys, a colere of syluer of the Kyngys lyuery, *and* a nobyll of viij s.
iiij d. the whych was Wykys. Item, a syde gowne of blewe of Wykys. Item,
a stokk gonne wyth iij chambers.

Gere taken owte of the Chauntré of ⌐Richard Calle⌐5

Item, a syde morrey gowne, a dobelet of blak satyn, a payre hosyn, a jakk,
40 the polrondys of a payre bryganders of rede sateyn fugre. Item, a payre of
large tabellys of box, price vj s. viij d.
Item, a staffe, price iij s. iiij d. Item, boke of Frensh, price iij s. iiij d.

Gere taken a-way of Margeré Pastons

Item, an vnce of gold of Venyse, di. pype of gold Damask, di. vnce of gold
45 of Gene, an vnce of sylk, a li. of threde, a close glasse of yvery, a grete
combe6 of yueré, a fyne kerchy of fyne holond cloth, a quarter of blak
velwet.

Gere of Johan Gayns

Item, a ryng of gold wyth a dyamaunt, a typet of sarsenet, a nobyll of x s.,
50 a nobyll viij s. iiij d.

Gere of John Wykys

Item, a dobelet of blak fusteyn, a hors harnys ⌐vj s.⌐, a gray hors price xl s.,
ij shertys price iiij s.

Will7 Bedford

55 Item, a Normandy byll *and* a bawe, price of them both vj s.

John Botelere

Item, a payre botys, a payre sporys, a shert, a cappe, a hatte, a dobelet, a
payre hosyn, a brydell, ij cropers, v ston of woll, xxx wolfellys, a spere staff.

Shepe

60 Item, taken a-way vppon Drayton grounde at on tyme by the baylly of
Cossey *and* othere, cc shepe callyd hoggys. Item, at a-nothere tyme vppon
the same grownd, iiijxx hoggys *and* xl theyves.
Item, at a-nothere tyme at Haylesdon, by the baylly of Cossey *and* Bottes-
ford *and* othere, viijc8 modere shype *and* cccc lambes.9

65 Memorandum, a gowne of Richard Calle pris ix s., j peyre hosen iij s., j
swerd iij s., ij bonetes ij s. ⟨. . .⟩10 j jakke11 xxvj s. viij d., j scherte iij s. iiij d.

---

5 *Interl. by Calle above* Ser John Pastons *canc.*   6 -e *repr. by stroke through* -b.
7 *Prec. by* John *canc.*   8 *MS.* viijcc.   9 *First part of verso, and* Wykes's *hand, end.*
10 *A few letters lost at torn corner; tail of one, probably* x, *remains.*
11 xvj s. viij d. *canc.*

Memorandum, the pullyng downe of the place at Heylesdon to the hurtes
and skathes of[11]
Item, the pullyng doune of the logge of[12] Heylesdon.
Item, the distroynge of the waryne at Heylisdon.   70
Item,[13] watt þe[14] maner *and* þe warreyn is werse in ʒerly wolew.
Item, memorandum þe rydynges *and* costes off suthe.
Memorandum þe assaw mad up-on Margery[15] Paston, Ser Jon Paston at
Heylysdon be-for þe place was[16] pullyd.
Memorandum þe inpresonment off Ser[17] Jon Paston in þe Flet *and* in þe 75
Kynges Benche.

B

This be þe parcellys[1] of suche gere as was borun awey at Heylesdon of John
Paston,[2] hys sounys *and* hys seruauntys by the Duke of Suffolk seruauntys
and tenauntys the xiiij day of Octobre the vte yere of Kyng E. the iiij[te], þe
weche day þe place of Heylesdon was brokyn *and* pullyd doune, &c.   5

John Paston

Item in primis,[3] ther was lost of beddyng ij fedrebeddys wyth þe traunsouns,
iiij dongys wyth the traunsounys, a grette seloure wyth the testoure, *and*
iij courteynes[4] of whit leynen clothe *and* a whitt kouerlytt of wourstede
longyng[5] þerto. Item, a seloure wyth þe testoure *and* iij courteynes of blewe 10
bokeram wyth a couerlytt of blewe wourstede longyng þerto.
Item, v pelowys of downe.
Item, vj couerlytys of werkys of dyuers colourys.
Item, vj peyre blankettys.
Item, ij peyre schetys of iij webbys *and* ij hedshetys of ij webbys *and* vj 15
peyre schetys of ij webbys.
Item, ij basounys of pewtyre *and* iij candelstykys of latoun for þe chaumbre.

The[6] Boterey

Item in primis, vj borde clothys, vj towellys, xij napkynys, vj candelstykys,
ij salttsalerys of syluer *and* ij salttsalerys of pewtyre, ij basounys, ij ewrys 20

---

[11] *End of line, no erasure or gap. These lines widely spaced as if additions were planned.*
[12] the *canc.*   [13] *Calle's hand ends.*   [14] þ- *in form of* y *throughout this hand.*
[15] *Abbr.* marg', *which could mean either* Margery *or* Margaret; *but from no. 196 it appears
that Margaret was not at Hellesdon at the time of the attack, and cf. B. l. 47.*
[16] was *repeated.*
[17] *Sic, in error; it was John Paston I who was in the Fleet at this time.*

195B. [1] -ll *crossed, as also in* towellys *l. 19,* vesellys *l. 30.*
[2] *At edge;* -s *perhaps lost.*
[3] *Here and later* -ri- *repr. by the usual* -re- *abbreviation,* -is *by the usual* -us *abbreviation.*
[4] *Divided by end of line at* courte.
[5] *Written* long, *curl on* g.   [6] botelere *canc.*

pewtyre, a barell of vynegre, a barell of vergyous, xij ⌈alle⌉[7] stondys, ij pantré kneyuys, a pece syluer, a pyppe for bredde, an alestole, xij spones ⌈of syluer⌉.

The Brewerne

25 Item in primis, a grett ledde to brewe v coumbe maltt wyth onys plawyng. Item, a macchefatt, ij geylyng fattys, ⌈vj kelers⌉, a taptrowe, a temps to clense wyth, a sckeppe to bere maltt, a seve to syft malt, a bultyng pype, ij knedyng fattys, and a moldyng borde.

The Kychyn

30 Item in primis, ij dozeyn pewtyre vesellys, iiij grett brasse pannys, iij pottys of brasse, j gredeyron, ij brochys, j dressyng knyff, j mortere of marble wyth a pestell, j lytell panne of brasse of di. galon, ij potthokys, ij rackys of yron, ij brenledys, an halmerrey to kepe in mette, j axe to cleyue wode, ij saltyngfattys to saltyn fleche.

35 ## Gerre takyn owt of þe Chyrche

Item, in the stepull ix cheff arrowes, ij handegownes, iiij chaumbres of gouns,[8] ij malles, ij jakkys, sawes, b[o]wes and arrowes. Item in þe chirche, a pursse wyth rynges and a colere of syluer wheche was Wekys. Item, vj bowes. Item, a stokke gounne wyth iij chaumbres.
40 Item, a seyde gowne of Wykys.

Ser John Pastounys gere hadde owt of þe Chaumbre

Furst, a seydde morrey gowne, a dowbelett of blake sateyn, a peyre hozyn, a jackke, the mahuturs of a peyre bryngaunderys[9] of welluett, and the perhawys of þe seyd bryngaunderys. Item, a peyre of large tablys of boxe, 45 price vj s. viij d. Item, a staffe pri[ce] iij s. vj d. Item, a boke of Freynsh[10] price xv d.

Margery Pastounys gere

Furst, an vnce[11] of golde of Venysse and di. pipe of golde of Damask. Item, di. vnce of golde of Gene. Item, j vnce sylke. Item, j li. of threde.
50 Item, a closse glasse[12] of yueré wyth a grett coumbe of yueré.[13] Item, a fyne cerche of hollonde clothe. Item, a quarter of weluett.

---

[7] Interl. above a letter heavily canc.
[8] -n- repr. by abbr. mark over -o- ; crowded at edge.
[9] Ends with the flourished -r used for -re, but the -ys abbreviation was presumably intended, as in l. 44.
[10] MS. freyngh.
[11] Written vn, -n tailed; usual abbreviation vnc with curl on -c as in l. 49.
[12] w canc.   [13] y- written over j.

Jone Gaynes ger*e*

Furst, a ryng of golde w*yth* a deamant. It*em*, a tepett of sarsanett.
It*em*, a noble of x *s*. Item, a noble of viij s. iiij d.

John Botelery*s* ger*e* 55

Furst, a peyr*e* bot*ys and* a peyre sporys. It*em*, a chirte p*rice* xij d. It*em*, a
cappe *and* an hatt, a dowbelett, a peyr*e* hozyn. It*em*, a brydell, ij crow-
per*e*s. It*em*, v ston of woulle. It*em*, xxx woulle fellys.

It*em*, taken at Heylesdon *and* at Drayton xj*c* scheppe *and* iiij*c* lambes be þe
balyff of Cossey M*aster* Philipp Lippieate *and* othre of þe Duke of Suff*olk* 60
men.[14]
Memo*randum* that Pers Waron saythe that ther was takyn awey by þe Duke
of Suff*olk* men vpon Drayton g[r]ownde at on tyme cc scheppe callyd
hogg*ys*.
It*em*, ther wer*e* takyn awey at anothir*e* tyme vpon the same grow*n*d iiij*xx* 65
hogg*ys and* xl theyves.
It*em*, at an-othyr*e* tyme at Heylesdon viij*c* modrecheppe *and* iiij*c* lambes.
It*em*, ther be takyn at Heylesdon for grenwaxe by þe vndre-schryf
farthare[15] cij scheppe, wherof ther be iiij*xx* xvj ewys, xx hogg*ys*, vj rammes.
v li. iiij s. ij d. 70

196. To John Paston I   1465, 27 October

Add. 34889, ff. 36*v*–37*r*. 11½ × 17 in. Wykes's hand.

Dorse: Continuation of text. Traces of red wax. Address in Wykes's hand:

*To my ryght wyrshypfull hosbond John Paston be thys delyu*eryd *in hast.*

The reference to the sack of Hellesdon fixes the date in 1465 (see no. 194). In that
year the Eve of SS. Simon and Jude fell on a Sunday (see note on l. 98).
    F. iv, p. 226. G. 534/617 (part). C. 43 (part).

Ryght wyrshypfull hosbond, I recomand me to you. Please it you to wyte
that I haue spoken w*yth* John Rus to doo your*e* erant*ys* to the p*a*rson of
Blowfyld for such maters as be cleymed for S*er* John Fastolf, but I cannot
send hym the byllys that ye send to me. I toke them to Arblastere for to
haue delyuerd to S*er* Thomas, *and* he told me that he had lefte the seyd 5
byll*ys*[1] at hom w*yth* Blaunch hys doghter*e*. I send to her*e* for hem, *and* they
cannot be founde; but I haue take John Rus the namys of them that clayme
the money, *and* he shall bryng you an aunswer*e* therof the wyke next after*e*
Hallawmasse.

---
    ¹⁴ *Recto ends.*   ¹⁵ *MS.* fatthare.
    196. ¹ *Crossed -ll here apparently serves as abbreviation.*

10   I send you a letter*e* by Gryne the lodere which was wryten vppon Wensday last, how that John Botelere *and* hys felowys were delyueryd owte of
prison. John Rus told me that Jenney ys sore be-hated w*yth* the Duches of
Suffolk *and* here sone for the matere that ys be-twyne John Straunge *and*
on of here men, *and* he dymeth, *and* othere moo, that it ys the ⌈chyff⌉ cause
15   of the brekyng vppe of houshold. It ys told me that Jenney wyll be betere
dysposyd to you ward*ys* then he hath be byfore yf he be spoken to of youre
maters.

Barthollomew Whyte hath be straungely entretyd, *and* hys brothere *and*
othere that com to record w*yth* hym, *and* they were betyn *and* putte in
20   prison *and* fovle revylyd by Harleston *and* the bayly of Ey *and* othere of
the Duck of Suffolk ys men. But yf such thyngys as thay haue don may be
chaystyd be-tyme men dyme that thay wyll do more harme in haste. I was
at Haylesdon vppon Thorsday laste passyd *and* sey the place there, *and*
in gode feyth there wyll no cryature thynke how fowle *and* orubelly it ys
25   a-rayed but yf they sey it. There comyth moch pepyll dayly to wondere
there-vppon both of Norwych ⌈*and*⌉ of other placys, *and* they speke shamfully therof. The Duck had be betere than a m¹ li. that it had neuer be don,
and ye haue the more gode wyll of the pepyll that it ys so foyll don. *And*
thay made youre tenauntys of Haylesdon *and* Drayton, w*yth* othere, to help
30   to breke down the wallys² of the place *and* the logge both, God knowyth
full evyll a-yenst there wyllys but that they derst no nothere wysse don for
ferre. I haue spoken w*yth* youre tenauntys of Haylesdon *and* Drayton both,
and putte hem in confort as well as I canne.

The Duck ys men rensackyd the church *and* bare a-way all the gode that
35   was lefte there, both of our*ys* and of the tenauntys, *and* lefte not so moch
but that they³ stode vppon the hey awtere *and* ransackyd the jmages *and*
toke a-way such as thay myght fynd, *and* put a-way the parson owte of the
church tyll thay had don, *and* ransackyd euery mans hous in the town v or
vj tymys. *And* the chyff maysters of robbyng was the baylly of Ey, the
40   baylly of Stradbroke, Thomas Slyford.⁴ *And* Slyford was the chyff robbere
of the cherch, *and* he hath most of the robbory next the baylly of Ey, *and*
as for lede, bras, pewtere, yren, dorys, gatys, *and* othere stuffe of the hous,
men of Coshay *and* Cavston haue it, *and* that thay myght not cary thay
haue hewen it a-sondere in the most dysspytuose wyse.⁵ Yf it myght be I
45   wold som men of wyrshop myght be send from the Kyng to see how it ys
both there *and* at the logge, ore than any snowys com, that thay may make
report of the troth;⁶ ellys it shall not mo be seyn so playnly as it may now.
And at the reuerens of God, spyde youre maters nowe, for it ys to orybell
a cost ⌈*and* trobell⌉ that we haue now dayly *and* most haue tyll ⌈it⌉ be
50   othere-wyse; *and* youre men dere not goo a-bowte to gedere vppe youre

lyfflode, *and* we kype her*e* dayly more then xxx p*er*sons for sauacyon of[7] ous *and* the place, for in very trowght *and* the place hadnot be kypyd strong the Duck had com hether*e*.

The mayer*e* of Norwych dede a-rest the baylly of Normand*ys*, Lovegold, Grygory Cordoner*e*, *and* Bartholomew Fuller*e* w*yth*-ovten any autoryté 55 saue only he sayth that he hath a comandement of ⌐the⌐ Duck to do so; *and* he wyll not lete hem ovte of p*ri*son tyll he had suerty for ache[8] of hem in iiij[xx] li. for to awnswer*e* to such maters as the Duck *and* hys counsell wyll put a-yenst hem at any tyme that thay be callyd, ⌐*and* so woll he do to other*e*, as many as he may gyte, that awe you any gode wyll⌐. *And* also the 60 mayer*e* wold haue had hem sworen that thay shold neu*er* be a-yenst the Duck nor non of hys, whych thay wold not do in no wyse. Pore Bartho*lomew* lyeth styll for defaute of suerty. He was som tyme moch tendyng to gode Edmond Clyre. Arblaster*e* thynketh verely that Hugh a Fen may do moch in your*e* maters, *and* he thynkyth that he woll do for you faythfully yf ye 65 wyll, &c.[9]

At the reuerens of God, yf any wyrshypfull *and* p*ro*fetabill mene may be take yn your*e* maters, for-sake it not in eschuyng of our*e* trobell *and* grete cost*ys* *and* charg*ys* that we haue *and* may growe her*e*-after*e*. It ys thoght here that yf my lord of Norff*olk* wolld take vppon hym for you, *and* that he 70 may haue a comyssyon for to enquer*e* of such ryott*ys* ⌐*and* robbory*es*⌐ as hath be don to you *and* other*e* in thys contray, that then all the contray wyll a-wayte vppon hym *and* s*er*ue your*e* entent, for the pepyll lovyth *and* dredyth hym more then any other*e* lord except the Kyng *and* my lord of Warwyk, &c. 75

It*em*, yf it please you, ther*e* ys on Harald of Haynford hath boght a bond tenantry of your*ys* of on John Whyte, *and* the p*ar*son had it in ferm be-fore that it was sold. *And* he sayth that yf it shold be sold that he had a p*ro*myse of the awner*e* that he shold by it be-fore any other*e* man; *and* the awner*e* sayth that he made hym neu*er* non soch p*ro*mys, nor*e* receyvd neu*er* peny 80 of hym for no bargyn. Wher-vppon I haue don hym examyn[10] a-fore the same p*ar*son[11] *and* all the parysh, *and* there he sware vppon a boke that he made neu*er* bargyng w*yth* no man saue only w*yth* Harald; *and* Harald hath payd hym ther*e*-fore by-fore suffycyaunt record *and* hath don coste vppon the hous sythen that he boght it, *and* by-cause of evyll wyll that the p*ar*son 85 awyth to hym he wold haue it from hym, but the p*ar*son hath no gode record of hys bargyn. I p*ra*y you thogh ye be enformyd by Ric*har*d Calle for the p*ar*son ys parte that ye yffe no credans to hym therin, for ye shall here the mater*e* your*e*-sylf when ye com[12] hom; for Ric*har*d holdyth more

---

[7] of *repeated*.

[8] *First letter seems to be* a, *but has been written twice and may have been meant to be corrected to* e.

[9] *Recto ends.*   [10] hym *interl. but canc.*   [11] MS. parsen.   [12] hym *canc.*

331

90 wyth the parson for hys love then for the troght of the matere, *and* I pray
you that Harald may ocupy the land tyll the[13] troght may be vnderstond.

And I pray you hertely send me word how ye do *and* how ye spyde in
youre maters in haste, *and* that I may haue[14] knowlych how youre sonnys
doth. I com hom thys nyght late, *and* shalbe hyre tyll I hyre othere
95 tydyngys from you. Wykys com hom vppon Satore-day, but he met not
wyth youre sonys.

God haue you in hys kypyng *and* send ous gode tydyngys from you.
Wryten in haste vppon the[15] Seynt Symon *and* Jude ys Evyn.

By yourys M. P.

197. Perhaps to JOHN BERNEY: draft　　　　Before May 1466

Add. 27444, f. 149. $11\frac{1}{2} \times 3$ in. Gresham's hand.

Dorse: Marks of folding, slightly soiled; but no seal or address.

The external appearance of this paper, as well as the numerous corrections, shows
it to be a draft. Despite the absence of signature or seal there is little doubt that it
was written for Margaret Paston. The reference to her cousin's having been blamed
for unlawful acts may possibly be connected with accusations that John Berney
(of Witchingham) was concerned in the murder of Thomas Denys in 1461 (see
Part II, no. 637, and cf. no. 161). Brandiston is close to Witchingham.

There is no indication of date except that John Paston I is alive, so that it must
be before his death in 1466. Gairdner plausibly suggests that infringements of the
Pastons' rights might perhaps be more readily made at the time when the Duke of
Suffolk was laying claim to Hellesdon and Drayton in 1465.

G. 516/597.

Cosyn, I recommaunde me to yow, letyng yow wete that I am informid
⌜that⌝ the parson of Brandeston is take be yowre sowdiors and led forth
wyth hem, and thay haue ryfelid his godis and svmme of myn[1] husbondis
also[2] and of his ballyes weche were left wyth[3] the seyd parson to kepe;
5 wherfore I avise yow and praye that he maye be lete goo a-gayn and to
haue ower godis as were take fro hym. Fore and yowre sowdioris be of
sweche disposicion that they wyll take that they may gete, it shall no
wurchip be ⌜to yow⌝ nor profite in tyme to come, and therof wolde I be[4]
sory. And if the[5] seyd parson be othirwyse disposid thanne he owth to be,
10 I wyll[6] helpe that he shall be chaysteysid as conciens *and* lawe requerith.

13 the *canc.*　　　　　　　　14 haue *canc.*
15 Sonday *canc.*
197. hvsbo *canc.*
2 that were left wyth the bally to kepe *canc.*
3 hym to kepe *canc.*
4 *A word heavily canc., apparently* full.
5 seyd the seyd *canc.*　　　　6 hespe *canc.*

I wolde ye shulde remember that[7] ye haue bore blame for sweche thyngis be-fore this tyme[8] ⌐that hath be do⌐ othirwise thanne lawe hath requerid. And God haue[9] yow in his kepyng. Wrete at Norwiche.

198. To JOHN PASTON II   1466, 29 October

Add. 34889, f. 46. 12×6 in. Wykes's hand.

Dorse: Traces of red wax. Address in Wykes's hand:

To my ryght wyrshypfull maystere Ser John Paston, kny3t, be thys lettere delyueryd in hast.

This was clearly written soon after the death of John Paston I in May 1466 (see no. 76).

    F. iv, p. 272. G. 560/649. C. 45.

I grytte you well, *and* send you God ys blessyng *and* myn, desyryng you to send me word how that ye spede in youre maters, for I thynk ryght long tyll I here tydyngys from you. *And* in alwyse I avyse you for to be ware that ye kepe wysly youre wrytyngys that ben of charge, that it com not in here handys that may hurt you heraftere. Youre fadere, wham God assole, 5 in hys trobyll seson set more by hys wrytyngys *and* evydens[1] than he dede by any of his moveabell godys. Remembere that yf tho were had from you ye kowd neuer gyte no moo such as tho be for youre parte, &c.

    Item, I wold ye shold take hyde that yf any processe com owte a-yenste me,[1] or a-yenst[2] any of tho that were endyted a-fore the coronere, that I 10 myght haue knowlych therof *and* to purvey a remedy therfore.

    Item, as for youre fader ys wyll, I wold ye shold take ryght gode counsell therin, as I am enformyd it may be provyd thogh no man take no charge thys twelfmonth. Ye may haue a lettere of mynystracyon to such as ye wyll, *and* mynestere the godys *and* take no charge. I avyse you that ye in no wyse 15 take no charge therof tyll ye know more than ye doo yet, for ye may verely knowe by that youre vnkell Will seyd to you *and* to me that thay wyll lay the charge vppon you *and* me for moo thyngys then ys exprest in youre fadere ys wyll, the whych shud be to grete for you or me to bere. But as for me, I will not be to hasty to take it vppon me, I ensure you. 20

    And at the reuerens of God, spede youre maters soo thys terme that we may be in rest heraftere, *and* lette not for no labour for the season; *and* remembere the grete cost *and* charge that we haue ⌐had⌐ hedyre-toward, *and* thynk verely it may not lange endure. Ye know what ye left when ye

---

7 ye shuld *canc.*   8 a *canc.*   9 haue *canc.*
198. 1 *Ampersand canc.*   2 of *canc.*
3 *Interl. above* haue *canc.*

25 were last at hom, *and* wyte it verely ther ys no more in thys countray to bere
owte no charge ⌐wyth¹. I avyse you to enquere wysely yf ye canne gyte any
more there as ye be, for els, by my feth, I feere els it will not be well *wyth*
ous. *And* send me word in hast hough ye doo, *and* whethere ye haue youre
laste dedys that ye fayled, for playnly thay ernot in thys contray. It ys told
30 me ⌐in consell¹ that Ric*hard* Calle hath nyere conqueryd youre vncle Will
wyth fayre promyse twochyng hys lyflode *and* othere thyng*ys* the whych
shold *p*revayll hym gretly, as he sayth. Be ware of hym *and* of hys felowe,
be myn avyse.

God send you gode spede in all youre maters. Wryten at Caster*e* the
35 moren next aftere Symon *and* Jude, where as I wold not be at thys tyme
but for youre sake, so mot I they.

By youre moder*e*

199. To JOHN PASTON II   1467, 11 July

Add. 34889, f. 63. $11\frac{1}{2} \times 8\frac{1}{4}$ in. Gloys's hand.

Dorse: Paper seal over red wax. Address in Gloys's hand:

To Ser John Paston, knyght, be þis deliuered in hast.

Sir John Paston was granted possession of Caister soon after his father's death.
A warrant of Edward IV dated 26 July 1466 instructed tenants, farmers, and
occupiers of the lands henceforth to pay all the issues and profits to him (copy in
Sandford's Genealogy: see Part II, no. 896 (G. 552/641)).[1] The Duke of Norfolk
claimed it, and finally attacked it, in 1469 (see, for example, nos. 202 and 203). In
1468 the two John Pastons were in Flanders for the marriage of Princess Margaret
to the Duke of Burgundy, but Daubeney was not with them (see no. 330). The
present letter must therefore be dated 1467.
    For Relic Sunday cf. nos. 78, 161.
    F. iv, p. 294. G. 576/671.

I grete you wele *and* send you Godd*es* blissyng *and* myn, letyng you wete
that Blykklyng of Heylesdon came fro London this weke, *and* he is right
mery *and* maketh his bost that *wyth*-in this fourtnyght at Helesdon ⌐shuld
be¹² bothe new lord*es and* new officer*es*. And also this day was brought me
5 word fro Cayst*er* that Rysyng of Freton shuld haue herd seid, in³ diu*er*se
plac*es* there as he was in Suff*olk*, that Fastolf of Coughhawe⁴ maketh all the
strenght that he may *and* *p*urposith hym to assaught Caystre *and* to entre
there if he may, in somych that it is seyd that he hath a v score men redy

199. ¹ *The associated letter from the King to the bailiffs of Yarmouth is misdated in
Gairdner's text* the xvijth *day of July. Sandford's manuscript reads* xxvijth.
    ² *Added in margin.*
    ³ such place as he [*changed to* there] was in *canc.*
    ⁴ maketh [*corr. from* make] all *canc.*

and sendyth dayly aspies to vnderstand what felesshep kepe the place. Be whos powere or favour or supportacion that he wull do this I knowe not, 10 but ye wote wele that I haue ben affrayd there be-fore this tyme whan that I had othere comfort than I haue now. *And* I can not wele gide ner rewle sodyour,[5] *and* also thei set not be a woman as thei shuld set be a man. Ther-fore I wold ye shuld send home your brothere or ell Dawbenye to haue a rewle *and* to takyn in such men as were necessary for ⌈the⌉ saffegard of the 15 place, for if I were there wyth-ought I had the more saddere or wurchepfull persones abought me, and there comyn a meny of[6] knavys *and* prevaylled in there entent, it shuld be to me but a vylney.

And I haue ben a-bought my liffelode to set a rewle there-in as I haue wretyn to you, which is not yet all parfourmed after myn desyre, *and* I wuld 20 not go to Cayster till I had don. I wull nomore days make there-abowtyn if I may; there-fore in any wyse send summe body home to kepe the place. And whan that I haue do *and* parfourmed that I haue be-gunne I shall purpose me thederward if I shuld do there any good, *and* ell I had leuer be thens. I haue sent to Nicholas *and* such as kepe the place that thei shuld 25 takyn in summe feles to assiste *and* strengh them till ye send home sum othere word ⌈or⌉[7] summe othere man to gouerne them þat ben there-in, &c. I marvayll gretly that ye send me no word how that ye do, for your elmyse be-gynne to wax right bold, *and* that puttith your frendes bothyn in grete fere *and* dought. There-fore purvey that thei may haue summe 30 comfort þat thei be no more discoraged, for if we lese our frendes it shall [be] hard in this troblelous werd to kete them ageyn.

The blissid Trynyté spede you in your materes[8] *and* send you the victory of your elmyse to your hertes eas *and* there confusyon. Wretyn at Norwich the[9] Saterday next be-fore Relyke Sonday in hast. 35

I pray you remembre wele the materes þat I wrote to you fore in the lettere þat ye had be James Greshams man, *and* send me[10] an answere there-of be þe next man þat comyth, &c.

By your moder M. P.

---

[5] *A plural ending may perhaps have been intended to be embraced in the abbreviation.*
[6] knaw *canc.*
[7] *Interl. above ampersand canc.*
[8] *Final loop incomplete, but apparently intended.*
[9] sad *canc.*   [10] am *canc.*

200. To JOHN PASTON II   1469, 12 March

Add. 34889, ff. 202ᵛ–203ʳ. 11½ × 15 in. Gloys's hand.

Dorse: Traces of red wax. Address in Gloys's hand:

To Ser John Paston, knyght, be this deliue̅red in hast.

The date appears partly from the Duke of Norfolk's claims to lands formerly Fastolf's. Several deeds of 1467 and 1468 are relevant: (*a*) on 2 October 1467 Sir John Paston released the manors of Cotton Hemnales and Hainford to Norfolk; (*b*) on 11 January 1468 Wainfleet, Yelverton, and other trustees of Fastolf released many of his manors, including Vaux, Bosoms, and Reedham in Caister, Guton, and Saxthorpe, to Sir John Paston; (*c*) on 1 October 1468 Yelverton, Howes, and Jenney, as trustees of Fastolf, enfeoffed the Duke of Norfolk in the manor of Caister and others. (Documents (*a*) and (*c*) in Magdalen College, Oxford, (*b*) in Bodl. MS. ch. Norfolk 746; abstracts in G. 579/677, 581/680, 658/764.) The report of the conduct of Grey and Burgess at Guton might seem to connect this letter with John III's no. 326 of 1467; but this cannot be of that year because George Neville, Archbishop of York, did not cease to be chancellor until 8 June 1467 (Scofield, i. 416). Further, Margaret's request for a kerchief for her daughter Anne is repeated in no. 201, which must be of 1469.

    G. LXXX/701.

I grete you wele *and* send you Goddes blyssyng *and* myn, desiryng you to recomaund me to my brothere William *and* to comune wyth hym *and* your councell in such materes as I wright to you, that there may be purveyd be summe writyng¹ fro the Kyng that my lord of Norffolk *and* his councell seas
5 of the wast that thei don in your lordsheps *and* in especiall at Heynford; for thei haue felled all the wood *and* this weke thei² wull carie it a-wey, *and* lete³ renne the wateres *and* take all the fyssh. And Ser William Yeluerton *and* his sone William, John Grey, *and* Burgeys, Will Yeluerton⁴ men, haue ben at Guton *and* takyn distresses, and wyth-ought that thei wull pay them
10 thei shall not set ought no plow to till there londe. Thei byd them lete there lond lye on-tilled ⌈but⌉ if thei pay them, so that if the tenauntes haue no remedy that thei may pesibily wyth-ought assaught or⁵ distresse takyng be the seid Yeluerton or his men, or of any þer in there names, at there liberté herye there londes wyth-in this vij days, there tylth in tho feldes
15 [shall] be lost for all thes yere and thei shall be on-doon. *And* though ye shuld kepe it here-after pesibilly, ye shuld lese the ferme of this yere, for thei may not pay you but if thei may occupie there londes. Thei set not so sone a plow ought at there gates but þer is a felesshep redy to take it. And thei ride wyth speres *and* laungegays like men of werre, so that the seid ten-
20 auntes arn a-ferd to kepe there owyn howses. Therfore purvey an redy remedye, or ell ye lese the tenauntes hertes *and* ye gretly hurt, for it is gret

---

    200. ¹ for *canc.*   ² -i *crowded in.*   ³ rent *canc.*
    ⁴ -n *tailed as usual when final, no loop for* -es.   ⁵ distresseyng *canc.*

pety to here the swemefull *and* petowse compleyntes of the pore tenauntes
that come to me for comfort *and* socour, sumtyme be vj or vij to-geder.
Therfore, for Goddes love, se that thei ben holpyn, *and* desire my brothere
William to geve you good councell here-in.   25

Also it is told me that my lady of Suffolk hath promysed you here good
will if your bargayn ⌐of the mariage¬ holdyth, to do as largely as she shall
be disired, or largelyere if there be any appoyntement takyn a-twix you
for any materes a-twix here *and* you. *And* thei wuld avyse you to geve any
money to here to make here refuse or disclayme here titill, me semyth[6] ye   30
may wele excuse you be the money that she had last *and* be the wronges
that were don be here *and* here men in ⌐fellyng of wood and¬ pullyng doun
of your place *and* logge at Heylesdon *and* takyn a-wey of the shep *and* your
faderes goodes which were takyn a-wey at the pullyng don of the seid
place;[7] whech wele considered she were wurthy to[8] recompense you. And   35
the Kyng *and* the lordes were wele enformed thei wuld considere[9] the
redilyere your hurtes. It semyth this Ser William Yeluerton hath comfort
that he is so bold, for [he] hath right prowde *and* fowle langage, *and* right
slaunderows, to the tenauntes, as thei haue reported to me; therfore be
right ware that ye bynde not your-self ner make non ensuraunce till ye be   40
suere of a pesibill possession of your londe, for oftyn tyme rape rueth, *and*
whan a man hath mad such a comenaunte he must kepit[10], he may not
chese;[11] there[fore] be not to hasty till your londe be clere. And labore
hastly a remedy for thes premysses, or ell Ser John Fastolfes[12] lyvelode,
thowgh ye entre it pesibilly, shall not be worth to you a grote this yere   45
wyth-ought ye wull on-do your tenauntes.

I pray you remembre a kerchye of cremyll for your suster Anne.

Remembre to labore sume remedy for your faderes will whill my lord
of Caunterbury lyvyth, for he is an old man *and* he is now frendly to you;
and if he happed to dye how shuld come after hym ye wote neuer. *And* if   50
he were a nedy man, in asmych as your fader was noysed of so greet valew
he wull be the more straunge to entrete; and lete this be not for-gete, for
were there[13] on that aught vs no good wyll he myght calle vs[14] vp to make
accounte of his goodes. *And* if we had not for to shewe for vs where-by we
haue occupied, he myght send doun assentence to curse vs in all the diosyse   55
and to make vs to deliuere his goodes, which were to vs a gret shame *and* a
rebuke. There-fore purvey hastly *and* wyssely þerfore whill he levyth, *and*
do not, as ye dede whill my lord of York was chancellor, make delays; for
if ye had labored in his tyme as ye haue do sith, ye had be thurgh in your

---

60 mater*es*. Be war*e* be that, *and* lete slauth nomor*e* take you in such diffaught. Thynk of after-clappes *and* haue p*re*vysion in all yo*ur* werk, *and* ye shall do the bett*er*.

God kepe you. Wretyn on Myd-lent Sonday in hast.

Be yo*ur* modre[15], M. P.

201. To John Paston II   1469, 3 April

Add. 34889, f. 74. 11⅜×9¾ in. Recto in Gloys's hand, dorse in hand of Edmond Paston (see also nos. 203, 205, 208).

Dorse: four manuscript lines and subscription. Traces of red wax. Address in Edmond Paston's hand:

To Ser John Paston.

The date appears from the expectation that the King would visit Norwich. He did so in 1469 (John II's letter no. 240 and John III's no. 333). The hand of the dorse is stiff and awkward, but recognizably that of Edmond Paston II, who appears here for the first time.

F. iv, p. 312. G. 601/704.

I grete you wele *and* send you Godd*es* blissyng *and* myn, thankyng you for my seall that ye sent me; but I am right sory that ye dede so grete cost þ*er*-vp-on, for on of xl d. shuld haue s*er*ued me right wele. Send me word what it cost you *and* I shall send you money ther*e*-for*e*. I send you a lett*er*
5 be a man of Yarmoth. Send me word if ye haue it, for I marveyll ye sent me non answer*e* ther*e*-of be Juddy. I haue non very knowleche of y*our* ensuraunce, but if ye be ensured I p*ra*y God send you joy *and* wurchep to-ged*er*, *and* so I trost ye shull haue if it be as it is reported of her*e*. And a-nemps God ye arn as gretly bownd to her*e* as ye were maried; and þer-
10 for*e* I charge you vp-on my blissyng that ⌜ye⌝ be as trew to her*e* as she wer*e* maried on-to ⌜you in all degrees⌝,[1] and ye shall haue the mor*e* grace *and* the bett*er* spede ⌜in all other*e* thynges⌝.[2] Also I wuld þat ye shuld ⌜not⌝ be to hasty to be maried till ye wer*e* ⌜more⌝ suer*e* of yo*ur* lyvelode, for ye[3] must remembr*e* what charge ye shall haue, *and* if ye haue not to mayntene it, it
15 wull be a gret rebuke; ⌜*and* therfor*e* labo*ur* that ye may haue releses of the lord*es and* be in more suerté of yo*ur* lond or than ye be maried⌝.[4]

The Duchesse of Suff*olk* is at Ewhelm in Oxford-shire, *and* it is thought be yo*ur* frend*es* here that it is do þat she myght be ferr*e*[5] *and* ought of the

---

[15] *Corr. from* moder.
201. [1] *Interl. above* here *canc.*   [2] *Interl. in place of some 22 words heavily canc.*
[3] y- *corr. from* þ.   [4] *Interl. below.*   [5] *Corr. from* fere.

wey, *and* þe rathere feyne excuse be-cause of age or sikenesse if þat the
Kyng wuld send for here for y*our* mater*es*. 20

Y*our* elmyse be as bold here as thei were before, wherfore I can not thynk[6]
but that thei haue su*m*me comfort. I sent to Cayst*er* that thei shuld be
ware in kepyng of þe place, as ye dede wright to me. Hast you to spede y*our*
mater*es* as spedily as ye can, that ye may haue lesse felesship at Cayst*er*, for
the exspenc*es* *and* cost*es* be grete *and* ye haue no nede þ*er*-of *and* ye 25
remembre you wele what charg*es* ye haue beside *and* how y*our* liffelode is
dispoyled *and* wasted be y*our* adu*er*saries.

Also I wuld ye shuld p*ur*vey for y*our* sust*er* to be w*yth* my lady of Oxford
or w*yth* my lady of Bedford or in su*m*me othere wurchepfull place where
as ye thynk best, *and* I wull help to here fyndyng, for we be eythere of vs 30
wery of othe*r*. I shall telle you more whan I speke w*yth* you. I p*ra*y you
do y*our* deveyre here-in as ye wull my comfort *and* welefare *and* y*our*
wurchep, for diu*er*se causes which ye shall vnd*er*stand afterward, &c.

I spake w*yth* the Lord Skales at Norwich, *and* thanked hym for the
good lordshep that he had shewed to you, *and* desired his lordshep to be 35
y*our* contynuall good lord. *And* he swore be his trought he wold do that he
myght do for you, *and* ⌐he⌐ told me that Yeluerton ⌐the justice⌐ had spoke
to hym in y*our* mater*e*, but he told me not what; but I trow *and* ye desired
hym to telle you, he wuld. Ye arn beholdyng to my lord of his good report
of you in this contré, for he reported bett*er* of you than I trow ye dese*r*ue. 40
I felt be hym that there hath be p*r*ofered hym large p*r*ofer*es* on y*our* ad-
u*er*saries p*ar*te ageyn you. Send me word as hastly as ye may aft*er* the
begynnyng of the t*er*me how ye haue sped in all y*our* mater*es*, for I shall
thynk right long till I here su*m*me good tidyng*es*.

It*em*, I p*ra*y you recomaund me to the good mayst*er* that ye gaffe to the 45
chapell of Cayst*er*, *and* thank hym for the gret cost that ⌐he⌐ dede on me
at Norwich; *and* if I were a grette lady he shuld vnd*er*stand that he shuld
fare the bett*er* fore me, for me semyth be his demenyng he shuld be right
a good man.

It*em*, I send you the nowche w*yth* the dyamaunth be the berere here-of.[7] 50

I pray yow[8] fore-gete not to[9] send me a kersche of cremelle fore nekker-
chys fore yowr syst*er* Anne, fore I am schente of þe good lady þat sche is
w*yth* be-cawse sche hathe non, *and* I can non gette i*n* alle thys towne. I
xuld wrythe more to yow but fore lakke of leysere.

God haue yow i*n* hys kepyng *and* send yow good spede i*n* alle yowr 55
mater*es*. Wretyn i*n* haste on Eestern Mu*n*day.

Be yowr mod*er*

---

[6] -k *over* g. [7] *Recto ends.*
[8] y- *in form of* þ *throughout this addition.*
[9] p *canc.*

202. To John Paston II   1469, 31 August

Add. 34889, f. 82. 11⅜×7¾ in. Gloys's hand.

Dorse: Traces of red wax. Address in Gloys's hand:

To Ser John Paston be this deliuered in ha⟨st⟩.[1]

The date is fixed by the Duke of Norfolk's siege of Caister. His safe conduct allowing John Paston III and the other defenders to leave after the surrender is dated 26 September 9 Edward IV (Part II, no. 786). Worcester dates the beginning of the siege 21 August (*Itineraries*, p. 186).

F. iv, p. 366. G. 616/720.

I grete you wele *and* send you God*des* blyssyng *and* myn, letyng you wete that S*er* John Heuenyngh*am* was at Norwich this day *and* spake w*yth* me at my moder*es*; but he wuld not þat it[2] shuld be vnderstand, for my lord hath mad hym on of the capteynes at Cayst*er* of þe pepill þat shuld kepe
5 the wetche abought the place þat no man shuld soco*ur* them if my lord dep*ar*ted. I desired hym to favo*ur* them if any man shuld[3] come to them fro me or you, *and* he wuld not gr*au*nte it; but he desired me to write ⌐to you⌐ to vnderstand if that my lord myght be mevyd to fynde suerté to recompense you all wrong*es* *and* ye wuld suffre hym to entre pesibilly and the lawe af*ter*
10 his entré wuld deme it you. Be ye avysed what answer*e* ye wull geve.

Item, sith that þat I spake w*yth* hym *and* the same day a feythfull frende of owr*es* came on-to me *and* mevyd me if þat my lord myght be entreted to suffre endifferent men to kepe[4] the place *and* take the profites for bothe p*ar*ties till þe right be det*er*myned be the lawe, *and* my lord for his p*ar*te
15 *and* ye for yo*ur* p*ar*te to fynde sufficient suerté þat yo*ur* nowther*e* shuld vex, lette, ner trobilled the seid endifferent men to kepe pesibilly the possession of þe seid place, *and* to take þe profight*es* on-to the tyme it be det*er*myned be þe lawe to his behowe þat the lawe demeth it. And þo[5] seid p*er*sones þat so endifferently kepe possession before ther*e* entré in-to the
20 seid place to fynde also sufficient suerté to answer*e* the p*ar*té þat the lawe demeth it to of þe profites, duryng ther*e* possession, *and* to suffre hym pesibilly to entre, or any in his name, whan so eu*er* thei be required be the p*ar*té to whom the right[6] is demyd. Of all þes pr*e*mysses send word how ye wull be demened be as good advyse as ye can gete, *and* make no lengere
25 delay; for thei must ned*es* haue hasty soco*ur* that be in the place, for thei be sore hurt *and* haue non help. And if thei haue hasty help it shall be the grettest wurchep þat eu*er* ye had, *and* if þei be not holpen it shall be to you a gret diswurchep, *and* loke neu*er* to haue favo*ur* of yo*ur* neybor*es* *and* frendes

---

202. [1] *End obliterated by dirt.*
   [2] *MS.* is.   [3] speke *canc.*
   [4] bothe *canc.*   [5] *Written* þ°.
   [6] id *canc.*

but if this spede wele. þer-fore prend it in your mend *and* purvey þer-fore
in hast, how so euer ye do.   30

God kepe you *and* send you the vittory of your elmyse, *and* geve you *and*
vs all *grace* to leve in peas. Wretyn on Sent Gyles Evyn at ix of þe belle
at nyght.

Robyn came home yester evyn, *and* he brought me nowthere writyng
from you ner good answere of this mater, which grevyth me right ill þat I   35
haue sent you so many⁷ massangeres *and* haue so febill answeres ageyn.

Be your modere

203. To John Paston II   1469, 10 or 11 September

Add. 34889, ff. 83ᵛ–84ʳ. 11½ × 16¾ in. Edmond Paston's hand.

Dorse: Marks of folding. Traces of red wax, and stitch-holes, but no
address. Note in unidentified fifteenth-century hand: *de obscidione manerij
de Castre.*

The year appears from the marriage agreement between Richard Calle and Margery
Paston, which was in 1469 (see John Paston III's letter no. 332). This is confirmed
by the endorsement, which shows that the reference at the end to 'the Duke' concerns the Duke of Norfolk's attack on Caister in the same year. The letter was
written before Michaelmas (see ll. 47–8), and must therefore precede no. 205, which
was begun on 22 September but not finished until the day after Michaelmas. It
must surely also precede no. 204, written on 12 September; for Margaret would
scarcely have failed, after that, to make some reference to the crisis of the siege of
Caister. On the other hand, the reference at the end to 'no duke in Ynglond' clearly
points to Writtle's mission on behalf of the Duke of Clarence, and so is later than
no. 202, of 31 August, which was a Thursday. The Friday of the Bishop's
interrogation must therefore have been 8 September.

F. iv, p. 358. G. 617/721. C. 55.

I grete ȝow wel *and* send ȝow Goddys blyssyng *and* myn, letyng ȝow wete
þat on Thurysday last was ⌈my moder *and* I⌉ where¹ wyth my lord of
Norwych, *and* desyerd hym² þat³ he woold⁴ nomore do in þe matere
towscheyng ȝowr syster tyl þat ȝe *and* my brothere, *and* othere þat wern
executors to ȝowr fader, mythe beyn here to-geder, fore they had þe rule   5
of here as weel as I. *And* he sayde playnly þat he ⌈had be⌉⁵ requeryd ⌈so
oftyn⌉ fore to exameyn here þat he mythe not, ⌈nore woold⌉, no lengare
delayyt, *and* schargyd me in peyn of cursyng þat sche schuld not be

---

⁷ *Here* be your modere *has been canc. The letter originally ended at* nyght *line 33, and the
last sentence, with a new subscription, was added at the foot later.*
203. ¹ -h- *over* e.   ² as I haue do bef *canc.*
³ þ *in form of* y, *as often though not regularly in Edmond's hand.*
⁴ not calle *canc.*   ⁵ *Interl. above* was *canc.*

deferred but þat sche xuld a-pere be-forn hy*m* þe nexte day. *And* I sayd
10 pleynly þat I woold nowd*er* bryng here nore send here; *and* þan he sayd
þat he woold send fore here hy*m*-sylfe, *and* schargyd þat sche schuld be at
here lyberté to cu*m*e wa*n* he sent fore here. *And* he seyd be hys trowthe þat
he woold be as sory fore here *and* sche ded not welle as he wold be *and* sche
were ⌐ryth nere⌐ of hys kyn, bothe fore my mod*er*ys sake *and* myn *and*
15 othere of ⌐here⌐[6] frendd*ys*; fore he woost welle þat here demenyng[7] had
stekyd soore at owr hart*ys*.

My mod*er* *and* I in-formyd hy*m* þat we kowd neu*er* ond*er*stond be here[8]
sayyng, be no language þat eu*er* sche had to hy*m*, þat neythere of he*m* were
bownd to othere, but þat they myth schese bothe. þan he seyd þat he woold
20 sey to here as[9] wele as he kowde be-fore þat he exameynd here; *and* so yt
was told me be dyu*er*se p*er*sones þat he ded as welle *and* as pleynly as sche
had be rythe nere to hy*m*, wych were to long to wrythe at thys tyme. Here-
afty[r] ʒe xalle wete, *and* hoo were laberers there-in. þe schanselere was not
so gylty there-in as I weend he had ben.

25   On Fryday ⌐the Bysschope⌐[10] sent fore here be Asschefeld *and* othere þat
arn ryth sory of here demenyng. And þe Bysschop seyd to here ryth pleynly,
and put here in re*m*emberawns how sche was born, wat kyn *and* frendd*ys*
þat sche had, *and* xuld haue[11] mo yf sche were rulyd *and* gydyd aftyre
them;[12] *and* yf sche ded not, wat rebuke *and* schame ⌐*and* los⌐ yt xuld be
30 to here yf sche were not gydyd be[13] the*m*, *and* cause of foresaky[n]g of here
fore any good ore helpe ore kownfort þat sche xuld haue of he*m*; *and* seyd
þat he had hard sey þat sche loued schecheon þat here frend were not
plesyd w*yth* þat sche xuld haue, *and* there-fore he bad here be ryth wel
a-vysyd how sche ded, *and* seyd þat he woold wndyrstond þe worddy*s* þat
35 sche had seyd to hy*m*, wheythere[14] yt mad matramony ore not. *And* sche
rehersyd wat sche had seyd, *and* seyd yf thoo worddy*s* mad yt not suhere,
sche seyd boldly þat sche wold make ⌐yt⌐[15] suerhere ore þan sche went
thens; fore sche sayd sche thowthe in here conschens sche was bownd, wat
so euere þe worddy*s* wern.[16] Thes leud worddy*s* gereue[17] me[18] *and* here
40 grandam as myche as alle þe remnawnte. *And* þan þe Bysschop *and* the
schawnselere bothe seyd þat there was neythere I nere no frend of hers
wold reseyuere. *And* þan Calle was exameynd ap*ar*te be hy*m*-sylfe, þat here

---

[6] *Interl. above* owr *canc.*
[8] saynyng *canc.*
[10] *Interl. above* he *canc.*
[12] -m *over* re.
[14] t *canc.*
[16] þat *canc.*

[7] was *canc.*
[9] were *canc.*
[11] *and* þe *canc.*
[13] hem *canc.*
[15] *Interl. above* hem *canc.*

[17] -re- *repr. by flourished* r. *The end has been altered so that the final form is uncertain:*
gereued *seems to have been written first, then* -d *corrected to* -th, *which in turn is struck out.*
[18] *Followed by* as mych, *of which* mych *canc.: the cancelling stroke ought to have deleted*
as *also.*

worddys *and* hys acordyd, *and* the tyme *and* where[1] yt xuld a[19] be don. *And*
þan þe Bysschop sayd þat he supposyd þat there xuld be fownd othere
thynggys ageyns hy*m* þat mythe cause þe lettyng there-of, *and* there-fore 45
⌈he⌉ say[d] he wold[20] not be to has⟨ty⟩[21] to ge⌈ue⌉[22] sentens there-vp-on, *and*
sayd þat he wold geue ouere day tyl þe Wodynsday ore Thursday aftyre
Mykylmes, *and* so yt tys delayyd. They woold an had here wyl p*ar*formyd
in haste, but þe Bysschop[23] seyd he woold non othere-wyse þan he had sayd.[24]
I was wy*th* my mod*er* at here plase wa*n* sche was exameynd, *and* wa*n* I hard 50
sey wat her*e* demeny[n]g was I schargyd my s*er*uantys þat sche xuld not be
reseyued in my*n* hows. I had ʒeue*n* here warny[n]g, sche mythe a be ware
afore yf sche had a be grasyows. *And* I sent to on ore ij more þat they xuld
not reseyue here yf sche ca*m*. Sche was browthe a-geyn to my place fore
to a be reseyued, *and* S*er* Jamys tolde the*m* þat browthe here þat I had 55
schargyd he*m* alle, *and* sche xuld not be reseyued; *and* soo my lord of
Norwych hath set here at Rogere Bestys to be there tyle þe day before
say[d], God knowyth fule euel ageyn[25] hys wyle *and* hys wyvys,[26] yf they
durst do othere-wyse. I a*m* sory þat they arn a-cu*m*yrd wy*th* here, but
ʒet I a*m* better payed þat sche is there fore þe whyle[27] þan sche had ben in 60
othere place, be-cause of þe sadnes ⌈*and* god dysposysion⌉ of hy*m*-sylfe *and*
hys wyfe, fore sche xal not be soue*r*d there to pleye þe brethele.
 I pray ʒ0w *and* requere ʒ0w þat ʒe take yt not pensyly,[28] fore I wot wele
yt gothe ryth nere ʒ0wr hart, *and* so doth yt to myn *and* to othere; but
reme*m*byre ʒ0w, *and* so do I, þat we haue lost of here but a brethele, *and* 65
setyt þe les to hart; fore and sche had be good, wat[29] so euere sche had be
yt xuld not a ben os jt tys,[30] fore *and* he were ded at thys owyre sche xuld
neu*er*e be at myn hart as sche was. As fore þe devors þat ʒe wrete to me of,
I[31] suppose wat ʒe ment, but I scharge ʒ0w vpon my blyssyng þat ʒe do
not, nere cause non othere to do, þat xuld offend God *and* ʒ0wr conschens; 70
fore and ʒe do, ore cause fore to be do, God wul take vengawns there-vpon
and ʒe xuld put ʒ0wr-sylfe *and* othere in gret joparté. Fore wottyt wele,
sche xal ful sor*e* repent here leudnes here-aftyre, *and* I pray God sche mute
soo. I pray ʒ0w, fore myn hard ys hese, be ʒe of a good cownfort in alle
thynngys. I trust God xal helpe ryth wele, *and* I pray God[32] so do in alle 75
owr[33] maters.
 I wuld ʒe toke hed yf there were[34] any labore mad in þe kort of Cawntyr-
bery[26] fore the leud mat*er*e fore sayd.

[19] *No space, as also below.*	[20] -ld *over* re.
[21] *Ink lost.*	[22] *Interl. above* u *canc.*
[23] he *canc.*	[24] tha*n* *canc.*
[25] -y- *over* g.	[26] *Ampersand canc.*
[27] -h- *crowded in.*	[28] yt g *canc.*
[29] *Abbr.* w^t. *The usual meaning 'wyth' makes no sense here.*	
[30] *Written* t *with loop, as in noun plurals; followed by ampersand canc.*	
[31] sch *canc.*	[32] help *canc.*
[33] *Initial* ʒ *canc.*	[34] *Written* wehere, he *canc.*

343

But yf the Duke be purveyd fore, he *and* hys wyse kow[n]sel xalle lese
80 thys cu*ntré*. Yt t*ys* told me þ*at* he sethe þ*at* he wul not spar*e* to do þ*at* he
is purposyd for*e* no duke in Ynglond. God helpe at nede.

204. To John Paston II   1469, 12 September

Add. 34889, f. 88. 11½ × 12¼ in. Gloys's hand.

Dorse: Marks of folding. Traces of red wax, and stitch-holes, but no
address.

For the date see no. 203.
F. iv, p. 382. G. 620/724. C. 56.

I grete you wele, letyng you wete that yo*ur* brother*e and* his felesshep stond
in grete jop*ar*té at Cayst*er and* lakke vetayll; *and* Dawbeney *and* Berney be
dedde *and* diu*er*se othe*re* gretly hurt, *and* thei fayll gonnepowder *and*
arrowes, *and* the place sore brokyn w*yth* gonnes of þe toder p*ar*te; so that,
5 ⌐but⌐ thei haue hasty help, thei be like to lese bothe there lyfes *and* the
place, to the grettest rebuke to you that eu*er* came to ⌐any⌐ᴵ jentilman, for
eu*ery* man in this countré marvaylleth gretly that ye suffre them to be so
longe in so gret jop*ar*té w*yth*-ought help or othe*re* remedy.
        The Duke hath be more fervently set þer-vp-on, *and* more cruell, sith
10 þ*at* Wretyll, my lord of Claraunce man, was ther than he was be-fore, *and*
he hath sent for all his tena*untes* from eu*ery* place, *and* othe*re*, to be
the*re* at Cayst*er* on Thorysday next comyng, that the*re* is than like to be the
grettest multitude of pepill þ*at* came þer yet. *And* thei p*ur*pose than to
⌐make a gret⌐ assaught, for thei haue sent for² gonnes to Lynne *and* othe*re*
15 place be the seeys syde, þ*at* w*yth* ther gret multitude of gonnes, w*yth*
othe*re* shoot *and* ordyna*unce*,³ ther shall no man dar appere in þe place.
Thei shall hold them so besy w*yth* ther gret pepill þ*at* it shall not lye in
the*re* pore w*yth*-in to hold it a-geyn them w*yth*-ought ⌐God⌐⁴ help them
or [thei] haue hasty⁵ soco*ur* ⌐from you⌐. There-fore, as ye wull haue my
20 blyssyng, I charge you *and* require you þ*at* ye se yo*ur* brother*e* be holpyn
in hast. And if ye can haue non meane, rathe*re* desire writyng fro my lord
of Clarens, if he be at London, or ell of my lord Archebusshop of York, to
þe Duke of Norffolk, þ*at* he wull gra*unte* them þ*at* be in þe place here
lyfes *and* ther good*es*. *And* in eschewyng of insurrecc*ions*, w*yth* othe*re*
25 inconuenyens þ*at* be like to growe w*yth*-in the shire of Norffolk, ⌐this⌐¹⁶

204. ¹ *Interl. above* anly *canc.*   ² gown *canc.*
        ³ þat *canc.*   ⁴ *In margin.*
        ⁵ socour *canc.*
        ⁶ *Inter. above* thys *corr. from* the *and canc.*

trobelows werd, be-cause of such conuenticles *and* gaderyng*es* w*yth*-in the seid shire for cause of þe seid place, thei shall suffre hym to entre vp-on such appoyntment, or othe*r* like, takyn be the advyse of yo*ur* councell there at London, if ye thynk this be not ⌈good⌉14, till the law hath deter-myned othe*r*e-wyse; *and* lete hym write a-nothe*r* lett*er* to yo*ur* brother 30 to deliu*ere* the place vp-on the same appoyntment. *And* if ye thynk, as I can suppose, that the ⌈Duke of Norff*olk*⌉ wull not aggré to this be-cause he gr*au*nted this a-forn *and* thei in the place wuld not accept ⌈it⌉, than I wuld the seid massangere shuld w*yth* the seid lette*res* bryng7 fro the seid lord of Clarence, or ell my lord Archebusshop, to my lord of Oxenford 35 ⌈othe*r*e lette*res*⌉ to rescue them forth-w*yth*, thoughe8 the ⌈seid Erle of Oxenford⌉ shuld haue the place duryng his lyffe for his labo*ur*. Spare not this to be don in hast if ye wull haue the*r*e lyves *and* be sett by in Norff*olk*, though ye shuld ⌈leys⌉9 the best man*er* of all for the rescue. I had lever ye lost þe10 lyffelode than the*r*e lyfes. Ye must gete a massangere of the 40 lord*es* or su*m*me othe*r* notabill man to bryng thes lette*res*.

Do yo*ur* devo*ur* now, *and* lete me send yow nomo*re* massange*res* for this mate*res*; but send me be the11 bere*re* here-of more certeyn comfort than ye haue do be all othe*r* that I haue sent be-fore. In any wyse, lete the lette*res* þat shall come to þe Erle of Oxenford comyn w*yth* the lette*res* ⌈that⌉ shall comyn to þe Duke of Norff*olk*, þat if he wull not aggree to the ton, that ye may haue redy yo*ur* rescue þat it nede nomo*re* to send þer-fore.

God kepe you. Wretyn the Tuesday next before Holy Rood Day, in hast.

Be yo*ur* modere

205. To JOHN PASTON II   1469, 22–30 September

Add. 34889, ff. 95ᵛ–96ʳ. 11½ × 14 in. Edmond Paston's hand.

Dorse: Traces of red wax. Address in uncertain hand, more formal than the letter, perhaps also Edmond's:

To Ser John Paston, in hast.

In John II's hand: *A Matre.*

This letter clearly refers back to no. 204 in answer to no. 243.
    F. iv, p. 396. G. 629/733. C. 60 (part).

I grete ʒow wele *and* send ʒow Godd*ys* blyssyng *and* my*n*, letyng ʒow wete1 þat me thynke be þe lett*er* þat ʒe sent me be Robeyn þat ʒe thynke þat

---

7 for *canc.*   8 -e *over* -t.
9 *Interl. above* leeys *canc.*   10 *From* þer.
11 thi *and incomplete* s *canc.*
205. 1 *Ampersand canc.*

I xuld wryte to ʒow fabyls *and* ymagynacyons. But I do not soo; I ⌈haue⌉ wrytyn[2] as yt haue be enformed me, *and* wulle do. It was told me þat bothe
5 Daubeney *and* Berney were dedee, but fore serten Daubeney is dede, God asoyle[3] hys sowle, where-of I am rythe sory, *and* yt had plesyd God þat yt mythe a be odere-wysse.

Remembyre ʒow ʒe haue had ij gret lossys wyth-yne thys towylemonthe, of hym *and* of Ser Thomas. God[4] wysythyt[5] ʒow as yt plesythe hym jn
10 sundery wyses.[6] He woold ʒe xuld knowe hym *and* serue hym better þan ʒe haue do be-fore ⌈thys⌉ tyme,[7] *and* þan he wule send ʒow ⌈þe more⌉ grace to do wele in alle othere thynggys. And fore Goddys loue, remembyreyt rythe welle *and* takeyt pacyentely, *and* thanke God of hys vysitacyon; *and*[8] yf any thyng haue be a mysse any othere wyse þan yt howte to haue ben
15 be-fore thys, owthere in pryde ore in laues expencys ore in any othere thyng þat haue offendyd God, amend yt *and* pray hym of hys ⌈grace and⌉ helpe, *and* entend welle to God *and* to ʒowr neybors; *and* thow ʒowr poore hereaftyre ⌈be⌉ to aquyte hem of here maleys, ʒet be mersyfulle to them, *and* God xale send ʒow þe more grace to haue ʒowr entente
20 in othere thynggys. I remembyre thys clawsys[9] be-cause of þe last letter þat ʒe sent me.

I haue sent to[10] Hary Halman of Sporylle to helpe to gette as ʒe desyerd me, *and* he canne not gette passyd v ore viij at the most, *and* ʒet yt wule not be but yf he cume þat ʒe trust vpon þat xuld cume, fore they long a
25 parte to hym. And Ryschard Schary⟨ls⟩[11] hathe a-sayed on hys parte, *and* he cane not gette passyd v, fore thoo þat long to vus ⌈there⌉ long[12] also to owr aduersarys, *and* they haue be desyerd be them *and* they woold nowte do fore hem; *and* there-fore they thynke to haue magery of þe todere parte. As fore þe jantylman þat ye[13] desyerd me to speke wyth, I spake wyth hys
30 wyfe *and* sche told me he was not in thys cuntré nere nowte woost wan he xuld be here; *and* as fore the toder man, he hath bowthe hym a leuery in Bromeholme Pryory *and* haue ʒeuen vpe þe woord, &c.

Item, as fore mony I kowde gette but x li. vpon pledgys, *and* þat is spent fore ʒowr materes here fore payeng of ⌈ʒowr men⌉[14] þat wern at Caster *and*
35 othere thynggys, *and* I woot not were to gette non, nowthere fore suerté ner fore pleggys. And as fore myn owyn lyuelod, I am so symppely payed

---

2 *From* wryte. 3 -y- *over* w.
4 so *canc.*
5 *Final reading uncertain owing to heavy blot on last two letters. First written* wysythe, *then* y *written over* -e *and apparently* -t *added.*
6 *From* weyes. 7 *Written* tymes, -s *canc.*
8 yt *canc.* 9 -ys *over* e.
10 s *canc.*
11 *Letters lost at damaged edge. The name meant is no doubt Charles.*
12 s *canc.*
13 y- *over* þ, e *raised.* 14 *Interl. above* them *canc.*

thereof þat I fere me I xale be fayn to borow fore my-sylfe ore ell to breke
vp howsold, ore bothe.

As fore þe 3elddyng of the place at Caster, I trowe Wretyll hathe told[15]
of the pow[n]tementys how yttys delyuerd. I woold þat had be so here thys 40
tyme, *and* 3an there xuld not a be do so[16] mykyle hurte as the⟨re⟩[17] ⌐is⌐[18] in
dyuerse weyes, fore ma[n]y of owr wele-wylleres arn putte to loosse fore
owr sakys. And I fare me yt xale be long here yt be recumpensyd a-geyn,
and þat xale cause othere to do þe lesse fore vus here-aftyre.

I woold 3e xuld [send] 30wr brothere woord, *and* sum othere þat 3e 45
truste, to see to 30wr owyn lyuelod, to sette yt in[19] a rule *and* to gader[20]
there-of þat may be had in haste, *and* also of Ser John Fastolffys[21] lyuelod
þat may be gadyrd in pesybyle wyse; fore as fore Ryschard Calle, he wulle
no more gadyre yt but yf 3e comaund hym, *and* he woold fayn make hys
acowntte *and* haue 30wr good maystyre-schepe, as yttys told me, *and* 50
delyuere þe euydens of Bekkeham and alle othere thynggys þat ⌐longgyth⌐[22]
to 30w þat he trusttythe þat 3e wylle be hys good maystere here-aftyre.
And he sethe he wylle not take non newe master tyle 3e refuse hys seruyse.
Remembyre þat 30wr lyuelod may be set in soche a rule þat 3e may knowe
how yttys *and* wat is owy⟨ng⟩[23] to 30w, fore be my feythe I haue holppyn 55
as mysche as I may, and more, sauyng my-sylfe. And therefore take hede
ere yt be weers.

Thys letter was begune on Fryday was vij nythe and enddyd thys day
nexte afftyre Mykylmes Day. God kepe 30w *and* 3eue 30w grace to do as
we⟨le⟩ as I woold 3e dede. And I scharge 30w be ware þat 3e sette no lond 60
to morgage, fore yf any auyse 30w there-to they arn not 30wr frenddys. Be
ware be ⌐tymes⌐ [be] myn a-vyse, &c. I trow yowr brothere wy⟨lle send⟩
30w tydyngys in haste.[24]

---

[15] þ, *then* 30w there of, *canc.*   [16] *No space.*
[17] *Letter lost at edge.*
[18] *Interl. above* was *canc.*   [19] a b *canc.*
[20] yt *altered to* yᵗ, *then canc.*
[21] *Ends* -ff *with unusually long downward flourish on cross-stroke, which seems likely to imply the* -ys *usually represented by a loop.*
[22] *Interl. above* lond *canc.*
[23] *Letters lost here and below at edge damaged by damp.*
[24] *Last sentence crowded in hastily at foot.*

206. To JOHN PASTON III   Probably 1470, 6 July

Add 34889, f. 107. 11⅜ × 5⅞ in. Gloys's hand.

Dorse: Paper seal over red wax and string. Address in Gloys's hand:

To John Paston þe yongere be þis deliuered in hast.

The date is probably between April 1469, when Margaret's daughter Anne was
living in a 'good lady's' household (see no. 201), and June 1472, when her marriage
to William Yelverton (grandson of the judge) had been arranged (see John III's
letter no. 352)—though it cannot have taken place until 1477, and not without some
intervals of doubt: cf. nos. 296, 369. At the date of John III's letter no. 374 she was
evidently still living with her mother, but by the time of Margaret's no. 226 she was
married to Yelverton.

'St. Thomas' is elsewhere used by Margaret to mean the Translation of St.
Thomas of Canterbury, 7 July (see nos. 127, 142, 160, 188). The year, then, is
unlikely to be 1469, when 7 July was itself a Friday and the previous Friday would
probably have been dated by reference to SS. Peter and Paul, the day before. In
July 1471 John III was in a position of some difficulty, in need of a pardon (see no.
347). The most likely year for this letter is therefore 1470.

F. iv, p. 288. G. 660/766.

I grete you wele *and* send you Godd*es* blyssyng *and* myn, letyng you
wete that sith ye dep*ar*ted my cosyn Calthorp sent me a lett*er* compleynyng
in his wrytyng that for asmych as he can not be payd of his ten*auntes* as he
hat be befor*e* this tyme he p*ur*posith to lesse his¹ howshold *and* to leve the
5   streytlyere; wherfor*e* he desireth me to p*ur*vey² for y*our* sust*er* Anne. He
seth she waxeth hygh, *and* it wer*e* tyme to p*ur*vey her*e* a mariage. I marveyll
what causeth hym to write so now: owther*e* she hath displeased hym or ell
he hath takyn her*e* w*yth* su*m*me diffaught. There-for*e* I p*r*ay you comune
w*yth* my cosyn Clere at London *and* wete how he is disposyd to her*e* ward,³
10 *and* send me word, for I shall be fayn to send for her*e and* w*yth* me she shall
but lese her*e* tyme; *and* w*yth*-ought she wull be the bett*er* occupied she
shall oftyn tymes meve me *and* put me in gret inquietenesse. Remembr*e*
what labo*ur* I had w*yth* your sust*er*. þerfore do y*our* p*ar*te to help her*e* forth
that may be to y*our* wurchep *and* myn.
15 Item, remembr*e* the bill þat I spake to you of to gete of y*our* brother*e* of
such money as he hath receyvid of me sith y*our* fader*es* disseas. Se y*our*
vnkyll Mautby if ye may, *and* send me su*m*me tydyng*es* as sone as ye may.
God kepe you. Wretyn the⁴ Fryday next be-for*e* Sent Thom*as* of
Caunt*er*bery in hast.
20   Be y*our* moder

---

206. ¹ how *blotted and canc.*   ² *MS.* pp-.
³ for I *canc.*   ⁴ thu *canc.*

207. To JOHN PASTON II   1470, 15 July

Add. 27445, f. 40. 11⅝ × 4 in. Pampyng's hand.

Dorse: Marks of folding. Paper seal over red wax, and stitch-holes, but no address.

The date appears from the similarity of this letter to one written to John II by Pampyng on his own account, and also dated on the Monday after Relic Sunday (the third Sunday after Midsummer; cf. no. 58). It refers to the situation in the year after the surrender of Caister (Part II, no. 765).

    G. 647/752.

I grete yow well and send yow Goddis blissyng *and* myne, letyng yow wete that y*our* fermo*ur*s have brought me a gret bille of rep*a*raci*o*n, the which I send yow w*yth* lx s. in mony. I wold haue had the residue of the mony of them, and they said it was y*our* agrement that this rep*a*raci*o*n shuld be do and alowed now at this payme*n*t, and so I coud get nomore mony of them. 5 And they say that the p*ar*son was prevy to the rep*a*raci*o*n. If ye were thus agreed *and* woll haue the rep*a*raci*o*n ⌈exami*n*ed⌉, ye may send word; but I wold ye shuld purvey for y*our*-self as hastely as ye may *and* come home and take heed to y*our* owne, *and* to myn therto, otherwise thanne ye haue do bifore this, bothe for my p*r*ofite *and* for your;[1] or ellis I shall purvey for 10 my-self otherwise in hast, so that I trust shall be more ease[2] *and* avayle for me *and* non ease nor pro⟨fi⟩te[3] to yow in tyme to come. I haue litell help nor comfort of non of yow yet; God geve me grase to haue heraftir.

I wold ye shuld assay whedir it be more p*r*ofitable for yow to serve me thanne for to s*er*ve such masters as ye haue servid afore this, and that ye 15 fynde moost p*r*ofitable theraftir do in tyme to come. Ye haue assayed the werld resonabilly; ye shall knowe y*our*-self the bettir heraftir. I pray God we may be in quyete *and* in rest w*yth* oure owne from hens forth. My power is nat so good as I wold it were for your[4] sake *and* other, *and* if it were we shuld not longe be in daungere. 20

God bryng vs oute of it, who haue yow in his kepyng. Wretyn w*yth* onhert*is* ease the Monday next aftir Relike Sonday.

                               By y*our* modir

---

207. [1] *No other letter visible, but ink smudged at end of line.*
  [2] for me *canc.*   [3] *Hole in paper.*   [4] sakys *canc.*

208. To JOHN PASTON II   1470, 28 October

Add. 34889, f. 206. $11\frac{1}{2} \times 9\frac{3}{4}$ in. Body of letter in Gloys's hand, postscript in Edmond Paston's.

Dorse: Postscript. Marks of folding. Paper seal (fleur-de-lis) over red wax and string, and stitch-holes; but no address.

From the tone of Margaret's rebukes, this letter was evidently addressed to John II, as his father's heir, rather than John III. The brothers were together when it was written, and in need of money. This was the position in October 1470, as appears from John III's letter no. 345.
     G. LXXXIII/761.

I grete you wele *and* send you Godd*es* blyssyng *and* myn, and I send you
be the berere here-of all the sylu*er* vessell that y*our* graundam maketh so
mych of, which she seid I had of myn husbond *and* myn husbond shuld
haue had it of his fader*e*. *And* where as she seid þ*at* I shuld had a garneys,
5 I had ner see neu*er* more than I send you; þ*at* is to say, ij plater*es*, vj
dysshes, *and* vj sawc*er*es. The ij plater*es* weyn xliij vnce¹ ⌈di.⌉, *and* þe vj
dysshes weyn lxxiiij² vnce di., *and* the sawc*er*es weyn xvij vnce j q*uar*ter; *and*
I marvayll that ye sent me not word what an vnce of sylu*er* is worth at
London, for it had be lesse jop*ar*té to haue sold it her*e and* haue sent you
10 the money than the plate. I myght haue sold it her*e* for iij s. an vnce, &c.,
⌈s*um*m*a* xx li. iiij s. iij d.⌉ Be war*e* how that ye spend it but in acquityng you
ageyn such as ye be in³ daunger*e* to, or abought the good speed of y*our*
mater*es*; for but if ye take oder*e* heed to y*our* exspenc*es* ye shall do your-
self *and* y*our* frend*es* gret diswurchep *and* enpoueryssh so them þ*at* non
15 of vs shall help other*e*, to owre elmys grete comfort.
     It is vnderstond right now in þis countré be such as cleyme to be frendly
to you in what grete daung*er*e *and* nede ye stande in, bothe to diu*er*se of
y*our* frend*es and* to y*our* elmyse. And also it is noysed þat I haue dep*ar*ted
so largely w*yth* you þ*at* I may nowther*e* help you my-self ner non of my
20 frend*es*, which is no wurchep *and* causeth men to set the lesse be vs. And
at þis tyme it compellith me to breke vp howshold *and* to sogeorn, which
I am right loth to haue do if I myght othere-wyse haue chosyn, for it caused
gret clamo*ur* in þis town þ*at* I shall do so, *and* it shuld not haue neded if I
had restreyned whan I myght. þ*er*-fore, for Godd*es* sake, take ⌈hede⌉ here-
25 to *and* be war*e* from hens forth, for I haue deliu*er*ed *and* sent you bothyn my
p*ar*te, the ded*es and* yowr*es*, *and* not restreyned nowther*e* for my-self ner*e*
the dede. Where-fore I thynk we spede *and* far*e* all the wers, for it is a fowle
slaunder*e* that he was so wurchepfull beried *and* his qwethword not p*ar*-
fourmed, *and* so litill do for hym sithen; and now though I wuld do for hym
30 I haue right not beside my lyffelode þ*at* I may make any chevyssans w*yth*

208. ¹ *Curl on* -c, *as elsewhere in this word, evidently represents* -e.
     ² di. *canc.*   ³ *No space.*

wyth-ought grete slaundere, *and* my lyffelode encreassith evill for I am fayn to takyn Mautby in myn owyn hand *and* to set vp husbondry þer, *and* how it shall profite me God knowyth. The fermo*ur* owyth me lxxx li. *and* more; whan I shall haue it I wote neu*er*. þerfore be neu*er* the boldere in yowre exspenc*es* for any help þ*at* [ye] trost to haue of me, for I wull fro hens-forth 35 bryng my-self ought of such daungere as I stond in for you*r*⁴ sak*es*, *and* do fore the dede *and* for them þat I haue my good*es* of. For till I do so I know for certeyn þat I shall fayll g*r*ace *and* displeas God, how haue you in his kepyng. Wretyn on Sent Symond*es* Day *and* Jud*es* in hast.

Be you*r* moder⁵ 40

It*em*, I send ȝow ij scherte clothys, iche of iij ȝard*ys* of þe fynest þat is in thys towne. I xuld a do³ he*m* mad here but yt xuld a be to long here ȝe xuld a*n* had he*m*. Ȝo*wr* awnte ore su*m* othere good woma*n* wule do here alm*es* vp-on ȝow fore þe makyng of the*m*. I thank ȝow fore the gowne þat ȝe gaue me. Halowmesse Day I hope xale be wurshuped ⌐there-wyt*h*⌐.⁶ At reuer*ens* of God, 45 be ware *and* take hed to soche thyngg*ys* as is wrety*n* wyt*h*-ynne thys lett*er*.

Telle ȝo*wr* brothere þat the mony is not ȝet cownyd þat I ⌐xuld⌐⁷ send hy*m* fore the⁸ sarsenet *and* damaske þat I spake to hy*m* foore. As fore the damaske, yt may be forebore tylle þe nexte terme, but as fore þe sarsenet, I woold haue yt *and* yt mythe be, fore I goo in my rent*ys*. Late ȝo*wr* 50 brothere see thys lett*er*. As fore ȝo*wr* syster, I ca*n* send ȝow no good tyd-yngg*ys* of here. God make here a good wooma*n*.

209. To JOHN PASTON III   1471, 5 November

A. Add. 27445, f. 50. 11½ × 8½ in. Draft, in two styles but evidently by the same unskilled hand, unidentified. Most of dorse covered by text. Marks of light folding, no seal or address.

B. Add. 34889, f. 113. 11⅝ × 8⅝ in. Fair copy in the second of the two styles of A, more carefully written. Dorse about half occupied by text. Marks of folding, soiled as if carried. No seal or address.

Despite the absence of seal or address there is little doubt that B, folded small and much stained on two of the folded sections, was actually sent. Since this is the only example of a letter of Margaret's surviving in both draft and fair copy, and since the versions differ at some points, both are given in full.

The date appears from the report of the death of John Berney of Witchingham, which occurred in 1471 (administration of his goods granted to his widow 23 January 1472: Consistory Court of Norwich, Reg. Jekkys, Pt. I, 36 d.). This letter answers John III's of 28 October (no. 347).

F. v, p. 10 (B only). G. 681/787 (A only).

---

⁴ say, *followed by loop, canc.*   ⁵ *Recto ends. Postscript in Edmond Paston's hand.*
⁶ *Interl. above* wyth alle *canc.*   ⁷ *Interl. above* may *canc.*
⁸ *A downstroke after the -e seems to have no significance.*

A

I grete you wele *and* send you God*des* blyssy*ng and* myn, letyng you wete that myn cosyn Clere hath sent to me for the c m*a*rc.¹ þat I borwed of her for your brother. It fortuned so that a frend of her*e* of late hath loste bett*er* than ccc m*a*rc., *and* he sent to her*e* for*e* money, *and* she had non þat she
5 myght comyn by *and* there-for she sent to me for þe seyd c m*a*rc. And I² knowe not how to do þer³-fore, ⌜by my⁴ torowth⌝, for I haue it not ner I can not make shyft þer-fore *and* I shuld go to p*re*son. þer-for comune w*y*th your*e* brother*e* her⁵-of *and* send me word how that he wull make shyft ther-for*e* in hast.⁶ I must ell ned*es* sell all my wood*es*, *and* that shall dysse-
10 avayll hym ⌜bett*er*⌝ than a cc m*a*rc. *and* I dey, ⌜*and*⌝⁷ if I shuld selle⁸ them now ther wull noman gewe so myche for*e* them be ner an c m*a*rc. as they be worth be-cause ther*e* be so many wood sales in Norfolke at thys tyme. þer-fore lete hym make purvyaunce þer-fore in hast, as he wull haue my good wyll *and* wull that I save hym the seyd wood*es* to þe bett*er* a-wayll,
15 *and* send me word here-of in hast if ⌜ye⌝⁹ wull my welfar*e*; for I shall neu*er* be i*n* quiete tille I k[n]owe an ende in thys, for*e* she hath þer-fore an obligac*i*on of an c li. and it is not kepte cloos—þer be many p*er*sones now k[n]owyn it, which me semyth a greet rebuke to me þat I dep*ar*tyd so largely w*y*th yowr brother*e* þat I res*er*uyd not to pay þat I was¹⁰ endaun-
20 gered for*e* hym, *and* so haue dyu*er*se seyd to me which of late haue k[n]owyn it. *And* whan I remembr*e*it it is to myn¹¹ hart a very sper*e*, consideryng that he neu*er* gaue me comfort*e* þer-in, ner of all þe money þat hath be reseyvyd wull neu*er* make shyft þer-for. *And* he had yet be-fore thys tyme haue sent me l m*a*rc. þer-of yet, I wuld haue thought þat he had had su*m*me
25 *con*sideracion of myn daunger*es* þat I haue put me i*n* for hym. Rcmembr*e* hym how that I haue excusyd hym of xx li. þat þe Prior of Bromholm had which shuld ell haue be in that daunger*e* þat it shuld haue be to vs a¹² grete ⌜rebwke to us⌝¹³ w*y*th-hought that he myght ⌜a⌝ ben holpyn w*y*th shuch money as he shuld haue had of your fadyrs bequest; *and* I payd to þe
30 shereffe for hym also money. All thes shuld haue holpe me wele þer-to, be-syde other*e* thyng*es* þat I haue bor*e* thys yer*es* þat I speke not of. There-for*e* lete hym helpe me now, or ell it shall dysawayll hym bett*er* than þe trebyll the money, whed*er* that I leue or dey, w*y*th-ought he hath bett*er* *con*sideracion to þe daunger*es* þat I stond in.

209A. ¹ *Curl on* -c, *as regularly in this hand in this word.*
  ² know *canc.*   ³ þ- *in form of* y, *as often in this hand.*
  ⁴ th *canc.*   ⁵ fore *canc.*
  ⁶ and I shall rather pay hym a-geyn in yer*es* *canc.*
  ⁷ *Interl. above* for *canc.*   ⁸ *Written* seelle, *first* e *canc.*
  ⁹ *Interl. above* he *canc.*   ¹⁰ end *and two other letters canc.*
  ¹¹ -n *seems to have been added later.*
  ¹² *No space.*   ¹³ *Interl. above* slaundere *canc.*

B

I grete yw wel *and* send yw God*dys* blyssy*ng and* myn, letty*ng* yw wete that myn cosyn Cler*e* hath sent to me fore þe c m*a*rc. that I borwed of her*e* fore ywyr*e* brother*e*. Yt fortunyd so that a frend of her*e* late hath lost bet*ter* than ccc m*a*rc., *and* he sent to her*e* fore money, *and* she had non þat she myth comyn by *and* there-fore she sent to me fore þe seyd c m*a*rc. *And* I k[n]ow 5 not how to do ther*e*fore, by my trowth, fore I haue it not ner*e* I can not make shyfth there-fore *and* I shwld go to p*re*son. þer-fore comune w*yth* ywyr*e* brother*e* here-of *and* send me woord how that he wull mak shyfth there-fore in hast. Fore I mwst ell ned*ys* sellyn all my wood*ys*, *and* that shall disawayll hym bet*ter* than cc m*a*rc. yf I dey, *and* yf I shwld sell them 10 now ther*e* wold non man geue fore hem[1] so mych by[2] ner*e* an c m*a*rc. as they ⌐be⌐[3] worth by-cause ther*e* be so many woodsalis in Norfolke at thys tym. *And* there-fore let hym mak p*ur*vyaunce there-fore in hast, as he wull haue myn good wyll *and* that I saue hym þe seyd wood*ys* to þe bet*ter* avayll in tym comy*ng*, *and* send me an answer*e* there-of in hast yf ye wull 15 my welfare; fore I shall neu*er* ben in quiete tyll I know an ende in thys, fore she hasth þer-fore an obligac*ion* of an c li. *and* yt ys not kepte cloos— þer ben many p*er*sonis now k[n]owyn it,[4] which me semyth a gret rebwke to me þat I dep*a*rtyd so largely w*yth* ywyr*e* brothyr*e* þat I r*e*servyd not to pay þat I was in daunger fore hym, *and* so haue diu*er*se seyd to me which 20 of lat haue knowyn it. *And* whan I remembret it is to myn hart a very sper*e*, consideryng that he neu*er* gaue me comforte þer-in, ner*e* of all þe mony þat ⌐he⌐ hath[5] reseyvyd wull neu*er* mak shyfth þer-fore. *And* he had yet be-forn thys tyme haue sent me l marc. þer-of yet,[6] I wold haue thowth that he had had som c*on*sideracion of myn daunger*e* that I haue put me in fore hym. 25 Remember hym that I haue excusyd hym of xx li. þat þe P*ri*ore of Brom- holm had which shwld ell haue be in that daunger*e* þat yt shwld haue be to ws a gret rebwke w*yth*-owt that he myth haue ben holpyn w*yth* shwch money as he shuld haue had of ywyr*e* fadyrs beqwest; *and* I payd ⌐to⌐[7] þe shreue fore hym also money. All thes shwld haue holpyn me well[8] þer-to, 30 by-syde othyr*e* thyng*ys* that I haue boryn these[9] yer*ys*[8] þat I speke not of. There-fore let hym helpe me now, or ell yt shall disawayll hym þe trebyll þer-of, qweder I leue or dey, w*yth*-owt that he haue bet*ter* consideracion to þe daunger*e* that I stond in.

209B. [1] by ner*e* an c *canc.*   [2] a *canc.*
[3] *Interl. above* arn *canc.*   [4] whws ch *canc.*
[5] be *canc.*   [6] *MS. punctuates here by oblique stroke.*
[7] *First interl. after* þe *but canc.*   [8] also *canc.*
[9] b *or* v *evidently canc.; not a numeral because not marked off by points or underlined.*

209 *A continued*

35   Also I wulde ye shuld meve hym to take[14] John Pampyng to hym, or el⸢
to gete hym a servyce in þe Chauncery or ⌜in⌝ summe other place wher[15] as
he myth be preferryd, for it ys pety þat he lesyth hys tyme so here, *and* i⸢
is[16] non a-wayll to non of ws; *and* for diuerse othyre thyngys whwsch ye shal⸢
know[12] her[17]-after I wolde that I ware hens in haste, fore all maner of
40 happys. Constrw ye, &c.

    I can yw thanke fore ywyre letter that ye sente me, *and* that ye haue
inquiryd of shwch thyngys as ye thynke that shwld plese me.[18] I send yw
þe[19] boxe *and* þe dedys that ye sente to me fore, but as fore þe key of þe
cofyre[20] in þe wtter chamber, I can not fyndyt.[21] Yf þe box had be ther-in
45 ye cwdnat haue haddyth but yf I had broke wp þe cofyre; there-fore
remember yw were ye haue do þe key. I kep styll þe key that ye sente me
tyll that ye cwm hom.

    As fore þe tydyngys here,[22] ywre cosyn Barney of Wychshynggam ys
passyd to Gode, hwm Gode asoyle. Veylys[23] wyfe *and* Londonys wyfe *and*
50 Pycard þe bacar of Twmlond ⌜ben gon also⌝. All thys hwlsold *and* thys
parych[24] ys as ye leftyd, blyssyd be Gode. We lewyn in fere, bwt we wut
not qweder to fle fore to be better than we ben here. I send yw demi a riale
for to by wyth swger *and* datys fore me. I pray yw do as wel as y⟨e c⟩an[25]
and send it me as hastely as ye may; *and* send me word qwat price a li. of
55 peper, clowys, masis, gingyr, *and* sinamun, almannys, rys, ganyngall,
safrwn, ⌜reysonys of corons⌝, grenys—of ych of these send me þe price of
ych of these, *and* yf[26] it be better shepe at London than yt ys here I shal
send yw mony to by ⌜wyth⌝ soch stwfe as I wull haue.

    Remember[27] that I spake to yw[28] to spek to ywyre brothcre fore þe seyd
60 c marc. wan ye departyd hcns; I trow ye[29] fore-gettyt that ye ⌜sent me⌝[30]
non answere ther-of. In ony wys lete me haue an answere ther-of in hast
and send me woord how ywyre brothere *and* ⌜ye⌝[31] sped in ywyre maters.

    And Goddys blissyng *and* myn mvt ye haue both, *and*[32] send yw good
sped in all ywyre maters. Wretyn in hast on Sentt Levnardys Eve.

65   By ywyre moder

---

[14] Jh *canc.*   [15] *Written* weher, *first* e *canc.*

[16] but a rebuke to vs that he ys non othere preferred *canc. First style ends here.*

[17] -r *added later.*   [18] *Recto ends.*   [19] þ- *in form of* y *usually in this style.*

[20] of *canc.*   [21] *Before* -t *incomplete* h *canc.*

[22] I ca *canc.*   [23] V- *interl. above* w *canc.*

[24] b *canc.*   [25] *Letters obliterated by blot.*

[26] þer *canc.*   [27] yw *canc.*   [28] of *canc.*

[29] dede n *canc.*   [30] *Interl. above* haue *canc.*

[31] *Interl. above* he *canc.*   [32] gode *interl. but canc.*

209 B continued

Also I wold[10] ye shwld meue hym to take Pampyng to hym, or ell to get 35
hym a serwyce in þe Chauncery or in summe othere place were as he myth
be proferryd,[11] fore it ys pety that he lesyth hys tyme here, *and* yt ys non
a-wayll to non of ws; *and* yf he were proferryd[11] by ws yt war wurchype to
ws, be-cause that he hathe be so long wyth ws. ⌐Helpe ye on ywyre parte¬,
and fore diuerse othere causese I wold he war hens in hast, fore all maner 40
⌐of¬ happys. Constrw ye, &c. I shall tell yw more her-after.

I can yw thank fore þe letter that ye sente to me, *and* that ye haue inquiryd of shwch thyngys as ye thynk[12] shwld plece me. I send yw þe box
and þe dedys that ye sente to me fore, but as fore þe key of þe cofyr in þe
wtter chamber I can not fyndyth. Yf þe box had be there-in ye kowd not 45
haue haddyt but yf I had brok vp þe cofyre; remember yw were þe key is.[13]
I kep styll þe key that ye sente me.

As fore tydyngys, my coseyn Barney of Wychshyngham,[12] Veylys wyfe,
Londonnys wyfe, *and* Pycard of Tumlond be passyd to God; God haue
here sollys. All thys howshold *and* this parych arn saue, blissyd be God. 50
We leuyn in fere, but we wut not qweder to fle fore to be better than we
arn here. I send yw v s. to by wyth swger *and* datys fore me. I wold haue
iij or iiij li. of swger, *and* be-ware þe remnont in datys *and* send hem to me
as hastely as ye may, *and* send me woord qwath price a li. of peper, clowys,
macys, gynger, sinamun, almannys, rys, reysonys of coranis, gannyngall, 55
safrun, grenys ⌐*and* comfytys¬—of ych of these send me word wath a li. ys
worth, *and* yf yt be better shepe at London than yt ys here I shall send yw
money to by such stufe as I wull haue.

Remember I spak to yw to spek to ywyre brothere fore þe forseyd c marc.
qwan ye departyd hens; I trow ye had foregettyt that ye sente me non 60
answere there-of. In ony wys let me haue an answere there-of in haste,
and send me word how ywyre brothere *and* ye spede in ywyre maters.

And Goddys blissyng *and* myn mut ye haue both, *and* send yw good
sped in all ywyre maters to his plesaunce *and* to ywyre wurchype *and*
profyth. Wretyn in hast on Sent Levnardys Evyn. I warn yw kepe þis letter 65
close *and* lese yt not, rathere brenyt.[14]

By[15] ywyre moder

[10] he ore *canc.*   [11] pro *repr. by the usual abbreviation.*
[12] -n- *has a minim too many.*   [13] *Recto ends.*
[14] *This last sentence seems to have been added later.*   [15] wy *canc.*

355

210. To JOHN PASTON II   Perhaps 1470, 15 November

Add. 34889, f. 99. 11½ × 10¼ in. Gloys's hand.

Dorse: Conclusion of text. Marks of folding, traces of red wax, and stitch holes, but no address.

The date is uncertain. It is before administration of John I's will had been granted; but though he died in May 1466 his will was evidently not proved until 1473 (see John II's letter no. 279). Margaret's anxiety to obtain a discharge for having prematurely administered her husband's estate is expressed in very similar terms in no. 211, which is almost certainly of 1471; yet no. 209 shows that she could not have sent money then. In late 1470 the brothers were together (no. 208), and the Chancellor (l. 27) was George Neville, a friend of John II's (no. 266).
    G. LXVII/629.

I grete you wele *and* send you Godd*es* blissyng *and* myn, letyng you wete that I send you be the berer*e* here-of xl li. of ryall,[1] which I haue chevysshed *and* borwed for you be-cause I wuld not take that was leyd ought for you at Norwich; for as I am enformed be Mayst*er* John Smyth, the chauncellere,
5 *and* other*e* that we ben all a-cursed that we haue thus mynystred the ded*es* godes w*yth*-ought licence or auctorité, *and* I wene we spede all the wers there-fore. At the reu*er*ence of God, gete you a licens of my lord of Caunt*er*bery, in dischargyng of my conscyens *and* yowres,[2] to mynystr*e* a certeyn su*m*me of iij or iiij[c] marc.,[3] enfo*ur*myng hym how that y*our*
10 lyffelod hath stond this ij yer*e* in such trobill þat ye myght right nought haue of it, ner yet can take of it w*yth*-ought ye shuld hurt y*our* ten*aun*tes. Thei haue so ben vexid be on-trew[4] meanes be-fore this tyme,[5] and ye haue many grete mater*es* on hand *and* ⌈may not⌉[6] haue to bere them ought ner to save y*our* right w*yth*-ought ye myght for a tyme takyn of y*our* fader*es*
15 ⌈godes⌉.[7] And this, I hope, shall discharge owre conscyens of þat we haue mynestred *and* spend be-fore; for we haue nomore to acquite[8] this xl li. *and* bere all other*e* charges but the xlvij li. that y*our* vnkyll ⌈and ye⌉[9] is prevy to, þat was leyd vp at Norwich.

    I wuld ye wer*e* war*e* of large yeft*es* *and* reward*es* gevyng, as other*e*[10]
20 folk*es* avyse you to do;[11] for though ye haue nede thei wull not be right redy to help you of ther*e* owyn, *and* þat ye may vnd*er*stond be that þat thei haue taken a-wey from you be-fore this tyme. I wuld not in no wyse ye shuld put y*our*-self in no daunger*e* to hym but as litill as ye may; for if ye do it shall be right wele remembred you her*e*-aft*er*. And be war*e* how ye
25 ben bownd in any obligac*i*on to any creature but if it be leyd in endifferent

210. [1] -ll *crossed as usual, perhaps here intended for* -lles.
    [2] ye may sey th *canc.*   [3] *Curl on* -c.   [4] meas, *and a second* meanes, *canc.*
    [5] *MS.* tymes.   [6] *Interl. above* haue *canc.*   [7] *Interl. above* stuffe *canc.*
    [8] ther *canc.*   [9] *In margin.*
    [10] *Ends in the loop meaning* -es, *but here presumably a miswriting for the common flourish on* -r *meaning* -e.   [11] so *canc.*

handes *and* trosty for yowre part; *and* remembre to gete the obligac*ion* þat ye mad to the Duchesse of Suff*olk*, for though it be in my lord Chauncelleres hande it ⌐is⌐ iopartows be-cause of p*er*ell of deth.

Item, vnderstand wele the poyntes that ben in my cosyn Arblasteres lettere that arn wretyn in yowre, *and* p*ur*vey redily there-fore for y*our* owyn a-vayll. 30

Item, send me home answeres of suche materes as arn now sent you bothen [by] mowth *and* wrytyng at this tyme as hastly as ye can, or ell it shall hurt you more than ye or I can yet vnderstonde.

Item, me semyth if ye shuld not comyn home this Crystmesse, or if ye 35 shuld be at my lady of Suff*olk*, it [were] necessary to haue Playtere there wyth you if ye shuld engroos any appoyntmentes wyth here at that tyme, for she is sotill *and* hath sotill councell wyth here; *and* þerfore it were wele do ye shuld haue su*m*me wyth you þat shuld be of y*our* councell.

If John Paston be wyth you at London, desire hym to take hede to 40 yowre[10] materes *and* in what case thei ben left at y*our* departyng, þat if nede be he may help you to labore for such causes as Wykes shall telle you be mowth; *and* if he be not wyth you *and* ye wull, I shall send hym to you.

Item, spare of[12] the xl li. asmych as ye may, that ye may p*ar*fourme vp the mony that the Duchesse of Suff*olk* shuld haue in cas[13] that it may not 45 be gadered of the lyvelode. Send home Wykes a sone as ye can, *and* how ye wull þat[14] I do in y*our* materes *and* lyvelode at home.

God haue you in his kepyng. Wretyn the Thursday next after Sent Martyn.

Be y*our* modere 50

211. To JOHN PASTON II 1471, 20 November

Add. 27445, f. 53. 11⅜×5¾ in. Edmond Paston's hand.

Dorse: Marks of folding. Paper seal over red wax, and stitch-holes; but no address.

John II and John III were together in London in November 1471 (see John III's no. 349). Margaret's reminder about spices and wine connects this letter further with nos. 209 and 212. Finally, the handwriting of this letter is so like that of Edmond's no. 394, of 18 November 1471, that it must be very close to it in date.

G. 684/790 (abstract).

I grete ȝow wel *and* send ȝow Godd*ys* blyssyng *and* myn, latyng ȝow wete þat I merevel þat ȝe send me no answere ageyn of þe letter þat I send ȝow be Rychard Raddeley; I woold ȝe schuld send me answere there-of in[1] hast.

---

¹² of *repeated.*   ¹³ *Recto ends.*   ¹⁴ w *canc.*
211. ¹ *No space.*

Item, remembyre I spake to ʒow þat ʒowr broder and ʒe schuld purvey
5 a mene to haue a dysscharge of my lord of Cawntyrebery fore ocapyeng or
ʒowr fadyres goodys. Yt is no jape. Yt woold be remembyrd and don, fore
and þe seyde lord foretyn to dyssesse ere we haue a dysscharge othere þat
schull² cum aftyre hym ⌈I suppose wul⌉³ be more hasty vp-on hus þan he
hath ben. I woold he schuld be informyd wat scharge and lossesys we haue
10 had þat hath causyd þe godys to be spent so þat we be not abyl to perform
hys wyll, wherefore þat ʒe desyere a dysscharge. Yt is not on-knowyn to my
seyde lord þe gret scharge and cost þat we haue had syn he dyssessyd, whom
God assoyle. Yf my seyde lord be inforemyd there-of and remembyrd, I
hope he schuld be þe b[e]tter lord to vus and dysscharge vs þe more hastely.
15 At reuerens of God, latte yt not be fore-ʒet; fore and any of vus foretunyd
to dye, there woold no man take no scharge fore vus but yf we haue a
dysscharge of hym fore þe seyde goodys. And as I am enformed but¹ late
my seyde lord hath ore schal in hast be remembyrd to calle vp-on vs
therefor to ʒe[ue] an answere of þe seyde goodys; where-fore I woold thys
20 were don in hast ore he calle vp-on yt.

Item, I pray ʒow remembyre þe spysys and þe malmesey þat I haue send
to ʒow fore.

Grete well ʒowr brodthere, and Goddys blyssyng⁴ and myn mut ʒe haue
bothe, and send ʒow good spede in alle ʒowr materes. I thynk long tyl I
25 here ho ʒe do. I may haue no leysere to wrytgh no more at thys tyme.
Wretyn on Sen Eddmond Day þe Kyng.

Be ʒowr modyre

212. To JOHN PASTON III 1471, 29 November

Add. 27445, f. 54. 11½ × 9⅛ in. Edmond Paston's hand.

Dorse: Traces of red wax. Address in Edmond's hand:

To John Paston, esquiere, be thys delyuerd in hast.

The date appears from the opening passage about the loan of 100 marks, which is
mentioned also at the beginning of no. 209, of 1471. Further, St. Andrew's Eve was
a Friday in that year.

G. 685/791. C. 65 (part).

I grete ʒow welle and send ʒow Goddys blyssyng and myn, letyng ʒow wete
þat I haue a letter from ʒowr brothere where-by I vndyrstand þat he cannot
nere may make no purvyans fore þe c mark¹; þe wyche causythe me to be
rythgh hevy, and fore othere thynggys þat he wrytht to me² of þat he is in

---

² -l over d.　　　　　³ wᵗ canc.　　　　⁴ haue canc.
212. ¹ A curved-back tail may imply suspension.　　² fore canc.

dawngere fore, remembereng wat we³ haue had before thys *and* ho symp- 5
pylly yt hath be spe*n*te, *and* to lytyl profythe to any of v*us*, *and* now arn i*n*
soche casse þat no*n* of v*us* may welle help othere w*yth*-owte þat we schuld
do þat were to gret a dysworeschup fore v*us* to do—owthere to selle wood
ore lond ore soche stuffe þat were nessessary fore v*us* to haue i*n* owr howsys.
So mot I a*n*swere a-fore God, I woot not how to do fore þe seyde mony *and* 10
fore othere thyngg*ys* þat I haue to do of scharge, *and* my worshup saued;
yt is a deth to me to thynk vp-on yt.⁴ Me thynkkyth be ʒ*o*wr brotheres
wrythtyng þat he thynkkyth þat I a*m* i*n*foremed be su*m*e þat be a-bowthe
me to⁵ do *and* to sey⁶ as I haue be-fore thys; but be my trowthe he demyth
a-mysse. Yt nedyth me not to be i*n*formed of no soche thengg*ys*. I co*n*strue 15
i*n* my owyn mend, *and* co*n*seyve j-now, *and* to myche; *and* wha*n* I haue
brokyn my co*n*seyte to su*m*e þat in happe he demytheyt too, they haue put
me i*n* cownforth more þa*n* I kowde haue be any jmajynasyon in my owyn
co*n*seythe.

He wrythetyth to me also þat he hath spend thys terme xl li. Yt is a gret 20
thyng. Me thynkkyth be good dyscresyon there mythe myche there-of ⌐a⌐
ben⌐ sparyd. ʒ*o*wr fadyre, God blysse hys sowle, hathe had as gret materes
to do as I trow he hathe had ⌐thys⌐ terme, *and* hath not spend ⌐halfe⌐⁸ þe
mony vp-on the*m* ⌐i*n* so lytyl tyme, *and* hath do ryth well⌐. At þe reuere*n*s of
God, avyse hy*m* ʒet to be ware of hys expe*n*cys ⌐and gydyng⌐, þat yt be no 25
schame to v*us* alle. Yt is a schame,⁹ *and* a thyng þat is myche spoky*n* of in
thys co*n*tré, þat ʒ*o*wr faders graue ston is not mad. Fore Godd*ys* loue, late
yt be reme*m*byrd *and* p*ur*veyde fore in hast¹⁰—there hathe be myche more
spend i*n* waste þa*n* schuld haue mad þat. Me thynkkyth be ʒ*o*wr brothere
þat he is wery to wrythe to me, *and* there-fore I wylnot a-ku*m*byre hy*m* 30
w*yth* wrythtyng to hy*m*. ʒe may telle hy*m* as I wryth to ʒ*o*w.

Item, I woold ʒe schuld reme*m*byre ʒ*o*wr brothere of Pekerengg*ys* matere,
if he cu*m* not hom hastely, þat ʒe *and* Townesend *and* Lu*m*nore may
⌐examynyt¹¹ and⌐ sette yt thorow. þe pore ma*n* is almost on-don there-by,
and hys brothere suethe hy*m* *and* trobylyth hy*m* sore ʒet. And also fore þe 35
plesure of my koseyn Clere *and* þe Lady Bolen I woold yt were sette
thorow.

As fore my ⌐rowndlet of⌐ wyne, I schuld send ʒ*o*w mony there-fore, but
I dare not putyt i*n* joparté, there be so many theves stereng. ⌐John⌐
Louedayes ma*n* was robbyd i*n*-to hys schyrte as he ca*m* hom ward. I trow 40
and ʒe assaye Towneshe[n]d ore Playtere ore su*m* othere good ku*n*tery ma*n*
of owyrs to lend yt ʒ⌐o⌐w fore me tyl they cu*m* hom, they wyl do so myche
fore me and I schal co*n*tente the*m* a-geyn.

---

³ w- *over* ha.   ⁴ ʒ*o*wr brothere t *canc.*   ⁵ w *canc.*
⁶ I *canc.*   ⁷ *No space.*   ⁸ *Interl. above* d¹ *canc.*
⁹ þat ʒ*o*wr *canc.*   ¹⁰ *The stroke of* -t *prolonged half an inch to end of line.*
¹¹ *Written* examyt, *with stroke above* -y-.

Item, Jamys Gressham hath ben passyng sekke, *and* ys ʒet. Judy tellythe
45 me þat ʒowr brothere is avysed fore to sue hym. Fore Goddys sake, late non
onkyndnesse be¹² schewed to hym, fore þat woold sone make an hend of
hym. Remembyre ho keynd *and* true hartyd he hath ben to vus, to hys
powre; *and* he had neuere takke þat offyce vpon hym þat he is in dawngere
fore¹³ ne had be fore owr sakkys. He hathe sold a gret parte of hys lond
50 there-fore, as I suppose ʒe haue knowlache of. Late yt be remembyrd, *and*
ellys owr enmyes wyl rejoysyt *and* there wyl no wurshup be there-in at long
way.

I schuld wryth more, but I haue no leysere at thys tyme. I trow ʒe wyl
sone kum hom, *and* there-fore I wryth the lesse. God kepe ʒow *and* send
55 ʒow good spede, &c. Wretyn þe Fryday, Sen Andrue Eue.

Be ʒowr modyre

213. To JOHN PASTON III   Probably 1471, 7 December

Add. 34889, f. 211. 11⅜×7¼ in. Gloys's hand.

Dorse: Remnants of red wax. Address in Gloys's hand:

To John Paston, esquyere, be þis deliuered.

There is no firm evidence of date, but Margaret wrote to John III with messages
for John II on St. Andrew's Eve 1471 (no. 212), and she might well have written
this a week later. The request at the end for sugar and dates seems to repeat that
in no. 209, of 5 November in the same year.
G. LXXXVI/792.

I grete you wele *and* send you Goddes blyssyng *and* myn, desyryng you to
send me word how that your brothere doth. It was told here that he shuld
haue be ded, which caused many folkes, *and* me bothyn, to be right hevy.
Also it was told me this day that ye were hurt be affray that was mad vp-on
5 you be feles disgysed. Ther-⌐fore⌐ in any wyse send me word in hast how
your brothere doth, *and* ye bothyn, for I shall not ben wele at eas till I know
how þat ye do. And for Goddes love lete your brothere *and* ye be ware how
þat ye walken *and* wyth what felesshep ye etyn or drynkyn, *and* in what
place; for it was seid here pleynly that your brothere was poysoned.¹
10 And this weke was on of Drayton wyth me, *and* told me that there were
diuerse of the tenauntes seid that thei wost not what to do if that your
brothere come home, and there was on of the Duk of Suffolk men by and²
bad them not feryn, for his wey shuld be shorted *and* he shuld come there.
Wherfore in any wyse be³ ⌐ware⌐ of your-self, for I can thynk thei⁴ geve no

¹² b- *over* s.   ¹³ but *canc.*
213. ¹ *MS.* poynsoned.   ² *Two letters, the second* a, *canc.*
³ *This* be *canc., evidently in error.*   ⁴ right *canc.*

fors what to do to ⌐be⌐ wenged *and* to put you fro y*our* entent that thei 15
myght haue her*e* wyll in Ser John Fastolf*es* lond. Thy⟨nk⟩e⁵ what gret
sorow it ⟨shu⟩ld be to ⟨m⟩e and any ⟨. . . you⟩. I had leu*er* ye had neu*er*
know þe lond. Remembr*e* it was þe distrucc*i*on of y*our* fad*er*. Trost not
mych vp-on p*ro*myses of lord*es* now a days that ye shuld be the suerer*e* of
þe favo*ur* of þ*er* men; for ther*e* was a man, *and* a lord*es* sone, seid but late 20
and toke it for an exampill, þ*at* S*er* Roberd Harecourt had the good will of
the lord*es* after þ*er* comyng in, *and* yet wyth-in short tyme aft*er* here men
kylled hym in his owyn place. A mannes deth is litill set by now a days.
þ*er*fore be war*e* of symulac*i*on, for thei wull speke right fayr⁶ to you þ*at*
wuld ye ferd right evyll.   25

The blissid Trynyté haue you in his kepyng. Wretyn in gret hast the
Sat*er*day next aft*er* Sent Andrewe. Lete this lett*er* be brent whan ye haue
vnd*er*stond it.

Item, I p*ra*y you send me iiij sug*er* lof*es*, ich of them of iij li., *and* iiij li.
of dat*es* if thei be newe. I send you x s. be the berer*e* here-of; if ye pay more 30
I shall pay it you ageyn whan ye come home. *And* forgete not to send me
word be þe berer*e* here-of how ye don, *and* remembr*e* þe bylles *and*
remembrauns for the man*er* of Gresham that I wrote to y*our* brother fore.⁷

Be y*our* moder*e*

214. To John Paston II   About 1472

Add. 34889, f. 116. 11⅞×8½ in. Gloys's hand (more carefully written than
usual).

Dorse: Marks of folding. Traces of red wax, and tape-slits, but no address.

The approximate date appears from John II's plan to sell Sporle wood. This is first
mentioned in John III's letter no. 350, late in 1471, and several times in 1472 (e.g.
John II's no. 267), but the sale was still under negotiation in April 1473 (no. 274).
By November 1473 John II writes of 'redeeming' Sporle (no. 282). There is no
means of knowing how soon Margaret may have heard of her son's intention.
    G. LXXXIV/794.

I grete you wele, letyng you wete that þ*er* was told me a thyng in y*our*
absens þ*at* goth right ner*e* myn hert, be¹ a wurchepfull man *and* such on as
ye wuld beleve *and* geffe credence to, and that owyth you right good wille,
which if it had comyn to myn remembr*a*unce at y*our* dep*ar*tere I wuld haue
spoke to you of it most specially befor all other*e* mater*es*; but I am so 5

⁵ *Several letters, and nearly half a line of writing, lost by damage to paper at a fold.*
⁶ MS. fary.
⁷ *The last paragraph crowded in later, above and beside the subscription.*
214. ¹ be *repeated.*

trobilled in my mende w*yth* yo*ur* mater*es*, that thei be so delayd *and* take no
bet*ter con*clusion, *and* w*yth* þe ontrowth þat is in s*er*ua*untes* now a days but
if þ*er* mayster*es* take bet*ter* heed to þ*er* hand*es*, that such thyng*es* as I wuld
rathest remembre I sonest for-g*e*te.

10   It was told me that ye haue sold Sporle wood, of a right credebill *and*
wurchep[full]² man; *and* þat was right hevy þat ye shuld be know of such
disposic*ion, con*sideryng how yo*ur* fader*e*, whos sowle God assoyll,
cherysshed in eu*er*y man*er* his wood*es*. And for the more preffe þat þis
shuld be trought, the forseid p*er*son told me þat it was told hym of on þat
15   was toward S*er* William Yelu*er*ton, to whom Richard Calle shuld haue seid
in thes term*es*, þat Sporle wood shuld be sold *and* þat it shuld comyn now
in-to Cristen menn*es* hand*es*; which if it wer*e* knowyn shuld cause bothyn
yo*ur*³ elmyse *and* yo*ur* frend*es* to thynk þat ye dede it for right gret nede,
or ell þat ye shuld be a wasto*ur and* wuld wast yo*ur* lyvelode. If ye had do
20   so in S*er* John Fastolfes lyffelode men shuld haue supposid that ye had do
it of good pollicé be-cause of þe onsuerté þat it stant⁴ in, to haue takyn þat
ye had myght of it⁵ duryng yo*ur* possession, to haue boryn ought the
daunger*es* of it w*yth* the same; but for to do þus of yo*ur* owyn lyffelode men
shall thyng þat ye do it for pure nede. And in asmych as it is so ner yo*ur*
25   most elmyse ere it shall be to you þe grettere vylney *and* shame to all yo*ur*
frend*es, and* the grettest coragyng *and* plesere þat can be to yo*ur* elmyse.
For if ye be thus disposid ye shall make them *and* all othere certeyn of þat
that be-for this tyme thei haue ben in dought, and cause them to p*ur*pose
the more cruelly ageyn you. Where-for*e*, in eschewyng of þe greet slaundr*e*
30   *and* inconveniens þat may grow þ*er*-of, I require you *and* more-ou*er* charge
you vp-on my blissyng, *and* as ye wull haue my good will, that if any such
sale or bargany be mad be yo*ur* assent or w*yth*-ought, be Calle or any
othere in yo*ur* name, that ⌈ye⌉ restreyn it; for I wuld not for a m¹ marc.⁶
þat it wer*e* vnd*er*stond þat ye wer*e* of þat disposic*ion*, ner that ye were
35   comyn to so gret nede which shuld cause ⟨y⟩ou⁷ to do so, for eu*er*y shuld
thynk þat it were thurgh yo*ur* owyn mys-gou*er*naunce. There-for*e* I charge
you, if any such bargayn be mad, that ye send a bill as hastly as ye can to
Herry Halman, þat he do all such as haue mad or takyn þat bargayn seasse,
and felle non of þe wood vp-on peyn that may falle þ*er*-of. And how so eu*er*
40   wull councell you the *con*[t]rary, do as I advyse you in this behalffe or ell
trost neu*er* to haue comfort of me. And if I may knowe ye be of such disposic*ion, and* I leve ij yere it shall disavayll you in my liffelode ccc m*ar*c.
There-for*e* send me word be þe berere here-of wheder ye haue assent to any

---

² *Over -p a circumflex which could be a suspension mark; but Gloys often writes it elsewhere
in positions where it cannot indicate omission of a suffix such as* -full.
³ y- *altered from* þ.
⁴ *Reading not quite certain, but very probable;* -a- *has an abnormally long off-stroke, as if
altered from* o, *and* -n- *is tailed, as if originally meant to be final.*
⁵ be *canc.*   ⁶ *Curl on* -c, *as also below.*   ⁷ *Hole.*

such thyng or nought, *and* how that ye be disposid to do ther*e*-in; for I shal
not be quiete in myn hert till I vnd*er*stond yow of þe *con*[t]*r*ary disposic*i*on. 45

Be yo*ur*[8] moder

215. To John Paston III 1472, 5 February

Add. 34889, f. 121. 11¾×8½ in. Gloys's hand.

Dorse: Paper seal over red wax and tape. Address in Gloys's hand:

*To John Paston, esquyere, be this deliue*red.

The date appears from the reference to the suit against John II by the widow of
one of the two men killed at the siege of Caister in 1469. From John II's letter of
28 September 1471 (no. 264) it seems that both widows were still preparing to sue
the appeal first projected in January 1470 (John III's no. 338). One disqualified
herself by marrying again (see Part II, no. 788, of 21 October 1471), but the other
went on with the case. The present letter must therefore date from early in 1472.
   Agas was an English form of *Agatha* (see, for example, *Promptorium Parvulorum*).
   F. iv, p. 424. G. 689/797.

I grete you wele *and* send you Godd*es* blyssyng *and* myn, letyng you wete
that the woman that sewyth the appell ageyn y*our* brother*e and* his men is
comyn to London to calle ther*e*-vp-on, and whan that she shuld come to
London ther*e* was deliu*e*red her*e* c s. for to sewe w*yth*; so that, be that I
her*e* in this countré,[1] she wull not leve it but that she shall calle ther*e*-vp-on 5
such tyme as shall be to y*our* most rebuke, but if ye ley the bett*er* wetch.
She hath evill councell, *and* þat wull see you gretely vtter*e*d, *and* þat ye may
vnd*er*stond be the money that was take her*e* whan she came vp; *and* ye
shuld fynd it, I knowe it wele, if thei myght haue you at avau*n*tag.[2] Ther*e*-fore,
for Godd*es* sake, make diligent serge be the advyse of y*our* councell that 10
ther*e* be no necglicens in you in this mater*e* ner other*e* for diffaught of
labo*ur*, *and* call vp-on y*our* brother*e and* telle hym that I send hym Godd*es*
blyssyng *and* myn, *and* desire hym that he wull now a while, whill he hath
the lord*es* at his entent, that ⌈he⌉ seke the meanes to make an ende of his
mater*es*; for his elmyses arn gretly coraged ⌈now of late⌉—what is the cause 15
I knowe not.
   Also I p*ray* you speke to Playter*e* that þ*er* may be fownd a meane þat the
shereffe or the gaderer*e* of the grene wax may be discharged of certeyn
issues that renne vp-on Fastolf for Mariott*es* mater*e*, for the balyffe was at
hym this weke *and* shuld haue streyned hym, but þat he p*ro*mysed hym þat 20
he shuld w*yth*-in this viij days labore[3] the meanes that he shuld be discharged or ell he must *con*tent hym, &c.

   [8] *Followed by* more *not canc.*
   215. [1] here *canc.*   [2] -g *at extreme edge of paper.*   [3] -d *canc.*

Also I send you be the berere here-of, closed in this letter, v s.[4] of gold, *and* pray you to bey me a sugere loffe *and* dates *and* almaundes *and* send it
25 me home, *and* if ye beware any more money, whan ye come home I shall pait you ageyn.

The Holy Gost kepe you bothyn *and* deliuere you of your elmyse. Wretyn on Sent Agas Day in hast.

Item, I pray you speke to Mayster Rogere for my sorepe, fore I had neuer
30 more nede there-of; *and* send it me as hastly as ye can.[5]

M. P.[6]

216. To John Paston II   1472, 5 June

Add. 27445, f. 58. 11½×8⅜ in. Edmond Paston's hand.

Dorse: Paper seal over red wax and string. Address in Edmond's hand:

To Ser John Paston, knythe, be thys delyuerid.

Under this in John II's hand: *per Matrem.*

The date must be later than the agreement in respect of the Fastolf lands between the Bishop of Winchester and John Paston II, set out in the indenture of July 1470, printed as no. 253. In June 1471 John II was still awaiting a pardon for his part in the battle of Barnet (see John III's letter no. 347), and would not be in a position to press his claim against the Duke of Norfolk. Margaret's request for a discharge for the Fastolf estate is repeated by John III in no. 353, and provision for Anne Paston's marriage is discussed both there and in no. 352. This is evidently of the same year as those letters, which are firmly datable in 1472. The state of development of Edmond's handwriting is in keeping with this date.

St. Petronilla's Day was 31 May.

G. 695/803.

I gret ȝow welle *and* send ȝow Goddys blyssyng *and* myn, latyng ȝow wet þat I spakke wyth frendys of myn wyth-yne thys fewe days þat told me þat I am lekke to be trobyld fore Ser John Fastolls goodys þe whyche were in ȝowr fadyrs possessyon; *and* as fore me, I had neuer non of them. Where-
5 fore I pray ȝow send me a kopy of þe dysse[1]-charge whyche ȝe haue of my lord of Wynschester ⌜þat⌝[2] ȝe told me þat ȝe had bothe fore my dyscharge *and* ȝowyrs, wat sum euer þat be callyd vpon of eythere of vus here-aftere.

Item, yt ys told me þat Harry Heydon hat bowthe of þe seyd lord bothe Saxthorpe *and* Tychewelle, *and* hathe takke possessyon there-in. We bette
10 þe busschysse, *and* haue ⌜þe⌝ losse *and* þe dy[s]worschuppe,[3] *and* othere

---

[4] *This sum underlined, and the four lines of writing embracing this sentence and the beginning of the next bracketed in margin.*

[5] *This last sentence crowded in at the foot to left of signature.*

[6] *Initials preceded by* be *canc.*

216. [1] *End of line.*   [2] *Interl. above* as *canc.*

[3] *Second letter apparently an imperfect* y, *crowded between* d *and* w.

men haue þe byrd*ys*. My lord hathe falsse kownselle *and* sympylle þat a-vyse⌐ythe⌐ hy*m* there-to. *And* as yt ys told me, Guton ys leke to goo þe same wey in hast; and as for*e* Heylysdon *and* Drayton, I trow yt is þere yt schalle be. Wat schalle falle of þe r*em*nant God k[n]owythe; I trow as evelle or*e* wher*e*sse. We haue þe losse a-mong v*us*. Yt owythe to be reme*m*byrd, 15 *and*[4] they þat be defawty to haue ko*n*syens[5] there-i*n*. *And*, so mot I thryve, yt was told me but latte þat yt is seyd in kownselle of them þat ben at Caster*e* þat I a*m* leke to haue but lytylle good of Mauteby yf þe Dukke of Norfolke haue possessyon stylle i*n* Cast*er*; *and* yf we lesse þat, we lesse þe fayere-este flowere of owr garlond. *And* there-fore helpe þat he may be owte 20 of possessyon ther*e*-of in haste, be myn a-vyse, wat so eu*er* fortune her*e*-aft*er*.

It*em*, yt is seyde here þat my lord arche¹-bysschoppe is ded; *and* yf yt be so, calle vp-on hys sueretés for*e* þe mony þat is owyng to v*us* i*n* hast be myn avyse. *And* at r*e*uerens of God, helpe þat I mythe be dyschargyd of þe 25 c mark[6] þat ȝe wot of, owd*er* be þat mene or*e* su*m* other, for*e* yt is to myche for*e* me to ber w*yth* othere charg*ys* þat I haue besyd þat. I a*m* to hevy wa*n* I thynk vp-on yt.

As for*e* yo*wr* syst*er* Anne, Mast*er* Godfrey *and* hys wyffe *and* W. Grey of Martyn arn vp-on a-powntme*nt* ⌐w*yth* me *and* yo*wr* brothere John⌐ so 30 þat ȝe wylle a-gre ther-to *and* be here good brother. Sche schalle haue to joyntor hys modyrs lyvelod aft*er* þe dyssesse of her*e* *and* here husbond, *and* I to pay x lj. be ȝer*e* to þe fynddyng of her*e* *and* here husbond tylle c lj. be payed. And yf hys[7] grawntsyers lyvelod falle to hy*m* here-aftere[8] he hathe p*ro*mysyd to amend her*e* joyntyre. Mast*er* Godfrey hathe p*ro*mysyd hy*m* 35 for*e* hys p*ar*te xl s. be ȝer*e*, *and* þa*n* lakkythe but iiij nobyls of xx mark be ȝere, þe wyche they hope ȝe wylle make vpe for*e* ȝo*wr* p*ar*te. ⌐Wyll*ia*m⌐[9] Grey told me he schuld speke w*yth* ȝow here-in wa*n* he kam to London thys terme.

God kepe ȝow. Wretyn i*n* hast[10] on Fryday nex⌐t⌐ after*e* Sen P*er*nelle. 40

Be yo*wr* modyre

---

⁴ teh *canc.*   ⁵ *From* ko*n*schens.
⁶ *Ampersand canc.*   ⁷ grauntsyer*e*s *canc.*
⁸ here w *canc.*   ⁹ *Interl. above* W *canc.*
¹⁰ of *canc.*

217. To JOHN PASTON III   Perhaps 1472, 23 October

Add. 34889, f. 108. 11⅜×6 in. Gloys's hand.

Dorse: Paper seal over red wax. Address in Gloys's hand:

To John Paston þe yongere be þis deliuered in hast.

The date must fall within the period of the duke of Norfolk's occupation of Caister. He seized it in 1469, and held it, with an interval during the restoration of Henry VI, until his death in 1476, when John Paston II recovered it (see nos. 294 and 300). The general situation is so like that described in no. 216 that it may well be of the same year.

G. LXXXVII/811.

I grete you wele, letyng you wete that on Saterday last past wyth-in nyght the felesshep at Cayster tokyn ought of Mautby[1] Cloos xvj shep ⌈of diuerse mennes⌉ þat were put there-in to pasture, and thei ledde them a-wey so that euery man ferith to put any bestes or catell þer-in, to my grete hurt and
5 discoragyng of my fermour þat is now of late come theder. And the seid evyll disposed persones affraid my seid fermour as he came from Yarmoth this weke, and shotte at hym, þat if he had not had a good hors he had be[2] like to haue ben in joparté of his lyfe; so that be thes rewle I am like to lese þe profite of þat lyfelode this yere but if there be purueyd the hastyere
10 remedy. Thei threte so my men that I dar send non theder to gadere it. Thei stuffe and vetaylle sore the place, and it is reparted[3] here that my lady of Norfolk seth she wull not leas it in no wyse. And the Duchesse of Suffolkes men sey that she wull not departe from Heylesdon ner Drayton, she wuld rathere departe from money; but þat shuld not be wurchepfull for you, for
15 men shull not than set be you. There-for I wuld[4] avyse you to haue rathere the lyvelod than the money. Ye shall mown excuse you be the college, which must contynue perpetuall, and money is sone lost and spent whan þat lyfelode abideth.

Item, I lete you wete that Hastynges hath entred ageyn in-to his fee of þe
20 constabyll-shep of þe Castell of Norwich[5] be the vertu of his patent þat he had of Kyng Herry, and I here sey he hath it graunted to hym and his heyeres. There was at his entres your vnkill Will and othere jentilmen dwellyng in Norwych. þis[6] was do be-fore þat ye sent me the letter be Pers. I had forgetyn to haue sent you word þer-of.

25 God kepe you. Wretyn þe Friday next after Sent Luke.

Be your moder

217. [1] Cl *canc.*   [2] *No space.*
　　[3] -ar- *abbr. exactly as in* departe *l. 13, etc.*   [4] -d *over* l.
　　[5] -w- *over* -ff-.   [6] *From* þᵗ.

218. To JOHN PASTON III   1472, 19 November

Add. 27445, f. 61. 11⅜ × 13½ in. Gloys's hand.

Dorse: Paper seal over red wax and string. Address in Gloys's hand:

To John Paston, esquyere.

The date appears mainly from the postscript, which implies that John III was in touch with the Duke of Norfolk. From no. 356 it is clear that he was at Framlingham in November 1472. The time of year also suits the report of attempts to upset the election; Edward IV opened his fourth parliament on 6 October 1472 (Scofield, ii. 39).

G. 705/814.

I grete you wele *and* send you Godde*s* blyssyng *and* myn, letyng you wete that I haue sent to Docto*ur* Aleyn wyffe to haue spoke w*yth* her*e* as ye desired me, *and* she was so syke that she myght not comyn. But she sent her*e* broder*e* elaw to me, *and* I lete hym wete the ⌐cause⌐ why that I wuld haue spoke w*yth* her*e* as ye desired me; *and* he told me that he shuld haue 5 brought me wrytyng this day from her*e* be vij of the belle how þ*at* she wull that ye shuld haue labored or do for her*e*, but he came nomor*e* at me. Neu*er*thelesse ⌐she sent me an nother*e* massanger*e* *and* lete me wete⌐¹ that her*e* husbond had sent her*e* a lett*er* the same nyght from London that she shuld come vp as fast as she cowde to labo*ur* to the lord*es* there in her*e* 10 pro*pre* p*er*son, wh⟨e⟩refore² she myght geve me non answer*e* ner send you word how that ye shuld do till ⟨that⟩ she had spokyn w*yth* her*e* husbond or had other*e* writyng from hym. Therfore I thynk t⟨hat s⟩he hath other*e* councell that avyseth her*e* to labo*ur* to other*e* than to you. I wuld not þ*at* ⟨ye were⟩ to besy in no such mater*es* ⟨t⟩ill the werd wer*e* mor*e* suer*e*, and 15 in any wyse³ that w⟨hile m⟩y lord þe Chauncellere is in ⟨ocu⟩pac*ion* labore to haue an ende of yo*ur* grete mater*es* *and* ⟨. . .⟩⁴mac*ion* *and* abide not vp-⟨on⟩ trost ⌐of⌐ an nother*e* seson, for so shall ye be disseyved a⟨s ye hau⟩e ben be-fore this tyme. ⟨I⟩ haue vnd*er*stand sith that ye dep*ar*ted that þ*er* ⟨. . .⟩⁵ mad to subplant yo⟨u⟩. þ*er*fore, for Godde*s* sake, in this 20 onstabil werd labore er⟨. . .⟩⁶ mater*es* that thei may hau⟨e⟩ su*mm*e good conclusion, and that shall make y⟨our elmyse⟩ fere you, *and* ell thei shall ⟨. . .⟩⁷ kepe you low *and* in trobill. And if any mater⟨. . .⟩⁶ be act of parlement *and* pro⟨fig⟩ht lete yo*ur* bill be mad redy, *and* lese not your ⟨ma⟩ter*es* fore other*e* mennes, for if yo*ur* elmyse may pro*fig*ht now at this tyme ye 25 shall be ⟨in⟩ wers case than eu*er* ye wer*e* be-fore. All the con⟨tra⟩y wenyth

---

218. ¹ *Interl. above* here seid brother*e* lawe told me that tyme that he was w*yth* me *canc.*
² *Missing letters and words here and below lost at three irregularly shaped holes in the paper.*
³ wy *canc.*   ⁴ *Room for seven or eight letters.*
⁵ *Room for about ten letters.*   ⁶ *Room for about twelve letters.*
⁷ *Room for three or four letters.*

that ye shuld now ouercomyn all your trobill, which if ye do not ye shall fall o⟨ug⟩ht of conceyte. I write as wele this to your brothere as to you. þerfore lete no diffaught be in you nowthere.

30 Item, it was lete me to wete syth that ye departed, of such as were your frendes and were conuersaunte wyth the toder parté, that þer was mad labore, and like to be concluded, that the eleccion of the knyghtes of þe shire shuld be chaunged and new certificat mad, and John Jenney set there-in. There-fore do your devour to vnderstond the trought as sone as ye 35 can, for the seid Jenney this day rideth vp to London ward, and I suppo⟨se be⟩cause of the same.

I pray you remembre your brothere to send me the evydence and remembraunce towchyng the maner of Gresham which that I wrote to hym be Juddy, and send them be sum suere man.

40 Item, take hede to the labour of your vnkyll, for he hath had right straunge langage of your brothere of late to right wurchepfull persones. þerfore werk wysely, and be ware wham that ye lete know your councell.

Item, remembre Lomnours matere as ye may do there-in, and send me word in hast. Mayster Roos shal be at London the next weke; there-fore ye 45 shall not nede to make my lord to write. But whan that he comyth, if my lord can make hym to put it in indifferent ⌈and wurchepfull⌉ men, than that it pleasith my lord to write to them that thei shuld take it vp-on them to set a rewle ther-in. Wyth-ought better advyse, me semyth it were wele do.

The Holy Gost be your gyde and send yow good spede and councell, and 50 deliuere you ought of all trobill and disseas to his plesere. Wretyn the Thursday next be-fore Sent Kateryn, in hast.

Recomaund me to my mastres Kateryn, and send me word how ye don, &c.

Be your moder

55 Do my lord on Sonday send for the shereffes debuté to wete how thei be disposid for certificate of þe knyghtes, and þer shall vnderstand if thei be eschaunged; for on Sonday at nyght or on Monday it shall be put in and ⟨after⟩ it is put in ther is no remedy. Geney seth he wull attempt the law there-in.

219. To JOHN PASTON III   1472, 23 November

Add. 27445, f. 63. $11\frac{1}{2} \times 3\frac{3}{4}$ in. Gloys's hand.

Dorse: Remnants of red wax. Address in Gloys's hand:

To John Paston, esquyere, be this deliuered.

The reference to Dr. Aleyn's wife connects this letter with no. 218.
    G. 707/816.

I grete you wele, letyng you wete that Docto*ur* Aleyn wyffe hath be w*yth*
me *and* desired me to write to you to desire you to be good mayst*er* to her*e*
husbond *and* to her*e* in her*e* mater*es*, for she tellith me that her*e* trost is
full in you, *and* if she myght haue walked she shuld haue come to haue
spoke w*yth* you or than ye dep*ar*ted. Therfor*e* I p*r*ay you do yo*ur* devo*ur* 5
for her*e*, for I conceyve that she feyneth not, notw*yth*stondyng that I had
her*e* in suspec*i*on, as I haue wretyn to you be-fore, be-cause that she came
not. But I conceyve now the trought, *and* þat sikenesse caused that she
absent her*e*. Therfor*e* I p*r*ay you help her*e*, for so God help me I haue
right gret peté on her*e* *and* it is right gret almes to help her*e*, *and* I trow she 10
wull put her*e* most trost *and* sewe speciall to you. Also I wuld ye shuld
desire yo*ur* brother*e* to be good mayst*er* on-to her*e*, for I suppose be that[1]
tyme ye haue herd her*e* excuse in such mater*es* as he shuld be displeased
w*yth* her*e* husbond ye shall hold you pleased.

God kepe you *and* send you hes blyssyng w*yth* myn. Wretyn on Sent 15
Clement*es* day at nyght, in hast.

Be yo*ur* mod*er*

220. Probably to JAMES GLOYS: draft   Probably 1473, 18 January

Add. 27445, f. 69. $11\frac{3}{4} \times 12$ in. Hand unidentified.

Dorse: Marks of rough folding only, no seal or address.

The epistolary forms, and the tone, are not those used by Margaret to her sons.
Since the person addressed was entrusted with escorting Walter Paston to Oxford,
and with writing a letter to him in Margaret's name, it was almost certainly meant
for her chaplain Gloys. He was evidently at this time in Norwich and Margaret not
far away in the country, since she expects him to be able to reach her the next day
(l. 54). She was probably at Mautby.

The date appears from the reference to the grave illness of 'my cousin Berney'.
Margaret sometimes referred in these terms to John Berney of Witchingham (e.g.
in no. 161); but he died, evidently of plague, in November 1471 (no. 209), and her
report of his death implies no long illness. From the time of year it is most likely
that the present reference is to Margaret's first cousin John Berney of Reedham,
who died on 20 January 1473 (*Inq. p.m.*, 13 Edward IV, no. 17, P.R.O. C 140/43).
Walter Paston took his degree at Oxford in June 1479 (see no. 404), so that this
would suit his going up well enough.

F. v, p. 152. G. 716/825. C. 70.

I recomaund me to you, and thanke you hertyly of youre letter*is* and
delygente labour*e* þat ye haue had in thoes mater*is* þat ye haue wretyn to me
of, and in all other*e* to my p*r*ofette and worschep, *and*[1] jn esspeciall atte
this sesons towchyng the mater*e* þat I sent[2] you þe jndenture of. Ye haue

5 lyghtyd myne hert þerin[3] by a pound, for I was in fere þat it wold not haue
bene doo so hastyly with-oute dangere. And as for the letters þat Thomas
Hollere son schuld haue brought me, I see nothere hym ne the letters þat
he schuld haue brought; wherefore I pray you hertely, yeue it be no dysese
to you, þat ye will take the laboure to bryng ⌜Walter⌝[4] theyr he schuld be,
10 *and* to poruaye[5] for hym þat he may be sette in good and sad rewle, for I
were loth to lese hym; for I trust to haue more joye of hym þan I haue of
them þat bene owlder. Though it be more coste to me to send you forth
with hym, I hold me plesed for I wote wele ye schall best porvaye[5] for hym,
and for suche thynges as is necessare to hym, than anothere schuld doo,
15 aftere myne jntent. And as for ane hors to lede hys gere, me thynke it were
best to porvaye one att Camberag, lesse than ye canne gytte ony carreours
from thens to Oxynforth more hastyly.

And I meruell þat the letters come not to me, and whethere I may laye the
defaute to the faudere or to the son þerof. And I wold Watere schuld be
20 copilet with a[6] bettere than Hollere son is þer as he schalbe. Howe beit, I
wold not þat he schuld make neuer the lesse of hym, by-cause he is ⌜his⌝
contré-man and neghboure.

And also I pray you wryte a[6] lettere in my name to Watere aftere þat ye
haue knowne myne entent by-fore this to hym ward: so þat he doo welle,
25 ⌜lerne well⌝, and be of good rowle[7] and disposycion, þer shall nothyng faylle
hym þat I may helpe with, so þat it be nessessare to hym. And bydde hym
þat he benot to hasty of takyng of orderes þat schuld bynd hym till þat he
be of xxiiij yere of agee ⌜or more⌝, thoff he be consaled the contraré, for
oftyn rape ⌜rewith⌝.[8] I will loue hym bettere to be a good seculare man þan
30 to be a lewit prest.

And I am soré þat my cosyn Bernay is seke, *and* I pray you yeff my white
wine, or ony of my wateris, or ony othere thyng that I haue þat ⌜is⌝ in youre
awarde may doo hym ony comforth, lette hym haue it; for I wold be right
sory yf ony thyng schuld comme to hym botte good. And for Godsake
35 advise hym to doo[9] make hys will, yeue it be not doo, *and* to doo well to my
cosyn his wiff, and els it were peté;[10] *and* I pray you to recomaunde me to
hyr, and to my nawnte, and to all the gentillmen *and* gentillwomen there.
And as for John Daye, and he ⌜be⌝ dede I wold be sory, for I know not
howe to comme by my mony[11] that he oweith me.

40 *And* I porpose þat Pacoke schall haue les to doo for me another yeree than
he haith had, if y may be bettere porvayed, with youre helpe, for he is for
hym-self bott not for me. And as for ony marchandes to my corn, I can

---

gytte none her*e*. þ*er*for I pray you doo ye als wele þ*er*in as ye canne. Also I
send you by the bereer*e* hereof the bill of myne resay*tes*, and yef ye go
forth with Walter*e* I pray you co*m*me to me als sone as ye may af*ter* ye be 45
co*m*myn home. *And* me lyketh myne abydyng *and* þe contré here right
well, and I trust whan somm*er* comith and fayre wether*e* I schall lyke it
better*e*, for I am cherysed here botte to well. And I constrew your lett*er*
⌐in¬12 other*e* mat*er*is well jnough, whereof I thanke you; *and* if it nede not
to send13 forth Walt*er* hastyly I wald ye myght come to me, ⌐thowe¬14 ye 50
schuld com opon one day *and* goo ayane on þe next day—⌐than¬15 schuld
I comon w*ith* you in all mat*er*is. *And* I hold best, if ye haue not þe lett*er*is
þat Holler*e* son schuld haue brough[t] me, þat ye send Sym ou*er* for them
this nyght þat I may haue them to-morowe, and yif ye may combe youre-
self I wold be þe bett*er* playsed. 55

And I remember*e* þat wat*er* of mynte or wat*er* of millefole were good for
my cosyn Bernay to drynke for to make hym to browke; *and* yeue thei send
to Dame Elesebeth Callethroppe, þ*er* ye shall not fayill of the tone or of
bothe. Sche haith other*e* wat*er*is to make folkis to browke.

God kepe you. Wrytyn on þe Monday next af*ter* Sent Hilleré. I haue no 60
lenger*e* leyser*e* atte this tyme.

221. To John Paston II   1475, 28 January

Add. 27445, f. 85. 11½×8½ in. Hand unidentified, appearing also in nos.
222 and 223.

Dorse: Continuation of text. Traces of red wax. Address in hand of letter:

*To Ser John Paston, knyght, be thys delyu*er*yd in hast . . . A° xiiij°.*

Dated.
F. v, p. 86. G. 752/863. C. 74 (part).

Jes*us*

Ryght welbelouyd son, I gret yow well and send yow Godd*ys* blyssyng and
myn, letyng yow wete þat I marveyle1 þat I have had no2 wrytyng from
yow sethyn ye sent me þe3 lettyr þat ye sent me be-for the Kyng*ys* comyng
to Norwych, in the wyche lettyr ye wrot to me þat ye shuld a wretyn a-geyn
to me or ye shuld de-part owt of London. It ys so þat yowyr hunkyll4 5
Willi*am* hath do payd to my cosyn Robard Clere but iiij^xx li. of the c li., and

he wol no mor pay but yff he hath delyueraunc of my pleggys,[5] the wych
war leyd to plegg for xx[ti] li., the wych ben bettyr. I wot well[6] be-cause of
the good well þat he owyt to me, as ye know, he wold ben in possessyon
10 ther-off. My cosyn ⌐Robard⌐ Cler was her wyth me thys weke and told me
þat yf he wold a deliueryd them he myth an had þe seyd xx li.; but he seyd
he wold nowt tyll he had spokyn wyth me. Be my trowth I fynd hym ryght
kyndly dysposyd to yow and to me bothe, and so I have desyryd hym to
kepe styll þe pleggys in hys possessyon tyll I have word from yow how ye
15 ar agreyd wyth yowyr hunkyll for the payment of the seyd mony. I wen
veryly ⌐þat⌐ ye have fownd hym swerté for alle; and yff ye have soo do, I
wold ye shuld wryt to yowyr hunkyll ther-for þat I myth have my pleggys
a-geyn, for I war loth that they shuld com in hys fyngyrs.
    ⌐Item⌐, as for[7] Sporyl wood, be-for the Kyngys comyng in-to Norffolk
20 I myth an had chapmen to a bowtyd a gret for xij[xx] mark, and now ther wol
no man ⌐by yt⌐[8] a gret by-cause of þe gret good þat the pepyll ys leyd to for
þe Kyng. Wer-for we ar a-bowth to retaylyt as well as we may, and as well
as yt can be browth too,[9] and[10] send yow word ⌐how we⌐[11] shall do⌐ as astely
as[12] I may.
25   As for yowyr barly in thys cuntré, yt cannot be sold a-bove x d. or xj d.;
þat ys the gretest prys of barly her, and but yt be at a bettyr prys I purpose
for to ⌐do⌐ yt malt. And as for[13] mony, I ⌐cowd⌐[14] not get ⌐yet⌐ of Pecok but
iij li., and he seth þat, be than þat þe ⌐owt⌐ chargys be boryn and þe
repracion of þe myll at Wyntyrton, we ar lyke to haue but lytyll[15] mor
30 mony be-syd the barly. Malt ys sold her but for xiij d., and whet ij s. or
xxvj d. at thys time and otys xij d. Ther ys non owtlod suffyrd to goo owth
of thys cuntré as yet; the Kyng hath comaundyd þat ther shuld non gon
owth of thys lond. ⌐I fer me þat we shall have ryth a straung ward⌐, God
a-mendyd whan hys wyll ys.
35   I thank yow for the flakons þat ye sent me; they be ryght good and plesyth me ryght well. I shall be as good an huswyff for yow as I can, and as I
wold be for my-selff. Send me word how ye doo of yowyr syknes þat ye
had on yowyr hey and yowyr lege; and yff God wol nowt ssuffyr yow to
have helth, thank hym ther-off and takyt passhently, and com hom a-geyn
40 to me, and we shall lyve to-gedyr[16] as God woll geve vs grase to do. And
as I have seyd to yow be-for thys, I wold ye war delyueryd of my Mastres
A. H., and than I wold trost þat ye shuld do the bettyr.[17]

[5] *The plural ending is apparently meant, both here and in other occurrences of this word
below; but there is only a small curl on the off-stroke of the -g, not the usual loop. The same kind
of curl has been corrected to the loop in* kyngys, *l. 19.*
[6] for the *canc.*   [7] *Written* forth, -th *canc.*   [8] *Interl. above* byyt *canc.*
[9] we shall do ther jn *canc.*   [10] I shall *canc.*
[11] do *canc.*   [12] we *canc.*   [13] P *canc.*
[14] *Interl. above apparently miswritten* cowd *canc.*   [15] MS. lykyll.
[16] *Written* geddyr, *first* d *seems to be canc. by overwriting.*
[17] *Recto ends. The sentence beginning* and than *is crowded into a separate line at the foot.*

As for the bokys that ye desyryd to have of Syr Jamys, the best of alle and the fayrest ys cleymyd, ner yt ys not in hys jnventory. I shall a-say to get yt for yow and I may. The prys of þe todyr ⌈bokys⌉ be-syd that ys xx s. 45 vj d., the wych I send yow a byll of. Yf ye lyk[18] be þe prys of them and ye wol haue them, send me word; and also I pray ⌈yow⌉ send me an answere of thys lettyr be-cause[19] I thynk long ⌈seth I hard⌉[20] from yow.

God have yow in hys kepyng. Wretyn at Mawdby on the Sattyrday nex be-forn the Purificacion of Owyr Lady the xiiij yer of Kyng Edward the 50 iiij^t.

Yowyr modyr

222. To JOHN PASTON III   1475, 28 January

Add. 27445, f. 84. $11\frac{1}{2}\times8\frac{1}{2}$ in. Hand of no. 221.

Dorse: Paper seal over red wax and string. Address in hand of letter:

To John Paston, sqwyer, be thys delyueryd in hast.

The date appears from the references to Robert Clere and to the King's coming to Norwich, which link this letter closely with no. 221. The two were written at Mautby by the same clerk on the same day.

F. v, p. 82. G. 751/862.

Jesus

I gret yow well and send yow Goddys blyssyng and myn, letyng yow wet þat my cosyn Robard Clere was her wyth me thys weke *and* told me þat he was nowt payd of the mony þat ye[1] know þat was borowd of hys modyr *and* of hym but iiij^{xx} li. þe xx li. þat my pleggys ly for ys on-payd. He seyd þat he was desyryd to delyuere my pleggys *and* to have be payd þe xx li., 5 but he wold not tyll he had spokyn wyth me be-cause of þe promys þat he had mad to me be-for þat he shuld not delyuer them to non wyth-owt my assent. I seyd to hym þat I suppose veryly þat yowyr brodyr hys a-greyd wyth yowyr hunkyll þat he shuld paye all the hole, for I suppose he hath a swerté for ale þat and more. I wold vndyrstond how yt ys, and how þat 10 my seyd cosyn shall be content, for I war loth to lese my pleggys. I wot yt well yowyr good hunkyll wold ben in possessyon wyth good well, but I wol not soo. I wold þat ye shuld speke wyth yowyr hunkyll ther-jn and send me word in[2] hast what he seet.

I marvyll, be my trowth, þat I had no wrytyng fro yowyr brodyr ⌈er⌉[3] he 15 departyd fro London, as he promysyd in the last lettyr þat he sent me, the wych was ⌈wretyn⌉ be-for the Kyngys comyng to Norwych. I went veryly

---

[18] *MS.* kyk.   [19] of my p *canc.*   [20] *Interl. above* tyll I have *canc.*
222. [1] no *canc.*   [2] a *canc.*   [3] *Interl. above* sethin he *canc.*

to have hard from hym ar thys tyme. I wold ye shuld send hym word of
yowyr hunkyly*s* delyng in thys seyd mater, and send me an answser ther-
20 off. Recomaund me to yowyr grauntd*am*. I wold she war her in Norf*folk* as
well at⁴ es as evyr⁵ I sy hyr, and as lytyll rewlyd be hyr son as evyr she was;
and than I wold hope þ*at* we⁶ alle shuld far the bettyr for hyr. Yt ys told
me þ*at* yowyr hunkyll hath mad gret menys *and* larg p*r*ofyrs to John
Bakton to make a relesse ⌜to hym⌝ of Oxinhed. Whedyr yt be don or nowt
25 I wot nowt yet, but I shall wot in hast yf I may. I wold ye shuld spekyn
w*yth* my lord of Norwych and a-say to get a lysen of hym⁷ þ*at* I may have
þe sacrement ⌜her⌝ in the chapell, be-cause yt ys far to þe chyrche and I am
sekly, and þe p*ar*son ys oftyn owt. For all man*er* of caswelté*s* of me and
myn I wold hauyt grauntyd yf ⌜I⌝⁸ myth⁹. Send me word yf ye her ony
30 tydyng*ys* from yowyr brodyr, how he doth ⌜of⌝¹⁰ hys seknes and in odyr
thyng*ys* as farforth as ye know, as astely as ye may. I thynk long tyll I her
from¹¹ hym for dyu*er*s causys.

God kepe yow. Wretyn in hast at Mawdby on þe Satyrday next be-for
Candelmes Day. Send me an answser of thys lettyr in hast, *and* odyr
tydyng*ys*, &c.

Be yowyr modyr

My cosyn Robard told me þat ther was mor than vij li. of þe mony þat
was payd hym þ*at* was ryght on-rysty and he cowd nowt havyt chaungyd;
he was on-goodly servyd ther-jn.

223. To John Paston III

1475, 5 March

Add. 43490, f. 15ᵛ. 11⅜×8½ in. Hand of no. 221.

This is written, without new address, on the back of John II's letter
no. 289.

The date is shown by the reference to twenty pounds owing to Clere, and by the
renewed request for a licence from the bishop, to be close to that of nos. 221 and
222, which are in the same hand.
F. ii, p. 178. G. 755/866.

John Paston, I send yow Godd*ys* blyssyng *and* myn, letyng yow wete þ*at*
I had non er thys lettyr than on Sent Mathu*ys* Evyn. Yf I myth a¹ had an
massengyr² or thys tym I had sent yt yow. I can yow thank for þe lettyr þ*at*
ye sent to my cosyn Calthorpp *and* me of þe tydyng*ys*;³ I wold ye shuld
5 do soo mor.

⁴ esse *canc.*   ⁵ *Written* hevyr, h- *canc.*   ⁶ alb *canc.*
⁷ to *canc.*   ⁸ *Interl. above* yt *canc.*   ⁹ b *canc.*
¹⁰ *Interl. above* wyth *canc.*   ¹¹ yow *canc.*
223. ¹ *and written,* nd *canc.*   ² to a *canc.*   ³ y *canc.*

As ye may remembyr þat I spak to yow for þe xx^{ti} li. for my cosyn Clere, spek to yowyr hunkyll ther-of *and* send me an ansswer ⌐ther of⌐ in⁴ hast, *and* for þe lycens þat I spak to yow for ⌐to have⌐ þe sacrement in my chapell. Yf ye cannot getyt of þe Busshop of Norwych getyt of þe Busshop of Caunterbery, for þat ys most swyr for all plas.⁵   10

God kepe yow. Wretyn on Myd-lent Sunday.

224. To JOHN PASTON II   1475, 23 May

Add. 27445, f. 89. 11½×8⅞ in. Hand unidentified.

Dorse: Paper seal over wax and string. Address in hand of letter:

Vn-to Syr John Paston be this delyuered in hast.

In John II's hand: *Mens' Maij A° xv°.*

The date after the address is confirmed by the fact that the Tuesday after Trinity Sunday was 23 May in 1475.

F. v, p. 104. G. 758/871.

Ryght welbelouyd son, I grete you well and send you *Crist*es blissyng and myne, desyringe to know how ye faire. I mervaile þat I haue herd no tydynges from you sythe ye sent me þe lettyr off an answere off þe xx^{ty} li. the which I haue layde pleages *fore* to my cosyn Cleere, the which lett*er* was wryten þe xxij^{ty} day off Febru*ar*. And as fore þat money, I can not 5 gete no lenger day þer-off þan Mydsomer, or fourte-nyght affter. And towardys þat money, and þe xx^{ty} li. þat I send yow by-syde to London by Sym, I haue receyued no more money off yowres but as moch as I send yow ⌐wryten in⌐¹ þis lett*er*. And as for any² discharge þat I promysed at þe boroeng³ off ⌐þe xx^{ty} li.⌐ whan I leyde the pleages þer-fore, I thought not but 10 þat your vncle shuld a boroed þem owte, and I to haue had my pleages as well as he his. Neu*er* þe less I shall be þe warere how I shall dele here-afftyr. By my trouth, I wote not how to do þer-fore.

The Kyng goth so nere vs in þis cuntré, both to pooere and ryche, þat I wote not how we shall lyff but yff þe world a-mend. God a-mend it whan 15 his wyll is. ⌐We⌐⁴ can noþer sell corne nere catell to no good preve. Malt is here but at x d. a comb, wheete a comb xxviij^{ty} d., ootes a comb x d. And þer-off is but lytell to geet here at thys tyme. Willi*am* Pecok shall send yow a byll what he hath payde for⁵ yow for ij task*es* at þis tyme, and how he hath purveyde ⌐for⌐⁶ þe remnaunte off y*our* corne and also off oþ*er* thyng*es* þat 20 be necessary þat shuld be purveyd fore in y*our* absence.

⁴ a *canc.*
⁵ *At edge of mount; but strong light shows that no other letter follows.*
224. ¹ *Interl. above* in a byll off wyth *canc.*
² *Apparently from* my.   ³ þer *canc.*   ⁴ *Interl. above* I *canc.*
⁵ þe *canc.*   ⁶ *Interl. above* off *canc.*

Send me word ⌈also⌉⁷ whome ye wyll desyre to do for yow in this contré, or ellys where, in your absence, and⁸ wryte to them to do for yow and they wyll be the better wylled to do for yow. And I wyll do my deuyr for yow
25 also as well as I can.

The somma off money þat I haue receyuyd off Wylliam Pecok: Fyrst— xl s. off Runnham. Item, off Bastwyk—xx s. Item, off Runnham—xx s. Item, ⌈off hym⌉ for barly at Runnham—xx s. Item, off þe fyschynge at Bastwyke—xiij s. iiij d. Item, for barely sold at Runnham—viij s. Summa
30 totalis—vj. li. xvj d. Item, I haue receyuyd off Richard Call off Sporle wodd—xxvj s. viij d. And more shall I hope here-afftyr wyth-in short tym. As I receyue for yow I hope to yeff yow a trew acownt; and þis is all þat I haue receyuyd for yow ȝytt sen ye departyd hens.

God bryng yow well a-geyn to þis contré, to his pleasans and to your
35 wurshyp and profyȝt. Wryten at Mawteby þe xxiijᵗʸ day of May and þe Tewsday next afftyr Trinyté Sonday.

For Goddes loue, and your breþer go ouer þe see, avyse them as ye thynk best for here sauegarde, for som off them be but yonge sawgeres and wote full lytyll what yt meneth to be as a saugere, nor for to endure to do as a
40 sowgere shuld do. God saue yow all and send me good tythynges off yow all. And send ye me word in hast how ye do, for I thynk longe to I here off yow.

Be youre modyr

Item, I wold not in no wyse þat ye shuld noþer sell nor sett to pleage þat ye haue in Runnham, what som euer fortune off þe remnaund, for yt is a praty thyng and resonable well payde and nere thys towne. I wold be ryght sory þat ye shuld for-bere that; I had leuer ye for-bore þat your vncle hath to morgage than þat.

225. To John Paston II   1475, 9 August

Add. 43490, f. 16. 12¼×9½ in. Calle's hand (MS. index attributes wrongly to W. Lomnor).

Dorse: Remnants of red wax over string. Address in Calle's hand:

To the right worshipffull Ser John Paston, knyght, in haste.

Dated.

F. ii, p. 180. G. 761/874 (part).

Right welbeloued son, I grete yow wele and sende you Godes blissyng and myn, desiryng to knowe how ye do and how ye fare. I mervell moche I here no word from you in writyng sith the letter I sent you be Symme weche he delyuerd you at London, wherin I sent you word that I desired

---

⁷ *Interl. above* ho *canc.*   ⁸ let *canc.*

to knowe how ye wold that I, and other weche ye wold, shulde do for you 5
here bothe for your liflode and for other thynges and also for the mater
be-twix your vncle and you, and also be-twix yow and other folkes; for, as
God defende, and ought come to[1] you but weele nowther I nor non other
that I knowe þat[2] owyth yow wery goode wille wot not[3] in what cace ye
stonde nor how ye wold it shulde be dalte wyth, nouther in lyfelode nor in 10
othyr thynges, weche is ryght hevy to me for to remembre concederyng
the viage weche ye be in nough at this tyme. I send to Spoorle to your
fermour for Midsomer pay last pasd,[4] and he sende me word that Tounesend wold haue ⌐it⌐ and charged your ⌐fermour⌐ to pay hym, and ell he
wold swe hes obligacion. I wend ye had ben through wyth Tounesend in 15
all thynges savyng for the ⌐c marke weche ye⌐ borewed of hym last. And
as for Sneylewell, I vndrestonde not who deleth for you there, wherof I
merwelle. And asfor suche money as I haue receyued of yours, non but for
the wode at Sporle xx li., and of Pecok for your lyfelode in Flegge ix li.
xv s. iiij d., nor no more is like to haue this yere, as he telleth me, but for 20
xx quarter barly be-cauce of suche charges as hath be leide vpon your lond
this[5] yere, as he sethe.

Item, on the Sonday next after Sein Jamys William Jenney come to Filby
and entred in-to Holme Halle londes, seyng that he entred in the ryght and
titell of his douterlawe weche was Boys doughter, and there openly[6] made 25
the tenauntes to retourne be j d. and charged them that they shulde not pay
no money nor ⌐no⌐ dewtés longyng to þat londe but only to hym or his son
or suche as they wol assigne, ⌐and he to saue them harmeles⌐ a-yen you and
all other. Wherfore I requere and prey you, as hastely as ye godely may, for
my hertes eace to sende me worde how ye[7] and your brethern fare, and how 30
ye spede in your viages, and a knowelege how ye wold that I and other shulde
dele for you in thes maters a-boue wreten, ar in any other that ye thynke
shuld be profitable for you; and þat I may do I wol do aswele as I can.

And as for tidynges here in this contré, we haue non but that the contry
is bareyn of money and þat my lady of Yorke and all her howsold is here at 35
Sein Benettes and purposed to a-bide there stille til the Kynge come from
be-yonde the see, and lenger if she like the eyre ther, as it is seide.

I thynke ryght longe tille I here som tidynges fro[8] you and from your
brethern. I prey God sende you and al your company goode spede in your
journayes to his plesure,[9] to your worshippes and profightes. Wreten at 40
Mauteby on Sein Laverens Even the xv yere of the regne of Kyng E.
the iiij^th.

Be your moder

---

225. [1] to *repeated.*   [2] þ- *in form of* y, *as also below.*
[3] how ye stonde *canc.*   [4] -d *over a vertical stroke.*
[5] lond *canc.*   [6] charged *canc.*
[7] fa *canc.*   [8] *MS.* for   [9] an *canc.*

226. To Dame Elizabeth Brews   1477, 11 June

Add. 27445, f. 112. $11\frac{1}{8} \times 6\frac{5}{8}$ in. Hand unidentified; the same as that of nos. 227 and 228, though much more regularly written than either.

Dorse: Paper seal. Address in hand of letter, rubbed and partly obliterated:

> *To þe ryght wurchy⟨pful⟩ and my very go⟨od lad⟩y ⟨and co⟩syn ⟨Dame El⟩yz⟨abeth B⟩rews.*

The date appears from the projected marriage of John Paston III and Margery Brews, which took place in 1477 (see especially no. 379).
F. v, p. 184. G. 799/913. C. 84.

Ryght wurchepful *and* my cheff lady *and* cosyn, as hertly as I can I recomaunde me to yow. Madam, lyeketh yow to vndyrstand that þe[1] cheff
cause of my wrytyng to yow at[2] thys season ys thys. I wot well yt ys not
vnreme*m*bred w*yth* yow the large comunycacyon[3] that dyuers tymes hathe
5 ben had towchy*n*g the maryage of my cosyn Margery yowyr dowghter *and*
my son John, of whyche I haue ben as glad, *and* now late-wardes as sory,
as euyr I was for eny maryage in my*n* lyve. And wher*e* or in whom the
defawte of þe breche ys, I can haue no p*ar*fyte knowlage; but, madam, yf
yt be in me or eny of myn, I prey yow assy*n*gne a day when my cosyn yowyr
10 husbond and ye thynk to be at Norwych to-ward*es* Salle, and I wyll com
theder to yow, and I thynk or ye and I departe þat þe defawte schall be
knowe wher*e* yt ys, and also that, w*yth* yowyr advyse and helpe *and* my*n*
to-gedyrs, we schall take some wey þat yt schal not breke; for yf yt dyd yt
wer non honoure to neyther p*ar*tyes, and in cheff to them in whom the
15 defawte ys, consyderyng that ⌐it⌐ ys so ferre spokun.

And, madam, I prey yow þat I may haue p*ar*fyte knowlage be my son
Yelu*er*ton, berar here-of, when thys metyng schall be, yf ye thynk it
expedyent, and þe soner the better in eschewy*n*g of worse; for, madam, I
know well yf yt be not co*n*cludyd in ryght schort tyme, that as for my son,
20 he entendyth to doo ryght well by my cosyn Margery *and* not so well by
hym-sylf, and þat schuld be to me, nor I trust to yow, no gret plesur*e* yf
yt so fortunyd—as God deffend, whom I be-seche to send yow your levest
desyers.

Madam, I be-sech yow þat I may be recomawndyd by þis bylle to my
25 cosyn yowyr husbond, and to my cosyn Margery, to whom I supposyd to
haue gevyn an othyr name or thys tyme. Wretyn at Mawteby on Seynt
Barnaby is Day.

By yo*ur* MARGARET PASTON

226. [1] þ- *in form of* y *regularly in this hand.*   [2] þ¹s *canc.*
     [3] *Dotted circumflex over final letter of this and several other words, apparently marking* n *and* m: son *ll. 6, 19,* them *l. 14,* hym *l. 21. Other superior strokes have doubtful value, as in* assyngne *l. 9 where the first* n *is apparently intended by a stroke above* -gn-.

227. To JOHN PASTON II: draft   1477, 11 August

Add. 27446, f. 2. 12¼ × 8⅜ in. Hand of no. 226.

Dorse: Marks of rough folding, no seal or address.

Dated. This is evidently a draft of Margaret's reply to no. 308.
    F. v, p. 200. G. 803/917.

Yt ys soo þat I vndyr-stonde be yowyr letter wretyn þe Thyrsday nexte
be-fore Seynt Lauerons þat ȝe wulde haue knowlage how þat I wuld[1] be
demenyd in Cokettys matere, qweche I send yow here-vndyr wretyn. I
putte yow in certeyn þat I wull neuyr pay hym peny of þat duty þat ys
owyng to hym thow he sue me for yt, not of myn owyn pursse, ⌐for⌐ I wul 5
nat be compellyd to pay yowyr dettys a-ȝens my well; and ⌐thow⌐[2] I wuld,
I may nat. Where-fore I a-wyse yow to see ⌐me⌐ sauyd harmelesse a-ȝens
hym for yowyr owyn a-wavntage in tyme cumyng, ⌐for⌐[3] yf I pay yt, at[4]
longe wey ȝe xall bere þe losse. And where ⌐as⌐ ȝe wryte to me þat I gaue
yow xx li. *and* promysyd odyr xx li., þat ys nat soo; for I wutte wele yf I 10
had soo doon ȝe wuld nat assynyd me, be yowyr letterys of yowyr owyn
hande-wrytyng þe whech I haue to schew, þat I schuld resseyue a-ȝen þe
same summe of Wylliam Pecok *and* of yowyr fermorys and byars of ⌐yowyr⌐[5]
wood of Sporle. And[6] take þis for a full conclusyon in thys matere, for yt
xall be noon othyr-wyse for me þan I wryte here to yow.   15

    I meruel meche þat ȝe haue delte aȝen soo symply[7] wyth Sporle, con-
syderyng þat ȝe *and* yowyr frendys had so mech to doo for to geetyt yow
a-ȝen onys, and ye hauyng noo gretter materes of charge þan ȝe haue had
sythyn[8] yt was laste pleggyt owte. Yt causyth me to be in gret dowte ⌐of
yow⌐ what yowyr dysposycion wul be here-aftyr for swheche lyfelood as 20
I haue be dysposyd ⌐be-fore þis tyme⌐ to leue yow after my decesse, for I
thynke veryly þat ye wulde be dysposyd here-aftyr to selle or sette to
morgage þe lond þat ye xulde haue after ⌐me⌐, yowyr modyr, as gladdly
and rathyr þan þat lyfelood þat ye haue after yowyr fadyr. Yt greuyth me
to thynke vpon yowyr gydeyng after þe greet good þat ȝe haue had in 25
yowyr rewle sythyn yowyr fadyr[9] deyyd, whom God ⌐assoyle⌐,[10] and soo
symply spendyt ⌐as yt hath ben⌐. God geue yow grace to be ⌐of⌐[11] sadde *and*
good dysposyn here-after, to hys plesans *and* conforte to me and to all yowyr
frendys *and* to yowyr wurchyp[12] *and* profyte here-after.

    And as for yowyr brothyr Wylliam, I wuld ye xulde purvey for hys 30
fyndyng, for as I told yow þe laste tyme ⌐þat⌐ ye ware at home I wuld no

---

227.   [1] -d *over* le.   [2] *Interl. above* yow *canc.*
     [3] *Interl. above* and *canc.*   [4] yᵉ *canc.*
     [5] *Interl. above* yᵉ *canc.*   [6] *Ampersand preceded by* and *canc.*
     [7] fo *canc.*   [8] ye *canc.*
     [9] dy *canc.*   [10] *Interl. above* absolue *canc.*
    [11] *Interl. above* as *canc.*   [12] *MS.* wurchyr.

lenger fynde hym ⌐at my cost *and* charge¬. Hys boord *and* hys scole hyer
ys owyng sythyn Seynt Thomas day a-fore Cristmesse, and he hathe greet
nede of gownys *and* odyr gere þat whare necessary for hym to haue in haste.
35 I wulde ȝe xulde reme[m]byrt *and* purvey þere-fore; as for me, I wul nat.

I thynke ȝe sette butte lytyl be myn blyssyng, *and* yf ye dede ye wulde a
desyyrdyt in yowyr wrytyng to me. God make yow a good man to hys
plesans. Wretyn at Mawteby þe day after Seynt Lauerons þe yere *and* þe
renge of Kyng E. þe iiijᵗᵉ þe xvij ȝere.

40   By yowyr modyr

228. To John Paston II: draft   1478, 27 May

Add. 43491, f. 24. 12×9⅞ in. Hand of no. 226.

Dorse: Marks of rough folding, no seal or address.

Dated.
  F. ii, p. 264. G. 818/933.

I greet yow wel *and* send yow Goddys blyssyng *and* myn, latyng yow wete
þat I haue sent yow be Whetelé þe clothe of golde, chargyng yow þat it be
not solde to non othere vse þan to þe performyng of yowyr fadyrs tovmbe,
as ȝe send me worde in wrytyng. Yf ye sellyt to any othyr vse, by my[1]
5 trowthe I xall neuer trost yow wyll I leue. Remembyr þat yt coste me xxᵗⁱ
marke þe pleggyng owte of yt, and yf I where nat glad to se þat made I
wolde not departe from it. Remembyr yow what charge I haue had wyth
yow of late, whyche wyl not be for my ease þis ij ȝere. Whan ȝe may better
I trost ȝe whyll remembyr yt.

10   My cosyn Clere dothe as meche coste at Bromhom as whylle drawe an
c li. vpon þe deskys in þe quere *and* in othyr placys, and Heydon in lyke
whyse; and yf þere xulde no thyng be don for ȝour fadyr, yt wolde be to
gret a schame for vs alle, and in cheffe to se hym[2] lye as he dothe.

Also as I vnder-stond þat my cosyn Robert Clere thynkyth gret on-
15 kyndenesse in delyng wyth hym of Pecoke for certeyn pasture þat ȝe
grawntyd hym to haue, *and* Pecok hath latyn it to othyr suche as he lyste
to lete yt to. Not wyth-stondyng my cosyn hath leyd þe pasture wyth hys
catell, *and* Pecok hathe strenyd them. I thynk þis delyng is not as yt xulde
be. I wolde þat iche of yow xulde do for othere, and leue as kynnysmen *and*
20 frendys; for suche seruawntys may make trobyll by-twyxe yow, wheche
where a-geynste cortesey, so nyhe newborys as ȝe be. He ys ⌐a¬ man of
substaunce *and* worchyp, *and* so wylle be takyn in thys schyre, and I were
lothe þat ȝe xulde lese þe good ⌐wylle¬ of suche as may do for yow.

228. ¹ trowth *canc.*   ² hy *canc.*

Item, where as ʒe haue begonne your cleyme in Heylysdon *and* Drayton, I pray God send yow good spede and foderaunce in yt. ʒe haue³ as good a ceason as ʒe wulde wysche, consyderyng þat your aduersary standys not in best ⌈favyr⌉ wyth þe Kynge. Also ʒe haue þe⁴ voyse in þis contré þat ʒe may do as meche wyth þe Kyng as ony knygth þat ys longyng to þe Corte; yf yt be so, I pray God contynuyt. And also þat ʒe xuld mary rygth nygth of þe Qwenys blood. Qwat sche ys we are not as certeyn, but yf yt be so þat yowyr lond schuld come a-gayne by þe reason of your maryage, and to be sett in rest, at þe reuerence of God for-sake yt nowt yf ʒe can fynde in your harte to loue hyr, so þat sche be suche on as ʒe can thynke to haue jssv by; or ellys by my trowth I had rathere þat ʒe neuer maryd in your lyffe. Also yf yowyr matere take not now to good effecte, ʒe *and* all yowyr frendys may repent them þat ʒe be-gan your cleyme wyth-owte þat ʒe haue take suche a suyr wey as may be to your intent, for many inconuenyens þat may falle þere-of.

God send yow good spede in all yowyr maters. Wretyn at Mawteby þe day after Seynt Austyn in May, þe xviij ʒere of Kyng Edward þe iiij^te.

Be yowyr modyr

229. Indenture of lease 1480, 1 August

Norfolk and Norwich Record Office, Bradfer-Lawrence Collection, vɪ b (iv). $15\frac{1}{4} \times 6\frac{3}{4}$ -7 in (top indented). Clerk's hand, unidentified; signature evidently autograph.

Dorse blank. Pendant seal of red wax, the device a capital H.

Unprinted.

This indenture made the first day of August the xx yer of the regne of Kyng Edward the iiij^th betwen Margaret Paston, late the wif of John Paston, squier, on the one part, and Thomas Brigge of Salle, gentilman, on the other part, witnesseth that the seid Margaret hath dimised and lete to ferme to the seid Thomas hir maner in Salle in the shire of Norffolk callid Kyrkhall, othirwise callid Flegge Halle, lying in Salle, Woddallyng, Oulton, Thyrnyng, Heydon, and other townys adioynyng, with the appurtenauntez, and hir maner in Briston and other townys adioynyng, with all the appurtenauntez, and all other londes and tenementez lying in the seid townys, to have and to hold the seid maners, londes, and tenementez, with the appurtenauntez, to the seid Thomas and to his assignes for the terme of vij yerys, the terme therof to begynne at the feste of Seint Michael th'arcaungell next comyng after the date of thise presentez indentures and to endure to the ende of vij yerys than next folowyng plenerly to be complete; paying therfore yerly vnto the seid Margaret or hir assignes xviij li. of laufull Englissh

³ be *canc.*   ⁴ wo *canc.*

money at too termes, that is to sey, ix li. at Crouchemasse next after the date forseid and ix li. at Halwemesse than next folowyng, and so forth yerly at Crouchemesse and Halwemasse by evyn porcions during the seid terme, and ix li. at Halwemasse next after the seid terme determyned. Ferthermore it
20 is accorded betwix the seid parties that the seid Thomas shall discharge the seid Margaret and hir heires of all sewtes, rentes, and seruices perteignyng to the seid maners or either of them during the seid terme at his coste, and he shall have vnderwode and hokeware growyng in the seid maners for the reparyng of the dekes, savyng the spryng, duryng the seid terme, and
25 levyng the dekes defensed sufficiently at the ende of his terme. Also the seid Thomas shall have the profitez of the courtes during his terme, and the courtes shall be holde and kept by the styward of the seid Margaret or hir depute at the costes of the seid Thomas, provided allewey that the seid Thomas shall take non avauntage ne goodes of the bondemen and women
30 belongyng to the seid maners save onely her chyvage, sutez to courtes, and amercymentes, and such seruice as is behouefull to the seid maners, they takyng resonable wages as they deserue during the seid terme by licence of the seid Margaret; but that the seid Margaret shall iustifie them and seise them and ther goodes and manumyse them at hir pleaser, and such as duelle
35 with hir or hir sones to be discharged of sewte, seruice, and chyvage whiles they duelle with them. Ferthermore, wher the seid Thomas and Thomas Herberd of Salle, chapman, are bounde to the seid Margaret by obligacion of xl marc.[1] bering date the day of the date of thise presentes, the seid Margaret graunteth and wulleth that if the seid Thomas paie or do paie to
40 the seid Margaret yerly xviij li. as is aboveseid, at such dayes as be lymyted and afore specifijd, that than the seid obligacion shall stande in no strength ne effect, and ellys it shall stande and remayne in strength and effect.

In witnesse wherof the parties beforseid have to thise presentez indentures alternatly sett ther sealles. Yevyn the day and yer aboveseid.

45   THOMAS BRYGGE

230. Copy of will   Nominally 1482, 4 February

Add. Charter 17253. Parchment roll, two skins stitched together, c. 12 × 66 in. Unidentified clerk's hand, marginalia in John Paston III's hand. No seal or signature.

Dorse blank except for modern notes.

This was evidently a working copy used by John III as executor, and was doubtless made after probate was granted in 1484. In addition to his marginalia recorded in the footnotes many paragraphs are marked in the margin with a cross in his hand as if he ticked them off as they were dealt with.

229. [1] Curl on c.

The will is registered in the Consistory Court of Norwich, Reg. A. Caston ff. 224^b–228^a, with record of probate at Norwich on 18 December 1484. The wording is almost identical, but there are many minor differences of spelling. A selection of the more significant variants is given in the notes, marked *R*.

Sandford's Genealogy, p. 18, contains the following passage which shows something of the relation between his copies of documents and the originals:

Her last Will and testament remaineth yet to be seen at Paston, sealed with Two seales of Arms, whereof the one is the coate of Mauteby and the other is the coate of Berry. In which Will are written these words. Item—I will that mine Executors provide a stone of marble to be laid aloft upon my grave, within a yeere next after my decease, and upon that stone I will have four Escocheons, sett at the Foure corners thereof; whereof I will the first scochen shall be of my husbands Armes and mine departed. The seconde of Mautebyes Arms and Berneyes of Redeham departed. The third of Mautebyes Armes and the Lord Lovyne departed. The fourth of Mautebyes Armes and Sir Roger Beauchamp departed, and in the middest of the said stone I will have a scochen set of Mautebyes Arms alone. (Cf. ll. 16–23 below.)

G. 861/978.

In the name of God, amen. I, Margaret Paston, widowe, late the[1] wiff of John Paston, squier, dought*er* and heire[2] to John Mauteby, squier, hole of spirit and mynde,[3] with p*ar*fite avisement and good delib*er*aci*on*, the iiij^{te} day of February in the yer[4] of our Lord God a m^{l}cccclxxxj, make my testament and last wille in this fourme folowyng.

First, I betake my sowle to God Almyghty[5] and to Our Lady his blissed moder, Seint Michael, Seint John Baptist, and to alle seintes, and my body to be beried in the ele of the cherch[6] of Mauteby byfore[7] the ymage of Our Lady there, jn which ele reste the bodies of diu*er*s of myn auncet*er*es, whos sowles God assoile.

It*em*, I bequethe to the high awter of the ⌜seid⌝ cherch of Mauteby xx s.[8]

It*em*, I wulle[9] that[10] the seid ele in which[11] my body shalbe[12] beried be newe roved,[13] leded, and glased, and the walles therof heyned conuenyently and werkmanly.[14]

It*em*, I wull that myn executo*ur*s p*ur*veye a[15] stoon of marble to be leyde alofte vpon my grave within a yer next aft*er* my decesse; and vpon that stoon I wulle have iiij scochens sett at the iiij corners,[16] wherof I wulle that the first scochen shalbe of my husbondes armes and myn dep*ar*ted, the ij^{de} of Mawtebys[17] armes and Berneys of Redham dep*ar*ted, the iij^{de} of

5

10

15

20

---

230. [1] *R* þ^e, *with* þ *in form of* y, *throughout.*   [2] *R* heyere.
[3] *R* sperite *and* mende.   [4] *R* ჳere.   [5] *R* almity.
[6] *R* chyrche (*usually*).   [7] *R* beforn.   [8] *In margin* xx s.
[9] *R* wille (*frequent, varying with* wylle, wull(e), wolle).
[10] *R* þ^t, *with* þ *in form of* y, *throughout.*   [11] *R* wyche (*frequently*).
[12] *R* schalle be.   [13] *R* newrouyd.   [14] *R* wark-.
[15] *No space, as often with* a *below.*   [16] *R* cornellys.
[17] *No space;* -s *of long form, unusual finally and apparently added later. So also below in this phrase.*

Mawtebys armes and the Lord Loveyn dep*a*rted, the iiij^te of Mawtebys
armes and Sir Roger Beauchamp dep*a*rted. And in myddys of the seid
stoon I wull have a scochen ⌈sett⌉ of Mawtebys armes allone, and vnder
the same thise wordes wretyn: 'In God is my trust'; with a scripture
25 wretyn in the verges[18] therof rehersyng thise word*es*: 'Here lieth Margret
Paston, late the wif of John Paston, dought*er* and heire of John Mawteby,
squier', and forth in the same scripture rehersed the day of the moneth and
the yer that I shall decesse, 'on whos[19] sowle God have m*er*cy'.

Item, I wulle that myn executo*urs* ⌈shall⌉ p*u*rveye xij pore meen of my
30 ten*a*untes, or other if they suffice not, the which I wulle shalbe apparailled
in white gownes with hodes according, to holde xij torches abowte myn
herse or bere at such tyme as I shalbe beried, during the exequies and
masse of my berying; which xij torches I wille remayne in the seid cherch
of Mawteby whil they may last[20] for my yerday. Which yerday I wull myn
35 heire kepe in the same cherch for me, my seid husbond, and myn aunce-
te*res* yerly during the t*er*me of xij yeres next aft*er* my decesse;[21] and I wull
that ich of the seid xij pore meen[22] the day of my beriing have iiij d. Also I
wull that iche p*re*ste being at my berying and masse have viij d. and ich
clerk in surplys iij d. Also I wull that the prest which shall berie me have
40 vj s. viij d., so that he seye ou*er* me at the tyme of my berying all the hole
s*er*uice that to the berying belongeth.

Also I wull that from the day and tyme that I am beried vnto the ende of
vij yeres than next folowyng be ordeyned a taper of wexe[23] of a li. to brenne
vpon my grave ich Sonday and haliday at all diuine s*er*uice to be seid or
45 sunge[24] in the seid cherch, and dailly at the masse of that preest that shall
singe there in the seid ele for my sowle.

It*em*, I wulle that vj[25] tapers ich of iiij li. brenne abowte myn herse ⌈the
day of my beryng, of which I wull that iiij yerly be kept to brenne abowte
myn herse⌉ whan my yerday shalbe kept aslong as they may honestly s*er*ue.
50 Item, I wulle have an honest seculer prest to synge and pray in the
seid ele for my sowle, the sowles of my father ⌈and mother⌉,[26] the sowle of
the seid John Paston, late my husbond, and for the sowlys of his aunceteres
and myn during the t*er*me of vij yeres next aft*er* my decesse.

It*em*, I wull that myn executo*urs* p*u*rveye a compleet legende[27] in oon
55 book and an antiphoner[28] in an other book, which bookes I wull be yeven
to abide ⌈ther⌉[29] in the seid cherch to the wursship of God aslonge as they
may endure.[30]

---

18 *R* werges.　　　　19 *R* hose.　　　　20 *R* lest.
21 *In margin* Memorandum v yer to come to kepe þe yerday.
22 *R* men.　　　　　　　　　　　　　23 *R* taper wax.
24 *R* soungon.　　　　　　　　　　　25 *R* vij.
26 *R* fader *and* modere.　　　　　27 *R* legent.
28 *Cross by John III above this word.*　29 *R* omits.
30 *In margin* v li. vj s. viij d. *above* vj li. xiij s. iiij d. *canc.*

Item, I wulle that euery houshold[31] in Mauteby, as hastily as it may be conuenyently doo[32] after my decesse, have xij d.

Item, to the emendyng of the cherch of Freton in Suffolk I bequethe a chesiple and an awbe.[33]

And I wull that ich houshold being[34] my tenaunt there have vj d.

And I bequethe to the emendement[35] of the cherch of Basyngham a chesiple and an awbe.[36]

And I wull that euery houshold there have viij d.

Item, I bequeth to the emendyng[35] of the cherch of Matelask a chesiple and an awbe.[37]

And I wull that euery pore houshold that are my tenauntes there have viij d.

Item, I bequethe to the emendyng of the cherch[38] of Gresham a chesiple and an awbe.[36]

And I wull that ich pore houshold that be my tenauntes there have vj d.

Item, I wull that ich pore houshold late my tenauntes at Sparham have vj d.

Item, to the reparacion ⌐of the cherch⌐[39] of Redham, there as I was borne, I bequeth v marc. and a chesiple of silk with an awbe with myn armes therupon, to the emendement of the same cherche.[40]

Item, to ich of the iiij houshes of freres in Norwich, xx s.

Item, to ich of the iiij houshes of freres of Yermouth and at the south toun to pray for my sowle I bequeth xx s.

Item, to the ankeres[41] at the Frere Prechours in Norwich I bequeth iij s. iiij d.

And[42] to the ankeres in Conesford I bequeth iij s. iiij d.

Item, to the anker at the White Freres in Norwich I bequeth iij s. iiij d.

Item, to ich hole and half susters at Normans in Norwich, viij d.

Item, to the Deen and his bretheren of the Chepell of Feld,[43] to the vse of the same place to seye a *dirige* and a masse[44] for my sowle, xx s.

Item, to the hospitall of Seint Gile in Norwich, also for a *dirige* and a masse for my sowle, xx s.

Item, to ich of the iiij pore meen and to either[45] of the susters of the seid hospitall, ij d.

Item, to the mother cherch[46] of Norwich for a *dirige* and masse, xx s.

Item, to iche lepre man and woman at the v yates in Norwich, iij d.

---

[31] *R* howsold.
[32] *R* conuenyently be do.
[33] *In margin* xvj s. viij d.
[34] *Dash over erasure.*
[35] *R* mendmente.
[36] *R* aube; *in margin* xvj s. viij d.
[37] *R* haube.
[38] *R* chyrche emendmente.
[39] *R on line.*
[40] *In margin* v li.
[41] *R* ankeresse.
[42] *R* Item.
[43] *R* chapelle a felde.
[44] *R* messe.
[45] *R* yche.
[46] *R* moder chyrche

And[42] to ich forgoer at euery of the seid yates, ij d.

95 Item, to ich lepre without the north gates at Yermouth, iij d., and to the[45] forgoer ther, ij d.

Item, to ich houshold of the parissh of Seint Peter of Hungate in Norwich that[47] wull receyve almes have iiij d.

Item, I wull have a *dirige* and a masse for my sowle at the parissh cherch
100 of Seint Michael[48] of Coslany in Norwich, and that euery preste ther havyng his stipend being therat have iiij d., and ich clerk in surplys of the same parissh than ther being have ij d.,[49] and the parissh clerk vj d., and the curat that shall seye high masse have xx d. And I bequeth to the reparacion of the bellys[50] of the same cherch vj s. viij d., and to the sexteyn there, to rynge
105 at the seid *dirige* and masse, xx d.

Item, I wull that myn executours shall geve to the sustentacion[51] of the parson or preste that shall for the tyme mynystre the sacramentez and diuine seruice in the cherch of Seint Petre of Hungate ⌈in Norwich⌉[39] xx li. ⌈of laufull money⌉,[52] which xx li. I wull it be putt in the rule and dispo-
110 sicion of the cherch reves of the same cherch for the tyme being, by the ouersight[53] of the substanciall persones of the seid parissh, to this intent that the seid cherch reves[54], by the ouersight as is befor-seid,[55] shall yerly yeve, if it so be that þe profites of the seid cherch suffice not to fynde a prest after ther discrecions, part of the seid xx li. to the seid parson or
115 preste vnto the seid xx li. be expended.

Item, I bequeth to Edmund Paston, my sone, a standing pece white couered, with a white garleek heed vpon the knoppe and a gilt pece couered with an vnicorne, a fetherbedde[56] and a traumsom[57] at Norwich and the costers of worsted that he hath of me.

120 Item, I bequeth to Katerine his wiff a purpill girdill herneisid[58] with siluer and gilt, and my ⌈bygge⌉ bras chafour, a brasen morter with an jren pestell, and a stoon morter of cragge.

Item, I yeve and graunte to Robert, sone of the seid Edmund, all my swannes morken with the merke called Dawbeneys merk and with the merk
125 late Robert Cutler, ⌈clerk⌉,[39] to have, hold, and enjoye the seid swannes with the seid merkes to the seid Robert and his heires for euermore.

Item, I bequeth to Anne, my doughter, wiff of William Yeluerton, my grene hangyng in my parlour at Mauteby, a standing cuppe with a couer gilt with a flatte knoppe, and a flatte pece with a couer gilt withoute,[59]
130 xij siluer spones, a powder boxe with a foot and a knoppe enamelled blewe, my best corse girdill, blewe herneised with siluer and gilt, my premer,[60] my

[47] R wyche	[48] R Sent Michill.	[49] *From* j d.; R j d.
[50] R bell *with* ll *crossed.*	[51] -st- *corr. from* ss.	[52] *In margin* xx li.
[53] R -sithe.	[54] R ryues.	[55] R afore rehersyd.
[56] R feder- (*usually*).		[57] R traunsom.
[58] her- *repr. by flourished* h; *spelt in full in l. 131.*		[59] R wᵗ on.
[60] R premere.		

bedes of siluer enamelled. It*em*, I bequeth to the seid[61] Anne my fetherbedde w*ith* sillo*ur*, curteyns, and tester in my p*ar*lo*ur* at Mauteby, w*ith* a
white cou*er*ing, a peir[62] blankett*es*, ij peir of my fynest shetes ich of iij
webbes, a fyne hedshete of ij webbes, my best garnyssh of pewter vessell, 135
ij basyns with ij ewres, iiij candelstek*es* of oon sorte, ij bras pottes, ij bras
pannes, a bras chafour to sett by the fyre,[63] and a chafour for colys.

Item, I require myn executo*urs* to paie to the seid William Yelverton
and Anne the money that I shall owe them of ther mariage money the day
of my decesse, of such money as shalbe receyved of such londes as I have 140
putte in feffement to accomplissh my wille.

Item, I bequeth to Willia*m* Paston, my sone, my standing cuppe chased
p*ar*cell gilt with a cou*er* with myn armes in the botom, and a flatte pece
with a traill vpon the cou*er*, xij siluer spones, ij siluer saltes wherof oon is
cou*er*ed, the hole bedde of borde Alisaundre as it hangeth on the gret 145
chaumber at Mauteby, with the fetherbedde, bolster,[29] blankett*es*, and
cou*er*yng[64] to the same, ij peir shetes, ij pilwes,[65] and my best[66] palet, a
basyn, an[67] ewre, and a[68] litel white bedde that hangeth ou*er* the gresyngg*es*
in the litell chaumber at Mauteby for a trussyng bedde.

Item, I bequeth an c m*ar*c. ⌈in money⌉[69] to be paied and bestowed tờ the 150
vse and byhoff of the seid Willia*m* Paston aft*er* this fo*ur*me folowyng, that
is to sey, in p*ur*chasyng of asmoch[70] lond to him and to his heir*es* as may
be had with the same money, or ellys to bye a warde to be maried to him if
eny[71] such may be goten, or ellys to be paied to him assone as it may be
conuenyently[72] gadered and receyved of succh londes as by me are put in 155
feffement as is beforseid, aft*er* the ele in Mauteby cherch be fynsshed and
p*ar*fourmed as is beforseid, and aft*er* the stipend of the p*re*ste lymyted to
singe for me be yerly levied, aswell as the money be[73] dispended vpon the
keping of my yerly obite. And if the seid William dye or he come to the age
of xxj yer, than the seid c m*ar*c. to be disposed for the wele of my sowle by 160
myn executours.

Item, I bequeth to John Paston, my sone, a gilt cuppe standyng with a
cou*er* and a knoppe lich a garleek[74] heed, vj gobelett*es* of siluer with oon
cou*er*.

Item, I bequeth to Margery Paston, the wif of the seid John, my pixt of 165
siluer with ij siluer cruett*es* and my massebook, with all myn awterclothes.

Item,[75] I bequeth to Willia*m* Paston, sone of the seid John Paston, and
Elizabeth his suster, c m*ar*c. whan they come to laufull age, to be take and
receyved of the lond*es* beforseid. And if either of them die[76] or they come

---

[61] *R* syde. [62] *R* peyere (*regularly*). [63] *R* fyour.
[64] *R* curyng. [65] *R* pyllows. [66] *R* peste.
[67] *R* And. [68] *R* the. [69] *R* mony *on line.*
[70] *R* as myche [71] *R* ony. [72] *R* conuenyenly be.
[73] *R* to be. [74] *MS.* garkeek *R* garleke.
[75] *In margin* c m*ar*ke solut' E P l m*ar*ke. [76] *R* dey *regularly.*

170 to the seid age, than I wull that the part of him or hir so deying remayne to
the survyver of them at laufull age; and if they bothe dye or they come to
the seid age, than I wull that the seid c marc. be disposed for the helth of
my sowle by th'avise of myn executours.

Item, I bequeth to Custaunce, bastard doughter of John Paston, knyght,
175 whan she is xx yer of age x marc., and if she die bifore the seid age, than I
wull that the seid x marc. be disposed by myn executours.[77]

Item, I bequeth to John Calle, sone of Margery ⌈my⌉ doughter, xx li.
whan he cometh to the age of xxiiij yer. And if the seid John dye or he
cometh to the seid age, than I wulle that the seid xx li. evenly be diuided
180 attwen[78] William and Richard, sones of the seid Margery, whan they come
to the age of xxiiij yer; and if either of the seid William and Richard dye
or he come to the seid age, than I wull that the part of him so dying remayne
to the survyver. And if bothe the seid William and Richard dye or the[79]
come to the seid age, than I wull that the seid xx li. be disposed by the good
185 advys[80] of myne executours for me and my frendes.

Item, I bequethe to Marie Tendall, my goddoughter,[81] my peir bedys of
calcidenys gaudied with siluer and gilt.

Item, I wull that ich of myn other[82] godchilder be rewarded by th'avyse
of John Paston my sone.

190 Item, I bequeth to Agnes Swan, my seruaunt, my musterdevelys gown
furred with blak, and a girdell of blak herneised[58] with siluer gilt and
enamelled, and xx s. in money.

Item, to Simon Gerard my siluer gobelet cured, and a flatt pece with
verges gilt, and myn hole litel white bedde in my chapell chaumber at
195 Mauteby,[83] with the fetherbedde lich as it is nowe in the seid chapell, with
a peir blankettes, a peir shetes, and a pilwe[84] of doun.

Item, to John Heythe a materas with a traunsom, a peir shetes, a peir
blankettes, and a couerlight.

Item, I wull that myn housholt[85] be kept after my decesse by half a yer,
200 and that my seruauntes wages be truly paied at ther departing, and also that
euery persone being my seruaunt the day of my decesse have a quarter
wages beside that they at her[86] departing have do seruice fore.

Item, I wull that all such maners, londes, and[29] tenementes, rentes, and
seruices which are descended vnto me by weye of inheritaunce immediatly
205 after my decesse remayne vnto myn heires accordyng to the last wille of
Robert Mauteby,⌈squier, my grauntfader⌉,[39] except such londes as I have
putte in feffement to accomplissh therof my last wille, and except v marc.

<hr>

[77] *In margin* x marke *erased.*
[79] *R* they.
[81] *R* godowghter.
[83] *R omits these two words.*
[85] *R* housholde.

[78] *R* be twen.
[80] *R* avyce.
[82] *R* oder.
[84] *R* pelowe.
[86] *R* ther.

of annuyté which I have graunted out of the maner of Freton in Suffolk to
Edmund Paston my sone, Katerine his wiff, and Robert ther sone, for
terme of ther lyves.　　　　　　　　　　　　　　　　　　　　　　210

Item, I bequeth to Anne, my doughter, x li. to hir propre vse.

And to Osbern Berney x marc. of the money comyng of the londes by
me put in feffement as is beforseid.[87]

Item, I wull that the residewe ⌐of the stuffe⌐[139] of myn houshold vn-
biquothen[88] be diuided equally betwen Edmund and William, my sones, 215
and Anne, my doughter.

The residewe of all my godes and catall,[89] and dettes to me owing, I
yeve and comitte to the good disposicion of myn executours to parfourme
this my testament and last wille, and in other dedes of mercye for my sowle,
myn aunceterez sowlez, and alle Cristen sowles, to the most pleaser[90] of 220
God and profit to my sowle.

Of this my testament I make and ordeyne the seid John Paston, squier,
my sone, Thomas Drentall,[91] clerk, Simon Gerard, and Walter Lymyngton
myn executours.

And I bequeth to the seid John Paston for his labour x li.　　　　225

And to iche of myn other executours for their labour v marc.

In witnesse wherof to this my present testament I have putto my seal.[92]
Yevyn[93] day and yer biforseid.[87]

---

[87] *R* be-fore rehersyd.　　　　　[88] *R* vnbequethe.　　　　　[89] *R* catallys.
[90] *R* plesour.　　　[91] *R* Trendall.　　　[92] *R* putt my sell.　　　[93] *R* yowyn.

JOHN PASTON II

231. To John Paston I   1461, 23 August

Add. 34888, ff. 189ᵛ–190ʳ. 11¼ × 16¾ in. Autograph.

Dorse: Conclusion of text. Traces of red wax. Address autograph:

To my rythg reuerent and worchypfoll fadere John Paston, esquyere, dwellyng
jn Heylysdon, be thys lettere delyueryd jn haste.

The date appears from the references to Edward IV's journeys. John II was
evidently with him in Sussex when this letter was written, and expected to go with
him to Wales. Edward was in Sussex in late August 1461 (Scofield, i. 198), and at
Ludlow from 18 to 26 September, though he did not himself go into Wales (Scofield, i. 202).

     F. iv, p. 46. G. 410/477. C. 27 (part).

Most reuerent *and* worschepful fadyre, I rekomawnd me hertylye, *and*
submytt me lowlely to yowre good faderhood, besechyng yow fore cheryté
of yowre dayly blyssyng. I beseche yow to hold me ascewsyd that I sente
to yowe none erste no wrythgtyng, fore I kowd not spede to myn jntent the
5 materys that ye sent to me fore. I¹ laboryd dayly my lord of Estsexe,²
treserere of Ynglond, to haue meuyd the Kyng bothe of the manere [of]
Deddham and of³ the byll copye of the corte rolle euerye mornyng ore he
went to the Kyng, *and* often tymys jnquieryd of hym and he had meuyd the
Kyng in these materys. He answeryd me naye,⁴ seyyng it was no tyme, *and*
10 seyd he wold it ware osse fayne spedd os I my-selfe; so³ offte tymys de-layeng
me that jn trowthe I thowt ta haue send yowe word that I felyd by hym
that he was not wyllyng to meue the Kyng there-in. Neuerthe-lesse I
lawboryd to hym contynually *and* prayed Baronners, hys man, to remembyre hym of it. I told offten tymys to my seyd lord that I had a man
15 teryyn jn⁵ town that I schuld a sente to yow fore othyre sundry materys,
and he teryid fore⁶ no thyng but⁷ that I⁵ mythg send yowe by hym an
answere of the seyd materys; othyre tymys⁸ besechyng hym to spede me in
thoys materys⁹ fore thys¹⁰ cawse that ye schuld thynke no defawte jn me

---

231. ¹ haue *canc.*   ² the the *canc.*   ³ of *canc.*   ⁴ *Ampersand canc.*
    ⁵ *No space.*   ⁶ m *canc.*   ⁷ for *canc.*   ⁸ I *canc.*
    ⁹ that *canc.*   ¹⁰ cla *canc.*

fore remember*yng*[11] jn the seyd mater*ys*. And nowe of late I, remember*yng* hym of the same mat*er*, jnq*u*iryd ⌐if⌐[12] he had meuyd the Kyng*ys* hythgnes 20 there-in; and he answeryd me þat he hadde felte and meuyd the Kyng there-in, rehersyng the Kyng*ys* answere þer-in: how þat, when he had meuyd the Kyng in the seyd man*er* of Dedh*am*, besechyng hym to be yowre good lord there-in, konsyderyng the seruyse *and* trewe hart[4] that ye haue done *and* owthg to hym, *and* jn espesyal the[13] rygth that ye haue 25 there-to, he seyd he wold be yowre good lord ther*e*in as he wold be to the[14] porest man jn Inglond. He wold hold w*yth* yowe jn yowre rygth; *and* as fore fauore, he wyll nogth be vndere-stand þat he schal schewe fauore more to one man then to anothyre, nowgth to on jn Inglond.

And as fore the bille copye of the cort rolle, when he meuyd to hym of it 30 he smylyd *and* seyd þat suche a bylle[15] there was, seyyng þat[16] ye wold an oppressyd syndrye of yowre contrémen of worchypfull men, *and* the[r]fore he kepyd it styll. Neu*er* the lesse he seyd he schuld loke it vppe in haste, *and* ye schuld haue it.[17] Baronners vndertoke to me[15] twyes ore thryes þat he sc[h]uld so a remembrid hys lord *and* mast*er* þat I schuld an had it w*yth*- 35 inne ij ore iij dayes. He is often tym*ys* absent, *and* there-fore I[5] haue it nowthg yyt. When I kan gete it I schall send it yowe, and of the Kyng*ys* mowth hys name þat toke it hym.

I scend yow home Pekok a-geyn; he is not fore me. God send grase þat he may do yow good seruyse, that be extymac*i*on js not lykelye. Ye schall 40 haue knowlyche aftyrward howe he hathe demenyd hym here w*yth* me. I wold, sauyng yowre dy[s]plesur*e*, that ye wer*e* delyueryd of hym, fore ⌐he⌐ schalle neu*er* do yow profyte nere[18] worchyp.

I suppose ye vnderstand[19] þat the monye that I hadde of yowe att Lundon maye not jndur*e* w*yth* me tyll that the Kyng[20] goo in-to Walys an 45 kome ageyn, fore I vndere-stand it schall be long[21] ore he kome a-geyn. Where-fore I haue send to[22] Lundu*n* to myn onkyl Clement to gete an c s. of *Cristofyre*[23] Hansom ⌐yowre seruau*n*t⌐, *and* send it me be my seyd seru*au*nt, *and* myn herneys w*yth* it whyche I lefte at Lundun to make klene. I beseche yowe not to be dysplesyd w*yth* it, fore I[24] kowd make non othyre 50 cheysaunce but I schuld a boruyd it of a strange man, sum of my felawys, whe[che] I suppose schold not lyke yowe and[25] ye herd of it a-nothyre tyme. I ame jn suerté where as I schall haue a-nothyre mann jn the stede of Pekoke.

My lord of Estsexe seythe he wyll do as myche fore yowe as fore any esquyere[26] in Inglond, *and* Beronners hys man tellyt ⌐me⌐, seyyng 'Yowre 55

---

[11] -er- *repr. by stroke through bow of* b*; so also below.*   [12] *Interl. above and* canc.

[13] y canc.   [14] *Two letters canc.*   [15] þat canc.

[16] þ- *in form of* y, *as occasionally elsewhere in this hand.*

[17] baruners canc.   [18] -re crowded in.   [19] strond canc.

[20] chome a canc.   [21] -g over d.   [22] lund canc.

[23] *Abbr.* xp- *with stroke above.*   [24] *Crowded in.*

[25] -d crowded in.   [26] e- crowded in.

fadyre js myche be-holdyng to my lord, fore he louyth hym well.' Baruners
meuyd me onys *and* seyd þat ye must nedys do sum-w⸢h⸣ate fore my lord
and hys; *and* I seyd I wost well þat ye wold do fore hym þat²⁷ laye jn yowre
poware. *And* he seyd þat ⸢þer⸣ was a lytyl²⁸ mony be-twyxe²⁹ yowe *and* a
60 jantylman of Estsexe callyd Dyrward, seyyng þat þer²⁴ is as¹³ myche
be-twejn my seyd lord *and* the seyd jantyilman, ⸢of⸣ the wyche mony he
desieryth³⁰ yowre part.

It is talkyd here howe þat ye *and* Howard schuld a streuyn to-gyddyre
⸢on þe schere daye⸣,³¹ *and* on of Howardys me[n] sc[h]uld a strekyn yow
65 twyess *wyth* a dagere, *and* soo ye schuld a ben hurt but fore a good dobelet
þat ye hadde on at that tyme. Blyssyd be God that³² ye hadde it on.³³

No more I wryth to yowre good faderhod ⸢at⸣³⁴ thys tym, ⸢but⸣ All-
mygthy God haue³⁰ yowe ⸢in⸣ hys kepyng *and* send yowe vyttorye of yowre
elmyse *and* worschyp jncressyng to yowre lyuys endyn. Wrytyn at Lewys
70 on Seynt Bertylmweys³⁵ Eue.

Be yowre *seruaunt* *and* eldere sone JOHN PASTON

232. To JOHN PASTON I 1462, 13 March

Add. 34888, f. 204. $11\frac{1}{4} \times 4\frac{5}{8}$ in. Wykes's hand, subscription autograph.

Dorse: Remnants of red wax over tape. Address autograph:

To myn ryth reuerent and *worschypful fadere John Paston, beyng jn the
Indere Temple.*

The date appears from Edward IV's presence in Stamford. He was there from 9 to
17 March 1462 (Privy Seal writs, noted by Gairdner).
F. iv, p. 126. G. 442/511.

Ryght reuerent *and* wyrshypfull fadere, I recom*m*and me vn-to you, besychyng you of youre blessyng *and* gode faderhode. Pleasyt it you to
vnderstond the grete expens¹ that I haue dayly travelyng *wyth* the Kyng,
as the berour here-of can enfourme you, *and* howe long that I am lyke to
5 tary here in thys countray or I may speke *wyth* you a-gayn, *and* howe I am
chargyd to haue myn hors *and* harnys redy *and* in hasty wyse; be-sykyng
you to consydere theys causes *and* so to remembre me that I may haue suche
thynges as I may do my maystere servys *wyth* *and* pleasure, trustyng in

---

²⁷ ye *canc.*
²⁹ -e *crowded in.*
³¹ when *also interl. before these words, but canc.*
³³ *Recto ends.*
³⁵ da *canc.*
232. ¹ *-e- repr. by dotted circumflex over -p-.*

²⁸ thyng þat ye *canc.*
³⁰ s *canc.*
³² euer ye bowte on *canc.*
³⁴ *Interl. above ampersand canc.*

God it schall be to youre wyrshyp[2] *and* to myn avayll.[3] In esspeciall,[4] I be-
syche you that I may be sure where to haue mony somwhat be-fore 10
Estern, other of you or by myn vncle Clement when nede ys. Of othere
causes the berour here-of can enfourme you.

No more to you at thys tyme, but God haue you in hys kepyng. Wryten
at[5] Stamford the xiij day of March.

By yowre sone *and* seruaunt JOHN PASTON þe oldere[6] 15

233. To JOHN PASTON I   1462, probably May–June

Add. 34888, f. 207. 12×4 in. Daubeney's hand, signature autograph.

Dorse: Paper seal over red wax and tape. Address autograph:

> *To my ryght wurschipfull fadre John Paston.*

The approximate date appears from a commission which, as Gairdner notes, was
granted on 29 May 1462 to Sir John Howard and Sir Thomas Walgrave to arrest
the ships *la Marie Talbot* and *la Marie Thomson*, of Lynn, and other vessels, 'for
the King's fleet against his enemies' (*Cal. Pat. Rolls, 1461–7*, pp. 203–4).
    F. iv, p. 100. G. 449/518.

Plesit you ⌐to wete¬ that I am at Leyn, and vnder-stande be dyuers
personys, as I am in-formed, þat þe Mayster of Carbroke wold take a[1] rewle
in the Mari Talbot ⌐as for capteyn¬, and to yeue jaketes[2] of his leuery to
dyuers personis qwych ben waged be oder ⌐men¬ and nouth be hym, beyng
in the said shep. Qwerfor, in as moch as I have but few sowdeors in myn 5
leuery here to strenketh me in þat qwych is the Kynges cummandement,
I kepe wyth[3] me yowre too men Dawbenney and Calle, qwich I purpose
shall seyle wyth me to Yermoth; for I have purueyed harneyse for hem,
and ye[4] shall well vnderstande, be þe grace of God, þat[5] the said Maystere
of Carbroke[6] shall have non rewle in the sheppes as I had purposid he shuld 10
haue had, be-cause of his besynesse, *and* for this is on of the specyall
causes I kepe yowre said men wyth me, besechyng you ye[4] takyt to non
dysplesour[7] of ther taryng wyth me. Nat wythstandyng þer herden[8] at

---

2 *Dotted circumflex over* -p, *apparently meaningless.*   3 *MS.* & vayll.
4 -c- *repr. by dotted circumflex over* -ei-.   5 London *canc.*
6 *Subscription and signature in Paston's hand.*
233. 1 *No space.*   2 j- *over* y.   3 you *canc.*
     4 *Written* yᵉ *as if* 'the'; *cf. no.* 172 *n.* 1.   5 nother he *canc.*
     6 nur no *canc.*   7 fo *canc.*
     8 *Evidently a local form of* errand; *cf.* erdon *in* Ludus Coventriae (*E.E.T.S. E.S. 120*),
p. 263, erdyn *in* Macro Plays (*E.E.T.S. 262*), *pp. 77, 88* (Castle of Perseverance).

Wyggenalle shall be*n* don this day, be the grace of God, whoo haue you
15 in kepyng.

Wreten at Leyn the morow after my dep*a*rtyng from you.

It*em*, as far such tydynges as be*n* her*e*, Th^t shall in-forme you.[9]

JOHN PASTON

234. To JOHN PASTON I   Probably 1464, 5 March

Add. 34888, f. 137. $11\frac{3}{8} \times 5\frac{3}{8}$ in. Autograph.

Dorse: Traces of red wax over tape. Address autograph:

To my ryght wyrschypful fadre John Paston, esquyere, be thys letter
delyueryd in hasty wyse.

The date of this appeal by John II to his father for forgiveness seems most likely
to be close to that of Margaret's letter no. 176. Fenn and Gairdner place both in
1459; but in addition to the points noted under no. 176 the handwriting of the
present letter is distinctly more mature than that of no. 231 of 1461.

    F. iii, p. 336. G. 323/375. C. 31.

Ryght worschypful syre, jn the most lowly wyse I comaund me to yowr*e*
good faderhod, besechyng yow of yowre blyssyng. Mut it plese yowr*e*
faderhod to remembre *and* concydre the peyn *and* heuynesse þat it hathe
ben to me syn yowr*e* dep*a*rtyng owt of thys contré, here abydyng tyl the
5 tyme it please yow to schewe me grace, and tyl the tyme[1] that by reporte
my demenyng be to yowre plesyng; besechyng yow to concydre þat I may
not ner*e* haue noo mene to seke to yow as I awght to do sauyng vndr*e* thys
forme, whych I besech yow be not take to no dysplesur*e*, ner am not of
power to do any thynge in thy[s] contré for worschyp or profyht of yow
10 ner*e* ease of yowre tena*u*ntys whych myght *and* scholde be to yowr*e*
pleasyng. Wherfor I beseche yow of yowre faderly pyté to tendre þe more
thys symple wryghtyng, as I schal owt of dowght her-afftere doo þat schal
please yow to þe vttermest of my power*e* *and* labor*e*. And if ther*e* be any
servyce þat I may do, if it please yow to comaund me or if I maye vnder-
15 stonde it, I wyl be as glad to do it as any thyng erthely, if it wer*e* any thyng
þat myght be to yowr*e* pleasyng.

    And nomore, but Allmyghty God haue yow in kepyng. Wretyn the v day
of Marche.

By yowr*e* older*e* sone JOHN PASTON

    [9] *This line written to left of signature, evidently later. The application of the abbreviation*
Th^t *is obscure.*
234. [1] An *canc.*

235. To JOHN PASTON I   1465, 27 September

Pembroke College, Cambridge, LC. II. 230, f. 5. 10½ × 6 in. Autograph.

Dorse: Paper seal over red wax. Address autograph:[1]

⟨To⟩ hys ryght worschypful ⟨fa⟩dre *John Paston, beyng* ⟨in t⟩he *Flete at London, be thys d*elyueryd.

The date appears from the reference to the Mautby living, which is discussed in Margaret's letter no. 192 of 1465. The two letters were written on the same day.
   G. LXII/612.

Ryght worschypful syr*e*, jn the most lowly wyse I recomand me to[2] yow. Pleasyth it yow to wete þ*at* I sente[3] yow a lett*er* but lat*e* agoo, in whych lett*er* I[4] let*e* yow haue vnderstondyng þ*at*, if it pleasyd yow to grante *and* assente ther*e*-to, Syr*e* Thom*a*s Howes wolde resyngne the benefyce of Mawteby to a ful prestly man of Norwych callyd S*yr* Thom*a*s Lyndys, 5 whom I suppose ye haue knolech of. Neuerthe-lesse I wote wele he[5] hath[6] not ben grettly aquentyd w*yth* yow. But I and he haue ben moch aquentyd to-geder*e*, *and* I vnderstond *and* knowe hys vertews leuyng *and* dysposicion ryght wele, whyche herafftere I wote wele scholde please yow ryght wele. And that lett*er* whyche I sent*e* yow, ⌈as⌉ I vnderstod syns, ⌈Nycholas 10 Colman⌉ the berer*e* ther*e*-of cam not owte of Norwych iiij or v dayes after*e* that the bylle was delyu*er*yd hym, wherfor I am jn dowte whyther*e* it is come to yowr*e*[7] handes o⟨r n⟩ot,[8] whyche cawsyth me to wryght to yow ageyn jn thys wyse; besechyng yow, if it plese yow þ*at* the seyd S*yr* Thom*a*s Lyndys schal be of yowr*e* promotyng jn þe wyse above[9] wretyn, 15 þ*at* then it lyke yow þ*at* I may haue answer*e* by the berer*e* herof, whych schal tary at London a day or ij *and* not passyng.
   Nomore to yow at thys tyme, but Alle-myghty God haue yow in guyd-yng. Wretyn at Heylesdon the Fryday next byfor*e* Sceynt Mychell.

                    By yowr*e* older*e* son JOHN PASTON 20

235. [1] *Some letters lost at torn edge.*   [2] to *repeated and canc.*
   [3] *First written* sende, *then* t *written over* d; *then the word canc. and written again.*
   [4] letter *canc.*   [5] h- *over* y.
   [6] -th *over* ue.   [7] p *canc.*
   [8] *Letters faded, paper complete.*   [9] reher *canc.*

236. To John Paston III   1467, probably March

Add. 34889, f. 57. 12×8¾ in. Autograph.

Dorse: Conclusion of letter. Traces of red wax. Address autograph:

To my brothere John Paston.

The approximate date appears from the reference to Lady Boleyn, which connects this letter with John III's letter no. 327. That was written soon after Easter 1467 (Easter Day was 29 March), and this is evidently a little earlier. But no. 327 is not a direct reply to this: John II does not here ask what his brother has done, but gives him advice. He evidently wrote another letter after this, which is now known only from a fragment in Sandford's Genealogy, p. 20 (G. 572/665):

'This Sʳ Iohn Paston Knᵗ . . . was one of the best men of Armes of his time, & at the great Torney that Kinge Edward the fourth helde at Eltham, he was chosen of the Kings side, as it doth appeare by a letter written to his brother Iohn Paston, wherein he writeth thus,

My hand was hurte at the Tourney at Eltham upon Wednesday last, I would that you had been there and seen it, for it was the goodliest sight that was sene in Inglande this Forty yeares of so fewe men. There was upon the one side within, the Kinge, My Lord Scalles, My selfe, and Sellenger, and without, my Lord Chamberlyn, Sʳ Iohn Woodvyle, Sʳ Thomas Mountgomery and Iohn Aparre &c.

By your brother Iohn Paston Mil:'

The spelling shows that this is not a minutely accurate copy of the original. Further, John II never used *you* as a nominative; he did not write 'By your brother' in the subscription of any surviving letter; and he appended 'K.' to his signature, not 'Mil.'. But the content is no doubt genuine, for it exactly fits John III's rejoinder in no. 327.

F. iv, p. 326. G. 570/662. C. 48.

Ryght worschypful *and* verrely welbelouyd brother*e*, I hertely comande me to yow, thankyng yow of yowre labor*e and* dyligence that ye haue in kepyng of my place at Castr*e* so sewerly, both w*yth* yowr*e* hert *and* mynde, to yowr gret bisynesse *and* troble; *and* I ageynwarde haue hadde so lytell
5 leyser*e* that I haue not spedde bot fewe of yowr*e* erendys, ner*e* kannot before thys tyme.

Asfor*e* my lady Boleynes dysposicion to yow werd*ys*, I kannot in no wyse fynde hyr*e* a-greable þat ye scholde haue her*e* dowter, for all the ⌈preuy⌉ meanes þat I kowde make; in so moche I hadde so lytell comfor*e* by all the
10 meanes þat I kowde make þat I dysdeyned in myn own p*er*son to comon w*yth* hyr*e* ther*e*-in. Neu*er*thelesse I vndre-stande þat sche seythe, 'What if he *and* sche kan agré, I wyll not lette it; but I will neu*er* advyse hyr*e* therto in no wyse.' *And* vppon Tewesday last past sche rood hom in-to Norfolke; wherfore as ye thynke ye may fynde the meane to speke w*yth*
15 hyr*e* yowre-selfe, for*e* w*yth*-owt that, in myn conceyt, it wyll nat be. And as for*e* Crosseby, I vndrestand not þat þer is no maryage concludyd betwen them; neu*er* thelesse there is gret langage þat it is lyke to be.

Ye be p*er*sonable, *and* p*ar* aue*ntur* yowr*e* beyng ones¹ in the syght of þe mayde, *and* a lytell descuu*er*yng of yo*ur* good wyl² to hyr*e*, byndyng hyr*e* to kepe it secret, *and* þat ye kane fynde in yowr*e* hert, w*yth* som co*m*fort of hyr*e*, to fynde the meane to brynge suche a mat*er* abowt as schall be hyr*e* pleas*ur and* yowr*ys*, but that thys ye kannot do w*yth*-owt som co*m*fort of hyr*e* in no wyse—. *And* ber*e* yor*e*-selfe as lowly to þe moder*e* as ye lyst, but to þe mayde not to lowly, ner*e* that ye be to gladde to spede ner*e* to sory to fayle. *And* I alweys schall be yowr*e* herault, bothe her*e* if sche com hydd*er* *and* at home when I kome hom, whych I hope hastyly w*yth*-in xl dayes at þe ferth*es*.³ My modr*e* hathe a lett*er* whych can tell yow more, *and* ye may lat Dawbeny se it.

JOHN PASTON, K.⁴

I suppose and ye kall welle vppon R. Calle he schall p*ur*uey yow mony. I haue wretyn to hym j-now.

237. Indenture of wager   1467, 1 May

Add. 39848, f. 56. 8½ × 4½ in. (indented). Text neatly written in Pampyng's hand, signature apparently autograph. Remnants of red wax.

Dorse: Marks of folding, soiled. Hastily written in unidentified hand: *pro John Paston 4 li. & 5 li. 3. 5 d.*, beside and below which, apparently in Paston's hand, twice, *Lomnore*.

Dated.
 G. 574/667.

This bille indentyd mad the first day of Maij the vij yere of the reigne of Kyng Edward the Fourthe bithwix John Paston, knyght, on the on p*ar*tie, and Thomas Lomno*ur* of London, mercer, on the othir p*ar*tie, witnessith that the said Thomas Lomno*ur* hath bargeyned, comena*un*tid and agreed w*yth* the seid John Paston in the forme folowyng, that is to say that the same Thomas hath sold to the said John an ambelyng hors vpon this condic*i*on that if the day of mariage bithwyx the lord Charles, sone *and* heire to the Duc of Burgon and my lady Margret, sustir to our*e* soue*re*yn lord the Kyng aboueseid, take effect, and the same lady Margret lawfully be maried to the said lord Charles w*yth*inne ij yere aftir the date of thes present, thanne and at the same day of mariage the said John Paston gra*u*ntith to pay to the said Thomas Lomno*ur* for the said hors vj m*ar*c. And if the said mariage take not effect w*yth*inne the seid ij yere, yet the

---

236. ¹ *wyth canc.*   ² *Crowded at edge.*
  ³ *At edge.*   ⁴ *Recto ends.*

397

seid John Paston grauntith to pay to the said Thomas Lomnour at any day
15 aftir the ij. yere aboueseid for the said hors xl s. and nomore.

In witnesse wherof the parties abouesaid to these billes enterchaungeably
haue set her seals the day *and* yere aboueseid.

JON PASTON, K.

238. To JOHN PASTON III   1468, 9 November

Add. 34889, ff. 67ᵛ–68ʳ. 11½ × 16¾ in. at full length, but the left-hand
bottom quarter was cut off before the letter was written. Autograph.

Dorse: Traces of red wax. Address autograph:

*To my ryght welbelouyd brothere John Paston, esquiere, beyng at Caster, or
to John Dawbeney per be thys letter delyueryd.*

The date appears from Paston's preparations for the defence of Caister, which the
Duke of Norfolk attacked in 1469 (see no. 202 and related letters). It is confirmed
by the report of Roger Ree's appointment as sheriff of Norfolk and Suffolk, which
dated from November 1468.

F. iv, p. 302. G. 592/691. C. 52 (part).

Ryght welbelouyd brother, I comand me to yow, letyng yow wete þat I
haue wagyd for to helpe yow *and* Dawbeney to kepe þe place at Castre iiij
wel assuryd *and* trew men to do al maner of thyng¹ what þat they be
desyiryd to do in saue-gard ore enforcyng of þe seyd place. *And* more-
5 ouyre they be prouyd men *and* connyng in the werre *and* in fetys of armys,
and they kan wele schote bothe gonnys *and* crossebowes and amende *and*
strynge them, *and* devyse bolwerkys ore any thyngys that scholde be a
strenkthe to þe place; *and* they wol, as nede is, kepe wecche *and* warde.
They be sadde *and* wel advysed men, sauyng on of þem whyche is ballyd
10 *and* callyd Wylliam Peny, whyche is as goode a² man as gothe on the erthe,
sauyng a lytyl he woll, as I vnderstand, be a lytel copschotyn; but yit he is
no brawlere, but ful of cortesye, meche vppon James Halman. The othere
iij be named Peryn Sale, John Chapman, Robert Jakys son; sauyng þat as
yit they haue non herneyse comyn, but when it komyth it³ schall be sent
15 to yow. And in the meane whyle I pray yow *and* Dawbeney to puruey them
some. Also a cople of beddys they most nedys haue, whyche I pray yow
by the help of my modre to puruey for them tyl þat I⁴ com home to yow.
Ye schall fynde them gentylmanly, comfortable felawes, *and* that they wol
and dare abyde be there takelyng. *And* if ye vndrestond þat any assawte
20 scholde be towardys, I sende yow thes men becawse þat men of þe contré

238. ¹ *A curl on -g, of unusual shape and uncertain significance.*
² *No space.*   ³ *MS.* is.   ⁴ go *canc.*

there abowt yow scholde be frayed for*e* fer*e* of losse of ther goody*s*; wherfor*e* if ther*e* wer*e* any suche thyng towardy*s* I wolde ye toke of men of the
contré but few, *and* that they wer*e* well assuryd men; for*e* ellys they myght
discorage alle the remenant.

And asfor*e* any wryghtyng fro the Kyng, he hathe promysyd þat þer 25
schall come non; *and* iff ther do hys vnwarys, yowr answer*e* may be thys,
how the Kyng hathe seyd, *and* so to delay them tyll I may haue worde, *and*
I schall sone p*ur*uey a remedy.

I vnderstond þat ye haue ben w*yth* my lorde of Norfolke now of late.
What ye haue don I wote not; we se þat he schal be her*e* ageyn thys daye. 30
More-ouyr*e* I trow John Alforde schall not longe abyde w*yth* my lorde. I
schall sende yow tydyng of other*e* thyngys in haste, w*yth* the grace of God,
who &c.

Wretyn on Wednysday nexte befor*e* Seynt Martyn.

JOHN PASTON 35

I fer*e* þat Dawbeney is not alther*e* best storyd to contenew howsolde
longe. Lete hym send me worde in hast, *and* I wyll releve hym to my
power*e*, *and* ore longe to I hope to be w*yth* yow. R[o]ger[5] Ree is scheryf of
Norfolke, *and* he schall be good j-now; th'exchet*er* I am not yit assertaynyd
of.[6]
40

Also þat thes men be at þe begynnyng entretyd as corteysly as ye can.

Also I pray yow to sende me my flowr*e* be þe nexte massanger*e* þat
comyth.

Also, as for*e* my Lorde Fytz-wat*er* oblygacion, I know non suche in myn
adward as yit.
45

Also þe obligacion of the Bisshop of Norwychys oblygacion, I neu*er* sye
it þat I rem*em*bre, wherfore I wolde *and* prey my modre to loke it vp.

Also as for*e* the byble þat the mast*er* hath, I wend the vtt*er*mest pryse
had not passyd v m*ar*k, *and* so I trowe he wyl geue it. Wet, I pray yow.

Also as for*e* Syre Wyll*ia*m Barbor*e and* Syre Wyll*ia*m Falyate, I wolde, if 50
they kan p*ur*uey for*e* them-selfe, folfayne be dyschargyd of them.

239. To JOHN PASTON III 1469, 17 March

Add. 34889, f. 73. 12×7⅛ in. Autograph.

Dorse: Paper seal over red wax and tape. Address autograph:

To my[1] *well belouyd brother*e *John Paston, or to John Dawbeney in hys absence.*

The date appears from the evidently recent death of Thomas Howes. John III's
letter no. 332 of May 1469 shows that he had died not long before.
    F. iv, p. 308. G. 600/703.

⁵ jee *canc.*   ⁶ *Recto ends.*
239. ¹ *MS.* myght.

Ryght worschypful *and* well belouyd brothere, I comand me to yow, letyng
yow wete þat S*yr* Thom*as* Howes hadde a free chapell in Cast*er*, ⌜where-of
þe gyfte longyth to me⌝, whyche chapell as I vnderstande scholde bee in
the olde tyme, er*e* the place at Cast*er* wer*e* bylte, w*yth*-in the motte;
5 wherfore I ame but the bett*er* pleased. *And* soo it is now þat at the speciall
request of the Qwen and other*e* especiall good lordes of myn I haue geuyn
it to þe berer*e* here-of, callyd Mast*er* John Yotton, a chapleyn of þe
Qwenys. Neu*er*thelle[s] in tyme passyd I p*ur*posyd that þe mast*er* of the
colegge scholde haue hadd it, *and* so er*e* longe to I hope he schall. Wher-
10 fore I thynke he most take possession, *and* that is the cawse of hys comyng;
wherfor*e* I pray yow make hym good cher*e*. He is informyd that it scholde
be worthe c s. be yer*e*, whyche I belyue[2] not; I thynke it der*e* jnow xl s.
by yeer*e*. He most haue it as it was hadde befor*e*.

Item, thys daye I vnderstonde that ther*e* be comen lett*er*is from my
15 moder*e* *and* yow *and* Dawbeney, wherin I schall send yow answer*e* when
I haue seyn them. No mor*e* at þis tyme, for w*yth*-in this iij dayes I schall
lette yow haue knolech of other*e* mat*er*is. Wretyn þe xvij day of Marche.

Whether*e* he nedyth indoccion or*e* institucion or*e* non I wot not. If it
nede, brother*e*, ye may seale any suche thynge as well as I. Mast*er* Steuyn
20 kan tell all suche thynges.[3]

JOHN PASTON, K.

240. To JOHN PASTON III   1469, early June

Add. 43489, f. 31. $11\frac{7}{8} \times 8\frac{1}{4}$ in. Autograph, very carelessly written; nearly
six manuscript lines added after signature.

Dorse: Paper seal over red wax. Address autograph:

*To my moodr*e* *and* to my brother*e* John Paston.*

The year 1469 appears from the fear expressed for the security of Caister (cf. no.
202). The month is determined by Edward IV's visit to Norfolk: he left London
for Bury St. Edmunds, Norwich, and Walsingham on 5 or 6 June of that year
(Scofield, i. 491–2).

F. ii, p. 22. G. 611/715 (omitting all the added matter except the last sentence).

Brother*e*, it is so þat the Kynge schall come in-to Norff*olk* in hast, *and* I
wot nat whethyr*e* þat I may com w*yth* hym or*e* nowt. If I come I most do
make a leuer*é* of xx[ti] gownes, whyche I most pyke owt by yowr*e* advyse;
and asfore[1] clothe for*e* suche *per*sones as be in þat contr*é*, if it myght be
5 hadd ther*e* att Norwyche or*e* not I wot not, *and* what *per*sonys I am nott

---

[2] -y- over another letter, apparently incomplete u.
[3] These last two sentences written beside the signature, evidently later.
240. [1] ch canc.

remembryd. Iff my modre be at Cast*er*, as ther schall be no dowt for*e* the kepyng of þe place whyl the Kynge is in that contré, than² I may haue the most p*a*rte at Cast*er*; *and* whether*e* ye woll offr*e* yowr*e*-selfe to wayte vppon my lorde of Norfolk or*e* not, I wolde ye dyd þat best wer*e* to do. I wolde do my lorde plesur*e* *and* s*er*uyse, *and* so I wolde ye dyde if I wyst 10 to be sur*e* of hys god lordeschyp in tyme to kome. He schall haue cc in a lyu*er*ye blew *and* taw⌐nye⌐,³ *and* blew on the leffte syde *and* bothe derke color*y*s. I pray yow sende me worde *and* yow[r] advyse be Juddy of what men *and* what horse I cowde be p*u*rueyd of if so be þat I most nedys kome, *and* of yowr*e* advyce in all thyng*y*s be wryghtyng; *and* I schall sende yow 15 hastil⟨y⟩⁴ other*e* tydyng*y*s.

JOHN PASTON, K.

And asfor*e* my mat*er*is my sariant*y*s haue no dowt in it,⁵ w*yth* þe grace of God, that þis t*er*me they schall do well j-now *and* haue an ende.

Also sende John Russe worde þat he hathe don in the best wyse, *and* þat 20 hys deposic*i*on *and* þe examynac*i*on in Cant*er*bury cort⁶ acorde in the best wyse, *and* so hath Fryre Moghte don passynly wele. I haue wr*e*t to myn oncle þat my moodr*e* kan tell hym mor*e* than I haue wret to hym. Late Sorell be well kepte.

241. To WALTER WRITTLE   1469, early September

Add. 34889, f. 85. 11¾×8¾ in. Autograph.

Dorse: Remnants of red wax over string. Address autograph:

*To Mastyr*e *Wryttyll.*

The approximate date is fixed by the negotiations for the raising of the Duke of Norfolk's siege of Caister, in which Writtle—who was in the service of the Duke of Clarence, and in this year sheriff of Essex and Hertfordshire—was acting for the Pastons; see nos. 203, 204. Since this letter was written the day after Writtle had left London it is evidently earlier than no. 242, dated 10 September, in which Paston comments on a letter received from Writtle in Norfolk.

F. iv, p. 370. G. 618/722.

Mast*er* Wryttyll, I recomande me to yow, besechyng yow hertely, as myn holl trust is in yow, that ye doo yowr*e* devoyr*e* to contynew trews tyll Fryday or*e* Sat*er*day in the mornyng, by whych tyme I hope the massang*er* shall come; *and* that ye be not dryuen to take an appoyntment iff ye kan vndrestand by any lyklyod that itt be able to be abydyn *and*¹ recystyd, *and* 5

² -n *over* t. ³ *At end of line.*
⁴ *Crowded at edge.*
⁵ *This sentence so far written to left of the signature, though certainly after it.*
⁶ ag *canc.*
241. ¹ resyst *canc. at edge.*

8124155   401   D d

that ye fele my brotherys dysposycion therin, as my trust is in yow; prayng
yow to remembre that it restythe, as God helpe me, on all my well. Fore
as God helpe me, I hadd leuyre the place were brennyd, my brother *and*
seruantys sauyd, than[2] the best appoyntment that euyre ye *and* I comonyd
10 of scholde be my goode wyll be takyn, iff thys massage from the Kynge
may reskwe it. And iff it be so that my lorde be remevyd by the Kynges
comandement whyche restythe *wyth* hys honore, I may in tyme to kome
do hym servyse as schall recompence any grodge ore dysplesure that he
euyre had ore hathe to me ore myn. *And* ye, iff it the rathere by yowre
15 wysdam *and* polesye the moene above wryten may be hadd, schall be as
sewre of the servyce of my trewe brothere *and* seruantys and me as ye kan
devyse, by my trowthe. Fore, in goode feythe, thys mat*er* stykyth more
nyghe myn hart *and* me than I kan wryght on-to yow, *and* to my brother
and seruantys more nere than, ⸢as⸣ God knowyth, they wot off. Wherffor,
20 Mast*er* Wryttyll, all owre welffare restyth in yow, besechyng yow to
remembre it, for thys mat*er* is to all vsse eyther makyng ore marryng.

Item, asfore Arblast*er* ore Louell,[3] I kan not thynke that they ore any
of them may be *wyth* yow; wherffore in yow is all, *and* God haue yow in
kepyng. Wretyn at London the day next afftre yowre depa*rt*yng.
25 I schall sende yow more knowleche to-morow, *wyth* Goddys grace.[4]

Yowr*ys*, JOHN PASTON, K.

242. To WALTER WRITTLE: draft or copy 1469, 10 September

Add. 34889, ff. 86ᵛ–87ʳ. 11⅝ × 16¼ in. Wykes's hand.

Dorse: Marks of folding, but not much soiled by carrying; no seal or
address. Faint endorsement: *M . . . Paston*, and some other words, in
unidentified hand.

The year is fixed by the siege of Caister; see also nos. 241, 243.
F. iv, p. 372. G. 619/723.

Ryght worshypfull syr*e*, I recomaund me to you, thankyng you of youre
grete labo*ure*, whych I haue no3t as yet but I shall dese*ru*e to my powere;
and forthermore lyke you to wyte that I haue thoght ryght long aftere you.
Neuyrthelesse I remembere well that ye delt wythe ryght delayous peple,
5 my lord Archbyshop *and* othere of my lord*ys*, *and* I dempte by-cawse of
youre long tarryng that by youre sad dyscrescyon all hadde ben sett
thorow. Neu*er* the lesse I vnderstond by youre wrytyng that my lord of
Norffolkys concell thynketh that hys entent whych ye sertefyed me by

---

² -n *over* t.   ³ -ll *over* r.
⁴ *The last line written beside the signature, evidently later.*

youre wrytyng sholde be more to hys wyrshop than the appoyntement*ys*
and rewll made by the lord*ys* of the Kyng*ys* concell whych be to my seyd 10
lord of Norf*folk* nere kyne, whych appoyntement*ys* sythen youre departyng
hath be largely remembryd a-mong*ys* the seyd lord*ys* here, thynkyng it in
hem-selff so honorabyll to my lord of Norf*folk* that there shuld non off my
lord*ys* concell well avysed mevyd to the contrary. Jamys Hobart was sent
fro my [lord] of Norf*folk* hedere, *and* spake w*yth* my lord Archbyshop, *and* 15
awnswere[1] he had of my seyd lord *and* howe my lord tendryd the matere
yet, *and* wyll. I trowe he haue told you, *and* yf he haue not the bryngere
her-of schall in-forme you. *And* he broght thys same appoynteme*nt* from
my lord that my lord was well aggryed that I shuld ocupye. For my parte,
jff I shud take no othere apoynteme*nt* but[2] acordyng to youre lett*er* it were 20
hard for me *and* for my tytell to putte my lord in that[3] possessyon, for
there ys thyng*ys* in erthe to myn esse in youre lett*er* gode for me in that
appoyntement, sauyng the suerty off my brothere lyffe *and* my s*er*uaunt*ys*
whych ye thynke dowtefull yf so be that thay lakke stuff, shotte, *and*
vytayll; mervaylyng sore *and* thynk it jnpossybell jn thys shorte season, or 25
in iiij tyme the season hedere-toward*ys* that thay shuld lakk, othere w*yth*-
owte it soo be that my lord*ys* men haue enterd owght the place *and* so
had there stuffe from hem, whych I cannot thynk.

Also, s*er*, for the tyme of youre comyng to my lord of Norf*folk* s*er*u-
auntys of ⟨. . .⟩[4] my modere at Norwych, mouyng to send to my brothere 30
hyre sone to delyu*er* the place vndere such a forme as youre lettere specefyeth, *and* so I cannot vnderstand what regard my*n* lord*ys* concell takyth
to my lord*ys* letter *and* to youre labo*ur* in thys behalf but that thay offeryd
as largely afore.

Ʒe wryteth in youre lettere that ye durst nat passe youre credens. 35
Please you to rememb*ere* that seyd youre credens affore the lord*ys* was
ryght large, *and* as large as myght well be in thys mat*ere* both to my lord*ys*
concell of Norf*folk* to w*yth*-drawe the seege, w*yth* moore othere mat*ere* as
ye knowe, *and* to the justic*e* of the peas *and* to the shyryff *and* hys offycers
youre awtoryté was grete j-now to jche of them. Wherfor, Mayster Wretell, 40
I neu*er* for thys nere ʒet wyll take appoyntment in thys matere but as my
lord*ys* wyll *and* my lord Archbyshop, whych as well as I my-selff haue holy
putte oure tryst to youre dyscrete dyreccyon; *and* my seyd lord ⟨syth⟩en[5]
youre dep*ar*tere, ʒoure goyng, thynkyng you all*ys* mete a man in executyng
there comaundement as cowde be chosyn. Neuer the lesse, for awnswere 45
to you at thys season my lord Archbyshop ys north-ward*ys* toward*ys* the
Kyng, how be it it ys seyd vppon a metyng w*yth* my lord of Clarens my
lord shuld reto*ur*ne a-yen; and as ʒest*er* euyn he send a s*er*uau*nt* of hys

---

242. [1] *MS.* anwswere.   [2] acr *canc.*
[3] suerty *canc.*   [4] *Paper decayed; room for about twelve letters.*
[5] *Hole in paper; extremities of letters visible.*

to me, wenyng to hys lordshyp that S*er* Humfray *and* ye were in Caster*e*
50 as was appoynted, *and* ye shuld send to hys lordshyp answer*e* of the gydyng
ther*e* by wrytyng, comaundyng me that yff any such wrytyng*ys* cam from
you yf hys lordshyp wernot past iij*ˣˣ*⁶ myle ⟨from Lon⟩don⁷ to com to hys
lordshyp; w*yth* the same vnderstandyng for sertayn that he ys nat yet so
ferr*e*. Wherfore I will in al⁸ the hast possybell ryde ny3t and day till I see
55 hys lordshyp, *and* after*e* cominicacyon had w*yth* hys lordshyp, as sone as
ys possybell that a man may go be-twext ye shall haue an aunswer*e* of hys
dysposicyon;⁹ for hys jntres is such that as I haue wryten I shall neu*er* do
therin w*yth*-oute hym, as my cosyn, brynger*e* herof, more playnly shall
enforme you. For I canne thynke ryght well that as¹⁰ 3e wryteth to me my
60 broder*e* wyll not delyu*er* the place to non erthly person but yf he see
wrytyng fro my lord.

It semyt be your*e* wrytyng that my lord of Norff*olk* consayll jntende not
that my lord Archbyshop shuld dele in thys mater*e*, for he ys not named
in your*e* lett*er*; wherof I mervayle, for it was movyd to you at your*e*
65 departyng hens the Kyng*ys* concell shuld haue take dyreccyon in thys
mater*e* or els my lord Cardenall, my lord of Clarens, my lord Archbyshop,
and my lord of Essex.¹¹ Neu*er* the lesse, Mayst*er* Wrytyll, all profytht,
man*er*, or lyfflod leyd apart, if it be so that thorow reklesnese my brother*e*
and seruauntys be in such jop*ar*té as ye haue wryten to me, whych shold
70 be half jnpossybell in my mynd that thay shold myssvse so moch stuff in
iiij tymes the space, *and* that ye haue euydent knowlych by my seyd
brother*e* hym-self therof, I wold praye yow to se hym *and* them in suerté
of ther*e* lyffys, what so eu*er* shold fall of the lyfflode. How be it, I woldnot
that my brother*e* *and* seruauntys shold gyff vpp the place, not for a m¹ li.,
75 yf thay myght in any wyse kepe it *and* save ther*e* lyves. *And* therfore, at
the reuerens of God, sytht it ys so that my lord Archbyshop *and* my lord*ys*
all *and* I haue putte *our* trust in you that ye wyll do y*our* deuoyere to haue
the verrey knowlych of my brother*e* hym-sylf, *and* not of my lord*ys* men,
wheder*e* he stante in such jop*ar*tye as your*e* lett*er* specefyeth or nat, for I
80 dowte not vppon the sy3th of thys lett*er* *and* of the letter that ye had before
that my brother*e* will put¹² no mystrust in you, consyderyng that he
knowyth that ye com from my lord*ys* *and* my lord Archbyshop *and* haue
my wrytyng. *And* as for my lord Archbyshop wrytyng an¹³ aunswer*e*,
such as it¹⁴ shalbe ye shall haue it in all the haste possybell; but I thynke
85 veryly that my lord eschewyth to telle you any thyng w*yth*out þat he

---

⁶ *This appears to be the right reading, though* xx *is on the line, and* iij *immediately below it.*
Fenn read xx.
⁷ *Paper decayed; some traces remain.*   ⁸ *No space.*
⁹ as my cosyn brynger*e* herof more playnly shall enforme you *canc.*
¹⁰ he *canc.*   ¹¹ it *written here, not canc.*
¹² you *canc.*   ¹³ *MS. ampersand.*
¹⁴ *Recto ends; verte folium written below.*

myght speke w*yth* you allone, *and* me thynketh v*er*yly that thay ought not
to lette you to speke w*yth* hym allone, consyderyng that ye haue auctoryté
and wrytyng from the lord*ys* so to do. *And* as for the justificacyon of
entryng the place *and* sege layng ⟨to t⟩he same, *and* the comaundement
of the justice of the pease *and* the sherewe to assyste my lord in thys 90
gydyng, I wote ye vnderstond that the lord*ys* knowe all that mater*e*, *and* ye
herd it comened, *and* how thay toke it in ther*e* consayt*ys*.

There ys no more, Mayst*er* Wryttell, but I co*m*mytt all thys wrytyng
vn-to your*e* dyscrescyon; and as ye thynk best acordyng to such me*n*nys
desyre as haue entretyd you therin, *and* for my moyst avayle, I p*r*ay you, 95
s*er*, soo doo, *and* I shall se vn-to your*e* besynes *and* labo*ur* that ye shall
haue cause to do for me in tyme comyng *and* as the brynger*e* herof shall
tell you.

And I p*r*ay God haue you in hys kypyng. Wryten at London the x day
of Septembr*e*. 100

By yo*ur* frend for ever*e*, JOHN PASTON, K.

243. To MARGARET PASTON 1469, 15 September

Add. 34889, ff. 89ᵛ–90ʳ. 11⅝ × 16¾ in. Autograph.

Dorse: Marks of folding, traces of red wax, and stitch-holes, but no
address. Various later endorsements, of which only *Oxnead* appears to be
in a fifteenth-century hand.

The date appears from the situation at Caister. This letter answers Margaret's
letter no. 204 of 12 September.
F. iv, p. 386. G. 621/725. C. 57 (part).

Moodre, vppon Sat*er*day last was Dawbeney *and* Bernay were on lyve *and*
mery, and I suppose ther cam no man owt of the place to yow syn that
tyme that cowde haue asserteynyd¹ to yow of ther*e* dethys. And as towchyng
the fyrsenesse of the Duke er*e* of hys peple schewyd syn that tyme ⌈that
Wryttel dep*a*rtyd⌉, I trowe it was concludyd that trews and abstynence of 5
werre scholde be hadd er*e* he dep*a*rtyd whych² shalle dewr*e* tyl Monday
next comyng. And by that tyme I trow þat trews schall be takyn tyll that
day vij nyght afftr*e*, by whych tyme I hope of a goode dyreccion schall be
hadde.

And wher*e* as ye wryght to me þat I scholde sewe for letter*is* from my 10
lordys of Clarance *and* Yorke, they be not her*e*; *and* iff they wrot to hym,
as þey³ haue don ij tymes, I trow it wolde nat advayle. *And* as fore to labor*e*
thois letter*is* *and* the rescu togedre, they ben ij sondry thyngys, for*e* when

---

243. ¹ it *canc.*   ² -e *canc.*   ³ þ- *in form of* y.

the rescu is redy that the cost there-of is don—for iff I be dreuyn therto
15 to rescu it ere they com there that scholde do it, it shall cost a m¹ escutys
and as moche afftre; whych wey were harde for me to take whyll þat I
maye do it otherwyse. But as to sey þat they schall be rescuyd iff all the
lande that I haue in Ing⟨elo⟩nd,⁴ and frendys, maye do it, they schall,
and God be frendly, and that as schortly as it may goodlely and wele be
20 browt abut. And the grettest deffaut erthly is mony, and som frendys
and neyborys to helpe; wherffore I besche yow to sende me comfort
what⁵ money ye coude fynde the menys to get ⌐ore cheuysche⌐ vppon
suerté sufficient ere vppon lyfflod to be jnmorgage⁶ ere yit solde, and what
peple by lyklyod, yowre frendys and myn, kowde make vppon a schort
25 warnyng, and to sende me worde in all the hast as it is nedffull.

But, moodre, I fele by yowre wryghtyng that ye deme ⌐in me⌐ I scholde
not do my deuyre wyth-owt ye wrot to me som hevye tydyngys; and,
modre, iff I had nede to be qwykynyd wyth a letter in thys nede I were
of my-selfe to slawe a felaw. But, moodre, I ensure yow þat I haue herde
30 x tymes werse tydyngys syn the assege by-gan than any letter that ye wrot
to me, and somtyme⁷ I haue herde ryght goode tydyngys both. But thys I
ensure yow, that they that be wyth-in haue no werse reste than I haue,
nere castyth⁸ more jupperté. But whethyre I had goode tydyngys er ill, I
take Gode to wittnesse þat I haue don my devoyre as I wolde be don fore
35 in case lyke, and schall doo tyll ther be an ende of it.

I haue sent to the Kynge to Yorke, and to þe lordys, and hope to haue
answere from them by Wednysday at þe ferthest; and affter that answere
shall I be rewlyd, and than send yow word, fore tyll that tyme kan I take
non dyreccion. And to encomfort yow, dy[s]peyre yow not fore lak of
40 vytayle ner of gonne-powdre, ner be natt to heuy ner to mery there-fore.⁹
Fore and heuynesse ore sorow wolde haue ben the remedy there-of, I
knew neuyre matere in my lyffe þat I kowde haue ben so heuy ore¹⁰ sory
fore. And¹¹ wyth Goddys grace it schall be remedyed well j-now; for by my
trowthe I hadde lever lose the maner of Caster than þe symplest mannys
45 lyffe therin iff¹² that may be hys saueacion. Wherfore I besche yow to
sende me worde wat mony and men ye thynke þat I am lyke to get in
that contré, fore the hasty purchace of mony and men schall be the getyng¹³
and rescu of it, and the sauevacion of most mennys lyffys, iff we take þat
weye.

50 Also thys daye I porpose to sende to Yorke to þe Kyng fore a thyng,
whych same only maye be lyklyod be the savacion of all. Ye must remembre
that the rescue of it is the last remedy of all, and how it is nat easy to get.

---

⁴ *Paper decayed.* maye *canc.*
⁵ what *repeated.*
⁶ *Abbr.* -morge *with superior a above g.*
⁷ tyme *repeated.*
⁸ -th *not quite clear, apparently written over another letter.*
⁹ Fore *canc.*
¹⁰ sek *canc.*
¹¹ *Ampersand over it.*
¹² th *canc.*
¹³ of *canc.*

And also ye sende me worde þat I scholde nat kome hom wyth-owt þat I kome stronke; but iff I had hadd on othere stronge place in Norffolke to haue comen to, thowe I had browt ryght fewe wyth me I scholde, wyth 55 Goddys grace, haue rescued it by thys tyme, ere ellys he scholde haue ben fayne to haue besegyd bothe placys ore yit, and the Duke had not kept Yarmoth owthe.

But, mother, I beseche yow sende me som mony, fore by my trowth I haue but x s. [I] wot not wher to haue more, *and* moreouy[r] I haue ben 60 x tymes in lyke case ore werse wyth-in thys x wekys. I sent to Rychard Call for mony, but he sendyth me non. I beseche yow to gyde the euydence þat Pekok can tell yow off, *and* to se it saffe, for it is tolde me þat Richard Call hath hadd right large langage of them; I wolde nat they com in hys fyngrys. I haue no worde from yow of them, ner whethere ye haue yit in 65 yowr kepyng the euydence of Est Bekham owt of hys handys, ner whethyre ye haue sent to my manerys that they schold not paye hym no more mony, ore not. Also þat it lyke yow to geve credence to Robyn in othere thyngys.

Wret the Fryday next affter Holy Roode Daye. 70

JOHN PASTON, K.

244. To JOHN PASTON III 1469, 18 September

Add. 34889, f. 93. 8⅜×9 in. Autograph.

Dorse: Traces of red wax. Address autograph:

To John Paston, and to noon othyre.

This clearly relates to the siege of Caister in 1469.
F. iv, p. 394. G. 625/729. C. 58.

I recomand me to yow, *and* promyse yow þat I haue *and* schall labore *and* fynde þe meane þat ye schall haue honore of yowre delyng, as ye haue hyddre-towardys, as all Ingelond *and* euery man reportythe. *And* moreouer I am in weye fore it by many dyuerse weys, wherof there schall be one exicutyd by thys day xiiij nyght at þe ferthest, ⌐and parauenture wyth-in 5 vij dayes⌐, *and* iff ye maye kepe it so longe I wolde ⌐be⌐ gladd. And afftre that, iff ye haue nott from me other wryghtyng, that than ye do there-in fore yowre saffgarde *and* yowre felaschep only, *and* to yowre worschypys; *and* asfore the place, no force therffore. Ye knowe thys hande, þerfore nedythe no mencion from whom it comythe. 10

And more-ouyre, they that be abut yow be in obloquy of all men, *and* more-ouyre they haue ben wretyn to by alse speciall wryghtyng as myght be afftre the worlde þat now is, and [I] promyse yow þat the Dukes

concell wolde þat they had neuyre be-gon it. *And* more-ouyr they be chargyd
15 in payne of there lyvys that, thow they gate the place, they scholde not
hurt on of yow. There is nowther ye ner none *wyth* yow but, and he knewe
what is generaly reportyd of hym, he ore ye—*and* God fortewne yow wele—
may thynke hym iiij tymes bettere in reputacion of all folk than euyre he
was.[1]

20 Be ware whom ye make a concell to thys mater. Also, I lete yow wete þat
I am in moche more comffort of yow þan[2] I maye wryght, *and* they þat
be abowt yow haue cawse to be more ferde than ye haue; and also beware
of spendyng of yowre stuffe of qwarellys, powdre, *and* stone, so that iff
they assawt yow ere we come that ye haue stuffe to dyffende yow of on[2],
25 *and* than of my lyffe ye get nomore; and that yowre felaschyp be euyre
ocopyed in renewyng of yowre stuffe.

Wretyn the Mondaye next afftre Holy Roode Daye.

I trow, thow ye be not preuy ther-to, ther is taken a trews new tyl
thys day vij nygh⟨t⟩.[3]

245. To MARGARET PASTON 1469, October

Add. 43491, f. 10. 8½ × 11¾ in. Autograph.

Dorse: Continuation of text. Paper seal over red wax and tape. Address
autograph:

To Mestresse Margret Paston be thys delyueryd.

The date is evidently soon after the surrender of Caister (see no. 334), for Daubeney,
who was killed in the siege, is spoken of as recently dead. The reference to the
approaching marriage of Margery Paston to Richard Calle confirms the year (see
no. 336), and the mention of 'evidence of Beckham' looks forward to no. 246; cf.
no. 335, and no. 10. Edward IV's privy seals show that he returned to London
from the north by 13 October (Scofield, i. 503).

F. i, p. 292. G. 632/736 (part).

Ryght worchypffull moodre, I comand me to yow *and* beseche yow of
yowre blyssyng, *and* God thanke yow fore yowre tendrenesse *and* helpe
bothe to me, my brothre, *and* servantys; besechyng yow to sende me worde
what is yowre plesure[1] *and* advyse how that ye thynke were best to do *wyth*
5 my servantys there *wyth* yow. Neuerthelesse somwhat I vndrestande by a
letter from my brothere John—*and* more-ouyre that he hathe myn euydence
of Bekham.

244. [1] Be wha *canc.*   [2] -n *has a superfluous minim.*
    [3] *This sentence written vertically in left-hand margin.*
245. [1] how *canc.*

Item, Dawbeney, God haue hys sowle, hadde in kepyng an oblygac*ion* in whyche Jam*es*[2] Gressham was bonde to me in an c m*ark, selyd w*yth*[3] Jam*es sele, osse I suppose of hys office, *and* w*yth* grene waxe. I haue lente 10 Jam*es and* payd for hym abut xl li., *and* haue non other sewerté. I praye yow late it be lokyd vppe be tymes. I deme it is amonge hys ge*re at Norwyche.

Item, that it lyke yow to speke to Jam*es Gressham that ⌈in any wyse⌉ he p*urey hym mony to save me harmelez he*re thys terme ageyn S*er Thom*as 15 Mongom*ery.

Item, myn oncle Will*iam scholde haue comen home eue*ry daye thys vij nyght, *and* thys daye or to-morow he comyth homward*ys. He and I be as goode as fallyn owt, for he hathe laten me pleynly wete þat he schalle haue alle my grauntdames lyfflod off ⌈here⌉ enherytance *and* of hyr joyntore also, 20 wherin I trust to God that he schall helpe. I woll not yit speke of it, ner I praye yow doo not. Also I beseche yow sende me worde of the delyng of my sustre Margery *and* Rycharde Calle. I wolde nat þat they we*re maryed of a whyle, iff it maye be, fore dyuers concideracions. Iff it lyk yow to speke on my behalffe, *and* yowr*ys bothe, to þe Bysshop to tary it tyll Crystmesse, 25 I hope by that tyme to fynde som remedye therffore; *and* to telle hym that I desyryd yow to speke to hym therin. And iff soo be that they sshall be maryed ⌈in haste⌉, þat than ye sende me worde þer-of whether it be don or nott, *and* whoghe he p*urposythe to dele w*yth* hyre, *and* how he woll gyde hyre *and* wher he woll dwelle. 30

Item, that it lyke yow to vndrestande what fellaschyp *and* what guydyng ys at Cast*er, *and* that ye haue alwey som spye that maye be grett w*yth* them *and* so to vndrestande it *and* to sende me worde.

Item, iff Ebysham come nat hom w*yth* myn oncle W. þat than ye sende me þe ij Frenshe bookys þat he scholde haue wretyn, þat he may wryght 35 them here.

JOHN PASTON, K.[4]

The Kynge is comyn to London, *and* there com w*yth* hym *and* roode ageyn hym the Duke of Glowcestr*e, the Duke of Suffolk, þe Erle of Aroundell, 40 the Erle of Northumbreland, the Erle of[5] Essex, the lordez Harry *and* John of Bokyngham, the Lord Dakrez, the Lorde Chambreleyn, the Lorde Montjoye, *and* many other knyghtys *and* sqwyerys, the meyr of London, xxij aldremen in skarlett, *and* of the crafftys ⌈men⌉ of the town to þe nombre of cc all in blewe. The Kynge come thorow Chepe, thowe it were 45 owt of hys weye, be-cawse he wold not be seyn; *and* he was acompanyed in all peple w*yth* m[1] horsse, som harneysyd *and* som nat. My lorde Arche-bysshop com w*yth* hym from Yorke *and* is at þe Moore, *and* my lorde of

---

[2] -es *abbr. by the sign usually meaning* -us; *so also below, and commonly in the name in* John II's *hand.*
[3] hys *canc.*   [4] *Recto ends.*   [5] essexe *canc.*

Oxenfford roode to haue mett þe Kyng, *and* he is w*yth* my lorde Arche-
50 bysshop at þe Moor*e and* com natt to town w*yth* þe Kyng. Som sey þat
they wer*e* yist*er*daye[6] iij myle to þe Kyng ward*ys* from the Moor*e, and* that
the Kyng sent them a massang*er* that they scholde come whan[7] þat he sent
for*e* them. I wot not what to suppose ther-in. The Kyng hym-selffe hathe
good langage of the lord*ys* of Claraunce, of Warwyk, *and* of my lord*ys* of
55 York, of Oxenfford, seyng they be hys best frendys. But hys howsolde men
paue other langage, so what schall hastily falle I cannot seye. My lorde of
Norffo*lk* schall be her thys nyght. I schall sende yow mor*e* when I knowe
more.

246. Indenture of sale (with provision for redemption)
1469, 6 November

Add. Charter 14526. Parchment, $12\frac{3}{8} \times 8\frac{5}{8}$ in. (indented, bottom turned
up, pendant seal). Hand unidentified.

Dorse: Marks of folding. Note in John Paston II's hand:

*Endent*ura *Rog*eri *Towneshend de man*erio *de Est Bekham.*

G. 634/738 (abstract).

This indenture made the vj[te] day of Nouembre the ix[th] yer*e* of the reigne
of Kynge Edward the Fourth bitwene Sir John Paston, knyght, on that one
partie and Roger Tounesende, gentilman, on that other partie, witnesseth
þat þe seid Sir John Paston hath graunted, bargayned, and solde to þe
5 seid Roger his manoir of Estbekham in the counté of Norffo*lk* and all his
londes and tenementes with þ'app*ur*tena*unces* in Estbekh*am*, Westbekham,
Bodham, Sheryngham, Beston iux*ta* mare, Routon, Shipden, Felbrigge,
Aylm*er*ton, Sustede, *and* Gressh*am* in the seid countee, which þe seid Sir
John purchased *and* hadde of the yifte *and* feffement of John Mariet the
10 elder of Estbekham, for an c marke of lawefull money of Englond, wherof
þe seide Sir John is payed in redy money in hande liiij li. by the handes
of the seid Roger. And so remayneth due to þe seid Sir John at þe makynge
of thise p*re*sentes of the seid c marke only xij li. xiij s. iiij d. to be payed to
þe same Sir John or his assignees by þe seid Roger or his assignees by þe
15 fest of Seint Luke next co*m*myng after the date of thise p*re*sentes. And for
the due execucion and accomplisshyng of þe seid bargayn and sale, þe
seid Sir John hath made a dede of feffement of the date of thise p*re*sentes
to þe seid Roger and other cofeffees of þe seid Roger named in þe seide
dede by þe seid Roger, to ther heires and assignees to þe vse of þe seid
20 Roger, his heyres *and* assignees, of þe seid manoir, londes, *and* tenementes

[6] yi- *apparently over* to.   [7] w- *over* h.

with þ'appurtenaunces, and a warrant of attourney in þe same dede to
make and deliuere an estate and season of and in the same manoirs,
londes, and tenementes, with th'appurtenaunces, to þe seid Roger and his
cofeffees after þe fourme *and* effecte of the seid dede. And þervppon þe
seid Sir John deliuered to þe seid Roger þe dede of þe seid purchase of the 25
seid Sir John and þe endentures of covenaunt and bargayne hadde *and*
made bitwene þe seid Sir John and John Mariett of and for þe seid manoir,
londes, and tenementes, and a dede made by James Andrewe to þe seid
John Mariett, and a-nother dede made by þe seid James and one William
Jamys to þe seide John Mariett and John Mariett of Runton of the 30
premisses. And by the seid last dede þer passed neuer liueré ne season, and
þerfore þe dede made by þe seide James Andrewe alone after þe decese of
þe seid cofeffees is good *and* effectuell, for therby passed liueré *and* season.
And where þe seid Sir John, by þe seide indentures of covenaunt made
bitwene him and þe seid John Mariett, graunted þat þe same John Mariett 35
and Elizabeth his wyf shuld haue þer dwellyng with-in þe mote of þe seid
manoir, and an annuité of x marke durynge þer lyves and þe lenger leuynge
of theym, þe seid Roger is aggreabill to þe same; and ouer that the seid
Roger is aggreabill þat, yf þe seid Sir John paye or do pay to þe seid Roger an
c marke of lawfull money of Englond by þe fest of All Seintes next commyng 40
after þe date of þise presentes, þat þanne þe seid Roger and his seid cofeffees, after dewe and resonable warnynge yeven vnto him at þe labour
and costes of þe seid Sir John, shall enfeffe þe seid Sir John and such as he
thanne will name in his dede withouten ony maner of warrantize.

In witnesse wherof þe parties beforneseid to thise endentures euery to 45
oþer haan sette þeire seals the day and yere aboueseid.

247. To ROGER TOWNSHEND, for another
Perhaps about 1470, 12 February

Add. 34889, f. 186. 11⅜×4 in. Text in Pampyng's hand, subscription
autograph.

Dorse: Paper seal over red wax and tape. Address autograph:

To the ryght worschypffull and hys best betrustyd frende, Rogere Townerende.

From the opening sentence it appears that this letter was intended for some unidentified person to whom Townshend was to pass it.

The date cannot be determined, except that it is apparently after the death of
John I. John II sold the manors of Beckham, Gresham, and other places to Townshend in 1469 (no. 246), and later borrowed money from him at various times. He
acted as counsel for the Paston brothers in a suit in 1470, and this letter may be of
roughly the same period.

G. LXXVI/699.

Right worshipfull sir, I comaunde me to yow, praying yow hertly to remembre that, by the award made by-twen yow *and* me by Roger Townesend for a tenement in Stratton in Norff*olk* callid Rees, I shuld delyuer yow all the evydens apperteynyng to the said plase, *and* not from thens
5 forth to chalenge ner interupte my lady y*our* wife ner yow of the said tenem*ent*; and that for thes said causes ye shuld *and* therto were agreyd to geve me an horse *and* x li. to an harneys. And moreovir, bifore Cristemasse in the Kynges chambre ye ther ageyn pr*o*mysed me that at such tyme as I send to yow home to yowr*e* plase by any ser*u*a*u*nt of myne er
10 any man from me that ye wold delyver it hym *and* send it me by hym. My brothir John hath send me word that he remembird yow therof on my behalfe, *and* that ye answerid hym that ye wold gyfe hym or me a fayre harneys at y*our* comyng to London. I deme in yow that ye thynke par case to bye a fayre harneys here for x mark; but, cosyn, as God help me, I bowte
15 an harneys syn that tyme for my-self which cost me xx li. But I can not desire of yow so moch; wherfore, cosyn, w*yth* all myn hert I pray yow acordyng to yowr*e* pr*o*myse that it like yow to send me by my ser*u*a*u*nt, berer herof, the said somme of x li., as my trust is in yow and as I wolde in like case haue don to yow, and as in the pr*e*mysses I delt feithfully w*yth*
20 yow *and* evir so shall dele, w*yth* the grase of God, who have yow in hys kepyng.

Wretyn at London the xij day of Feveryer.

Yowre JOHN PASTON, K.

248. To JOHN PASTON III   1470, about 20 February

Add. 43491, f. 14. 11⅝ × 17½ in. Autograph.

Dorse: Continuation of text. Paper seal over red wax. Address autograph:

*To John Paston, esquiere, beyng at Norwyche, be thys lett*er *delyu*eryd.

The approximate date appears from the mention of (*a*) the Bishop of Winchester's administration of Fastolf's will, and (*b*) the King's projected expedition to Lincolnshire. (*a*) On 13 February 1470 Thomas Bourchier, Archbishop of Canterbury and Cardinal, granted to William, Bishop of Winchester, administration of Fastolf's estate, 'nullis alijs executoribus in testamento dicti defuncti nominatis ad administracionem bonorum eiusdem de jure admittendis protunc existentibus' (Magdalen College, Fastolf Paper 93). (*b*) In March 1470 Edward IV led a force to Lincolnshire against rebels under Sir Robert Welles (Scofield, i. 511–14).

From several details (the clock, oranges, Dr. Pykenham, Townshend's indenture) it is clear that this letter is answered by John III's letter no. 339 of 1 March, so that it must have been written perhaps a week earlier. See also Part II, no. 787.

This letter is set out in paragraphs, most of them preceded by a mark in the margin.

F. ii, p. 28. G. 637/742 (part).

I comande me to yow, letyng yow wete that I haue receyuyd yowre letter[1] in þe boxe, *and* the byllys also off yowre receytys where-in ye refferre yow to a rekenyng whyche ye made to me last, whyche I remembre nat, nere haue no byllys off it that I remembre. But thys was it that I desyred off yow to haue wreten ore asserteynyd me off in rekenyng off all the receyt, 5 asswell olde as newe, off all that was be-hynde *and* owyng off the tenantys by the seyng *and* wryghtyng off Richard Call, and off whom *and* in what place *and* what daye *and* whyther off the olde arreragys ore ellys off the last yere.

Item, ye wryghte to Osberne Berney vij li., refferryng yow to þe last 10 rekenyng, *and* I haue not þat I knowe no suche rekenyng, nere I knowe nat wher that vij li.[2] was payed nere where a-bowt spendyd. I praye yow iff ye haue any leysere to make bothe rekenyngys in on, *and* that I maye vndrestande what I owe in yowre conceyte in Norffolk, *and* what is owyng me.

Item, I prey yow sende me the wryghtyng be-twen Townesende *and* me 15 by the next massanger.

Item, I haue not all the crosse bowez; I lak the tylere fore[3] the mydell bowe, jtem a wyndase fore the bowe that was broken, *and* the Normandy byll. I praye yow sende them me in hast, fore I mervaylle that they come natt wyth þe othere gere. 20

Item, I praye yow sende hydder a bowe þat wasse Dawbeneys, wyth a crokyd horn, how so euer ye doo fore Tom Stompys.

Item, as fore Mestresse Kateryn Dudlé, I haue many tymez recomandyd yow to hyre, and sche is noo thynge dyspleasyd wyth itt. She rekkythe nat how many gentylmen love hyre—sche is full off love. I haue betyn the 25 mater for ⌐yow⌐ yowre onknowleche, as I tolde hyre. She answerythe me þat sche woll noon thys ij yere, and I beleve hyre, for I thynke sche hathe the lyffe þat sche can holde hyr content wyth. I trowe she woll be a sore laboryng woman þis ij yer for mede off hyre sowle.

And Mestresse Gryseacresse is sure to Selengere wyth my lady off 30 Exestre, a fowle losse.

Item, I praye yow speke wyth Harcort off the Abbeye fore a lytell clokke whyche I sent hym by James Gressham to amend, *and* þat ye woll get it off hym, and it be redy, *and* sende it me; and asfore mony for hys labore, he hathe another clokk off myn whyche Syr Thomas Lyndez, God haue 35 hys sowll, gaue me. He maye kepe that tyll I paye hym. Thys klok js my lordys Archebysshopis, but late not hym wete off it, *and* þat itt [be] easely caryed hyddre by yowre advyse.

Also, as for orengez I schall sende yow a serteyn by the next caryere.

And asfor tydynge, the berere heroff schall infforme yow; ye most geue 40 credence to hym.

248. [1] -s *seems to be written over final loop, and both canc.*
[2] wha *canc.*   [3] for *repeated.*

Asfor my goode spede, I hope well I am offryd yit to haue Mestresse
Anne Haulte, *and* I schall haue helpe j-nowe, as some seye.

Item, ther is a weye mevyd by the meane off my lorde off Wynchest*er*
45 betwen S*yr* William Yelu*er*ton *and* me, *and* bothe S*yr* William Yelu*er*ton
and I agreyd to abyde hys awarde; wherffore I hope thys next *ter*me ther
schall be a weye taken *and* an ende; *and*, in concell be it, I fere not the
adwarde. I may not wryght my goode hope ner suerté there-off, iff S*yr*
William Yelu*er*ton will abyde by that he hathe seyde; *and* iff he do natt
50 he is begyled, for my lorde off Wynchest*er* hathe take admynest*r*acion off
S*yr* J. Fastolff*ys* testment *and* S*yr* William Yelu*er*ton is excludyd. S*yr*
William Yelu*er*ton wotythe nat her-off, and I rek not thowe ye tell hym
not ther-off. But thys ye may sey to Wyll*i*am Yelu*er*ton, whyche hathe
by-foore thys tyme feynet that he ment well *and* wold that we hadd ben
55 acordyd, that ye vndrestand that suche a tretye is hadd be-twen hym *and*
me, *and* that ye preye God make an ende betwen vs, *and* than schall we
all be goode felawez ageyn; *and* that ye vndrestande þ*at* Heydon woll be
a gret lett*er* her-off, for he louythe nowthe S*yr* W. Yelu*er*ton in conclusion, nor me nowther, *and* that he hathe a gret whyle lawhyd at vs
60 bothe; *and* iff[4] we tweyn wer agreyd that nowther*e* of vsse bothe hathe
no nede in tyme to kome to dele w*yth* hym, for off olde malyse he louyth
vs nowthe but hatythe vs bothe. *And* more ouyr*e* he hathe reportyd hym-
selff off S*yr* Wyll*i*am Yelu*er*ton þ*at* he hathe not delt wyselye *and* that he
hathe auenturyd, for malyse of me, hys welffar*e*; *and* he had kowde haue
65 knowen what he hadde don, but he seyde he was not wyse, seyng that
and I hadde recuueryd ageyn hym in the Chancerye that he wer verrely
ondon. But I ensure yow I rek not whethyr*e* the tretyse take effecte er*e*
nott, for*e* the[r] schall be a lyfft at it er*e* owght longe to, w*yth* the grace off
God. I may not wryght the secretnesse heroff. Thys mat*er* maye not be
70 wyst to noo body but to my moodre *and* yowe onlye, nowther to S*yr* Jam*es*
ner noo bodye.[5]

Item, I preye yow remember the oblygac*i*on that Dawbeney, God haue
hys sowle, hadde off Jam*es* Gresham how he was bonde to me in c m*ar*k.

Item, I vnderstande þ*at* Thom*as* Wyngffelde *and* ye were at Walsyng-
75 ham to-gedr*e*; God speede yow.

Item, asfore them that were jndyghtyd w*yth* me off forcyble entré, ther
schall no processe goo owt ageyn them, for*e* I haye p*ur*ueyd an attorny
for them in the Kynges Benche *and* haue jmp*ar*lyd for them tyll the next
terme.

80 Item, I praye yow to comon wyth myn oncle Wyll*i*am *and* to haue a byll
off hym what þ*at* is betwen hym *and* me, *and* what I owe hym *and* vppon
what pledgys, *and* to tell hym that thoys pledgys þ*at* he thynkythe lest
worthe þ*at* he woll sende me worde, þ*at* they may be fyrst pledgyd owt,

---

4 wh *canc.*   5 *Recto ends.*

for I may not well all at onez. But I preye yow sende me worde off hys
dysposy*ci*on heryn, and also whether*e* he be off the same dysposic*i*on in 85
my grantdamez londe as he was at hys last beyng here,[6] at whyche tyme
he tolde me *þat* he scholde *and* wolde haue suche lond as I loked afftre,
rehersyng moreouyr*e* that myn oncle[7] Clement had laboryd the same.

Item, I praye yow to speke w*yth* the chancelere Docto*ur* Pykenam so
that I may haue the mony that was oweng me for S*yr* Thom*a*s Lyndys, 90
wheroff I toke a byll to S*yr* W. Marrys. It is a-bowt the some off v m[a]rke.
Item, Doct*ur* Pykenh*a*m tolde me at hys laste beyng here *þat* suche goodez
as wer*e* S*yr* Thom*a*s wer*e* yit r*e*seruyd for*e* me, *and* noo thynge don for
hym tyll that I be payd off my dewté; *and* sende me worde.

Item, it is soo *þat* I am halffe in p*ur*pose to com hom w*yth*-in a monythe 95
her*e*-afftre, or a-bowt Med-lente or*e* beffor*e* Esterne, ondyr*e* yowr*e* corec-
c*i*on, iff so be that ye deme *þat* my mood*er* wolde helpe me to my costys,
x m[a]rk or ther-a-bowt. I praye yow feele hyr*e* dysposic*i*on and sende me
worde.

Item, I cannot telle yow what woll falle off the worlde, for the Kyng 100
verrely is dysposyd to goo in-to Lyncoln-schyre *and* men wot nat what
wyll falle ther-off ner*e* there-afftr*e*. They wene my lorde off Norffolke
scholde brynge x m[l] men.

Item, ther is comen a newe litell Torke, whyche is a wele vysagyd felawe
off the age off xl yer*e*, *and* he is lower*e* than Manuell by an hanffull *and* 105
lower then[8] my lytell Tom by the scholderys,[9] *and* more lytell above hys
pappe. *And* he hathe, as he seyde to *þe* Kyng hym-selffe, iij or iiij ⌜sonys⌝
chyldr*e*, iche on off hem as hyghe *and* asse lykly as the Kynge hym-selffe.
And he is leggyd ryght j-now, *and* it is reportyd that hys pyntell is asse
longe as hys legge. 110

It*em*, I praye yow schewe or*e* rede to my moodre suche thyngez as ye
thynke is for*e* here to knowe, afftr*e* yowr*e* dyscression, *and* to late hyre
vndrestonde ⌜off the article⌝ off the treté betwen Syr*e* Wyll*i*am Yeluerton
and me.

Item, my lorde off Warwyk, as it is supposyd, schall goo w*yth þe* Kynge 115
in-to Lyncolne-schyre. Som men seye *þat* hys goyng shall do good, *and*
som seye that it dothe harme.

I praye yow euyr*e* haue an eyghe to Cast*er* to knowe the rewle ther*e*,
and sende me worde; and whyther my wyse lorde *and* my lady be yit as
sottyt vppon it as they wer*e*, *and* whether my seyd lorde resortythe thyddr*e* 120
as offte as he dyd or nott, *and* off the dysposyc*i*on off the contré.

J. P., K.

---

[6] *First written* there, t- *canc.*   [7] Wy *canc.*
[8] *MS.* them.   [9] *MS.* schorderys.

249. To the BISHOP OF WINCHESTER: draft

1470, between February and July

Add. 39848, f. 58. $8\frac{1}{4} \times 11\frac{1}{2}$ in. Autograph, except for one sentence.

Dorse: Marks of folding, no seal or address. Note in Pampyng's hand:

The copy of the request to the Bisshop of Wynchester by Ser John Paston, knyght.

This is a partial draft, very hastily written and with numbers in the margin indicating a revised order of the paragraphs. The date appears from the negotiations with the Bishop of Winchester. It is evidently not long after the grant to him of the administration of the Fastolf estate (see no. 248), and before the disposal of the various manors according to the agreement embodied in no. 252. That agreement also contains the 'acquittance' requested in the first paragraph of the present draft.
G. 698/806 (abstract).

Fyrst, Syr J. P. compleyneth ⌜and desyrethe, as⌝¹ he hathe dyu*er*se
xiij   tymes dessyred, my lorde to make hym an aq*ui*taunce of m¹m¹m¹m¹m¹
mark² whyche myght haue been claymed by vertu of wordes rehersed
in the bergayne be-twyen Syr J. Fast*olf* and John Past*on*, esq*ui*ere,
5   fader, &c.
xiiij   *And* also off all goodes are any³ that weer Syr J. Fastolff, that come
[to] hys handes, hys faderys, or anye other ⌜to⌝ the vse off J. Paston,
esqu*i*er, acordyng to an endent*ur*.
ix   Item, he desyrethe hys⁴ ⌜fefféys sholde⌝ be dyschargyd off any
10   entresse in any londes þat weer Syr J. Fastolff in⁵ Flegge, in as moche
as ⌜all⌝ they excede nott þe valur*e* off 1 li. yerlye ⌜acordyng⁶ to
þ'endent*ur*⌝, as þe seyd Syr John is redy to make goode *and* preeff as
reason wyll *and* concyence, ore⁷ ellys, &c.
vj   Item, he desyrethe that my lorde off Wynchest*er and* othere feffyes
15   schulde make astate off the tenement callyd Fayrchyldes, parcell off
the man*er*s, londes, or ten*ementys* callyd⁸ Heylesdon, Drayton, Tol-
vij   thorp, ⌜ore⌝ ten*ementys* in Norwyche to Guy Fayrffax, Roger Townesend, William Dau*er*se, *and* other to þe vse off the seyde⁹ lorde *and*
þe seyde Syr John.
20   Also þe seyde Syr J. Paston desyrethe to¹⁰ be pr*e*uye *and* see the
xj   bullys off dyspensac*i*on for the alteryng off the coledge to be fondyd
nowe at Oxenforthe, wher it sholde *and* most ellys be at Castre. And

---

249. ¹ *Interl. above* þat *canc.*   ² *Superior* a *superfluously written above* -ar-.
³ revenewes *canc.*   ⁴ *Over another word, apparently* to.
⁵ *Some letters, apparently* estffle, *canc.*
⁶ *MS.* agordyng.   ⁷ o- *over diagonal stroke of punctuation.*
⁸ heylesto *at edge, canc.*   ⁹ reuere *canc.*
¹⁰ see *and canc.*

þes be sufficienth bothe in lawe *and* conscience accordyng to þe prom[e]sse[11] of þe[12] said Busshop mad to hym.[13]

Ante Also he desyrethe to be aserteyned *and* to se the letter off admynestra- 25
j.   cion whyche my[14] lorde most gete on-to hym-se⌐l⌐ffe approuyd executur off þe wyll *and* testement off Syr J. Fast⟨olf⟩.[15]

Item, as for the maner of Guton, Syr J. Paston thynkythe that he oweth[16] not to assent as yit that W. Passton shold relese, for ij causis: on for hys penalté for Caster, *and* þe second fore the entresse off my 30 lorde off Canterbury.

Item, as for the maneris off ⌐Saxthorpe⌐, Heynfforthe, Burnevyles in Nakton, ⌐Cotton⌐, the seyd John Paston owythe to haue a preffer-ment *and* to haue theym or any parte off them byffor the amortyse-ment for londys off lyke valew. As for the maneris off Calkotys, 35 Browston, Spitelyngys, Hablond, Leystoffte in Suffolk,[17] *and* off the maneris off Beyton, Tychewell, Esexe in Hyklyng, if[18] the lysense be hadde off dyspensacion to þe vse specefyed in the endentur, savyd on-to Syr J. Paston hys profferment off exchaunge, he is ag⟨re⟩yd[19] as the cort wyll awarde. 40

250. Indenture pledging plate   1470, 3 July

Add. 27445, f. 38. Parchment, 12¼×4½ in. (indented). A formal clerk's hand.

Dorse blank except for *Schawe* in unidentified hand.

G. 643/748 (abstract).

This indenture witnessith that Sir John Paston, knyght, being possessed of xx disshes and a sawser of siluer weying by Troy weight xxvij lb. ix vncis and di. in playn and open market in the Citee of London, hathe bargayned, sold, and deliuered the day of the date of thise indentures to Edmund Shaa, citezein and goldsmyth of London, the saide xx disshes and sawser 5 for l li. sterlinges by the said Edmund to the forsaid Sir John Paston afore-hand paid, wherof the same Sir John Paston knowlachith him-self truly contented and satisfied by thise presentes, to haue and to hold the forsaid xx disshes and sawser to the said Edmund, his executours and assignees as

---

[11] -e *repr. by flourish on* -ss.   [12] þ- *in form of* y.
[13] *This last sentence in another hand.*   [14] my *repeated.*
[15] *At edge.*   [16] -th *apparently over another letter.*
[17] *A diagonal stroke here and a line under the next three words seem intended to mark off a new section, noted also by a mark in margin.*
[18] *MS.* is.   [19] *Middle obscured by blot.*

10 theire propre godes foreuermore; which bargayn, sale, and delyueree not-
withstondyng, the same Edmund grauntith by thise presentes, if the said
Sir John Paston pay or doo to be paid to the forsaid Edmund, to his
executours or assignees, l li. sterlinges the xiijth day of Octobre next commyng after the date of thise indentures, or at any tyme byfore the same
15 day, than the said xx disshes and sawser shalbe deliuered by the saide
Edmund or his assignees to the forsaid Sir John Paston or to his attourney
makyng the saide payment. And if defaulte be made in payment of the saide
l li. in parte or in all at the saide xiijth day of Octobre, than the saide
graunte made by the forsaid Edmund of reliueree of the saide xx disshes
20 and sawser be void and of noon effect. But that than the saide Sir John
Paston grauntith and byndith him by thise indentures and promiseth vpon
his honoure and worship to warant the said xx disshes and sawser and the
sale of the same to the said Edmund, his executours and assignees, ayenst
almaner people foreuer.
25   In witnesse wherof the parties aforsaid to thise indentures entierchaunge-
ably haue sette theire sealles. Youen the third day of July in the xth yere of
the reigne of Kyng Edward the Fourth.

251. Indenture pledging plate   1470, 8 July

Add. Charter 17249. Parchment, $5\frac{1}{2} \times 6\frac{1}{4}$ in. (indented); traces of red
wax. Hand unidentified, appearing also in no. 257.

Dorse: Blank except for *Kelke* in contemporary hand, and later notes.

   G. 644/749 (abstract).

This endenture made at London the viij day of Julij the x^{the} yere of the
regne of Kyng Edward the iiij^{the} by-twyxt Syr John Paston, knyght, of the on
partye and Sthephen Kelke, citeseyne *and* goldsmyth of London, on the
other partye, bereth witnesse[1] þat the said Syr John the day of this present
5 wrytyng hathe bargayned, delyuered, *and* solde to the forsayd Sthephen
xvj potengers, weying of Troy weyght xxij li. x vnc. of seluer di. vnc., for
xl li. of laufull money of Englond receyued by þe same Syr John for the
same bargayne. And the said Sthephen graunteth by this presentes that
and the said Syr John, his executors or assignez, pay or do to be payed to
10 þe said Sthephen xl li. of laufull money of Englond by-fore þe feste of
Witsontyde[1] next comyng, þat than the same Sthephen shall selle *and*
delyuer a-yen to the said Syr John alle the forsaid dysshes *and* potengers of
seluer; prouyded that, *and* the same potengers be take a-wey by any open

robberye, that than þe said Sthephen be not bounden her-by to þe latter
sale or relyueré. 15

In witnesse wher-of the partyes a-bouesayd to þis endentures enter-
chaungeabully haue set to theire seales þe day and yere a-foresaid.

252. Indenture of agreement on Fastolf estate   1470, 14 July

Magdalen College, Oxford, Norfolk and Suffolk 29. Parchment, 21 × 15 in.
(indented); pendant seal of John Paston II. Clerk's hand, appearing also
in nos. 254, 262, John Paston III's declaration no. 344, and in other documents related to these negotiations.[1]

Dorse: In a coarser hand: *Magna indentura conuencionum factarum inter
dominum episcopum Wintoniensem et J. Paston militem de qua materia tamen
dictus Johannes generaliter relaxauit.* In another hand: *E. iiij^{ti} x^{mo}.*

This is one of the final sealed copies of the agreement, partial drafts of which exist
in other Magdalen documents, Norfolk and Suffolk 36 and 51. The former of these
is a long paper roll (three sheets joined to form a roll about 49 in. long) in the hand
of no. 260 and some other associated papers, containing most of the material in the
agreement but in a different order and with some variations of detail, as well as
many differences of spelling, and also a draft of no. 254.

G. 645/750 (note only).

This indenture made betwene the right reuerend fader in God William
Wayneflete, Bisshop of Wynchestre, on the oone party, and John Paston,
knyght, on the other party, wittenesseth that where John Fastolf, knyght,
nowe dede, late beyng seised in his demene as of fee of dyuers maners,
londis, and tenementes in the countees of Surré, Essexe, Suffolk, and 5
Norfolk, and in the cité of Norwich, and beyng also possessed of right grete
and notable summes of money, jowelex, plate, aras, and other godez
and catallez qvyk and dede, caused a feoffement of the said maners,
londes, and tenementez to be made to the seid reuerend fader and other,
to haue to them and to theire heyres foreuermore to parfourme thereof 10
the wille and entent of the seid Syr John Fastolf, the same Syr John Fastolf
also made his testament and named and ordeyned the seid reuerend fader
and other to be executoures of the same testament; which Syr John
Fastolf, amonge othere pitueux and charitable dedes, willed and ordeyned
vij prestys and vij poore folkes to be endowed perpetuelly to praye for the 15
soulez of the same Syr John Fastolf and of Dame Millicent his wife and

252. [1] Norf. and Suff. 40 is a receipt by Sir William Yelverton for £87 paid by William,
Bishop of Winchester, in settlement of claims against Fastolf's estate by Jacquette, Duchess
of Bedford, 'yeuen in the Priory of Saynt Marye Ouerey in Suthwerk' on 20 November
1469. Norf. and Suff. 48 is a receipt by John, Duke of Norfolk, for 100 marks paid by the
Bishop on account of a total of 250 to be paid 'as soone as the saide bisshop shal haue
certeyne knowlege of the delyueré of possession of the maner of Castre', dated 24 December 1470.

other of his frend*es* and benefact*ours*. After the decesse of which S*yr* John
Fastolf grete variance hathe growen betwene John Paston, sqwyer, fader
of the seid John Paston, knyght, on the oon p*ar*ty, and dyue*res* of the seid
20 feofféz on the other p*ar*ty, for a bargayne alleged to be made betwene the
said John Fastolf, knyght, *and* John Paston, sqwyer, of the seid maneres,
lond*es*, *and* ten*emen*tez in the countéz of Norfolk, Suffolk, and in the citee
of Norwich; by occasion of which variance dyvers of the seid feofféz of the
seid man*er*es, lond*es*, *and* ten*emen*tez haue thereof made estat, su*mm*e to
25 oon p*er*sone *and* su*mm*e to other, and grete su*mm*es ⌐of money⌐ *and* also
grete substaunce of the said good*es* and catallex *and* of th'issues and
profett*es* growen and co*mm*en of the seid man*er*s, lond*es*, *and* ten*emen*tez,
and the wod*ez* of the same, haue be wasted, decaied, and spent, the verey
wille of the seid S*yr* John Fastolf in many grete p*ar*ties thereof delaied
30 and not p*ar*fouremed yet nor executed, and the seid troublez co*n*tynued
neu*er* likly in tyme cu*m*myng to be executed. Wherefor the seid reue*r*end
fader, seyng that all the seid named executo*urs* nowe in life, excepted
hymself oonely, what for renownecyng of admi*n*istracion of the seid testament, what for other cawses, may not now take vpon them the admi*n*istra-
35 cion thereof, considered also of the seid grete substance of lond and good*ez*
the grete waste, destruccion, *and* p*er*plexité, havyng pité and co*m*passion
that of so blessed *and* charitable entent of the seid John Fastolf no co*m*-
mendable effect shuld ensue, remembryng the singuler trust which the
same John Fastolf to hym had, bothe in the seid feoffament and in th'
40 execucion of the testament and of the p*re*myssez, hathe taken vpon hym
th'execucion of the seid testament, entendyng by the grace of God, bothe
of the seid lond*es* as farforthe as he may and also of such good*ez* of the
seid John Fastolf as yet re*m*ayne ⌐vnspent⌐ and shal com to the hondys of
the seid reue*r*end fader*e*, that the wille of the same John Fastolf therof
45 shalbe executed.

Ther*e*fore in ceesyyng of variances, pleez, and trowblez which haue
fallen and hereaftir by likliode shuld be co*n*tynued, *and* in accomplesme*n*t
of p*ar*ty of the will of the ⌐said⌐ John Fastolf, ⌐it is aggreed betwene the
said p*ar*ties in maner and fourme foloyng⌐: that is to witt that the said John
50 Paston and all other p*er*sonez by hym or to his vse havyng any title, possession, or int*er*esse in any maners, lond*es*, ten*emen*tez, or other possessions
which wer*e* of the seid John Fastolf in the counteez and citee aforesaid,
except certeyn man*er*s, lond*es*, ten*emen*tez, *and* possessions w*ith* thaire
appurtenauncez vnder writen, that is to wite the man*er* of Castre w*ith*
55 appu*r*tenance in the counté of Norf*olk*, and all the londys and ten*emen*tez
called Vaux, Redh*am*, or Bosoms in Castr*e*, the man*er* called Spencers in
Haryngby, except also the man*er*s of Hailesdon, Drayton, Tolthorp, *and*
ten*emen*tez in the citee of Norwich,[2] shal relenxe before the fest of

[2] *Curl on* -c.

Cristmasse to the seid reuerend fadere and ⌐to his⌐ heires foreuermore all
theire right and interesse which thei haue in all the seid maners, londes, *and* 60
tenementez, or in ony of them, excepted before excepted, discharged of
any rent, reconusaunce, execucion, or ony charge by them or ony of them
made, other than the same maners, londes, tenementez, and possessions or
any parcell of them were charged tyme of the first estat thereof made to
the said John Paston or to ony person or persones to th'use of the said 65
John Paston.

Also the said reuerend fader shal, before the said fest of Cristmasse, do
to be made to þe seid John Paston, knyght, or such personez as the same
John wol assigne, and to theire heires foreuermore, a lawfull and sufficiant
dymysse of estate of fee symple of the said maner of Castre *and* of the seid 70
maner called Spensers in Haryngby *and* of all the londes and tenementez
in Castre and also the londes *and* tenementes in Haryngby called Spensers
which were of the seid John Fastolf, and which the seid reuerend fadere
to-gedir with John Beauechampe, knyght, Lord Beauechamp, *and* other
had of the feoffament of Rauf Lord Suydeley and other such,[3] *and* the hole 75
estat as the seid reuerend fader *and* Lord Bewchamp have or had by reson
of the same feoffement discharged of any rent, reconusaunce, execucion,
or any charge by theym or either of them made, other than the same
maners, londes, and tenementez or any parcell of them were charged tyme
of the same feoffement made. Also the seid reuerend fader graunteth to 80
doo his effectuell deuoure[4] ⌐to cause[5] William Paston to make dymyss of his
estat of fee theryn to the seid John Paston, knyght, in the same fourme
discharged, *and* that by sub pena if the case require. And forthermore the
seid reuerend fader promitteth vpon his honoure to do his effectuell
deuoure⌐ that before the feste of Witsontide next comyng John, Duke of 85
Norfolk, *and* all other personez by the same Duke or to his vse beyng feoffed
in the seid maner of Castre or in any of the seid londes *and* tenementes in
Castre aforeseid, shal make laufull *and* sufficient dymysse of theire estat,
title, and interesse thereof to the seid John Paston, knyght, or to such
personez as the same John Paston wol assigne and to theire heires foreuer- 90
more, discheirged of any rent, reconusaunce, execucion, or any charge
other than the same maners, londes, and tenementes or any parcell of them
were charged tyme of the first estat thereof made to the seid Duke or to
any person to th'use of the same Duke. And if William Yeluerton, knyght
and justice, or William Geney, seriaunt, haue not relessed or graunted 95
theire estat in the seid maner of Castre to the seid John, Duke of Norfolk,
nor to none other persone to th'use of the same Duke, than the said reuerend
fader shal doo his effectuell deuoure to cause the said William Yeluerton

---

[3] *Last six words, except* -ley, *on eras.*
[4] *Ending repr. by superior* r *with additional flourish.*
[5] *These two words on eras.*

421

and William Geney to graunte theire said estat to the seid reuerend fader
100 or to the seid John Paston, knyght, or to such personez as the seid John
Paston wol assigne and to theire heires foreuermore, or relesse in-to theire
possession before the seid fest of Cristmasse, discharged of any rent,
reconusaunce, execucion or any charge by theym or either of them made
other than the same maners, londes, and tenementez or any parcell of them
105 were charged tyme of the first estat thereof made to the seid William
Yeluerton *and* William Geney.

   And if th'estat of the seid maner[6] of Castre to the seid John Paston,
knyght, be not so made by the seid Duke and other to his vse possessed
thereof, the said reuerend fader graunteth that withyn iij monethes next
110 foloyng the said fest of Witsontide to do make a laufull and sufficient estat
of fee symple of the maner of Guton with th'appurtenaunce to the said
John Paston, knyght, or to such personez as the same John wol assigne *and*
to theire heires, discharged as it was tyme of the feoffement made thereof
to the seid reuerend fader, or elles to paye and content to the same John
115 Paston, knyght, or to his assignez withyn the same iij monethes dccxl
markez laufull money of Englond. Also it is aggreed that if the seid John
Paston, knyght, haue not the seid maner [of] Guton to hym and to his heires
as is aforesaid, than the same reuerend fader shal discharge the seid John
Paston of promys of bargayne of the seid maner of Guton by the seid John
120 Paston, knyght, made to Thomas, Archebisshop of Canterburye.

   Also, as to the said maners of Halysdon, Drayton, Tolthorp, *and*
tenementes in the cité of Norwich with theire appurtenaunces,[7] it is aggreed
betwene the seid parties that the seid reuerend fader *and* John Paston,
knyght, shal sue for the obteynyng thereof by laufull and resonable menes
125 by aduyse of theire counseill *and* at theire owne cost; and suche thynge
theryn as thei[8] haue, or shalbe recouered, goten, or obteyned by them or
any of them, or by any other havyng therein[9] title or interesse to th'use of
any of them, shalbe equally dyvided betwene the said reuerend fader *and*
John Paston, knyght, *and* theire bothe heyres, how be it that any of the
130 seid reuerend fader *and* John Paston, knyght, decesse before the same
recoueryng, getyng, or obteynyng. And neither of the same partiez, heyres,
or executours shal take advauntage by the survyuer, butt oonely haue the
halfdele of such thyngez as shalbe recouered, goten, or obteyned. Also
neither of the same partiez shal theryn take nor make ende nor relesse
135 withoute assent of other. And it is also aggreed that the seid reuerend fader
of the said maners of Drayton, Tolthorp, and tenementes in the citee of
Norwych and londes, tenementez, and possessions in Drayton, Tolthorp,
and Norwich with theire appurtenauncez[10] which were of the said John

---

6 -s *erased.*   7 *Loop for* -es *written over curl on* -c.
8 -i *added later.*   9 -in *smaller, on eras.*
10 -z *added later.*

422

Fastolf, knyght, shal thereof[11] before the said fest of Cristmas enfeffe Guy
Fairefaxe, serieant at lawe, John Paston, sqwyer, Roger Tounesend, 140
Nicholas Hervy, *and* William Danvers, to haue to them *and* to theire
heires, to th'use of the seid reuerend fader *and* John Paston in fourme
abouesaid.

And ouer this, as to the seid maner of Wynterton called Begvilez, the
maner of Reppes in Bastwik, londes *and* tenementes called Cattes in Haryng- 145
by, the thirde part of the maner of Rounham, londes *and* tenementez in
Yernemouthe, londes *and* tenementez called Billez in Stokesby, with theire
membres, possessions, hereditamentes, *and* appurtenauncez, it is aggreed
betwene the said parties that the said reuerend fader[12] ⌈shal there-of⌉
before the seid fest of Cristmas cause to be made to the said Guy Fairefaxe, 150
John Paston, sqwyer, Roger Tounesend, Nicholas Hervy, *and* William
Danvers a lawfull *and* sufficiant dymyss of estat of fee symple, aswell such
and the hoole estat *and* partez of the same as the seid reuerend fader and
the seid Lord Beauechamp now haue or at any tyme had by reson of the
feoffement thereof made by the seid Rauf Lord Suydeley *and* other to the 155
seid reuerend fader, Lord Beauchamp, *and* other, as such *and* the hole
estat *and* partez of the same as the seid reuerend fader hathe or shal haue
by relesse of the feoffés of the seid John Paston, knyght, or by the seid
Duke or ⌈other⌉ to his vse, or by the seid William Yeluerton *and* William
Geney or any of [the] feoffés of the seid John Fastolf. 160

Also the seid reuerend fader graunteth to doo his effectuell deuoure to
cause William Paston to make thereof dymyss of his estat of fee in the
same fourme, *and* that by sub pena as the case requyreth, which feoffement
of the seid reuerend fader thereof in fourme aboueseid shalbe made to
th'entent that the seid John Paston, knyght, *and* his heires shal haue thereof 165
as much londes *and* tenementez as to-gedir with the seid maner of Castre,
londes *and* tenementes in Castre, the said maner, londes, *and* tenementez
called Spencers[13] in Haryngby, shal atteyne to the yerely value of l li. ouer
all chargez and reprises at eleccion of the seid J. Paston. And the residue
thereof aboue l li. yerely shalbe to th'use of the seid reuerend fader *and* his 170
heires, to be disposed for the sowle of the seid John Fastolf. And that as
wel the seid maners of Castre and Haryngby, the seid londes and tenementez
in Castre *and* Haryngby, as the said maners of Wynterton, Reppes, the
iij[d] [14] part of the maner of Rounham, londes and tenementez called Cattys
in Haryngby, londes *and* tenementes in Yernemouth, londes *and* tenementez 175
called Billes in Stokesby, with theire membres, possessions, hereditamentes,
and appurtenauncez, shalbe extended to an yerly value by the discrecion
of Roger Tovnesend and William Danvers,[15] the same extent to be made
in writyng before the fest of Candelmas next foloyng; and if the seid Roger

---

[11] -of *on eras.*   [12] *Last four words on eras.*   [13] *MS.* Spenes.
[14] *MS.* iij[the].   [15] *Short eras.*

180 and William or any of them decesse before the seid extent made, than it is
aggreed betwene the said partiez that euerych of þem[16] shal for theire part
name oone persone to make the same extent before the fest of Estre than
next foloyng aftir the date of these presentez. And if the seid Roger and
William, or if thei decesse before extent made the seid other personez

185 named in fourme aboueseid, can not accord in makyng of the seid extent,
than the seid partiez bethe aggreed that the same Roger and William, or
if they decesse the seid other personez named, shal chese an vmpere to
make the seid extent before the fest of Witsontide next foloyng; vnto which
extent in any of the seid fourmez made bothe the seid parties shal stond.

190 And if noone extent be made in any of the seid fourmez before the seid
fest of Witsontid, than[15] the seid feofféz shal suffre the seid John Paston,
knyght, to haue thereof, and of Castre and Haryngby as is aforeseid, to the
yerly value of l li., and the seid reuerend fader shal haue the residue thereof
ouer l li.

195 Also the seid reuerend fader is aggreed att his owne charge[15] to obteyne
of the Pope a sufficiant dispensacion for chaungyng of the place and fundacion of the seid perpetuel prestes and poore folkes fro the seid maner of
Castre. Also, withyn vj monethes next foloyng the seisyn and possession
of þe same reuerend fader obteyned and had of all the seid maners, londes,

200 and tenementes, excepted before excepted, the same reuerend fader graunteth to exhibit and fynd perpetuelly in his college att Oxonford vij prestys
and vij poore scolers to praye for the sowles of the seid John Fastolf and
of Dame Milicent his wife, his frendys and benefactoures. Also the same
reuerend fader graunteth to acquyte and discharge the seid John Paston,

205 knyght, and th'executoure of John Paston, sqwyer, of m[1]m[1]m[1]m[1] marcz
which mought be claymed by the seid reuerend fader for the bargayne
pretented to be made betwene the seid John Fastolf and John Paston,
sqwyer; and ouer this the same reuerend fader graunteth to acquyte and
discharge the same John Paston, knyght, of all summez of money, jowelx,

210 plate, aras, and all goodes and catallex quyk or dede which late were of
the seid John Fastolf and com to the hondes or to th'use of the seid John
Paston, sqwyer, John Paston, knyght, or any of them, or any other persone to
th'use of the said John Paston, sqwyer, John Paston, knyght, or any of them.
Also, if any of the seid maners, londes, and tenementes which shal re-

215 mayne or be to th'use of the said reuerend fader lye to the pleasure of the
seid John Paston, knyght, þe same reuerend fader graunteth byfore th'
amortezement thereof þe said John Paston to haue them to hym or to his
heires by wey of eschaunge for othere maners, londes, and tenementez of
suere title and like value.

220 Also the same John Paston vpon his feith, knyghthode, and honesté

---

[16] *End of line, which may have encouraged use of* þ- (*though it is fairly common below*).
The writing becomes smaller towards the end.

promytteth to delyvere before þe said fest of Cristmas to þe seid reuerend
fader all dedes, chartres,[17] euydences,[18] *and* munimentz concernyng soolly
any of þe said maners, londes, *and* tenementes which by vertu of this[19]
aggrement shal remayne toward þe said reuerend fader *and* which þe same
John Paston, or any other person to his vse, now hathe or by the seid fest 225
of Cristmas shal haue. And all such dedes, chartres, munimentz, *and*
euidencez which the same John Paston, or any other person to his vse, hathe
concernyng aswel the seid maners, londes, *and* tenementes which as is foresaid shal remayne to the said reuerend fader, as to þe said maners, londes,
and tenementes which by the seid aggrement shal remayne to þe said John 230
Paston, knyght, the same John Paston as aboue promitteth to do bryng
before the seid fest of Cristmas all the seid dedes, chartres, munimentz, and
euidences[18] to þe Priory of Seynt Marie Ouerey in Suthwerk, there to be
delyuered *and* putt in a chest lokked with ij lockes *and* ij keyes, whereof
oon key shal remayne with the seid reuerend fader *and* a-nother key shal 235
remayne with the seid John Paston, knyght, to th'entent that bothe þe
seid partiez may haue recourse to the seid euidences[18] whan any of theire
possessions be putt in plee or trowble; vnto which recourse so to be had
bothe the seid partiez shalbe aggreable, aftir the trwe entent hereof declared
by writyng endented *and* triparted, whereof oone part shal remayne with 240
þe seid reuerend fader *and* a-nother part thereof shal remayne with the
said John Paston, knyght, and þe iij part thereof shal remayne with the
Priour of Seynt Marie Ouerey.

And in like wise the seid reuerend fader promytteth on his honoure[4] to
delyuere to the seid John Paston, knyght, before the seid fest of Cristmas 245
all dedes, chartres, euidences, *and* munimentz concernyng soolly any of
the seid maners, londes, *and* tenementez which by vertu of ⌜this⌝ aggrement
shal remayne toward the seid John Paston, knyght, and which the seid
reuerend fader, or any persone to his vse, ⌜nowe⌝ hathe or by the seid fest
of Cristmas shal haue. And all such dedes, chartres, munimentz, *and* 250
euidences[18] which the seid reuerend fader, or any persone to his vse, hath
concernyng[20] aswel the seid maners, londes, and tenementz which shal
remayne to þe seid reuerend fader as to þe seid maners, londes, *and* tenementez which shal remayne to þe seid John Paston, knyght, the seid
reuerend fader as aboue promitteth to do bryng before þe seid fest of 255
Cristmas all þe seid dedes, chartres, munimentes, *and* euidences to þe seid
Priory of Seynt Marie Ouerey, there to be delyuered *and* putt in-to the
seid chest to th'entent aforesaid.

In witnesse whereof the seid partiez vnto thies indentures chaungeablé

---

[17] *Abbr. here and regularly below* chres *with long curve.*
[18] *Written* -cz, *evidently as abbr.; elsewhere both* -es *and* -ez *are used.*
[19] t- *inserted later.*
[20] concer *on eras.*

260 haue putt their*e* sealez. Date is the xiiij^{the} daye of Jule the x^{the} yere of the
reyne of Kyng Edward the iiij^{the}.

253. Indenture of release and quitclaim of Fastolf manors
1470, 14 July

Magdalen College, Norfolk and Suffolk 28. Parchment, $16\frac{1}{4}\times8\frac{1}{2}$ in. (indented). Clerk's hand, different from no. 252. Signature autograph; seal.

Dorse: In hands of endorsements of no. 252: *Indentura inter dominum
episcopum Wintoniensem et J. Paston militem de acquietancia et relaxacione.
E. iiij^{ti} x^{mo}.*

G. 645/750 (abstract).

This endenture made bitwene the right reu*er*ent fader in God, William
Wayneflete, Bisshop of Wynchestr*e*, executo*ur* of the testament of Sir
John Fastolf, knyght, on the oon parte and John Paston, knyght, son and
heire of John Paston, squyer, and executoure of the testament of the same
5 John Paston, squyer, named to be oon of th'executours of the testament
of the said John Fastolff, on the other parte, witnesseth that where in other
endentures made bitwene the same parties, wherof the date is the day of
makyng of thiez p*r*esentz, of disposicion and departyng of alle the man*er*s,
londez, tenementz, possessions, and hereditament*es*, with their*e* app*ur*-
10 tena*u*ncez, whiche were of the said John Fastolf, knyght, in the counteez
of Surré, Essex, Suff*olk* and Norff*olk*, and in the citee of Norwich, the
said John Paston, knyght, hath oonly therof taken and shall have toward
hym-self *and* his heires and other to his vse the man*er*e of Castr*e* with th'
app*ur*tena*u*ncez and the londes and tenementz called Vaux, Redh*a*m, and
15 Bosoms in Castr*e*, the man*er*e called Spencers in Haryngby, and the londes
and ten*em*entz called Spensers in Haryngby with their*e* app*ur*tena*u*ncez,
and also to have to hym and to his heires *and* other to his vse of the said
man*er*s, londez, *and* ten*em*entz, togider with the man*er*e of Wynterton
called Begvyles, the man*er*e of Reppes in Bastwyk, the third parte of the
20 man*er*e of Rounh*a*m, londes and ten*em*entz called Cattes in Haryngby,
londez and ten*em*entz called Billes in Stokesby, londes and ten*em*entz in
Yernemouth with their*e* membres, possessions, hereditamentz, and app*ur*-
tena*u*ncez to the yerly value of l li. over all charges and reprisez at eleccion
of the said John Paston accordyng to the saide other indentures, and of
25 the man*er*ez of Haylesdon, Drayton, Tolthorp, and ten*em*entz in the cité
of Norwich with their*e* app*ur*tena*u*ncez the said reu*er*ent fader and John
Paston, knyght, to have as in the said endent*ur*es more playnly may appiere,
the said John Paston, knyght, not to have more of any of the man*er*s,
londes, tenementz, possessions, and hereditament*es* whiche were of the

426

said John Fastolf, but vtterly to leve theym to the said reuerent fader, to 30
parfourme therof the wille and entent of the said John Fastolf, but if the
said John Paston like to have of theym by waye of eschaunge as in the saide
endentures more playnly may appiere. Therfore the said reuerent fader
relesseth and quietclaymeth by thiez presentz to the¹ said John Paston
m¹m¹m¹m¹ marc. by reason of the bargayne allegged to be made bitwene 35
the said John Fastolf and the said John Paston, squyer. The said reuerent
fader also relesseth, dischargeth, and quietclaymeth by thiez presentz to
the said John Paston, knyghte, and his heires the fundacion or makyng
of [a] college and endowyng of vij preestes and vij poure men to praie
perpetuelly for the sowles of the said John Fastolf *and* of Dame Milcent 40
his wif and theire benefactours, whiche fundacion, makyng, and endowyng
the said John Paston, squyer, by reason of the said allegged bargayn was
bownde and sholde have made. The said reuerent fader also relesseth and
quietclaymeth by thiez presentz to the said John Paston, knyght, alle
manere of accions, claymes, *and* demaundes whiche the said reuerent fader 45
hath or may have ayenst the said John Paston, knyght, his heires or executourz, or ayenst th'executourz of the testament of the said John Paston,
squyer, or any of theym by reason of the testament of the said John Fastolff
and of the godes or catelles whiche were of the said John Fastolf *and* whiche
cam to the handes of the said John Paston, squyer, John Paston, knyght, 50
or any other persone to the vse of theym or of any of theym. And the same
John Paston, knyght, relesseth and quietclaymeth by thiez presentez
to the said reuerent fader alle maner accions, claymes, and demaundez of
londez, possessions, or godes whiche were of the said John Fastolf whiche
the same John Paston hath, or may have by reason of the said allegged 55
bargayn, or by reason of any agreement bifore tyme had or made bitwene
the said reuerent fader and the same John Paston, or by any other reason
or cause growen bifore the makyng of the saide other indentures; alwey
forseen that this present endenture nor no graunte nor relesse therin conteyned extend not to the avoydyng or dischargyng of any promys, coven- 60
aunt, penalité, paiement of money, estate, or relesse of londez or tenementz,
or liueree of evidences² to be made, or graunte to be parfourmed or caused
to be parfourmed by any of the saide partiez to oþer or any to their³ vse to
be parfourmed herafter, conteyned in the said other indentures, but that
all the poyntes and articles in the saide other indentures conteyned be 65
truely parfourmed and kepte after the true intent of the same.

   In wittenesse wherof the said partiez vnto thies endentures have chaungeably putte theire seales the xiiij day of Juyll the xᵗʰ yere of the reigne of
Kyng Edward the iiijᵗʰ.

John Paston, K. 70

253. ¹ to the *repeated*.   ² *These three words on eras.*
³ *From* or caused *to* their *on eras.*

254. Indenture of agreement concerning Fastolf manors
1470, 14 July

Magdalen College, Norfolk and Suffolk 11. Parchment, 18⅜ × 6 in. (indented). Clerk's hand, the same as no. 252.

Dorse blank. Pendant seals of the Bishop of Winchester and Paston.

G. 645/750 (abstract).

This indenture triparted made betwene the right reuerend fader in God, William, Bisshop of Wynchestre, on the oone part, and John Paston, knyght, Guy Fairfaxe, serieant at lawe, John Paston, sqvyer, Roger Tovnesend, Nicholas Hervy, and William Danvers on the other part, witnesseth
5 that where the said reuerend fader, by his chartre ⌈indented⌉ whereof date is þe daye of makyng of thies presentez, hathe enfeoffed þe said Guy, John Paston, sqvyer, Nicholas, and William of þe maners of Drayton and Tolthorp in þe counté of Norfolk and of all þe londes, tenementez, possessions, and hereditamentez in Drayton, Tolthorp, and in the cité of Norwich
10 with theire appurtenauncez which sumtyme were of John Fastolf, knyght, and which þe said reuerend fader, togedir with other late ioyntly had to them, theire heirs[1] and assignez, of þe dymysse and feoffement of Rauf Boteler, knyght, Lord Suydeley, and other as in the said chartre may appiere, th'entent of þe said feoffement is that such thyng as by the said
15 reuerend fader and John Paston, any of them or theire heirs, shal thereof be recouered, goten, or obteyned shalbe equally dyvided betwene þe said reuerend fader and John Paston, knyght, and theire both heires, and nethir of þe said parties shal take advauntage by the survyver of other, but oonely haue the halfedele of such thynge as shalbe recouered, goten, or obteyned.
20 And forthermore, where the said reuerend fader by oon other chartre ⌈indented⌉, whereof date is also the day of makyng of thies presentez, hathe enfeoffed the said Guy, John Paston, sqvyer, Roger, Nicholas, and William of þe maner of Wynterton called Begvilez, þe maner of Reppys in Bastwik, þe thirde part of the maner of Rowneham, londez and tenementez called
25 Cattes in Haryngby, londes and tenementes called Billez in Stokesby, and all the londes, tenementes, possessions, and hereditamentez in Wynterton, Bastwik, Rounham, and Yernemouthe, with appurtenauncez, which sumtyme were of þe said John Fastolf and wich the said reuerend fader togedir with other late ioyntly had to them, theire heires and assignes, of þe dymysse
30 and feoffement of þe said Rauf Lord Suydeley and other as in the said chartre[2] maye appiere, th'entent of the said feoffement is that ⌈of⌉ þe maners of Wynterton and Reppys, the iij part of the maner of Rounham,

----

254. [1] *Abbr, hrs with stroke above ; so again later.*
[2] *Abbr. chre with stroke above.*

428

londez and tenementez called Cattes in Haryngby, londes and tenementez
called Billez in Stokesby, and all þe londez, tenementez, and possessions
and hereditamentez in Wynterton, Bastwik, Rounham, and Yernemouth 35
abouesaid, *with* th'appurtenauncez, the said John Paston, knyght, and his
heirs shal haue as muche of maners, londes, *and* tenementez, togedir *with*
the maner of Castre, londes and tenementez called Vaux, Redham, *and*
Bosoms in Castre, the maner, londes, *and* tenementez called Spencers in
Haryngby, shal atteyne to þe yerely value of l li. ouer all charges and 40
reprises att eleccion of the said John Paston, and the residue thereof aboue
l li. yerely shalbe to th'use of the said reuerend fader and of his heirs to be
disposed for the soule of the said John Fastolf, alwey foreseen if any extent
thereof be made in any fourme conteyned in other indentures thereof made
betwene þe said reuerend fader and John Paston, knyght, or theire heyres 45
⌈that⌉ bothe the said partiez stond to the same extent so made.

   In witness whereof þe said partiez vnto thies indentures haue chaungeablé putt theire seales, the thirde part hereof ensealed *with* þe seales of the
said reuerend fader and John Paston, knyght, remaynyng *with* the said
Guy Fairefaxe. Date is the xiiij^the^ day of Juyll the xth yere of þe reigne of 50
Kyng Edward the iiij^th^.

255. To Lord Beauchamp: draft   1470, July

Add. 35251, f. 25. 11½ × 4¼ in. Text and signature in an unidentified hand,
the same as that of the draft of no. 252;[1] marginal notes autograph.

Dorse: Marks of folding, no seal or address. Rough notes in Paston's hand:
dominus de Bewchamp and *therffor in non wyse.*

This is part of a corrected draft, clearly of about the same date as no. 252.
   G. LXXV/674.

And[2] forasmoch as I am credibly[3] enfourmed that my lord of Winchestre
hath sent to you desiring that ye shold ensele dyuers writingys of[4] graunt
and relesse of your estat in alle such maners, londys, *and* tenementys as
late wer of[3] J. Fastolf, knyght, and wheryn[5] ye, togider wyth other, be
iointly enfeffed to th'use of the seid J. Fastolf[6] I,[7] considering the honor- 5
able disposicion *and* gret sadnesse of my seid lord of Winchestre, which ⌈is

---

255. [1] *At the foot Blomefield wrote* The Hand-Wrighting of Sr Iohn Paston; *but, except
for the marginalia, this cannot be accepted.*
   [2] *In margin opposite* To þe Lord Bechamp (*with dotted circumflex over* -mp), *and a little
lower,* to myn oncle Wylliam in lyke forme, *autograph.*
   [3] *This word underlined.*   [4] re *canc.*   [5] And wheryn *underlined.*
   [6] to . . . Fastolf *underlined.*   [7] therfor *canc.*

feffé of the seid therin *and*[18] hath now taken vpon [hym] th'administraci*o*n of testament of the seid J. F., trusting verryly that my seid lord wol as conscience requireth consider my title *and* interese in that behalf, pr*ai*e
10 you right hertely that, not wy*th*stonding any labo*ur* or mocion on my p*ar*t or for me ⌈in tyme passed⌉ made to you to ensele any writyng of gr*au*nt or relesse of yo*ur* seid estat to me or to myn vse, that ye wol now ensele *and* p*ar*fourme the entent *and* desir of my seid lord of Win*ch*estre now made vnto you.

15 Ser JOHN PASTON, K.

256. To JOHN PASTON III 1470, 5 August

Add. 43491, f. 15. 12 × 10¼ in. Autograph.

Dorse: Traces of red wax over tape. Remnants of an address not certainly in Paston's hand: *Paston &c.*

The date is evidently very shortly before Clarence and Warwick landed at Dartmouth in September 1470 and restored Henry VI to the throne.
 F. ii, p. 46. G. 648/753 (part).

Brother, I comand me to yow, letyng yow wete þat I sende yow a lett*er* in a boxe by Corby, *and* a nother by Gulmyn the gonn*er*e whyche I wote well is nat comen yit to yow; wherffor I praye yow to remembre the lett*er* broght to yow by Coorby, *and* in cheff that the euydence whyche ye wote
5 offe be her*e* in all the haste, for by my trowthe *and* they be not her by Sat*er*daye itt is to me a r*e*proche, I haue so largely appoyntyd *and* promysed ther-in.
　　Item, I thynke þat Mestresse Kateryn Dodlee hathe lettyd yow, wherffor iff it soo be þat Dauerse com in-to Norffolke er*e* than ye haue serchyd for*e*
10 the seyde euydence, he woll p*ar*case desyr*e* to helpe yow, whyche nedythe nat to doo, for I haue seyde by the assent off Dauerse to my lorde off Wynchest*er* that he scholde helpe yow; neuyr*e* the lesse Dauerse seythe he woll nowther desyr*e* it nor besy hym abowt it. He schall com thedyr*e* for other cawsesse, noo-thyng ageyn myn aduantage, wherffor I praye yow
15 make hym goode cheer *and* holde hym company in that ye maye. Also telle Johne Pampyng that the mayde at þe Bulle at Cluddys at Westm*in*ster sent me on a[1] tyme by hym to the Moor*e* a rynge off goolde to a tookne, whyche I hadde not off hym; wherffor I wolde he scholde sende it hyddre, for sche most haue itt ageyn, or*e* ellys v s., for it was not hyrrys.

---

[8] *How much of this interlineation is intended to remain is doubtful. After* feffé, and *also is* canc., *after* seid, J. F. and *also;* feffé and *also is underlined.*
256. [1] *No space.*

Item, I praye yow be redye, the mater qwykennythe bothe for yowe *and* 20
yowres as well as for vs *and* howrys. As for tydynges, my lorde Erche-
bysshop is at the Moore, but ther is beleffte wy*th* hym dyuerse off the
Kynges s*er*uantes,² and as I vnderstond he hathe lysence to tarye ther tyll
he be sente foore. Ther be many folkes vppe in the Northe, soo þat Percy
is not able to recyst them; *and* soo the Kyng hathe sente for hys feeod men 25
to koom to hym, for³ he woll goo to putt them down,⁴ *and* soom seye þat
the Kynge ssholde come ageyn to London *and* that in haste, *and* as itt is
sayde Cortenayes be londyd in Deuenschyre *and* therre rewle.

Item, that þe⁵ Lordes Clarance *and* Warwyk⁶ wooll assaye to londe in
Ingelonde euyrye daye, as folkes feere. I praye yow late not John Mylsent 30
be longe from me, wy*th* as moche as can be gaderyd, *and* also that ye
wryght to me off all thynges that I haue wretyn to yow fore, so that I maye
haue answer*e* off eu[er]y thynge. Other thynges Bachelere Walter*e*, berere
here-off, schall informe yow.

Wretyn at London the Sondaye nexte beffor Seynt Lawrence Daye. 35

Also my brother Edmonde is not yit remembryd. He hathe not to lyff
wy*th*; thynke on hym, &c.

JOHN PASTON, KN.

257. Indenture pledging plate 1470, 7 August

Add. Charter 17250. Parchment, 6 × 6¼ in., top indented and foot irregularly cut; traces of red wax. Hand of no. 251.

Dorse: Blank except for *Richard Rawlyns* in contemporary hand.

G. 649/754 (abstract).

This endenture made at London the vij^the day of August in þe x^the yere of
the regne of Kyng Edward þe iiij^the bytwene S*yr* John Paston, knyght, on
the o¹ p*ar*tye, and Ric*hard* Rawlyn of London, grocer*e*, on the other p*ar*tye,
witnesseth² that þe said S*yr* John hathe þe day *and* yere afore said solde,
bargayned, *and* delyu*er*ed to þe said Ric*hard* ij chargers, iiij potengers, 5
weying xj li. Troy weyght on vnc. *and* iij q*uar*ter of seluer, for xx li. of
lawfull money of Englond receyued by the said S*yr* John the day of makyng
of this present*es*. And the said Ric*hard* graunteth þat and the said S*yr* John,
his execut*ors* or assigneez pay or do to be payed to the said Ric*hard*, his
execut*ors* or assigneez xx li. of lawfull money of Englond by-fore þe 10

---

² *and* iff *canc.* ³ *Over ampersand.* ⁴ *MS.* dowm.
⁵ *Inserted later.* ⁶ -k *over* ll.
257. ¹ *Uncertain because damaged.* ² wit- *abbr.* w^t.

feste of Wythsonday next comyng, that than he shall doo delyuer to the said S*yr* John or his assigneez so paying the said xx li. all the foresaid dysshes of seluer.

In wytnesse wher-of the p*ar*tyes aboue said to this endentures haue set
15 to there seles the day *and* yere a-boue wreten.

258. To JOHN PASTON III   1470, 15 November

Add. 34889, ff. 105ᵛ–106ʳ. 12 × 16¾ in. Recto autograph, verso in Wykes's hand, signature autograph.

Dorse: Continuation of text. Traces of red wax. Address in Wykes's hand:

To John Paston, esquyere, in haste.

The date appears, as Gairdner notes, from the position of the Earl of Oxford. He took a leading part in the temporary restoration of Henry VI in 1470, and was charged with organizing the defence of the eastern counties against Edward's return (Scofield, i. 568, and his letters Add. 43489, ff. 41, 42, G. 663/769 and 664/770). The autograph part of this letter is hastily written, with many more errors, corrections, and defective constructions than usual in John II's writing.

F. iv, p. 450. G. 656/762.

Brother, I comand me to yow, prayng yow þat thys be yow[r] guydyng iff other folkys wy[ll] agré to þe same: þat M*aster* Roos, olde Kneuett, ye, *and* the worshypffullest þat wyll do for owre sake, as Arblast*er*, John Gyneye,[1] Wodhows, *and* al other gentelmen þat at the daye wyll be in
5 Norwyche, þat ye all holl os on bodye come to-gedre þat my lorde off[2] Oxenfforde maye ondrestande þat som strenkethe[3] restyth ther, by whyche iff it be well handely[d] *and* proue in the handely[ng] I trow Heydonnes parte woll be but an easy comparyson. Neu*er* the lesse ye than most ye[4] be ware off on payn, *and* that is thys: Heydon wyll off crafft e sende amonge yow
10 p*ar* case vj or more w*yth* harneyse for*e* to sclandr*e* yowre felawschep wyth sey⟨in⟩g[5] that they be ryotous peple *and* nott of substance. Requer*e* the gentelmen aboue wretyn that iff any men be in Norwyche off the contré that ber*e* any suche harneyse to do them leue it, or*e* any glyst*er*yng byll. The meyr*e and* siteseynes off Norwyche wher wonte to haue a sertayne
15 in harneyse off men off the town to þe nombre off ij or*e* iij or*e* vᶜ, whyche iff they[6] now do in lyke case those woll owe bett*er* wyll to M*aster* Roos *and* yow þan to othere folkys; *and* iff it be so þat the thowte nat to haue non

258. [1] *MS.* gymeye.   [2] off *repeated.*
     [3] *MS.* strenkethethe.
     [4] *Repeated* ye *retained because it is uncertain which Paston would have deleted.*
     [5] *Hole in paper.*   [6] be *canc.*

suche at thys tyme I thynke the meyre[7] woll do it at þe request off[8] Master
Roos *and* yow, iff lak off tyme cawse it not.

Item, be well ware off Clopton, fore he hathe avysed my lorde to be all 20
to-gydre rewled by Heydon, in so moche he hathe reportyd that all thyng
and all materys off my lordes, *and* in all the contré, scholde [be] guydyd by
Heydon. Iff Clopto*n* ore Hygham[9] or*e* Lowes John be besy, prese in to my
lorde byffor the[m], fore the[r] be no Suffo*lk* materys, *and* tell the raylyng,
prayng them not to cawse my lorde to owe hys fauore for*e* there plesere ⌈to 25
som folkes ther*e* present⌉, fore iff my lorde fauoryd, or*e* theye owther*e*, by
lyklyod my lorde *and* they myght lose vj tyme as many frendes as he scholde
wynn by ther*e* meanes. Also iff ye cowde fynde the menes, Master R. *and*
ye, to cawse [the] meyr*e* in my lordes ere to telle hym, thow he scholde
bynde my lorde to concell, that the loue of the contré *and* syté restyth[10] on 30
owre syde, *and* that other folkys be not belouyd ner*e* neuyr*e* wer*e*, thys
wolde do nonn harme, iff it be soo þat all thynge go olyuer[11] currant; w*yth*
mor*e* to remembre[12] that ther*e* is owt off that contré that be nat at[13] Nor-
w*ych*, besyde[14] me, that be ryght worshypfull *and* as [15]worshypffull as few
be-longyng to Norffo*lk* that woll *and*[16] schall do my lorde s*e*ruyse, the 35
rather for*e* my sake *and* Master Rossys,[17] *and* the rather*e* iff my lorde remytt
nat moche thynge to Heydon guydyng. Also the goodely menes[18] wherby
ye best can entrete my cosyn ⌈Syr W.⌉ Calthorpe[19] at the seyde day, wse
them to caw[s]e ⌈hym⌉, iff itt wyll be, to come, ye in hys companye *and* he
in yow[r] in cheff at yow[r] cheff schew, *and* Master Roos *and* he in com- 40
pany; latyng my seyde cosyn wete þat I tolde hym ones þat I scholde meue
hym off a thyng I trostyd scholde be[20] encressyng bothe to hys honor*e and*
well.

I sende yow a lettyr*e* com to Norwyche by lyklyod to yow on Monday
last past; it come some-what the lattre, for*e* I wende haue dyed nat longe 45
by-foore it. Also I receyued on from yow by ⌈Master⌉ Blomvyle yist*er* euyn.
Tell my cosyn W. Yelu*e*rton that he may not appyre off a whylle in no
wyse; I trow my cosyn hys fadr*e* schall sende hym worde off the same. Do
þat ye can secretly that my lorde be nat heuy lorde on-to hym. It is vndrestande þat itt is doon by the craffte off Heydo*n*[21]—he gate hym in-to that 50
offyce to haue to be ageyn me, *and* nowe he sethe that he hathe done[22] all
þat he can ageyn me *and* now may doo no mor*e*, nowe he wolde remeve
hym. The daye is comen þat he fastyd the euyn fore, as an holye yonge

[7] ande si *canc.*		[8] yow *canc.*	
[9] J *and incomplete* o *canc.*		[10] restythe *follows* restyth.	
[11] *This, though unintelligible, appears to be the correct reading.*			
[12] *MS.* remememembre.		[13] at *repeated.*	
[14] my bro *canc.*		[15] as *repeated.*	
[16] and *follows ampersand.*		[17] *and* that owe me the *canc.*	
[18] thatt *canc.*		[19] ⌈do⌉ iff to *canc.*	
[20] the *canc.*		[21] *Abbr.* (*at end of line*) heyd, -d *tailed.*	
[22] *Written* don, *with unusually elaborate tail on* -n.			

monke[23] fastyd more than all the couent, afftre that fore hys holynesse[24] *and*
55 fastyng hopyd to be abbott, whyche afterwarde was abbot, than leffte he
hys abstynens seyng the daye was come þat he fast the eeuyn fore.[25]

Brothere, I *pray* you recomand me to my lord of Oxfordes gode lordshyp,
and where as I told my lord that I shuld haue awayted vppon hys lordshyp
in[26] Norffolk, I wold that I myght soo haue don leuer then a hundred li.;
60 but in godefeth[27] thos maters that I told my lord [I] trowed shold lette me
wer not fynyshed tyl yesterday, wherfor y[e]f that cause. *And* also syn
Halowmasse euery othere day my3tnot hold vppe myn heed, nor yet may,
insomoch that sythen the seyd day in Westm*inster* Hall *and* in othere place
I haue goon w*yth* a staffe as a goste, as men sayd, more lyke that I rose owte
65 of the erth then owte of a fayre laydys bedd; *and* yet am in lyke case,
sauyng I am in gode hope to amende. Wherfore I beshyche hys lordshyp
to pardon me, *and* at a-nothere tyme I shall make dobell a-mend*es*, for
by my trouth a man cowydnot haue hyred me for v[c] markis[28] w*yth* so gode
will to haue ryden in-to Norffolk as to haue at thys season, there to haue
70 awaytyd un hys lordshyp; and also I wold haue ben glad, for my lord
shold haue knowyn what seruys that I my3t haue don hys lordshyp in
that contray.

It*em*, youre geere ys send to you, as Thom*as* Stompes sayth, sauyng
Mylsent*es* geere *and* the shaferon, whych I cannot entrete Thom*as* Stompes
75 to goo therefore thys iij or iiij days, wherfore I knokkyd hym on the crowne,
&c.

It*em*, loke that ye take hyde that[29] the lettere wernot broken or that it
com to youre hand*es*, &c.

Wryten at London on Thursday next aftere Seynt Erkenwold*es* Day, &c.
80   JOHN PASTON, K.

259. Inventory   Probably 1470

Add. 39848, f. 54. 8½ × 12 in. Pampyng's hand.

Dorse: Continuation of text (left unfinished).

The approximate date appears from the heading and from John Paston II's petition
of 1475 (no. 294). This inventory is probably concerned with the 'stuf and ordinaunces' which the petition says were taken by Norfolk during his first occupation
of Caister, ending in 1470. John III had made an inventory of the contents of
Caister when he was forced to leave it in September 1469 (see his letter no. 336);

23 *and* feynyng grett sympless *canc.*
24 *Last five letters hasty and imperfectly inked.*
25 *Recto ends. The rest, except signature, in Wykes's hand.*
26 thys contray *canc.*
27 *Tail of -h brought back through and above -t-, perhaps intending insertion of -y-.*
28 -is *above line, at end.*   29 that (*end of line*) *repeated.*

but the present one cannot have been made until the Pastons had regained possession, since they could not have known earlier what had been removed.
  G. 630/734 (note only).

These vndirwretyn be the good*es and* stuffe of howsold lefte in the maner
plase of Caster by Sir John Paston at the entré of my lord of Norff*olk* in-to
the same maner, and born and led awey duryng my lord*es* possession there.[1]

First, xxiij barres of jron lying overthwart the jnner gate and the bakhows
gate, ich worth ij s. iiij d.   5

Item,[2] ij gret fowlers w*yth* vj chambirs lying in the jnner gates.
Item, a lesse fowler and a s*e*rpentyne w*yth* vj chambirs lying in S*er* John
Stilles chambir.
Item, a gret s*e*rpentyne w*yth* iij chambirs lying vpon a carte.
Item, a short potte gonne w*yth* ij chambirs lying in the chapell.   10
Item, iiij gonnes lying in ij stokk*es* callid orgon gonnes, w*yth* ix chambirs.
Item, a gret fowler lying in Bedford*es* Towre w*yth* iij chambirs.
Item, a small s*e*rpentyn w*yth* iij chambirs lying in Penys Towre.
Item, a gret fowler w*yth* iij chambirs lying in the lavendré.
Item, a s*e*rpentyne w*yth* ij chambirs lying in the somer halle.   15
Item, a fowler w*yth* iij chambirs lying in the kechyn.
Item, a small s*e*rpentyne w*yth* iij chambirs lying in the botery.
Item, ij smale s*e*rpentynes w*yth* vj chambirs lying in the gret towre.
Item, a gret fowler w*yth* iij chambirs lying in the larder.
Item, over the bakhows gate a small fowler w*yth* iij chambirs.   20

It*em*, in the overmest chambir of the gret ⌈towre⌉[3] a gret standard and a
peyre gardevyand*es*.
It*em*, in the tresory ij standard*es* bounde w*yth* jron.
Item, in the warderobe a gret standard *and* a cofir w*yth* quarell hed*es* a
busshell.   25
Item, iij panes of glasse of xviij fete wele wrought w*yth* jmages *and* armes
and other besy werk set in the chambir wyndowe over the chapell.
Item, ij panes of glasse of xij fete in the same chambir wrought w*yth* armes
and other devises.
Item, ij panes of glasse of ij fete w*yth* armes in the somer halle.   30
Item, in the same halle *and* chambir next vj plates of coper *and* gilt w*yth*
armes vpon, set in the walle for wax or candell to stonde on.
Item, in the same halle ij longe tabils, on grene, a nothe[r] yelough.
Item, ij peyre trostelis poyntid[4] reed.
Item, iij chayris, wherof ij were poyntid reed *and* on grene.   35
Item, in Daubeneys chambir a cuppebord w*yth* a rennyng leed.

259. [1] *A word erased, apparently* first.
  [2] *This and the next 13 items bracketed together, and in margin* Gonnes xx.
  [3] *Interl. above* chambir *canc.*   [4] *Sic, here and later.*

Item, in the nethermest chambir of the gret towre a falt tabill.
Item, a peire trostelis on-poyntid.
Item, a long chayre poyntid reed in the chambir next the somer halle.
40 Item, a long chayre onpoyntid in Inglose chambir.
Item, a cuppebord *and* a long chayre poyntid in the prest*es* halle.
Item, xij formes standyng in dyvers chambirs.[5]

Item, a morter of brasse set in a long stokke w*yth* a pestell therto.
Item, a tornyng morter of free stoon w*yth* iiij holis.
45 Item, ij gret spittis callid standard*es*.
Item, a peyre quernes to grynd w*yth* mustard.

Item, a gret leed to brewe w*yth* iiij co*m*b malt.
Item, a gret vessell of brasse set in a forneys to sethe in growte.
Item, a gret gylyng fat for iiij co*m*b malt.
50 Item, ix led*es* set in iij stokk*es* to cole in worte, ich conteynyng xx galons
and more.
Item, xij stond*es* to tonne in ale, ich conteynyng xxiiij gal.

Item, ij spyndyls of jron for the hors mille.
It*em*, ij ryngis for the same.
55 Item, ij trendils for the same.

Item, a pese of lede that coverid on of the rounde torett*es* of the jnner gate.
Item, a-nother pese of leed that coveryd a litell toret comyng oute on to the
clokke lede ouer S*ir* James chambir.
Item, a pese of lede of a spowte of ij yard*es* long comyng by the gresis next
60 the chapell.
Item, a cranke of jron to wynde w*yth* the clokke.
Item, xxv lokk*es*.
Item

260. Declaration concerning the Fastolf estate 1471, 12 February.

Magdalen College, Oxford, Norfolk and Suffolk 50. $12\frac{1}{8} \times 8\frac{7}{8}$ in. Hand
unidentified, appearing also in the draft of no. 252, etc.; signature
autograph. Remnants of red wax.

Dorse blank, marks of rough folding.

G. 661/767 (abstract).

5 *Recto ends.*

To alle *Cristen*[1] people whom this p*resent*[2] writing shal come vnto John Paston,[3] knyght, sendeth greting in *our* Lord God euerlasting. Where it is so that certein agrement*es and* accord*es* beth had betwene the right reue*r*end fader in God, W*illiam*, Bisshop of Winchestre, on the oon p*art*, and me the seid J. Paston on the other p*art*, of the man*er*s, lordshippes, londes, ten*ementes*, possessions, *and* hereditament*es* which sumtyme wer of J. Fastolf, knyght, as in endentures therof betwene vs made may appier; where also sithen the making of the same indentures iugement hath be yoven for me ayenst W. Yelu*er*ton, knyght, in the Kyng*es* Chauncerie vpon a bille sued by me in the same Chauncerie ayenst the seid W. Yelu*er*ton *and* W. Genney, s*er*ieant; and ou*er* this where the seid *reuerend fader*[4] hath sued ayenst W. Paston, vncle of me the seid J. Paston, a writte sub pena in the seid Chauncerie; know ye me the seid John Paston, knyght, feithfully to promytte *and* gra*u*nt by thiez p*resentes* and bynd me by the order of knyghthode *and* myn honesté as ferforth *and* as straitly as I can to p*ar*fou*r*me *and* fulfille on my behalf alle *and* euerich of the appointement*es* made betwene the seid *reuerend*[5] fader *and* me, natwithstonding the seid iugement, suyt*es*, or any other cause or occasion what so euer it be.

In witnesse wherof I haue vnto thies p*resentes* put my seale xij day of February the xlix yer of the regne of *our* soue*r*ain lord King Henry the vj^{the}.

JOHN PASTON, K.

261. To MARGARET PASTON 1471, 18 April

Add. 43489, f. 44. 11⅜×8½ in. Autograph.

Dorse: Conclusion of text. Remnants of red wax and tape. Address autograph:

To my Moodre.

The date is clearly four days after the battle of Barnet on 14 April 1471.
F. ii, p. 62. G. 668/774. C. 61.

Moodre, I recomande me to yow, letyng yow wette þat, blyssed be God, my brother John is a lyffe *and* farethe well, *and* in no p*er*ell off dethe. Neu*er* the lesse he is hurte w*yth* an arow on hys ryght arme be-nethe þe elbow, *and* I haue sent hym a sorion whyche hathe dressid hym, *and* he tellythe me þat he trustythe þat he schall be all holl w*yth*-in ryght schort tyme. It is so þat John Mylsent is ded, God haue m*er*cy on hys sowle, *and*

260. [1] *Abbr.* xpen *with stroke above.* [2] *Abbr.* pnt *with stroke above.*
[3] se *canc.* [4] *Abbr.* R F.
[5] *Abbr.* R.

Wyll*i*am Mylsent is on lyffe *and* hys other*e* seruant*ys* all be askapyd by all lyklihod.

Item, as for me, I ame in good case, blyssyd be God, *and* in no jopart*é*
10 off my lyff ⌐if⌐ me lyst my-selffe, for*e* I am at my lybert*é* iff nede bee.

Item, my lorde Arche-bysshop is in the Towr*e*. Neu*er* the lesse I trust to God þ*at* he schall do well j-noghe. He hathe a saffe-garde for hym *and* me bothe. Neu*er*thelesse we haue ben troblyd syns, but nowe I vndrestande þ*at* he hathe a pardon, *and* so we hope well.

15 There was kyllyd vppon the felde halffe a myle from Bernett, on Esterne Daye, the Erle off Warwykk, þe Marqweys Montacu, S*y*r Willi*a*m Terell, S*y*r Lowes John, *and* dyu*e*rse other esqui*e*r*ys* off owr*e* contr*é*, Godm*e*rston *and* Bothe. *And* on the Kyng Edwardes p*ar*tye, the Lorde Cromwell, þe Lorde Saye, S*y*r Omffrey Bowghshere off owr*e* contr*é*, whyche is a sore
20 moonyd man her*e*, *and* other peple off bothe p*ar*tyes to þe nombre off more then a m[1].

As for other*e* tythynges is vndrestande her*e* þ*at* the Qwyen Margrett is verrely londyd, *and* hyr*e* sone, in the west contr*é*, *and* I trow þ*at* as to-morow er*e* ellys þe next daye the Kyng Edward*e* wyll dep*ar*t from hense
25 to hyr*e* warde to dryve her owt ageyn.

Item, I beseche yow þ*at* I maye be recomandyd to my cosyn Lomnor*e*, *and* to thanke hym for*e* hys goode wyll to me wardes iff I had hadde nede, as I vndrestoode by the berer heroff. *And* I beseche yow on my behalue to advyse hym to be well ware off hys delyng or*e* langage as yit, for the
30 worlde, I ensur*e* yow, is ryght qwesye, as ye schall knowe w*yth*-in thys monythe. The peple heer*e* feerythe it soor*e*. God hathe schewyd hym-selffe marvelouslye, lyke hym þ*at* made all *and* can vndoo ageyn whan hym lyst; *and* I kan thynke þ*at* by all lyklyod schall schewe hym-sylff as mervylous ageyn, *and* þ*at* in schort tyme, *and* as I suppose offter*e* then onys in casis
35 lyke.

Item, it is soo that my brother*e* is on-p*ur*veyed off monye. I haue holpyn hym to my power *and* above, wherffore, as it pleasythe yow, remembre hym, for [I] kan not p*ur*ueye for my-selffe in þe same case.

Wretyn at London the Thorysdaye in Esterne Weke. I hope hastely to
40 see yow. All thys bylle most be secrett.[1]

Be ye nat adoghted off the worlde, for I trust all schall be well. Iff it thusse contenewe I ame not all vndon, ner*e* noon off vs; *and* iff otherwyse, ⌐then⌐, &c.

261. [1] *Recto ends.*

262. Schedule to release of lands   1471, 12 July

Magdalen College, Oxford, Norfolk and Suffolk 5. Strip of parchment
$13\frac{1}{4} \times 3\frac{1}{4}$ in., attached by strip and seal to another piece $13\frac{1}{2} \times 5\frac{1}{2}$ in. Both
in the same clerk's hand as no. 252.

The main document is a release in Latin, in the usual form:

Nouerint vniuersi per presentes me, Johannem Paston, militem, remisisse,
relaxasse, ac omnino pro me et heredibus meis imperpetuum quiete-clamasse
Dauid Husband, clerico, et Willelmo Gifford, clerico, heredibus et assignatis eorum
imperpetuum totum ius meum, titulum, interece, et demandam . . . de et in
manerijs de Saxthorp, Tichewell, Hayneford, Essexe in Hiklyng, Beyton, Coton
Hempnales, Burneviles in Naketon, Calcote, Leystoft, Habelond, Broweston,
Gorleston alias dict' Spitlynges. . . .

It is dated 12 July 11 Edward IV, with autograph signature *John Paston, K.* It is
endorsed in another clerk's hand: *Relaxacio Johannis Paston militis post iudicium
redditum pro ipso contra Willelmum Yeluerton in cancellaria H. vj*ti *A° xlix°.*

G. 673/779 (abstract).

I, John Paston, knyght, haue do this writyng of reles hereto annexed to be
writen. And also I haue sealed the same writyng and delyuered hit to
Robert Anketill to kepe as a cedule, and nott my dede as yet, vnto tyme
that Dauid Husband and William Gifford, named in the same writyng, or
oone of them, requyre the said Robert to delyuere to them or to oone of 5
them the said writyng; att which tyme I wol that the same Robert delyuere
to the said Dauid and William, or to oone of them, the foresaid writyng as
my dede, the same writyng att the same delyuerance so to be made by the
said Robert first to take effect as my dede and not before.

263. To JOHN PASTON III   1471, 15 September

Add. 43491, f. 16. $11\frac{5}{8} \times 11\frac{3}{4}$ in. Autograph.

Dorse: Traces of red wax. Address autograph:

To Mestresse Margret Paston or to John Paston, esquier, hyr sone, in hast.

The date appears from the reference to John III's pardon, which connects this
letter with no. 348. It is confirmed by the mention of the execution of Thomas
Nevill, 'the Bastard of Fauconberg', who was beheaded at Middleham on 22 September 1471 (see *D.N.B.*).

F. ii, p. 72. G. 675/781 (part). C. 63 (part).

Ryght well belouyd brother, I comande me to yow, letyng yow wete þat I
am in wellffare, I thanke God, *and* haue ben euyre syns þat I spake last
wyth yow; *and* mervayle sore þat ye sent neuer wryghtyng to me syns ye

departyd. I herde neuyre syn þat tyme any worde owt off Norffolk. Ye
5 myght att Bertelmev¹ Feyre haue had massengerys j-nowe to London, *and*
iff ye had sent to Wykys he scholde haue conveyd it to me.

I herde yister-daye þat a worsted man off Norffolk þat solde worstedys
at Wynchester seyde þat my lord off Norffolk *and* my lady wer on pylgrymage at Owre Lady on foote, *and* so they went to Caster; *and* þat at Norwyche
10 on scholde haue had large langage to yow *and* callyd yow traytore, *and*
pyked many quarellys to yow. Sende me worde ther-off. It were well doo
þat ye wer a lytell sewrere off yowr pardon than ye be. Auyse yow; I deme
ye woll her-afftre ellys repent yow.

I vndrestonde þat Bastarde Fauconbryg is owther hedyd or lyke to be,
15 *and* hys brother bothe. Som men seye he wolde haue deseruyd it, *and* som
sey naye.

I purpose to be att London the fyrst daye off the terme. Sende me worde
whethyre ye schall be ther or nott.

Item, I wolde wete whether ye haue spokyn wyth my lady off Norffolk
20 or not, *and* off hyr dysposicion, *and* the howsoldys, to me *and* to yow
wardes, *and* whether it be a possible to haue Caster ageyn *and* ther goode
wyllis, or nott. *And* allso I praye yow vndrestande what felaschyp *and*
guydyng is in Caster, *and* haue a spye resortyng in *and* owt; so maye ye
know the secretys a-monge them.

25 Ther is moche adoo in the Northe, as men seyn. I pray yow be ware off
yowr guydyng, *and* in chyff off yowre langage, so þat fro hense forthe by
yowr langage noo man parceyue þat ye fauor any person contrary to þe
Kynges plesure.

I vndrestonde þat þe Lord Ryuers hathe lycence off þe Kynge to goo to
30 Portyngale, now wyth-in thys vij nyght. I pray yow recomande me to my
moodre, *and* beseche hyr off hyr blyssyng on my be-halue. I herde not from
hyre thys x wekys, nowther² I wote not whether sche be payed off x li. at
Sporle ore nott. I deme yis; neuerthelesse Harry Halman is a false schrew.
For all my spekyng wyth hym my-selffe, *and* þer-to þe [daye] assyngnyd by
35 hym-selffe, wher as he scholde haue payed at Candelmes ⌈to paye me⌉, he
hadd daye to ⌈paye Townesend tyll⌉ Fastyngonge; *and* at Mydsomer I
vnderstonde he had not payed Townesende, as hym-selffe tolde me. He
hathe don me an hurte þerby more than he wenythe. Iffe he haue not payed
my moodre I praye yow see þat sche be payed, *and* scende to hym for it;
40 *and* sende me worde how it is.

Item, I praye yow scende me worde iff any off owre frendys or well-
wyllerys be dede, fore I feer þat ther is grete deth in Norwyche *and* in other
borowghe townese in Norffolk; for I ensure yow it is the most vnyuersall
dethe þat euyre I wyst in Ingelonde, for by my trowthe I kan not her by

---

263. ¹ *Cramped at edge, so that the last two letters are uncertain.*
² *An oblique stroke here can hardly be intended to indicate a new sentence.*

pylgrymes þat passe þe contré, ner noon other man þat rydethe er gothe 45
any contré, þat any borow town in Ingelonde is free from þat sykenesse.
God sease it whan it pleasyt hym. Wherffor, for Goddysake, late my
moodre take heede to my yonge brytheryn, that they be nat in noon place
wher that sykenesse is regnyng, nor that they dysport not *wyth* noon other
yonge peple whyche resortythe wher any sykenesse is. *And* iff þer be any 50
off that syknesse ded or enffecte in Norwyche, for Goddes sake lete hyre
sende them to som frende off hyrse in-to þe contré, *and* do ye þe same, by
myn advyce. Late my moodre rather remeve hyr howsolde *in*-to þe co*n*tré.[3]

Euyn now Thyrston browt me worde fro Lundon þat it was Doctore
Aleyn þat cawsyd yowre troble þat ye had at Norwych, *and* þat John 55
Pampyng roode for a dyscharge for*e* yow *and* þat he hathe sped well; but
hoghe, þat wot I nott. Iff ye be cleer owt off ⌐Doctor*e* Aleyn⌐[4] danger, kepe
yow ther *and* here-afftre ye maye schoffe as well at hys carte. I praye yow
sende me worde of ⌐all⌐ the forme off hys delyng *wyth* yow.

I had almost spoke *wyth* Mestresse An Hault, but I dyd not. Neuyre 60
thelesse thys next terme I hope to take on weye *wyth* hyr*e* or*e* othere. Sche
is agreyd to speke *wyth* me, *and* sche hopythe to doo me ease, as sche
saythe. I praye yow sende me worde hoghe ye doo *wyth* my lady Elysabeth[5]
Boghscher*e*; ye haue a lytell chaffyd it, but I can not tell howe. Sende me
worde whether ye be in bett*e*r hope or*e* werse. 65

I her seye þat the Erle off Oxenffordys bretheryn be goon owt off
sceyntewarye. Syr Thom*a*s Fulfforthe is goon owt off sceyntewarye *and* a
gret felaschyp fettchyd hym, a iij^{xx}, *and* they sey þat wyth-in v myle off
London he was [*wyth*] cc men, *and* no man wotethe wher*e* he is become
not yit. The Lordes Hastyng*ys and* Howerd be in Caleys *and* haue it 70
pesebely, *and* Syr Walter Wretteslé *and* Syr Ieffrey Gate be comyn thense
and woll be at London thys daye, as it is seyde.

Wretyn at Waltham besyd Wynchest*er* the daye nex Holy Roode Daye.

J. P., K.

---

[3] *Recto ends.*   [4] *Interl. above* hys *canc.*
[5] *MS.* -betȝ, *influenced by the common abbreviation; cf. no. 264 n. 14.*

264. To JOHN PASTON III   1471, 28 September

Add. 43489, f. 47. 12×8½ in. Autograph.

Dorse: Continuation of text. Paper seal over red wax and tape. Address autograph:

To hys well belovyd John Paston, esquier, at Norwyche, or to Mestresse Margret hys moodre.[1]

The references to John III's pardon and to Fauconberg show that this letter was written soon after no. 263.

F. ii, p. 80. G. 676/782 (part).

I comande me to yow, letyng yow weet þat I vndrestonde þat þe Duchesse off Suff*olk and* þe Duke of Norff*olk* concelle jntend verrely thys terme in the begynnyng to comence a-geyn the appelys ageyn me *and* yow *and* other off[2] owr s*e*rua*n*tys, wherffor itt is full convenyent þat we take goode
5 heede *and* ryght goode advyc*e* how to guyde vs for itt, *and* whether it is co*n*venyent for me to appyre or nott; wher-in I wolde, as well as in other mater*ys*, fayne knowe yowr*e* advyce *and* comon w*yth* yow *and* other off my frendes er I jop*ar*te any s*er*tayn weye, for in my conseyt I most thys terme take oon wey or other. Wherffor I praye yow, iff ye maye in any wyse, þat
10 ye wolde ⌐be¬ her at London w*yth*-in iiij dayes afftr*e* Seynt Feythe, as well for the mater*ys* above wretyn as for a fynall co*n*clusion to be taken w*yth* Mestresse An Hault *and* w*yth* all other folkys.

Item, I vndrestande be Juddy þat he hathe spoken w*yth* yowr cosyn Sampson at þe Barse, *and* he p*ro*myttyd Juddy þat he scholde hym-selffe
15 haue spoken w*yth* yow[3] er thys tym. He seyde alsso þat he hathe wretyn to yow twyes or thryes; howe it is syns I wote not.

I wolde fayne haue the mesur*e* wher my fadre lythe at Bromholm, bothe the thyknesse *and* co*m*pase off the peler at hys hed *and* from that the space to þe alter, *and* the thyknesse off that awtr*e*[4] *and* jmagery off tymbre werk,
20 *and* what hyght the arche is to þe gronde off þe jlde, *and* how hye the grovnde off the qwyr*e* is hyer than the grownde off the jlde.

Item, I praye yowe late the mesur*e* by pakthred be taken, or ell mesured by yerde, how moche is from the northe gate ther the brygge was at Gressham to þe sowthe wall, *and* in lyke forme from the este syde to þe west; also
25 the hyght off the este wall *and* the hygh[t][5] off the sowthest towr*e* from þe grownde, iff ye maye easely. Alsso what breede eu*er*y towr*e* is w*yth*-in þe wall, *and* whych towr*e* is moore than other w*yth*-in; also how manye fote or what brede eche towre takythe, w*yth*in jche cornere off þe quadrate[6]

264. [1] *Abbr. moo with flourish, at edge of fold.*   [2] ther *canc.*
   [3] hy *canc.*   [4] -w- *from* l.   [5] *At edge.*
   [6] *Here, and interrupting the following two lines of writing, is a rough plan about an inch square of a quadrangle with four round towers, of varying diameter, at the corners, and a square gatehouse attached to the right-hand wall.*

ovyrethwert the dorys, *and* how many taylorys yerdys is from þe moote syde
wher the brygg[7] was to þe hyghe weye, or to þe heddge all a-longe the 30
entré, *and* what brede the entré is be-twyen þe dykys. I praye yow, iff ye
haue a leyser in any wyse, se thys doone yowr-selffe iff ye maye; or ellys
iff Pampyng do it, or who þat ye thynke can doo it, I wolle spende xx d.,
or as ye seme, to haue the sertayn off euery thyng her-in. And as for my
faderys tombe, I charge yow se it yowre-selffe, *and* when I speke wyth yow 35
I woll tell yow the cawses why þat I desyre thys to be doon.

As for tydyngys,[8] the Kyng *and* þe Qwyen *and* moche other pepell ar
ryden *and* goon to Canterbury, neuyr so moche peple seyn in pylgrymage
her-to-foor at ones, as men seye. Alsso it is seyde þat þe Erle off Penbroke
is taken in-to Brettayn, *and* men seye þat the Kyng schold haue delyueré 40
off hym hastely; *and* som seye þat the Kynge off France woll se hym saffe
and schall sett hym at lyberté ageyn.[9]

Item, Thom*a*s Fauconbrydge hys hed was yesterdaye sett vppeon London Brydge lokyng in-to Kent warde, *and* men[10] seye þat hys brother was
sore hurte *and* scope to seyntwarye to Beuerlé. Syr Thom*a*s Fulfforthe 45
escapyd owt off Westm*i*nster wyth an c sperys, as men seye, *and* is in-to
Deuenshyre, *and* ther he hathe strekyn off Syr John Crokkerys hed *and*
kylt an[11] other knyght off the Corteneys, as men seye. I wolde ye hadd
yowre verrey p*a*rdon at onys, wherffor I praye yow fayle not to be at
London wyth-in iiij daye afftre Seynt Feythe. Ye schall do goode in many 50
thynges, *and* I praye yow sende me worde her-off by the next[12] massenger,
and iff it come to Mestresse Elysabeth[13] Hyggens at þe Blak Swan sche
schall comveye it to me, for I woll not fayle to be there at London ageyn
wyth-in thys vj dayes. Mestresse Elysabeth[14] hathe a son, *and* was delyueryd
wyth-in ij day[15] afftre Seynt Bertelmew, *and* hyre dowtre A. H. was þe 55
next daye afftre delyueryd off an other sone, as sche seythe xj wekys er
hyre tyme. It was crystened John, *and* is ded; God save all.

Nomore tyll I speke wyth yow. Wretyn at London on Mychellmesse
Euyn.

J. P., K. 60

Item,[16] I praye yow late som wytty felaw, or ellys yowre selff, goo to þe
townes ther as thes ij women dwelle, *and* inquire whether they be maryed

---

[7] -g *over* h.
[8] *The ending* -ys *is probably meant, though the loop on* -g *is incomplete.*
[9] *This word, in a separate line at right-hand bottom corner, ends the recto.*
[10] *MS.* mer.
[11] *Corr. from* a, *which was followed by* kr *and another letter, later canc.*
[12] -x- *over* s.   [13] -th *repr. by* 3.
[14] -beth *repr. by* b3.
[15] *Near edge, against mount; no other letter visible against light.*
[16] *This paragraph begins without interval, and the first fifteen words complete the line above the signature. But it continues below, and was written with a different pen and ink, so is patently a postscript.*

syns and ageyn, or not; for I holde the hoorys weddyd, *and* iff they be than
the appelys wer abbatyd ther-by. I reme*m*ber not ther names; ye knowe
65 them bett*er* than I. Alsso in þe schreffvys bookys ther maye ye fynde off
them.

265. Inventory of papers   After 1470

Add. 27445, f. 48. 8⅜×11½ in. Autograph.

Dorse: Marks of folding, no seal or address. Along the upper left side an
unidentified hand has written *caste*.

Of the dates mentioned in the inventory, one is 9 Edward IV and two 10 Edward
IV; so that 10 Edward IV (4 March 1470–3 March 1471) was evidently past, but
probably not long. Gairdner plausibly suggests that the coffer in question may be
that mentioned by John III in no. 349.
    The principal negotiations between Paston and the Bishop of Winchester, which
are likely to be meant by the 'acta' of l. 6, took place in 1470 (see nos. 252–4).
    G. 679/785.

In þe sqar*e* trussyng coff*r*e

A boxe w*yth* euydence off my place in Fletstrett.
A lytell box w*yth* obligac*i*ons off þe Archbisshop off York *and* W. Je*n*nyes
obly*gacion.*
A box w*yth* euydence off Tytlyshall.
5 A box w*yth* þe lett*er* off attorney off Fastolff*ys* londes by S*yr* John Paston.
I, a box de act*is* int*er* Ep*iscopu*m Wynt*on*iensem *et* J. P. milit*em.* Item,
endentur*a* de argento mutuat*o* t*er*mi*no* T*r*initat*is* A° x° *et* testam*entum*
W. Paston Justic*iarij.*
Item, ij pixides de nouis cartis de terr*is* Fastolff*is.*
10 Item, a litell box w*yth* þe obligac*i*on off T. Fastolff, *and* on off Jam*es*
Gresh*am.*
Item, a box w*yth* the dede off gyfft off J. P. *and* þe byll assy*n*gnyd for þe
dyama*n*t.
Item, the bagge de placit*is* in vsu.
15 Item, the bagge w*yth* ger taken owt off my caskett.
Item, a bagge w*yth* the bondell wher-on was wreten 'London'.
Item, a bagge w*yth* euydence off Est Bekkh*am.*
Item, a bondell de act*is* parlime*n*t*i et* de excambia in Paston.
Item, a bondell de act*is* Ca*n*tuariens*ibus.*
20 Item, a bondell de fyrma Cast*er* Berdolff*is.*
The endent*ur* off Snaylwell by Wylleys.
A bondell off Gresh[a]m, Moleyns.

444

A bondell off pr*oce*sse off þ'eschekyr*e*, lett*er and* byllys sirca f*estu*m Joh[ann]is, A° ix°.

Item, th'endent*ur* off W. Jeney.   25

Item, a bondell off lett*er*is *and* byllis, A° x°.

A bondell wyt*h* jnqu*is*ic*io*ns nott ret*ur*nyd in-to þe Chanceri.

Copia voluntat*is* Fastolff vltim*a et* pr*o*bata.

Enventoriu*m* apu*d* Cast*er* p*er* Ep*iscopu*m Norwic*ensem et* do*mi*nu*m* de Scales, *et* alia ad redisesinam.   30

Apu[n]ctamentu*m* regis *et* lit*er*a amici. Endent*ur*a de Fennes p*er* patrem Hugon*is* Fenne.

The verray endent*ur* off my mariage.

Item, a bondell off lett*er*is from my brother John.

Item, iij billis, þe endent*er* off W. Jeñney for Nacton, a byll off Wylleys, 35 *and* on off J. Owen.

Item, a bondell wyt*h* þe names off them þat had stoff from Heylesdon.

Item, a byll off Sweynesthorp.[1]

Item, a byll off Brok off Dedh*a*m off þe p*ur*chace þeroff.

A qu*i*tance pr*o* Scaccario.   40

A bonde towchyng the pr*o*batte off Fastolffis will, wyt*h* mj olde testament.

A copie off a gen*er*all releffe de t*er*ris Fastolff*is*.

266. To MARGARET PASTON   1472, 8 January

Add. 43491, f. 17. 12 × 10⅜ in. Autograph.

Dorse: Paper seal over red wax and tape. Address autograph:

To my most honorable[1] *and tendre moo⟨dre⟩, Margrette Paston, be thys lett*er *d*elyueryd.

Dated.
   F. ii, p. 86. G. 687/795 (part).

Most worschypffull *and* kynde moodr*e*, I comande me to yow *and* beseche yow off yowr*e* dayly blyssyng *and* remembraunce. Please it yow to wete thatt I haue my pardon, as þe berer*e* heroff can jnfforme yowe, for com*ff*ort wheroffe I haue been the merier thys Crystmesse, *and* haue been parte ther-off wyt*h* S*yr* George[2] Browen *and* wyt*h* my lady myn aunte hys wyffe. 5 *And* be-for Twelthe I come to my lorde Archebysshope, wher I haue hadde as greete cheer, *and* ben as welkom, as I cowde devyse, *and* iff I hadde ben in sewerté þat Castre weer*e* hadde ageyn I wolde haue comen homewardes

265. [1] *First -e- over* y.
266. [1] *This word uncertain owing to damp-stains.*   [2] *MS.* Geroge.

thys daye; wherffor I sende thys man home nowe to late yow haue know-
10 leche theroff, *and* my brother bothe, in chyeffe for thys cause, that iff theer
be any crafftye delaye by Sothewell or Brandon, thatt than my brother
maye late them haue knowleche ther-off, soo thatt my lordes concell off
Norff*olk* maye vndrestand³ thatt my lorde neer noon other maye haue it
off þe Kynges ⟨. . .⟩ as they ha⟨u⟩e been halffe ⟨. . .⟩ off heer-to-foo*re*;
15 besechyng⁴ yow to hast my brother in laboryng ther-abowt iff ⟨. . .⟩⁵ be
⟨. . .⟩⁶ soo thatt itt maye ones ageyn come to Crysten mennes handes. *And*
by the latt*er* ende off thys terme, iffe itt be hadde ageyn, I *p*urpose to come
home *and* see yow thys Lente *and* sette my londe in bett*er* rewle than itt
hathe been heer-to-foo*re and* repayre vppe my howses. *And* I beseche
20 yow to rememb*er* my brother to doo hys deueyr*e* thatt I maye haue ageyn
my stuffe, my bookes *and* vestm*entỹs, and* my beddyng, how so euyr*e* hee
doo, thoghe I scholde gyffe xxᵗⁱ scutes by hys advyse to my lady Brandon
or som other goode felawe.

As for any tydynges, ther be noon heer saffe þat the Kynge hathe kepte
25 a ryall Crystmesse, *and* now they seye þat hastelye he woll northe, *and*
some seye þat he woll in-to Walys, *and* some seye þat he woll in-to þe
west contré. As for Qween Margrett, I vndreston þat sche is remeuyd from
Wyndeshor*e* to Walyngfforthe nyghe to Ewhelme, my lady off Suff*olk*⁷
place in Oxenfforthe schyr*e. And* men seye þat the Lorde Ryu*er*se schyppyd
30 on Crystmesse euyn in-to Portyngale warde; I ame nott serteyn. Also the[r]
schalle be a convocac*i*on off the clergye in all haste, whyche men deeme
wyll avayle the Kynge a dyme *and* an halffe, some seye.

I beseche Gode sende yow goode heele *and* ⟨mo⟩re joye in on yeer than
ye haue hadde thys vij. Wretyn att the Moor*e* the viij daye off Janeu*er* A°
35 E. iiij xj°.

By yowr*e* soone J O H N   P A S T O N, K.

---

³ -*e may have been written. The paper is a good deal decayed in several places, and a large*
hole affecting three lines just touches the end of this word.
⁴ *Upper part of first six letters lost, but lower part clear.*
⁵ *Two or three letters lost.*
⁶ *Perhaps ten letters lost.*
⁷ *Abbr.* Suff, *with tag, as usual, with no indication of ending.*

267. To JOHN PASTON III   1472, 17 February

Add. 43489, f. 49. 11⅜×7⅝ in. Autograph.

Dorse: Traces of red wax. Address autograph:

A Jehan Paston, esquiere, soit doné.

The date appears from the reference to strained relations between the dukes of Clarence and Gloucester. Gloucester married Anne Neville, younger daughter of the Earl of Warwick and widow, or fiancée, of Edward Prince of Wales, in 1472. Clarence had married Warwick's elder daughter Isabel, and resented Gloucester's claim to part of Warwick's lands (Scofield, ii. 6, 26–7; Jacob, p. 571).

    F. ii, p. 90. G. 690/798.

Brother, I comande me to yow *and* praye yow to loke vppe my *Temple off Glasse, and* sende it me by the berer heroff.

    Item, as for tydyng*ys*, I haue spoken w*yth* Mestresse Anne Hault at a praty leyser *and*, blyssyd be God, we be as ferfforthe as we weer to-foore, *and* soo I hoope we schall contenew; *and* I promysed hyr*e* that at the next 5 leyser that I kowd fynde ther-too *þat* I wolde come ageyn *and* see hyr*e*, whyche wyll take a leyser*e* as [I] deeme. Now syn thys obseruance is ones doon I p*ur*pose nott to tempte God noo moor*e* soo.

    Yister*d*aye the Kynge, the Qween, my lordes off Claraunce *and* Glowcest*er* wente to Scheen to pardon, men sey nott alle in cheryté. What wyll falle 10 men can nott seye. The Kynge entretyth my lorde off¹ Clarance for my lorde off Glowcest*er*, *and* as itt is seyde he answerythe that he maye weell haue my ladye hys sust*er* in lawe, butt they schall parte no lyvelod, as he seythe; so whatt wyll falle can I nott seye.

    Thys daye I p*ur*pose to see my lady off Norff*olk* ageyn, in goode howr*e* 15 be it. Ther is proferyd me marcha*un*tys for Sporle woode, God sende me goode sale whan I be-gynne; *þat* poor*e* woode is soor*e* manased *and* thrett. Yitt woote I nott whethyr I come home beffoor*e* Est*er*ne or nott; I schall sende yow worde.

    No moor, &c. Wretyn the fyrst Tewesdaye off Lenton.   20

JOHN PASTON, K.

267. ¹ glowcest*er* *canc.*

268. To John Paston III 1472, 30 April

Add. 43491, f. 9. 11¾ × 10⅞ in. Autograph.

Dorse: Traces of red wax. Address autograph:

To Master John Paston, or to my mestresse hys moodre, be thys letter delyueryd in hast.[1]

The date is fixed by the report of the death of Sir Thomas Waldegrave, which occurred on 28 April 1472 (*Inq. p.m.*, 12 Edward IV, no. 4). On the arrest of the Archbishop of York (George Neville), and his imprisonment at Hammes near Calais, see Scofield, ii. 28.

F. i, p. 288. G. 692/800.

Brother, I comand me to yow, prayng yow þat ye late William Barker weet þat I wolde þat he made hys acompt, *and* that acompt I wolde that eythere Geffrey Spyrlyng or som other auditore off Norwyche, wyth John Pampyng, toke itt off hym. And as for any presedentys ther-off, but iff Spyrlyng ore
5 William Berker haue any them-selff, ellys I cann non puruey as yitt. Neuerthelesse I suppose that Goodknape off Ormessby hathe owther be experyence or ellys in wrytyng mater j-nowe to charge hym wyth. And as for the rent in Rakhythe longyng to Runham, I had levere itt wer respigtyd than þat ther scholde as yitt be any troble for itt. I praye yow that thys
10 maye be doon, *and* thatt Pampyng in alle hast goo her-abowt. *And* as for the costys or audytorys rewarde that schalle growe off the same, it maye be payed by Barker. Also that he delyuer the remenant off the mony that is fonde in hys hande, soo that itt maye be sent me hyddre. Also I praye yow remembre þe mony for Syr Thomas Lynde. The daye þat Master John
15 Smythe assyngnyd is past; *and* sende me word by Juddy.

I sende yow a letter by Corby wyth-in iiij dayes byffor thys, *and* ther-wyth ij pottys off oyle for saladys, whyche oyle was goode as myght be when I delyueryd itt, *and* schall be goode at þe reseyuyng iff it be nott mysse-handelyd ner mysse-karyed.

20 Item, as for tydyng, the Erle off Northomberlonde is hoome in-to þe Northe, *and* my lorde off Glowcester schall afftre as to-morow, men seye. Also thys daye Robert off Racclyff weddyd the Lady Dymmok at my place in Fleetstrett, *and* my ladye *and* yowrys Dame Ely[sa]beth[2] Bowghcher is weddyd to þe Lorde Howardys soone *and* heyre. Also Syr Thomas Wal-
25 graue is ded off þe syknesse þat reygnyth, on Tewesdaye. Now theer for yowe.

Also my lorde Archebysshope was browt to þe Towre on Saterday at nyght, *and* on Mondaye at mydnyght he was conveyd to a schyppe *and* so in-to þe see, *and* as yitt I can nott vndrestande whedyre he is sent nere

---

268. [1] *Last two words added, smaller.* [2] *MS.* -betȝ.

whatt is fallyn off hym. Men seye þat he hathe offendyd; but as John ₃₀
Foster seythe, som men sey naye. But all hys meny are dysparblyd, euery
man hys weye, *and* som þat are greete klerkys *and* famous doctorys of hys
goo now ageyn to Cambrygge to scoolle.

As for any other tydyng, I heer noon. The Cowntesse off Oxenfford is
stylle in Seynt Martyns; I heer no worde off hyre. The Qween hadde ₃₅
chylde, a dowghter, but late at Wyndeshor; ther-off I trow ye hadde worde.
And as for me, I am in lyke case as I was. And as for my lorde chamberleyn,
he is nott yit comen to town. When he comythe, than schall I woote whatt
to doo. Syr John off Parre is yowre freende and myn, *and* I gaffe hym a
fayre armyng sworde wyth-in thys iij dayes. I harde somwhatt by hym off ₄₀
a bakk freende off yowrys; ye schall knowe moore here-afftre.

Wretyn the last daye off Aprylle.

269. To JOHN PASTON III 1472, 4 November

Add. 43491, f. 18. 11⅝ × 13¾ in. Autograph.

Dorse: Traces of red wax. Address autograph:

A Johan Paston, esquyere, soit doné.

Dated.
   F. ii, p. 112. G. 703/812. C. 69 (part).

Worshypffull *and* weell belovyd brother, I recomaund me to yow, letyng
yow weet þat I sente yow a letter *and* a rynge wyth a dyamand, in whyche
letter ye myght well conceyue what I wold ye scholde do wyth þe same
ryng, wyth manye other tydyngys *and* thyngys whyche I prayed yowe to
haue doon for me; whyche letter Boton[1] had the beryng off. It is soo nowe ₅
þat I vndrestond that he is owther deed ore ellys harde eskapyd, wheroff I
am ryght heuye, and am not serteyn whethyre the seyd letter *and* rynge
come to yowre handys ore nott. I wolde nott that letter were seyn wyth som
folkys, wherffor I praye yow take goode heede hoghe thatt letter comythe
to yowre handys, hooll or brokyn; *and* in especiall I praye yow gete it iff ye ₁₀
haue it nott.

Also I praye yow feele my lady off Norffolkys dysposicion to me wardys,
and whethyre she toke any dysplesure at my langage, ore mokkyd ore
dysdeyned my wordys whyche I hadd to hyre at Yarmothe be-twen the
place where I fyrst mett wyth hyre *and* hyre lodgyng. Fore my lady Brandon ₁₅

---

269. [1] *Fenn and Gairdner read* Botoner (*William Worcester's alternative name*). *But the
tail on -n is usually without significance in John II's hand, and the Pastons certainly had a
servant called Boton at this time* (see *John III's letter no. 346*). *They do not appear to have
called Worcester 'Botoner'.*

and Syr Willi*am* also axhyd me what word*ys* I had had to hyr*e* at that tyme. They seyde þ*at* my lady seyde I gaff hyr*e* ther-off, *and* þ*at* I sholde haue seyde þ*at* my lady was worthye to haue a lord*ys* soon in hyr*e* belye, fore she cowde cheryshe itt *and* dele warlye w*yth* it. In trowthe, owther the

20 same or*e* word*ys* moche lyke I had to hyr*e*, whyche wordys I ment as I seyde. They leye to þ*at* I seyde she toke hyr*e* ease. Also I scholde haue seyde þ*at* my ladye was off s[t]atur*e* goode *and* had sydes longe *and* large, so that I was in goode hope she sholde ber*e* a fayr*e* chylde; he was nott lacyd nor*e* bracyd jne to hys peyn, but þ*at* she lefft hym rome to pleye hym in. They

25 seye that I seyde my lady was large *and* grete, *and* that itt sholde haue rome jnow to goo owt att. *And* thus whyther my lady mokk me or theye I woote nott. I mente weell, by my trowthe, to hyr*e* *and* to þ*at* she is w*yth*, as any he þ*at* owythe heer*e* best wyll in Ingelond. If ye can by any mee*n*e weete whethyr*e* my ladye take it to dysplesure or[2] nowt, or whether she thynke I

30 mokkyd hyr*e*,[3] or iff she wyght it but lewdnesse off my-selffe, I praye yow sende me worde, for I woot nott whethyr*e* I maye trust thys Lady Brandon or*e* nott.

Item, os for*e* tydynges, nowe heer be but fewe saff that, as I vndrestande, jmbassator*ys* off Bretayn shall come to London to-morowe, and men seye

35 that the Lorde Ryuerse and Scalys shall hastelye come hom, *and* men seye þ*at* ther is many off the sowdeor*ys* þ*at* went to hym in-to Bretayn been deede off the flyxe and other*e* jpedemye, *and* þ*at* the remenant sholde come hom w*yth* the Lorde Skalys; *and* som seye þ*at* thees jmbassator*ys* come for moor*e* men. *And* thys daye rennyth a tale þ*at* the Duke off Bretayne

40 sholde be ded. I beleeff it nott.

I sent yow worde off an hawke; I herde nott from yow syns. I do *and* shall doo þ*at* is possible in suche a neede.

Also I canne nott vndrestond that my lorde off Norff*olk* shall come heer*e* thys tyme, wherffore I am in a greet angonye howe js best for*e* me to sywe[4]

45 to hym for*e* rehauyng off my place. þ*at* goode lorde woot full lytell how moche harme he doothe me, *and* how lytell goode or*e* worshyp it dothe hym. I praye yow sende me yowr*e* advyce.

No moor*e* to yowe at thys tyme, but God haue yow in hys kepyng. Wretyn at London þe iiij daye off Novembre A° E. iiij^{ti} xij°. I feere me þ*at*

50 jdelnesse ledythe yowr*e* reyne. I praye yow rather*e* remember S*yr* Hughe Lavernoys tyll yowr*e* hauke come.

JOHN PASTON, K.

---

[2] *MS.* on.   [3] iff o *canc.*
[4] *Second letter blotted; y seems to be written over* e.

270. To John Paston III   1472, 8 November

Add. 43491, f. 19. 9 × 11¾ in. Autograph.

Dorse: Continuation of text. About 2 in. below the end, upside down in relation to the letter, *pryncysse* in John II's hand. Traces of red wax. Address autograph:

A John Paston, esquyer, soyt doné.

Dated. Some of the subjects treated take up matters mentioned in letters written by John III some weeks or even months earlier: the hawk in nos. 354 and 355, the ring for Jane Rodon in no. 354, the acquittance for Fastolf's property in no. 353.

    F. ii, p. 118. G. 704/813 (part).

Brother, I comand me to yow, letyng yow weet þat wheer my moodre desyreth þat I sholde sende worde to my fermor*ys* off Sporle that they sholde paye to my moodre x marke for my brother Will*i*am, it weere nowe to short a warnyng, for I haue assyngnyd it to Townesende, the hoole as fore the yeer past. I haue alweyis offryd it hyr*e and* she was neu*y*re ar nowe 5 abowt to receyue it, *and* as yitt it nedyth not greetlye fore no charge þat she hathe moor*e* than she was wont to haue abowt hym. Sche spendythe[1] nott v mark by yeer on hym, as I conceyve. Neverthelesse, as for the next yeer I promyse yow she shall haue it for me, or ellys I shall p*u*rueye as weell for hym.   10

    Item, as for the aqwytance[2] off the Bysshop off Wynchest*er*, I shall doo for hyr*e* as my part is to doo. I shall gete it iff I can, *and* iff I cannott, iff it be pr*o*ffitable for hyr*e* I wolde hyr*e* consell had som other meene to gete it. Iff I gete it I am worthy thanke, *and* iff I gete it nott I am worthy no magrye. I shall doo as I can.   15

    Item, as for my sust*er* Annys comyng hyddr, I shall p*u*ruey for hur*e* wy*th* myn aunt iff I can, iff my moodr*e* will dep*ar*t wyth c s. be[3] yere, wher-off I am not serteyn. Iff she wer heer at my settyng *and* my moodr had onys payed c s. for on yeer, I feer me she wolde be weery *and* lothe to paye an other c s. for the next. Neu*er*thelesse I woll p*u*rueye for hyr*e* thoghe I 20 sholde paye the c s. by yeer my-selffe, *and* yit she is nott my dowtre. As for the[4] c li. to be payed in x yer, it is a strange proffre to a ientylwoman*ys* mariage ward. By my trowthe, I offryd c marke ⌐wyth hyre⌐, to be payed on a daye, besyde þat þat my moodr*e* woll dep*ar*t wyth, to haue had on that I soppose ye knowe, but it is not lyke to bee; it greuys me to remembr*e* 25 the onkyndnesse off the worlde. Neu*er*thelesse I hope to see a remedye ther-in. Folkys weene to be ther owne best freend*ys and* are there owne[5]

270. [1] hyr*e* *canc.*   [2] *MS.* aqwytantance.
    [3] *MS.* ber.   [4] c ly *and another letter, perhaps* u, *canc.*
    [5] best *canc.*

moost fooys. Folkys be roonne so ferre ther-on that they woot not wher they be and growe paste shame.[6]

30 As ⌜fore⌝ the delyueraunce off the rynge to Mestresse Jane Rothon, I dowt nott but it shall be doon in the best wyse so þat ye shall geet me a thank moore than the rynge and I are worthe ore deserue.

And wheer ye goo to my laydy off Norffolkys ⌜and wyll be theere⌝ att the takyng off hyre chambre, I praye God spede yow,[7] and Owre Ladye hyre 35 to hyre plesure, wyth as easye labore to overkom that she is abowt as euyre had any lady or ⌜gentyll⌝-woman saff Owre Lady heer-selffe. And soo I hope she shall to hyre greet joye and all owres, and I prey God it maye be lyke hyre in worshyp, wytt, gentylnesse, and euery thynge excepte the verry ⌜verry⌝ thynge.

40 As for the hawke þat I sende yow, thanke me for it, God save it, for I trow she woll neuer be nowght, as Cromer seythe. Neuerthelesse it is the best þat I can geet,

> wherffor prennes en gree,
> þer is noon othere remedee

45 as yit, but iff I kan geet a better ye shall it habbe.

I praye yow sende me worde off the ij letteris þat I sent yow.

Item, I praye yow recomand me to Sampson. I am glad that he is ageyn in favore wyth my lorde and my ladye.

> Neuerthelesse I am sorye þat Rygge
> 50 hathe bytyn hym soo by the bygge,
> and that lytell Qwayll
> pynchyd hys pendaunt so nyghe hys tayle.

And as fore the pye that ye sent me worde off I remytt it to yowre dyscrecion.

55 No moore to yow at thys tyme,[8] but I woll sleepe an howre þe lengere to-morow by-cawse I wrote so longe and late to-nyght. Wretyn betwyen þe viij and þe ix daye off Novembre A° xij° E. iiij[ti].

J. P., K.

[6] Recto ends.   [7] and hyre as neer canc.
[8] MS. at thyme.

271. To Margaret Paston or John Paston III

1472, 22 November

Add. 27445, f. 62. $11\frac{3}{8} \times 11$ in. Autograph.

Dorse: Continuation of text. Traces of red wax. Address autograph:

To Mestresse Margret Paston, or to John Paston, esquiere, or to Roose dwyllyng affore ther gate to delyuer to them.

The date is shown by the reference to John III's intention to visit the Duchess of Norfolk, and to her approaching confinement, to be close to that of no. 270.
F. v, p. 28. G. 706/815.

Please it yow to weete þat I have opteyned letter*ys* from the Kynge to my lorde off Norffolke, to my lady off Norff*olke, and* to ther concell, whyche letter to ther*e* concell is nott sup*er*scrybyd for cawse we wyst nott serteyn whyche off the councell sholde be present when the massenger*e* cowme. I therffor thynke þat thoos namys most be somwhatt by yowr*e* advyce, 5 *and* for-get nott Gornaye, nor yitt Brome, iff ye thynke so best, nor Sowthewelle. I trust to my cosyn Gornaye *and* on-to Brom *and* Barnard in cheffe, *and* as to Bernarde brother*e* I praye yow to take hys advyce, for I hope he is my welwyller, as ye know; *and* iffe he do me parffyght ease in thys mater I thynke verrely in tyme to come to gyff hym xx scutys, 10 *and* yit a goode turne whan so eu*er* it lythe in my power. The Kynge hathe specially doon for me in thys case *and* hathe pitte me, *and* so have þe lordys, in ryght greete comfort þat iff thys fayle þat I shalle haue ondelayed justyce; *and* he hathe sente a man off worshyp *and* in greet favore w*yth* hym on thys massage, whyche hathe nott offte ben seyne, whyche gentyl- 15 man kan well do hys mastrys massage *and* brynge trywe reporte. I have gevyn hym v li. for hys cost*ys*; God sende hym *and* yow goode spede in thees werk*ys*. I feere thatt he shall nott speke w*yth* my lady, for þat she hathe takyn hyr*e* chambr*e*. Iff she be my verry goode ladye, as she hathe seyde hertoffore þat she wolde be, I hope þat she wolle speke w*yth* hym. 20 Neu*er*thelesse I praye yow by the mean*ys* off Mestresse Jahne Rothen that [ye] will have my ladye mevyd for*e* me, *and* wher þat herre-to-fore I wolde have dep*ar*tyd wyth c m[a]rke to have hadde hyr*e* goode helpe *and* to be restoryd to my place, whyche nott[1] acceptyd I tolde my seyde lady þat I feeryd þat my power sholde natt be ther-afftre to gyff so large a plesyr*e*; 25 for at þat tyme I was in hope þat the Bysshop off Wynchest*er* sholde have payd it, thoghe it hadde drawen a c li. Yit, for as moche as men may nott lure none hawk*ys* w*yth* empty handys, I wolde yitt agré to gyffe my lady xx li. for an horse *and* a sadell so þat I be restoryd to my place, *and* thatt doone to have a relesse off my lorde *and* my goun*ys and* bok*ys* to be 30

---

271. [1] e *and the beginning of* x *canc.*

restoryd iff it maye bee. Neuerthelesse thys mony is nott yit redy wyth me.
I remytte thys to yowre dyscressyonys.

Item, iff it be soo þat itt be thowte behovefull, I thynke þat thoghe
nowthere Slyfelde nore ye, brother John, maye come in-to my ladyes
35 chambre, þat my moodre, iff she weer at Norwyche, she myght speke wyth
hyre, for þat she is a woman and off worshyppe. I thynke þat my moodre
sholde meve my lady moche. I thynke þat ther most be som body for me
havyng auctoryté to conclude for me, or ellys ⌐knowyng myn entente¬; ellys
they myght make delaye, and seye they wolle at þe Kyngys enstance comon
40 wyth me, neuer the lesse I was nott ther present. Wherffor, rather than fayle
yff neede be I wolle wyth-owte any abode iff I heere from yow come home,
and Slyfelde is agreyd to tary the[r] a vij nyghte for my sake so þat the
mater take effecte. I praye yow make hym goode cheere, and iff it be so
that he tarye, I most remembre hys costys. Therffor iff I shall be sent for
45 and he tery at Norwyche ther-whylys it wer best to sette hys horse at þe
Maydes Hedde, and I shalle content for ther expencys.²

Item, ye maye largely sey on my behalve for suche servyse þat I sholde
do to my lorde and lady hereaffter, whyche by my trowthe I thynke to doo.
Neuerthelesse to sey þat I woll be hys sworyn man, I was neuer yitt lordys
50 sworyn man, yit have I doone goode seruyce and nott leffte any at hys most
neede nere for feere. But as Gode helpe me I thynke my lady shalle have
my servyce a-bove any lady erthely, wheche she scholde weell have knowyn
had I been in suche case as I hadde nott been alweye þe werse welkome
for that on off myn herandys alweye was vndrestande þat it³ was for Caster,
55 whyche was nott acceptable and I euyre the werse welkome.

Item, brother, I ame concludyd wyth my lorde for yow þat ye shalle be
at Caleys iff ye list, and have iij men in wagys vndre yow, wheroff my lorde
seythe þat William Lovedaye most be on tyll tyme þat he have purveyd
othere rome for hym. Iff ye be dysposyd to goo, as I tolde hym þat ye
60 weer, yitt wer it nott best þat ye lete it be knowe tyll thys mater be doone,
and than ye maye acordyng to yowre promyse lete my ladye have knowleche ther-off. Neuer þe lesse my lorde shall be here wyth-in xx dayes or
ther-abowt; iff ye come thys weye ye maye speke wyth hym. Neuer the
lesse ye shall nott lose no tyme iff ye weer at Caleys at thys owre, for my
65 lorde promysed me þat he wolde wryght to Elkenhed, þe tresorer at Caleys,
for yow by the next massenger thatt went.

Item, ther hathe Perauntys wyffe wryte to me þat Bernaye seruyth hyre
onkyndely. He owythe hyre xxxij s. and she is in noon hope þat euyre he
woll come ther ageyn. Sende me worde iff he wyll. He shall nott lyff so
70 weell and trywly to-geedr, I trowe, but iff he goo thyddre. I hadde comen
home butt þat I⁴ ame nott yitt verrely purveyd for payment for my oncle

---

² *Recto ends.*   ³ *MS.* is.
⁴ I *repeated.*

William þe xxvj daye off thys mony[th],[5] *and* he dothe me harme he delythe so oncurteysly *wyth* Towneshende, for he wille nott yitt paye hym the c m[a]rke payeable att Halowmesse whyche he hadde a monythe affore; wherffor I feer*e* þat Towneshende wille nott do for me ageyn. I shall doo as I kan.

Wretyn on Sondaye next[6] Seynt[7] Clement.

J OHN P ASTON, K.

272. T O J OHN P ASTON III 1473, 3 February

Add. 43489, f. 55. 11⅞×8½ in. Autograph.

Dorse: Traces of red wax. Address autograph:

To John Paston, esqwyere, ore to Mestresse Margret Paston hys moodre, be thys letter delyueryd.

Dated.

F. ii, p. 120. G. 717/826 (part).

Weell belovyd brother, I comand me to yow, letyng yow weet þat I wrote yow a lett*er* þe xxij daye off Januar*e* whyche was delyu*e*ryd to Thomas Elys at Caleys the seyde daye, wenyng to me þat he sholde haue ben in Norff*o*lk wyth-in vj or vij dayes afftr*e*, but now I vndrestand that thys lett*er* is lyke to be wyth yow as sone as it. 5

It is so now þat I suppose verrely to be at London by the xiij or xiiij daye off Feverer*e* but iff wynde or*e* wedre cawse it; at whyche daye, acordyng as the other lett*er* spekyth off, I beseche[1] my moodre þat Playtere[2] maye mete wyth me ther*e*, lyke as he and I comonyd towchyng the man*er* off Sporle, *and* I trust to God that that mat*er* shall be easyd. 10

Item, I praye yow take goode heed to þe lett*er* þat yonge Thomas Elys hathe the beryng off, to weete whether it hathe been oponyd or*e* nott; þe worde is full false.

As for tydyng*ys* heer, ther bee but fewe saff þat þe Duke off Borgoyn *and* my lady hys wyffe farethe well; I was wyth them on Thorysdaye last 15 past at Gawnt. Peter Metteney farethe weell *and* Mestresse Gretkyn bothe, *and* Babekyn recomand hyr*e* to yow. She hathe ben verry seke,[3] but it hathe doon hyr*e* goode for she is fayrer *and* slenderer than she was. *And* she cowde make me no cheer*e*, but alwey my sawse was 'How faret Mast*er* John yowr*e* brother?', wher-wyth I was wrothe *and* spake a jalous worde ar*e* too, 20 dysdeynyng þat she shulde car*e* so moche for yow when þat I was present.

---

[5] *Cramped at edge.*	[6] -x- *over* s.	[7] Arke *canc.*
272. [1] -th *canc.*	[2] *Name underlined.*	[3] -e *over* y.

I pray yow make a goode bargeyn for my ferme barly in Fledge, so that I myght haue mony now at my beyng in Ingelond, whyche shall not contynew past a monyth by lyklyhod.

25 Item, I pray yow take goode heede to myn olde stuffe at Norwyche soo that it appeyre nott, and sende me worde to Hoxonys in wrygtyng what goode þe bysshop ded ⌐fore⌐ me att Framynham *and* how my lorde, my lady, *and* all the cort are dysposyd to me wardys.

I herd also seye þat my ladye *and* yowrys, Dame Margret Veere, is ded, 30 God haue hyre sowle. Iff I weer not sorye for herre I trowe ye haue been.

No moore to yow at thys tyme, but All-myghty Good haue yow in kepyng. Wretyn at Caleys þe iij daye off Februarye A° r.r. E. iiij xij°.

J. P., K.

273. To JOHN PASTON III 1473, 2 April

Add. 43490, f. 4. 9⅞ × 5¼ in. Autograph.

Dorse: Paper seal over red wax and tape. Address autograph:

A soun treschere et ben amé freere, John de Paston, esquiere.

Dated. This answers John III's letter no. 361.
F. ii, p. 122. G. 721/830.

Weell belovyd brother, I recomand ⌐me⌐ to yow, letyng yow wete þat at the request off Mestresse Jane Hassett *and* yow I haue laboryd bothe þe knyghtys off þe sheere off Norffolk *and* the knyghtys off þe shyre off Suffolk. I vndrestod theere had ben made labore þat suche a thyng shulde haue ben 5 as ye wrotte to me off, but now it is saff. Raff Blaundrehasset[1] were a name to styrte an hare. I warant the[r] shall come no suche name in owre bokys nere in owre howse; it myght par case styrt xxti harys at onys. 'Ware that', quod Perse. I redde there ⌐in the bylle off Norffolk⌐ off on John Tendall, esquiere, but I suppose it be not ment by owre Tendall, *and* iff it be he 10 shall not rest theere iff I maye helpe it.

As fore tydynges, the werst that I herde was that my moodre wyll not doo so moche fore me as she pit me in comffort off. Othere tydyngys, I herd sey fore serteyn þat þe Lady Fytzwater is ded *and* þat Master Fytzwater shall haue cccc m[a]rke a[2] yere more than he had. I am not sory therffore. 15 As fore the worlde, I woot nott what it menyth. Men seye heere, as weell as Hogan, þat we shall haue adoo in hast. I know no lyklyhod but that suche a rumore there is. Men sey the Qwyen ⌐wyth the Prynce⌐ shall come owt off Walys *and* kepe thys Esterne wyth the Kyng at Leycetre, *and* som seye nowthere off them shall com there.

<hr>

273. [1] *Both names underlined.*   [2] *No space.*

Item, off beyond þe see it is seyd þat the Frense Kyng*ys* host hathe 20
kyllyd the Erle off Armenak *and* all hys myry mene, som seye vndre
appoyntment *and* som seye they wer*e* besegyd *and* gotyn by pleyn assault.
Ferthermoore men seye that þe Frenshe Kynge is w*yth* hys ost vppon the
wat*er* off So*m*me a lx myle froo Caleys. I leve them wheer I fand them.

I made yowr*e* answer*e* to þe frendys off Mestresse Jane Godmerston 25
acordyng to yowr*e* instruc*cion*. As for me, I am nott serteyn whether I
shall to Caleys,[3] to Leysetr*e*, or come hom in-to Norffo*lk*, but I shall hastely
send yow worde. I pray*e* yow be nott hasty vppon Will*ia*m Berker for S*yr*
John Stille ner for John Koke, for by my feythe I may not forber it.

Wretyn þe ij daye off Aprill A° E. 4. xiij°. 30

274. To John Paston III 1473, 12 April

Add. 27445, f. 71. 11½×16⅝ in. Autograph.

Dorse: Continuation of text. Traces of red wax. Address autograph:

*To John Paston, esqu*i*ere.*

Dated.
F. v, p. 50. G. 722/831.

Best belovyd brother, I recomand me on-to yow, letyng yow weet þat I
receyuyd on Wednysday last past yow[r] angry lettr*e* towchyng the troble
þat Sandre Kok is in, wherin I haue largely comonyd w*yth* John Russe *and*
advysed hym to take a curteys weye w*yth* Sandre for yowr*e* sake *and* myn.
He seythe he wold nott dysplease yow by hys wyll, *and* that he p*ur*posythe 5
to entrete yow *and* wolde deser*ue* it to yowe. He vndrestod þat ye had large
langage to þe jurye þat passyd ageyn Saundre. I lete hym weete þat ye weer*e*
wrothe, *and* that he shall nowther please yow ner*e* me but iff he dele
curteyslye w*yth* Saundre. I tolde hym as for*e* the condempnac*ion* vppon
the ac*cion* off trespasse, I thoght it nowther*e* good ner worshypffull. Also 10
I haue wretyn to þe person off Maultby to dele curteyslye w*yth* Sawndre
iff he woll please yow or*e* me.

Item, I sende yow herwythe the[1] *supercedyas* for*e*[2] Saundre so that, iff
ye fynde any meane for the condempnac*ions*, þat than ye maye ease ther-
wyth the suerté off pease. John Russe, as I suppose, is att home thys daye. 15

Item, as for tydynges heer*e*, the Kynge rydeth ⌈fresselye⌉ thys daye to
Northamton warde, ther*e* to be thys Esterne; *and* afftre Esterne he p*ur*-
posythe to be moche at Leysettr*e* and in Leysettr*e* shyre. Euery man seythe
þat we shall have adoo or*e* Maye passe. Hogan the prophet is in the Towr*e*.

---

[3] orto *canc.*
274. [1] *Some five letters heavily canc.* [2] Shaundre *canc.*

20 He wolde fayne speke w*yth* þe Kyng, but the Kynge seythe he shall not
avaunt þat euyr*e* he spake w*yth* hym.

Item, as for*e* me, I most nedys to Caleyse warde to-morowe. I shall be
heer*e* ageyn iff I maye thys next terme. John Myryell, Thyrston, *and* W.
Woode be goon from me, I shrewe them. My modre dothe me moore
25 harme than good. I wende she wolde haue doon for me.[3] Playter wroot to
me þat she wolde haue leyde owt for me c li. *and* receyuyd it agey*n* in v yere
off the man*er* off Sporle, wherto I trustyd; whyche iff she had p*er*fformyd
I had nott ben in no jup*ar*té off the man*er* off Sporle. Neu*er*thelesse I shall
do whatt I kan, yit I preye yow calle vppon hyr*e* for*e* the same; remembr*e*
30 hyr*e* off that promyse.

Item, I preye yow remembr*e* hyr*e* for my fadrys tombe[4] at Bromholme.
She dothe ryght nott; I am afferde off hyr*e* þat she shall nott doo weell.

Bedyngffelde shall mary S*yr* John Skotty*s* doghtr*e*, as I suppose.

Item, Janor*e* Lovedaye shall be weddyd to on Denyse, a fuattyd[5] gentyl-
35 man w*yth* S*yr* G. Brown, nowther to weell ner to ylle.

Item, as for me, iff I had hadd vj dayes leyser mor*e* than I hadd, *and*
other also, I wolde haue hopyd to haue ben delyu*er*yd off Mestresse Anne
Hault. Hyr frend*ys* the Quyen *and* Att⟨cl⟩if agreyd to comon *and* conclude
w*yth* me iff I can fynde the mean*ys* to dyscharge hyr*e* concyence, whyche
40 I trust to God to doo.

j.[6] Item, I praye yow that ye take a leyser*e* thys Estern halydayes to ryde
to Sporle *and* sende for John Osberne, *and* I wolde ye sholde conclude a
bergayn wyth on Bochere,[7] a woode byer*e*, whyche Mendham þat was my
fermor*e* ther*e* can fecche hym to yow.

45 ij. *And* thys is myn entent. I wolde haue the dyk*ys* to stonde stylle acordyng
as John Osberne *and* I comonyd, I trow xij foothe w*yth*-in the dyke.

iij. Item, þat þe standard*ys* off suche mesur*e* as he *and* I comonyd off maye
also be reseruyd; I suppose it was xxx inche abow*t* a yerde from the
grownde.

50 iiij. Item, that it be surely fencyd at þe cost off þe woode byer*e* in any
wyse w*yth* ⌈a⌉ sure hedge, bothe hyghe *and* stronge.

v. Item, that ther*e* be a weye taken w*yth* the fermory*s* for*e* the vndrewood
so þat I lesse nott the ferme therffore ⌈yerly⌉. Item, John Osbern can[8] telle
yow the meanys howe to entrete the fermory*s*, for Herry Halman hathe
55 pleyed the false shrowe *and* fellyd my woode vppon a tenement off myn
to þe valew off xx m[a]rke, as ⌈it⌉ is tolde me. I praye yow enquire that
matr*e* *and* sende me worde, ⌈*and* dele w*yth* hym ther-afftre⌉.

---

[3] pr *and part of another letter canc.*

[4] *Dotted circumflex over* -om-, *of doubtful significance.*

[5] *Sic; presumably miswritten, but how is not apparent.*

[6] *This and following numerals in margin, opposite the line in which each item respectively*
begins. The opening words of each item are underlined except when they begin a line.

[7] *Name underlined.*   [8] -n *over* l.

vj. Item, iff the seyde wood, clere above all chargys excep as is above, be
made any better than cc m[a]rke I woll seye that ye be a good huswyff. John
Osberne seythe þat he woll doo me a frendys turne ther-in *and* yitt gete 60
hym-selff an hake-neye.

vij. Memorandum that he haue nott past iij ore iiij yere off vutraunce at þe
ferthest.

viij. Item, that I haue payement off the holl as shortly as ye kan, halffe in
hande, the remenant at halffe yeere ore ellys at ij tymes wyth-in on yere, at 65
þe ferthest by Mydsomere xij monyth.

ix. *And* that ye make no ferthere bergayn than Sporle woode *and* the lawnde,
not delyng wyth noon other woode nowther in the maner nor ellys wher
in non other tenement.

x. Item, that ye haue sufficient sewerté for the monye, wyth penaltés iff 70
nede be, som othere men bonden wyth hym for the payement.

xj. Item, I wolle well be bownde to waraunt it to hym. Item, I sende yow
herwyth a warant[9] to yow *and* John Osberne joyntlye to bergayn, comone,
and conclude that bergayn.

xij. Item, I suppose he woll, iff he conclude wyth yow, desyre to felle thys 75
Maye *and* I to haue mony soon afftre. I reke not[10] ⌈thowe he fellyd
not⌉ tyll thys wynter,[11] but iff he woll nedys begyn thys Maye, therffor
I wryght yow thus hastelye. Entrete hym iff ye can that he felle not tyll
wynter.

xiij. Item, be ware howe ye bergeyn so þat he felle nott butt in sesonable 80
tyme *and* sesonable wood, for he maye felle no vndrewood thys Maye,[12]
as I trowe.[13]

Item, as for yowre costys, late th⟨. . .⟩[14] newe fynde yow mete *and* I woll
allow it them,[15] ore ellys make me a bylle what it dra⟨. . .⟩nce yow.[16]

Item, I praye yow iff ye g⟨. . .⟩[17] for me as ye can. I made my lady heer 85
but easy cheer; neuerthelesse I gaff hyre ⟨. . .⟩ys.

I promysed hyre to purueye hyre a⟨. . .⟩[18] weselys, but I was deseyuyd; yit
I wend to haue had on.

My lord of Norffolk hathe ben mevyd for Caster by my lord Cardenall[19]
and the Bysshop off Wynchester, but it woll take non effecte ⟨. . .⟩y lady 90
com. God gyff grace þat she brynge auctoryté when she comythe thys next
terme to common ther-in *and* conclude, *and* so I prey yow advyse hyre.
Itt may haply paye for hyre costys.

---

[9] -t *over* d.   [10] iff the bergeyn myght not be executyd *canc.*
[11] as for hys fellyng *canc.*   [12] me *canc.*
[13] *Tear at foot of leaf affects this line, but nothing seems to be lost.*
[14] *Words lost here and later at tear more than two inches long; extent of loss uncertain
because the writing becomes smaller here at foot.*
[15] *Last letter uncertain.*   [16] *Recto ends.*
[17] *Words lost at tear, since the paper was reversed for the writing on verso.*
[18] *Vestiges suggest* peyre.   [19] *MS.* Cor-.

Nomore to yow, but wretyn at London the xij daye off Apryll A° E.
95 iiij^ti xiij°.

I sende yow herwyth ij letteris from John Osbern to me, wherby *and* by
hys billes ye may vndrestond þe verry valewe[20] off the wood. I praye yow
sende me wryghtyng ageyn by the Mondaye vij nyght afftre Estern. Iff
Hoxon ore[21] the goode man off the Goot haue it they shall conveye it to me.

275. To John Paston III   1473, 16 April

Add. 43490, f. 6. 11⅝×8 in. Autograph.

Dorse: Traces of red wax. Address autograph:

To John Paston, esquiere, in Norffolk.

Under the address, autograph:

I prey yow iff W. Mylsent go froo yow þat he myght come to me to Caleys.
I woll haue hym.[1]

Dated.
    F. ii, p. 130. G. 723/832.

Wyrsshypffull *and* ryght hertyly belowyd brother, I recomande me on-to
yow, letyng yow wete þat on Wednysdaye last past I wrote yow a letter
wheroff John Garbalde had the beryng, promyttyng me þat ye shold haue
it at Norwyche thys daye ore ellys to-morowe in the mornyng; wherin I
5 praye yowe to take a labore acordyng afftre the tenure off the same, *and* þat
I maye haue an answere at London ⌐to Hoxon¬ iff any massenger come, as
eu[er]e I maye doo fore yow. As for tydyngys, there was a truse taken at
Brussellys ⌐abut the xxvj daye off Marche last past¬ be-twyn the Duke off
Borgoyn *and* þe Frense Kyngys jmbassatorys *and*[2] Master William Atclyff
10 for the Kyng heere, whyche is a pese be londe *and* water tyll the fyrst daye
off Apryll nowe next comyng, betwyen Fraunce *and* Ingelond *and* also þe
Dukys londes. God holde it for euere *and* grace be.

Item, the Erle off Oxenfford was on Saterdaye at Depe,[3] *and* is purposyd
in-to Skotlond wyth a xij schyppys. I mystrust that werke.

15 Item, there be in London many flyeng talys seyng that þer shold be a
werke, *and* yit they wot not howe.

Item, my lorde chamberleyn sendyth now at thys tyme to Caleys þe
yonge Lorde Sowche *and* Syr Thomas Hongreffordys dowtre *and* heyre,

---

[20] ther *canc.*   [21] *Corr. from* off.
275. [1] *Last word uncertain owing to soiling.*   [2] the *canc.*
[3] *Name marked off and underlined.*

and som seye þe yonge Lady Haryngton. Thes be iij grett jowellys. Caleys
is a mery town; they shall dwell ther*e*, I wot not whyghe.   20

No mor*e*, but I haue ben *and* ame troblyd wy*th* myn ouer*e* large *and*
curteys delyng wy*th* my seruant*ys and* now wy*th* ther onkyndnesse. Plattyng, yowr*e* man, wolde thys daye byd me far*e*-well to to-morow at Dou*er*,
not wy*th*stondyng Thryston, yowr*e* other man, is from me *and* John
Myryell *and* W. Woode, whyche promysed yow *and* Dawbeney, God   25
haue hys sowle, at Castr*e* þat iff ye wolde take hym in to be ageyn wy*th*
me þat than he wold neu*er* goo fro me; *and* ther-vppon I haue kepyd hym
thys iij yer*e* to pleye Seynt Jorge *and* Robynhod *and* the shryff off Notyng-
ham, *and* now when I wolde haue good horse he is goon in-to Bernysdale,
and I wy*th*-owt a keper*e*.   30

Wretyn at Cant*er*burye, to Caleys warde on Tewesday *and* happe be,
vppon Good Frydaye þe xvj daye off Apryll A° E. iiij^{ti} xiij°.

Yowr*e* J. P., K.

Item, the most part*e* off the sowdyor*ys* þat went ou*er* wy*th* Syr Robert
Green haue leeff *and* be comyn hom, the hyghe-weye full. My cariage was 35
be-hynd me ij howres lengere þan I lokyd afftre, but j-wysse I wende þat
I myght haue etyn my part*e* on Good Frydaye, all my gownes *and* pryde
had ben goon; but all was saffe.[4]

---

276. To JOHN PASTON III   1473, 18 May

Add. 43490, f. 7. 11½×8½ in. Autograph.

Dorse: Continuation of text. Traces of red wax. Address autograph:

To John Paston, esquyer, in Norwyche.

Dated; but 18 May is St. Dunstan's Eve, not Day.
  This letter is unusually carelessly written, becoming hastier as it goes on.
  F. ii, p. 136. G. 724/833 (part).

Ryght wershypffull brother, I recomand me to yow, letyng yow weet þat
I receyuyd a lettr*e* yisterdaye þat com fro yow, wretyn the viij daye off
Maye, wherby I vndrestond þat the troble þat John Osberne has had hathe
lettyd the bargeyn off the woode in Sporle, wheroff I make no grett forse
so þat it maye be weell her-afftre. And as for John Osbernes beyng her*e*,   5
I heer*e* no worde off hym. I wolde be glad to weet ones what I weer the
rycher for*e* that woode.

Item, I thynke, iff I haue leyser*e*, to com *and* speke wy*th* my moodre.
Bothe she *and* Playter*e* haue promysed me so largely þat[1] it is shame for

---

⁴ *The postscript begins above the signature.*
276. ¹ *þ, exceptionally in John II, in form of* y.

10 them to goo balke w*yth* it; *and* iff she wolde helpe me as she hathe promysed, þan all shall be weell. Sende me worde what wey ye haue taken for
Saundr*e* Cok. Ye weere at Yarmothe—on Nycoll, a man off R. Racclyffys,
tolde me þat he spake w*yth* yow there, *and* þat ye promysed hym to haue
sende me a lett*er* by hym, but ye dyd nott.

15   As for tydyng*ys*, the Erle off Wylshyr*e and* the Lord Sudelé be ded, *and*
it was seyd þat S*yr* W. Stanlé was deed, but now it is seyd naye.

    As for W. Melsent, I woll nott haue hym but iff he had goon from yow,
as it was tolde me that he was. As for Burgeys, iff I haue verry greet nede
I shall sende yow worde; feell hys dysposic*ion and* sende me worde by
20 Juddy.

    Item, as for Mast*er* John Smythe, he delys² harde w*yth* me. Late Juddy
receyue off hym what he can geet; a m*a*rke is passyng lytell fo[r] vj m[a]rke.

    Item, the Fryres heer most be remembryd ⌐for there xx s. þat he bar-
gayned for*e* hy[s] grownde there⌐, also a stoon for hym. Take what ye
25 maye *and* afftre thatt cometh mor*e*.

    Item, as for Fastolff, he is nott curteyse. I praye yow deell w*yth* hym
ther-afftr*e*. Axe it as on-curteysly iff ye mete w*yth* hym.

    Item, I preye yow remembre the mat*er* off John Kendall, so þat I maye
haue a goode astate *and* relesys in my lond in Fylbye. Inqu*ire* afftr*e* goode
30 amblyng horse.

    Item, as for yowr*e* goyng to Seyn Jam*es*, I beleve it but atwyen ij.³

    Item, John Osbern com to town thys afftre-non, *and* ryght now I spake
w*yth* hym. He promysed me to doo þat in hym lythe when he comythe
hom, whyche shall be in all hast, as he seythe. He wyll dep*art* homward*ys*
35 to-morow.

    I herd seye that a⁴ man was thys daye examyned *and* he conffessed þat
he knewe greet tresor*e* was sende to þe⁵ Erle off Oxenfford, wheroff a m¹ li.
sholde be conveyd by a monke of Westm*inster and* som sey by a monke
off Chartrehows.

40   Item, that the same man schulde acuse c gentylmen in Norff*olk and*
Suff*olk* þat have agreyd to assyst the seyd Erle at hys comyng ⌐thyddre⌐,
whyche as itt is seyd sholde be w*yth*-in viij dayes afftr*e* Seynt Donston, iff
wynde *and* weddr*e* serffe hym—flyeng tales.

    No more at thys tyme, but God haue yow in kepyng. Wretyn at London
45 on Seynt Donstones Daye, þe xviij daye off Maye A° E. iiij*ti* xiij°.

JOHN PASTON,⁶ K.

---

² hade *with* r *over* d *canc.*
³ *Recto ends. The verso, even more hastily written, is evidently later.*
⁴ *No space.*   ⁵ duk *canc.*
⁶ *Abbr. by curl on* -t.

277. To John Paston III 1473, 3 June

Add. 43490, f. 8. 11¾×8¾ in. Autograph.

Dorse: Continuation of text. Remnants of red wax and tape. Address autograph:

> *To John Paston, esquiere, be thys delyveryd.*

Dated.
> F. ii, p. 138. G. 725/834. C. 71 (part).

Ryght wyrshypffull brother, I comand me to yow, latyng yow weet þat thys daye I was in verry *p*urpose to Caleys warde, all redy to haue goon to þe barge, saff I teryed for a yonge man þat I thoght to haue had w*yth* me thyddr*e*, on that was w*yth* Rows whyche is in the cowntr*é*. *And* becawse I cowde not geet hym, and þat I have nomore heer w*yth* me butt Pampyng, 5 Edward, *and* Jak, therffor Pampyng remembryd me that at Caleys he tolde me þat he *p*urposed to be w*yth* the Duchesse off Norff*olk*, my lady *and* yowr*ys*; *and* Edward is syke[1] *and* semythe nott abydyng—he wolde see what shold falle off thys worlde. *And* so I am as he that seythe, 'Com hyddr*e*, John, my men'. *And* as happe was yisterday Juddy went a-fore to 10 Caleysward;[2] wherffor I am nowe ille *p*urueyd, whyche for owte þat I knowe yit is lyke to kepe me heer*e* thys Wytsontyd.[3] Wherffor, iff ye knowe any lykly men *and* fayre condyc*i*oned *and* good archer*ys*, sende hem[4] to me, thowe it be iiij, *and* I wyll have them *and* they shall haue iiij m[a]rke by yer*e and* my lever*é*. He maye com to me hyddr*e* to þe Gott, or yit to 15 Caleys, w*yth* a riall iff he be wyse, whyche iff nede bee I wolde þat Berker*e* toke hym to com vppe w*yth*, iff it be suche on as ye tryst.

Item, I suppose bothe Pytte *and* Kothye Plattyng shall goo from me in hast. I wyll neu*er* cherysshe knaves soo as I have don for ther sakys.

Item, I praye yow sende me a newe vestment off whyght damaske for*e* 20 a dekyn, whyche is among myn other geer at Norwyche, for he shall ther-too as ye woot off. I wyll make an ⌐armyng⌐ doblett off it, thow I sholde an other tyme gyff a longe gown off velwett for*e* an other vestment; ⌐*and* send it in all hast to Hoxon to send me.⌐ I hopyd to have been verry mery at Caleys thys Whytsontyd, *and* am weell apparayled *and* apoyntyd saff that 25 thes folkys fayle me soo; *and* I have mat*er* there to make off ryght excellent. Som man wolde have hasted hym to Caleys thowe he had hadd no bett*er* erand, *and* som men thynke it wysdom *and* profyght to be theer now, weell owt off the weye.

---

277. [1] -y- *over* e.
   [2] *Written without space and with long s, which John II does not use finally. In l. 2 the same combination is divided, and has 'sigma' s.*
   [3] *Slit for tape damages last three letters.*   [4] -e- *over* y.

30 Item, as for the Bysshop *and* I, we bee nerr*e* to a poynt than we weer*e*, so that⁵ my part is nowe all the londes in Flegge holly, the man*er* off Heyles-don, Tolthorpe, *and* ten[*emen*]tys⁶ in Norwyche *and* Erlham excepte Fayrechyld*ys*; but farweell Drayton, the devyll doytt them!

Item, large *and* ferre comynycac*io*n hathe ben bytwyen S*yr* John Fogge, 35 Ric*h*ard Hawlte, fore ther sust*er and* me, byffore Doctore Wynterborne *and* ellys wher*e*, so that I am in bett*er* hope than I was by Seynt Lawrens that I shall haue a delyu*er*aunce.⁷

Item, as for tydyng*ys* heer, I trow ye have herde yowr*e* part*e* howe þat þe Erle off Oxenfford londyd at⁸ Seynt Osyes in Esexe⁹ þe xxviij daye off 40 Maye, saff he teryed nott longe; for iff he hadd the Erle off Essexe rod to hym wardys, *and* the lord*ys* Denham *and* Durasse *and* other mor*e*, whyche by lyklyod sholde have dystrussyd hym. But yit hys comyng savyd Hogan hys hed, and hys profesye is the mor*e* belevyd, for he seyde that this troble sholde begyn in Maye, *and* þat the Kyng sholde northwardys *and* that þe 45 Scott*ys* sholde make vs werke *and* hym batayle. Men loke afftre they wot not what, but men by harneys fast. The Kyng*ys* menyall men *and* þe Duke off Clarauncys¹⁰ ar*e* many in thys town; þe Lord Ryu*er*se com to-daye, me[n] sey to p*ur*ueye in lyke wyse.

Item, how þat þe Cowntesse off Warwyk is now owt off Beweley seynt-50 warye, *and* S*yr* Jam*es* Tyrell conveyth hyr*e* northwarde, men seye by the Kynges assent, wherto som men seye þat the Duke of Clarance is not agreyd.

Item, men seye þat the Erle off Oxenfford is abowt the jlde off Tenett hoveryng, som seye w*yth* grett companye *and* som seye w*yth* fewe.

55 No mor*e*, but God kepe yow. Wretyn at London the iij daye off June A° ⌜E. iiij⌝ᵗⁱ xiij°.

JOHN P., K.

278. To EDMOND PASTON II   1473, 5 July

Add. 43490, f. 9. 12×8½ in. Autograph.

Dorse: Continuation of text. Remnants of red wax and tape. Address autograph:

*A Edmond Paston, esquyer*e, *a Caleys soyt donné—A° xiij°.*¹

Dated.

F. ii, p. 146. G. 727/836.

⁵ that *repeated.*   ⁶ *Usual mark of contraction omitted.*
⁷ *Recto ends.*   ⁸ a- *over another letter.*
⁹ *Ampersand canc.*   ¹⁰ lythe *canc.*
278. ¹ *Date added later.*

Brother*e* Edmond, I grete yow weell, letyng yow weete þat abowt thys daye vij nyght I sende yow a lett*er* by Nycholas Bardeslee, a sowdyor*e* whyche is wont[2] to be at borde [at] Perauntys, and also an hoseclothe[3] off blak for*e* yow. I wende þat ye sholde haue hadde itt w*yth*-in ij dayes, but I am afferde þat he deseyued me. 5

Item, I lete yow weet þat Plattyng is comen hyddr*e*, *and* he seythe þat ye gaffe hym leve to fetche hys geer*e and* Pittys, *and* that is hys erande hyddr*e and* noon other*e*; ner*e* he thowt neu*er* to goo fro me, ner*e* he wyll nott goo fro me, as he seythe. Wherffor I praye yow sende me worde off hys condyc*i*ons, *and* whyghe[4] ye thynke þat he sholde neu*er* do me worshypp. 10 He seythe also þat he *and* Pytte weer at þe takyng off the Est*er*lyngys, *and* that he was in the *Pakker*e *and* Pytte in the *Crystoffre*. I praye yow sende me worde howe bothe he *and* Pitte quytte them, by the report off som jndyfferent trewe man þat was ther*e*. Iff they quytte them weell[5] I wolde love them the bett*er*, wherffore the next daye afftre the[6] syte off thys lett*er* 15 I praye yow wryght ageyn, *and* sende it by the next passage.

Item, I sende a lytell praty boxe herwith whyche I wolde þat Juddy sholde delyu*er* to þe woman þat he wotyth[7] off, *and* praye hyr*e* to take it to þe man þat she wotyth off; þat is to seye as moche as ye know all well j-now, bot ye maye nott make yow wyse in no wyse. 20

Item, I praye yow sende me worde as ye wer*e* wont to do off heere well-ffare, *and* whether I weer*e* owt *and* other jnne, ore nott; *and* whether she shall forsake Caleys as sone as ye sende me worde off, or nott. By God, I wolde be w*yth* yow as fayne as yowr*e*-selff, *and* shall be in hast, w*yth* Godd*ys* grace. 25

Item, as for my brother John, I hope w*yth*-in thys monyth to see hym in Caleys, for by lyklyhod to-morowe or ellys the nexte daye he takyth shyppe at Yarmothe *and* goothe to Seynt Jam*es* warde, *and* he hathe wretyn to me þat he wyll come homwarde by Caleys.

Item, I suppose þat Jam*es* Song*er* shall com w*yth* me to Caleys þe rather 30 for yowre sake.

Item, Mestresse Elysabett fareth well, but as yit Song*er* knoweth nott so parffytly all þat ye wolde weet þat he woll nott wryght to yow off thees ij dayes tyll he knowe moore. But iff she hadde ben bolde, *and* durst have abydyn styll at hyr*e* gate *and* spoken w*yth* me, so God helpe me she had 35 hadd thys same þat I sende nowe[8] where ye woot off, whyche ye shall see woryn heer afftr*e*. Itt is a praty ryban w*yth* praty aglett*ys and* goodlye. Make yow nott wyse to Juddy, nowther not þat ye wolde weet any thynge, for*e* I maye sey to yowe at hys comyng ovr*e* he browt goodly geer*e* resonablye.

---

[2] *Repeated as* wonte.   [3] *MS.* -chothe.
[4] -y- *over* e.   [5] -ll *over* r.   [6] shy *canc.*
[7] -o- *slightly looped at the top, so resembling* e ; *but* wotyth *a few words later is clear.*
[8] *Recto ends and* turne *is written in the corner below.*

40   Item, as for my byll þat is gylt, I wolde it weer taken heed too. Ther is on in the town þat can glaser[9] weell j-nowe, as I herde sey. Also ther is on comythe euery markett daye fro Seynt Omerys ⌈to Caleys⌉, *and* he bryng-ethe[10] dagerys *and* fecchyth; also he maye haue it *wyth* hym *and* brynge it ageyn the next markett daye for xij d. or xvj at þe most; *and* ellys late it

45   be weell oylyd *and* kepte tyll I come.

No more. Wretyn at London þe v daye off Jull A° E. iiij^{ti} xiij°.

279. To Margaret Paston   1473, 30 July

Add. 34889, f. 125. 11⅜×8⅜ in. Autograph.

Dorse: Continuation of text. Remnants of red wax over tape. Address autograph:

To my ryght wyrshypful Moodre, Margret Paston.

The date appears from the reference to Sporle, especially to the promise John II claimed to have received through Playter; for the same points are made in his dated letters nos. 274 and 276 of 12 April and 18 May 1473. Further, in no. 278, dated 5 July 1473, he expects to be in Calais within a month.

    G. LXXXVIII/837.

Ryght[1] wyrshypffull *and* my ryght tendre modre, I recomaunde me to yow, besechyng yow off yowre dayly blessyng. Please it yow to weet þat I herde nott from yow off longe tyme, whyche cawsythe me to be ryght hevye; nere at þe last tyme þat I sende to yow in wryghtyng I hadde from yowre-selffe

5   noo wryghtyng ner answere ageyn saff by Playtere on tym *and* by my brother an other tyme, whyche answer off Playtere was noo-thyng acord-yng but cont*r*aryaunt to other wryghtyng more comfortable þat he had sent me nott longe byffore thatt, on yowre behalve as he wrotte, whyche God amende. Neuerthelesse to my more heuynesse I herde seye þat ye sholde

10 have been passhyng hevy for my sake, *and* in cheffe fore that I was lyke to late goo the maner off Sporle, wherin I was pytte in comffort to have had relyffe by the meanes off yow; *and* syns it was tolde me þat iff I leete it goo þat ye wolde therfore dysavauntage me more londe in tyme to come off syche as by poscybylyté myght com to mee off yowrys. Vppon whyche

15 corage my grauntdame *and* myn oncle to-gedre gaffe me an answere on hyr part moche lyke, *and* so my fadre, God have hys sowle, leffte me scant xl li. londe in rest, *and* ye leffe me as pleasythe yow, *and* my grauntdame at hyre plesure. Thus maye I have lytell hope off the worlde. Neverthelesse I beseche yow to be my good moodre, how so euer ye doo *wyth* yowre londe,

20 fore I feell weell þat iff I have on losse I am lyke[2] therffor to have three. But

---

       [9] -r *of unusual shape, evidently added later.*
       [10] dake, *with* g *over* -k-, *canc.*
  279. [1] *Abbr. by flourish on* g.   [2] *MS.* lyffe.

as for Sporle, it shall nott goo iff I maye ner*e* by my wyll, *and* iff ther hadde
b*e*n performed me as largelye as was promysed me by Playter*e* I wer*e*
sewre it sholde nott have goon nor³ yit sholde nat goo. Neu*er*thelesse, iff
ye *and* all my frendys *and* yowr*y*s in Norff*olk* myght haue lende me so
moche monye, *and* to haue takyn it vppe in v yer*e*, I suppose they sholde 25
*p*ar auent*ur* have ben payed ageyn in a yere or*e* ij iff I had solde any woode.

Neu*er*thelesse, plese yow to weet þ*at* I have provyd my fadres wyll *and*
testement, wherin I maye nowt dele on-to þe tyme that all the executor*y*s
have reffused, wherffor*e* ther most be sende sitac*i*ons⁴ to yow *and* alle⁵
other that weer namyd my fadris executor*y*s, wherin iff ye lyst not to take 30
admynystrac*i*on, as I woot well ye woll nott off olde, ye most than make
a proctor*e* that must on yowr*e* behalve byffor my lorde off Cant*er*bury,
w*y*th a sufficiant warant *and* autoryté, vndr*e* a notarys syngne ther in the
corte reffuse to take admynestrac*i*on; *and* thys jnstrument and aultoryté
I beseche yow maye be redy *and* at London by the fyrst daye off þe terme. 35
And iff ye be not aqueyntyd w*y*th non suche at London, iff it please yowe
to take *and* avowe for yowr*e* proctor*e* *and* sende hym auctoryté, on Master
John Halsnothe, whyche was a clerke off Mast*er* Robert Cent*y*s *and* was
so trusty to my fadr*e*, God have hys sowle, *and* to sende me a lett*er* off yowr*e*
wylle ther-in, I vndretake þ*at* he shall nott do but as ye sende me worde. 40
Plese it yow to gyff credenc*e* to Juddy her-in.

No mor*e* to yow at thys tyme, but Jeshu have yow in hys kepyng. Wretyn
att Caleys the last daye saff on off Julle.

Yowr*e* s⟨one⟩⁶ J. P., K.

280. To JOHN PASTON III: draft　　　　　1473, late

Add. 27445, f. 25. 11½×6⅝ in. Autograph.

Dorse: Marks of rough folding, and tape slits; but no seal or address.

This is evidently a fragment of a draft. It must have been written to John III. It is
dated by Gairdner 1466, on the ground that it refers to the administration of the
will of John Paston I, who died in that year. But from no. 279 it appears that the
will was not proved until 1473. There John II writes of the need for the other
executors to decline administration and appoint 'proctors' to make a declaration to
that effect, and suggests that Margaret should appoint Master John Halsnothe.
The matter of the present note is so similar that it cannot be far distant in time.
See also no. 282, ll. 79–81 and no. 283, first paragraph.

G. 566/655.

Item, Arb[l]ast*er* must mak a procty*r* by yowr*e* advyce, *and* iff he lyst to
make the seyd Mast*er* John Halsnothe he maye; ell he must sende vppe an

other, *and* he must also make a let*ter* off warant to þe seyde Mast*er* John
Halsnothe vndr*e* hys sell by yowr*e* advyce in thys forme:

5   Mast*er* John, &c., I recomande me &c., letyng yow weet þat I haue made
yow my proctor*e* towchyng the[1] testement off John Paston, esq*uiere*,
wherffore I praye yow þat ye on my behalve r*e*ffuce the admynyst[r]ac*io*n
off hys[2] seyde testamen[t], fur*e* I woll nowt have ado ther-w*yth*. Wher-
ffo[r] loke þat ye on my behalve r*e*ffuce all admynestrac*io*n, entresse, or*e*
10   besynesse þat I myght have there-by, *and* thys shewys yow my wyll
her-in *and* shall be to yow a dyscharge att any tyme. No moore, &c.

                                   Yowr*e* frend Jame*s* Arblaster[3]

I wolde nat þat myn oncle Will*i*am scholde cawse hym to take on hym as
hys felaw, for iff myn oncle Will*i*am doo thus moche in the corte I suppose
15 it may her-afftr*e* doo ease; for as God helpe me I cannot say ver*re*ly iff my
fadr*e*, God haue hys sowle, ag[r]eyd that he shold be on, but in my sowle
he neu*er* thowt þat he sholde be, for he neu*er* namyd no moore butt my
modr*e* *and* me, *and* afftre yow whan I rehersyd myn oncle Clement, yow,
and Arblast*er*, *and* than he chase yow, seyng he thoght þat ye wer*e* good
20 *and* trewe. Kepe thys secrett. Iff myn oncle be noon execut*ur* it maye
happely brynge ageyn a trussyng coffre w*yth* cc old peyse noblis whyche
he toke from me as execut*ur*.

281. To JOHN PASTON III   1473, 6 November

Add. 43490, f. 5. 11¾×8¾ in. Autograph.

Dorse: Continuation of text. Paper seal over red wax and tape. Address
autograph:

> *To John Paston, esquiere, at Norwych be thys d*elyueryd.

Dated. The vestment (l. 46) recalls no. 277, l. 20.
    F. ii, p. 126 (misdated 15 April). G. 731/841 (part).

Wyrshypffull *and* well belovyd brother, I comand me to yow, letyng yow
weet þat the worlde semyth qweysye heer, for*e* the most part that be abowt
the Kyng haue sende hyddr*e* for ther harneys; *and* it [is] seyd for serteyn
that þe Duke of Claraunce makyth hym bygge in that he kan, schewyng as
5 he wolde but dele w*yth* the Duke of Glowcest*er*. Butt the Kyng ententyth[1]
in eschyewyng all jnconvenyent*ys* to be as bygge as they bothe, *and* to be a
styffelere atwyen them. *And* som men thynke þat vndr*e* thys ther sholde

---

280. [1] will *and canc.*   [2] *Corr. from* thys.
   [3] *This draft is marked off from the rest of the text by horizontal lines above and below.*
281. [1] -th *apparently over* d.

be som other thynge entendyd *and* som treason conspyred, so what shall falle can I nott seye.

Item, it is seyde þat yisterdaye ij passagerys off Dovre were takyn. I fere 10 þat iff Juddy had noon hasty passage, so þat iff he passyd nott on Sondaye or Mondaye, þat he is taken *and* som geer off myn þat I wolde nott for xx li. I hope *and* purpose to goo ⌐to Caleys⌐² warde on Sonday ore Mondaye, or nyghe bye, for I ame nott acompanyed to do any seruyse heer, wherffor it were better for me to be owt off syght. 15

Item, I praye yow calle vppon Doctore Pykenham *and* Master John Bulman, Hubberd, *and* other fore to make redy þe c li. þat I sholde haue off them. They grantyd³ me onys ⌐by the advyce of Fowlere⌐ þat I sholde have had it, so þat I hadd delyueryd them the oblygacion *and* fonde them sewerté to save them harmeles, whyche suerté was redy, *and* I neuer the⁴ 20 neere.⁵ I shall preue my fadrys wyll *and* have a letter off admynestracion, *and* nott beer grett perell; whyche I nedyd nott to have don iff Doctore Pykenham had ben kynde *and* just. Wherffor I thynke they shall paye for parte off my costys iff I sewe them. Neuerthelesse I preye yow entrete them that iff I sende them the oblygacion *and* heer-afftre fynde them sewerté 25 to saff them harmlesse, þat than I maye wett where to have my mony herin. I pray yow sende me answer in all the hast.

Item, Sprynge, þat wayted⁶ on my fadre when he was in jowelhows, whom my fadre at hys dyeng besett xl s., he cryethe euyr on me for it, *and* in weye off almesse he wolde be easyd thow it wer but xx s. or x; wherffor 30 he hathe wretyn to my modre, *and* most have an answer ageyn. I wolde þat my moodre sende hym as thoghe she lende hym som whatt, *and* he woll be pleasyd, *and* ellys he can seye as shrewdely as any man in Ingelonde.⁷

Item, the Kynge hathe sent for hys greet seall. Som seye we shall have a newe chavnceler, but som thynke þat the Kynge dothe as he dyde at the 35 last feldys: he wyll have the seall wyth hym. But thys daye Doctor Morton, Master off þe Rollys, rydethe to þe Kyng *and* berythe the seall⁸ wyth hym.

Item, I had neuer more nede off mony than now, wherfore Fastolffys v m[a]rke *and* the mony off Master John Smythe wolde make me holl.

Item, I praye yow remembre alwey my moodre *and* Playtere bothe off 40 ther promyse þat they made me off c ly. *and* to receyve it ageyn at Sporle off the ferme in v yere.⁹ Neuerthelesse iff I sell my wode I shall paye hyr in o yeere; jff I passe¹⁰ Mychelmesse I lose xx li., whyche wyll nott becom me in no wyse. I praye yow calle on [them].

---

² *Interl. above* thyddre *canc.*

³ *Uncertain:* g, *superior* r, *and* n *clear, the rest cramped at edge, and* t *apparently written over* y.

⁴ *MS.* ther.

⁵ *A word or two heavily canc.*   ⁶ *MS.* wayten.

⁷ *After this, in right-hand bottom corner,* turn, *marked off by angular line. Recto ends.*

⁸ *MS.* sease.   ⁹ v yere *underlined.*   ¹⁰ *Superfluous* I.

45 Wretyn on Seynt Lenard*ys* Daye A° r.r. E. iiij^{ti} xiij°.

Item, sende me my vestment acordyng to þe lett*er* I sent yow by Symond Dam in all hast.¹¹

J. P., K.

282. To JOHN PASTON III 1473, 22 November

Add. 27445, f. 73. 11⅝ × 16½ in. Autograph.

Dorse: Continuation of text. Traces of red wax. Address autograph, faint and mutilated:

⟨*T*⟩*o John Paston,* ⟨*e*⟩*squyer*e, *be thys d*elyuery*d.*

Dated.
F. v, p. 54. G. 732/842. C. 72 (part).

Ryght wyrshypfull *and* hertyly belovyd brother*e,* I comand me to yow, letyng yow wet þ*at* I receyuyd a lett*er* that com from yow wretyn sirca viij Mychaelys, wherin ye leet me weet off þe decesse off S*yr* Jam*es, and* þ*at* my moodr*e* is in p*ur*pose to be at Norwyche; *and* I am ryght glad þ*at*
5 sche wyll now doo somwhat by yowr*e* advyce. Wherffor be war*e* fro hense forthe¹ þ*at* noo suche felawe crepe in be-twyen hyr*e and* yow, *and* iff ye lyst to take a lytell labor*e* ye may lyff ryght well, *and* she pleasyd. It is as good that ye ryde w*yth* a cople off horse at hyr*e* cost as Syr*e* Jam*es* or*e* Richard Calle. Ye sende me word*e* also þ*at* she in noo wyse wyll p*ur*ueye thyr*e* c li. for þe
10 redemyng off Sporle. Late it goo. As towchyng that mat*er*,² John Osbern tolde me that he comonyd w*yth* yow at Sporle off that mat*er.* Ferre, he devysed þ*at* Kokett or*e* suche an other man sholde, to haue it the bett*er* cheppe, leye owt the valewe off vj yer*e* for to haue it vij yer*e,* wherto I wolde agr*é; and* for Goddys sake iff thatt maye be browt a-bowt late it be doon.
15 As ye woot off, it is laten for xxij li. by yer*e,* yit þe fermor*ys* graunt but xxj; but to Kokett it wolde be worthe xxv li., yea *and* bett*er.* Neu*er*the lesse, iff Kokett wyll delyu*er* vj^{xx} li. I wolde he had it for vij yeer*e,* w*yth* thys that my moodr*e* be agreable to þe same by-cawse off th'entresse that she hathe for my brother Will*i*am, whyche shall nott be off age thys vij yeer*e.*
20 Neu*er*the lesse, as ye know myn olde entent, I p*ur*pose to p*ur*uey for hym in an other plase bett*er* than theer*e,* off whyche graunte off my moodr*e* I praye yow to be my solycytore, in why⟨c⟩h⟨e iff⟩³ it be browt abowt Sporle shall be in as goode case as euyr*e* he was. John Osbern willyd me to make yow a sufficiaunt⁴ waraunt to selle and felle wood at Sporle, whyche I

---

¹¹ *The last sentence, forming a full MS. line, evidently added after the signature.*
282. ¹ *Ampersand canc.* ² *After this* Sporle *written in margin.*
³ *Paper decayed.* ⁴ *MS.* -aunce.

remembre ye have in as ample forme as can be. Neuerthe lesse iff thys 25
meane above wretyn, off letyng to ferme, maye be hadde, it shall I hope
nat nede to felle nere selle moche; but I remytte that geere to yowre
dyscrescion. But iff ye haue suche comfforte I praye yow sende me worde.
I maye seye to yow John Osbern flateryd me, fore he wolde haue borowyd
mony off me. Item, jn retaylyng off woode theere it weere harde to tryst 30
hym, he is nedye.⁵ Iff Kokett ore whoo so euyre had that maner to ferme
for vij yere *and* payd therffor but vjˣˣ li. he sholde, to lete it ageyn, wynne
xxxvj li., whyche we[re] moche; wherffore, iff it myght bee, yt were more
resenable vjˣˣ vij li. to be reseyuyd, *and* yit is there lost xxix li., ore ellys iff
ye take lesse mony *and* fewere yerys so it be afftre the rate, so there be 35
purueyd c li. at þe lest. Send worde.

Item, ye wroot þat lyke a trewe man ye sende me xviij s. by Richarde
Radlé. Ye weere to trewe, but he semys to be a false shrewe, fore he browt
me noon yitt. Whethyr he be owt off town ore nott kan I nott seye.

Ye prayed me also to sende yow tydyngys how I spedde in my materis, 40
and in cheff off Mestresse Anne Hault. I haue answere ageyn froo Roome
that there is the welle off grace *and* salve sufficiaunt fore suche a soore, *and*
that I may be dyspencyd wyth. Neuerthe lesse my proctore there axith
a mˡ docatys, as he demyth, but Master Lacy, an other Rome-rennere
heere, whyche knowyth my seyde proctore theere, as he seythe, as weell 45
as Bernard knewe hys sheeld, seythe þat he menyth but an c docatys, ore
cc at þe most; wherffor afftre thys comythe moore. He wrote to me also
q*uod* Papa hoc facit hodiernis die*bus* multociens.

Item, as towchyng Caster, I tryst to God þat ye shall be in it to myn vse
ore Crystmesse be past.   50

Item, yowre ost Brygham recomand hym to yow, *and* when he *and* I
rekenyd I gave hym ij noblis fore yowre borde whyll ye weere theere in hys
absence; but in feythe he wolde, fore nowth þat I kowde doo, take j d.,
wherffore ye most thanke hym ore charge me to thanke hym on yowre
behalve in som nexte epystyll þat ye wryght to me to Caleys. He leete me 55
weet þat he wolde do moore for yow than soo.

Item, my Lady Bowgchere was almost deed but she ⟨is⟩ amendyd. I
trowe they com in-to Norffolk.

Item, as for W. Berkere, I heere no worde from hym. I praye yow comon
wyth Berney ther-in; he knoweth⁶ myn conceyt. *And* also I praye yow hast 60
Berney ageyn. I wold not þat he pleyed the fooll nere wastyd hys tyme
nere hys syluer.

Item, as for the brace off growndes, ore on verry goode ore in especiall
þe blak off Germynys, I can nott seye but ye be a trewe man, but Will*iam*

---

⁵ *Following sentence marked off by a right-angled sign, its horizontal stroke under the first*
word; a similar sign marks off send worde *l. 36, which is at end of line, perhaps added.*
⁶ knowe *at end of line,* eth *at beginning of next.*

65 Mylsent isse a false shrewe, so mote I thee; *and* I trow hys master
is[7] too.

Item, I most haue myn jnstrument*ys* hydd*er* whyche are[8] in the chyst
in my chambre at Norwyche, whyche I praye yow *and* Berney to-gedre,
joyntly but natt seu*er*ally*e*, to trusse in a pedde *and* sende them me hyddr*e*
70 in hast, *and* a byll ther-in how many pec*ys*. Thys most be had to avoyde
jdelnesse at Caleys.[9]

Item, I preye yow take heed among thatt my stuffe take noon harme,
ner*e* that myn[10] euydence wher ye wott off be owt off jop*ar*té.

Item, I praye yow doo for Berney*e* as ye kan so þat he maye be in
75 sewerté for hys annywyté, *and* that it be nott costi*us* fro hense forthe to
hym any mor*e* to come or*e* sende for it. I pray yow wynn*e* yowr*e* sporys in
thys mat*er*.[11]

Item, I p*ur*posed to haue sent heer*e-wyth* the testament off my fadr*e*
and the scytac*i*ons to my moodr*e*, to yow, *and* Arblaster, but they be nott
80 redy. W*yth*-in ij dayes afftr*e* the comyng off thys I suppose they shall be
w*yth* yow, *and* than I shall wryght mor*e* to yow.

As for other tydyng*ys*, I trust to God thatt the ij Dukes off Clarans *and*
Glowcester[12] shall be sette att on by the adward off the Kyng.

Item, I hope by the mean*ys* off þe Duke of Glowcest*er* þat my lord
85 Archebysshop shall com hom.

Item, as towchyng my sustr*e* Anne, I vndrestand she hathe ben passyng
seek, but I wende þat she had ben weddyd. As for*e* Yelu*er*ton, he seyde but
late þat he wold haue hyr*e* iff she had hyr*e* mony, and ellis nott; wherffor me
thynkyth that they be nott verry sewr*e*. But amonge all other thyng*ys* I
90 praye yow be war*e* þat þe olde love off Pampyng renewe natt. He is nowe
fro me; I wott nat what he woll doo.

No more. Wretyn at London the xxij daye off Novembr*e* A° r.r. E.
iiij[ti] xiij°.

JOHN PASTON, K.

[7] *MS.* þis.
[8] a- *over* b.
[9] Caleys *at end of following line, marked off.*
[10] euydens *canc.*
[11] *Recto ends.*
[12] -l- *over* r.

283. To JOHN PASTON III   1473, 25 November

Add. 27445, f. 74. $11\frac{5}{8} \times 10\frac{1}{4}$ in. Autograph.

Dorse: Traces of red wax. Address autograph:

To John Paston, esquiere.

The date appears from the reference to the siege of the Earl of Oxford. He seized
St. Michael's Mount in September 1473, and held out until February 1474 (Scofield, ii. 85–8). The mention in the opening paragraph of Master John Halsnothe
as prospective 'proctor' connects this letter with nos. 279 and 280; and the reference
to Arblaster at the end is also probably to be connected with no. 280.

F. v, p. 62. G. 733/843.

Ryght wyrshypffull *and* well belovyd brother, I recomaund me to yow, letyng
yow weet þat I sende yow herw*yth* j sitacion[1] where[2]-in[3] ben my moodre
and yee, wheroff I praye yow þat I maye haue hasty answeere. The effeccte
theroff is no moore bute ye bothe most sende answere *and* make yow a
proctore heere, *and* that most come hyddre ondre a notaryes syngne afferm-   5
yng that ye make suche a man Mast*er* John Halsnothe, ore ellis yff ye will
do þe cost to sende som other hyddre[4] yowre proctore to take admynystra-
cion ore to reffuse, *and* what so he dothe ye to holde it for ferme *and* stable.
Than most my moodre *and* ye wryght a letter vndre my moodr*ys* seall *and*
yowre syngne manuell to me *and* Master John Halsnothe jn thys forme: 10
'We gret yow well, letyng yow weet þat we haue made yow, Mast*er* John
Halsnoth, owre proctore in the testament off John Paston, husbond *and*
fadre to yow,[5] wherin we wyll þat on owre behalff ye reffuse the admynestracion off the seyde testament; *and* thys wryghtyng is to yow warant
and dyscharge, *and* also the verry wyll off vsse.' Thys most we haue for   15
owre dyscharge.

Item, I pray yow take good hedde to my soster Anne lesse the olde love
atwyen hyr*e and* Pampy*ng* renewe.

Item, I pray yow sende me worde howe my moodre is dysposyd to hyr
wardys, *and* iffe so weer that a[6] good mariage myght be had, what she wolde   20
depart wyth.

Item, I praye yow þat ye remembre hyr for the tombe off my fadre at
Bromholme, *and* also the chapell at Mavteby, *and* sende me worde how she
is dysposyd her-in.

Item, iff I have Caster ageyn whethyre she wolle[7] dwelle ther or nott,   25
and I wyll fynde hyr a prest towardys at my charge *and* geve hyr the

---

283. [1] *Last four letters written over an earlier form ending in -s ; preceding numeral corr.
from* ij *to* j.

  [2] *Corr. from* wheroff.   [3] the on *canc.*

  [4] *and* ellis ye *canc.*   [5] *Error for* vsse.

  [6] *No space.*   [7] *Apparently corr. from* wolde.

dovehowse *and* other comodytés ther; *and* iff any horsekeper off[8] myn lye
ther I wolle paye for hys borde also, as weell as for the prest*ys*.

Item, iff my modr*e* sholde haue a new prest I thynk þat my brother S*yr*
30 J. Goos weer*e* a metly man to be ther. He wolde also doo as ye wolde haue
hym. Nowe ber*e* the cuppe euyn, as whatcalle-ye-hym seyde to Aslake. Be
war*e* off myner*ys* fro hense forthe, *and* sende me worde how ye trist Doctor*e*
Pykenh*a*m. I wolde, iff he wolde doo owght[9] for my moodr*e*, that he hastyd
the so*n*ner to paye me the c li. so þat I myght pledge owt Sporle.

35 Item, as for*e* other tydyng*ys*,[10] the Erle off Oxenforthe is stille besegyd.
Neu*er*thelesse onys he issued owt *and* toke a jentilman *and* hant[6] hym
w*yth*-in, but now off late he was besye *and* on espyed hym *and* shott at hym
and strake in the ⌈verry⌉ fase w*yth* an arowe. I sye thys daye þe same man,
and theer I leeff hym.

40 Iff Arblast*er* come to yow ye maye see hys lett*er* sente to hym by me,
wherin I have wretyn þat he scholde take yowr*e* advyc*e*; but I pray yow
above all thyng*ys* that ye[11] make hast so þat I heer from yow ageyn by thys
day vij nyght.

At London the xxv daye off Novembr*e*.

45
JOHN PASTON,[12] K.

284. To MARGARET PASTON   1474, 20 February

Add. 43490, f. 11. $8\frac{3}{4} \times 7\frac{1}{8}$ in. Autograph.

Dorse: Continuation of text. Traces of red wax. Address autograph:

Mestresse Margrett Paston, at Norwyche.

Dated.
   F. ii, p. 154. G. 736/846.

Ryght honorable *and* most tendr*e* good moodr*e*, I recomand me to yowe,
besechyng yow to haue, as my tryst is þat I have, yowr*e* dayly blessyng;
and thanke yow off yowr*e* good moderhood, kyndenesse, cheere, charge,
and coste whyche I had *and* pvtte yow to att my last beyng w*yth* yow,
5 wh[y]che God gyffe me grace her-afftre to deserve. Please it yow to weet
þat I thynke[1] longe þat I heere nott from yow, or*e* from Pekok yowr*e*
seruaunt, for*e* the knowlege howe he hathe doon in þe sale off my ferme
barlye, ner*e* what is made there-off. Wherffore I beseche yow, iff it be not
answeryd by that tyme þat thys bylle comythe to yowe, to hast hym *and*

---

[8] *MS.* on.   [9] *Corr. from* owt.
[10] *Abbr. by stroke above instead of usual loop.*   [11] *MS.* me.
[12] *Abbr. by curl on* t.
284. [1] *MS.* thynge.

itt hyddreward*ys*, fore iff þat had nott taryed me I deme I had ben at 10
Caleys by thys daye. For it is soo, as men seye, þat þe Frense Kynge w*yth*
a gret hoste is at Amyas, but iij^{xx} myle from Caleys, *and* iff he or*e* hys roode
byffor*e* Caleys *and* I nott theer*e*, I wolde be sorye.

Item, men seye þat the Erle off Oxenfford hathe ben constreynyd to sewe
for*e* hys pardon only off hys lyffe, *and* hys body, ⌈goodes, londes⌉, w*yth* all 15
þe remenaunt at þe Kynges wyll, *and* soo sholde in all haste nowe com in
to þe Kyng. *And* som men seye þat he is goon owt off þe Mownte, men wot
not to what plase, *and* yit leffte a greet garnyson theer*e* weell fornysshyd in
vytayll *and* all other thyng.

Item, as for*e* the hauyng ageyn off Castr*e*, I trust to have good tydyng*ys* 20
theroff hastelye.²

Item, my brother John farethe weell, *and* hathe doon ryght delygentlye
in my cosyn Elisab*eth*³ Berneys mater*ys*, wheroff hastely I trust he shall
sende hyr*e* tydyng*ys* þat schall please hyr*e*; *and* as to-morow⁴ he p*ur*posyth
to take hys jurneye to Walys warde to þe Lord Ryverse. 25

Nomor*e* at thys tyme, but Jeswe haue yow in hys kepyng. Wretyn at
London the xx daye off Feu*er*ere A° E. iiij^{ti} xiij°.

Yowr*e* sone J. PASTON, K.

---

285. To MARGARET PASTON   1474, probably November

Add. 27445, f. 82. 11½ × 11½ in. Autograph.

Dorse: Paper seal over red wax. Address autograph:

*To Mestresse Margrett Paston at Norwyche, er to J. Paston in hyr*e* absence.*

The date appears from the references to John II's paying off of his debt to Towneshend, and to the books left by James Gloys. The state of affairs is clearly only a
little earlier than that of no. 286, which is dated.
    F. v, p. 72. G. 745/856. C. 73 (part).

Ryght wyrshypfull *and* my moste kynd *and* tendre moodre, I recomaund me
to yow, thankyng yow off the grete cost *and* off the greet cher*e* þat ye dyd
to me *and* myn at my last beyng wyth yow*e*; whyche cheer*e* also hathe
made me p*er*ffyghtly hooll, I thanke God *and* yow, in so moche þat where
as I feeryd me þat for weykenesse, *and* so green recuv*e*ryd off my syknesse, 5
þat I scholde have apeyryd by the weye, but, God thanke yow, I toke soo
my crommys whyls I was w*yth* yow þat I felyd my-sylffe by the weye that
God *and* ye had made me strong*er* than I wenyd þat I had ben, jn so moche
þat I feell my-selffe eu*er*y daye holler*e* than other.

---

² *Recto ends.*   ³ *Abbr. -b3.*   ⁴ *Third -o- over y.*

10   It was soo that I mett wyth myn onkle William by the weye, and there in
the felde I payed hym the iiij li. whyche I had borowyd off hym, and he was
passyng jnquisytyff howe þat I was purueyd fore recompensyng off Towneshend. I tolde hym I hopyd weell. He tolde me þat he vndrestood þat I
had the c li. off the Bysshopys executorys, and he had herd seye þat I had

15 also borowyd an other c li. off a marchaunt, and so I lakyd but an c marke.
I deme he herde thys off T. Lovell, fore I tolde hym þat I was in hope to
fynde suche a freende þat wolde lende me c li. He axed me who was that;
I answeryd hym an olde marchaunt, a freende off myn; but myn oncle
thowte þat sholde be by weye off chevyshanse and to myn horte, wherffore

20 I was pleyne to hym and tolde hym that ye were sewerté therffore and
purueyed it off suche as wolde doo for yowe. And as for the forte c mark,
he seyde to me þat as for that he wolde, rather than joparté sholde be,
purvey it by weye off chevyshaunce at London, jn so meche þat ere he
come fro London he had for my sake leyde v c markys worthe off plate

25 wyth Hewghe Fenne. The place at Warwykys Inne is large and my grawnt-
dame is agyd; it had ben jopartous to leve moche plate wyth hyre, thoghe
halffe were hyre owne. But iff I maye doo other wyse I purpose nott to
chevyshe any mony by hys meane.

Item, I have delyueryd yowre botell to Courbye þe caryere thys same
30 daye, and he promysed me to be wyth yow on Mondaye nyghte ore ellys
on Towesday tymely. He hathe also xl d. to paye for the thryd hyryd horse,
and he bryngythe the iij horse wyth hym and is contente for hys labore
and for the mete largely. They be delyueryd hym in as good and rather
better plyght than whan I had them forthe, and nott gallyd[1] nore hurte.
35 He hat[h]e also ij sadelys, on off my brotherys and an other hyred, as ye
woot off. Item, he hathe a peyre botys off Edmond Reedys þe shomakere,
whyche Saundre borowyd off hym. I beseche yowe that William Mylsent
ore Symme maye se þat euery man have hys owne.

Item, as fore my brother Edmond, blyssyd be God he is weell amendyd.
40   Item, as fore Hankyn owre dogge, I am a-ferde neuer to see hym but iff
yowre good helpe bee.

Item, as for the bookys þat weer Syr James, iff it lyke yow þat I maye
haue them I ame not able to by them; but som-what wolde I gyffe, and the
remenaunt, wyth a goode devowte herte by my trowthe I wyll prey for hys
45 sowle. Wherffor iff it lyke yow by the next massenger ore karyere to sende
hem, in a daye I shall have them dressyd heer; and iff any off them be
claymyd here-afftre in feythe I wyll restoore it.[2]

Wretyn on Saterdaye.

JOHN PASTON, K.

---

285. ¹ -yd *over other letters, perhaps* ey.
  ² *Last sentence crowded into bottom corner to right of subscription, which itself is cramped
at foot.*

286. To Margaret Paston   1474, 20 November

Add. 27445, f. 83. 11¾×8½ in. Autograph; see Plate VI.

Dorse: Traces of red wax. Address autograph:

To Mestresse Margrete Paston, ore to Roose dwellyng byffore hyre gate at Norwyche.

Dated.
   F. v, p. 78. G. 746/857.

Afftre dew recomendacion, my most tendre *and* kynde moodre, I beseche yow off yowre dayly blessyng. Please it yow to weete þat I reseyvyd a lettre that¹ come from yowe, wretyn þe xxvj daye off Octobre, non erst but on Wednysday last past; wherby I conceyvyd þat at þe wryghtyng off þat letter ye weere nott serteyn off the delyng betwyn Towneshende *and*   5 me. It was so þat, God thanke yow, I receyvyd þe xx li. broght by Syme *and* also the mony browght by my brothere, wyth whyche mony, *and* wyth moore þat I had my-selff, I redemyd the maner off Sporle *and* payed Towneshend bothe þe cccc m[a]rke ther-fore *and* also x li. þat I owte hym besyde; *and* have off hym an aqwytaunce off all bargaynes   10 ⌜*and*⌝ off all other dettys. Neuerthelesse, I assayed hym iff he wolde, iff nede hadde ben, gyvyn me a xij monyth lenger respyght, whyche he grauntyd to do. But in conclusyon I can nott entrete hym but þat he woll have the vttremest off hys bargayn, *and* thys xx li. payeable at Candelmesse *and* Esterne. I kan entrete hym noon other wyse as yit; wherfore I thynke   15 iff I had passyd my daye it had ben harde to have trustyd to hys cortesye, jn so moche I fynde hym also ryght loose in the tonge. For Bekham, he spekyth no-thyng comfortably ther-in; what he wyll doo can I nott seye.

   Item, as for Castre, it nedyth nott to spore nore prykke me to doo owghte ther-in. I doo þat I can wyth goode wyll, *and* somwhat I hope to doo   20 hastely þer-in þat shall doo goode.

   Item, as for the bokes þat weere Syre James, God haue hys sowle, whyche it lykethe yow þat I shall have them, I beseche yow þat I maye have them hyddre by the next massenger; *and* iff I be goon, yit that they be delyueryd to myn ostesse at þe George at Powlys Wharff, whyche wolle kepe them   25 saffe, *and* þat it lyke yow to wryght to me whatt my peyne ore payment shall be for them.

   Item, it lyked yow to weet off myn heelle. I thanke God nowe þat I am nott greetly syke nere soore but in myn heele, wherin alle men know nott whatt peyne I feele. *And* wher ye advysed me to hast me owt off thys towne,   30 I wolde full fayne be hense. I spende dayly more than I sholde doo iff I were hense, *and* I am nott well porveyed.

       286. ¹ *MS.* thhat.

Item, blessyd be Good my grauntdam is amendyd by suche tyme as myn oncle W. come hyddre, but my yongest cosyn Margret, hys doghtre, is ded
35 *and* beryed er he come hom. I am as moche a-ferde off thys londe þat is in hys hande as I was off that þat was jn Towneshendys hande.

I hope to wryght yow moore serteyntés wyth-in iiij ore v dayes. Nomore, &c. Wretyn þe xx daye off Novembre A° E. iiij xiiij°.

Yowre sone J. PASTON, K.

287. To JOHN PASTON III 1474, 20 November

Add. 43490, f. 13. 11¾×8½ in. Autograph.

Dorse: Continuation of text. Traces of red wax. Address autograph:

To John Paston, esquyere, at Norwyche, ore to Roose dwellyng affore Mestresse Pastonys gate in Norwych.

At right angles, in John III's hand:

> j d. clowys *and* masys
> swgyr—quart.
> quart. tyer
> quart. muskadell.

Dated.
F. ii, p. 164. G. 747/858.

Ryght wyrshypfull *and* weell belovyd brother, I recomaunde me to yow, letyng yow weet þat I have comonyd wyth yowre freende Dawnson *and* have receyvyd yowre rynge off hym, *and* he hathe by myn advyce spoken wyth hyre ij tymes. He tellythe me off hyre delyng *and* answerys, whyche
5 iff they were[1] acordyng to hys seyng a feynter lovere than ye wolde, *and* weell aghte to, take ther-in greet comffort, so þat he myght haply slepe þe werse iij nyghtys afftre. And suche delyng in parte as was by-twyen my Lady W. *and* yowre freende Danson he wrote me a bylle theroff, whyche I sende yow herwyth; *and* that þat longythe to me to doo therin it shall
10 nott fayle, to leeve all other bysynesse a-parte. Neuerthelesse, wyth-jn iiij dayes I hope so to deele here-in þat I suppose to sette yow in serteynté hoghe þat ye shall fynde hyre[2] fore evyre heer-afftre. It is so, as I vndrestande, þat ye be as besy on yowre syde fore yowre freende Dawnson wheer as ye be. I praye God sende yow bothe goode spede in thees werkys,
15 whyche iff they be browte abowte, jche off yowe is moche be-holden to other. Yit weere it pyté þat suche craffty wowerys as ye be bothe scholde speede weell but iff ye love trewly.

287. ¹ Corr. from be.   ² -y- over incomplete o.

Item, as fore Stoctonys doghtre, she shall be weddyd in haste to Skeerene, as she tolde hyre-selffe to my sylkemayde whyche makyth parte off suche as she shall weere, to whom she brake hyre harte *and* tolde hyre þat she 20 sholde have hadde Master Paston, *and* my mayde wende it had been I þat she spake off;[3] wyth moore, þat the same Master Paston[4] kome where she was wyth xx men *and* wold have taken hyre aweye. I tolde my mayde þat she lyed off me, and þat I neuer spake wyth hyre in my lyff, nere þat I wolde not wedde hyre to have wyth hyre iij^{ml} marke. 25

Item, as for Ebortonys dowghtre, my brother Edmonde seythe þat he herde neuer moore speche þer-off syns yowre departyng, *and* þat ye wolde þat he sholde nott breke nore doo no-thynge ther-in but iff it come off theere begynnyng.

Item, I had answere from my lorde þat he is my speciall goode lorde, 30 *and* þat by wryghtyng; *and* as for Bernaye, he sette hym in hys owne wagys for my sake, *and* þat whan so euer I come to Caleys I shall fynde all thyng there as [I] woll have it, *and* rather better than it was heere-tofor.

Item, þe Kynge come to þis towne on Wednysdaye. *And* as for the 35 Frenshe enbassate þat is heere, they come nott in þe Kynges presense, by lyklihod, for men seye þat þe chyeff of them is he þat poysonyd bot⟨he⟩[5] þe Duke off Berry *and* þe Duke off Calabre.

Item, there was neuer more lyklyhood þat þe Kyng shall goo ouy⟨re⟩[5] thys next yere than it is nowe.[6] 40

I praye yow remembre þat I maye have þe pewtre vessell hyddre[7] by þe next karyer by the lattre ⟨ende⟩[8] off thys weke.

Item, I praye yow remembre so þat I maye have the bokys by the same tyme whyche my moodre seyde she wolde sende me by the next cariere.

Wretyn at London þe Sondaye þe xx daye off Novembre A° E. iiij^{ti} 45 xiiij°.[9]

JOHN PASTON, K.

---

[3] *Ampersand canc.*   [4] *A word canc., perhaps* konne.
[5] *Letters lost at tear in corner.*   [6] *Recto ends;* turne *is written in the corner.*
[7] *First line of verso covered by binder's mount, but visible against strong light. After* vessell, she *canc.;* -y- *in* hyddre *over* e.
[8] *Fenn's reading, now lost at corner.*   [9] *From* A° *in a separate line, underlined.*

288. To John Paston III 1474, 11 December

Add. 43490, f. 14. 8–9×6 in. (right side irregularly torn before writing). Autograph.

Dorse: Continuation of text occupies all but a 2½×3-in. space left for address and seal. Remnants of red wax. Address autograph:

To John Paston, esquiere.

Dated.

F. ii, p. 170. G. 749/860 (part).

Brother, I recomaunde me to yow, letyng yow weete þat I have, lyke as I promysed yowe, I have doon my devoyre to knowe my Lady Walgraues stomake, whyche, as God helpe me *and* to be pleyn to yowe, I fynde in hyre no mater nere cawse þat I myght take comfort off. Sche wyll in no
5 wyse receyve nere kepe yowre rynge wyth hyre, *and* yit I tolde hyre þat she scholde not be any-thynge bownde therby but þat I knew by yowre herte off olde þat I wyst weell ye wolde be glad to forbere the levest[1] thyng þat ye had in the world whyche myght be dayly in here presence þat sholde cawse hyre onys on a daye to remembre yow; but itt wolde not be. She
10 wolde nott therby, as she seyde, putte yow[2] nere kepe yow in any comffort ther-by, *and* more-ovyre she preyed me þat I sholde neuer take labore moore heere-in fore she wolde holde hyre to suche answere as she hadd gevyn yow to-foore; wherwyth she thowght bothe ye *and* I wolde have holde vs contente had nott been the wordys off hyre suster Geneffyeff.
15 When I vndrestoode all thys, *and* that ouer nyght ⌈she bad⌉ hyre þat weent bytwyen hyre *and* me byd me brynge wyth me hyre muskeball whyche, &c., than I aftre all thys axid iff she weere dyspleasyd wyth me for it, *and* she seyde naye. Than I tolde hyre that I had nott sent it yowe fore synne off my sowle, *and* so I tolde hyre all how I had wretyn to yow
20 why that I wold nott sende it yow by-cawse I wyst weell ye sholde have slepyd the werse. But nowe I tolde hyre, as God helpe me, þat I wolde sende it yow, *and* gyffe yow myn advyse nott to hope ouyre moche on hyre whyche is ovyre harde an hertyd lady for a yonge man to tryst on-to, whyche I thowght þat for all my wordys ye cowde nott nere wolde nott do
25 fore all myn advyce. Yitt ageynwardys, she is nott dyspleasyd nor forbad me nott but that ye sholde have the kepyng off hyre mvskball.[3] Wherffor do ye wyth itt as ye lyke. I wolde it hadd doon weell. By Good, I spake fore yow soo that in feythe I trowe I kowde nott seye so weell ageyn; wherffor I sende yow herwyth yowre rynge *and* the onhappy muskeball
30 also. Make ye[4] mater off it herafftre as ye kan. I am nott happy to wow,

288. [1] -v- *over* f. [2] *Ampersand canc.*
[3] *Recto ends; from* that *crowded into bottom corner.*
[4] *About three letters, apparently* mat, *canc.*

480

nowther for my-selff nere noon othere. I tolde hyre all þe process off the
Lorde Howarde *and* off yowre grewndys as I kowde; all helpys notte.

Item, I praye yow late my brothere Edmonde vndrestonde þat as for þe
chevysshaunce þat myn oncle W. spake off, as God helpe me itt canne
nott be, I cannott chevyshe for my-selffe. I feer þat I am lyke to be 35
deseyuyd by hym; by God I had lever than c noblys þat I weer qwyte off
hym. I can se noon other as yit, but that I ame nott lyke to goo to Caleys
byffore Crestmesse but iff I wolde jopart it at hys curtesye. I am in an
agonye wyth hym þat vexithe all my spyrytys. I heer no woorde from my
brother E. ner fro R. Lynsted howe they have sped wyth Towneshende. 40
Iff ther be any answere sent to myn oncle W. he makyth me nott prevye
ther-to, whe[r]for I have to grett an hurte jff I wote nott in all haste howe
þat Lynsted hathe doon wyth Towneshend *and* also att Snaylwell; wherffor
in hast sende worde to me or to myn ostesse at þe George. I here no worde
off my vessell nere off my bokys. I mervayll. 45

No more. Wretyn at London the xj daye off Decembre A° E. iiij^{ti} xiiij°.

J. P., K.

289. To John Paston III 1475, 17 January

Add. 43490, f. 15. 11⅜×8½ in. Autograph.

Dorse: Traces of red wax. Address autograph:

To þe ryght worshypfull John Paston, esquiere, at Norwych, ore to hys
moodre Margreet Paston in hys absence, in haste.

Margaret's letter no. 223 fills the blank space.

Dated.
F. ii, p. 174. G. 750/861.

I recomande me to yow, prayng yow hertely þat I maye have weetyng
whan þat my lorde *and* ladye off Norffolk shalle be at London, *and* howgh
longe they shall tery theere, *and* in especiall my lorde off Norffolk, for
vppon there comyng to London were it for me to be guydyd. Neuerthelesse
I wolde be soory to come theere but iff I nedys most. I thynke it wolde be 5
to yow ouyre erksom a labore to solycyte the materys a-twyen them *and*
me but iff I weere theere my-selffe; wherffore iff ye thynke it be convenyent
that I come thyddre, I praye yow sende me worde as hastely as ye maye,
and by what^1 tyme ye thynke most convenyent þat I sholde be theere, *and*
off all suche counfforte as ye fynde ore heere off the towardnesse ther-off, 10
and whan also þat ye shall be theer yowre-selffe. Fore it is so þat as to-
morow I purpose to ryde in-to Flaundrys to purveye me off horse *and*

289. ^{1} *MS.* whhat.

herneys, *and* p*ar*case I shall see the assege at Nwse er*e* I come ageyn iff
I have tyme, wherffor jff I so doo by lyklyhod it woll be a xiiij dayes er I
15 be heer ageyn. *And* afftre as I heer*e* from yowe *and* other, then vppon
that at þe next passage, *and* God woll, I p*ur*pose to come to London warde,
God sende me goode spede, jn cheff for þe mat*er* above wretyn *and*
secondly for*e* to appoynt w*yth* the Kynge *and* my lorde for suche retynwe
as I sholde have now in thees werrys in-to Frawnce. Wherffore I praye
20 yow in Norffolk *and* other places[2] comon w*yth* suche as ye thynke lykly
for*e* yow *and* me þat ar*e* dysposyd to take wag*ys* in gentylmenn*ys* howsys
and ellys where so þat we maye be the moor*e* redy whan þat nede is.
Neu*er*thelesse at thys owr*e* I wolde be gladde to have w*yth* me dayly iij or*e*
iiij mor*e* than I have suche as weer*e* lykly, for I lakke off my retynwe þat
25 I have heer*e* so[3] many.

I praye yow sende me som tydyng*ys* suche as ye heer*e*, *and* howghe þat
my brother Edmonde dothe, for as for tydyng*ys* heer*e*, theer*e* be but fewe
saffe þat the assege lastyth stylle by the Duke off Burgoyn affoor*e* Nuse[4]
and the Enp*er*ore hathe besegyd also, not ferr*e* from thense, a castell *and*
30 an other town in lyke wyse ⌜wher-in⌝[5] þe Dukys men been. *And* also þe
Frenshe Kynge, men seye, is comyn nyghe to þe wat*er* off Somme w*yth*
iiij[m] sper*ys*, *and* som men trowe þat he woll[6] at þe daye off brekyng off
trewse, or ellys byffoor*e*, sette vppon the Duk*ys* contreys heer*e*. When I
heer*e* moor*e* I shall sende yowe moor*e* tydyng*ys*. The Kyng*ys* jnbassator*ys*,
35 S*yr* Thom*as* Mongomer*é* *and* þe Mast*er* off the Roll*ys*, be comyng homward*ys* from Nuse,[4] *and* as for me I thynke þat I sholde be seke but iff I
see it. Syr*e* John off Parre *and* Will*i*am Berkeley com thys weys to Flaundr*ys* ward to by them horse *and* herneys, *and* [I] made S*yr* J. Parre goode
cheer*e* as I cowde for yowr*e* sake, *and* he tolde me þat ye made hym haulte
40 cheer*e* &c. at Norwyche.

No moor*e*. Wretyn at Caleys the xvij daye off Janeu*er* A° Edwardi iiij[ti]
xiiij°.

2 *A word, perhaps* feele, *canc.*   3 *MS.* se.
4 *Dot over* u *evidently intentional, since it occurs twice.*   5 *Interl. above* off *canc.*
6 *MS.* well.

290. To JOHN PASTON III or others   1475, 5 February

Add. 27445, f. 86. 11⅝×8½ in. Autograph.

Dorse: Traces of red wax. Address autograph:

To hys brother John Paston, ore to hy[s] oncle William Paston in Werwykk
Lane, ore to Edmond Paston at þe George at Powlys Wharffe: to delyuer
any of them.
A few incomplete words in John III's hand.

Dated.
F. v, p. 92. G. 753/864.

Ryght worshypfull, I recomaunde me on-to yow, letyng yow weete þat I
thynke longe þat I heere nott from yow syns Crystmesse nere have no
serteyn knowleche whether þat Towneshend hathe performyd hys promysse ore nott, nere off my brothere Johnys beyng at London, nere off
my lord ore lady off Norffolkys comyng to London, at whoys comyng 5
sholde be þe cheffe labore *and* sewte þat I or any for me sholde labore.
It was soo, God thanke yow bothe, þat iche off yow at my last beyng wyth
yow grauntyd me to take labore vppon yow *and* iche off yow for the hauyng
ageyn off my place in Castre. Now is it soo þat wher my verry purpose
was to have comyn to London now, wyth the Master of the Rollys *and* 10
Syr Thomas Mongomeré, demyng to fynde the Kyng at the parlement,
and also þat my lorde *and* lady off Norffolk sholde nott by lyklyhod fayle
to be theere also,[1] wherffore me thoght the tyme was convenyent; but it
happyd so þat suche tydyngys come hyddre off the Frenshe Kyngys hasty
comyng in-to thees marchys off Pykardye whyche cawsyd my lordys deputé 15
and cownsell heere to desyre *and* charge me soo streyghtly þat in noo wyse
I maye, tyll I heere othere tydyngys, departe from hense. Notwythstondyng
the marchall *and* counsell heere have wretyne to my lorde lywe-tenant for
me, *and* moore-ouer desyryd both ⌐þe¬ Master off þe Rollys *and* Syr T.
Mongomeré to remembre my materys both to þe Kynge *and* to my lorde, 20
in so moche þat iff the season be convenyent bothe þe seyd Master *and*
Syre T. Mongomeré wille labore bothe the Kynge *and* my lorde to entrete
my lorde of Norffolk, my lady hys wyff, *and* ther consell to do for me all
that reason wyll, off whoys good willys ⌐*and* labore here-in¬ I ame better
ensuryd off than I kan, for lakke off leysere at thys tyme, wryght yowe 25
wetyng off. Wher-for I praye yow *and* iche off yow, iff the season be
convenyent, to take the labore that theese jentyllmen maye do for me *and*
to my[2] proffyght like as I feelle them dysposyd to doo; *and* moore-ouer
I have somwhatt informyd them bothe ther-in. *And* also þat I maye

290. [1] *and soo canc.*   [2] f *and another letter canc.*

30 hastyly heer from yow; *and* jff it come to þat any mony most be geuyn to
my lorde ore lady off Norffolk for a plesyre herffore, I woll vppon as I
heer from yow come to yow in alle hast possible, all thyng*ys* leyde a-parte.

Item, iff any lett*er* be requeryth[3] to be hadde, jn lyke forme as onys ther
was from the Kyng to my lorde off Norffolk, S*yr* T. Mongomeré will by
35 yowre advyc*ys* opteyne yow suche on off yowre entent*ys* to my pr*o*ffyghte
in the premyssys, *and* by thys my wryghtyng I bynde me to repaye yowe
iff any suche lett*er* ore wryghtyng be opteynyd, what so eu*er* it coste.

No more for lakke off leyser. Wretyn at Caleys the v daye off Feu*er*ere
A° E. iiij xiiij°. As for tydyng*ys* heer, my mast*er*is th'embassator*ys*, S*yr*
40 T. Mongomeré *and* the Mast*er* of the Rollys, kom streyght from the Duke[4]
at hys assege at Nywysse, whyche wyll nott yit be wo*n*ne.

Yowr*e* J O H N   P A S T O N, K.

291. To M A R G A R E T   P A S T O N   1475, 22 February

Add. 27445, f. 87. 11½×8 in. Autograph.

Dorse: Traces of red wax. Address autograph:

*To Mestresse Margret Paston at Norwyche be thys delyu*e*ryd.*

Two lines in an unidentified hand:
M*emorandum* þat S*yr* John Paston owthe to Will*i*am Paston acordyng
to þe endent*ur* made be-twex þem -- viij*xx* ij li. xiij s. iiij d.
Wheroff payable þe firste day of Octobre for Townsend -- c m*a*rkes. Item
the xxvj day off Nouembre -- iiij*xx* xvj li.

Dated. This answers Margaret's letter no. 221.
F. v, p. 96. G. 754/865. C. 75 (part).

Please it yow to weete þat I receyuyd a lett*er* from yow wretyn þe Saterdaye
next byffor*e* Candelmesse, for answer*e* wheroff lyke it yow to weete þat,
as for the bokys þat weer S*yr* Jam*es*, God haue hys sowle, I thynke best
that they be styll w*yth* yow tyll þat I speke w*yth* yow my-selff. My mynde
5 is now nott most vppon bok*ys*.

Item, as for xx li. þat ye sey þat yowre plate lythe fore, it is so þat I
fownde my oncle Will*i*am no sewerté therffore. As Playter*e and* my brother
John bothe cowde enfforme yowe, it was neu*er* desyryd off me, nere the
tolde me nott þat[1] any suche pledge laye for it, but þat ye hadd dyschargyd
10 me off xx li. *and* chevysshyd it, *and* þat ye sholde repaye it in hast; wherin
I woll do as ye woll, *and* as it pleasyth yow to sende me wetyng.

---

³ *MS.* requesyth.   ⁴ *Ampersand canc.*
291. ¹ euyr*e canc.*

Item, I ame sory þat ye be no bettre payd off þe xx li. þat I had off yowe, whyche ye sholde haue receyuyd ageyn off my londys in Flegge; iff the markett be nott goode yit I hope jt shall be better. Neuer the lesse my wyll is that ye sholde have yowre holl xx li. ageyn *and* nott lose j d.; wherffor iff 15 it be soo þat ye be mysse seruyd there, I beseche yowe off pacyence tyll the begynnyng off the next yeere, *and* iff aught be behynd ye shall receyue vppe the remenaunt then, for as God helpe me I wolde be sory þat ye lost moore for me. I have pytte yow to cost, charge, *and* losse j-nowge, God thanke yowe off it, thoughe ye lose no more; wherffor jff Sporle woode sprynge any 20 syluer ore golde it is my wyll þat fyrst off alle ye be yowre owne payere off all þat is be-hynde, *and* next thatt to paye myn oncle William vij^xx vj li. xiij s. iiij d., *and* besyd that xvj li. lost vppon the chevysshaunce offe iiij^xx li.; *and* so I owe viij^xx ij li. xiij s. iiij d. Wherfor I beseche yow to make hast in repayment heroff as fast as it woll growe, as my trost is in yowe. 25

Item, wher it pleasyd yow to weete off myn heele *and* a-mendyng, I thanke Godde I ame in goode case, *and* as goode a[s] full hooll bothe off the fevre agwe, off myn je, myn legge, *and* myn heele, saff þat I ame tendre off all theese *and*, were nott goode rewle, full like to feell off iche off them ryght soone. Neuerthelesse God thanke yow off yowre large profre, wheroff 30 I wolde be ryght gladde iff I myght, fore trobles *and* other labore that I have takyn on me nowe in-to Fraunce warde. For the goode spede off me *and* þat jorneye I beseche yow off yowre preyerys *and* remembrance; *and* thatt jorney wyth Goddys grace onys doon, I purpose verrely wyth Goddys grace therafftre to daunce atendaunce most abowt yowre plesure *and* ease. 35 *And* wyth Goddys grace soone vppon Esterne, ere euyre I goo forthe, I hope to se yow *and* fecche yowre blessyng.

No moore at thys tyme, but Jesus have yow in hys kepyng. Wretyn at Caleys the xxij daye off Feuerere A° E. iiij^ti xiiij°.

Yowre sone JOHN PASTON, K. 40

292. To EDMOND PASTON II   1475, 13 June

Add. 27445, f. 90. 11½ × 4⅞ in. Autograph.

Dorse: Traces of red wax. Address autograph:

To *John Paston ore to hys brother Edmond Paston at þe George at Powles Wharff.*

The date cannot be later than 1475, for the Duke of Norfolk died in January 1476 (see no. 295). The Bishop of Lincoln, Thomas Rotherham, was chancellor from 27 May 1474 until 1483, though from 10 June to 28 September 1475 the Bishop of Rochester, John Alcock, took his place while he attended the King in France (*Handbook of British Chronology* (2nd edn., 1961), p. 86). Margaret Paston's letter no. 224

of 23 May 1475 speaks of the intention of John II's younger brothers to go overseas, and no. 293 reports their return to England. Cf. also no. 395.

F. v, p. 110. G. 760/873.

Brother Edmonde, it is soo þat I heer telle þat ye be in hope to come hyddre *and* to be in suche wag*ys* as ye schall can lyve lyke a jentylman, wheroff I wolde be gladde. Wherffor for yowre bett*er* speede I lete yow weete þat Heugh Beamond is deed, wherffor I wolde ye had hys roome, 5 nowe or*e* neu*er* iff ye can brynge it a-bowt. Ellys, iff ye dyspose yowe to abyde in Inglonde, syns it is so þat the Bysshop of Lynkolne is chaun-celere, hys seruyse is the meter for yow—he is next neyghbor*e* to Norff*olk* off any astate. God sende yow som good warde off hys.

I praye yow iff yowr*e* leyser be ther-afftr*e* to remembr*e* Towneshende 10 þat he w*yth* the advyse *and* assystence off my Mast*er* off þe Rollys have[1] on daye off Marche w*yth* þe slawe Bysshope off Wynchest*er*, þat he maye kepe me hys promyse; þat is to seye to entrete þe Duke *and* Duchesse off Norff*olk* for Cast*er*. He p*r*omysed to doo it, *and* to ley owt an c li. for þe same.

15 Item, I praye yow sende me som tydyng*ys* w*yth*-in v dayes afftre þat ye see thys bylle. Wretyn at Caleys þe xiij daye off June.

JOHN PASTON, K.

293. To MARGARET PASTON   1475, 11 September

Add. 27445, f. 91. 11⅝ × 5⅞ in. Autograph.

Dorse: Traces of red wax. Address autograph:

To Mestresse Margret Paston, at Norwyche.

The date appears from the account of Edward IV's return to England. He landed at Calais on 4 July 1475 and returned in September after the conclusion of the Treaty of Picquigny on 29 August (Scofield, ii. 131, 140, 148–9).

F. v, p. 112. G. 762/875.

Ryght reu*er*end *and* my most tendr*e and* kyynde moodre, I recomaunde me to yow. Please it yow to weete þat, blessyd be God, thys wyage off the Kyng*ys* is fynysshyd for thys tyme, *and* alle the Kyng*ys* ost is comen to Caleys as on Mondaye last past, þat is to seye þe iiij daye off Septembr*e*, 5 *and* at thys daye many off hys host be passyd þe see in-to Inglond ageyn, *and* in especiall my lorde off Norff*olk and* my bretheryn.

Item, I was jn goode hope to have hadde Cast*er* ageyn. þe Kynge spake to my lorde off Norff*olk* for it *and* it was full lyke to have comyn, but in conclusyon it is delayed tyll þis next terme, by whyche tyme the Kynge

292. [1] a daye *canc.*

486

hat[h]e comaundyd hym to take advyce off hys councell *and* to be sywere 10
þat hys tytle be goode, ore ellys þe kyng hathe asserteynyd hym þat for
any favore he most do me ryght *and* justyce, &c. And iff Caster hadde
comen, by my feythe I had comyn streyhte home. Notwytstondyng, iff I
may do yow servyce or ease, as ye *and* I have comonyd heere-to-foore,
afftre as I heere from yow, as God helpe me, I purpose to leeffe alle heere 15
and come home to yow *and* be yowre hosbonde *and* balyff; wher-in I spake
to my brothere John to telle yow myn advyce.

I also mysselyke somwhat the heyre heer, for by my trowt[h]e I was in
goode heele whan I come hyddre, *and* all hooll, *and* to my wetyng I hadde
neuer a better stomake in my lyffe; *and* now wyth-in viij dayes I am crasyd 20
ageyn. I suppose þat I most be at London at Mychelmesse *and* ther to
purveye for payment for myn oncle William, by whyche tyme I praye yow
þat I maye heer from yow, *and* off yowr advyce *and* helpe iff any thynge be
growyn off Sporle woode. For had nott yit that danger have been, I mygh[t]
yit have ben at home wyth yow at thys daye or wyth-in vij dayes afftre. 25

No more, but I beseche Jesus have yow in kepyng. Wretyn at Caleys
the xj daye off Septembre.

JOHN PASTON, K.

294. Petition to EDWARD IV 1475

Bodl. MS. Charters Norfolk a.8, no. 728. Parchment, 15 × 6 in. (top edge
mutilated). Unidentified clerk's hand.

Dorse: Incomplete remnants of notes, the clearest . . . *Paston mil. Regi
pro . . .*

The approximate date appears from the account of the Duke of Norfolk's seizure
of Caister Castle. He took it in September 1469 (see John III's letter no. 334), gave
it up during the restoration of Henry VI, but took it again on 23 June 1471 (William
Worcester, *Itineraries*, p. 252). The present petition was made four years later
'and more', so that it must have been in the latter part of 1475. Norfolk died on
17 January 1476 (see no. 295).
　　G. 766/879.

⟨To þe King⟩[1] our souuerain lord

⟨Sheweth⟩ vnto your highnesse your feythful liegeman and seruaunt John
Paston, knight, that where Ser William Yeluerton, William Jenney, and
Thomas Howes were infeffed in certain ⟨. . . to þe⟩ vse of youre said
suppliaunt, they of great malice, confetered with oon or ij of þe counsell
of my lord þe Duc of Norffolk, caused the[2] same Duc to clayme tytle vnto 5

---

294. [1] *Top left-hand corner torn off, affecting heading and three MS. lines.*
　　[2] *Corr. from* them.

⟨þe mano⟩ire of Caster and other land*es* of yo*ur* said suppliant, wherinne þe
said Yelu*er*ton and his coofeffees wer*e* infeffed, contrary to þ'entent and
wille þat þei wer*e* enfeffed for*e*; vpon whiche³ title the said Duc w*ith* great
force assegid and entred þe said manoir*e* of Castre and other land*es* of yo*ur*
10 said suppliant, putting ⌈hym⌉ from þe lawful possession and estate þat he
had in þe same, and also take from him vjᶜ shepe and xxx nete, and þe same
w*ith* other stuf and ordin*au*nces longing to þe same manoir*e* of þe value of
c li. toke and caryed awey, and þe said manoir*e* diffacid, hurt, and appeired,
so þat it coude not be repaired w*ith* cc marc. Also þe revenues of þe said
15 land*es* by þe space of iij yer*es* to þe value of vijˣˣ li. þe same my lord the
Duke⁴ receyued and þe owt rent*es* of þe same never payed; whiche great
trouble was like to be þe vndoing of yo*ur* said suppliant. Wherfore he was
fayn to sue to þe said Duc and lord by þe meanes of his godsip þe Bisshop
of Wynchestr*e*, whiche was in his sp*eci*al favo*ur*; at whos contemplac*i*on,
20 and for vᶜ marc whiche þe same yo*ur* suppliant payed vnto the same Duc,
he gr*a*unted him to haue ayen his said manoir*e* and land*es* and to restore
him to þe possession of the same, whiche was so doon. And yo*ur* said suppliant being in peasible possession, my said lord þe Duc and his cofeffees,
S*er* William Brandon, Thomas Hoo, Rauf Ashton, and other, at þe desire
25 of my said lord relessed þeir*e* estate and int*er*esse aswel vnder my said
lord*es* sele as vnder þeir*e* own seles; wherupon yo*ur* said besecher continued in possession but half a yer*e*, at whiche time he was chargid in
repar*a*cions to þe so*m*me of c marc, and payed þe owt rent*es* dewe by þe
space of þe said iij yer*e* to þe so*m*me of xl li.
30 That doon, my said lord, by sinistr*e* moc*i*on and aduice w*ith* force ayen
entred þe said manoir*e* and other land*es* aforsaid, w*ith* alle stuf of howshold
being in þe same manoir*e* to þe value of c marc, and so long time hath kept
and reioysed þe revenues of þe said land*es*, and in chief þe said manoir*e*,
to þe value of vjˣˣ li., by þe space of iiij yer*e* and mor*e*. For redresse wherof
35 yo*ur* said suppliant hath þis said space of iiij yer*e* sued to my said lord and
his counsell, and of alle þat time þe same my lord wold never suffr*e* him
to co*m*me in his pr*e*sence ne her*e* him, ne noon other for him, to declare
or shewe his grief. And forthermore, whanne yo*ur* said besecher hath sued
to þe counsel of my said lord and desired þe*m* to moue his lordship þerinne,
40 and to ansuer*e* him resonably and according to right, they ansuered þat
þei haue shewed my said lord his request, and þat he was, and is alwey,
so moved and displesid w*ith* þe*m* þat þei dar nomor*e* move him þerinne.
And þus yo*ur* said suppliant hath loste alle his coste and laboure, to his
charge, by his feyth, this iiij yer*e* in his sute þe so*m*me of vᶜ marc, and now
45 is owt of remedye w*ith*out youre habundant gr*a*ce be shewed in þat behalue,
in somoche as he is not of power t'attempte youre lawes ayenst so mighty
and noble estate, nor t'abide þe disples*er* of him.

³ pretensed *canc.*   ⁴ *These four words on eras.*

Wherfor*e* please it y*our* moost noble gr*a*ce, at þe reu*er*ence of God, to move my said lord to wi*th*drawe þe affecci*on* whiche he so hath to þe said manoir*e* and land*es*, and to suffr*e* y*our* said besecher to haue and enioye 50 þe possession of þe same according to right; and he at youre commandment shal relesse vnto my said lord alle þe da*m*mag*es* aboue wretyn, whiche amounte to þe so*m*me of m¹ccc liij li. vj s. viij d., and in time to co*m*me, with God*des* gr*a*ce, be þe more hable to do you s*er*uice, and also sp*e*cially preye to God for þe conseruaci*on* of youre moost noble p*er*sone and estate royall. 55

295. To Margaret Paston   1476, 17 January

Add. 43490, f. 18. 8¾ × 5½ in. Autograph.

Dorse: Marks of folding, slight traces of red wax, and stitch-holes, but no address.

This letter must have been written from the Duke of Norfolk's seat at Framling-ham. The writing is hasty, and the absence of the usual forms of greeting and con-clusion suggests that it was composed too hurriedly for ceremony. Fenn remarked: 'This Letter has no Direction, but it is written either to John Paston, Esquire, or Margaret Paston.' Gairdner preferred the former, because John III's letter no. 367 shows that the brothers were indeed together in Norwich three days later, as the last paragraph of this letter might be supposed to presage; whereas John II paid no visit to his mother, who seems to have been living at Mautby. (Whether she was living there continuously is uncertain, for the address of no. 298 shows that she was expected to be in Norwich in March; but at any rate she was not with John III, who wrote no. 367 to her only four days later.) But the British Museum MS. index rightly comments that this letter cannot have been intended for John III in view of the terms in which he wrote to Margaret about the cloth of gold in no. 367. (The cloth is mentioned again in no. 311 and in Margaret's no. 228.) The word interlined in John III's hand (note 1) points in the same direction. The most likely explanation of it is that the brothers were at Framlingham together, and that John III, reading the letter over, found one of his brother's words not immediately intelligible because of the unusual way in which it was abbreviated, and wrote a clear transcription of it above. It may be added that Symme (l. 13) was evidently a personal servant of Margaret's (see, e.g., John III's nos. 364 and 374).

    Dated.

    F. ii, p. 186. G. 768/881.

Lyke it yow to weete þat not in þe most happy season ⌐for me¬ jt is so for-tunyd þat wher as my lorde off Norffolke yist*er*daye beyng in good heele, thys nyght dyed a-bowte mydnyght; wherffor it is for alle þat lovyd hym to doo *and* helpe nowe that that may be to hys ⌐honoure¬¹ *and* weell to hys sowele. *And* it is soo þat thys contré is nott weell p*ur*veyd off² clothe off 5

295. ¹ *Interl. in the hand of John Paston III, above what seems to have been* honure *(abbr. by superior* r *and a flourish) canc.*
  ² T *canc. (cf.* tyssywe *l. 10 below).*

golde for the coveryng for hys bodye *and* herse, wherffor, eu*er*y man helpyng to hys powere, I putte the cowncell off my lorde in cownffort þ*at* I hopyd to gete on for that daye if it weer so þ*at* it be nott broken or putt to other vse. Wherffor please it yow to sende me worde iff it be so þ*at* ye

10 have or kan kom by the clothe off tyssywe þ*at* I bowte for my fader*ys* tombe; *and* I vndretake it shall be saffyd ageyn for yowe on-hur[t] at my perell. I deeme herby to gete greet thanke *and* greet assystence in tyme to come; ⌐*and* that owther Sy*m*me or Mother Broun maye delyu*er* it me to-morow by vij off þe clokke⌐.³

15 Item, as for other meany*s*, I have sente my servant Richard Tornor to London, whyche I hope shall brynge me goode tydyng*ys* ageyn; *and* wyth-in iiij dayes I hope to see yowe. Wretyn on Wednysdaye the xvij daye off Janyuer*e* A° E. iiij^ti xv°.

JOHN PASTON, K.

296. To John Paston III   1476, 27 January

Add. 43491, f. 20. 11¾ × 10¼ in. Autograph.

Dorse: Continuation of text. Traces of red wax. Address autograph:

To John Paston, esquiere, at Norwyche be thys delyueryd.

This answers John III's letter no. 368, and is answered by no. 369. John Hastings (l. 4) was sheriff of Norfolk and Suffolk in 1474–5.
Dated.
F. ii, p. 190. G. 771/884.

I recomaunde me to yow, letyng yow weete þ*at* I was jnfformyd by Ric*har*d Radlé þ*at* on Scarlett, þ*at* was vndrescheryff to Hastyng*ys*, wolde sywe to me on yowre behalff for*e* thatt ye weer*e* dyspleasyd w*yth* a retur*n*e off *Nichyll* vppon yow in þe seyde Hastyng*ys* tyme; wherffor Ric*har*d Radlé

5 thoghte þ*at* the seyde Scarlett wolde be gladde to gyff yow a noble or a riall for a sadell to amendy*s*, so þ*at* ye wolde sease *and* stoppe the bylle whyche ye entende to putt in to þe corte ageyn hys maste*r* Hastyng*ys*. Wherffor the seyde Scarlett com to me *and* prayed me to helpe in the same, *and* so I have don my devoyr*e* to feele off hym the most þ*at* he can fynde

10 in hys stomake to dep*ar*te w*yth* to please yow; *and* in conclusyon I trowe he shall gyff yow a doblett clothe off sylke, price xx s. ore þ*er*-abowte, whyche vppon suche answeere as I heer from yowe I deme þ*at* Bysshop the atornye shall, iff I conclude w*yth* hym on yow*re* behalve, paye in mony or otherwyse to whom þ*at* ye woll assyngne heere. I shall by the meany*s* off

---

³ *This clause written at the foot, above the signature, and marked by crosses for insertion here.*

Raddelé weete at whoys sywte it was takyn owte. I deme it som-thynge 15
doon by craffte by the meanys off them þat have entresse in yowre lond
to þ'entent to noyse itt therys, or to make yow past shame off the sellyng
ther-off.

Item, I have receyvyd a letter from yowe, wretyn on Tywesdaye last.

Item, wher þat som towardys my lady off Norffolk noyse þat I dyd 20
onkyndely to sende so hastely to Caster as I dyd, þer is no dyscrete person
þat so thynkyth; fore iff my lorde hade ben as kynde to me as he myght
have ben, *and* acordyng to suche hert *and* seruyce as my grauntffadre, my
fadre, yowre-selff, *and* I have owght *and* doon to my lordys off Norffolk
þat ded ben, *and* yitt iff I hadde weddyd hys dowghtre, yitt most I have 25
doon as I dydde. *And* moore-ovyre, iff I ⌐had⌐ hadde any demyng off my
lordys dethe iiij howrys ore he dyed, I most nedys, but iff I wolde be
knowyn a foolle, have entryd it¹ the howre byffore hys dyscesse.² But in
effecte theygh³ that in þat matere have alweye ment onkyndely to me, they
feyne þat rumore ageyn me; but there is noon thatt ment truly to hym þat 30
dede is þat wolde be sory þat I hadde itt, *and* in especiall suche as love hys
sowle.

Item, wher it is demyd þat my lady wolde herafftre be the rather myn
hevy lady for þat delyng, I thynke þat she is to resonable so to be, fore I
dyd it nott onwyst to hyre cowncell. þer was no man thoght⁴ þat I sholde 35
doo otherwysse, an as to seye þat I myght have hadde my ladyes advyce
ore lyve,⁵ I myght have teryed yitt or I cowde have speken wyth hyre, ore
yitt have hadde any body to have mevyd hyre on my be-halve. As ye wote,
I dydde what I cowde. Moreouyre I taried by the advyce off Syr Robert
Wyngffelde iij dayes þer for þat he putte me in comffort þat þe Lorde 40
Howard *and* hys brother Syr John sholde have comyn to Norwyche, att
whoys comyng he dowtyd nott but þat I sholde have a goode dyreccion
takyn for me in thatt mater. They leyhe to me onkyndenesse for ouyr-
kyndenesse.⁶

Item, as for my mater heere, itt was thys daye beffoore alle the lordes 45
off the cowncelle, *and* amonge them ale it was nott thowght þat in my
sendyng off Whetley thyddre in-mediatly afftre the dyscese off þe Duke
þat I dalte onkyndly ore onsyttyngly, but þat I was moore onresonably
dalte wyth. Wherffor, late men deme whatt they wylle, grettest clerkys are
nott alweye wysest men; but I hope hastely to have on weye in it ore othere. 50

Item, I wende to have fownde a gowne off myn heere, but it come home
the same daye þat I come owte, browght⁷ by Herry Berker, lodere. I wolde
in alle hast possible have thatt same gowne off puke furryd wyth whyght

296. ¹ it *apparently crowded in later.*   ² *Rest of recto written much smaller.*
³ *Another letter, now indistinguishable, canc.*   ⁴ *Ending smudged.*
⁵ -y- *over* e.   ⁶ *Recto ends.*
⁷ -gh- *apparently over* te.

lambe. Item, I wolde have my longe russett gowne off þe Frenshe russett
55 in alle hast, for I have no gowne to goo in here.

Item, I praye yow recomande me to my moodre, *and* late vs alle preye
God sende my lady off Norffolk a soone, fore vppon þat restythe moche
mater. For iff þe Kyngys soone mary my lordys dowghtre, the Kynge wolde
þat hys soone sholde have a fayre place in Norffolk, thowhe he sholde gyffe
60 me ij tymes þe valywe in other londe, as I am doon to weete. I praye yow
sende me worde off my ladyes spede as soone as ye kan.

Item, as for Bowen, I shall fele hym, *and* sholde have doon thowghe ye
hadde nott sente.

Item, ther is offryd me a goode mariage fore my suster Anne, Skypwyth-
65 thys sone *and* heyre off Lynkolneshyre, a man v or vjᶜ m[a]rke by yeere.

No more. Wretyn at London þe xxvij daye off Janyvere Aº E. iiijᵗⁱ xvº.

Item, my lady off Excester is ded, *and* it was seyde þat bothe þe olde
Dywchesse off Norffolk *and* þe Cowntesse off Oxenfforde weere ded, but
itt is nott soo yitte.
70 Item, I shall remembre Caleyse bothe for horse *and* alle.

Item, Phylypp Lovedaye is heere comyn thys daye, *and* wyll be wyth
yow in hast. He comythe home for goode *and* alle.

297. To JOHN PASTON III or MARGARET PASTON
1476, 12 March

Add. 27445, f. 100. 11⅝×6 in. Autograph.

Dorse: Traces of red wax. Address autograph:

*To John Paston, esquiere, ore to Mestresse Margrett Paston hys moodre,
in Norffolk.*

Dated.
F. v, p. 130. G. 775/888.

I recomande me to yow, letyng yow wete þat, blessyd be God, vppon
Saterdaye last past my lorde *and* wee toke the see *and* come to Caleyes þe
same daye. *And* as thys daye my lorde come to Guynesse, *and* theere was
receyvyd honourablye wyth-owt any obstaklys; wheer as I fownde Master
5 Fytzwalter *and* other, whyche wer ryght hevye fore the dethe off þe noble
man thatt was theere to-foore. Itt happyd soo þat my seyd Master Fytzwalter axid me ryght hertely fore yow, *and* I lete hym weete þat I demyd
ye wolde be heere in haste, wheroffe he seyde he was ryght soory, fore soo
moche þat he entendyth to come in-to Englonde; *and* as I conceyve he
10 wyll come to Attylborogh *and* brynge my mestresse hys wyffe wyth hym,
and theer to stablysshe hys howse contynuall. Wherffor he thynketh þat
he sholde have as grete a lakke off yow as off any on man in þat contré,

willyng me to wryght on-to yowe *and* to late yow weete off hys comynge.
He also hathe tolde me moche off hys stomake *and* tendre fau*ur* þat he owythe
to yow, wherffore I asserteyn yow þat he is yow*r*e verry especiall goode   15
mast*er, and* iffe ye weer*e* abydynge in thatt contré whylse he weer*e* theer*e*,
he is dysposyd to doo largely for*e* yowe in dyu*e*rse wyse whyche weer*e* to
longe to wryght; in so moche þat I feele by hy*m* þat he thynkyth þat itt
sholde be longe er*e* he scholde be wery off yowr*e* expenc*ys* off horse or*e*
man. Now I remytte alle thynge to yowr*e* dyscresion. Ye woote best what   20
is for*e* yow.

As for my lorde, I vndrestande nott yitt whethyr*e* he wylle in-to Ingelonde the weke to-for*e* Est*er*ne or*e* ellys afftr*e*. I pray yow recomande me to
my moodr*e*; I wolde have wretyn to hyr*e*, but in trowthe I ame some-whatt
crasyd, what w*yth* the see *and* what wythe thys dyet heer*e*.   25

Nomoor*e* to yow, but wretyn at Gynes the xij daye off Marche A° E. xvj.

By J OHN P ASTON, K.

298. T O M ARGARET P ASTON or J OHN P ASTON III
1476, 21 March

Add. 43490, f. 20. 12 × 8¾ in. Autograph.

Dorse: Traces of red wax. Address autograph:

*To Mestresse Margrete Paston at Norwyche, or*e *hyr*e *sone John Paston,*
*esquyer*e*, and to eu*erych off them.*

Dated.
F. ii, p. 198. G. 776/889.

I recomande me to yowe. Like it yow to weete þat I am nott sertay[n]e
yitte whether*e* my lorde *and* I shall come in-to Ingelonde þe weke byffoor*e*
Est*er*ne or*e* ellys the weke afftr*e* Est*er*ne; wherffor, moodr*e*, I beseche yow
to take noo dysplesyr*e* w*yth* me for my longe tarijnge, for I durst doo noon
otherwyse for*e* dysplesyng off my lorde. I was[1] noo-thynge gladde off thys   5
jornaye iff I myght goodely have chosen. Neu*e*rthelesse, savyng þat ye
have cawse to be dyspleasyd w*yth* mee for the mat*er* off Kokett, I am ellys
ryght gladde, for I hope þat I ame ferre moore in favor*e* w*yth* my lorde
than I was to-foor*e*.

Item, I sende yow, brother John, a lett*er* herw*yth* whyche was browte   10
hyddr*e* to Caleys from þe George at Powles Wharff; I deme it comythe
from my brother Wat*er*.

Item, iff ye entende hyddrewarde itt weer*e* weell doon þat ye hyghed[2]
yowe, for I suppose þat my lorde wille take the vywe off alle hys retynywe

298. [1] *Some letters canc., perhaps* fore.   [2] -g- *apparently over* t.

15 heere nowe byffoore hys departyng, *and* I thynke þat he woolde be better
contente wyth yowre comyng nowe than an other tyme. Doo as ye thynke
best, *and* as ye maye. Item, wher Master Fytzwalter made me to wryght
to yowe to advyse yow to tarye, I remytte thatt to yowre dyscrescion.

As for tydyngys heere, we here from alle the worlde. Fyrst, the Lord
20 Ryverse[3] was at Roome right weell *and* honorably, *and* other lordys off
Ynglonde, as þe Lorde Hurmonde *and* þe Lorde Scrope, *and* at there
departyng xij myle on thyse[4] halff Roome the Lorde Ryverse was robbyd
off alle hys jowellys *and* plate, whyche was worthe m¹ marke or better, *and*
is retornyd to Rome for a remedy.

25 Item, þe Duke off Burgoyne hathe *conqueryd* Loreyn, *and* Quene
Margreet shall nott nowe be lyklyhod have it; wher-for the Frenshe Kynge
cherysshyth hyre butt easelye. Butt afftre thys conquest off Loreyn the
Duke toke gret corage to goo vppon the londe off þe Swechys to *conquere*
them; butt the berdyd hym att an onsett place, *and* hathe dystrussyd hym
30 *and* hathe slayne the most parte off hys vamwarde *and* wonne all hys
ordynaunce *and* artylrye, *and* more-ovyre alle ⌐stuffe⌐ thatt he hade in hys
ost wyth hym exceppte men *and* horse þat fledde nott. But they roode þat
nyght xx myle, *and* so the ryche salettys, heulmettys, garter nowchys gelte,
and alle is goone, wyth tentys, pavylonys, *and* alle, *and* soo men deme hys
35 pryde is abatyd. Men tolde hym that they weer frowarde karlys, butte he
wolde nott be-leve it; *and* yitt men seye þat he woll to them ageyn. Gode
spede them bothe!

Item, Syr John Mydelton toke leve ⌐off þe Duke⌐ to sporte hym, but he
is sett in pryson att Brissellys.

40 I praye yowe sende me som worde iff ye thynke likly þat I maye entre
Castre when I woll, by the nexte massenger.

Wretyn at Caleys in resonable helthe off bodye *and* sowle, I thanke
Good, the xxj daye off Marche A° E. iiij^ti xvj°.

J. P., K.

299. To MARGARET PASTON or JOHN PASTON III

1476, 27 May

Add. 27445, f. 102. 11¾×7½ in. Autograph.

Dorse: Traces of red wax. Address autograph:

To Mestresse Margret Paston att Norwyche, ore¹ to hyre sone John Paston.²

This letter must have been written in 1476, not long after the death of the Duke of
Norfolk in January, while John II was trying to establish his claim to Caister.

---

³ d *and some other letters canc,*   ⁴ *No space.*
299. ¹ *ore repeated.*   ² *Followed, obviously wrongly, by* K. (*the abbr. for* knyght).

Letter no. 300, which is precisely dated, reports the successful conclusion of his efforts. His dating of the present letter is therefore wrong, for the Monday after Ascension Day in 1476 was 27 May, not 26. (It is true that the reading is not quite certain, for the numeral is at the edge of the paper and the last *j* is incomplete at the top; but there seems to be no room for a preceding *i*.)

F. v, p. 144. G. 778/891.

Please it yow to weete þat as for my mater*ys*, *and* theye appeyr*e* nott, the doo, blessyd be Godde, as weell as I wolde they dyd, saffe that it shalle cost me grett mony *and* it hathe cost me moche laboor*e*. It is soo þat the Kynge most have c m[a]rke, *and* other cost*ys* will draw xl marke. *And* my mat*er* is examynyd by the Kyng*ys* cowncell *and* declaryd affoore all the lord*ys*, 5 *and* nowe lakkythe noo-thynge bu⟨tt pre⟩vy[3] seal*ys and* wryghtyng to Master Colv⟨i⟩ll to avoyde. For th⟨e Kynge hathe pro⟩mysed[4] me as moche as I wolde he scholde fulleffille, *and* alle the lord*ys*, jug*ys*, seriaunt*ys*, have affermyd my title goode. Nott w*yth*stondyng Sowthewell, Jam*es* Hubberde, *and* Syr W. Braundon wher*e* at ther*e* owne desyr*ys* offryd to afferme *and* 10 advowe my tytell for goode, *and* þat my lorde off Norff*olk* þat ded is hadde noo tytell thatt they knywe, they tolde my tale as ille as they cowde, *and* yitt a lye or*e* too to helpe it, *and* yit it seruyth them nott. They be knowen as they ar*e*, in cowncell be it seyde, *and* so most all thys lett*er* be. I have moche payne to gete so moche mony. Neu*er*the lesse, but iff myn oncle 15 schewe hym-selffe werse than eu*er* he was, I shalle nott fayle iff he kepe me promyse, *and* thatt is but as he dyde last, þat is butt to be my sywerté *and* I to make hym sywerté ageyn.

The Kynge dep*ar*tythe thys daye *and* wille nott be[5] heer tyll Frydaye, whyche lettyth me, or*e* ellys by thatt daye I wolde have hopyd to have 20 comen homeward*ys*, *and* erst p*ar* aventur.

Nomoor*e*, but J*esus* have yow in kepyng. Wretyn at London þe xxvj daye off Maye, the Mondaye next Holy Thurrysdaye þe[6] Assenc*i*on. þe Kynge wold⟨e⟩ have bowte it, but he was enfformyd off the trowthe *and* þat it was nott for a prynce, *and* off the greet pryse þat I wolde selle it att for 25 þat I myght nott for-ber it, for he scholde have payed m¹m¹ m[a]rke or*e* moore iff he hadde hadde itt.

Yowr*e* sone J. P A S T O N, K.

[3] *Letters lost here and later where paper has decayed at a fold.*
[4] *Fenn's conjecture fits the fragments.*
[5] *MS.* se.   [6] *No space.*

300. To JOHN PASTON III   1476, 30 June

Add. 27445, f. 103. $11\frac{1}{4} \times 8\frac{3}{8}$ in. Autograph.

Dorse: Traces of red wax. Address autograph:

To John Paston, esquiere, beyng at the syngne off the George at Powles Wharff.

Dated.

F. v, p. 148. G. 779/892.

I recomaunde me to yow, letyng yow weete þat I hav receyvyd yowre letter
wretyn the next daye aftre Mydsomer; for answer wheroff I thynke þat to
be bownde in v^c m[a]rke I thynke it is to moche, where-as I felt by yow ye
sholde have wyth þe gentylwoman but $iiij^c$. Neuer the lesse I agree. But ye
5   shall vndrestande þat I wyll nott be bownde for yow þat ye shall make hyre
joyntoure past xx li. by yere wyth-in a sertayne daye lymyted, be it j yere
ore ij; þat is þe¹ largest þat ye maye performe. For as fore the maner² off
Sparham, my moodre *and* ye acorde nott in yowre sayngys. She wyll
nowght graunte yow ther-in whylse she levyth, saff, as she seythe to me,
10 she hathe grauntyd yow x m[a]rke by yeere tyll xl li. be payed, þat is but
vj yeere. *And* afftre hyre dyscease she woll agree wyth goode will, so þat
it maye be yowre proferment þat ye sholde have þat maner in joyntur wyth
yowre wyffe to þe lenger lyvere³ off yow bothe, payng x m[a]rke by yeere,
soo ⌜ore there⌝ as she wyll þat it shall be. Therfore as for l m[a]rke joyntur,
15 I pray yow bynde me in no suche clawse butt iff it be for xx li. by a resonable daye, *and* xx m[a]rke afftre the dyssease off my moodre. Take example
at Derby.

Item, ye make yow sywerere than I deme yow bee, for I deme þat here
frendes wyll nott be content wyth Bedyngffeldys sywerté nore yowrys. I
20 deme thys mater will ocopy lenger leysere than ye deme ⌜fore⌝.

Item, I remembre thatt thys mony þat she sholde have is nott redy, but
in the handes off marchauntys off the Estaple, whyche at a prove ye shall
fynde par case so slakke payerys þat ye myght be deseyvyd ther-by. I
knowe dyverse have lost mony er they cowde gete ther dywtés owte off th'
25 Estaple. God spede yow *and* sende yow þat ye wolde have. I sende yow þe
obligacion her-wyth acordyng to yowre desyre, *and* a letter to Bedyngffelde
thankyng hym for yow, *and* more-ouer letyng hym know off myn entent.
Opyn it *and* close it ageyn iff ye lyst.

Item, wher I tolde yow þat the gowne clothe off olde chamlott⁴ I wolde
30 have it hoome for my suster Anne, ye for-gate it. I praye yow sende it home
by the next massenger, *and* a letter wyth it off suche tydyngys as ye knowe.

Item, blissed be God, I have Castre at my will.

---

300. ¹ þ *in form of* y.   ² *Corr. from* mater.
   ³ -y- *over* e.   ⁴ -o- *blind ;* e *might have been meant.*

God holde it bett*er* than it [was] doone her-to-foore.

No moor*e*, but wretyn the next daye afftr*e* Seynt Petre, A° E. iiij*ti* xvj°.

J. PASTON, K. 35

301. To MARGARET PASTON — Probably 1476, 30 August

Add. 34889, f. 188. 11⅜×6¾ in. Autograph.

Dorse: Remnants of red wax. Address autograph:

To Mestresse Margret Paston.

The date is hard to determine. The only illness of John Paston III mentioned else-where is that after his return from Calais in 1475 (see no. 365); but the brothers had then both been at Calais at the material time. From no. 297 it appears that John III meant to go to Calais again in March 1476, but from no. 298 it is doubtful whether he did so. As Gairdner observes, the fact that he was ill at Attleborough suits 1476, for 'Master Fitzwalter' is said in no. 297 to be about to take up permanent residence there and to be anxious to have John III with him.

G. XCI/893. C.77.

Please it yow to wete þ*at* I was vppon Tywesdaye, the daye þ*at* I dep*ar*tyd froo yowe, w*yth* my brother*e* John at Atelborow by viij off the clokke at euyn, *and* founde hym in suche case as iff ye had seyn hym than ye wolde nowe be as gladde ⌈of hym⌉ osse off a nywe sone. I wenyd nott þ*at* he scholde ⌈not⌉ have levyd tyll þe mornyng, in so moche þ*at* by my trowthe I 5 dare seye þ*at* iff it had nott fortunyd vs to have comyn to hym, he had no⟨t⟩¹ been on lyve on Wednysdaye; for*e* syns Sat*er*daye slepyd he nott iiij howr*ys*, *and* yitt iij off them was syns I come thydyr*e*, on-to thys nyght. *And* thys nyght, blessyd be God, he hathe slepyd well, *and* w*yth* Goddys grace I dowte nott but thatt he shall do weell, for*e* hys agywe is goone, *and* 10 alle þ*at* laye in hys stomake *and* vndre hys syde it weryth aweye. *And* w*yth*-in a daye or*e* ij I hope he shall be so stronge þ*at* I maye come from*e* hym, *and* he hopyth to see yowe w*yth*-in fewe days afftr*e*, as he seythe.

On Wednysdaye I wysshyd to hym þ*at* he *and* I hadde been at Nor-wyche; whervppon he harpyd all ⌈þat⌉ nyght, *and* for*e* caw[s]e he hadde 15 nott so goode rest as he wolde, it fylle in hys brayne to come to Norwyche, *and* he in an angre wolde nedys to horse—he wolde no*n* horsse litt*er*, he was so stronge. Neu*er*thelesse we wenyd nott þ*at* he sholde have been able to have redyn a myle, *and* wenyd þ*at* it had nott been possible to have passyd Wyndh*am*. Bott whan he was vppe for*e* þ*at* we seyde he roode so welle he 20 ledde vss a dawnce fast*er* than alle we cowde weell folowe. He was at Wyndham, by my trowthe, in lesse þan an howr*e*, by a large q*u*arter*e*, *and* ther restyd hym an howr*e*, *and* to horse ageyne *and* was heer*e* in lesse than

301. ¹ *At edge.*

an howre *and* on halffe. *And* now he dowtyth nott to slepe weell, fore he
25 seythe þat he neu*er* faylyd to[2] slepe weell in that bedde þat he hathe chosyn
now at Frenshys; *and* thusse I hope he be sauffe. *And* I ame in dowte
whethyr*e* I shall w*y*th-in ij dayes owther come home to yow or*e* ellis to
goo forthe as ye woote off.

No moore, &c. Wretyn on Frydaye next the Decollac*i*on off Seynt John
30 Baptyst.

Item, I have the wryghtyng*ys* off Ric*h*ard Calle.[3]

Yowr*e* sone J. PASTON, K.

302. To JOHN PASTON III   1477, 14 February

Add. 43490, f. 21. 12×6 in. Autograph.

Dorse: Remnants of red wax. Address autograph:

To John Paston, esquyer, at Norwyche in hast.

Dated.

F. ii, p. 204. G. 786/900.

I recomaunde me to yow, letyng yow weete þat yister*d*aye beganne the
grete cowncell to whyche all the astat*ys* off þe londe shall com to, butt iff
it be for gret *and* resonable excusis. *And* I suppose þe cheffe cawse of thys
assemblé is to comon what is best to doo n⟨o⟩w[1] vppon þe greet change
5 by the dethe off þe Duke of Burgoyne, *and* for þe kepyng off Caleys *and* the
Marchys, *and* for the *p*reseruac*i*on off þe amytéys[2] taken late as weell w*y*th
Fraunce as now w*y*th the membrys off Flaundr*ys*; wher-to I dowt nott þ*er*
shall be jn all hast bothe þe Duk*ys* off Clarance *and* Glowcestr*e*, wherof
I wolde þat my brother E. wyst.
10   Item, I feele butt litell effecte in the labor*e* off W. Alyngton; neu*er*thelesse I deme it is nott for yow. She shall nott passe cc m[a]rke, as ferr*e* as
I can vndrestand ap*a*rte.

Item, I will nott forget yow other-wyse. Itt is so þat thys daye I heer
grett liklyhood þat my Lorde Hastyng*ys* shall hastely goo to Caleys w*y*th
15 greet company. Iff I thynke it be for*e* yow to be on, I shall nott for-geet
yow.

Item, thys daye the mat*er* by-twyen Mestresse Anne Haulte *and* me
hathe ben soor*e* broken bothe to þe Cardynall, to my Lorde Chamb*er*leyn,
and to my-selffe, *and* I am in goode hope. When I heer *and* knowe moor*e*,
20 I shalle sende yow worde. It semythe þat the worlde is alle qwaveryng. It
will reboyle somwher, so þat I deme yonge men shall be cherysshyd; take

---

[2] sly *canc.*

302. [1] *Damaged by damp.*

[3] *This last sentence crowded in later.*

[2] -y- *apparently over beginning of* e.

yowre hert to yow. I feer þat I can nott be excusyd, but þat I shall forthe
wyth my Lorde Hastyngys ouyre þe see; butt I shall sende yow worde in
hast, *and* iff I goo I hope nott to tary longe.

Item, to my brother Edmond: I am like to speke wyth Mestresse Dyxon 25
in hast, *and* som deme þat þer[3] shall be condyssendyd[4] þat iff E.P. come
to London þat hys costys shall be payed fore.

I shall hastely sende yow worde off more thyngys. Wretyn at London þe
xiiij daye off Feuerere A° E. iiij^{ti} xvj°, þe Fryday a-fore Fastyngong.

JOHN PASTON, K. 30

303. To JOHN PASTON III   1477, 9 March

Add. 27445, f. 106. $8\frac{1}{2} \times 4\frac{7}{8}$ in. Autograph.

Dorse: Traces of red wax. Address autograph:

To John Paston, esquyere, in hast.

Dated.

F. v, p. 164. G. 789/903.

I have receyvyd yowre letter *and* yow[r] man J. Bykerton, by whom I knowe
all þe mater off Mestresse Brews, whyche iff it be as he seythe I praye
Godde brynge it to a goode ende.

Item, as for thys mater off Mestresse Barly, I holde it butt a bare thynge.
I feele weell þat itt passyth nott ⟨. . .⟩[1] marke. I syghe hyre fore yowre sake. 5
She is a lytell onys; she maye be a woman heere-afftre, iff she be nott olde
nowe: hire person semyth xiij yere off age, hyre yerys men sey ben full
xviij. She k[n]owyth nott off the mater, I suppose. Neuerthelesse she
desyryd to see me as gladde as I wasse to se hyre.

I praye yow sende me som wryghtyng to Caleys off yowre spede wyth 10
Mestresse Brewys. Bykerton tellyth me þat she lovyth yow weell. Iff I
dyed I hadde lever ye hadde hyre than the Lady Wargrave; neuerthelesse
she syngeth weell wyth an harpe. Clopton is aferde off Syr T. Greye, for
he is a wydowere now late, *and* men sey þat he is aqueyntyd wyth hyre of
olde.   15

Nomore. Wretyn on Sondaye the ix daye off Marche A° E. iiij^{ti} xvij° to
Caleys warde.

J. PASTON, K.

Iff ye haue Mestresse Brews *and* E. Paston Mestresse Bylyngford, ye be
lyke to be bretheryn.[2]   20

---

³ *Corr. from* þᵉ.
⁴ -yss- *apparently written over the loop which commonly abbreviates* -ys.
303. ¹ *Perhaps four letters lost at hole.*
² *This sentence crowded in at left of signature.*

304. To Margaret Paston   1477, 28 March

Add. 43491, f. 23. 11⅝ × 9½ in. Autograph.

Dorse: Remnants of red wax over tape. Address autograph:

To my ryght worshypfull moodre Margret Paston.

Dated.
    F. ii, p. 238. G. 797/911.

Please it yow to weete þat I have receyvyd yowre letter wherin is remembryd the gret hurte þat by liklihod myght falle to my brother John iff so
be þat thys mater betwyn hym *and* Syr Thomas Brewses doghtre take nott
effecte, wheroff I wolde be as sory as hym-selffe reasonably; *and* also þe
5 welthy *and* convenyent mariage þat scholde be iff it take effecte, wheroff
I wolde be as gladde as any man, *and* ame better content nowe þat he
sholde have hyre than any other þat euyre he was hertoffoore abowte to
have hadde—concyderyd hyre persone, hyre yowthe, *and* the stok þat she
is comyn offe, þe love on bothe sydes, þe tendre fauore þat she is in wyth
10 hyre fadre *and* moodre, the kyndenesse off hyre fadre *and* moodre to hyre
in departyng wyth hyre, the favore also *and* goode conceyte þat they have
in my brothere, the worshypfull ⌈*and* vertuous⌉ dysposicion off hire fadre
and moodre, whyche prenostikyth þat of lyklihod the mayde sholde be
vertuous *and* goode. All whyche concyderyd, *and* the necessary relyffe þat
15 my brother most have, I mervayle the lesse þat ye have departyd ⌈*and*
geuyn⌉¹ hym ⌈the maner of Sperham⌉ in suche forme as I haue knowleche
off by W. Gornay, Lomnore, *and* Skypwyth; *and* I ame ryght gladde to se
in yow suche kyndenesse on-to my brother ⌈as⌉² ye have doon to hym, *and*
wolde by my trowthe levere than c li. þat it weere fee symple londe, as it
20 is entaylyd, whyche by liklyhood scholde prospere wyth hym *and* hyis
blode the better in tyme to come *and* sholde also neuer cavse debate in
owre bloode in tyme to come, whyche Godde dyffende for that weere on-
naturell.

    Item,³ ⌈an⌉ other jnconvenyence is, wher as I vndrestande þat the maner
25 is gevyn to my brother *and* to hys wyff *and* to þe issywe bytwen them
bygoten, iff the case weer soo þat he *and* she hadde yssywe togedre a
dowtre ore moo, *and* hys wyffe dyed *and* he maried afftre an othere *and*
hadde issywe a sone, þat sone sholde have noon londe, *and* he beyng hys
fadris heyre. *And* for th'enconvenyence þat I have knowe late in vre in case
30 lyke, *and* yit enduryth, in Kente by-twyen a jentylman *and* his sustre, I
wolde ye toke the advyce off yowre concell in thys poynt. *And* that þat is
past yow by wryghtyng ore by promyse I deme verrely in yow þat ye dyd
it off kyndenesse *and* in eschywyng off a moore yll þat myght befall.⁴

304. ¹ *Interl. above wyth canc.*   ² *Interl. above ampersand canc.*
        ³ *Over An.*   ⁴ *Last three words crowded in at end of line.*

Item, where as it pleasyth yow that I sholde ratefye,[5] grawnt, ore conferme the seyde gyfte on-to my brother, it is so þat wyth myn honesté I may nott, 35 and for other cawses. The Pope will suffre a thyng to be vsyd, but he will nott lycence nor grant it to be vsyd ner don; and soo I. My brother John knowyth myn entent weell j-now heer-to-foore in thys mater. I will be fownde to hym as kynde a brother as I maye be.

Item, iff it be soo þat Syr T. Brews and hys wyff thynke þat I wolde 40 troble my brother and hys wyff in the seyde maner, I can fynde no meene to putte them in sywerté þer-off but iff it weere to be bownde in an obligacion, wyth a condicion þat I shalle nott[6] trowble ner inquiete them ther-in.

Item, I thynke þat she is made sywer j-now in astate in the londe, and 45 that off right I deme they shall make noone obstacles at my wryghtyng, for I hadde neuer non astate in the londe, nere I wolde nott þat I had hadde.

No mor to yow at thys tyme, but All-myghty God have yow in kepyng. Wretyn at Caleys the xxviij daye off Marche A° E. iiij xvjj°.

By yowr sone J. PASTON, K. 50

305. To JOHN PASTON III   1477, 14 April

Add. 43490, f. 31. 11¾×7⅝ in. Autograph.

Dorse: Paper seal over red wax and tape. Address autograph:

To John Paston, esquyere.

Dated.
    F. ii, p. 244. G. 798/912.

Ryght worshypfull and hertely belovyd brother, I recomaunde me to yow, letyng yow weete þat as by Pyrse Moody when he was heer I hadde no leysere to sende answere in wryghtyng to yow and to my cosyne Gurnaye off yowre letteris; butt for a conclusion, ye shalle fynde me to yowe as kynde as I maye be, my conciense and worshyp savyd, whyche when I 5 speke wyth yowe and them ye bothe shall weell vndrestande. And I praye God sende yow as goode speede in þat mater as I wolde ye hadde, and as I hope ye shall have er thys letter come to yow; and I praye Gode sende yow yssywe betwyne yow þat maye be as honorable as euer was any off yowre ancestris and theris, wheroff I wolde be as gladde in maner as off myn 10 owne. Wherffor I praye yow sende me worde how ye doo, and iff Godde fortune me to doo weell, and be off any powere, I woll be to Syr Thomas Brewse and my lady hys wyffe a verry sone in lawe for yowre sake, and take

---

[5] *Second letter smudged, superior a written above it.*   [6] j canc.

them as ye doo, *and* doo for them as iff I wee*r*e in case lyke w*yth* them as ye
15 bee.

No moore, but Je*sus* have yow in kepyng. Wretyn at Caleys the xiiij daye
off Aprill A° E. iiij^{ti} xvij°.

As for tydyng*ys* her, the Frenshe Kynge hathe gothen many off the
town*ys* off the Duk*ys* off Borgoyne, as Seynt Quyntyn*ys*, Abevyle, Motrell,
20 *and* now off late he hathe goten Betoyne *and* Hedynge w*yth* þe castell ther,
whyche is on off þe ryallest castell*ys* off the worlde; *and* on Sonday at euyn
the Ameralle off Fraunce leyde seege at Boloyne, *and* thys daye it is seyde
þat þe Frenshe Kynge shalle com thyddr*e*, *and* thys nyght it is seyde þat
ther was a vysion seyne abowte þe wally*s* off Boloyne, as it hadde ben a
25 woman w*yth* a mervylowse lyght; men deme þat Owr*e* Lady the*r*e will
shewe hyre-selffe a love*r*e to þat towne. God forfende þat it weer Frenshe;
it weer worthe xl m*l* li. þat it we*r*e Englyshe.

J. Paston, K.

306. To John Paston III   1477, probably April

Add. 27445, f. 110. 11¾×8¼ in. Autograph.

Dorse: Paper seal over red wax. Address autograph:

To hys weell belovyd brothre John Paston, esquyere.

This letter is evidently a reply to an appeal by John III for help in reaching a
marriage settlement with Sir Thomas Brews. The approximate date appears from
other letters dealing with the subject which are dated in March and April 1477
(see nos. 303–5). The place of this letter in the series appears from the reference in
l. 6 to Piers Moody as messenger. Moody had taken a letter to Margaret Paston
(probably no. 304), but in no. 305 John II says that he had had no time to write
to his brother by the same means. The present letter is therefore evidently later
than no. 305, but not much.

The sheet is cut across below the last line of writing, and no subscription or
signature remains.

F. v, p. 180. 795/909. C. 83.

I recomande me to yow, letyng yow weete þat I receyvyd a let*ter* off yowr*ys*
⌐by⌐¹ Edward Hensted ij dayes aff*tr*e þat Whetley was dep*artyd* from me,
whyche he hadde forgetyn in hys caskett, as he seyde; wher[o]ff I sholde
have sente yow answe*r*e by Whetley iff I had hadde it to-fo*r*e he wente.
5 Notw*yth*stondyng I am ryght lothe to wryghte in that mat*er* offte, fo*r*e for
a conclusion I wrote to my moodr*e* by Peerse Moody alle þat I myght and
wolde doo ther-in. Ye have also nowe wretyn ageyn. Yow neede nott to
praye me to doo þat myght be to yowre profyght *and* worshyp, þat I myght
doo, offter than ⌐onys, or⌐ to late me weete theroff; for to my powe*r*e I

306. ¹ *Interl. above* off *canc.*

wolde do for yow *and* take as moche peyne for yowr*e* weell, *and* remembr*e* 10
itt when p*ar* case ye sholde nott thynke on it yowr*e*-selffe. I wolde be as
gladde þat one gaffe yow a man*er* off xx li. by yeer*e* as if he gave it to my
selffe, by my trowthe.

Item, wher ye thynke þat I may w*yth* concience recompence it ageyn
on-to owr*e* stokke off other londys þat I have off þat valywe in fee symple, 15
it is so þat Snaylwell, by my grauntefadr*ys* will on*ys* *and* by my fadris
will sceconder*e*ly, ⌈is⌉ entaylyd to þe issyw off my fadr*ys* body.

Item, as for Sporle xx li. by yeer, I hadde ther-off butt xx m[a]rke by
yer*e*, whyche xx m*a*rke by yeer*e* *and* the x m[a]rke ouyr*e* I have endanger*e*yd,[2]
as ye weell knowe off þat bargayne, whyche iff itt be nott redemyd I most 20
recompence som other man*er* off myn to on off my bretheryn for the seyde
x marke ouyr[3] xx m[a]rke þat longith to me; wherffor I kepe the man*er* off
Runham. Than have I fe symple londe þe man*er* off Wynt*er*ton, w*yth*
Bastwyk *and* Billys, whyche in alle is nott xx m[a]rke by yeer*e*, whyche[4]
is nott to þe valywe off þe man*er* off Sp*ar*ham. And as for Castre, it weer 25
noo convenyent lond to exchange for suche a thyng, nor*e* it weer*e* nott
polesy for me to sett þat man*er* jn suche case, for alle man*er* off happis. I
nede nott to make thys excuse to yowe but þat yowr*e* mynde is troblyd.
I praye yow reioyse nott yowr*e*-sylffe to moche in hope to opteyne ⌈thynge⌉
þat alle yowr*e* freendys may nott ease yow off; for iff my moodr*e* wer*e* dys- 30
posyd to gyve me *and* any woman in Ingelande the best man*er* þat she
hathe, to have it to me *and* my wyffe *and* to þe heyr*ys* off owr*e* too bodyes
begotyn, I wolde nott take it off hyr*e*, by God. Stablysshe yowr*e*-selffe
vppon a goode grownde, *and* grace shall folowe. Yowr*e* mat*er* is ferre spoken
off *and* blowyn wyde, *and* iff it preve noo bett*er* I wolde þat it had neu*er* 35
be spoken off. Also, þat mat*er* noysyth me þat I am so onkynde þat I lette
alle togedr*e*. I thynke notte a mat*er* happy, nor*e* weell handelyd, nor*e*
poletykly dalte w*yth*, when jt can neu*er* be fynysshyd w*yth*-owte an
inconvenyence, *and* to any suche bargayne I kepe neu*er* to be condescen-
tyng ner*e* off cowncell. Iffe I weer*e* att the begynnyng off suche a mat*er*, 40
I wolde have hopyd to have made a bett*er* conclusyon, iff they mokke yow
notte. Thys mat*er* is drevyn thus ferforthe w*yth*-owte my cowncell; I
praye yow make an ende w*yth*-owte my cowncell. Iffe it be weell, I wolde
be glad; iff it be oderwyse, it is pité. I praye yow troble me no moor*e* in
thys mat*er*.[5] 45

---

[2] it *canc.*   [3] -r *flourished, but the flourish struck through.*
[4] In *and two other words heavily canc.*
[5] *Sheet cut across after this line. Traces of the extremities of tall letters below show that more
was written.*

307. To John Paston III 1477, 23 June

Add. 43490, f. 32. 11⅝ × 5¾ in. Autograph.

Dorse: Remnants of red wax. Address autograph:

To John Paston, esqwyere.

Dated.
    F. ii, p. 248. G. 800/914.

I recomand me to yow, letyng yow weete þat I have spoken w*yth* Herry
Colett *and* entretyd hym in my best wyse for yow, soo þat at þe last he is
agreyd to a resonable respyght¹ for þe xv li. þat ye sholde have payd hym
at Mydsom*er,* as he seyth, *and* is gladde to do yow ease or plesyr*e* in all
5 þat he maye. *And* I tolde hym þat ye wolde, as I supposyd, be heer*e* at
London herr*e* nott longe to, *and* than he lokyth afftr*e* þat ye sholde com
see hym, for he is sheryff *and* hathe a goodely hows.

    Item, my lady off Oxenfforth lokyth afftr*e* yow, *and* Arblast*er* bothe. My
lorde off Oxenfford is nott comen jn-to Inglonde þat I can p*er*ceyve, *and*
10 so þe goode lady hathe nede off helpe *and* cowncell howe þat she shall doo.

    No moor*e* at thys tyme, butt God have yow in kepyng. Wretyn att
London on Seynt Awdryes Daye A° E. iiij^{ti} xvij°.

    Tydyng*ys,* butt þat yist*er*daye my lady Marqueys off Dorset, whyche is
my Lady Hastyng*ys* dowtr*e,* hadd chylde a sone.

15   Item, my Lord Chamb*er*leyn is comyn hyddr*e* fro Caleys *and* redyn w*yth*
þe Kynge to Wyndeshor*e, and* þe Kynge wille be her*e* ageyn on Mondaye.
                                J. P., K.

308. To Margaret Paston 1477, 7 August

Add. 27446, f. 1. 8½ × 11⅞ in. Autograph.

Dorse: Traces of red wax. Address autograph:

To þe ryght worshypfull Mestresse Margret Paston.

This letter is answered by Margaret's no. 227.
  Dated.
    F. v, p. 196. G. 802/916.

Please it yow to weete þat I have receyvyd yowr*e* lett*er* wretyn þe Tywes-
daye nexte afftr*e* Seynt Jam*es* Daye, wherin ye desyr*e* me to rem*em*bre
Kokett, and also to be helpyng to my brother John*ys* mariage. As for*e*
Kokett, as God helpe me I knowe nott yitt the mean*ys* possible þat I myght

paye hym by thatt daye; for thoos mater*is* þat be off grettest wyght *and* 5
charge *and* þat stonde nerrest my weell, þat is to seye the sywerté off þe
maner off Castr*e, and* the mat*er* bytwen Anne Hault *and* me, shall w*yth*
Godd*ys* grace thys terme be at a p*er*ffyght ende, whyche will charge me
ferther*e* than I have mony as yitt, or*e* lyke to have byffor*e* that tyme off
myn owne, *and* as God helpe me I wote nott wher*e* to borow.   10

Item, I most paye w*yth*-in thys iij yeer*e* iiij*c* m[a]rke to Towneshende ore
ellis forffett the man*er* off Sporle, *and* thus my charg*ys* be grett*er* than I
maye a-weye w*yth*, concidryd suche helpe as I have. And iff it fortunyd
þat I forffetyd the man*er* off Sporle, ye weer*e* neu*er* lyke to se me myry
afftr*e*, so God helpe me. Ye gave me on*ys* xx li. to it ward*ys, and* ye pro- 15
myttyd as moche, whyche I receyvyd; *and* synnys off my mony off seyde
man*er* growyng þat come to yowr*e* hand*ys* was rec*eyvyd* by yow ageyn the
seyde xl li., whyche when Kokett scholde be payed was nott yowr*e* ease
to dep*ar*te wyth. Neu*er*thelesse ye maye yitt, when yow lyketh, perfform*e*
yowr*e* sayde gyffte *and* promyse, *and* thys somme owyng to Kokett is nott 20
so moche. Neu*er*thelesse I suppose þat ye be nott so weell p*ur*veyd; wherffore, iff it please yow at yowr*e* ease here-afftr*e* to p*er*forme yowr*e* seyde
gyffte *and* promysse, so þat I maye have it w*yth*-in a yer*e* ore ij, or*e* yitt iij, I
sholde p*ar* case gete yowr*e* obligac*i*on to yow ageyn from Kokett, *and* he
pleasyd. Wherffor I beseche yow þat I maye have an assyngnement off 25
suche dett*ys* as been owyng yow, payeable at leyser*e* off suche mony as is
owyng for the woode at Basyngham or*e* ellys-wher, for so God helpe me I
sholde ellys wylfully ondoo my-selffe; wherin I beseche yow to sende me an
answer*e* in hast.

Item, as towchyng the mariage off my brother John, I have sente hym 30
myn advyce *and* tolde hym wherto he shall truste, *and* I have grauntyd hym
as moche as I maye. I wolde þat I weer*e* at on comunycacion atwyen them
for hys sake, whyche I sholde iff I myght.

As for*e* my comyng home, I ame nott yitt sertayn theroff. I shalle hast
me as faste as I canne, w*yth* þe grace off God, who have yow in hys kepyng. 35
I beseche yow to remem*bre* the p*re*myssis *and* to helpe me, *and* w*yth*
Godd*ys* grace thes ij mater*is* above wretyn, bothe off Castr*e and* Mestresse
Anne Hault, shall be endyd to my profyth *and* rest, *and* moore-ovyre er*e*
awghte longe to, w*yth* Godd*ys* grace, the man*er* off Sporle to be owte off
dangere; promyttyng yow þat I shall doo jn Kokett*ys* mat*er* as moche as 40
is possible for me to doo to yowr*e* plesyre. It shall neu*er* neede to prykk
nor threte a free horse. I shall do whatt I can. Wretyn the Thorysdaye
next byffor*e* Seynt Lawrence A° E. iiij^{ti} xvij°.

By yowr*e* sone J OHN P ASTON, K.

309. Copy of will   Nominally 1477, 31 October

Add. 27446, f. 4. About 8½ (torn) by 15⅝ in. Hand of the clerk who wrote
Add. 45099: see no. 10.

Dorse blank.

The left of the sheet has been torn off, taking with it several words at the beginning
of every line. It was evidently a full sheet, so would be about 11 in. wide or a little
more. The approximate position of the writing margin can be judged from the first
line, which must have begun 'I John Paston knyght'; and since this clerk wrote
comparatively regularly it is possible to form some notion of the loss in later parts.
But the tear is very irregular, leaving only the first seven lines roughly equal. These
have lost about 15 letter-spaces; the tear slopes inwards to the thirteenth line, where
the loss is twice as great; then out again to the twentieth line, where it is of perhaps
12 letters; then irregularly to the forty-third line, where it is of more than 50
letters; and finally out again to the fifty-fifth and last line where it is about the same
as at the beginning. There is also a small tear at the top, a hole at the beginning of
the second paragraph, and slight wear at the right edge.

The text is carefully written in a formal style, with few corrections. It is evidently
a copy rather than a draft, for even a late draft would be likely to show some correction of a more substantial kind and probably autograph. John II presumably never
read it, for he would not have left uncorrected the clerk's 'Swaywell' in l. 29, which
must be a miscopying of 'Snaylwell'. This copy, in fact, was probably not made in
his lifetime; the clerk wrote no other of John II's papers, but he was working for
John III in 1484.

G. 806/920.

⟨I, John Paston, k⟩nyght, in the last day of O⟨ctober anno⟩ *Domi*ni
m⟨¹ccclxxvij°, will, *graunte*, and be-queth my sowle to All-myghty God
and to the ⟨. . .⟩ Marye, Seint John Baptist, Seint Gorge, Seint Cristofur*e*,
and Seint Barbara, and my body, yf I dyghe ny the cyté of London, ⟨. . .⟩

5 of Owre Lady in the Whithe Frerys there, at the northe-est corner*e* of the
body of the chyrche, and there to be made an orator⟨y⟩¹ ⟨. . .⟩d or muche
leke as ys ou*er* S*yr* Thomas Browne in the Frere Prechours, to the valour
of xx li., so that it may cause ⟨. . .⟩ there prayours there the rather*e* to
remenbr*e* my sowle and to pray therefore; and that there be geuyn to the

10 behoff ⟨. . .⟩at plotte of grounde be made suer*e* vnto me for eu*er* the some
of xx marc.
   ⟨. . .⟩ dayly be the space of an holl yere by sou*m*me well disposed brother*e*
of the same howse, and that the seyd brothe⟨r⟩¹ ⟨. . . notw⟩ithstonding yf
I decesse in the counté of Norff*olk* or there nye abouute, I wolde my bodye

15 were buried at the prio⟨ry⟩¹ ⟨of Bromholm ny⟩ vn-to the founders toumbe,
which arche is vn-to the northsyde and ryght agayn my fadyr*e* toum⟨be⟩¹
⟨. . . w⟩ith an awter*e* and a toumbe for me to the value of xx li., and that
the howse there have a² reward*e* ⟨. . .⟩ to the Frerys of London, and that

309. ¹ *At right edge; paper decayed.*   ² *No space.*

there be also a brod*er* of that howse to synge for my sowle by one ⟨. . .⟩s
salarye.   20

⟨. . .⟩ a closette made at my cost ou*er* my faders body there ⟨to the
val⟩ue of xx li. so that owre cousyns ⟨. . .⟩y have the more deuocion to that
place and the rather*e* reste there bodyes there the encresse of the ⟨. . .⟩
encrese and pr*o*fite of the howse and reste on the religeus³ thereof lyke as
owre auncetours have ⟨. . . a⟩nd to the entent that I have disclosed but 25
on-to fewe p*er*sons concernyng the fee ferme that is payed ⟨. . . t⟩he Duke
of Suff*ol*k.

⟨. . . bro⟩ther*e* John, yf I dye with-owth yssue leffull of my bodye, have
the man*er* of Swaywell to hym and ⟨. . .⟩ accordyng to the willez both of
myn graunfadere and of my fader*e*, on whos sowles God have m*er*cye 30
the ⟨. . .⟩esse.

⟨. . .⟩ Bysshope of Wynchester*e* or his assygnes woll and fynde suerté
to do founde at the lyste iiij prestys ⟨. . .⟩ of John Fastolf and his frendys,
&c., at Caster, and that there be⁴ bylded loggyng conueniant for those
⟨. . .⟩r⁵ adioynyng vppon the bakhous ou*er* the gardeyn withouuth the mote 35
on the weste syde of my ⟨. . .⟩es in the seid man*er* or man*er*s yn Cast*er*
gr*a*unt by chart*our* grounde, space, and londe conuenyant for such ⟨. . .⟩
entré and yssue therunto and to that entent and byldyng or purchasyng of
license of the Kyng ⟨. . .⟩ pr*o*fitez of the seid man*er*s holly be expendid the
terme of vij yerez next aft*er* my dissece, and moreou*er* ⟨. . .⟩ resorte ther*e* 40
in his owne p*er*sone to ou*er*-see the werkys or byldyng or establyssyng of
the seyd howse ⟨. . . h⟩ave playn lyberté to dwell with-jnne my seid man*er*
and fortresse the seid t*er*me of vij yerez and that t⟨. . .⟩¹ ⟨. . . p⟩restys.⁶

⟨. . . cha⟩pell of Seint John Baptyst withyn the seyd towne of Cast*er*, with
all the pr*o*fitez yerly of that same, be geuy*n* ⟨. . .⟩ed to the seyd college 45
or howse for eu*er*more, with lycence therunto had of the Kyng and of the
Pope with ⟨. . .⟩ in Castre beforeseyd, which londis with the seyd chapell
schalbe of the yerly value of vij⁷ li. yerly ⟨. . .⟩ment of one prest aboue the
charge that the Bysshope will do to pray for the sowles of my fader*e*
⟨. . .⟩ Thomas Lyndys, clerk, and of S*yr* John Dawbeney, and that aft*er* 50
this aboue wretyn be p*er*formed, yf that⁸ ⟨. . .⟩es make astate by fyne
reryd and enrolled in the Kynges courte of the seid man*er* and man*er*s in
Castre ⟨. . . th⟩e yssue of his bodye lauffully comyeng.⁹ And for defaute of
yssue of his body lawfully ⟨. . . rem⟩ayne to the issue of my moders lawfully co*m*mynge. And for defaute of yssue of here body lawfully co*m*myng 55
⟨. . .⟩ my*n* vncle Edward Maudeby and to the yssue of his body lawffully
co*m*mynge. And that for defau⟨te⟩¹ ⟨. . . com⟩yng that the seyd man*er*s

---

³ *Second -e- perhaps over* o.   ⁴ -e *over* y.
⁵ for *canc.*   ⁶ *Five or six letters, the last* th, *erased.*
⁷ yere *canc.*   ⁸ *Four minims, at edge, canc.*
⁹ that the seyd man*er*s *canc.*

remayn to my cousyn S*yr* William Calthorpe and to the right eyrez ⟨. . .⟩
for defaute of issue of his body lawfully co*m*myng the seyd man*er*s to
60 reuerte to the ⟨. . .⟩[10]

⟨. . . chap⟩ell of the seyd collage be presented by the lordys of my seid
man*er* ⟨. . .⟩gned by Syr John Fastolff.

⟨. . .⟩eryng de eadem villa vendatur per executores meos ad perimplen-
dum et persoluendum ⟨. . .⟩em inuenerit securitatem ad redimendum
65 manerium de Sporle predictum quod si ipse ⟨. . .⟩ x acre terre de eisdem
perquesite de Johanne Kendall tempore debito dentur predicto Johanni
fratri ⟨. . . legitti⟩me procreatis. Et defectu exitus legittimi de predicto
Johanne fratre meo tunc predicte terre et tenementa remaneant ⟨. . .⟩y
triaui mei legittime procreatis; et pro defectu exitus legittimi predicti
70 triaui mei tunc remaneant Willelmo ⟨. . .i⟩psius Willelmi legittime procreatis. Et pro defectu exitus legitt[i]mi predicti Willelmi tunc omnia predicta terre et tenementa ⟨. . .⟩ assignatis imperpetuum, proviso quod[11]
executores testamenti Willelmi Pekering habeant x marcas pro ⟨. . .⟩ habeat
xxxvij acras terre de predictis terris sibi per voulountatem patris eius
75 assignatis siue legatis si tante ⟨. . .⟩ terre que idem Johannes vendidit sint
de numero illarum acrarum sibi limitatarum per Nicholaum patrem
predicti Johannis ac⟨. . .⟩ recompensacionem eo quod idem Johannes forte
credidit quod ipse iuste potuit vendere queque terras et tenementa in
feofame*nt*⟨o⟩[I] ⟨. . . pat⟩ris, non obstante quod pater predictus non declar-
80 auit quicquid faciendum de dictis terris suis vltra certas acras ⟨. . .⟩*na*
ipsius patris.

310. To John Paston III and Osbern Berney

1478, 5 May

Add. 27446, f. 11. 12 × 8¼ in. Autograph.

Dorse: Traces of red wax over tape. Address autograph:

To John Paston, esquiere, ande to Osberne Berney and to eueryche off them
*be thys lett*er *delyu*e*ryd.*

Dated.
  G. 814/929.

I reco*m*aunde me to yowe, *and* thanke yow off yowr*e* labor*e* þat ye hadde
at. Heylesdon *and* Drayton in seyng þe woodys ther*e*; *and* it is soo heere
þat Ric*hard* Ferore seyde þat he repentyd hym þat euyr*e* he dalte w*yth*
any woode theer*e*, *and* iff I hadde sente hym but þe leest chylde þat I hadde
5 to have warnyd hym to leve he wolde notte have dalte ther-wyth. *And* he

---

[10] *End of paragraph lost at deep tear.*   [11] ille terre *canc.*

fonde noo comfforte in the Chancery but þat he is lyke to contente me for the¹ harmes *and* hurte þat is doone, *and* moore-ovyr*e* he hathe an injoncyon þat he shall felle noo moor*e*.

Item, wheere as he desyryd me to be freendly to hym, I dalte so w*yth* hym þat I trowe he wylle reporte þat I seyde *and* dalte moor*e* cortesly w*yth* hym 10 than he demyd þat I woolde doo. Yitt for alle inco*n*venyenc*ys* þat myght falle, I wolde be gladde to have a weell stomakyd felawe þat wolde for my sake eu*e*rye daye see the seyde wood*ys* off Heylesdon *and* Drayton *and* to knowe iff any weer*e* fellyd heer-afftr*e*, *and* iffe ther*e* be any fellyd syns that Whetley was theer*e*, *and* I can preve it by wytnesse, I sholde have 15 bett*er* recompence for eu*e*ry tree ⌜than⌝² iiij trees weer*e* worthe.

Item, it is so þat he hathe answeryd to my bille, wheryn he seythe þat he neu*er* knywe byfor the subpena delyu*er*yd hym þat I hadde any clayme or entrest in the man*er* off Heylesdon, but þat it was peasyblé my lord*ys* off Suff*olk*. Wherffor I suppose þat ther*e* be many men in Norwyche þat 20 comonyd w*yth* hym off the byenge off that woode er*e* evyr he made hys fulle bergayne; *and* p*ar* aventu*r* some freendys off hys gave hym warnyng ther-off and off myn entrest. Iff any suche credyble man*e* þat hadde hadde any suche langage to hym, or in hys companye, er*e* than he bargayned, or any man þat he laboryd to be halffe marchant or byer*e* w*yth* hym, ar any 25 man þat refusyd to bye the seyde woode bycawse off myn entrest in the pr*e*sence off Feror*e*, any such credyble man maye, iff he wyll wytnesse ther-in w*yth* me or þat dar*e* avowe it, sholde be to me a remedy off alle that is fellyd. I praye yow iff ye can heer*e* any suche þat ye will in the pr*e*sence off them make a bylle off remembraunce theroff, *and* off ther 30 sayng, so þat they maye her-afftr*e* wytnesse in þe mat*er*. Neu*er*thelesse trowthe it is that he hadde knowleche theroff j-nowe, *and* soo hadde eu*er*y man off hys havor*e* in Norwych, I dowt nott. *And* as for hym, I ame sure he hadde knowleche, for so moche as he desyryd at hys bargayn to have a sywerté to be savyd harmeles ageyn me, whyche was grawntyd hym butt 35 nott executyd.

No mor, butt ⌜I⌝ hope w*yth* Goddys grace to have hastely goode remedy for the hole man*er*, *and* off Drayton therto *and* alle the remenaunte. Wretyn a[t] London the v daye off Maye Aº E. iiijᵗⁱ xviijº.

310. ¹ hurst *canc.*   ² *Interl. above ampersand canc.*

311. To Margaret Paston 1478, 13 May

Add. 43490, f. 35. 12 × 6⅞ in. Autograph.

Dorse: Traces of red wax. Address autograph:

To my ryght worshypfull moodre Margrete Paston be thys delyueryd.

Dated.

F. ii, p. 260. G. 815/930.

Please it yow to weete þat, where as I entendyd to have ben at home thys
Mydsomer, *and* purposyd wyth yowre goode helpe to have bygonne vppon
my fadrys tombe so þat it myght have ben endyd thys somyre, it is soo þat
fore suche cawsys as are nowe bygvnne by-twyen my lorde off Suffolk *and*
5 me for the manerys off Heylesdon, Drayton, &c., for whyche materis I
most nedys be heere thys nexte terme, therffor I deme jt wolle be afftre
Mydsomer ere than I can see yowe. Please it yow also to weete þat I comonyd
wyth Master Pykenham to weete iffe he wolde bye the clothe off golde
fore soo moche as he desyryd onys to have bowte it, *and* he offryd me onys
10 xx marke therffore. Neuerthelesse it coste me¹ xxiiij li.; yit nowe when þat
I spake to hym ther-off he refusyd to bye it, *and* seyde þat he hadde nowe
so many chargys þat he maye nott. Butt it is soo þat the Kynge dothe make
sertayne copys *and* vestymentys off like clothe whyche he entendyth to
gyve to the coledge at Foodryngeye wher my lorde hys fadre is nowe
15 buryed, *and* he byethe at a grete pryce. I comonyd wyth the vestment
maker for to helpe me forthe wyth xij yerdys, *and* he hathe grauntyd me to
doo, as Whetleye can telle yow; wherffor, iff it plese yow that it be bystowyd for to make a towmbe for my fadre at Bromholme, iff ye lyke to
sende it hyddre, iffe it be solde I vndretake or Mychelmesse þat ther shalle
20 be a tombe *and* somwhatt ellys ovyre my fadris grave, on whoys sowle God
have mersye, þat ther shalle noone be lyke it in Norffolk, *and* as ye shalle be
gladde herafftre to see it. *And* Gode sende me leyser þat I maye come home;
and iff I doo nott, yit the monye shalle be pitte to noon other vse butt kepyd
by some þat ye trust tylle þat it maye be bystowyd acordyng as is above
25 wretyn; *and* ellys I gyve yow cawse neuyre to trust me whylle ye *and* I
lyve. When I was last wyth yow ye grauntyd þat the seyde clothe off golde
sholde be bywaryd abowte thys werke þat is above wretyn, whyche iff ye
wylle perfforme, I vndretake þat ther shalle be suche a towmbe as ye shalle
be pleased wyth, thowghe it cost me xx marke off myn owne purse besyde,
30 iff I onys sette vppon it.

No more, but I beseche Goode have yow in hys kepyng. Wretyn at
London þe Wednysdaye in Whyghtsonweke Aº E. iiijᵗⁱ xviijº. Please it
yow to sende me worde by Whetleye off yowre plesyre her-in.

By yowre sone JOHN PASTON, K.

311. ¹ onys *canc.*

312. To JOHN PASTON III   1478, 25 August

Add. 43491, f. 25. $11\frac{3}{4} \times 10\frac{3}{4}$ in. Autograph.

Dorse: Traces of red wax. Address autograph:

*To John Paston, esquyere, be thys lettre delyueryd, ore to my mestresse hys
wyffe at Norwych to delyuer to hym.*

Dated.

F. ii, p. 270. G. 821/936.

Brother John, I recomaund me to yow, *and* I thanke God, my sustre yowre
wyffe, *and* yow off my fayre nevywe Crystofre whyche I vndrestande ye
have, where-off I ame ryght gladde *and* I praye God sende yow manye iff[1]
it be hys plesyre. Neuerthelesse ye be nott kynde þat ye sende me no wetyng
ther-off; I hadde knowleche by footemen ore euer ye kowde fynde any   5
massanger on horsbak to brynge me worde ther-off.

Syr, it is soo þat the Duke off Bokyngham shall come on pilgrymage to
Walsyngham, *and* so to Bokenham Castell to my[2] lady hys sustre, *and*
then it is supposyd þat he shalle to my lady off Norffolk; *and* myn[3] oncle
William comythe wyth hym. And he tellyth me þat ther is like to be troble   10
in the maner off Oxenhed, wherffore I praye yow take hede[4] lesse þat the
Duke off Suffolk councell pley therwyth now at the vacacion off the bene-
ffyse as they ded wyth the beneffice off Drayton, whyche by the helpe off
Master John Salett *and* Donne hys man ther was a qweste made by the
seyde Donne þat fownde þat the Duke off Suffolk was verrye patrone,   15
whyche was false yitt they ded it fore an euydence. But nowe iff any suche
pratte scholde be laboryd it is, I hope, in bettre case, for suche a thynge
most needys be fownde byffore[5] Master John Smyth, whyche is owre olde
freende; wherffor I praye yow labore hym þat iff neede bee he maye doo
vsse a freendys torne ther-in.   20

Item, bothe ye ande I most nedys take thys matere as owre owne, *and* it
weere for noon other cawse butt for owre goode grawntdames sake. Neuerthe lesse ye woote well thatt ther is an other entresse longyng to vsse afftre
here dysceasse. Iffe ther be any suche thynge begune ther by suche a
fryere or prest, as it is seyde, I mervayle þat ye sente me no worde ther-off;   25
butt ye haue nowe wyffe *and* chylder, *and*[6] so moche to kare fore thatt ye
forgete me.

Asfor tydyngys here, I her telle þat my cosyn Syr Robert Chamberleyn
hathe entryd the maner off Scolton vppon yowre bedffelawe Conyerse,
wher-off ye sende me no worde.   30

312. [1] *MS.* it.   [2] my *repeated.*
    [3] *Three or four letters canc.*   [4] -e *over* d.
    [5] the *canc.*   [6] *Ampersand crowded in later.*

Item, yonge William Brandon is in warde *and* arestyd fore thatt he
scholde have by[7] force ravysshyd *and* swyvyd an olde jentylwoman, *and*
yitt was nott therwyth easyd but swyvyd hyr oldest dowtre *and* than wolde
have swyvyd the othere sustre bothe, wher-fore men sey fowle off hym,[8]
35 that he wolde ete the henne *and* alle her chekynnys; *and* som sey þat the
Kynge entendyth to sitte vppon hym, *and* men seye he is lyke to be hangyd,
for he hathe weddyd a wedowe.

Item, as for the pagent þat men sey þat the Erle off Oxenforde hathe
pleyid atte Hammys, I suppose ye have herde theroff, itt is so longe agoo.
40 I was nott jn thys contré when the tydyngys come, therfor I sent yow no
worde ther-off; butt for conclusion, as I here seye, he lyepe þe wallys *and*
wente to þe dyke *and* in-to þe dyke to þe chynne, to whatt entent I cannott
telle—some sey to stele awey *and* some thynke he wolde have drownyd
hym-selfe, *and* so it is demyd.

45 No more, butt I ame nott sertayne whether I shall come home in hast
ore nott. Wretyn at London the daye nexte Seynt Bartelmewe A° E.
iiij[ti] xviij°.

JOHN PASTON, K.

313. To MARGARET PASTON   1479, about May–June

Add. 34889, f. 47. $11\frac{5}{8} \times 11$ in. Autograph.

Dorse: Traces of red wax. Address autograph:

To Mestresse Margrete Paston be thys delyueryd.

The approximate date appears from the report that 'my uncle Mautby's' will had
been proved. This must be Edward, younger brother of John Mautby, Margaret
Paston's father; see his letter to Margaret, Part II, no. 730. John II left the reversion
of some property to him in his will (see no. 309, l. 56). He is presumably the
Edward Mautby, of Garlickhythe in London, whose will is recorded in P.C.C.,
Reg. Wattys 36. The will was made on 15 April and proved on 11 May 1479,
administration being granted to his widow Maud.

F. iv, p. 264. G. 563/652 (part, undated). C. 89 (part).

Please it yow to weete þat I sende yow by Barkere, the berere heroff, iij
triacle pottes off Geane, as my potecarie swerytht on-to me, *and* moore-
ouyre that they weer neuer ondoo syns þat they come from Geane; wheroff
ye shalle take as many as pleasyth yow. Neuerthe lesse my brother John
5 sente to me for ij; þerfore I most beseche yowe þat he maye have at þe leste
on. There is on potte þat is morkyn ondre þe bottome ij tymes wyth thyes
letteris, 'M.P.', whyche potte I have best truste on-too, *and* nexte hym to
þe wryghe potte; *and* I mystruste moost þe potte þat hathe a krotte abovyn

---

[7] -y *over* e.   [8] *Ampersand canc.*

in the toppe, lesse þat he hathe ben ondoone. *And* also the other ij pottys
be prentyd w*yth* þe marchauntys marke too tymes ⌜on the coueryng*ys*⌝, 10
and that other potte is butt onys morkyn but w*yth* on prente. Notwythstondyng I hadde lyke othe *and* promyse for on as well as for alle.[1]

Item, it was soo þat I was yister*daye* w*yth* myn oncle Mautebyes wyffe,[2]
and delyuer*yd* yowre lett*er*, *and* lete her wete also þat ye had wretyn to me
to speke w*yth* hyr*e and* to have delyuer*é* off suche euydenc*ys* as she hathe. 15
And in effecte she is nott dysposyd to delyu*er* them on-to þe tyme þat she
be in sywert*é* off her mony off the arrerag*ys* on-to myn oncle her*e* husbonde, whyche she seythe is abowte þe somme off xx li.; *and* that doone
she woll delyu*er* them, *and* ellys nott. *And* than I prayed hyr*e* to se them,
and soo at þe laste she grauntyd me to see them, *and* so yister*daye* I sawe 20
them; *and* ther come iiij off her neyborys *and* wer ther present, whyche as
I *cons*eyuyd wer but shewyd *and* browte vppe for þat I sholde thynke þat
she lakked noon helpe; *and* many suche soleyn toyes she hathe, *and* she
hopyth þat ye sholde dep*art* w*yth* her w*yth* a fee off x m[a]rke or xx m[a]rke
by yeer. Bott as God helpe me I thynke, contrary to her promyse made to 25
me, she hathe laten other folk*ys* see thos[3] euydenc*ys*, for she knywe eu*ery*
dede weelle j-nowe *and* browte me forthe fyrst iij box*is* w*yth* olde euydenc*ys*,
I syghe neu*er* older, but as to seye þat ther be any þat will avayle, as God
helpe me I deme nott there is nott paste x ore xij olde dedys þat I wolde
gyffe for a grote, *and* yit ther be abowte an hou*n*dred olde dedys in alle iij 30
box*is*. And than for a seconde corse she browte me iij other deedys endentyd off suche astate as was made to myn ij oncl*ys* off Sall, Wynt*er*ton,
&c., *and* off them wolde she speke no worde tyll þat I tolde heer þat she
most needys have suche; *and* soo she wolde graunte noo mor*e*, saff þat I
bare hyr*e* soo on hande þat I wost weell ther wer*e* more, so at þe last she 35
seyde þat she shalle delyu*er* alle iff she have her monye. It is a peyne to
deele w*yth* hyr*e*.

I sawe the wylle *and* testament off myn oncle her hosbonde, whyche is
prowyd *and* vndre my lorde Kardynall*ys* sealle, *and* she provyd sool
executryse *and* hathe taken admynestrac*io*n; I syghe it vndre sealle. 40
Wherffor I thynke beste þat ye *p*urveye the on halffe off her arrerag*ys and*
sende it hyddr*e*, *and* at þe receyvyng off that halffe I hope þat she shalle
delyu*er* alle the euydenc*ys and* truste yow for þe other halffe tylle Candelmesse or*e* Esterne, as I deme. But jn effecte she moste be sworyn, *and* other
bothe whyche as I shalle devyse, whyche I deme hathe ouyre-lokyd the 45
euydenc*ys*; and soo we shall make the best ther-off þat can be, *and* ellys,
as she seythe her-selffe *and* as she lokythe afftr*e*, þat ye scholde cause her*e*
to be hadde byffor the Chauncelere. She is in many thyng*ys*[4] full lyke a

---

313. [1] *A flourish fills in the line. Fenn and Gairdner print only to here.*
   [2] *and saw canc.*
   [3] *Apparently first written* thoos, *then second* o *canc.*   [4] *-g- over* k.

wyffe off London *and* off Londone kyndenesse, *and* she woll needys take
50 advise off Londoner*ys*, wheche I telle her*e* can nott advyse her howghe she
scholde deele weell w*yth* any[5] body off worshyp. *And* I tolde her*e* þat she
owghte[6] off ryght to truste bett*er* to yowr*e* promyse than ye sholde on-to
herys, but ther-in she woll compare w*yth* a bett*er* woman than her-selffe
as off her promyse, *and* yit I deme it is broken. I praye yow sende me worde
55 her-off by the next massenger*e*. I tolde her also þat but iffe she pleasyd
yow þat she wer neu*er* lyke to have peny ther-off, for she canne nott
dystreyne ther-for, *and* as for yow, ye neu*er* receyvyd peny theroff.
Neu*er*the lesse yowr*e* wryghtyng to her *and* yowr*e* promyse is j-nowghe to
her to be in suerté þat she shalle be payed.
60   I hope to doo welle, *and* the bett*er* for that þat ye sente me, jn alle my
mater*ys*.[7]

314. Memoranda   1479, August

Add. 27446, f. 29. $5\frac{1}{2}$ (irregular) $\times 8\frac{1}{8}$ in. Autograph.

Dorse: Marks of folding; no seal or address. Note, apparently autograph:
Bill off M*e*moran*d*a.

The date appears from the reference to Agnes Paston's death. She died about
18 August 1479 (see Edmond II's letter no. 397), and since John does not know
whether she has yet been buried this must have been written very soon after.
    G. 838/954.

M*e*moran*dum* vppon the presse at þe ferther ende is a box w*yth* ij ore ii⟨j⟩[1]
bondellis w*yth* euydence off Oxenhed *and* Hauteyn.
M*e*moran*dum* that ther is rollis tytelyd vppon them 'cont*r*a Will*ia*m
Pas⟨ton⟩', and they be owther vppon the presse or on the cowntre[2] or on
5 the shelffe by the cowntr*e*, or ellys in the cowntre on[2] that syde next the
shelffe.

To enq*ui*re off myn oncle Will*ia*m, off Jane, off my grauntda⟨mys⟩ wylle,
and whoo wrot itt, *and* whether she be buried or noo, *and* who weer
present at hyr*e* wylle makyng, *and* iff she spake[2] owte off her londes.

10 Inq*ui*re
off the Kynge
the Chaunceler

---

[5] *Corr. from* ony.   [6] *Corr. from* owthe.
[7] *The rest (if any) lost at torn corner; room for only one or two words.*
314. [1] *Edge torn.*
[2] *Room for four or five letters at torn edge, but nothing appears to be lost.*

Milorde Chamberleyn
Syr Thomas Mongomeré
Mi lorde Cardynall   15
Master Bele *and* hys clerke for my fader*ys* wille.

315. To MARGARET PASTON   1479, 29 October

Add. 43490, f. 38. 12×9 in. Autograph.

Dorse: Traces of red wax. Address autograph:

*To þe ryght worshypfull Mestresse Margret Paston be thys delyu*er*yd.*

Dated.
   Though addressed to Margaret this letter was intended for John III as well (see last sentence), and he answered it in no. 381. John II's 'fear of the sickness' was justified: he died a little over two weeks later.
   F. ii, p. 276. G. 840/956.

Please it yow to weete þat I have ben heer at London a xiiij nyght,
wher[o]ff the first iiij dayes I was in suche feer*e* off the syknesse, *and* also
fownde my chambr*e and* stuffe nott so clene as I demyd, whyche troblyd
me soor*e*; and as I tolde yow at my dep*a*rtyng I was nott weell monyed,
for I hadde nott paste x m[a]rke, wher*o*ff I dep*a*rtyd xl s. to be delyu*er*yd 5
off my olde bedfelaw*e*, *and* then I rode be-yonde Donstaple *and* there
spake w*y*th on off my cheffe wittnessis, whyche pr*o*mysed me to take labor*e*
and to gete me wryghtyng*ys* towchyng thys mat*er* bytwyen me *and* þe Duke
off Suff*olk, and* I rewardyd hym xx s.; *and* then as I jnformyd yow I payed
v m[a]rke jncontynent vppon my comyng hyddr*e* to replegge owte my 10
gow[n]e off velwett *and* other geer. And then I hopyd to have borowyd some
off Towneshe[n]d,[1] and he hathe foodyd me forthe euyr*e* synys, *and* in
effecte I cowde have at þe most *and* at þe soneste yisterdaye xx s.; wherffor
I beseche yow to p*ur*veye me c s., and also to wryght to Pekok þat he
p*ur*veye me as moche, c s., whyche I suppose þat he hathe gaderyd[2] at 15
Paston *and* other plac*ys* by thys tyme. Fore w*yth*-owte I have thys x li., as
God helpe me, I fer*e* I shalle doo butt litell goode in noo mat*er*, nor yitt I
woote nott howe to come home but iff I have it. Thys geer hathe troblyd
me so þat it hathe made me moor*e* than halffe seke, as God helpe me.
   Item, I vndrestande þat myn oncle Will*i*am hathe made labor to þ'ex- 20
chetor,[3] *and* þat he hathe bothe a wrytte off *diem*[4] *clawsyth extremu*m *and*
also a *supercedeas.* I have wretyn to þe exchetor th⟨e⟩r[5]-in off myn entent.

---

315. [1] *Cramped at edge.*   [2] *MS.* goderyd.
   [3] *Abbr. by superior* r. *Spellings in full in ll. 30 and 35 show that* -or *was meant.*
   [4] -i- *apparently over* jj.   [5] *Letter lost at hole.*

Iff myn oncle hadde hys will in that, yitt sholde he be neu*er* the nerre the londe, butt in effecte he shold have thys avauntage whyche is behovefull
25 for a weyke mate*re*, to have a coulou*re* o*re* a clooke o*re* a botrase. But ⌐on Tywesdaye [16] I was w*yth* þe Bysshop off Hely, whyche shewyth hym-selffe goode and worshypfull, *and* he seyde þat he sholde sende to myn oncle Will*iam* þat he sholde nott procede in no suche mat*er* till þat he speke w*yth* hym; and moore-ouyre þat he scholde cawse hym to be heer hastelye. In
30 whyche mat*er* is no remedy as nowe, butt iff it wer*e* soo þat þe exchetor, iff he be entretyd to sytte by myn oncle Will*iam*, whyche p*ar* case he shall nott, þat iff my brother John *and* Lomnor*e* have knowleche off the daye, *and* they myght be ther*e*, Lomnor*e* can geve euydence j-now in that mater w*yth*-owte þe boke. And more-ouyre þat they see bothe the lett*er* *and* the
35 other noote þat I sente to þe exchetor, *and* w*yth* helpe off th'exchetor all myght be as beste is. And iff my brother *and* Lomnor take labor her-in, I shall reco*m*pence ther cost*ys*.

Wretyn in hast*e* w*yth* schort advisemen[t] on the Frydaye next Seynt*ys* Symond *and* Jude A° E. iiij[ti] xix°. Late my brother John se thys bille, for
40 he knoweth mor off thys mater.[7]

JOHN PASTON, K.

316. Inventory of Books   Not after 1479

Add. 43491, f. 26. About 5 (irregular)× 17 in. Autograph.

Dorse blank.

The paper has decayed along the whole of the right side so that part of the text is lost. The extent of loss can be approximately judged from the heading, and from some of the titles. The top line probably ended 'John Paston knyght' (but possibly only 'k.'). The third item must have contained 'The Legende off Ladyes, (?La) Bele Dame saunce Mercye, þe Parlement off Byrdys, þe Temple off Glasse'. The exact form and spelling of some of the titles is uncertain—in item 5 there is no 'la' before 'bele da⟨me⟩', and 'Mercy' is written out, not abbreviated—but clearly not very much has been destroyed. The list was evidently written on a strip of paper about 6 in. wide, made by cutting a sheet roughly in half lengthwise; and while rolled up it was damaged by damp.

The items are set out separately, with an arabic numeral preceding each of the first eleven: see Plate VII.

Fenn concluded from William Ebesham's account for copying (see Part II, no. 751) that this inventory was that of the library of 'John Paston'. He must have meant John Paston II, for Ebesham specifies 'Sir John'. Gairdner thought it 'most probably' belonged to John III. But (as A. J. Collins first pointed out in *The Times*, 7 July 1933, 15–16) the hand is unquestionably John II's. Since he died on 15

---

[6] *Interl. above in* and another word *heavily canc.*
[7] *Last sentence crowded in later.*

November 1479 it cannot be later than that, nor can it be earlier than the publication of Caxton's first edition of *The Game and Playe of the Chesse* (item 4) in 1475.
F. ii, p. 300. G. 869/987.

The Inventory off Englysshe bokis off Joh⟨. .⟩
made þe v daye off Novembre A° r.r. E. iiij^ti ⟨. . .⟩

1. A boke had off myn ostesse at þe George ⟨. . .⟩
off þe Dethe off Arthur[1] begynyng at Cassab⟨. . .⟩
Warwyk, Kyng Richard Cure delyon,² a croni⟨. . .⟩
to Edwarde þe iij, pric——

2. Item, a boke off Troylus whyche William Bra⟨. . .⟩
hathe hadde neer x yer *and* lent it to Da⟨. . .⟩
Wyngfelde, et jbi ego vidi; valet³

3. Item, a blak boke wyth The Legende off Lad⟨. . .⟩
saunce Mercye, þe Parlement off Byr⟨. . .⟩
Glasse, Palatyse *and* Scitacus, The Med⟨. . .⟩
the Greene Knyght,⁴ valet—

4. Item, a boke jn preente off þe Pleye of þe⟨. . .⟩

5. Item, a boke lent Midelton, *and* therin is Bele Da⟨. . .⟩
Mercy, þe Parlement off Byrdys, Balade ⟨. . .⟩
off Guy *and* Colbronde, Off the Goos, þe⟨. . .⟩
þe Dysput[i]son bytwyen Hope *and* Dyspeyre⟨. . .⟩
Marchauntys, þe Lyffe off Seint Cry⟨. . .⟩⁵

6. A reede boke þat Percyvall Robsart gaff m⟨. . .⟩
off the Medis off þe Masse, þe Lamentacion ⟨. . .⟩
off Chylde Ypotis, A Preyer to þe Vernycle⟨. . .⟩
callyd The Abbeye off þe Holy Gooste⟨. . .⟩

7. Item, in quayerys Tully de Senectute in d⟨. . .⟩
wheroff ther is no more cleere wretyn⟨. . .⟩

8. Item, in quayerys Tully or Cypio de Ami⟨. . .⟩
leffte wyth William Worcester, valet—

9. Item, in quayerys a boke off þe Polecye off In⟨. . .⟩

10. Item, in qwayerys a boke de Sapiencia⟨. . .⟩
wherin þe ij parson is liknyd to Sapi⟨. . .⟩

316. ¹ *Apparently first written* Artur, *then* h *written over* u *and superior* r *added.*
² *Titles underlined separately.*
³ *At least two words, the first beginning with* M, *canc.*
⁴ *Titles underlined separately, but the usual initial oblique stroke omitted except before* Palatyse.
⁵ *Interl. above* Seynt Cry *is* 'and pl⟨. . .⟩', *with no surviving indication of where it should be inserted.*

11. It*em*, a boke de Othea, text *and* glose, valet⟨. . .⟩
in quayer*ys*——

M*emorandum*, myn olde boke off blasonyng*ys* off a⟨. . .⟩
It*em*, the nywe boke portrayed *and* blasonyd⟨. . .⟩
35 It*em*, a copy off blasonyng*ys* off armys *and* t⟨. . .⟩
names to be fownde by lett*er*——————————
It*em*, a boke w*yth* armys portrayed in paper   v[6] ⟨. . .⟩

M*emorandum*, my boke off knyghthod *and* ther-in[7] ⟨. . .⟩
off makyng off knyght*ys*, off just*ys*, off torn⟨. . .⟩
40 fyghtyng in lyst*ys*, paces holden by sou⟨. . .⟩
and chaleng*ys*, statut*ys* off weer *and* de Regimi⟨. . .⟩
valet——

It*em*, a boke off nyw statut*ys* from Edward⟨. . .⟩
the iij——

---

[6] *Though this numeral is almost opposite* paper *it is linked by an angled line with the previous line. It may have been part of the total figure for this section.*
[7] *Part of another letter, like* n *or* u, *remains.*

JOHN PASTON III

317. Perhaps to THOMAS PLAYTER: draft   1461, March

Add. 43489, f. 6. 12 × 8½ in. Lomnor's hand (see p. lxxvii).

Dorse: Marks of folding but not soiled by carrying. No seal or address.

Fenn and Gairdner attributed authorship to John III, but the manuscript index assigns it, with a question mark, to John II. Only the contents show that it was written on behalf of one of John Paston's sons. The brother whom John I thought of sending to London would surely be John II, at this time about 19, rather than John III, who was two years younger—in fact by August 1461 John II was in the King's household. Yet this draft can hardly have been composed by John III himself, for its style is much more mature than that of his earliest autograph letters (e.g. no. 318). It may have been composed by Lomnor, who wrote it; but it seems at least to have been checked by John I, for the words 'my broþer' in l. 23 are interlined, above a cancelled 'me', in a hand that is not Lomnor's, or that of either of the sons, but looks like John I's. It appears therefore as if he meant, perhaps for reasons of discretion, to send this letter in John III's name (originally John II's, hence the cancelled 'me'). William Paston II and Playter were acting for John I in London about this time, and the tone of the letter is appropriate to Playter, the family servant, rather than to William Paston, the nominal writer's uncle.

The date appears from the mustering of troops. On 6 March 1461 Edward IV issued a proclamation calling on men between the ages of 16 and 60 to come to him prepared to fight, and the Duke of Norfolk was charged with the raising of men in Norfolk (Scofield, i. 154–7). It is probably before the battle of Towton on 29 March (see William II's letter no. 90).

F. i, p. 226. G. 384/449.

I recomawnde me to yow, and lete yow wete þat¹ notwythstandyng tydyng*ges* come downe, ⌈os ye knowe⌉, þat pepill shuld not come vp tyll thei were sent fore, but to be redy at all tymes, this notwithstandyng ⌈mech⌉² pepill³ owt of this cuntré⁴ have take wag*es*,⁵ seying thei woll goo vp to London. But⁶ thei have no capteyn ner rewler assigned be the   5 comissioneres to awayte vp-on, and so thei stragyll abowte be them-self and be lyklynes arn not leke to come at London, half of them. And men that come from London⁷ sey there have not passid Thetford not passyng

317. ¹ þ *in form of* y *throughout.*
    ² *Interl. above a cancelled word which may be* such.
    ³ gooth vp *canc.*   ⁴ for thei *canc.*
    ⁵ but thei stragyl *canc.*
    ⁶ non *canc.*   ⁷ and have not *canc.*

cccc[8] and yet the townes and the cuntré that have waged hem shall thynk
10 thei be dischargid. And therfor if this lordes above wayte aftyr more
pepill ⌜in this cuntré⌝, be lyklynes it woll not be easy to get wyth-owt a
newe comission and warnyng; and yet it woll be thought ryght straunge
of hem that have waged pepyll to wage any more, for euery towne hath
waged and sent forth, and arn redy to ⌜send⌝[9] forth as many as thei ded
15 whan the Kyng sent for hem be-fore the feld at Lodlowe, and thoo that
arn not goo be in goyng in the same forme.

Item, ther was shrewd rewle toward in this cuntré, for ther was a
certeyn person ⌜forth-wyth aftyr the jurny at Wakefeld⌝ gadered felaship[10]
to have mordered John Damme, as it is seyd; and also ther is at the castell
20 ⌜of⌝ Rysing and in other ij plases made gret gaderyng of pepill and hyryng
of harneys, and it is wele vndyrstand ⌜they be⌝[11] not to the Kyng ward, but
rather the contrary[12] and for to robbe.[13] Wherfore my fadyr is in a dowte
whedir he shall send ⌜my broþer⌝[14] vp or not, for he wold have his owne
men abowte hym ⌜if nede were here⌝;[15] but[16] notwythstandyng he wyll
25 send vp Dawbeney,[17] his spere and bowes wyth hym, as Stapilton and
Calthorp or other men of worship of this cuntré agree to doo. Wherfore
demene yow in doyng of yowre erandes ther-aftyr, and if ye shall bryng
any masage from the lordes take writyng, for Dancortes massage is not
verely beleved be-cause he browt no wrytyng.
30 Item, this cuntré wold fayne take these fals shrewes[18] that arn[19] in
oppynion contrary to the Kyng and his counsell, if they had any auctorité
from the Kyng to do so.

Item, my brother is redyn to Yarmowth for ⌜to lette⌝[20] brybours that[21]
wold a robbed a ship vndyr colour of my lord of Warwyk, and longe no-
35 thyng to hem ward.

[8] and fewe be *canc.*
[9] *Interl. above* goo *canc.*
[10] and *canc.*
[11] *Interl. above* it is *canc.*
[12] or el *canc.*
[13] in the, *and a blotted word which may be* weye, *interl. but canc.*
[14] *Interl. in another hand, probably John I's, above* me *canc.*
[15] *Interl. above* and where as Syr Miles Stapilton *canc.*
[16] *Superfluous* not.
[17] at *canc.*
[18] and *canc.*
[19] of *canc.*
[20] *Interl. above* there arn *canc.*
[21] t- *over* y.

318. To JOHN PASTON I   Probably 1461, 10 November

Add. 27445, f. 14. 10¼ × 5½ in. Autograph.

Dorse: Paper seal over red wax. Address autograph:

To my most reuerent and worchepfull fadyr John Paston be thys delyueryd in hast.

The date is not fixed by any particular event mentioned, but can be estimated from several circumstances. Since John Paston I died in May 1466 this letter cannot be later than 1465. In the latter part of that year John I was in prison (no. 77), and in November 1464 he had lately been convicted of trespass and outlawed (MS. Add. 27444, ff. 132–6); so that in those years John III could not reasonably hope 'to hear of his welfare and prosperity' and would surely have used a different formula. From November 1462 until after March 1464 John III was with the Duke of Norfolk in Wales. This letter is therefore likely to have been written earlier than that. This suits the handwriting and setting out, which are nearest to those of nos. 163 and 164, written by John III for Margaret on 2 and 16 November 1461. Further, no. 164 mentions Geoffrey Sperling, a former servant of Fastolf's who appears often in the letters during Fastolf's lifetime but rarely afterwards. This is the only letter while his father was alive in which John III signs himself 'the younger'; in no. 319 he is 'junior', but after that 'the youngest'.

G. 545/633 (abstract).

Most reuerent *and* worchepfull fadyr, I recomande me to yow lowly,[1] preying yow of yowyr[2] blyssyng *and* hertly desyiryng to her of yowyr welfare *and* prosperyté, the whyche I prey God preserue *and* kepe to hys plesans *and* to yowyr hertys desyir. Plesyt yow to haue knowlage þat I haue spoke wyth Warwyk *and* Stwklé fore the plase *and* þe londys in Arleham, 5 *and* they wyle not geue but vj d. for an acre, *and* they to kepe the reparacion of the plase; but so I wold not lete heme haue it. But Stwklé hathe promysyd me þat all the[3] londys schalle be purveyd for as for thys yer. Warwyk was wyth my modyr as thys day, *and* he desyiryth to haue the londys in Arleham for vij d. an acre as for thys yer. And in as myche as Stwklé had promysyd 10 me to purvey for the londys for thys yer, I cownselyd my modyr þat he schuld not haue heme wyth-owt he wold tak hem for a[4] longer terme. As for Kook, he wole no lenger hold[5] the plase *and* the xviij acrys nowthyr for[6] vij nor viij d. an acr *and* to kepe the reparacion of the plase. He wole geue but vj d. for an acr, *and* he to kepe the reparacion of the plase; *and* yet 15 he wole not be bownde to repare the plase. *And* so he wole no lenger haue it but he may haue it for vj d.

I haue spoke wyth Dame Alys Neche *and* Jaferey Spyrlyng, *and* ⌐they⌐ haue agreyd bothe þat ther schall be set a tenaunt by bothe ther assenttys

---

318. [1] d *canc.*   [2] -r *crowded in.*
[3] *Written* thes, -s *apparently canc.*   [4] *Crowded in.*
[5] hys l *canc.*   [6] vj *canc.*

20 for ⌜to⌝ ocwpye the londys that they be at debat for tyll ye come home, *and* as ye de*ter*myne the ma*ter* when ye come home they bothe hold hem wele payid.

And All-mythy[7] God haue yow in hys kepy*ng*. Wretyn in hast on Seynt Martynys Evyn.

25   Yow*yr* sone *and* ser*ua*unt J OHN P ASTON þe yo*ng*er

319. To J OHN P ASTON I   1462, 1 November

Add. 43489, f. 18. 11½×3½ in. Autograph.

Dorse: Paper seal over red wax and tape. Address autograph:

*To my ryth reu*e*rent and worchepfull fadyr John Paston be thys delyu*e*ryd in hast.*

The date appears from the reference to Bamburgh Castle. Margaret of Anjou invaded Northumberland from France on 25 October 1462, and soon captured the castles of Bamburgh and Alnwick. Sir Richard Tunstall was Henry VI's chamberlain. (Scofield, i. 165, 261–2; Jacob, p. 529).

    John Paston III was in the retinue of the Duke of Norfolk at Holt Castle in Denbighshire. Framlingham in Suffolk (l. 10) was the Duke's seat.

    F. i, p. 266. G. 463/532.

Ryth reu*er*ent *and* worchepfull fadyr, I recomand me on-to yow, besechy*ng* yow lowly of yo*wyr* blyssy*ng*. Plesyt yow to haue knowlage þat my lord is p*ur*posyd to send for my lady, *and* is lyke to kepe hys Crystmas her in Walys, for þe Ky*ng* hathe desyiryd hym to do þe same. Wherfor I beseche
5 yow þat [ye] wole wychesaue to send me some mony by the berer herof, for in good feythe, as it is not onknowy*ng* to yow, þat I had but ij noblys in my purse whyche þat Rychard Call took me by yo*wyr* comandement when I[1] dep*ar*tyd frome yow owt of Norwyche. The[2] berer her-of schuld bye me a gowne w*yth* pert of the mony, if it plese yow to delyu*er* hym[3] as myche
10 mony as he may bye it w*yth*; for I haue bot on gowne at Framy*ng*ham *and* an othyr her, *and* þat is my leu*er*é gowne *and* we must wer hem eu*er*y day for þe most p*ar*t, *and* on gowne w*yth*-owt change wyll sone be done.

    As for tydy*ng*ys, my lord of Warwyk yed forward in-to Scotlond as on Saterday last past w*yth* xx m[l] men, *and* Syr Wylli*am* Tunstale is tak
15 w*yth* þe garyson of Bamborowhg, *and* is lyke to be hedyd,[4] by þe menys of S*yr* Rychard Tunstale is owne brodyr.

[7] J *and apparently* shu *canc.*
319. [1] rod ow *canc.*   [2] brear *canc.*
  [3] hym *repeated.*   [4] for *canc.*

522

As sone as I her ony more tydy*n*gys I schall send hem yow, by þe *grace* of God who haue yow in hys kepy*n*g. Wretyn in hast at the casty[l] of þe Holt vp-on Halowmas Daye.

Yo*wyr* sone *and* lowly seru*au*nt J. P A S T O N, Jun*ior*⁵ 20

320. To J O H N   P A S T O N   I I   1462, 11 December

Add. 43489, f. 20. 11½ × 8¾ in. Autograph.

Dorse: Continuation of text. Traces of red wax. Address autograph:

To my ryth worchepfull brodyr ⟨John⟩¹ Paston the older, sone of John Paston, esqwyer, be thys delyueryd in hast.

The date appears from the account of affairs in the north. Alnwick, Dunstan-burgh, and Bamburgh castles were in the hands of Margaret of Anjou and be-sieged by Warwick late in 1462, and Edward IV was at Durham in December of that year (Scofield, i. 264; Jacob, pp. 529–30).

F. i, p. 272. G. 464/533.

Ryth worchepfull brodyr,² I recomand me to yow. Plesyt yow to wet þat as thys day we had tydyngys her that the Scottys wyll come in-to Inglond wyt*h*-in vij days aftyr the wryttyng of thys lettyr for to rescue these iij castellys, Alnewyk, Donsamborowe, and Bameborowe, whyche castellys wer besegyd as on yesterdaye. And at the sege of Allnewyk lythe my lord ⁵ of Kent *and* þe Lord Scalys, *and* at Donsameborow castyll lythe the Erle of Wyrcetyr,³ Syr Rafe Grey, *and* at the castyll of Bameborow lythe the Lord Montagwe *and* þe Lord Ogyll *and* othyr dyu*er*s lordys *and* gentylmen that I knowe not; *and* ther is to hem owte of Newe-castyll ordynans ⌐jnowe⌐ bothe for the segys *and* for the feld in cas that ther be ony feld takyn, as I 10 trowe ther sc[h]all none be not yet, for the Scottys kepe no promes. My lord of Warwyk lythe at þe castyll of Warcorthe but iij myle owt of Alne-wyk, *and* he rydyth dayly to all thes castelys for to ou*er*-se the segys, *and* if they want vetaylys ⌐or⌐ ony othyr thyng he is redy for to p*ur*uey it for them to hys power. The Kyng comandyd my lord of Norfolk for to condyth 15 vetalys *and* the ordynans owt of New-castyll on-to Warcorthe castyll to my lord of Warwyk, and so my lord of Norfolk comandyd Syr John Howard, Syr Will*ia*m Peche, Syr Rob*er*t Chamberleyn, Rafe Ascheton, *and* me ⌐and⌐⁴ Calthorp *and* Gorge ⌐and othyr⌐ for to go forthe wy*th* the vytalys *and* ordynans on-to my lord of Warwyk, *and* so we wer wy*th* my 20 lord of Warwyk wy*th* þe ordynans *and* vytalys⁵ yest*er*daye.

---

⁵ *Abbr.* Jun *with the curl that usually represents* er.
320. ¹ *At tape-slit. The name was evidently written on the tape.*
  ² *MS.* brododyr.   ³ *No gap.*
  ⁴ *Interl. above and* othyr *for canc.*   ⁵ as *canc.*

The Kyng lythe at Durham *and* my lord of Norfolk at New-castyll; we haue pepyll j-now her. In cas we abyd her I pray yow p*ur*uey þat I may haue her more mony by Crystmas Evyn at the ferthest, for I may get leue
25 for to send non of my wagyd men home ageyn. No man can get no leue for to go home but if they stell a-wey, *and* if they myth be knowe they schud be scharply ponyschyd. Mak as mery as ye can, for ther is no joperté toward not yet; *and* ther be ony joperté I schall[6] sone send yow word, by the grase of God. I wot well ye haue more tydyngys than we haue her, but
30 thes be trewe tydyngys. Yeluerton *and* Geney ar lek for to[7] be gretly ponyschyd for be-cause they come not hedyr to the Kyng; they ar morkyn well j-now, and so is John Bylyngforthe *and* Thomas[8] Playter, wher-for I am ryth sory. I pray yow let them haue wetyng ther-of, þat the may p*ur*uey ther excuse in hast so that the Kyng may haue knowlage[9] why that
35 they come not to hym in ther one *per*sonys. Let them come or send ther excuse to me in wrytyng, *and* I schall p*ur*uey that the Kyng schall haue knowlage of ther excuse; for I am well aqueyntyd w*yth* my Lord Hastyngys *and* my Lord Dakarys whyche be now gretest a-bowt the Kyngys person, and also I am well aqweyntyd wyth[10] the yonger Mortymer *and* Fererys,
40 Hawte, Harpor, Crowmer, *and* Bosewell of the Kyngys howse.[11]

I pray yow let my grandam ⌐*and* my cosyn Cler¬[12] haue knolage how that ⌐I¬ desyiryd yow to let hem haue knowlage of the tydyngys in thys letyr, for I promysyd for to send them tydyngys. I pray[13] yow let my modyr haue cnowelege howe þat I *and* my felawsc[h]ep *and* your serua*un*tys are at þe
45 wrytyng of þis lettyr in good hell, blesyd be God. I pray ⌐yow¬ let my fadyr haue knowlage of thys lettyr *and* ⌐of¬ the todyr ⌐lettyr¬ þat I sent to my modyr by Felbryggys man, *and* how that I pray bothe hym *and* my modyr lowly of her blyssy*n*gys. I pray yow that ye wole send me some lettyr how ye do, *and*[14] of yow*yr* tydyngys w*yth* yow, for I thynk longe that I her
50 no word fro my modyr *and* yow. I pray yow þat thys byll may recomand me to my systyr Margery *and* to my mastres Jone Gayne *and* to all god mas-tyrys *and* felawys w*yth*-in Castyr. I sent no lettyr ⌐to¬ my fadyr neuyr syn I dep*ar*tyd fro yow, for I kowd get no man to London, *and* neu*er* sythe.

I pray yow in cas ye spek w*yth* my cosyn Margaret Clere recomande me
55 to hyr; and All-mythy God haue yow in hys kepyng. Wretyn at Newcastyll on S*aterday* next aftyr þe Consepsion of Owyr Lady.

Yow*yr* JOHN PASTON the yongest.

I pray yow let Rychard Call se thys lettyr.

---

[6] s- *over* c. [7] to *repeated*. [8] pal *canc*.
[9] ther-of or ellys they be lek to be schent, *and* Sternyng is morkyn a *canc*.
[10] mo *canc*. [11] *Recto ends*.
[12] *Words interlined, with caret, now covered by the binder's mount but legible against strong light.*
[13] *Abbr.* pay *with superior* a, *as again below*. [14] of *canc*.

321. To J OHN P ASTON I   1464, 1 March

Add. 43489, f. 22. $11\frac{1}{2} \times 9\frac{1}{4}$ in. Autograph.

Dorse: Traces of red wax. Address autograph:

To my ryȝte reuerent and worchepfull fadyr John Paston, dwellyng in Castyr, be thys delyueryd.

The date appears from the reference to 'the Duke of Somerset's going' (l. 12). This must refer to his desertion of the King and departure from Wales to Bamburgh at the end of 1463 (Scofield, i. 312–13). He had fled to Scotland also in 1462; but John Paston I was in London in March of that year (see no. 232, address), and John III's letter no. 319 shows that the Duchess was not yet at Holt Castle.

F. i, p. 284. G. 486/560.

Ryth reuerent *and* worchepfull fadyr, I recomand me on-to yow, besechyng yow lowly of youyr blyssyng, desyiryng to her of youyr wellfar *and* prosperyté, the whyche I[1] pray God preserue on-to hys plesans *and* to yowyr hertys desyir; besechyng yow to haue me excusyd þat ye had no wrytyng fro me syth þat I departyd frome ⟨y⟩ow,[2] ⌈for⌉ so God me helpe, I send 5 yow a lettyr to London a-non aftyr Kandylmas by a[3] man ⟨of⟩[2] my lordys and he for-gat to delyuer yt to yow, *and* so he browt to me the lettyr a-yen, and sythe þat tyme I kowd get no messenger tyll now.

As for tydyngys, syche as we haue her I send ⌈yow⌉. My lord[4] and my lady ar in good hele, blyssyd be God, and my lord hathe gret labor *and* cost 10 her in Walys for to tak dyuers gentyll-⌈men⌉ her[5] whyche wer consentyng *and* helpyng on-to þe Dwke of Somersettys goyng; *and*[6] they wer apelyd of othyr se[r]teyn poyntys of treson. *And* thys mater, *and* by-cause the Kyng sent my lord woord to keep[7] thys contré, is cause that my lord terythe her thus longe. And now the Kyng hathe geue my lord power 15 whedyr he wole do execussyon vpon thes gentyllmen or pardon hem, whedyr that hym lyst; *and* as fertheforthe as I kan vndyrstand yet they schall haue grase. *And* as sone as thes men be com in, my lord is porposyd to come to London, whyche ⌈I⌉ supose schall be wyth-in thys fortnyth. The menys namys þat he apechyd ⌈ar thes⌉:[8] John Hanmer *and* Willi*am* 20 hys sone, Roger Pulyston *and* Edward of Madok. These be men of worchepe þat schall come in. The comonys in Lancasher *and* Chescher wer vp to the nombyr of a x m[l] or mor, but now they be downe a-yen, *and* on or ij ⌈of⌉ hem was hedyd in Chestyr as on Saterday last past. Thomas Danyell is her in Chesscher, but I wot not in what plase. He hathe sent 25

---

321. [1] pray *canc.*
[2] *Letters covered by tape.*
[3] fela *canc., followed by a repeated.*
[4] is in goo *canc.*
[5] in Walys *canc.*
[6] of othyr *canc.*
[7] *Second* -e- *inserted later.*
[8] *Interl. above* wyll *canc.*

iij or iiij letyrys to Syr John Howard syn my lord come hedyr. And othyr
tydyngys her we none her but þat I supose ye haue herd be-for.

I supose veryly þat it schall be so⁹ nye Estern er euer my lord come to
London þat I schal not moue come home to yow be-for Estern, wher-for
30 I beseche yow þat ye wole wychesaue that on of youyr men may send a
byll to myn oncyll Clement or to some othyr man, who þat ye wole, in
youyr name, ⌐þat⌐ they may delyuer me the mony tha[t] I am be-hynd of
þis quarter syne Crystmas, *and* for the next qwarter in parte of þat some
þat it plesyd yow to grant me by yer, for by my¹⁰ trowthe the felawchep
35 haue ⌐not⌐ so myche mony as ⌐we⌐ wend to haue had be ryth myche, ⌐for
my lo[r]d hathe had gret cost syn he cam hedyr⌐; wherfor I beseche yow¹¹
that I may haue þis mony at Estern, for I haue borowyd mony þat I must
paye a-yen at¹² Estern.

And I pray to All-myty God haue yow in kepyng. Wretyn in þe castyll
40 of the Holte in Walys the fyrst day of Marche.

     Youyr sone *and* lowly seruant ⌐JOHN⌐¹³ PASTON þe yongest

322. To JOHN PASTON I   Probably 1464, 2 June

Add. 34889, ff. 190ᵛ–191ʳ. 17 × 8¼ in. (unusually written along the length
of the paper, not across). Autograph.

Dorse: Marks of folding, slits for tape, remnants of red wax; no address.

The probable date appears from the reference to a dispute between John Paston I
and Jenney. Paston was convicted of trespass against William Jenney and William
Hogan on 10 September 4 Edward IV (1464) (G. 494/572, iii summarizes a copy
in MS. Add. 27444 f. 134 of a *supersedeas* giving these particulars). The terms used
in the present letter are best suited to the time before the action, when the parties
were seeking support. Paston failed to appear before the county court at Ipswich
on 21 May, 18 June, 16 July, and 13 August 1464 (see G. 494/572, iv).
 G. LX/586.

Ryth reuerent *and* worchepfull fadyr, I recomand me on-to yow, bes[e]ch-
yng yow lowly of youyr blyssyng. Plesit yow to haue knowlage how þat I
haue be in Sowthefolk for syche materys as my cosyn Dawbeney took my
modyr a byll of towchyng the materys be-twyx¹ yow *and* Jenney, and of all
5 the jentylmen that ye wold my modyr schold send to for thys mater ther
ar no more at home bot John Aly[n]gton; *and* I schewyd hym the byll of
the² namys of the jnqwest, *and* [he] knew no more of hem all bot thes:
John Depden, Thomas Wodborne, John Donemowe, Herry Chesten, *and*
Adam Wrene.³ And to all them Aly[n]gton sent a man of hys for to fele

⁹ *No space.*   ¹⁰ th *canc.*   ¹¹ *In margin.*
¹² *MS.* ast.   ¹³ *Interl. above* Jhon *canc.*
322. ¹ Jenney *and canc.*   ² j *canc.*
 ³ *Each name marked off and underlined.*

hem how they wer dysposyd. Thys was the answer of John Depden *and* 10
Thom*a*s Wodborne: they seyd the last tyme they wer at London iche of
ther costys stood hem on x s., *and* they seyd they wold no mor come at
London bot if they knew who schod pay for ther costy*s*; bot me thowt by
Alyngtonys man that they wold haue had a brybe of yow, be-syd þe
payi*ng* for ther issuys, for to haue bedyn at home, for they haue non othyr 15
leuy*ng* but brybys. As for John Donemow *and* Herry Chesten, so that ther
issuys may be payd they wyll not come ther, nor ⌐in⌐trowthe they schall not
come ther; wher-for Aly[n]gton prayith yow þat ther issuys may be payid.
Adam Wrene was not spok to, for ⌐he⌐ is Jenneys baly or hys fermo*ur*. As
for the quest, they are not yet somonyd to aper, *and* but if they be somonyd 20
þer schall non of hem all aper. The most part of the todyr dwell a-bowt
Ippyswyche, *and* they be Debnamys tena*u*ntys *and* Brewsys; *and* I kowd
get no man to spek w*yth* hem but if I schold⁴ haue spok w*yth* hem my-
selue, *and* my spekyng w*yth* hem schold rather apeyryd the mat*er* than
a-mendyd it. 25

And also I hyid me the faster home a-geyn for I lay at my cosyn Loue-
days on Corp*us* Cristi⁵ Day at nyth, *and* he told me that the Duches of
Sofokys consell wold entre in-to Calcot Hall, *and* they wold kep it tyll the
Duches knew who schold be her tena*u*nt, ⌐owthyr ye or Debnam⌐. Thus
told on of the men of the seyd cowncell to Loueday, whyche man schold 30
ryd thedyr w*yth* hem, *and* thys schold be do as to-morow at aftyr non;
bot I trow they wole but tak a distres for the seruys of the man*er* whyche
is dwe, but I haue sent word to Rysyng *and* to the tena*u*ntys that they
schold dryue a-wey ther catell. And as for the man*er*, my brodyr *and* I schall
kepe it so þat they schall not entyr as that ⌐daye⌐, by the grase of God, nor 35
aftyr nowthyr *and* we may knowe of it, but if ye send vs othyr-wys word. As
for the namys that ye wold haue for to pase vpon the mat*er* betwyx⁶ yow
and Hogan, I spak to Aly[n]gton *and* Loueday ther-of,⁷ *and* Loueday seyd
he knew⁸ non þat wold ⌐pas⌐ vp-on ony jnquest for hym, for he medylyd
w*yth* no syche men; *and* Alyngton seyd that he kowd assyne me non men 40
for serteyn, not tyll he had spok w*yth* some, whyche he seyd wold aske gret
leyser for he knew bot fewe in Sofolk—if it had be in Cambryge-schyre he
kowd haue get yow j-nowe. My modyr spak w*yth* old ⌐Banyard of Sibton
Abbey⌐⁹ for the same mat*er*, *and* ⌐he⌐ knew non þat wold pase vpon þe mat*er*
at his desyir, but he asygnyd dyu*er*s men þat loue not ⌐Jeney⌐, whyche he 45
kowd thynk wold pase vpon it at yowr desyir if ye spak w*yth* hem youyr-
selue or at þe lest iche of hem kowd get yow ij or iij men that wold sey as
they wold in cas ye spak w*yth* hem youyr-selue, whoys namys I send yow
in a byll by Loueday.

---

⁴ s- *over* c.   ⁵ *Abbr.* xpi *with stroke above.*
⁶ -e- *crowded in later;* Hog *canc.*   ⁷ *and* they seyd *canc.*
⁸ -n- *over* e.   ⁹ *Interl. above* Banyad *canc.*

50   Item, ⌐as¬ for þe gape at Nakton, Rychard Call seyth ⌐that¬¹⁰ it was a ⌐thorn¬¹¹ busche was leyd in ⌐wyth-owt a stake¬ be-twyx ij thornys þat grew; *and* as for Jeneys net, ther was not on lost her calfe that I¹² can jnquer of.

    And I¹² pray God forther yow in all youyr materys to hys plesans *and* 55 to youyr hertys desyir. Wretyn in hast at Hallysworthe the¹³ Saterday next aftyr Trinité Sonday.

    My cosyn Heueny[n]gham is at London, ⌐and¬ he kowd asygne yow men that wold sey as he wold, mor than Syr John Wy[n]gfeld, Aly[n]gton, *and* all.¹⁴

60   Youyr sone *and* lowly seruant JOHN PASTON þe yongest

323. To MARGARET PASTON   1465, 14 September

Add. 34889, f. 32. 10½ × 4⅝ in. Autograph.

Dorse: Paper seal over red wax and string. Address autograph:

To my mastras Margaret Paston be thys delyueryd in hast at London.

The date appears from Margaret's being in London. John I's letter no. 77 and Margaret's letter no. 192 show that she visited him there in September 1465, and there is no record of any other visit. Connection with no. 192 is confirmed by the reference to Cotton.
    F. iv, p. 224. G. 526/607.

Aftyr all humbyll *and* most dwe recomendacion, as lowly as I can I beseche yow of youyr blyssyng. Plesyt yow to wet þat I haue sent to my fadyr to haue an answer of syche maters as I haue sent to hym for in hast, of whyche materys the grettest of substans is for the maner of Cotton; 5 besechyng yow to remembyr hym of the same mater, þat I may haue an answer in þe most hasty wyse. Also I pray yow that myn ante Poonyngys may be desyiryd to send me an answer of syche materys as sche wotyth of by hym þat schall brynge me an answer of þe mater of Cotton.

    Also, modyr, I beseche yow þat ther may be purueyd some meane þat 10 I myth haue sent me home by þe same mesenger ij peyir hose, j peyir blak *and* an othyr peyir of roset, whyche be redy made for me at the hosers wyth þe crokyd bak next to þe Blak Freyrs gate wyth-in Ludgate; John Pampyng knowyth hym well j-now. I suppose *and* þe blak hose be payid for, he wyll send me þe roset vnpayd for. I beseche yow þat þis ger be not forget, for 15 I haue not an hole hose for to do on. I trowe they schall cost bothe peyr viij s.

¹⁰ *Interl. above* th *canc.*   ¹¹ *Interl. above* thon *canc.*
¹² *Crowded in later.*   ¹³ Fryday *canc.*
¹⁴ *This last sentence in a new line to left of subscription, probably added later.*

My brodyr *and* my sustyr Anne *and* all þe garyson of Heylysdon fare
well, blyssyd be God, *and* recomand hem to yow eue*r*ychon. I pray yow
vysyt þe Rood of Northedor, *and* Seynt Sauyour at Barmonsey amonge
whyll ye abyd in London, and ⌈let⌉ my sustyr Margery goo w*yth* yow to 20
prey to them þ*at* sche may haue a good hosbond or sche com hom ayen.

And now I pray yow send vs some tydyngys as ye wer wonte to comand
me. And the Holy Trinyté haue yow in kepyng, *and* my fayir mastras of
þe Fleet. Wretyn at Norwyche¹ on Holy Rood Daye.

Yo*uyr* sone *and* lowly seru*a*unt J. P A S T O N þe yongest 25

324. To J O H N P A S T O N I   1465, 3 October

Add. 34889, f. 34. 11¾ × 13 in. Autograph.

Dorse: Traces of red wax. Address autograph:

*To my ryth reue*r*end and worchepfull fadyr John Paston be thys delyu*e*ryd.*

The date appears from the account of John III's activities at Cotton. Margaret's
letter no. 192 reports that she entered Cotton on the Sunday before Michaelmas,
i.e. 22 September, and that she left John III in charge of it.

Fenn attributed this letter to 'John Paston, the son', and referred the signature
to one of his facsimile plates reproducing John II's signature from an unspecified
letter. Gairdner was deceived by this into assigning the present letter to John II.
He discovered the mistake, and corrected it in a footnote to his introduction (1901
edn., p. cclxi, 1904, p. 229), but even in the edition of 1904 he allowed the wrong
heading to remain in the text.

F. iv, p. 80. G. 531/613.

Aftyr all humbyll *and* most dwe recomendacion, as lowly as I can I beseche
yow of yo*uyr* blyssyng. Plesyt yow to haue knowlege þ*at*, as on Sonday
next be-for Myhelmas Day, as my modyr came fro London ward sche cam
homward by Cotton; *and* sche sent for me to Heylysdon to come to hyr
thedyr, *and* so I haue ben in the plase eue*r* sethyn. And as sone as Myhel- 5
mas Day was past I be-gane to dystreyne the ten*a*unt*ys and* gadryd some
sylluyr, as myche I trowe as wyll pay for ou*y*r costys, *and* yet I cepe here
ryth a good felawschep, *and* mor wer p*r*omysyd me whyche þ*at*¹ came not
to me, wherby I was ner deseyuyd; for when² Debnam herd sey how þ*at*
I began to gadyr syluyr he reysyd many men w*yth*-in j daye *and* an halfe, 10
to þe nombyr of iij^c men, as I was credebly assartaynyd by a yeman of þe
chambyr of my lordys³ ⌈that co*n*nythe me good wyll, whech⁴⌉ yeman, as

---

323. ¹ þe *canc.*

324. ¹ *This ends a line, and the next and many following lines are marked in the margin by
lines and sometimes in the text by brackets, with some brief Latin notes, very carelessly written,
in the hand of John Paston I.*

² Debnam *canc.*   ³ whyche *canc.*

⁴ whech *in the hand of John Paston I.*

sone as he had sene ther felauschep, rod streyth to my lord *and* jnformyd
hym of it; *and* also he informyd my lord how þat I had gadryd a-nothyr
15 gret felawschep, whyche felawschep he namyd more then we wer by jᶜ
and an halfe *and* yett more. *And* he seyd on-to my lord *and*⁵ my lady *and*
to ther consell þat wy*th*-owt that my lord took a dyreccyon in the mate*r*
that ther wer leek to be do gret harme on bothe ou*y*r pertyes, wheche⁶ wer
a gret dysworchep to my lord, consederyng how þat he takyth vs bothe for
20 hys men *and* so we be knowyn ⸢well⸣ j-now; vpon whyche jnformacion *and*
dysworchep to my lord þat⁷ tweyn of hys men schold debat so ner hym,
contrary to þe Kyng*ys* pese, consedryd of my lord *and* my lady *and* ther
cownsell, my lord sent for me *and* Syr Gylberd Debnam to come to hym
to Framlyngham bothe. *And* as it fortunyd well, my modyr come to⁸ me
25 to Cotton not half an owyr ⸢be⸣-for þat the mesenger cam to me fro my
lord, wheche was late vpon Twysday last past at nyth, *and* the next day
on the mornyng I rod to my lord to Framlyngham, *and* so ded Syr Gylberd
also. *And* as sone as we wer come we wer sent for to come to my lord, *and*
when we came to my lord he desiyryd of vs bothe þat we schold neythyr⁹
30 gadyr no felawschep, but syche men as we had gadryd þat we schold send
hem home a-yen *and* þat the coort schold be contenuyd in-to the tyme
þat my lord, or syche as he wold asyngne, had spok bothe wy*th* yow *and*
Yelue*r*ton *and* Jenney,¹⁰ *and* þat on jndeferent man chosyn by us bothe
schold be assynyd to kep the plase in-to þe tyme þat ye *and* they wer spook
35 wy*th*. And then I answ[er]ed my lord *and* seyd how þat at that tyme I had
my mastyr wy*th*-in þe man*er* of Cotton, whyche was my modyr, *and* in-to
the tyme þat I had spook wy*th* hyr I cowd geue none answer; *and* so my
lord sent Rychard Fulm*er*ston, berer her-of, to my modyr thys day for
an answer, whyche answer he schold bryng to my lord to London, for my
40 lord rod to Londonward as yesterday, *and* þe soner be-cause he trustyd to
haue a good end of þis mate*r* ⸢*and* alle othyr⸣ be-twyx yow, whyche¹¹ he
takyth for a gret worchep to hym ward *and* a gret auantage bothe *and* he
cowd bryng þis mate*r* abowt; for then he wold trust to haue you*y*r seruyse
alle, whyche wer to hym gret tresou*r* and auantage. And þis was the answer
45 þat my modyr¹² and I gaue hym, þat at þe instans of my lord *and* my ladye
we wold do þus myche as for to put þe coort in contenuans *and* no more
to receyue of þe profyt*ys* of þe man*er*¹³ than we had, *and* had dystresid for,
tyll in-to þe tym that sche *and* I had word ayen fro my lord *and* yow if so
wer þat þey wold neythyr mak entreys nor dystreyn the ten*au*ntys nor cepe
50 no coort more then we wold do; *and* ⸢we told Rychard Fulm*er*ston that⸣
thys my modyr *and* I ded at þe jnstans *and* gret request of my lord be-

---

⁵ la *canc.* ⁶ wh *canc.* ⁷ the *canc.*
⁸ se *canc.* ⁹ *MS.* neythythyr.
¹⁰ *and* they þat spe   *and* when þat they spek wy*th canc.*
¹¹ wyche *canc.*   ¹² gaue þat at the i *canc.*   ¹³ ty *canc.*

cause my lord intendyd pes, whyche resonably we wold not be ayenst, *and* yet we seyd we knew well þat we schold haue no thank of yow when ye knew of it *wyth*-owt it wer be-cause we ded it at my lordys jnstans. But be-for thys answer we had receyvyd[14] as myche syluyr full nye as Rychard 55 Calle sent vs bokys of for to gadyr[15] yt bye, *and* as for þe possessyon of þe plase, we told hym þat we wold kepe it, *and*[16] Syr Gylberd agreyd so that Yelu*er*ton *and* Jeney wold do þe same, for it was tyme for hym to sey so for my lord told hym þat he wold set hym fast by the feet ellys to be suyr of hym þat he schold make non jnsurreccions in-to þe tyme þat my lord came 60 ayen fro London. I wene, *and* so dothe my modyr bothe, þat thys appoynt-ment was mad ⌈in good tyme⌉, for I was deseyuyd of bettyr than an c men and an halfe þat I had promyse of to haue come to me when I sent for hem. Thys promes had I be-for þat I sent to yow the last lettyr the daye aftyr Sey*nt* Myhell. Jenney herd sey ow þat I cepyd Cotton, *and* he rod to 65 Nacton *and* ther held a cort *and* receyuyd þe profytys of the man*er*.

I beseche yow þat I may haue knowlage in hast fro yow how ye wyll þat I be demenyd in thys mat*er* and in all othyr, *and* I schall aplye me to fulfyll you*yr* intent in them to ⌈my⌉ power, by the grace of God, whom I beseche haue yow in guydyng *and* sende yow yow*yr* hert*ys* desyir. Wretyn 70 at Hemnalle Halle in Cotton the Thursday next be-for Seynt Feythe.

My modyr recomandyth hyr to yow, *and* preyith yow to hold hyr excusyd that sche wrytyth not to yow at thys tyme for sche may haue no leyser.

The berer her-of schall informe yow whedyr Jeney wyll agré to thys 75 appoy[n]tment or not. I thynk he dar do non othyr wyse.[17]

Yow*yr* sone *and* lowly seruu*nt* JOHN PASTON

325. To JOHN PASTON II   1467, 27 January

Add. 33597, f. 3. $11\frac{3}{8} \times 8\frac{3}{8}$ in. Autograph.

Dorse: Paper seal over red wax and string. Address autograph:

To my mastyr Syr John Paston logyng in Fletstret be thys delyueryd.

The date is after the death of John Paston I in 1466, but apparently not long after. The report of the behaviour of Grey and Burgess connects this letter with no. 326. It is true that they appear again in Margaret's letter no. 200, which is evidently two years later; but the reminder in no. 326 seems to be a direct reference to ll. 26–41 below. 'My lord' who claims lands is the Duke of Norfolk, whose father had claimed Caister in 1461 (see Part II, no. 636) and who afterwards seized it.

G. LXX/659. C. 46.

¹⁴ syl *canc.*   ¹⁵ *No space.*   ¹⁶ De *and incomplete* b *canc.*
¹⁷ *The last two paragraphs written to left of subscription, evidently later.*

Syr, lyekyth it yow to wet þat thys day my modyr sent me your lettyrs, wer-by I vndy[r]stand, blessyd be God, all thyng standyth in good wey. Also I vndyrstand by your lettyr sent to my modyr *and* me þat ye wold haue your lyuelod gadyrd as hastyly as we myght do it. Syr, as to that, *and*

5 othyr folk do no wers ther deuer in gaderyng of othyr manerys then[1] we haue don in Caster, I tryst to God that ye schall not be long vnpayid; for thys day we had in the last comb of barly that eny man owyth in Caster towne, not wyth standyng Hew Awstyn *and* hys men hathe crakyd many a gret woord in the tym þat it hathe ben in gaderyng. *And* twenty comb

10 Hew Awstyns man had don cartyd, redy for to haue led it to Yermowth, *and* ⌜when⌝ I herd ther-of I let slype a sertyn of whelpys, that gaue the cart *and* the barly syche a torn þat it was fayne to tak couert in your bakhous systern at Caster Halle; *and* it was wet wyth-in an owyr aftyr þat it cam hom, *and* is nye redy to mak of ⌜good malt[2] ale, ho ho⌝.[3] William Yeluerton

15 hathe ben at Gwton, *and* hathe set in a new bayly ther *and* hathe dystreynyd the tenauntys, and hathe[4] gen hem day tyll Candyllmas to pay syche mony as he axyth of hem. Also the seyd Yelluerton hathe ben at Saxthorp, *and* hathe dystreynyd the fermour ther *and* takyn of hym swerté to paye hym. And thys day the seyd Yeluerton *and* viij men wyth hym, wyth jakys *and*

20 trossyng dobletys all þe felawshep of hem, wer redy to ryd, *and* on of the sam felawshep told to a man that sye hem all redy þat they shold ryd to tak a dystres in serteyn maners þat wer Syr John Fastolffys. Wher-for I suppose veryly that they be to Gwton *and* Saxthorp, wher-for to-morow I purpose to send Dawbeney thedyr to wet what they do, *and* to comand

25 the[5] tenauntys *and* fermors that they pay no mony to no body bot to yow.[6]

John Grey, othyrwyse callyd John de les Bay,[7] *and* John Burgeys, they be Yeluertons kapteyns, *and* they ryd *and* go dayly, as well in Norwyche as in othyr plasys of yours *and* othyr menys in the contré, in ther trossyng dowbelettys, wyth bombardys *and* kanonys *and* chaseueleyns,[8] *and* do what

30 so euer they wyll in the contré.[9] Ther dar no pore man dy[s]plese theym, for what so euyr they do wyth ther swordys they[10] make it lawe, *and* they tak dystressys owt of menys[11] howsys, horse or catell or what they wyll, thow it be not on that fee that they ask the dwté for. Wher-for me thynkys wyth esy menys ye myth get a preuy seall of the Kyng to be dyrectyd to

35 the meyir of Norwyche, as for the towne of Norwyche, *and* for the contré a-nothyr preué seall dyrect to me ⌜and⌝[12] to som othyr good felaw, ⌜Syr Will[ia]m Calthorp, for he hatyth Grey⌝, for to arest the seyd felaws for

---

325. [1] wh then *canc.*   [2] *MS.* mall.
  [3] *Interl. above* ale *canc.*   [4] h- *over* d.
  [5] the *repeated.*   [6] B *canc.*
  [7] *Name marked off and underlined.*
  [8] -s- *long, written over a partly formed round* s.
  [9] -r- *over* e.   [10] -y *crowded in.*
  [11] *Loop for* -ys *over tail on* n *originally final.*   [12] *Interl. above* or *canc.*

syche ryot, *and* to bryng hem to the next *p*reson ther to abyed w*yth*-owt
bayle[13] tyll syche tym as the Kyng sendyth othyrwyse woord; *and* they
that the pre*ué* sale shall be dyrect to to be chargyd vpon peyne of ther 40
alegeans to execut *þ*e Kyng*ys* comandment. *And* thys done I warant *your*
lyuelod *þ*at my lord delys not w*yth* shall be gadyrd pesybylly. As to *þ*at
lyuelod *þ*at my lord clemys, I schall do my deu*er*, ⸢ou*yr*⸣ logyng kep, to
tak as myche *p*rofyt of it as I may, by the grase of God, whom I pray send
yow the acomplyshement of *y*our hert*ys* desyir, *and* othyr *p*or folys thers. All 45
my felawshep ar mery *and* well at ease, blyssyd be God, *and* recomandyth
hem all on-to yow. Wretyn the Twysday next be-for Kandylmas.

Y*our* brodyr J. P.

I pray yow let me *and* my felawshep not be long w*yth*-owt tydyng*ys* from
yow.[14]   50

326. To John Paston II   1467, 7 February

Add. 34889, f. 56. 11¼ × 6½ in. Autograph.

Dorse: Marks of folding, stitch-holes, traces of red wax; no address.

The date is after the death of John Paston I, and at a time when witnesses were still
being examined during the inquiry before probate of Fastolf's will. John Clerk had
already given evidence, and Bartholomew Ellis was often mentioned, at the exam-
inations held in May 1466 (MS. Add. 27450, abstract in G. 550/639). Probate of the
will was granted to John Paston and Thomas Howes on 26 August 1467 (Magdalen
College, Oxford, Chartae regiae et concessae 50. 8. ii (H.M.C. 4th Report (1874),
p. 458; K. B. McFarlane, 'William Worcester', *Studies presented to Sir Hilary
Jenkinson* (Oxford, 1957), p. 201 n. 5)). This letter must evidently be earlier than
that.
    F. iv, p. 276. G. 569/661.

Syr, it is so *þ*at thys Sate*r*day John Rus sent me word by Robert Botler *þ*at
Willi*a*m Yelu*er*ton hathe ben thys iij dayis in Yermothe for to get new
wytnessys vp to London, *and* it is thowt by the seyd John Rus *and* Robert
Botler ther wytnessyng ⸢is⸣[1] for to proue *þ*at[2] it was S*yr* John F. wyll *þ*at
ther schold be morteysyd iij*c* mark by yer to *þ*e colage, *and* also *þ*at syche 5
astat as my fadyr took[3] her at Cast*er* at Lames next be-for *þ*at S*yr* John
F. dyid was delyu*er*yd to my fadyr to *þ*e intent for to perfo[r]m *þ*e seyd wyll.
Barthol*om*ew Elys, John[4] Appylby, *and* John Clerk ar the[5] wytnessys. And
as for Barthol*om*ew Elys, he is owtlawyd, *and* also men sey in Yermowthe
*þ*at he is bawde be-twyx a clerk of Yermowthe *and* hys owne wyfe. And as 10

---

[13] bayle *marked off and underlined.*   [14] *This postscript vertically in left margin.*
326. [1] *Interl. above* be *canc.*   [2] is *canc.*
    [3] th *canc.*   [4] Appilby, *crowded at edge, canc.*
    [5] wytnj *canc.*

for John Appylby, he is halff frentyk, *and* so take in the towne, not w*yth*-standyng he is an attorny, as Barthol*om*ew Elys is, in the baylys coort of Yermowthe. And as for John Clerk of Gorleston, he is owtlawyd at S*yr* John Fastolfys swte, *and* ⌐at⌐[16] dyu*er*s othyr menys, not w*yth*standyng he
15 is thorow w*yth* S*yr* T. Howys for S*yr* J. F.,[7] for thys cause þat the seyd clerk was on of S*yr* T. Howys last wytnessys ⌐be-for thys⌐. I trow John Loer shall be a-nothyr wyttnesse. As for Barthol*om*ew Elys *and* John Appylby, they lye thys nyht at Blyborowgh onward on her wey to London-ward; ⌐make good weche on hem⌐.
20 I pray yow send vs some good tydyng*ys*. Wretyn the Sater*day* lat at nyght next aftyr Kandylmas Day. I pray yow rememb*yr* John Grey *and* John Burgeys. We haue hom the ⌐most part⌐[18] of yo*ur* barly saue fro Wynt*er*ton, *and* þat I trost to haue þis next wek, or ellys we wyll scrat for it, by the grace of God, whom I beseche mak yow good. I thynk ther
25 comyng vp is for to dysproue yo*ur* wyttnessys þat ye had in-to the Chancery.[9]

J. P.

327. To John Paston II   1467, April

Add. 34889, f. 58. 11½×8½ in. Autograph.

Dorse: Marks of folding and slight soiling, traces of red wax; no address.

The date is after the death of John Paston I and before probate of Fastolf's will, and so in the same year as nos. 325 and 326. The season is soon after Easter (see l. 36); Easter Day in 1467 was 29 March.
    This answers John II's letter about the tourney known from the extract copied by Sandford and given in the headnote to no. 236.
    F. iv, p. 330. G. 573/666. C. 49 (part).

Syr, plesyth yow to weet þat my modyr *and* I comonyd þis day w*yth* Freyr Mowght to vndyrstand what hys seyi*ng* shall be in the coort when he comyth vp to London, wheche is in þis wyse. He seyt*h*[1] at syche tyme as he had shreuyn Master Brakley *and* howsyllyd hym bothe, he let hym wet
5 that he was enformyd by dyu*er*s personys that the seyd Master Brakley owt for to be in gret consyens for syche thyngys as he had doone *and* seyd, *and* causyd my fadyr, whom God asoyle, for to do *and* seye allso, in prouy*ng* of S*yr* John Fastolfys wyll; to whom the seyd Masty*r*[2] Brakley answerd thus agayne: 'I am ryght glad that it comyth to yow in mynd for
10 to meue me w*yth* thys mater in dyschargyng of my consyens ayenst God,'

---

⁶ *Interl. above* of *canc.*   ⁷ for *canc.*
⁸ *Interl. above the same words blotted and canc.*   ⁹ *This last sentence* **added later.**
327. ¹ *Abbr.* sey *and raised* t.   ² *Above* -yr *is the curl usually representing* er.

seyi*ng* ferther-mor to the seyd Freyir Mowght, be the wey þat hys sowle shold to, that the wyll þat my fadyr put in to the coort was as veryly Syr John Fastolfys wyll as it was trew that he shold onys deye.

Thys was seyd on the Sonday, when þe seyd Brakley wend to haue deyid. Then on the Monday he revyvyd³ a-yen *and* was well amendyd⁴ tyll on the Wednysday. And on the Wednysday he sekynd a-yen, sup-posy*ng* to haue dyeyd forthe-w*yth*; and in hys syknes he callyd Freyr Mowght, whyche was⁵ conffessor on-to hym, of hys owne mosyon, sey*ng* on-to hym in thys wyse: 'Syr, ⟨wh⟩er⁶ as of your ⌐owne⌐ mosyon ye meuyd me the last day to tell yow aftyr my consyens of *Syr* John Fastolfys wyll lyek wyse as I knew, *and* now of myn owne mocyon *and* in dyschargy*ng* of my sowle, for I know well þat I may not askape but þat I must dye in hast, wherfor I desyir yow that [ye] wyll report⁷ aftyr my dethe þat I took it vpon my sowle at my dyi*ng* þat that wyll þat John Paston put in to be prouyd was Syr John Fastolfys wyll.' *And* ⌐the seyd Brakley⌐⁸ dyid the same Wednysdaye.

And wher as ye wold haue had Rychard Calle to yow as on Sonday last past, it was thys Twyisday or I had yo*ur* lettyr; and wher as it plesyth yow for to wyshe me at Eltam at the tornay for the good syth þat was ther, by trowththe I had leuer se yow onys in Cast*er* Halle then to se as many ky*ng*gys tornay as myght be betwyx Eltam *and* London.

And, syr, wher as it lyekyth yow to desyir to haue knowlage how þat I haue don w*yth* þe Lady Boleyn, by my feythe I haue don nor spokyn nowght in þat mater, nor not wyll do tyll tyme þat ye com hom, *and* ye com not thys vij yer. Not w*yth*standy*ng*, þe Lady Boleyn was in Norwyche in the week aftyr⁹ Estern, fro the Saterday tyll¹⁰ the Wednysday,¹¹ *and* Heydons wyfe *and* Mastras Alys bothe; *and* I was at Cast*er and* wyst not of it. Hyr men seyd þat she had non othyr erend to the towne but for to sport hyr; bot so God help me I supose þat she wend I wold haue ben in Norwyche for to haue sen hyr dowghtyr.

I beseche yow w*yth* all my hart, hye yow hom, thow ye shold tery but a day; for I promyse yow yo*ur* folk thynk þat ye haue forgetyn hem, *and* the most ⌐part⌐¹² of them must depart at Whytsontyd at the ferthest, they wyll no¹³ lenger abyd.

Your J. PASTON

And as for R. Calle, we can not get half a q*uarter* þe mony þat we pay for þe bare housold, besyd menys wagys. Daube nor I may no mor w*yth*-owt coynage.

---

³ -v- *apparently over* u *in both cases.*   ⁴ th *canc.*   ⁵ hys *canc.*
⁶ *Only parts of* wh *visible, the rest lost at wormhole.*   ⁷ to all folk *canc.*
⁸ *Interl. above* he *canc.*   ⁹ aftyr *repeated.*
¹⁰ tyll *repeated.*   ¹¹ hyr men w *canc.*
¹² *Interl. above* pass *canc.*   ¹³ *No space.*

328. To MARGARET PASTON   Perhaps 1467, about October

Add. 34889, f. 196. 11¾×6¾ in. Autograph.

Dorse: Marks of folding, paper seal over red wax and string; no address.

The precise date does not appear from the contents. Gairdner suggested 1467, on the ground that the two John Pastons are together and in good health, and that John II has not yet sold Beckham, as he did in November 1469 (see no. 246). This seems likely to be right. It is certainly later than John Paston I's death in May 1466, and does not make the impression of being of the same year. In 1468 the brothers were in Flanders (see no. 330). During most of 1469 they seem to have been apart. Margaret's letter no. 199 shows that they were together at any rate in July 1467. If this were the year, the reference to the uncertain relations between the King and the lords would apply to Warwick's growing dissatisfaction with Edward's policies in that year (see for example Scofield, i. 429–35).

There is nothing in the language of the letter that conflicts with this date.

G. LXXIV/673.

Ryght worchepfull modyr, I recomand me on-to yow,[1] lowly besechyng yow of your blyssyng. Plesyt yow to we[t] þat my brodyr and I be in good hele, blyssyd be God, and all ouyr felawshep; and as for me, I tryst to God to ⟨se⟩[2] yow by Halowmes or wyth-in iiij dayis aftyr at the ferthest, at
5 whyche tyme I tryst to fynd þe menys ⟨to⟩[2] dyscharge yow of syche folk as ye kepe of my brodyrs. And þat must I do by myn owne menys, for as for my brodyr, by my trowthe he is not of power to do it; for þis I ensure yow, so God help me, he hathe at thys season not a peny in hys purs nor wotys ⌈not⌉ wher to get eny.
10   And as for Bekham,[3] I warant and ye wyll send the plate whyche ye and I comond of for to helpe to paye hys dettys and for to swe forthe for hys jwgement thys terme, it shall neythyr be morgagyd nor sold. Wherfor, modyr, I and he bothe beseche yow þat ye wyll send hym the plate by Jwdé, or ellys, so God help me, I wot not how he shall do; for by the feythe þat
15 I ow to God he lokyth euery day to be arestyd, and so I wene he shall, so God helpe me. Jwdé had ned to be sped hastyly lest syche arestys falle in the tyme.
    And as for my lord of Norffolk,[4] jt is promysyd me to haue hys good lordshep, but I must tery a whylle,[5] as my lady told yow, for the maners
20 sake.
    And as for tydyngys her, so God help, neythyr the Kyng nor the lordys can as yet vndyrstand no serteynté whedyr they shall go to-gydyr a-yen by the werre or not. When I here þe serteynté I shall send yow word. Ye may send mony by Jwdé for my sustyr Annys hood and for þe tepet of
25 sersenet, viij s. a yerd of damask and v s. for sarsenet; hyr hood wyll take iij quarters.

328. [1] besy canc.   [2] *Letters lost at torn edge.*
   [3] I warant *at end of line,* warant canc.   [4] I trust canc.   [5] -h- *over* y

No mor for lak of leyser; but I pray God send you y*our* hert*ys* desyir *and* othyr pore folys thers.

Y*our* sone *and* humbyll seruant J. P A S T O N

329. To J O H N P A S T O N I I   Probably 1468, March

Add. 33597, f. 4. $11\frac{3}{8} \times 7\frac{1}{8}$ in. Autograph.

Dorse: Paper seal over red wax. Address autograph:

To my mastyr Syr *John Paston, knyght, in Fletstret.*

The date is evidently earlier than the Duke of Norfolk's seizure of Caister in September 1469 (see no. 334). The reference to releases suggests that it is soon after Fastolf's trustees released Caister and other manors to John Paston II; see headnote to no. 200. From the subscription the letter seems to have been written early in Lent; Ash Wednesday in 1468 was 2 March.

G. LXXVII/700.

Syr, &c., jt is so that w*yth*-owght ye haue hasty reparacyon doon at Cas*ter* ye be lyek to haue doubyll cost in hast, for the reyn hathe so moystyd the wallys in many plasys that they may not[1] tylle ⌜the howsys tyll⌝[2] the wallys be reparyd, or ellys ye shall haue doubyll cost for to vntylle y*our* howsys ayen at syche tyme as ye shall amend the wallys; and if it be not do thys 5 yer many of the wallys wyll lye in the moot or longe to. Ye knowe the febyllnesse of the vtter coort[3] of old. John Pampy*ng* hathe had home to Caster as good as x*ml* tylle fro the plase at Yermouthe, and it wer peté that the tyll wer lost, *and* the lenger þat it lythe vnleyd the wers it wyll be. I haue thys day bespok as myche lyme as wyll serue for the tyll, ⌜wherfor⌝[4] 10 I prey you reme*m*byr the cost of the werkmanshep *and* puruey the money by oo mean or othyr, what shefte so euyr ye make.

And for your owne profyte reme*m*byr to goo thorow w*yth* Hwghe of Fen, for by my trowthe ye wyll ellys repent yow or owght longe, for bothe ye shall loose hys good wyll and lett p*ar* auenture[5] that auantage that he 15 myght do yow in y*our* lond recouery*ng*, wher as he may do yow harme *and* he wyll, and then to late wyse.

I*tem*, that ye reme*m*byr y*our* relesys *and* gounys of my lord of Norff*olk* er ye com hom.

I*tem*, I send yow by the berer herof a lettyr ⌜dyrect to yow⌝ that a man 20 of my lord of Oxenfortheys delyuerd me,[6] whych lettyr comyth fro the Kyng.

---

329. [1] haue *canc.*   [2] *Interl. above* in many plasys tyll *canc.*
[3] af *canc.*   [4] *Interl. above* whero *canc.*
[5] hys *canc.*   [6] fro t *canc.*

Item, that ye remembyr in eny wyse to serche for the fyne in syche plasys as my modyr sent yow woord of in a lettyr, for myn oncyll *and* my graunt-
25 dam report that they haue serchyd in all plasys ther as it shold be, but they can not fynd no thyng of it. Also that ye look whedyr the fyne was reryd to eny feoffeys mor then to my grauntfadyr *and* my grauntdam ⌈*and* ther issu⌉, for *and* ther wer eny feoffeys namyd in the fyn it is the bettyr for yow. My lady *and* my grantdam be com to London for the same mater, wherfor
30 it wer well do that the jwgys wer enformyd of your mater befor they spak wyth theym.

I prey yow hye yow hom hastyly *and* se your owne profyt your-sylf. Pampyng *and* I shall clowt vp your howsys as we may wyth the money þat we haue tyll more com, but ye[7] shold do bettyr your-sylf. I prey red thys
35 byll onys on a day tyll ye haue sped thes maters wretyn her-in. Thowe it be to your peyne to labore theym, remembyr your profyt. Nomor, &c., but God kep yow thys Lent fro lollardy of fleshe.

Wretyn at Norwyche the Twysday next aftyr that I depertyd fro yow.

J. P.

330. To Margaret Paston 1468, 8 July

Add. 43491, f. 11. 12¼ × 11¾ in. Autograph; see Plate VIII.

Dorse: Two paper seals over red wax and string. Address autograph:

To my ryght reuerend and worchepfull modyr Margaret Paston, dwellyng at Caster, be thys delyueryd in hast.

The date is fixed by the account of the marriage of Margaret of York, youngest sister of Edward IV, to Charles Duke of Burgundy, which took place in 1468. The Paston brothers went to Bruges in the princess's retinue.

F. ii, p. 2. G. 585/684. C. 50.

Ryth reuerend *and* worchepfull modyr, I recomand me on-to you as humbylly as I can thynk, desyiryng most hertly to her of youyr welfare *and* hertys ese, whyche I pray God send yow as hastyly ⌈as⌉ eny hert can thynk. Plesyt yow to wet þat at the makyng of thys byll my brodyr *and* I
5 *and* all ouyr felawshep wer in good helle, blyssyd be God.

As for the gydyng her in thys contré, it is as worchepfull as all the world can deuyse it, *and* ther wer neuer Englyshe-men had so good cher owt of Inglond that euer I herd of.

As for tydyngys her, but if it be of the fest I can non send yow, sauyng þat
10 my Lady Margaret was maryd on Sonday last past at a towne þat is callyd The Dame, iij myle owt of Brugys, at v of the clok in the mornyng. *And*

---

7 -e *crowded in.*

sche was browt the same day to Bruggys to hyr dener, *and* ther sche was
receyuyd as worchepfully as all the world cowd deuyse, as w*yth* presessyon
w*yth* ladys and lordys best beseyn of eny pepyll that eu*er* I sye or herd of,
and[1] many pagentys wer pleyid in hyr wey in Bryggys to hyr welcomyng, 15
the best þat eu*er* I sye. And the same Sonday my lord the Bastard took
vpon hym[2] to answere xxiiij knyt*ys* ⌐*and* gentylmen⌐ w*yth*-in viij dayis at
jostys of pese; *and* when þat they wer answeryd they xxiiij *and* hym-selue
schold torney w*yth* othyr xxv the next day aftyr, whyche is on Monday next
comy*ng*. And they that haue jostyd w*yth* hym in-to thys day haue ben as 20
rychely beseyn, *and* hym-selue also, as clothe of gold *and* sylk *and* syluyr
and goldsmythys werk[3] myght mak ⌐hem⌐; for of syche ger, *and* gold *and*
perle *and* stonys, they of the Dwkys coort, neythyr gentylmen nor gentylwomen, they want non, for w*yth*-owt þat they[4] haue it by[5] wyshys, by my
trowthe I herd neuyr of so gret plenté as her is.   25

   Thys day my Lord Scalys justyd wyth a lord of thys contré, but nat
w*yth* the Bastard, for ⌐they⌐ mad promyse ⌐at London⌐ that non of them[6]
bothe shold neuer dele w*yth* othyr in armys. But the Bastard was on of the
lordys þat browt the Lord Scalys in-to the feld, *and* of mysfortwne an
horse strake my lord Bastard on the lege, *and* hathe hurt hym so sore that 30
I can thynk he shalbe of no power to acomplyshe vp hys armys, *and* that
is gret peté, for by my trowthe I trow God mad neu*er* a mor worchepfull
knyt.

   And asfor the Dwkys coort, as of lordy[s], ladys, *and* gentylwomen, knyt*ys*,
sqwyirs, *and* gentyllmen, I herd neu*er* of[7] non lyek to it saue Kyng Artourys 35
cort. By my trowthe, I haue no wyt nor reme*m*brans to wryte to yow halfe
the worchep that is her; but þat lakyth, as it comyth to mynd I shall tell
yow when I come home, whyche I tryst to God shalnot be long to; for we
depert owt of Brygys homward on Twysday next comyng, *and* all folk þat
cam w*yth* my lady of Burgoyn owt of Inglond, exept syche as shall abyd 40
her styll w*yth* hyr, whyche I wot well shall be but fewe. We depert the
soner for the Dwk hathe word that the[8] Frenshe Kyng is p*ur*posyd to mak
wer vp-on hym hastyly, *and* that he is w*yth*-in iiij or v dayis jorney of
Brugys; *and* the Dwk rydythe on Twysday next comyng forward to met
w*yth* hym. God ⌐geue⌐ hym good sped, *and* all hys, for by my trowthe they 45
ar the goodlyest felawshep tha[t] eu*er* I cam among, *and* best can behaue
them, *and* most lyek gentyllmen.

   Othyr tydyng*ys* haue we non her, but that the Dwke of Som*er*set ⌐*and*
all hys bend⌐ depertyd welbeseyn owt of Brugys a day be-for that my lady
the Dwches cam thedyr; *and* they sey her that he is to Qwen Margaret þat 50
was, *and*[9] shall no mor come her a-yen no⌐r⌐ be holpyn by the Dwk.

330. [1] may may *canc.*   [2] th *canc.*   [3] mygth *canc.*
  [4] cowd *canc.*   [5] why *canc.*   [6] t- *crowded in.*
  [7] the *canc.*   [8] kyng *canc.*   [9] *Ampersand crowded in.*

No mor, but I beseche yow of youyr blyssyng as lowly as I can, whyche I beseche yow forget not to geue me euery day onys. And, modyr, I beseche yow þat ye wolbe good mastras to my lytyll man, *and* to se þat he go to
55 scole. I sent my cosyn Dawbeney v s. by Callys man for to bye for hym syche ger as he nedyth. And, modyr, I pray yow thys byll may recomand me to my sustyrs bothe, *and* to þe mastyr, my cosyn Dawbeney,[10] Syr Jamys, Syr John Stylle, *and* to pray hym to be good mastyr to lytyll Jak *and* to lerne hym well; *and* I pray yow þat thys byll may recomand me to
60 all youyr folkys *and* my well-wyllers.

And I pray God send yow youyr hertys desyr. Wretyn at Bruggys the Fryday next aftyr Seynt Thomas.

Your sone *and* humbyll seruaunt J. PASTON þe yonger

331. To JOHN PASTON II   1469, 7 April

Add. 34889, f. 75. $11\frac{1}{4} \times 4\frac{1}{4}$ in. Autograph.

Dorse: Traces of red wax. Address autograph:

To master Syr John Paston.

The date appears from the reference to Edward IV's projected visit to Norfolk. He was in Norwich in June 1469 (see John II's letter no. 240).

F. iv, p. 318. G. 602/705.

Syr, I pray yow recomand me to my Lord Scalys good lordshep, *and* to let hym weet þat ⌈in lyek wyse as hys lordshep gaue ⌈me⌉ in comandement⌉ I haue enqweryd what þe gentyllmanys answer was that my lord of Norffolk sent to, to awayte vp-on hym at the Kyngys comyng in-to thys contré.
5 Hys answer was to my lord of Norfolkys messenger ⌈that⌉ he had promysyd my Lord Scalys to awayte vp-on hym at the same seson, *and* in as myche as he had promysyd my Lord Scalys he wold not false hys promesse for no man on lyue. I fond the menys[1] that the seyd gentyllmanys wyfe meuyd hyr husbond wyth the same mater as thow she had axyd hym of hyr awne hed,
10 *and* he[2] told hyr that he had geuyn thys answer. Thys gentylman is Syr W. Calthorp, but I pray yow tell my Lord Scalys that ye vndyrstand not who it is, for he preyid me to be secret ther-in.

I pray wyth all my hart[3] hye how hom in hast, for we thynk longe tyll ye coome. And I pray yow send me woord whedyr ye shall be mad a crysten
15 man or ye com home or nowt. And if so be þat ye send eny man hom hastely,[4] I pray yow send me an hat *and* a bonet by þe[5] same man, *and* let

¹⁰ -y *crowded in.*
331. ¹ that *canc.*   ² gaue h *canc.*   ³ I *canc.*
     ⁴ h- *over* a.   ⁵ *Raised* e *over* t.

hym bry*ng* the hat vp-on hys hed for mysfacyony*ng* of it. I haue ned to bothe, for I may not ryd nor goo owt at þe doorys wy*th* non þat I haue, they be so lewde: a murry bonet *and* a blak or a[6] tawny hat.

And God send yow[7] yo*ur* desyr. Wretyn[8] at Cas*ter* the vij day of Apryll. 20

Your J. PASTON

332. To JOHN PASTON II   1469, May

Add. 34889, f. 77. 13¾×6⅛ in. Autograph.

Dorse: Conclusion of text. Marks of folding, red wax seal over string. No address.

The year appears from the Pastons' fear of action against Caister by the Duke of Norfolk; cf. especially John II's letter no. 238, which also mentions Robert Jackson. Richard Calle's attempt to gain the brothers' approval for his marriage to Margery Paston fits the same period (see e.g. Margaret's letter no. 203).

The season is apparently near Whitsuntide (ll. 36 and 40); the mention of Easter in l. 49 seems to contradict this, but must be a jocular reference to the following year. Whit Sunday in 1469 was 21 May.

F. iv, p. 344. G. 607/710. C 53 (part).

Syr, plesyth it to vndyrstand that I conceyue by yo*ur* lettyr whyche þat ye sent me by Jwdé þat ye haue herd of R. C. labor whyche he makyth by ouyr vngracyous sustyrs assent; but wher as they wryet that ⌈they⌉ haue my good wyll ther-in, sauy*ng* yo*ur* reue*r*ence þey ⌈falsly⌉[1] lye of it, for they neuer spake to me of þat mater, nor non othyr body in ther name. Louell 5 axyd me onys a qwestyon whedyr þat I vndyrstood how it was betwyx R. C. *and* my sustyr. I can[2] thynk þat it was by Callys menys, ⌈for⌉[3] when I axyd hym whedyr C. desyird hym to meue me þat qwestyon or not, he wold haue gotyn it aweye by hu*m*mys *and* by hays. But I wold not so be answeryd, wherfor at þe last he told me þat hys oldest sone desyird hym 10 to spere whedyr þat R. C.[4] wer swyr of hyr or nowt, for he seyd þat he knew a good maryage for hyr. But I wot he lyeyd, for he is hole wy*th* R. Cale in þat mater; wher-for, to þat entent þat he nor they shold pyek no comfort of me, I answerd hym þat *and* my fadyr, whom God asoyle, wer a-lyue *and* had consentyd ther-to, *and* my modyr *and* ye bothe, he 15 shold neu*er* haue my good wyll for to make my sustyr to selle kandyll *and* mustard in Framly[n]gha*m*; *and* þus, wythe mor whyche wer to longe to wryet to you, we dep*ar*tyd.

<hr>

⁶ tawny *canc.*   ⁷ *Superior* r *above* o, *canc.*
⁸ wretyn *repeated.*
332. ¹ *Interl. above same word miswritten and canc.*   ² *Repeated as* kan.
   ³ *Interl. above* fo *but canc.*   ⁴ w *and incomplete* h *canc.*

And wher as it plesythe yow in yo*ur* lettyr to crye me mercy for þat ye
20 sent me not syche ger as I sent yow mony for, I crye yow mercy þat I was
⌜so⌝ lewde to encomber yow w*yth* eny so sympyll a mater, consyderyng the
grette maters *and* weyghty þat ye haue to doo; but need compellyd me, for
in thys contré is no syche stuffe as⁵ I sent⁶ to yow for.

Also, wher as it plesyth yow to send to Rychard Calle to delyuer me monye,
25 so God help me I wyll non axe hym for my-sylfe, nor non had⁷ I of hym,
nor of non othyr man but of myne owne, syne ye depertyd; but þat lytyll
þat I myght for-bere of myn owne I haue delyu*er*yd to Dawbeney for
howsold, *and* payd it for yow in menys wagys. *And* ther-for who eu*er* sendys
yow word þat I haue spent yow eny mony syne ye went hens, they must
30 geue yow an othyr reknyng, sauyng in met *and* drynk, for I eete lyek an
horse of p*ur*pose to eete yow owte at the dorys; but þat nedythe not, for
ye com not w*yth*-in them, whe[r]for, so God help me, the felaushep her
thynkys þat ye haue forgetyn vs alle. Wherfor, *and* eny thyng be ille⁸ rewlyd
when ye come home, wyet it yo*ur*-selfe for defawt of ou*er*-syght.

35 Also I vndyrstand for v*er*ry se[r]teyn, *and* it is sent me so woord owt of
my lordys howse, that thys Pentcost is my lordys consell at Framlyngham,
and they p*ur*pose thys week *and* the next to hold coortys her at Cast*er and*
at all othyr man*er*s þat wer S*yr* John F., p*ur*chasyd of Yellu*er*ton *and* of
S*yr* T. H., whom God asoyle; *and* how that my demenyng shalbe it is to
40 late to send to yow for auyse, wherfo⟨r⟩ *and* I do well I axe no thank *and*
if I do ille I pray yow ley the defawt on ou*yr*⁹ lytyll wyte. But I p*ur*pose
to vse the fyrst poynt of hawkyng, to hold fast *and* I maye; but so God help
me, *and* they myht pulle downe þe howse on ou*yr* hedys I wyet hem not,
whyche I trust to God to kep hem from. For, by God that bowght me, the
45 best erle in Inglond wold not dele so w*yth* my lord *and* my lady as ye do
w*yth*-⌜owt⌝ makyng of some menys ⌜to⌝ them; so God help me, who so
eu*er* auyse yow to do so, he is not yo*ur* frend. And I may, I tryst to God to
se yow a-bowght Mydsom*er* or be-for, for in good feythe I wene ye p*ur*pose
yow þat it shall be Estern er ye come hom; for all yo*ur* seruau*n*tys her wen
50 that ye p*ur*pose no more to dele w*yth* them, but to leue hem her in ostage to
my lord of Norfolk.

A[l]so, syr, I pray yow p*ur*uey what ⌜jne⌝¹⁰ þat my brodyr Edmu[n]d
shall be in, for he losyth sore hys tyme her, I promyse yow. I pray yow send
me word by the next messenger þat comyth, *and* I shall eythyr send hym or
55 bryng hym vp w*yth* me to London.¹¹

---

⁵ ye *canc.*   ⁶ th *canc.*
⁷ h- *over* I.   ⁸ wh *canc.*
⁹ *This abbr., with superior* r, *usually means* 'our' (*as in ll. 3 and 43*), *which written in full is* ouyr (*or* owyr); *but sense here requires* 'over'. *The superior* r *might be a slip for the* -er *curl* (*as in* ouer- *l. 34*), *but since John III often spells such syllables* -yr *it may well be deliberate; cf. no. 333 l. 66.*
¹⁰ *Interl. above* in *canc.*   ¹¹ *Recto ends.*

Also, syr, we pore sanz deners of Cast*er*[12] haue brook iij or iiij stelle
bowys; wherfor we beseche yow, *and* ther be eny maker of steelle bowys
jn London whyche is v*er*ry ku*nn*yn*g*, þat ye ⌈wyll⌉ send me woord,
⌈and⌉ I shall send yow the bowys þat be brokyn, whyche be yo*ur* owne
greet bowe *and* Roberd Jaksonys bowe *and* Johon Pampyn*g*⟨ys⟩[13] bowe. 60
Thes iij haue kast so many caluys þat they shall neu*er* cast qwarellys tyll
they be new mad. I praye yow fynd the menys that my lord may haue
some resonable meane profyrd so þat he *and* my lady may vndrystand that
ye desyir to haue hys good lordshep. I promyse yow jt shall do yow ease,
and yo*ur* tena*u*ntys both. *And* God preserue. 65

J. P.

333. To JOHN PASTON II   1469, June

Add. 34889, ff. 80ᵛ–81ʳ. 11¼ × 16¾ in. Autograph.

Dorse: Marks of folding, paper seal over red wax and string. No address.

The date appears from the report of Edward IV's visit to Norwich. Cf. John II's
letter no. 240.

F. iv, p. 334. G. 612/716.

To begyn, God yeld yow for my hatys.
The Ky*ng* hathe ben in thys contré *and* worchepfully receyuyd in[1]-to
Norwyche, and had ryght good cher *and* gret gyftys in thys contré, wher-
wythe he holdyth hym so well content that he wyll hastyly be her agayn,
and the Qwen allso; ⌈wyth⌉ whom, by my power auyse, ye shall com if so 5
be that the terme be do by þat tym þat she com in-to þis contré. And as for
yowr maters her, so God help me, I haue don as myche as in me was in
laboryn*g* of theym as well to my Lord Reuers as to my Lord Scalys, Syr
John Wydvyll, Thom*as* Wyngfeld, *and* othyr abowt the Ky*ng*. And as for
the Lord Reuers, he seyd to myn oncyll Will*ia*m, Fayirfax, *and* me that he 10
shold meue the Ky*ng* to spek to the two dwkys of Norf*folk and* Suf*folk* that
they shold leue of ther tytyls of syche lond as[2] wer Syr John Fastolff*ys, and*
if so be þat they wold do nowt at the Kyng*ys* reqwest, þat then the Ky*ng*
shold comand theym to do no wast*ys* nor mak non assawtys nor frayis vpon
yow*yr* tena*u*ntys nor plasys tyll syche tym as the lawe hathe determynd 15
w*yth* yow or ayenst yow. þis was seyd by hym the sam day in the morny*ng*
that he depertyd at noon; whedyr he meuyd the Ky*ng* w*yth* it or nowt I
can not seye. Myn oncyll Wyll*ia*m thynkys naye, *and* the same aftyr-none

---

[12] of Cast*er* *repeated, canc.*
[13] *Crowded at edge, but tail below line shows that the -ys loop existed.*
333. [1] *to Norwyche, apparently miswritten, canc.*   [2] is is *canc.*

folowy*ng* I told my Lord Scalys that I had spokyn w*yth* my lord hys fadyr
20 in lyek forme as I haue rehersyd, *and* axyd hym whedyr that my lord hys
fadyr had spokyn to the Ky*ng* or nowt; *and* he gaue me thys answer, ⌐that⌐
whedyr he had spokyn to the Ky*ng* or nowt þat³ the mater shold do well
j-now. Thomas⁴ Wy[n]gfeld told me *and* swore on-to me that when⁵
Brandon meuyd the Ky*ng and* besowght hym to shew my lord fauour in
25 hys maters ayenst yow, that the Ky*ng* ⌐seyd on-to⌐⁶ hym a-yen, 'Brandon,
thow thou can begyll the Dwk of Norffolk, *and* bryng hym abow[t] the
thombe as thow lyst, I let the wet thow shalt not do me so, for I vndyrstand
thy fals dely*ng* well j-now.' And he seyd on-to hym more-ouer that if my
lord of Norffolk left not of hys hold of that mater that Brandon shold
30 repent itt eu*ery* veyn in hys hert; for he told hym that he knew well j-now
that he⁷ myght rewyll my lord of Norffolk as he wold, *and* if my lord dyd
enythy*ng* that wer contrary to hys lawys,⁸ the Ky*ng* told hym he knew well
j-now that it was by no bodys menys but by hys; *and* thus he depertyd fro
the Ky*ng*.
35 Item, as by wordys the Lord Scalys *and* Syr John Wydvyll tak tendyr
y*our* maters mor then the Lord Reuers.
Item, Syr John Wydvyll told me⁹ when he was on horsbak at the Ky*ng*gys
deperty*ng* that the Ky*ng* had comandyd Brandon of p*ur*pose to ryd forthe
fro Norwyche to Lyne for to tak a conclusyon in¹⁰ y*our* mater for yow,¹¹
40 and he bad me þat I shold cast no dowghtys but þat ye shold haue y*our*
entent; *and* so dyd the Lord Scalys also. *And* when þat I preyd them at
eny tyme to shew ther fauor to y*our* mater, they answerd that it was ther
mater as well as y*our*, consydery*ng* the alyans betwyx yow. Comon w*yth*
Jakys Hawt, *and* he shall tell yow what langage was spokyn be-twen the
45 Duk of Suffolkys consell *and* hym *and* me. It is to long to wryght, but I
promyse yow ye ar be-hold to Jakys, for he sparyd not to spek.
Item, the Kyng rod thorow Heylysdon Waren towa[r]d*ys* Walsy[n]gham,
and Thomas¹² Wyngfeld promysyd¹³ me that he wold fy⟨nd⟩¹⁴ the menys
that my lord of Glowsestyr, *and* hym-sylf bothe, shold shew the Ky*ng* the
50 loge þat was broke ⟨down⟩, and also þat they wold tell hym of þe breky*ng*
down of þe plase. Contrary to thys maters *and* all t⟨he⟩ comfort that I had
of my Lord Scalys, Syr John Wydvyll, ⌐and⌐ Thomas Wy[n]gfeld, myn
oncyll Wyll*iam* seythe that ⌐þe⌐¹⁵ Ky*ng* told hym hys owne mowthe when
he had redyn forby the loge in Heylysdon Waren that he supposyd as well
55 þat it myght falle downe by the self as be plukyd downe, for if it had be
plukyd down he seyd þat we myght haue put in ou*yr* byllys of it when¹⁶ hys

jugys sat on the oyeer determyner in Norwyche, he beyng ther.[17] And then myn oncyll seythe how that[18] he answerd the Kyng that ye trustyd to hys good grace that he shold set yow thorow wyth bothe þe dwkys by mene of treté, *and* he seyth þat the Kyng answerd hym[19] that he wold neythyr tret 60 nor spek for yow but for to let the lawe proced; *and* so he seyth that they depertyd. And by my trowthe, *and* my lord Tresorer encorage yow not more then he dyd vs her, ye shall haue but esy help as on þat party; wherfor labor your maters effectually, for by my trowthe it is ned, for, for all ther[20] woordys of plesur, I cannot vndyrstand what ther labor in thys contré hathe 65 don good; wherfor be not ouyr swyft tyll ye be swyr of your lond, but labor sore þe lawe, for by my trowthe tyll that be passyd wyth yow ye get but esy help, as I can vndyrstand.

I had wyth me on day at dener in my modyrs plase, she beyng owt, the Lord Scalys, Syr John Wydvyll, Syr John Haward, Nycolas Howard, John 70 of Parr, Thom*as* Garnet, Fostwe Cheyny,[21] Trussell þe knyghty*s* son, Thom*as* Boleyn, q*ua* propter,[22] Brampton, Bernard, *and* Brom, Perse Howse,[23] W. Tonstale, Lewes de Bretayll, *and* othyr, *and* mad hem good cher so as they held them content.

It*em*, my lord of Norff*olk* gaue Bernard, Broom, nor me no gownys at 75 thys seson, wherfor I awaytyd not on hym; notwythstandyng I ofyrd my seruyse for þat seson to my lady, but it was refusyd, I wot by auyse. Wherfor I p*ur*pose no more to do so. As for Bernard, Barney, Broom, *and* W. Calthorp ar sworn my lord of Glowsetyrs men, but I stand yet at large not wythstandyng my Lord Scalys spak to me to be wyth the Kyng; but I 80 mad no promes so to be, for I told hym þat I was not woorthe a groote wyth-owt yow, *and* therfor I wold mak no promes to no body tyll they had your good wyll fyrst; *and* so we depertyd.

It was told me þat ther was owt a preué seall for yow to attend vpon the Kyng northeward, *and* if it be so I thynk v*er*yly it is do to haue yow fro 85 London be craft, þat ye shold not labor your maters to a conclusyon thys terme but put them [in] delaye. I pray yow p*ur*uey yow on it to be at hom as sone as the terme is doone, for be God I take gret hurt for myn absence in dyuers plasys; and the most part of your men at Cast*er* wyll deperte wythowt abod *and* ye be not at hom wyth-in thys fortnyght. I pray yow 90 bryng hom poynt*ys* *and* lasys of sylk for yow *and* me.

J. P.

---

[16] *MS.* wehn.
[17] *The rest written with a different pen, much blotted and hastier in style. Insignificant corrections are not noted.*
[18] the Kyng *canc.* [19] -y- *over* e. [20] -r *crowded in.*
[21] W. Trusess, *and another partial attempt, canc.*
[22] *These two words marked off and underlined.* [23] *and* othy *canc.*

334. To John Paston II   1469, about 25 September

Add. 34889, f. 94. 8¾×4¾ in. Autograph.

Dorse: Marks of folding, traces of red wax, and stitch-holes. No address.

On a section shown by soiling to have formed part of the outside of the folded letter, in a hand unlike Paston's but unidentified:

Caystre yelded J. P.

Note in John II's hand, cancelled (cf. no. 245, ll. 8–9):

the obligacion of J. Gressham of c mrk lefft wyth Dawbeneye.

The date is fixed by the report of the surrender of Caister. The Duke of Norfolk issued a safe conduct to the surrendered garrison dated at Yarmouth on 26 September (MS. Add. 43489, f. 32: Part II, no. 786; also no. 909).
F. iv, p. 410. G. 628/732. C. 59.

Ryght worchepfull syr, I recomand me on-to yow. And as for the serteynté of the delyuerance of[1] Caster, John Chapman can tell yow how þat we wer enforsyd therto as well as my-sylf. As for John Chapman *and* hys iij felaws, I have purueyd that they be payid iche of them xl s., wyth the mony
5 þat they had of yow *and* Dawbeney, and þat is j-now for the seson that ⌈they⌉ haue don yow seruys. I pray yow geue them ther thank, for by my trowthe they haue as well deseruyd it as eny men þat euer bare lyue; but as for mony, ye ned not to geue hem wyth-owt ye wyll, for they be plesyd wyth ther wagys.
10 Wryttyll promysyd me to send yow the serteynté of the apoyntment. We wer, for lak of vetayll,[2] gonepoudyr, menys hertys, lak of suerté of rescwe, dreuyn ther-to to take apoyntement.

If ye wyll þat I come to yow, send me woord *and* I shall poruey me for to tery wyth yow a ij or iij dayis. By my trowthe, the rewardyng of syche
15 folkys as hathe ben wyth me dwryng the sege hathe putt me in gret danger for the monye.

God preserue yow, *and* I pray yow be of good cher tyll I spek wyth yow; *and* I trust to God to ese your hert in some thynggys.

J. Paston

334. [1] of *repeated* (*in following line*).   [2] -ll *crowded in*.

335. To JOHN PASTON II 1469, 5 October

Add. 34889, f. 97. $11\frac{1}{2} \times 8\frac{3}{8}$ in. Autograph.

Dorse: Paper seal over red wax and string. Address autograph:

To my master Syr John Paston in Flettstret.

The date is evidently soon after the surrender of Caister, for John III seeks instructions for the men who had helped in the defence, and Daubeney is dead (see nos. 205, 334). For the 'evidence of Beckham' cf. nos. 245-6.

F. iv, p. 412. G. 631/735.

Ryght worchepfull s*y*r, I recomand [me] on-to you, prayi*n*g yow that ye wyll in all hast send me word how þat ye wyll þat S*y*r John Styll, John Pampyng, W. Mylsent, Nycolas Mondonet, T. Tomson shall be rwlyd, *and* whedyr þat they shall sek hem newe seruysys or not, ⌐*and* Mathewe⌐¹ *and* Bedford also, for he hathe be w*yth* me þis seso*n and* is fro my modyr. 5 And if so be þat ye wyll haue thes to abyd w*yth* yow, or eny of them, send word whyche þat they be; for² be-twyx thys *and* Halowmas my modyr is agreyd that they shall haue met *and* drynk of hyr for syche a serteyn wekly as my modyr *and* ye *and* I can acord when we met. Notw*yth*standy*n*g, if ye kowd get Barney, or eny of thes seyd folkys whyche þat ye wyll not kepe, 10 eny seruyse in the mene seson it wer more worchep for yow then to put them from yow lyek masterles hondys,³ for by my trowthe they ar as good menys bodys as eny leue, *and* spescyally S*y*r John Stylle *and* John Pampy*n*g. And I wer of power to kepe them, ⌐*and* all thes befor rehersyd⌐, by trowthe they shold neuer depert fro me whyll I leueyd. If ye send me word that I 15 shall come to yow to London for to comon w*yth* yow of eny mater, so God help me I haue neythyr mony to com vp w*yth* nor for to tery w*yth* yow when I am ther but if ye send me some; for by my trowthe thes⁴ werkys haue causyd me to ley owt for yow bettyr then x or xij li. besyd þat mony þat I had of my modyr, whyche is abowt an viij li. God amend defawt*ys*, 20 but þis I warant yow, w*yth*-owt þat it be Mathew whyche ⌐ye⌐ sent woord by John Thressher that ye wold haue to awayt on yow, ther is no man þat was hyryd for the tyme of thys sege that wyll axe yow a peny.

Also I pray yow send downe a comandment to Stutvylle or to some awdytor to take acomptys of Dawbneys byllys, for hys executors ar sore 25 callyd vpon for to admynyst*er* by þe⁵ Byshop, or ellys he seythe that he wyll seqwest*er*. Dawbeney set in hys dett*ys* that ye owt hym xij li. *and* x s. Whedyr it be so or nowt hys byllys of hys owne hand wyll not lye, for he mad hys byllys clere or then the sege cam abowt vs.

---

335. ¹ *In margin, with no reference mark to show where it should be inserted.*
² and *canc.*   ³ b *and part of* y *canc.*
⁴ -s *crowded in.*   ⁵ *repeated as* bythe.

30 · As for the euydence of Bekham, my modyr sent to Calle for hem and he
sent hyr woord that he wold make hys acompt*ys and* delyu*er* the euydence
and all to-gedyr. My modyr hathe sent to hym ayen for hem thys day. If
she sped they shall be sent to yow in all hast, or ellys *and* ye send for me I
shall bryng hem w*yth* me. Send my modyr *and* me word who ye wyll þat
35 haue the rwyll of yo*ur* lyuelod her in thys contré, *and* in[6] what forme þat
it shall be delt w*yth*. I wyll not make me mastyrfast w*yth* my lord of
Norffo*lk* nor w*yth* non othyr tyll I spek w*yth* yow; *and* ye thynk it be to be
don, get me a mastyr.

Dell corteysly w*yth* the Qwen *and* þat felawshep, *and* w*yth* Mastras
40 Anne[7] Hawte for wappys tyll I spek w*yth* yow. Wretyn on Seynt Feythys
Euyn.

                                                                    J. PASTON

I pray yow in all hast possybyll send[8] me answer of eu*er*y thyng in thys
bylle, for it reqweryth hast.
45   My modyr had answer fro Calle er I had wret thys byll, *and* Call seyth
so þat he may haue swerté to saue hym harmeles for the anuyté that he
standyth bownd for, *and* for the oder mony þat he is suerté to pay for
Maryot (I trow it be xv or xvj li.) he wyll delyu*er* the euydense, or ellys
not. He wyll not haue yow bownd,[9] and as for ⌈me⌉ I had leuer he wer
50 hangyd ⌈then⌉[10] to be bond to hym. Send me word how thys mater shall
be handyld, *and* also I pray yow send me tydyng[11] of[12] the Kyng *and* the
lord*ys*, and of yo*ur* mast*er*, how he is in fauor *and* ye w*yth* hym.

By Sent George, I *and* my felawshep stand in fer of my lord of Norffo*lkys*[13] men, for we be thret sore, not w*yth*standy*ng* the saue gardys þat
55 my felawshep haue. As for me, I haue non, nor non of yo*ur* howsold men,[14]
nor non wyll haue; it wer shame to take it.[15]

336. To JOHN PASTON II   1469, after September

Add. 27445, f. 37. 11⅜ × about 6⅜ in. (irregularly torn at foot). Autograph.

Dorse: Marks of rough folding. No seal or address, but stitch-holes (nine
groups of three).

The date is after the surrender of Caister, and after Calle had fallen out of favour
with the Pastons (see especially Margaret's letter no. 205).
    G. 633/737 (abstract).

[6] what *canc.*	[7] hwte *with* h- *over* A, *and* f, *canc.*	[8] *MS.* sent.
[9] *and* w *canc.*	[10] *Interl. above ampersand canc.*	
[11] *An abnormal tail on* g *may be meant to stand for* -ys.		[12] *MS.* or.
[13] not *canc.*	[14] m- *has a superfluous minim.*	
[15] *This paragraph written vertically in left margin.*		

Syr, I recomand me, &c. And as for Maryot, I haue reknyd wy*th* ⌐hym⌐ *and* payid ⌐hym⌐ syche mony that he is owy*ng* but v mark for hys anuyté, *and* all oþ*er* rekny*ng*ys in-to thys owyr; whyche v mark ⌐*and* as myche more as Calle is bond for as for Halowmes paye⌐ is owy*ng* in the same maner of Bekh*a*m, *and* he is agreyid to take it as it may be gadryd. As for 5 the aqwetans of W. Bakton *and* John Maryot, I spak not yet wy*th* Bakton, but I p*ur*pose to do er then I com in Norwyche ayen. As for syche euydens as John Maryot hathe of Bekh*a*m, he wyll delyu*er* them to me when I com to Bekh*a*m, whyche I p*ur*pose to take in my wey homward to Norwyche.

Item, I send yow ⌐closyd her-in⌐ the copye of the condycyon whyche ye 10 be¹ bownd for to John Maryot.

Item, I can not redyly tell yow what ye be endettyd for John Maryot, ⌐wher-for I send yow the copy of the byll of hys dett*ys* closyd her-in⌐.²

Item, as for S*yr* T. Mongomerés man, John Maryot seyth that as for the dett þat he owt ⌐to⌐ Symkyn Symond*ys*, husbond to the same woman that 15 hathe hym condempnyd, he was onys sewyd for it by on Gargraue, mastyr,³ *and* in that mater attorny to the seyd Symkyn, vp-on whyche swte the seyd John Maryot was owtlawyd, of whyche owtlawry he hathe hys chartyr whyche is alowyd not wy*th* standy*ng*, *and* ye can agré for xiij s. iiij d. or for xx s. J. Maryot woll well, but he wyll not passe that in no wyse. 20

Item, in eny wyse remem*b*yr to sew J. Maryott*ys* chartyr for hys last owtlawry for hys det to John Sherman, fyshemonger of Norwyche, or ellys by my trowthe ye do yo*ur*-sylf a shame *and* vndo hym.

Item, as for Rychard Call hathe delyu*er*yd me, as he seythe, all syche wrytyng*ys* as he had of y*our*, sauy*ng* an endentur of lety*ng* of þe maner of 25 Saxthorp whyche is but a jape; but all that he hathe delyu*er*yd me⁴ sauy*ng* a rentall of Snaylewell ar but acomptys *and* byllys of rekny[n]g*ys* wretyn wy*th* hys owne hand, sauy*ng* an old bagge wy*th* as old wryty[n]g*ys* whyche be of no substans. And as I trow he hathe delyu*er*yd me a iiij or v coort rollys of S*yr* J. Fastolff*ys* londys, of hys own hand also, *and* ij or iij rollys 30 of y*our* owne cort*ys* in dyu*er*s plasys.

Item, as for the lety*ng* me haue knowlage of the areragy*s* of yo*ur* lyuelod, he hathe don resonably well hys deuer, as I haue p*ro*uyd.

As for hys abydy*ng*, itt is in Blakborowgh nonry a lytyll fro Lynne, *and* ouyr vnhappy sustyrs also;⁵ and as for hys seruyse, ther shall no man haue 35 it be-for yow *and* ye wyll. I her not spek of non othyr seruys of no lord*ys* þ*a*t he shold be in.

Item, as for Dawbneys executors, I spak not yet wy*th* them for yo*ur* oblygacyon nor for hys byllys, but I p*ur*pose to tak it in my wey homward.

---

336. ¹ bonwnd *canc.*

  ² *Interl. above* but I suppose it may be payid of the same in-to a [*short numeral illegible*] noblys *canc.*

  ³ to th *canc.*   ⁴ is but *canc.*   ⁵ a- *over ampersand.*

40 Item, I send yow ⌐her-in⌐ a copy of the inventory whyche I mad at my
depertyng fro Caster.

Item, I purpose to be at Sporle to-morow or on Thorsday, *and* ther to
se what may be mad of the wood, *and* he þat wyll geue most for it in hand
and of þe ⟨. . .⟩[6] yow woord what þat he wyll geue, *and* tyll I haue answer
45 fro yo⟨w . . .⟩ no percillys[7] *and* ⟨. . .⟩

337. To JOHN PASTON II   1469, December

Add. 34889, f. 98. $11\frac{1}{2} \times 8\frac{1}{8}$ in. Autograph.

Dorse: Traces of red wax. Address autograph:

> *To master Syr John Paston, knyght.*

The date is apparently soon after the Christmas immediately following the siege of
Caister (see especially no. 334).
F. iv, p. 416. G. 636/740 (part).

Ryght worchepfull syr, I recomand me to yow, &c. It is so þat thys day ther
⌐cam⌐ a good felaw to me, whyche may not be dyscoueryd, *and* let me wet
that my lord of Norffolkys consayll hathe thys Crystmas gotyn the two
wydows[1] whoys husbondys wer slayn at þe sege of Caster, *and* haue hem
5 bowndyn in a gret some þat they shall swe a peell ayenst me, *and* syche as
wer ther wyth me wyth-in the plase; *and* they be bownd also þat they shall
relese no man wyth-in the apell namyd tyll syche tyme as my lord of
Norffolk wyll lycence them.

Item, the cawse is thys, as it is told me by dyuers, that ye make no more
10 swte to my lord for your-sylf then ye do, *and* ther-for they do þe wers to
me for your sake.

Item,[2] Sandyr Fastolff was her wyth me thys day, *and* seythe that the
sheryff of Suffolk hathe dystreynd hym for isswys that he lost for Maryottys
mater of Bekham, so that ⌐he⌐ hathe payid x s. *and* must pay othyr x s. at
15 Candylmas, *and* he thynkyth to be sauyd harmeles by yow ayenst Candylmas, *and* to haue recompense ayen of the x s. þat he hathe payid. *And* also
he preyth yow þat he may haue þe mony at that day at the ferthest, for he
thynkyth þat he hathe deserueyd it in othyr maters.

Item, it is also let me wet þat my lord of Norffolk wyll send a man or two
20 in pesybyll wyse for to entre the maner of Gwton, *and* if so be þat they
that be ther ⌐of your men⌐ wyll not auoyd possessyon by them, then to send

---

[6] *The sheet is irregularly torn across, mutilating the last two lines of writing; room for some
40 letters here.*
[7] *Third letter over-written, reading uncertain.*
337. [1] *of canc.*   [2] fa *canc.*

thydyr mor pepyll so þat yo*ur* men shall be of no power to a-byd ther malys. I wyll thydyr my-sylf *and* ned be, *and* kep possessyon as longe as[3] I may.

As for Bekham, Townysend[4] man *and* I wer ther yersterday *and* took 25 possessyon[5] bothe, for lesse suspessyon.

As for yo*ur* gowne, yo*ur* mantyll, crosbowys, *and* yo*ur* Normandy byll, Corby shall bryng hem yow thys week at the ferthest, and I shall send yow my byllys as hastyly as I can ⌐make hem vp⌐, I tryst w*yth*-in thes iiij dayis.

Ite*m*, I pray you labor effectwally for poore Pykry*n*g, berer her-of; hys 30 tryst is all in yow *and* in non othyr man.

Ite*m*, the person of Heynforthe is sore trowblyd by W. Yeluerton for the oblygacyon of viij li. that he is bownd in, whyche viij li. was payid to Call be-for the makyng of the oblygacyon to W. Yelu*er*ton, ⌐*and* he hathe hym at[6] an exigent⌐. 35

Ite*m*, as for my comy*n*g vp to London, so God help me *and* I may chose I com not ther, for *argent me fawlt*, w*yth*-owt a pell or an jnkyr of som specyall mater of yo*ur* cawse it.

Ite*m*, I pray yow reme*m*byr Caleys, for I am put owt of wagys in thys contré. 40

Ite*m*, I pray yow send me some tydy*n*gy*s* how the world gothe, *ad con-fortandu*m *stomacu*m.

Ite*m*, ye must puruey a newe atorny in thys contré as for me, for ou*yr* maters *and* clamore is to gret *and* owr purse *and* wytte to slendyr; but I wyll rubbe on as longe as I maye, bothe w*yth* myn owne *and* othyr menys 45 þat wyll do for me, tyll bettyr pese be.

Wretyn thys Sate*r*daye at Norwyche.

J. P.

338. To John Paston II   1470, 23 January

Add. 34889, f. 120. $11\frac{3}{8} \times 11\frac{3}{4}$ in. Autograph.

Dorse: Traces of red wax. Address autograph:

To my ryght worchepfull brodyr Syr John Paston, knyght, be thys delyueryd.

The date appears from numerous circumstances. It is evidently not long after the loss of Caister—'the place' of l. 63, and it is before no. 342 (the date of which is fixed) because John III here says 'there is no man of us indicted' (l. 62) whereas in no. 342 the indictment has been made. Further, the possibility of negotiations with the Bishop of Winchester about Fastolf's estate (l. 47) must be earlier than the settlement of July 1470 (see no. 252). Yelverton's suit against the parson of Hainford (l. 36) is described in closely similar terms in no. 337. The crossbows and

---

³ Ima *canc.*   ⁴ *At edge; the loop for* -ys *may have been lost.*

⁵ *MS.* possesessyon.   ⁶ *No space.*

other equipment (ll. 39–41) are evidently those referred to in no. 337, and also in
John II's letter no. 248. The year must therefore be 1470.

This was Fenn's dating. Gairdner, working from Fenn's very incomplete and
dislocated text, altered it to 1472. But this is additionally unsuitable because of the
dating on 'the Tuesday next after St. Agnes the first'. 'St Agnes the first' is 21
January; her second feast, called also her Nativity, is exactly a week later, 28 January. In 1472 21 and 28 January fell on Tuesday, and it is incredible that anyone
would date a letter written on 'St. Agnes the second' by reference back to the earlier
feast. (Gairdner took over Fenn's date 23 January, which suits 1470, without
noticing that it does not fit 1472.)

F. iv, p. 420. G. 688/796 (part).

Ryght worchepfull syr, I recomand me to yow in my best wyse. Lyekyth
it yow to wet that, acordy*ng* to yow*yr* desyir[1] in dyuers of y*our* lettyrs sent
on-to me, I haue spook w*yth* Heydon for the deed of Bekh*am* whyche he
hathe; and he answeryth me that John Maryot owyth hym xxx li., *and*
5 at syche tym as he is payid of that mony he seyth he is redy to delyuer the
deed, *and* in-to syche tyme as[2] he ⌈be⌉ payid of þ*at* monye he wyll no deed
delyuer to no man.

It*em*, I haue spook w*yth* Storour, the vndyrsheryff of Norff*olk*, *and* am
acordyd w*yth* hym for all maner of proses a-yenst yow or eny of yo*ur*
10 seru*auntys* tyll the next proses com owt, sauy*ng* for a *fieri facias* is awardyd
owt of the Chekyr vp-on your londy*s* of lviij s. whyche is geuyn to the Blak
Freyrs of Oxenforthe. *And* that haue I fownd swerté *and* am bownd to hym
in v mark that he shall be payid by viij dayis aftyr Kandyllmas.

It*em*, ye must tak good heed that ye *and* yo*ur* ⌈meen⌉[3] may be[4] in swerté
15 w*yth*-owt[5] arest for the forsybyll entré thys terme er eny more proses com
owt ayenst yow or them, or ellys they that ⟨b⟩e[6] in thys contré ar lyek to
be trowblyd hastyly.

It*em*, yerstyrday W. Gornay entryd in-to Saxthorp, *and* ther was ⌈he⌉
ke⟨py⟩*ng* of a coort, *and* had the ten*auntys* attornyd to hym. But er the
20 coort was all doon I cam thedyr, w*yth* a man w*yth* me *and* no more, *and*
ther be-for hym *and* all hys felawchep, Gayne, Bomsted, Hoppys, *and* iij
or iiij mor, I chargyd the ten*auntys* that they shold proced no ferther in
ther coort vp-on peyn þ*at* myght falle of it; *and* they lettyd for a season,
but they sye that I was not abyll to make my pertye good, *and* so they
25 prosedyd forthe. *And* I sye that, *and* set me downe by the stward *and*
blottyd hys book w*yth* my fyngyr as he wrot, so that all the ten*auntys*
afermyd that the coort was enterupte by me as in yow*yr* ryght; *and* I
reqweryd them to record that ther was no pesybyll coort kepet, *and* so they[7]
seyd they wold. W. Gornay *and* I dynyd to-gedyr the same daye, *and* he
30 told me that he had spokyn to yow of the same mater.

338. [1] *I canc.*   [2] *MS. ampersand.*   [3] *Interl. above* man *canc.*
[4] dyschad, *et edge, canc.*   [5] *-t raised.*
[6] *Letters here and below lost at hole.*   [7] *-y crowded in.*

Item, ye must take hed for[8] on Reed swyth dyue*r*s of þe tenauntys of
Gwton for ocupyi*n*g of serteyn lond*ys* in Gwton callyd ⌈Bullys⌉[9] londys,
and he hathe them at an exigent at thys terme, so þat the seyd tenauntys
dar not paye yow nor ocupye non of the seyd lond*ys*, *and* they wer letyn
for xxx s. be yer ⌈*and* more⌉, *and* serteyn barly.   35

Item, the person of Heynforth is swyd[10] by W. Yelue*r*ton, *and* is at an
exygent also for viij li. whyche he payid to Rychard Calle. Ye must se that
he be sauyd harmles, bothe for consyens *and* shame.

Item, I haue thys day delyueryd yo*ur* mantyll, yo*ur* raye gowne, *and* yo*ur*
crosbowys w*yth* telers *and* wyndas, *and* yo*ur* Normandy byll to Korby to   40
bryng w*yth* hym to London. Item, in eny wyse, and ye can, axe the probate
of my fadyrs wyll to be geuyn yow w*yth* the bargayn þat ye make w*yth* my
lord of Cante*r*bery, *and* I can thynk that ye may haue it; *and* as soone as it
is prouyd ye or I may haue a lettyr of mynystracyon vp-on the same *and* a
qwetance of my lord Cardnalle euyn foorthe-w*yth*, *and* thys wer on of the   45
best bargaynys that ye mad thys ij yer, I enswyr yow. *And* he may make
yow a qwetance, or get yow on of the Bysheop of Wynchestyr, for S*yr* John
Fastolfys goodys also; *and* in my reson thys wer lyght to be browght
a-bowght w*yth* the same bargayn. And ye p*ur*pose to bargayn w*yth* hym
ye had need to hye yow, for it is told me that my lord of Norffolk wyl   50
entyr in-to it hastyly, *and* if he so doo it is the wers for yow, *and* it wyll
cawse them to profyr the lesse syluyr.

Item, I pray yow send me some secret tydy*n*gys of the lyklyod of the
world by the next messenger that comyth betwen, that I may be eythyr
myryer or ellys mor sory then I am, *and* also þat I may gwyd me ther-   55
aftyr.

Item, as for S*yr* R. Wyngfeld, I can get no x li. of hym, but he seyth þat
I shall haue the fayirest harneys thatt I can bye in London for syluyr; but
mony can I non get. I can not yet make my pesse w*yth* my lord of Norf*olk*
nor my lady by no meane, yet eu*er*y man tellyth me that my lady seyth   60
passy[n]gly well of me allweys. Notw*yth*standy*n*g I trowe þat they wyll
swe the apell thys term, yet ther is no man of vs jndytyd but if it wer doon
afor the crowners or then we cam owte of þe plase. Ther is now but iij men
in it, *and* the bryggys alwey drawyn.

No mor, but God la*n*t yow, myn her. Wretyn ⌈the⌉ Twysday nex aftyr   65
Sey*n*t Agnet þe fyrst.

J. P.

Thys day Edmu[n]d Reed, sowter of Norwyche, sone *and* heyir to Red
that swyth yo*ur* tenauntys at Gwton, cam to Gwton *and* as to-morow he
p*ur*poseyth to entre Bullys lond*ys*; but I wyll lett hym *and* I can, I tryst   70

---

[8] byf *canc.*   [9] *Interl. above* Redys *canc.*
[10] for *canc.*

to God, who preserue yow. And need be I com to yow, or ellys nowt; *and* all the lord*ys* com [to] London I pray yow recomand [me] to John Leuenthorp *and* Penne *and* all good felaws. Send tydy*ngys* in hast, I pray yow.

339. To John Paston II   1470, 1 March

Add. 34889, ff. 192ᵛ–193ʳ. 11½ × 14 in. Autograph.

Dorse: Marks of folding, only lightly soiled. No seal or address.

In a corner, in John II's hand: *J. P. lett*er. At right angles, in John III's hand: *Pers Ley.*[1]

The date must be soon after 1469, because of the reference to the executors of John Daubeney, who was killed at the siege of Caister. The year is confirmed by comparison with John II's letter no. 248, to which this is an answer.
'My Lady Anne' (l. 28) is William Paston II's wife, Lady Anne Beaufort.
G. LXXXII/741.

Ryght worchepfull syr, I recomand me to yow aftyr þe old maner, sertyfy*ing* yow þ*at* I haue comonyd w*yth* my modyr for y*our* comy*ng* hom, but I can not fynd by hyr þ*at* she wyll depert w*yth* eny syluyr for y*our* cost*ys*, for she *and* hyr cwrate alegge mor pou*er*té then eu*er* wasse.

5   Item, as for y*our* clok at Harcort*ys*, it wyll be nye Est*er*n er it be redy, for ther is stolyn owt of hys chambyr some of the ger þ*at* belongyd therto, *and* þ*at* must haue leyser to be mad ayen.

Item, the caryer forgat y*our* byll behynd hym, but it was delyu*er*yd all to-gedyr;[2] but it shall be browght yow, *and* þe wyndas w*yth* þe teler, by

10   the next caryer, as myn orang*ys* shall com to me, I tryst. Dame Elyzabet Calthorp is a fayir lady *and* longyth for orang*ys*, thow she be not w*yth* chyld.

Item, I pray yow that ⌈ye⌉ wyll make aqwetance on-to[3] the person of Mawtby *and* to John Seyne as executors to John Dawbeney, for they[4] wyll

15   take non admynystracyon of hys good*ys* tyll they be aqwetansyd of you *and* my modyr. Ye maye do it well j-nowgh, so God help me, for I wot well ye owt hym mony *and* he nat yow, if so be þ*at* he wer trewe when he dyid, *and* I wot well we fond hym neuyr ontrew in hys lyue. But hys frendys *and* othyr of the contré putt grett defawt in me þ*at* ther is no-thynk don for

20   hym, seyi*ng* that he myght do no more for vs but lose hys lyfe in y*our* seruyse *and* myn, *and* now he is half forgotyn among vs; wherfor I pray yow let thys be sped.

---

339. [1] *End uncertain, perhaps incomplete.*   [2] Item *canc.*
[3] Jo *canc.*   [4] -y *crowded in.*

Item, as for Doctor Pykenh*a*m, J. Pampy*n*g⁵ can tell yow he is not in Norwyche. When he comyth I shall spek w*yth* hym *and* send yow hys answer. 25

Item, as for myn oncyll Wyll*ia*m, I haue grant to haue a byll of hym what eu*er*y thyng lythe for, but all thyng is not yet in rest ayen þ*a*t was remeuyd for the chyrchy*n*g of my Lady Anne. As sonne as I haue the byll I shall send it yow, *and* hys answer whyche he wyll fyrst haue plegyd owght, *and* also whethyr he p*ur*posyth to do as he seyd by my gr*au*ndamys lond. 30

Item, Gefrey Spyrlyng hathe ofte spokyn to me to send to yow for to vndyrstand how ye wyll deell w*yth* hym for hys place in Norwyche, for he seythe that he had leuer haue y*our* good mastyrshep ther-in then eny othyr manys good lordshep; for *and* ye wyll be hys good mastyr he wyll swe no ferther, or ellys he must. 35

Item, a[s] for⁶ myn old rekny*n*g, I shall make it vp in hast *and* send it yow for y*our* bettyr rem*e*mbrance, for as me thynkyth by y*our* wrytyng ye haue nye forgetyn it; but I am rype j-now in it⁷ for myn owne dyscharge.

Item, I pray yow take in-to y*our* a-ward a short murry jornade of myn whyche Jacobyn, Wyk*y*s woman, hathe, lest that she be flyttyng *and* þat it 40 be exchetyd.

Item, I prey yow send me swyr tydy[n]g*ys* of the world in hast.

As for the Bysheop of Wynchestyr, W. Wyrcetyr told my modyr⁸ that he had takyn charge x dayis or then Pampy*n*g cam hom, but he wenyth that the Byshop wyll be a-yenst yow, in so myche that [he] auysyd my 45 modyr to consell yow that ye shold labor to my lord Cardynall þat þe seyd Byshop shold not be amyttyd to take admynystracyon.

No mor, &c. Wretyn at Norwyche the fyrst daye off Marche.

J. P.

I pray get vs a wyfe somwher, for 'meli*us* est nubere in d*o*m*i*no qu*am* 50 vrere' (c*a*p*i*t*u*lo pr*imo*).⁹

Nouerint vniu*er*sy per pr*esentes* me J. P. ⌈mylit*em*⌉¹⁰ remisisse, &c., Roberto¹¹ Cotteler, p*er*sone eclesie de Mawtby in com*ita*tu Norffolk et Joha*n*ni Seyne de Rollysby in eodem com*ita*tu, executores¹² testam*en*ti *et* ultim*e* voluntatis Joha*n*nis Dawbeney, armyg*er*i, nup*er* defu*n*cti, omni- 55 *m*adas acc*i*ones tam reales, &c., qu*as* v*er*sus eundem Robertu*m* siue Joha*nn*em Seyne h*a*bui, habeo, &c., rac*i*one alicui*us* debyti dicti Joha*n*nis Dawbeney ⌈iam defu*n*cti⌉¹³ mychi dicto J. Paston debite a principio mu*n*di vsq*ue i*n die*m*, &c. In cui*us*, &c. Datu*m*.¹⁴

---

⁵ -ham *canc.*   ⁶ for *repeated.*   ⁷ it *repeated.*
⁸ of *canc.*   ⁹ *Reference marked off and underlined.*
¹⁰ *Interl. above* K *canc.*   ¹¹ *MS.* Roberoto.   ¹² *MS.* executorer.
¹³ *Interl. above* jn cuius &c. *canc., and after* michi debite *also interl. but canc.*
¹⁴ *This Latin draft marked off by a bracket in margin, extended to include the next two lines.*

60 As for the yer of þe Kyng, let it be set in; but[15] as for the daye *and* þe
monyth, let it be owt, for the day must be ⌐aftyr⌐[16] þe probate of the wyll
and the admynistracyon takyng. I pray yow let thys be sped in all hast
possybyll, *and* as[17] for your obligacyon *and* syche ger as belongyth to yow,
I shalbe swyr of it er[18] they haue the aqwetance.

65 It*em*, as for owyr afrayis her, J. Pampy*ng* can tell yow; but and they get
me ye loose a brodyr, *quod iuratum est*. It is good to do by the comandment
of your mastyr. Whyll I am so well boryn owte thys my lord of Norffolkys
galantys send me woord dayly *ad confortandum stomacum*. Ye must spek
w*yth* your mastyr *and* comon some remedye hastyly, or be God I enswyr

70 yow whyll owyr Dwk is thus cherysheid w*yth* the Kyng ye nor I shall not
haue a man vnbetyn or slayn in thys contré, ⌐nor ouyr-sylfe nowthyr, as
well ye as I⌐, *quod iuratum est* onys ayen. The Dwke, the Dwches, *and*
ther consell ar wrothe that ye make no meanys to them your-sylfe.

It*em*, I send yow Townysendys endentwre ⌐by⌐ John Pampyng.

340. To John Paston II — 1470, 14 May

Add. 27445, f. 56. $11\frac{1}{2} \times 6\frac{7}{8}$ in. Autograph.

Dorse: Paper seal over red wax. Address autograph:

To mastyr Syr John Paston, knyght, in hast.

A brief account, in an uncertain hand and partly illegible, scribbled in
top left corner; the first line is 'Wyn pottell ij d.'

The date appears both from Paston's difficulties with Gurney at Saxthorpe, which
recall the events described in no. 338, and from the mention of Gresham's bond
which forms a link with no. 341. The strange Dutch greeting in l. 38 is close to the
form in no. 338, l. 65.

G. 693/801 (dated 1472).

Syr, I recomand me to yow, &c.[1] W. Gorney *and* I ar apoyntyd that ther
⌐shall⌐ no mony be takyn at Saxthorp tyll thys terme be past, for he hathe
promysyd me to spek w*yth* yow *and* your consell *and* þat ye shall tak a wey
be-twyx yow so þat ye shall be bothe plesyd. He had warnyd a coort at

5 Saxthorp[2] to haue be kep vpon Holy Rood Day last past, *and* ther he wold
haue gadyrd the half yer ferm; but it fortunyd me to be ther er the coort
was half don, *and* I took syche a wey w*yth* hym that the qwest gaue no
verdyt, ner they procedyd no ferther in ther cort nor gadyrd no mony
ther, nor not shall do tyll syche tym as ye spek to-gedyr *and* ye be at

---

[15] *and for canc.*   [16] *Interl. apparently above the same word miswritten.*
[17] *MS. af.*   [18] *No space.*
340. [1] *gorne canc.*   [2] *Ampersand canc.*

London thys term. ⌜But⌝ *and* ye be not at London I wold auyse yow to 10
let Townysend tak a wey w*yth* hym, for it lyeth not in my power
to keep werr w*yth* hym; for *and* I had not delt ryght corteysly vp-on Holy
Rood Day I had drownk to myn oystyrs, for yowng Heydon had reysyd
as many men as he kowd mak in harneys to haue holp Gornay, but when
Heydon sye þat we delt so corteysly as we ded he w*yth*drew hys men *and* 15
mad hem to go hom a-yen. Not w*yth*-standyng they wer redy *and* ned had
be, *and* also my lord of Norffolkys men wyll be w*yth* hym ayenst ⌜me⌝, I
wot well as yet, tyl bettyr pesse be.

Item, as for myn ownkyll Will*iam*, I haue spook w*yth* hym *and* he seyth
þat he wyll make a byll in all hast of iche percell be-twyxt yow, *and* send 20
yow word in wryghty*n*g how that he wooll deell w*yth* yow; but I can not
se þat he besyth hym a-bowght it not w*yth*standy*n*g I call vpon hym dayly
for it.

As for mony, I can non get neythyr at Snaylewell nor at Sporle tyll
Mydsomer, thow I wold dryue all the³ catell ⌜they⌝⁴ haue. I ⌜was⌝⁵ bond 25
to the shreuys for grenwax *and* for a *fyeri facias* þat is awardyd owt of
yow*yr* lond⁶ wyche drawyth in all bettyr than v mark, *and* I am fayn to
borow the mony to pay it, by þat Lord I beleue on, for I cowd not gadyr
a nobyll of areragys syn I was w*yth* yow at London of all the lyuelod
ye haue. 30

As for John⁷ Maryot, he is payid of hys anuyté in-to a nobyll or x s. at
the most but, as for all hys dettors, I can not pay hem tyll I can gadyr more
mony, so God help me. I pray ⌜yow⌝ send a byll to John Pampy*n*g that ⌜he⌝
may ryed w*yth* me ouyr all yo*ur* lyuelood *and* take a cler rekny*n*g what is
owy*n*g *and* what þat I haue receyuyd, that ye may haue a cler rekny*n*g of 35
all that ye owe in thys contré *and* what yo*ur* tenauntys owe yow.

Item, I pray yow send me woord as hastyly as ye can how the⁸ world
goothe. No more, but God lant yow, lansman; *and* rather then to stand in
dowght reme*m*byr what peyn it is a man to loose lyberté. The Flet is a
fayir preson, but ye had but smale lyberté ther-in, for ye must nedys aper 40
when ye wer callyd.

Item, I haue fownd Jamys Greshamys oblygacyon. It*em*, he comyth to
London ward thys day. Wretyn þe xiiij day of Maye.

J. P.

---

³ *Written* they, -y *canc.*   ⁴ *Interl. above* I *canc.*
⁵ *Interl. above* am *canc.*   ⁶ if *canc.*
⁷ Maryett *canc.*   ⁸ we *written and not canc.*

341. To John Paston II   1470, 25 May

Add. 27445, f. 57. $11\frac{1}{2} \times 8\frac{3}{8}$ in. Autograph.

Dorse: Marks of folding and soiling, no seal or address. In a hand evidently
John II's, *John Paston.*

The date must be after the loss of Caister. John Milsent, who is referred to (l. 38),
was killed at the battle of Barnet in April 1471 (see John II's letter no. 261). 1470
is therefore the only possible year.
G. 694/802 (dated 1472).

Ryght worche[p]full syr, I recomand me to yow, sertyfyi*ng* yow þat I was
p*ur*posyd to haue com to London to haue mad my pese w*yth* my lady of
Norf*f*olk, but I vndyrstand she is not in London. Notw*yth*standy*ng* that
is no cause of my*n* abydy*ng*[1] at hom, but thys is the cause, so God help me:
5 I can get no mony, neythyr of y*our* lyuelod ner of myn, to pay for my
cost*ys* nor for to ease yow w*yth* at my comy*ng*. Not w*yth*standy*ng* I am
promysyd som at Snaylewell, *and* if so be þat John can take eny ther he
shall bryng it yow w*yth* þis byll. I send yow her ij of my rekny*ng*gys that I
haue rec*eyuyd and* payd syn I delt w*yth* yow*yr* lyuelod, *and* by thes ij *and*
10 by þat rekny*ng* þat I sent yow to London ye may know what is rec*eyuyd*
by me, *and* what I haue payid *and* howgh; *and* when so euyr ye wyll let
y*our* tenaunt*ys and* fermo*ur*s at all plasys be examynd,[2] ye shall fynd it non
othyr-wyse. So God help me, as y*our* lyuelod is payid it can not paye y*our*
dett*ys* in thys contré, for it drawyth vp-on a x li. that ye owe yet in thys
15 contré ⌐besyd the xij li. to Dawbney¬, *and* wyth-in thes vij dayis I shall
send yow a cler byll what ye owe, for ther ar axyid many thyng*ys* þat I
knewe not of when I was w*yth* yow.
   Also I enswyr yow by my trowthe I saw my modyr neuyr sorer meuyd
w*yth* no mater in hyr lyue then she was when she red the byll that ye gaue
20 me warny*ng* in that Perker had atamyd an axyon ayenst yow *and* me, for
she supposyth v*er*yly þat it is doon by my*n* oncyll Will*i*am meanys, to
make yow to sell your lond. But thys she comandyd me for to send yow
⌐word¬, that *and* ye sell eny lond but paye y*our* dett*ys* wyth syche good as
my lord Archebyshop owyth yow, and eny law in Inglond can put fro yow
25 eny of hyr lond she sweryth by þat feyth that she owyth to God she wyll
put fro yow dobyll as myche lond as ye selle. *And* ther-for I wold auyse
yow call sharply vpon my lord þe Archebyshop, for ye ar not bond to vndo
y*our*-sylf for hym.
   Item, I pray yow se þat I tak no hurt by Parker. As for my*n* oncyll W.,
30 I can not mak hym to send yow the byll of syche stuff as he hathe of yow*yr*.
He seythe he woll, but he comyth no[t] of w*yth* it. He *and* I ar fowly fallyn

341. [1] *Altered from* my bydyng; *-n repr. by abbreviating stroke, a crowded in.*
   [2] *Ampersand canc.*

owght thys same day for a mater betwyx Louell *and* John Wallsam *and* hyr sustyr. Louell hathe bowt Jone Walshamys part of hyr lyuelod *and* maryd hyr to a knaue, *and* myn oncyll W. hath oft spok w*yth* my modyr *and* me for to delyuer Jone Walsh*a*mys euydence to Louell whyche[3] I haue in 35 kepy*ng*; *and* be-cause I wyll not delyuer Louell the euydence therfor we fyll[4] owt, in so myche þ*at* he seyth he wyll stryp me fro the maner of Sweynstho[r]p. Wherfor I pray yow in eny wyse send me ⌐by John Myl-sent¬ a copye of the deed that I sent yow to London. Ther is in the same deed Gresh*a*m *and* Snaylewell *and* Sporle *and* Sweynsthorp all to-gedyr, I 40 trow; ⌐*and*¬ I prey yow let the date *and* the feoffeys namys *and* all be set in. *And* ⌐I¬ trust to God to mak[4] yt so sewyr that he shall do me lytyll harm.

Gefrey Spyrly*ng* cally*th* oft vpon me to vndyrstand how ye wyll dell w*yth* hym for hys plase in Norwyche. I pray you send me woord by John 45 what answer I may geue hym. He dely*th* alwey ryght frendly w*yth* yow.

It*em*, I send yow her-wyth Jamys Gresh*a*mys oblygacyon.

It*em*, I pray yow send serteyn woord how þe world gothe.

Wretyn þe xxv day of May.

J. P.[5] 50

342. To John Paston II 1470, 22 June

Add. 34889, f. 101. 11¼ × 10½ in. Autograph.

Dorse: Paper seal over red wax and string. Address autograph:

To Syr John Paston, knyght, or to Thomas Stompys to delyuer to þe seyd
Syr John.

The date is fixed by the reference to fighting at Caister in the preceding August (cf. no. 334).

F. iv, p. 428. G. 641/746.

Ryght worchepfull syr *and* my specyall good brodyr, I recomand me to[1] yow. And for as myche as I can not send yow good tydy[n]g*ys*, ye shall haue syche as I knowe. It is so þ*at* on Wednysday last past ye *and* J.[2] Pam-py*ng and* Edmu[n]d Broom wer endyttyd of felonye at the sessyons her in Norwyche for shoty*ng* of a gonne at Caster in August last past, whyche 5 goone slowghe two men: J. Pampy*ng and* Broom as pryncypall *and* ye ⌐as¬ accessary. Notw*yth*standy*ng* Townysend *and* Lomnor hold an oppynyon that the v*er*dytt is voyd, for ther wer ij of th'enqwest that wold not agré to th'endyttment, *and* in as myche as they ij wer agreyd in othyr maters

---

³ my modyr *and canc.* ⁴ *No space.*

⁵ *Last line and initials vertically in margin.*

342. ¹ *to repeated.* ² *Written over another letter, and much obscured.*

10 *and* not in that, *and* that they two wer not dyschargyd[3] fro the remnant at
syche tym as that verdyth of yowyr endytment was gouyn, ther oppynyon
is that all the verdyght is voyde, as well of all othyr maters as of yowyr.
Whedyr ther opynyon be good or not I can not determyne, nor them-sylf
neythyr. I pray yow let not thys mater be slept, for I can thynk that my
15 lord of Norffolkys consaylle wyll cawse the wedows to tak an apell and to
remeue it vp in-to the Kyngys Benche at the begynyng of thys term.
Townysend hathe promysyd me that he shall be at London on Twysday
next comyng, *and* then ye may comon wyth hym in that mater *and* take
hys auyse.

20 Item, Townysend *and* Lomnor thynk that *and* ye haue good consayll ye
may justyfye the kepyng of the plase for the pesybyll possessyon that ye
haue had in it mor then iij yeer. But in conclusyon all thys is doo for nowght
ellys but for to enforse yow to take a dyreccyon wyth my lord of Norffolk,
I vndyr-stood by R. Sothewell, for he *and* I comonyd in thys mater ryght
25 largely betwyx hym *and* me; in so myche he tellyth me that *and* I be at
London in the week next aftyr Seynt Petyr,[4] at whyche tyme he shall be
ther hym-sylff, he seyth þat my lady hathe promysyd me hyr good ladyshep
and sent me woord by hym, in as myche as he spak for me to hyr, that she
wold remembyr myn old seruyse *and* for-get the gret dysplesyr, in syche
30 wyse that I shall vndyrstand that the swtte þat I haue mad to my lord hyr
husbond *and* hyr shall torne to your auantage, *and* myn bothe, more then
we weene as yett or shall vndyrstand tyll syche tyme as I haue spokyn
wyth hyr good grace. *And* vpon thys promesse I haue promysyd[5] Sothewell to meet wyth hym at London that same week next aftyr Seynt Petyr;
35 wherfor I wold passyngly fayne þat ye wer in London at þat season, or nye
abowght London, so that I myght vndyr-stand at your plase wher þat I
myght spek wyth yow or then I spek wyth my lady.

I purpose to go to Canterbery on foot thys next week, wyth Goddys
grace, *and* so ⌐to⌐ com to London fro thense. I pray yow se þat I be safe for
40 Parker *and* Herry Colettys mater. Sothewell told me thys, that if so be þat
ye wyll your-sylff, ye shall haue bothe good lordshep *and* ladyshep *and*
mony or lond or both, *and* all your maters[6] set cler. What þat he menyth I can
not sey.

As for all othyr maters in thys contré, I shall do as well as I[7] may, for
45 fawt of monye, ⌐tyll I spek wyth yow⌐. I haue many callers on, as I shall
tell yow when I come.

No more, bot God preserue yow *and* your. Wretyn at Norwyche Fryday
next afftyr Corpus Cristi[8] Daye.   J. P.

I ded as myche as I kowd to haue lettyd th'endyttment, but it wold not be,
50 as I shall enform yow; *and* Townysend knowyth the same.

---

[3] at *canc.*   [4] he seythe þat *canc.*   [5] sy *canc.*
[6] -s *added later.*   [7] *Crowded in.*   [8] *Abbr.* xpi *with dotted circumflex.*

343. To John Paston II   1470, 25 June

Add. 34889, f. 102. 11⅛×7¼ in. Autograph.

Dorse: Paper seal over green wax and tape. Address autograph:

To Syr John Paston, knyght, or to Thomas Stomppys to delyuer to the seyd
Syr John.

The date appears from the similarity of the opening to that of no. 342.
    F. iv, p. 434. G. 642/747.

As I sent yow woord by a lettyr that John Wymondham browght to London, J. Pampyng is endyghtyd ⌐of felony⌐, *and* Edmu[n]d Broom as
principallys, and ye as axcessary, for schotyng of a gonne in Awgust last
past, whyche gonne kyllyd ij men; *and* I trowe that my lord of Norffolkys
consayll wyll¹ make on of the wedows, or bothe, to swe an apell vp-on the 5
same endyghtment thys terme. Wherfor I pray yow se well to thys mater,
that when it is sertyfyid in-to the Kyngys Benche, Broom *and* Pampyng
may haue warnyng that they may puruey for hem-self ⌐if¹²⌐ ther com eny
capyas owght for hem. Townysend can tell yow all the mater.
    Also ye must in eny wyse be ware, for my grauntdam *and* myn Lady 10
Anne *and* myn oncyll Wylliam shall be at London wyth-in thes viij or x
dayis, and I wot well it is for nowght ellys but to make myn oncyll William
swyr of hyr lond. Notwythstandyng, she hath reryd a fyn of it be-for
Goodreed³ the justyse in my grauntfadyrs dayis, and my modyr tellyth
me that ye⁴ haue the copye of the same fyne. I wold auyse yow to haue it 15
redy, what so euyr betyd. I trow they wyll be the more besy abowght the
same mater be-cause they thynk that ye dar not com in London nor at
Westmestyr to lett them. But if so be þat ye haue not the copy of the same
fynne, look that ye spare for no cost to do serche for itt, for it wyll stand
yow on hand, I feell by the werkyng.   20
    Thys day seuennyght I trust to God to be forward to Caunterbery at
the ferthest, and vp-on Saterday com seuennygh[t] I tryst to be in London,
wherfor I pray yow leue woord at yowyr plase in Fleetstrett wher I shall
fynd yow, for I purpose not to be seyn in London tyll I haue spook wyth
yow.   25
    I pray yow remembyr thes maters, for all is doon to make yow to drawe
to an ende wyth thes lordys that haue your lond fro yow.
    No more, but I pray⁵ God send yow your herttys desyir in thees maters
and in all othyr. Wretyn at Norwyche the Monday next aftyr⁶ Seynt John
Baptyst.   30

                                                                        J. P.

343. ¹ ta *canc.*   ² *Interl. above ampersand canc.*
    ³ *Name marked off and underlined.*   ⁴ hame *canc.*
    ⁵ yow *canc.*   ⁶ sy *canc.*

344. Declaration concerning the Fastolf estate

1470, 27 August

Magdalen College, Oxford, Norfolk and Suffolk 4. Parchment, $13\frac{5}{8} \times 10\frac{1}{4}$ in. Clerk's hand, unidentified, appearing also in nos. 252, 254 (John II); signature autograph.

Dorse blank. Pendant seal of red wax.

G. 652/757 (abstract).

Be it knowen by thies presentez that where the right reuerend fader in God William Wayneflete, Bisshop of Wynchestre, oone of þe feoffés of Ser John Fastolf, knyght, and also oon of th'executoures of the testament of the same Ser John Fastolf, now sole hathe taken vpon hym th'execucion of þe
5 same testament, and also to parfourme þe wille of þe said Ser John as far-forthe as it may be parfourmed of suche maners, londes, and tenementez in þe counteez of Surré, Essexe, Norfolk and Suffolk and in the citee of Nor-wich, and of suche goodez of the said Ser John Fastolf ⌜which⌝ may be obteyned and cum to þe hondys of þe said reuerend fader, I, John Paston,
10 sqvyer, son of John Paston, sqwyer, which John Paston my fader was also named oone of þe feofféz of þe said Ser John Fastolf and oone of th'exe-cutoures of his testament, remembryng the grete busynesse and trowble which my said fader had in his dayes bothe with þe maners, londes, tene-mentez, and goodez of þe said Ser John Fastolf which haue beene wasted,
15 expended, and deuowred, the will of þe same Ser John in many parties and most substaunce thereof nott yet[1] parfouremed, trustyng by the grace of God that þe said reuerend fader wol doo his effectuall deuoure to þe verry parfouremyng therof in discharge of þe sowle of my fader aforesaid, and for that þe said reuerend fadere hathe rewarded me to shew my verry
20 gode will to my power to þe full parfouremyng of þe will of þe said Ser John Fastolf, promytt by my trouthe and faithe which I owe to Almyghty God, and also bynd me by thiese presentez, to doo trwe and faithfull seruyce vnto þe said reuerend fader, and to be aydyng and assistyng to þe said reuerend fader, his heyres and executoures, and to his college of Saynt
25 Marye Mawdeleyne sett withoute þe est gate of Oxon., and to all officers, stiwardes, receyuoures, bailliez, and other minystrers, fermers, and[2] ten-auntez of þe said reuerend fader, his heirs and executoures, or of þe said college and theire successoures, or of any other personez or persone hauyng any thynge to th'use of the said reuerend fader, his heires or executours, or
3⟩ to th'use of þe said college or theire successoures, in any of the said maners, londes, and tenementez, so that þe said maners, londes, and tenementez, ind euery parcell of them, shal now be occupied and leten to theire grettest

344. [1] *MS.* þet.   [2] *From* minystrers *on eras.*

562

profitt and þe rentez and commoditeez of the same truly and dwly gedered and com to þe handys of þe same reuerend fadere, his heirs *and* executours, and to þe handys of þe ministres of þe said college for þe tyme beyng or to 35 þe hondis of such persones or persone as the same reuerend fader wol thereto assigne accordynge to the prouysion and ordynaunce of þe same reuerend fader made or to be made in that behalf. And forthermore I, the said John Paston, vpon my said trouthe and faithe promytt and bynd me by thies presentez to delyuere to þe said reuerend fader, before þe feste of 40 All Sayntez next foloyng aftere þe date of these presentez, all maner of chartres, dedes, euydencez, munimentez, court rollez, rentallez, *and* rollez of accomptes, skrowes, writyngez, and copiez concernyng or specifiyng any of þe said maners, londes, *and* tenementez which I, þe said John Paston, or any persone to my vse now haue; alway foreseen that þis promyss 45 extende nott to delyuerance of any chartres, dedes, euydencez, muny-mentez, court rollez, rentallez, rollez of accomptes, or copiez of them con-cernyng sooly þe maner of Castre with th'appurtenauncez, which by couenant made betwene the said reuerend fader and Ser John Paston, knyght, brother of me the said John Paston, sqwyer, most remayne with 50 the same Ser John[3] Paston. And if att any tyme aftir þe said fest of All Sayntez any dedes, chartres, munymentez, court[4] rollez, rentallez, rollez of accomptez, or copyez, other than soolly concernyng þe maner of Castre with th'appurtenauncez as aboue, com to the hondys of me þe said John Paston, or of any other to myne vse, I faithfully promytt and bynde me by 55 thies presentez to make of þem delyuerance to þe said reuerend fader in all conuenyent hast after thay so com to my hondis.

In witnesse whereof to thiese presentez I putt to my seale. Yeuen att Esshher the xxvij^the daye of August the x^the yere of þe reigne of Kyng Edward the iiij^the. 60

J. PASTON

345. To MARGARET PASTON 1470, 12 October

Add. 43489, f. 40. 11¾×8¼ in. Autograph.

Dorse: Paper seal over red wax and tape. Address autograph:

To my ryght worchepful¹ modyr Margaret Paston by thys delyuerd.

The date is in the midst of the upheaval accompanying the restoration of Henry VI in 1470; he was recrowned on 13 October. The Earl of Worcester was executed on 18 October (Scofield, i. 542, 546–7). 'St. Edward's Eve' is the eve of the Translation of Edward the Confessor, 13 October.

F. ii, p. 50. G. 654/759.

³ *Small erasure.*   ⁴ *r flourished in error.*
345. ¹ *Fold. by a patch.*

Aftyr humbyll *and* most dew recomendacyon, as lowly as I can I beseche yow of y*our* blyssyng. Plesyt yow to wet þat, blyssyd be God, my brodyr *and* ⌈I⌉ be in good hele, *and* I tryst that we shall do ryght well in² all owyr maters hastyly, for my lady of Norffolk hathe promysyd to be rewlyd by
5 my lord of Oxynforthe in all syche maters as belonge to my brodyr *and* to me. *And* as for my lord of Oxynforth, he is bettyr lord to me, by my trowthe, then I can wyshe hym in many maters, for he sent to my lady of Norffolk by John Bernard only for my mater *and* for non othyr cawse, my*n* onwetyng ⌈or wythowt eny preyer of me⌉, for when he sent to hyr I was at London
10 *and* he at Colchestyr, *and* þat is a lyeklyod he remembyrthe me. The Dwk *and* the Dwchess swe to hym as humbylly as euyr I dyd to them, in so myche that my lord of Oxynforth shall haue the rwyll of them *and* thers by ther owne desyirs *and* gret meanys.

As for the ofyceys that ye wrot to my brodyr for, *and* to me, they be for
15 no poore men; but I tryst we shall sped of othyr ofyseys metly for vs, for my mastyr the Erle of Oxynforthe bydyth me axe *and* haue. I trow my brodyr S*yr* John shall haue the constabyllshep of Norwyche Castyll w*yth* xx li. of fee; all the lordys be agreyd to it.

Tydyng*ys*, the Erle of Wyrcestyr is lyek to dye þis day, or to-morow at
20 the ferthest. John Pylkyngton, M*astyr* W. Attclyff, *and* Fowler ar takyn *and* in the castyll of Pomfrett, *and* ar lyek to dye hastyly, w*yth*-owte þey be ded.³ S*yr* T. Mongomeré *and* Jon Done be takyn; what shall falle of hem I can not sey. The qwen þat was *and* the Dwchesse of Bedford be in seyntuary at Westmestyr. The Bysheop of Ely w*yth* othyr bisheopys ar in
25 Seynt Martyns. When I here more I shall send yow more.

I prey⁴ God send yow all your desyirs. Wretyn at London⁵ on Seynt⁶ Edward*ys* Euyn.

Your sone *and* humbyll seru*au*nt J. P.⁷

Modyr, I beseche yow þat Brome may be spokyn to to gadyr vp my
30 sylluyr at Gwton in all hast possybyll, for I haue no mony. Also þat it lyek yow þat John Mylsent may be spokyn ⌈to⌉ to kep well my grey horse *and* he be a-lyue, *and* þat he spare no met on hym *and* þat he haue konnyng lechys to look to hym. As for my comyng hom I knowe no serteynté, for I terry tyll my lady of Norffolk com to go thorow w*yth* tho maters, *and*
35 s⟨he⟩⁷ shall not be here tyll Sonday.

² in *repeated*.   ³ *Double long s canc.*   ⁴ -d *canc.*
⁵ of *canc.*   ⁶ MS. seynd.
⁷ *Subscription marked off, and postscript written to left of it and below it.*
⁸ *Tear at foot.*

346. To MARGARET PASTON   1471, 30 April

Add. 27445, f. 45. 11½×9⅛ in. Autograph.

Dorse: Paper seal over red wax. No address.

The date is soon after the battle of Barnet, fought on Easter Day, 14 April 1471, in which John Paston III had been wounded (see John II's letter no. 261). The signature 'J. of Gelston' occurs only here. 'Gelston' is Geldeston; but there is no evidence that John III held property there. The manor belonged to Margaret Paston's stepfather. She wrote her letter no. 127 from Geldeston in 1444, and John III was born in that year. It is therefore likely enough that he was born there, and used this designation as a kind of private code to his mother to conceal his identity from strangers who might read the letter. The absence of address confirms the impression that the letter was meant to be confidential.

F. v, p. 2. G. 670/776. C. 62 (part).

Aftyr humbyll *and* most dew recomendacyon, jn as humbyll wyse as I can I beseche yow of yo*ur* blyssyn*g*, preyin*g* God to reward yow wy*th* as myche plesyer *and* hertys ease as I haue latward ⌈causyd⌉[1] you to ⌈haue⌉ trowbyll *and* thowght. And wy*th* Godys grace it shall not be longe to or then my wrongys *and* othyr menys shall be redressyd, for the world was neuyr so 5 lyek to be owyrs as it is now; werfor I prey yow let Lomnor no[t] be to besy as yet.

Modyr, I beseche yow, and ye may spare eny money, þat ye wyll do yo*ur* almesse on me *and* send me some in as hasty wyse as is possybyll, for by my trowthe my lechecrafte *and* fesyk, *and* rewardys to them that haue 10 kept me *and* condyt me to London, hathe cost me sythe Estern Day more then v li. And now I haue neythyr met, drink, clothys, lechecraft, nor money but vp-on borowyn*g*, and I haue asayid my frendys so ferre that they be-gyn to fayle now in my gretest ned that euyr I was in.

Also, modyr, I beseche yow, *and* my horse þat was at lechecraft at the 15 Holt be not takyn vp for the Kyn*g*ys hawkys, that he may be had hom *and* kept in yo*ur* plase, *and* not to go owght to watyr nor no whedyr ellys, but that the gat be shet *and* he to be chasyd aftyr watyr wy*th*-in yo*ur* plase, *and* that he haue as myche met as he may ete. I haue hey j-now of myn owne, and as for otys, Dollys wyll p*ur*uey for hym, or who that dothe it ⌈I wyll paye⌉. 20 And I beseche yow þat he haue eu*er*y wek iij boshell of otys, *and* eu*er*y day a peny worthe of bred. *And* if Boton[2] be not at Norwyche and Syme kep hym I shall geue hym well for hys labore. Also þat Phelypp Loueday put the ⌈othyr⌉ horse to gresse ther as he *and* I wer acordyd.

It*em*, that Boton send me hyddyr the two shyrtys that wer in my casket, 25 *and* þat he send me hydyr xl s. by the next messenger þat comyth to London.

346. ¹ *Interl. above* put *canc.*

    ² *Fenn and Gairdner read* Botoner; *but the tail on* -n *is of the form used commonly without significance, and differs from the* -er *mark. Cf. no. 354, n. 25, and John II's letter no. 269, n. 1.*

I*tem*, that Mastress Broom send me hedyr iij longe gownys and ij doble*tty*s, *and* a jaket of plonket chamlett, *and* a morey bonet owt of my cofyr—S*yr* Jamys hathe the key—⌜as I sent hyr word be-for thys⌝.

30 I*tem*, that syche othyr wryghty*ng*ys *and* stuff as was in my kasket be in you*r* kepy*ng*, *and* þat no body look my wryghty*ng*ys.

I*tem*, that the horse þat Purdy hathe of myne be put to some good gresse in hast.

And if it plese yow to haue knowlage of ouy*r* royall person, I thank God 35 I am hole of my syknesse, and trust to be clene hole of all my hurttys wyth-in a seue*n*nyght at the ferthest, by wyche tym I trust to haue othyr tydy*ng*ys. And those tydy*ng*ys onys had, I tryst not to be longe owght of Norf*olk*, wyt*h* Godys grace, whom I beseche pr*e*serue yow[3] *and* you*r* for my part.

Wrety*n* þe last day of Apryll. The[4] berer her-of can tell you tydy*ng*ys 40 syche as be trew for v*er*y serteyn.

Your humbylest seruau*n*t J. OF GELSTON

347. To MARGARET PASTON   1471, 5 July

Add. 34889, f. 111. $11\frac{3}{4} \times 7\frac{3}{4}$ in. Autograph.

Dorse: Marks of folding, traces of red wax, and stitch-holes. No address.

The date appears from Paston's need of a pardon after the battle of Barnet. Gairdner notes that the King signed the bill for his pardon on 17 July 1471 but it did not pass the Great Seal until 7 February 1472 (Pardon Roll 11 E.IV, m.9). See no. 346, and also John II's letter no. 263, l. 12.

Anthony Woodville, Lord Scales, became Earl Rivers in 1469, but Paston still uses his old title.

F. iv, p. 116. G. 672/778.

Most worchepfull *and* my ryght specyall good modyr, as humbylly as I can I recomand me on-to yow, besechyng yow of youy*r* blyssyng. Please[1] it yow to vndyrstand that thys day I spake wyt*h* Bacheler Water, whyche let me haue vndyrstandyng of you*r* welfare, wherof I thank God wyt*h* all my hert. 5 Also he leet me haue knowlage[2] that the Lord Scalys had g*r*auntyd yow to be my good lord, wherof I am no-thyng prowd for he may do leest wyt*h* the gret mastyr, but he wold depert ouyr the see as hastyly as he may. And because he wenyth that I wold go wyt*h* hym, as I had promyseyd hym euyr[3] *and* he had kept[4] foorthe hys jornay[5] at that tyme, thys is the cause 10 that he wyll be my good lord *and* help to get my pardon. The Kyng is not best pleaseyd wyt*h* hym for that he desyerthe to depert, jn so myche that

³ MS. yoʳ, *exactly as your following.*   ⁴ berer *miswritten canc.*
347. ¹ *No space.*   ² wyth all *canc.*
³ MS. euys.   ⁴ promyse *canc.*
⁵ MS. jormay.

the Kyng hathe seyd of hym that wen so euyr he hathe most to do, then
the Lord Scalys wyll sonest axe leue to depert, and weenyth that it is most
be-cause of kowardyese. As for perdon, I can non get w*yth*-owght I shold
paye to myche money for it, and I am not so p*u*rueyd. As for Herry Hall- 15
man, my brodyr wyll axe hym no syluyr tyll ye be payeyd; therfor ye may
send to hym and haue it.

It*em*, I am sory that ye haue fadyrd my hors þat was at Caster to be my
brodyr Edmu*n*dys, for I had leueer þat they had hym styll then owght ellys;
wherfor thow they⁶ profyr hym yow fro hense foorthe, let not my brodyr 20
Edmu*n*d take hym but let hym sey, whedyr they wyll let hym haue hym or
not, that I haue promyseyd my brodyr Edmu*n*d a bettyr hors for hym so
that he wyll not cleyme⁷ the same for hys.

As for tydyng*ys*, her be non but þat the Scottys *and* Walyshe men be
besy. What they meane I can not seye. My cosyn John Loueday can tell 25
yow *and* ther be eny odyr flyeyng talys, for he hathe walkyd in London,
and so do not I.

When I may I wyll com hom, w*yth* Godys grace, whom I beseche to
send you y*our* hertys desyeyr. Wretyn the v daye of Julle.

By y*our* humblest sone *and* seru*au*nt J. P. 30

348. To MARGARET PASTON   1471, 22 July

Add. 27445, f. 46. $11\frac{1}{4} \times 5\frac{3}{4}$ in. Autograph.

Dorse: Traces of red wax. Address autograph:

To my most worchepfull modyr Margaret Paston be thys delyueryd in hast.

The date is fixed by the grant of John III's pardon (see no. 347, headnote).
   F. v, p. 6. G. 674/780.

Ryght worshepfull modyr, I recomand me to yow, and as lowly as I can
I beseche yow of y*our* blyssyng. Please ⌐yow⌐ to vndyrstand that thys
Wednysday S*yr* Thom*as* Wyngffeld sent to me *and* let me wet that the
Kyng had syngnyd my bylle of perdon, whyche the¹ seyd S*yr* Thom*as*
delyueryd me; *and* so by Fryday at the forthest I tryst to haue my perdon 5
ensealyd by the Chanceler. And soone aftyr so as I can fornyshe me I tryst
to se yow, if so be that eny of the Kyng*ys* hows² com in-to Norwyche. I
wold fayne my gray horse wer kept in mewe for gnattys.

Also, modyr, I beseche yow that Dollys *and* hys felawe may be sent to
that I may haue my money redy ayenst that I com hom, whyche is dew 10
to ⌐be⌐ payid, for thys mater hathe cost me the settyng ou*er*. Also that it

---

⁶ -y *crowded in.*   ⁷ hym for hys *canc.*
348. ¹ *Altered from* he *and fold. by* ha *canc.*   ² S*yr* Thomas Wy *canc.*

may please yow that Purdy at Heylysdon maye be sent to for the horse
that he hathe of myne, *and* that the horse may be kept well *and* haue as
myche met as he wyll eate be-twyx thys *and* þat I com hom; *and* þat
15 Jakys nage haue met j-now also.

Also, *and* Syr Thom*a*s Wyngfeld com to Norwyche, that he may haue
as good cher as it please yow to make on-to that man that I am most be-
hol⟨d⟩³ to for hys gret kyndnesse *and* good wyll; for he takyth full my part
ayenst my gretest enmyeys, Brandons *and* hys brodyr Will*ia*m. For at my
20 fyrst comy*n*g to S*y*r Thom*a*s Wyngfeld bothe Will*ia*m Wyngfeld *and*
Will*ia*m Brandon the yonger wer w*y*th S*y*r Thom*a*s, and had gret wordys
to my owne mowthe, *and* in cheff W. Wyngfeld; *and*⁴ wher so euyr he may
met me on euyn grownd he wyll do myche, but *and* we met euynly no fors,
so I haue yo*ur* blyssy*n*g.

25 I prey yow w*y*th-owght it be to my Lady Calthorp let ther be but fewe
woordys of thys p*er*don.

No more, but I prey God p*re*serue yow *and* yours. Wretyn the Wednysday n[e]xt be-fore Mary Mawdelen.

By yo*ur* humblest sone J. P.

349. To M ARGARET P ASTON   1471, 28 October

Add. 27445, f. 47. 11⅝×5½ in. Autograph.

Dorse: Badly damaged by damp. Traces of red wax. Address autograph,
but only *rgaret* remains.

The date appears from the prospect of a general pardon, which was offered in the
autumn of 1471 (Scofield, ii. 21).
    This letter is answered by Margaret's of 5 November (no. 209).
    G. 678/784.

Ryght worchepfull m⟨odyr, as lowly as⟩¹ I can I recomand me to yow,
besechy*n*g yow of yo*ur* dayly blyssy*n*g, prayi*n*g yow to take thys key, *and*
S*y*r Jam⟨ys w*y*th y⟩ow ⟨and m⟩y broder E. or J. Pampy*n*g, *and* to ondo þe
kofyr þat standith at my bedys feet, *and* ther jn a ly⟨tyll s⟩qware box ye
5 shall fy⟨nd two de⟩dys wher-of the seallys be wownd in whyght paper;
my brodyr E. sye when I wond them vp. The ton ⟨. . . begy⟩nyth '⌈Sciant
&c. q*uod* ego⌉ Matilda Bigota',² and the todyr begynyth 'Sciant &c. q*uod*

---

³ *Small hole in paper. From the off-stroke to the right of it only* d *seems to have been lost.*
⁴ *Crowded in.*
349. ¹ *Much lost here and later at large irregular holes in the paper, mainly between the first
and second of the three vertical folds.*
    ² *Name marked off and underlined.*

ego Roger*us* ⟨. . .⟩.³ I ⟨pre⟩y yow let ⟨them be⟩ sealyd *and* sent me by
Radley² w*yth* the deed*ys* ther-in. S*yr* Jamys knowyth the ⟨. . .⟩. But ⟨if so
be⟩ that ye fynd not thys box w*yth* thes two deed*ys* in þat cofyr, then I   10
prey yow take the k⟨ey . . .⟩teye of the same cofyr *and* opyn the cofyr that
standyth in þe vtter chambyr, *and* ther ye shall fynd ⟨. . .de⟩edys.

My brodyr S*yr* John recomandyth hym to yow, *and* besechyth yow of
yo*ur* blyssyng. And as for hys mater⟨ther is yet no conclu⟩syon⁴ of no
poynt, but I tryst ther shall be w*yth*-in thes ij dayeys. Jenney W. trowbly⟨th 15
. . . my⟩ brodyrs seru*aunt*ys w*yth* old accyons *and* all syche thyng*ys* as he
can renew to stoppe the oblygacio⟨ns w⟩hyche he is bownd in on-to my
broder, but all shall be easeyd, I tryst. As for M*astres* A. Hawlt, the mater
is mevyd ⟨by dyu⟩ers of the Qwenys consayll, and of ferre by R. Hault;
but he wold it shold be fyrst of ou*yr* mocyon *and* we wold ⟨it⟩ shold com 20
of theym fyrst. Ou*yr* mater shold be the bettyr.

Tydyng*ys*, ther is a gen*er*all p*er*don mevyd whyche my brodyr ⌐*and* I⌐
trystyth to haue the preue⟨leg⟩e of as soone as it is grantyd, whyche shall
be a-bowght All Halow Tyed at the ferthest. I haue spok w*yth* my L⟨ord
Ryue⟩rs *and* w*yth* all myn old aqweyntance, *and* haue good cheer of theym, 25
hold as it maye. When we be conclud⟨yd in⟩ eny poynte of ou*yr* maters
ye shall haue knowlage⁵ howhe, to put yow in ⟨comfo⟩rt er we haue eny
⟨. . .⟩ but in veyn; when we haue comfort ye shall haue parte.

Newe tydy*ngys*, datys v ⟨. . .s⟩vgyr of iij kwte x d. ⌐a li.⌐⁶ *and* bettyr I
tryst. No more, but I beseche God preserue yow *and* yours. Wretyn on 30
⟨Seint⟩ Symond*ys* Day *and* Jwde.

Yo*ur* humblest sone *and* seru*aunt* J. PASTON

350. To JOHN PASTON II   1471

Add. 27445, f. 55. 11¾×4¾ in. Autograph.

Dorse: Marks of folding, no seal or address. In a hand evidently John II's,
John Paston.

This is only the latter part of a longer letter. The year appears from the reference
to Lord Rivers's projected voyage to Portugal, mentioned also in John II's letter
no. 266 of 8 January 1472. The reference to Sporle wood also connects this with
John II's letter no. 267.
    G. 686/793.

The v*er*y valew of Sporle wood passyth not c mark of no manys mony that
I can spek w*yth*, *and* to be payid by dayis as the byll that Jwdé shall

---

³ *This name is marked off and underlined, and the second oblique stroke, which followed the
surname, is visible.*
    ⁴ but *canc.*   ⁵ ther *canc.*   ⁶ *Top of l lost.*

delyu⟨er yow⟩[1] rehers, *and* ther-ayenst ye shold loose iij li. of the ferme of
þe maner yerly, whych standyth by vndyr-wood, *and* yet the fense must
5 stand yow on[2] xij mark by the lest wey; but by God, *and* I wer as ye I wold
not sell it for c m[a]rk more then it is woorthe.

Syr John Styll recomandyth hym to your good mastyrshep, *and* seyth
pleynly if ye wyll he wyll com vp to yow *and* awayte on yow whersoeuer ye
be, coort or othyr. By Seynt Mary, he is owyng more mony then I wend,
10 for he is owyng for a twelmonthe *and* a quarter at thys Crystmas, sauyng
for hys boord xij d. a wek for iij quarters. *And* he seythe pleynly that ye *and*
R. Call bothe bad hym syng styll for Syr John Fastolf as he dyd be-fore,
but I haue bodyn hym þat he shall get hym a seruyse now at thys Crystmas, *and* so he shall wyth-owt that ye send hym othyr-wyse woord, or
15 ellys that ye or I may get hym som benefyse or fre chapell, or som othyr
good seruyse, whyche I praye yow enqwer for.

Item, *and* ye werk wysly, your mater mrght com in wyth othyr maters of
the lordys in ther apoyntmentys wyth the Kyng, but it wold be labord to
a porpose þis Crystmas whyll ye haue leyser to spek wyth your mastyr.
20 Item, myn aqweyntans[3] wyth þe Lord Reuers is non othyrwyse but as
it hathe ben alweys, sauyng *and* he go no[w] to Portygall to[4] be at a day vp-
on the Serasyns I purpose *and* haue promysyd to be ther wyth hym; *and*
that jorney don, as Wykys seythe, farwell he. He purposyth to go forward
a-bowt Lent,

25 But Fortune wyth hyr smylyng contenans strange
Of all our purpose may mak a sodeyn change.

I ensuer yow he thynkyth all the world gothe on ther syd ayen. *And* as for
my comyng vp at the begynnyng of thys next term, wyth-owt ye send me
othyr-wyse woord þat I myght do yow som good when I wer com, by my
30 feyth I com not ther, for it shold put yow to a cost *and* me to a labor *and*
cost bothe; but [if] ye send for me I com streyght, thow I tery the lesse
whyll ther, *and* so I shall wyth-owt I may do yow som good, by my feythe.
I purpose to make vp my byllys cler, *and* send yow the copyse as hastyly
as I can.

35 Yonge Wyseman, othyrwyse callyd foole, told me that Syr W. Yeluerton
is abowt to make a bargayn wyth the Dwches of Suffolk or wyth my lord of
Norffolk, whyche he may get fyrst, fo[r] the maner of Gwton. I reseyue
all yet, God hold it. I praye yow recomand me to my brodyr Molyenewx
and all othyr good felaws.

40   J. P.

350. [1] *Corner lost.*   [2] on *repeated.*
        [3] *An extra minim after the second* a.   [4] by *canc.*

351. Verses: draft   Date uncertain; probably after 1471

Add. 43491, f. 27. Paper L-shaped, a sheet with about a quarter cut out: $8\frac{3}{8} \times 11\frac{1}{2}$ less $3\frac{1}{8} \times 6\frac{3}{4}$ in. Autograph.

Dorse: Last two stanzas. Marks of folding, no seal or address.

Fenn, followed by Gairdner, described this document as 'Verses written by a Lady in the reign of Henry VI. or Edward IV. To an absent Lord with whom she was in love.' Gairdner suggested that 'they may have been from the Countess of Oxford to her husband after he escaped abroad in 1471. . . . Or they may have been the production of Lydgate writing in the name of a lady parted from her lord.' But from the many corrections and hesitations the manuscript is clearly a draft of an original composition, and it is entirely in John III's hand. It may well be a mere exercise in the fashionable mode of the literary 'epistle'; but it is not impossible that the poem was meant more or less seriously by Paston, for the expressions are not necessarily those of a woman. If that were so the lord might most probably be the Earl of Oxford, and the date 1471 or later as Gairdner suggested.

Such a date would, at any rate, suit the linguistic forms. John III does not spell *ryght*, *knyght*, etc. with *gh* until 1467, but after 1468 uses it regularly: cf. *ryth*, *knyt*, *browt* still in no. 330; the extension of *gh* to *wryght*, *owght*, etc. begins in 1469; cf. *wryght*, *dowghtys* in no. 333, *owght* in no. 339; *shall* appears from 1467—in no. 325, beside *schall*; *sylf(e)* appears from 1469—in no. 332, earlier *selue* as in no. 330; *theym* appears first in 1467 (no. 325), but does not prevail until after 1471 (from no. 349 onwards)—*them* is still normal in no. 345). The general style of writing is like that of letters written in the early seventies, though there is little difference to be observed until no. 389.

F. ii, p. 304. G. 870/988.

My ryght good lord, most knyghtly gentyll knyght,
On-to yo*ur* grace in my most[1] humbyll wyse
I me comand, as it is dew *and* ryght,
Besechyng yow at leyser to aduyse
Vp-on thys byll, *and* p*er*don myn empryse   5
Growndyd on foly ⌐for lak of prouydence⌐[2]
On-to yo*ur* lordshep to wryght wy*th*-owght lycence.[3]

But wher a man is wy*th* a feuyr shake,
Now hot, now cold, as fallyth by auenture,
He in hys mynd coniecte wyll *and* take   10
The nyghest meane to worche for hys cuyre,
More pacyently hys peynys to endure;[4]

351. [1] *Interl. above* my most *is* euery humbyll, *of which* humbyll *is canc.*

[2] *Interl. above* and on jnsolence, *the last two words canc.*

[3] *This line replaces the following, written above it:* Thus for to wryght ⌐owght⌐ youy*r* lycence, *the first three words canc.*

[4] *This line replaces the following cancelled line, above it:* ⌐And⌐ Ryght so I whyche dayly do endure. *Below, in position of the line-beginning, is* W, *the rest of the line blank.*

And ryght so I,[5] so it not yow[6] dysplease,
Wryght in thys wyse my peynys to apease.

15 For when I cownt *and* mak a rekny*n*g
Betwyx my lyfe, my dethe, *and* my desyer,
My lyfe, alas, it seruyth of no thyng,
Sythe w*yth* yo*ur* pertyng depertyd my plesyer.
Wyshyng youy*r* presence setyth[7] ⌈me⌉ on fyer,
20 But then yo*ur* absence dothe my hert so cold
That for the peyne I not me wher to hold.

O, owght on absence, ther foolys haue no grace—
I mene my-sylf—nor yet ⌈no⌉ wytt to gwye
Theym owt of peyne to com on-to that place
25 Wher as presence may shape a remedye
For al dysease; now fye on my folye,
For I dyspeyryd am of yo*ur* ⌈soone metyng⌉[8]
That ⌈God⌉ I prey me to yo*ur* presence bryng.

Farwell, my lord, for I may wryght no more,
30 So trowblyd is my hert w*yth* heuynesse.
Envye[9] ⌈also it⌉ gremyth me most sore
That thys rwde byll shall put hym-sylf in presse
To se yo*ur* lordshepe of hys[10] *p*resumptuousnesse
Er ⌈I my-sylf⌉;[11] but ⌈yett⌉[12] ye shall not mysse
35 To haue my hert ⌈to⌉-for[13] my byll, j-wys.[14]

Whyche I comytt, *and* all my hole seruyse
In-to yo*ur* hand*ys*, demeane ⌈it⌉[15] as you lyst.
Of it I kepe to haue no more franchyse
Then I hertlesse swyrly me wyst,
40 Sauy*n*g only þ*at* it may be as tryst
And ⌈to yow⌉[16] trew as euyr was hert, *and* pleyn,
Tyll cruell dethe dep*ert*[17] yt vp-on tweyn.

---

[5] *Erasure large enough to cover some three letters.*
[6] not *interl. superfluously.*
[7] -yth *crowded in; before set,* dothe *and interl.* me *canc.*
[8] *Interl. above* geyn comy*n*g *canc.*
[9] *This line originally began with* but yet, *which is canc.*
[10] symp *canc.*   [11] *Interl. above* then may I, *first two words canc.*
[12] *Interl. above* thys *canc.*   [13] then *canc.*
[14] *This line and the next stanza written vertically to the right, on the projecting part of the L-shaped sheet.*
[15] *Interl. above* theym *canc.*
[16] *Interl. above* verry *canc.*   [17] *No space. This line ends recto.*

351. *Verses: draft, probably after 1471*

⟨A⟩dew¹⁸ dysport, farwell good companye,
⟨I⟩n all thys world ther is no joye, I weene,
For ther as whyleom ⌐I sye *wyth* myn jee⌐¹⁹   45
A lusty lord leepyng vp-on a grene,
The soyle is soole, no knyght*ys* ther be seen,
No ladyse ⌐walk⌐ ther they wer wont to doone.
Alas, ⌐some folk⌐²⁰ depertyd hense to soone.

Som tyme also me*n* myght a wageor make,   50
And *wyth* ther bowys a feld haue it tryed
Or at the paame ther ther plesure for to ⟨take⟩.²¹
Then wer they loose *þat* now stand as tyed.
I not wher to thys world may be a-plyed
For all god cher on euyn *and* on morow   55
Whyche then was ⌐mad⌐²² now tornyth me to sorowe.

352. To John Paston II   1472, 5 June

Add. 43489, f. 50. 11½×8½ in. Autograph.

Dorse: Continuation of text. Traces of red wax. Address autograph:

To my ryght worchepfull brodyr Syr John Paston, knyght.

The date is fixed by the pregnancy of the Duchess of Norfolk, whose daughter
Anne was born on 10 December 1472 (Scofield, ii. 203).
    F. ii, p. 92. G. 696/804 (part). C. 66 (part).

Ryght worchepfull s*yr*, I recomand me to yow, sertyfy*ing* yow *þat*, as God
help ⌐me⌐, I wend *þat* Will*ia*m Barker had ben *wyth* yow thys Whyghtson-
tyd at London *and* browght yow monye, for so he promysyd bothe Judé
and me *þat* he shold do, and also at hys comy*ng* to London *þat* he shold
make yow ther a clere rekny*ng* what mony he had rec*eyuyd and* delyuerd.   5
And tyll thys day that I spak *wyth* hys son I wend he had ben *wyth* yow
be-cause I herd not fro yow the contrary syn Jwdé was her. Hys son
hathe promysyd me that he shall be *wyth* me thys nyght or to-morow at
the ferthest, *and* if ⌐he⌐ com syche monye as he hathe I shall cause hym to
send it ⌐yow⌐, *and* a vewe of hys acompte to-gedyr by the next messenger   10
that we can get to London, I promyse yow *wyth*-owght slawthyng.¹ As for

---

¹⁸ *First letter of this and next line lost at torn edge.*
¹⁹ *Interl. above* a man myght espye *not canc. This line replaces the following cancelled line
above it:* I leef to longe alas what remedye.
²⁰ *Interl. above* the lord *canc.*
²¹ *Lost at edge.*   ²² *Interl. above* had *canc.*
352. ¹ for *canc.*

an hole aco*m*pte, Gefrey Spyrly*n*g can not charge hym w*yth* non wyth-
owght a *p*resedent. I trow ye haue aco*m*ptys of Wynterton *and* Bastwyk
and Runha*m* amo*n*g yo*ur* euydence of Cast*er*, *and* if ye send me woord
15 to look among yo*ur* euydence for syche I schall, *and* then we may charge
hym w*yth* hys hole aco*m*pte *and* I fynd onys a *p*resedent. I haue yest*er*day
sent to Herry Hallman to make yo*ur* money[2] redy a-yenst Mydsomer, *and*
as sone as I her fro hym ayen I shall send yow suyr woord when ye shall
send to hym for monye *and* not fayle.

20   It*em*, Mastyr John Smythe telly*th* me þat S*yr* T. Lyndys goodys ar not
abyll to paye a q*ua*rter of hys detty*s* þat be axyd hym, wherfor syche money
as is be-left it most be devydyd to eu*er*y man a *p*arte aftyr the quantyté,
whyche dyuysyon is not yet mad; but when it is mad he hathe promyseyd
me þat yo*ur* pert shalbe worthe iij þe best. I meuyd hym to[3] haue sent yow
25 some monye befor the dyuysyon to haue pleasyd w*yth* the apotycary *and* þe
freers for a season, *and* I haue halfe a promesse that he wyll do so; I ensuer
yow by my trowthe, he nor S*yr* W. Marrys shall not forget it for lak of
cally*n*g on. I tryst v*er*yly ye shall haue the most parte þat ye get of theym
w*yth*-in thes vj dayis, for I fynd Mast*er* J. Smyth well wylly*n*g ther-to.

30   It*em*, as for J. of Barneys hors, who so haue leest need to hym he shall
cost hym xx mark,[4] not a peny lesse. Ye send me woord of þe maryage of
my Lady Jane; o maryage for an other—ou*yr* norse *and* Bedford wer axid
in the chyrche on Son-day last past. As for my syst[er] Anne, my modyr
wyll not remeue fro W. Yellu*er*ton for Bedyngfeld, for she hathe comond
35 ferther in þat mater syn ye wer in þis contré, as it aperyth in hyr lettyr þat
she sendyth yow by Thyrston.

    Tydyng*ys* her, my lady of Norff*olk* is w*yth* chyld, she wenyth hyr-sylf,
and so do all þe women a-bowght hyr, in so myche she waytys the qwyk-
ny*n*g w*yth*-in thes vj wekys at the ferthest. Also W. Gornay wenyth that
40 Heydon is swyr of Saxthorp *and* þe Lady Boleyn of Gwton. John Osbern
auysythe yow to take brethe for yo*ur* wodsale at Sporle, for he hathe cast
it that it is woorthe as good as ix^xx li.[4] Be war of Montayn, for he may not
pay yow so myche mony w*yth* hys ease.

    I prey yow recomand ⌜me⌝ to S*yr* John Parre w*yth* all my seruys, *and*
45 tell hym by my trouthe I longyd neuer sorer to se my lady then I do to se
hys mast*er*shepe. And I prey God that he aryse neuer a[5] morny*n*g fro my
lady his wyff w*yth*-owght it be ageyn hyr wyll tyll syche tyme as he bryng
hyr to Ou*yr* Lady of Walsy*n*gham. Also I prey ⌜yow⌝ to recomand me in
my most humbyll wyse on-to þe good lordshepe of þe most corteys,
50 gentylest, wysest, kyndest, most compenabyll, freest, largeest, *and* most
bowntefous knyght, my lord the Erle of Arran,[6] whych hathe maryed the

---

2 *Ampersand canc.*   3 *as canc.*
4 *Sum written larger than the rest, marked off, and underlined.*
5 *Recto ends.*   6 *-n written with tail like y, corrected.*

352. *To John Paston II, 5 June 1472*

Kyng*ys* sustyr of Scotlon. Her-to, he ⌜is⌝ on the lyghtest, delyuerst, best
spokyn, fayirest archer, deuowghtest, most p*er*fyght *and* trewest to hys
lady of all the knyghtys that euer I was aqweyntyd w*yth*; so wold God my
lady lyekyd me as well as I do hys person *and* most knyghtly condycyon,   55
w*yth* whom I prey yow to be aqweyntyd as you semyth best. He is lodgyd
at þe George in Lombard Strete. He hath⁷ a book of my syster Annys of
þe Sege of Thebes. When he hathe doon w*yth* it he promysyd to delyuer
it yow. I prey yow lete Portlond brynge þe book hom w*yth* hym. Portlond
is loggyd at þe George in Lombard Stret also.   60

And thys I promysse yow, ye schall not be so longe a-yen w*yth*-ought
a byll fro me as ye haue ben, thow I shold wryght how ofte the wynd chan-
gyth; for I se be yo*ur* wryghtyng ye can be wrothe *and* ye wyll.⁸ Wretyn
the v day of June. As for Rysy[n]g, I shall send hym woord to kepe hys
day *crastino Johannis*.⁹   65

J. PASTON

353. TO JOHN PASTON II   1472, 8 July

Add. 27445, f. 59. 11½ × 12⅛ in. Autograph.

Dorse: Traces of red wax. Address autograph:

To my ryght worchepfull brodyr Syr John Paston, knyght.

This letter is closely linked to no. 352 by references to several matters, especially
the Duchess of Norfolk's pregnancy, the estate of Thomas Lyndys, and provision
for Anne Paston's marriage.

F. v, p. 16. G. 697/805. C. 67 (part).

Ryght worchepfull s*yr*, I recomand me to you, sertyfyi*ng* yow that I haue
spokyn w*yth* Mastyr John Smyth for S*yr* T. Lyndys, and he hathe shewyd
me yo*ur* byll whyche ye axe to be content ⌜of⌝. Yo*ur* byll ⌜a-lone⌝ drawyth
iiij mark *and* ode monye, for ye haue set in yo*ur* byll for wax a-lone xx s.,
whyche to Mastyr John S. jmagynacyon, *and* to all other ofycers of the   5
coort, shold not drawe past xx d. at hys beryi*ng*. The byllys that be put
in to the coorte of S*yr* T. Lynys dett*ys* drawe¹ xxx li. xviij s. vj d.², *and* all
the money that can be mad of hys house *and* goodys in thys contrey drawyth
but v li. Maste*r* J. Smyth wold ye shold send hym in to the coort an
jnventory of syche goodys as S*yr* T. had at London when he dyeid, *and* þat   10

---

⁷ *At edge*; -th *under mount but visible.*
⁸ for lytyll *struck through, and also marked by four small crosses above and four below, with
the words* crosse it *interl. above.*
⁹ *This last sentence added later in paler ink.*
353. ¹ drawe xxx li. *canc.*
² xxx li. *marked off and underlined; the rest unmarked.*

jnventory onys had ye shall haue as comyth to your part, *and* more also.
Ye must send þe serteynté whedyr the wax be xx s or xx d. And as for the
freers, Mast*er* John wyll not alowe theym a peny, for he seyth wher þe
dett*ys* may not be payeid, set þe beqwest*ys* at nowght. He is agreid to pay
15 the potycarye aftyr that he haue þe jnventory fro yow. Rysyng I trowe hathe
be w*yth* yow.

Item, as for John Maryot, I haue sent to hym for þe xl s., but I haue non
answer.

Item, I haue spok w*yth* Barker, *and* he hathe no money nor non can get
20 tyll haruest, when he may dystreyn the cropp vp-on þe grownd. He seyth
ther is not owy*ng* past v mark, and on Sat*er*day next comy*ng* he shall send
me a vewe of hys acompte whyche I shall send yow as sone as I haue it. As
for Fastolff*ys* v mark, J. Wyndh*am* hathe be spokyn to by me half a doseyn
tymys to send to hym for it, *and* he seyth ⌈he⌉ hathe doon so.

25 Item, S*yr* John Styll hathe told Jwdé when ye shall haue the chalys. Ax
Jwdé of yo*ur* crwet*ys* allso.

Item, the prowd, pevyshe, *and* euyll dysposyd prest to vs all, S*yr* Jamys,
seyth þat ye comandyd hym to delyuer þe book of vij Sagys to my brodyr
Water, *and* he hathe it.

30 Item, I send yow the serteynté her-w*yth* of as myche as can be enqweryd
for myn oncyll W. cleym in Cast*er*. Those[3] artyclys þat fayle, the ten*auntys*
of Cast*er* shall enqwer theym *and* send theym to me hastyly. They haue
promysyd *and* they com ye shall haue theym sent yow by the next messenger þat comyth to London.

35 Item, my modyr sendyth yow woord that she hathe neyther Mast*er*
Robard Popyes oblygacyon nor the Byshopys. It*em*, my modyr wold ye
shold in all haste ⌈gete⌉[4] her aqwetance of the Byshop of Wynchest*er* for
S*yr* John Fastolff[5] good*ys*. She preyid yow to make it swyr by þe auyse of
your consayll, *and* she wyll pay for the cost*ys*. It*em*, she preyith ⌈yow⌉ to
40 spek to þe seyd Byshop for to get Mast*er* Clement Felmy[n]gham the viij
mark be yer dwry*ng* hys lyffe that S*yr* J. Fastolff be-set hym. She preyid
yow to get hym an asygnement for it to som maner in Norff*olk* or in
Lothynglond.

Item, she wold ye shold get yow an other house to ley in youyr stuff
45 syche as cam| fro Cast*er*; she thynkyth ⌈on of⌉ the freerys is a fayir house.
She p*ur*poseyth to go in-to the contré *and* ther to soiorn onys a-yen. Many
qwarellys ⌈ar⌉[6] pyekyd to get my brodyr E. *and* me ought of hyr howse.
We go not to bed vnchedyn lyghtly. All þat we do is ille doon, *and* all that
S*yr* Jamys *and* Pekok dothe is well doon. S*yr* Jamys *and* I be tweyn. We

---

³ *Uncertain*: -o- *apparently corr. from* e.

⁴ *Interl. above* haste, *with caret after, which is followed by* do mak *canc.;* haste *also canc.,
clearly in error.*

⁵ -ff *has the off-flourish usual when final, not the loop representing* -ys.

⁶ *Interl. above ampersand canc.*

fyll owght be-for my modyr wyth 'Thow prowd prest' *and* 'Thow prowd 50
sqwyer', my modyr takyng hys part, so I haue almost beshet þe bote as for
my modyrs house. Yet somer shalbe don or I get me eny mastyr.

My modyr purposeith hastyly to take estate in all hyr londys, *and* vp-on
that estate to make hyr wyll of þe seyd londys: parte to geue to my
yonger brethyrn for term of her lyuys *and* aftyr to remayn to yow, pert 55
to my syster Annys maryage tyll an c li. be payid, part for to make hyr
jle at Mawtby, parte for a prest to syng for hyr *and* my fadyr *and* ther
ancestrys. And in thys angyr⁷ betwen Syr Jamys *and* me she hathe promyseid me that my parte shall be nowght; what your shalbe I can not sey.
God sped the plowghe! I feythe ye must puruey for my brodyr E. to go 60
ouer wyth yow, or he is on-don. He wyll bryng xx noblys in hys purse. My
modyr wyll nowthyr geue nor lend non of you bothe a peny forward.
Puruey a meane to haue Caster ayen or ye goo ouyr; my lord *and* my lady—
whyche for serteyn is gret wyth chyld—be wery ther-of, *and* all þe housold
also. 65

If ye wyll eny othyr thyn[g] to be don in thys contré, send me woord
and I shalldo as well as I can, wyth Godys grace, who preserue yow.

Wretyn the viij day of Julle. I pray yow recomand me to my lord
of Aran, Syr John Par, ⌐Syr George Browne⌐, Osbern Berney, R. Hyd,
J. Hoxson, my cosyn hys wyfe Kate, W. Wood, *and* all. I prey brenne 70
thys by[ll] for losyng.⁸

Your J. P.

354. To JOHN PASTON II   1472, 21 September

Add. 43489, f. 52. 11¾×8½ in. Autograph.

Dorse: Entirely covered with text. Marks of folding and soiling, and stitch-
holes, but no seal or address. From the soiling it appears that part of the
text must have been exposed when the paper was folded.

Dated at the end (in a lighter ink) by John II.
  F. ii, p. 102. G. 701/809.

Ryght worchepfull syr, I recomand me to yow, letyng yow wet þat your
desyer as for the knyghtys of the shyer was an impossybyl ⌐to⌐ be browhgt
a-bowght, for my lord of Norffolk *and* my lord of Suffolk wer agreid more
then a fortnyght go to haue Syr Robert Wyngfeld *and* Syr Rychard Harcort; and that knew I not tyll it was Fryday last past. I had sent ⌐or I rod 5

---

⁷ *Dotted circumflex above -n-.*
⁸ *Last sentence written more lightly and hastily, evidently later.*
354. ¹ *In margin.*

to Framly[n]gham⌐ to warne as many of your frendys² to ⌐be⌐ at Norwyche
as thys Monday to serue your entent as I koud; but when I cam to Framly[n]gham *and* knew the apoy[n]tment that was takyn for the ij knyghtys,
I sent warnyng ayen to as many as I myght to tery at hom. *And* yet ther
10 cam to Norwyche thys day as many as ther costys drewe to ix s. j d. ob.,
payid *and* reknyd by Pekok *and* R. Capron, *and* yet they dyd but brak ther
fast *and* depertyd. And I thankyd hem in your name *and* told them that
ye wold haue noo voyse as thys day, for ye supposyd not to be in Inglond
when the perlement shold be. And so they cam not at the sherhous, for
15 ⌐if⌐ they had it was thowght by syche as be your frendys her that your
aduersarys wold haue reportyd þat ye had mad labor to haue ben on,³ and
þat ye koud not bryng your purpose a-bowght.⁴

I sent to Yermowthe, *and* they⁵ haue promysyd also to Doctor Aleyn
and John Russe to be mor then iij wekys goo. Jamys⁶ Arblaster hathe
20 wretyn a letter to the baylé of Maldon in Essex to haue you a borgeys ther.
Howe Jwdé shall sped let hym tell yow when ye spek to-gedyr.⁷

Syr, ⌐I⌐ haue ben twyis at Framly[n]gham sythe your departyng, but now
the last tym the consayll was ther I sye yowyr lettyr, whyche was bettyr
then well endyghtyd. R. T. was not at Framly[n]gham when the consayll
25 was ther, but I took myn owne auysse *and* delyuerd it to the consayll, wyth
a propocysion ther-wyth as well as I kowd spek it; and ⌐my⌐ wordys wer
well takyn, but your letter a thowsand fold bettyr. When they had red it
they⁵ shewyd it to⁸ my lady. Aftyr that⁸ my lady had sen it I spak wyth my
lady, offyryng to my lord *and* hyr your seruyse, *and* besyd þat ye to do my
30 lord a plesur *and* hyr a bettyr, so as ye myght depert, wyth-ought eny some
specyfyid. She wold not dell⁹ in that mater, but remyttyd me a-yen to the
consayll, for she seyd *and* she spake in it tyll my lord *and* the consayll wer
agreid they wold ley the wyght of all the mater on hyr, whyche shold be
reportyd to hyr shame; but thys she promyseid, to be helpyng so it wer
35 fyrst meuyd by the consayll. Then I went to¹⁰ the consayll *and* offyrd
befor them youyr seruyse to my lord, and¹¹ to do hym a plesure for þe
haueing ayen of your place *and* londys in Caster xl li., not spekyng of your¹²
stuff nor thyng ellys. So they answerd me your offyr was more then resonabyll, *and* if the mater wer thers they seyd they wyst what conscyence wold
40 dryue hem to. They¹³ seyd they wold ⌐meue⌐¹⁴ my lord wyth it, *and* so they
dyd; but then the tempest aros *and* he gaue hem syche an answer that
non of hem all wold tell it me. But when I axid an answer of hem they seyd
and som lordys or gretter men meuyd my lord wyth it the mater wer your.
⌐Kepe consayle.⌐ *And* wyth thys answer I depertyd; but Syr W. Brandon,

---

² fo *canc.*   ³ and *canc.*   ⁴ I send *canc.*
⁵ -y *crowded in.*   ⁶ h *canc.*   ⁷ *Five oblique strokes.*
⁸ my lord *and canc.*   ⁹ d- *apparently corr. from* t.   ¹⁰ to *repeated.*
¹¹ *Written in full over ampersand.*   ¹² -ur *raised.*
¹³ -y *crowded in before* sy *canc.*   ¹⁴ *Interl. above* me *canc.*

Sothewell, Tymperley, Herry Wentworthe, W. Gornay, *and* all other of 45
consayll vndyrstand that ye haue wronge, in so myche that they meuyd me
that ye shold take a recompence of other lond to the valew. But they wold
not avowe the offyr, for I anserd hem that if þey had ryght they wold haue
ofyrd no recompence. Dyscwyr not thys;[15] but in my reason, *and* my lord
Chamberleyn wold send my lady a letter wyth some p⟨re⟩uy[16] tokyn betwyx 50
theym, and allso to meue my lord of Norffolk when he comyth to the
perlement, serteynly Caster is yours.

If ye mysse to be burgeys of Maldon and my lord Chamberleyn wyll, ye
may be in a-nother plase. Ther be a doseyn townys in Inglond that chesse
no borgeys whyche ought to do, *and* ye may be set in for on of those townys 55
and ye be frendyd. Also in eny wyse fo⌈r⌉get not in all hast to get some
goodly ryng, pryse of xx s., or som praty flowyr of the same pryse *and* not
vndyr, to geue to Jane Rodon, for she hathe ben the most specyall laborer
in your mater *and* hathe promysyd hyr good wyll foorthe, *and*[17] she dothe
all wyth hyr mastresse. And my lord Chamberleyn wyll, he may cause my 60
lord of Norffolk to com vp soner to ⌈the perlement⌉[18] then he shold do, *and*
then he may apoynt wyth hym for yow or þe ferm corn be gadryd. I
profyrd but xl li., *and*[19] if my lord Chamberleyn profyr my lady the remenaunt I con thynk it shall be takyn; my lady must haue somwh⟨at⟩[20] to
bye hyr kouercheffys be-syd my lord. A soper þat I payd for wher all the 65
consayll was at Framly[n]gham ij s. iij d., *and* my costys at Framly[n]gham,
twyis lyíng ther by viij dayis, wyth ix s. j ob. for costys of þe contré at
Norwyche, drawyth a-bowght xx s., I trowe more, by Ouyr Lady—if it be
lesse, stand to your harmys; *and* sic remanet v li. xiij s. iiij d.[21]

I axe no more god of you, for all the seruyse þat I shall do yow whyll the 70
world standyth, but a gosshawke, if eny of my lord Chamberleyns men or
yours goo to Kaleys, or if eny be to get in London—that is a mewyd hawk,
for she may make yow sporte when ye com in-to Inglond a doseyn yer hens,
and to call vp-on yow owyrly, nyghtly,[22] dayly, ⌈dyner, soper⌉[23] for thys
hawke. 75

I pray noo mor, but my brodyr E., J. Pampyng, ⌈Thyrston⌉, J. Myryell,
W. Pytte, T. Plattyng, Jwdé, Lityll Jak,[24] Mastyr Boton,[25] *and* W. Wood
to boote, to whyche persons I prey yow ⌈to⌉ comand me; and if all thes
lyst to spek to yow of thys mater when Syr[26] George Browne, W. Knyuett,
R. Hyd, or eny folkys of worchepp[27] and of my aqweyntanse be in your 80

---

[15] *Recto ends.*   [16] *Abbr. mark covered by mount.*
[17] ye *canc.*   [18] *Interl. above* London *canc.*
[19] he *canc.*   [20] *At edge.*
[21] *Only* v li. *marked off and underlined.*   [22] *Ampersand canc.*
[23] *Interl. above* but *canc.*   [24] B *canc.*
[25] *Fenn and Gairdner read* Botoner; *but the tail on* -n *is regular, not the* -er *abbr.; cf. no.*
346, n. 2.   [26] Jeorge *canc.*
[27] or *canc.*

company, so þat they may helpe forthe, for all is lytyll j-nowe *and* ye be not
very well wylly*ng*, I shall so p*u*ruey for ⌐hem⌐, *and* euer ye com to Norwyche *and* they w*yth* yow, that they⁵ shall haue as deynté vytayll *and* as
gret plenté ther-of for j d. as they shall haue of the tresorer of Caleys for
85 xv; and ye p*a*rauenture a pye of Wymondham to boote. Now thynk on me,
good lord, for jff I haue not an hawke I shall wax fatt for default of labor
and ded for defawlt of company, by my trowthe.

Nomore, but I pray God send you all your desyers, *and*²⁸ me my mwyd
gosshawk in hast; or rather þen fayle a sowyr hawke. Ther is a grosser
90 dwelly*ng*²⁹ ryght ouerayenst the well w*yth* ij bokettys³⁰ a lytyll fro Seynt
Elyns hathe euyr hawkys to sell. Wretyn at Norwych the xxj day of
September.³¹

J. P.

Rather then faylle a tarssell prouyd wyll ocwpy the tyme tyll I com to
95 Caleys.

354ᴀ. Letter in the name of JAMES ARBLASTER to the Bailiff of Maldon 1472, 20 September

Add. 43489, f. 51. 11½×c. 7 in. John III's hand.

Dorse: Traces of red wax, tape-slits, folded and soiled as by carrying.
Address in John III's hand:

To my ryght trusty frend John Carenton, Baylye of Maldon.

Under this in John II's hand *A° E. iiijᵗⁱ xij°.*

This letter is placed here because, though it is subscribed in Arblaster's name, it is
wholly in the hand of John Paston III. It is evidently the letter he mentions in no.
354, and the address shows that it is the original, not a copy. It is not apparent why
John III should have written on behalf of Arblaster, or how he or John II recovered
the letter; but the state of the paper requires the conclusion that this was what
happened.
F. ii, p. 98. G. 700/808.

Ryght trysty frend, I comand me to yow, preying yow to call to y*our* mynd
that, lyek as ye *and* I comonyd of, it wer necessary for my lady *and* you all,
hyr seru*aun*tys *and* ten*aun*tys, to haue thys p*er*lement as for on of the
burgeys¹ of the towne of Maldon syche a man of worchep *and* of wytt as²
5 wer towardys my seyd lady, and al⟨so⟩³ syche on as is in fauor of the Kyng
and of þe lordys of hys consayll nyghe abought hys p*er*sone; sertyfyei*ng*

---

²⁸ my *canc.*   ²⁹ -g *with stroke above crowded in.*   ³⁰ ha *canc.*
³¹ *The year* A° E. iiijᵗⁱ xij° *added in John II's hand.*
354ᴀ. ¹ of the *canc.*   ² my *canc.*   ³ *At edge.*

yow that my seyd lady for hyr parte, *and* syche as be of hyr consayll, be most agreabyll that bothe ye *and* all syche as be hyr fermors *and* tenauntys *and* wellwyllers shold geue your voyse to a worchepfull knyght *and* on of my ladys consayll, S*yr* John Paston, whyche standys gretly in favore w*yth* my lord Chamberleyn, *and* what my seyd lord Chamberleyn may do w*yth* the Kyng *and* w*yth* all the lordys of Inglond I trowe it be not vnknowyn to yow, most of eny on man alyue. Wherfor by the meanys of the seyd S*yr* John Paston⁴ to my seyd lord Chamberleyn bothe my lady *and* ye of the towne kowd not haue a meeter man to be for yow in the perlement to haue your needys sped at all seasons. Wherfor I prey yow labor all syche as be my ladys seruauntys, tenauntys, *and* wellwyllers to geue ther⁵ voyseys to the seyd S*yr* John Paston, and that ye fayle not to sped my ladys jntent in thys mater, as ye entend to do hyr as gret a⁶ plesur as if ye gaue hyr an c li.

And God haue yow in hys⁷ keping. Wretyn ⌐at Fysheley⌐ the xx day of Septembyr.

J. ARBLASTER

I prey yow be redy w*yth* all the acomptanttys belongyng to my lady at the ferthest w*yth*in viij dayis⁸ next aftyr Perdon Sonday, for then I shall be w*yth* yow, w*yth* God*y*s grace, who haue yow in keepyng.

355. To JOHN PASTON II   1472, 16 October

Add. 27445, f. 60. 11½×9½ in. Autograph.

Dorse: Traces of red wax. Address autograph:

A monser J. Paston, cheualler.

Under this in John II's hand *A° E. iiijᵗⁱ xij°*. Along the edge, in an uncertain hand, *Jenkyn* and some numerals.

The date is fixed by John II's endorsement, and confirmed by John III's repeated request for a hawk, already made in no. 354.
F. v, p. 24. G. 702/810. C. 68 (part).

Ryght worchepfull s*yr*, I comand me to yow, sertyfyi*ng* yow that Pekok hathe receyuyd of S*yr* John Stylle by a bylle all syche stuff as¹ he had of your; and as for Kendallys mater, he hathe doon as myche in it as can be doon. But as for Richard Calle, he hathe geuyn hym a pleyn answer þat he wyll not seale to the lease þat ye haue mad to Kendalle, for he seyth he wottyth not whether it be y*our* wylle or not, notw*yth*standyng he sye yore sealle vp-on it. I wold be sory to delyuer hym a subpena *and* ye sent it me.

⁴ to my *canc.*	⁵ wyse *canc.*	⁶ *Crowded in.*
⁷ kepeing *canc.*	⁸ afty *canc.*	
355. ¹ ye sent *canc.*		

I send yow herw*yth* the endenture betwyx yow *and* Townesend. My
modyr hathe herd of that mater by the reporte of old Wayte, whyche
10 rennyth on it w*yth* opyn mowthe in hys werst wyse. My modyr wepyth *and*
takyth on meruaylously, for she seythe she wotyth well it shall neu*er* be
pledgyd ought; wherfor she seythe that she wyll p*ur*uey for hyr lond þat
ye shall non selle of it, for she thynkys ye wold *and* it cam to yowr hand.
As for hyr wyll, *and* all syche maters as wer in hand at y*our* last bei*ng* here,
15 they thynk that it shall ⌜not⌝ lye in all oure porys to let it in on poynt.

S*yr* Jamys is euyr choppy*ng* at me when my modyr is present, w*yth* syche
wordys as he thynkys[2] wrathe ⌜me⌝ and also ⌜cause⌝[3] my modyr to be
dyspleaseid w*yth* me, evyn as who seyth he wold I wyst that he settyth not
by the best of vs. And when he hathe most vnsytty*ng* woordys to me, I
20 smylle a lytyll *and* tell hym it is good hery*ng* of thes old talys. S*yr* Jamys is
p*ar*son of Stokysby by J. Bernays gyft. I trowe he beryth hym the hyeer.

I*tem*, ye must sende in haste to W. Barker a warant[4] to pay John Kook
xxxjj s., *and* to the woman of Yermothe for otys x s., ⌜*and* Syr John Styll
hys[5] money⌝, for they call dayly vp-on it.

25 I*tem*, I prey yow send me some tydyng*ys* howgh the world gothe, *and*
whether ye haue sent eny of y*our* folk to Caleys. Me thynk*ys* it costyth yow
to myche money for to kepe hem all in London at y*our* charge.

I*tem*, whethyr ye haue eny thyng spokyn of my goi*ng* to Caleys.

I*tem*, as for a goshawk or a terssell, I wend to haue had on of yours in
30 kepyng or thys tyme; but fere fro jee, fer fro hert. By my trowthe, I dye
for defawlt of labore. And it may be by eny meane possybyll, for God*ys*
sake let on be sent me in all hast, for ⌜if⌝ it be not had by Halowmess the
seson shall passe a-non. *Memento mei*,[6] and in feythe ye shall not loose on
it—nor[7] yet myche wyne on it, by God, who p*r*eserue yow.
35 Wretyn on Seynt Mychell Day in Monte Tomba.

J. P.

[2] me *canc.*   [3] *In margin.*
[4] *Off-flourish on -t written over o.*   [5] *Three letters, perhaps* bra, *canc.*
[6] *These two words marked off and underlined.*   [7] by, *and* h *written over* g, *canc.*

356. To John Paston II   1472, 24 November

Add. 27445, f. 64. 11⅜×8⅜ in. Autograph.

Dorse: Traces of red wax. Address autograph:

To master Syr John Paston, knyght.

Under this in John II's hand, *Aº xijº E. iiijᵗⁱ*. Beside this, on the corresponding soiled panel which must have formed the other outside surface of the
folded letter, is the postscript, in John III's hand.

The date is given by John II's note at the end, repeated in the endorsement; but it
is clear also from the news of the Duchess of Norfolk, and of the hawk (cf. no. 355).
    F. v, p. 36. G. 708/817.

Ryght worchepfull syr, I recomand me to yow, thankyng yow most hertly
of your dylygence[1] and cost whyche ye had in gettyng of the hawk whyche
ye sent me, for well I wot *your* labore *and* trowbyll in that mater was as
myche as thow she had ben the best of the world. But so ⌈God⌉[2] help me,
as ferforthe as the most connyng estragers that euer I spak w*yth* can 5
jmagyn, she shall neuer serue but to ley eggys, for she is bothe a mwer de
haye *and* also she hathe ben so brooseid w*yth* cariage of fowle[3] that[4] she
is as good as lame in boothe hyr leggys, as euery man may se at jee; wherfor
all syche folk as haue seen hyr auyse me to cast hyr in-to some wood wher
as I wyll haue hyr to eyer. But I wyll do ther-in as ye wyll, whedyr ⌈ye 10
wyll⌉ I send hyr yow[5] a-yen or[6] cast hyr in Thorp wood *and* a tarsell w*yth*
hyr, for I woot wher on js. But now I dar no more put yow to the cost
of an hawke; but for God*ys* sak, *and* ther be eny tersell ⌈or⌉[7] good chep
goshawk that myght be gotyn, that the berer herof may haue hyr to bryng
me. And I ensuer yow be my trowthe ye shall haue Dollys *and* Browne 15
bonde to paye yow at Kandyllmas the pryse of the hawke. Now, and ye
haue as many ladyse as ye wer wont to haue, I reqwere yow for hyr sake
that ye best loue of theym alle, onys trowbyll yowr-syllf for me in thys
mater, *and* be owght of my clamor.

    Item, as for the ryng, it is delyuerd, but I had as gret peyn to make hyr 20
take it as euer I had in syche a mater; but I haue promyseid yow to be hyr
knyght, *and* she hathe promyseid me to be more at yowr comandment then
at eny knyght*ys* in Inglond, my lord reseruyd, *and* that ye shall well vnderstand if ye haue owght to do wherin she may be an helper, for ther was
neuer knyght dyd so myche cost on hyr as ye haue doo. 25

    I meruayll that I her no woord of the lettyrs that my lord Chamberleyn
shold send to my ⌈lord *and* my⌉ lady for Cast*er*. It is best that my lord

---

356. ¹ whyche *canc.*   ² *Interl. above* gold *canc.*
  ³ *First part of* -w- *apparently written over a second* o.
  ⁴ that *repeated, but canc.*   ⁵ yow *repeated.*
  ⁶ MS. of; *cf. next note.*   ⁷ *Interl. above* of *canc.*

Chamberleyn wryght to my lady by som preuy tokyn betwyx theym *and* let a man of hys ⌐com wyth⌐[18] the lettrys. My lord Chamberleyn may speed
30 wyth my lady what maters he wyll, sauyng the gret mater, *and* if ye inbyll me for a solysitor, I shalbe a vouster comandment a touz iours.

Item, me thynkyth that ye do euyll that ye go not thorowgh wyth my lady of Suffolk for Heylysdon *and* Drayton, for ther shold growe mony to yow whyche wold qwyte yow ayenst R. T. *and* all other, *and* set yow befor for
35 euer. I prey yow, for your ease *and* all others to yow ward, plye thes maters.

As for all othe[r] thyngys, I shall send yow an answer when I com to Norwyche, whyche shall be on Thorsday, wyth Godys grace. I haue teryd her at Framly[n]gham thys s[e]uennyght, for [my] lady took not hyr chambyr tyll yersterday.
40 A dewe. Wretyn on Seynt Kateryns Euyn.

J. P.[9]

I sye ⌐the⌐ pye *and* herd it spek, *and* be God it is not worthe a crowe. It is fer wers then ye wend. Be God, it wer shame to kep it in a cage.[10]

357. To John Paston II   1472, late November

Add. 27445, f. 67. $8\frac{1}{2} \times 6\frac{1}{4}$ in. Autograph.

Dorse: Paper seal. Address autograph:

To Syr John Paston, knyght.

On the corresponding outside panel, written partly over the sealing paper, apparently though not certainly by John II, a large *A° xv mens' novemb'*.

The date is fixed by the reference to the approaching birth of the Duchess of Norfolk's child (cf. no. 356, end). This must be her daughter Anne, born on 10 December 1472 (see no. 352). John II's letter no. 296 of 27 January 1476 refers to a later pregnancy, but that cannot be in question here because the Duke—who died on 16–17 January 1476—is alive, and the birth is expected within a week; cf. also no. 358. The reference to letters from the King to be brought by Slyfeld links this letter with John II's no 271, which must be a little earlier. The date given in the endorsement is therefore wrong, for November 1472 fell in 12 Edward IV. Perhaps John II wrote it when sorting his papers some years later, and associated this letter with the Duchess's later pregnancy, which was in 15 Edward IV.
F. v, p. 40. G. 712/821.

Syme recomandyth hym to your good mastyrshep *and* preyeth yow that ye wyll not forget, though he be a boye, to let hym were the same lyueré that your men do. And if it pleased yow to lete hys gowne clothe be sent hym

---

[8] *Interl. above* on delyuer *canc.*
[9] *Recto ends. In right-hand bottom corner, in John II's hand, is* A° E.iiij[ti] xij°.
[10] *This postscript on the verso, in a cramped space beside the address.*

hom, that it myght be mad a-yenst y*our* comei*ng* in-to thys contré, he wold
be as prowd as eny man ye haue.   5

S*yr*, as h*er*tly as I can I thank yow for the hatt whyche ⌈is comy*ng*, as⌉ I
vndyrstand by y*our* wryty*ng*, sent by John the Abottys man of Seynt Benet.

My modyr sendys yow God*ys* blyssy*ng* and hyrs, *and* preyes yow to get a
new lycence of my lord of Norwyche that she may haue the sacrement in
hyr chapell. I gat a lycence of ⌈hym⌉ for a¹ yere *and* it is nyghe woryn   10
ought. Ye may get it for the Byshoppys lyue *and* ye wylle.

As for the lettyrs that Slyfeld shold get newe of the Kyng, whyche ye
shold bryng to my lord of Norff*olk*, it is myn avyse that ye shall come home
y*our*-sylff as hastyly as ye maye so that ye may be at the crysteny*ng* of the
chyld that my lady is w*yth*. It shall cause yow gret thank, *and* a gret fordell   15
in y*our* mater. And as for the lettres, leue a man of y*our* to awayte on Slyfeld to bryng ⌈theym⌉ aftyr yow; of whyche lettres I avyse ⌈yow⌉ to haue
on dyrect fro the Kyng to yow, comandy*ng* yow to be the messeng*er and*
bryng*er* of the other lettres to my lord, my lady, *and* ther consayll, for
your owne mater. And thys me thynkyth shall do well, for then shall ye   20
mou shewe to my lord*ys* consayll the lettre dyrect to yow, that ye haue
awtoryté to be your owne solycytour; and also it shall be thought that the
Kyng tendryth yow *and* y*our* mater, when he wryghtyth to y*our*-sylff for it.

My lady wayteth hyr tyme w*yth*-in viij dayes at þe ferthest.²

358. To John Paston II   1472, 18 December

Add. 43489, f. 38. 13¾ × 6¾ in. Autograph.

Dorse: Paper seal over red wax and tape. Address autograph:

To my mastyr S*yr John Paston, knyght, be thys delyu*er*yd.*

Under this apparently in John II's hand, *A° x°.*

The year must be 1472 (see no. 352): the endorsement, like that of no. 357, is wrong.
The day is the first Friday on which the christening could be held after the child's
birth on 10 December.
    F. ii, p. 42. G. 714/823 (part).

Ryght worchepfull s*yr*, I recomand me to yow, thanky*ng* yow most hertly
of y*our* gret cost whyche ye dyd on me at my last bei*ng* w*yth* yow at London, whyche to my power I wyll recompence yow w*yth* the best seruyse
that lythe in me to do for your plesure whyll my wytt*ys* be my*n* owne.

Syr, as for the mater of Cast*er*, it hathe be meuyd to my ladys good grace   5
by the Byshope of Wynchest*er* as well as he kowd jmagyn to sey it, con-
sedery*ng* the lytyll leyser that he had w*yth* hyr. And he told me that he had

───

357. ¹ yerre *canc.*   ² *Last sentence crowded into right bottom corner.*

ryght an agreabyll answer of hyr, but what hys[1] answer was he wold not
tell me. Then I axyd hym what answer I shold send yow, in as myche as
10 ye mad me a solysyter to hys lordshep for that mater. Then he bad me
that vndyr consayll I shold send yow woord that hyr answer was more to
your plesure then to the contrary, whych ye shall haue more pleyn knowlage of thys next terme, att whyche tyme bothe my lord *and* she shall be at
London. The Byshop cam to Framlyngham on Wednysday at nyght, and
15 on Thursday by x of the clok be-for noon my yong lady was krystend and
namyd Anne.[2] The Byshop crystynd it *and* was godfadyr bothe, and wyth-
in ij owyrs *and* lesse aftyr the crystenyng was do, my lord of Wynchest*er*
departyd towardys Waltham. A lytyll be-for the Byshopys departyng my
lady sent for Thom*as* Davers, and ther he spak wy*th* hyr of dyuers thyng*ys*;
20 so a-mong all he remembryd hyr of Cast*er*, besechyng hyr to be good lady
in that mater as she had promysyd, *and* as he knewe well that she had[3] ben
in tyme past, for he told hyr that it was a thyng that towchyd gretly the
honour of my lord of Wynchest*er* in as myche as he p*r*omyseid yow the
pesybyll possessyon ther-of, whyche ye had not as yet. Then my lady
25 answeryd a-yen that thys next terme bothe my lord *and* she shold be at
London, and she knewe well that soone aftyr that they[4] wer com to London
my lord *and* my lord of Wynchest*er* shold meete, and aftyr thys lytyll
aqweyntance ⌐heere⌐ ther they shold haue more; at qwhyche tyme she
hyr-sylff wold devyse to my lord of Wynchest*er* syche a wey to brek in
30 to my lord of that mater that he shold speed of hys entent. But er eu*er*
T. Dau*er*s wold tell me what hys answer was of hyr, he mad me to be
sworyn that I shold neuer dy[s]cou*er* it but to yow, *and* þ*at* ye shold kepe
it secrett. And I let yow pleynly weet I am not the man I was, for I was
neuer so roughe in my mastyrs conseyt as I am now; *and* þ*at* he told me
35 hym-sylff before Rychar d Sothewell, Tymp*er*ley, S*yr* W. Brandon, *and*
twenty more, so that they þ*at* lowryd nowgh laughe vpon me.

No mor, but God look. Wretyn ⌐at Framly[n]gham⌐ the Fryday next
aftyr þ*at* I depertyd fro yow. Thys day my lord is towardys Walsyngham,
and comandyd me to ou*er*take hym to-morow at þe ferthest.[5]
40   J. P.

I prey yow recomand me to mastyr Josephe in my best wyse, *and* Sampson
dothe þe same.

---

358. [1] hys *repeated and canc.*   [2] *Name marked off by oblique strokes.*
   [3] *Second letter botched, resembles e.*   [4] -y *crowded in.*
   [5] *This last sentence to left of initials, written smaller and evidently added later.*

586

359. To the DUKE OF NORFOLK: copy   1472, late

Add. 27445, f. 68. $11\frac{5}{8} \times 6\frac{1}{4}$ in. Autograph.

Dorse: Marks of folding, soiling, and stitch-holes. No seal or address.

This is evidently a copy, though it is unusually carefully, even formally, written and
the state of the paper shows that it must have been sent—perhaps to John II for
information. The date appears from the statement that the Duke had been in
possession of Caister for three years and more (see no. 334).
    F. v, p. 44. G. 715/824.

To the right hyghe and myghty prince and my right good and gracious
            lord, my lord the Dwke of Norffo*lk*

Mekly besechyth your hyghness your poore and trew contynuall seru*a*unt
and oratour John Paston the yonger that it myght please your good grace
to call on-to your most discret and notabyll remembrance that lateward, 5
at the cost*ys* and charge of my brodyr John Paston, knyght, whyche most
entendith to do that myght please your hyghness, the ryght nobyll lord
the Bysshopp of Wynches*ter* entretyd so and compouned w*yth* your lordshepp that it liekyd the same to be so good and gracyous lord to my seyd
brodyr that, by forsse of serteyn dedys, relessis, and lettrys of attorney 10
selyd w*yth* the sealys of y*our* good grace and of other serteyn p*er*sonys
jnfeoffyd to your vse in the maner of Castre, late John Fastolff*ys*, knyght,
in the conté of Norffo*lk*, my seyd brodyr and I, w*yth* other enffeoffyd to
my seyd brodyrs vse in the seyd maner, wer peasably possessyd of and in
the same tyll syche tyme as serteyn p*er*sonys, seru*a*unt*ys* on-to your good 15
grace, entred in to the seyd maner, and therof haue takyn the jssues[1]
and p*ro*fitys in the name of your seyd hyghnesse by the space of thre yer and
m⟨ore⟩,[2] to the gret hurt of my seyd brodyr and me, your seyd seru*a*unt and
oratour. Wherfor, as I ⌐haue¬ oft tymys befor thys, I beseche your good
grace, at the reu*er*ence of God and in the wey of charyté, that my seyd 20
brodyr may by your hyghness be a-yen restoryd in-to the possessyon of
the sey[d] maner accor⟨dyng⟩[2] to the lawe and good conscyence. And we
shall prey to God for the p*re*seruacyon of your most nobyll estate.

        358. [1] *MS.* jssuses.   [2] *Ink faded owing to damp, traces visible.*

360. To John Paston II

1473, 8 March

Add. 39848, f. 59. 12⅛ × 7¼ in. Autograph.

Dorse: Paper seal over red wax and string. Address autograph:

A mysyr John Paston, scheualler, soyt doné.

Under this in John II's hand, *Mens' Marcij A° xiij°.*

The date at the end confirms the endorsement. Ash Wednesday in 1473 was
3 March.

G. 719/828 (abstract).

Ryght worchepfull syr, I recomand me to yow, sertyfyi*ng* yow that, in
lyek wyse as I promysyd yow in the lettyr that Playter sent yow, I haue
be wy*th* my modyr, *and* as well as I cowde, *and* Playter bothe, we aduer-
tyseid hyr to make cheuesance for the c li.; but we bothe kowde not remeue
5 hyr fro hyr purpose, whyche Playters lettyr specyfyeth. Wherfor looke ye
tryst aftyr non other comfort as for hyr, *and* so she bad me send yow woord.

As for Barker, Jwdé can tell yow hys answer. As for John Kook, ye[1]
promyseid hym payment your-sylff, *and* to Syr John Stylle v mark in
partye of payment; *and* therfor spake I to Barker. My modyr hathe sold
10 hyr[2] barlye for xiiij d., *and* so I told Barker. As for Maste*r* John Smythe, I[3]
meet non ofter wy*th* hym then I speek wy*th* hym of it, but I can not geet
yeet; but if I can geet it by eny meane possybyll I shall assay thys week,
for he shall keepe hys coort*ys* heer in Norwyche all thys week *and* the next
bothe. *And* as for Fastolff, I can not do but speke to Wymondham, hys
15 fadyr in lawe, *and* that do I as ofte as I meet hym; I can no more do.

But as to the gret mater that requyryth an hasty answer lest the kok be
in perayle *and* that other shold be hyndyrd by reason of my slowthe, I wold
no syche jnconuenye*n*ce shold ⌐falle¬ thorought me. Me thynkys Edmu[n]d
Fastolff was a resonabyll man to Robert of Lyne, wherfor let my brodyr
20 Edmu*n*d swe for the same, for on wyffe may serue for vs bothe tyll bettyr
pesse be. So God help me, ye maye alegge a pleyne excuse, I reke not who
knoweith it, that thees dyrk werrys haue so hyndyrd me ⌐that¬ hyr lyuelode *and* myne bothe shold be to lytyll to leue at oure ease tyll I wer
ferther befor the hand than I kowde be thys two yer, *and* she fownd aftyr
25 hyr[4] honourre *and* my poore apetytt; wherfor I had leuer forbere that I
wold haue then to bryng hem in peyn that I wold haue. Sey bettyr for me,
for ye can *and* ye wylle. Thys mater must be honestly handyld, for I wot
well my yong lady of Oxenforthe shall heere of it.

We haue here no tydy*n*gys, but a fewe Frenshemen be whyrly*n*g on the
30 coost*ys* so þat ther dare no fyshers go owght but vndyr saue co*n*dyth.

---

360. [1] pros *canc.*   [2] malt *canc.*
      [3] meet *canc.*   [4] *A word of some six letters heavily canc.*

I prey yow *and* ye haue eny more orangys then ye ocupye, that poore men may haue p*ar*te for a gret-belyed lady. And we shall prey to God for yow. Wretyn the fyrst Monday of Cleene Lent, A° E. iiij*ti* xiij°.

J. P.

361. To JOHN PASTON II 1473, 26 March

Add. 27445, f. 70. 11 × 4⅜ in. Autograph.

Dorse: Traces of red wax. Address autograph:

*To my mast*er *Syr John Paston, knyght, be thys delyuerd in hast.*

Under this in John II's hand, *xxviij° die Marcij A° xiij° E. iiij*ti.

The date given in the text and endorsement is confirmed by John II's letter no. 273, which answers this.

F. v, p. 46. G. 720/829.

Syr, it is so that my cosyn John Blenerhasset is enformyd that for verry serteyn he is chosyn to be on of the colectours of the taske in Norf*folk*, wher in v*er*ry trowthe he hathe not a foot of lond w*yth*-in the shyer. Wher-for I beseche yow that as hastyly as ye may aftyr þe syght of thys bylle þat it may please yow to take the labore to comon w*yth* Syr Rychard Harre- 5
corte, *and* to let hym haue knowlage þat thys gentyllman hathe nowght w*yth*-in the shyer, and þat ye tweyne may fynd the meane to get hym owght of þat thanklesse offyce; for I promyse yow it encomberthe ⌈hym⌉ evyll, *and* my mastresse hys wyffe *and* alle ⌈vs⌉ hys frendys here. And if so be þat ye *and* Syr R. Harcorte may not fynd the meane betwyx yow, that 10
then it may please yow to meue my lord Chamberleyn w*yth* thys mater. And so ⌈prayithe yow⌉ Mast*er* Harsset *and* Mastresse Jane hys wyff also, for she lyekyth no-thyng by the¹ ofyce. It is thowght her amonge vs þat Heydons be þe causers þat he was set in. I prey yow enqwer of Syr R. Harcort who was the cause, *and* þat it may be wyst in þe next byll þat 15
ye send me; for if they wer the causers it lythe in my cosyn Harsett*ys* power to qwytte theym.

We haue no tydy*ng*ys to send but þat our Frenshemen whyche kepte our costys her ar home in-to France, for lake of vytayll we saye. Hogan is put in þe gyldhalle in Norwyche, *and* shalbe browght vp to London for 20
reporty*ng* of hys old talys; he varythe not.

No more, but I prey God send yow the Holy Gost amonge yow in the p*ar*lement howse, *and* rather þe devyll,² we sey, then ye shold grante³ eny

---

361. ¹ offyc *and flourish canc.*   ² then ye *canc.*
³ -ran- *uncertain, apparently written over something else.*

more taskys. Wretyn þe day next aftyr Ou*yr* Lady Day the Anuncyacyon
25 A° xiij E. iiij^{ti}.

Yonge Heydon laborythe all þ*at* he can to ma⌐r⌐y on of hys doughtyr to
yonge John Barney by þe mean of W. Calthorpp.

J. P.

As I was wryghty*ng* þis bylle Mastresse Jane Harsset comandyd me
30 streyghtly that I shold recomand hyr to yow in hyr best wyse, *and* she
sendyth yow word she wold be as fayne to here fro yow as an other poore
body.⁴

362. To 'Mistress Annes' 1474, 22 July

Add. 43490, f. 43. 11⅜ × 5¼ in. Autograph.

Dorse: Marks of folding and soiling, traces of red wax, and slits for tape.
No address.

The date appears, as the manuscript index notes, from the reference to John Lee
and his wife, who are mentioned again in no. 363. 'Mistress Annes' (i.e. Agnes)
must be the 'thing' at Blackfriars, and may possibly be 'Stocton's daughter' of John
II's letter no. 287 of the same year. How John III recovered the letter does not
appear.

Fenn assigned this letter to 'John Paston', referring the signature to a facsimile
of John II's. He suggested that 'Mistress Annes' was either Anne Haute (to whom
John II was for some time engaged), or 'some lady abroad at Calais'. Gairdner, who
had not seen the manuscript, followed and enlarged upon this, and dated the
letter 1468.

F. ii, p. 294. G. 588/687.

Sythe it is so that I may not, as oft as I wold, be ther as I¹ myght do my
message my-sylff, myn owne fayir Mastresse Annes, I prey yow ⌐to⌐
accepte thys byll ⌐for⌐ my messanger to recomand me to yow in my most
feythefull wyse, as he that faynest of all other desyerth to ⌐kn⟨o⟩we⌐ of
5 yowr welfare, whyche I prey God encresse to your most plesure. And
mastress,² thow so be³ that I as yet haue govyn yow bot easy cause to
reme*m*byr me for lake of aqwey*n*tance, yet I beseche yow let me not be
forgotyn when ye rekyn vp all your seru*a*untys, to be sett in the nombyr
w*yth* other. And I prey yow, Mastresse Annes, for that servyse that I owe
10 yow, that in as short tyme as ye goodly may that I myght ⌐be⌐ assarteynyd
of⁴ your entent, and of your best frend*ys*, jn syche maters as I haue brokyn
to yow of, whyche bothe your and myn ryght trusty frend*ys* John Lee or

---

⁴ *This sentence crowded in at the head of the page after the rest of the letter was written.*
362. ¹ wold *canc.*   ² -a- *over* e.
³ be *repeated, canc.*   ⁴ *Crowded in.*

ellys my mastresse hys wyff promysyd befor yow and me at our fyrst and
last being togedyr, that as sone as they[5] or eyther of theym knewe your
entent and your frendys that they shold send me woord. And if they do 15
so I tryst sone aftyr to se yow.

And now farwell, myn owne fayir lady, and God geue yow good rest,
for in feythe I trowe ye be in bed. Wretyn in my wey homward on Mary
Maudeleyn Day at mydnyght.

Your owne JOHN PASTON 20

Mastresse Annes, I am prowd that ye can reed Inglyshe, wherfor I prey
yow aqweynt yow *wyth* thys my lewd hand, for my purpose is that ye
shalbe more aqweyntyd *wyth* it or ellys it shalbe ayenst my wyll. But yet
when ye haue red thys byll I prey yow[6] brenne it or keepe it secret to your-
sylff, as my feythefull trust is in yow.   25

363. TO JOHN PASTON II   1474, 25 July

Add. 27445, f. 76. $12\frac{1}{8} \times 6\frac{3}{4}$ in. Autograph.

Dorse: Remnants of red wax over paper tape. Address autograph:

> *To Syr John Paston, knyght, or to hys brodyr Edmu[n]d in hys[1] absence,*
> *lodgyd at the George by Powlys Wharff in London.*

Under this in John II's hand, *A° xiiij°.*

The date given in the endorsement is confirmed by the reference to Eberton's
daughter in John II's letter no. 287.
F. v, p. 66. G. 739/850.

Ryght worchepfull s*yr*, I recomand me to yow, prey*i*ng yow to reme*m*byr,
or ye depert ought of London, to spek w*yth* Herry Ebertonys wiff, draper,
and to enforme hyr that I am profyrd a maryage in London whyche is
woorthe vj^c mark *and* bettyr; w*yth* whom I preyid yow to comone in as
myche as I[2] myght ⌈not⌉ tery in London my-sylff, alweys reseruy*n*g that 5
if so be that Mastresse Eberton wyll dele w*yth* me, that ye shold not
conclud in the other place thow so wer that Eberton wold not geue so moche
w*yth*[3] Mastress Elyzabet hys dowghtyr as I myght haue w*yth* the other, for
syche[4] fantazy as I haue in the seyd Mastress Elyzabet Eberton; and that
it lyek yow to sey to Ebertons wyff that syche as I spak to hyr of shalbe 10
bettyrd rather then enpeyryd, as for my part, and if it lyek hyr to deele w*yth*
me I wylbe at London for that cawse only w*yth*-in xiiij dayis aftyr the

---

⁵ -y *crowded in.*   ⁶ eythyr *canc.*
363. ¹ y *over something else, apparently the* -es/-is *abbr.*
² I *repeated at beginning of line.*   ³ mastress *canc.*
⁴ fantay *canc.*

wryghty*ng* of thys byll, w*yth* God*ys* grace, who p*re*serue yow and yours.
Wretyn at Norwyche on Sey*nt* Jamys Day.

15 Also, s*yr*, I prey yow that ye wyll, as I desyerd yow, comon ⌜w*yth*⌝ John
Lee or hys wyf, or bothe, and to vndyrstand how the mater at the Blak
Freerys dothe, and that ⌜ye⌝ wyll⁵ see *and* spek w*yth* þe⁶ thyng your-syllf,
⌜and w*yth* hyr fadyr *and* hyr modyr,⌝ or ye depert; and that it lyek yow to
desyer John Leeis wyff to send me a byll in all hast possybyll how fer-
20 forthe the mater is and whedyr it shalbe necessary for me to come vp to
London hastyly⁷ or not, or ellys to kast all at the kok. Also, s*yr*, I prey yow
that Pytt may trusse in a male whyche I lefft in your chambyr at London
my tawny gowne furyd w*yth* blak and the doblet of porpyll sateyn *and* the
doblet of blak sateyn, and my wryghty*ng* box of sypresse, and my book of
25 the mety*ng* of the Dwke and of the Emperour; and when all thys gere is
trussyd in the male to delyuer it to the berer herof to bryng me to Norwyche.
J. P<small>ASTON</small>

Item,⁸ I send yow herw*yth* the pylyon for the male and x s. for the hyer,
whyche is vsery, I tak God to rekord. Also that it lyek ⌜yow⌝ to spek w*yth*
30 your apotycary ⌜whyche⌝ was somtyme the Erle of Warwyk*ys* apotycary,
and to weet of hym what the wedow of the Blak Freiris is woorthe, *and* what
hyr husbond*ys* name was. He can tell all, for he is exce*c*utore to the wedous
husbond. I prey yow forget me not, no more then I do yow. I haue spokyn
thys day w*yth* Jamys Hubberd and Herry Smyth, and to-morow I shall
35 haue an answer of theym. Also, my modyr wyll labore thys mater w*yth*
effect that the cc mark may be had for the wood.

Also, brodyr Edmu[n]d, I prey yow and my brodyr S*yr* John be not in
London, that ye wyll labore ⌜all⌝ thys maters⁹ w*yth* effect, as my trust is
in yow, jn ev*er*y poynt as is aboue wretyn. Also I assartayn yow that I was
40 w*yth* Ferrour thys day, and he had no leyser to comon w*yth* me, but I wyll
be w*yth* hym ayen to-morow by apoyntment bytwyx hym and me; and so
as I speed I shall send yow woord by the next man that comyth to London.

Also, I sent John Leeis wyff a lettyr by on Crawethorn, dwelly*ng* in
Wood Street or ellys in Sylu*er* Street at the end of Wood Street. I prey
45 yow weet whedyr she had it or nought. And she had it not, brodyr Edmu[n]d,
I prey yow go to the same Crawethorn and tak the lettyr of hym and
delyuer it hyr in all hast.

---

⁵ de *canc.*   ⁶ *Crowded in.*   ⁷ or nat *canc.*
⁸ *This sentence, as far as* male, *written above the signature.*
⁹ -s *crowded in.*

364. To M ARGARET P ASTON   Probably 1475, 29 March

Add. 34889, f. 129. 11⅝×6 in. Autograph.

Dorse: Almost complete seal of red wax. Address autograph:

To my ryght worchepfull modyr Margaret Paston, at Mawtby.

The probable date is suggested by the reference to wages and retinue. Margaret's letter no. 224, of May 1475, shows that some of John II's younger brothers had left home and intended to go to Calais. Letter no. 365, which is dated, shows that John III had indeed been there.

F. iv, p. 444. G. 757/868.

Ryght worchepfull modyr, aftyr all humbyll recomendacyons as lowely as I can I beseche yow of your blyssyng. Pleasyt yow to wet that late yester-nyght¹ I cam to Norwyche purposeing to haue been as thys day wyth yow at Mawtby, but it is so that I may not hold my purpose, for he that shall pay me my quarter wagys for me *and* my retenew is in Norwyche and waytyth ourly² when hys money shall com to hym. It is oon Edmu[n]d Bowen of the Cheker, a specyall frend of myn, and he avysyth me to tery tyll the money be com lest þat I ⌐be⌐ vnpayed; for who comyth fyrst to the mylle fyrst must grynd. And as I was wryghtyng thys byll on of the gromys of my lordys chambyr cam to me and told me that my lady wyll be here in Norwyche to-morow at nyght, towardys Walsy[n]gham, whyche shall I wot well be a-nother lett to me,³ but I had more need to be other-wyse ocupyed then to awayte on ladyse; for ther is as yett, I trowe, no sperre that shall go over the see so evyll horsyd as I am. But it is told me that Rychard Call hathe a good horse to sell, and on John Bocher of Oxborough hathe an other; and if it myght please yow to geue Syme leve to ryd in-to that contré at my cost and ⌐in⌐ your name, seyng that ye wyll geue on of your sonys an horse, desyiryng hym that he wyll geue yow a penyworthe for a peny, and he shall, and the pryse be resonabyll, hold hym pleasyd wyth yowr payment ought of my purse ⌐thow he knowe it not⌐ or hys horse depert fro hys handys. Modyr, I bese[che] yow, and itt may please yow, to geue⁴ Syme leue to ryde on thys message in your⁵ name, that he may be here wyth me to-morow in the mornyng betymys; for wer I onys horsyd I trowe I wer as ferforthe redy as some of my neyghborows.

I herd a lytyll word that ye purposeid to be here in Norwyche thys ⌐next⌐ week. I prey God it be thys week. Modyr, I beseche yow that I may haue an answer to-morow at the ferthest of thys mater, and of eny other seruyse that it please yow to comand me, whyche I wyll at all seasons [be] redy to

---

364. ¹ late *canc.*   ² *Superior* r *above* -ur-.
³ that *canc.*   ⁴ -ue *crowded in.*
⁵ *A short word, like* name, *interl. but heavily canc.*

accomplyshe, wyth Godys grace, whom I beseche to preserue yow *and*
30 yours. Wretyn at Norwyche thys Wednysday in Estern week.

By your sone and seruaunt J. P.

365. To John Paston II   1475, 10 October

Add. 27445, f. 92. 11¾ × 10 in. Autograph.

Dorse: Paper seal over red wax and string. Address autograph:

To the ryght worchepfull Syr John Paston, knyght, lodgyd at the George by
Powlys Wherff in London.

Dated.

F. v, p. 116. G. 763/876.

Ryght worchepfull syr, I recomand me to yow, sertyfyi*n*g yow that I haue
comonyd wyth Barnard *and* other your wellwyllers wyth my lord of
Norffo*lk*, whyche avise me that ye shold for your nyghest meane to get
Caster a-yen labore to get a lettre¹ fro the Kyng dyrect to R. Sothewell,
5 Jamys Hubbard, and oþer of my lordys consayll bei*n*g, *and* to jche of
theym; and in the seyd letter to lete theym haue knowlage that the Kyng
mevyd to my lord of the seyd mater beyond þe see, *and* hough ⌐my¬ lord
answerd the Kyng that at hys comy*n*g in-to Inglond he wold meue to hys
seyd consayll of the seyd mat*er* and geue the Kyng an answer. Wherfor
10 the Kyng in the seyd lettyr must streyghtly charge theym, *and* iche of
theym, to comon wyth my lord in the seyd mater in syche wyse that the
Kyng may be sertyfyed of an answer fro my lord *and* theym at the ferthest
by *Crastino Animarum*, for Suthewell nor Jamys Hubbard shall not be at
London befor Halowmass. And thys is the best wey that ye may take, as
15 we thynk here. My lady sweryth, *and* so dothe Barnard on hyr byhalff,
that she wold as fayne ye had it as eny body; notwythstandyng she seyd
not so to me sythe I cam hom, for I spak not wyth hyr but onys sythe I
sye yow last. Yet she lythe in Norwyche, *and* shall do tyll she be delyuerd.

But I haue be seek ever sythe I cam on thys syd the see, but I trust
20 hastyly to amend, for all my seknesse that I had at Caleys, *and* sythe I cam
ouer also, cam but of cold; but I was never so well armyd for the werre as
I haue now armyd me for cold. Wherfor I avyse yow take exampyll by me
if it happyn yow to be seek, as ye wer when I was at² Caleys: in eny wyse
kepe yow warme. I weene Herry Woodhous nor Jamys Arblaster ware
25 never ⌐at onys¬ so many cotys, hose, *and* botewx as I doo, or ellys by God
we had gone therfor. What we shall yet I can not sey, but I bere me bold
on ij dayes amendy*n*g.

365. ¹ *Dotted circumflex over -r-.*   ² Caly *canc.*

My modyr sendyth yow God*ys* blyssi*ng and* hyrs, and she wold fayne haue yow at hom w*yth* hyr; *and* if ye be onys mette she tellyth me ye shall not lyghtly dep*art* tyll dethe dep*art* yow. 30

As I was wryghty*ng* thys lettyr on told me that the Kyng shold be at Walsy[n]gh*a*m thys next [weke]; if it be so it wer best for yow to awayte on the Kyng all the wey, *and* if ye haue not men *and* horse j-nowghe I shall send yow. Do as ye thynk best, and as ye wyll haue me to do send me your avyse *and* I shall accomplyshe it to my power, w*yth* God*ys* grace, who 35 p*r*eserue yow.

Wretyn at Norwyche the x day of Octob*er* A° xv° E. iiij^ti.

P. J.

366. To John Paston II   1475, 23 October

Add. 43490, f. 17. $11\frac{1}{2} \times 7\frac{1}{2}$ in. Autograph.

Dorse: Traces of red wax and tape. Address autograph:

To Syr John Paston, knyght, lodgyd at the George by Powlys Wherff in London.

Dated.

    F. ii, p. 182. G. 764/877.

Aftyr all dwtés of recomendacyon, please it yow to vndyrstand that I haue spokyn w*yth* my lady sythe I wrot to yow last, and she told me that the Kyng had no syche woordys to my lord for Cast*er* as ye told me; but she seyth that the Kyng axid my lord at hys dep*ar*tyng ⌈fro Caleys⌉ how he wold deele w*yth* Cast*er*, and my lord answerd nevyr a woord. S*yr* 5 W. Brandon stood by, and the Kyng axid hym what my lord wold do in that mater, seyi*ng* that he had comandyd hym be-for tyme to meue my lord w*yth* that mater. And S*yr* W. Brandon gaue the Kyng to answer that he had doone so. Then the Ky*ng* axid S*yr* W. B. what my lordys answer was to hym, and S*yr* W. B. told the Kyng that my lord*ys* answer was that the 10 Kyng shold as soone haue hys lyff as that place. And then the Kyng axed my lord whedyr he seyd so or nought, *and* my lord[1] seyd yee. And the Kyng[2] seyd not o woord ayen, but tornyd hys bak *and* went hys wey. But my lady told me and[3] the Kyng had spokyn eny woord in the world aftyr that ⌈to⌉ my lord, ⌈my lord⌉ wold not haue seyd ⌈hym⌉[4] nay. And I haue gevyn my 15 lady warny*ng* that I wyll do my lord no more servys; but or we p*ar*tyd she mad me to make hyr promess that ⌈I⌉[5] shold let hyr haue knowlage or I fastonyd my-⌈sylff⌉[6] in eny other servysse. And so I dep*ar*tyd, and sye hyr not syness nor nought p*ur*pose to doo tyll I spek w*yth* yow.

---

366. [1] seyd ya *canc.*   [2] a *and incomplete* n *canc.*
[3] my *canc.*   [4] *Interl. above* a woord *canc.*
[5] *Interl. above* she *canc.*   [6] *Interl. above* sylff, *where* -ff *is written over* l, *canc.*

20 I prey yow bryng hom some hattys *wyth* yow, or and ye come not hastyly
send me on by Corby, whyche[7] shall com homward on Fryday or Saterday
next comy*ng* at the ferthest, and I shall pay yow for it a comb otys when
ye com hom. My modyr wold fayn haue yow at Mawtby. She rod thydyr
ought of Norwyche on Saterday last past to p*ur*vey yo*ur* lodgy*ng* redy
25 ayenst yo*ur* comy*ng*.

I haue been ryght seek a-yen sythe I[8] wroote to yow last, and thys same
day haue I ben passy*ng* seek. It wyll not ought of my stomak by no mean;
I am vndon. I may not ete halff j-nough when I haue most hungyr. I am
so well dyettyd, *and* yet it wyll not be. God send yow heele, for [I] haue
30 non iij dayes to-gedyr, do the best I can.

Wretyn at Norwyche the Monday next be-for Seynt Simond *and* Jude
A° E. iiij^{ti} xv°.

J. P.

Myn oncyll told Calle when he payed hym the money that I had ben at
35 London *wyth* hym to compasse hym. He ment that I cam thedyr to pr*ou*e
hys kyndness to yow ward. I prey yow tell hym that[9] I dyd nor seyd to
hym other-wyse then ye desyerd me to doo. I promyse yow he is v*er*ry[10]
wrothe *wyth* me, by Symys seyi*ng*.[11]

367. To MARGARET PASTON   1476, 21 January

Add. 27445, f. 95. $8\frac{1}{2} \times 7\frac{5}{8}$ in. Autograph.

Dorse: Remnants of red wax. Address autograph:

To my ryght worchepfull modyr Margaret Paston.

The date can be fixed by the reference to the departure of John Paston II. It is later
than the Duke of Norfolk's death on 17 January 1476 (John II's letter no. 295).
John III's next letter (no. 368) shows that John II had left Norwich before Tuesday
23 January; and since the present letter was written on Sunday the only possible
date is 21 January.

F. v, p. 138. G. 769/882.

Aftyr all dewtés of recomendacyon, pleasyt yow to weet that as yest*er*day
att noon my brodyr Syr John dep*ar*tyd fro Norwyche toward*ys* London,
for as now all the sped is *wyth* the Kyng for the swerté of the maner of
Cast*er*, consydery*ng* the dyei*ng* seasyd of my lord of Norffolk. He trustyth
5 to be in thys contré ayen *wyth*-in x or xij dayes. And at hys dep*ar*ty*ng* he
seyd to me that ye sent hym woord to selle the clothe of gold if he myght

---

7 is *canc.*   8 *Crowded in.*
9 y *canc.*   10 *Written* vrry, *with* -er *curl.*
11 *This paragraph follows on after the date, to the left of the initials, but continues below them for two lines.*

selle it well, whyche clothe I thynk may be sold iff ye wyll agré.[1] Not wyth-
standy*ng* I wylle make no bargayn for it tyll ye send me woord of the
serteyn some, what ye wyll haue for it or ellys ye to haue it a-yen. S*yr*
Robard Wyngfeld offyrd me yest[er]day xx mark ⌐for it⌐, but I wot well   10
ye shall haue more for it if ye wyll sell it; wher-for as ye wyll deele in thys
mater I prey yow send me woord to-morow be tymys, for if thys bargayn
be forsakyn I trow ⌐it⌐[2] wyll be longe ⌐or⌐[3] ye kan get ⌐an other bargayn to⌐[4]
selle it eny thyng aftyr that it is woorthe.

Modyr, in as humbyll wyse as I can I beseche yow of y*our* blyssy*ng*. I   15
trust fro hense foorthe that we shall ⌐haue⌐ our chyldyr in rest w*yth*-ought
rebwky*ng* for ther pley*ing* wanton, for it is told me your ostass at Freton
hathe gotyn ⌐hyr⌐ syche a thyng to pley w*yth* that our other chyldyr shall
haue leue to sporte theym. God send hyr joye of it. Wrytyn at Norwyche
thys Sonday.   20

Y*our* sone and humbyll seru*au*nt J O H N P A S T O N

368. To J O H N P A S T O N I I   1476, 23 January

Add. 27445, f. 96. 11¼×6⅛ in. in full, rough rectangle about 2×4¼ in. torn
out at right before writing. Autograph.

Dorse: Traces of red wax. Address autograph:

To Syr John Paston, knyght, at þe George at Powlys Wharffe.

Under this in John II's hand, *Aº xvº.*

The date given at the end and in the endorsement is clearly right, for the letter must
have been written very soon after the Duke of Norfolk's death and close to no. 367.
    F. v, p. 120. G. 770/883.

Aftyr all dewtés of recomendacyon, lyeketh yow to weet that I ensuer yow
your se*n*dy*ng* to Cast*er* is evyll takyn among my lord*ys* folk*ys*, in so myche
that some sey that ye te*n*dryd lytyll my lord*ys* dethe in as myche as ye wold
so sone entre vp-on hym aftyr hys dyssease w*yth*-ought avyse[1] *and* assent
of my lord*ys* consayll. Wherfor it is thought here by syche as be y*our*   5
frend*ys* in my lord*ys* house that, if my lady haue onys the gra*u*nt of the
wardshepp of the chyld, that she wyll ocupye Cast*er* w*yth* other lond*ys* *and*
ley the defaute on your vnkynd hastyness of entré w*yth*-ought hyr assent.
Wherfor in eny wyse gete yow a patent of þe Kyng ensealyd be-for hyrs,
and ye[2] may by eny meane possybyll.   10

367. [1] *Two words heavily canc.*   [2] *Interl. after if canc.*
    [3] *Interl. above of canc.*   [4] *Interl. above eny to canc.*
368. [1] *of canc.*   [2] *Crowded in.*

Also, I prey yow comon *wyth* my lord Chamberleyn for me, and weet hough that he wyll haue me demeanyd. ⌐It⌐ iss told me for serteyn that ther is non hey to gete at Caleys;³ wherfor if I mygh[t] be pardond for eny kepy*ng* of horse ⌐at Caleys⌐ tyll myd-somer⁴ it wer a good torne.

15 The berer heroff shall com home ayen fro London *wyth*-in a day aftyr that he comyth thedyr. If ye wyll ought comand hym I prey yow send me woord by hym⁵ hough ye do *wyth* your maters, *and* I prey yow in eny wyse lete me vndyrstand ⌐by the berer heroff⌐ hough Bowen of the Cheker wyll dele *wyth* me; vj^{xx} *and* x li. it is nough, *and* I wold haue vij^{xx} li. *and* x li., 20 and I to plege it ought in iiij or v yer or ellys to forfet the maner.

Wretyn at Norwyche the Twysday next aftyr your departy*ng* thens.⁶

JOHN PASTON

369. To John Paston II 1476, 3 February

Add. 27445, f. 97. 11¾×8½ in. Autograph.

Dorse: Traces of red wax. Address autograph:

To Syr John Paston, knyght, at the George by Powlys Wharff in London.

Under this in John II's hand, *M' Februarij A° xv°.*

The date given in the endorsement is confirmed by John II's letter no. 296, which this answers.

G. 772/885.

Aftyr all dwtés of recomendacyon, lyeketh yow to wette that w*yth*-in thys owyr past I recey[uy]d your let*ter* wretyn the xxvij day of Januar, by whyche I vndyrstand that Scarlet wold haue an end w*yth* me; but lesse then xl s. is to lytyll, for if I wold do¹ the vttermost to hym I shold recouer by the 5 statwte, I trow, xl li. or more, but lesse then xxx⌐iij⌐ s. ⌐iiij d.⌐ I wyll in no wyse. *And* ye may sey that ye of your owne hed wyll geue hym the ode nobyll of xl s., *and* if ye haue the v noblys I prey yow let Parker of Flett-stret haue ther-of xxx s., *and* lete Pytte *and* Rychard *and* Edward drynk the xl d. As for your gownys, they shalbe sent yow in as hasty wyse as is 10 possybyll.

Thys must be consayll: it ⌐is⌐ promysyd my lady by my lord Chamber-leyn that the² *diem clausit extremu*m for my lord shall not be delyuerd tyll she be of power to labore hyr-sylff her³ most aua*u*ntage in that mater, wherfor ye ned not to dele ouer⁴ largely w*yth* th'exchetour. Also consayll:

---

³ -s *crowded in.* ⁴ it wer *canc.* ⁵ hym *repeated, canc.*
⁶ *Inserted in another hand, apparently John II's:* xxiij die Januarij A° E. iiij^{ti} xv°.
369. ¹ d- *over* t. ² dy *canc.* ³ *Written* ther, t- *canc.*
⁴ la⌐r⌐gely *canc.*

Robard Brandon *and* John Colevyle haue by meanys enformyd my lady 15
that ye wold haue gotyn Caster fro hyr by stronge hand now thys frost,
whyll the mote is frosyn, in so myche that she was *pur*posed to haue sent
thedyr R. Brandon *and* other to haue kept the place tyll syche tyme as she
made axe me the questyon whedyr ye entendet that wey or not. And I
auysed hyr that she shold rather sofyr R. Brandon *and* hys retenew to lye 20
in Norwyche of hys owne cost then to lye at the tav*er*ne at Yermouthe on
hyr cost; for I lete hyr haue knowlage that ye neuer entend[5] non entré in-to
that place but by hyr assent *and* knowlage, I wost well.

S*yr*, for God*ys* sake, in as hasty wyse as is possybyll send me woord how
ye feele my lord Chamb*er*leyn *and* Bowen dysposed to me ward*ys*, for I 25
shall neuer be in herty*s* ease tyll I vndyrstand ther twoy*s* dysposysyon.

Also I prey yow let Symond Dame haue knowlage, as soone as ye haue
red thys lettyr, that I wold in eny wyse that he swe forthe the axions a-yenst
Darby *and* other for Byskley, notw*yth*standy*ng* the bylle that I sent hym to
the contrary by Edmu[n]d Jeney, for[6] Darby *and* I ar brokyn of of our 30
entreté whyche was apoyntyd at Thettford. God sped yow in thes maters,
and in all other.

Ye send me woord of a good maryage for my syst*er* Anne. I prey yow
aspye some old thryffty draffwyff in London for me. Thom*a*s Brampton
at the Blak Fryers in London, wyth syche other as he *and* I apoyntyd, wyll 35
helpe yow to aspye ⌈on⌉ for me on ther part. I prey yow *þat* I may be
recomandyd to hym, *and* prey hym that[7] he wyll in as hasty wyse as he can
comforte me w*yth* on letter fro hym *and* fro the other person[8] that he
and I comond of; *and* I prey yow, as ye se hym at the P*ar*uyse *and* ellys
where, calle on hym for the same letter, *and* telle hym that ye must nedys 40
haue on to me, *and* when ye haue it breke it, *and* ye lyst, or ye send it me.

370. To Lord Hastings   1476, 2 March

Add. 27445, f. 98. 12⅜ × 10¼ in. Autograph.

Dorse: Traces of red wax, tape-slits, marks of folding and soiling. Address
autograph:

To my lord.

The lord to whom this is addressed must have been Lord Hastings, Lieutenant of
Calais from 1471. The date appears from John II's letter no. 297, reporting that
Hastings and his retinue sailed for Calais on 9 March 1476.
    Though it appears strange that John III should have been able to recover this
letter, its condition shows that it must have been sent. Yet it is too untidily written

---

    [5] -yd *written but canc.*   [6] t *and part of* h *written and not clearly canc.*
    [7] hym *canc.*   [8] -n- *has an extra minim.*

to be appropriate for delivery to Hastings himself. Perhaps it was sent to John II to be copied fair.

F. v, p. 124. G. 773/886.

My most doughtyd and singuler good lord, aftyr most humble *and* dew recomendacyon please it your good lordshepp to have knowlage that, accordyn̄g to your comandement,[1] jn my wey homeward I reme*m*bred me of a p*er*sone ⌈whyche[2] to⌉ my ⌈thynkyng is⌉[3] meetly to be clerk of ⌈your⌉
5 kechyn, whyche ⌈p*er*sone is⌉ now[4] in seruyse w*yth* Mast*er* Fitzwater, and was befor that w*yth* Whethyll at Gwynes and purveyor for hys house, and at syche tyme as the Kyngy*s* grace was ther last in hys vyage towardes France. Thys man is meane of stature, yonge j-nough, well wittyd, well manerd, a goodly yong man on horse *and* foote. He is well spokyn jn
10 Inglyshe, metly well in Frenshe, and verry p*ar*fite in Flemyshe. He can wryght *and* reed. Hys name is Rychard Stratton. Hys modyr is Mastress Grame of Caleys. And when I had shewyd hym myn jntent he was agreable *and* verry glad if that it myght please your lordshepp to accept hym in-to your servyse, wherto I pr*o*mysed[5] hym my poore helpe as ferforthe as I
15 durst meve your good lordshepp for hym, trustyn̄g that I shold have knowelage of your plesure her-in or I departed towardes your lordshep ought of this contrey. Wherfor I advysed ⌈hym⌉ to be redy w*yth*-in xiiij dayes of Marche at the ferthest, that if[6] it pleasyd y*our* lordsheppe to accept hym or to haue a syght ⌈of⌉ hym be-⌈for⌉ your dep*ar*tyn̄g to Caleys, that ther shold
20 be no slaughthe in hym. He desyred me to meve Mast*er* Fitzwater to be good mastyr to hym in thys behalve, and so I dyd; and ⌈he⌉ was v*er*ry glad *and* agreable ther-to,[7] seyin̄g if hys sone had ben of age, and all the seruau*n*tis he hathe ⌈myght be in eny wyse⌉[8] acceptabell to y*our* lordshepp, that they all, *and* hym-silff in lyek wyse, shall be at y*our* comandment whyll
25 he leveth.

And at my comyn̄g hom to my poore house I sent for Robart Bernard and shewid on-to hym that I had mevyd your lordshepp for hym, and he in lyek forme is agreable to be redy by the xiiij day of[9] Marche to awayte on y*our* lordshepp, be it to Caleys or ellys where, and fro that day ⌈so
30 foorthe⌉ for ever whyll hys lyff wyll last, w*yth*-ought grugein̄g or contrarying your comandement *and* plesure in eny wyse that is in hym possibyll t'accomplishe. I shewed on-to hym that I had preyed Mast*er* Talbot to be a mean to y*our* good lordshepp for hym, and if so wer that Mastyr Talbot thought that y*our* lordshepp wer content to take hys servyse then, that it
35 wold please M*astyr* Talbot to meve my lady of Norff*olky*s grace to wryght

---

370. [1] *First written* comand *with flourish on* -d, *over which* e *written and* ment *added.*
[2] *Interl. above* in-canc.; *following* to *in margin.*   [3] *Interl. above* mynd *canc.*
[4] is *canc.*   [5] -d *crowded in.*
[6] if *repeated in next line.*   [7] if it *canc.*
[8] *Interl. above two words heavily canc.*   [9] Marhe *canc.*

or send to Bernard putty*ng* ⌐hym⌐ in knowlage that hyr *grace* is content that he shall become yo*ur* menyall seru*au*nt; wherof he was passy*ng* well pleasyd. But that not w*yth*standy*ng*, as I enformed yo*ur* lordshepp, he is not so reteyned neyther by fee nor pro*m*ess but that he may let hym-sylff loose to do yo*ur* lordshepe seru*y*se ⌐when ye wyll receyue hym⌐, and so wyll he do;[10] but your lordshepe so pleasid, leve wer bettyr. 40

Rychard Stratton told me that whyll he was in servyse w*yth* Whethyll, John Redwe mocyond hym onys myche aftyr thys jntent, but at that tyme Whethyll wold not be so good mastyr to hym as to meve your lordshepe for hym. 45

My lord, I trust that yo*ur* lordshepe shall lyek bothe ther *per*sones *and* ther condicyons, and as for ther ⌐trowthes⌐[11], if it may please yo*ur* good lor[d]shepe to accept my ⌐poore⌐ woord w*yth* thers, I wyll depose largely for that. And as it pleasyth yo*ur* good lordshepe to comand me in thes maters and all ⌐other⌐, jf it may please yo*ur* lordshepe to shewe[12] the same 50 to my brodyr Nessfeld, he knowith who shall sonest ⌐be w*yth* me to⌐ putt me in knowlage of yo*ur* plesure, whyche I shall be at all seasons redy t'accomplyshe to my poore power, w*yth* God*ys* grace, whom I beseche longe to contenue the pr*os*perous astate of yo*ur* good lordshepp.

Fro Norwyche the second day of Marche, w*yth* the hand of yo*ur* most 55 humble seru*au*nt *and* beedman

JOHN PASTON

371. To MARGARET PASTON   1476, probably late March

Add. 27445, f. 93. 11⅝×6½ in. Autograph.

Dorse: Marks of folding only once each way. No seal or address.

The date must be before Easter 1476. John III was clearly in the Duchess of Norfolk's household, and from the absence of reference to the Duke (contrast no. 357) this must have been written after his death on 17 January 1476 (John II's letter no. 295). It is therefore to be connected with John II's letter no. 296, of 27 January, hoping for the birth of a son to the Duchess, whose pregnancy in 1475 is also mentioned in no. 365, l. 18. The expected child evidently did not live, for the Duke's sole heir was his daughter Anne, born in 1472. The present letter cannot refer to the Duchess's confinement in 1472 because Margaret Paston apparently did not go to live at Mautby before the end of 1474. Further, the 'wrong way' (l. 20) must refer to John II's attempt to establish his right to Caister as soon as the Duke of Norfolk died, without applying to the Duchess and her advisers; see his letter no. 296 and John III's no. 369 (in which Robert Brandon and John Colvyll also appear). It is likely that the reference to 'the latter end' of a letter of John II's is to his no. 298, ll. 40–1. The suggested date would be consistent with the request for

---

10 if all *canc.*   11 *Interl. above* trow *canc.*
12 *your canc.*

a new cloth for John Paston I's tomb 'against Easter', which implies that Easter
was not far away; in 1476 Easter Day was 14 April.

F. v, p. 134. G. 765/878. C. 76 (part).

Aftyr all dewtés of recomendacyon, in as humbyll wyse as I can I beseche
yow of your blyssyng. The cheff cause that I wryght[1] to yow for at thys
season is[2] for that I vndyrstand that my lady wold be ryght glad to haue
yow a-bought hyr at hyr labore, jn so myche that she hathe axyd the
5 questyon of dyuers gentyllwomen whedyr they thought that ye wold awayte
on hyr at that season or nought. And they answerd that they durst sey that
ye wold wyth ryght[3] good wyll awayte on hyr at that tyme and at all other
seasons that she wold comand yow. And so I thynk that my lady wyll send
for yow; and if it wer your ease to be here I wold be ryght glad that ye
10 myght be here, for I thynk yowr being here shold do gret good to my
brodyrs maters that he hathe to sped wyth hyr. Wherfor, for Godys sake,
haue your horse and all your gere redy wyth yow wherso euer ye be, ought
or at home. And as for men, ye shall nott need many, for I wyll come for
yow and awayte on yow my-sylff, and on or ij wyth me.[4] But I had nede to
15 vndyrstand wher to fynd yow, or ellys I shall[5] happyly seeke yow at
Mautby when ye be at Freton; and my lady myght then fortune to be ferforthe on hyr jorney or ye cam, if she wer as swyfte as ye wer onys on Good
Fryday.

And as for the mater in the latter end of my brodyr Syr Johnys lettyr,
20 me thynk he takyth a wronge wey if he go so to werk; for as for the peopyll
here, I vndyrstand non other but that all folkys here be ryght well dysposyd
towardys that mater, fro the hyghest degré to the lowest, except Robart
Brandon and John Colvyll. And it is a grete lyklyhod that the grettest body[6]
is well dysposyd towardys that mater, in as myche as they wold put yow to
25 the labore aboue wretyn; and if they wer not, I thynk they wold not put
yow to that labore.

Also, here was here wyth me yesterday a man fro the Priour of Bromholme to lete me haue knowlage of the ille speche whyche is in the contré
now of new that the tombe is not mad. And also he seythe that the clothe
30 that lythe ouer the graue is all toryn ⌜and rotyn⌝, and is not worthe ij d.,
and he seythe he hathe pachyd it onys or twyis; wherfor the Pryour hathe
sent to yow at the leest to send thedyr a newe clothe a-yenst Estern.

Also, Mastyr Sloley preyith yow for Godys sake, and ye wyll do non
almess of tylle, that he myght borow some of yow tyll he may bye some,
35 and pay yow a-yen, for on the fayir⌜e⌝st chambyrs of the Fryers standyth
halff oncouerd for defaulte of tylle, for her is yett non to get for no money.

And the Holy Trynyté haue yow in kepyng. At Norwyche thys Twysday.

Your sone and humbyll seruaunt J. PASTON

371. [1] -yng canc.   [2] th canc.   [3] good canc.
    [4] also canc.   [5] mo canc.   [6] -r canc.

372. To John Paston II   1476, 6 May

Add. 27445, f. 101. 7⅛ × 5¼ in. Autograph.

Dorse: Paper seal over red wax and string. Address autograph:

To the ryght worchepfull Syr *John Paston, knyght, lodgyd at the George by*
Powlys Wharff in[1] *London.*

Dated. 'Shene' is evidently used as a jocular code for Caister, which John II was
still considering seizing by force; cf. nos. 298, 371.
    F. v, p. 140. G. 777/890.

Aftyr all dewtés of recomendacyon, lyeketh yow to wet that to my power
ye be welcom a-yen in-to Inglond. And as for the castell of Shene, ther is
no mor in jt but Colle *and* hys mak, *and* a goose may get it; but jn no wyse
I wold not that wey, *and* my modyr thynkyth the same. Take not that wey
if ther be eny other.   5
    I vndyrstand that Mastres Fytzwater hathe a syst*er*, a mayd, to mary. I
trow *and* ye entretyd hym she myght come in-to Crysten menys handys.
I prey yow spek w*yth* Mastyr Fytzwater of that mater for me. And ye may
telle ⌈hym⌉, synse that he wyll haue my servyse, it wer as good, *and* syche
a bargayn myght be mad, that bothe she *and* I awaytyd on hym *and* my   10
mastress hys wyff at oure owne cost, as I a-lone to awayt on hym at hys
cost; for then he shold be swer that I shold not be flyttyng and I had syche
a qwarell to kepe me at home. And I haue hys good wylle it is non jnpossy-
byll to bryng a-bowght.
    I thynk to be at London w*yth*-in a xiiij dayes at the ferthest, *and* par- 15
auenture my mastress also, in consayll be it clatryd.
    God kepe yow *and* yours. At Norwyche the vj day of May A° E. iiij^ti xvj°.
                                                                        J. P.

373. To an unknown lady: draft   Probably 1476

Add. 27445, f. 99. 11⅝ × 6¾ in. Autograph.

Dorse: Marks of folding but not as regular as usual. No seal or address.

The text is much corrected, obviously a draft. The likely date appears from Paston's
use as messenger of Richard Stratton, whom he had recommended to Lord Hastings
in no. 370. It cannot be later than his marriage to Margery Brews in 1477 (see no.
379).
    G. 774/887.

Mastresse, thow so be that I, vnaqweyntyd w*yth* yow as yet, tak vp-⌈on⌉
me to be thus bold as to wryght on-to yow w*yth*-ought your knowlage *and*

---

372. ¹ *in* repeated.

leue,¹ yet, ⌐mastress⌐,² for syche pore seruyse as I now in ⌐my⌐¹³ mynd owe
yow, purposyng, ye not dyspleasyd, ⌐duryng my lyff⌐ to contenu the same,⁴
5 I beseche yow ⌐to pardon my boldness and⌐ not to dysdeyn but to accepte
thys sympyll bylle to recomand me to yow in syche wyse as I⁵ best ⌐can
or may jmagyn to your ⌐most⌐ plesure⌐⁶; and, mastress, ⌐for⌐ syche report
as I haue herd ⌐of yow by many and⌐⁷ dyuerse ⌐persons⌐, and specyally
⌐by⌐¹⁸ my ryght trusty⁹ frend Rychard Stratton, berer her-of, to whom I
10 beseche yow to geue credence ⌐in syche maters as he shall on my behalue
comon wyth yow of, if it lyke you to lysten ⌐hym⌐¹¹, and¹⁰ that ⌐report⌐
causythe me to be the more bold to wryght on-to yow ⌐so as I do⌐ for ⌐I
haue herd oft tymys⌐ Rychard Stratton sey that ye can and wyll take euery
thyng well that is well ment; whom I beleue and trust as myche as fewe
15 men leueing, I ensuer yow by my trowthe. ⌐And⌐,¹¹ mastress, I beseche yow
to thynk non other-wyse in me but that I ⌐wyll and⌐ shall at all seasons¹²
be redy¹³, wythe Godys grace, to acomplyshe all syche thyngys as I haue
enformyd and desyerd ⌐the seyd Rychard on my behalue⌐ to geue yow
knowlage of, but if it so be that a-geyn my wyll it ⌐come of⌐¹⁴ yow that I
20 be cast off fro yowr seruyse and not wyllyngly by my desert; and that I am
⌐and wylbe⌐ yours and at your comandmen[t] in every wyse dwryng my lyff.

Her I send yow thys bylle wretyn wyth my lewd hand and sealyd wyth
my sygnet to remayn wyth yow for a wyttnesse ⌐ayenst me⌐, and to my
shame and dyshonour if I contrary it. And, mastress, I beseche yow in
25 easyng of the poore hert ⌐that somtyme was⌐¹⁵ at my rewle, whyche now
is ⌐at⌐ yours, that in as short tyme as ⌐can be⌐¹⁶ that I may haue knowlage
of your entent and hough ye wyll haue me ⌐demeanyd⌐¹⁷ in thys mater. And
I wylbe at all seasons redy to parforme ⌐in thys mater and all others⌐ your
plesure as ferforth as lythe in my poore power to do, or in all thers that
30 ought wyll do for me, wyth Godys grace, whom I beseche to send yow the
accomplyshement of your most worchepfull desyers, myn owne fayer lady,
for I wyll no ferther labore but to yow ⌐on-to the tyme ye geue me leue
and⌐ tyll I be suer that ye shall take no dysplesu[r]e wyth my ferther labore.

---

373. ¹ by me or some other for me axyd of yow be fore, and also of you befor interl., canc.
² Interl. above mastress I beseche yow canc. ³ In margin.
⁴ I mastress canc. ⁵ Crowded in.
⁶ Interl. above may please yow canc. ⁷ Interl. above of canc.
⁸ Interl. above of canc. ⁹ frend canc.
¹⁰ Crowded in. ¹¹ Interl. above wherfor canc.
¹² dwryng my lyfe canc. ¹³ why canc.
¹⁴ Interl. above be a longe on canc. The rest of the line (to yours) is written at the height of
the interlineation and the normal line left blank.
¹⁵ Interl. above was wont to be canc., before which that stands uncanc. in error.
¹⁶ Interl. above I may canc. ¹⁷ Interl. above to dele canc.

374. To Margaret Paston   1477, 8 March

Add. 43490, f. 26. $11\frac{3}{4} \times 4\frac{3}{8}$ in. Autograph.

Dorse: Conclusion of text. Remnants of red wax over paper tape. Address autograph:

To my ryght worchepfull modyr Margaret Paston.

The date appears from the negotiations for John III's marriage to Margery Brews, which took place late in 1477 (see no. 379). Topcroft (ten miles south of Norwich), where this letter was written, was the seat of Sir Thomas Brews.

F. ii, p. 220. G. 787/901. C. 81.

Ryght ⌜worschepfull⌝ modyr, aftyr all dwtés of recomendacyon, jn as humble wyse as I can I beseche yow of y*our* dayly blyssy*ng*. Modyr, pleasyt you[1] to wett that the cause that Dam Elyzabeth Brews desyreth to mete w*yth* yow at Norwyche, and not at Langley[2] as I apoyntyd w*yth* yow at my last bei*ng* at Mawtby, is by my meanys; for my brodyr Tho*m*as Jermyn,[3] 5 whyche knowyth nought of the mate[r], tellyth me that the causey or ye can come to Bokenh*a*m Fery is so over-flowyn that ther is no man that may an-ethe passe it, though he be ryght well horsyd; whyche is no mete wey for yow to passe ouer, God defend it. But all thyng*ys* rekynyd, it shalbe lesse cost to yow to ⌜be⌝ at Norwyche ⌜as⌝ for a day or tweyn, *and* 10 passe not, then to mete at Langely wher every thyng is dere; and y*our* horse may be sent hom ayen the same Wednysday.

Modyr, I beseche yow for dyuers causys that my syst*er* Anne may come w*yth* yow to Norwyche. Modyr, the mater is in a resonable good wey, *and* I trust, w*yth* God*ys* mercy *and* w*yth* y*our* good help, that it shall take 15 effect bettyr to myn aua*u*ntage then I told yow of at Mawtby; for I trow ther is not a kynder woman leuei*ng* then I shall haue to my modyr in lawe[4] if the mater take, nor yet a kynder fadyr in lawe then I shall haue, though he be hard to me as yett. All the cyrcumstancys of the mater, whyche I trust to tell yow at y*our* comy*ng* to Norwych, cowd not be 20 wretyn in iij levys of paper, *and* ye know my lewd hed well j-nough—I may not wryght longe; wherfor I fery ouer all thyng*ys*[5] tyll I may awayte on yow my-selff.

I shall do tonne[6] in-to y*our* place a doseyn ale, *and* bred acordy*ng*, ayenst Wednysday. If Syme myght be forborn, it wer well don that he 25 war at Norwyche on Wednysday in the morny*ng* at markett.[7]

Dam Elyzabeth Brewse shall lye at Jon Cookys. If it myght please yow, I wold be glad that she myght dyne in y*our* howse on Thursday, for ther

---

374. [1] *Repeated as* yow.   [2] -y *crowded in.*
  [3] te *canc.*   [4] -e *added later.*
  [5] th *canc.*
  [6] *Curve above four minims probably indicates simply* -nn-.
  [7] *Recto ends.*

shold ye haue most secret talkyng. And, modyr, at the reuerence of God,
30 beware that ye be so purveyd for that ye take no cold by the wey towardys
Norwyche, for ⌐it⌐ is the most peraylous marche that euer was seyn by
eny manys dayes that now lyueth.

And I prey to Jesu preserue you *and* yours. Wretyn at Topcroft the
viij day of Marche.

35
Your sone *and* humbyll seruaunt J. P.

375. To JOHN PASTON II   1477, 9 March

Add. 27445, f. 107. 12 × 6¼ in. Autograph.

Dorse: Paper seal and red wax. Address autograph:

Thys bylle be delyuerd to Thomas Grene, good-man of the George by Powlys
Wharffe, or to hys wyff, to send to Syr John Paston wherso evere he be, ⌐at⌐
Caleys, London, or other placys.

Dated.
F. v, p. 166. G. 790/904.

Ryght worchepfull s*yr and* my most good *and* kynde brodyr, in as humbyll
wyse as I can I recomand me to yow. S*yr*, it is so that I haue, sythe John
Bekurton dep*ar*tyd fro hens, ben at Toppcrofft at S*yr* Thom*as*[1] Brewse.
And as for the mater that I sent yow word of by Jon Bekurton towchy*ng*
5 my-sylff *and* Mastress Margery Brews, I am yet at no serteynté, hyr fadyr
is so hard; but I trow I haue the good wyll of my lady hyr modyr and hyr.
But as the mater provyth I shall send yow woord, w*yth* God*ys* grace, in
short tyme. But as for John Bekurton, I prey yow dele w*yth* hym for suerté
as a[2] soudyor shold be delt w*yth*. Trust hym never the more for the bylle
10 that I sent yow by hym, but as a man at wylde, for eu*er*y thyng that he
told me is not trewe; for he dep*ar*tyd w*yth*-ought lycence of hys mastyr
S*yr* Thom*as* Brewse, *and* is fere endangeryd to dyuers in thys contrey. I
prey God that I[3] wryht not to yow of hym to late; but for all thys I knowe
non vntrowthe in hym, but yet I prey yow trust hym not ouer myche,
15 vpon my woord.

Syr, Perse Mody recomandyth hym to yo*ur* mastyrshep *and* besecheth
yow to send hym word ⌐in hast⌐ hough he shall be demeanyd at yo*ur* place
at Cast*er*, for he is asygnyd to no body[4] as yet to take of mete *and* drynk, nor
yet wher þat he shall haue money to paye for hys mete *and* drynk; *and* now
20 is the cheff replenysheí*ng* of yo*ur* waren[5] there ⌐the auauntage of the dove
howse wer well for hym tyll ye come hom your-sylff.⌐[6]

375. [1] *MS.* Tohm*as*.   [2] soyed *canc.*   [3] wryght *canc.*
          [4] at *canc.*   [5] -t *written but canc.*   [6] *Interl. below.*

Syr, I prey yow pardon me of my wryghtyng, hough so ever it be, for carpenters of my crafte that I vse now haue not alderbest ther wyttys ther owne. And Jesu preserue yow. Wretyn at Norwyche the ix day of Marche A°. E. iiijᵗⁱ septimodecymo.

35

J. P.

376. Memorandum of marriage terms: draft   1477

Add. 27445, f. 108. 8½ × 12 in. Autograph.

Dorse: Marks of folding, No seal or address.

From its interlineations this has the appearance of a draft made by Paston to be submitted to Sir Thomas Brews for adoption as the terms on which he would give his daughter in marriage. A copy by Paston of a document written by Brews would surely have been tidier.

F. v, p. 170. G. 791/905.

Memorandum to let my cosyn Margaret Paston vndyrstand that for a jonter to be mad in Sweynsthorp in hand, *and* for a jontore of no more but x mark ought of Sparham, I ⌜wylle⌝ depart wyth cc mark in hand, *and* to geue theym ther boord free as for ij or iij yer in serteyn, or ellys ccc mark wyth-ought ther boord payable by l mark yerly tyll the some of ccc mark be full 5 payed.

Item, I wyll geve cccc mark, payable l li. in hand at the day of maryage and l li. yerly tyll the some of cccc mark be full payed, vpon thes con-dycyons folowing:

wher-of on condycyon is thys, that[1] I wyll lend my cosyn John Paston 10 vjˣˣ li. ⌜besyd hys maryage money⌝ to pledge ought[2] the maner of Sweyns-thorp[3] so that he may fynd syche a frend as wyll paye me a-yen the seyd vjˣˣ li. by xx mark a yer, so that it ⌜be⌝ not payed of the maryage money nor of the propre goodys of my seyd cosyn John;

or ellys an other condycyon is thys: if it be so that my seyd cosyn John 15 may be suffred fro the day of hys maryage to my doughter to take the hole profites of the maner of Sparham ⌜besyde⌝[4] the maner of Sweynsthorp for terme of ther two lyves *and* the longest of theym leveing, yet wyll I be agreable to depart wyth the seyd cccc mark, ⌜payable a-yen⌝ in forme above seyd.[5] And if thes or eny of the conclusyons may be takyn, I am 20 agreable to make the bargayn swer, or ellys no more to be spokyn of.[6]

376. [1] the *canc.*   [2] that I wy *canc.*
[3] now in hand *canc.*   [4] *Interl. after* as well as of *canc.*
[5] *and* to geve theym ther boord for a yer or two *canc.*
[6] for no man he *canc., and followed by a flourish.*

377. Memorandum on marriage negotiations 1477

Add. 27445, f. 111. 5¼×11½ in. Autograph.

Dorse: Marks of folding. No seal or address.

The date is clearly in the course of John III's marriage negotiations, and probably not far from that of John II's letter no. 304 of 28 March.

F. v, p. 172. G. 796/910.

Memorandum to kepe secret fro my moder that the bargayn is full concludyd.

Item, to let hyr haue fyrst knowlage that in the chapell, wher as ye wold had ben no book nye by x myle, that when Mastyr Brews seyd that he wold
5 shortly haue eyther more lond in joyntour ⌜then Sweynsthorp and x ma[r]k ought of Sparham⌝, or ellys that some frend of myne shold paye the vj^xx li. so that it shold not be payed of the maryage money, that ⌜then⌝ I sware on a book to hym that I wold never of my mocyon endanger moder nor broder ferther then I had done, for I thought that my modyr had done myche
10 for me to geue ⌜me⌝¹ the maner of Sparham ⌜in syche forme⌝² as she had done, but Mastyr Breus wyll not agré wyth-ought that my mastress hys doughter and I be mad swer of it now in hand, and that we may take the hole profytes what so euer fortune.

Item, to enforme my moder that, if so be that we may be ⌜pute⌝ in
15 possessyon of all the hole maner duryng oure two lyues and the lengest of vs leveing, þat then Mastyr Brews wyll geve me in maryage wyth my mastresse hys doughter cccc markys, payable in hand l li.; and so yerly l li. tyll the some of cccc mark be full payed.

Item, that wher as he had leyd vp c li. for the maryage of a yonger
20 doughter of hys, he wylle lend me the same c li. ⌜and xx li. more⌝ to pledge ought my lond, and he to be payed³ ayen hys c li. and xx li. by x li. by yer.

Item, to avyse my modyr that she brek not for the yerly valew of Sparham aboue the x mark dwryng hyr lyve.

378. To MARGARET PASTON 1477, probably 28 June

Add. 27445, f. 113. 11⅝×16¼ in. Autograph.

Dorse: Remnants of red wax over string. No address.

The year is apparent from the marriage negotiations. The date 'St. Peter's Day' (29 June) in the two drafts intended for Margaret to have copied should, if Paston were careful, be a day later than that of this letter. He was at Sall in the Brews household, and this letter had to reach Mautby, Margaret's home, and be copied. (The

377. ¹ Interl. above of canc.
² Interl. above so myche canc.; as she also interl. but canc. ³ in hand canc.

manor of Stinton in Sall, about five miles west of Aylsham, was Brews's residence before he acquired Topcroft. It is about 25 miles from Mautby in a straight line.)
F. v, p. 188. G. 801/915.

Ryght worchepfull *and* my most good and kynd moder,[1] in as humbyll wyse as I can or may I[2] recomand me to yow and beseche yow of y*our* dayly blyssy*ng*. Moder, please it yow to vndyrstand that tyll thys day Dame Elyzabeth Brews hathe ben so syke that she myght nevyr, sythe she cam to Salle, haue leyser to comon of my mater w*yth* Master Brews tyll thys 5 day; and thys day w*yth* gret peyn, I thynk the rather because Heydon was ther, the mater was comond. But other answer than she hathe sent yow in hyr lettre closed her-in can she not haue of hyr husbond; wherfor modyr, if it please yow, myn advyse is to send hyr answer a-yen in thys forme folowi*ng*, of some other manys hand:[3] 10

Ryght worchepfull and my v*err*y good lady and cosyn, as hertly as I can I recomand me to yow. And, madam, I am ryght sory, if it myght be otherwyse, of the dysease[4] as I vndyrstand by the berer herof that my cosyn yo*ur* husbond *and* ye also haue had a season, whyche I prey God[5] soone to redresse to your bothe easeis. And, madam, I thank yow hertly 15 that ye haue reme*m*bred the mater to my cosyn your husbond that I spak w*yth* yow of at syche tyme as I was last w*yth* yow at Norwyche, to my gret comfort. And j-wyse, mada*m*, I am ryght sory that John Paston is no more fortunate then he is in that mater; for, as I vndyrstand by yo*ur* lettyr, my cosyn yo*ur* husbond wyll geue but an c li., whyche is no 20 money lyek for ⌈syche⌉ a joyntore[6] as[7] is desyred of my son, thow hys possybylyté wer ryght easy. ⌈But⌉, madam, when I mad[8] that ⌈large⌉ grant in the maner of Sperha*m* that I haue mad ⌈to⌉ hym and my cosyn yo*ur* doughter, he told me of an other some that he shold haue w*yth* hyr then, of an c li. He ⌈hathe⌉ befor thys be wont to tell ⌈me⌉ non vntrowthe, and 25 what I shall deme in thys mater I can not sey; for me thynkyth, if more then an c li. wer promysed on-to hym by my cosyn yo*ur* husbond *and* yow, that ye[9] wold not[10] lett to geve it hym[11] w*yth*-ought so wer that I or he abryggyd eny thyng of ou*yr* p*r*omess, whyche I wot well neyther I nor he intend to do, if I may[12] vndyrstand that hys seyi*ng* to me was 30 trowthe and that it may be p*ar*formyd. But wyst I that he told me other-wyse then my cosyn your husbond and ye p*r*omysed hym, to deseyue me of Sp*ar*ham, by my trowthe thow he haue it he shall lese as myche for it, jff I leve, *and* that shall he well vndyrstand the next tyme I se hym. And,

378. [1] moder *repeated.*
[3] *These last five words added later.*
[5] sooe *canc.*
[7] ye *canc.*
[9] wyll no more *canc.*
[11] more then he and I and he wyll *canc.*
[2] bese *canc.*
[4] that *canc.*
[6] of *canc.*
[8] hym *canc.*
[10] for *canc.*
[12] se that wet that hy *canc.*

35 madam, I prey God send vs good of thys mater, for as for hys broder Syr
John ⌐also⌐, I sent ones to hym for it to haue[13] mad good the same
graunt that I grauntyd yow wyth hys assent ⌐to them and to⌐[14] ther issu
of ther ij bodyes lawfully comyng, and he dyd not ther-in as I desyred
hym; and ther-for I prey ⌐yow⌐ pardon me for sendyng on-to hym eny
40 more, for, madam, he is my sone and I can not fynd in my hert to becom
a dayly petycyoner of hys sythe he hathe denyed me onys myn axing.
Parauenture he had ben better to haue parformyd my desyer; and what
hys answer was vn-to me John Paston can tell yow as well as I. But,
madam, ye ar a moder as well as I, wher I prey tak it non other-wyse
45 bot well that I may not do by John Paston as ⌐ye⌐[15] wyll haue me to do;
for, madam, thow I wold he dyd well, I haue to purvey for more ⌐of my⌐
chylder then hym, of whyche some be of that age that they can tell me
well j-now that I dele not evenly wyth theym, to geve John Paston so
large and theym so lytyll. And, madam, for syche[16] grwgys and other
50 causys I am[17] ryght sory[18] that the graunte is knowyn that I haue mad
wyth-ought it myght take effect.

And therfor, madam, fro hensforthe I remyght all thyng to yowr
dyscressyon, besechyng yow the rather for my sake to be my son Johnis
good lady. And I prey God preserue yow to hys plesure, send yow hastyly
55 yowr hele a-yen, and my cosyn your husbond also, to whom I prey yow
that I may hertly be recomandyd, and to my cosyns Margery and
Margaret Byllyngforthe. Wretyn at Mawtby on Seynt Petrys Day.

Your MARGARET PASTON

An other lettyr to me that I may shewe.

60 I gret yow well and send you Godys blyssyng and myn, letyng yow wet
that I vndyrstand well by my cosyn Dame[19] Elyzabeth ⌐Brewsys⌐[20]
lettyr, whyche I send yow her-wyth wherby ye may vndyrstand the
same, that they entend ⌐not to⌐[21] parforme thos ⌐proferys⌐[22] that ye told
me they promysyd yow, ⌐trustyng that ye told me non other-wyse then was
65 promysed yow⌐; wherfor I charge yow on my blyssyng that ye be well
ware how ye bestow your mynd wyth-ought ye haue a substance wher-
vpon to leve, for I wold be sory ⌐to⌐ wet yow myscary, ⌐for if ye do in
your defawt looke neuer aftyr helpe of me⌐. And also ⌐I wold be as sory⌐[23]
for hyr as for eny genty[l]woman leveing,[24] jn good feythe; wherfor I

---

13 conf canc.

14 Interl. above in the canc.

15 Interl. above he canc.

16 gruggeys canc.

17 not canc.

18 of canc.

19 At edge, abbr. by stroke over -m.

20 Interl.; Elyzabeth first written with -ys ending, which is canc.

21 Interl. above to and part of another letter canc.

22 Interl. above promessys canc.

23 for hyr also interl. but canc.

24 by canc.

warne yow be ware ⌈in eny wyse⌉, and look ye be at Mawtby w*yth* me as 70
hastyly as ye can, and then I shall tell yow more.

And God kepe yow. Wretyn at Mawtby on Seynt Petrys Day.

Yo*ur* modyr M. P.

379. To John Paston II   1478, 21 January

Add. 27446, f. 8. 11¼×8¼ in. Autograph.

Dorse: Traces of red wax. Address autograph:

To my ryght worchepfull broder Syr John Paston, knyght.

Under this in John II's hand, *J. P. A° xvij°.*

Dated.
F. v, p. 208. G. 811/925.

Syr, aftyr all dutés of recomendacyon, lyeketh yow to vndyrstand that I
haue comond w*yth* dyuers folkys of the Dwk of Suff*olk* now thys Crystmass
and sythen, whyche let me in seccret wyse haue knowlage, lyek as I wrott
on-to yow, that he must mak a shefft for money, and[1] that in all hast.
Wherfor, s*yr*, at the reu*er*ence of God, let it not be lachesyd, but w*yth* effect 5
aplyed now whyll he is in London, *and* my lady hys wyff also; for I assarteyn yow that c mark wyll do more now in ther need the*n* ⌈ye⌉ shall
p*ar*auenture do w*yth* cc marky*s* ⌈in tyme comy*ng*⌉ and thys season be not
takyn. And alweys fynd the meane that my lady of Suff*olk* ⌈*and* Syr R.
Chamberleyn⌉ may be yo*ur* gwyd in thys mater, for as for my lord he 10
nedyth not to be mevyd w*yth* it tyll it shold be as good as redy to the
sealyng.

Syr, lyeketh yow also to reme*m*ber that I told yow ⌈that⌉ Mastyr Yotton
had, as I cam last toward*ys* London, desyred me by a lettre of attorney
wryttyn w*yth* hys owne hand to se th'enprowment of syche p*ro*fytes as ar 15
growi*ng* of hys chapell in Cast*er* that ye gaue hym. And at syche season
as I told yow of it ye seyd on-to me that ye wold asay to make a bargayn
w*yth* hym so that ye myght haue a prest to syng in Cast*er*. S*yr*, me thynk
ye can not haue so good a season to meve hym w*yth* it as now thys p*ar*lement tyme, for now I thynk he shalbe awaity*ng* on the Quen. And also, if 20
ye myght compone w*yth* hym or he wyst what the valew wer, it wer the
better. And I haue p*ro*mysed hym to send hym woord thys terme of the
v*er*ry valew of it, and also syche money as I cowd gader of it. Wherfor, s*yr*,
I prey yow that by the next messeng*er* that ye can get to Pekok that ye wyll
send hym woord to paye me for the lond in xxx acres, as it hathe ben 25
answerd befor tym.

379. [1] th⌈a⌉t *canc.*

And as for tydy*ng*y*s* here, we haue non, but we wold fayne here of all
yo*ur* royalté at London, as of the maryage of my lord of York *and* other
p*ar*leme*n*t mater; and so I prey yow that I may doo when ye haue leyser.
30 Syr, I prey yow that Whetley may haue knowlage that my broder
Yelu*er*ton hathe p*ro*mysed me to take hym xl d. he owyth me by reason of
hys fermore at Cast*er* more then that.

And s*yr*, as for my huswyff, I am fayne to cary² hyr to se hyr fadyr and
hyr frend*ys* now thys wynter, for I trow she wyll be³ ought of facyon in
35 somer. And so jn my p*ro*gresse fro my fadyr Brews on-to Mawtby I took
Mast*er* Playter in my wey, at whoys hows I wrot thys bylle the xxj day of
January A° E. iiij^{ti} xvij°. And I beseche God to p*re*serue yow *and* yours.

Your J. Paston

380. To Margaret Paston 1478, 3 February

Add. 27446, f. 9. 11¼ × 13¼ in. Autograph.

Dorse: Traces of red wax. Address autograph:

To my ryght worchepfull modyr Margaret Paston.

The date appears from the reference near the end to Paston's wife's taste for dates
'at this season'. This presumably implies pregnancy, and the general tone of the
letter suggests that it was her first. John III's son Christopher was born in 1478;
see John II's letter no. 312.

F. v, p. 212. G. 812/926.

Ryght worchepfull modyr, aftyr all dwtés of humble recomendacyon, in as
humble wyse as I can I beseche yow of y*our* dayly blyssy*ng*. Pleasyt yow
to wett that at my bei*ng* now at London, lyek as ye gaue me in comand-
me*n*t I mevyd to Mastyr Pykenh*a*m *and* to Jamys Hubart for ther bei*ng*
5 at Norwyche now thys Lent, that ye myght haue ther avyses in syche
maters as ye let me haue vndyrstandy*ng* of. And as for Mastyr Pykenh*a*m,
he is now Juge of the Archys, and also he hathe an other offyce whyche is
callyd *Auditor causar*um, and hys besyness is so gret in bothe thes offyces
that he can not tell the season when that he shall haue leyser to come in-to
10 Norff*olk*; but I left not tyll I had gotyn Jamys Hubbart *and* hym to-gedyrs,
and then I told theym yo*ur* jntent. And then Mastyr Pykenh*a*m¹ told Jamys
and me hys jntent, and he preyed Jamys that he shold in no wyse fayle to
be w*yth*² yow thys Lent. Not w*yth*standy*ng* it was no gret ned to prey hym
myche, for he told Doctore Pykenh*a*m that ther was no gentylwoman in
15 Inglond of so lytyll aqueyntance as he had w*yth* yow that he wold be³

² hym *canc.*   ³ g *and the beginning of* r *canc.*
380. ¹ pu *canc.*   ² yow *canc.*   ³ s *canc.*

glader to do servyse on-to, and myche the glader for he purposeth[4] fro
hensforthe duryng hys lyff to be a Norffolk man *and* to lye wyth-in ij myle
of Loddon,[5] whyche is but viij or x myle at the most fro Mautby. And in
conclusyon he hathe appoyntyd to awayte on yow at Norwyche the weke
next aftyr Mydlent Sonday, all the hole weke if nede be, all other maters   20
leyd apart. Also I comond wyth my brodyr Syr John at London of syche
maters as ye wold haue amendyd in the bylle that he sent on-to yow, and
he stake not gretly at it.

Also, modyr, I herd[6] whyle I was in London wher was a goodly yong
woman[7] to mary whyche was doughter to on Seff, a merser, and she shall   25
haue cc li. in money to hyr maryage *and* xx mark by yer of lond aftyr the
dyssease of a steppe-modyr of hyrs whyche is vpon l yer of age. And or
I departyd ought of London I spak wyth some of the maydys frendys, and
haue gotyn ther good wyllys to haue hyr maryd to my brodyr Edmund.
Notwythstandyng those frendys of the[8] maydys that I comond wyth avysyd   30
me to get the good wyll of on Sturmyn, whyche is in Mastyr Pykenhamys
danger so myche that he is glad to please hym. And so I mevyd thys mater
to Mastyr Pykenham, and jncontynent he sent for Sturmyn and desyred
hys good wyll for my brodyr Edmu[n]d, and he[9] grantyd hym hys good
wyll so that he koud get[10] the good wyll of the remenaunt that wer execu-   35
tours to Seff, as well as the seyd Sturmyn was; and thusferforthe is the
mater. Wherfor, modyr, we must beseche yow to helpe vs forward wyth a
lettyr fro yow to Mastyr Pykenham to remembyr hym for to[11] handyll well
and dylygently thys mater now thys Lent. And for I am aqueyntyd wyth
your condycyons of old, that ye reke not who endytyth more lettres then   40
ye, ther-for I haue drawyn a note ⌜to⌝ yowr secretarys hand Freir Perse,
whyche ⌜lettre⌝ we must prey yow to send vs by the berer herof, *and* I
trust it shall not be longe fro Mastyr Pykenham.

Your doughtyr of Sweynsthorp *and* hyr soiornaunt E. Paston recomandyth hem to yow in ther most humble wyse, lowly besechyng yow of your   45
blyssyng. And as for my brodyr Edmu[n]d Sweynsthorp, for non jntreté
that hys ostas your doughtyr nor I koud jntrete hym myght not kepe hym
but that he wold haue ben at home wyth ⌜you⌝ at Mautby on Sonday last past
at nyght; *and* as he was departyng fro hens had we word fro Frenshes wyf
that, God yeld yow, modyr, ye had govyn hym leve to dysporte hym her   50
wyth vs for a vij or viij dayes. And so the drevyll lost hys thank of vs, *and*
yet abod nevyr the lesse. Youyr doughtyr sendyth yow part of syche poore
stuff as I sent hyr fro London,[12] besechyng yow[13] to take it ⌜in⌝ gree though
it be lytyll plenté that she sendyth yow. But as for datys, I wyll sey trowthe

[4] -th *crowded in.*	[5] *First* d *over* n.
[6] -d *crowded in.*	[7] *Ampersand canc.*
[8] mady *canc.*	[9] grandyd *canc.*
[10] the remnant *canc.*	[11] to *repeated.*
[12] besy *canc.*	[13] th *canc.*

55 ye haue not so many by ij pownd as wer ment on-to yow, for she thynkys at thys season datys⁷ ryght good mete, what so ever it mea[n]yth.

I prey God send vs good tydyngys, whom I beseche to preserue yow *and* yours *and* to send yow your most desyred joye. At Sweynsthorp on Ashe Wednysday.

60   *Your* sone *and* humble seruaunt J. PASTON

Modyr, pleasit yow to remember that ye had need to be at Norwych v or vj dayes befor that Jamys Hubbart *and* your consayll shall be ther wyth yow, for to look vp your evydence *and* all other thyngys redy. Also, if ye thynk that thys bylle that I send yow herwyth be good j-now to send to
65 Doctore Pykenham, ye may close vp the same *and* send ⌜it⌝ sealyd to me ayen ⌜and⌝ I shall convey it forthe to hym.

381. To JOHN PASTON II   1479, 6 November

Add. 27446, f. 32. 11¼×12⅜ in. Autograph.

Dorse: Traces of red wax over string. Address autograph:

To Syr John Paston, knyght.

The date appears from the reference to business with the escheator. This links up with John II's dated letter no. 315, to which this is an answer.

Edmond Paston's 'bargain' with Mistress Clippesby led to their marriage shortly after this; see his letter no. 399.

F. v, p. 254. G. 841/957.

Syr, aftyr all¹ dutés of recomendacyon, pleasyt to vndyrstand that, acordyng to your lettre sent me by Wyllson, Lomnore and I mett at Norwyche and drew ought a formable bylle ought of your, and sent it a-yen to th'exchetore Palmer by my brodyr Edmund, whyche had an other erand in-to that
5 contré to spek wyth H.² Spylman to get hys good wyll towardys the³ bargayn lyek to be fynyshed hastyly betwyx Mastress Clyppysby and hym. And, syr, at the delyueré of the bylle of jnquisicyon to th'exchetour, my brodyr Edmu[n]d told hym that, accordyng to your wryghtyng to me, I spak wyth myn oncle Willam and told hym that I vndyrstood by yow that my lord of
10 Elye had aswell desyred hym in wryghtyng as you by mouthe that non of you shold swe to haue the jnquisycion fond aftyr your jntentys tyll other weyes of pese wer takyn betwyx yow; wherfor my brodyr Edmu[n]d desyred hym that wyth-ought myn oncle labord to haue it fond for hym, ellys that he shold not proced for yow. But th'exchetour answerd hym⁴ that
15 he wold fynd ⌜it⌝ for you aftyr your byll of hys owne autorité, and so it was

381. ¹ all *repeated.*   ² *Crowded in.*
³ *Some six or seven letters heavily canc.*   ⁴ that he wold *canc.*

fond. But, syr, ye must remembre that[5] my lord of Ely desyred myn oncle
as well as you to surcease, as I putt my oncle in knowlage. And myn oncle
at the fyrst agreid[6] that he wold make no more sute a-bought it, ⌐in¬ trust
that ye wold do the same acordy*ng* to my lord of Elys desyer; wherfor ye
had ned to be ware that th'excheter slyppe not fro yow when he comyth   20
to London *and* sertyfye it or ye spek w*yth* hym. Th'excheter shalbe at
London by Twysday or Wednysday next comy*ng*, ⌐at John Leeis house¬,
for he shall ryd forwardys as on Monday next comy*ng* betymys, &c.

Syr, your ten*auntys* at Crowmer sey that they know not who shalbe ther
lord; they marvayll that ye nor no man for yow hathe not yet ben there.   25
Also, when I was w*yth* myn oncle I had a longe pystyll of hym that ye had
sent Pekok to Paston and comandyd the ten*auntys* ther that they shold pay
non areragys to hym but if they wer bond to hym by oblygacyon for the
same. Myn oncle seythe it was other-wyse apoyntyd be-for the arbytrorys.
They thought, he seyth, as well my Mastyr Fytzwalter as other, that he   30
shold receyue that as it myght be gadryd; but now he seythe that he wottyth
well some shall renne awey *and* some shall wast it, so that it is nevyr lyek
to be gadryd, but lost. And so I trow it is lyek to be of some of the dettors,
what for casuelté of dethe and thes other causes befor rehersyd. Wherfor
me thynkyth if it wer apoyntyd[7] be-for the[8] arbytrors that he shold   35
receyue theym as he seythe,[9] it wer not for yow to brek it; or ellys if he be
pleyn executor to my gr*au*ntdam then also he ought to haue it. I spek lyek
a blynd man. Do ye as ye thynk, for I was at no syche apoyntme*nt* befor
th'arbytrors, nor I know not whethyr he is executor to my gr*au*ntdam[10] or
not ⌐but¬ by hys seyi*ng*.   40

Also, syr,[11] ye must of ryght, consydery*ng* my brodyr Edmu*n*dys dili-
gence in y*our* maters sythe y*our* depa*r*tyng, helpe hym forwardys to myn
oncle S*yr* George Brown, as my brodyr Edmu[n]d preyid yow in hys lettyr
that he sent on-to yow by Mondys sone of Norwyche, dwelly*ng* w*yth* Thom*as*
Jenney, that myn oncle S*yr* George may gett to my brodyr Edmu*n*d of the   45
kyng þe wardshepp of John Clyppysby, son *and* heyer to John Clyppysby,
late of Owby in the conté of Norff*olk*, sqwyr, dwry*ng* the nonnage of my
lord *and* lady of York, thow it cost iiij or v mark the swte. Let myn oncle
S*yr* George be clerk of the hamper and kepe the patent, if it be gr*a*ntyd,
tyll he haue hys moné, *and* that shall not be longe to. Myn oncle S*yr* George   50
may enforme the Kyng for trowthe that the chyld shall haue no lond
dwry*ng* hys yong modyrs lyff, and ther is no man her that wyll mary w*yth*
hym wyt*h*-ought they haue some lond w*yth* hym; and so the gyft shall not
be gret that the Kyng shold geve hym. And yet I trow he shold get the

---

[5] that *repeated, canc.*   [6] that *canc.*
[7] tha *canc.*   [8] *Written* they, -y *canc.*
[9] me th *canc.*   [10] of *canc.*
[11] *A rough line is drawn under the line of writing which ends here, and in the margin a little
below is* no *and raised* t *ending in a flourish, i.e.* 'nota'.

55 modyr by that meane, and in my conseyt the Kyng dothe but ryght if he
graunt my brodyr Edmu[n]d Clyppysbys son in recompence for takyng
my brodyr Edmu*n*dys son, otherwyse callyd Dyxsons, the chyldys fadyr
being alyve. Dyxson is ded, God haue hys sowle, whom I beseche to send
you your most desyred joye.

60   Wretyn at Norwyche on Seynt Leonard*y*s Day.

J. PASTON

Syr, it is told me þat Nycolas Barlee, the scyuer, hathe takyn an axion
of dett ayenst me thys terme. I prey yow let Whetley or some body spek
wyt*h* hym and lete hym wet that if he swe me softly thys terme¹² that he
65 shall be payed or the next terme be at an end. It is a-bought vj li., and in
feythe he shold haue had it or thys tyme and our threshers¹³ of Sweynsthorp had not dyed vpp. And if I myght haue payed it hym a yer ago, as
well as I trust I shall sone aftyr Crystmass, I wold not for xij li. haue brokyn
hym so many p*ro*messys as I haue.

70   Also, s*yr*, I prey yow send me by the next man that comyth fro London
ij pottys of tryacle of Jenne—they shall cost xvj d.; for I haue spent ought
that I had wyt*h* my yong wyff *and* my yong folkys *and* my-sylff. And I
shall pay hym that shall bryng hem to me, *and* for hys caryage. I prey yow
lett it be sped. The pepyll dyeth sore in Norwyche, *and* specyally a-bought
75 my house; but my wyff *and* my women come not ought, *and* fle ferther we
can not, for at Sweynsthorp sythe my dep*ar*tyng thens¹⁴ they haue dyed
and ben syke nye jn¹⁵ ev*er*y house of¹⁶ the towne.

382. Account   1479, after 25 November

Add. 27446, f. 35. 4¼ × 6¼ in. Autograph.

Dorse blank.

The year is fixed by the reference to the death of Walter Paston (see Edmond II's
letter no. 397). The day of writing was probably a little later than the receipt of the
money mentioned in the first sentence.
    F. v, p. 252. G. 845/961.

Rec*eyuy*d at Cressi[n]gh*a*m the Thursday nex aftyr Seynt Edmu[n]d at the
corte ther v li. x s. by the handys of me John Paston, sqwyer

Wherof payed to my modyr for costys don vp-on the bery*ng*
of Walter¹ Paston and whyll he lay sek, *and* for the hyer of a man   xxix s.
5 comy*ng* wyt*h* the seyd Water fro Oxn.² xx d.   xj d.³

---

¹² terme *repeated, canc.*   ¹³ *Uncertain; apparently first written* ther-, *then* e *canc.*
¹⁴ thy *canc.*   ¹⁵ *Corr. from* nyen.   ¹⁶ thys *canc.*
382. ¹ -l- *crowded in.*   ² -n *tailed.*   ³ v *canc. before* x.

Item, payed to William Gybson for j horse sadyll *and* brydyll
lent to[4] Water Paston by the seyd William   xvj s.

Item, gevyn the seyd man comy*ng* fro Oxn.[2] wyt*h* the seyd
Water by the handys of J. Paston   xx d.

Item, payed for dyuers thyng*ys* whyll Water Paston lay sek   iiij d. 10

Item, for the cost*ys* of John Paston rydy*ng* to kepe the coort at
Cressi[n]gham a*nn*o supr*ad*icto, whych was iiij dayes in doi*ng*
for the styward mygh[t] not be ther at þe day p*r*efyxid.   iij^s· iiij^d·

383. To Margaret Paston   1479, November

Add. 43490, f. 39. 11¾×6½ in. Autograph.

Dorse: Postscript. Paper seal over red wax. Address autograph:

*To my ryght worc⟨he⟩pfull modyr Margarett Paston at Sey*nt *Peters*[1] *of
Hundgate.*

The date is immediately after the death of John Paston II, which took place in
November 1479. (The writ to the escheator requiring an inquisition to be held is
dated 30 November; the record of the inquisition itself is lost—*Inq.p.m.*, 20
Edward IV, no. 15. Fenn gives the date of death as 15 November, but cites no
authority.)
    F. ii, p. 280. G. 846/962. C. 92 (all without postscript).

Ryght worchepfull modyr, aftyr all dwtés of humble recomendacyon, as
lowly as I can I beseche yow of yo*ur* dayly blyssy*ng and* preye[r]s. And,
modyr, John Clement, berer heroff, can tell yow the mor pité is, if it
pleasyd God, that my brodyr is beryed in the Whyght Fryers at London,
whych I thought shold not haue ben, for I supposyd that he wold haue   5
ben beryed at Bromholme. And that causyd me ⌈so⌉[2] sone to ryd to London
to haue p*ur*veyd hys bryngi*ng* hom; and if it had ben hys wylle to haue leyn
at Bromholm, I had p*ur*posyd all the wey as I haue redyn to haue brought
hom my gr*aun*tdam *and* hym to-gedyrs, but that p*ur*pose is voyd as now.
    But thys I thynk to do when I com to London, to spek wyt*h* my lord   10
Chamberleyn *and* to wynne by hys meanys my lord of Ely if I can. And if
I may by eny of ther meanys cause the Kyng to take my servyse *and* my
quarell to-gedyrs, I wyll; and I thynk that S*yr* George Brown, S*yr* Jamys
Radclyff, and other of myn aqueyntance whyche wayte most vpon the
Kyng and lye nyghtly in hys chamber wyll put[3] to ther good wyllys. Thys   15
is my wey as yet. And, modyr, I[4] beseche yow, as ye may get or send eny
messengers, to send me yo*ur* avyse, *and* my cosyn Lomenors, to John

    ⁴ the *canc.*
  383. ¹ *Written* pe *with* t, er *abbr.,* and s *all raised.*   ² *Interl. above* the *canc.*
    ³ *No space.*   ⁴ *Crowded in.*

Leeis hows, taylore, w*yth*-in Ludgate. I haue myche more to wryght, but myn empty hed wyll not let me re*m*ember it.

20   Also, modyr, I prey that my brodyr Edmu[n]d may ryd to Marly[n]g-forthe, Oxenhed, Paston, ⌐Crowmer⌐, *and* Cast*er* and in all thes maners to entre in my name, *and* to lete the ten*au*ntys of Oxenhed *and* Marly*n*gfor[the] know that I⁵ sent no word to hym to take no mony of theym but ther attornement; wherfor ⌐he⌐ wyll not, tyll he her fro me ayen, axe hem non,

25 but let hym comand theym to pay to ⌐no⌐ seru*a*unt of myn oncles, nor to hym-sylff nor⁶ to non othyr to hys vse, in peyne of payment a-yen to me. I thynk if ther shold be eny money axid in my name, p*ar*auenture it wold ⌐make⌐ my lady of Norff*olk* ayenst ⌐me⌐ *and* cause hyr to thynk I dellt more contrary to hyr plesure⁷ than dyd my brodyr, whom God p*ar*don of hys

30 gret mercy. I haue sent to entre at Stansted *and* at Orwellbery, *and*⁸ I haue wretyn a bylle to Anne Montgomery and Jane Rodon to mak my lady of Norff*olk* if it wyll be.

                      Y*our* sone *and* humble seru[au]nt J. Paston⁹

If myn vnkynd oncle make eny mastryes to gadre money, areragys or 35 other, my Mastyr Fytzwater, S*yr* Robart Wyngfeld, S*yr* Thom*a*s Brew[s], my brodyr Yelu*er*ton, my brodyr Harecort, *and* other of my frendys I trust wyll sey hym naye, if they haue knowlage.

384. To Margaret Paston   1479, December

Add. 27446, f. 39. 11½ × 8⅜ in. Autograph.

Dorse: Traces of red wax. Address autograph:

   To my ryght worchepfull and most kynd modyr Margaret Paston.

The date is not long after the death of John Paston II. A letter from Lomnor here referred to is dated 28 November (Part II, no. 793), so that this must have been written early in December.

   F. v, p. 266. G. 849/965.

Ryght worchepfull modyr, aftyr all dutés of humble recomendacyon, as lowly as I can I beseche yow of your dayly blyssy*n*g *and* preyer. Pleasyt yow to vndyrstand that, wher as ye wyllyd me by Poiness to hast me ought of the heyer that I am jn, it is so that I must put me in God, for her must 5 I be for a season; and in good feyth I shall never, whyll God sendyth me lyff, dred mor dethe then shame. And thankyd be God, the sykness is well seasyd here; *and* also my besyness puttyth a-wey my fere. I am drevyn to

⁵ I de *canc.*   ⁶ -r *crowded in.*
⁷ thyn *canc.*   ⁸ *Capital* A, *with ampersand above.*
⁹ *Recto ends.*

labore in lettyng of th'execucyon of myn vnkynd onclys entent, wher-in I
haue as yet non other dyscorage but that I trust in God he shall fayle of it.

I haue spokyn wyth my lord of Ely dyvers tymys, whyche hathe put me
in serteynté by hys woord that he wyll be wyth me ayenst myn oncle in
iche mater that I can shewe that he entendyth to wrong me in. And he wold
fayne haue a resonable end be-twyx vs, wher-to he wyll helpe, as he seythe.
And it is serteyn my brodyr, God haue hys soule, had promysed to a-byde
the reule of my lord Chamberleyn *and* of my lord of Ely, but I am not
yett so ferr forthe, ⌈nor⌉ not wyll be tyll I know my lord Chamberleyns
intent. And that I purpose to do to-morow, for then I thynk to be wyth
hym, wyth Godys leve.

And sythe it is so that God hathe purveyd me to be the solysytore of thys
mater, I thank hym of hys grace for the good lordys, mastyrs, *and* frendys
that he hathe sent me, whyche haue parfytely promysyd me to take my
cause as ther owne; and those frendys be not a fewe. And, modyr, ⌈as⌉ I
best can *and* may I thank yow *and* my cosyn Lomenore of the good avyse
that ye haue sent ⌈me⌉, and I shall aplye me to do ther-aftyr. Also, modyr,
I beseche ⌈you⌉ on my behalff to thank myn cosyn Lomnorre for þe[1]
kyndness that he hathe shewyd on-to me in gevyng of hys answer to myn
onclys seruaunt whyche was wyth hym.

Modyr, I wryght not so largely to yow as I wold do, for I haue not most
leyser. And also, when I haue ben wyth my lord Chamberleyn, I purpose
not to tery longe aftyr in London, but to dresse me to yow wardys; at
whyche tyme I trust I shall brynge yow more serteynté of all ⌈the⌉ fordell
that I haue in my besyness then I can as yett ⌈wryght⌉. I am put in serteynté by my most specyall good mastyr, my Mastyr of the Rollys, that my
lord of Ely is *and* shalbe bettyr lord to me then he hathe shewyd as yet; and
⌈yet⌉ hathe ⌈he⌉ delt wyth me ryght well *and* honourably.

Modyr, I beseche yow that Pekok may be sent to to purvey me as myche
money as is possybyll for hym to make ayenst my comyng hom, for I haue
myche to pay her in London, what for the funerall costys, dettys, *and*
legattys that must be content in gretter hast then shalbe myn ease. Also I
wold the ferme barly in Flegge, as well as at Paston if ther be eny, wer
gadryd, and iff it may be resonably sold, then to be sold or putt to the
maltyng; but I wold at Caster that it were ought of the tenauntys handys,
for thyngys that I here. ⌈Kepe ye consell thys fro Pekok *and* all folkys⌉[2];
whyche ⌈mater⌉ I shall appese if God wyll geve me leve.

384. [1] *Crowded in.*   [2] *Interl. in a hasty scribble.*

385. Memorandum of complaints against WILLIAM PASTON II: draft
After 1479

Add. 27446, f. 40. $7\frac{3}{4} \times 6\frac{1}{2}$ in. Autograph.

Dorse: Marks of folding but not soiled by carrying. No seal or address. Endorsement autograph:

Copyes of draughtes[1] of the wrongys don by W. Paston to J. Paston ⌈fadyr⌉, Syr J.P. and J.P.

The date is after the death of John Paston II.
  G. 850/966.

Thes be th'eniuryes[2] *and* wrongys don by Wil*l*iam Paston to John Paston[3] hys nevew.

Fyrst, the maners of Marly[n]gforthe, Stansted, and Horwellbery was gev⟨en . . .⟩[4] Wil*l*iam Paston, justyce,[5] and to Agnes hys wyff *and* to th'eyers
5 of ther[6] tw⟨o bodyes⟩, to whom the seyd John Paston is cosyn *and* heyer, that is to sey ⟨. . .⟩ son ⌈to⌉[7] John, son ⌈*and* heyer⌉ to the seyd Wil*l*iam[8] *and* Agnes.

Item, wher ⌈Ed*mund* Clere wy*th* other jnfeoffyd to the vse of the seyd Will⟨*iam* Paston⟩[9] *and* of hys heyres, the whyche Wil*l*iam mad hys wyll
10 that th⟨e seyd Agnes⟩ ⌈hys⌉[10] ⟨wyff⟩ shold haue the seyd maner for terme of hyr lyff, and aftyr th⟨e seyd Wil*l*iam⟩ dyed and the seyd Agnes occupyed for terme of hyr seyd lyff ⟨. . .⟩ of the seyd feoffés the seyd maner; and aftyrwardes the seyd ⟨Agnes dyed⟩, afftyr whoys dethe Syr John Paston, knyght, as cosyn *and* heyer to t⟨he seyd Agnes⟩ in-to the seyd
15 maner entred, *and* dyed wy*th*-ought issue of hys bodye ⟨. . .⟩ John as brodyr *and* heyer to the seyd Syr John[11] ⟨. . .⟩ seyd maner entred, and is lettyd to take the pro*f*ytys of the same by ⟨. . .⟩ of the maners of Marly[n]gforthe, Stansted, *and* Horwelbery befor r⟨ehersyd⟩ by the meanys of the seyd Wyll*i*am.

---

385. [1] *These three words crowded in; after them, M canc.*
  [2] *-s added later.*   [3] squyer *canc.*
  [4] *Paper decayed at right edge, with irregular loss at ends of most lines.*
  [5] &c. *canc.*   [6] t- *crowded in.*
  [7] *Interl. above* of *canc.*   [8] justys *canc.*
  [9] *Interl. above* the seyd Wil*l*iam Paston was seasyd of the maner of *canc.*
  [10] *Below the* th *preceding the mutilation.*
  [11] and cosyn *and* heyer is lett *canc.*

386. To M A R G A R E T   P A S T O N   Between 1482 and 1484

Add. 27446, f. 48. 11½ × 8 in. Autograph.

Dorse: Traces of red wax. Address autograph:

> *To my ryght worchepfull modyr Margaret Paston.*

The date is after Margaret Paston made her will. The version of her will which took effect, and of which copies survive (see no. 230), was made on 4 February 1482 and proved on 18 December 1484. According to John II's servant Whetley she had made a will as early as 1478 (see his letter of 20 May 1478, Part II, no. 782); but the reference here must be to the later one because the general circumstances are obviously later than the death of John II.

F. v, p. 296. G. 862/979. C. 95.

Ryght worchepfull modyr, jn my most humble wyse I recomand me to yow, besechyng yow of your dayly blyssyng; and when I may, I¹ wyll with as good wyll be redy to recompence yow for the cost that my huswyff *and* I haue put yow to as I am now bond to thank yow for it, whyche I do in the best wyse I can. And, modyr, it pleasyd yow to haue serteyn woordys to my 5 wyff at hyr depertyng towchyng your² remembrance of ⌈the⌉ shortness that ye thynk your dayes of, and also of the mynd that ye have towardys my brethryn *and* systyr, your chyldyr, and also of your seruauntys, wher-in ye wyllyd hyr to be a meane to me that I wold tendyr and favore the same. Modyr, savyng your plesure, ther nedyth non enbasatours nor meanys 10 betwyx yow *and* me, for ther is neyther wyff nor other frend shall make me to do that that your comandment shall make me to do, jf I may have knowlage of it. And if I haue no knowlage, jn good feyth I am excuseabyll bothe to God *and* yow. And well remembred, I wot well ye ought not to haue me in³ jelusye for on thyng nor other that ye wold haue me to accom- 15 plyshe if I overleve yow, for I wot well non oo man a-lyve hathe callyd so oft vpon yow ⌈as I⌉ to make your wylle and put iche thyng in serteynté that ye wold have don for your-sylff *and* to your chyldre *and* seruauntys. Also, at the makyng of your wylle, and at every comunycacyon that I haue ben at wyth yow towchyng the same, I nevyr contraryed thyng that ye wold 20 have doon *and* parformyd, but alweys offyrd my-sylff to be bownde to the same.

  But, modyr, I am ryght glad that my wyff is eny-thyng [in] your favore or trust, but I am ryght sory that my wyff or eny other chyld or seruaunt of your shold be in bettyr favore or trist wyth yow then my-sylff; for I wyll 25 *and* must forbere *and* put fro me that that all your other chyldre,⁴ ser- uauntys, prestys, werkmen ⌈and⌉ frendys of your that ye wyll ought bequethe to shall take to theym. And thys haue I *and* evyr wylbe redy

---

386. ¹ *Crowded in.*   ² *Some three words heavily canc.*
    ³ no *canc.*   ⁴ *Ampersand canc.*

on-to whyll I leve, on my feyth, and nevyr thought other, so God be my
30 helpe, whom I beseche to preserve yow and send yow so good lyff and
longe that ye may do for youre-sylff, *and* me aftyr my dyssease. And I
beshrewe ther hertys that wold other, or shall cause yow to mystrust or to
ne vnkynd to me or my frendys.

At Norwyche thys Monday, w*yth* the hand of your sone and trwest
35 seru*au*nt

JOHN PASTON

387. Bill of complaint against WILLIAM PASTON II: draft
1484

Add. Charter 17257. Each of the eighteen paragraphs surviving (the
beginning lost) written on a separate slip; the slips originally stitched
together, now pasted, forming a roll of width 11¾ to 12¼ in. and length 36 in.
Each except the fifth and last two marked in margin by a large, often
capital, letter; some of these mutilated by damage to the paper. They are
in the order: F, H, ampersand, S, S, ?T (defective), one unidentifiable,
M, O, P, Q, R, T, V, þ.

First and third paragraphs in the same unidentified hand, small and
rather irregular, with wide space between lines (especially para. 1, which
has half-inch spaces) to allow for corrections. Other paragraphs except the
last two in the large upright hand of the copy of John II's will in no. 309,
with some corrections in the first hand and some by John III. The last two
paragraphs in John III's hand.

The date appears from the 'five years save a quarter' during which John III had
suffered alleged injuries at the hands of his uncle William II. He would have been
the victim only after the death of John II in November 1479.

G. 880/998.

All-so the seyde John Paston now compleynaunt seyth ⌐that⌐ John Paston,
fadyre off the ⌐same⌐[1] John,[2] was seased off the maner*e* callyd[3] Hollwellhalle
wyth th'appurt*e*naunces in Estodenham joyntly wyth all the londis,
tenement*es*, rent*es*, *and* ser*ui*ces whyche sume tyme wer*e* John Jerham,
5 Ewstase Rows, John[4] Davy, vikere off the chyrche off[5] Estodenham, ande
Water*e*[6] Danyell, or any off thers, ⌐lyeng⌐ in the townys off[7] Estodenham,
Mateshalle, Mateshaleberghe, *and* othire townys adyoynyng; ande off
all the londis,[8] tenement*es*, rent*es*,[8] ser*ui*ces *and* lybertés, wyth ther

---

387. [1] *Interl. above* seyd *canc.*   [2] now complaynaunt on lyff *canc.*
[3] Passtons ore *canc.*   [4] Davye *canc.*
[5] estto *canc.*   [6] danyellis *canc.*
[7] Todenham *canc.*   [8] *Ampersand canc.*

appur*tenaunces*, callyd Toleys lyeng in the townys off[9] Wymondham *and*
Carleton, *and* othir*e* townys adyoynyng[10] whyche sume tyme were Will*i*am   10
Thuxston; and off the scite off on mese[11] wyth a pece londe[12] lyenge in a
croffte to the same mese adyoynyng wyche[13] is accomptyde xiiij acres off
londe wyth th'appur*tenaunces* callyd Colneys,[14] othyre-wys callyd Whynnes
in[15] Carleton,[16]   in hys demene[17] as off fee; ande so beyng[18] seased
ther-off ⌐up-on trust⌐ enffeffede Will*i*am Yelu*e*rton, justys, John Fastolff,   15
knyght, Myles Stapelton, knyght, *and* othir*e* to be hadde to them *and* to
theyr*e* heyrs for*e* eu*e*r, be the fores wher-off they were ther*e*-off seased in
theyr*e* demeane as off fee; ande aff*tyre* ⌐the seyd feffm*ent* in forme afforseyd mad the seyd John Paston the fadyr disseassed⌐.[19] The ryght off the
whyche maner, londis,[8] *tenementes, and* othir*e* the premysses aff*tyr* the   20
desses of the seyd John the fadyr owith to ⌐come⌐[20] to the seyd John now
compleynaunt[21] as sone *and* heyr*e* off the seyd John Paston[22] for as myche
as the seyd John the fadyr*e* made no wylle ⌐nor mencyon of the aforseyd
maner, londis,⌐[23] *tenementes*, nor*e* off other the pr*e*mysses,[24] whyche man*e*r,
londis,[8] *tenementes and* othir*e* the premysses the seyd Will*i*am Paston hath   25
and agenst the cours of the lawe ocupyeth.

Item,[25] the seid John requerith an astate to be takyn in those londys
lymyted to Will*i*am ⌐the sone⌐ ⌐for deffaut of issu off⌐[26] Clement Paston
by the will of there fadir*e* accordyng to the seid will aswell as in those
londis that ar or shuld be purchased w*yth* the m[l] mark[27] accordyng to   30
th'endenture mad by-twyn th'exec*utors* of Will*i*am Paston, justice, that is
to sey to the seid Will*i*am ⌐the son⌐[28] and to the eyres of his body, and for
defaute of yssue of his bodye to remayn to th'eyers of Will*i*am Paston,
justice, which the seid John is.

All-so[29] the seyd John Paston now compleynaunt seyth that ther*e* be   35
decayed at Marlyngfford and Oxenhed, be meane off th'enterupsion off the
seyd Will*i*am, tweyn water melles,[30] wher-off jche was letyn for x marke be

yere, and all-so othire howsyng be the same ockasion at Oxenhed, ⌐Mar-
lyngfford⌐, Stansted, *and* Orwelbury decayed to the[31] hurt of the seyd John
40 Paston off v c mark, whech the seyd John Paston desyreth to be recom-
pensede.

Item,[32] the seid John axith of the seid Will*i*am for wast don in the man*er*
of Paston for lak of reparac*i*on xl li.

Item, the seid Will*i*am hath[33] takyn awey owth of the man*er*s of John
45 Paston, that is to sey of hes man*er*s of Paston, Oxened, Marlyngford,
Stansted, and Horwelburye, siche stoff and greynys, catell, and hotilemen-
tis of the seid man*er*s ⌐as⌐ were ⌐agreyd be th'executors of the seyd Will*i*am
Paston, justyse⌐,[34] to be left and latyn with the seid man*er*s, to the value
of xl li.

50 Item, the seid John axith to be restored to all the euydence longyng to
the man*er*s aforesaid, ⌐and othire the premysses⌐,[35] which the seid Will*i*am
wrongfully witholdith.

Item, the seid John ax⟨it⟩h[36] to hys possession which he hath of ⟨*and*⟩[37]
in the man*er* of Caster*e* and other*e* man*er*s adyongnyng the relesse of all
55 such title ⌐and⌐[38] interest as the seid Will*i*am hath be wey of feffement in
the foresaid man*er* and man*er*s jn like forme as other*e* his cofeffés have in
tyme past relassed to Sir John Paston, whoos eyre the seid John is.

Also the seid John Paston desireth the p*er*formance of diu*er*se comen*au*ntis
and articles conteyned in diu*er*se indentures and writynges mad be the
60 avise of the reu*er*end fadir*e* in God Will*i*am, Bisschoppe of Lyncolne,
sup*er*visour of the testement of the seid Will*i*am Paston, justice, bytwix
th'exec*ut*ors of the same Will*i*am Paston for kepyng of the trewe jntent and
will of the seid Will*i*am Paston, justice, as by the same jndentures and
writynges redye to be schewed more[39] pleynlye shall appere, the entent
65 and p*er*forma[n]ce of which writyng[40] is jnt*er*vpted and brokyn by the seid
Will*i*am Paston and his meanys[41] to the hurt *and* damage off the seyd
John Paston now compleynaunt off

Item, the seid Will*i*am hath contra[r]ye to trouuth and conscience vexed
and trouubled and put to ⌐cost *and*⌐[35] charge[42] the seid John nowe be the space
70 of ⌐v yere saffe a quarter[43] ⌐and hath distorbede⌐[44] the same John to take *and*
perceyue th'issus *and* p*ro*fetes off the ⌐same⌐[28] man*er*s ⌐to the hurt *and* damage off the seyd John⌐[45] jn defendyng of his right ⌐off *and*⌐[35] in the ⌐maners

---

[31] gret *canc.*   [32] *Second hand again.*
[33] dispoyled and *canc.*   [34] *Interl. by first hand above* acostomed *canc.*
[35] *Interl. by first hand.*   [36] *Paper decayed.*
[37] *Caret indicates interlineation, lost at join in paper.*
[38] *Interl. above* ar *canc.*   [39] pleyl, *with stroke over* y, *canc.*
[40] -es *canc.*   [41] *Rest of sentence (and line) by first hand.*   [42] to *canc.*
[43] *Interl. by first hand above* ayere and more *canc. From here to* off the seyd John *interl.
by first hand with a second phase of interlineations.*
[44] *Interl. above* in distorbyng *canc.*   [45] *Interl. above* afforeseyd and *canc.*

afforeseyd⌐146 ⌐of ij m¹ mark⌐147 be-syde greffe, ⌐gret laboure⌐135 and⁴⁸ disseace
that the seid John ⌐hath dayly ⌐be putt on-to⌐ by th'okcasion afforseyd⌐.⁴⁹

Item, accordyng to the will of Will*i*am Paston, justice, the seid John axith 75
to be restored to parth of such goodis as hath ben dispendid by John
Paston the fader*e*, Sir John Paston, and the seid John nowe compleyn*au*nt,
in defence, kepyng, and recoveryng of such londis as were Will*i*am Paston,
justice, which draweth aboue the *summa* of m¹ li.

Item, where on   ⁵⁰ Lomnore had a cofur*e* in kepyng ⌐and v m¹ mark in the 80
same be extymasion⌐135 to the vse of John Paston, fadir*e* of the forsayed Sir
John and John, the seid Will*i*am Paston fraudelently atteyned the seid
cofur*e* ⌐wyth the seyd sume off money⌐135 aft*er* the dissece of the seid John
the fadir*e*, and had it in his kepyng serteyn dayes and did with it his
pleasur*e* vnknowyn to the seid Sir John Paston and John Paston his 85
brother*e*,⁵¹ and aft*er* at Herry Colett*es* house the seid Will*i*am brought the
seid cofur*e* to the seid John Paston, knyght, and there openyd the seid
cofur*e*, where was then lefte but cc old⁵² noblis⁵³ which wer*e* by extimac*i*on
in value c li., ⌐and⌐ the seid Will*i*am toke ther*e* the seid gold awey with
hym ageyn the will of seid Sir*e* John, and witholdith the same ⌐wherof the 90
seyd John preyeth to be restored⌐.²⁸

Item, the seid Will*i*am atteynyd⁵⁴ and gate a peyer*e* of basons of siluer and
parte or all gilt from the seid Sir John Paston and John Paston ⌐now com-
pleynant⌐135 abouuth such season as he toke the cofur*e* and coyne afore-
rehersed, which basons wer*e* in value c mark; and the seid Will*i*am yet 95
witholdith the seid basons, ⌐to the whyche the seyd John preyeth also to
be restored⌐.⁵⁵

Item, the seid Will*i*am gate in-to his possession a chargere of siluer, in
value x mark*e*, and iij bollys of siluer that were in kepyng of Bachelere
Water*e*, a frier*e* Carmelit of Norwich, to th'entent that a certeyn coost 100
shuld have ben doon vpon the liberarye of the Friers Carmelites aforesaid
for the sowlis of Will*i*am Paston, justice, and Angnes his wiff, which
chargere and bollys the seid Will*i*am yet with-holdith⁵⁶ and kepith to his
owne vse, and therefore the seid charges ar not fulfylled.

---

⁴⁶ *This, prec. by* same *canc., interl. by first hand above* maner*s* londes and tenementes
aforesaid *canc.*

⁴⁷ *Interl. above* to the *summa* of cc mark *canc.*   ⁴⁸ grette *canc.*

⁴⁹ *Interl. by first hand, with secondary interlineation above* sufferyd *canc., above the*
following, canc.: daylye sufferith in as mech as for lake of takynge of the profitz of the ⌐seyd⌐
[*Paston*] maners the seid John may not doo ⌐as he wolde⌐ [*first hand*] for the sowlis of
Will*i*am Paston, justice, and Angnes his wiff, John Paston ⌐the⌐ [*Paston*] fadere and Sir
John Paston, brothere to the seid John compleynaunt. *After* afforseyd, and mor ou*er* be
the seyd occasions and *also interl. by first hand and canc.*

⁵⁰ *Blank space of* ½ *in.*

⁵¹ whath was in the seid cofure savyng by extimac*i*on v m¹ mark *canc.*

⁵² Edward*es* canc.   ⁵³ all excepte right fewe *canc.*

⁵⁴ -d *crudely written over* th.   ⁵⁵ *Added by Paston.*

⁵⁶ with *ends line.*

105   Item, the seid John axith restitucion[57] of suche jnportable charges as the seid William ⌐hathe⌐[35] put the forsaid Sir John on-to by the space of many yeres as ⌐in⌐[35] plesures doyng ⌐and rewardis⌐,[28] which apperith by writyng of the hande of the seid Sire John, which pleasures and charges the seid Sir John was constreyned to doo in defence of the seid William; where-of
110 the seid John ⌐axeth to have amendys of cc mark⌐.[55]

    Item, by the occacion[58] and meanys of the seid William the seid Sir John was ⌐constreyned⌐[59] to lende on-to the reuerende fadere in God George, late Archeb[i]sschop of York, m[1] mark, whech was nat payed ageyn by the summa of c li. The seid John axith to be restorid ⌐ther-of⌐.[60]

115   Item, the seid William hath fellyd tymbre and wodys in the maners[61] of the seid John, that is to sey the maners of Oxened and Marlyngford, to the hurth of the seid John of xx li.[62]

    Item, the seyd John ⌐Paston⌐ complaynaunt axith to be restoryd to all syche money as hathe be takyn *and* dyspendyd by all ⌐siche persones⌐ as haue
120 ben[63] assigned by meanes of the seyd Wylliam to distorbe *and* jntervpt the seyd John[64] compleynaunt of ⌐hys⌐ ryght, tyghtyll, possessyon, entrest of *and* in the maners, londis, *and* tenementes *and* other ⌐the⌐ premysses dwryng the seyd v yer ⌐sauff⌐[65] a quarter, as well as to all syche money as hathe ben dyspendyd dwryng the seyd v yer sauff a quarter[66] by the seruauntys of the
125 seyd compleynaunt by hym assigned to tery *and* abyd vp-on the seyd maners, londes, *and* tenementis ⌐and other the premysses⌐, ther to kepe the possessyon of the seyd compleynaunt, whyche extendith to the some of xl li. *and* above.

    Item, the seyd John compleynaunt axith to be restoryd to all syche money
130 as hathe ben receyved by meanys of the seyd William dwryng the seyd v yer sauff a quarter of syche as ar or haue ben fermors or tenauntes of the maners, londis, *and* ten[eme]ntis aforseyd duryng the seyd season, as well as to all syche money as is not levyable of[67] dyvers of the seyd fermors *and* tenauntes fallyn in poverté sythe the trowblows season of the v yer sauff a quarter
135 befor rehersed, whyche extendith to the some of cc li. or above.

---

[57] *MS.* restistucion.   [58] -cc- *doubtful because of blot.*
[59] *Interl. by Paston above* stryined (*or* strynied) *canc.*
[60] *Interl. by first hand above* as executour to Sire John *canc.*
[61] -s *added by Paston.*
[62] *Second hand ends here; all the rest by Paston.*
[63] sett *to canc., and* -n *added to* be.
[64] *Part of a letter, presumably* P, *struck out with long dash.*
[65] *Interl. above* saffe *canc.*
[66] vp, *prec. by another letter, canc.*   [67] th *canc.*

388. Draft letter from ELIZABETH BROWNE
1485, before 23 September

Add. 27446, f. 60. $8\frac{1}{2} \times 8\frac{5}{8}$ in. Autograph.

Dorse: Marks of folding but not soiled by carrying. Endorsement autograph:

The copye of a lettre of Dame E. Brow⟨n⟩e[1] ayenst William Paston.

This is a corrected draft, evidently composed by John III for his aunt to have copied. The date first written was 19 May, but this was changed to 23 September. (Henry VII succeeded on 22 August.) To allow time for dispatch and copying the draft must have been finished a few days before this date.

F. v, p. 304. G. 885/1003.

To my ryght worchepfull *and* hertly beloved nevew John Paston, sqwyer.

Right worchepfull and my ryght hertly beloved nevew, I recomand me to yow. And wher as ye desier me to send yow woord whether my brodyr John Paston y*our* fadyr was w*yth* my fadyr *and* hys, wh⟨om⟩[1] God assoyle,[2] dury*ng* hys last syknesse *and* at the tyme of hys diss⟨ea⟩se[1] at Seynt Brydis 5
or nowght, nevew, I assarteyn yow vpon my feythe *and* poore honor⟨e⟩[3] that I was ⌐xiiij, xv yer, or xvj yer old ande⌐[4] at Seynt Brydis w*yth* my fadyr *and* my modyr when my fadyrs last syknes took hym, and tyll he was disseassid. And I dare depose befor eny *per*sone honorable that ⌐when⌐[4] my fadyrs last siknesse tooke hym my brodyr your fadyr was in Norff*olk*, 10
and he came not to London tyll aftyr that my fadyr was disseassid. And that can S*yr* Will*ia*m Cootyng *and* Jamys Gressh*a*m record, for they[5] bothe were my fadyrs clerkys ⌐at that tyme⌐. And I remembre *and* wot ⟨w⟩ell[6] that Jamys Gressham was w*yth* my fadyr at Seynt Brydys ⟨dur⟩yng[6] all hys[7] siknesse and at hys disseasse. And thys wyll I wyttnesse whyle I 15
leve for[8] a trowthe, as knowith God, whom I beseche to *pre*serue you *and* yours.

   And, nevew, I prey yow recomand [me] to my neese your wyff, whom I wold be glad to se onys a-yen in London, wher thys bylle was wretyn, signed w*yth* myn hand, *and* sealid w*yth* my seale[9] the xxiij daye of Septem- 20
ber the first y*er* of the reyngne of Kyng Herry the vij[th].
            Your lovei*ng* awnte EL⟨IZA⟩BETH[10] BROWNE

388. [1] *Hole in paper.*   [2] at eny *canc.*
   [3] *At edge, which has crumbled slightly; a small trace of another letter, doubtless -e.*
   [4] *Interl. above one or two letters canc., perhaps* er.
   [5] -y *crowded in.*   [6] *Second hole.*
   [7] last *interl. but canc.*   [8] for *repeated.*
   [9] the Thursday next befor Whyghtsonday the second yer of Kyng Richard the Thred *canc. The revised date is crowded in above the subscription.*
   [10] *Third hole.*

389. To MARGERY PASTON — Between 1487 and 1495

Add. 27446, f. 68. 8¾ × 6⅛ in. Autograph.

Dorse: Traces of red wax and seal embossed on the paper. Address autograph:

To Dame Margery Paston at Oxenhed.

The title 'Dame' was normally given to the wife of a knight. The date of this letter is therefore later than the battle of Stoke in June 1487, at which John Paston III was knighted. This fits the reference to James Hobart, who became King's Attorney in 1486 (*Cal. Pat. Rolls, 1485–94*, p. 138). Margery died in 1495 (see p. lxi).
F. v, p. 346. G. 898/1019.

Mastress Margery, I recomand me to yow, and I prey yow in all hast possybyll to send me by the next swer messenger that ye can gete a large playster of y*our flose vngwentoru*m for the Kynges Attorney Jamys Hobart; for all hys dysease is but an ache in hys knee. He is the man that brought
5 yow and me togedyrs, and I had lever then¹ xl li. ye koud w*yth* y*our* playster depart hym and hys peyne. But when ye send me the playster ye must send me wryghty*ng* hough it shold be leyd to *and* takyn fro hys knee, and hough longe it shold abyd on hys kne vnremevyd, and hough longe the playster wyll laste good, and whethyr he must lape eny more clothys
10 a²-bowte the playster to kepe it warme or nought.
  And God be w*yth* yow.

Y*our* JOHN PASTON

390. To LORD FITZWALTER: draft — Between 1487 and 1495

Add. 27446, f. 82. 11⅜ × 5 in. Autograph.

Dorse: Marks of folding, but not soiled by carrying. No seal or address.

As Fenn noted, this is a draft of a letter evidently intended for Sir John Radcliff, who was summoned to Parliament in 1485 as Lord Fitzwalter in right of his mother Elizabeth, the heir of Walter Lord Fitzwalter. He was lord of the manor of Billingford, about three miles east of Diss, and the James Radcliffe mentioned was presumably a relative. The date is after Paston's knighthood in 1487 and before Fitzwalter was attainted, for his association with Perkin Warbeck, on 14 October 1495. (See *Inq.p.m., Henry VII*, ii, no. 10; *Chronicles of London*, ed. C. L. Kingsford (Oxford, 1905), pp. 207, 212.)
F. v, p. 382. G. 919/1042.

Humbly besecheth y*our* good lordshepe y*our* dayly seru*aunt and* beedman John Paston, more kayteff than knyght, that it may please yow of y*our*

389. ¹ *MS.* ther.   ² bouth *canc.*

specyall grace to dyrect ought y*our* lettres sygned w*yth* your hand and
sealid w*yth* your seall to the dreedfull man Jamys Radcliff of Bylli*n*gforthe,
sqwyer, fermo*ur* of y*our* wareyn ther—⌐ought of⌐ whoys wareyn no maner 5
of man nor vermyn dare take on hym for dought of y*our* seyd dredfull
[man] to¹ take or carye a-wey eny of your game ther for ⌐fere⌐² of³ hangyd
vp among other mysdoers and forfaytours, as wesellis, lobsters, polkattys,
bosartys, *and* mayne currys—thatt the seyd Jamys shall vpon the
syght of y*our* seyd wryghty*n*g delyver or cause to be delyverd to y*our* seyd 10
besecher or to hys deputé delyuerer of your seyd lettres ⌐at hys fyrst syght
of ⌐the same⌐⁴⌐ vj coupyll blake conyes or renny*n*g rabettys, or some blake
and some whyght to the seyd nombre, to store w*yth* a newe grownd of y*our*
seyd besechers at Oxenhed, more lyeke a pynnefold then a⁵ parke.

And y*our* seyd besecher shall daylye prey to God for the p*r*eservacyon 15
of y*our* noble estate longe t'endure.

391. To RICHARD CROFT   Probably about 1500

Add. 27446, f. 54. 12×8¼ in. Autograph.

Dorse: Marks of folding but not soiled by carrying. No seal or address.

This is evidently a draft. If the flourish under the signature is in fact meant for 'K',
as it seems to be, it must be later than June 1487 when John III was knighted.
But the general effect of the contents suggests a date well on in his life, when he
was fully established as head of the family; and the style of handwriting supports
this.

William, Lord Mountjoy, 1485–1534, was born about 1478 and studied under
Erasmus in Paris in 1496 and 1498–9 (*Complete Peerage*).

G. 871/989 (abstract).

Richard Croft, the wedyr is siche that I wyll ⌐not⌐ jopart to ryde as yet, for
I am not best at ease and a lytill colde myght mak me worse. I send yow by
this berer iij byllis that John Calle tooke me, whiche shewe every receyte
of John Callis *and* Robert Salles, *and* payment*ys* also. I can not fynde the
newe fermall of Caster here, wherfor I haue takyn to this berer the key of 5
my cofir at Yermouthe. I thynk *and* ye wyll ryde thedyr w*yth* hym ye
shall fynd in my cofir the last fermall of Caster, *and* other bokys w*yth* it.
And if need be, ⌐*and* ellis not⌐, ye may cause Robert Salle *and* John Carter
to come hydyr on Fryday or Saterday next comyng and end ther acomptes
her at Norwyche.   10

I sye John Wynnys byllis that his man brought me yesterday, Twysday,
wherby I vndyrstand that he desyreth to be alowyd v li. for Byshoppis of

Yermouthe, *and* for heri*ng* delyuerd to myn cosyn Loveday; wherto I am agreid, but I wyll not that John Wynne shall selle non of my ferme barly
15 to paye theym, for I woll haue all the barly in John Wynnys charge maltyd for my Lord Mountioye. If he haue not money jnow of myn when he hathe acomptyd to paye Byshopes ther v li. I wyll make vppe ther money ought of myn owne purse.

I*tem*, I send yow a waraunt fro the shreve to do warne those pe*r*sones in
20 Flegge *and* Yermouthe that ar enpanellid betwyx the Kynge *and* me to be at Thettford at the assises on Wednysday next comy*ng*. I prey yow take the warant to Symond Gerrard and[1] prey hym in my name to send for the bayly of the hundred *and* to cause hym to geve warny*ng* to theym that be enpanellid to kepe ther day at Thettfford. And prey Symond Gerrard to
25 speke w*yth* as many of the quest hym-selff as he can, and to shew theym that I haue ought my *nisi prius* by assent of the Kyng*ys* Attorné, and he hym-silff comandid it ought.

And if the wedyr amend by none I wyll se yow this *nygh*t, w*yth* God*ys* grace. Fro Norwyche this Wednysday, by yo*ur* frend
30   J. PASTON, K.[2]

392. To WILLIAM PASTON III and RICHARD LIGHTFOOTE
Probably 1503, after April

Add. 27446, f. 99. $8\frac{5}{8} \times 10\frac{3}{8}$ in. Autograph.

Dorse: Traces of red wax. Address autograph:

*To my brother Will*iam Paston *and* my cosyn Richard Lightfoote, *and* to iche
of theym.

This letter was written while William Paston III was in the service of the Earl of Oxford. The date appears from the reference to John III's wife and 'the widow, her daughter Leghe'. John's second wife was Agnes, daughter of Nicholas Morley of Glynde, Sussex, who by a previous marriage had a daughter Isabel. She married John Legh of Addington, Surrey, who died on 24 April 1503 (*Inq. p.m.*, *Henry VII*, ii, no. 684. See *Notes and Queries*, 5th ser., ix (1878), 326, 370, 414.) John III himself died in August 1504 (see p. lxi). He would be more likely to write of his stepdaughter in these terms fairly soon after she was widowed.

The reference to Sir Robert Clere (ll. 22 ff.) does not help in dating. He was knighted in 1494, and made his will in 1529. His son William married Elizabeth, daughter of John III (Blomefield, xi. 237).

G. 939/1071.

391. [1] he to *canc.*
[2] *Name marked off and underlined, the line ending in a flourish that seems to be a form of* K *with a mark of suspension.*

Mastyrs bothe, I recomand me to yow and send yow closid her-in a booke of the seying of dyvers folkis whiche testyfiee ayenst Thomas Rutty and other. I prey yow shewe it to my lordys good lordshepe, and that I may know hys plesur ferther in as hasty wyse as may be that I may ordere me ther-aftyr. I had gret labore to come by the woman that was in servyse wyth 5 Rutty, whiche sie all ther conversacyons many yeris. She is now in servyse wyth Richard Calle. And I haue Thomas Bange in prison at Norwyche wyth the shrevys of Norwych. The woman seythe he is as bold a theffe as eny is in Ingland, but he wyll nowghte conffesse, nor I hand⟨e⟩lyd¹ hym not sore to cause hym to confesse, but and Ruty knowe that he ⌐and the 10 woman be⌐² in hold and hathe told talis I thynke it wyll cause Rutty to shewe the pleynesse.

Clerk *and* Roger Heron ar endightid at this sessyons at Norwyche, last holdyn on Twysday last past ⌐for robbing of the pardoner⌐, and so is Rotty and all his felaw-shepe³ that the woman hathe apechid. According to hir 15 apechement Raff Taylour is over the see, Robert Fenne is dede, John Bakor *and* William Taylour ar yett vntakyn. If my lord send for T. Bange or the woman some of my lordis seruauntys had need to come for theym, for I can not do in the cause for lake of men *and* horse, for my wyff ridith this next week in-to Kente to the wydow hir doughtir Leghe. 20

And as for Ramesey, liek a prowde, lewde, obstynat foole, he wyll not come befor my brothe[r] Syr R. Clere nor me, but he seythe he wyll be wyth my lord hastyly and shewe his mynde to his lordshepe, whiche I beleve not. The substancyall marchantys of Norwyche hathe shewid ther myndys to my brother Syr R. Clere *and* me that he entendith ⌐to⌐ William 25 Bayly gret wronge in his reknyngys.

393. To an unknown knight: draft After 1485

Add. 34889, f. 138. 8¼ × 12 in. Autograph.

Dorse blank, but about half soiled as if folded outside, and some irregular slits.

Neither the date nor the occasion of these facetious verses emerges from the content, except that they must be later than the Earl of Oxford's return from exile in 1485 (cf. no. 401). Fenn suggested that the 'Black Knight' may have been Sir John Paston, and Gairdner thought it was 'most probably the later Sir John Paston, whose services the Earl of Oxford continually made use of'. But since the lines are in John Paston III's hand, with his own corrections in the fifth and sixth stanzas, this cannot be so. He must have written them, whether on his own account or for a colleague in Oxford's service.

F. iv, p. 458. G. 948/1073.

392. ¹ *Fifth letter obliterated by blot.* ² *Interl. above* is *canc.*
   ³ *Divided at line-end.*

Non decet sinescallo tam magni comitis
Vt Comes Oxonie verbis in anglicis
S⟨c⟩ritter[1] epistolas vell suis in nuncijs
Aliquid proponere si non in latinis.

5   Igitur ille pauperculus predicti Comitis
Magnus sinescallus magni comitatis
Nuncupatur Norffolk latin[i]s in verbis
Apud Knapton in curia in forma judicis.

Tibi Nigro Militi salutem, ⌐et⌐ omnibus
10   Notifico quod Langdon ille homunculus
Nullam pecuniam liberare vult gentibus,
Quod est magnum jmpedimentum nostris operibus.

Idcirco tibi mando sub pena contemptus
Quod tu indilate proprijs manubus
15   Scr[i]bas tuas littras quod ille homunculus
Copiam pecunie deliberet gentibus.

Sin autem per littras has nostras patentes
Ego et operarij qui sunt consencientes
Omnes vna voce pravemus suos dentes
20   Nisi ⌐liberet⌐[2] pecuniam cum sumus egentes.

Teste meipso apud Knapton predicta,
Est ⌐et⌐ michi testis Maria benedicta,
Quod vicesimo die Julij non inderelicta
⌐Erat summa solidi⌐,[3] res hec non est ficta.

393. [1] *Paper slightly decayed.*   [2] *Interl. above* dederit *canc.*
[3] *Interl. above* Erant decem denarie, *of which* Erant *is corr. to* erat *and the rest canc.*

EDMOND PASTON II

394. To JOHN PASTON III   1471, 18 November

Add. 34889, f. 130 and 27445, f. 52. Two fragments, original dimensions
11¾×12¼ in., irregularly torn across. Autograph.

Dorse: Traces of red wax. Address autograph:

> *Tho my rytgh wurshfull brothere John Paston, jn hast.*

In John III's hand:

In *pri*mis to þe pryncypall of Stapyll In	v s.
It*em*, for iiij lasys[1]	viij d.
It*em*, for iij doseyn poynt*ys*	vj d.
It*em*, for a plonket ryban	vj d.

The date appears from Margaret Paston's request for a runlet of malmsey, of which
she reminds John III in nos. 211 and 212—both of which are in Edmond's hand.
   G. LXXXV/789. C. 64 (part).

Rytgh wurshupful ⌐brothere⌐, I recu*m*mawnd me to ʒow, prayeng ʒow
hartely þat[2] ʒe wyl reme*m*byre soche maters as I wryth to ʒow. I send ʒow
⌐now⌐ be the brynggare here-of[3] mony, wyche mony I prey ʒow þat [ʒe]
be-stowe ⌐yt⌐ as I wryth to ʒow. I wend a don yt my-sylf,[4] but co*n*syderyng cost*ys and* othere dyue*rs* thyngg*ys* I maynot bryng yt abowthe; 5
where-fore I pray ʒow hartely to take þe labore vp-on ʒow, and I trust to
dese*r*vyt.
   I pray ʒow be-stow thys mony thus:[5] to *Cry*stofyre[6] Hanyngton v s.; to
þe Pry*n*spall of Stapyl In v s. i*n pa*rte of payme*n*t; also, I pray ʒow to bye
me iij ʒerddys of porpyl schamlet, price þe ʒerd iiij s.; a bonet of depe 10
murry, pryce ij s. iiij d.; an hose clothe of ʒelow carsey of an ellyn, I trow
yt wyl cost ij s.; a gyrdyl[7] of plunkket ryban, p*r*ice vj d.; iiij lac*ys* of sylke,[8]
ij of on colore *and* ij of an othe*r*e, price viij d.; iij doseyn poynttys, wythe,
red, *and* ʒelow, p*r*ice vj d.; iij peyere of pateyns—I pray ʒow late Wylli*a*m

---

394. [1] viij d. *canc.*
  [2] þ *in form of* y *throughout, as regularly in Edmond II's hand.*
  [3] thys *canc.*   [4] but I haue *canc.*
  [5] *Each item in the following list marked off by a cross.*
  [6] *Abbr.* xpo- *with stroke above.*   [7] -l *over* d.
  [8] of d *canc.*

15 Mylsant purvey fore þem. I was wonte to pay but ij d. ob. fore a payere,
but I pray ȝow late them not be left behynd⁹ þow I pay more. They must
be lowe pateyns; ⌜late them⌝¹⁰ be long j-now and brod vp-on þe hele.

Among alle othere I pray ȝow recummawnd me to Masteres Elyzabet
Hygouns. I may sey pouerté partys feleschepe; yf þat I¹¹ had ben so well
20 purveyde as I wend, I trowst ⌜to⌝¹² have ben wyth ȝow here thys. Also I
pray ȝow recummawnd me to my brothere ⌜Ser John⌝. I fere lesse he wyl
take¹³ a dysplesure wyth me þat I send hym no mony; I pray ȝow excuse
me as wel as ȝe can. I trust to send hym sum a-bowth Candylmesse.

I had a promyse of Masteres Elyzabet of a typet of welve⟨t⟩,¹⁴ but and
25 I myth haue a hatlase I woold thynk me well. I pray ȝow sey thus myche
on ȝour owyn hed, and yf ȝe can not spede of þe hatlase I pray ȝow bye me
on of xij d. ore xvj d. Also, ser, I send Parkare hys mony be the brynggare
hare-of, and I haue desyered hym to lend me a gown of puke, and I haue
send hym a typet of welvet to boredyre yt ⟨rown⟩d¹⁵ a-bowthe; and I pray
30 ȝow be at schesyng there-of. And yf þat he wyl not, be Cryst calkestokke
on hys hed! þat is schoryle in Englyshe; yt is a terme ⌜new⌝¹⁶ browthe vp
wyth my marschandys of Norwyche.

Ser, John Pamppyng recummawnd hym to ȝow, and pray ȝow þat ȝe
wyl remembyre hys harnes, and yf þat ȝe can get þe mony he pray ȝow to
35 delyuer Parkare x s. þat he howyth hym.

Also, ser, my modyre gretys ȝow wel and send ȝow Goddys blyssyng and
heres, and prays ȝow þat ȝe wyl bye here a runlet of malmesey owthe of
þe galey; and yf ȝe haue no mony sche byd þat ȝe schuld borow of my
brothere Ser John ore of sum othere frend of ȝowers, and send h⟨e⟩re woord
40 as hastely as ȝe haue yt and sche schale send ȝow mony. And yf þat ȝe send
yt home sche byd þat yt schuld be woond in a canmasse fore brochyng of
þe caryars, fore sche sethe þat sche hath knowyn men serued soo ⌜be-fore⌝.

Also I pray ȝow, yf ȝe speke wyth Master Rogere, tell hym þat yf he
cum in-to thys cuntré thys Crystem[a]s he schal haue hys x s., and yf þat
45 he cum not I schal send yt hym be xij day at þe fardest. I pray ȝow hartely
remembyre my gere, and þat ȝe wyl desyere Wylliam Mylsant on my behalue to purvey fore þe caryage in as hasty wyse as yt can. Also I pray ȝow
þat þe weluet þat levyt of my typet may be send hom a-geyn, fore I woold
strype a dobelet there-wyth. As fore Masteres Blakeny, I trow sche be in
50 ȝour quarters. I woold I had þe same entyrepryce vp-on hyre þat John
Bramppton of Atylborowe had¹⁷ vp-on Mastere Bryston.

Alle þe coorte recummawnddys hem to ȝow. I pray ȝow, and ȝe can get
me any profytabyl servyce, a-saye. My brothere Ser John was meved of my

---

⁹ MS. behyng.
¹⁰ Interl. above þat the canc.
¹¹ Written over h.
¹² In margin, replacing I canc.
¹³ MS. tate.
¹⁴ Letter lost at hole.
¹⁵ Parts of several letters lost at the tear.
¹⁶ In margin.
¹⁷ h- over d.

hawnt Ponynggys to haue ben wyth here. I woold haue rytgh an hesy
seruyse tyl I were owthe of detys.   55

God haue 30w in hys kepyng. Wretyn at Norwyche þe Munday nex
be-fore Sen Edmond þe Kyng.

EDMOND PASTON

395. To JOHN PASTON III   Probably 1472, 16 May

Add. 34888, f. 22. 12 × 5⅞ in. Autograph; see Plate IX.

Dorse: Remnants of red wax. Address autograph:

To John Paston, esquyere.

The date cannot be fixed with certainty, but Gairdner's suggestion of 1475 cannot
be right because Gloys, who must be the person meant in ll. 15–20, died early in
October 1473 (see John II's letter no. 282). Edmond's attitude to Gloys recalls the
situation described in John III's letter no. 353 of 8 July 1472, and that is the most
likely year for the present letter. (Edmond was in Calais from perhaps late 1472
to July 1473; see nos. 278, 354, 360. He was back in England in July 1474, as the
address of John III's letter no. 363 shows, but evidently returned in 1475 in
accordance with his indenture to the Duke of Gloucester; see nos. 224, 293, 396.)
This date suits the handwriting and the linguistic forms, which agree in several
particulars with those of no. 394 against the later letters from 1479 onwards.

F. iii, p. 426. G. 58 (and *errata* in vol. iii)/870.

Syre, I recummawnd me to 30w. Please yt 30w to wette þat my[1] modyre
hathe causyd me to putte Gregory owte of my seruyse; as God help, I
wrythe to 30w the very cause why. Yt happyd hym to haue a knavys loste,
in pleyn termes to swhyve a quene; *and* so dyd in þe konynere-closse.[2] Yt
foretunyd hym to be a-spyed[3] be ij plowemen of my modyrs, whyche werene   5
as fayne as he of þat matere, *and* desyerd hym to haue parte; *and* as
kompany requereyd, seyd not nay, jn so myche þat þe plowemen had here
alle a nythe in there stabylle *and* Gregory was clene delyuerd of ⌐here¬ and,
as he swhereys, had not a do wyth here wyth-in my modyres place. Not
wyth-standdyng my modyre thynkkys þat he was[4] grownd of þat matere,   10
where-fore there is no remedy but he moste a-voyde. And in so myche þat
⌐at¬ þe laste tyme þat 3e were here [3e] desyerd hym ⌐of me¬ yf þat he
schuld departe from me, I send 30w þe very cawse of hys departyng as my
modyre sethe. But I am in serteyn þe contrary is true—yt is nomore but
þat he can not plese alle partys; but þat jantylman is hys woordys lord: he   15
hathe seyd þat he woold lyfte[5] whom þat ⌐hym¬[6] plese,[7] *and* as yt scheweyt
welle he lyftyd on xiiij myle in a morenyng, *and* now he hathe ben cawsare

---

395. ¹ *No space.*   ² *Written as one word* ('rabbit-warren-yard').
     ³ *in canc.*   ⁴ w *canc.*   ⁵ hom *canc.*
     ⁶ *Interl. above* yt s *canc.*   ⁷ hym *canc.*

of hys lyfte I wot not how far*e* but yf þat ʒe be hys bett*er* mast*er*. But ⌐and⌐[18] we a-mong v*us* geue ⌐not⌐[19] hy*m* a lyfte, I pray God þat we neu*er* thryve,
20 *and* þat is hys i*n*-tente I trowe to bryng v*us* to. Where-fore I requer*e* ʒow, yf þat yt plese ʒow to haue hy*m*, þat ʒe wylle be þe bett*er* mast*er* to hy*m* for*e* my sake, fore I a*m* he þat js as sory to dep*ar*te from hy*m* as any ma*n* on lyue from hys s*er*ua*nt*; *and* be my trowthe, as farforethe as I knowe ⌐he is⌐ as true as any on lyue. I troste my foretu[n]e schale be bett*er* þa*n* eu*er* to
25 leue thus her*e*, but yf I wer*e* hens ward*ys* I ensuer*e* ʒow I woold not schange ⌐fore no*n* þat I knowe⌐. He is p*ro*fytabylle on dyu*er*s thyngg*ys*, as ʒe knowe welle.

There has ben a gre[t] br*e*ke be-twyx Calle *and* me, as I schal enform*e* ʒow at my comyng, wyche schalle be[10] on Wedynsday next, be þe grace
30 of[11] God,[12] who p*re*s*er*ue ʒow. Wretyn at Mawteby on Wyteson Eue.

EDMOND PASTON

396. Indenture for military service   1475, 7 April

Pierpont Morgan Library, Thane Collection. $14\frac{1}{2} \times 7\frac{1}{4}$ in. Unidentified clerk's hand, Gloucester's signature apparently autograph.

Dorse blank except for notes by Blomefield and the sixteenth-century annotator.

Dated.
    This document was first printed by Curt F. Bühler in *R.E.S.* xiv (1938), 8–10. Notes in Blomefield's hand on both front and back show that it had been in his possession before Thane acquired it.
    Bühler observed that the indenture is a form in which spaces were left for the insertion of the retained person's name and of the number of archers to be furnished. The spaces were in this case filled in by the clerk who wrote the form. Gloucester signed it in the top left corner, opposite the first line.

This endenture made the vij daye of Aprile the xv[th] yere of the reigne of Kyng Edward the iiij, betwixt the right high and mighty prince Rychard, Duc of Gloucestr*e*, Constable and Admirall of Englond, on the on partie, and Edmond Paston, squyer, on that othyr partie, wyttenessith that the
5 sayd Edmond ys reteyned and wit*h*holden w*ith* the sayd Duc to do him seruice of werre w*ith* the Kyng oure souu*er*ayn lord now in his viage ouir the see for an hol yere at his spere, weell and sufficyently horsed, armed, and arrayed as it apperteyneth to a man of armes, and thre archers, well and sufficiently horsed, herneised, habilled, and arrayed as it app*er*teyneth
10 to archers, takyng for hym-self xviij d. a daye and for eu*er*y archer vj d. by

---

    ⁸ *Interl. above* yf þat *canc.*   ⁹ *In margin.*   ¹⁰ of *canc.*
    ¹¹ of *repeated, canc.*   ¹² h *canc.*

the daye, of the whiche wages the sayd Edmond hath reseyued for the first quarter of the sayd hol yere the daye of the sealing of these presentes, at whiche day the sayd Duc hath yeven knowleche to the sayd Edmond that he shal make moustres of hymself and hys sayd retenue at Portesdown in Hampshire the xxiiij^ty day of May next commyng or the same daye 15 at any othyr plase vpon resounable warnyng. At that day and tyme the sayd Edmond byndeth hym by thise presentes to appere in hys propyr personne with his sayd retenue. And if it happen the sayd Edmond, aftyr the reseyte of his sayd fyrst paiement, to dicesse or be in suche sykenesse or disease that he may nat be able to come to the sayd moustresse in hys 20 propyr personne, that thanne he shal fynd an able man in his sted with hys sayd retenue to performe his sayd seruise accordyng to the tenure of this endenture, or ellys to repaye to the sayd Duc that money by hym reseyued for hym and hys sayd retenue for the sayd quartere. And for the seconde quartere of the sayd yere the sayd Edmond shalbe payed by the sayd Duc 25 of the wage of hym and of yche of his sayd retenue at the makyng of the mostres of hym and the same his retenue afore such comissioners as ⌜shal⌝ be deputed ther by the Kyng oure souuerayn lord, at wiche tyme shal be-gynne the terme of the sayd hole yere and nat affore. And aftyr the sayd moustresse and payement, with Goddes grase, to go to shyp at suche tyme 30 as the Kyng and the sayd Duc shal comaunde theim. And for the othyr half of the sayd yere the sayd Edmond shalbe payed by the sayd Duc for hym-self and hys said retenue on the yondyr syd on the see, monethly in Englyshe money or in money there rennyng to the valu of Englysshe money, so all-waye that the same wages be payed with-in x days aftyr the 35 end of eueryche of the sayd monethes or ell the sayd Edmond to be quited and discharged ayenst the Kyng and the sayd Duc of eny covenaunt specifeyd in these endenture, the same endenture nat withstandyng. And the sayd Edmond shal dvely and truely obeye al the Kynges proclamaciouns and ordinaunces and fulfylle the comaundment of the sayd Duc to his 40 power, and shal make wacche and warde of hym-self and his sayd retenue frome tyme to tyme, whene and as ofte duryng the tyme aboue sayd as he ther-to shall dvly be warned and required by the sayd Duc or hys comiser.[1] And in cas that any moustresse to be mad be-yond the see by the sayd Edmond of hys sayd retenue lakketh any of his nombre of the same othyr- 45 wyse than by dethe or sikenesse proued, thane the sayd wages of theim that so shal fayle shalbe rebated vp-on the payement to be made to the sayd Edmond frome tyme to tyme as the cas shall require. Also the sayd Duc shal haue the iij^de parte of wynnynges of werre aswell of the sayd Edmond as the iij^de of iij^dz where-of iche of hys retenue shalbe answeryng vnto hym 50 of there wynnynges of werre duryng the tyme aboue said, be yt prysoners,

---

396. [1] *Expansion not quite certain. The last letter is* s *of sigma form, with off-curl, different from the scribe's usual final* s.

prayes, or othyr goode*s* or catall*es* what-soeu*er* thei be. And the sayd Edmond, or he or thay that shal so take suche prisoners or prayes, shal shewe
vnto the said Duc w*ith*-in vj dayes aftir*e* the so takyng² aswell the names
55 of the sayd prisoners as th*e*ire estate, degré, or condicio*un*, and the qua*n*tité
and valu of the said gettynge*s* bi estimacion, vpon payn*n*e of forfactur*e* of
the sayd prysoners and wynnynge*s* aboue sayd. Also the sayd Edmond shal
haue alman*er* prysoners to hys p*ro*pre vse that shal happ*e* to be takyn by
him or by ony of his sayd retenue dury*n*g the tyme aboue sayd, except the
60 iij^de of iij^dz aboue sayd, the Kynge oure souu*e*rayn lorde*s* adu*e*rsary, and
all kynge*s* and kynge*s* sonnes, his adu*e*rsariers of Fraunce, and also all
lieueten*au*ntz and chifteyns hauyng the sayd adu*e*rsariers power*e*, whiche
shalbe and abyd prisoners to o*ur* sayd souu*e*rayn lord, for the whyche he
shal make resounable aggrement w*ith* the takers of theym, except also all
65 othyr*e* kynge*s*, kynge*s* sonnes, prynces, duke*s*, erles, and chyef capitaynes
nat hauyng the sayd adu*e*rsariers power, whiche shalbe and abyde prisoners
to the said Duc, for the whiche he shal make resounable aggrement w*ith* the
takers of theim. And if it happe*n* the sayd Duc w*ith*-in the sayd yere to
dicesse, then the sayd Edmond and hys sayd retenue shal s*er*ue out the
70 yere aboue sayd vndyr suche a capitaigne as the Kynge shal assyne and
appoynt to haue the rule of hym and hys sayd retenue; and if the sayd Duc
be takyn, hurt, or diseased w*ith*-in the sayd tyme so that he shal nat be able
to do the Kynge s*er*uise of werre, then the sayd Edmond and his retenue
dury*n*g the tyme of hys enp*ri*soun*n*ent, hurt, or disease shal s*er*ue oute the
75 same tyme vndir his lyeueten*au*nt or comys*er*.¹ And that all these coven-
*au*ntz aboue sayd by the sayd Edmond wele and truly to be obs*er*ued and
kepte the same Edmond byndeth hym-self, his heires and executours to
the sayd Duc in the so*m*me of c li. sterlynge*s* by these p*re*sente*s*. In wittenesse wher*e*-of the parties aboue sayd to thise p*re*sent endenture*s* enter-
80 chaungeably haue put³ to their*e* seales the day and yer*e* aboue sayd.

R. Gloucestre⁴

397. To John Paston III 1479, 21 August

Add. 27446, f. 27. 8⅜ × 4⅛ in. Autograph.

Dorse: Marks of folding and soiling. No seal or address. In John III's
hand, *dies mortis A. P.*

Dated.
   F. v, p. 250 (attributed to 'John Paston'). G. 836/952. C. 91.

---

² *MS.* tokyng.   ³ *No space.*
⁴ *Written at top left.*

Suere¹ dydyng*ys* arn com to Norwyche þat my grandam i s dyssessyd, whom God² assoyle. My*n* vncle had a messeng*er* ʒesterday þat she shuld not escape, *and* this day cam a-nothere, at suche tyme as³ we wer*e* at⁴ masse for*e* my brother*e* Water*e*, whom God assoyle. My*n* vncle was comyng to haue offer*ed*,⁵ but þe last messeng*er* retornyd hy*m* hastely, so þat he toke⁶ 5 hys hors incontyne*nt* to enforme mor*e* of ow*ur* hevynes.

My syst*er* ys delyu*er*d, *and* þe chyld passyd to God, who send v*us*⁷ hys g*r*ace.

Dokkyng told me sekretly þat for*e* any hast⁸ my*n* vncle shuld ryde by my lady of Norff*olk* to haue a iij skor*e* p*er*sons. Whyther*e* it is⁹ to co*n*vey my 10 grandh*am* hydere or*e* nowght¹⁰ he cowde not sey. I deme it is rathere to put them in possessyon of some of her*e* lond*ys*.

Wretyn the Saterdaye the xxj¹¹ daye of August Aº E. iiij^ti xixº.¹²

398. To WILLIAM PASTON III Perhaps after 1480, January

Add. 27446, f. 46. 8½×4½ in. Autograph.

Dorse: Traces of red wax and of embossed seal. Address autograph:

> *To my brother*e *Wylliam Paston be this delyu*erd.

The date cannot be determined. William Paston III did not come of age until 1480 (see John II's letter no. 282), and Gairdner suggests that concern for his marriage is not likely to be earlier than this; but William's own letter no. 407 is sufficient to show that this need not be so. Yet it is doubtless more probable that he was of age, especially in view of the age of the 'gentlewoman'. The linguistic forms and the style of the handwriting cannot be distinguished from those of nos. 397 and 399.

F. v, p. 282. G. 858/974.

I hartely recomawnd me to ʒow. Her*e* is lately fallyn a wydow i*n* Woorstede whyche was wyff to on Boolt, a¹ worstede marchant, *and* worth a m¹ li., *and* gaff to hys wyff a c mark*e* i*n* mony, stuffe of howsold² and plate to þe valew of a*n* c mark*e*, *and* x li. be ʒer*e* i*n* land. She is callyd a¹ fayer*e* ia*n*tylwoma*n*. I wyll for*e* ʒo*ur* sake se her*e*. She is ryght systyre of fad*er and* modyre to 5 Herry Ynglows. I p*ur*pose to speke wyt*h* hy*m* to gett hys good wyll. This³ ja*n*tylwoma*n* is abowght xxx ʒer*es*, *and* has but ij chyld*er*en whyche shalbe

---

397. ¹ *Preceded by* Syre *heavily canc.*   ² god *repeated in next line, canc.*
  ³ as *repeated, canc.*   ⁴ at *repeated, canc.*
  ⁵ *Ampersand canc.*   ⁶ hys *canc.*
  ⁷ of *canc.*   ⁸ he s *canc.*
  ⁹ -s *over* t.   ¹⁰ -g- *over* h.
  ¹¹ *Corr. from* xxiij, *and* ·21· *interl. above.*   ¹² *This last line in a different ink.*
398. ¹ *No space.*   ² to þe v *canc.*
  ³ *This appears to be the form intended, though a small loop beginning* -s *gives the preceding letter some appearance of* e.

at þe dedys charge. She was hys wyff but v ʒere. Yf she be eny better þan I wryght fore, take it in worthe⁴ I shew the leeste. Thus lete me haue know-
10 lache of ʒour mynde as shortly as ʒe can, and whan ʒe shall movn be in this cuntré.

And thus God send ʒow good helth and good auenture. From Norwyche þe Saterday after xijᵗʰᵉ Day.

ʒour E. PASTON

399. To MARGARET PASTON   1481, 27 January

Add. 27446, f. 47. 8¾×9 in. Autograph.

Dorse: Paper seal over red wax and string. Address autograph:

To my ryght wurchypfull and especiall good mothere Margaret Paston.

The date is evidently soon after Edmond's marriage to Katherine, daughter of John Spelman, Esq., and widow of William Clippesby, Esq., of Oby. Margaret Paston, in her will made in February 1482 (no. 230), made bequests to Robert, son of Edmond and Katherine. They must therefore have been married by 1481. (Margaret also granted an annuity of 5 marks out of her manor of Freton, Suffolk, to Edmond and Katherine and their son Robert on 9 October 1482 (Add. MS. 27446, f. 50, G. 864/981).) Clippesby died on 24 September 1479 (Blomefield, xi. 148 (misprinted 144), quoting his gravestone in Ashby church); Katherine, as his relict and executrix, proved his will, which is dated 20 September 1479, on 18 May 1480 (ibid., and *Norwich Wills*, i. 91). The marriage was being negotiated as early as November 1479: see John III's letter no. 381.

F. v, p. 276. G. 859/975.

Ryght worchypfull and moste especialle good modyre, jn my moste vmble wyse wyth alle my duté and seruyse I recomawnd me to yow, besechynge ʒow of ʒour blyssyng, whyche is to me moste joy of erthely thynge.¹ And it plese ʒow to be so good and kynde modyre² to forgeue me and also my wyffe
5 of owur leude offence þat we haue not don owur duté, whyche was to haue seyn³ and aue⁴ waytyd vp-on ʒow ore now.⁵ My huswyffe trustythe to ley to ʒow here huswyferey fore here excuse, wyche I muste beseche ʒow not to accepte; fore jn good faythe I deme here mynde hathe ben othereweys ocapyed þan as to huswyfery, whyche semyth welle be þe latchesnes of þe
10 tylthe of here landdys. I beseche God, ⌈fore þe forderawnce⁶ of them as now⌉, rewarde ʒow and þe good parson of Mautby, and ⌈also⌉ Mastyre Baley, who I wende woold not haue balkyd this pore loggeyng to Norwyche wardys. I vndyrestand by þe brynngere here-of þat ʒe entende to ryde to Walsyngham. Yf it please ʒow þat I may wete þe seayson, as my duté is I
15 shalle be⁴ redy to awayte vp-on ʒow.

⁴ *MS.* woothe.

399. ¹ I *canc.*   ² to me *canc.*   ³ ʒow *canc.*
   ⁴ *No space.*   ⁵ w *canc.*   ⁶ -d- *over* b.

Plese it ȝow þat þe[7] brynggare here-of cam to me fore[8] x s. viij d. whyche
I shuld ow hys fadyre. Trew it was at my laste departyng ⌈from hym⌉ I
owte hym so[4] mych, but sertaynly ore I cam at Thetfford homewardys I
thowt of concyence he owte to haue restoryd me as myche. I had my horsse
wyth hym at lyvery, and amonge alle ⌈on⌉[9] of them was putte to gresse and 20
to labure, so þat he dyed of a laxe by þe wey. I payed fore hard mete euer
to hym.[10] Plese it ȝow to delyuer Kateryn v s. wyche I send ȝow in this
bylle. I am not assartaynd how she is purveyde of mony towardys here
jornay. Yf[11] here fadyre cowde not a[4] cleymed j d. of me I woold not se
here dysporveyd yf I myght, nore[12] þe poreste chyld þat[13] is belonggyng to 25
hys loggeyng.

Modyre, my wyffe is boold to send ȝow a[4] tokyn. I beseche ȝow pardon
alle thynggys not don acordyng to duté. I beseche God send ȝow þe
accomplyshment of ȝour moste woorchypfull desyers. At Owby, þe Saterday nex⌈t⌉ before Candylmes. 30

ȝour vmble son and seruant EDMOND PASTON

400. To JOHN PASTON III Between June 1487 and February 1493

Add. 27446, f. 93. 11½ × 16½ in. Autograph.

Dorse: Marks of folding, but no seal. Address autograph:

To the ryght wurshupfull Ser John Paston, knyght, be þis delyuerid.

The date is later than the battle of Stoke (16 June 1487) at which John III was
knighted. It is not later than February 1493 because Elisabeth Clere, mother of
Robert Clere of Ormesby, the 'cousin' of l. 2, is still alive (l. 17); she died on
1 March that year (*Inq. p. m.*, *Henry VII*, i, no. 914). Sir Roger Townshend (l. 13)
died in the same year (*D.N.B.*). It seems likely to be later rather than earlier
in the period, for William Paston IV cannot have been born before 1479, and it is
his marriage that is in question in l. 4; but prospective marriages of minors were
often sold when they were very young, so that this is of little weight. William IV in
fact married Bridget, daughter of Sir Henry Heydon of Beconsthorpe.

'Hynengham' is Hedingham in Essex, the residence of the Earl of Oxford; John
III was a member of his council at least as early as 1487 (Part II, no. 807).

F. v, p. 432. G. 933/1056.

Ryght wurshypfull ser, I recomawnd me to ȝow. As ȝesterday I was wyth
my cosyn Clere. He lythe at Borow, and my mastres hys wyveffe, be-cause
the plage reygnyth at Ormysby. And so of hys own mocyon he mevyd to
me of the maryage of my nevew ȝour soon, and as glad foolkys woold be
to bargayn as euer ȝe wyste; and soo hathe shewyd me that ȝe shuld haue 5

---

[7] þ, *not* y.   [8] mony *canc.*   [9] *Interl. above* j *canc.*
[10] *Some six short words heavily canc.*   [11] s *canc.*
[12] *Flourished* -r *over* t.   [13] h *canc.*

as myche as Ser E. Bedyngfelld, whyche was v c marke. Moore-ouer he
shewyd that he woold depart wyth it to Ser Rogere T. ore to Harry Colett,
whyche he shewyd 3e woold not of but to haue the mony at 3our dysposys-
syon. And me semys¹ be hys report that he knowyth well that yf 3e delle
10 wyth Ser H. H. he wyll be in a² suerté that the mony that he shuld depart
wyth shuld goo to the redemyng of 3our landys and othere 3our dawngeres.
More-ouer he shewyd me that the mony whyche 3e skyftyd of³ H. Colett
was th⟨oug⟩ht⁴ be Ser Harry H. that ⌐Ser R.⌐ Townesend shuld haue ben
contentte wyth it, whyche is knowyn the contrary, and causyd hym to geue
15 delaye in that be-halffe⁵ to 3ow.

I know well this jantylman berythe 3ow as good mynde as any man alyve,
my mastres hys mothere and allso ⌐my mastres⌐ hys wyve in lyeke wyesse;
and me semys he makys not the dowghttys to delyuer 3ow hys mony that
othere men do of the delyuerye of thers. Foore trowthe he shewythe me
20 hys mynde, whyche is thus. Yf 3e wyll putt lande in feffement fore 3eres,
to the full contentacyon of Townesend, Colett, ⌐and⌐⁶ ⌐of⌐ my vncle,
whyche he and all men thynke 3e muste be charged to ore euer 3e goo
thorow, and that 3our next frendys haue the receyte of it tyll it be full
contente and payed, thus ore⁷ suche a suere weye ⌐to be had⌐⁸ fore the well
25 of all parteys, I darre say he is not alyve wyll indevoure hym⁹ wyth better
wyll to deele wyth 3ow, and, as my mynde seruys me, streytte hym-sylffe
as it may be booryn, be-syde my mast[r]es hys modyres v c. My mastres
hys wyffe on my faythe¹⁰ I darre say the moste harty body to 3ow wardys
in this be-halffe that is alyve, and the fayneeste body woold be to haue it
30 accomplyshyd.

Ser, I thenke 3e be to-wardys London, and well I woot 3owur mynde is
to ease 3our-sylffe as hastely as 3e may. I pray God 3e do to 3our honure
and to 3our ⌐moste⌐ well to-gederys. Marchandys ore new jantylmen I
deme wyll proferre large. Noon othere dyspreysed, 3e know the contyn-
35 ewance of this man and how he is alyed. Well I woott yf 3e depart to London 3e shall haue proferes large. Yf 3our jornay be not but to ease 3ow in
that be-halffe, be my poore avyce slake fore iij ore iiij days, fore euer me
semys I shuld not haue ben brokyn to ⌐so largely⌐ but that they entende it
hastely to¹¹ say to 3ow.
40 Sythe I was there I vndyre-stande yf it had not happyd me to haue seyne
them as 3esterday she woold this day¹² haue made here cowntenance¹³ to

---

400. ¹ he and Ser Harry *canc.*   ² *No space.*
  ³ *Ser canc.*   ⁴ *Letters lost at hole.*
  ⁵ *Interl.* to *and* 3w *on line, canc.*   ⁶ *In margin.*
  ⁷ *Flourished* -r *over* f.   ⁸ *Interl. above* he w *canc.*
  ⁹ glad *canc.*   ¹⁰ as *canc.*
¹¹ *In margin opposite the line beginning with this word is a paragraph mark, which presum-*
ably indicates a new paragraph at Sythe.   ¹² hue *canc.*
¹³ *Beginning with this word the lines, so far beginning nearly an inch and a half from the*
left edge, are lengthened to fill the whole width of the paper.

haue seyn her*e* nes, ⌈Bothes dowter*e*⌉, wyche is at Pallyng*ys* for*e* fer*e* of the plage, and haue comyn seyne my wyffe,[14] and specyallly[15] to haue de-syred vus to meve 30w toward*ys* them; and i*n* trowthe so she hasse. I pray God 3e do as well to 30*ur* honur*e* as I woold do my-sylffe. Yf 3e wyll tery thys 45 lytell season be-foor*e* r*e*hersyd, yf 3e lyste, I woott well 3e may haue the mat*er* moor*e* largely comyned; and yf 3e tary tyll Monday I wull awayte on 30w to Hynengh*a*m, w*y*th God*ys* grac*e*, who eu*er* pr*e*seru*e* 30w and 30*ur*s.

3o*ur* E. PASTON

401. Claim for allowances: draft   Between 1489 and 1492

Bodl. MS. Douce 393, f. 80 b. $8\frac{1}{2} \times 5\frac{7}{8}$ in. Hand unidentified.

Dorse: Marks of folding one way, soiled at one end. Note in hand of text: *Billa Edmu*n*di Paston.*

This document is unfinished. The approximate date appears from the affairs of the Earl of Oxford, who appointed Edmond Paston receiver of the Scales lands. These were part of the estate of Thomas, Lord Scales, which after the death of his widow passed to William Tyndale, a relative of Oxford. Oxford returned from exile after the accession of Henry VII in August 1485. His letter appointing Paston (Part II, no. 855), is dated 7 April, so must be of 1486 or later but not after 1489, because it names Tyndale without mentioning the knighthood given him on 30 November of that year. Since this document says that Paston had held the receivership for three years, it cannot be earlier than 1489 and could be as late as 1492.

G. 912/1035.

Edmu*n*d Paston, receyvo*ur* of the Scalys landes, askyth to be allowed of xij li. xij s. viij d. whiche hangith ou*er* his hede in his accompte made bifore Robert Sharp at the Feste of the Pureficacion of O*ur* Lady laste paste for his costes ⌈*and* expenses⌉ for two yeres as hyt apperith in the sayd accomptes.   5
Item, the sayde Edmu*n*d askyth to be allowed for his costes *and* expenses of this yere—cxviij s. iiij d., beside his costes com*m*ynge and goynge to this accompte.
Item, for his rewarde of the saide iij yeres *ad placitu*m *d*omi*n*or*um, whereof ys allowed ⌈for his costes⌉ by the comandeme*n*t of my lorde—x li.   10
Ite*m*, allowed by the

---

14 *Written apparently* wyffee, *the first* e *struck out.*
15 ade *canc.*

WALTER PASTON

402. To Margaret Paston   Before 1479, 19 May

Add. 27446, f. 12. $11\frac{7}{8} \times 6\frac{5}{8}$ in. Autograph; see Plate X.

Dorse: Traces of red wax. Address autograph:

To his worchypfull ⟨m⟩oder[1] *Margaret Paston, ⟨d⟩wellyng in Mawtby, ⟨b⟩e*
*þis lett*er *delyv*eryd *in hast.*

The year is uncertain. Walter died in 1479, between the making of his will on
18 August and the report of his death on 21 August in Edmond II's letter no. 397.
He took his degree at Oxford in June of the same year, and since there is no word
of this in the present letter it must be at least a year earlier.
    F. v, p. 224. G. 816/931. C. 85.

Rytgh rev*er*ent *and* worchypfull mod*er*, I recomavnd me on-to yowr*e* good
moderchypp, besechyng yow to geve me yowr*e* dayly ben*e*dyiccyon,[2] desyeryng hartyly to heer*e* of yowr*e* prosperyté, whych God p*r*eserve to hys
plesure *and* to yowr*e* hartys desyyre, &c. I marvel soor*e* that yow sent me
5 noo word of the lett*er* wych I sent to yow by Mast*er* Wyll*ia*m Brown at
Est*er*. I sent yow word that tym that I xold send yow myn exspe*n*ses[3]
p*ar*tyculer*e*ly, but as at thys tym the berar*e* here-of had a lett*er* sodenly
that he xold com hom, *and* there-fore I kowd have noo leysure to send
them yow on that wys; *and* there-fore I xall[4] wryt[5] to yow in thys lett*er*
10 ⌜the⌝[6] hool som of my exspense*s* sythyns I was w*yth* yow[7] tyll Est*er* last
paste, *and* also the reseytys, rekenyng the xx s. that I had of yow[8] to Oxon.[9]
wardys, w*yth* the Buschopys fyndyng.
    The hool som of[10] reseytys ys v li. xvij s. vj d., *and* the holl som of
exspense*s* ys vj li. v s. v d. ob. q*ua.*; *and* that comth ⌜over⌝[11] the reseytys in
15 my exspe*n*ses I have borowd of Mast*er* Edmu*n*d, *and* yt drawyth to viij s.,
and yet I recon non exspe*n*ses sythyns Est*er*; but as fore them they be not
grete. *And* there-fore I besech yow to send me mony by Syre Richard

402. [1] *The missing initial letters were on the sealing tape, now lost.*
  [2] bene *abbr.* bn *with stroke above.*
  [3] -es *in this word repr. throughout by cross on long* s, *as usually for* ser.
  [4] send *canc,*   [5] y *canc.*   [6] *Interl. above* my *canc.*
  [7] th th *canc.*   [8] hydyre *canc.*   [9] *Suspension shown by tail on* -n.
  [10] exspenses *canc.*   [11] *Interl. above* of *canc.*

Cotman, bryng*er* of thys lett*er*, or*e* ellys by the next maseng*er* that yow kan have to me.

I besech yow that he that I sent by thys lett*er* to yow may have good 20 scher*e* yf he bryng yt hym-selfe, as he telth me that he woll, for*e* he ys a good lov*er* of myn. Mast*er* Edmu*n*d Alyard *r*ecomavnd hym specyaly to yow, *and* to all my brodyrn *and* systyrs *and* to all yowr*e* howsold,¹² *and* I besech yow that I may be *r*ecomavndyt¹³ to all them also, *and* specyaly to my brodyr*e*¹⁴ John þe yong*er*. 25

No mor*e* to yow at thys tym, but Allmythy Ie*s*us have yow in hys kepyng, ame*n*. Wret*y*n at Oxonforth¹⁵ on Seynt Du*n*stonys Day *and* þe¹⁶ xix day of May.

By yowr*e* soun *and* scoler*e* WALTE*R* PASTON

403. To JOHN PASTON II   1479, 22 May

Add. 27446, f. 23. $11\frac{3}{8} \times 2\frac{3}{4}$ in. Autograph.

Dorse: Traces of red wax and embossed seal. Address autograph:

*To hys ryth reverend brod*er *Ser John Paston at Cast*er *Hall in Norfolk.*

Under this in John II's hand, *A° xix°.*

The year is given by the endorsement.
    This letter is written on a narrow slip of paper in exceptionally small script, only a quarter as large as that of no. 402.
    F. v, p. 244. G. 830/945.

After all dw rever*ens and* recome*n*dac*i*ons, likyth yt yow to vnd*er*stond that I reseyvyd a lett*er* fro my brod*er* John wher-by I vnd*er*stod that my mod*er and* yow wold know what þe costys of my p*r*ocedyng schold be. I sent a lett*er* to my brod*er* John c*er*tyfyyng my costys *and* þe causys why that I wold p*r*ocede; but as I have sent word to my mod*er* I p*ur*pose to tary now 5 tyll yt be Mychylmas, for yf I tary tyll than sum of my costys schall be payyd for. I supposed¹ whan that I sent þe lett*er* to my brod*er* John that þe Qwenys brod*er* schold² have p*r*ocedyd at Mydsom*er*, but he woll tary now tyll Michylm*a*s; but, as I send word to my mod*er*, I wold be inceptor be-for Mydsom*er*, *and* ther-for I besechyd her to send me sum mony, for*e* 10 yt woll be sum cost to me, but not mych. *And*, Syr, I besech yow to send me word what answer ye have of þe Buschopp of³ Wynchest*er* for that mat*er* whych ye spak to hym of for me whan I was w*yth* yow at London. I

¹² *Ampersand canc.*   ¹³ -yt *crowded in, very small.*
¹⁴ John *with* -n *tailed canc.*   ¹⁵ th *canc.*
¹⁶ þ- *in form of* y.
403. ¹ -d *crowded in.*   ² schold *repeated, canc.*
    ³ wh *canc.*

thowth fore to have had word ther-of or thys tym. I wold yt wold com, for
15 owr⁴ fyndyng of þe Buschopp of Norwych begynnyth to be slake in payment. *And* yf ye know not whath thys ⌜term⌝ menyth, 'inceptor', Master
Edmund, that was my rewlere at Oxforth, berar her-of,⁵ kan tell yow, or
ellys any oder gradwat.

Also I pray yow send me word what ys do wyth þe hors I left at Totnam,
20 *and* whyder þe man be content that I had yt of or nat.

Iesu preserve yow to hys pleswr *and* to yowr most hartys desyyr. Wretyn
at Oxforth þe Saturday next after Ascensyon of Owr⁶ Lord.

WALTER PASTON

404. To John Paston III   1479, 30 June

Add. 27446, f. 24. 11¼×3 in. Autograph.

Dorse: Traces of red wax and of embossed seal. Address autograph:

To hys ryth trusty and *hartyly belovyd brod*er *John Paston, abydyng at þe
Georg¹ at Powlys Qwharfe in London, be þis lett*er *deluyeryd.*

The date appears from no. 402.
   F. v, p. 248. G. 831/946. C. 90.

Rygth worchypfull *and* hartyly belovyd broder, I recomaund me on-to yow,
desyeryng feythfoly to here of yowr prosperyté, qwhych God preserve;
thankyng yow of dyverse letterys that yow sent me. In the last letter that
yow sent to me ye wryt that yow schold have wryt in the letter that yow
5 sent by Master Brown how that I schold send yow word what tym that I
schold procede; but there was non such wrytyng in that letter. The letter
is yet to schew, *and* yf yow com to Oxon.² ye schal see the letter, *and* all
the leterys that yow sent me sythynnys I cam to Oxon.

And also Master Brown had that sam tym mysch mony in a bage, so
10 that he durst nat bryng yt wyth hym, *and* that sam letter was in that sam
bage, *and* he had for³-gete to take owt the letter, *and* he sent all to-geder by
London; so that yt was þe next day⁴ after that I was m⌜a⌝ad bachylere ore
than þe letter cam, *and* so þe fawt was not in me.

And yf ye wyl know what day I was maad baschylere, I was maad⁵ on
15 Fryday was sevynyth, *and* I mad my fest on the Munday after. I was
promysyd⁶venyson a-geyn my fest of my Lady Harcort *and* of a-noder man

⁴ *Written* yowr, y- *canc.*   ⁵ of *repeated, canc.*   ⁶ *MS.* yowr.
404. ¹ *At edge.*
   ² *Here and later suspension shown by flourish carried back from tail of* -n.
   ³ g, *another letter, and* t *canc., perhaps* got.   ⁴ after *canc.*
   ⁵ on Fryday *canc.*   ⁶ -m- *written first* n, *then a minim interlined.*

to, but I was deseyvyd of both; but my gestys hewld them plesyd wyth such mete as they had, blyssyd be God, hoo have yow in hys kepyng, amen.[7]

Wretyn at Oxon. on the Wedenys-day next after Seynt Peter.

W. PASTON 20

405. Copy of will   Nominally 1479, 18 August

Add. 27446, f. 26. $7\frac{1}{4} \times 9\frac{3}{4}$ in. Hand unidentified.

Dorse: In John III's hand, faint, ⟨V⟩ltima voluntas Walteri Paston, after which in another hand and darker ink, *clerici*.

The year is fixed by Edmond Paston II's dated report of Walter's death in no. 397. This copy is neither holograph nor signed, so that there is nothing to prove exactly when it was written; but from the style of the hand it might well have been near or on the date of composition.

G. 834/950.

In Dei nomine, amen. Ego Walterus Paston,[1] clericus, in bona et sana memoria existens, condo testamentum meum apud Norwicum xviij° die mensis Augusti in hunc modum.

In primis lego animam meam Deo Omnipotenti, Beate Marie, et omnibus sanctis, et corpus meum ad sepeliendum in ecclesia Sancti Petri de Hunde- 5 gate coram ymagine Sancti Johannis Baptiste. Item, lego summo altari prefate ecclesie iij s. iiij d. Item, lego reparacioni ecclesie supradicte ij s. vj d. Item, Fratri Johanni Somerton, bachalaureo, v s. Item, lego Magistro Edmundo vnam togam penulatam cum manicis de mynkys. Item, lego Roberto Wulff vnam togam viridem [2] cum chamelet. Item, lego Roberto 10 Holand, filio spirituali, togam meam curtam. Item, lego Magistro Roberto Hollar vnam togam penulatam cum gray. Item, lego Johanni Parkere mantellum meum rubeum. Item, lego Magistro Roberto Hollere vnum puluinar vocatum le bolstar. Item, lego Magistro Edmundo Alyard vnum puluinar. Item, lego Ricardo Richardson vnam togam penulatam ad manus 15 cum menyver. Item, ⌈volo⌉ quod residuum[3] bonorum meorum in Oxonia sit ad vsum Magistri Edmundi Alyard, sic quod soluat principali Johanni Skelton et Thome Coco. Item, volo quod oues mee quas habet Willelmus Bataly senior in villa de Mawteby diuidantur equaliter inter fratrem meum Edmundum Paston et sororem meam Annam Yeluerton et sororem meam 20 Margeriam Paston vxorem fratris mei Johannis Paston. Item, lego terras et tenementa manerij mei de Cressyngham, si possum dare, fratri meo Johanni Paston, armigero, sibi et heredibus suis, sub condicione ista quod

---

[7] *Abbr. by tail on* -m.

405. [1] armiger *erased*.   [2] *Blank space in MS.*

[7] sit ad vsum Magistri Edmundi Alyerd *canc.*

si contingat fratrem meum predictum Johannem Paston esse heredem
25 patris mei quod nullo modo habeat terras et tenementa predicta, sed quod
frater meus Edmundus Paston habeat terras et tenementa predicta sibi et
suis heredibus. Residuum vero bonorum non legatorum lego et do dis-
posicioni executorum meorum vt et ipsi fideliter disponant pro anima mea.

Huius autem testamenti mei executores condo per presentes fratrem
30 meum Johannem Paston, armigerum, pro ista patria et Magistrum Edmundum Alyard pro bonis meis remanentibus Oxonie.

WILLIAM PASTON III

406. To JOHN PASTON III   Probably 1478, 7 November

Add. 27446, f. 18. 11½ × 3¾ in. Autograph.

Dorse: Remnants of red wax. Address autograph:

> *To hys worchepful brodyr John Paston be thys delyuered in hast.*

The date is clearly not much earlier than no. 407.

    F. v, p. 236. G. 824/939. C. 87.

Ryght reuerent *and* worchepful brodyr, I recomaunde me on-to yow, desyrynge to here of yowre welfare *and* prosperité, letynge yow wete that I haue reseuyd of Alwedyr[1] a lettyr *and* a nobyll in gowlde þer-in.[2] Ferthermore, my creansyr Mayster Thomas hertely recomaundyd hym to yow, *and* he praythe yow to sende hym su*m* mony for my comons[3] for he seythe 5 ye be xxᵗⁱs. in hys dette, for a monthe was to pay for[4] whe[n] he had mony laste.

    Also I beseche yow to sende me a hose clothe,[5] on for þe halydays of su*m* colore *and* a-nothyr for þe workyng days,[6] how corse so eu*er* it be it makyth no matyr; *and* a stomechere, *and*[7] ij schyrt*ys*, *and* a peyer of sclyppers. *And* 10 if it lyke yow that I may come wyt*h* Alwedyr be watyr *and* sporte me[8] wyt*h* yow at London a day or ij thys terme tyme, than ʒe may let all thys be tyl þe tyme that I come. And than I wol telle you when I schall be redy to come from Eton, by þe grace of God, whom haue yow in hys kepyng.

    Wretyn the Saturday next[9] aftyr All Halown Day, wyt*h* þe hand of yo*ur* 15 brodyr

WYLL*IA*M PASTON

406. ¹ *Ampersand canc.*

    ² þ- *in form of* y *throughout, as usually in William III's hand.*

    ³ *Written in full, but dotted circumflex above* -n-, *as elsewhere in William III's hand, notably his signature.*

    ⁴ fo *canc.*   ⁵ -t- *over long* s.   ⁶ what *canc.*

    ⁷ a *canc.*   ⁸ me *repeated.*   ⁹ aftyr *canc.*

407. To JOHN PASTON III   Probably 1479, 23 February

Add. 43489, f. 25. 11×7 in. Autograph; see Plate XI.

Dorse: Traces of red wax. Address autograph:

To ⌈his⌉ worchepfull broder John Paston be thys delyuered in hast.

The date appears from certain small circumstances. The letter was written on
the Eve of St. Mathias, 23 February, and the following Monday was the first
Monday of Lent (l. 23). This happened in 1479. It was true also of 1474, and since
William was born probably in 1459 (see John II's letter no. 282, l. 19) that might
seem more suitable to the age of a boy at Eton. But Thomas Stevenson was a fellow
of Eton from 12 July 1479 to 1486 (Sir Wasey Sterry, *The Eton College Register
1441–1698* (Eton, 1943), p. xxix), and William's critical interest in a young woman
of 18 or 19 is much more appropriate to the later year.

F. i, p. 296. G. 827/942. C. 88.

Ryght reuerent and worchepfull broder, aftyr all dewtés of recomendacion
I recomaunde me on-to yow, desyryng to here of your prosperité and welfare, whych I pray God long to contynew to hys plesore and to your hertys
desyre; letyng yow wete that I receyued a letter from yow, in the wyche
5 letter was viij d., wyth þe¹ whyche I schuld bye a peyer of slyppers;
ferthere-more certyfyyng yow as for þe xiij s. iiij d. whyche ȝe sende by a
jentylmannys man for my borde, cawlyd Thomas Newton, was delyuered
to myn hostes, and soo to my creancere Master Thomas Steuenson²; and
he hertely recomended hym to yow.

10 Also ȝe sende me worde in the letter of xij li. fyggys and viij li. reysons.
I haue them nott delyuered, but I dowte not I schal haue, for Alwedyr tolde
me of them *and* he seyde þat they came aftyr in an other barge.

And as for þe yong jentylwoman, I wol certyfye yow how I fryste felle
in qweyntauns wyth hyr. Hir fader is dede. Ther be ij systers of them, þe
15 elde⟨r . . .⟩³ þe whych weddyng I was wyth myn hostes, and also desyryd
by þe⁴ jentyl-man hym-selfe, cawlyd Wylliam Swanne,⁵ whos dwellynge⁶
is in Eton. So it fortuned that myn hostes reportyd on me odyrwyse than
I was wordy, so þat hyr moder comaundyd hyr to make me good chere,
and soo in good feythe sche ded. Sche is not a-bydynge ther sche ys now,
20 hyr dwellyng is in London; but hyr moder *and* sche cam to a place of hyrs
v myle from Eton, were þe weddyng was, for be-cause it was nye to þe
jentylman whyche weddyd hyr dowtyr. And on Monday next comyng, þat

407. ¹ *This þ- in traditional form; in the rest of the letter y is used.*
² *Dotted circumflex above -n.*
³ *Words lost at hole, tail presumably of r remaining. A modern hand has supplied* is just
weddyd at, *written on a patch.*
⁴ *Written ye, -e canc. and another written above the line.*
⁵ *Name partly touched up, apparently by the modern hand of n. 3.*
⁶ *MS. dewllynge.*

is to sey þe fyrst Monday of Clene Lente, hyr moder and sche wyl goo to þe pardon at Schene, and soo forthe to London, and there to a-byde in a place of hyrs in Bowe Chyrche-yerde.   25

And if it plese yow to inquere of hyr, hyr modyrs name is Mestres Alborow. þe name of the dowtyr is Margarete Alborow, the age of hyr is be all lykelyod xviij or xix ʒere at þe fertheste. And as for the mony *and*[7] plate, it is redy when soo eu*er* sche were weddyd; but as for the lyuelod,[8] I trow not tyl aft*er* hyr modyrs desese, but I ca*n* not telle yow for very certeyn 30
⟨. . .⟩[9] but yow may know by inqueryng. And as for hyr bewté, juge yow that when ʒe see hyr, yf so be that ʒe take þe laubore; and specialy beolde hyr handys, for and if it be as it is tolde me sche is dysposyd to be thyke.

And as for my comynge from Eton, I lake no-thynge but wersyfyynge, whyche I troste to haue wy*th* a lytyll co*n*tynua*n*ce. *Queritur*: *Quomod*o no*n* 35
valet hora, valet mora? Vnde d*icitur*:

> Arbore ia*m* videas exemplu*m*. No*n* die possu*n*t
> Om*n*ia supleri; s*et* ta*m*en illa mora.

And thes too *ve*rse a-fore seyde be of myn own makyng.

No more to yow at thys tyme, but God haue yow in hys kepyng. Wretyn 40
at Eton the Euen of Seynt Mathy the Apostyll, in haste, wy*th* the hande of yo*ur* broder

W YLL*IA*M P ASTON

408. To E DMOND P ASTON II   After 1480, 22 February

Add. 27446, f. 42. 12×6½ in. Autograph.

Dorse: Traces of red wax. Address autograph:

*To hys right worchepfull brodyr Edmu*n*de Paston be thys lettyr delyu*eryd.*

The latest date required by the contents is that of Edmond's marriage (l. 16), which took place probably in 1480 or at the beginning of 1481 (see no. 399). The style of the handwriting might suggest that this letter was in fact several years later than this, for it is much more fluent and practised than that of nos. 406 and 407, and similar to the letters of 1488 and later; but the reference to 'my brother's will' makes it unlikely to be very long after John II's death in 1479.

G. 853/969 (abstract).

Aftyr all dewtés of recomenda*c*ion I recomau*n*de me on-to yow, letynge yow wett that here is closid in thys same byll the wyll of my fadyr, suche as my brodyr hathe, *and* he seyth that it is the very wyll of my fadyr *and* that he had it owt of the regestyr. And as for towchynge of my mater, I

---

[7] b *canc.*   [8] *Written* -lond, -n- *canc.*
[9] *Some words lost at hole, to the right of which* r bewte *canc.; the missing passage would seem to be* and as for hy, *canc. and transposed to follow six words later.*

5 can haue no*n* othe[r] ende than I had whan I dep*a*rtyd fro yow, sauynge
that my brodyr hathe gotyn a p*a*rdon for þe alyenac*i*on þat the Bochop of
Wynchestyr alyenyd. And as for the estate that I schold haue in it, I can
gete no*n*¹ but acordynge to my fadyrs wyll, whyche is to me and to my
heyers malys as is specyfyed in the wyll. And as for my brodyrs wyll is no*n*
10 other but that I schuld haue Runh*a*m, whyche is viij li. a ʒere *ad*² *min*us,
in recompense of the x me*r*ke owt of the man*er* of Sporle, so that I relessyd
all my ryght that I haue in the man*er* of Sporle. And as towchynge yow in
my brodyrs wyll, there is no-thyng; for I redde it ou*er and* woll wright it
also, so that I woll haue the same for my copye that he wrote w*yth* hys owne
15 hande.³

Also I beseche yow to recomau*n*de me hertely to my sustyr y*our* wyff.
No more to yow at thys tyme, but God haue yow in hys kepynge. Wretyn
at London the xxij day of February, be yowre brodyr⁴

W*YLLIA*M P*ASTON*

409. To J*OHN* P*ASTON* III $\qquad$ 1487, 7 March

Add. 43490, f. 12. 11¼×8 in. Autograph.

Dorse: Continuation of text. Marks of folding and soiling, no seal discernible. On the soiled panel only traces of the address legible, apparently
autograph: *Paston be thys* ⟨. . .⟩*yuered*. Above this the paper has crumbled
away.

The date appears mainly from the account of the King's council at Sheen and his
intended progress through Essex and Suffolk to Norfolk at Easter, which took place
in 1487 (G. Temperley, *Henry VII* (London, 1917), p. 62). This is confirmed by
the reference to Edward Hexstall of Dover (ll. 29 ff.), who is described as 'rebel' on
14 March of the same year, but received a general pardon on 4 May (*Cal. Pat. Rolls,
1485–94*, pp. 158, 172). A letter of Richard Fox thirty-four years later places the
Earl of Northumberland's indenture (ll. 23 ff.) in the first year of Henry VII's
reign (ending 21 August 1486) (A. Conway, *Henry VII's Relations with Scotland and
Ireland 1485–1498* (Cambridge, 1932), p. 34). This does not fit the present report
ideally; but Fox's recollection may not have been minutely accurate (he was uncertain about the sum involved), or the agreement may have been made earlier than
the meeting described here.

Fenn printed the address as *To hys broder, Sir John Paston, be thys letter delyvered.*
If this were right it would conflict with this dating, for John III was not knighted
until the battle of Stoke in June 1487. (Fenn took the reference to be to John II and
dated the letter 1474, which as Gairdner observed is for several reasons impossible.)
But the first part of the address seems unlikely to have been much more distinct in
Fenn's day than it is now, and he probably reconstructed it from other letters—as
he certainly did in other cases.

F. ii, p. 158. G. 908/1031 (part; dated 1489).

408. ¹ in it *canc.* ² my *canc.* ³ I *canc.* ⁴ wyl *canc.*

Syr, I recomaunde me on-to yow, latynge yow wete that, as for John Petyr-sons mater, as ʒett it is nott spedde. I spake on-to Mayster Secretory of it, *and* promysyd hym that ʒe badde me; *and* he aunswerd me that he wold nott geue ⌐yowe⌐[1] non[2] cowmfortt in it for wynnyng of yo*ur* money ⌐other⌐ than ye schuld fyend trew, *and* so he wold nott vndyrtake it thow ʒe wold 5 spende abowt it c m*e*rke. And so vp-on thys aunswere I went on-to my lord *and* toke hym on of the byllys, *and* so he aunswerd me that at the fyrst worde the Kynge asched hym l li. And where as ʒe reqwere to haue it grauntyd w*yth*-owt fyne[3] or fee, I wold ʒe had it w*yth* ⌐the payment of þe⌐[4] fyne or[5] fee, for it schall nott coste past xx s. or iiij nobyls more than ʒe 10 offerd to þe secretory; *and* also in nowthyr of those byllys ther is non clawse in it wherby it scholde be grauntyd w*yth*-owt fyne or fee, *and* thow ther were it is tolde me it p*ro*fyte nott, they of the Chauncery woll nott lose ther dewtés for Kynge nor other. And as for the generall lycens, I haue asked my lord[6] of it, *and* he aunswerde me that he wott well ther schall be[7] 15 non g*r*auntyd of a gode whyle, *and* it schall come fyrst to yo*ur* handy*s*, for I tolde hym how that ʒe were begylyd whan ʒe were at London.

As for to speke w*yth* Mayst*er* Schypton, or yet w*yth* my lorde Treserer, I cowd not brynge it a-bowt, for my lord entendyd to ryde the next morow aftyr the makynge of thys lett*er*; but I aduysyd Edmond Dorman to speke 20 w*yth* Mayst*er* Shypton as he went homewarde. As for my lord Treserer, he was not w*yth* the Kyng of all the counsell tyme, þe whyche was endyd on the iij^de day of Marche. And theder came my lorde of Northethomyrlond the fyrste day of Marche, *and* dep*ar*tyd the euen afore þe makyng of thys lett*er*, *and* hathe endentyd w*yth* the Kynge for the kepynge owt of the 25 Schottys and warrynge on them, *and* schall haue large money, I can nott telle þe some for certeyn.

Also the[r] is an[8] rover takyn at Brystowe, on Cowper ⌐as⌐ I[9] wene, *and* he is lyke to be hanged, *and* he confessythe more of hys felawis. Also Edwarde Hecstowe of Douere[10] is apechyd of treson of many straunge poynty*s*, *and* 30 hys accusere *and* he wer*e* bothe afore the Kynge, *and* then they were takyn apert and he hym-sylfe c*on*fessyd it that hys accusere accusyd hym of, *and* many other thyng*ys* more than[11] he was accusyd of. And ⌐he had⌐ many lord*ys and* gentylmen to aunswere for hys trowthe *and* hys demenynge afore-tyme,[12] for as I hard sey bothe the Kynge in a maner, nor non of the 35 tother lord*ys* nor gentylmen, beleuyd not hys accuser tyl þat he confessyd it hym-selfe; *and* so he is in the Towre *and* lyke to be dede.[13]

As for the Kyng*ys* comynge[14] in-to the contré, on Monday come forte-nyght he woll lye at the Abbey of Stratteforde *and* so to Chelmnsford, þan

409. ¹ *Interl. above* me *canc.*

² *A short word lost at a tear; but from the remaining traces it seems to have been canc.*
³ of *canc.* ⁴ *Interl. above* owt *canc.* ⁵ *Corr. from ampersand.*
⁶ lord *repeated, canc.* ⁷ now *canc.* ⁸ baner *canc.* ⁹ *No space.*
¹⁰ -r *canc.* ¹¹ -n *over* t. ¹² *Recto ends.* ¹³ at *canc.* ¹⁴ it *canc.*

40 to Syr Thomas Mongehombrey, þan to Heuenyngham, than to Colchestyr,
þan ⌈to⌉ Ipswyche, þan to Bery, þan to Dame Anne Wyngfeldys, *and*
soo to Norwyche; *and* there woll he be on Palme Sonday Euyn, *and* so tary
there all Ester *and* þan to Walsyngham. Wher-fore ʒe had nede to warne
Wylliam Gogyne *and* hys felawes to puruey them off wyne j-now, for euery
45 man berythe me on hande that þe towne schalbe dronkyn drye as Yorke
w⟨as⟩[15] whan the Kynge was there.

Syr, Mayster Sampson recomaunde hym on-to yow, and[16] he hathe
sende yow a rynge be Edmonde Dorman; and besyds that he requeryd
me to wryte on-to yow þat it were best for yow to puruey yow of some
50 gentyl-many[s] thynges ageyns the Kyngys comyng, for suere he woll
brynge yow gestys j-now, *and* therfore puruey yow þer-aftyr. Also he
sendythe yow worde that it is my lordys mende þat my syster, wyth all
other godely folkys þer-abowte, scholde acompeny wyth Dame Elsebethe
Calthrop, be-cawse there is noo grete lady ther-a-bowte, ageyns the Kyngys
55 comynge, for my lorde hathe made grete boste of the fayre *and* goode gentylwomen of þe contré *and* so the Kynge[17] seyd he wolde see them sure. Syr,
my lorde hathe sente on-to þe most[18] part of the gentyl-men of Essex to
wayte vp-on hym at Chelmnysford, where as he entendythe to mete wyth
the Kynge, *and* þat they be well apoyntyd ⌈þat þe Lankeschere men may
60 see⌉ þat ther be gentylmen of so[19] grete sobestaunce þat þei ⌈be⌉ able to bye
alle Lankeschere. Men thynke that ʒe amonge yow wol doo þe same. Your[20]
contré is gretely bostyd of, and also the jnabytours of þe same. I beseche
yow to remembre my hors that ye promysyd me.

God kepe yow. Wretyn at Schene in haste þe vij^te day of Marche wyth
65 the hande of your brodyr

WYLLIAM PASTON

410. To the BAILIFF OF MAUTBY   1487

Add. 34889, f. 137. 11⅞×3½ in. Autograph.

Dorse: Remnants of red wax, and embossed seal. Address autograph:

To the Baly of Mawlteby.

The date is shown by the reference to the prospective visit by the King to be close
to that of no. 409. For 'Henyngham' see no. 400.
　　F. iv, p. 310. G. 910/1033.

Mayster Baly, I recomaunde me on-to yow, praynge yow that ye woll
sende me be ⌈Wylliam Kokkys⌉[1], berer her-of, iiij nobylles in golde putt

15 *At edge, partly covered.*　16 *Corr. from* hande.　17 kynge *repeated.*
18 -he *canc.*　19 *Corr. from* as.　20 Y *in form of* þ.
410. 1 *Interl. above the canc.*

654

in to the[2] same boxe that thys byll is in as thow it were euydens, for I haue
tolde the masengere that he schulde brynge me nothynge butt euydens;
for he[3] is in a[4] manere dep*ar*tyng owt of my s*er*uyse, wherfore I wold nott 5
he knew so myche of my counsell. *And* as for the remenaunte,[5] I wollde ʒe
schulde kepe it tyll I come my-selfe. And if Bayard be on-solde I pray yow
late hym be made ⌐fatte⌐[6] ageyns the Kynge come in-to the contré, what
so eu*er* I pay for the kepyng of hym. *And* I schall wete how goode a corser
I schall be my-selfe at my comyng in-to the contré, be the grace of God, 10
who haue yow in kepyng.
  Wretyn at Henyngh*a*m be y*our*

           W YLL*IA*M P ASTON

411. To J OHN P ASTON III   1488, 13 May

Add. 27446, f. 73. 11⅝×8¼ in. Autograph.

Dorse: Paper seal over wax. Address autograph:

  *To S*yr *John Paston be thys lettyr dely*u*ered.*

The date appears from the report of 'my lord Woddevyle's' expedition to Brittany.
Edward Woodville, Lord Scales, went to help the Duke of Brittany against the
French in May 1488 (J. D. Mackie, *The Earlier Tudors* (Oxford, 1952), p. 87). This
is confirmed by the reference to the King of Scots: the son of James III rebelled
against him in the same year (A. Conway, *Henry VII's Relations with Scotland and
Ireland*, pp. 13–18).
  F. v, p. 366. G. 904/1026.

Aftyr all dewe recomendac*i*on, pleasyt yow to vndyrstonde that my lorde
hathe ben w*yth* the Kynge in Wyndeso*ur* at Seynt Georgys Feste, *and* ther
at the same feste were bothe þe jnbaceto*ur*s of Breten and of Flaundyrs as
well fro the Kynge of Romayns as fro the yonge Duke. But I can not schew
yow þe certeyn whedyr we schall haue w*yth* them warre or pease. But I 5
vndyrstonde for certeyn that all suche capeteyns as wente to þe see in
Lente, þat is to sey S*yr* Charlys Som*er*sett, S*yr* Rich*ard* Hawte, *and* S*yr*
Wyll*ia*m Vampage, makythe them redy to goo to the see ageyn as schortely
as they can, to what jntente I can not sey. Also, where as it was seyde that
my lord Woddevyle and other schulde haue gone ou*er* in-to Breten to 10
haue eyded the Duke of Breten, ⌐I can not tell of non suche eyd. Butt⌐
vp-on that seynge ther came many men to Sowthehamton, where it was
seyd that he schulde haue takyn schyppyng to haue waytyd vpon ⌐hym⌐
ou*er*, *and* soo whan he was[1] countyrmaundyd thos that resortyd thedyr to
haue gon ou*er* ⌐w*yth* hym⌐ taryde there styll, in hope þat they schuld haue 15

    [2] sane *canc.*   [3] hath *canc.* [4] *No space.*
    [5] *Ampersand canc.* [6] *Interl. above* faste *canc.*
  411. [1] sch *canc.*

ben lycensyd to haue gone ouer, *and* whan they sey no lykeleod that they
schuld haue lycens there² was ij c of them that gete them in-to a Breten
schyppe þe whyche was late come ouer wyth salte, *and* bad the mayster sett
them a lond in Breten. *And* they had nott seylyd not paste vj legys butt
20 they aspied a Frencheman, *and* the Frencheman ⌐mad⌐ ouer to them, *and*
they ferde as thow they wolde not haue medylde wyth them, *and* all the
Englysche-men ⌐went⌐ vndyr the hetchys soo that ⌐they⌐ schewyd no more
but those that came to Sowthehamton wyth the schype, to cawse the
Frenche-men to be the more gladder to medyll wyth them. *And* soo the
25 Frencheman burdyd them, *and* then they that were vndyr the hetches
came vp and soo toke þe Frencheman *and* caryed þe men, schyppe, and
all in-to Breaten. Also ther was ther an jnbacetour fro the Kynge of
Schottys who is now ⌐put⌐ in grete trobyll be hys son *and* other of³ the
lordys of hys londe.
30   Syr, as I came homewerde be London I spake there wyth Emonde
Dormand, *and* he ⌐seyd that he⌐ had wretyn onto yow but he had non
aunswere; wherfor he prayd me that if I knew ony man comynge towerdys
Norwhyche *and* I wolde wrythe on-to yow þat he ferythe if ye see non
other dyreccion that he schall be comittyd to þe Flete. Also he schewyd me
35 that Herry Wyott wholde fynde the mene to haue yow condemnyd *and*
recouer þe obligacion of xl li. ageyns yow. *And* soo he seythe he whote nott
how to doo, for he is halfe dysmayd. He ferythe lesse that he schall neuer
come home; but he intendythe to plede the obligacion fulfylyd⁴ at
Norwyche, for he seythe ther is non other remedy to saue yow fro the
40 condemnacion tyl that he herythe otherwyse from yow, whyche he thynk-
ethe ⌐longe⌐ aftyr.
   Wretyn at Henyngham ye xiij^te day of May wyth the hand of your brodyr

WYLL*I*AM PASTON

412. To JOHN PASTON III, sending copy of a letter from
    Henry VII to the Earl of Oxford   1489, April

Add. 27446, f. 77. 11⅛ × 12¼ in. Copy of the King's letter in unidentified
hand; last sentence and signature autograph.

Dorse: Paper seal over red wax. No address, but the brother for whom it
was intended would certainly be John III.

The date appears from the account of operations in Brittany under Sir Richard
Edgecombe, whose expedition is mentioned in Margery Paston's letter no. 420.
This copy was probably made soon after the King's letter, dated 22 April, was
received at Hedingham.
   F. v, p. 370. G. 913/1036.

² -re *over* y.   ³ hys *canc.*   ⁴ *Second* -y- *crowded in.*

Right trusty and entierly beloued cousin, we grete you wele. Inasmoch as it hath liked God to sende vs good tiding*es* oute of Bretayn such as we dought not but that ye be desirous to vndrestonde, we wryte vnto you of them as thay be comen to our*e* knowlage, and as foloueth.

The Lord Malp*er*tuis, now late w*yth* vs in ambassade from our*e* dere cousine the Duchesse of Bretayne, shippid at our*e* porte of Dortmouth and arriued at Saynt Powle de Lyon in Bretayn on Palmesonday at iiij after*e* noone, from whens he wrote vs the dispos*i*cion and the state of the countré there, and of the landyng and the demeanyng of our*e* armee. We receiued his wrytyng on Monday last at evynsong tyme, and be-cause he was of 10 Bretayn borne and favorable to that p*ar*tie we ne gave[1] such trust to his tiding*es* as was thought to vs sureté to wryte[2] to you theruppon.

This day aftre High Masse comyth vnto vs from oute of Bretayne forsaid, and w*yth* a new ambassade from our*e* said cousine, Fawcon, oon of our*e* pursiuant*es*, that ratifieth the newes of the seid Lord Malp*er*tuis, which 15 ben these.

After the garysson of Frenshmen in the towne of Gyngh*a*m had certeinté of the landyng of oure armee thei drwe downe the fabours of Gyngh*a*m and made thayme mete to defende a siege, but assone as thei vndirstode that our*e* seid armee jornayned toward*es* theim thei left the same Gyngh*a*m, 20 where our*e* said armee arriued the Thursday next be-fore Palmesonday and was receiued w*yth* p*ro*cession, logged and receiued, refreshed in the town iiij dayes; and goyng toward*es* the said Duchesse thei must passe to the castell and borugh of Monconter. In that castell was also a garnisson of Frenshemen, which incontinently vpon worde that our*e* said armee drwe 25 toward*es* theym the Frenshmen did cast downe gret parte of the walles and fled from thens. In that castell and borugh our*e* seid armee kept thair*e* Estre. The castell of Chawson adioy[n]ing ner to the towne of Saynt Bryak was also garnisond w*yth* Frenshmen.[3] That castell they set on fire and soo fled. And[4] the townes of Henebone and Vannes were garnisond w*yth* 30 Frenshmen, which breke downe the walles of the townes and putte them-selff to fligth. Th'inhabitau*n*tes a-bought Brest haue layd siege th*er*eunto, and goten the base courte of the Frenshmen or the departyng of our*e* said pursiuau*n*t. The garnison of the towne of Concarnewe, which is oon of the grettest strenghes of all Bretayn, was besieged in like wyse and drevyn to 35 that necessité that thei w*yth*-in offerid, ar his said dep*ar*tyng, to avoyde the towne w*yth* staffe in hande. How that is takyn or what is more done sithens he cannot telle. Oure said cousine the Duchesse is in her citee of Raynes, and our*e* right trusti knyght and counsellour*e* Sir Richard Eggecombe there also, hauyng cheeff rule a-bowte her*e*. And the Marchall of Bretayn 40 arredieth hym to joyne w*yth* them in all haste w*yth* a gode band of men.

---

412. [1] no *canc.*   [2] to wryte *repeated, canc.*
[3] which breke downe the walles *canc.*   [4] *MS.* In.

Mony noble men of that countree repaire to oure said armee to take their partie.

These premisses in substaunce we haue be wryting aswell from the cheff
45 capytaynes of oure said armee as from oure comptrollour forsaid, and that oure said armee, blessid be God, hath among theyme-self kepte such love and accorde that no maner of fray or debate hath bene bitwene theym sithens the tyme of thair departing out this oure reame.

Youen vnder oure signed at oure castell of Hartford the xxij day of Aprill.

50 Syr, thys js the copye of the lettyr that þe Kynge sente my lorde of Oxynford of tydynges owte of Breten. Be yowre brodyr

WYLLIAM PASTON

413. To John Paston III   1489, between 6 and 10 May

Add. 27446, f. 79. $11\frac{1}{2} \times 12\frac{5}{8}$ in. Autograph.

Dorse: Traces of red wax, paper seal. Address autograph:

To hijs brodyr Syr John Paston.

The date appears from the news of rebels in the north against whom the King was preparing to march. This must refer to the insurrection of 1489 in which the Earl of Northumberland was killed on 28 April (see Margery's letter no. 420)—'this unhappy deed' (l. 5) no doubt means the murder. A letter from the Earl of Oxford dated from Hedingham on 6 May (see Part II, no. 819) asks John Paston III, as the Earl's 'right well-beloved counsellor' to present himself at Cambridge 'upon Tuesday next coming', which would be 12 May. The request is repeated in the present letter (l. 24); 'on Tuesday' implies writing after Tuesday 5 May, and presumably not later than 10 May to allow time for the journey.

F. v, p. 360. G. 916/1039.

Syr, I recomaunde me on-to yow. And where as ye desyre that I schulde sende yow worde of suche tydyng as Phylyp Lewes *and* Wyndesor bryng-ythe fro the corte, they be come thens bothe; but we here of no tydyng*ys* that they brynge but that yondyr folkys abyde stylle abowte þe place where
5 as thys onhappy dede was done, *and* not wyth no grete nowmbyr, they sey not paste wyth v or vj c when[1] they were moste.[2] Howbeyt they haue made proclamacions in þe cuntrey to mete wyth oder of ther affynyté as on Tuesday last past, as it aperythe in the copy of ther proclamacion heraftyr folowyng. Also they schew the Kynge intendythe to holde on hys jurney,
10 and Phylyp Lewes is redyn ageyn to the Kyng, *and* schall brynge wyth hym money for all ther wagys that schall be in my lordys retynew, as yow[3] and vj of Syr Wylliam Bolens seruauntys *and* od⟨yr⟩.[4]

413. [1] -e *apparently canc.*   [2] w *canc.*
[3] *and* odyr *canc.*   [4] *Letters lost at hole.*

Syr, Mastyr Clopton sye yowre lettyr, and a seythe he knew my lord*ys* mende suche that he⁵ durste not meue hym w*yth* it. Ther was S*yr* Wyll*ia*m Say, but Clopton wolde not it schulde be knowen of non other but your- 15 selfe. He sent my lorde⁶ be a s*er*ua*u*nt of hys xl li. to haue excusyid hym, *and* it wolde not be takyn; *and* þ*a*t I m*er*vell of. Howbeyt he brake thus fer to my lorde: he asched hym how many he apoyntyd yow to brynge w*yth* yow, *and* he answerde⁷ hym xx*ti*, *and* than he schewyd hym yowr*e* charg*ys* þ*a*t ye haue had.⁸ My lorde ⌜seyd ye⌝⁹ myght haue men a-nowe, *and* ther 20 wag*ys* schalbe payd for. Clopton aunswerde how that it wolde coste yow large money besyde þ*er* wag*ys* to hors them *and* harnes them, *and* how that¹⁰ to sey the trowthe ye were not well at ese. Not w*yth*standynge all thys my lorde wyllyd that ye schulde come to hym to Cambryge on Tuesday at nyght, w*yth* as many as y⌜e⌝e myght, *and* ye *and* he schulde do well j-now. 25 Soo Clopton thyngyth that and ye brynge a dosen w*yth* yow it is suffy-cyent,¹¹ howbeyt þ*a*t S*yr* Emonde Bedyngfeld, S*yr* Thomas Tyrell, *and* S*yr* Rych*ar*d Lewes haue ben w*yth* my lorde, *and* yche of them haue offyrde to mete w*yth* my lorde at Cambryge w*yth* xxx me*n* apese of them. So I wolde not ye¹² schulde be to ferre vndyr them. Wherfor I thynke best that 30 ye puruey yow so as and ye¹² schulde goo forthe ⌜yor-selfe⌝, for I can p*er*seue non othyr wyse.

My bedfelawe Cornwaleys is maryed in the northe, and he came as yesternyght to my lorde, streyt owt of the contré, *and* he scheythe non othyrwyse but as I haue wretyn here afore in thys lettyr.¹³ Ye schall haue 35 for yor-self *and* for yche of y*our* s*er*uaunt*ys* horsyd *and* hernessyd xx s. in hande at Cambryge for a monthe. *And* I truste we schal haue done or xx days to an ende, w*yth* þe grace¹⁴ of God, who haue yow in kepynge. At Heny[n]gham.   Be yo*ur* brodyr WYLL*IA*M PASTON

To be knowyn to all the Northe p*a*rty*s* of England to eu*er*y lorde, knyght, 40 esquyer, gentylman, and yeman, that they schalbe redy in ther defensable aray, jn the Est p*ar*te on Tuysday next comyng on Aldyrton More, and in the West p*ar*te on Gateley¹⁵ More the same day, vpon peyne of losyng of ther goody*s* *and* bodyes, for to geynsstonde suche p*er*sons as is abowtward for to dystroy owre suffereyn lorde the Kynge and the Comowns of 45 Engelond for suche vnlawfull poynty*s* as Seynt Thomas of Cauntyrbery dyed for. And thys to be fulfyllyd and kept by eu*er*y ylke comenere apon peyn of dethe.

And thys is in the name of Mayster Hobbe¹⁶ Hyrste,
Robyn God-felaws brodyr he is, as I trow.   50

⁵ druste dust *canc.*   ⁶ my lorde *repeated.*
⁷ *First written* aunswerde, *then* he a *written over* au-.
⁸ *Two words, apparently* wher of, *and* seyd *interl. canc.*
⁹ *Interl. above smudged* s *canc.*   ¹⁰ y *canc.*
¹¹ hu *and apparently incomplete double* b *canc.*   ¹² *Written* y*e*.   ¹³ y*e* *canc.*
¹⁴ *MS.* grage.   ¹⁵ *Second* -e- *over* y.   ¹⁶ *Incomplete* C *canc.*

414. To John Paston III   1492, 18 February

Add. 27446, f. 89. 8⅝ × 12⅛ in. Autograph.

Dorse: Traces of red wax. Address autograph:

To the ryght worchepfull Syr John Paston, knyght.

The date appears from the account of Henry VII's preparations to invade France.
He eventually did so in October 1492 (Mackie, p. 108).

  F. v, p. 412. G. 929/1053.

Aftyr all dew recomendac*i*on, lyke it yow to vndyrstond that S*yr* Herry
Heydon schewyd me that it is agreyd be S*yr* Edmond Bedyngfeld that the
mater betwyx hym *and* my brodyr Yelu*er*ton schalbe comynd at Norwyche,
and there a dyrecc*i*on to¹ be takyn in the same mater mete for them bothe.
5   Syr, þe Kyng sendythe ordynaunce dayly to þe see syde, *and* hys tent*ys*
and alys be a-makyng faste *and* many of them be made. And there is also
grete p*r*ouysyon made be gentylmen þat scholde goo wythe hys grace for
hors, harnes, tent*ys*, halys, gardyuyans, cart*ys*, *and* othyr thyng*ys* that
scholde s*er*ue them for thys jurney that the Kynge entendythe to take on¹
10 hand, soo that be¹ lykelyod hys grace wolbe goyng sone vpon Ester. And
so I entende, aftyr that I here he[r]aftyr, to goo to Caleys to p*u*ruey me of
harneys and suche thyng*ys* as I schall nede besydes hors, vndyr that forme
þat my cost*ys* schalbe payd fore. Syr, I am as yet no bettyr horsyd than I was
whan I was wythe yow, nor I wote not where to haue none, for hors flesche
15 is of suche a price here that my p*u*rce is schante able to bye on hors; wherfor
I beseche yow to herkyn for some in yowre contré. Syr, my cosyn John
Heydon tolde me that þe Prior of Waburnes horse was rially amendyd, and
that þe Abott of Seynt Benet*ys* schewed hym there was a bay hors off a
p*a*rsons nygh² onto Seynt Benetis and þat þe Abot wolde gete hym for my
20 cosyn Heydon at a resonable price. Syr, my cosyn John Heydon woll geue
me hys entrest in that hors if the Abot haue bowght hym, *and* so ye³ may
lete þe Abot haue knowlege; *and* if he haue not bowght hym, I beseche
yow sende to see hym, for I wote not how to do w*yth*-owt yowre help aswell
in horsyng of me as in other thyng*ys*. At the makyng of thys lettyr I canot
25 acerteyn yow what p*a*rson it is that owythe thys hors. If I can know I wolle
send yow worde in a bylle I sende to Thomas Jullys be the berer herof.
    Syr, as towardy*s* my jurney to Caleys, the whyche I entende to haue tane
at my laste beyng w*yt*h yow, jt was so I was dysapoyntyd⁴ of Thomas Dey
and an other man I scholde haue had be hys menys, as ye haue had know-
30 lege of or now. *And* also I had went to haue had ⌐folkys a⌐ mette w*yt*h me
⌐at Hedyngham⌐⁵ whyche dednott. My lorde, seyng me dysesyd and also

---

414. ¹ *No space.*   ² *MS.* nyght.   ³ *Written* yᵉ.
    ⁴ -p- *over beginning of a* b.   ⁵ *Interl. above* folk *canc.*

non otherwyse p*ur*ueyd, wyllyd me in ony wyse to tary ⌜on-tyl hys comyng
to London⌝, and sent myn excuse to my Lorde Dawbeney vndyr thys
forme, how that I was ⌜sore⌝ disesyd, notwythestondyng I was welewyllyd
to haue come to fulfyll my p*ro*messe, but he cowde not sofyr me seyng me ₃₅
soo dysesyd. And so my Lord Dawbeney⁶ was sory of my dysese *and* content that I taryd.

Syr, I beseche yow to holde me excusyd for kepyng of Thomas Lynsted,
yow*re* s*er*ua*u*nt, *and* hym bothe. It is soo that he *and* I bothe haue ben in
hande w*yth* my vnkyll for hys mater, *and* yett wee haue hym at noo good ₄₀
poynt, but I troste we schall haue. Syr, if I take thys jurney to Caleys I
moste beseche yow to forbere hym lenger, *and* jf ⌜I⌝ goo not to Caleys,
thow I be lothe to forbere hym yet I schall brynge hym w*yth* me schortly
in-to Norfolke, ye to haue hym if ye lyste, w*yth* þe grace of God, who haue
yow in kepyng. ₄₅

Wretyn at London þe xviij day of February w*yth* the hande of yowre
pore brodyr

WYLL*I*AM PASTON

⁶ *Two words, apparently* seyd he, *heavily canc.*

MARGERY PASTON

415. To John Paston III   1477, February

Add. 43490, f. 23. 11⅞ × 4½ in. Hand of Thomas Kela, a clerk of Sir Thomas
Brews (see Part II, nos. 773, 792).

Dorse: Traces of red wax. Address in Kela's hand:

> *Vn-to my ryght welbelouyd Voluntyn John Paston, squyer, be þis bill*
> *delyuered, &c.*

The date is most likely in the year of John III's marriage to Margery; see his letters
nos. 374–9.
 F. ii, p. 210. G. 783/897. C. 79.

Ryght reuerent and wurschypfull and my ryght welebeloued Voluntyne, I
recommande me vn-to yowe full hertely, desyring to here of yowr welefare,
whech I beseche Almyghty God long for to preserue vn-to hys plesure and
ȝowr hertys desyre. And yf it please ȝowe to here of my welefare, I am not
5 in good heele of body ner of herte, nor schall be tyll I here from yowe;

> For þer wottys no creature what peyn þat I endure,
> And for to be deede I dare it not dyscure.

And my lady my moder hath labored[1] þe mater to my fadure full delygently,
but sche can no more gete þen ȝe knowe of, for þe whech God knowyth I
10 am full sory.

But yf that ȝe loffe me, as I tryste verely that ȝe do, ȝe will not leffe me
þerfor; for if þat ȝe hade not halfe þe lyvelode þat ȝe hafe, for to do þe
grettyst labure þat any woman on lyve myght, I wold not forsake ȝowe.

And yf ȝe commande me to kepe ⌈me⌉ true where-euer I go
15 Iwyse I will do all my myght[2] ȝowe to love and neuer no mo.
And[3] yf my freendys say þat I do amys, þei schal[4] not me let so for to do,
Myn herte me byddys[5] euer more to love ȝowe
Truly ouer all erthely thing.
And yf þei be neuer so wroth, I tryst it schall be bettur in tyme commyng.

415. [1] to fa *canc.*
 [2] and neuer no mo *canc., and followed by full stop which should also have been canc.*
 [3] tho *canc.*   [4] *Corr. from* schuld.   [5] *First -y- over* e.

No more to yowe at this tyme, but the Holy Trinité hafe ȝowe in kepyng. 20
And I besech ȝowe þat this bill be not seyn of non erthely creature safe
only ȝour-selfe, &c. And thys lettur was jndyte at Topcroft wyth full heuy
herte, &c.

Be ȝour own M. B.

416. To JOHN PASTON III   1477, February

Add. 43490, f. 24. 11⅝ × 5½ in. Kela's hand.

Dorse: Paper seal over red wax. Address in Kela's hand:

> *To my ryght welebelouyd cosyn John Paston, swyere, be this lettur*
> *delyueryd, &c.*

The date is close to that of no. 415, but seems to be a few days later. The letter from
John III referred to in l. 3 may well have been an answer to no. 415.
     F. ii, p. 214. G. 784/898. C. 80.

Ryght wurschypffull and welebelouyd Volentyne, in my moste vmble wyse
I recommande me vn-to yowe, &c. And hertely I thanke yowe for þe
letture whech that ȝe sende ⌈me⌉ be John Bekurton, wherby I vndyrstonde
and knowe þat ȝe be purposyd to com to Topcroft in schorte tyme, and
wyth-owte any erand or mater but only to hafe a conclusyon of þe mater 5
betwyx my fadur and ȝowe. I wolde be most glad of any creature on lyve
so þat the mater myght growe to effect. And ther as ȝe say, and ȝe com
and fynde þe mater no more toward þen ȝe dyd afortyme ȝe wold no more
put my fadur and my lady my moder to no cost ner besenesse for þat
cause a good wyle afture, weche causyth myn herte to be full hevy; and 10
yf þat ȝe com and the mater take to non effecte, þen schuld I be meche
more sory and full of heuynesse.

     And as for my-selfe, I hafe don and vndyrstond in the mater þat I can
or may, as Good knowyth. And I lete yowe pleynly vndyrstond þat my
fader wyll no more money parte wyth-all in that behalfe but an c li. ⌈and 15
l marke⌉, whech is ryght far fro the acomplyshment of ȝowr desyre. Wherfor, yf þat ȝe cowde be content wyth þat good and my por persone, I wold
be þe meryest mayden on grounde. And yf ȝe thynke not ȝowr-selfe so
satysfyed, or þat ȝe myght hafe mech more good, as I hafe vndyrstonde be
ȝowe ⌈afor⌉, good, trewe, and lovyng Volentyne, þat ȝe take no such labure 20
vppon ȝowe as to com more for þat mater; but let it¹ passe, and neuer more to
be spokyn of, as I may be ȝowr trewe louer and bedewoman duryng my lyfe.

     No more vn-to yowe at thys tyme, but Almyghty Iesus preserve ȝowe
bothe body and sowle, &c.

Be ȝour Voluntyne MERGERY BREWS 25

     416. ¹ *MS.* is.

417. To JOHN PASTON III   Perhaps 1481, 1 November

Add. 27446, f. 51. $11\frac{7}{8} \times 8\frac{1}{2}$ in. Letter and postscript in Calle's hand, subscription autograph.

Dorse: Paper seal over black wax. Address in Calle's hand:

To my right worshipful master John Paston, in haste.

The date is uncertain except that it is between the death of John Paston II in November 1479 and that of Margaret Paston in 1484. All Saints' Day was a Thursday in 1481, which would suit the contents well enough.
F. v, p. 288. G. 865/982. C. 93 (part).

Right reuer[e]nt[1] and worshipfull ser, in my moste vmble vice I recomaunde me vnto yow as lowly as I can, &c. Plese yow to wete John Howes, Alexander Qwharteyn, John Fille, wyth the parson and the newe myller of[2] Marlyngforth, haue goten Thom at Welles carte of Estetodenham, ⌜fermor⌝[3] to myn
5 vncle William ⌜Paston⌝, Herry Herby of Meelton Magna, fermour and baly to my seide vncle, Richard Barkers carte of the seide towne of Meelton, late fermour and yette is in daunger to my seide vncle, and William Smythes carte of Brandon iuxta Bernham Broom, late fermour and baly and also in daunger to my seide vncle, on Monday[4] and Twesday last past caryed a-
10 wey from Merlyngforth in-to the place at Seint Edmondes in Norwich xij of your greete plankes, of the weche they made vj loodes, beryng a-bowte the seide cartes bowes and gleves for feere of takyng a-wey.

Ser, as for your tenauntes of Marlyngforth, they wythholde her catell and hem-selfe bothe from the coorte and come not wythin the lordship
15 nor make noon attornment,[5] exept Thom Davy and John Water, weche absentyng of the tenauntes is to them a greet hurt and los for lak of sedyng of ther londes wyth ther wynter corn; besechyng you for Godes sake to remembre som remedy for them.

My Lady Caltorp hath ben at Geppeswich on pilgry-mache, and
20 came homward be my lady of Norffolk, and ther was moche cominicacion of your mater be-twix you and myn vncle, seyng[6] to my Lady Caltorp ye nede not a go[7] to London, ye myght haue ⌜had⌝ an ende at home, remember-beryng to my seid Lady Caltorp of the mocion that he made towchyng the maner of Sporle, promyttyng[8] to my lady to a-bide þat and to write and
25 seale as largely as any man wol desire hym; and at hes departyng from my lady he was not mery, what the cauce was I wot not.[9] My Lady Calthorp desireth me to write to yow to haue ende, for he intendes[10] largely to haue

417. [1] *Abbr.* reunt *with* er-*curl rising from cross on* t.   [2] myller *canc.*
[3] *Interl. above for canc.*   [4] last *canc.*
[5] sen ye departed *canc.*   [6] ye *canc.*
[7] *Written* gonne, *but* -nne *canc.*   [8] on *canc.*
[9] but he was not mery of your departyng *canc.*   [10] -t- *over* d.

a peace w*yth* you, as he seth, but truste hym not to moche for he is not goode.

My mother in lawe thynketh longe she here no word from you. She is in ³⁰ goode heele, blissed be God, and ⌐al⌐ yo*ur* babees also. I mervel I here no word from you, weche greveth me ful evele. I sent you a lett*er* be Brasio*ur* sone of Norwiche, wher-of I here no word.

No more to you at this tyme, but Almyghty Je*s*u haue you in hes blissed kepyng. Wreten at Norwich on Allowmes Day at nyght.   ³⁵

Be your*e* ser*u*a*u*nt *and* bedewoma*n* M ARGER Y PASTON¹¹

S*er*, I prey you if ye tary longe at London þat it wil plese [you] to sende for me, for I thynke longe sen I lay in yo*ur* armes.

418. To JOHN PASTON III   Perhaps 1481, 4 November

Add. 27446, f. 52. 11⅞ × 6⅝ in. Hand of nos. 19, etc.; subscription autograph; see Plate XII.

Dorse: Traces of red wax. Address in hand of letter:

*To my ryght wurchupfull mayst*er *John Paston, esquyer, be this lett*er *delyuerd in hast.*

The date is clearly only a few days after that of no. 417.
  F. v, p. 292. G. 866/983. C. 94 (part).

Myne owyn ⌐swete hert⌐, jn my most humyl¹ wyse I recomaund me on-to you, desyryng hertly to her*e* of your*e* welfar, the wheche I beseche Allemyghty God p*re*ser*u*e *and* kepe to his ples*er and*² your*e* hert*ys* desyer. Sere, the cause of my wrytyng to you at this³ tyme: on Friday att nyght last past come Alexand*er* Wharton, John Hous, *and* John Fylle, w*yth* ij good cart*ys* ⁵ well mannyd *and* horsyd w*yth* hem, to Marlyngford, and there⁴ at þe man*er* of Marlyngford *and* at the mille lodyn bothe cart*ys* w*yth* mestlyon *and* whete, and betymys on Saturday i*n* the mornyng they departyd fro Marlyngford towardy*s* Bongey, as it is seyd; for the seyd cart*ys* come fro Bongey, as I soppose by the sendyng of Bryon, for he goth hastyly ou*er* þe se, as it ¹⁰ is seyd, and as I suppose he wyll haue the mestlyon ou*er* w*yth* hym, for the most part of the cart lood*ys* was mestlyon, &c.

Item, ser, on Saturday last past I spacke w*yth* my cosyn Gornay, and he seyd if I wold goo to my lady of Norf*f*olk *and* besech hyr good gr*a*ce to be your*e* good *and* gracyous lady, she wold so be; for he seyd that on word of ¹⁵ a¹ woman shuld do mor*e* than the word*ys* of xx men, yiffe I coude rewyll

───────────────

¹¹ *Subscription in different hand, very unskilled; doubtless Margery's own.*
418. ¹ *No space.*   ² *to and beginning of* h *canc.*
    ³ d *and part of another letter canc.*   ⁴ th *canc.*

my tonge *and* speke non harme of myn vnkyll. And if ye comaund me so
for to do, I trist I shuld sey nothyng to my ladys displesu*re*, but to youre
p*ro*fyt; for me thynkyth by the wordy*s* of them, *and* of youre good fermore
20 of Oxned, that they wyll sone drawe to an ende; for he cursyth the tyme
that eu*er* he come i*n* the ferme of Oxned, for he seyth þ*at* he wotyth well
that he shall haue a grette losse, and yet he wyll not be aknowyn whed*er* he
hathe payd or nought; but whan he seth his tyme he wyll sey trowth. I
vnderstond by ⌈my seyd cosyn Gornay⌉⁵ that my lady is ner*e* wery of hyr
25 p*ar*te, ⌈*and*⌉⁶ he seyth my lady shal¹ come on pylgremage i*n*-to this towne,
but he knowyt*h* not whed*er* afor*e* Cristmes or aftyr; and if I wold thanne
gete my Lady Calthorpe, my moder i*n* lawe, *and* my moder *and* my-selfe,
and come before my lady besychyng hyr to be youre good *and* gracyous
lady, he thynkyth ye shull haue an ende, for fayne she wold be redde of it,
30 wyt*h* hyr ⌈onowre⌉ sauyd, but yette money she ⌈wold⌉ haue.

Nomor*e* to you at this tyme, butte I mervell sor*e* that I haue no lett*er*
from you.⁷ I prey God p*re*serve you *and* send me good tydyngy*s* from you,
and spede you well in youre mater*ys*. And as for me, I haue gotyn me
anothyr logyn felawe; the ferst lett*er* of hyr name is Mastras Byschoppe.⁸
35 She recomaundyth hyr to you by the same tokyn that ye wold haue had
a tokyn to my mayst*er* Bryon.

Att Norwych the Sonday next aft*er* the fest of All Seynty*s*.

Be yowr*e* s*er*uaunt *and* bedewo*m*a*n* MARGERY PASTON⁹

419. To JOHN PASTON III   1486, 21 January

Add. 27446, f. 62. $11\frac{1}{2} \times 3\frac{3}{4}$ in. Hand unidentified.

Dorse: Traces of red wax and of embossed seal. Address in hand of letter:

To my mastyr John Paston be this delyvird.

Dated.
    F. v, p. 314. G. 888/1007.

Ryght reu*er*ent and wortschepfull syre, jn my most vmbill weysse I recomaunde me to you, desyryng to here of your welfare, the wytche I besche
God to¹ preserve to his plesur and to your harty*s* desyir. Syr, I thank you
for the venyson that ye sent me. And youre schepe is seylyd ⌈owte of þe⌉
5 havene as this daye.

    ⁵ *Interl. above* hym *canc.*   ⁶ *Interl. above* for *canc.*
    ⁷ but *canc.*   ⁸ the *canc.*
    ⁹ *Subscription in same han.. .is that of no. 417.*
    419. ¹ his *canc.*

Syr, I send you be my brodyr ⌐Wyllem⌐ your stomachere of damaske.
As for youre teppet of velvet, it is not here; An seythe that ye put yt jn your
casket at London.

Syr, your chyldryn be jn goode helle, bellsside be God.

Syr, I prey you sende me the gowild that I spak to you of be the nexst 10
man that comythe to Norwytche.

Syr, your mast that laye at Yermowythe is letyn to a scheppe of Hull for
xiij s. iiij d.; *and* if the⌐r⌐² fawyll ony hurt ther-to ye schall have a new mast
ther-for.

No mor to you at this tyme, but Almyty God have you in his kepyng. 15
Wretyn at Castyr Hawill the xxj daye of Janeuer jn the furst yere of Kyng
Harry the vij^{th}.

Be your *ser*uaunt MARGERY PASTON

I prey God no ladyis no more ovyr-com you that ye geve no lenggar
respyt jn your materys. 20

420. To JOHN PASTON III   1489, 10 February

Add. 27446, f. 76. 11⅜×16⅞ in. Hand unidentified; subscription autograph.

Dorse: Traces of red wax. Address in hand of letter:

*To my rygth wurchypful maystyr Syr John Paston, knyth, þis lettyr be
delyveryd in hast.*

The date appears from the report of an impending expedition to Brittany. Commissions to inquire into the raising of archers for this purpose were issued on 23
December 1488, and to take musters on 28 February 1489 (*Cal. Pat. Rolls, 1485–
94*, pp. 278, 282). The Earl of Northumberland was killed by a mob near Thirsk on
28 April 1489 (*Complete Peerage*, ix. 718); cf. William Paston III's letter no. 413.

F. v, p. 350. G. 907/1030.

Rygth reu*er*ent and worchypfull s*yr*,¹ in þe² most owmble wyse ⌐I⌐ recomand me vn-to yow, desyryng to here of yowre welfare, þe qwech God long
contynew. S*yr*, myn brodyr Wyllyam recomawnd hym on-to yow, and as
for þe³ lettyr þat ȝe sent on-to hym, he hath schewyd my⁴ lord þe entent
þer-off and ⌐he⌐ thynkyth hym-self þat it is⁵ no part of hys duté to have 5
any part of þe fysch or*e* any mony þat schuld grow þer-of. Never þe lasse
my lord, acordyng as yowr*e* desyre was in þe lett*er*, had qwestyond John
a⁶ Lowe of⁷ thys fych, a-for þe comyng of John Danyel,⁸ what he had doon

---

² *Interl. above* -y *canc.*
420. ¹ I *canc.*   ² þ *in form of* y *throughout.*   ³ led *canc.*
⁴ *Written* myn, -n *canc.*   ⁵ non *canc.*   ⁶ *No space.*
⁷ þe *canc.*   ⁸ wat, *with flourish on stroke of* t, *canc.*

wyth-all, and he aunswerd as for þe nedyre chavyll þer-of he had put it in
10 sewrté and leyd it in a howse be-cawse yowre debyté seasyd it to my⁴ lordys
vse tyll it⁹ myth be vndyrstond wedyre þe propyrté ware in þe Kyng or in
my⁴ lord. And so my lord held hym well content it schud be so, in so moch
as þe Kyng and my⁴ lord ⌐have⌐¹⁰ comawndyd John a Lowe þat thys forsayd chavyll schuld be browth vp to þe Kyng in all goodly hast. Fardermore
15 my⁴ brodyr Wyllyam perseyvyd be yowre wrytyng þat ye cowd make þe¹¹
remnawnth of þe fych¹² worth a iiij li. to my⁴ lord. My lord wold ʒe schuld
not trobyll yowre-self no more wyth-all be-cawse he thynkyth þat þe
propyrté is not in hym. And also⁶ an⌐o⌐dyre, my brodyre Wyllyam heryth
sey in þe corte þat þe Kyng and my lord be content þat þe remenavnt of
20 þe fych be to þe vse of them of þe cuntré, þe wech ʒe schall here þe more
serteyn þer-of here-after.

Also my broder Wyllyam seyth þat my lord wyllyd yow þat ʒe schuld
send þe retorne of þe comyscion as hastyly as ʒe can, and mervell þat ʒe
hath not sent it vp or thys.

25 As tovardys þe brekyng vp of þe parlement, many lykelywoodys þer be
þat it schuld contynew no wyle, and thes be they. My lord ⌐þe⌐ Arche-
byschop of Yorke departyd as¹³ ʒysterday, and my⁴ lord of Northethomyrlond schall goo as on Fryday, and also all schuch folkys as schall goo in-to
Breten schall be at Portysmowth on Satyrday cum forthnyth, and þe Munday
30 after on see bord, at wech seassun þe Kyng intentyd to be þer to take þe
mustyrs.

And as for thos jantylmen that toke schippyng to a gon over in-to Breten
vp-on a fortnyth a-goo, þat is to sey Syr Richard Egecum þe cowntrollere,
Syr Roberd Clyfford, Syr John Trobylvyll, and Johon Motton, sariant
35 porter, be a-ryvyd a-geyn vp-on þe cost of Yngland, save all-only Syr
Richard Egecum wech londyd in Breten and þer was in a towne callyd
Morleys, wech a-non vp-on hys comyng was besegyd wyth þe Frenchmen,
and so skapyd hardly wyth hys lyff; þe wech towne þe Frenchemen have
gotyn, and also þe towne ⌐callyd⌐¹⁴ Bre⌐e⌐st, how-be-it þe castell holdyth
40 as we here say. And þer be apoyntyd serteyn captens as thys seasun, wech¹⁵
be Lord Bruke, Syr John Cheney, Syr John of Arundell, Syr John Becham,
Syr John Gray, myn broder Awdley,¹⁶ myn vnkyll Syr Gylberd Debnam,
and Thomas Stafford and many odyr knytys and esqwyrys.

And, syr, I thanke yow for þe lettyr þat ʒe sent me. Also, syr, I¹⁷ have
45 fulfyllyd myn pylgremage, thanke-it be God. Also, syr, we vndyrstond¹⁸
þat it is anactyd of euery x merke of mevable goodys xxd. to þe Kyng,
be-syd þe tennyth of euery mannys londys.

9 myn *canc.*   10 *Interl. above* hath *canc.*
11 rema *canc.*   12 wyth a *canc.*
13 hyst *canc.*   14 *Interl. above* of *canc.*
15 ben *canc.*   16 s *canc.*
17 *Beginning of* f *canc.*   18 -o- *over part of another letter.*

And, syr, my[4] brodyre Heydon schall send yow þe serteyn of all odyre thyngys grawntyd at thys parlement, for he hath cawsed John Danyell to tery all thys day for hys letter, be-cawse he was wyth þe Kyng at West- 50 mestre þat he myth not entend to wryth it tyl nyth.

Also, syr, Master Calthorp hath payd j c merke to þe Kyng.

Also, syr, I have delyuerd þe x li. to Master Hawes and reseywyd of hym þe oblygacion. Also I have delyuerd þe xx[ti] merke to Edmund Dorman be my brodyr Heydons comawndment. 55

No more to yow at thys tyme, but God and þe Holy Trinyté have yow in here[19] kepyng; and myn syster Anne wyth all þe company recomawnd hem on-to yow. Wretyn at London þe x day of Februare.

Be yowre seruaunt MARGERY PASTON[20]

[19] -e- *over* i.   [20] *Subscription as in nos. 417, 418.*

WILLIAM PASTON IV

421. To John Paston III   Perhaps about 1495

Add. 27446, f. 98. 8¾ × 5½ in. Autograph.

Dorse: Traces of red wax, and embossed seal. Address autograph:

To my most special good father Ser John Paston, knyght.

William Paston IV was born probably about 1479. John III's first son Christopher was born in 1478 (see John II's letter no. 312), but must have died before 1482 since he is not mentioned in Margaret's will (no. 230). It is likely that William would be at Cambridge about the age of 15. 'Pamsborow' is evidently Ponsbourne in Hertfordshire, the first element of which is commonly *Pomes-*, *Pomeles-* in early documents (*The Place-Names of Hertfordshire* (E.P.N.S., 1938), p. 218).

F. v, p. 410. G. 938/1062.

After most humbyl wyse of reco*m*mandacion, jn my most lovyngly wyse I beseche yow of *your* dayly blyssyng, showyng yow þat[1] I am at S*er* John Fortescu place be-cause they swet so sor at Cambryg. Also I shew yow þat M*aster* Thomas Clark ys desessyd, hows sowle God haue m*er*cy.

5   Also, I beseche yow that ye wol se a remedy for the comun of Snaylwel, for[2] the bayly of Snaylwel *and* on of *your* fermors war w*yth* my tutor *and* me and shevyd me þat all the comun shuld a be takyn a-way butt for M*aster* Cotto*n* and the vecur of Fordan, hom I beseche yow to thank.

Fro[3] Pamsborow, be *your* most humbyl s*er*uant

10   W*i*ll*i*am Pasto*n*

421. [1] þ- *in form of* y *throughout.*   [2] y *canc.*   [3] -r *canc.*

PART OF NORFOLK AND SUFFOLK

Names of places containing Paston residences are underlined.

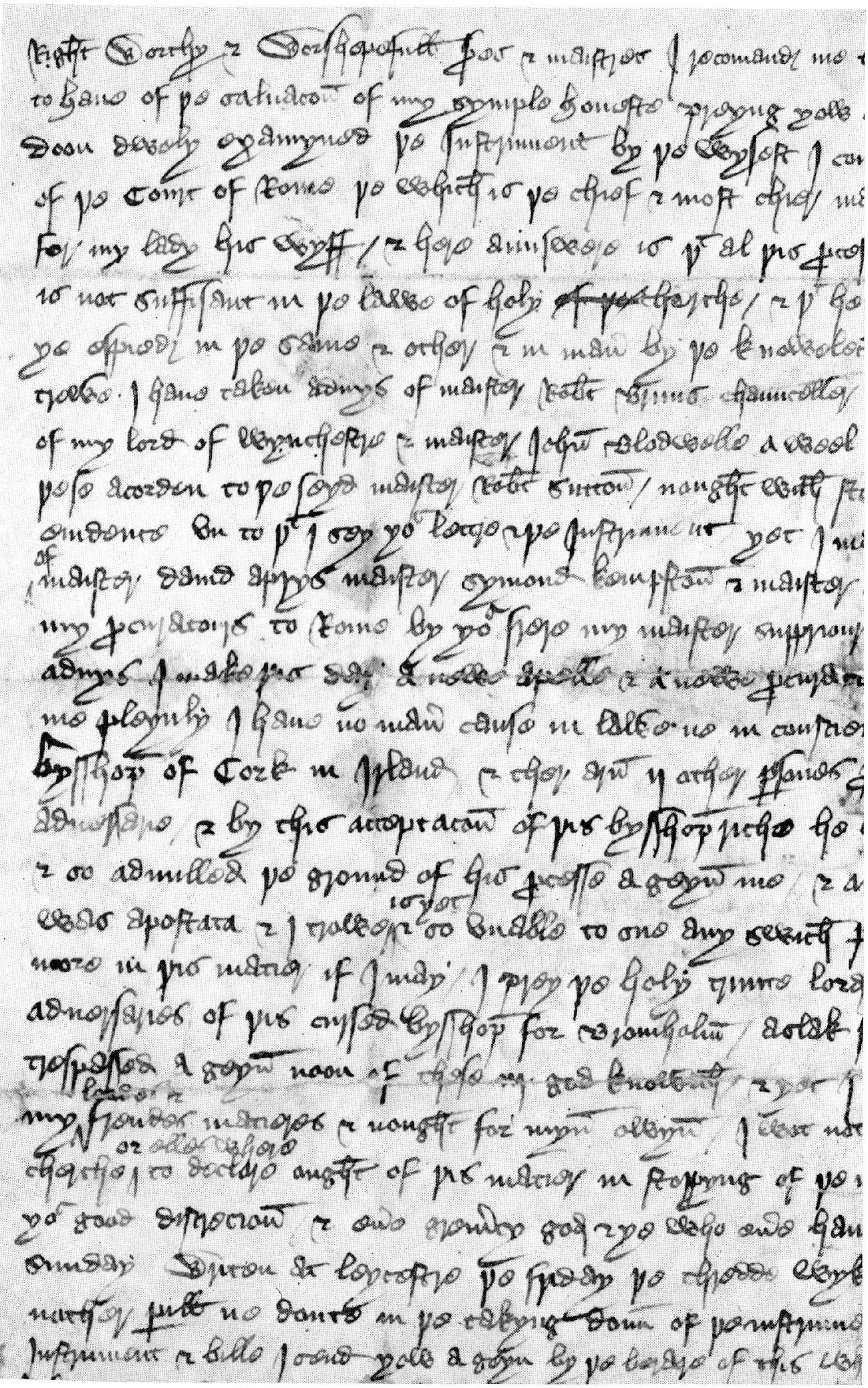
Right worthy & worshipfull sir & maister I recomaunde me to
to haue of ye saluacion of my symple honeste preyng yow
Yow derely examyned ye instrument by ye whiche I con
of ye court of Rome ye which is ye chief & most chief me
For my lady his wyff / & here aunswere is yt al ye proc
is not sufficient in ye lawe of holy ~~of ye~~ chirche / & yt ho
ye errour in ye same & other & in man by ye knowlech
clerkes. I haue taken aduys of maister Robt Sutton chauncellor
of my lord of Wynchestre & maister John Blodwelle a wol
here acorden to ye seyd maister Robt Sutton / nought with st
condiciones vn to yt I sey ye lawe & ye instrument yet I ma
of maister Dauid Aprys maister Symond Kempston & maister
my proctours to Rome by ye whiche my maister suppose
aduys I wolde yis day a nother appele & a nother procur
me pleynly I haue no man cause in lawe ne in consci
bysshop of Cork in Irlond & ther ben ii other p̄sones
admissiones / & by this acceptacion of yis bysshop which he
& so admitted ye grounde of his processe a geyn me / & a
wolde apostata & I walker is yet so vnable to one day seruich
were in yis matier if I may / I prey ye holy trinite lord
admissiones of yis cursed bysshop for Emlyhalm / wolde
ressayued a geyn noon of these iii. god knoweth / & yet
lawer &
my frendes maistres & nought for myn owne / I dar no
or other clerkes
chirche / to declare aught of yis matier in stoppyng of ye
yor good discrecion / & ouer yis matier god & ye lawe and han
Sunday Dpison at leycestre ye spede ye grete clerk
matier ~~putt~~ no doute in ye takyng doun of ye instrume
instrument & bille I send yow a geyn by ye berer of this lett

B.M. MS. Add. 27443, f. 80
Letter no. 4, hand of WILLIAM PASTON I, 1426

B.M. MS. 43488, f. 4 (× ¾)

Letter no. 13, written for AGNES PASTON, probably 1440

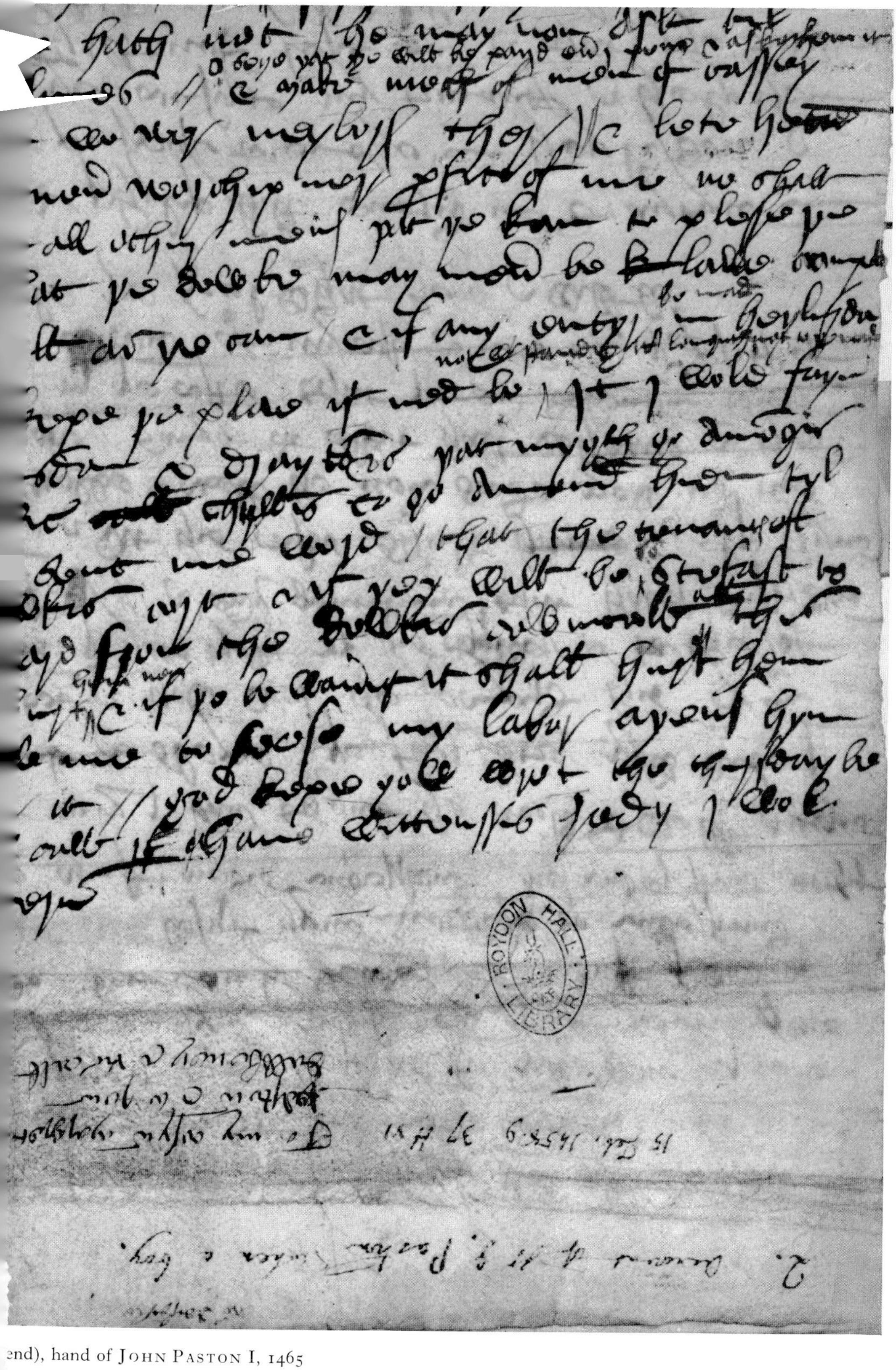

end), hand of JOHN PASTON I, 1465

B.M. MS. Add. 33597, f. 5 ($\times \frac{7}{8}$)

Letter no. 85, hand of WILLIAM PASTON II, probably 1458

V

B.M. MS. Add. 34888, f. 191

Letter no. 116, hand of CLEMENT PASTON, 1461

B.M. MS. Add. 27445, f. 83
Letter no. 286, hand of JOHN PASTON II, 1474

B.M. MS. Add. 43491,
f. 26 ($\times \frac{9}{16}$)
Inventory, no. 316,
hand of JOHN PASTON II

answeryd they a pay... salue sipylor tarney w oth
and they that haue lofyd w hym w to thys day haue ben
sotwyd be goldsmythys h warb my g... my g... ma... f... for of
corth neythyr gentylmen ner gentylwomen they want
by my trowthe I haue nevyr off so grete plente as here
but nat w the bastard for thed promyss that now the
bastard was ow of the logge I brow the lord scalyd w t
bastard ow the loge z gothe qurt hym do ore that
demyd that w grett pete fo by my trowthe I have
ow... corth ad oth lordys ladys z gentylwomen buyff of
same thyng a sewryd corth by my trowthe I haue no wyth
qur but y lastyth ad itz comyth to myn... I shall tell
be long to for we depart owt of bryg... q... ward
of burgoyn owt of ynglond ex ept suape as shall abyd
depart the sater fr the duke gothe word that the ky
gastyly z that he w w w my ob dayes germey of om...
to mete w hym god hym good spede z all thys for by
a mery z besy can besyn... hym... z mafter lyf g...
z... off so... by w... belefyw owt of brug...
they say... cryt he... to quen margareta I wadd...
no mor but I beseche yow of you blyssyng ad low
me every day onys and modyr I beseche yow y ye w the
I have my cosyn danb... by tallyd... fo to
pray yow thys byll may recom... me to my lord yd
joh styll z to pray hym to be good mafter to me that I
may recomand me to all you folkys z my wel wy the
at brugg the fryday next afyr sayt ... p...

8 July
1468.
8 Ed. IV.

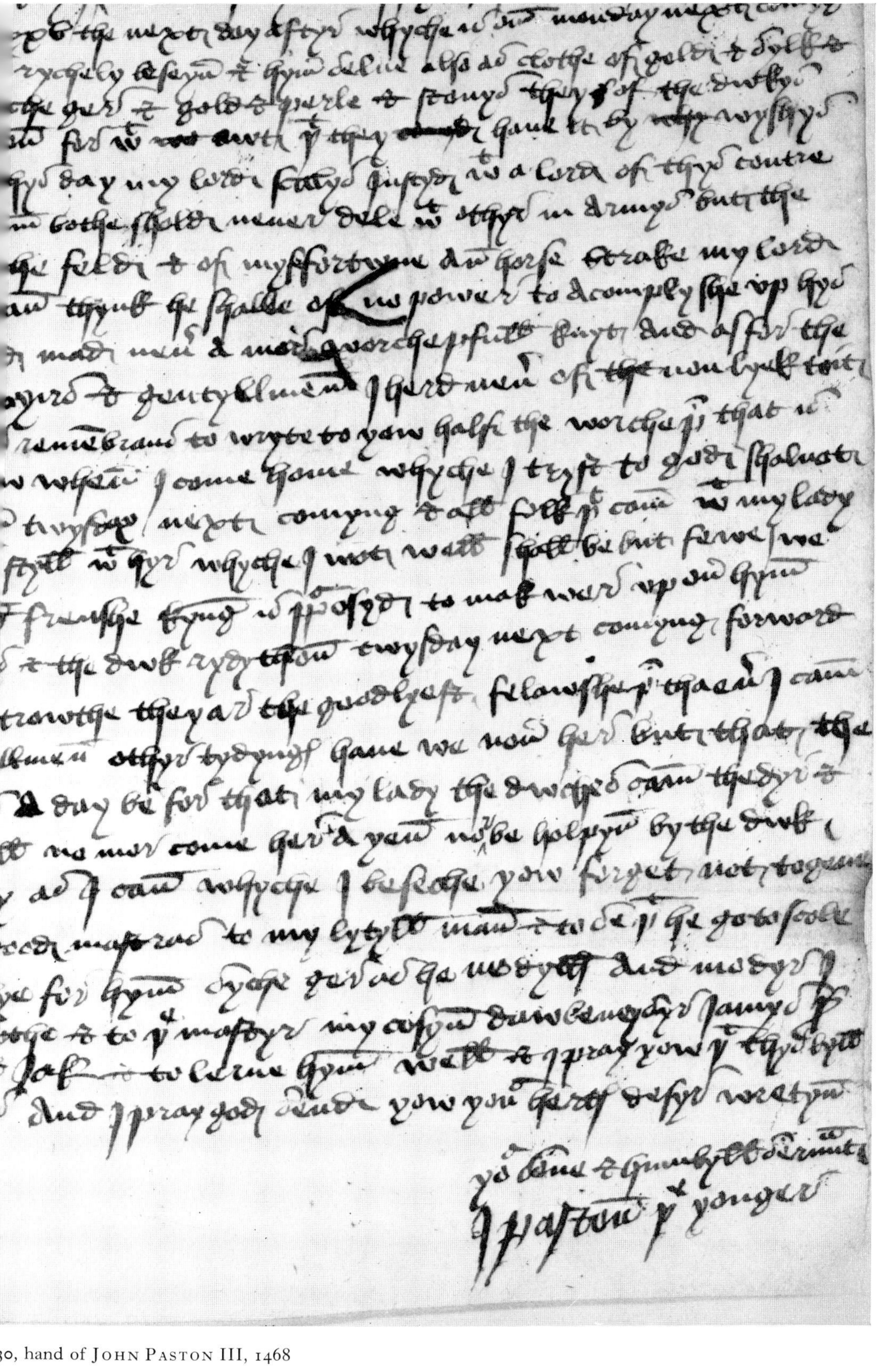

330, hand of JOHN PASTON III, 1468

B.M. MS. Add. 27446, f. 12 (×¾)

Letter no. 402, hand of WALTER PASTON, before 1479

B.M. MS. Add. 43489, f. 25 (×¾)

Letter no. 407, hand of WILLIAM PASTON III, probably 1479

B.M. MS. Add. 27446, f. 52 (×⅓)

Letter no. 418, written for MARGERY PASTON, with autograph subscription, perhaps 1481